Textbook on Contract Law

Textbook on
Contract Law

10th Edition

Jill Poole

LLB, LLM, FHEA, FRSA, FCI Arb, Barrister
Professor of Commercial Law and
Head of Aston Law
Aston Business School, Aston University.

OXFORD
UNIVERSITY PRESS

OXFORD
UNIVERSITY PRESS

Great Clarendon Street, Oxford OX2 6DP

Oxford University Press is a department of the University of Oxford.
It furthers the University's objective of excellence in research, scholarship,
and education by publishing worldwide in

Oxford New York

Auckland Bangkok Buenos Aires Cape Town Chennai
Dar es Salaam Delhi Hong Kong Istanbul Karachi Kolkata
Kuala Lumpur Madrid Melbourne Mexico City Mumbai Nairobi
São Paulo Shanghai Taipei Tokyo Toronto

Oxford is a registered trade mark of Oxford University Press
in the UK and in certain other countries

Published in the United States
by Oxford University Press Inc., New York

British Library Cataloguing in Publication Data

Data available

Library of Congress Cataloging in Publication Data

Data available

Typeset by Newgen Imaging Systems (P) Ltd., Chennai, India
Printed in Great Britain
on acid-free paper by
Ashford Colour Press Ltd, Gosport, Hampshire

ISBN 978-0-19-957436-0

1 3 5 7 9 10 8 6 4 2

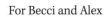

For Becci and Alex

Guide to using the book

Textbook on Contract Law includes a range of tools and features to help you establish a well-rounded appreciation of the subject. This guide shows you how to fully utilize your textbook to get the most out of your studies.

Summary of the issues

This chapter examines the legal treatment of those mistakes which are claimed to m basis that, although the parties have reached agreement, both parties entered into th same fundamental mistake.

• In order to protect the interests of third parties and to ensure certainty in transa of common mistake in English law has traditionally been very narrowly defined. I frustration doctrine, if the parties have allocated the risk of the event in the terms of th allocation clause will govern.

• There will be a fundamental common mistake in instances of true impossibilit

Chapter summaries

Each chapter starts with a list of key issues that will be discussed, so you are aware of what will be covered and can check your understanding.

---

debt so that the creditor could sue for the balance, arguing (at p

All men of business...do every day recognise and act on the groun their demand may be more beneficial to them than it would be to in ment of the whole. Even where the debtor is perfectly solvent, and s Where the credit of the debtor is doubtful it must be more so.

Such reasoning recognizes that there may be a factual ben Indeed, promises to accept less might seem to be no differer

Extracts

Short extracts from cases and legislation are highlighted for easy identification.

---

support them. The best example of the operation of the doctrine is the leadi *Metropolitan Railway Co.* (1877) 2 App Cas 439.

A lease contained a covenant requiring the lessee to repair upon notice from the lessor, gave notice requiring repair within six months. The railway company, the le offering to sell back to the lessor the company's remaining interest in the prope Negotiations continued for some two months before breaking down. Hughes subs be entitled to possession of the property on the basis that, since the company ha the required repairs within six months of the original date of the notice requiring r been forfeited. The company claimed that there was a tacit understanding (or an ir the repairs need not be carried out if the negotiations came to a successful conclu meantime the period of notice would not start to run. In the House of Lords the exist promise was not really in doubt. Nevertheless, it was unsupported by consideration ably unenforceable. However, the House of Lords refused to accept that argument.

Case summaries

Summaries of the cases discussed appear in blue font so you can easily pick out the salient facts and details.

Inntrepreneur Pub Co. v East Crown Ltd [2000] 2 Lloyd's Rep 6

 Question

Was it the statement maker's intention to make a binding promise a that if the statement were inaccurate it would result in automatic bi *Symons and Co. v Buckleton* [1913] AC 30)?

Another way of putting this question is simply to ask whethe maker was to guarantee the truth of their statement.

Questions

Some of the questions that students ask most frequently on various points of contract law have been selected to appear in these question boxes, together with clear and succinct answers and explanations.

described as 'past', and the rule is easily explained by the theor
given in exchange for the promise.

 Example

I am drowning in a lake. You rescue me. **Then** I promise to pay yo
consideration you have provided is your act of rescuing me but th
ation because it pre-dates my promise and is therefore not given ir

The past consideration rule is well illustrated by the classic ca

Examples

Key points of law are illustrated by reference to
everyday situations so you can see how the law
operates in practice.

Roffey consideration and the relationship with duress

 Key point

In *Roffey*, Glidewell LJ had sought to state the applicable le
proposition:

1. if A has entered into a contract with B to do work for, or to supp
   return for payment by B and
2. at some stage before A has completely performed his obligatio
   son to doubt whether A will, or will be able to, complete his sid
3. B thereupon promises A an additional payment in return for A's

Key points

Points of particular significance are featured in key
point boxes, so you can check your understanding
of these fundamental principles during learning
and revision.

✳ Summary

Terms implied in fact must be:

1. implied on a 'one-off' basis into this particular contract
2. based on construing the contract so that it reflects what a rea
   it to mean
3. necessary to achieve that construction.

Summaries

Some of the more complex principles are summed
up in summary boxes within chapters to provide
additional clarification and further aid the learning
process.

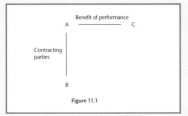

Figure 11.1

Figures

Line diagrams offer visual representations of
contractual relationships to help you understand
this often complex subject.

Further reading

Reform

Adams and Brownsword, 'Privity of contract: That pestilential nuisance' (1993) 56 MLR 722.
Adams, Beyleveld, and Brownsword, 'Privity of contract: The benefits and burdens of law refor
Burrows, 'Reforming privity of contract: Law Commission Report No. 242' [1996] LMCLQ 46
Flannigan, 'Privity: The end of an era (error)' (1987) 103 LQR 564.
Kincaid, 'Privity reform in England' (2000) 116 LQR 43.
Law Commission Consultation Paper, LCCP No. 121, *Privity of Contracts: Contracts for the be*
(1991).
Law Commission Report No. 242, *Privity of Contracts: Contracts for the benefit of third partie*
Smith, 'Contracts for the benefit of third parties: In defence of the third party rule' (1997)17

Further reading

These recommendations for further reading will help
you to broaden your understanding and ensure your
study is efficient and well directed.

---

should reduce much of the complexity of the law governing third-party enf
tion clauses.

The 1999 Act may also provide a direct right of enforcement in situatio
Southern Water Authority v Carey and ***Norwich City Council v Harvey*** (see
the clarity of the risk-allocation clauses and because the Act specifically states
(i.e., the subcontractor)' need not be in existence when the contract is entered

However, it would not be available in factual situations such as ***Scruttons***
because of the absence of an **express** identification of the third party as an i
of the clause. The same problem would exist on the facts in ***London Drugs v***
namely the fact that the clause does not **expressly** confer a benefit on the em
can be said to be **expressly** identified as members of a class of 'warehousen
ity is that this can be achieved only by fairly generous implication. ***The Eu***
operate in either of these cases because the first criterion specified by Lord I
The 1999 Act effectively keeps this first requirement and dispenses with tl

Cross references to *Casebook on Contract Law*

Cases that are the subject of extended extracts in Jill
Poole's *Casebook on Contract Law* are highlighted
in bold, blue italics for easy cross reference between
the two texts.

Guide to using the Online Resource Centre

Textbook on Contract Law is accompanied by an Online Resource Centre providing students and lecturers with ready-to-use teaching and learning resources.

www.oxfordtextbooks.co.uk/orc/poole/

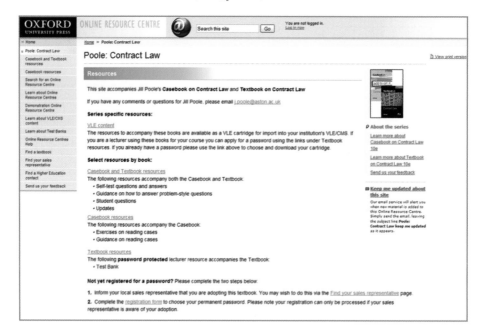

For students

These resources are accessible to all, with no registration or password required, enabling you to get the most from your textbook.

Regular updates

This valuable resource allows you to access changes and developments in the law that have occurred since publication of the book. They allow you to keep up to date while continuing to benefit from Jill Poole's insightful analysis.

> There have been two recent important decisions of the House of Lords: one to deal with a matter omitted from legislative coverage and the other, more fundamentally, to confirm the applicable measure of damages for breach as compensation for ACTUAL losses *suffered*, even if this means taking account of matters that might have limited loss after the date of

Guidance on answering questions

This advice on how to answer problem questions will stand you in good stead when you start your contract law course. It covers fundamental issues such as the organization of answers, use of facts, and statements about the law.

Guidance on writing answers to problem questions in contract law

General organisation
Introduction and conclusion
Use of facts
Statements about the law
How to be successful

One important point at the start - Do not treat a problem question as an invitation to write an abstract essay about the legal issues involved in the

Self-test questions and answers

You can download a series of questions on each topic to test your knowledge and understanding, before downloading the sample answers for reference.

QUESTIONS: TERMS AND BREACH OF CONTRACT

1. What distinguishes a pre-contractual statement that is a term from a pre-contractual statement that is only a mere representation? (2)

2. What is the basic test for determining if a pre-contractual statement is a contractual term or mere representation? (1)

For lecturers

This resource is password protected to ensure only lecturers can have access.
Registering is easy: click on 'Lecturer resources' on the Online Resource Centre, complete a simple registration form which allows you to choose your own username and password, and access will be granted within 48 hours (subject to verification).

Test bank

This is a fully customizable resource containing 300 multiple choice questions, all with answers and feedback. This test bank can be used for formal assessment, revision, or ongoing learning support for your students.

Chapter 02 - Question 18
Which **one** of the following statements **most accurately** describes the decision in *Byrne & Co v Van Tienhoven*
  A telegraphed acceptance became effective when received by the offeror.
  An offeree could not accept an offer after the offeror has posted a letter revoking the offer.
  Revocation of an offer by post would only become effective when received by the offeree.
  Once an offer was accepted and a letter of confirmation followed the acceptance, any revocation of the offer

1 out of 1
Correct. This was what was decided in *Byrne & Co v Van Tienhoven*. The postal rule does not apply to acceptances (provided use of the post is reasonable). Thus, revoking an offer by post is only effective
Page reference: 76-7

Outline contents

Detailed contents

xv

Preface

It seems no time at all since I was writing the Preface for the ninth edition of *Textbook* but the intervening years have seen no let up in the volume of interesting, if not always helpful, contract case law and new developments. Whoever foretold the death of contract (it was Grant Gilmore) could not have been more wrong. The development of principle continues to flourish, although it sometimes appears that its technicality continues to grow—and, as my daughter (Becci) is fond of telling me—I had it easy as a law student in the late 70s/early 80s since just look how much law has 'happened' in the meantime. She has a point—and you have my sympathies!

As my students will testify, I will happily discuss the latest decisions and their potential implications—at some length. I suspect I may be more familiar with contract case law than any other subject, although football would be a close call. If all else fails I want Gaby Logan's job! (This may be a surprising revelation to anyone who knows my ethnic origins and can recall my particular affinity with Rugby Union as a student; not a terribly pleasant experience in the days of television lounges in halls of residence when studying at an English University in the early 80s). I therefore have my uses in pub quiz teams—although I have yet to be asked any pub quiz questions about contract case law (strange that).

It has also been another exciting period for the development of Contract law, particularly in terms of contractual construction and remedies. The Privy Council in *Attorney General of Belize v Belize Telecom Ltd* had confirmed construction as the determinative test for implication of terms in fact and rejected the officious bystander and business efficacy tests. Such an implied term is not 'added' to give effect to the presumed intentions of the parties but has been a term of the contract all along, had we only bothered to take the trouble to construe the contract terms as a reasonable person would. The 'reasonable person' has taken on an even greater significance in determining formation (*Maple Leaf Macro Volatility Master Fund v Rouvroy*) and content, and the courts have shown a greater willingness to interfere where something 'must have gone wrong with the language' (using a similar argument to that first advanced by the House of Lords in *Schuler v Wickman Machine Tools* in the 1970s) on the basis of what the reasonable person, having all the background knowledge that would have been available to the parties, would have understood the parties to have meant (*Chartbrook Ltd v Persimmon Homes Ltd* (HL)). Despite this intervention, the House may have taken a step back from abolition of the 'exclusionary rule' in relation to the relevance of pre-contractual negotiations in the process of contractual interpretation. This is one of the decisions of the highest court that raises as many questions as it answers. Another in a line of controversial decisions is the decision in *Transfield Shipping Inc. v Mercator Shipping Inc., The Achilleas* on remoteness and ability to recover damages in contract. It seems reasonably clear that there is a tension and diverging opinions, although bank charges seems to be the exception, on matters contractual in what is now the Supreme Court (see e.g. *Shogun Finance v Hudson, The Golden Victory*). Such decisions make life more interesting for some—and more complex for the unfortunate law student who has to struggle to identify any commonality of argument and then await the fall-out in terms of subsequent decisions of the lower courts and academic analysis of the cases. If it is any consolation, I feel sure that the helpfulness of the limbs in *Hadley v Baxendale*, not to mention their practical relevance in terms of pleadings and limiting the scope of possible evidence, will ensure that they are not so easily discarded, if such was indeed the intention of Lord Hoffmann in *Transfield*. General principles can be helpful but guidance in terms of how the principles are to be applied is invariably sought.

The Supreme Court caused something of a surprise for commentators in 'the bank charges' case in November 2009. Submission of the manuscript for this edition had to wait until the following day in order to accommodate discussion. The decision may be more significant in terms of what it did not say than what it did, although there were some interesting observations concerning banking practice in the UK which displayed some insight—and courage given the consumer context. As I was originally (many years ago) a graduate trainee with one of the major banks (probably a lucky escape) and have taught banking law, I have a particular interest in banking operations and have watched this litigation, and the arguments, with some interest.

Other interesting new case law includes *Tekdata Interconnections Ltd v Amphenol Ltd* (battle of forms in a relational contract); *Statoil ASA v Louis Dreyfus Energy Services LP, The Hariette N* (mistakes as to terms compared with collateral matters); and case law examining quantum in cases of fraudulent misrepresentation (a increasingly recurrent theme in the case law), *4Eng Ltd v Harper, Dadourian Group International Inc. v Simms (Damages),* and *Parabola Investments Ltd v Browallia Cal Ltd*. However, these provide only a flavour of the many recent developments covered in this book.

This edition includes reference to the provisions of the Draft Common Frame of Reference (if only for comparative purposes) and to the CRPs (Consumer Protection from Unfair Trading Regulations 2008). It also refers to the Law Commission's 2009 Consultation on The Illegality Defence and the potentially significant proposal for a Consumer Rights Directive which has important implications for contractual remedies. Details of subsequent developments, case law and other, are posted on the website.

As always, I am happy to answer emails from readers relating to the content of this *Textbook* or the *Casebook*. *Textbook* is designed to provide greater levels of explanation and discussion than are possible in a casebook but *Casebook* is an essential support tool in terms of ensuring understanding by enabling readers to see the development and statements of principles for themselves. The blue bold on case names throughout this text is intended to indicate that the case is the subject of fuller treatment in *Casebook on Contract Law* so that immediate cross reference can be made. This edition also makes a number of important structural changes to improve the structure of content and to reduce the size of some chapters to something more manageable. Formalities and capacity now appear in Chapter 5, leaving Chapter 4 to consideration and promissory estoppel. Classification of terms (conditions, warranties and innominate terms), previously in Chapter 6, has been moved to Chapter 8 (Breach) where it has application. Chapter 8 has been extensively rewritten to terms of examining the election on repudiatory breach and the issues surrounding the election following an anticipatory breach.

This edition contains a number of other presentational devices designed to improve the visual impact of the text and reinforce understanding by highlighting key points and illustrative examples. I have also continued, and improved, the popular summaries at the beginning of each chapter and the indicators of further reading at the end have been broken down in order to be of maximum assistance to readers. On many occasions the arguments within specific important articles are mentioned or rehearsed in the text. I fully appreciate the danger that such lists of readings may be reproduced as readings for assessed work and have therefore deliberately listed only the surname of each author in an effort to discourage this practice. Finally, as someone who makes notes in colour, I regard the use of multi-colour text as extremely helpful in highlighting key points, headings, and case details.

I have chosen to continue references to 'plaintiffs' rather than claimants when discussing specific plaintiffs in pre-CPR case law on the basis that the judgments and speeches extracted in *Casebook* contain references to plaintiffs and it would therefore be confusing to use both terms. However, abstract comments on the current legal position will obviously make reference to claimants. Finally, and for the avoidance of doubt, abstract references to the masculine in this text are also intended to include the feminine.

I hope to retain something of the 'unique' and personal nature of my prefaces whilst avoiding further embarrassment to my 'children', now both adults. The writing and proof reading period has coincided with limb issues (although different limbs to those in *Hadley v Baxendale*). My father broke his ankle, then my brother was involved in a skiing accident when he was hit (seems to be something of an understatement) by a snowboarder (fractures various), and even Alex, my son, who plays American football at university—and appears to think he is the last line of defence, managed to end up with a problem with his leg (necessitating the reinvention of mum's taxi). I am tottering on my high heels with care! Fortunately, only one of my offspring is now at university (and in need of a drip infusion of cash), Becci is now 'a graduate trainee' who seems to know more about employment law than I ever will and who has organizational skills to be envied. The entire family, friends and colleagues, have been supportive of my writing, whilst perhaps not always appreciating the enormity of the task and its continuing nature. They have long since become accustomed to periods when I am 'working nights' to get through the many box files of case law and new developments required for each new edition—and now leave me well alone while paper flies in all directions.

This is the 26th year in which I have been lecturing Contract law and researching in this area. In that time I have had the pleasure of conveying the joys of Contract law to many thousands of students—both in person and through the books. It is simply not true to say, as I sometimes hear, that 'anyone can teach contract law'; anyone can teach contract law badly, without enthusiasm, insight and knowledge of its practical application and relevance. Lecturing is invariably a two-way process and I continue to learn from my students. Over the years this interaction has helped me to judge where extra help may be required and better explanations provided. I hope that as part of this process I have managed to transfer some, if not all, of my enthusiasm for this fascinating area of law and the delights of a structured approach to legal study with a view to promoting understanding of the complexities of legal reasoning.

The team at Oxford University Press has, as always, coped with my little eccentricities with tolerance and humour and I am particularly indebted to Sarah Viner, for her support over a number of years; Helen Davis who somehow has to manage and organize me; Rekha Summan (who has to transform the manuscript into the finished product); and Jeremy Langworthy for his excellent copy editing and banter. I think I may have convinced Jeremy that it is judges who avoid the use of hyphens where they would normally appear! Finally, I am grateful to all those tutors and students who recommend and use my books and for the many generous email messages received since the last edition. As always, I welcome any comments or questions about the content in *Textbook* or on the companion website—j.poole@aston.ac.uk

Jill Poole
Aston Law, Aston Business School, Birmingham

Table of cases

Table of statutes and statutory instruments

Statutes

Statutory instruments

Table of international legislation

Introduction to the law of contract

1

Summary of the issues

- Contracts are legally enforceable agreements which represent a vehicle for planned exchanges. In our society these exchanges are regulated by the principles of contract law in a way which is designed to meet the needs of society and should reflect the theoretical basis for the chosen regulatory approach. This chapter explains some of the main theories underpinning the development of English contract law and notes that, in order to be a satisfactory theory, the theory must explain how the law has developed to the point it is at today as well as providing the basis for establishing how the law may develop in the future by indicating general principles capable of giving rise to specific rules.

- This chapter also examines the nature of contractual liability as a prelude to the more specific treatment of the components of that liability examined in subsequent chapters. Contractual obligations derive from party agreement and it is this feature which distinguishes contractual liability from liability in tort. The relationship between contract and tort is considered, highlighting the fact that a set of facts may give rise to concurrent liability in contract and tort and assessing the distinctions between such claims and remedies.

- In order to fully appreciate the development of contract law principles it is necessary to have some understanding of the history of the law of contract and how the contextual background has impacted on those principles. This chapter therefore contains a brief historical explanation.

- Contracts for the sale of goods feature as illustrations of the application of general contractual principles throughout this book. Such contracts provide a practical example of contracts to which it is easy for students to relate. However, such contracts are also regulated by specific legislation and common law principles so that it is necessary to explain this legislation and principles in the broadest terms and, in particular, to explain the basic distinction between contracts which are void and voidable and the effect of this on third parties.

- The movement towards the globalization of contract law proved important in the latter stages of the twentieth century and will inevitably have a profound effect on contract law in the twenty-first century. This chapter therefore examines these issues, including the various attempts to produce a set of harmonized principles, including a Common Frame of Reference for European Contract Law, and the impact of other international developments such as the growth in e-commerce and electronic communications and the significance in a shrinking world of the principles of contract law applied in other jurisdictions. It also notes the UK's adoption of Rome I, determining the governing law where the parties have failed to provide which jurisdiction's law is to govern their contractual disputes.

- In recent years European directives have had a marked influence on the development of English contract law, especially in the context of consumer contracts. The most significant of these directives are noted and new developments highlighted for future reference. Perhaps the most significant outcome of the implementation of these European directives has been the introduction of the concept of 'good faith' into English contract law. The debate surrounding the meaning and significance of this concept is outlined and briefly assessed (see also the examination in the context of unfair contract terms in **Chapter 7**).

- This chapter also examines the proposal for a Consumer Rights Directive in the context of the review of the Consumer Acquis (i.e. the body of European law and directives).

- Finally, the other recent development which is likely to influence the future development of English contract law is the implementation of the European Convention on Human Rights into English law by means of the Human Rights Act 1998. There is some debate concerning the scope of this Act in the context of relationships between private individuals and also in relation to the applicability of Convention Rights to contract legislation and disputes. This chapter considers two illustrative contract-based cases where the application of the Act has been discussed, namely *Wilson v Secretary of State for Trade and Industry* (formalities and the Consumer Credit Act 1974) and *Shanshal v Al-Kishtaini* (recovery of money or property under a contract tainted by illegality).

1.1 The nature of contractual liability

Contracts are legally enforceable agreements.

- To say that an agreement is 'legally enforceable' is merely a shorthand way of saying that it is an agreement to which the law gives its sanction, as opposed to mere social arrangements which exist outside the framework of the law and which are binding only in the sense of moral obligation or social convention.

- Liability for breach of contract is, therefore, liability for failure to keep to the terms of such an agreement.

This definition of contract implies (at least) three distinct fields of legal rules relating to contracts. There must be:

- rules relating to the formation and content of agreements
- rules relating to the enforcement of agreements and
- rules distinguishing those agreements which are legally enforceable from those which are not.

1.1.1 Essential ingredients of enforceability

The rules determining whether an agreement is to be regarded as enforceable are the subject of Chapters 4 and 5. They embrace three separate elements: consideration (see 4.2), intention (5.1), and form (5.4). Thus, an agreement will be classed as a contract only if it satisfies the requirements of consideration, if the parties intend legal consequences to result from it and it meets any special rules of evidence which are applicable to this type of contract.

1.1.1.1 The consideration requirement

Of the above elements the most important is consideration, which is a distinguishing feature of common law contract not found in civil law systems. **Consideration will be defined below (see 4.2.1) as the action, inaction, or promise thereof by one party which induces the action, inaction, or promise of another.** Consideration for one promise may therefore be provided by another promise, and so a contract may be constituted out of nothing more than an exchange of promises. There are good functional reasons for the enforceability of promises which have induced the reliance of another, but it has sometimes been suggested that liability upon a promise which has not yet induced another's reliance is an unnecessary feature of the law. The reason for that suggestion is that where there has been no reliance, no harm will be caused by failure to keep the promise. Despite the apparent logic of this reasoning, the law has rightly rejected it for practical reasons of evidence. That is, it may in some circumstances be extremely difficult to prove reliance on a promise.

 Example

If A promises to sell B 100 tonnes of grain, and B agrees to buy it, but before A commences delivery or B makes any payment one of them backs out of the agreement, it might be said that no harm will be done by cancellation of the contract since neither party has done anything in reliance on it. However, what if B has already sold the grain to C, or A has turned down the opportunity to sell the grain to D, on account of the contract?

Rather than put the parties to the proof of their reliance, the law assumes that promises have a tendency to induce reliance, and so liability attaches to the mere act of reciprocal promising. Contracts in which performance on both sides remains in the future are described as 'executory', and the binding nature of such agreements is an important element in the commercial value of the device of contract.

1.1.2 Agreement

The rules relating to the formation and the substance of agreements are the subjects respectively of **Chapter 2** and **Chapter 6**. In defining contracts as being based on agreements, it is implicit that we are concerned with obligations which are consensually (or voluntarily) undertaken. Moreover, it follows from the description of consideration given above (see 1.1.1.1) that agreements usually consist of reciprocal promises. It is important, however, to give an early warning about the limits of the notion of agreement.

- Not all undertakings are completely voluntary, in that the law imposes certain obligations on those who enter particular types of agreement (see 6.4). Thus, the fact of entering the agreement may be voluntary, but the substance of the agreement is to some extent dictated by law (e.g., undertakings as to the quality of goods sold).

- Not all agreements are consensual if by that term we are to understand a precise symmetry between the real intentions of the parties.

It was once common to speak of agreements being formed by a 'meeting of the minds' of the parties, which suggests that their **subjective** intentions must coincide. It is of course almost impossible to discover a person's real or subjective intentions, and for this reason the law regards agreements as formed by a coincidence of **objectively ascertained** intentions. That is, what each party actually intended is irrelevant if to all outward appearances the parties are in agreement. The objective test of formation of contracts, and especially the meaning of 'objectivity' in this context, is considered in more detail below (see 2.1).

1.1.3 Enforcement

When we consider the necessity of enforcing the obligations created by those agreements which qualify as contracts, it is inevitable that our attention will primarily be focused on those remedies for breach of contract which are available in the ordinary courts. Our understanding of the rules of the law of contract, including those rules relevant to enforcement, is largely derived from judicial statements. The enforcement of contractual obligations by legal proceedings is the subject of Chapters 9 and 10. It is necessary here only to summarize what is explained in more detail in the introduction to Part 3 (pp. 335–8). Although we speak of the enforcement of contractual obligations, the paradigm remedy for breach of contract is compensation for non-performance rather than compulsion of the performance promised in the contract. Moreover, although in the field of criminal law the idea of 'law enforcement' involves the imposition of penalties for non-compliance, the law of contract denies any role to penalties in securing performance of contracts (although see *Attorney-General v Blake* [2001] 1 AC 268 and the remedy of accounting for profits in exceptional circumstances).

1.2 Relationship between contract and tort

English law maintains a fairly strict division between contract and tort, which represents one of the major divisions of legal classification between obligations voluntarily assumed and obligations imposed by law.

- **Contractual obligations are voluntarily assumed, in that they derive from agreements which individuals are free to make or refrain from making.**
- **Tortious obligations arise independently of the will of those involved, and derive from standards of behaviour imposed by law.**

In this section reference will be made exclusively to the tort of negligence, which imposes an obligation not to breach the duty of care (i.e., the duty to behave as would a reasonable person in the circumstances) which the law says is owed to those who may foreseeably be injured by any particular conduct or activity. The leading case on the law of negligence is *Donoghue v Stevenson* [1932] AC 562, which involved the notorious snail in the bottle of ginger beer. The manufacturer and bottler of the ginger beer was held to owe a duty of care to consumers (see further 11.1).

It is ironic that a marked distinction is maintained between contract and tort, since the action for breach of contract was originally a sub-species of an early form of action for tort (see 1.3). The strictness of the distinction appears to owe much to nineteenth-century developments. The prevailing philosophy of the time, sometimes summarized under the epithet '*laissez-faire*', regarded man as master of his own destiny, and believed that, if given free rein, man's intelligence would operate to the benefit of all. This philosophy gave rise to two specific legal notions relevant to contracts:

- The first, and more important, is 'freedom of contract' (see 1.4.2.2).
- The second was that, being based in free will, contract was the **superior** norm. That is, contractual obligations were supposedly superior to all others because of the manner of their generation. Thus, obligations which might otherwise be imposed by law, would give way to obligations contractually agreed between the parties.

Modern writers have been deeply sceptical of this second notion. Some have gone as far as to talk of the 'death of contract'—e.g., Gilmore, *The Death of Contract* (Ohio State University Press, 1986)—suggesting that the law is moving progressively to a system of imposed obligations even in those fields traditionally regarded as the exclusive domain of the law of contract. Reports of the death of contract are no doubt greatly exaggerated, but there is no denying that there has been a marked retreat from the high point of contractual superiority. In ***Henderson v Merrett Syndicates Ltd*** [1994] 3 All ER 506 at p. 532, Lord Goff, deprecating analysis which 'involves treating the law of tort as supplementary to the law of contract', affirmed the modern trend, saying that 'the law of tort is the general law, out of which the parties can, if they wish, contract'.

Where they do contract, the existence of a contract between the parties will normally militate against any duty of care in tort since the contract will be 'inconsistent with an assumption of responsibility which has the effect of short-cutting the contractual structure so put in place by the parties' (per Lord Goff in ***Henderson v Merrett Syndicates Ltd***). However, in ***Riyad Bank v Ahli United Bank (UK) plc*** [2006] EWCA Civ 780, [2006] 2 All ER (Comm) 777, which was a very different case to *Henderson* on the facts, the defendant, a Kuwaiti bank, had provided advice on an investment fund under a contract with the general advisor to the Riyad bank which had set up this fund. There was therefore no contract between the fund and the defendant. The fund suffered losses as a result of the defendant's negligent advice. The Court of Appeal held that the contractual background, and decision not to have a direct contract between the fund and the defendant, did not mean that there could never be any duty of care in tort (assumption of responsibility) owed to the fund. It depended on the facts and here the advice was given directly to the fund and the fund suffered loss in consequence. Longmore LJ stated (at [32]): 'There cannot be a general proposition that, just because a chain exists, no responsibility for advice is ever assumed to a non-contractual party.'

1.2.1 Overlap of contract and tort

That there is nothing which makes contractual obligations necessarily superior to tortious obligations appears to be a logical conclusion from the fact that there are many instances where the two may overlap. A simple example should suffice to demonstrate that the same factual situation may give rise to both contractual and tortious liability.

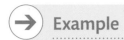 **Example**

A student (A) arranges with a haulier (B) to send his case of belongings to a college, paying in advance for the service to be provided. In the course of performance of this service, the case is placed in an open truck and, as the truck goes round a sharp bend, one side comes down and the case falls off the truck into the river. A has a contract with B. There are reciprocal, voluntarily assumed obligations (A to pay: B to deliver the case). A may therefore bring an action for breach of contract against B. Alternatively, if A can prove negligence on B's part (which may not be difficult, since the assumption must be that it is not normal for a case to be lost in this way), A may sue in tort, since B will be in breach of a duty to take proper care of A's case. Thus, the same facts may give rise to a claim either for breach of contract, or for breach of a duty of care arising in tort.

At first sight it may seem curious to regard the contractual obligation in this situation as superior to that arising in tort, since they are identical. **It is possible, however, because contractual obligations are agreed, to agree to modify the nature of the obligation by contract, for example by inserting an exemption clause in the contract which limits or excludes B's liability** (see generally 7.4 and 7.5). It is the potential for the parties to stipulate the substance of the obligation which led to the belief in the superiority of contractual obligations. So, in ***Henderson v Merrett Syndicates Ltd*** (above), Lord Goff said:

Approached as a matter of principle, therefore, it is right to attribute to that assumption of responsibility, together with its concomitant reliance, a tortious liability, and then to enquire whether or not that liability is excluded by the contract because the latter is inconsistent with it.

To this extent Lord Goff acknowledges the superiority of contract.

Nevertheless, the potential for a contractual term to exclude liability is today seriously diminished. For example, a clause purporting to limit B's liability in the above situation would be valid only if it were reasonable under the Unfair Contract Terms Act (UCTA) 1977 (see 7.6.2), and the exclusion may also be an unfair term under the Unfair Terms in Consumer Contracts Regulations 1999, SI 1999/2083 (see 7.7). Thus, absolute freedom of contract, if it ever existed, has given way to a much more limited freedom which must coexist with many rules of contract law which impose obligations on the parties and limit the substance of a contract.

1.2.2 Remaining significance of the division

Despite the blurring of the distinction between contract and tort which has taken place in recent years, it is easy to identify ways in which contract and tort remain separate.

- An obligation of positive performance some time in the future can normally be created only by contract, even if some of the substance of that obligation will be defined by legal imposition.

- The standard of performance required under a contract is often strict (see 8.2.1.1), while liability for the tort of negligence depends upon the claimant being able to prove that the defendant acted unreasonably.

Nevertheless, the blurring of the distinction between contract and tort has led to the disappearance of, or uncertainty over, differences traditionally regarded as fundamental.

1.2.3 Measure of loss recoverable

The traditional distinction between damages for breach of contract and damages for negligence was that, in the case of the former, damages for loss of profit might be recovered (see **Part 3, p. 337**); while in the latter, lost profit (or pure economic loss) could not be recovered, and the claimant was limited to the recovery of reliance loss (the amount necessary to restore the claimant to the position it was in before the tort took place).

It has been accepted for some time that a claimant bringing proceedings for breach of contract may claim reliance losses rather than lost profits in some circumstances (see **9.4**). If the claimant is unable to establish what the lost profit would have been, because it is too speculative, it may even be forced to claim reliance loss damages (see **9.3.4**). Although English law has flirted with the converse rule, that a person bringing a claim in tort may recover expectation loss (or 'pure economic loss'), this has occurred only in limited circumstances (see **11.5.1**). These restrictions have important repercussions for subcontractors. Therefore, in this field, at least, the notion that contract is the superior norm still prevails to some extent.

1.2.4 Remoteness of damage

In both contract and tort, damages may not be recovered for losses which are too remote a consequence of the breach of contract or breach of duty. **It has been traditional to assert that the test of remoteness is stricter in relation to contract claims than it is in relation to claims in tort, in that the test in contract is one of reasonable contemplations whereas the test in tort is reasonable foreseeability** (*The Heron II* [1969] 1 AC 350). However, in *H. Parsons (Livestock) Ltd v Uttley Ingham & Co. Ltd* [1978] 1 QB 791, the members of the Court of Appeal were unable to agree whether there was any difference at all in the remoteness tests of contract and tort, or whether such difference as there was lay not between contract and tort but between expectation (profit) and reliance (physical) losses. The respective merits of these potential rules, and the policies they may be taken to represent, are discussed below (see generally **9.9.2.5**). There are also signs of some blurring of the distinction as to the remoteness rules in the speeches of Lords Hoffmann and Hope in *Transfield Shipping Inc. v Mercator Shipping Inc., The Achilleas* [2008] UKHL 48, [2009] 1 AC 61, following the adoption of a test of whether there was an 'assumption of responsibility' for the loss in contract, albeit that subsequent decisions at first instance have denied that there was any intention to alter existing principles.

1.2.5 Limitation of actions

Under the Limitation Act 1980, a standard limitation period of six years applies to claims both in contract (s. 5) and in tort (s. 2), with the exception of personal injury cases in tort when the period is three years (s. 11 of the 1980 Act). Nevertheless, a distinction remains between contract and tort, since the time at which the limitation period begins to run varies. In contract it begins to run at the time of breach (i.e., this is the time when the cause of action accrues). In tort it does not begin to run until some damage occurs, because there is no cause of action up to this time. This difference was roundly condemned by Mustill LJ in *Société Commerciale de Reassurance v ERAS (International) Ltd* [1992] 1 Lloyd's Rep 570 at p. 602:

> The different treatment for limitation purposes of claims in contract and in tort is already unsatisfactory because: (1) whatever the legal logic, the fact that claims in contract and in tort between the same parties arising out of the same facts become time-barred on dates which may well be years apart offends common sense;...(3) so far as limitation is concerned, the rules regarding the accrual of the cause of action tend to push the evolution of substantive law in the wrong direction. In most if not all cases a plaintiff will be better off framing his action in tort, whereas, in our judgment, if a contract is in existence this is the natural vehicle for recourse.

Since the decision of the House of Lords in *Hendersen v Merrett Syndicates Ltd* [1995] 2 AC 145 which accepted the existence of an independent or concurrent cause of action in tort, a claim may be brought in tort within six years of the date when the claimant first sustains damage, albeit that if the claim were in contract, e.g. a claim against a surveyor or other professional in respect of a failure to exercise reasonable care and skill, the six-year limitation period would have started when the breach occurred.

1.3 History of contract law

The history of the law of contract is complex and contentious, and those who seek a comprehensive account must refer to specialist works (e.g., Simpson, *A History of the Common Law of Contract* (Oxford University Press, 1987)); Simpson also wrote the historical introduction to Furmston, *Law of Contract* (Cheshire, Fifoot, and Furmston), 15th edn (Oxford University Press, 2007). The intention in this section is to provide a brief historical explanation of some elements of the law of contract, since it is an inevitable feature of the common law, based as it is in the system of precedent, that ancient doctrines sometimes return to haunt the modern law.

Two periods of history are especially significant in the development of the law of contract:

- the period of some three hundred years, ending in the early years of the seventeenth century, when the action for breach of contract first developed
- the second period covers the late eighteenth and nineteenth centuries, which saw the climax of the philosophy of freedom of contract and which laid the foundations upon which our modern law is built.

At the beginning of the thirteenth century the royal courts did not hear actions relating to contracts. Of course, many transactions took place which we would today recognize as contracts, such as sales and loans, but they were left to be regulated by the many specialist or local jurisdictions which existed at the time.

- The first common law action for breach of contract was that of **covenant**. However, it was unable to develop into a general law of contract, because it was restricted to contracts made under seal (see **4.1**).

- A further action of **debt** was developed which applied in the case of informal agreements, and which enabled the recovery of a specific sum of money owed to the claimant on the fiction that the claimant was recovering his own money. Debt nevertheless had its limitations. It did not allow the recovery of an unliquidated sum by way of damages for failure to perform a promised action (as opposed to the mere payment of money). In addition, trial procedures for debt were open to abuse by defendants, making success in such actions something of a lottery.

- When the royal courts finally sought to expand their jurisdiction by taking control over contract actions, they did not seek to develop either of the existing writs (or claims) which today we recognize as contractual in nature. Rather, they turned to a more flexible writ, which was the forerunner of the modern tort of negligence, known as **trespass on the case**. The advantage of the trespass action was that the procedure was far more secure against abuse than was the case for the action of debt. By the end of the fourteenth century the courts would allow claims based on trespass for defective performance of an undertaking, which in the medieval Latin of court pleadings was known as an *assumpsit*.

    Assumpsit is the real foundation of the law of contract, but it developed relatively slowly, since in the early period it was available only for defective performance of an undertaking, and was not available for non-performance. This discrepancy can be explained in terms of formal procedure, but in practical terms was clearly illogical, and it was finally removed in *Thoroughgood's Case* (1584) 2 Co Rep 9a, 76 ER 401. The remaining obstacle to the development of *assumpsit* as a complete contract doctrine was the action for debt, since some courts would not allow an action to recover a specific sum of money on assumpsit, but insisted on the action being brought in debt, with its associated procedural difficulties. This obstacle was removed, and the law of informal contracts brought within the unified cause of action of *assumpsit,* by *Slade's Case* (1602) 4 Co Rep 92a, 76 ER 1072.

In the peculiar way of the common law, the establishment of a unified remedy for all types of contract action was the catalyst for the development of general principles of contract law. The most important, and yet the most baffling to scholars, was the development of the doctrine of consideration. There are broadly two schools of thought as to how consideration came into English law:

- The first attributes it to the doctrine of *causa* found in Roman and civil law, and which is said to have made its way into the common law via Canon law and then the Chancery court.

- The second attributes it to an analogous (but far from identical) requirement of the action of debt, and the requirement of detriment in the action of trespass, which were somehow transferred to the action of *assumpsit* to give it form.

Whichever may be the true explanation, the precise mechanics of the development of the doctrine of consideration are obscure. All that may be said with confidence is that by the seventeenth century the requirement of consideration in informal contracts was in place, and the law of contract began to take on a shape which we still recognize today.

1.4 **Role of contract and contract law**

The central role of contract in our legal and economic systems is not accidental. If lawyers, judges, and (more latterly) Parliament have worked at refining, honing, and polishing the law, and litigants continue to rely on it, it is because contract serves important purposes in society. Indeed, it appears that the device of contract is put to important uses in many diverse societies, and it would be wrong to assume that contract law as we know it is the only model, or is of universal application.

It is essential to distinguish between the device of contract, which has universal qualities, and the law of contract, which is the vehicle for adapting those universal qualities to the particular needs of a given society.

1.4.1 **Role of contract**

All societies require a vehicle through which **planned exchanges** can be made. Societies require methods of ordering existence so that such cooperation as is deemed necessary may take place. The role of planning embraces the need people have to project reliable courses of action into the future. The idea of **exchange** includes not only 'one-off' contracts, but also long-term business relationships comprising perhaps many hundreds of individual contracts; it may also include interpersonal relationships, and even the individual's relationship with the state. There is a relationship of mutual support between societal stability, the idea of planning, and the existence of exchange. The ability to plan ahead is an important factor in creating stability, while a stable society, in which it can be predicted that exchanges will take place, is an essential ingredient of reliable planning.

What may seem to be an entirely theoretical description of the role of contract may be put into context by a simple example. For many readers, the only experience of contracting will be as an ultimate consumer, so that each contract made seems isolated and discrete. In that sort of situation the planning element in contracts is not self-evident.

 Example

When a student purchases a book in a shop there is no doubt that the machinery by which the purchase is executed is a contract, but there is little sense of being merely one link in a chain, since the student is the last link. A moment's consideration will reveal, however, that the particular contract of sale can be achieved only within a complex matrix of other contracts. If it is an academic textbook, it is likely to have been commissioned by a publisher from the author. Both parties derive planning benefits from such a contract. The author knows that the time spent labouring on the book will be rewarded by publication and (she hopes) the payment of royalties on sales. The publisher is able to fill a gap in the list of books it publishes, in the secure knowledge that it will have such a book to offer to booksellers after a certain period. Before the decision to go ahead with the book is made, the publisher's employees will probably have carried out some market research, and a decision will have been reached on the price at which such a book will sell. The publisher will seek to meet that price target by making contracts with printers and binders which will keep costs at the estimates made when fixing the price of the book. The printers and binders will in turn make long-term contracts with their »

raw material suppliers, so that they too may be sure that their costs remain within estimates. Delivery services, wholesalers, and retail bookshops will all be involved in the process of delivering the book to the ultimate consumer.

Businessmen do not assume that the link between author and reader will be achieved by a catalogue of fortunate accidents: they plan every stage of the marketing of a book, and they achieve confidence in the planning by securing it with contracts. **This matrix of contractual relationships, against which any particular contract must be viewed, explains why the first instinct of contract lawyers is to seek to preserve an agreement under threat, since much more is at stake when one contract fails than just the relationship between the two contracting parties.**

1.4.2 **Role of contract law**

If the role of the device of contract is to provide for confident planning of exchanges, the role of contract law is to mould those planned exchanges to the particular society the law serves. Thus, English contract law reflects the politico-economic philosophy prevailing in this country. Theories of the law of contract, which in recent years have been a fashionable subject of academic debate, are simply the reflection of these politico-economic philosophies. Just as few claim that any single such philosophy has a monopoly of the right answers for any given society, so it is difficult to claim that any single contract theory provides all the right answers as far as the development of the law of contract is concerned. But that does not mean that contract theory is without value.

1.4.2.1 The significance of theory

There are many judges and practising lawyers who would deny the existence of any theory underlying the common law of contract, or who would dismiss theory as unrelated to the real world. This attitude may be understandable, since judges and lawyers must decide individual cases on their merits in accordance with the law, and are not primarily concerned with the elaboration of theory. Nevertheless, it may also be shortsighted. The law does not stand still, but rather has its own internal dynamism. In particular, changes in the law may result from judicial reasoning by reference to values where the court perceives the need to make a choice of how the law should develop to meet a situation not previously encountered, or where the scope of a particular rule has not been precisely defined. Consistent development of the law, so that such changes 'fit' within the existing scheme of things, assumes that judges have a sense of what the scheme of things is. Thus, an understanding of the theory of contract is essential to rational choices in developing the law, and should provide students of law with criteria by which to assess the appropriateness of choices made. A satisfactory theory must explain how the law has developed to the point it is at today, and must provide the basis for establishing how the law may develop in the future by indicating general principles capable of giving rise to specific rules. Dissatisfaction with theory in general may have been caused by the growing inability of classical theory, which has been the dominating theory, to account for some of the existing rules of the law of contract. The question remains whether there is any more satisfactory theory which can take its place.

The discussion in this section inevitably refers to the substance of the law, which is examined later in this book. Readers may therefore find it beneficial to return to this section after completing their study of the substantive law.

1.4.2.2 Classical theory

The roots of classical theory go back at least as far as the eighteenth century. In seeking to explain the somewhat adventitious development of contract law in England, nineteenth-century commentators borrowed from the writings of French legal theorists, who by 1804 had succeeded in embodying in the French civil code a highly individualist conception of contract. The parties were regarded as having the power and the unrestricted freedom to determine how their relationship was to be governed. This French approach, which was the product of the political liberalism of the eighteenth century, fell in with the economic liberalism of nineteenth-century England to produce an equally individualist theory of contract law in this country. Nevertheless, the realities of the process of adjudication meant that the substantive law was obliged to move away from a purely individualist or subjective approach to contract, so that the much vaunted sanctity of individual autonomy in contracting, which made contract immune from judicial interference, was much more a theoretical ideal than a rule of law.

When we talk about the classical theory of contract today—see Fried, *Contract As Promise: A theory of contractual obligation* (Harvard University Press, 1981)—we must consider a modified form of the theory which has tried to account for the way the law has developed. **Nevertheless, at the core of this 'modern' classical theory is the binding nature of the promise which has been voluntarily made.**

The crucial element in contract, which marks it out as different from most other areas of the law of obligations, is that it is more than reactive: it is creative. It does not merely provide the means of resolving disputes which may arise when certain events happen: it provides the mechanisms whereby things can be made to happen. For early contract scholars it was a crucial observable phenomenon that without any reliance by either party the law regarded the mutual exchange of promises as, without more, sufficient to create a binding obligation (see **4.2.1.1**).

Tort and restitution were obligations produced by a reaction to events; but contract produced obligation as the result of the mere *exercise of will* in the form of promise. It was not surprising, therefore, that promise became the core of the theory, since it appears to be the essential ingredient marking contract out as separate from the rest of the law of obligations.

Before we examine how classical theory fits with the law of contract, we should examine why the mere fact of promise (or voluntary undertaking) produces obligation.

1. A first explanation, which owes much to political liberal theory, is that there is a *moral obligation* inherent in promising which is derived from the social convention of creating expectations by one's undertaking (Fried, *Contract As Promise* (1981), pp. 14–17). The social convention came into being because the liberal ideal of respect for persons and property could be achieved only if reliable cooperation could be established. There is support for this idea in the rule that the measure of damages for breach of contract is the amount necessary to put the non-breaching party into the position they would have been in had the contract been performed (see **9.2**), which is generally regarded as protecting that party's expectation under the contract. We know that this protection of expectation is restricted by rules relating to remoteness (see **9.9.2**) and the fact that it is not possible to recover for loss of

expectation where that expectation loss is too speculative (see 9.3.4). However, a cogent argument can be made that these doctrines are no more than necessary limits to cope with procedural problems such as the fallibility of the means of proof, and do not take away from the basic premise that the promisee's actual expectation is to be protected. A more serious objection arises out of the fact that the objectivization of contract apparent in the formation of contracts (see 2.1) and in remedies for breach of contract (see 9.3) appears to be more than procedural, and seems to substitute for the actual expectation a collective appraisal of what the expectation should have been.

2. A second explanation of the binding nature of promise, not entirely distinct from the first, derives from the liberal economic theories of the nineteenth century. **Here, individual autonomy is not the goal itself, but it is a pivotal tool in the achievement of the actual goal of *maximization of wealth* to the greater good of all in society.** Maximization of wealth is achieved by market exchanges, where both or all the parties involved count themselves as benefited by the exchange which has taken place. The concept of market depends upon the binding nature of bargains made in the market, so that the individual's promise is required to be binding for the market system to work. Support for this version of classical theory can be found in the existing English rules relating to exemption clauses in genuinely freely negotiated contracts (see 7.2). The purpose of such devices is said by economists to be to provide a mechanism whereby the parties may allocate the risks of the enterprise between them: if they are both wealth-maximizers they may be assumed to have allocated those risks in a mutually beneficial way. To refuse to enforce exemption clauses in such circumstances would be wrong, since the effect would be to reallocate the risk away from what the parties had calculated was mutually beneficial. Nevertheless, classical theory is ill-equipped to account for such intervention in freedom of contract as is provided, for example, by UCTA 1977 (see 7.6). On the other hand, the recent trend to accept the parties' own allocation of the risks in the context of commercial contracts (see 7.6.6.2) indicates a return to the basic principles of classical contracting in this sector.

It is not surprising that classical theory provides a coherent explanation of the rules of formation of agreement (**Chapter 2**). Promise is the essence of the theory. Promises create expectation, and can only do so if clear lines of communication are established. These rules do no more than set out the means whereby promises are made. Nevertheless, the fact that the rules are consistent with the theory cannot hide the fact that there is increasing doubt, even among the judiciary, about whether the existing rules really conform to what business people do in practice (see below).

It is perhaps surprising that classical theory should cavil at the doctrine of consideration (Fried, *Contract As Promise* (1981), pp. 28–39, especially at p. 35). After all, the paradigm of consideration is usually said to be the mutual exchange of promises. Perhaps the consideration doctrine is no more than a trace of the Protestant work ethic in the common law: a rule against getting something for nothing! More probably, it shows that the common law idea of contract is founded in economic rather than political liberalism: wealth maximization results from mutual exchange, and there is no exchange involved in gratuitous promising.

Beyond the rules relating to the formation of contracts, the position of classical theory is less secure. Where the law must react to events which are outside the scope of the will of the parties, or to which the parties have for whatever reason given no attention, the insistence of classical theory on the autonomy of the will of the parties is inconsistent with some of the rules of the law of contract as they have developed. Thus in relation to mistake (**Chapter 3**), illegal contracts (Chapter 16), implied terms (see **6.4**), and frustration (**Chapter 12**), the approach of contemporary law had developed in such a way as to impose a solution, often based on the criterion of what is reasonable in the circumstances, and to abandon the fiction of searching for and complying with the will of the parties. However, the most important development in recent years has been a reversion to greater recognition of the parties' intentions as expressed in their agreement and as understood by the objective bystander so that there is no need to 'add' to give effect to the parties' intentions since the parties' intentions can be construed to reveal their agreement, e.g. Lord Hoffmann's approach to the question of terms implied in fact in ***Attorney General of Belize v Belize Telecom Ltd*** [2009] UKPC 10, [2009] 1 WLR 1988, although terms implied in law remain an externally imposed solution. It follows that classical theory is not wholly without relevance, and may be experiencing something of a revival in English contract law, albeit in an objective sense of seeking to give effect to the parties' intentions. There is no doubt that classical theory shaped the law in a crucial period of its development, and that it draws attention to an important element in modern contract law, the binding nature of mutual promises. However, it cannot be regarded as an entirely satisfactory theory when it is unable to account for some important areas of the law. Its failure in this regard probably reflects the fact that the politico-economic philosophy which inspired it, is no longer the philosophy underlying our contemporary law. Nevertheless, the doctrine of binding precedent ensures that cases decided during the period when the classical concept of contract was at its height remain influential today, and it is for this reason that classical theory continues to make a significant contribution to existing law.

In recent years two separate perceptions have generated the belief among many commentators that classical theory is unable to explain the entirety of modern contract law.

- **The first is that contract law is not merely a response to the exercise of will by the contracting parties. Contract law also responds to events, often by imposing an obligation generally regarded as nevertheless contractual, or by modifying an already existing obligation. In each case the reaction of the law is independent of the will of the parties.**

  Examples of this response to events may be found in the law relating to promissory estoppel (see generally **4.8**) and other areas of law.

- **The second perception is that the limited empirical evidence available (see Beale and Dugdale (1975)) suggests that in practice business people do not behave in a manner consistent with the classical conception of contract.**

  For example, only in a formal sense could their contractual undertakings be regarded as promises, or the product of an exercise of will, since they frequently had little knowledge of the detailed undertakings contained in contractual documents. Moreover, business people frequently do not seek to avail themselves of the full remedy available for breach of contract (damages for lost profit) in cases of mutual exchange of promises but no performance. Thus, where an order was cancelled before any work had been done, most of the firms surveyed would accept the cancellation without seeking compensation. Where there had been some, but not complete, performance by the time of cancellation, a charge would be made, usually based on the cost of work actually done, and an allowance for profit related not to the entire contract but solely to the means of computing actual costs incurred.

1.4.2.3 Reliance-based theories

The most significant post-classical theory of contract is based on the notion that obligation results from the fact of reliance (and its most eloquent exponent has been Professor Atiyah: see especially (1978) 94 LQR 193). Both the practice of business people and some of the legal doctrines noted above (especially promissory estoppel) suggest that the important factor is not the promise made, but the fact of reliance on it. Promise remains important in providing evidence of what has been undertaken, but it is not the source of obligation. Even in the field of formation of agreements, where classical theory is relatively secure, the analysis is sometimes improved by considering reliance as the source of obligation. This view is certainly a more rational explanation of the cases relating to what are known respectively as the 'battle of forms' (see **2.4.2.3**) and 'agreements to agree' (see **3.1.4.2**).

In general it seems that our instinct of obligation (or its absence) lies not in the mere fact of promise, but in the quality of the reaction to the promise. Consider this well-known example:

Example

A says to B, 'Let's go out for dinner. I'll pay for the meal; you buy the wine.' B agrees, and they arrange to meet at the restaurant. A does not keep the date, preferring to go to the cinema with C. It is almost universally accepted that A's behaviour should not be regarded as a breach of contract actionable in the courts.

For classical theory, that conclusion presents a problem, since there appears to be no difference in moral terms between this promise and a promise of a more commercial nature (e.g., to deliver goods for payment). The social convention of keeping promises applies equally to both. Neither is there an absence of exchange: A's promise is not gratuitous, and therefore appears to meet the wealth-maximizing criterion. Why then is it our first instinct that A's promise did not give rise to a contractual obligation? The answer appears to lie in the quality of our reaction to the promise, which involves weighing the extent and nature of the reliance placed upon it. Thus, serious consequences are likely to result from the failure to deliver goods which have been promised in return for payment, but it is not easy to predict very serious consequences resulting from the failure to keep a dinner date. Notice, however, that our reaction is not in terms of what actually happened: it is a generalized reaction based upon what in our experience would normally be the case, or what would be reasonable in the circumstances. It seems clear, therefore, that in some circumstances reliance may provide a better explanation of the source of contractual obligations than does classical theory.

Nevertheless, it also seems that, like classical theory, reliance alone cannot account for the whole of the law of contract.

- There is the problem of wholly executory contracts, which are enforceable after the mere exchange of promises. They may be less significant in real life than the place given to them in the textbooks, but there is no denying that the law does enforce contracts which exist in the absence of any reliance.

- There is the problem of promissory estoppel, which although a source of obligation is only a qualified source: it does not create any new obligations where none existed previously (see **4.8.3.2**). How can reliance be the major source of obligation when the principal reliance-based doctrine does not itself create active obligations?

- There is the problem of those rules of contract law which are based on criteria independent of the parties to the contract. A weakness of the reliance theory is that it is as much based in the relationship between the contracting parties as is classical theory. In respect of classical theory it was suggested that one flaw was its inability to cope with those rules of contract law which permit judicial intervention in the agreement between the parties according to what is reasonable rather than according to what is presumed to have been their intention. The same criticism applies to reliance theory, in that it is unable to account for the court's intervention in the contract on grounds of reasonableness which does not derive from the dealings between the parties but from a collective or community sense of what is right in the circumstances.

1.4.2.4 A collective theory of contract

A somewhat different response to the inadequacy of classical theory has been the suggestion that contractual obligation is derived from the need to protect reasonable or legitimate expectation (e.g., Reiter and Swan, 'Contracts and the protection of reasonable expectation' in *Studies in Contract Law* (Toronto: Butterworths, 1980), pp. 1–23 and Steyn, 'Contract law: Fulfilling the reasonable expectations of honest men' (1997) 113 LQR 433).

This theory is similar to classical theory in seeing expectation as the essence of contract, but it goes beyond classical theory in recognizing that promise is not the only means of creating expectation. **Indeed, it assumes that in many circumstances society (through the courts) will regard one party's expectation as reasonably held and so deserving of protection irrespective of the will of the other party.** So, some expectation will be created by promise, some by reliance, some by other means, including perhaps the protection of certain classes within society and 'fairness'. The essence of the collective approach to contract and its basis in reasonable expectation is that it endeavours to be sufficiently flexible to account for most, if not all, observable instances of contractual obligation.

This theory rests heavily on the roles both of the device of contract and of contract law. Contract law, it was suggested above, is the vehicle which adapts the device of contract, which is important for its facilitation of planned exchanges, to the need of a particular society. Classical contract law, therefore, reflected the use made of planned exchanges in the aggressively free enterprise society of the nineteenth century. It would not be surprising to find classical ideas of contract law unsatisfactory if the nature of society had itself changed. Most people accept that there has indeed been a change in the nature of society since the nineteenth century, from out-and-out free enterprise to mixed economy. That is, in our society today resources are allocated partly through the decisions of private individuals and companies, and partly through the decisions of government (including the courts). The precise balance of the mixture changes from time to time, and since the 1980s there has been a swing away from a more collectivist approach to one which is more individualist.

In this context 'allocation of resources' involves the redistribution of wealth between the more and less powerful in society by means other than taxation and welfare legislation. Thus, the law administered by the courts does not strive only for allocative efficiency, as a free-market approach would prescribe. It also contains an element of distributive justice which cannot be explained in terms of market economics. The law, whether it is a judicial creation or the creation of Parliament, attempts to redress the balance between the weak and strong elements in society, protecting the former against the latter. On the other hand, the very idea of a *mixed* economy means that where the functions of balance and protection are not required, the legal system must enable private ordering of exchange. Thus, the law must assess the level of intervention required according to the type of contract confronting it. It is able to do so by amending the nature of what it deems to be a reasonable expectation according to the circumstances of the case.

The relevant circumstances to be consulted in evaluating what are the reasonable expectations in any given situation will include the nature of the parties, and especially their relative positions. However, they will also include the nature of the subject matter of the contract, the manner in which the contract was entered into, and relevant public policies of the society in which the contract was made. The result is that we should have general principles of the law of contract, but also specific rules tailored to particular types of contractual activity. This theoretical breaking down of contractual activity into distinct groups, to which distinct rules may apply because of the different assumptions we make about what would be a reasonable expectation within each particular type of activity, appears to have been reflected in more recent developments in the substantive law. Although there is still a common core of principles of contract law, many discrete areas of contractual activity have developed their own specialized rules. Employment contracts, contracts for the sale of goods (see 1.5), contracts made by consumers, contracts of insurance, contracts of international trade, are all examples where it is necessary to proceed from an understanding of the general law of contract to more specific rules relevant to the particular context alone. A detailed example will serve to illustrate the point.

Example

In contracts for the sale of goods there is no blanket implied term guaranteeing the quality of goods sold, but there is such an implied term where the seller is selling 'in the course of a business' (Sale of Goods Act (SGA) 1979, s. 14(1) and (2): see 6.4.2.4). This implied term about quality can be excluded by express words in the contract of sale where the buyer is also in business, but it is not possible to exclude the guarantee of quality in the case of a sale to a consumer (UCTA 1977, s. 6(2) and (3): see 7.6.4.1).

Thus, we find that within the law relating to the sale of goods there are differing rules which apply according to the nature of the contracting parties. The rules which apply between business people exist to enforce the bargain made between them by their express promises (see, e.g., **Photo Production Ltd v Securicor Transport Ltd** [1980] AC 827 and case law on reasonableness under UCTA 1977 in the context of commercial contracts), but the rules applicable in the case of contracts with consumers impose standards of 'fair' contractual behaviour intended to prevent the stronger party taking advantage of the weaker, and those standards reflect the collective values of society as a whole.

1.4.2.5 Formalism and realism

One further theory, which also reflects the practical distinction in approach to commercial and consumer contracts, merits some mention here. Adams and Brownsword ('The ideologies of contract' (1987) 7 LS 205, *Understanding Contract Law,* 5th edn (Sweet and Maxwell, 2007), and

Brownsword, *Contract Law: Themes for the twenty-first century,* 2nd edn (Oxford University Press, 2006), Ch. 7) argue that there are competing ideologies in the approach of the judiciary to contract cases. They believe that these competing ideologies assist both in explaining contract decisions and in predicting future decisions, although the ideologies lead to tensions in what Adams and Brownsword refer to as the contract 'rule book'.

- **Formalism** regards the rule book as a closed system of principles which are to be mechanically applied, and it is therefore divorced from the results in individual cases.

- However, most modern judges tend to adopt a **realist approach** which may involve challenges to the rule book where it stands in the way of achieving justice. The realist approach can itself be broken down into:

  (a) market-individualism

  (b) consumer-welfarism.

The philosophy behind the *market-individualist* approach is essentially commercial and focuses on contract as the means to facilitate competitive exchanges. Therefore certainty is a vital influencing factor for market-individualists, who in this context seek to defend the reasonable assumptions of the parties. On the other hand, the *consumer-welfarist* approach is more interventionist (e.g., consumer protection) and focuses on questions of fairness and reasonableness. As a result it is far more flexible and protectionist in its approach compared to market-individualism. As Brownsword states in *Contract Law: Themes for the twenty-first century,* 2nd edn (2006), at p. 137:

> Putting the contrast very generally, whereas the former ideology insists upon contractors being held to their freely agreed exchanges, the latter seeks to ensure a fair deal for consumer contractors and, more generally, to relieve against harsh or unconscionable bargains.

It is possible to identify these differing approaches in individual judgments and *ratios* of cases: see Adams and Brownsword, *Understanding Contract Law,* 5th edn (Sweet and Maxwell, 2007).

1.4.2.6 Conclusion

If any single theory can explain the disparate elements of current contract law, it is perhaps the chameleon-like theory of protection of reasonable expectations. It has been argued that the theory rests on a circular argument, since the expectation exists only by virtue of the fact of its protection, and so the theory is no more than a self-fulfilling prophecy. This argument neglects the importance of the role of the device of contract (see 1.4.1), which suggests that the function of confident forward planning which is facilitated by contract would continue to be used by the great majority of contracting parties whether or not contracts were legally enforceable. Equally, the mere fact that contracts are enforceable would not cause parties to contract unless the device of contract was perceived to be socially useful. In other words, like classical theory, the theory of protection of reasonable expectations derives its sense of obligation from social convention, from the socially practised habit of contracting in order to provide for planned exchanges.

The important difference between classical, promise-based theory and the protection of reasonable expectation is that under the latter theory the content of the expectation may be dictated by something other than an individual's voluntary undertaking. Of course, in many contracts, especially those of a commercial nature, the law allows the dimension of individual autonomy to govern the expectation, and in those situations this theory may be little different from classical theory. Thus, in commercial matters the law must be the servant and not the master of those engaged in business. But in many other types of contract the law imposes limits on the dimension of individual autonomy in contracting, and contractual expectations are shaped by collective evaluations of what the content of obligations should be.

1.5 Contract and the sale of goods

Contracts for the sale of goods are amongst the most common types of contract encountered. For many readers, their main experience of contracting will have been in purchasing goods. For that reason, many of the hypothetical examples of contracts used in this text are based on simple sales transactions. Nevertheless, it is important to enter a note of caution about contracts for the sale of goods. Such contracts have developed as a distinct category, to which the general principles of contract law apply, but on top of which have been grafted special rules applicable to sales transactions alone. This law was originally codified in 1893, and subsequent amendments have been consolidated in the SGA 1979, as amended. A detailed study of these rules requires a separate book (e.g., Atiyah, Adams, and MacQueen, *The Sale of Goods*, 12th edn (Pearson Longman, 2010). Particular rules applicable to the sale of goods are noted throughout this text, but it is necessary here to explain the important impact of the notion of 'property' which is central to such contracts.

1.5.1 The central role of property rights

Section 2(1) of the SGA 1979 defines a contract of sale of goods as a 'contract by which the seller transfers or agrees to transfer the property in goods to the buyer for a money consideration'. 'Property' here means ownership, and so the legal effect of a sales transaction is to transfer the ownership of the goods from seller to buyer. When dealing with sales contracts it is important to keep that legal effect in mind, since it has important consequences for the rest of the law.

The overriding importance of the transfer of ownership is well demonstrated by the decision in ***Rowland v Divall*** [1923] 2 KB 500.

> The plaintiff had bought a car from the defendant. He then resold the car to a third party. The police repossessed the car after a period of four months, the car having been stolen by a person who had sold it to the defendant. The plaintiff repaid the money he had received from the third party, and then claimed back the price he had paid to the defendant, on the ground of total failure of consideration (see **10.5.1**). That is, he claimed that he had received nothing of what he was entitled to receive under the contract of sale. The defendant sought to resist this claim by saying that the failure of consideration was not total, since the plaintiff had had the (potential) use of the car for four months. His defence failed, because the plaintiff was entitled under a contract of sale not merely to use of the car but to legal ownership. Since the car was stolen, the defendant was not in a position to transfer legal ownership and this meant that the whole contract failed.

1.5.2 The power to transfer ownership

The general rule is that the seller can transfer only such title to goods as the seller himself enjoys (SGA 1979, s. 21(1)). Therefore, where the seller is not the owner, he cannot transfer ownership to the buyer. Unfortunately, lawyers and judges often still refer to this rule by its Latin name, so it is necessary to give it here: *nemo dat quod non habet*. The rule is subject to a number of important exceptions, which are of particular importance in the law of agency.

The operation of the rule can be demonstrated by reference to the facts of ***Rowland v Divall*** [1923] 2 KB 500 (above). The plaintiff was obliged to refund the money to the third party to whom he thought he had sold the car, because he had not been able to pass the ownership of the car to that third party. The reason for his inability to pass on ownership was that he had not been the owner, since the defendant, who had purported to sell the car to him, was also not the owner at the time of the sale. Thus, a defect early in the chain of sales (the defendant did not acquire ownership when he unwittingly bought the car from a thief) caused all the subsequent sales to be defective because ownership was not transferred by the transaction. Of course, had one of the exceptions to the general rule applied to any one of the chain of transactions, ownership would have been transferred even if the seller had not himself been the owner, and from that point on subsequent sales would not have been defective. For example, if the thief had been a mercantile agent who was known regularly to sell cars on behalf of others, and had been in possession of the car with the consent of the owner before he misappropriated it, the defendant would have acquired good title (Factors Act 1889, s. 2(1)) and the subsequent sales in the chain would have been unaffected by the early defect in title.

The *nemo dat* rule is clearly an obstacle to the free flow of goods in commerce, especially where it necessitates the unravelling of complex chains of sales, and the exceptions to the rule have been developed precisely to avoid, if possible, the need to unravel contracts which at the time of the transaction neither contracting party knew to be affected by a defect in title to the goods purportedly sold.

1.5.3 Void and voidable contracts and sales to third parties

The rule relating to the power to transfer ownership is further complicated by the distinction which must be made between void and voidable contracts.

- **A void contract is automatically no contract at all; it is treated as if it had never been made, so that a void contract can have no effect.** An agreement which is affected by a fundamental 'common mistake' is, for example, void: the contract fails from the very beginning and no consequences can ensue from it (see 13.1).

- **On the other hand, a voidable contract remains a valid contract until the party who has the right to complain takes steps to have it set aside. Should that party choose not to have the contract set aside, the contract is valid and all the usual effects of contract flow from it.** An example of a voidable contract is an agreement affected by misrepresentation (see Chapter 14).

These differences of effect between void and voidable contracts have an impact on the power to transfer ownership. Since a void contract can have no effect, it is impotent to transfer ownership between the purported seller and buyer. Thus, if a contract of sale from A to B is void, a third party (C) who subsequently purports to buy the goods from B cannot obtain ownership of the goods since B is not the owner. This consequence can be avoided only if one of the exceptions to the rule about transfer of ownership applies (see 1.5.2).

On the other hand, since a voidable contract is of full effect until actually set aside, it can transfer ownership between seller and buyer. Thus, if a contract of sale from A to B is merely voidable, a third party (C) who subsequently purports to buy the goods from B does obtain ownership of the goods provided the sale by B to C takes place before A takes steps to have the contract set aside. This rule is embodied in s. 23 of the SGA 1979. A close corollary of the rule is that once third-party rights have intervened in the case of a voidable contract, the party who had the right to have the contract set aside (rescind it) loses that right (see, e.g., **3.2.2.2** and 14.5.2.4).

1.6 **The globalization of contract law**

There are a number of international influences on the principles of English contract law which have had a considerable impact on its development over recent years. These developments have in the first place meant that some changes to substantive principles have been necessary, e.g. to implement European legislation. In addition, English contract law needs to adapt to the demands of contracting in an electronic age which is necessarily international. The growth of e-commerce poses considerable challenges for existing principles. Alongside these developments, there have been a number of projects the objective of which has been the harmonization of contract and commercial law principles. Given the increasingly international dimension of contracting, it is seen as important to address differences in principles and treatment of specific issues arising in contractual formation, performance, and breach.

1.6.1 **Harmonized statements of principle**

In the latter part of the twentieth century, there were a number of attempts to harmonize or produce statements of principles in an effort to rationalize the distinctions apparent between jurisdictions. In the context of international sales contracts, the United Nations Commission on International Trade Law (UNCITRAL) was responsible for the 1980 Vienna Convention on Contracts for the International Sale of Goods (CISG). As an international convention, this can have effect only if ratified by the country concerned. To date the Vienna Convention has not been ratified by the UK, although it has been ratified by most other significant trading nations and now forms part of the legal principles applicable to international sales contracts within those jurisdictions.

In 1994, UNIDROIT, the International Institute for the Unification of Private Law, produced its *Principles of International Commercial Contracts* in an attempt to provide a uniform set of principles (or articles) which might be adopted for use in any jurisdiction. The intention is that these principles can be adopted by the parties as governing their contractual dealings. The principles are truly international, in the sense that the participants to the discussions who devised the principles come from a range of backgrounds: common law, civil law, and socialist traditions (see Furmston, 'Unidroit General Principles for International Commercial Contracts' (1996) 10 JCL 11).

At the same time the Lando Commission produced a set of contract law principles for Europe which might be used as the basis for harmonization of contract and commercial law within the

European Union (experience with the implementation of relevant European directives having highlighted the fundamental differences between the legal backgrounds in Member States) and, in the meantime, might also be explicitly adopted by the parties. These *Principles of European Contract Law* (PECL) were published in three parts and Parts 1 and 2 form part of a single volume (Lando and Beale, *Principles of European Contract Law: Parts I and II* (Kluwer Law International, 2000) and Lando, *Principles of European Contract Law: Part III* (Kluwer Law International, 2003)). As we shall see, there are many similarities between the UNIDROIT principles and PECL. However, neither have any legal force and their use will depend upon adoption by the parties. Both UNIDROIT and PECL have been cited as examples of alternative approaches and how the law might develop; for example, discussions of such principles are included in Law Commission Consultation Papers as a matter of course. It is therefore important that students should both be aware of their existence and have some exposure to examples of relevant articles in individual instances. For this reason, individual articles are referred to in this text. Since the articles of the new *Draft Common Frame of Reference* (DCFR), intended as the European 'toolkit', appear to be based on and overlap with the provisions of PECL, it will be interesting to see whether PECL is subsumed by the DCFR. There are some clear differences, e.g. scope (DCFR is much broader in its coverage), level of detail, and differences in language (DCFR refers to 'party autonomy' whereas PECL uses 'freedom of contract'). This text now makes reference to UNIDROIT, PECL, and DCFR provisions for academic and comparative interest.

Where relevant and of interest, this book also highlights some decisions of Commonwealth courts, e.g. the High Court of Australia and the Supreme Court of Canada, and principles of substantive law, e.g. § 90 of the American Restatement of Contracts (2d), for the purposes of indicating how these jurisdictions have approached a particular issue or legal dilemma, e.g. alteration promises (see **4.8.6**) and privity (see **11.3.3** and **11.6.4**). It has become common practice for judges to refer to a range of sources as justifying their decisions. This factor alone is further evidence of the internationalization of contract law.

1.6.2 Europeanization of contract law: European directives and the Common Frame of Reference

1.6.2.1 Directives and harmonization

The European Union has introduced a number of measures, essentially in the field of consumer protection, as directives, which have required implementation by Member States. These have had considerable influence on the law of consumer protection and, less directly, on general approaches to contracting. The most significant in terms of general contract law is probably Directive 1993/13/EC on unfair terms in consumer contracts (implemented and now in force as the Unfair Terms in Consumer Contracts Regulations 1999, SI 1999/2083, discussed at 7.7). Although the central importance of this directive is its scope and challenge to the fairness of terms in consumer contracts, it also introduced the concept of 'good faith' as a principle of English contract law (see **1.6.3**). Another example of a directive discussed in this text is the Distance Selling Directive 1999/7/EC, which protects consumers in distance sales or services contracts (implemented as the Consumer Protection (Distance Selling) Regulations 2000, SI 2000/2334). This directive is relevant to contracts concluded through the electronic medium, e.g. Internet contracts. There have also been directives aimed at achieving an effective basis for e-commerce in the European Union, namely the Electronic Signatures Directive 1999/93/EC (implemented in part by the Electronic Communications Act 2000 and in part by the Electronic Signatures Regulations 2002, SI 2002/318) and the E-Commerce Directive 2000/31/EC (implemented by the Electronic Commerce (EC Directive) Regulations 2002, SI 2002/2013; and discussed at **5.4.6**). The Injunctions Directive 1998/27/EC (implemented by Part 8 of the Enterprise Act 2002) has ensured that in the consumer context there is an effective enforcement mechanism to ensure the effectiveness of these measures (discussed at 7.7.7.1).

The Consumer Protection from Unfair Trading Regulations 2008, SI 2008/1277 (CPRs), which came into force on 26 May 2008, implement the EU Unfair Commercial Practices Directive (UCPD) 2005/29/EC. This directive is designed to combat unfair behaviour in business to consumer contracts by prohibiting certain marketing and selling practices. The CPRs prohibit traders in all sectors from engaging in unfair commercial (mainly marketing and selling) practices against consumers and set out rules that determine when commercial practices are unfair (reg. 3). Regulation 5 covers misleading actions (including false or deceptive information) and reg. 6 is aimed at misleading material omissions. Regulation 7 seeks to prohibit aggressive commercial practices involving harassment, coercion, or undue influence. The CPRs create various offences relating to these unfair commercial practices (enforceable via the Enterprise Act 2002, Enterprise Act 2002 (Part 8 Community Infringements Specified UK Laws) Order 2003/1374, as amended) but do not impact directly on 'the rules on the validity, formation and effect of a contract' and do not provide individual consumers with the ability to claim damages in the event of infringements of the CPRs.

The UCPD is a maximum harmonization directive so that Member States may not adopt measures which are more restrictive, i.e. which impose higher standards of consumer protection. This was confirmed in *VTB-VAB NV v Total Belgium NV*, C-261/07 [2009] 3 CMLR 17.

The 'Europeanization' of contract law (in the sense of general principles) has been fairly limited because it has largely been aimed at consumer transactions (although the Directive on Self-Employed (Commercial Agents) 1986/653/EC, has a more general impact on agency law in the commercial context and see also the Late Payment Directive 2000/35/EC (**10.1.3.2**)).

1.6.2.2 Review of the acquis and 'The Way Forward'

The Commission has been reviewing a number of existing consumer protection directives having an impact on contract law as part of 'The Way Forward' (see 1.6.2.1) and has confirmed its intention to move away from minimum harmonization via directives (leaving Member States free to fix a higher level of protection) to maximum harmonization (or exact harmonization) as the only way of ensuring consistency in application across Member States. In February 2006 the then DTI issued a consultation and report by academics on the review of the EU consumer acquis. In February 2007 the Commission issued its delayed Green Paper on the Review of the Consumer Acquis. This document set out various options for reform of the directives and suggested areas that could be revised with a view to creating an improved framework for consumer protection and simplifying consumers' rights and responsibilities. In October 2008 the European Commission published a proposal for a new Consumer Rights Directive, *Proposal for a Directive on Consumer Rights*, COM (2008) 614 final. This framework directive would repeal four existing European consumer directives—the Doorstep Selling Directive 85/577/EEC, the Unfair Terms in Consumer Contracts Directive 93/13/EEC, the Distance Selling Directive 97/7/EC, and the Consumer Sales and Guarantees Directive 1999/44/EC—and replace them with a single horizontal directive: <http://ec.europa.eu/consumers/rights/cons_acquis_en.htm>.

In November 2008, the government published a consultation on this proposal and a full response in July 2009. A White Paper, 'A Better Deal for Consumers: Delivering real help now and change for the future' was published in July 2009. Chapter 4, 'Modernising consumer law' covers the implementation of the proposed directive in the UK. The House of Lords published its report in July 2009 (HL Paper 126-I and II) recommending that the government should not agree to the proposal as drafted and called for further research on consumer behaviour. In particular, the report called for any directive to set minimum standards so that existing consumer protection should not be reduced (see. e.g. the proposal to remove the existing English law ability to reject faulty goods, discussed at 8.5.3.1).

1.6.2.3 European contract law: *Draft Common Frame of Reference*

In 1989 and 1994 the European Parliament adopted two resolutions advocating the creation of a European Code of Private Law as the most effective method to achieve harmonization and complete the internal market. In 1999 the Pavia Group produced a preliminary draft containing valuable comparative information and models for a potential future code ('European Civil Code—Preliminary Draft, Study Group for a European Civil Code, Academy of European Private Lawyers'). In the same year the European Parliament determined that there should be 'greater convergence in civil law' and in March 2000 the European Parliament asked the Commission to study this possibility. In July 2001 the Commission issued a 'Communication on European Contract Law' (Communication from the EU Commission to the Council and European Parliament on European Contract Law, 11 July 2001, COM (2001) 398 final). The Commission stated that its aim was to broaden the debate, i.e. to move beyond the purely academic. The Commission's communication contained a number of options for action, ranging from doing nothing, the promotion of non-binding common principles and standard forms, rationalization and improvement of existing legislation, and finally, to the pivotal issue of adoption of a new instrument at European level (a European contract code). The Commission consulted on these possible options and issued its action plan in February 2003 ('A More Coherent European Contract Law', COM (2003) 68 final). In this action plan the Commission appeared to back away from the option of an imposed European contract code in favour of improving the coherence of existing instruments concerning contract law and promoting the wider use of standard contract terms across the EU. Both measures would appear to be necessary precursors to the more radical step of devising a contract code at some later date. **The aim therefore is to produce 'The Common Frame of Reference for European Contract Law' (CFR) or 'toolbox' (fundamental principles, key definitions, and model provisions) to be used when revising existing legislation or producing new legislation covering contract law.**

In 2004 the Commission issued a further document ('The Way Forward', COM (2004) 651 final) relating to its aims in producing the Common Frame of Reference, including improving the existing contract law legislation, providing guidance to Member States so that greater consistency could be achieved when devising and drafting legislation on contract law and, perhaps the real agenda, acting as the basis for an optional European contract code in the medium term. This was followed by a *First (Annual) Report on Contract Law and the Acquis Review* in 2005 and the Commission's *Second Progress Report on the Common Frame of Reference* (CFR) was published at the end of July 2007: <http://ec.europa.eu/consumers/cons_int/safe_shop/fair_bus_pract/cont_law/index_en.htm>.

An interim outline edition of the Academic Version (Study Group on a European Civil Code and Research Group on EC Private Law (Acquis Group)) of the *Draft Common Frame of Reference* (DCFR) was published in early 2008, and the Draft CFR in early 2009. It is the provisions of the DCFR which are referred to in this text as they are likely to be adopted as the CFR 'toolbox' should this be progressed. The Commission is expected to issue a White Paper containing its plans for the Academic CFR. The intention is that the CFR should be a non-binding legal instrument that may be used on a voluntary basis and serve as a common source of inspiration or reference. The DCFR did not receive a favourable response from the House of Lords in its twelfth report for the 2008–9 session published in June 2009, *European Contract Law: The draft common frame of reference* (HL Paper 95). The priority for the House of Lords Sub-Committee is advancing mutual understanding of diverse systems rather than any opt-in set of European rules or an EU-wide set of standard terms of contract. (See also Eidenmüller, Faust, Grigoleit, Jansen, Wagner, and Zimmermann, 'The Common Frame of Reference for European private law: Policy choices and codification problems' (2008) 28 OJLS 659.)

1.6.2.4 Good faith in English contract law

Arguably the most significant contribution to general English contractual principles resulting from European directives and influence has been the introduction of the concept of 'good faith'. (For an excellent discussion of the issues and arguments, see Brownsword, *Contract Law: Themes in the twenty-first century*, 2nd edn (Oxford University Press, 2006), Ch. 6. The discussion here is merely intended to give some background to the current debate.)

Traditionally, unlike civil law jurisdictions and several common law jurisdictions, English law has not recognized any general concept of good faith contracting in terms of negotiation, content, or performance of contracts. 'Good faith' was recognized by Bingham LJ in **Interfoto Picture Library Ltd v Stiletto Visual Programmes Ltd** [1989] 1 QB 433 as being 'in essence a principle of fair and open dealing'. However, many commentators regard its major deficiency as the inability to provide a clear definition of what it encompasses.

While English law has not recognized any general principle of good faith, it has, to use the words of Bingham LJ, 'developed piecemeal solutions in response to demonstrated problems of unfairness'. For example, the regulation of exemption clauses (Chapter 7), the penalty rule (see 9.10), duress and undue influence (Chapter 15), and the rule governing incorporation of onerous and unusual terms (see 6.3.1.5). However, this is not the same thing as adoption of a general principle.

There has been some scepticism about the desirability of adopting a general principle of good faith in English contract law (e.g., Lord Ackner in **Walford v Miles** [1992] 2 AC 128 at p. 138, who, in the context of negotiations, regarded such a concept as too vague and 'inherently repugnant to the adversarial position of the parties when involved in negotiations'). Commercial lawyers, concerned to ensure that England retains its primary role in the resolution of international commercial disputes, have worried about the inherent uncertainty of such a general concept and the restrictions that it may impose on commercial dealings. Of course, this may be unduly to underestimate the ability of the English courts to give effect to vague principles and notions. For example, it is accepted that English law gives effect to 'reasonable expectations' of the contracting parties, which some would argue can be equally difficult to identify with precision. In any event, it would appear to be easier for English contract lawyers to accept a concept of good faith in relation to performance of a contract than in relation to its negotiation, and it is in this context that the concept of good faith has now been explicitly incorporated into English law in the Unfair Terms in Consumer Contracts Regulations 1999. In the context of these regulations, the House of Lords examined the concept of 'good faith' in **Director General of Fair Trading v First National Bank plc** [2001] UKHL 52, [2002] 1 AC 481 and treated 'good faith' as an overarching concept of 'fair and open dealing' requiring both procedural and substantive fairness in contracting (good faith is discussed further in relation to the regulations at 7.7.3). It therefore appears that English judges have experienced fewer difficulties with the concept than the sceptics would have anticipated.

Given that the concept of good faith appears to be an integral element of European consumer protection, we are likely to see its significance grow in this context in particular. Its relevance in the context of commercial contracts will always be more controversial. The DCFR, PECL, and the UNIDROIT *Principles of International Commercial Contracts* all contain a general principle requiring that the parties act in accordance with fair dealing and good faith (DCFR I-1:103; Art. 1:201, PECL; Art. 1.7, UNIDROIT). This broad principle is applied in other articles throughout each set of principles, and the good faith requirement applies to formation, performance, and enforcement (e.g. DCFR II-3:301(2)–(4) negotiating in good faith). The concept is therefore seen as an essential underlying principle against which the parties' dealings are to be judged and in the light of which future principles will need to develop.

1.7 The Human Rights Act 1998 and contract law

The Human Rights Act 1998 came into force in October 2000 so that there has been some opportunity to evaluate the impact of the Act on English contract law, and specifically, to assess any case law involving a claim or defence based on this Act. The Human Rights Act 1998 incorporates the European Convention on Human Rights into English law so that these Convention Rights can be enforced under English law.

There are two issues of debate relating to the Act and its impact on contract law:

1. the question of whether the Act applies to private law obligations

2. the scope of Convention Rights and whether they can extend in a practical sense to interference with contractual obligations.

There has been some academic debate relating to the first of these questions, i.e. the impact of the Act in the area of private law obligations (between two individuals or between an individual and a company) (see Buxton, 'The Human Rights Act and private law' (2000) 116 LQR 48 and Bamforth, 'The true "horizontal effect" of the Human Rights Act 1998' (2002) 118 LQR 203). **The debate turns on the interpretation of s. 6 of the Act which states that it is 'unlawful for a *public authority* to act in a way which is incompatible with a Convention Right'** (emphasis added). This implies that the Act does not apply as between private individuals. However, since 'public authority' in this context includes a court or arbitral tribunal, it can be argued that there is considerable scope of the application of the Act in the area of private law. The House of Lords in ***Aston Cantlow v Wallbank*** [2003] UKHL 37, [2004] 1 AC 546, defined 'public authorities' as having functions of a public nature and as bodies 'whose nature is governmental in the broad sense of the expression'. This definition may well limit the scope of application of the Act in the contractual context (see, e.g., ***R (West) v Lloyd's of London*** [2004] EWCA Civ 506, [2004] 3 All ER 251, discussed below). There are significant implications in terms of contracting arising from the absence of a legislative definition of 'public authority'. In *YL v Birmingham City Council* [2007] UKHL 27, [2007] 3 WLR 112, the House of Lords 3:2 held that a 'private, profit-earning company' which provided residential and nursing care to individuals under a contract was not acting as a public authority, despite the fact that the company was so acting under a contract with the local authority in fulfillment of the local authority's statutory duties. However, when terminating a social tenancy a publicly funded body was acting as a 'public authority' so that the Act applied (*R (on the application of Weaver) v London and Quadrant Housing Trust* [2009] EWCA Civ 587, [2009] 4 All ER 865: majority of Court of Appeal: Rix LJ dissenting). The difficulties of definition persist.

The second issue relates to whether contract law and specific contracts violate Convention Rights.

Article 1 of the First Protocol states that:

every natural or legal person is entitled to the peaceful enjoyment of his possessions. No one shall be deprived of his possessions except in the public interest and subject to the conditions provided for by law and by the general principles of international law.

This article arose for consideration in the context of the treatment of illegality in English contract law. English law principles prevent a person who was a party to an illegal contract from recovering any money or property passing under that contract (see the discussion at 16.6). At first sight, therefore, there is the potential for conflict with Art. 1 of the First Protocol although, as recognized by the Law Commission (LCCP No. 154, 'The Effect of Illegality on Contracts and Trusts', 1999), Art. 1 does contain a 'public interest' exception.

The Court of Appeal in *Shanshal v Al-Kishtaini* [2001] EWCA Civ 264, [2001] 2 All ER (Comm) 601 (for more detailed discussion, see 16.6.1), relied on this 'public interest' exception in rejecting an argument that the English common law principles on non-recovery were incompatible with the Human Rights Act. However, although the common law principle of non-recovery was justified in the public interest on these facts it by no means follows that it will be justified in all instances of illegality. The decision in *Wilson v Secretary of State for Trade and Industry, sub nom Wilson v First County Trust (No. 2)* [2003] UKHL 40, [2004] 1 AC 816 (see also 5.4.4.2 and formalities requirements), represented the first examination by the House of Lords of the application of the Act in the contractual context.

The Court of Appeal had declared that s. 127(3) of the Consumer Credit Act 1974 was incompatible with rights guaranteed by Art. 6(1) and Art. 1 of the First Protocol of the Convention. Section 127(3) provided that where, in the context of regulated consumer credit agreements, the debtor did not sign the document containing all the prescribed terms, the credit agreement would be unenforceable by the creditor. It was alleged that this ban represented a disproportionate response and therefore infringed the rights of the creditor, in this case a pawnbroker.

The House of Lords held that the Court of Appeal had been wrong to make such a declaration on the basis that the facts and the cause of action in the particular case had arisen before the 1998 Act came into force and the Act did not have retrospective effect. Article 6(1), which guaranteed procedural fairness by providing for fair and public hearings in the determination of civil rights and obligations, was not infringed since, although the effect of s. 127(3) was to restrict the rights of creditors under regulated agreements, the section did not prevent access to the court in order to determine whether the agreement in question fell within the legislation as a regulated agreement. In any event, if the section had the effect of interfering with the creditor's property rights under Art. 1 of the First Protocol, that interference was justified given the policy underpinning the consumer protection legislation.

Quite apart from the issue of the non-retrospective effect of the Act, this decision appears to indicate that the highest court was in no great hurry to adopt a liberal and embracing response to attempts at intervention in existing domestic legislation based on alleged contraventions of the Human Rights Act. No doubt the coming years will see a greater willingness to accept such challenges but perhaps not in the context of attempted denial of consumer protection measures already adopted by Parliament.

Interestingly, however, the case is concerned with the scope of Convention Rights and does not deny the potential for the application of the Convention in the context of private law rights. The fact that the human rights question reached the House of Lords in *Wilson* and the Court of Appeal in *Shanshal* would appear to indicate that the Act will in many instances be treated as having horizontal effect. However, it was held that decisions of Lloyd's of London as part of a voluntary and contractual relationship with syndicate members did not fall within s. 6 of the 1998 Act since the objectives of Lloyd's were commercial rather than governmental. Therefore the terms of the contract governed the relationship. Lloyd's was itself regulated by the Financial Services Authority which was therefore the answerable public authority. It followed that the Act did not apply to a claim that the decision to approve minority buy-outs was prejudicial to the right of possession of property in Art. 1 of the First Protocol (*R (West) v Lloyd's of London* [2004] EWCA Civ 506, [2004] 3 All ER 251).

Notwithstanding the decision in *Wilson*, the Human Rights Act would appear to have potential implications for contractual principles in a number of contexts, but especially in the context of employment contracts and confidentiality obligations.

1.8 The governing law in contractual disputes

The choice of governing law is often an issue for contracting parties who are domiciled in different jurisdictions or where the performance of the contract is to occur in different jurisdictions. What happens if the parties have not chosen the governing law?

The Law Applicable to Contractual Obligations (England and Wales and Northern Ireland) Regulations 2009, SI 2009/3064, give effect to Regulation (EC) No. 593/2008 on the law applicable to contractual obligations ('Rome I'). Rome I applies to contracts concluded from 17 December 2009 and establishes uniform choice of law rules in the field of contractual obligations. The regulations give effect to this European law by requiring the English courts to apply Rome I. Rome I will not apply to 'obligations arising out of dealings prior to the conclusion of a contract' (Art. 1(2)(i), Rome I) but, that apart, the usual rule will be that the governing law will be the law of the place where the party required to effect the characteristic performance of the contract has his habitual residence, e.g. the seller in a sale of goods contract.

Article 19(1) of Rome I defines habitual residence for companies and other bodies, incorporated or not, as 'the place of central administration', while the habitual residence of a natural person acting in the course of their business activity is defined as being their 'principal point of business'. In determining the habitual residence, 'the relevant point in time shall be the time of the conclusion of the contract' (Art. 19(3), Rome I). However, the 'habitual residence' test specified under Art. 4(1) and (2) will not apply where it is clear from the circumstances that a contract is 'manifestly more closely connected' with a country, when the 'law of that other country shall apply' (Art. 4(1)(3)). If it is not possible to determine the governing law using Art. 4(1) or (2) the 'contract shall be governed by the law of the country with which it is most closely connected' (Art. 4(1)(4), Rome I; *Intercontainer Interfrigo SC(ICF) v Balkenende Oosthuizen BV*, C-133/08).

Further reading

General and theory

Adams and Brownsword, 'The ideologies of contract' (1987) 7 LS 205.

Adams and Brownsword, *Understanding Contract Law*, 5th edn (Sweet and Maxwell, 2007).

Atiyah, 'Contracts, promises and the law of obligations' in *Essays on Contract* (Oxford University Press, 1986) or see (1978) 94 LQR 193.

Atiyah, 'The modern role of contract law' in *Essays on Contract* (Oxford University Press, 1986).

Baker, 'From sanctity of contract to reasonable expectations' [1979] CLP 17.

Brownsword, *Contract Law: Themes for the twenty-first century* (Butterworths, 2000), Chs 5 and 6.

Burrows, 'Contract, tort and restitution: A satisfactory division or not?' (1983) 99 LQR 217.

Coote, 'The essence of contract' (1988) 1 JCL 91 and 183.

Eisenberg, 'Relational contracts' in Beatson and Friedmann (eds), *Good Faith and Fault in Contract Law* (Oxford University Press, 1995).

Fried, *Contract as Promise: A theory of contractual obligation* (Harvard University Press, 1981).

Gilmore, *The Death of Contract* (Ohio State University Press, 1986).

McKendrick, 'English contract law: A rich past, an uncertain future?' [1997] CLP 25.

Mitchell, 'Leading a life of its own? The roles of reasonable expectation in contract law' (2003) 23 OJLS 639.

Reiter and Swan, 'Contracts and the protection of reasonable expectation' in *Studies in Contract Law* (Toronto: Butterworths, 1980).

Smith, *Contract Theory* (Clarendon Press, 2004).

Steyn, 'Contract law: Fulfilling the reasonable expectations of honest men' (1997) 113 LQR 433.

History

Atiyah, *The Rise and Fall of Freedom of Contract* (Oxford University Press, 1979).

Simpson, *A History of the Common Law of Contract* (Oxford University Press, 1987).

Contract law in practice

Beale and Dugdale, 'Contracts between businessmen: Planning and the use of contractual remedies' (1975) 2 Brit J of Law & Soc 45.

Principles of international commercial contracts and uniform principles

Furmston, 'Unidroit general principles for international commercial contracts' (1996) 10 JCL 11.

Hobhouse, 'International conventions and commercial law: The pursuit of uniformity' (1990) 106 LQR 530.

UNIDROIT, *Principles of International Commercial Contracts* (Rome: Unidroit, 2004).

European directives and harmonization

Bridge, 'Good faith in commercial contracts' in Brownsword, Hird, and Howells (eds), *Good Faith in Contract* (Dartmouth, 1999).

Brownsword, '"Good faith in contracts" revisited' [1996] CLP 111.

Lando, 'Principles of European contract law: An alternative to or a precursor of European legislation' (1992) 40 Am J of Comp Law 573.

Lando, *Principles of European Contract Law: Part III* (Kluwer Law International, 2003).

Lando and Beale, *Principles of European Contract Law: Parts I and II* (Kluwer Law International, 2000).

Twigg-Flesner, 'Deep impact? The EC Directive on unfair commercial practices and domestic consumer law' (2005) 121 LQR 386.

European contract: *Draft Common Frame of Reference*

Eidenmüller, Faust, Grigoleit, Jansen, Wagner, and Zimmermann, 'The Common Frame of Reference for European private law: Policy choices and codification problems' (2008) 28 OJLS 659.

Miller, 'The Common Frame of Reference and the feasibility of a common contract law in Europe' [2007] JBL 378.

Whittaker, 'A framework of principle for European contract law?' (2009) 125 LQR 616.

Contract law and the Human Rights Act 1998

Bamforth, 'The true "horizontal effect" of the Human Rights Act 1998' (2002) 118 LQR 203.

Buxton, 'The Human Rights Act and private law' (2000) 116 LQR 48.

Part 1

Formation

This Part looks at the making (or formation) of contracts. **A contract is a legally binding agreement and this has a number of elements: there must be agreement and that agreement must be legally enforceable.**

Chapter 2 examines the process of determining whether an agreement has been reached between the parties. This raises the preliminary question of how we determine the existence of agreement. The law usually requires the existence of an offer and a corresponding acceptance. In order to be effective any offer or acceptance must also be properly communicated and will take effect from the time that communication is effective. Chapter 2 examines the interrelationship of the various legal principles determining agreement, including the issue of communication in an electronic age. One of the most interesting—and commercially essential—questions for contract formation is whether the existing principles can be adapted to the needs of electronic contracting, particularly as English contract law has taken some time to devise principles governing communications by facsimile and telephone; even now there remains uncertainty in terms of contracting through these media, e.g. the point at which acceptance messages left on telephone answering machines are effectively communicated. In the wider context, the contract formation principles contained in the *Draft Common Frame of Reference* (DCFR), the *Principles of European Contract Law* (PECL), and the UNIDROIT *Principles of International Commercial Contracts* may suggest that some of the tensions in the law of formation in English law might be better addressed by other principles.

The process of negotiating to reach agreement can be protracted, and on occasions the parties may well fail to reach agreement on all the terms of their contract, or may agree to negotiate or deliberately leave gaps in their agreement. Chapter 3 examines the principles determining when an agreement is sufficiently certain to be capable of enforcement and what happens when no agreement has been reached. It also examines mistakes which prevent the parties from reaching agreement and mistakes whereby the contractual document fails accurately to reflect what the parties agreed.

The factors determining the enforceability of agreements and promises are examined in Chapters 4 and 5, namely, the general requirement in English law to provide consideration in order to enforce a contractual promise (Chapter 4), and the existence of an intention to create legal relations and specific requirements of form, such as writing, in order for an agreement to be legally binding (Chapter 5). The consideration requirement (Chapter 4) is relevant both to formation and alterations to existing contracts, but both are examined within this Part for ease of understanding.

Agreement

Summary of the issues

This chapter examines the process of determining whether an agreement has been reached between the parties.

• The existence of agreement is determined objectively on the basis of the impression given by the parties' words and actions. However, the actual assumptions made by the promisee (i.e., the person to whom the promise (offer) is made) are relevant in the sense that if the promisee knows, or ought reasonably to know, that an offer on these terms was not intended, that promisee cannot 'snap up' the offer. This legal principle has particular practical relevance where goods are advertised at dramatically reduced prices on retailers' websites in circumstances where it is clear that there is no obvious special offer, e.g. a television set normally retailing for £499 which is advertised for sale on a website at £4.99.

• Traditionally, the objective evidence of agreement is the existence of an offer and corresponding acceptance. However, this approach has been criticized as artificial and inflexible and on occasions the courts have found agreement in the absence of these traditional criteria, particularly where there has been performance.

• An offer is an expression of willingness to contract on the specified terms without further negotiation and must be distinguished from an invitation to treat (or invitation to negotiate). Generally, advertisements, displays in shop windows and on supermarket shelves, and invitations to tender are all invitations to treat. However, some advertisements or invitations to tender may amount to offers and the legal status of a website is unclear.

• An acceptance is a final expression of assent to the terms of the offer made in response to that offer. The operation of the mirror image rule (requiring that the acceptance must mirror the terms of the offer) has given rise to some practical difficulties in the form of the 'battle of forms'.

• Offer and acceptance must be properly communicated in order to be effective. The general rule is that **actual communication** is required. **Actual communication** is interpreted to mean that the communication has to **reach** the intended recipient. However, the dispatch rule is the general rule applicable to postal acceptances (i.e., a postal acceptance is treated as communicated when it is posted) and there may be implied waiver of the communication requirement in the case of most unilateral offers.

• An offer may be terminated by rejection, by counter offer, by lapse of time, and in some circumstances by the death of the other party. An offer may also be terminated by revocation (withdrawal) of the offer before acceptance occurs. Generally a revocation of an offer must be actually communicated (received) to be effective but there are special rules applying to the question of whether it is possible to revoke a unilateral offer once performance has commenced (***Errington v Errington***) and with regard to the communication requirement for revocation of a unilateral offer (***Shuey v US***).

2.1 Determining the existence of agreement: The objective approach

In order to be able to conclude that there is a contract giving rise to enforceable obligations, we must first identify the existence of a binding **agreement** between the parties.

It is the fact that the obligations are voluntarily agreed which distinguishes contract from other areas of law, such as tort, where the obligations are imposed by law. However, although it is often said that for agreement there must be a *consensus ad idem* (or meeting of minds), this does not mean that subjectively the parties' intentions must coincide. The existence (and indeed the content) of an agreement, and whether that agreement was intended to be legally binding, are not determined on the basis of what the parties themselves thought or intended. Instead, the courts look at external evidence (what the parties said and did at the time) as objectively indicating the parties' intentions and ask whether, on the basis of this evidence, the reasonable man would say that the parties were in agreement. As Lord Denning stated in ***Storer v Manchester City Council*** [1974] 1 WLR 1403 at p. 1408:

> In contracts you do not look into the actual intent in a man's mind. You look at what he said and did. A contract is formed when there is, to all outward appearances, a contract. A man cannot get out of a contract by saying: 'I did not intend to contract', if by his words he has done so.

It follows that the 'voluntary' (consensual) nature of contractual liability may be more apparent than real. This conclusion raises difficult theoretical questions when seeking to justify the primacy of contractual obligations, as compared, for example, to tortious responsibility, on the basis that contractual obligations are voluntarily assumed. In addition, it makes it difficult to support contractual theories which rest on the premise of respect for contractual obligations as consensual and which therefore seek to resolve issues by reference to the parties' 'intentions' (discussed in Chapter 1). Such intentions must also be determined objectively and so are also more apparent than real.

Nevertheless, it is clear that from a pragmatic perspective that the objective approach is preferable to a purely subjective approach, for a number of reasons:

- A subjective approach would create uncertainty. It would not be safe to rely on any promise if the promisor (i.e., the person making the promise) could later deny that s/he ever intended to make such a promise. Security of transactions is an essential characteristic of contract law.

- It would be totally impractical. As the parties may later say whatever suits their purpose at that time, in evidential terms it is clearly preferable to look only at what the parties said and did at the time of the agreement.

As Adams and Brownsword (*Understanding Contract Law*, 5th edn (Sweet and Maxwell, 2007), p. 48) have stated: 'To found contract on a subjective approach, therefore, would impede commerce, invite fraud, and unfairly defeat good faith reliance on the natural meaning of a promise.'

It is clear, therefore, that determining the existence and content of an agreement—and whether it is intended to be legally binding—depends not on the parties' subjective intentions but on the impression which they have given by their words and actions. (For a recent statement to this effect see Lord Phillips in *Shogun Finance Ltd v Hudson* [2003] UKHL 62, [2004] 1 AC 919, [123]–[125].) Steyn LJ, in *Trentham Ltd v Archital Luxfer Ltd* [1993] 1 Lloyd's Rep 25 at p. 27, said, 'the governing criterion is the reasonable expectations of honest men' or what a reasonable man has been led to believe the position to be.

In *Maple Leaf Macro Volatility Master Fund v Rouvroy* [2009] EWHC 257 (Comm), [2009] 1 Lloyd's Rep 475, the defendants alleged that they did not intend to enter into any contract because they did not think the document they were signing, a termsheet, was a legally binding document. They believed they were signing no more than a non-contractual commitment to continue negotiations and the judge accepted this evidence. However, applying the objective approach to contract formation, the applicable test was 'how a reasonable man versed in business would have understood the exchanges between the parties' and 'whether, objectively assessed, the parties evinced in their exchanges an intention to conclude a contract'. The judge concluded that the wording and presentation of the termsheet indicated an intention to be legally bound, and particularly the words 'Please sign to acknowledge agreement and acceptance of the terms of the transaction.'

The importance of determining the parties' intentions on contractual content by reference to objective criteria was also stressed by the Privy Council in *Attorney General of Belize v Belize Telecom Ltd* [2009] UKPC 10, [2009] 1 WR 1988, (discussed **6.4**). Lord Hoffmann stated (at [16]) that the decision on whether to imply a term was a process of construction and that a court:

> is concerned only to discover what the instrument means. However, that meaning is not necessarily or always what the authors or parties to the document would have intended. It is the meaning which the instrument would convey to a reasonable person having all the background knowledge which would reasonably be available to the audience to whom the instrument is addressed: see *Investors Compensation Scheme Ltd v West Bromwich Building Society* [1998] 1 WLR 896, 912–913. It is this objective meaning which is conventionally called the intention of the parties…

Of course, this gives rise to a further question: whose views determine the impression given? Who is the reasonable person for this purpose? There is no agreed view on this question.

2.1.1 The objective approach interpreted

Howarth ('The meaning of objectivity in contract' (1984) 100 LQR 265) argued that there are three different interpretations of what is meant by objectivity depending upon the standpoint of the reasonable man:

1. 'promisor objectivity', which involves an assessment from the point of view of the reasonable promisor

2. 'promisee objectivity', which involves an assessment from the point of view of a reasonable promisee to whom the words were conveyed

3. 'detached objectivity', involving an assessment of the position from the point of view of an independent external person (so-called 'fly on the wall' objectivity).

In particular, 'promisee objectivity' must be understood as referring to a reasonable promisee in the context of the actual promisee, e.g. business person or consumer (Bradgate, *Butterworths' The Law of Contract*, M. P. Furmston (ed.), 3rd edn (LexisNexis Butterworths, 2007), p. 401). For example, in **Bowerman v ABTA Ltd** [1996] CLC 451, the majority of the Court of Appeal held that the ABTA notice would reasonably have been read by a member of the public (in the position of the promisee) as containing an offer of protection. Equally, the objective determination of the formation question would require an assessment based on the understandings of commercial parties in the commercial context (**Covington Marine Corporation v Xiamen Shipbuilding Industry Co. Ltd** [2005] EWHC 2912 (Comm), [2006] 1 CLC 624).

There has been much academic disagreement on the question of the preferred meaning of objectivity, particularly between promisee objectivity and detached objectivity. For example, Spencer, 'Signature, consent and the rule in *L'Estrange v Graucob*' [1973] CLJ 104 and Vorster, 'A comment on the meaning of objectivity in contract' (1987) 103 LQR 274, support promisee objectivity; whereas Howarth ((1984) 100 LQR 265 and (1987) 103 LQR 527) supports detached objectivity as being impartial and providing for greater scope for judicial intervention to promote 'the needs of justice'. Lord Brightman's statement in **The Hannah Blumenthal** [1983] 1 AC 854 at p. 924 ('To entitle the sellers to rely on abandonment, they must show that the buyers so conducted themselves as to entitle the sellers to assume…that the contract was agreed to be abandoned', may be interpreted as supporting promisee objectivity (the 'promisee' being the sellers in this context); and the classic statement of Blackburn J in **Smith v Hughes** (1871) LR 6 QB 597 at p. 607:

If, whatever a man's real intention may be, he so conducts himself that a reasonable man would believe he was assenting to the terms proposed by the other party, and that other party upon that belief enters into the contract with him, the man thus conducting himself would be equally bound as if he had intended to agree to the other party's terms.

is often cited as supporting promisee objectivity, but seems equally capable of being cited to support detached objectivity.

There are two points that need to be made relating to Howarth's interpretations of objectivity:

1. Terminology

Howarth used the terms 'promisor' and 'promisee'. This terminology has caused problems for some commentators (see, for example, Vorster (1987) 103 LQR 274 at 276–8) who point to the fact that in a bilateral sale contract the seller may be a promisor (in relation to the promise to sell the goods) and a promisee (in relation to the buyer's promise to pay for the goods). However, if the objectivity test is being applied to determine the existence of agreement between the parties and whether they intended to be legally bound, the objectivity test will look at the correspondence and conduct within the structure of offer and acceptance. The promisee is therefore the recipient of the relevant correspondence or conduct. For example, the question of whether there is agreement depends upon whether there has been an offer and whether there has been a corresponding acceptance of that offer. In each case the assessment can take place from the point of view of a reasonable person in the position of the recipient of that 'offer' or 'acceptance', i.e. in terms of promisee (recipient) objectivity this would involve asking:

- What would a reasonable recipient in the position of the offeree understand the communication or conduct to mean?
- What would a reasonable recipient in the position of the offeror interpret the response to mean?

Spencer ([1973] CLJ 104), who advocated promisee (recipient) objectivity, put the matter succinctly: 'Words are to be interpreted as they were reasonably understood by the man to whom they were spoken, not as they were understood by the man who spoke them.'

2. The context for determining objectivity: Formation or content?

The meaning of objectivity would appear to vary according to the context in which the test of objectivity is applied and there appears to be a distinction between formation objectivity and content objectivity. Formation objectivity encompasses two situations. Objectivity is the applicable test to determine both the existence of agreement between the parties and whether the parties intended to be legally bound (see 5.2). In addition, objectivity is also the test when determining the **interpretation** to be given to the contractual terms (see **Chapter 6B**) ('content objectivity'—see *Investors Compensation Scheme Ltd v West Bromwich Building Society* [1998] 1 WLR 896 and *Attorney General of Belize v Belize Telecom Ltd* [2009] UKPC 10, [2009] 1 WLR 1988). Whereas it would seem that 'promisee objectivity' (from the point of view of a reasonable promisee in the position of this promisee) can be seen to be an appropriate test on formation questions, the determination of content may require determination based on both promisor and promisee objectivity—or even detached objectivity. Evidence of such a distinction can be seen in the UNIDROIT principles, the *Principles of European Contract Law* (PECL), and in the Draft Common Frame of Reference (DCFR) (see 1.6.1).

Article 4.2(2) of the UNIDROIT *Principles of International Commercial Contracts* provides that a party's statements and other conduct 'shall be interpreted according to the meaning that *a reasonable person of the same kind as the other party* would give to it in the same circumstances'. This article therefore provides for promisee objectivity and the commentary states that this test will be applicable in the context of formation of contracts (i.e., in relation to the question of whether there is an agreement and an intention to be legally bound). By comparison, the substantive content of a contract should reflect the intentions of *both* parties so that where a common intention cannot be established 'the contract shall be interpreted according to the meaning that reasonable persons of the same kind as the parties would give to it in the same circumstances' (UNIDROIT, Art. 4.1). This refers to reasonable persons (in the plural) and would appear to require the contract to be interpreted from the point of view of both a reasonable promisor and a reasonable promisee in the same circumstances. This would appear to be different to detached objectivity, since the approach of a reasonable bystander is detached from the parties, whereas in Art. 4.1, UNIDROIT, the party context is clearly relevant.

The *Principles of European Contract Law* adopt a similar distinction. In order to have a concluded contract the parties must intend to be legally bound and it must be possible to identify sufficient agreement on the terms (Art. 2:101). Intention of a party to be legally bound turns upon that party's statements or conduct 'as they were reasonably understood by the other party', i.e. promisee objectivity. By comparison, interpretation of substantive content of the contract is determined, as under UNIDROIT, by reference to the meaning that 'reasonable *persons* of the same kind as the parties would give to it in the same circumstances' (Art. 5:101(3)). The DCFR adopts a similar approach: II-4:102 (formation) and II-8:101 (interpretation of content).

Although Vorster's support for such an interpretation involving the duplication of the reasonable person (reasonable promisor and reasonable promisee) was decisively rejected by Howarth (1987) 103 LQR 527 at p. 530, as 'an unhelpful confusion', it is clearly the approach favoured by UNIDROIT, PECL, and the DCFR, at least in the context of interpretation of the contractual content, and has the advantage of reflecting the actual context and **these parties** rather than the detached view of the court which may well have the effect of imposing content on the parties which neither of them wanted.

An evaluation of the case law provides further support for a difference in the meaning of objectivity dependent on the context of formation or content. For example, ***Bowerman v ABTA Ltd*** [1996] CLC 451 and ***Edmonds v Lawson*** [2000] QB 501 concerned intention to be legally bound (see **5.2.2.1** and **5.3**) so that it may not be surprising that promisee objectivity is applied to the determination of this intention. By comparison, at first instance in ***Thake v Maurice*** [1984] 2 All ER 513, Peter Pain J at p. 519, stated that: 'The test as to what the contract in fact was does not depend on what the plaintiffs or the defendant thought it meant, but on what *the court* objectively determines that the words used meant.' But how does the court determine this meaning? Denning LJ's reference to 'an intelligent bystander' in ***Oscar Chess Ltd v Williams*** [1957] 1 WLR 370 at p. 375, when interpreting the statement that a particular car was a '1948 model', may suggest that 'detached objectivity' is to be applied to content questions. In ***Investors Compensation Scheme Ltd v West Bromwich Building Society ('West Bromwich')*** [1998] 1 WLR 896 (Chapter 6B), Lord Hoffmann accepted that, although the starting point for interpretation will be the words used by the parties themselves in an effort to ascertain the parties' reasonable intentions, a wider category of evidence (the matrix of facts) was available in interpreting content, i.e. 'absolutely anything which would have affected the way in which the language of the document would have been understood by a reasonable man' or, as later qualified and explained, 'anything which a reasonable man would have regarded as relevant' (***BCCI v Ali (No. 1)*** [2001] UKHL 8, [2002] 1 AC 251). The content test in ***Attorney General of Belize v Belize Telecom Ltd*** [2009] UKPC 10, [2009] 1 WLR 1988, also focuses on interpretation by 'a reasonable person' with knowledge of the matrix or background. Thus the factual matrix ensures that any interpretation will take account of more 'detached' factors such as market conditions and practices. (For further discussion of the meaning of contractual intention, see DeMoor, 'Intention in the law of contract: Elusive or illusory?' (1990) 106 LQR 632.)

2.1.2 The residual subjective element

Of course, subjective intentions are relevant in the general sense that they may well coincide with the objectively ascertained intentions of the parties. However, does subjective intention have any **other** relevance?

The Court of Appeal in ***The Leonidas D (Allied Marine Transport Ltd v Vale do Rio Doce Navegacao SA)*** [1985] 1 WLR 925, adopted the formulation of Lord Brightman in *The Hannah*

Blumenthal. Robert Goff LJ (at p. 936) in *The Leonidas D* explained Lord Brightman's formulation in the following terms:

[I]f one party, O, so acts that his conduct, objectively considered, constitutes an offer, and the other party, A, believing that the conduct of O represents his actual intention, accepts O's offer, then a contract will come into existence, and on those facts it will make no difference if O did not in fact intend to make an offer, or if he misunderstood A's acceptance, so that O's state of mind is in such circumstances irrelevant.

Whereas the conduct of the promisor is judged objectively and what the promisor may subjectively have intended is irrelevant, the actual assumptions made by the promisee are relevant where the promisee:

1. either knows or
2. *ought reasonably to know*

that the promisor did not intend to make an offer (or did not intend to make an offer in those terms). It is only in this sense that subjective considerations are relevant to determining the existence of agreement.

There will therefore be no contract where the promisee actually knows that the promisor has no intention to contract with him on those terms. Peel, *Treitel's The Law of Contract*, 12th edn (Sweet and Maxwell, 2007), p. 1, makes clear the reasoning for this exception when he states that the purpose of the objective approach 'is to protect B [the promisee] from the prejudice which he might suffer as a result of relying on a false appearance of agreement. There is clearly no need in this way to protect a party who knows that the objective appearance does not correspond with reality'.

Of course, this reference is to positive *actual* knowledge of a different intention on the part of the promisee, when clearly there will be no prejudice to the promisee. However, will something less than actual knowledge suffice? Will it suffice that the promisee 'could not have been unaware' of the true position, or 'ought reasonably to have known'? In other words, is it also the case that the promisee is not considered as prejudiced where the **reasonable** promisee **ought reasonably to have known** the true position?

In *Maple Leaf Macro Volatility Master Fund v Rouvroy* [2009] EWHC 257 (Comm), [2009] 1 Lloyd's Rep 475, Andrew Smith J referred (at [228]) to the possibility that the defendants would not be bound, despite objective appearances if the claimants actually or reasonably believed that it was not the defendants' intention to be bound and not, in the judge's view, if the claimants had 'simply formed no view one way or the other as to whether the defendants so intended'. The judge concluded that the defendants had the burden of establishing this and they had not done so.

By comparison, in *Hartog v Colin and Shields* [1939] 3 All ER 566 (for facts see **3.3.2.2**) the evidence was established and it was held that, on the basis of the pre-sale negotiations, the plaintiff (offeree) could not reasonably have supposed that the offer contained the offeror's true intention as to the contract terms. However, at first sight this decision is difficult to reconcile with that of the Court of Appeal in *Centrovincial Estates plc v Merchant Investors Assurance Company Ltd* [1983] Com LR 158 (for facts see **3.3.2.2**). It can be argued that in *Centrovincial* the defendants, the tenants, ought to have known of the plaintiffs' mistake because the rent review clause indicated that in no circumstances should the rent fall when reviewed. However, the Court of Appeal did not consider that the plaintiffs had satisfied the necessary burden of proof on this issue, i.e. they had not shown that the defendants ought to have known of the mistake. (In this situation the person making the offer alleges that he made a mistake with regard to the contract terms which the other **ought to have known about** and so cannot be allowed to 'snap it up'. 'Snapping up' is discussed in the context of agreement mistake at 3.3.2.) However, there is an important limitation on the relevance of subjective intentions in that the promisee must know or the promisee ought to know that the promisor is making a mistake as to the terms of the contract. If the mistake relates to an ancillary (or collateral) matter, the subjective position of the promisee is irrelevant (*Smith v Hughes* (1871) LR 6 QB 597). In *Statoil ASA v Louis Dreyfus Energy Services LP, The Harriette N* [2008] EWHC 2257 (Comm), [2008] 2 Lloyd's Rep 685, [2009] 1 All ER (Comm) 1035 (see also 3.3.2.1 and 13.5.3), Aikens J stated (at [88]): 'if one party has made a mistake about a fact on which he bases his decision to enter into a contract, but that fact does not form a term of the contract itself, then, even if the other party knows that the first is mistaken as to this fact, the contract will be binding'. By comparison, in the Singapore decision of *Chwee Kin Keong v Digilandmall.com Pte Ltd* [2005] 1 SLR 502, 3.3.2, the mistake related to a term, namely the price of goods being sold on an Internet site.

2.1.3 Traditional and non-traditional approaches to identifying agreement

The objective approach looks for external evidence of agreement, i.e. the words and conduct of the parties. Traditionally, agreement must be demonstrated by an unequivocal offer made by one party (the offeror) and by complete acceptance of that offer by the other party (the offeree). This approach is, of course, neat and designed to promote certainty. However, it is clearly artificial and inflexible, and may well ignore the reality of the situation by dictating that no agreement has been reached for purely technical reasons. As a result, there have long been instances of the courts either 'finding' the necessary offer and acceptance, or ignoring the traditional approach and simply recognizing the existence of agreement by means of other external evidence.

Lord Wilberforce, in *New Zealand Shipping Co. Ltd v A M Satterthwaite & Co. Ltd, The Eurymedon* [1975] AC 154 (for facts see 4.4.2), admitted that it was a recognized practice to seek to 'find' the necessary offer and acceptance when he said (at p. 167): 'English law, having committed itself to a rather technical and schematic doctrine of contract, in application takes a practical approach, often at the cost of forcing the facts to fit uneasily into the marked slots of offer, acceptance and consideration.' This statement was later used by Lord Denning MR to support his view that on occasion a different approach to determining the existence of agreement was called for. In *Butler Machine Tool Co. Ltd v Ex-Cell-O Corporation (England) Ltd* [1979] 1 WLR 401, Lord Denning suggested that the circumstances as a whole (i.e., all the documents and the parties' conduct) should be examined in an attempt to discover agreement. It seems that he wished to replace what was a question of law (subject to precise and sometimes detailed rules) with a pure question of fact. Although Lord Denning applied this approach in both *Butler Machine* and in the Court of Appeal in *Gibson v Manchester City Council* [1978] 1 WLR 520, the House of Lords in *Gibson* ([1979] 1 WLR 294; see the judgment of Lord Diplock at p. 297) made it clear that offer and acceptance remained the normal analysis and applied that analysis to the facts before them (involving a contract said to have been entered into as a result of exchange of correspondence).

Of course, it does not follow that the House of Lords in *Gibson* was accepting that offer and acceptance was the *only* mechanism for determining the existence of a contract. Lord Diplock said 'there may be certain types of contract, though I think they are exceptional, which do not fit easily into the normal analysis of a contract as being constituted by offer and acceptance'.

2.1.3.1 In what circumstances might a different analysis of agreement be appropriate?

Steyn LJ, in *Trentham Ltd v Archital Luxfer Ltd* [1993] 1 Lloyd's Rep 25, considered that the normal analysis would apply 'in the vast majority of cases', and specifically gave a contract alleged to be made by exchange of correspondence as an example of the application of this approach. However, he added that this 'is not necessarily so in the case of a contract alleged to have come into existence during and as a result of performance'. Therefore, agreement may be found to exist using other means where the alleged agreement is based on the conduct of both parties (i.e. an executed agreement), despite the inability to analyse the performance in terms of offer and acceptance.

These difficulties presented themselves in *J Murphy & Sons Ltd v Johnston Precast Ltd* [2008] EWHC 3024 (TCC), in that it was clear that there was an executed agreement and the issues related to whether terms and conditions had been incorporated (so necessitating a highly artificial analysis of offer and acceptance whereby the faxing of an order was held to constitute the point 'at which the contract was made' since that was the moment when the parties had acted as if there was a contract and production had commenced). However, the Court of Appeal in *Tekdata Interconnections Ltd v Amphenol Ltd* [2009] EWCA Civ 1209, [2010] 1 Lloyd's Rep 357, [2009] 2 CLC 866, also considered that whereas it was technically possible that the context of a long term relationship and the conduct of the parties might displace the traditional offer and acceptance analysis, this was unlikely and would be difficult to establish on the facts. In addition, since the *Trentham* principle appears to be part of a more general policy-based approach to recognize executed agreements wherever possible (see 3.1.3.3), it cannot be said that the decision in *Trentham* provides unqualified general support for the alternative analysis determining the existence of agreement.

However, there is clear acceptance in both the UNIDROIT *Principles* and PECL of the fact that agreement can be reached without the traditional analysis of offer and acceptance (e.g., Art. 2.1; UNIDROIT (conduct sufficient to show agreement) and Art. 2:211, PECL). Further, there are recognized situations in case law where the offer and acceptance analysis does not work very well and may come to be abandoned. These are situations which involve one or more third parties in the negotiating process (see *Clarke v Dunraven* [1897] AC 59), or instances where an offer is made more generally than to a single, identified offeree (see *Wilkie v London Passenger Transport Board* [1947] 1 All ER 258) or instances where the court is using the vehicle of contract to impose an obligation (see *Upton-on-Severn RDC v Powell* [1942] 1 All ER 220).

2.1.3.2 Conclusion

Although there are instances where the traditional offer and acceptance analysis has not been employed, the House of Lords in *Gibson* regarded them as 'exceptional' and this has since been confirmed by the Court of Appeal in *Tekdata Interconnections Ltd v Amphenol Ltd*, so that, for purposes of application, the traditional offer and acceptance analysis should be the starting point.

2.2 **Traditional approach: Offer and acceptance**

Determining the existence of agreement using offer and acceptance is inevitably to some extent a technical process. There must be a *valid and communicated* offer and acceptance of that offer before any effective revocation (or withdrawal) of the offer occurs. The analysis or application therefore involves two steps:

1. Identification of the correspondence

The first question to address is whether the offeror has made an 'offer'; this involves an examination of what can constitute an offer (see **2.3**). Other questions then arise, such as: did the offeree accept that offer (and what is needed to constitute an acceptance—see **2.4**), or was the offer withdrawn before acceptance could occur (see **2.5**)?

2. Does that correspondence satisfy the relevant communication rule, i.e. is it effective and when does it take effect?

It is necessary to determine whether the correspondence in question, be it offer, acceptance, or revocation, has been effectively communicated since, until such time, it cannot take effect (see **2.3.3** and **2.4.5**). This involves:

- identifying the applicable principle for communication, for example, the general rule may apply and the communication may need to be actually communicated to the recipient
- then determining whether this in fact happened
- if so, determining at what point in time it occurred.

The interrelationship of the applicable principles will determine whether the offer and acceptance (and hence agreement) have occurred. Adams and Brownsword, *Understanding Contract Law*, 5th edn (2007), p. 49, have likened this process to learning the rules of chess, i.e. it is necessary to learn the ways in which each piece (principle) can be moved and the impact that each move will have on the other pieces (principles) and eventual outcome.

2.3 **Offers and invitations to treat**

2.3.1 **Making the distinction**

An offer is an expression of willingness to contract on the specified terms without further negotiation, so that it requires only acceptance for a binding agreement to be formed. The formulation in the DCFR (II-4:201) has much to recommend it: 'A proposal amounts to an offer if (a) it is intended to result in a contract if the other party accepts it; and (b) it contains sufficiently definite terms to form a contract.'

An offer must be distinguished from all other statements made in the course of negotiations towards a contract (so-called 'invitations to treat') since only an offer is capable of immediate translation into a contract by the fact of acceptance.

A technical definition of an invitation to treat would be restricted to statements indicating the maker's willingness to receive offers. However, the expression is commonly used to describe any negotiating statement falling short of an offer which furthers the bargaining process, e.g. 'Would you be interested in buying my car?' is an invitation to treat and not an offer. Such statements may take the form of attempts to stimulate interest, requests for the supply of information, or any other stage in the sometimes lengthy progress to agreement.

On many occasions, offers and invitations to treat are easy to distinguish. On the other hand, there are times when the distinction is a fine one. In particular, it should not be assumed that correspondence described as 'an offer' will be considered as such. In practice the courts look to the individual facts of each case in making the distinction, although there are recognized instances when a communication is more likely to be regarded as only an invitation to treat (discussed below at 2.3.2).

The starting point for any determination of this issue must be that in order to constitute an offer the communication must be both:

- **sufficiently specific in terms of the main obligation and price to be capable of immediate acceptance**
- **made with an intention to be bound by the mere fact of acceptance (i.e., a definite promise to be bound).**

The language used

This intention to be bound by the mere fact of acceptance is determined objectively, so that it amounts to examining the language used. In *Gibson v Manchester City Council* [1979] 1 WLR 294, the House of Lords examined the language of the correspondence between the parties in order to determine whether there was the necessary intention to be bound.

> The council had a policy of selling council houses to tenants. Mr Gibson was such a tenant and he applied for details. The city treasurer had replied that the council 'may be prepared to sell the house to you' and invited Mr Gibson to complete an application form if he wished to buy. Mr Gibson did this, but the council changed its policy and the question arose as to whether there was already a concluded contract of sale between Mr Gibson and the council. The House of Lords held that there was no concluded contract because the language of the city treasurer's letter made it clear that the council did not intend to make a binding promise to be bound. The letter was not an offer which Mr Gibson had accepted, rather it was inviting Mr Gibson to make an offer to buy. Although Mr Gibson had made such an offer to buy, his offer had not been accepted at the time of the change of policy.

This decision is normally contrasted with that of the Court of Appeal in *Storer v Manchester City Council* [1974] 1 WLR 1403, where the court held that a binding contract had been concluded because the language used—namely, '[i]f you will sign the Agreement and return it to me, I will send you the Agreement signed on behalf of the [Council] in exchange'—indicated that it was the council's intention to be bound and therefore constituted an offer.

A further useful illustration is provided by the decision in *Harvey v Facey* [1893] AC 552, where the plaintiffs had asked the defendants whether they would sell a particular property and requested that the defendants telegraph their lowest price. The defendants' reply, stating that the lowest price was £900, was held not to constitute an offer but was only an indication of the minimum price if the defendants decided to sell. This case also illustrates that in contracts for the sale of land, the courts will look for clear evidence that the process of negotiation is complete, and that a definite promise to be bound is being made, before it determines that there is an offer capable of being accepted. For example, in *Clifton v Palumbo* [1944] 2 All ER 497, the words 'I am prepared to offer you my estate for £600,000' was held not to constitute an offer.

In more general terms, the context in which the communication is made can affect whether it is interpreted as an offer or an invitation to treat. In *iSoft Group plc v Misys Holdings Ltd* [2003] EWCA Civ 229, unreported, 28 February 2003, the Court of Appeal approved the first instance interpretation of a term of an agreement for the acquisition of a company ([2002] EWHC 2094 (Ch)) which provided that the vendor was to 'offer to sell' to the purchaser 'after-acquired competing businesses for fair market value and on fair and reasonable conditions'. The parties, and the business community, could not reasonably be taken to have envisaged that this term meant that the vendor had to present the buyer with an offer capable of acceptance which could thereby become an immediately binding contract. The term required only that the vendor should indicate a willingness to sell for a fair market value. (In any event, the term was no more than an agreement to agree or was too uncertain to be enforced: see 3.1.4.2.)

2.3.2 Recognized instances of offer or invitations to treat

Case law has established that there are some recognized instances when a particular communication is more likely to be regarded either as an offer, or as an invitation to treat. These operate as a starting point for consideration by the court, but it is quite possible that the normal principle may be found to be inappropriate, being at odds with the intention of the parties as revealed by the facts and the language used.

2.3.2.1 Advertisements, brochures, and price lists

1. The general rule: advertisements, brochures, and price lists amount to invitations to treat

In *Partridge v Crittenden* [1968] 1 WLR 1204, the appellant had placed an advertisement indicating that he had certain wild birds for sale. It was an offence to offer such birds for sale. The advertisement did state a price, but gave no details about delivery or quantities available. **On appeal the appellant's conviction was quashed, because the court held that the advertisement did not amount to an offer but was merely an invitation to treat.** In the words of Lord Parker, there was 'business sense' in treating such an advertisement as no more than an invitation to treat.

Such a conclusion makes 'business sense' because construing such an advertisement as an offer would mean that the seller might find himself unable to supply all those who replied to the advertisement (the 'limited stocks' argument). In *Grainger and Sons v Gough* [1896] AC 325, a wine merchant's catalogue and price list were considered to constitute no more than an invitation to treat on precisely that ground. If, however, the catalogue had been addressed to a limited group of customers, or had made it clear that unlimited supplies were available then, other things being equal, it might have been sufficiently specific to amount to an offer. In any event, it is possible to meet the 'limited stocks' argument by arguing that there is an implied term that the 'offer' is available only while stocks last (see, for example, DCFR II-4:201(3) which adopts this position). It can be avoided more explicitly by an express term to this effect.

2. The exception: Where the advertisement is unilateral

A unilateral contract (discussed in detail at **2.6**) (or so-called 'if' or 'reward' contract) is a contract where one party (the promisor) binds itself to perform a stated promise upon performance of the requested act or condition by the promisee. However, the promisee gives no commitment to perform the act or condition but rather is left free to choose whether to perform or not.

If a reward is advertised for the performance of a specified act, such as supplying information, that advertisement will constitute a unilateral offer, assuming that the language is sufficiently definite to be viewed as such. The acceptance of such an offer is the performance of that act and it cannot be accepted by making a promise (which is the position in the case of bilateral contracts, such as simple sale of goods contracts).

In ***Carlill v Carbolic Smoke Ball Co.*** [1893] 1 QB 256, the defendants had placed an advertisement in which they promised to pay £100 to any person catching influenza after using their smoke ball remedy three times a day for two weeks. The advertisement stated that £1,000 had been placed in a separate bank account in order to meet any claims made. The plaintiff had caught influenza after using the smoke ball in the required manner but the defendants denied any liability to pay £100. The Court of Appeal held that the advertisement constituted an offer since it requested performance of an act as the acceptance (using the smoke ball as directed and catching influenza). In addition, the Court of Appeal treated the deposit of money as an indication of a willingness to be bound by the terms of the advertisement, thereby confirming the intention to be legally bound. It followed that the £100 was payable.

Similarly, in ***Bowerman v ABTA Ltd*** [1996] CLC 451, the majority of the Court of Appeal held that an ABTA notice, which was displayed on the premises of travel agents who were ABTA members, constituted an offer (or promise) of ABTA protection for customers performing an act, namely booking holidays with those ABTA members. This was because the notice requested the performance of an act as the acceptance, i.e. booking a holiday through an ABTA member. The notice was intended to be read, and would reasonably have been read, as an offer.

A further illustration is provided by the facts in ***O'Brien v MGN Ltd*** [2001] EWCA Civ 1279, [2002] CLC 33, where the advertisement in the *Daily Mirror* of a scratch card game with a prize of £50,000 was held to constitute an offer which was accepted when those with winning scratch cards telephoned the hotline to claim their prize.

The fact that such advertisements are regarded as offers makes practical sense, in that if a notice of a reward for performance of a particular act were to be regarded as an invitation to treat, the response (namely performing the act) would be the offer which could be accepted or rejected at will. People offering a reward would therefore have the benefit of seeing the requested act performed and yet not be bound to pay the reward.

That an advertisement requesting performance of an act constitutes an offer can be seen by examining the US decision in ***Lefkowitz v Great Minneapolis Surplus Store*** 86 NW 2d 689 (1957). Here the advertisement was in the following terms: 'Saturday 9 a.m. sharp: 3 brand new fur coats, worth to $100. First come first served. $1 each.' This was held to be an offer. Such an advertisement requested performance of an act (being one of the first three customers on Saturday morning). Performance of this act constituted the acceptance and therefore entitled the customer to purchase one of these fur coats at this sale price.

However, if such an advertisement is to constitute an offer it must be clear and definite in its terms and leave nothing open for negotiation. It may also need to relate to a limited quantity of the specified goods, as in *Lefkowitz*. To illustrate this point, and for amusement, see the terms of the Pepsi promotion in the United States (discussed in Graw, 'Puff, Pepsi and "that plane"—The John Leonard saga' (2000) 15 JCL 281). Under the terms of a promotional campaign, Pepsi points could be redeemed for prizes. The advertisement in question appeared to promise the chance to win a Harrier Jump Jet by collecting 7 million points. Although it can be argued that this amounts to requesting performance of an act as the acceptance, the US court held that the advertisement was an invitation to treat. The court reasoned that the advertisement was not in terms which could be construed as a definite and clear promise to be bound; for example, there was no mention of the action required to claim the prize. In addition, there were no words of limitation to limit the potential liability to supply. This advertisement was therefore construed as requesting a promise, in the form of accepting the terms of the promotion. However, this con-clusion must be viewed as an artificial interpretation designed to avoid the existence of a binding contract to supply the jet.

? Question

Is the promise requesting performance of an act?

The identification of an advertisement as an offer or as an invitation to treat appears to generate confusion (and many emails asking for assistance). Despite the time devoted to unilateral contracts on contract law modules, there are relatively few unilateral contracts in practice. The vast major-ity of contracts are bilateral, i.e. they involve a promise in exchange for a promise. The contract will be bilateral if it is possible to respond to the initial promise, in a way which attracts legal conse-quences, simply by making a promise. On exchange of such promises each party is bound, although performance of those promises will occur later. For example, I may promise to pay you £100 for your bicycle if you deliver it, payment on delivery. You promise (agree) to sell and deliver your bicycle next Monday. We are bound on exchange of promises although payment and delivery will not occur until 'next Monday'.

The fact that I have requested that you deliver the bicycle does not render this unilateral since it is possible to accept by promising to do this. **The promise will only be requesting an act (and there-fore will be unilateral) if it is only possible to respond by actually performing the act in ques-tion.** This will be the case in reward scenarios, e.g. in *Carlill v Carbolic Smoke Ball Co.* it would not have been possible to respond by *promising* to perform the requested act of using the smoke ball as directed and catching influenza; the act itself must be performed in order for the promise to pay to be enforceable. Similarly, if I promise to pay a reward of £50 to anyone who finds and returns my lost dog, it is not possible to claim this reward by simply promising to find and return the dog; performance of the act itself is essential.

In *Intense Developments Ltd v Development Ventures Ltd* [2006] All ER (D) 346 (Jun), the judge rejected an argument that an offer to take a loan for the development of a site, which would be repaid on completion with 50 per cent of the profit of the sale, amounted to a unilateral offer. This was a bilateral offer of a loan which would normally be accepted by promising to make the loan on the terms indicated, although acceptance by conduct in transmitting the loan amount to the account des-ignated in the offer terms constituted acceptance by conduct on the facts (*Brogden v Metropolitan Railway Co.* (1877) LR 2 App Cas 666). This is not the same as requiring performance of an act as the only means of acceptance. On these facts it was possible to accept by promising to repay the loan on completion on the proposed terms.

The crucial question, therefore, is whether it is possible to accept by promising to perform (bilat-eral) or whether it is only possible to accept by performing the requested act (unilateral).

2.3.2.2 Shop displays—shop windows or supermarket shelves

In *Fisher v Bell* [1961] 1 QB 394, it was held that to display a flick-knife with a price marker in a shop window did not amount to commission of the offence of *offering* such a knife for sale. In ***Pharmaceutical Society of Great Britain v Boots Cash Chemists (Southern) Ltd*** [1953] 1 QB 401, it was held that the display of goods on shelves in a self-service store did not amount to an offer of the goods for sale, so that no contract was formed merely by the customer removing the goods from the shelf. The facts were as follows:

> It was a legal requirement that certain drugs and medicines could be sold only under the supervision of a registered pharmacist. Boots had introduced self-service stores where the cash desks were supervised by such a person. Therefore an offence was committed if any sale contract relating to these drugs and medicines was formed **before** the customer reached the cash desk, e.g. if the sale contract was formed when the goods were removed from the shelves, since there was no supervision at that point. It was held that no offence had been committed. The display of goods on supermarket shelves constituted an invitation to treat and not an offer so that there was supervision at the point of sale.

Analysis of the *Boots* case

There is no consensus on what would constitute the offer by the customer since although Lord Goddard, at first instance, appeared to consider that the offer was made when the goods were selected and put into the basket, there are strong grounds for arguing that the offer does not occur until the customer presents the goods to the cashier at the cash desk, thereby communicating a definite intention to be bound to the shopkeeper. The acceptance (on behalf of the shopkeeper) would appear to be the cashier's act of 'acceding to the sale', constituted by 'accepting the price' (see the judgments of Lord Goddard CJ and Somervell LJ in the Court of Appeal).

It appears to have been imperative to the future operation of self-service systems for the courts in the *Boots* case to conclude that the contract was made 'at the cash desk' and not before—and therefore to be able to conclude on the facts that Boots had not committed the offence. The decision, that a display amounted to an invitation to treat, was justified on two grounds: (1) the shopkeeper's freedom of contract (by analogy with an ordinary shop) and (2) the unfortunate practical consequences considered to follow if the display was held to constitute an offer.

1. Shopkeeper's freedom of contract

In an ordinary shop, such as a bookshop, the shopkeeper reserves the right to refuse to sell (subject to anti-discrimination legislation), and that option is exercised in each case by the cashier on the shopkeeper's behalf when the goods are presented for payment at the cash desk. In the self-service scenario, in order to achieve the objective of preserving the shopkeeper's freedom of contract (i.e., controlling acceptance), the court considered that the offer to buy must come from the customer. Accordingly, the offer could not be the shopkeeper's display of the goods.

On the other hand, it could be argued (e.g., Unger (1953) 16 MLR 369) that the price of instituting a self-service system with its associated cost savings should be that the shopkeeper loses this freedom of contract and that it makes more sense to analyse the display as a standing offer, as in the case of the deckchairs in ***Chapelton v Barry UDC*** [1940] 1 KB 532, below, and other displays where further negotiation is not envisaged. The acceptance, and control of the contract, would then rest with the customer. This is the preferred approach of the DCFR since a display of goods is generally to be treated as an offer to sell the goods displayed until the stock of those goods is exhausted, i.e. a standing offer.

2. Practical consequences for customers if a display were held to amount to an offer

The courts in the *Boots* case appear to have assumed that if they found the display to be an offer then the customer's acceptance would have been the act of removing the goods from the shelves. This would have been extremely inconvenient in a practical sense since customers would not have been able to select goods from the shelves, put them in baskets or trolleys, but subsequently change their minds about the purchase.

However, this does not necessarily follow. If the display were to constitute an offer, the acceptance could occur much later, e.g. the act of presenting the goods to the cashier (see the US case of *Lasky v Economy Grocery Stores* 65 NE 2d 305 (1946)). The argument is that on this interpretation there would be supervision before the contract is concluded, although arguably the pharmacist could not prevent such a sale if control over the conclusion of the contract (acceptance) rested with the customer. On the other hand, it would allow some flexibility prior to that time, since the shopkeeper could withdraw such an offer at any time before acceptance and customers would retain the ability to change their minds before their own act of acceptance.

> ## ? Question
>
> **If there is a non-self-service counter inside a supermarket, where is the contract of sale made?**
>
> This point has arisen indirectly in the context of the criminal law where the goods in question have deliberately been priced at a lower price as a result of an arrangement between the customer and the counter assistant, leading to a charge of theft. It has been assumed in such a case that the contract of sale occurs at the counter although property in the goods would not pass until payment of the price at the cash desk (see, e.g., Jackson (1979) 129 NLJ 775 at 777, interpreting comments in *Pilgram v Rice-Smith* [1977] 2 All ER 658). Jackson assumes that the customer is making an offer to *buy* the selected goods, e.g. a joint of meat, and that the assistant accepts that offer by marking up the goods so that the price can be paid. The important distinguishing factor is considered to be 'having dealt with another human agent'.
>
> However, it must be questioned whether this interpretation is correct. The point is unlikely to be litigated and supermarkets accept that customers will change their minds about selected products. It would seem that this 'transaction' is no different to any other *selection* of goods in a supermarket, e.g. putting a tin of baked beans into the shopping trolley but later changing one's mind. The customer does not make an offer to buy until such time as the shopping is complete and the customer decides to check out. Such a position would also equate with the website shopping experience, i.e. it is possible to remove selected items from the cart at any time before the checkout process.
>
> *Note*: The making of a sale contract and the passing of property (i.e., ownership) in the goods which are the subject of that contract may occur at different times. In a supermarket, the property in the goods does not pass until the price is paid (*Lacis v Cashmarts* [1969] 2 QB 400 at p. 407, *Davies v Leighton* (1979) 68 Cr App R 4, [1978] Crim LR 575).

Despite the decision in the *Boots* case, it is possible to imagine a situation in which the display of goods in a shop would amount to an offer; for example, if it were made clear that the shopkeeper was willing to sell to anyone paying the displayed price. On this basis it is also possible to explain the conclusion in *Chapelton v Barry Urban District Council* [1940] 1 KB 532, that a display of deckchairs constituted an offer. It followed that the contract to hire the deckchair could already have been concluded before a ticket containing an exemption clause was issued. Accordingly, the exemption did not protect the local council from liability when the deckchair collapsed resulting in injury to the hirer. Thus, there may have been policy reasons which explain why the display was treated as an offer in this case.

Similarly, in *Thornton v Shoe Lane Parking Ltd* [1971] 2 QB 163 (discussed at 6.3.1.4) Lord Denning MR analysed automatic machines, e.g. vending machines, as constituting standing offers on the basis that as soon as the machine was activated there was no possibility of negotiation. The 'standing offer' approach also enables commercial sense to be realized by accepting the conclusion that in a self-service petrol station the customer accepts the garage's offer of petrol by putting petrol into the vehicle's petrol tank and is therefore liable to pay the amount shown on the pump (*Re Charge Card Services Ltd (No. 2)* [1989] Ch 497).

2.3.2.3 Websites

It would seem that websites are the electronic equivalent of displays, advertisements, or catalogues of products for sale. In English law this should mean that, in general, a website constitutes an invitation to treat. From a practical perspective this is important, since, as discussed above, the result is that that the site provider will retain freedom to contract as the offer will come from the customer. The site provider can therefore avoid entering into contracts with online buyers in excluded jurisdictions. In addition, the provider's stock may be limited and if the website is an invitation to treat so that customers make offers to buy, the provider can manage its stock and will not find itself bound to supply all those online buyers who seek to place orders (although see earlier observations concerning DCFR II-4:201(3) suggesting that a display of goods is an offer). Regulation 12 of the Electronic Commerce (EC Directive) Regulations 2002, SI 2002/2013, may imply that a website will be treated as an invitation to treat since it provides that the customer's 'order *may be* the offer'. However, the language used is hardly conclusive on this point and this is badly thought out if the DCFR is suggesting the opposite, although the final say on steps to electronic contract formation will rest with the retailer which is placed under a duty to provide details of the process (reg. 9(1) and DCFR II-3:105(1)).

If the website does constitute an invitation to treat, the offer will presumably be made by the customer at the checkout stage when the customer clicks the relevant instruction to process the order. The retailer may, however, wish to provide all the order and payment details and provide for acceptance to be made by the customer (thereby ensuring it is received in the retailer's jurisdiction). DCFR II-3:202 may well anticipate that acceptance may come from the customer when it provides for the retailer to acknowledge receipt of this 'acceptance' communication.

Pricing mistakes on websites

A particular problem for website providers is the inadvertent mispricing of goods. In this context the status of the website, and whether a binding contract has been made, will be highly relevant. If a website constitutes no more than an invitation to treat, mispricing will not result in the supplier having to fulfil a contract at the misquoted price. For example, in September 1999, Argos advertised Sony television sets on its website at £3 instead of £299. On New Year's Eve 2001 a particular camera was incorrectly advertised on the Kodak website at £100 instead of the actual price of £329. Kodak had sent customers an automated order confirmation stating that £100 would be charged to their credit card. There was a similar incident in March 2003 when the Amazon website offered a pocket PC for sale at £7.32 instead of the retail price of £274.99 and a television normally retailing for £350 was displayed at a price of 49p on the Argos website on the August bank holiday weekend in 2005.

The legal position might be thought to differ depending upon what happened to individual customers: in the 1999 Argos incident some orders were placed and also confirmed by Argos while, on discovering the mistake, Argos advised other customers trying to place orders that there had been a mistake and that no orders could be accepted at the stated price. In the case of customers whose orders were not accepted or confirmed, there could be no binding contract of sale if the website constituted an invitation to treat. These online buyers would need to argue that the website was an offer, which would be a theoretical possibility only if performance of an act is requested (see 2.3.2.1) and where it is clear that the stock is limited. Something similar to the factual scenario in *Lefkowitz* would be required, e.g. a television set at £3 to the first ten online buyers after 6 a.m. GMT on Thursday 1 March. However, a normal sale of goods contract is bilateral, involving an exchange of promises and not the performance of an act.

What about those customers whose orders had been confirmed and whose credit cards had been charged?

It might be thought that their 'offers' had been accepted by the retailer. However, there are two legal hurdles facing such customers.

The first difficulty facing those customers whose orders had been confirmed was the fact that Argos had made a very clear mistake as to the price term, which online buyers either knew or ought reasonably to have known had been made. This was surely the whole point of the attempts to secure the television sets at the bargain price; online buyers knew very well that a mistake had been made and were seeking to 'snap it up'. The case law establishes that there will be no binding contract in this situation (***Hartog v Colin and Shields*** [1939] 3 All ER 566: see **2.1.2** and **3.3.2**). In ***Chwee Kin Keong v Digilandmall.com Pte Ltd*** [2004] SLR 594, the High Court of Singapore had indicated that suspicious pricing on an Internet site, when compared with the known market value of the goods, would lead to the conclusion that a person in the position of a reasonable prospective purchaser 'ought to have known' of the mistake and would therefore be seeking to snap it up (see **3.3.2**). This leaves open the possibility that it is not 'snapping up' where the goods are priced incorrectly but not noticeably so, e.g. a television set at £200 instead of the normal retail price of £300. In addition, in the example above where a television set is offered for £3 to the first ten online buyers, it is clear that a special offer was intended and that there is no mistake as to the price term.

Of course, if the website is not an 'offer' or if the acceptance does not come from the buyer, then acceptance comes from the retailer and the customer's so-called 'snapping up' offer can be rejected by the retailer on those terms. It is only the offeree's subjective position that is relevant, and not that of the offeror (see **2.1.2**). However, it is the principle of seeking to take advantage that the courts object to and the balance may have swung in favour of the retailer in any event by the practice of retailers delaying acceptance (see below).

Secondly, an electronic confirmation of an order may be no more than this (reg. 11 of the Electronic Commerce (EC Directive) Regulations 2002), i.e. it may not constitute an acceptance of the order but serve only to identify and warn customers of orders placed unintentionally.

Increasingly, online retailers have complied with the duty to indicate to consumers 'in a clear, comprehensible and unambiguous manner…the different technical steps to follow to conclude the contract' (reg. 9(1)) so that the site provider's terms and conditions normally spell out precisely what action will constitute the acceptance. For example, terms and conditions may specify that acceptance will not occur, and a contract will not be formed, until the goods are dispatched

(Argos incident, August 2005). It follows that the retailer can withdraw the advertisement prior to dispatch of the goods.

As a final point, it should not be assumed that there is no liability on suppliers in this situation. First, there may be criminal liability since the Consumer Protection from Unfair Trading Regulations, SI 2008/1277 (in force 26 May 2008), e.g. reg. 5 (prohibiting a range of actions misleading consumers), make it a criminal offence to engage in such prohibited activity (see 1.6.2.1). In addition, reg. 13 of the Electronic Commerce (EC Directive) Regulations 2002, allows for an action seeking damages for breach of statutory duty where, for example, the site provider has not complied with the reg. 9(1) requirement to indicate clearly, before an order is placed, the steps that will result in a concluded contract.

The important point is that there will be *no contractual liability* (and hence no compensation with which to purchase the goods which have been denied) in the vast majority of instances of price mistakes on websites.

2.3.2.4 Tenders

Request for tenders is normally an invitation to treat (inviting tenders)

The request for tenders (or quotations) is a negotiating device common in the world of major commercial contracts. A company seeking to purchase a major item or service, such as a piece of equipment or some construction work, will invite tenders (or quotations) from those interested in supplying the goods or service sought. Such an invitation may be published generally or in a trade journal, or circulated to companies likely to be interested. In normal circumstances the invitation for tenders is not treated as an offer, since the company issuing it may have criteria other than price which it wishes to take into account in awarding the contract. In that case the tenders themselves are the first offers made (see *Spencer v Harding* (1870) LR 5 CP 561) and the person requesting the tenders has the freedom to determine which (if any) they will accept.

Exceptions where the request can also constitute an offer (or promise)

There are, however, two situations where the request to submit tenders (or bids) can *also* constitute an offer which, if accepted, will form a binding contract containing a specific promise.

1. Express contractual promise to accept the most competitive bid

Where the request for bids commits the person issuing the invitation to tender to accept the most competitive bid, either the highest or the lowest bid, that promise to accept the most competitive bid will bind the person making it to do just that. There are *obiter* statements to this effect in *Spencer v Harding* (above) and the legal position was analysed in *Harvela Investments Ltd v Royal Trust Co. of Canada (CI) Ltd* [1986] AC 207.

In *Harvela* the vendors of a plot of land sought a 'single offer' for the whole plot from each of two interested parties, promising to accept the highest offer received provided it met other conditions stipulated. Both parties submitted bids complying with the conditions, but while one merely stated a price it was prepared to pay, the other stated both a concrete sum and a referential bid (i.e., '$101,000 in excess of any other offer'). The question for the House of Lords was which of the two bids was the higher, thus constituting the acceptance necessary for the formation of the agreement. In one sense the referential bid was the higher offer, but such a conclusion was possible provided only one party made such a bid.

The House of Lords considered that as one of the main purposes of competitive tender bargaining is to ensure that negotiations come safely to fruition, allowing unrestricted use of referential bids risked such bargaining being abortive. The House of Lords therefore implied into the request for bids a stipulation that referential bids would not be accepted. In the opinion of Lord Templeman, with whom all their Lordships agreed, it was open to the vendors to initiate a process of bargaining by referential bids (which would be a form of auction), but such an interpretation would not be placed on a request for competitive tenders in the absence of express words to that effect.

The unilateral contract

In *Harvela*, Lord Templeman faced a conceptual difficulty in respect of the implied stipulation against referential bids, in that there was no contract immediately apparent into which that stipulation could be implied. It could not be implied into any eventual contract to buy the land, since such a term would be too late and would bind only one party. Lord Diplock overcame the problem by describing the tendering process as being governed by a unilateral contract (see 2.6) under which:

- the invitation to submit tenders was a unilateral offer (promise), to accept the highest bid and to abide by the other tendering conditions
- this offer was accepted by submitting the highest bid.

This analysis is equally useful where the person inviting bids has committed themselves to accept the highest (or lowest) bid but then sells the goods to a bidder who did not submit the highest (or lowest) bid. In order to hold a person to their promise, to give effect to the bidder's reasonable expectations and possibly also on the basis of reliance on the promise, some legal analysis is called for if such a promise is to bind. As a general principle English law does not recognize pre-contractual liability, i.e. it does not impose any liability on the person requesting the bids prior to the making of the contract to sell or to award work—and then, only with the person who buys the goods or is awarded the work. However, the courts can avoid recognition of 'pre-contractual' liability by creating a separate (unilateral) contract to enforce the promise to accept the highest (or lowest) bid in favour of the person fulfilling that condition.

Although there will be a unilateral contract with the highest (or lowest) bidder, the only remedy for breach of that promise to sell to the highest (or lowest) bidder will be an award of damages. The highest bidder will not be entitled to receive the goods or work that were bid or tendered for because this question is governed by the bilateral contract (see *Spencer v Harding*, above).

	Main bilateral contract awarding goods or services	Unilateral contract based on the promise to accept most competitive tender
Invitation to tender	Invitation to treat	Offer promising to accept most competitive tender, e.g. lowest tender for work
Tenders	Each tender is an **offer**	Submitting lowest tender **accepts** the offer and results in a contract based on that promise
Requestor decides on successful tenderer	Acceptance of a tender results in a contract with that person by which they are awarded the work.	If the person awarded the contract under the bilateral contract is not the lowest tenderer, awarding the contract under the main bilateral contract will breach the unilateral contract and entitle the lowest tenderer to damages to compensate to its loss.

2. Contractual obligation to consider tenders which conform to the bid conditions

Similarly, a fictional unilateral contract was employed in ***Blackpool and Fylde Aero Club Ltd v Blackpool Borough Council*** [1990] 1 WLR 1195 in order **to impose an obligation to consider tenders (or bids) which conformed to bid conditions.**

> The council ran an airport, and granted a single concession to operate pleasure flights from the airport. The licence had been held by the plaintiff club but when the concession came up for renewal, the council determined to invite competitive tenders for it. Tenders were to be submitted by 12 noon on a specified day. On that day the council's letter box was not cleared between the time when the club posted its tender and the closing time for bids, with the result that the club's tender was not considered. The club claimed that the council was in breach of an implied obligation to consider all conforming tenders received before the deadline.
>
> The Court of Appeal agreed. There was an implied unilateral offer (promise) to consider conforming bids, which was accepted by submitting such a bid.

Bingham LJ recognized that no one would go to the trouble and expense of preparing a tender and submitting it in time if they thought that it would not even be considered, so that in recognizing the implied unilateral contract based on an implied promise the Court of Appeal was giving effect to the reasonable expectations and reliance of those submitting tenders.

However, the court also stressed that the only contractual obligation was to *consider the bid*. Thus, as in the ***Harvela*** analysis, the only liability for breach of the contractual obligation to consider conforming tenders will be in damages (and it is likely that the damages award would compensate for wasted expenditure, or possibly damages for loss of the chance to be awarded the contract: 9.4 and 9.3.4).

Although based on the same unilateral contract analysis, the ***Harvela*** and ***Blackpool*** scenarios can be distinguished since, whereas in *Harvela* the obligation forming the basis of the unilateral contract was an *express* promise to accept the highest bid, in ***Blackpool Aero Club*** the obligation to consider confirming tenders was *implied* from the circumstances, namely the fact that only a limited number of contractors were invited to tender and that there was a detailed procedure to be followed for the submission of tenders. These factors were said to justify the implication of a promise to consider conforming tenders. Since these factors are hardly exceptional, it is likely that such an implication can be made in the vast majority of tendering situations.

Post *Blackpool*

This analysis of an implied unilateral contract was accepted by the Court of Appeal in ***Fairclough Building Ltd v Port Talbot BC*** (1992) 62 BLR 82, but the ***Blackpool Aero Club*** case was distinguished on its facts. In *Blackpool Aero Club*, the council had wholly failed to consider the bid, whereas in *Fairclough* the bid was ruled out after preliminary consideration because of a risk of conflict of interest. As a result, no breach of the implied unilateral contract had occurred.

In ***J & A Developments Ltd v Edina Manufacturing Ltd*** [2006] NIQB 85, QBD (NI), the High Court of Justice in Northern Ireland applied the ***Blackpool*** analysis to imply an obligation that the tendering procedure would be conducted in accordance with the principles of a Code of Procedure for tendering. These principles involved an obligation not to seek to alter or reduce any tender once submitted. It followed that by entering into a process of negotiation by which those who had submitted tenders were invited to reduce their tenders, the defendants had acted in breach of contract and were liable in damages. Following this reduction process, the contract had been awarded to the second lowest tenderer who had reduced his price so that it became the lowest, rather than to the plaintiff, who had been the original lowest tenderer. However, given that there was no obligation to award the contract to the lowest tenderer, the decision to award damages based on full expectation loss (i.e., with no discount at all for loss of the chance of being awarded the contract) seems surprising and appears to be based on the conclusion that it was 'a matter of high probability that if the defendants had observed the Code the plaintiff would have been awarded the contract' (at [102]).

In the context of public sector contracts, the courts appear willing to accept an implied obligation of greater scope, namely an implied obligation to act fairly in the tendering process (***Harmon CFEM Facades (UK) Ltd v Corporate Officer of the House of Commons*** (1999) 67 Con LR 1 and ***Pratt Contractors Ltd v Transit New Zealand*** [2003] UKPC 83, [2004] BLR 143). The tendering and award of contracts by public sector bodies is subject to special legislative regulation (see, e.g., the Public Contracts Regulations 2006, SI 2006/5 and the Utilities Contracts Regulations 2006, SI 2006/6) and this appears to distinguish these types of contracts. Nevertheless, the Northern Irish courts have indicated that similar obligations may exist by virtue of the ***Blackpool*** case in parallel with the statutory context (***Natural World Products Ltd v ARC 21*** [2007] NIQB 19 (HC(NI))). This suggests that the requirements of fairness and good faith in the tendering process derive from the common law and can be inferred from the tendering process itself. This authority and the decision in ***Scott v Belfast Education Library Board*** [2007] NI Ch 4, [2007] CILL 2510 (High Court of Justice of Northern Ireland), which have persuasive authority before the English courts, indicate that these obligations will apply in the public sector where the threshold for the application of the statutory regime has not been met. This leaves open the question of whether, on the basis of the ***Blackpool*** case, similar obligations can apply in relation to tendering in the private sector.

2.3.2.5 Auctions

An advertisement that an auction is to be held is not an offer to hold it and a request for bids at an auction is generally no more than an invitation to treat (***Harris v Nickerson*** (1873) LR 8 QB 286), even if the auction advertisement refers to lots being 'offered for sale' (***British Car Auctions Ltd v Wright*** [1972] 1 WLR 1519). Therefore, each bid is an offer, and acceptance occurs when the auctioneer indicates acceptance of a bid with the fall of his hammer (Sale of Goods Act (SGA) 1979, s. 57(2)). ***Harris v Nickerson*** is authority for the fact that if an advertised auction fails to take place, or if the lots advertised are withdrawn from the sale, since the advertisement was only an invitation to treat, the auctioneer will incur no liability.

Auctions without reserve

However, the position is different where an auction is advertised as being 'without reserve' (i.e., involving a promise to sell to the highest bidder and promising not to apply any reserve price or allow the vendor to bid in order artificially to push up the price).

In ***Warlow v Harrison*** (1859) 1 E & E 309, the court dealt *obiter* with the question of whether the next highest bidder has any remedy where the owner successfully bids for the property at an auction without reserve. The court stated that there would be a remedy for breach of contract. The basis for this appears to be the implication of a unilateral contract based on the promise that it will be an auction without reserve.

- This promise (that there will be no reserve) constitutes a unilateral offer.
- The unilateral offer is accepted by the highest genuine (bona fide) bidder at the auction.

If the promise not to apply a reserve is broken then the auctioneer will be liable in damages to the highest genuine bidder who suffers loss. However, the highest genuine bidder will not be entitled to the property sold, because his offer has not been accepted by the fall of the auctioneer's hammer.

Warlow v Harrison, and this analysis, was applied by the Court of Appeal in ***Barry v Davies (Trading as Heathcote Ball and Co.)*** [2000] 1 WLR 1962.

> The case concerned the sale of two machines at an auction without reserve. The plaintiff was the only bidder for the two machines, worth about £14,000 each. The auctioneer withdrew the machines from the sale on the basis that the bids (of £200 for each machine) were too low. The plaintiff claimed damages representing the cost to purchase the machines elsewhere, less the amount of his auction bids.
>
> The Court of Appeal allowed this damages award (of £27,600) on the basis that there was a collateral (separate but linked) contract between the auctioneer and the highest bidder whereby the auctioneer promised to sell to that bidder. The auctioneer had breached this contract by withdrawing the machines from the sale.

The consideration for this collateral (unilateral) contract was the detriment suffered by the bidder whose bid was open to be accepted by the auctioneer, and it was a benefit to the auctioneer through increased attendances pushing the bidding up (although on the facts in *Barry v Davies* this clearly did not have the desired effect since the plaintiff was the only bidder). The other consequence of this decision, as explained by Stuart-Smith LJ, is that by withdrawing the goods, the auctioneer is bidding on behalf of the seller, which is unlawful under s. 57(4) of the SGA 1979. This may have consequences for the seller and, by s. 57(5), the buyer may treat a sale in contravention of s. 57(4) as fraudulent.

 ## Summary

This analysis means that at an auction without reserve:

1. There is a **bilateral contract selling the goods** to whoever makes the bid which the auctioneer accepts by the fall of the hammer. On this analysis, the advertisement of an auction without reserve (or requests for bids at such an auction) is an invitation to treat and each bid is an offer. The acceptance comes from the auctioneer. This contract determines the person who is entitled to the goods.

2. **The promise that the auction is 'without reserve' constitutes a unilateral offer (promise) to that effect which is accepted by the highest genuine bidder.** If a reserve is applied and the goods withdrawn from the sale, or if the owner is permitted to bid and artificially pushes up the price, there is a breach of this unilateral contract and the highest genuine bidder is entitled to be compensated by the payment of damages. That person is not, however, entitled to the goods since this matter is governed by the bilateral contract of sale.

? Question

Is it possible to withdraw a bid at an auction without reserve?

This depends on what constitutes the acceptance of the unilateral offer or promise not to apply a reserve. Clearly, if the unilateral offer were capable of being accepted by all those who bid (although » only the highest genuine bidder would claim damages for suffering loss), it would not be possible to withdraw a bid at such an auction. However, following **Barry v Davies** it is clear that the offer is accepted only by the highest genuine bidder and, since this fact cannot be determined until the fall of the hammer or when the auctioneer withdraws the goods from the sale, it follows that a bid can be withdrawn until that point.

2.3.3 Communication of the offer

An offer does not take effect unless and until it is actually communicated to the offeree; and it is not possible for an offeree to accept unless the offeree had knowledge of the offer (see 2.4.4). Thus, the point of communication of the offer is important because it is only then that the offer can be accepted. This gives rise to the question of what will constitute 'actual communication' (which is also a question of relevance when considering acceptances and revocations). What, for example, would the position be if the offer letter (or email) were delivered to the offices of the offeree but not immediately opened by the offeree? This issue is considered below at 2.4.5.3 and 2.4.5.4, but it is interesting to note that the Vienna Convention for the International Sale of Goods 1980 (CISG), has a 'receipt' rule for offers (Art. 15.1) and helpfully defines 'receipt' as occurring when an offer 'is made orally' to the offeree or is 'delivered by any other means to him personally, to his place of business or mailing address' (see also Art. 1.10, UNIDROIT; Art. 1:303, PECL; DCFR 1–1:109(4)). Where a person has no mailing or business address, receipt will occur when the offer is delivered to that person's 'habitual residence'. Therefore, 'receipt', in these contexts, does not require that the communication should actually have been read by the person to whom it is addressed.

However, it would not be possible to accept without knowledge of the offer so that although an offer might be communicated without the offeree having read or listened to it, any acceptance of that offer would not then be given in exchange for it and so would be invalid as an acceptance (see further 2.4.4).

2.4 Acceptance

2.4.1 Requirements for a valid acceptance

Acceptance is what turns a specific offer, made with the intention to be bound, into an agreement.

How do we identify whether such an acceptance has occurred? The general principles applying to acceptances are as follows:

- To constitute acceptance (and thus agreement), the offeree's unequivocal expression of intention and assent must be made in response to, and must exactly match, the terms of the offer. This concerns the fact of acceptance, i.e. whether we can recognize the correspondence or action as a valid acceptance.

- The matching acceptance must be communicated to the offeror in order to be effective.

These principles are so well established as to need little general comment. Such difficulties as exist arise out of the application of the principles to the realities of everyday contract negotiation.

In simple consumer transactions it is common that only one offer is made, and acceptance is straightforward. No detailed negotiation of terms is involved. Taking the example of a sale in a self-service shop (see **2.3.2.2**), the customer takes a price-displayed item off the shelf and presents it to the cashier, thus making an offer to buy it for the displayed price. The cashier accepts the offer on behalf of the shop, payment is instantaneous, and terms as to quality are left to be implied under the SGA 1979 (see **6.4.2.4**). The role of acceptance in this case is crucial but without legal difficulty.

Commercial contracts, especially for non-standard goods, may be very different. Frequently more than one offer will be made before negotiations are complete, and the language of 'acceptance' may be used before a technical legal analysis would identify acceptance as having been made.

2.4.2 The mirror image rule: Identifying a valid acceptance

An acceptance must be unconditional and correspond with the exact terms proposed by the offeror.

2.4.2.1 Counter-offers

If when responding in a form purporting to be an acceptance, the offeree alters the terms contained in the offer or adds a new term, that response will constitute a *counter-offer*. This counter-offer cannot constitute an acceptance of the original offer. Instead:

- As the counter-offer is itself an offer on the revised terms being made by the offeree, agreement will result only if there is acceptance of the counter-offer by the original offeror.
- The further effect of a counter-offer is to operate in the same way as a rejection, namely to destroy the original offer and so prevent the original offeree from changing its mind and accepting that original offer. This effect is clearly demonstrated in relation to a price term in the case of *Hyde v Wrench* (1840) 3 Beav 334.

> A offered to sell land to B for £1,000. B replied offering £950. Clearly that was not an acceptance but a counter-offer. A rejected the counter-offer, whereupon B purported to accept the original offer of £1,000. A denied that any contract had been made, and the court agreed. It was not open to B to revive A's offer unless A was willing to revert to those terms.

Where the variation in terms is in relation to something less central than the price clause, it is common for the reply to the offer to be described as an 'acceptance'. However, in this situation the reply is also only a counter-offer. In *Jones v Daniel* [1894] 2 Ch 332:

> A offered £1,450 for land belonging to B. Purporting to accept the offer, B sent a document for signature to A containing terms additional to those proposed by A, relating to method of payment, proof of title, and final performance. Although there was nothing unreasonable about the terms, they could not be part of an agreement until A had assented to them. Since A did not agree, there was no contract.

Thus, even where there is agreement on the major terms (e.g., price and subject matter) there may still be no contract because of failure to agree on the ancillary terms.

This counter-offer rule can lead to difficulty where the parties are not particularly concerned about the details of the ancillary terms, and fail to notice discrepancies between the offer and the purported acceptance. This difficulty is illustrated by ***Brogden v Metropolitan Railway Co.*** (1877) 2 App Cas 666.

> The appellant had for some time supplied coal as and when required to the respondent company. The parties decided to enter into a more formal long-term agreement. After negotiations, a draft contract was drawn up by the respondent and sent to the appellant. The appellant filled in the name of an arbitrator, marked the draft as 'approved' and returned it to the respondent. In technical terms the appellant's communication was a counter-offer, but the respondent's manager, being satisfied with the draft, merely put it in a file. He did not communicate his acceptance of the additions made. The parties then commenced performance under the agreement. Subsequently, a dispute arose in which it was questioned whether in fact any long-term contract had come into existence. The House of Lords held that the commencement of performance by the respondent, which had ordered and taken delivery of coal consistently with the terms of the alleged agreement, was acceptance by conduct of the appellant's counter-offer.

Brogden is authority for the fact that a bilateral offer need not be expressly accepted by words but can be accepted by conduct. However, it is clear that the conduct must be referable to the offer and be identifiable as acceptance of the offer terms (*Day Morris Associates v Voyce* [2003] EWCA Civ 189, (2003) 12 EG 129 (CS)).

2.4.2.2 Identifying a counter-offer

A counter-offer, which purports to accept but in fact operates to reject the original offer, must be distinguished from a request for further information *before the offeree decides whether to accept*.

1. Requests for further information

If there is no more than a request for further information, the offer will remain available for acceptance. ***Stevenson, Jacques and Co. v McLean*** (1880) 5 QBD 346, concerned negotiations for the sale of a quantity of iron.

> The defendant had offered to sell at a price of '40s net cash per ton'. The plaintiffs had replied asking whether the defendant would accept '40 for delivery over 2 months, or if not, the longest limit you could give'. It was held that this reply did not operate to reject the defendant's offer but was only an inquiry to determine whether there was any flexibility in the offer terms. Therefore, it remained possible for the plaintiffs to accept that offer.

? Question

Is the response a counter-offer or a request for further information?

This is perhaps the most frequently asked student question in the initial weeks of study.

It is not too difficult to make the distinction between counter-offer and request for more information on the facts in ***Stevenson v McLean*** since the plaintiffs had not reached the stage where they were purporting to accept and their response could not be interpreted as sufficiently specific and definite to constitute a counter-offer. However, other cases may prove more difficult. »

As indicated above, there are two key factors in making the distinction:

1. Is the offeree purporting to accept but at the same time changing the terms (counter-offer) or is he trying to decide whether he can accept by seeking to negotiate on the offer terms (request for further information)?

2. How certain is the language used in the response? For example: A offers to sell B his car for £1,500. B replies: 'I agree, but I'm only prepared to pay £1,400' (counter-offer).

    Compare this with the following: A offers to sell B his car for £1,500. B replies by asking whether A might be prepared to accept £1,400 (request for further information before deciding whether to accept).

2. The effect of qualifying covering letters

What is the position if the response purports to accept in unconditional terms but a covering letter sent with this 'acceptance' indicates that the performance required for that acceptance will not occur? Is this a counter-offer?

This question arose for decision in *The Society of Lloyd's v Twinn* (2000) 97 (15) LSG 40, *The Times*, 4 April.

The defendants alleged that they had not accepted a settlement agreement offered to Lloyd's Names in July 1996, and therefore could not be in breach of the agreement because, although they had completed the application forms, their covering letter had asserted that they would not be able to pay the sums that would be due from them under the terms of the settlement. The Court of Appeal rejected this argument and concluded that there was an unconditional acceptance of the offer in the form of the completed application forms. The covering letter sought to obtain a concession, but it was separate and collateral to the concluded contract rather than a condition of the acceptance, and this fact was borne out by subsequent correspondence in which the defendants clearly accepted that they had signed and returned valid acceptances of the offer.

Scott V-C expressed the position as follows:

An acceptance which seeks an indulgence will be effective if it is clear that the offeree was unconditionally accepting the offer. In a case where the terms of the offer held out a considerable benefit to the offeree, the offeree might well want to accept notwithstanding that in some respect or other he, the offeree, would not be able to perform. Suppose an offer with a stipulation requiring performance by a specified date...Why should the offeree not give an unconditional acceptance but, at the same time, try to agree an extension of time, warning the offeror that his (the offeree's) performance would anyway take place later than the specified date?

He added that the question of whether there was an unconditional acceptance and a collateral counter-offer, or a counter-offer preventing acceptance, would depend on the facts of the particular case, and that 'the intended effect of a purported acceptance' would need to be 'judged objectively from the language used and the surrounding circumstances'.

2.4.2.3 The battle of forms

With the increasing use of often conflicting standard terms of business, each party to a sale or supply contract will send its own terms in an effort to ensure that those terms and conditions prevail. The question in such a case is to determine whose terms govern in this 'battle of forms'. The problem here is that if the traditional analysis of offer, counter-offer, and acceptance is applied, there may well be no contract at all, because of the absence of a matching offer and acceptance, or there may be a contract referable to the last set of terms to be sent before performance. If there is no contract, it may be possible to obtain payment for goods or services on a restitutionary basis (on the basis that otherwise the receiving party would be unjustly enriched by receiving goods without having to pay for them) (*Peter Lind & Co. Ltd v Mersey Docks and Harbour Board* [1972] 2 Lloyd's Rep 234 and *British Steel Corporation v Cleveland Bridge & Engineering* [1984] 1 All ER 504; see **3.1.5**). However, in both situations it is likely that neither party would have appreciated the legal effect.

Despite the consequences that can result from the application of the traditional analysis, the courts have tended to follow it. For example, it was adopted by the majority of the Court of Appeal in *Butler Machine Tool Co. Ltd v Ex-Cell-O Corporation (England) Ltd* [1979] 1 WLR 401, although Lord Denning MR suggested a more radical approach.

> In *Butler Machine*, the sellers sent a quotation for the supply of a machine to the buyers. This quotation was issued on the basis of the sellers' conditions which were to 'prevail over any terms and conditions in the buyer's order', and which included a price variation clause. The buyers placed an order, and their letter contained conflicting conditions which, in particular, contained no price variation clause (i.e. a fixed-price contract). At the bottom of the order was a tear-off confirmation slip expressly subject to the buyers' terms, which the sellers completed and returned. The sellers claimed to be entitled to vary the contract price. The Court of Appeal rejected that claim on the basis that the sellers had expressly accepted the buyers' terms when they completed and returned the acknowledgement slip. In other words, the sellers had accepted the buyers' 'last shot'.

However, whereas Lawton and Bridge LJJ analysed this last shot as a counter-offer, Lord Denning MR adopted a different approach, which involved separating the question of formation of a contract from the determination of its content. Lord Denning considered that a contract was formed where the parties were agreed on the material points even if there were conflicting terms in their forms. He then turned to the question of content and whose terms would govern, and stated:

> In some cases, the battle is won by the man who gets the blow in first. If he offers to sell at a named price on the terms and conditions stated on the back: and the buyer orders the goods purporting to accept the offer—on an order form with his own different terms and conditions on the back—then if the difference is so material that it would affect the price, the buyer ought not to be allowed to take advantage of the difference unless he draws it specifically to the attention of the seller. There are yet other cases where the battle depends on the shots fired on both sides. There is a concluded contract but the forms vary. The terms and conditions of both parties are to be construed together. If they can be reconciled so as to give a harmonious result, all well and good. If differences are irreconcilable—so that they are mutually contradictory—then the conflicting terms may have to be scrapped and replaced by a reasonable implication.

Last shot prevails

The 'last shot' invariably appears to be the significant document in determining who wins (or loses) the battle of forms because of the possibility of acceptance of this counter-offer by conduct, e.g. *Sauter Automation Ltd v Goodman (Mechanical Services) Ltd* (1986) 34 BLR 81, *Chichester Joinery v John Mowlem and Co.* (1987) 42 BLR 100, and *Nissan UK Ltd v Nissan Motor Manufacturing (UK) Ltd*, unreported, 26 October 1994.

However, the interesting question is to what extent the Denning approach in *Butler Machine Tool* can be adopted or should the courts generally focus on the traditional offer and acceptance analysis?

In *Tekdata Interconnections Ltd v Amphenol Ltd* [2009] EWCA Civ 1209, [2010] 1 Lloyd's Rep 357, [2009] 2 CLC 866, in the context of a 'battle of forms' in a long term contracting arrangement the seller appealed a first instance decision that the buyer's terms governed the contracting relationship. The process was that the buyer would send purchase orders containing its own terms and conditions. The seller would acknowledge the purchase orders by sending an acknowledgement stating that its own terms and conditions (including an exemption clause) would prevail. This should have been analysed as an offer by the buyer with the last shot sent by the seller so that conduct (delivery) would result in a contract on the seller's terms. However, the judge at first instance adopted the comments made by Lord Denning in the *Butler Machine Tool* case and analysed the parties' relationship. He therefore concluded that the buyer's terms prevailed because that had been the parties' intentions all along. The Court of Appeal upheld the appeal and applied the traditional analysis. Longmore LJ put the position thus (at [21]):

> although I am not saying that the context of a long term relationship and the conduct of the parties can never be so strong as to displace the result which a traditional offer and acceptance analysis would dictate, I do not consider the circumstances are sufficiently strong to do so in the present case. Indeed I think it will always be difficult to displace the traditional analysis in a battle of forms case, unless it can be said there was a clear course of dealing between the parties. That was never proved.

Dyson LJ noted (at [25]) that this approach 'has the great merit of providing a degree of certainty which is both desirable and necessary in order to promote effective commercial relationships'. It follows that the Court of Appeal was not saying that a Denning contextual approach would never be applicable but it was not the starting point for any analysis and would be difficult to establish on the facts. In particular, Longmore LJ appears to have been influenced by argument to the effect that whatever Lord Denning said in *Butler Machine Tool*, he actually applied a traditional analysis, i.e. that the acknowledgement slip had been expressly accepted by the seller.

If a party wishes to avoid contracting on the other's terms it seems that it will need to make this explicitly clear. For example, although in *Butler Machine* the sellers had tried to ensure that their terms were paramount by drafting a clause stating that their terms and conditions would prevail over those in the buyers' order, this proved ineffective in the face of their express acceptance of the buyers' counter-offer (the last shot). The sellers had also claimed that their terms were in fact the last document, because in sending the acknowledgement slip they had again referred to their quotation. This argument failed because the Court of Appeal regarded this reference as relevant only to the issue of the price and not as an attempt to incorporate the sellers' standard terms of supply. More recently, in *Balmoral Group Ltd v Borealis (UK) Ltd* [2006] EWHC 1900 (Comm),

61

[2006] 2 Lloyd's Rep 629, [2006] 2 CLC 220, although orders had been placed on the purchaser's own terms (which included a requirement for compliance with the quality terms in the sales legislation), the purchaser had not produced a copy of these terms. A reference 'in poor typescript' at the bottom of purchase orders did not amount to *clear* notice that the purchaser intended only to contract on its own terms (ineffective first shot). If the purchaser wished to avoid contracting on the supplier's terms it needed to make this explicitly clear. By comparison, the supplier had put its terms (excluding liability for breach of the statutory quality terms) on the back of its invoices and these had been seen and initialled by the managing director of the purchasing company and no objection had been made. Accordingly, by purchasing the materials at the quoted prices from the supplier, the purchasing company had accepted the supplier's terms (i.e., the last shot was the only effective shot).

It is nevertheless important to analyse whether the differing form is obviously conflicting before applying the last-shot doctrine. In *Sterling Hydraulics Ltd v Dichtomatik Ltd* [2006] EWHC 2004 (QB), [2007] 1 Lloyd's Rep 8, it was argued, in an attempt to rely on a limitation clause in the defendant's 'general terms of sale', that the acknowledgement of the claimant's purchase order referring to these terms for the first time, amounted to a counter-offer which had been accepted when the claimant took delivery of the goods (a last-shot argument). However, the judge rejected this argument and considered that the acknowledgement *did not make it clear* that the terms were in conflict with those in the purchase order since there was no real difference in the payment terms (both referred to payment within two months of delivery), and because the defendant had failed to supply a copy of its sales terms with the acknowledgement of order. Accordingly, the acknowledgement was correctly interpreted as an acceptance rather than as a counter-offer and a binding contract existed on the claimant's standard terms of purchase (the first shot). The judge concluded that this 'battle of forms was barely a skirmish'. (See 6.3.1.2 for discussion of the failure to incorporate by reference on these facts.)

Interestingly, the judge in *Sterling Hydraulics Ltd v Dichtomatik Ltd* also referred to Lord Denning's approach in *Butler Machine Tool* of separating the formation of a contract from a determination of its content and, applying that approach, came to the conclusion that there was a binding contract on the basis of all the correspondence passing between the parties. Nevertheless, Lord Denning's suggestion in *Butler Machine Tool* for determination of content in cases of conflicting terms, by replacing such terms with terms based on reasonable implication, was far ahead of what was then, and is currently, acceptable to English law (see *Tekdata Interconnections Ltd v Amphenol Ltd* [2009] EWCA Civ 1209, above), and we shall have to go some way further down the road to judicial intervention in the process of contracting before the courts will construct a contract on behalf of the parties out of the conflicting terms and conditions in the various documents passing between them (but see § 2–207 of the Uniform Commercial Code in the United States and Art. 19 of the CISG 1980).

Article 2.1.22 of UNIDROIT, Art. 2:209 of PECL, and now DCFR II-4:209 all broadly accept that a contract is formed in a battle of forms situation unless one party has explicitly notified the other (either in advance, or without delay) that it does not intend to be bound if there are conflicting terms. In accordance with these principles, where a contract is formed despite the conflicting terms, its content will comprise those terms which are common in substance, and the implication is that the courts will fill any gaps. Each set of principles also contains a provision addressing 'modified acceptances' 'which do not materially alter the terms of the offer' (Art. 2.1.11, UNIDROIT; Art. 2:208, PECL; DCFR II-4:208). These articles state the general rule, i.e. that a modified acceptance is a counter-offer. However, 'modified acceptances' will be acceptances unless the offeror makes speedy objection to the discrepancy (UNIDROIT, PECL, and DCFR), or the offer expressly limited acceptance to the terms of the offer (PECL and DCFR), or the offeree's acceptance was conditional upon the offeror's assent to the differing terms and the assent was not received within a reasonable time (PECL and DCFR). Where there is such an acceptance, the terms of the contract will be the offer terms as modified by the acceptance.

Lord Denning's approach to formation of the contract, like the formulations in the UCC (Uniform Commercial Code (United States)), Vienna Convention, UNIDROIT, PECL, and the DCFR, placed great emphasis on material terms or terms which 'materially alter' the offer. This raises the question of identification of 'material terms' and hence 'material alterations'. Article 19(3) of the CISG 1980 defines 'material alterations'. However, this definition is extremely broad and only the most trivial of alterations would be regarded as not materially altering the offer. In particular, if the response contains any changes to price, payment terms, delivery, liability, and any dispute mechanism, the response would constitute a rejection. There is some explanation of 'material' terms and modifications in the commentary to the UNIDROIT *Principles* and PECL, but the idea of a list as in Art. 19(3) of the CISG 1980 is expressly rejected by PECL in favour of the retention of flexibility, given that any list could not be exhaustive. Instead, Art. 1:301(5) of PECL contains a definition of 'material' as a matter 'which a reasonable person in the same situation as one party ought to have known would influence the other party in its decision whether to contract on the proposed terms or to contract at all'.

2.4.3 Failure to follow the prescribed method of acceptance: A valid acceptance nevertheless?

The offer may stipulate that the offeree is to respond using a particular method of communication or is to respond to a particular address. Where the offeree has failed to comply with the stipulated method for accepting prescribed by the offeror, it might be thought, on the basis of the mirror-image rule, that where the offeree uses a different method that 'acceptance' would be invalid. However, where the offeror has not made it clear that the stipulated method is mandatory and that no other will suffice, a pragmatic approach has been taken in the case law.

1. Explicit words are required in order for a stipulated method to be considered mandatory, e.g. an explicit statement that the prescribed method must be followed and that no other will suffice.

2. In *Manchester Diocesan Council of Education v Commercial & General Investments Ltd* [1970] 1 WLR 241, Buckley J stated that where the offeror has not made it very clear that the stipulated method is mandatory and that no other will suffice, the following principles applied so that the acceptance might nevertheless be valid:
   - Any equally efficacious method of acceptance will be valid if it fulfils the purpose in prescribing the method. For example, if the offeror wants a quick response and prescribes acceptance by fax, then as long as this method is not mandatory, any acceptance that is just as quick as a fax acceptance will suffice.
   - Alternatively, if the method was prescribed in order to benefit, the offeree, the offeree can waive (give up) a stipulation for his benefit and use a different method as long as this method does not disadvantage the offeror. In *Yates Building Co. Ltd v Pulleyn &*

Sons (York) Ltd (1975) 119 SJ 370, the offer stipulated that the acceptance should be sent by registered or recorded post. This was intended to enable the offeree to prove that the acceptance had been posted (see **2.4.5.2**). Accordingly the offeree could waive this requirement and take the risk of the ordinary post.

The facts of ***Manchester Diocesan*** are slightly unusual.

It was the offeree who had required that the offer specify that the offeree's acceptance letter was to be sent to the particular address given in the tender. The intention was to ensure that there would be a binding acceptance on posting to the prescribed address (see postal rule of acceptance at **2.4.5.2**). However, the plaintiff offeree had in fact sent the acceptance to the offeror's surveyor and not to the address specified in the offer.

Buckley J held that since the stipulated method was intended to benefit the offeree, the offeree could waive compliance with this if the method used was no less advantageous to the offeror. On the facts the method used was no less advantageous to the offeror since the acceptance had been actually communicated.

(?) Question

If an offer is sent by post, must the acceptance be sent by post?

No. The acceptance would not necessarily need to be sent by post unless the offeror had made it quite clear that acceptance by post was mandatory. That apart, where an offer is sent by post and the parties are at a distance, the post will be considered as *one* of the envisaged methods for a response (***Henthorn v Fraser*** [1892] 2 Ch 27: offer communicated by hand but the parties were at a distance from one another) but need not be the only one. It will be necessary to consider the context and the evidence of the offeror's objectives in making the offer by post. For example, it may be clear from the terms of the offer that the offeror contemplates a quicker response, e.g. by email or fax, than is possible using the postal service.

2.4.4 **Acceptance in response to the offer**

The rule that acceptance must be made in response to the offer is a close relative of the principle requiring communication of an offer and also the principle which defines consideration as the price for which the promise of the other is bought. The fact that a claimant is not entitled to a reward when his performance of the act requested takes place in ignorance of the reward offer can be explained either in terms of an absence of consideration or in terms of an absence of agreement (see **4.2.1.1**: ***R v Clarke*** (1927) 40 CLR 227). That is, either the performance was not induced by the offer, or the acceptance (which in such a contract is constituted by the performance of the requested act: see **2.6** below) was not made in response to the offer.

However, it is clear from the decision in ***Williams v Carwardine*** (1833) 5 C & P 566, that as long as the offeree did have knowledge of the offer, and thus accepted in response to it, his motive in so doing is irrelevant. The decision in ***Gibbons v Proctor*** (1891) 64 LT 594 might be considered to be at odds with the principle that there must be knowledge of the offer in order to be able to claim the reward. However, this decision has been explained as turning on the particular requirements of the offer, which required the information to be given to a particular person, Superintendent Penn. Although the information was initially given to another colleague at a time when there was no knowledge of the reward, the offeree had the necessary knowledge at the time when the information reached Superintendent Penn and the decision can therefore be interpreted as reflecting accepted principle.

Critique

The rule that acceptance must be in response to, and with knowledge of, the offer has a number of unfortunate consequences:

First it may leave parties without a contract, despite the fact that they are in fact subjectively agreed on all matters, if they cannot objectively be shown to have gone through the process of agreement. If two parties both make offers to each other more or less simultaneously (i.e., before receiving the other's offer) [cross-offers] then, even if the offers are made in identical terms, there is no contract. The offers may correspond, but there is no agreement because there is no acceptance made in response to the other's offer (***Tinn v Hoffman*** (1873) 29 LT 271). In practice, the apparent harshness of this rule is mitigated by the fact that any small act of performance by one party may well be regarded as acceptance by conduct and so establish agreement (see **2.4.2.1**).The finding of no contract in the absence of some act of performance was explained in ***Tinn v Hoffman*** as a rule of convenience to avoid uncertainty over whether a contract had come into existence.

Secondly, as Hudson ((1968) 84 LQR 503) has argued in the context of rewards and the decision in ***Gibbons v Proctor***, an offeror could obtain the benefit of performance of an act and yet not have to pay the reward simply because the particular offeree happened not to see the offered reward. It is at least arguable that there are strong policy grounds for encouraging the giving of information by those who act under a sense of moral duty but may not have seen the published reward.

2.4.5 Communication of acceptance

The second general principle of acceptance is that the acceptance needs to be communicated to the offeror (in the sense of being actually received).

There are two important exceptions to this general rule:

1. implied waiver of the communication requirement in the case of unilateral contracts

2. acceptances by post, where the parties are necessarily not in each other's presence.

2.4.5.1 Implied waiver of the need to communicate acceptance in unilateral contracts

In a unilateral contact, performance of the act constitutes the acceptance and there is therefore no need to communicate the fact that you are *attempting to perform* that act. Authority for this principle is the decision in ***Carlill v Carbolic Smoke Ball Co.*** [1893] 1 QB 256 and, in particular, the statement by Bowen LJ:

> In the advertisement cases it seems to me to follow as an inference to be drawn from the transaction itself that a person is not to notify his acceptance of the offer before he performs the condition, but if he performs the condition notification is dispensed with.

Bowen LJ gave the example of a reward for the return of a lost dog to a particular place. The acceptance is the act of returning the dog to that place and there is no need to communicate an intention to perform the act. Of course, the particular offer may expressly provide that communication is a necessary part of the acceptance (requested act), e.g. where there is a reward for supplying information. In addition, although it may not be necessary to communicate an intention to seek to perform the requested act, it may still be necessary at a practical level to communicate the fact of that performance in order to notify the offeror that the reward is being claimed. However, that is not part of the acceptance itself.

Silence in bilateral contracts

By comparison, in standard bilateral negotiations, the general rule is that the offeror cannot waive the need for communication and stipulate that silence will constitute acceptance. The authority for this is said to be the decision in *Felthouse v Bindley* (1862) 11 CB NS 869.

An uncle and nephew had been negotiating the sale of the nephew's horse to his uncle, but they could not agree on the price. In the end the uncle had written, saying that if he heard no more he would assume that the nephew agreed to his proposal of a price of £30 15s. The nephew appears to have been satisfied with this arrangement, since he instructed an auctioneer to withdraw the horse in question from a sale. However, he did not communicate this fact to his uncle. When the auctioneer mistakenly sold the horse, the uncle sued him for conversion, claiming to be the owner of the horse under a contract with his nephew. The court did not accept his claim, stating as one of its reasons that 'the uncle had no right to impose upon the nephew a sale...unless he chose to comply with the condition of writing to repudiate the offer'.

As Miller ((1972) 35 MLR 489) argued, the actual decision on the facts in *Felthouse v Bindley* appears to be incorrect since neither of the grounds said to justify the silence principle applied on the facts:

1. Silence will often be equivocal and the silence principle is said to protect offerees from contracts where they had no intention to accept. However, the nephew's conduct in instructing the auctioneer not to include the horse in the auction sale would appear to indicate that there was an intention to accept.

2. It would be difficult to argue that the problem was that the nephew had not communicated this intention to his uncle since, in imposing the silence requirement, the uncle had waived the need for that communication.

Nevertheless, the silence principle itself is valid and underpins the rules on inertia selling, i.e. where an offeror, without any previous course of dealing, seeks to force an offeree to reply in order to avoid the formation of a contract. In the case of such inertia selling to consumers, reg. 24 of the Consumer Protection (Distance Selling) Regulations 2000, SI 2000/2334 applies, so that unsolicited goods sent to consumers become an unconditional gift with immediate effect. The Consumer Protection from Unfair Trading Regulations 2008, SI 2008/1277, may also be relevant since Schedule 1 refers to demanding payment for unsolicited goods as an unfair commercial practice within reg. 3(4). Such an unfair commercial practice will constitute an offence within the provisions of Part 3 of these Regulations (reg. 12). The previous legislation aimed at deterring inertia selling, the Unsolicited Goods and Services Act 1971, continues to apply in the business context.

Exceptions

However, it is certainly not the case that silence can never be acceptance. In some contexts, especially where there has been a continuing course of dealing, silence (or conduct) can be sufficient acceptance.

1. If there has been a course of dealing whereby the offeree has taken the benefit of services offered, the offeree's silence (or conduct) can constitute acceptance

If A operates a coal delivery (or window cleaning) round, and regularly delivers two bags of coal to B or cleans B's windows, either collecting the money on delivery or leaving an invoice to be paid later, without any formal order being placed, B would be unable to deny the existence of a contract for coal actually delivered or for the cleaning of his windows. B would be bound by his own silence, which would constitute a sufficient acceptance.

Equally, many people have relied upon the automatic annual renewal of their insurance policies to ensure that the required cover starts as soon as the previous year's cover comes to an end. Yet it is not uncommon, at the crucial date, for the policyholder not to have replied to the company's proposal, which is no more than an offer needing acceptance.

2. If it is the *offeree* who is attempting to hold the *offeror* to the offeror's stipulation of silence then the offeree's silence will constitute acceptance

In *Felthouse v Bindley*, the particular form of the action (against the auctioneer) may have been significant. If the facts had been different, and it had been the uncle who had refused to take delivery of the horse on the basis that there had been no communication of acceptance to him, his nephew should have been able to rely on the uncle's stipulation and his own silence as establishing the existence of the contract (see Peel, *Treitel's The Law of Contract*, 12th edn (Sweet and Maxwell, 2007), pp. 35–6 and Miller (1972) 35 MLR 489). In this situation the offeror would be bound by the offeree's silence, and arguably the basis for this would be estoppel (i.e., the fact that the offeror expressly formulated his offer so that silence should be acceptance and therefore cannot deny this position where the offeree has relied on it). The technical difficulty here is that Kerr J in *Fairline Shipping Corporation v Adamson* [1975] QB 180 held that this would amount to using the estoppel as a cause of action, which is not permitted in English law. However, it must surely be the case that the estoppel would operate to prevent the defendant (offeror) from raising lack of communication of the acceptance as a defence to the offeree's claim for payment.

3. If it was the offeree, rather than the offeror, who initiated the proposal that the offeree's silence would constitute acceptance

In *Re Selectmove Ltd* [1995] 1 WLR 474 at p. 478, Peter Gibson LJ suggested, in *obiter* comments, that an offeree would be bound by his silence where he has given an undertaking to speak:

Where the offeree himself indicates that an offer is to be taken as accepted if he does not indicate to the contrary by an ascertainable time, he is undertaking to speak if he does not want an agreement to be concluded. I see no reason in principle why that should not be an exceptional circumstance such that the offer can be accepted by silence. But it is unnecessary to express a concluded view on this point.

On the facts in this case, the tax payer had been in negotiations with the Revenue over tax arrears. In August 1991 he had made an offer to the tax collector that he would pay future amounts as they fell due and arrears by monthly instalments commencing in February 1992. The collector indicated that he would have to seek approval for this proposal but that he would advise the tax payer if the proposal was unacceptable. There was no further communication between them until October 1991 when the Revenue demanded payment in full. The tax payer argued that there was a binding agreement for the Revenue to accept payment by instalments. The Court of Appeal rejected this argument on the basis that the tax collector had no authority to commit the Revenue to the suggested contract.

However, it was accepted that the position may be different where the offeree does possess the necessary authority to contract. Any other position would defeat the legitimate expectations of the offeror. In addition, there can be no objection on policy grounds since there is no question of a duty to speak being *imposed* by the offeror on the offeree. (If there had been the necessary authority and if the tax payer had paid the arrears in accordance with the proposal, there might have been an issue of estoppel since the proposal terms would then have been relied upon.)

Nevertheless, the circumstances may make it quite clear that the silence is not to be taken as acceptance or as involving any binding promise or variation, e.g. **Northstar Land Ltd v Brooks** [2006] EWCA Civ 756, [2006] 2 EGLR 67. The claimant purchaser had served notice to complete following the exercise of an option to purchase land for development. This notice required completion on 2 January. However, the claimant later offered to extend the deadline for completion to 9 January in light of the Christmas and New Year break. On 2 January, solicitors for the defendants (vendors) were asked to agree to completion being deferred to 9 January. The solicitors stated that they would need to take instructions and would revert back. However, they did not do so. Having received no response, the claimant assumed that the completion date had been deferred and so did not complete on the schedule date of 2 January. The Court of Appeal confirmed that there was no obligation on the vendors' solicitors to respond so that the claim for specific performance had to fail.

2.4.5.2 The postal rule of acceptance

When the parties negotiate to a conclusion in each other's presence there is little problem. There is little danger of uncertainty as to whether agreement has been reached, although recollections may differ as to its content if it has not been recorded. The general rule is that words of acceptance must not only be spoken, they must be heard by the offeror. Thus, if words of acceptance are drowned by a loud noise they must be repeated before the contract is concluded (see the judgment of Denning LJ in **Entores Ltd v Miles Far East Corporation** [1955] 2 QB 327).

However, when the parties are not in each other's presence communication becomes a more critical issue, especially when the agency of a third party, such as the Post Office, or of a machine is involved. The law has developed a distinction of potentially fundamental importance between instantaneous and non-instantaneous communications. Instantaneous communications are treated more or less as if the parties were in each other's presence, whereas special rules apply to non-instantaneous communications.

Acceptance and the risk of the post

The problem with contract negotiation by post is that letters may either be delayed or lost. The central question is who should bear this risk of loss or delay? In **Adams v Lindsell** (1818) 1 B & Ald 681, the defendants offered to sell wool to the plaintiffs, asking for a reply 'in course of post'. The defendants' letter was misdirected, so that the plaintiffs' reply was delayed beyond the normal course of post, and the defendants sold the wool to someone else. Nevertheless, the plaintiffs had sent a letter of acceptance on the day that the offer had been received, and claimed that there was an enforceable contract. The court upheld that claim, and since this case the general rule has been that where acceptance is communicated by post, the contract is formed as soon as the letter is sent, without need for it ever to reach the offeror. This rule applies even if the postal acceptance never arrives and the offeror is ignorant of the fact that an acceptance was posted: ***Household Fire and Carriage Accident Insurance Co. Ltd v Grant*** (1879) 4 ExD 216. In ***Household Fire v Grant*** the postal acceptance never arrived but the Court of Appeal held there to be a binding contract on posting. The postal rule therefore places the risk of loss or delay squarely on the offeror since it follows that the offeror will be bound by a contract despite the non-receipt of an acceptance sent by post.

Justifications for the postal rule of acceptance

Attempts have been made to justify the rule on all kinds of grounds.

1. It is said that without such a rule offerees would never know whether a contract had been formed. In other words, if actual communication of a postal acceptance is required, the offeree would not be safe in relying on the acceptance until receipt of written notification that the acceptance had arrived and such confirmation would also be necessary for the notification of the fact of receipt of the acceptance, and so on. Such a position was considered to be commercially inconvenient.

2. It has also been argued that the postal rule prevents offerees from speculating by posting an acceptance and then (if the market changes) withdrawing it by speedier means (e.g., telephone), although see further the discussion on retraction (or overtaking) of a postal acceptance, below.

3. It could be argued that the offeror, unlike the offeree, will not be prejudiced by delays or loss in the post, since the offeror is expecting a response and will check if a reply is not received.

4. Alternatively, it is argued that if the offeror has indicated that use of the post is permissible, then it is the offeror who should bear the risks of that system. This last explanation is borne out by ***Henthorn v Fraser*** [1892] 2 Ch 27, in which it was made clear that the postal rule is applicable only where it was reasonable in all the circumstances for the offeree to have used the post; such would most obviously be the case where the offer had been sent by post.

The truth of the matter is almost certainly that whenever one of the risks of the use of the post materializes, whatever conclusion the court reaches will be harsh on one of the parties. The postal rule is no more than a rule of convenience adopted in the interests of certainty. The basic argument is that offerors should know the risks inherent in use of the post and can protect themselves if they so wish. Indeed, the fact that the postal rule can be avoided in practice is often used as a reason to justify its existence!

Criticisms of the postal rule

The postal rule has been the subject of much criticism.

- Where a postal acceptance has been lost in the post, the offeror may believe that, since no reply has been received, the offeree does not wish to accept. The offeror may therefore believe that there will be no question of breach if a contract relating to the same subject matter is made with someone else.

- A further criticism made by Bramwell LJ in a powerful dissent in *Household Fire and Carriage Accident Insurance Co. Ltd v Grant* (1879) 4 ExD 216, was that the operation of such a rule is arbitrary since it does not apply to non-postal acceptances and little conscious thought may have been given to the decision to communicate the acceptance using one form of communication rather than another, e.g. the post compared to hand delivery or acceptance by faxed letter. Bramwell LJ would therefore have preferred the ordinary rule of communication to apply equally to acceptance by post. The most significant part of his judgment is where he says that the harm he perceives in the postal rule 'will be obviated only by the rule being rendered nugatory by every prudent man saying "Your answer by post is only to bind if it reaches me"'.

1. Avoiding the postal rule

It is sensible, therefore, for the offeror to seek protection against the risks posed by the postal rule by stipulating that a particular means of acceptance (other than the post) is required, or wording the offer to require actual communication of any acceptance. This is precisely what the offeror achieved in *Holwell Securities Ltd v Hughes* [1974] 1 WLR 155.

> The defendant granted the plaintiff an option for the purchase of certain land, which was said to be exercisable by notice in writing to the defendant at a given address within six months. An option is no more than an offer, and although the plaintiff posted a letter accepting the offer in question within the six-month period, it failed to arrive. The Court of Appeal held that the option had not been validly exercised and, accordingly, there was no contract. The main finding was that the mere words 'notice in writing to' were sufficient to oust the postal rule. These words amounted instead to a stipulation that notice must reach the offeror, thus reinstating the general principle of actual communication.

It would seem relatively straightforward, in the light of this interpretation of what are fairly common words, to avoid the operation of the postal rule. For example, the words 'let me know' your answer may suffice as emphasizing the need for actual communication. Thus, the significance of the postal 'rule' as a practical principle may well be overstated. In his judgment Lawton LJ referred to football pools coupons as an example of a familiar situation where the postal rule is ousted.

Although *Holwell* provides authority for the fact that it is possible to oust the operation of the postal rule of acceptance by using *express* words, Lawton LJ also stated that the postal rule 'probably does not operate if its application would produce manifest inconvenience and absurdity', and he interpreted this to mean that the rule can be ousted if it is clear from the subject matter and the circumstances that the parties cannot have intended that there should be a binding agreement until there has been actual communication of an acceptance. This again provides ample scope for the avoidance of the postal rule in practice.

2. Retraction of (or overtaking) a postal acceptance

Is it possible to retract a postal acceptance before it reaches the offeror? In other words, could the offeree post an acceptance but then change his mind and telephone the offeror to tell him that he does not want to accept and that the offeror should therefore disregard any acceptance letter?

There is no English case authority; and a Scottish case (*Countess of Dunmore v Alexander* (1830) 9 S 190) is highly dubious authority, although it is sometimes cited in support of the conclusion that it is possible to overtake a postal acceptance. This Scottish case is of questionable authority because:

- The majority appears to be treating the letter being overtaken as an offer and offers are revocable before they are communicated and accepted.

- The case is complicated by the fact that communications take place through an agent or intermediary.

- It is not strictly speaking an 'overtaking' case because both communications arrived at the same time.

Despite the absence of authority, there has been much academic discussion of this question of whether it is possible to overtake a postal acceptance. There are two opposing positions:

(a) It is not possible to retract (or overtake) a postal acceptance

It might be assumed that if the postal rule is in fact a 'rule' then logic would dictate that it would not be possible to retract a postal acceptance since it would be binding on posting. This conclusion is frequently supported by asserting that to allow any other conclusion would permit the offeree to be able to 'play the market', i.e. to accept an offer to purchase goods at one price and later to withdraw that acceptance by a quicker method if market conditions make the contract less profitable.

(b) It is possible to retract (or overtake) a postal acceptance where the offeror is not disadvantaged

It can be argued that the postal 'rule' is nothing more than a rule of convenience to determine who should bear the risk of loss or delay in the post. As such, its operation should focus on the question of inconvenience, and it can be argued that logically any offeror will accept and act upon the communication received first, so that as long as a postal acceptance is retracted before that postal acceptance arrives, the offeror suffers no disadvantage, (see Hudson, 'Retraction of letters of acceptance' (1966) 82 LQR 169). Not only does the offeror suffer no disadvantage, but it might equally be considered unreasonable for the offeror to rely upon a postal acceptance which he knows has been retracted. A further justification for allowing the offeree this latitude is the fact that the offeror can always oust the operation of the postal rule if s/he wishes by the use of express words requiring that the post should not be used or requiring actual communication of any acceptance sent by post.

2.4.5.3 Instantaneous methods of communicating but non-instantaneous messages

The post is very obviously a method of non-instantaneous communication, and therefore the law has recognized that there needs to be a principle to determine who should bear the risks of transmission. On the other hand, it is generally accepted that telephone negotiation is a form of instantaneous communication, so that the parties are treated as if in each other's presence and no contract will be formed unless the words of acceptance are clearly heard by the offeror ('the receipt rule'). A similar approach was taken to telex communications (*Entores Ltd v Miles Far East Corporation* [1955] 2 QB 327). On the facts of *Entores*, it was necessary to decide *where* the contract was formed in order to determine whether the contract was made within the jurisdiction.

> A Dutch company sent an offer by telex to an English company. The English company sent a counter-offer response by telex and the Dutch company responded by telexing an acceptance of the counter-offer. The Court of Appeal held that the contract was made in England where the acceptance was received. The telex message took effect where it was received.

By analogy with telex messages, an acceptance by fax has also been held to amount to an instantaneous communication which takes effect on receipt (*JSC Zestafoni Nikoladze Ferroalloy Plant v Ronly Holdings Ltd* [2004] EWHC 245 (Comm), [2004] 2 Lloyd's Rep 335 at [75]: the agreement was made in England where the fax acceptance was received). Of course, the sender of a fax receives a message informing them that the message has been received, although it does not always follow that the fax communication has been received in its entirety—or legibly.

What if an instantaneous method is used but the actual communication is non-instantaneous?

In *Entores*, Denning LJ had recognized that there were occurrences which could affect the instantaneous nature of the transmission, e.g. if the telephone or telex line went dead during transmission but the offeree was unaware of this fact and thought the acceptance message had got through. If the offeror, knowing that a message was being sent, did not ask for it to be repeated, Denning LJ (at p. 333) considered that 'the offeror...is clearly bound, because he will be estopped from saying that he did not receive the message of acceptance. It is his own fault that he did not get it.'

Summary

Summary of the principles in the judgment of Denning LJ as they apply to communication of acceptance by an instantaneous method:

- In general, the onus is on the communicator (offeree) to get his message through.
- If the line goes dead and the communicator (offeree) knows this, then the offeree must repeat the message and ensure that it is received.
- If the recipient (offeror) knows that a message is being sent and that it has not been received but the offeree believes the message has got through, then the offeror must ask for the message to be repeated. If he does not do so, the offeror will not be able to deny that the acceptance was effectively received.
- If no one is at fault (i.e., the offeree believes the message got through and the offeror does not know that any message was being sent), then the acceptance will not have been communicated and there will be no contract.

That there are instances when the actual communication would be non-instantaneous, despite the use of an instantaneous method of communication, was explicitly recognized in *Brinkibon Ltd v Stahag Stahl und Stahlwarenhandelsgesellschaft GmbH* [1983] 2 AC 34. Lord Wilberforce stated that messages are frequently sent by telex out of business hours, leaving messages stored until the following day. (The same can be said of fax communications and email.) In such non-instantaneous cases, Lord Wilberforce stated (at p. 42) that:

No universal rule can cover such cases: they must be resolved by reference to the intentions of the parties, by sound business practice and in some cases by a judgment where the risks should lie.

In effect Lord Wilberforce was saying that there is no rule for such cases. **However, a general principle appears to be identifiable, namely that if the offeree has done all that he might reasonably be expected to do to get his message through, that acceptance should take effect when the offeree might reasonably expect it to be communicated to the offeror.**

1. Communication to a business during office hours

It follows that if an acceptance has been communicated to a business during office hours, the offeree could reasonably expect the offeror to be monitoring the (say) fax machine, and would expect communication to occur when the message was received by the machine. Accordingly, in this situation, communication to the machine would suffice as 'actual communication'. Authority for this principle is provided by:

- the decision in *The Brimnes* [1975] QB 929 (although the case itself concerned a notice of withdrawal rather than an acceptance)
- comments by Lord Fraser in *Brinkibon Ltd v Stahag Stahl* that messages would be at the risk of the recipient if the recipient failed to man its telex (or fax) machine.

2. Communication to a business outside office hours

The converse position was considered by Gatehouse J in *Mondial Shipping and Chartering BV v Astarte Shipping Ltd* [1995] CLC 1011. The judge suggested that receipt of a contractual notice should be deemed to occur at the start of the next working day if it was in fact received and stored outside normal working hours (in this case the opening for business on the following Monday, since the message was sent and received at 23.41 hours on a Friday). Gatehouse J also indicated that he viewed this result as consistent with Lord Wilberforce's approach, which was to consider each case on its particular facts.

The meaning of 'ordinary business hours'

This raises a difficult question concerning the definition of 'ordinary business hours' and how this will be determined. In *The Brimnes* [1975] QB 929, a message received between 17.30 and 18.00 was considered to be received within 'ordinary business hours'. Will the meaning of 'ordinary business hours' vary according to the knowledge of the parties in any particular case (e.g., if the offeree knows that the offeror always closes at 16.00 hours on a Friday), or should this question be determined objectively and a general definition provided? The first solution might fit more easily with the principles set out by Lord Wilberforce, although those who seek certainty in their commercial dealings would probably regard a more objective formulation as preferable.

Messages left on telephone answering machines

Even these principles leave open some difficult questions, such as: when is there communication of an acceptance message left on a telephone answering machine?

- If we apply the general principle of what the offeree could reasonably expect, the conclusion might be that the message will not be communicated until actually played back, since anyone leaving a message should reasonably assume that, as the machine is switched on, the message will not be communicated immediately. (This ignores the practice of using an answering machine to screen calls.)

- On the other hand, Coote ((1971) 4 NZULR 331) argued, by analogy with the postal rule, that where the machine appears to be working, in leaving the message the offeree has put the matter out of his control so that this should be the point of communication. In addition, in inviting communication using this method, the offeror may be taken to have accepted the risk of being bound by an acceptance of which he has no knowledge. Such a position might be preferable for evidential reasons since many machines will record the time of receipt of the message; and it is also a good deal more convenient for the offeree since it avoids the possibility of numerous repeat telephone calls.

2.4.5.4 Electronic means of communicating

Electronic communications are covered by the Consumer Protection (Distance Selling) Regulations 2000, SI 2000/2334, so that certain information must be provided to the consumer **before the conclusion of the contract**. This makes it important to determine when the contract is concluded. It is also vitally important to decide whether the postal rule ('the dispatch rule') or 'the receipt rule' applies to these communications, because this in turn will determine the place, and time, of contracting. A distinction exists between contracts made on a retailer's website and contracts made exclusively by the exchange of email messages. Whereas the Electronic Commerce (EC Directive) Regulations 2002, SI 2002/2013, apply to website contracting, their application is expressly excluded from applying to contracts made exclusively by exchange of emails (regs. 9(4) and 11(3)).

1. Email

On the facts, it may be the case that despite the use of email communications during the negotiation stage, the parties did not intend that there was to be a binding contract reached by the exchange of emails, e.g. *Pretty Pictures v Quixote Films Ltd* [2003] EWHC 311 (QB) where a signed written contract was contemplated by the parties.

Email acceptance messages raise complex questions since the expression 'electronic mail' may suggest that they are a replacement for posted letters of acceptance, so that the postal rule should apply. This view may be supported by the fact that such messages are sent via a server and may not be immediately received.

Accordingly, there are two possible approaches to the communication of email **acceptance** messages:

(a) Postal analogy

It can be argued that such messages are similar to postal acceptances. The sender of the message puts it out of their control by pressing the 'send message' key and there will inevitably be some, albeit very short, interval before the message reaches its destination. If the postal rule applied, the email contract would be binding the moment the message of acceptance was sent. This would be important, assuming the customer makes the offer, for suppliers of goods or services who send acceptances by email, since the contract would then be formed in the jurisdiction of that seller or supplier.

(b) The receipt rule

However, given the complexities of individual email systems, it would seem preferable to apply an actual communication (or 'receipt' rule), in particular because the sender will know if the message has not been sent and can resend it. By analogy with *Entores*, that ought to mean that responsibility for getting the message through to its destination should lie with the communicator. This approach is supported by the decision of the High Court of Singapore in *Chwee Kin Keong v Digilandmall.com Pte Ltd* [2004] SLR 594, [97]–[99], on the basis that the receipt rule has greater global acceptance and because email is in some respects very different to a postal communication.

Nevertheless, there are two obvious problems with the receipt solution:

- It will mean that if the customer makes the offer and the supplier accepts, the contract will be formed in the customer's jurisdiction (place of receipt of the acceptance), which may suit the customer but will be too risky for suppliers.

- The second problem with such a solution is the same difficulty affecting all communications to which the receipt rule applies, namely to determine what is meant by 'receipt' or 'actual communication'. Is it communication to the mail server, to the computer, or when the acceptance message is actually read?

As mentioned at 2.3.3, the CISG 1980, UNIDROIT *Principles*, and PECL, all adopt a definition of 'receipt' to assist with certainty, and a similar rule might be usefully devised to cover electronic communications if the receipt principle is adopted. Such a definition is expressly included in the DCFR since I-1:109(4)(c) refers to notice transmitted by electronic means being received 'when it can be accessed by the addressee'. Expert evidence would be required to identify this.

2. Website (or Internet) contracting

Internet contracting (i.e., offer and acceptance at the website, also discussed at 2.3.2.3) is instantaneous so that the receipt rule should apply. The Electronic Commerce (EC Directive) Regulations 2002, SI 2002/2013, apply to such contracts. In practical terms, the transmission of messages is controlled by clicking on various responses to messages. The online buyer initially clicks on a 'checkout' or 'send order' button. The retailer then checks stock availability and will usually confirm this by a message displayed on the screen. This is not intended to constitute acceptance, because it is clear to the customer that further action on his part is required by entering credit or debit card details. Only after these details have been transmitted and accepted does the retailer send a message confirming that the order has been received. This is unlikely, however, to be regarded as the retailer's acceptance which is often expressly delayed until the dispatch of the goods themselves. It may be interpreted as an offer, leaving it to the customer to accept by confirming (and thereby ensuring that the contract is made in the retailer's jurisdiction where the acceptance is received).

Although what constitutes the acceptance is not identified in the E-Commerce (EC Directive) Regulations 2002, reg. 11(2) does provide that, unless the parties are businesses and agree otherwise, the order and the acknowledgement of receipt of order 'will be deemed to be received when the parties to whom they are addressed are able to access them'. This appears to confirm that the receipt rule is appropriate in this context and that receipt will occur when the message has been downloaded from the server and is therefore capable of being accessed by the addressee. This approach receives explicit support in the decision of the High Court of Singapore in **Chwee Kin Keong v Digilandmall.com Pte Ltd** [2004] SLR 594 at [101].

Logically, the receipt principle ought to apply equally to the order, acknowledgement of the order and to whatever constitutes the acceptance communication.

Conclusion

Although the Electronic Commerce (EC Directive) Regulations which accept the receipt rule do not apply to email contracting, it would be very strange if the 'receipt' rule applied to Internet contracting and to all email correspondence apart from email acceptances so that it seems preferable for the receipt rule to be adopted generally in this context. There is now some support for this conclusion in the definition of receipt in the DCFR.

2.5 Termination of offers

To be capable of acceptance an offer must not only be specific and have been made with the intention of being bound (see **2.3.1**), it must also be current. Acceptance made after an offer has ceased to be valid is ineffective to form a contract. This section examines the means by which offers terminate so that they are no longer available for acceptance.

2.5.1 Lapse of time

Where an offer is left open indefinitely, there may come a time when the offeree can no longer accept.

> In *Ramsgate Victoria Hotel Co. Ltd v Montefiore* (1866) LR 1 Ex 109, the defendant had applied for shares in the plaintiff company in early June 1864. Shares were allotted to him in late November 1864. The defendant refused to pay for the shares, although he had not withdrawn his application at the time when the shares were allotted. It was held that he was not obliged to go through with the purchase of the shares. The company's response to the defendant's offer had not been made within a reasonable time.

It is not possible to give any indication of what is a reasonable time, which will be a question of fact in each case. Where the offer is expressly stipulated to be open for a limited period ('a firm offer') the offer will automatically lapse at the end of this fixed period.

Interestingly, the DCFR would allow late acceptances to operate if the offeror is prepared to treat it as an acceptance and informs the offeree of this fact without undue delay (II-4:207(1)). Under the DCFR where the acceptance has been dispatched and delayed in the transmission process but ought to have been received in due time, the offeree can rely upon it as acceptance unless the offeror has promptly informed the offeree that the offer has lapsed (II-4:207(2)). This would provide similar protection to the postal rule to an offeree unless the offeror has been prompt in indicating that the offer has lapsed.

2.5.2 **Death**

The death of either party may terminate an offer, although the English authorities are far from clear as to the precise circumstances in which an offer will lapse on death.

Death of the offeror

Where the contract is for the performance of a personal service by the offeror which depends upon some skill which is exclusive to the offeror, the offeror's death automatically terminates the offer. Thus, an offer by a concert pianist to perform at a concert could not be accepted after the death of the pianist.

However, where the subject matter is something available in an open market, there is no difficulty about obtaining substitute performance of what had been offered. Then the issue is whether the executor of the dead offeror's estate should have to arrange such substitute performance. The orthodox view is that the burden should not fall upon the executor provided notice of the death of the offeror has been given to the offeree, so that in the case of an offer to give a guarantee it has been held that an offeree cannot accept it after he has been informed of the death of the offeror (*Coulthart v Clementson* (1879) 5 QBD 42). But where the offeree has no notice of the death of the offeror at the time when the acceptance is made, the deceased's estate will be bound. There are *obiter dicta* to this effect in *Bradbury v Morgan* (1862) 1 Hurl & C 249.

Death of the offeree

Although there are *obiter* statements in *Reynolds v Atherton* (1921) 125 LT 690 suggesting that in this situation the offer ceases to be an offer at all, the position is probably that the offeree's representatives can accept the offer if it is of a non-personal nature.

2.5.3 **Revocation**

An offer may be expressly terminated (or revoked), or the revocation may occur by implication, e.g. where the response to the offer is a counter-offer (*Hyde v Wrench* (1840) 3 Beav 334: see **2.4.2.1**). In addition, an offer may be impliedly revoked by the offeror making a second offer. The decision in *Pickfords Ltd v Celestica Ltd* [2003] EWCA Civ 1741 provides authority for the fact that where A makes an offer to B (the first offer or price quotation) and then makes a second (differing) offer, without expressly revoking the first, the second offer may automatically revoke the first if in making the second offer the offeror 'clearly indicates an intention…to withdraw the first offer'. This can be compared with the situation where B asks for a second (additional) quotation based on different facts, e.g. a fixed-price quotation. In this situation B has a choice between the two offers or quotations because the second quotation was requested and provided on the basis of providing greater choice rather than rejecting the original offer.

Express revocation of an offer

In negotiations towards a bilateral contract, the general rule is that the offeror is free to withdraw the offer at any time before acceptance (*Offord v Davies* (1862) 12 CB NS 748). It follows that revocation of an offer after the time of acceptance is ineffective.

2.5.3.1 'Firm offers'

It is not uncommon for an offer to be expressed as 'open' for a given period of time. It follows that the offer cannot be accepted once that period has elapsed (see **2.5.1**). It might also be thought that the offeror is promising that he will not revoke the offer within that period of time. However, this is no more than a pre-contractual promise and English law is clear that such a promise is no different from any other promise and is unenforceable unless supported by separate, valuable consideration (e.g., such as an option to purchase: see **Holwell Securities Ltd v Hughes** [1974] 1 WLR 155). **Routledge v Grant** (1828) 4 Bing 653 provides authority for the fact that a firm-offer promise is freely revocable in English law unless supported by consideration.

> In **Routledge v Grant** the defendant offered to take a lease of premises belonging to the plaintiff, at the same time promising to hold his offer open for six weeks. After only three weeks the defendant purported to revoke this offer, while at the end of the six weeks the plaintiff purported to accept it. The court held that there was no contract. In the absence of consideration to support the promise to keep the offer open for a specified period, the offer may be withdrawn at any time, even before expiry of that period.

Critique of the firm-offer rule in English law

The English rule on firm offers is not accepted by most other legal systems. Even most American states, whose contract law is derived from English law, have abandoned the rule, at least in the case of firm offers made by those in business in relation to potential sales of goods (see Uniform Commercial Code, §2–205). Since the firm offer is a valuable tool in forward planning, especially where a firm wishes to be able to rely on prices quoted by potential subcontractors when tendering for a major contract, it might be thought desirable for the English rule to be abandoned so that it would not be possible to revoke such an offer during the period stated. Article 2.1.4, UNIDROIT; Art. 2:202, PECL; and DCFR II-4:202(3) provide that an offer cannot be revoked if it states a fixed time for acceptance and it is clear from the commentary to PECL that this would cover the firm offer.

Such a reform of English law might be achieved simply by identifying a very small reciprocal benefit to the offeror in making the firm offer promise, such as might amount to consideration under the approach adopted in the context of alteration promises to pay more in **Williams v Roffey Bros & Nicholls (Contractors) Ltd** [1991] 1 QB 1 (described as a 'practical' or 'factual' benefit: see 4.4.4). There might, for example, be some factual benefit to the offeror in having an identified offeree carefully considering his offer, even if it may not be converted into the benefit of an actual contract. However, the **Williams v Roffey Bros** principle **cannot be applied** in this context because it applies only to promises altering *existing* contracts (see 4.4.4).

2.5.3.2 Communication of a revocation

In all types of negotiation, whether instantaneous or not, revocation is ineffective until actually communicated to the offeree, and until that time the offer is open for acceptance.

1. A revocation must be actually communicated. The postal rule of acceptances does not apply to revocations of offers

The fact that the postal rule applies in the case of acceptance (see 2.4.5.2) but does not apply in the case of revocation (see 2.5.3), means that the courts must pay close attention to the timing of communications.

If a letter of acceptance is posted after a letter of revocation has been posted, but before that revocation is received, the acceptance will be effective to form a binding contract although it was dispatched after the revocation. This was exactly what happened in **Byrne and Co. v Van Tienhoven and Co.** (1880) 5 CPD 344.

A letter of revocation of an offer was sent from Cardiff to New York on 8 October. Acceptance of the original offer was telegraphed on 11 October from New York to Cardiff, followed on 15 October by a letter of confirmation, each being sent before the letter of revocation had arrived. The court held that a contract had come into existence on 11 October (the postal rule also applying to acceptances by telegram), because the revocation was ineffective until communicated to the offeree.

A further example is provided by the facts of *Henthorn v Fraser* [1892] 2 Ch 27 where the revocation of an offer posted at 12 noon did not reach the offeree until 5 p.m. However, since the offeree posted the acceptance at 3.50 p.m., there was a binding contract from that time. The revocation has to be communicated in order to be effective and was therefore too late.

The UNIDROIT *Principles*, PECL, and the DCFR all contain potentially useful provisions which aim to protect the offeree against intervening revocation in the case of postal acceptances, given that both sets of principles apply the receipt rule to postal acceptances. Although an acceptance is not effective until it reaches the offeror (Art. 2.1.6(2), UNIDROIT; Art. 2:205, PECL; DCFR II-4:205(1)), the offeror can revoke only if the revocation reaches the offeree before he has dispatched his acceptance (Art. 2.1.4(1), UNIDROIT; Art. 2:202, PECL; DCFR II-4:202(1)).

Revocation of unilateral offers made to the whole world

There is a special rule applicable in the case of revocations of unilateral offers made to the whole world where the offerees are necessarily unidentified so that actual communication of a revocation to individual offerees cannot occur (*Shuey v United States* 92 US 73 (1875); discussed at 2.6.4).

2. The revocation need not be authorized by the offeror, provided the offeree ought reasonably to believe it

In *Dickinson v Dodds* (1876) 2 ChD 463, the defendant had offered to sell a house to the plaintiff, and had promised to leave the offer open for three days, although the plaintiff had given no consideration for the promise. The plaintiff had decided to accept the offer, but had taken no steps to communicate his decision to the defendant when he was informed by Berry, an apparently reliable person, that the defendant had been offering or agreeing to sell the property to a third party. The plaintiff then attempted to communicate his acceptance to the defendant, and claimed that there had been no effective revocation of the offer before his communication of acceptance.

The Court of Appeal held that the manner of communication of revocation was irrelevant, provided that the plaintiff knew that the defendant no longer intended to sell the property to him by the time his purported acceptance was made.

This conclusion means that an offeree will have to decide whether to believe revocation information which is communicated by a third party. There is a risk that the source is unreliable and the information is incorrect. The safest course of action, if possible, will be for the offeree to check directly with the offeror in such circumstances.

2.6 Unilateral contracts

A unilateral contract is a contract where one party (the promisor) binds himself to perform a stated promise upon performance of a stated act by the promisee, but under which the promisee gives no commitment to perform the act but rather is left free to choose whether to perform or not.

Such contracts are sometimes referred to as 'if contracts', since they take the form of the following well-known example first cited in *Great Northern Railway Co. v Witham* (1873) LR 9 CP 16: 'If you will go to York, I will give you £100.' Examples of unilateral contracts are option contracts, estate agency contracts, and reward contracts (which can include rewards for information, return of property, and for collecting tokens in an advertising promotion). This kind of bargain is outside the standard contracting situation, usually described as bilateral or synallagmatic where there are two identified contracting parties who exchange promises and are both bound from the moment of that exchange.

Unilateral contracts can be explained in terms of offer and acceptance, but sometimes only with difficulty. It was in the context of just such a contract that Lord Wilberforce commented upon the artificiality of the offer and acceptance analysis in *The Eurymedon* [1975] AC 154 (see **2.1.3**).

2.6.1 Unilateral offer

There are two different types of unilateral offer:

1. A unilateral offer (requesting performance of an act) may be made to an identified individual

In *Great Northern Railway Co. v Witham* (1873) LR 9 CP 16, the defendant argued that a unilateral offer (promise requesting performance of an act in exchange) could not result in a contract because there was no reciprocity from the promise, i.e. only the promisor is bound when this promise is made. That argument was roundly rejected by the court, which saw such offers as a matter of everyday practice.

2. Alternatively, the offer may be made to the public at large, or to a particular class of persons

The classic example of such offers is the offer of a reward in return for the performance of some service, such as the apprehension of a criminal or the finding of lost property. In *Carlill v Carbolic Smoke Ball Co.* [1893] 1 QB 256 (the facts are given at **2.3.2.1**), the defendants sought to avoid having to pay the promised sum, although the plaintiff had caught influenza after apparently proper use of the smoke ball, by saying that there could be no contract because there would otherwise have been a unilateral contract with the whole world. Bowen LJ rejected this argument, saying:

It is not a contract made with all the world. There is the fallacy of the argument. It is an *offer* made to all the world; and why should not an offer be made to all the world which is to ripen into a contract with anybody who comes forward and performs the condition? It is an offer to become liable to anyone who, before it is retracted, performs the condition, and, although the offer is made to the world, the contract is made with that limited portion of the public who come forward and perform the condition on the faith of the advertisement.

This authority was relied on by the majority of the Court of Appeal in *Bowerman v ABTA Ltd* [1996] CLC 451, in deciding that an ABTA notice, displayed by travel agents and containing a promise to reimburse the cost of holidays when ABTA members ceased to operate, constituted an offer to customers which was accepted by anyone booking a holiday with an ABTA member.

2.6.2 Acceptance and consideration in the unilateral contract

Acceptance must be made *in response to* the offer (see **2.4.4**). This principle has particular application in the context of unilateral offers made to the whole world, such as offers of rewards, and much of the case law is concerned with these offers. The requested act must be carried out in response to the offer of a reward so that there can be no acceptance where there was no knowledge of the offer.

The general rule is that in unilateral contracts performance of the requested act constitutes both the acceptance and the consideration to support the offeror's promise to pay the reward. Thus, in *Daulia Ltd v Four Millbank Nominees Ltd* [1978] Ch 231, Goff LJ said: '[T]he true view of a unilateral contract must in general be that the offeror is entitled to require full performance of the condition which he has imposed and short of that he is not bound.'

However, there is an argument (Winfield, *Pollock's Principles of Contract*, 13th edn (Stevens, 1950), p. 19, adopted by the Law Revision Committee in its Sixth Interim Report in 1937, Cmnd 5449) which suggests that for some purposes acceptance may be constituted by commencing performance of the stipulated act, so that any attempt to revoke the offer after the commencement of performance will be too late (see **2.6.3.2**). It follows that both parties are bound on acceptance. But, no reward would be payable until the complete performance of the act since, until that time, the consideration for the promise of the reward will not have been provided. There are considerable difficulties in accepting this analysis which are discussed at **2.6.3.2** below.

2.6.3 Revocation

Revocation presents particular difficulties in the case of offers of unilateral contracts due to the fact that acceptance in a unilateral contract is constituted by performance of the act requested in the offer promise. It follows that in theory it would be open to the offeror to revoke the offer at any time before completion of that performance, even where the offeree had gone to effort or expense in attempting performance, since the revocation would have occurred before the moment of acceptance (*Petterson v Pattberg* 161 NE 428 (1928) and see **2.5.3**).

It has long been recognized that application of the normal rule in this situation can cause hardship and injustice. Nevertheless, attempts to overcome the rule have run into conceptual difficulties. It is generally accepted that it would be desirable for the power to revoke to be lost once the offeror has notice that an offeree has unequivocally embarked upon performance. Loss of the power to revoke would not affect the rule that acceptance is constituted only by full performance of the act requested in the offer. There are *dicta* to that effect from Goff LJ in *Daulia Ltd v Four Millbank Nominees Ltd* [1978] Ch 231. This legal position was recently affirmed by the Court of Appeal in *Soulsbury v Soulsbury* [2007] EWCA Civ 969, [2008] 2 WLR 834, also discussed at **16.4.2**, in relation to a promise of £100,000 on the death of an ex-husband in exchange for the ex-wife refraining from enforcing a county court order in her favour. The Court of Appeal considered that once she acted on this promise by not suing to enforce the maintenance order, the promise could no longer be revoked. However, if she gave up and sued for the maintenance then clearly she would not have accepted and could not claim the £100,000. (See the discussion of this unilateral contract by Longmore LJ at [48]–[50].)

The difficulty is in finding a conceptual explanation for such a principle.

2.6.3.1 Promissory estoppel

Perhaps the most obvious explanation lies in the doctrine of promissory estoppel (see **4.8.2**), since it is not difficult to identify both a representation that the offer would be held open long enough for performance to be completed and a reliance by the other party on that representation.

> In ***Errington v Errington and Woods*** [1952] 1 KB 290, a father had bought a house for his son and daughter-in-law to live in, promising that although the house and accompanying mortgage were in his name he would transfer the house to their names once they had paid off all the mortgage instalments. The father died and the son left the daughter-in-law, who continued to live in the house and to pay the instalments. The question arose of whether the daughter-in-law could be forced to surrender possession of the house.

Denning LJ said:

> The father's promise was a unilateral contract—a promise of the house in return for their act of paying the instalments. It could not be revoked by him once the couple entered on performance of the act but it would cease to bind him if they left it incomplete and unperformed…They have acted on the promise and neither the father nor his widow, his successor in title, can eject them in disregard of it.

There is a hint in the passage quoted that Denning LJ viewed the inability to revoke the promise as based on estoppel, since he referred expressly to the fact that the couple had acted on the promise. In many cases, however, such analysis will not work, because there is no pre-existing legal relationship and because in English law the doctrine cannot currently be used to found a cause of action (see **4.8.3.2**). Since ***Errington v Errington*** involved the expenditure of money on land belonging to another, it may be justified on the basis of the analogous doctrine of proprietary estoppel (see **4.9**), but that places a serious limitation on the case as explaining the loss of the power to revoke.

2.6.3.2 Acceptance upon commencement

An alternative explanation is to question the usual rule that in unilateral contracts acceptance and consideration are synonymous and simultaneous (see **2.6.2**). Instead, it is argued that acceptance in a unilateral contract can occur by commencing performance of the requested act although there is no entitlement to the reward until the consideration (full performance of the act) has been supplied.

However, the main difficulty with such a simple rule is that, pending complete performance of the requested act, it has always been accepted that an offeree is entirely free to decide whether or not to perform, and indeed free to commence performance and then stop before completion without fear of any penalty other than the loss of the opportunity to earn the promised reward. If acceptance were to be constituted by starting performance, then the contract would, of course, be in existence from that moment. The offeree would then be obliged to complete performance or face a claim for breach of contract. To tie the offeree in by such a rule would be to defeat one of the objects of the unilateral contract, which is to avoid the need for initial reciprocity inherent in the consideration doctrine as it is applied to bilateral contracts. ('Unilateral' means that only one party is bound on the giving of the promise; the offeree is not bound until complete performance of the act.)

2.6.3.3 Collateral contract

A third explanation rests on the identification of two contracts in such cases.

1. The main unilateral contract, with acceptance and consideration furnished in the ortho-dox way by performance of the act stipulated in the offer, and until complete performance of the act no reward would be payable.

2. An additional collateral (or ancillary) unilateral contract which consists of an offer (implied promise) not to revoke the main offer once the offeree has commenced performance of the stipulated act, and this offer would be accepted by that act of commencing this performance (see McGovney (1914) 27 Harv LR 644 at p. 659). There would then be an enforceable promise to keep open the main offer (and not to revoke). There is no real conceptual difficulty with this explanation, since commencing performance can be the consideration for the collateral contract not to revoke because it is the performance impliedly requested in the offer.

However, this explanation is highly artificial and bears no resemblance to the manner in which unilateral offers are in fact made. It also possesses one significant drawback, namely that this mechanism will not actually prevent revocation of the main unilateral offer. It only means that there will be a breach of the collateral contract and the remedy would be damages for that breach. Nevertheless, more recent developments in respect of implied contracts (see, for example, *Harvela Investments v Royal Trust Co. of Canada Ltd* [1986] AC 207 and *Blackpool and Fylde Aero Club v Blackpool Borough Council* [1990] 1 WLR 1195 at 2.3.2.4) may lend support to 'the two contract' approach as the solution to the conceptual dilemma.

Furthermore, there is clear support in the case law for 'the two contract' approach to revocation since both the House of Lords in *Luxor v Cooper* and the Court of Appeal in *Daulia v Four Millbank Nominees* considered the question of whether revocation was possible by first deciding whether there was an implied promise not to revoke once performance had commenced. The existence of such an implied promise acts as the basis for the collateral unilateral contract. On the facts no such promise could be implied in *Luxor v Cooper* since the context envisaged an offer that should be freely revocable until completion of the sale.

> *Luxor (Eastbourne) Ltd v Cooper* [1941] AC 108 involved an estate agency contract on terms whereby the agent was to be paid £10,000 on completion of the sale of two cinemas to a purchaser for at least £185,000. Although such a purchaser was found, the sale did not take place. The House of Lords refused to imply a term to the effect that the owners had undertaken not to prevent the sale (i.e., there was no implied promise not to revoke) on the basis that the terms of the offer made it clear that it was to be freely revocable at any time before completion.

2.6.3.4 Conclusion

None of the above explanations is entirely satisfactory. It is likely that future courts will continue their reticence to explain why they are prepared to hold that a unilateral offer can no longer be revoked once performance has commenced. On the other hand, it may be that in the promissory estoppel explanation (and the removal of some of its current limitations) lie the seeds of the wider development of that doctrine into a principle of full liability.

Despite the difficulties in legal analysis, it seems fairly safe to predict that the courts will continue to find offers of unilateral contracts to be irrevocable after performance has begun. However, there will be instances where the offer may make it clear that the parties intended that revocation might occur at any time before complete performance of the act, as in *Luxor (Eastbourne) Ltd v Cooper* [1941] AC 108, so that the principle cannot be stated in all-embracing terms.

In *Schweppe v Harper* [2008] EWCA Civ 442, Waller LJ made the following comment in the context of passages from *Chitty on Contracts* which clearly support the 'acceptance' on commencement approach:

Where there is an offer to pay for the performance of a certain task, part performance can produce a contract under which that offer cannot be withdrawn. That should be the more so where there has not only been part performance but there is a real benefit being accepted by the offeror from that part performance. In such a case the court should be reluctant to find that the offeror has reserved a right to withdraw the offer after part performance.

This suggests that part performance constitutes acceptance of the contract, or possibly a collateral contract promising not to withdraw. The difficulty with the first interpretation, although arguably not the second, is that this would also preclude the performing party from changing its mind and withdrawing. The Court of Appeal seems clear that instances when the right to revoke is reserved, e.g. as in *Luxor v Cooper*, should be rare.

2.6.4 Communication of revocation of a unilateral offer

In relation to offers made to the whole world, there are particular problems in applying a rule which states that a revocation of an offer must be communicated to the offeree since the offerees will be unidentified. Practical considerations would therefore suggest that it would be appropriate to follow the approach taken in the American case of *Shuey v United States* 92 US 73 (1875). In this case it was held to be sufficient that the 'same notoriety be given to the revocation that was given to the offer'. Therefore, if the same channel is used and the same level of publicity achieved, the fact that an individual offeree has not seen the revocation would be irrelevant.

The DCFR includes this principle on revocation of offers to the whole world since II-4:202(2) provides that such an offer 'can be revoked by the same means as were used to make the offer'.

2.6.5 Function of unilateral contracts

The typical unilateral contract is usually regarded as being the offer of a reward for the performance of some service (see *R v Clarke* (1927) 40 CLR 227), or the repeat option for the supply of goods provided in a long-term contract to deliver goods as and when ordered (see *Great Northern Railway Co. v Witham* (1873) LR 9 CP 16). These functions are well known and well documented, and require no further comment.

The unilateral contract device

In addition to these typical functions, as we have seen throughout this chapter (e.g., **2.3.2.4**), unilateral contracts are sometimes used by the courts to manipulate the facts of situations of negotiation into binding contracts where instinct suggests that a contractual relationship exists but the facts do not lend themselves to a conventional analysis of a bilateral contract. Two House of Lords cases will serve to illustrate the point:

1. *The Eurymedon*

The facts of **New Zealand Shipping v Sattherthwaite (The Eurymedon)** [1975] AC 154 are related elsewhere (see **4.4.2** and **11.6.4**). The essential point is that the court found a contract to exist between a shipper and a stevedore although the two had not dealt directly with each other but each had a separate contract with the carrier in the case. Lord Wilberforce explained the existence of the contract between shipper and stevedore in the following way:

> The bill of lading brought into existence a bargain initially unilateral but capable of becoming mutual, between the shippers and the stevedore, made through the carrier as agent. This became a full contract when the stevedore performed services by discharging the goods. The performance of these services for the benefit of the shipper was the consideration for the agreement by the shipper that the stevedore should have the benefit of the exemptions and limitations contained in the bill of lading.

There is little doubt that this analysis owes more to the court's legitimate desire at that time (before the Contracts (Rights of Third Parties) Act 1999: see **11.4**) to avoid the doctrine of privity of contract than it does to any genuine description of the nature of the negotiations between the three parties.

2. *Harvela Investments Ltd v Royal Trust Co. of Canada*

In **Harvela Investments Ltd v Royal Trust Co. of Canada** [1986] AC 207 (see **2.3.2.4**), Lord Diplock adopted a 'two contract' analysis in order to 'create' a contract comprising a promise to accept the highest offer received (and into which could be implied term ruling out the adoption of a referential bid).

It seems highly probable that the implication of such unilateral contracts will continue as a pragmatic means of solving existing deficiencies in English contract law.

Further reading

General on agreement and unilateral contracts

Adams and Brownsword, *Understanding Contract Law*, 5th edn (Sweet and Maxwell, 2007).

Furmston, Norisada, and Poole, *Contract Formation and Letters of Intent* (John Wiley and Sons, 1998).

Goodhart, 'Unilateral contracts' (1951) 67 LQR 456.

Graw, 'Puff, Pepsi and "that plane"—The John Leonard saga' (2000) 15 JCL 281.

Simpson, 'Quackery and contract law: The case of the *Carbolic Smoke Ball*' (1985) 14 JLS 345.

Winfield, 'Some aspects of offer and acceptance' (1939) 55 LQR 499.

Approach to identifying existence of agreement

De Moor, 'Intention in the law of contract: Elusive or illusory?' (1990) 106 LQR 632.

Howarth, 'The meaning of objectivity in contract' (1984) 100 LQR 265.

Howarth, 'A note on the objective of objectivity in contract' (1987) 103 LQR 527.

Vorster, 'A comment on the meaning of objectivity in contract' (1987) 103 LQR 274.

Offers and invitations to treat

Adams and Brownsword, 'More in expectation than hope: The Blackpool Airport case' (1991) 54 MLR 281.

Gower, 'Auction sales of goods without reserve' (1952) 68 LQR 457.

Jackson, 'Offer and acceptance in the supermarket' (1979) 129 NLJ 775.

McKendrick, 'Invitation to tender and the creation of contracts' [1991] LMCLQ 31.

Montrose, 'The contract of sale in self-service stores' (1954) 4 Am J Comp Law 235.

Phang, 'Tenders and uncertainty' (1991) 4 JCL 46.

Scott, 'The auction house: With or without reserve' [2001] LMCLQ 334.

Slade, 'Auction sales of goods without reserve' (1952) 68 LQR 288 and (1953) 69 LQR 21.

Unger, 'Self-service shops and the law of contract' (1953) 16 MLR 369.

Acceptance

Adams, 'The battle of the forms' (1979) 95 LQR 481.

Hudson, *'Gibbons v Proctor* revisited' (1968) 84 LQR 503.

McKendrick, 'The battle of the forms and the law of restitution' (1988) 8 OJLS 197.

Miller, *'Felthouse v Bindley* revisited' (1972) 35 MLR 489.

Mitchell and Phillips, 'The contractual nexus: Is reliance essential?' (2002) 22 OJLS 115.

Rawlings, 'The battle of forms' (1979) 42 MLR 715.

Effective communication

Capps, 'Electronic mail and the postal rule' (2004) 15 ICCLR 207.

Coote, 'The instantaneous transmission of acceptances' (1971) 4 New Zealand UL Rev 331.

Evans, 'The Anglo-American mailing rule' (1966) 15 ICLQ 553.

Gardner, 'Trashing with Trollope: A deconstruction of the postal rules in contract' (1992) 12 OJLS 170.

Hudson, 'Retraction of letters of acceptance' (1966) 82 LQR 169.

Mik, 'The effectiveness of acceptances communicated by electronic means, or—Does the postal acceptance rule apply to email?' (2009) 26 JCL 68.

Murray, 'Entering into contracts electronically: The real WWW' in Edwards and Waelde (eds), *Law and the Internet: A framework for electronic commerce*, 2nd edn (Hart Publishing, 2000).

Murray, 'Articles 9–11, ECD: Contracting electronically in the shadow of the E-Commerce Directive' in Edwards (ed.), *The New Legal Framework for E-Commerce in Europe* (Hart Publishing, 2005).

Revocation of offers

Law Commission, Working Paper No. 60, 'Firm offers', 1975.

McGovney, 'Irrevocable offers' (1914) 27 Harv L Rev 644.

Agreement problems

Summary of the issues

This chapter examines two issues:

1. Those principles determining when an agreement is sufficiently certain to be capable of enforcement and asks whether there can be any liability in the absence of agreement.
2. Mistakes preventing agreement or which result in a contractual document failing accurately to reflect what the parties agreed.

• As a general principle, it is for the parties to make their agreement and ensure that the terms are sufficiently certain to be enforced. As a result, the court will generally refuse to fill any gaps and such an agreement will be void as a contract because of the uncertainty. However, this has to be balanced with the need to avoid the parties using allegations of uncertainty to escape from bad bargains, especially where the alleged uncertain agreement has been executed, i.e. performed. Therefore, in practice the courts may rescue the agreement if some objective evidence is available to fill the gaps. The courts therefore use commercial practice and previous performance to determine the meaning of vague terms on the basis of reflecting the obvious intentions of the parties. If there is no such evidence, there will be no contract.

• As an alternative, if an uncertain clause is meaningless, as opposed to still to be agreed, it may be possible to sever that clause (remove it) and enforce the remaining terms of the agreement.

• Agreements for the parties to agree a matter, such as the price, will generally lack the necessary certainty. If nothing is said as to price, then statute will imply a reasonable price. If the parties have provided a mechanism for fixing the price and that mechanism operates, there is no certainty problem. However, where such a mechanism for fixing the price breaks down, the courts will need to decide whether the mechanism is integral and essential for fixing the price and whether any of the parties is at fault in relation to this breakdown.

• If there is uncertainty so that no contract results, in some circumstances there may nevertheless be an obligation to pay the reasonable value for requested performance that has been received on the basis that otherwise the recipient would be unjustly enriched (i.e., a *quantum meruit* claim).

• A formation mistake will occur where one or both of the parties allege that they made a fundamental mistake which prevents agreement. However, the doctrine of mistake is very narrow and limited; in part this is because of the effect on third parties of a finding that the agreement is void. In particular, the mistake must be a mistake as to terms, as opposed to a mistake as to a collateral matter.

• The parties may be at cross-purposes so that objectively there is no agreement. A contract will only be void if there is no element of fault, i.e. the mistake was not provoked by, or the responsibility of, one of the parties.

- As a result of the decision of the House of Lords in **Shogun Finance Ltd v Hudson**, in the case of unilateral mistakes as to identity there is a distinction between contracts concluded via written documents and contracts made in face-to-face dealings. Where the contract is made via written documents, identity is important to the decision to contract so that the offer made to the party named in the writing can be accepted only by that named person. It follows that a rogue will acquire no title under such a contract and the mistaken party can recover the property. However, where a contract is concluded via face-to-face dealings, there is a presumption of an intention to contract with the person physically present. Such a contract will therefore not be void but will be voidable for the fraudulent misrepresentation as to identity. The result is that the innocent third-party purchaser can keep the goods where the contract is voidable.

- Mistakes in transcribing the parties' agreement can be rectified to conform to that agreement but the circumstances when this can happen are tightly circumscribed.

- The defence of *non est factum* (not my deed) may very rarely be available if (a) a party can show that they were unable, through no fault of their own, to understand the effect of the document they were signing and (b) that the document signed is fundamentally different in nature to the document they believed they were signing.

General background

Despite the apparent existence of agreement between the parties, the agreement may be void as a contract (automatically of no effect from the very beginning) due to uncertainty in its terms, or because the parties have made a fundamental mistake as to a term of the agreement.

However, because the effect of a contract being void is so drastic:

- The courts have limited the circumstances in which an allegation of mistake will lead to this result on the basis that mistake is not to be used as an excuse to escape from bad bargains and should not detract from the core principle of the security of transactions.

- The courts have employed the same approach in the context of curable uncertainty. They are keen, recognizing the need for precision in business contracts, to find a concluded contract despite allegations of uncertainty as long as they are able to determine the meaning of vague terms or resolve a problem of a missing term. This is particularly the case where the agreement in question has been executed by the parties. As Lord Tomlin stated in **Hillas & Co. Ltd v Arcos Ltd** (1932) 147 LT 503 at p. 512, the purpose is to ensure that 'the dealings of men may so far as possible be treated as effective, and that the law may not incur the reproach of being the destroyer of bargains'.

3.1 Certainty of agreements

3.1.1 The background

More complex than the issue of the existence of an agreement is the problem raised where the existence of an agreement in formal terms is not disputed, but one party alleges either:

- that important terms have not been agreed upon or
- that a term or terms is or are too vague, so that the contract is unenforceable.

In practice there is considerable overlap between these possibilities since, if an essential term is omitted, the agreement will necessarily be vague; and if certain terms are vague, in the sense that their meaning is unclear, this will lead to uncertainty as to the meaning of what has been agreed.

This is clearly an area where there is at least potential for conflict between the relational nature of contracting and the once-and-for-all focus inherent in judicial intervention in contracts. To adopt the words of Lord Wright in *Hillas & Co. Ltd v Arcos Ltd* (1932) 147 LT 503 at p. 516, it is accepted that when business people make:

> big forward contracts for future goods over a period…in general in such contracts it must be impossible…to specify in advance all the details of a complicated performance.

Parties sometimes leave trivial details to be worked out later, or in long-term contracts leave the price to be agreed from time to time, or otherwise consciously leave gaps in their agreements because the information and transaction costs of negotiating an agreed allocation of any particular risk are out of proportion to the likelihood of the risk maturing. Sometimes, as a safety net, they put in an arbitration clause for the resolution of matters which cannot be worked out amicably between them. In nearly all cases they rely on their goodwill at the time of contracting and their mutual interest in maintaining the relationship (which almost certainly extends beyond the individual contract in question) to iron out any problems not covered by the agreement.

It can be the case that loosely drafted contracts may be some way into performance before this vagueness or lack of provision is appreciated or considered an issue. At that point, any court which becomes involved will be left with an invidious task. If asked to enforce the agreement between the parties where they have left some matters deliberately unspecific, the court may feel that it has nothing tangible to enforce. At that stage, of course, if the matter has got as far as litigation, there is a danger that the goodwill on which the parties once relied may have evaporated. Yet, if there has been more than trifling performance by one or both of the parties, it is a drastic step to say that the supposed terms are too vague for there to be any real agreement, and thus to conclude that there is no contract.

3.1.2 The approach of the courts

The task of the court is to walk the narrow line between:

- writing the parties' agreement for them (which has traditionally been viewed as beyond the power of the judges and an infringement of freedom of contract)
- maintaining the contract by supplying 'reasonable' terms to be implied from the perceived intentions of the parties (on the implication of terms see generally 6.4).

In *Hillas & Co. Ltd v Arcos Ltd*, Lord Wright made it clear that the role of the court (at least where there has already been some performance) is to preserve the contract whenever possible. He stated (at p. 514):

> [T]he court is [not] to make a contract for the parties…except in so far as there are appropriate implications of law, as for instance, the implication of what is just and reasonable to be ascertained by the

court as a matter of machinery where the contractual intention is clear but the contract is silent on some detail. Thus in contracts for future performance over a period, the parties may neither be able nor desire to specify many matters of detail…Save for the legal implication I have mentioned, such contracts might well be incomplete or uncertain.

Much depends upon the facts of each case. There are no clear lines dividing certain agreements from uncertain agreements. Rather it is often a question of degree coupled with the extent of the willingness of the particular court to intervene to rescue the contract.

The general principle can probably be stated as follows: to be enforceable as a contract an agreement must be sufficiently precise (taking into account the whole context of the negotiations) for the court to be confident that what it is enforcing complies with the parties' actual intentions (objectively ascertained, of course: see 2.1) rather than any imputed to them by the court itself.

The problem, ironically, is that this principle is itself vague and an invitation to the exercise of a considerable amount of judicial discretion. It is possible, however, to discern certain guidelines.

3.1.3 Agreements where essential terms are vague

3.1.3.1 Ambiguity

In *Raffles v Wichelhaus* (1864) 2 Hurl & C 906, 159 ER 375, the level of ambiguity was such that there could be no agreement between the parties.

> The plaintiff had promised to sell and deliver to the defendants 125 bales of cotton at a given price 'to arrive ex *Peerless* from Bombay'. There were two ships called *Peerless*, and one left Bombay in October while the other left Bombay in December. When the defendants refused to accept the plaintiff's cotton, which had been shipped on the December ship, the plaintiff brought an action against the defendants alleging breach of contract. The defendants alleged that they understood the ship in the agreement to be the ship sailing in October. At the time of contracting, the fact that there were two ships of this name sailing from Bombay within this time period seems not to have been known by either party. The court found for the defendants.

Understanding the case is not easy, since the court gave no reason for its decision. The case is cited by some as one of the last vestiges of a subjective approach to intention (see 2.1). The real intentions of the parties (assuming the court had discovered their real intentions) did not coincide, so that there was never really any agreement. On the other hand, it seems likely that neither a detached bystander nor a reasonable man in the defendants' shoes would have had any way of knowing from the words used by the parties which of the two ships was intended. Lord Phillips MR in *Great Peace Shipping Ltd v Tsavliris Salvage (International) Ltd* [2003] EWCA Civ 1407, [2003] QB 679 treated *Raffles v Wichelhaus* as a case of latent ambiguity and on the facts the court in *Raffles* also recognized this ambiguity, which in this case could not be resolved by resort to any objective standard. The court was therefore left with no alternative other than to conclude that there was no contract.

3.1.3.2 Objective basis for determining the meaning of terms

Even where there is no total ambiguity, it must be possible to ascertain a meaning which would satisfy the objective bystander.

> In *Scammell & Nephew Ltd v Ouston* [1941] AC 251, the House of Lords was faced with an agreement to purchase a van on 'hire purchase terms', but details of these hire purchase terms, such as amount of

any deposit and the amount and frequency of repayments, had not been agreed. The House of Lords considered that there were so many possible interpretations of this expression that it was impossible to say which one the parties had intended, and it was necessary for the parties in each case to agree upon the relevant terms.

However, it is equally clear that where a court can resort to clear commercial practice or to previous dealings between the parties in order to ascertain the meaning of a particular contractual expression, it will do so, thereby giving effect to what must have been the 'obvious' intentions of the parties.

For example, Lord Wright, in **Scammell v Ouston** (at p. 273), referred to the example of a sale contract 'on cif terms', which he regarded as having 'a definite and complete meaning under the law merchant'. By contrast, there are a number of different meanings of a contract made on 'fob' terms.

The need for some objective basis on which to determine the terms of the contract is essential.

In **Baird Textiles Holdings Ltd v Marks & Spencer plc** [2001] EWCA Civ 274, [2002] 1 All ER (Comm) 737 (see **4.8.3.1**), the alleged term was that Marks & Spencer would acquire garments from Baird 'in quantities and at prices which in all the circumstances were reasonable' but there was no objective criteria for assessing any reasonable quantity or price. The Court of Appeal held that it could not make an agreement for the parties in the absence of any objective basis for determining its terms.

The absence of objective criteria was also fatal in **Durham Tees Valley Airport Ltd v Bmibaby Ltd** [2009] EWHC 852 (Ch), [2009] 2 Lloyd's Rep 246. The contract in question required the airline to base and fly aircraft from a particular airport over a ten-year term. However, it did not specify any objective criteria for determining whether this obligation was performed, i.e. it did not specify number of flights and passenger numbers. When the airline shut its base at the airport, the claimant sought damages based on an alleged implied term that the airline should operate from the airport in a manner that was reasonable in all the circumstances. Davis J refused such an implied term as being too vague and amounting to imposing an agreement which objectively the parties could not be taken to have intended.

The existence of expert evidence as to the recognized meaning of 'fair and reasonable specification' was regarded as one of the factors rescuing an option in **Hillas and Co. v Arcos Ltd** (1932) 147 LT 503.

The plaintiffs had agreed to buy '22,000 standards of softwood goods of fair specification' from the defendants during the 1930 season, and had also been granted an option to enter into a contract 'to purchase 100,000 standards for delivery during 1931'. The option clause did not specify the kind, size, or quality of goods to be supplied. The plaintiffs made a valid exercise of the option but the defendants had already sold their entire season's production of timber and so claimed that there was no option contract because it was too vague to be enforceable. However, the House of Lords held that the option contract was complete and binding.

Their Lordships were forced to go to considerable lengths in implying terms in order to make sense of the agreement. This was achieved by implication from the terms of the 1930 contract, which had already been performed, and by expert evidence regarding recognized commercial practice in interpreting 'fair specification'. The option clause had been part of what the plaintiffs had paid for, and to have found it unenforceable as being too vague would have been to deprive the plaintiffs of part of their bargain. Therefore the preferable course was clearly to rescue this agreement if at all possible.

3.1.3.3 The significance of performance

The other significant factor in *Hillas v Arcos* was the fact that part of the contract, relating to supply in the 1930 season, had already been performed and, in general, **case law suggests that there is a reluctance to come to the conclusion that there is no valid agreement where there has been performance.** Instead, in such circumstances, the courts strive to maintain a contract whenever possible. After all, if the parties have managed to perform an apparent agreement it would appear odd for a court to conclude that it is too vague to be capable of performance. Where there has been no performance (and the agreement is executory) a different attitude prevails.

The importance of the 'executed agreement' factor in influencing the decision of courts was recognized by Cohen LJ in *British Bank for Foreign Trade Ltd v Novinex Ltd* [1949] 1 KB 623 at pp. 629–30, quoting Denning J, the judge at first instance. It was also more fully articulated in *Trentham Ltd v Archital Luxfer Ltd* [1993] 1 Lloyd's Rep 25 at p. 27, when Steyn LJ stressed that where both parties have partly or fully performed the apparent agreement it will be 'unrealistic' to argue that an apparent agreement is void for vagueness or uncertainty. He added that:

> the fact that the transaction is executed makes it easier to imply a term resolving any uncertainty, or, alternatively, it may make it possible to treat a matter not finalized in negotiations as inessential.

However, it must be clear from the decision in *British Steel Corporation v Cleveland Bridge & Engineering Co. Ltd* [1984] 1 All ER 504 (see **3.1.4.1**) that this 'executed factor' will enable a court to avoid a conclusion of vagueness or uncertainty only where there is a sufficient basis for 'gap filling'. In *British Steel Corporation v Cleveland Bridge* Robert Goff J had concluded that there was too much which had still to be agreed on the facts.

A similar conclusion was reached in *J. Murphy & Sons Ltd v ABB Daimler-Benz Transportation (Signal) Ltd* [1999] CILL 1461, where the defendant had authorized the plaintiff subcontractor to commence a phase of the works and this work had been carried out. Nevertheless, the judge concluded that there was no agreement because at least two material terms remained to be settled between the parties.

3.1.3.4 Severing meaningless clauses

Where a particular inessential term is vague, it may be possible to sever (remove) that term and enforce the rest of the agreement.

In *Nicolene Ltd v Simmonds* [1953] 1 QB 543, the agreement in question referred to acceptance as being on 'the usual conditions of acceptance' when there were no such 'usual conditions of acceptance'. The plaintiffs, the buyers in the case, sought damages for breach of contract by the seller, and the seller argued that no contract had been concluded because of the uncertainty as to this term.

However, the Court of Appeal rejected this argument, holding that as this clause was meaningless, it could be severed from the rest of the agreement. Denning LJ expressly distinguished a meaningless clause (capable of being severed) from a clause on which agreement had not yet been reached (see **3.1.4**).

There is a discernible policy objective in this decision, namely that without the application of severance in such circumstances, a party would be able to insert a meaningless clause in order to allow for a later escape route from the contract.

3.1.4 **Agreements where essential terms are missing**

3.1.4.1 General principle

As a general principle, there needs to be agreement on all important terms or the agreement will be too uncertain to be enforceable. If important matters have still to be agreed between the parties, the assumption must be that the parties are still negotiating and do not yet intend to be legally bound. For example, in ***British Steel Corporation v Cleveland Bridge & Engineering Co. Ltd*** [1984] 1 All ER 504, important terms had still to be agreed between the parties so that the court held there to be no concluded agreement.

> Negotiations were entered into in anticipation of concluding a contract whereby the plaintiffs would manufacture steel nodes for the defendants. Although all the elements of the contract had not been agreed, both parties confidently expected that a contract would result. The defendants requested the plaintiffs to commence the work before complete agreement was reached. However, agreement was never reached on some matters and no formal contract was concluded. The plaintiffs had delivered all but one of these nodes and so sued the defendants for the value of the nodes on the basis of a *quantum meruit* (reasonable value). The defendants counterclaimed for breach of contract.
>
> Robert Goff J found that so much remained to be agreed (such as price, delivery dates, and liability for consequential loss and delay) that it was 'very difficult to see' how a contract had been formed. Accordingly, there could be no counterclaim for breach of contract.

This conclusion is probably explained by the fact that the judge clearly considered the defendants largely responsible for the failure to agree. To have found a contract in the circumstances might have exposed the plaintiffs to an action for breach of contract by the defendants, penalizing the plaintiffs for something which, in the judge's view, was not their fault. However, it was held that the plaintiffs could recover on a *quantum meruit* because the defendants would otherwise have been unjustly enriched at the plaintiffs' expense (see **3.1.5**).

The case is significant because it indicates that, despite the fact of performance, a court will not, and cannot, create a contract where it is clear that there is no agreement on important terms and further negotiation is essential (see also *Jackson (Trustee in Bankruptcy of Subhash Kanji Thakrar) v Thakrar (a Bankrupt)* [2007] EWHC 271 (TCC), 113 Con LR 58: the trustee had not agreed to be bound by any settlement, there was a claim by HM Customs & Excise that remained outstanding and there was no agreement on the security to be given).

3.1.4.2 Agreements to agree

If a matter is left to later agreement between the parties then it will lack the necessary certainty.

> In ***May & Butcher v R*** [1934] 2 KB 17n, an agreement had been made for the sale of surplus war equipment to the plaintiffs, the price being left to be agreed between the parties 'from time to time'. The parties were unable to agree, and the plaintiffs sought to enforce the agreement at a 'reasonable price' to be determined by the court. The House of Lords refused to do this.

The point was not articulated as part of the reasoning, but there can be little doubt that the court's conclusion that no contract had come into existence was made much easier by the fact that no performance under the agreed terms had taken place.

However, what appears to be a matter left open for later agreement, may not be. In *Bell Scaffolding (Aust.) Pty Ltd v Rekon Ltd* [2006] EWHC 2656 (TCC), [2007] CILL 2405, the judge concluded that a reference to 'agreed prices' was a reference to the claimant's price list. It did not mean 'prices to be agreed' and could therefore be clearly distinguished from an agreement to agree.

A further example of the reluctance of the English courts to enforce 'agreements to agree' where there has been no performance under the terms of the alleged contract, is provided by the decision of the House of Lords in *Walford v Miles* [1992] 2 AC 128.

> The parties, negotiating for the sale and purchase of a business, had entered into a 'lock-out agreement', the purported effect of which was to prevent the respondent prospective sellers from negotiating with anyone other than the appellants. Negotiations were unsuccessful, and after a time the respondents decided to sell to a third party. The appellants then brought an action for breach of the 'lock-out agreement'. The agreement was found to be unenforceable.

According to Lord Ackner, who gave the only substantial speech in the House of Lords, the fatal weakness of the agreement was that it was indefinite in length. It was a bare agreement to negotiate, and therefore without legal force.

The House of Lords rejected the argument that such an agreement could be made sufficiently certain because there was an implied duty placed on a party who had agreed to a lock-out to negotiate in good faith with the other party in order to reach agreement. Such a position was regarded as 'irreconcilable with the adversarial nature of the parties when involved in contract negotiations' (per Lord Ackner at p. 138).

Lock-out agreements

The House of Lords had concluded that had the 'lock-out agreement' stipulated a period of time during which exclusive negotiations were to take place, it would have been enforceable, because the element of uncertainty would have been removed. Lord Ackner's *dictum* was followed by the Court of Appeal in *Pitt v PHH Asset Management Ltd* [1994] 1 WLR 327, in relation to a 'lock-out' agreement for a two-week period. In the case of enforceable 'lock-out agreements', the remedy for breach will focus on the purchaser's wasted costs (see 9.4) and since the transaction may not have proceeded in any event, the measure of damages might be restricted to the additional costs wasted as a result of the vendor's breach of the 'lock-out'.

In *Chilli Developments Ltd v Commission for the New Towns* [2008] EWHC 1310 (QB), [2008] NPC 72 a developer had entered into negotiations with a regeneration agency. An exclusivity agreement provided that during a three-month period the agency would not invite tenders or enter into negotiations in relation to the land. A mutual obligation of good faith was incorporated. When the first lock-out expired it was extended by four months. However, once that period had expired the agency sold the land elsewhere. The developer claimed the agency had never genuinely intended to enter into the final development contract with it and sought damages. The judge was clear that once the lock-out ended, the agency was free to negotiate and sell elsewhere and there was no evidence of bad faith in the negotiations during the lock-out period.

Express provisions requiring parties to negotiate in good faith

It is important to bear in mind that the decision in *Walford v Miles* that there could be no *implied* duty to negotiate in good faith was made in the context of negotiations which were expressly made 'subject to contract'. Unlike in *Walford v Miles*, where the argument had been to *imply* a duty to negotiate in good faith, in *Petromec Inc. v Petroleo Brasileiro SA Petrobas (No. 3)* [2005] EWCA Civ 891, [2006] 1 Lloyd's Rep 121, the Court of Appeal had to consider whether the courts should enforce an *express provision in a commercial contract* requiring the parties to negotiate in good faith in respect of the cost of certain contractual extras. The arguments against such recognition, based on *Walford v Miles*, were that:

1. The obligation was no more than an agreement to agree.

2. It was too uncertain to be enforced.

3. It was difficult or impossible to say whether any termination of negotiations was the result of bad faith.

The Court of Appeal (see, in particular, the judgment of Longmore LJ at [115]–[121]) considered that:

1. The argument that this was an agreement to agree was irrelevant since this was an obligation contained in an agreement which was itself legally enforceable.

2. It would be relatively easy to determine the actual costs in question and therefore it ought not to be difficult to determine what the result of good faith negotiations would be. This disposed of the argument that it could never be known whether agreement would have been reached and what its terms would have been so that it would have been impossible to assess loss caused by breach of the obligation.

3. Although 'bad faith' withdrawal from negotiations (and hence identification of a breach of such a duty) was 'somewhat elusive' as a concept, this case could be clearly distinguished from *Walford v Miles* where there had been no concluded agreement between the parties, where all negotiations were 'subject to contract' and where there was no express undertaking to negotiate in good faith. Here the express agreement to negotiate was contained in a complex commercial agreement reached between the parties and it would defeat the expressed intentions and reasonable expectations of the parties to deny the enforceability of that express obligation.

On the facts, it was held that there had been no breach of this clause to negotiate in good faith with respect to these extra costs.

It is clear that item 2 is significant in accepting an express provision to negotiate in good faith, i.e. it must be possible for the court to conduct the exercise of fixing the cost or price in question. For this reason in *BBC Worldwide Ltd v Bee Load Ltd (T/A Archangel Ltd)* [2007] EWHC 134 (Comm) the judge held that an agreement to consider in good faith any request by the defendant to extend the scope of the agreement was unenforceable (*Walford v Miles*) since there were no criteria in this clause enabling a court to determine whether 'in good faith' any particular form of extension should be viewed favourably. In *Butters v BBC Worldwide Ltd* [2009] EWHC 1954 (Ch), where Peter Smith J expressly adopted the approach of Longmore LJ in the *Petromec* case as applicable to the facts before him, stressing that the 'good faith clause' would have been 'carefully drafted by large commercial organisations (no doubt equipped with the usual array of lawyers) as an attempt to address the possibility that a clause might unintentionally be invalid'. By comparison in *Tramtrack Croydon Ltd v London Bus Services Ltd* [2007] EWHC 107 (Comm), unreported, 31 January 2007, the obligation to agree compensation arrangements in good faith and acting reasonably whenever Tramtrack agreed to accept certain tickets and passes as valid, was sufficiently certain precisely because it was not an abstract obligation to act in good faith. The parties had agreed to act reasonably when agreeing and, if they failed to agree, the agreement contained a provision for expert determination in the event of just such disputes.

Thus, although English law does not recognize a general duty to negotiate in good faith (but see comments by Lord Steyn in 'Contract law: Fulfilling the reasonable expectations of honest men' (1997) 113 LQR 433 at p. 439), it will, it seems, be prepared to recognize an express provision in a concluded contract to negotiate in good faith on a particular issue where there are criteria on which to make the calculation in question. For example, in *Petromec* it was accepted that the court could have conducted the exercise of fixing the reasonable cost of the contractual extras but the necessary criteria were absent in the *BBC* case.

This position may usefully be compared with the recognition of a duty to negotiate in good faith in other jurisdictions, such as Germany, and the provisions of attempted codifications of contractual principles (see 1.6.1). The *Draft Common Frame of Reference* (DCFR) II-3:301 provides that although a person is free to negotiate and is not liable for failure to reach agreement, 'a person who is engaged in negotiations has a duty to negotiate in accordance with good faith and fair dealing and not to break off negotiations contrary to good faith and fair dealing'. This duty is mandatory and cannot be excluded or limited. If a person breaches this duty they become 'liable for any loss caused to the other party by the breach. II-3:301(4) specifies one such instance where it is 'contrary to good faith and fair dealing' as being where a person enters into or continues negotiations 'with no real intention of reaching an agreement with the other party'. Article 2:301 of the *Principles of European Contract Law* (PECL) is in the same terms, as is Art. 2.1.15 of the UNIDROIT *Principles of International Commercial Contracts*. A contract to negotiate in good faith is also recognized in the United States (see *Channel Home Centers Division of Grace Retail Corporation v Grossman* 795 F 2d 291 (1986)).

3.1.4.3 Agreements to agree a price: The significance of performance

However, in English law, even where there is only an agreement between the parties to agree a price, it seems that the courts will enforce that agreement if at all possible once performance has begun.

> In *Foley v Classique Coaches Ltd* [1934] 2 KB 1, the parties had made an agreement for the supply of the defendants' petrol requirements, at a price to be agreed from time to time. The contract included an arbitration clause, and was linked to a deal whereby the defendants purchased a parcel of land from the plaintiff. Performance continued without incident for three years before the defendants argued that this contract was unenforceable because the price clause was uncertain.
>
> The Court of Appeal found that the agreement was enforceable, the defendants having to pay a 'reasonable price' for petrol supplied. What was reasonable in the circumstances might be determined, if necessary, by arbitration.

In part it seems that it was the fact of actual performance, including the conveyance of the parcel of land, and the danger of depriving the plaintiff of one important element of the bargain, which persuaded the Court of Appeal. It is interesting to note that the court did not allow the decision of the House of Lords in *May and Butcher v R* (3.1.4.2 above) to dissuade it from reaching this conclusion. It seems, therefore, that uncertainty as to price is not as a matter of law always fatal to an agreement; rather, it is a question of construction of the contract in each case. The most obvious distinguishing feature between the two cases, however, is the lack of performance in one and the substantial performance in the other.

Similar principles were at work in *Alstom Signalling Ltd v Jarvis Facilities Ltd* [2004] EWHC 1232 (TCC), 95 Con LR 55.

There was an agreement between the main contractor and subcontractor to agree pain/gain sharing. However, since this was a commercial contract which had been performed, the court concluded that it was not an unenforceable agreement to agree. Instead, the court should seek to find a fair and reasonable mechanism to determine the sharing. If this failed, the terms of the subcontract gave the court the power to make a determination on any differences.

The judge stated:

Once parties have contracted, the commercial considerations which need to be weighed are quite different from those which fall to be considered when negotiations are broken off before a transaction is agreed or before performance of a project is commenced.

It is also clear that as long as there is initial agreement on the price in a continuing contract, the contract is sufficiently certain.

In *Mamidoil-Jetoil Greek Petroleum Co. SA v Okta Crude Oil Refinery (No. 1)* [2001] EWCA Civ 406, [2001] 2 Lloyd's Rep 76, the fee for the first two years of a ten-year contract was fixed at the outset. The fee for the remaining eight years of the term was left to be fixed, although the evidence was that agreement had in fact been reached for four of these years. On this basis the Court of Appeal rejected the argument that there was an 'agreement to agree' the fee so that the agreement was uncertain. Instead, the court held that, in the event of a failure to fix the fee in the latter years of the term, a term would be implied allowing for a reasonable fee to be fixed.

This decision represents a practical recognition of the fact that in the case of continuing contracts it may not be practical or feasible to fix all matters at the outset of the contractual term. The important fact was that there was a sufficiently certain contract at the outset and on that basis 'the courts will seek to make it work' (per Rix LJ). This point was also approved in *Bell Scaffolding (Aust.) Pty Ltd v Rekon Ltd* [2006] EWHC 2656 (TCC), [2007] CILL 2405 (**3.1.4.2** above), in that although it was envisaged that the prices in the price list might change over time, those prices would remain as the applicable prices until new agreement was reached and the court 'would strive to preserve the contract once there had been performance' (per Ramsey J).

3.1.4.4 Mechanisms for determining the price

No mechanism for fixing the price

Section 8 of the Sale of Goods Act (SGA) 1979 provides:

(1) The price in a contract of sale may be fixed by the contract, or may be left to be fixed in a manner agreed by the contract, or may be determined by the course of dealing between the parties.

(2) Where the price is not determined as mentioned in subsection (1) above the buyer must pay a reasonable price.

In *May and Butcher v R*, Lord Dunedin suggested that s. 8(2) (and the ability to fix a reasonable price) applies *only* where the contract is silent as to price, and does not apply where a price-fixing mechanism has failed to work. Such an interpretation seems to be unduly narrow and to fly in the face of logic. To say nothing at all about price is surely less certain than to attempt to make a flexible provision, which takes into account the changing value of money through time.

Price-fixing mechanism fails to work

1. The principle in *Sudbrook Trading Estate Ltd v Eggleton*

May and Butcher was distinguished in *Sudbrook Trading Estate Ltd v Eggleton* [1983] 1 AC 444.

> In **Sudbrook Trading v Eggleton** a lease contained an option to purchase the land in question at a price to be agreed by two valuers, one to be nominated by each party. The lessors refused to appoint a valuer and claimed that the option clause was unenforceable because the price term was uncertain.
>
> The House of Lords refused to find the clause unenforceable and held that if the parties have provided sensible but subsidiary and non-essential machinery for fixing a fair price, and that machinery had for some reason broken down, then the court should attempt to take the place of that machinery by identifying a fair and reasonable price which was reasonable in all the circumstances.

Lord Diplock's speech distinguishes this position from a case where an individual is specifically named in the clause as being given the responsibility to determine the important matter, where the contract would be frustrated if that person was then unable to make a determination through no fault of either of the parties, e.g. death of the person named.

No doubt their Lordships were influenced in their conclusion that this clause was inessential by the fact that there had been considerable performance of the main contract and there was a danger of the lessee being deprived of an important part of its bargain had a contrary result been reached. Lord Fraser also highlighted the fact that it was the lessors who, in not making the appointment, were preventing the machinery from operating thereby deriving the lessees of this benefit. In addition, as Lord Fraser stressed, although it might appear logical for the courts to refuse to substitute their own machinery for that provided by the parties, such a practice would be commercially inconvenient as the inevitable consequence would be that such an agreement would be void.

2. Limiting the principle in *Sudbrook v Eggleton*

Sudbrook v Eggleton was distinguished by the Court of Appeal in *Gillatt v Sky Television Ltd* [2000] 1 All ER (Comm) 461 in the context of an argument to enforce a single payment provision. The Court of Appeal in *Gillatt* had no such incentive to substitute its own machinery since the agreement itself would not be rendered void. **In addition, the party requesting the court to substitute its own machinery had the ability (but had failed) to make the necessary appointment itself.**

> In **Gillatt v Sky Television Ltd**, by an agreement Sky had acquired shares in Tele-Aerials Satellite Ltd (TAS), and by clause 6 of this agreement it had been agreed that if Sky sold or disposed of this shareholding then Sky would pay Mallard Ltd '55 per cent of the open market value of such shares…as determined by an independent chartered accountant'. Mallard Ltd had subsequently assigned (transferred) this right to Gillatt. Sky later transferred its shares to a wholly owned subsidiary, and Gillatt claimed that clause 6 applied so that he was entitled to the payment. However, neither Gillatt, nor Sky nor Mallard had taken any steps to appoint the independent accountant to determine the value of the shares and, since a reasonable time had elapsed, it was no longer possible to do so.

Gillatt argued that this requirement to appoint an independent accountant to determine the value of the shares was only intended as a description of the machinery to be applied if there was any dispute between the parties relating to entitlement under the clause and was not an essential pre-condition to the existence of any entitlement under the clause. This argument relied on *Sudbrook* as authority to support the principle that 'where the machinery is not essential, if it breaks down for any reason the court will substitute its own machinery'.

However, the Court of Appeal concluded that:

1. The valuation requirement in *Gillatt* was both integral and essential, and the clause did not contain any other objective criteria in order to determine the value of the shares as there was no definition of 'open market value' (despite the fact that there were many ways of calculating this).

2. This indicated that the parties had agreed to leave this to the independent chartered accountant, and it was the duty of the court to give effect to this intention rather than to make its own valuation.

3. This was also not a case involving a breakdown of the contractual machinery, since the claimant had not attempted to make the necessary appointment.

It would seem, therefore, that the principle in *Sudbrook* will in future be confined to cases where the breakdown in the machinery is attributable to the fault of *one* of the parties in not cooperating.

It had also been thought that where a particular person was not named in the clause, that machinery was more likely to be regarded as non-essential on the basis that a decision to name a person indicated that this machinery was regarded as essential because certain skills, which this individual possessed, were required by the parties. This was strongly argued by counsel for Mr Gillatt, but was not regarded as significant by the Court of Appeal in the light of the other evidence. More fundamentally, it is clear that the principle in *Sudbrook* cannot be relied upon in the absence of any evidence of objective criteria intended by the parties to be used in determining the price (*Gillatt v Sky Television Ltd* and *Baird Textiles Holdings Ltd v Marks & Spencer plc* [2001] EWCA Civ 274, [2002] 1 All ER (Comm) 737: see 3.1.3.2).

Gillatt v Sky Television was followed by the Court of Appeal in *Infiniteland Ltd v Artisan Contracting Ltd* [2005] EWCA Civ 758, [2006] 1 BCLC 632 in preference to *Sudbrook Trading Estate v Eggleton* because (a) the machinery for price adjustment was considered to be essential and (b) it had not broken down since, as in *Gillatt,* it had failed to operate due to the failure of the party seeking the adjustment to operate the machinery provided for in the clause.

Chadwick LJ (at [59]) stated:

I can see no reason, in principle, why a party, say 'A', who chooses not to allow the contractual machinery to operate should be able to ask the court, nevertheless, to enforce the contract against the other party, say 'B'. It is no answer, in such a case, to say that the machinery is non-essential. It is the machinery upon which the parties agreed when they made their bargain. A cannot be heard to insist on the agreed machinery—as a defence to a claim made against him—if it is he who has not allowed it to operate. But, equally, as it seems to me, in such a case A cannot insist on imposing on B other machinery to which B has never agreed. B is not to be denied the benefit of the machinery to which he has agreed—in resisting a claim made against him—by A's unilateral refusal to allow that machinery to operate.

Infiniteland, as the purchaser, was required by the clause to produce a calculation of net asset value as the first step in the procedure and it had failed to do so. Therefore, *Sudbrook* was inapplicable and it was not possible for the court to substitute its own machinery, particularly as that machinery required any disputes to be resolved by an independent chartered accountant who was an expert in such matters.

Sudbrook was also distinguished in *Bruce v Carpenter* [2006] EWHC 3301 (Ch), unreported, 29 November 2006, where the valuation of a shareholding was to be determined by an expert. When the expert considered that an issue fell outside her area of expertise, the shareholder argued that the court could intervene as the contractual machinery had broken down. However, it was held that the parties had fixed this machinery for valuation by the named expert, who was therefore essential. If the court interfered it would be acting in direct conflict with the parties' agreement for private valuation. In any event, the machinery had not broken down as the expert could still carry out a valuation.

Thus, the scope of the *Sudbrook* principle is extremely limited in practice.

Conclusion on the approach to certainty

In conclusion, it can be stated on the basis of an assessment of the case law that ultimately it will be a question of fact in each case whether the contract is sufficiently clear for the court to be able to enforce by reasonable implication the apparent agreement between the parties.

3.1.5 Recovery where a contract fails to materialize

As was seen in *British Steel Corporation v Cleveland Bridge and Engineering* [1984] 1 All ER 504 (see **3.1.4.1**), even where the court concludes that no agreement was reached between the parties because essential terms are missing, it may still be prepared to order that the recipient should pay a sum to cover the reasonable value of the performance received where that performance was requested by that party.

The basis for this award is restitution, namely that to allow the recipient to retain the promised performance would result in that party being unjustly enriched at the expense of the performing party.

The Court of Appeal in *Whittle Movers Ltd v Hollywood Express Ltd* [2009] EWCA Civ 1189, 11 November 2009, transcript available via Westlaw, expressly considered that courts should 'not strain to find a contract' where the parties were still negotiating as to terms but some performance had commenced. A restitutionary solution was the appropriate response.

3.1.5.1 Generally no recovery for expenses incurred during the negotiation process

However, this possibility of recovery may not apply generally to expenses incurred during the negotiation process in preparation for the contract. This was made clear in the decision of Rattee J in *Regalian Properties plc v London Dockland Development Corp.* [1995] 1 All ER 1005. The judge stated that, in the absence of a express contractual undertaking to cover such costs, the words 'subject to contract' made it clear that each party was free to withdraw from negotiations at any time and that each party incurred pre-contractual costs at their own risk. In addition, it was possible to distinguish *British Steel Corporation v Cleveland Bridge* on the basis that in that case the plaintiffs had sought to recover for the 'accelerated performance of the anticipated contract' where that performance had been requested by the defendants, whereas in *Regalian* the plaintiffs had incurred expenses in the form of payment of professional fees for designs to enable them *to obtain and perform the contract.* There was therefore not the same benefit to the defendant.

On the facts in **Regalian**, the judge also found that the contract did not materialize because of the failure to agree on the price and not, as had been alleged by the plaintiffs, because the defendant decided to abandon the project. Rattee J did not deal with the position where the negotiations were not 'subject to contract' and where they broke down because of the unilateral decision by one party to abandon the project. However, in **Countrywide Communications Ltd v ICL Pathway Ltd** [2000] CLC 324, there was fault.

3.1.5.2 Exceptional cases where it is possible to recover for expenses incurred in anticipation of a contract which does not materialize: *Countrywide Communications Ltd v ICL Pathway Ltd*

The plaintiff in **Countrywide Communications Ltd v ICL Pathway Ltd** had carried out public relations work in connection with a successful bid which had been made by the defendant to supply a system for the payment of benefits to the Benefits Agency and Post Office Counters Ltd. The plaintiff had been assured that it would be appointed if the bid succeeded, but on the success of the bid the defendant appointed another consultancy. It was held that the plaintiff was entitled to payment (£38,370) for the time it had spent and to cover its costs on the basis that (a) there was fault on the part of the defendant and (b) the services in question were of benefit to the defendant.

The judge, Nicholas Strauss QC, stressed that this did not allow for any general recovery of costs incurred in tendering or preparing for a hoped for contract (although see **Blackpool and Fylde Aero Club v Blackpool Borough Council** [1990] 1 WLR 1195 at **2.3.2.4,** where an obligation to consider conforming tenders was implied and, in the event of breach of this promise, contractual damages would be available which might be based on reliance loss).

The judge in **Countrywide Communications** (at p. 349) identified a number of factors to consider in deciding whether it was possible on a particular set of facts (referred to as 'exceptional cases') to recover for expenditure incurred in anticipation of a contract which did not materialize:

1. whether the services were of a kind which would normally be given free of charge

2. the terms in which the request to perform the services was made may be important in establishing the extent of the risk (if any) which any claimants may fairly be said to have taken that such services would in the end be unrecompensed. (This was linked to the issue of whether the parties were expressly or impliedly negotiating 'subject to contract', or whether one party had given an assurance that they would not withdraw in these circumstances.)

3. whether the services were of real benefit to the defendant so that he could be said to be unjustly enriched at that claimant's expense (clearly important in the light of *Regalian Developments,* although Denning LJ in *Brewer Street Investments Ltd v Barclays Woollen Co Ltd* [1954] 1 QB 428 had regarded the fact that the services were requested as being a benefit in itself)

4. the circumstances in which the contract failed to materialize (i.e., any fault on the part of the defendant so that the circumstances are outside the risk undertaken by the claimant).

In addition, the judge stressed that recovery was unlikely if the expense was not incurred in the course of providing services requested by the defendant, and that the weight to be given to each

of these factors would vary from case to case. This decision is therefore helpful in rationalizing existing case law to provide a set of guiding principles concerning when recovery may be possible.

A further example of an award of a *quantum meruit* occurred in *Yule v Little Bird Ltd,* unreported, 5 April 2001.

> The claimant alleged that he had been engaged by the defendant to direct a documentary film and had worked on the project for some months before being dropped and replaced by another director. It was found as a fact that no formal contract had ever materialized between the parties and that this practice was usual in the industry. However, as the defendant had requested, or at least accepted, services from the claimant in furtherance of the project, he could not expect the services of the claimant to go unrewarded and a *quantum meruit* was therefore appropriate.

Therefore, although English law does not expressly recognize any general duty of good faith in contract negotiations, there are clear indicators here that there is some recognition of principles of fair dealing through the use of restitutionary principles to recompense a party who has performed services at the request of the other party, where that party has been expressly led to believe that they will be awarded the contract to which those services relate.

3.2 Agreement mistake

By agreement mistake we mean that one or both of the parties made a fundamental mistake relating to the terms of the contract (i.e., an 'offer and acceptance' mistake) which prevents the formation of an agreement, although the parties may well subjectively believe that they are in agreement. Peel (in *Treitel's The Law of Contract,* 12th edn (Sweet and Maxwell, 2007), p. 310) refers to these mistakes as negativing consent.

There is another category of mistake in English law which does not relate to the issue of reaching agreement. This occurs where both parties do not deny that they reached agreement but allege that this agreement is impossible to perform because they both made a fundamental mistake (see common or shared mistake: Chapter 13).

3.2.1 The doctrine of mistake in English law

The word 'mistake' may be misleading if it is taken to indicate a single coherent doctrine. In practice it indicates no more than a loose association of doctrines often connected in no other way than that they are called into play in factual contexts in which one or both parties may in everyday language be said to have been mistaken. In fact, it has been argued that English law really knows no independent doctrine of mistake, and that those cases in which apparent mistake has resulted in a contract being set aside involve the application to the particular situation of established rules of the law of contract, such as the rules of offer and acceptance. While the rules of offer and acceptance play an increasingly important role, there is evidence of identifiable principles relating to mistake. What is clear, however, is that these principles recognize that any such doctrine of mistake is extremely limited in English law.

In English law, much of what passes for mistake can be explained in terms of other rules of English law which have been dressed up in language borrowed from the civil law and which are arguably inappropriate to the common law conception of contract. The reason for this civil law influence appears to be that the writing of systematic legal treatises began in France much earlier than it did in England, and at the end of the eighteenth century and the beginning of the nineteenth century the writings of the celebrated French lawyer, Pothier, gained a certain currency in England. The transference of the notion of mistake from one legal system to the other was misguided, however, since French law at the time was committed to a much more subjective approach to the formation of contracts than ever prevailed in England. An allegation of mistake is inevitably much more serious where the test of agreement is subjective.

3.2.2 The effect of mistake

One reason for the limited doctrine of mistake in English law is that where mistake operates it usually makes the contract void. More precisely, the effect is that there is no contract and the law takes the view that there never has been a contract. The wider impact of this conclusion is such that the courts appear to have been unwilling to extend the mistake doctrine.

The fact that the contract is void is of fundamental importance in the context of sale of goods:

- If no contract ever existed, title to the property (i.e., ownership rights and the ability to transfer ownership and possession) which is the subject matter of the sale, cannot have passed between seller and buyer.

- By contrast, if a sale contract is voidable, i.e. valid until set aside, as for example in the case of a contract induced by misrepresentation (see generally Chapter 14), title does pass.

It is the fact that title does not pass under contracts which are void for mistake that has made mistake an attractive doctrine to claimants but left the courts uneasy about its application.

3.2.2.1 The effect if the contract is void for mistake

Where a contract is void for mistake, the seller has not lost title to the goods in question and is therefore entitled to the return of the actual goods by virtue of possessing rights of ownership. Where the original buyer remains present and solvent, the impact of the fact that a contract affected by mistake is void is slight, since if, for example, the original seller seeks redress then it is unlikely in most circumstances to matter whether the seller recovers the actual goods or their monetary equivalent. Where, however, the original buyer has disappeared, or is insolvent, the seller will seek a remedy by recovering the actual goods, if entitled to do so.

If the contract is void, the seller is entitled to the return of the actual goods even where they have passed out of the hands of the original buyer into the hands of a third party who knows nothing of the dealings between seller and buyer (a so-called 'innocent' third party).

3.2.2.2 The effect if the contract is merely voidable

However, if the contract were merely voidable (liable to be set aside by the remedy of rescission), and before the time of the seller's claim the buyer had disposed of the goods to an innocent third party, the third party would be protected from recovery of the goods by the original seller because rescission is a personal remedy and not available against a third party.

3.2.2.3 Two 'innocent' parties

It is true that both the original seller and the third party into whose hands the goods have passed are 'innocent', so that it is unfortunate that either should suffer. Nevertheless, it is generally considered that the original seller is in a better position to guard against mistake than the third party, who played no part in the transaction between seller and buyer. It would be somewhat harsh therefore, for the third party to be the person who suffers. However, this will be the inevitable result where the original seller retains title to the goods because the contract was void. It is probably for this reason that traditionally the English courts have been unwilling to extend the doctrine of mistake beyond its narrow bounds and have generally preferred to avoid the conclusion that the contract is void for mistake (although see the impact of policy and contextual considerations in ***Shogun Finance Ltd v Hudson*** [2003] UKHL 62, [2004] 1 AC 919).

3.3 Types of mistakes negativing agreement

Agreement mistakes occur where, despite what one or other party may assert, it is impossible to identify objective evidence of agreement from what has passed between the parties (see **2.1**). For that reason these mistakes are sometimes called 'mistakes negativing consent'. If both parties are willing to recognize that they have failed to come to any final agreement, they may usually extricate themselves without recourse to the courts. Problems occur, and litigation ensues, when one of the parties asserts that an agreement exists on the basis of the terms as *that party* understood them. Cases fall into two categories:

1. those where the parties are genuinely at cross-purposes, so that each party makes a mistake but the mistakes are different (see **3.3.1**)

2. unilateral mistakes, where only one party is mistaken but the other either knows of the mistake or ought to know of it (see **3.3.2**).

Instances of both kinds of mistake being claimed successfully are rare, and the conclusion must be that, in this context, mistake is a very narrow doctrine unlikely to afford relief in the majority of cases.

3.3.1 Cross-purposes mistake

Mistakes of the kind where the parties are at cross-purposes are sometimes referred to as 'mutual mistakes', although care must be taken with this expression because it has also been used, especially by nineteenth-century courts, to describe shared or common mistakes. (In the case of shared or common mistake the parties do not deny that they reach agreement but it is alleged that the contract is impossible to perform because both parties entered into the contract on the basis of the same fundamental mistaken assumption.)

In the case of mutual or cross-purposes mistakes, the problem is that although one or both parties may assert that a contract exists, each on terms favourable to that party, on an objective interpretation it is impossible to resolve the ambiguity over what was agreed, so that the only possible conclusion is that there is no contract. In fact, when stated in this way, it is clear that the rule is not peculiar to the law on mistake. It is the same rule examined in relation to the formation of agreements and certainty of terms (see **2.1** and **3.1.3.1**). Thus, the famous old case of ***Raffles v Wichelhaus*** (1864) 2 Hurl & C 906 (two ships named 'Peerless' sailing from Bombay) has been treated as an instance of cross-purposes mistake (for a full discussion, see **3.1.3.1**).

In ***Scriven Bros and Co. v Hindley and Co.*** [1913] 3 KB 564, two lots taken from the cargo of a single ship were put up for sale by auction. Inspection would have revealed that one was hemp and one was tow, but the auction catalogue did not reveal this. The lots carried the same shipping marks, and the custom of the trade was that different cargoes would not normally have the same marks. The buyers bid for both lots, having inspected the hemp but not the tow, in the mistaken belief that both lots were hemp. The buyers had therefore agreed to pay well over the market price for the lot which was tow. The sellers brought an action against the buyers to recover the price of the tow, and the buyers alleged that they had not agreed to buy the tow and that a mistake had been made.

After considering the evidence, the court allowed the defendants to avoid the contract on the basis that there had been no agreement. Both parties' interpretations were equally plausible in an objective sense.

A reasonable person in the position of the defendant buyers would reasonably have concluded that the lots being sold with the same shipping marks were the same and the evidence was that the auctioneer realized only that the defendants had made a mistake as to the value of the goods being sold, but would not have realized that the defendants thought both lots were hemp. Since it was impossible to say what should have been understood from the lots on display, the decision that there was no contract is justifiable.

3.3.1.1 The objective test

Thus, the courts apply the objective test to the question of the existence of agreement and ask whether one party's interpretation is more reasonable than the other's.

Smith v Hughes (1871) LR 6 QB 597 (see **3.3.2.1**), the leading case on the meaning of objectivity, involved an allegation of cross-purposes mistake but the court concluded that since, on an objective assessment, there was symmetry between what was offered and what was accepted, the contract should be upheld.

In **Smith v Hughes**, the plaintiff offered to sell oats to the defendant. The defendant examined a sample, and agreed to take the whole consignment. On delivery it was discovered that the oats were 'new', and thus of no use to the defendant who required 'old' oats (that is, the previous season's oats). The defendant then refused to pay, claiming that the contract was void for mistake. The court rejected this defence. The mere fact that one party had deluded himself into entering into a contract, which was of no advantage to him, did not enable the court to say that there was no contract in the absence of any express mention by the defendant that he required 'old' oats.

Thus, a true cross-purposes mistake will only avoid the contract where there is latent ambiguity. Such an argument failed in *NBTY Europe Ltd (formerly Holland & Barrett Europe Ltd) v Nutricia International NV* [2005] EWHC 734 (Comm), [2005] 2 Lloyd's Rep 350, as it was held that the meaning of the correspondence was clear.

This case concerned an agreement to buy shares in a company where there was a particular method of fixing the consideration payable by reference to an adjustment related to the value of the net assets, although the maximum adjustment was set at £2.5m. The parties could not agree on the net assets figure and so could not agree the adjustment figure. The purchaser had sent an email offering to accept £2.5m 'in full and final settlement'. The vendor had replied accepting that this discharged 'all and any claims' relating to the sale contract and this had then been confirmed as correct by the purchaser. The vendor then claimed that it had not agreed as the parties were at cross purposes on the question of precisely what had been 'settled' by the email correspondence, i.e. the vendor alleged that it believed the agreement related only to settlement of the adjustment figure and excluded the debt amount.

It was held that by referring to 'settlement of all and any claims' the vendor had made a counter-offer covering both the adjustment and debt amounts and this had been accepted by the purchaser. The evidence was that the vendor had not believed that the figure excluded the debt. Therefore the meaning of the email was clear and, distinguishing *Raffles v Wichelhaus*, there was no latent ambiguity because one party's understanding of the meaning was objectively more justifiable on the facts.

3.3.1.2 A fault doctrine?

It is difficult in relation to these cases to resist the inference that the courts sometimes (although not always) apply an unarticulated fault doctrine. **Where a genuine situation of cross-purposes is seen to exist and one party is seen as responsible for provoking the mistake, the court will decide in favour of the other party.**

In *Scriven Bros and Co. v Hindley and Co*. [1913] 3 KB 564, the auctioneer who sought to enforce the contract had provoked the mistake by failing to make clear the distinction between the bales of hemp and tow, although they had the same shipping marks, and producing a catalogue which was unclear and misleading.

The court refused to enforce the contract, Lawrence J stating:

> [I]t was peculiarly the duty of the auctioneer to make it clear to the bidder…which lots were hemp and which lots were tow…[A] contract cannot arise when the person seeking to enforce it has by his own negligence, or by that of those for whom he is responsible, caused, or contributed to cause, the mistake.

Of course, the defendants had not investigated both lots, but the court recognized that the defendants owed no *duty* to examine the samples of tow.

The decision to enforce the alleged contract in **Smith v Hughes** (1871) LR 6 QB 597 can be explained in similar terms. The party seeking to resist enforcement of the contract (the buyer) had contributed to, or provoked, the mistake by not indicating clearly that 'old' oats were required, and could not then be heard to say that there was no contract.

Similarly, in **Tamplin v James** (1880) 15 ChD 215, the defendant clearly misunderstood the offer which he accepted. He thought he was buying an inn and adjoining gardens of a property well known to him. In fact, the sale particulars were clear that the gardens were not included in the property on offer, but the defendant had not bothered to examine these particulars and so was at fault. It followed that objectively there was agreement and at first instance Baggallay LJ granted specific performance (i.e., an order enforcing performance of the contract in accordance with its terms) against the defendant, saying:

> [W]here there has been no misrepresentation, and where there is no ambiguity in the terms of the contract, the defendant cannot be allowed to evade the performance of it by the simple statement that he has made a mistake. Were such to be the law the performance of a contract could rarely be enforced upon an unwilling party who was also unscrupulous.

The plaintiff was unaware of the mistake being made by the defendant and if specific performance had been refused would have been forced to find another buyer as a result of the reckless conduct of the defendant buyer.

3.3.2 **Unilateral mistake**

In some situations it is said that only one of the parties is mistaken. However, as can be seen from the discussion of the case law concerning cross-purposes mistake (at **3.3.1**), this is in fact no more than another way of saying that one party's understanding and the objectively observed agreement coincide, and the other party's understanding is out of line.

In such circumstances, the objectivity principle determines that there is a contract on the objectively observed terms, which will be enforced by the courts. However, the courts will ignore the objectivity principle where it appears that the party whose understanding coincides with the objective agreement was aware that the other party was labouring under a mistake and failed to draw the attention of that other to that mistake. Indeed, the courts will go further and assume that a party is aware of the other's mistake where a reasonable person in that party's place would have been so aware. In *Chwee Kin Keong v Digilandmall.com Pte Ltd* [2005] 1 SLR 502, the Singapore Court of Appeal considered 'ought reasonably to have known' to constitute a reasoning process in reaching the conclusion that there was in fact knowledge of the mistake, e.g. if the price of goods on an Internet site 'is so absurdly low in relation to its known market value, it stands to reason that a reasonable man would harbour a real suspicion that the price may not be correct or that there may be some troubling underlying basis for such a pricing' (quoting the judge at first instance [2004] SLR 594).

This very limited mistake doctrine of unilateral mistake applies where:

1. one party is genuinely **mistaken as to a term of the contract** and the mistake is one without which that party would not have entered into the contract

2. that mistake ought reasonably to have been known to the other party and

3. the mistaken party is not in any way at fault.

3.3.2.1 It must be a mistake as to term rather than a mistake as to a collateral matter

Condition 1 is particularly important since, if the mistake does not relate to a term of the contract but affects a so-called 'collateral' matter, such as a quality of the subject matter or a fact on which the decision to enter the contract was based, **it will not prevent agreement as it is not a mistake relating to what has been offered and accepted.**

In *Smith v Hughes* (see **3.3.1.1**), in the absence of an express stipulation for 'old' oats, whether the oats supplied were 'old' or 'new' was only a collateral matter concerning a quality of the oats.

In *Clarion Ltd v National Provident Institution* [2000] 1 WLR 1888, the defendant did not appreciate that the terms of the agreement meant that the claimant was aware of prices before making the decision to switch units between pension funds. Although the claimant was aware of this mistaken understanding, it was held that this was a mistake relating to the commercial effect of the agreement rather than its terms and therefore relief was refused.

In *Statoil ASA v Louis Dreyfus Energy Services LP, The Harriette N* [2008] EWHC 2257 (Comm), [2008] 2 Lloyd's Rep 685, [2009] 1 All ER (Comm) 1035 (see also **2.1.2** and **13.5.3**), Aikens J stated (at [88]) and expressly relying on *Smith v Hughes*: 'if one party has made a mistake about a fact on which he bases his decision to enter into a contract, but that fact does not form a term of the contract itself, then, even if the other party knows that the first is mistaken as to this fact, the contract will be binding'. On the facts it was not a term of the compromise agreement covering the amount of demurrage (freight) that was payable under the contract of sale, that discharge of the cargo was erroneously thought to have been completed (so ending the laytime) on 13 October when it had not occurred until 24 October. The mistake merely concerned a fact on which the decision had been made to enter into the compromise agreement and that was not a mistake as to a term. The judge compared this with the position in the decision of the Court of Appeal in Singapore in **Chwee Kin Keong v Digilandmall.com Pte Ltd** [2005] 1 SLR 502, **3.3.2** above, where the mistake related to the price term of goods on an Internet site.

3.3.2.2 The difficulty of meeting the requirements for an operative unilateral mistake

Examples of all the conditions being met are rare.

> In **Hartog v Colin and Shields** [1939] 3 All ER 566, the defendants offered to sell to the plaintiffs certain hare skins at 10¼d per pound. In fact, the defendants intended to sell at the same price per piece. The trade custom was to sell by the piece, and there were about three pieces to the pound, so that the defendants' offer was at about one-third of the normal price. The plaintiffs claimed to have accepted the offer so that there was a binding agreement based on the contract price as mistakenly offered. They claimed to be entitled to damages when the defendants failed to perform. The court found for the defendants. Singleton J made it clear that the crucial element for any defendant to establish was that the other party must have realized the mistake. In other words, a party cannot 'snap up' an offer when that party is aware that the other has made a mistake relating to the offer terms.

This is recognition of a principle of fair dealing in contractual negotiations in English law which prevents a party taking advantage of an obvious error by the other party (see also the discussion of mispricing on websites: **2.3.2.3**).

However, in many instances the impact of the mistake will be much less clear, in which case the mistaken party may find it impossible to satisfy the burden of proof. This occurred in **Centrovincial Estates plc v Merchant Investors Assurance Company Ltd** [1983] Com LR 158.

> The defendants were tenants of offices with an annual rental of £68,320, subject to review from 25 December 1982. The rent review clause provided that on that date the rent should be increased to the current market rental value, as agreed between the parties, and in no circumstances should the rent be lower than the figure payable immediately before the review. Agreement was reached on a figure of £65,000 before the plaintiffs realized that they had made a mistake, since they claimed that they had intended to propose a figure of £126,000.
>
> The Court of Appeal refused to grant a declaration to the effect that there was no legally binding agreement on the figure of £65,000 on the ground that it had not been established that the defendants knew or ought reasonably to have known of the plaintiffs' error when they reached agreement on the figure of £65,000.

The court appears to have considered it 'at least arguable' that the defendants considered that the rent might be reduced, despite the existence of the proviso in the rent review clause.

3.3.3 Unilateral mistake: Mistake as to identity

The situation in which unilateral mistake has most often been relied upon is that of mistake of identity. It is nearly always the case that the mistake as to identity has been provoked by conduct on the part of the other party which amounts to fraudulent misrepresentation (see **14.4.1.1**). The disadvantage of a claim based on misrepresentation is that its effect is to make the contract merely voidable, and since rescission is a purely personal remedy, it may be sought only against the person making the representation. However, in mistake of identity cases the usual situation is that property is acquired and immediately resold to a third party. The dishonest party (the 'rogue') then disappears, making the misrepresentation remedy worthless and leaving the original owner trying to recover the property from the third party. (See Figure 3.1.)

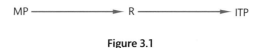

Figure 3.1

Thus the mistaken party (MP) is induced by the rogue (R) to transfer possession of goods under a contract. R immediately resells the goods to a third party who knows nothing of the fraudulent inducement and so is an 'innocent third party purchaser' (ITP).

If the contract between MP and R is void for mistake as to identity, R will not have acquired any title to pass onto the ITP so that MP can recover the goods from the ITP or sue the ITP for damages in the tort of conversion. On the other hand, if the contract between MP and R is merely voidable for the fraudulent misrepresentation, R obtained title to the goods which R can pass on to the ITP. Since MP's remedy is a personal remedy of rescission (setting aside the contract) as against R, it is lost once an ITP purchases the goods (s. 23 of the SGA 1979). The goods cannot then be recovered from the ITP.

The result is that the courts are faced with having to decide which of two 'innocent parties' should suffer as a result of the fraud by the rogue:

- If mistake can be proved the contract is void (see 3.2.2) and the original owner will succeed in recovering the property from the third party, even where that third party may be wholly innocent.

- In order to avoid this conclusion, Lord Denning suggested that the effect of mistake of identity ought to be to make the contract voidable (see **Lewis v Averay** [1972] 1 QB 198), on the basis that the innocent third party is generally more 'innocent' than the mistaken party and in need of greater protection.

This suggestion has its attractions, and had been recommended by the Law Reform Committee in its *Twelfth Report on Transfer of Title to Chattels,* Cmnd 2958 (1966), para. 15). However, the legal position had been to restrict the circumstances when a contract would be void for mistake as to identity by adopting a complicated distinction between 'true mistakes as to identity' and mistakes as to attributes, which can be said to represent the distinction between mistakes as to terms and collateral matters (see **Smith v Hughes** and discussion at 3.3.2.1). A mistake as to attributes, e.g. creditworthiness, was not regarded as sufficiently fundamental to render the contract void. Thus, the approach was to take a very limited interpretation of 'identity' as a term of the contract. In addition, a mistake as to identity had to be crucial to the decision to contract. Although there was a decision of the House of Lords which had held identity to be crucial where a contract had been concluded by written correspondence (**Cundy v Lindsay** (1878) 3 App Cas 459), in accordance with the central policy objective, where the contract was made in a face-to-face situation the presumption was that identity was not crucially important to the parties and that they intended to deal with the person physically present. Even in this context, there were apparently irreconcilable decisions which appeared to turn on whether the court in question had presented the identity question as an 'offer and acceptance' analysis, i.e. MP intended to offer the goods for sale to the person whose identity was assumed by R, rather than to R. Accordingly, R could not accept the offer.

It had been hoped that the House of Lords in *Shogun Finance Ltd v Hudson* [2003] UKHL 62, [2004] 1 AC 919 would inject some clarification and certainty into the law on mistake as to identity by resolving these apparent inconsistencies in approach, e.g. by introducing a general principle that 'mistake' as to identity rendered the contract voidable and so abolishing the identity/attributes distinction and the emerging distinction between face-to-face and written contracting. However, if anything, the split decision of the House of Lords in terms of result, and to some extent in terms of analysis, has added to the complexity of the applicable law and reinforced arbitrary distinctions of principle.

In order to identify and evaluate the decision in *Shogun Finance Ltd v Hudson*, it is vital to appreciate the state of the law immediately prior to the decision.

3.3.3.1 Testing the fundamental importance of identity: The face-to-face case law prior to the decision in *Shogun Finance v Hudson*

In a face-to-face situation, where the parties negotiate in each other's physical presence, the actual decision to sell does not normally rest on the question of the identity of the buyer. It is the decision to allow the goods to be taken away on credit which will be influenced by the attributes of the buyer, but this is a collateral issue. Accordingly, in face-to-face situations, the courts generally concluded that the contract was not void for mistake as to identity because of the presumption that the parties intended to deal with the person physically present.

There has always been a recognized exception to this position in face-to-face contracts where identity can be shown to be crucial, namely where the intention is to contract with a particular company and the contract purports to be made by a person on behalf of that company (a so-called 'bogus official') where that person has no such authority to act (*Hardman v Booth* (1863) 1 H & C 803, 158 ER 1107). In such situations the clear intention is to deal with another person, i.e. the company, so that no personal contract can be concluded with the rogue official.

However, this apart, in face-to-face contracting it is generally presumed that identity is not crucial to the decision to contract. Two cases, in particular, are cited as authorities to support this conclusion.

> In *Phillips v Brooks Ltd* [1919] 2 KB 243, a rogue went into a jewellery shop and examined some jewellery. He wrote out a cheque for some pearls and a ring, and announced that he was Sir George Bullough, giving an address in St James's Square. He was allowed to take away a ring without paying for it after the plaintiff had checked that the name and address tallied. The court was unwilling to allow the plaintiff to recover the ring from the third party to whom it had been pledged, since in its view the contract was not void. The plaintiff had intended to contract with the person who had been present in the shop. It was a judgement as to creditworthiness, rather than the person's identity, which had persuaded the plaintiff in this case to allow the contract to proceed on credit terms.

The same rationale explains *Lewis v Averay* [1972] 1 QB 198.

> In *Lewis v Averay* the plaintiff had advertised his car for sale. The rogue offered to buy it. He said that he was the well-known actor, Richard Greene, and wrote out a cheque, signing it 'R.A. Green'. The plaintiff was unwilling to allow him to take the car away until the cheque had cleared, but the rogue showed him an official pass for Pinewood Studios with his photograph on it in the name of 'Richard A. Green'. At that point the plaintiff allowed the rogue to take the car and the log book. The rogue sold the car to the defendant (an innocent purchaser), and his cheque proved to be worthless. The plaintiff was unable to recover the car from the defendant.

Lord Denning's reasoning in the case has already been explained (see 3.3.3). Megaw LJ proceeded by a more orthodox analysis to reach the same conclusion. Megaw LJ felt that the plaintiff had not been concerned about the identity of the person with whom he was dealing. He had been misled by the rogue into believing that he was dealing with a person of substance, but this was merely a mistake as to creditworthiness.

Case analysis

In both *Phillips v Brooks* and *Lewis v Averay* the presumption of an intention to contract with the person physically present had not been rebutted. In addition, in both cases it can be argued that the decision to contract had already been made before the issue of identity was raised, and in neither case was the sale 'called off' when the purchaser proposed to pay on credit. In both cases it is possible to argue, therefore, that at the point when the question of identity was raised it related only to the issue of creditworthiness prior to the decision to allow the person present to take the goods away on credit before the cheque payment had cleared.

This was often the basis used to explain and distinguish the decision of the Court of Appeal in *Ingram v Little* [1961] 1 QB 31, i.e. based on the argument that the plaintiff in *Ingram v Little* had made it clear at the outset that she was not prepared to let the car be taken away before the cheque had cleared and changed her mind only after checking identity. On this reasoning, it was at least arguable, even in face-to-face contracts, that if the rogue introduced himself at the outset as someone else, this might make identity crucial to the decision to contract. On the other hand, all three cases appear essentially to turn on a judgement about ability to pay and creditworthiness, and so ought to have reached the same basic conclusion on the effect of the mistake. In addition, and in any event, the reports of *Phillips v Brooks Ltd* are ambiguous as to the precise point at which the rogue mentioned that he was Sir George Bullough.

> In *Ingram v Little* [1961] 1 QB 31, two spinster sisters had negotiated for the sale of their car to a rogue masquerading as one Hutchinson. At first they would not accept his cheque, but they later relented having checked the name, initials, and address he had given them against a telephone directory entry. They then allowed him to take the car away immediately, and later sought to recover it from the innocent third party to whom it had been sold.
>
> The majority in the Court of Appeal appears to have been satisfied, on rather flimsy evidence, that the plaintiff had intended to deal with the person the rogue had pretended to be rather than with whoever was present before her.

In the light of the very limited check on his identity made by the plaintiff the decision is a little surprising. **The reasoning rested on concluding that the offer to sell had been made only to the *real* Hutchinson so that only he could accept it.** However, this offer and acceptance analysis presupposes the fundamental importance of identity to the decision to contract when this had to be established separately. In other words, the offer will only be made to the real Hutchinson if that identity was so important to the decision to contract that it became a part of the offer terms so that only the *real* Hutchinson could accept.

> For example, in *Boulton v Jones* (1857) 27 LJ Ex 117, the defendant sent an order for goods to the shop of Brocklehurst. The same day Brocklehurst had sold his business, including current stock, to the plaintiff, his former foreman. The plaintiff supplied the goods, but the defendant was unwilling to pay for them on the basis that he had ordered from Brocklehurst because he had a set-off against him. The court found for the defendant, because it was not open to the plaintiff to substitute himself for the original offeree

without first informing the offeror (which would amount to making a counter-offer). The identity of the contracting party was vitally important to the defendant because of the existence of the right of set-off and the plaintiff was aware that the defendant intended to deal with his predecessor. Accordingly, the plaintiff could not accept an offer that he knew was intended for another.

On these facts, it was clear that identity was vital to the terms on which the offer was placed, but in other cases this fact may be less obvious.

In *Lewis v Averay*, *Ingram v Little* was treated as anomalous (even though strictly binding on the court). Lord Denning stated that he considered the 'material facts' in all three cases to be 'quite indistinguishable'. It may be that the decision is explicable as one based on policy in that, in normal circumstances, where an allegation of mistaken identity is made, the courts are concerned to protect the innocent third-party purchaser who acquired the goods from the rogue. However, in *Ingram v Little* that innocent third party was a car dealer, and the Court of Appeal may have felt more sympathy towards the elderly plaintiff.

The majority of the Court of Appeal in *Shogun Finance Ltd v Hudson* [2001] EWCA Civ 100, [2002] QB 834, rejected an argument based on the application of the presumption that a contracting party intends to contract with the person in front of them in face-to-face negotiations (in this case the contract between the rogue and the finance company had been entered into at the premises of a car dealer). The majority reached their conclusion on the basis that the car dealer was not acting as agent for the finance company so that this was not a face-to-face contract. However, more generally, the majority also considered that the face-to-face presumption applied only to oral contracts, whereas the contract in question was written. There was a strong dissent from Sedley LJ who considered that the presumption applied so that the finance company had contracted with the rogue.

The majority decision of the Court of Appeal in *Shogun Finance v Hudson* also adopted the offer and acceptance analysis which had been used by the majority of the Court of Appeal in *Ingram v Little*, i.e. focusing on the question of 'to whom should the offeree (the rogue) reasonably have interpreted the offer as having been made?' Sedley LJ advocated that Parliament should look at this area of the law because development at common law was effectively curtailed by the decision of the House of Lords in *Cundy v Lindsay*. Therefore, before examining the decision of the House of Lords on appeal in *Shogun Finance v Hudson*, it is first necessary to examine the earlier decision of the House in *Cundy v Lindsay* and the limitations it imposed.

3.3.3.2 The decision of the House of Lords in *Cundy v Lindsay*

This decision is authority for the fact that where the parties negotiate at a distance it may be easier to establish an identity mistake because the identity of the person placing an order has to be known in order to dispatch the goods. It should therefore be easier to prove that identity was of crucial importance to the making of the contract. To put it in terms of offer and acceptance: the offer must be made to the person named on the written order form, so that only that person can accept.

In **Cundy v Lindsay** (1878) 3 App Cas 459, the rogue set up business under the name Blenkarn at 37 Wood Street. A very respectable company called Blenkiron and Co. traded at 123 Wood Street. The rogue ordered goods from the plaintiffs, making his signature look as though it read Blenkiron. The plaintiffs sent the goods without payment to 'Blenkiron and Co.' at the rogue's address, and the rogue sold them to the defendants, innocent purchasers. The success of the plaintiffs' plea of mistake, and thus their ability to recover the goods from the defendants, depended upon whether they intended to deal with whichever firm traded at 37 Wood Street, or whether they intended to deal specifically with Blenkiron and Co. The court of first instance took the former view, but the Court of Appeal and the House of Lords took the latter, so that the plaintiffs succeeded in establishing that the contract was void for mistake.

The consequence of the finding that the contract was void for mistake as to identity was that it was the defendants, as innocent third-party purchasers, who suffered the loss because they were found to have converted goods (tort of conversion) to which they had no title.

It seems a reasonable inference from the facts that the plaintiffs intended to deal with a particular firm by name, as opposed to dealing with an address, which would be of no great significance to them. However, this gives rise to the question why the name of the firm would be important to them. It may well be because they thought they were dealing with the respectable Blenkiron and Co. which was likely to pay for the goods supplied on credit. The decision may also be questionable because of the emphasis placed on the need for a subjective meeting of minds in the speeches in the House of Lords.

Nevertheless, the analysis of their Lordships that the plaintiffs intended to contract with Blenkiron and Co., as named in the written document, was subsequently relied upon to underpin the decision of the majority of the House of Lords in **Shogun Finance v Hudson**.

3.3.3.3 Mistaking one existing person for another

The decision in **Cundy v Lindsay** illustrates the principle that to operate to render the contract void, any mistake must involve the mistaken party mistaking the rogue for another existing entity. In **Cundy v Lindsay** it was key that the plaintiffs knew that there was a reputable firm named Blenkiron and Co. operating from Wood Street; otherwise, the use of any fictitious name might suffice. However, and ironically, it is the fact that they had heard of Blenkiron and Co. which provides evidence to support the conclusion that the decision to contract may have been motivated by considerations of creditworthiness. As Lord Denning noted in **Lewis v Averay**, it is very difficult to distinguish a person's identity and his attributes (referring to it as a 'distinction without a difference'); indeed, a person may be identified by means of his attributes (e.g., 'the wife of Van der Borgh' in *Lake v Simmons* [1927] AC 487).

Nevertheless, it is clear that the mistake must relate to another existing entity—and an offer cannot be made to a non-existent person.

113

In **King's Norton Metal Co. Ltd v Edridge, Merrett and Co.** (1897) 14 TLR 98, a rogue, named Wallis, established a bogus business called 'Hallam and Co.', and had written to the plaintiffs on headed paper depicting a large factory and suggesting that it was a well-established and thriving firm. The plaintiffs supplied goods to Hallam and Co. on credit. These goods were immediately sold to the defendants, innocent purchasers. The plaintiffs claimed that the contract was void for mistake and sought to recover the goods from the defendants.

The Court of Appeal rejected their claim. The plaintiffs had intended to deal with the writer of the letter, whoever that was. In order for a mistake as to identity to operate, one existing entity had to be mistaken for another existing entity. There was only one existing identity here (the rogue using an alias) and the plaintiffs must have intended to deal with that person.

In fact, the mistake made by the plaintiffs was as to the writer's ability or willingness to pay for the goods. In other words, it was merely a mistake as to creditworthiness, or an error of judgement, which will not negative agreement.

3.3.3.4 The decision of the House of Lords in *Shogun Finance Ltd v Hudson*

The decision of the House of Lords in **Shogun Finance Ltd v Hudson** represents the latest statement of principle, although the decision is striking in terms of the differences in approach adopted by the majority and the minority—and even within the majority speeches.

> The rogue had visited a Mitsubishi motor dealer and had expressed an interest in purchasing a Mitsubishi Shogun. The rogue had then identified himself as Mr Dulabh Patel and had produced Mr Patel's stolen driving licence as proof of his identity and address. The dealer had agreed the price for the car (£22,500) and had then faxed a copy of the proposed hire purchase agreement to the claimant finance company, together with a copy of the driving licence. This agreement named Mr Patel as the customer but the rogue had signed by forging Mr Patel's signature. The finance company carried out the usual checks on credit rating and approved the finance. Therefore, the dealer allowed the rogue to take away the vehicle. The rogue then sold the vehicle to the defendant for £17,000 and disappeared.
>
> When the finance company brought a claim against the defendant for damages in the tort of conversion, the defendant claimed that he had acquired good title under s. 27 of the Hire Purchase Act 1964 because the rogue was a 'debtor' under the terms of that section and so could pass good title to the defendant.
>
> The majority of the Court of Appeal had held that the rogue was not a 'debtor' because the hire purchase agreement had been made with the real Mr Patel who was named in the written document. The real Mr Patel could not be liable on that agreement because his signature had been forged. The majority also rejected the defendant's alternative argument that the dealer had acted as agent for the finance company so that this was a face-to-face contract made between the finance company and the rogue. It had been argued that on this basis it was a face-to-face contract to which the presumption applied and the finance company had therefore contracted with the rogue.
>
> The House of Lords dismissed the appeal by a majority of 3:2, Lords Nicholls and Millett dissenting. The majority held that there was a written agreement made between the finance company and the rogue which was a nullity because Mr Patel's signature had been forged.

The result on these facts was that, contrary to the traditionally assumed policy on this matter, the innocent third-party purchaser was not protected. This appears to be because the majority of the House of Lords relied heavily on another, competing policy argument, namely the primacy of written documents and the fact that this writing records the parties' names. To have gone behind this was considered to be dangerous practice and would expose the finance company to the dangers of fraud by those who were able to steal identity and assume the identity of that other.

Majority: Lord Hobhouse

Lord Hobhouse considered that the question arising for determination related only to the construction of the written hire purchase agreement rather than the law as to mistake as to identity. He applied the parol evidence rule (6.2.1) and concluded that since the written contract named Mr Patel, it was Mr Patel who had made the offer to take the vehicle on hire purchase terms. It followed that the acceptance related only to that offer. It was not possible to go outside the terms of the written document. Lord Walker also purported to agree with the speech of Lord Hobhouse.

Majority: Lords Phillips and Walker

Lord Phillips focused on the 'offer and acceptance' analysis in mistake as to identity cases (i.e., the question of agreement) and reaffirmed the distinction in the previous case law between face-to-face contracting and contracting via written correspondence so that in face-to-face contracting there is a presumption that the offer is intended to be made only to the person physically present and only that person can accept it, whereas in contracts made by means of written documents, such as the present case, the offer-and-acceptance questions were determined solely by focusing on those written terms. Accordingly, he came to the same overall conclusion as Lord Hobhouse, whilst expressly maintaining the face-to-face presumption for non-written contracts.

Lords Nicholls and Millett (dissenting)

In the dissenting speeches the distinction between written and face-to-face contracting is considered to be arbitrary and their Lordships favoured a policy approach which protected the innocent third-party purchaser (ITP) since:

[t]he loss is more appropriately borne by the person who takes the risks inherent in parting with his goods without receiving payment [per Lord Nicholls at [35]]

and

[i]t is surely fairer that the party who was actually swindled and who had an opportunity to uncover the fraud should bear the loss rather than a party who entered the picture only after the swindle had been carried out [per Lord Millett at [82]].

Not surprisingly, therefore, given this policy approach of the minority, the conclusion must be that there is a voidable contract. To achieve this there must be two steps to the analysis:

- determine the existence of a contract
- assess the effect of the fraud to see whether it renders the contract unenforceable.

On the view of the minority, there was a contract in existence between the finance company and the rogue based on the presumption that you intend to contract with the person with whom you are 'dealing'. (It follows that on the minority analysis there will always be a contract with the person with whom a mistaken party (MP) is dealing.) The fraud would render such a contract voidable.

3.3.3.5 Analysis

Thus, the real distinction in the approaches is between reliance on objective determination of agreement via offer and acceptance (the 'offer and acceptance' analysis) and reliance upon the fraud which induced a mistake. However, identity must be crucially important in order for the rogue offeree to know that the offer is intended for someone else so that the rogue offeree cannot accept it. Equally, the offeror must consider that the identity of the offeree is so important that the offer is made only to the 'real' offeree. The difficulty is that the cases do not provide a satisfactory answer to determine this and the analysis tends to be circular. The results in the face-to-face cases should remain true, i.e. identity was not the vital factor as the decision to contract was not affected by any mistake—only the decision to let the goods be taken away on credit. (This may be the accepted position of all members of the House of

Lords, albeit that Lord Hobhouse does not consider this case law to be relevant on the facts.) The difficulty in **Shogun Finance v Hudson** is that, in the context of the hire purchase agreement, the offer has to be made to the person named in the document, making it difficult to argue that someone else was the intended contracting party. However, the facts require a different approach since had the rogue handed over counterfeit cash for the Mitsubishi car the contract to sell the car would have been made between the dealers and the rogue. Shogun Finance would inevitably make decisions on whether to agree hire purchase terms based on the credit rating of a named individual and it is the fact that the name carries with it a credit rating which is significant rather than the 'identity' of the person named in the written document.

Therefore, what is needed is some coherent principle to determine when identity is important to the decision to contract. The alternative approach is to conclude that, apart from factual scenarios such as that in **Boulton v Jones**, identity is rarely important to *the decision to contract,* just to the credit terms—and therefore to conclude that it is the fraud which is important, rather than the existence of agreement on an offer and acceptance analysis.

The fault question

It is interesting to consider whether there is any residual 'fault' question after the decision of the House of Lords in **Shogun Finance v Hudson**.

The position prior to **Shogun Finance v Hudson** was that the claimant had to show that it was not at fault by demonstrating that reasonable steps were taken to check the identity of the person with whom they were dealing. This was considered to provide an alternative explanation of the 'face-to-face' case law. For example, in **Phillips v Brooks Ltd** [1919] 2 KB 243 (see 3.3.3.1), merely to have checked in a directory that Sir George Bullough lived at the address given did not establish that the man in the jewellery shop was in fact Sir George Bullough. This would not explain the different conclusion on the effect of the mistake in **Ingram v Little** [1961] 1 QB 31, where the plaintiff had checked that the person who the rogue purported to be lived at the address given, but no more. In **Lewis v Averay** [1972] 1 QB 198, checking the pass to Pinewood Studios, displaying a photograph of the rogue, ought arguably to be regarded as reasonable steps to confirm identity, since there is then a connection between the identity claimed and the evidence to establish that the person in question has that identity. This would seem to be fairly typical as a means of checking identity. However, on the facts, the Court of Appeal regarded this as insufficient.

On this basis it might be considered that the dissenting view of Sedley LJ in the Court of Appeal in **Shogun Finance Ltd v Hudson** [2001] EWCA Civ 1000, [2002] QB 834 (see 3.3.3.1) has much to recommend it since, although the claimants carried out a credit check for the person named on the driving licence, they did not check that the person before them was in fact the licence holder.

It is more likely that fault is irrelevant where the contracting is achieved on the basis of written documents. The House of Lords in **Cundy v Lindsay** (see 3.3.3.2) did not even consider any requirement to check identity. At the time such a check might have considerably delayed the process of reaching agreement because communications at a distance could not be achieved via instantaneous methods. Of course, nowadays, no such argument could be sustained and it would seem to be appropriate practice to carry out some sort of check before dispatching goods on credit. Inevitably, however, this may necessarily be a credit check rather than a true check to establish identity.

The majority of the House of Lords in **Shogun Finance v Hudson** was keen to protect lending and credit bodies who carried out a traditional identity check of asking to see an identity document but who were happy to allow a £22,500 car to be taken away on the basis of a driving licence and a signature which resembled that of the licence holder. By comparison, in the Court of Appeal, Sedley LJ had expressed dissatisfaction with the checks carried out by the finance company, given the value of the transaction, and had concluded that 'if there was ever a seller who ought to be treated as having assumed the risk of loss, it was…the present claimants'. That said, the ITP had purchased a car worth £22,500 for £17,000 but would have felt reasonably confident since the seller had both the car and the relevant paperwork. The fraud in **Shogun Finance** would have been more difficult to achieve with photographic identity and some agencies are insisting on this as a means of identification rather then an old paper-style driving licence.

Conclusion

1. The decision in **Shogun Finance v Hudson,** which had been so eagerly awaited, has proved to be a huge disappointment in terms of clarifying the applicable principles to determine when a contract will be void for mistake. Contracts made in writing are likely to be void and contracts made face to face are likely to be voidable. However, to the parties it might appear far from clear whether the contract is face-to-face or written, e.g. the dealings with the car dealer in **Shogun Finance**, followed by the making of a written hire purchase contract with the finance company. A customer might well consider that the contract was made by the dealer, although the agency argument was rejected in **Shogun Finance v Hudson**.

2. It appears that there will be no contract with the rogue where the real intended party is named in a written document. However, where the parties contract in a face-to-face situation, it appears that the contract is likely (and even almost certain) to be voidable for fraud. The answer for lenders and vendors is therefore to insist on a written contract whenever this is practical, but there seems no obvious method of protection available to ITPs, although some checks may be possible where pressures of time permit. The significance, or otherwise, of any degree of fault on the part of the MP or the ITP should have greater significance in determining which of these two innocent parties should suffer the loss caused by the actions of the rogue.

3. Arguably the void/voidable distinction is not the most appropriate one since it is an 'all or nothing' approach, i.e. either the contract is void for mistake so that the mistaken party can recover the goods (and the innocent third-party purchaser suffers the loss), or the contract is voidable for fraud so that the innocent third party can keep the goods (and the mistaken party suffers the loss). An alternative suggestion of apportioning the loss between these two innocent parties in accordance with their respective degrees of fault was suggested by Devlin LJ in **Ingram v Little** [1961] 1 QB 31 and would be similar to the apportionment of losses having an extrinsic cause seen in the Law Reform (Frustrated Contracts) Act 1943, discussed at **12.8.2**. However, this solution did not find favour when it was considered by the Law Reform Committee, *Twelfth Report on Transfer of Title to Chattels,* Cmnd 2958 (1966). The reason given was that apportionment was considered to leave too much to judicial discretion and was too complex, thereby leading to uncertainty.

3.4 **Mistakes in documents**

Types of document mistakes:

- The remedy of *rectification* of a written document may be available in some limited instances where a transcription mistake has been made in recording the parties' oral agreement in writing (see **3.4.1**).

- Another type of mistake relating to a document may raise the question of the applicability of the plea of *non est factum*. It is important to appreciate that this plea will be applicable only in exceptional cases. It involves a party asserting that, although a document contains that party's signature, it is not the document that the party thought they were signing so that it should not bind them (see **3.4.2**). This plea of *non est factum,* although in one sense reflecting a mistake by the party signing, also bears some relationship to fraud (see **14.4.1.1**).

3.4.1 **Rectification**

Rectification was defined above as providing a remedy where there has been a simple transcription mistake in recording an oral agreement in writing.

3.4.1.1 Operation of the doctrine

1. The remedy is normally available only when the document said to incorporate the agreement fails to reproduce the *common intentions* of the parties.

In **Joscelyne v Nissen** [1970] 2 QB 86, a daughter owned a house, which was also occupied by her father and mother. Her father had agreed to transfer his car hire business to his daughter, and in return she had agreed to pay him a weekly sum and to pay household expenses, including the gas, electricity, and coal bills and the cost of a home help. However, the eventual written agreement referred to the payment of the weekly sum and that the daughter was to 'discharge all expenses in connection with the whole premises'. Following a dispute, the daughter had stopped paying the fuel bills and costs of home help. The father sought rectification of the document containing their agreement to make explicit their original intention that such bills should be paid by the daughter.

The court was satisfied that the father's version of the agreement did reflect what had actually been agreed between the parties. Indeed, the daughter's defence focused more on pursuing a legal argument against rectification (see below) than on denying the terms of this agreement. The contract was rectified in line with the interpretation originally placed on the contractual document by the daughter.

The most difficult obstacle confronting a claimant seeking rectification is to prove that the document does not truly reflect what was agreed. Courts are understandably reluctant to change the terms of a written agreement, since in the great majority of cases the contractual document is the most secure evidence there is of what was agreed by the parties (often referred to as representing 'the cogent evidence of the parties' intention'). In **Joscelyne v Nissen**, the Court of Appeal stated that 'convincing proof' would be required to counteract that 'cogent evidence', indicating that by this expression they intended a high burden of proof to fall on any claimant. The burden of proof was explained in similar terms by Brightman LJ in *Thomas Bates & Son Ltd v Wyndham's (Lingerie) Ltd* [1981] 1 WLR 505 at p. 521 and by Peter Gibson LJ in *Swainland Builders Ltd v Freehold Properties Ltd* [2002] 2 EGLR 71 at p. 74.

It was made clear by Lord Hoffmann in *Chartbrook Ltd v Persimmon Homes Ltd* [2009] UKHL 38, [2009] 3 WLR 267, that evidence of the continuing common intention had to be assessed objectively, i.e. in terms of whether a reasonable observer would consider there to be such an intention and not what the parties later claim their intention to have been.

In *KPMG v Network Rail Infrastructure Ltd* [2007] EWCA Civ 363, [2007] Bus LR 1336, a draft lease attached to the original agreement for a lease of commercial office premises had contained a break clause providing for the tenant to determine the lease only in specific circumstances. The lease was executed some ten years later following negotiations with an amended, and more generous, break clause in favour of the tenant. The lessor sought rectification arguing that it had always been intended that the terms of the break clause in the draft lease should apply. At first instance the judge agreed and the tenant appealed arguing that this intention should not have been assumed and that it thought the clause had been deliberately amended in its favour.

The Court of Appeal considered that since the tenant's solicitor had explained the effect of the final clause and had accepted the change, the lessor had not established that there was a common continuing intention at the date of the execution of the lease that the break clause should be in the terms contained in the original draft. In addition, selective rectification of those parts of the clause which met common intentions, whilst ignoring those parts that did not, was not possible.

2. If all the objective evidence is that the parties *did* agree in the terms used in the document, it will not avail the claimant to insist that they misunderstood the meaning of the words used.

In *Frederick E. Rose (London) Ltd v William H. Pim Junior & Co. Ltd* [1953] 2 QB 450, the plaintiffs were asked to supply 'Moroccan horse beans described as "feveroles"'. They did not know what feveroles were, and asked the defendants, who said they were simply horse beans. The plaintiffs therefore entered into a contract to purchase the requisite number of horse beans from the defendants. They then discovered that 'feveroles' were a superior type of horse bean, and the buyers of these 'feveroles' sought damages from the plaintiffs. The plaintiffs sought rectification of their agreement with the defendants.

However, the Court of Appeal refused rectification on the basis that the contract as written down reflected what had been agreed orally. (In fact, both parties had mistakenly thought that 'feveroles' were the same as horse beans, but on the facts there was no remedy in mistake: see 13.4.1.3.)

3. It was once thought that rectification would be available only where there was already an 'antecedent concluded contract' on the basis of the oral negotiations between the parties, and that rectification would not be available where the document itself represented the first point of contracting between the parties. However, this theory was rejected in *Joscelyne v Nissen,* the Court of Appeal holding that firm agreement short of contract (an 'outward expression of accord') was sufficient, provided that the common intention of the parties continued up to the moment of recording their agreement in writing. This 'outward expression of accord' is more of an evidential factor than a strict requirement in some cases of rectification. In *Munt v Beasley* [2006] EWCA Civ 370, it was clear that both parties had a continuing common intention on the basis of the agent's particulars of sale of a lease that the lease included the loft, although this was not stated in the lease itself. Rectification was therefore ordered and the landlord's claim for damages for trespass and breach of covenant four years after the tenant started a loft conversion necessarily failed.

3.4.1.2 Rectification if the contractual document fails to accurately record the intentions of only *one* party

There were authorities, culminating in *A. Roberts & Co. Ltd v Leicestershire CC* [1961] Ch 555, which suggested that even where the document failed to record the intentions of only one of the parties, rectification might be available. However, those authorities were largely overruled by *Riverlate Properties Ltd v Paul* [1975] Ch 133 where a lessor had made a mistake in drafting a document containing a proposed lease, and subsequently sought to amend it in a way that would have increased the burden on the lessee. The Court of Appeal refused to rectify the lease in those circumstances since at the time of contracting the lessee did not know about the lessor's mistake, still less had there been any kind of sharp practice.

The significance of these factors was made clear in ***Thomas Bates & Son Ltd v Wyndham's (Lingerie) Ltd*** [1981] 1 WLR 505.

> Tenants had taken a lease from the plaintiffs on two previous occasions, and on each occasion an option for renewal in the lease contained a price term leaving the matter to be agreed between the parties, or to be fixed by arbitration. A further lease omitted provision for arbitration in the event of any dispute over fixing the rent, a fact noted by the tenants but not drawn to the attention of the plaintiffs. The plaintiffs sought rectification of the lease after it had been executed.
>
> The Court of Appeal dismissed the tenants' appeal against the trial judge's order for rectification. **Rectification would be allowed even where the mistake was one-sided, provided the other party knew of the mistake but failed to draw it to the attention of the mistaken party; and provided there was some inequitable benefit to the party conscious of the other's mistake (not necessarily amounting to sharp practice).**
>
> *Roberts v Leicestershire CC* was good law because it rested on precisely this principle.

This line of authority was considered again in ***Commission for the New Towns v Cooper (GB) Ltd*** [1995] Ch 259. Stuart-Smith LJ suggested that rectification in the one-sided mistake cases turned upon the existence of 'unconscionable conduct'. **This in turn raised the subsidiary question of whether rectification could ever be granted in such circumstances if the party seeking to rely upon the terms as written did not know of the other's mistake.**

Stuart-Smith LJ was satisfied that the existence of unconscionable conduct would be established if it could be shown that a party intended the other to be mistaken, and so conducted himself as to divert that other's attention from discovering the mistake. He was also satisfied that in such circumstances the suspicion that the other may indeed be mistaken would be sufficient to amount to actual knowledge of the mistake. In so deciding he relied upon the classification of Peter Gibson J in *Baden v Société Générale pour Favoriser le Développement du Commerce et de l'Industrie en France SA (1982)* [1993] 1 WLR 509 at pp. 575–6, which treats 'wilfully shutting one's eyes to the obvious' as actual knowledge.

Rectification was ordered on this basis in ***Hurst Stores & Interiors Ltd v ML Europe Property Ltd*** [2004] EWCA Civ 490, [2004] BLR 249. A final version of a statement of account was different from all previous versions seen by the parties and did not reflect the agreement which the parties had reached on the basis for the valuation of certain works. The project manager for the construction company had signed this final version of the statement without the difference being drawn to his attention. The Court of Appeal held that the employer's construction manager, who had prepared the final document, had actual or 'shut eye' knowledge of this mistake so that rectification was appropriate. By comparison, the Court of Appeal in ***George Wimpey UK Ltd v VI***

Components Ltd [2005] EWCA Civ 77, [2005] BLR 135, rejected a claim for rectification based on unilateral mistake concerning the formula for the calculation of an extra payment because there was insufficient evidence of actual knowledge of the mistake (even on the extended definition of actual knowledge in *Baden v Société Générale*) or that the vendor had failed to draw the purchaser's attention to the last minute change to this formula. The Court of Appeal stressed the exceptional nature of the jurisdiction in *Commission for the New Towns* to rectify a contract on the basis of unilateral mistake and the considerable contracting experience of this purchaser when compared to that of the vendor.

In general terms it will be extremely difficult to succeed in proving both the requirement of actual knowledge and unconscionable conduct on the part of the other party so that rectification based on unilateral mistake will be rare. In *Rowallan Group Ltd v Edgehill Portfolio No. 1 Ltd* [2007] EWHC 32 (Ch), [2007] NPC 9, Lightman J reiterated the conclusion in *George Wimpey* 'that the remedy of rectification for unilateral mistake is a drastic remedy, for it has the result of imposing on the defendant to the claim a contract which he did not, and did not intend to, make. Accordingly, the conditions for the grant of such relief must be strictly satisfied.'

The judge spelt out the need to establish that the defendant had actual knowledge of the claimant's mistake, which included 'wilfully shutting one's eyes to the obvious and wilfully and recklessly failing to make such inquiries as an honest or reasonable man would make'. However, 'if the Defendant intended that the Claimant should be mistaken in this regard and deliberately set about diverting the Claimant's attention from discovering the mistake, it is unnecessary that the Claimant actually knew that the Claimant was mistaken: it is sufficient that the Defendant merely suspected that it was so'. On the facts, however, the defendant had no actual knowledge of factors influencing the making of the amendment and there was no reason why it should have known of the mistake or suspected it. It was therefore, to use the judge's words, a 'hopeless case'.

It may even be difficult for those claiming rectification based on unilateral mistake to succeed in establishing their own belief at the time and that they made a mistake.

In **Ahmed v Wingrove** [2006] EWHC 1918 (Ch), [2007] 1 P & CR D15, the original option agreement in January 2001 referred to the condition that the defendant obtain planning permission within twelve months. The agreement needed to be redrafted in July 2001 to reflect the fact that the claimants' property was in joint names and referred again to the need for planning permission to be obtained within twelve months. The planning permission was secured in June 2002 and the defendant sought to exercise the option in the same month. The claimants argued that the July 2001 agreement should be rectified to insert January 2001 as the start date for the twelve-month period because (a) either that was the common intention of both parties, i.e. that the start date was to remain unaltered, or (b) the defendant knew that the period for planning permission had not been extended by the July 2001 agreement and it would therefore be unconscionable for the defendant to resist rectification.

It was held that the argument based on mutual mistake could not succeed because the defendant had intended the July agreement to have a new start date. To succeed in the alternative claim based on unilateral mistake the claimants needed to establish (a) that they believed the twelve-month period ran from January 2001, (b) that the defendant had actual or shut eye knowledge of this belief and (c) that the defendant's conduct had been so unconscionable that it would not be unfair to hold him to the terms of the agreement that he knew or suspected the claimants thought they were entering. However, the claim failed at the first hurdle as the claimants could not establish that they intended or believed the July agreement was to run from January 2001.

Alternatively, there may be evidence of a mistake but it must be a mistake as to a term (provision) of the agreement rather than as to its quality. In **Connolly v Bellway Homes Ltd** [2007] EWHC 895 (Ch), the parties were agreed on the figure that represented the estimated sales price that the claimant later sought to have rectified. The judge noted:

> This is in truth a case where one party has subsequently come to appreciate that it should not have agreed to the inclusion of a particular term. But that is not the sort of error which enables a court to rectify the agreement. The court cannot remake the parties' bargain just because it has turned out to be significantly to the detriment of one party, and significantly to the benefit of the other.
>
> This case, it seems to me, is just the sort of case which Sedley LJ had in mind in his judgment in the *George Wimpey* case…when he said (at para. 62): 'There are at least two kinds of mistake. One is a literal misunderstanding of some fact material to the proposed contract. The other is an error of judgment in entering into the contract. I find it difficult to think that the second kind has any relevance to the law of unilateral mistake' [paras 109–10].

3.4.2 The plea of *non est factum*

The Latin phrase *non est factum* literally means 'It is not my deed'. As a rule of the law of contract, it affords a defence to a party against whom a claim is brought in reliance upon a signed written agreement, where that party is able to show that they were unaware of the true meaning of the document when signing it. It is a very limited exception to the rule that a person's signature on a document irrevocably binds the person to its contents (see 6.2.2).

The rule developed at a time when adult literacy was far from commonplace (*Thoroughgood's Case* (1584) 2 Co Rep 9a). The classic example of the operation of the rule is *Lewis v Clay* (1897) 67 LJ QB 224.

> The plaintiff asked the defendant to witness some deeds for him. He showed the defendant some papers, over which he held a piece of blotting paper with a number of holes cut in it, his explanation being that the content of the deeds must remain private. The defendant signed in the spaces. In fact, the papers were promissory notes made out to the plaintiff, to the value of £11,000. It was found as a fact that the defendant had not been negligent, and he was therefore able to resist the plaintiff's action.

Later, the advent of universal education and general adult literacy put the continued existence of the rule in doubt. The matter eventually came before the House of Lords in **Saunders v Anglia Building Society** (also known as **Gallie v Lee**) [1971] AC 1004.

> An elderly aunt intended to give her house to her nephew so that he could use it as security for a loan, on condition that she be allowed to remain living there. A friend of the nephew, known to be assisting him to obtain a loan, asked her to sign a document, which the friend said was a deed of gift of the house to the nephew. The aunt had broken her glasses, and so signed without reading the document, which turned out to be a deed conveying the house to the friend. The friend then mortgaged the property but defaulted on the payment of the mortgage instalments, so that the building society sought possession of the house. The House of Lords declined to abolish the plea of *non est factum* but considered that the aunt's plea failed on these facts.

The narrow *ratio* of their Lordships' decision is that the difference between what the aunt signed and what she thought she was signing was not so great as to establish beyond doubt that she did not consent to it. She thought she was signing a document transferring owner-ship of the house, which is precisely what she signed. Thus, the *non est factum* defence is not available except in cases where:

> the transaction which the document purports to effect is essentially different in substance or in kind from the transaction intended [per Lord Wilberforce].

Their Lordships did, however, consider the extent of the rule. Lord Wilberforce thought it would be rare today for a literate adult to succeed in a plea of *non est factum*. In the case of those who were illiterate, or blind, or lacking in understanding, the position was less clear. According to Lord Wilberforce (at p. 1027):

> The law ought…to give relief if satisfied that consent was truly lacking but will require of signers even in this class that they act responsibly and carefully according to their circumstances in putting their signature to legal documents.

That the rule has been severely restricted by the decision in ***Saunders v Anglia Building Society*** was confirmed by the peremptory dismissal of the plea of *non est factum* by the Court of Appeal in ***Avon Finance Co. Ltd v Bridger*** [1985] 2 All ER 281 (and for continuing evidence of judicial reluctance to invoke the doctrine, see ***Norwich and Peterborough Building Society v Steed (No. 2)*** [1993] Ch 116). Remedies may, nevertheless, be available in a *non et factum* scenario depending on the facts based on misrepresentation (See Chapter 14) or undue influence (15.2). However, misrepresentation and undue influence render the contract voidable which is less drastic a remedy and offers some protection for third parties.

Further reading

Agreements to agree

Brown, 'The contract to negotiate: A thing writ in water' [1992] JBL 353.

Buckley, '*Walford v Miles*: False certainty about uncertainty—an Australian perspective' (1993) JCL 58.

Neill, 'A key to lock-out agreements?' (1992) 108 LQR 405.

Steyn, 'Contract law: Fulfilling the reasonable expectations of honest men' (1997) 113 LQR 433.

Failure of anticipated contracts to materialize

Ball, 'Work carried out in pursuance of letters of intent: Contract or restitution?' (1983) 99 LQR 572.

Barker 'Coping with failure: Reappraising pre-contractual remuneration' (2003) 19 JCL 105.

McKendrick, 'Negotiations "subject to contract" and the law of restitution' [1995] RLR 100.

Agreement mistake
General

Brownsword, 'New note on the old oats' (1987) 131 SJ 384.

Simpson, 'Contracts for cotton to arrive: The case of the two ships *Peerless*' (1989) 11 Cardozo L Rev 287.

Identity

Chandler and Devenney, 'Mistake as to identity and the threads of objectivity' (2004) 1 JOR 7.

McLauchlan, 'Mistake of identity and contract formation' (2005) 21 JCL 1.

Macmillan, 'Mistake as to identity clarified?' (2004) 120 LQR 369.

Macmillan, 'Rogues, swindlers and cheats: The development of mistake of identity in English contract law' [2005] CLJ 711.

Enforceability of promises: Consideration and promissory estoppel

Summary of the issues

Chapters 4 and **5** examine the criteria necessary to establish the existence of a binding contract, namely that (1) either there is consideration to support the promise which it is sought to enforce, or that promise is contained in a deed (**Chapter 4**), and (2) there is an intention to be legally bound (**Chapter 5**). In general, English law enforces bargains and not gratuitous promises. **Accordingly, in general terms, a promise will be unenforceable unless it is contained in a deed (indicating that any promise is taken seriously) or it must be supported by consideration.** Consideration means an act or a promise given in exchange for the promise (i.e., the price for which the other's promise was bought).

• Consideration need not be adequate but must be sufficient. **In other words, the courts will not examine whether what has been given in exchange is of equivalent value but some acts or promises are not recognized by the law as being good consideration, e.g. past consideration, performance of an existing legal duty.**

• The consequence is that, since consideration is also required to support a promise to alter an existing contract, traditionally it was the case that simply performing the existing contractual duty was not recognized as a good consideration because there was no fresh benefit or detriment to support the new alteration promise. However, in the context of an alteration promise to pay more, the Court of Appeal in *Williams v Roffey Bros* held that consideration to support an alteration promise would exist where *factual* benefits arose to the promisor from the making of the alteration promise.

• This contrasted with the decision of the House of Lords in *Foakes v Beer*, in the context of alteration promises to pay less, where factual benefit to a creditor arising from a promise to accept part payment in full satisfaction and not to sue for the balance, was not considered sufficient, and fresh consideration was held to be required. **The result is a discrepancy in the treatment of different alteration promises since an alteration promise to pay more may be supported by consideration (factual benefit to the promisor) whereas factual benefit cannot suffice as the consideration to support an alteration promise to accept less.**

• Where an alteration promise is not supported by consideration, that promise may have some binding effect (although not the same binding effect as where consideration is present) on the basis of the doctrine of promissory estoppel. This estoppel is based on reliance and prevents a promisor going back on his promise where that would be inequitable in circumstances where the promisee has relied upon that promise. The difficulty with promissory estoppel in English law is that it operates only as a defence and cannot create a cause of action. A more flexible approach to estoppel has been evidenced in Australia and this has led to academic arguments supporting the use of the Australian approach in English law. The future of consideration and its relationship with the doctrine of estoppel is therefore particularly interesting at the present time.

4.1 Introduction

In Chapter 1, a contract was defined as a legally enforceable agreement (see 1.1). We have already considered the process of finalizing agreement (see **Chapter 2**) and problems relating to uncertain terms and agreement mistakes, which may result in the agreement having no effect (see **Chapter 3**). Later we shall also be examining factors which may vitiate consent and which relate to the actual making of the agreement, such as misrepresentation (see Chapter 14) and duress and undue influence (see Chapter 15).

It is an implicit assumption of the definition, however, that not all agreements are contracts. There must therefore be a body of legal rules by which it is possible to determine whether or not an agreement amounts to a contract. This chapter and **Chapter 5** examine the principles determining the circumstances in which an agreement will be treated as enforceable (i.e., treated as a legally binding contract).

It was suggested in Chapter 1 that, in its formative period, English law developed by the curious means of first identifying remedies and then inductively developing the rights which gave rise to those remedies. In the case of contract, the result was that once a remedy for breach of an undertaking was identified, the courts still had to develop a test for distinguishing enforceable agreements from those which the courts were unwilling to enforce (see 1.3). The major indicator of enforceability adopted by the common law was that of mutual exchange of (at very least) promises of value. In the terminology of the law, where a promise in an agreement was given in return for something of value (including another promise), the first promise was given for *consideration* and could be enforced by legal action.

A promise given without consideration (gratuitous promise) was unenforceable unless made in a deed under seal. This strange expression means no more than that the promise had to be contained in a document on which the promisor had fixed an impression in wax of some identifying mark, such as a crest. Right up to the present day, documents have been made under seal, particularly for the conveyance of land which has been sold, but the traditional wax seal has given way to a modern red sticker, and sometimes not even as much as that. The formal requirements for the form of deeds were altered by s. 1 of the Law of Property (Miscellaneous Provisions) Act 1989 so that deeds no longer require a seal to be valid, and need no longer be written on parchment, although there are stricter requirements for the attestation of signatures, and the deed must be 'delivered' by the person making it (although this does not require physical transfer, but merely recognition that it legally binds the deliverer) (see 5.4.3).

4.1.1 The debate about the consideration requirement

It is easy to understand how consideration became the cornerstone of contracts at common law since those seeking to make promises enforceable could avoid quite considerable formality simply by providing evidence of an exchange of things of value. On the other hand, consideration has frequently been the source of much academic debate. There are two reasons for this:

1. Many legal systems in the world have efficient and just rules of contract law without any requirement of consideration as a precondition of enforceability.

2. Some agreements which are acknowledged to satisfy the requirement of consideration are said nevertheless to be unenforceable, because either:

   (a) the court is unwilling to believe that the parties ever intended that they should be enforced by legal action (see **Chapter 5**)

   (b) the court is not satisfied that there is adequate evidence of the alleged agreement (see 5.4).

In consequence, some commentators have suggested that the requirement of consideration should be abandoned, on the ground that the task of sorting enforceable from unenforceable agreements is already achieved by principles requiring that an intention to create legal relations be established and by essential formalities for certain types of contract. (Intention is recognized as the applicable criterion in the *Draft Common Frame of Reference* (DCFR), II-4:101 and see *Principles of European Contract Law* (PECL), Arts 2:101 and 2:102.) Article 3.2 of the UNIDROIT *Principles of International Commercial Contracts* makes it clear that the only requirement for a contract is agreement. In determining whether there is agreement, Art. 2.1.2 provides that intention to be bound is regarded as relevant. Article 3.2 expressly excludes consideration or the continental requirement of 'cause' as requirements of enforceability. This position is also reflected, at least in the context of alteration promises, in the approach of the Court of Appeal of New Zealand in *Antons Trawling Co. Ltd v Smith* [2003] 2 NZLR 23 where Baragwanath J, giving the judgment of the court, stated:

> The importance of consideration is as a valuable signal that the parties intend to be bound by their agreement, rather than an end in itself. Where the parties who have already made such intention clear by entering legal relations have acted upon an agreement to a variation, in the absence of policy reasons to the contrary they should be bound by their agreement.

On the other hand, other commentators, such as Williston in the United States, have suggested that principles determining intention to create legal relations and evidential formality are themselves redundant since the consideration doctrine ('the test of bargain') embraces such functions (see Hepple [1970] CLJ 122).

Nevertheless, the orthodox view remains that intention to create legal relations, consideration, and (in some cases) evidential formality are *all* essential ingredients of enforceability (see *Edmonds v Lawson* [2000] QB 501; 5.3).

4.1.2 Is the promise supported by consideration?

The terminology changes in this chapter because the question is focusing on enforceability of promises rather than on the making of agreements. The presence or absence of consideration to support a promise will become an issue where the promise has not been performed and it is sought to enforce it (i.e., to sue for its breach). The person seeking to enforce the promise is (ignoring third-party questions for the present) the person to whom the promise was made. This person is the *promisee* and the person making the promise is the *promisor*.

This can be confusing.

 ## Example

In a sale of goods (a contract by the exchange of promises) the seller (S) has promised to deliver the goods and the buyer (B) has promised to pay for them on delivery.

1. S, in breach of its promise, fails to deliver and B wants to sue for breach. In relation to the delivery promise, S is the promisor and B is the promisee who is now seeking to enforce that promise and B therefore needs to show that it has provided consideration to support S's promise. B can do this since B promised to pay for the goods on delivery.

2. However, what if B is the party in breach? S has delivered the goods and B has failed to pay for them, in breach of its promise to do so. S is seeking to enforce B's promise so this time S is the promisee and B is the promisor. S can demonstrate the necessary consideration to support B's promise since S promised to deliver the goods.

4.1.3 Formation and alteration promises

A formation promise is a promise made where there is no existing contract between the parties and it is sought to create one. Formation promises must be distinguished from alteration promises where a party (or parties) to an existing contract seeks to alter (vary) its terms.

As a general rule, both types of promise must be supported by consideration if the promise is to be enforceable (assuming that it is not contained in a deed). However, a more relaxed approach to the enforceability of alteration promises can be detected because either:

1. It is easier to find consideration to support some alteration promises (i.e., in some circumstances it can take the form of a factual benefit to the promisor which arises from the making of the alteration promise).

2. Despite the absence of consideration, the doctrine of promissory estoppel operates as a defence to prevent the promisor from going back on his promise.

It should not, however, be thought that it is difficult to identify consideration to support a formation promise; on the contrary, all sorts of trivial exchanges have sufficed. However, the law takes a strict approach to some acts or promises which it generally considers to be insufficient as consideration.

4.2 Identifying consideration

4.2.1 Definitions of consideration: Benefit/detriment or the price for which the promise of the other is bought

Traditional analysis has usually considered the existence of consideration to be demonstrated by proof of a **benefit and/or a detriment**. For example, in *Currie v Misa* (1875) LR 10 Ex 153 at 162, Lush J stated that:

> A valuable consideration, in the sense of the law, may consist either in some right, interest, profit or benefit accruing to the one party, or some forbearance, detriment, loss or responsibility, given, suffered, or undertaken by the other.

Although the act or promise said to constitute the consideration may be both a detriment to the promisor and a corresponding benefit to the promisee, it is not necessary to have both benefit and detriment, as was made clear in the statement by Lush J.

Modern English law has largely abandoned the benefit/detriment analysis, preferring the definition of consideration provided by Sir Frederick Pollock (in *Pollock's Principles of Contract,* Sir Percy Winfield (ed.), 13th edn (Stevens, 1950), p. 133) to the effect that consideration is constituted by 'an act or forbearance of one party, or the promise thereof', being 'the price for which the promise of the other is bought'. This statement was adopted by Lord Dunedin in ***Dunlop Pneumatic Tyre Co. Ltd v Selfridge & Co. Ltd*** [1915] AC 847.

It is, of course, still possible to detect elements of benefit and detriment in this definition, but what is most important is the emphasis upon exchange. A simple benefit and detriment analysis cannot account for some of the decisions of the courts, but it is important to be familiar with the formulation given above, in part because some of the cases still use the language of benefit and detriment, but more especially because some sub-rules of the doctrine of consideration owe their existence to the traditional formulation (see 4.3). A good example of the continuing influence of the language of benefit and detriment is the important decision of the Court of Appeal in ***Williams v Roffey Bros and Nicholls (Contractors) Ltd*** [1991] 1 QB 1, which caused a thorough re-evaluation of the doctrine of consideration (see especially 4.4.4 and 4.6.1). However, in analysing in a contemporary problem whether consideration exists in an agreement, it would be much better to rely on the notion of exchange.

The essential test is whether what is provided by the one party (be it action, inaction, or merely a promise thereof) induced the action, inaction, or promise of the other.

4.2.1.1 Acts or promises given in exchange: The bilateral/unilateral distinction

Consideration has been defined both in terms of acts done (or not done) and in terms of promises, so that there are two ways in which the other's promise is 'bought'.

The great value of contract as a commercial device is that it provides for liability on an obligation even where performance on both sides remains in the future (see 1.1.1.1). It is in this facility that the strength of contract as an instrument of planning lies.

1. Bound on the exchange of promises

In a bilateral contract, consideration is provided by the exchange of promises.

The classic example of consideration involving an exchange of promises is a contract for the sale of goods, where the seller agrees to deliver the goods at some time in the future and the buyer agrees to pay for them either on delivery, or by some credit arrangement. At the time of the agreement neither side has done anything towards the performance of the promises made, but the agreement still has contractual force. Both parties have subjected themselves to a potential claim for breach of contract in the event that they fail to perform, and in this sense there is a clear benefit or detriment at the time the promises are given. This type of consideration is described as *executory.*

If the seller failed to deliver, the buyer would have a claim for breach of contract (i.e., the delivery promise) since this promise is supported by consideration provided by the buyer (i.e., the buyer's promise to pay on delivery). The contract exists from the moment of the exchange of the promises although performance is to occur later.

2. Consideration as the performance of the requested act

Where consideration consists of an exchange of a promise for an act then it is described as *executed*. This type of contract is a unilateral contract (see 2.6), e.g. a promise of a reward in exchange for the act of supplying certain information, as in *R v Clarke* (1927) 40 CLR 227.

> The government of Western Australia offered a reward for information leading to the arrest of certain criminals. Clarke gave information which led to a conviction and sued to recover the reward, although he admitted that at the time of giving the information his only motive had been to clear his own name. It was held that he was unable to recover.

The case is usually described as being an example of the need to know about an offer before being able to accept it. Clarke, however, had seen the reward offer but had forgotten about it. The better view may therefore be that his action was not induced by the promise of reward, and therefore consideration was absent. The element of exchange is vital.

Executed consideration consists of a promise followed by an act. Care must be taken to distinguish the situation where an act is followed by a promise, which does not amount to consideration (see 4.3.3: past consideration).

4.2.1.2 Consideration distinguished from conditions imposed upon the recipients of gifts

This distinction can be difficult to explain. Peel, in *Treitel's The Law of Contract,* 12th edn (Sweet and Maxwell, 2007), pp. 79–80, argues that in *Carlill v Carbolic Smoke Ball Co. Ltd* [1893] 1 QB 256, the consideration provided by the plaintiff was her use of the smoke ball as requested by the defendants. The need to catch influenza was interpreted as only a condition enabling her to enforce the promise. This may be because catching influenza cannot be controlled directly by the plaintiff, and therefore cannot be seen as something of value provided by the plaintiff. Similarly, in *Thomas v Thomas* (1842) 2 QB 851, the requirement that the widow should remain a widow and not remarry was a condition entitling her to enforce the promise and not the consideration to support the testator's promise to leave her his house.

These examples of conditions are very different in nature to the requirement to supply three chocolate wrappers in *Chappell & Co. Ltd v Nestlé Co. Ltd* [1960] AC 87 (for facts, see 4.3.2). The House of Lords rejected an argument to the effect that the wrappers were not part of the consideration but merely a condition for the supply of the record for 1s 6d. As Lord Reid stated, the wrappers were supplied by the applicant at the request of the defendants and **were of benefit** (albeit in the loosest sense of this word) to the defendants. On the other hand, in the case of conditional gifts there is no direct benefit to the requestor from performance of the condition entitling the party to enforce the promise, e.g. catching influenza or remaining a widow.

This distinction may be considered largely redundant if the *Chappell v Nestlé* approach to the definition of consideration is adopted, i.e. if the consideration to support a promise consists of whatever has been requested in exchange by the promisor. On this basis catching influenza (*Carlill*) and remaining a widow (*Thomas*) would be part of the consideration to support the promise rather than a condition or entitlement to enforce it, since these acts are part of the **requested exchange**.

4.2.1.3 Consideration must be distinguished from the motive for the making of the promise

The exchange theory of consideration also requires the giving, in exchange for a promise, of something of value, so that mere motive in making a promise, unattached to any element of value, is not sufficient consideration.

> In **Thomas v Thomas** (1842) 2 QB 851, a dying man had expressed the wish to the executors of his will that his wife should be able to live in his house for as long as she should wish to and remained a widow. On the strength of this wish the executors promised the house to the widow. The court was unanimous in its view that, whatever the moral obligation, in such a situation the mere motive of satisfying the wishes of the deceased testator could not constitute consideration.

In addition, satisfying the testator's desire could not be consideration to support the executors' promise enabling the widow to enforce their promise since consideration had to move from the promisee and this was not consideration supplied by the promisee (the widow).

4.2.2 Does consideration need to 'move from the promisee'?

Thus, traditionally it was considered that the consideration to support a promise had to move from (i.e., be supplied by) the promisee (which was itself interpreted to mean that the consideration had to *move* from the claimant or person enforcing the promise—see *Thomas v Thomas* (1842) 2 QB 851). However, if this interpretation were to be adopted it might prevent a third party from enforcing a promise. The Contracts (Rights of Third Parties) Act 1999 now provides for third-party enforcement in certain circumstances and it is clear that in the light of this legislative measure and comments by the Law Commission in its report, *Privity of Contract: Contracts for the benefit of third parties,* Cm. 3329 (1996), Part VI, consideration need not be provided by a claimant (see **11.2.2**). However, consideration to support a promise must be supplied **by someone** if the promise is to be enforceable—and that person will usually be the promisee (i.e., the person to whom the promise was made).

4.3 Consideration must be sufficient but need not be adequate

4.3.1 Need not be adequate (equivalent)

Once something of value can be shown, the court makes no inquiry into whether the thing offered is a genuine equivalent of the promise made.

At some early point in its history the doctrine of consideration might have developed as a means to police bargains between parties, requiring the exchange of things of equivalent value. As such it would have been part of the law's armour against duress and fraud (see **4.4.4** and Chapter 15). In fact, the doctrine of freedom of contract, and no doubt the mere practical difficulty of proving equivalence, intervened to prevent such a development. There is no investigation of whether the value given in return for the promise is any real benefit to the promisor or any real detriment to the promisee, let alone of whether the promises exchanged are of equivalent value. All that is required is that actual value be given. Thus, in *Thomas v Thomas*, the widow to whom the house was promised had in turn promised to pay £1 per annum as ground rent, and to maintain the property in good and tenantable repair. This return promise was found to be of actual value, and thus to amount to sufficient consideration. This rule finds frequent expression in the provision in leases for peppercorn rents.

Although the Unfair Terms in Consumer Contracts Regulations 1999, SI 1999/2083 (for the scope, origin, and general impact of the Regulations, see 7.7) give a broad jurisdiction to overturn contract terms which are unfair, they do not apply to terms which concern the adequacy of the price or remuneration as against the goods or services sold or supplied, provided such terms are in plain, intelligible language (reg. 6(2)). So this basic principle of the common law is largely unaffected by the new law, provided the consumer contract is drafted in clear terms.

4.3.2 Sufficiency: Something of value in the eyes of the law

In saying that in *Thomas v Thomas* (1842) 2 QB 851 there was an exchange of things of value, it is possible, though not particularly revealing, to analyse that exchange in terms of benefit and detriment. Such analysis fails altogether in the case of *Chappell & Co. Ltd v Nestlé Co. Ltd* [1960] AC 87.

> The case involved a promotional scheme for a brand of chocolate whereby records of a song were offered to the public for 1s 6d (7.5p) and three chocolate wrappers, whereas the normal price was 6s 6d (32.5p). Manufacture and sale of the records constituted a breach of copyright in the song unless royalties were paid to the copyright owners, who in this case were the plaintiffs. Under a statutory scheme a copyright owner was not entitled to object if informed and paid a royalty of 6.25 per cent of the ordinary retail selling price. The defendant gave notice, stating the ordinary retail selling price to be 1s 6d, and the plaintiffs objected.
>
> The House of Lords took the view that whether the chocolate wrappers were part of the price paid depended upon whether they were part of the consideration for the sale of the records to the public. A minority of their Lordships found evidence of motive in the promotional scheme but not consideration. Lord Reid, making the leading speech for the majority, conceded that the wrappers could not be seen as either benefit or detriment in one sense: the chocolate company threw them away as soon as they arrived, and no doubt the consuming public would have thrown them away before that but for the offer. However, what mattered was that the company saw fit to require the delivery of the wrappers in exchange for its delivery of the record. The company's motive for so doing was of no interest to the court, but the requirement of exchange demonstrated the existence of consideration.

By comparison, in *Lipkin Gorman v Karpnale Ltd* [1991] 2 AC 548, gaming chips were held not to constitute consideration for the money paid for the chips by a member of a gaming club on the basis that the chips were 'worthless'. It seems that the chips were regarded as merely facilitating the gambling process, and therefore not as having any value to the parties involved. This is difficult to justify, and the true basis of the decision would seem to be the desire to protect the victim of the theft of the money in question who was trying to recover it from the gaming club. (The Gambling Act 2005, s. 335(1) means that in future the casino or gaming club will be legally bound in the normal way by its promise to pay out.)

This minimalist approach to the identification of benefit in **Chappell v Nestlé** was again evident in **Williams v Roffey Bros** [1991] 1 QB 1 (the facts are given at **4.4.4**). In **Williams v Roffey Bros** the Court of Appeal had to decide whether a promise to pay more money to achieve performance under an existing contract was enforceable, despite the fact that the plaintiff had apparently given nothing additional in return for this promise. Two members of the Court of Appeal (Glidewell and Purchas LJJ) were willing to find consideration, despite its absence on a legal and objective analysis, in the subjective (factual) benefit to the promisor arising from making the promise. Detriment was not a required part of the equation (and this position has subsequently been confirmed by the recognition of consideration only in the form of benefit in **Edmonds v Lawson** [2000] QB 501). The other member of the Court of Appeal in **Williams v Roffey Bros**, Russell LJ, took a more radical, normative approach and considered that the existence of consideration was to be determined in the light of the view taken on the desirability of enforcing the promise in question. On the facts, Russell LJ was influenced by the commercial nature of the relationship between the parties, and the unconscionable result of not enforcing the promise.

The majority reasoning in **Williams v Roffey Bros** was followed by Hirst J in *Anangel Atlas Compania Naviera SA v Ishikawajima-Harima Heavy Industries Co. Ltd (No. 2)* [1990] 2 Lloyd's Rep 526. This was another case involving a promise altering a term of the existing contract, and the judge found that consideration was constituted by the 'practical conferment of benefit or a practical avoidance of disbenefit'. Despite the existing contract between the parties, the judge found the defendants to have admitted that there was a factual (or practical) benefit to them in holding the plaintiffs to the original delivery date under the contract in market conditions in which many clients were seeking to cancel contracts or to postpone delivery dates. By promising amendments to the contract advantageous to the plaintiffs, in return for their taking delivery on the due date, the defendants hoped to influence other clients to keep to their contracts. Consequently, the amendments were legally enforceable (see also *Lee v GEC Plessey Telecommunications* [1993] IRLR 383).

Thus, the definition of consideration in **Chappell v Nestlé** and in **Williams v Roffey Bros**, may be regarded as coinciding with Sir Frederick Pollock's definition of consideration as 'the price for which the promise of the other is bought' (see **4.2.1**), provided it is realized that price here means anything of actual subjective value to the promisor.

It is worth giving some attention to the test by which the courts determine whether something is of sufficient value to amount to consideration. It appears to embody elements of both law and fact. There seems to be a rule excluding mere sentiment from constituting consideration, and consideration cannot involve a promise to give up a right which is not possessed (see **White v Bluett** (1853) 23 LJ Ex 36; son's promise not to complain about his father's distribution of his property could not be consideration because the son had no right to complain). The objectivization of contract (see **2.1**) means that the court is the ultimate arbiter of each party's intentions (see, in particular, the discussion of the meaning of practical benefit in Chen-Wishart, 'Consideration: Practical benefit and the Emperor's new clothes' in Beatson and Friedmann (eds), *Good Faith and Fault in Contract Law* (Oxford University Press, 1995), pp. 131–2). However, subject to these obvious legal limitations, it seems that anything may be of sufficient value to amount to consideration if the party receiving it regards it at the time as a sufficient inducement to give his return promise, which is an essentially factual test. This idea of mutual inducement as the most basic kind of exchange is at the heart of the majority opinion in **Chappell v Nestlé**, and many of the more difficult English cases on consideration fit more comfortably with that analysis than with any other.

4.3.3 Past consideration: The necessity for exchange

It was suggested at **4.2.1.1** that where it is alleged that a contract exists on the basis of an act followed by a promise, the courts will not enforce such a promise. In such cases the consideration is described as 'past', and the rule is easily explained by the theory of exchange since the act is not given in exchange for the promise.

 Example

> I am drowning in a lake. You rescue me. **Then** I promise to pay you £100 for your trouble. The only consideration you have provided is your act of rescuing me but that act cannot be a good consideration because it pre-dates my promise and is therefore not given in exchange for that promise.

The past consideration rule is well illustrated by the classic case of *Roscorla v Thomas* (1842) 3 QB 234.

> The plaintiff had negotiated the purchase of a horse from the defendant for a given price. When the negotiations had been completed and agreement reached, the defendant assured the plaintiff that the horse was sound and free from vice. The horse failed to match that description, and the issue was whether any enforceable warranty (i.e., promise) had been given that the horse was sound. There would now be an implied statutory warranty that the horse was of satisfactory quality under s. 14 of the Sale of Goods (SGA) 1979 but at the time of this case the plaintiff's only remedy rested on the express warranty. However, this express warranty was given *after* the making of the contract and therefore could not be the consideration to support the promise to buy as it was not given in exchange for that promise.

Re McArdle [1951] Ch 669 provides a further illustration of the past consideration rule.

> The children of a family were by their father's will entitled to a house after their mother's death. During the mother's lifetime one of the married children lived in the house and his wife paid for several improvements to be made. Subsequently, all the children signed a document in which they promised that the wife should be repaid £488 out of the estate for the work done. This promise was held to be unenforceable because the work had been executed before the promise was made, so that the work was not given in exchange for the promise and amounted to past consideration.

4.3.3.1 Sidestepping past consideration: The previous-request device

There is a device which can be used to avoid (or sidestep) the past consideration rule in cases in which it can be said that there was an understanding that goods or services were to be paid for, but no express agreement had been reached as to the amount payable before the time for performance. In such cases, a subsequent promise to pay a stated sum might well appear to be past consideration. On the other hand, it would be undesirable as a matter of policy for such understandings not to be enforceable, not least because many professional people such as accountants and solicitors operate on the basis that their services are to be paid for but that a precise fee will not be stated until after performance.

This example makes it clear that this device is not an exception to the past consideration rule; it is merely a way of reinterpreting the factual situation in order to sidestep that rule. Using the 'device', the subsequent promise to pay is no more than quantification and evidence of an obligation to pay, which had already arisen by virtue of a simple contract between the parties. As we saw in **Chapter 3**, s. 8 of the SGA 1979 makes express provision for the price to be left unspecified in a sale of goods contract and fixed at a subsequent date.

In *Pao On v Lau Yiu Long* [1980] AC 614, Lord Scarman provided the following definition of the conditions for operation of the exception:

> The act must have been done at the promisor's request: the parties must have understood that the act was to be remunerated either by a payment or the conferment of some other benefit: and payment, or the conferment of a benefit, must have been legally enforceable had it been promised in advance.

Pao On v Lau Yiu Long extended the scope of this device to apply not just to requested acts but also to situations where the making of a promise is requested.

 ## Summary

1. I **request** that you perform an act (or make a particular promise).
2. That request carries with it an **implied promise to pay** (the promise).
3. The **act** is performed (or requested promise made).
4. There is a **later express promise** which fixes the amount of the reward (reward promise).

Performing the act (3) can be a good consideration to support the earlier implied promise to pay (2) because the act comes after that promise and is performed in exchange for that implied promise.

The earliest example of the device is *Lampleigh v Brathwait* (1615) Hob 105.

> Brathwait killed a man, and asked Lampleigh to intercede with the King to obtain a pardon. Lampleigh did as he was asked, and was successful in obtaining the pardon. Brathwait *then* promised him £100. There is no doubt that Lampleigh's performance was executed before the promise was made, but the court said that the fact that the service had been requested meant that the promise was nevertheless supported by consideration, namely the performance by Lampleigh.

In other words, in making the request Brathwait must be taken impliedly to have promised to pay for the service rendered, and in relation to that promise consideration was not past. The later express promise merely fixed the amount of the reward.

This explanation of *Lampleigh v Brathwait* was put forward in *Re Casey's Patents* [1892] 1 Ch 104 by Bowen LJ (at pp. 115–16):

> Even if it were true…that a past service cannot support a future promise, you must look at the document and see if the promise cannot receive a proper effect in some other way. Now, the fact of a past service raises an implication that at the time it was rendered it was to be paid for, and, if it was a service which was to be paid for, when you get in the subsequent document a promise to pay, that promise may be treated either as an admission which evidences or as a positive bargain which fixes the amount of that reasonable remuneration on the faith of which the service was originally rendered.

4.3.3.2 Does the previous request device apply on the facts?

There are two core requirements.

1. Was there a request to perform the act or make the promise?
2. Can it be said that this request carries with it an implied promise to pay or compensate?

In addressing these questions, and particularly the second question, some assistance may be gained by distinguishing commercial and domestic agreements since there is some evidence that a court may be more willing to find a request, and to imply a promise to pay, in the case of a commercial relationship than in a domestic one.

In *Re McArdle* [1951] Ch 669 (for facts, see **4.3.3**), the court did not find in this domestic situation any implied promise to pay dating from before the time when the work was done. There could be no earlier implied promise to compensate because there had been no request by the promisors that the work be carried out. However, if the context is domestic, even where a request can be found, it will inevitably be more difficult to argue that the request carries with it an implied promise to pay for the services. For example, if I ask my neighbour to help me to take out my rubbish for the rubbish collection, although I have made a request we would not anticipate any remuneration for this service, in the absence of some express promise to this effect.

By comparison, in the commercial context, where there is a request of some kind, it will be much easier to establish an implied promise to pay for the services simply because in the commercial context people do not generally do things for nothing.

Re Casey's Patents [1892] 1 Ch 104 is an example in the commercial context. A manager promoted a particular invention for the owners of the patent rights for a two-year period. The owners then promised him a share in those rights in consideration for his previous services for them. It was alleged that the promise was unenforceable as being supported only by past consideration. In finding the promise to be enforceable, Bowen LJ found evidence on which to base the implication of a promise to pay in the entirety of the circumstances as the manager must always have assumed that his work would be remunerated in some way. The subsequent promise merely fixed the form of that remuneration.

The facts of *Pao On v Lau Yiu Long* [1980] AC 614 provide a further example of the implication of a promise to pay (or indemnify) arising from a request in the context of a commercial contract.

The case concerned the enforceability of a promise of indemnity in favour of the plaintiffs, which had been made by the defendants, the majority shareholders in the Fu Chip Investment Company. This indemnity document referred to the main agreement between the Fu Chip Company and the plaintiffs, whereby the plaintiffs had promised not to sell 60 per cent of their shares in Fu Chip before 30 April 1974. It was clear that the plaintiffs' promise in the main agreement had been made at the request of the defendants who wished to ensure the stability of the market price for shares in Fu Chip. The Privy Council considered that the promise had been made on the understanding that the plaintiffs were to be compensated by the defendants for agreeing to this restriction on their ability to sell their shares. Accordingly, the plaintiffs' promise in the main agreement, whereby they promised to retain the shares, constituted a valid consideration for the defendants' implied promise to compensate them. The later indemnity promise merely fixed the nature of that protection.

Lord Scarman (at p. 634), giving the judgment of the court, laid great stress upon the fact that this case involved businessmen bargaining at arm's length:

> It seems clear, therefore, that where the whole arrangement is couched in terms of commercial exchange, the courts may be more willing to interpret circumstances as amounting to a request to perform a service, despite the absence of anything as express between the parties, and they may be more willing to find that the request carries with it an implied promise to pay.

 ## Summary

Pao On v Lau Yiu Long

1. The defendants request a promise from the plaintiffs (i.e., that the plaintiffs will retain their shares for one year).
2. This request is coupled with an understanding that the defendants were to give the plaintiffs some form of protection (or indemnity) against a fall in the value of those shares in this period.
3. The plaintiffs make the promise to retain the shares for a year.
4. The defendants give the indemnity promise fixing the exact protection.

In relation to the defendants' promise to give an indemnity (2), the plaintiffs' promise (3) is not past consideration.

4.3.3.3 Genuine exception for negotiable instruments

A negotiable instrument is a document containing a promise of payment which when transferred gives the transferee for value a right to enforce the promise against the promisor free of any defences which would have been available to the promisor against the transferor (see **11.5.4**). A good example is a cheque.

Section 27(1) of the Bills of Exchange Act 1882 provides that valuable consideration for a bill of exchange may be constituted either by consideration as normally defined in contract law, or by 'an antecedent debt or liability' (s. 27(1)(b)). Goods or services may have been supplied and these goods or services are paid for by cheque. The consideration for the promise of payment contained in that cheque would be past consideration were it not for the statutory exception in s. 27(1). This is because the cheque is used as payment to satisfy an existing debt, albeit that the debt may have just been created (e.g., employing a cleaner and writing a cheque in payment).

4.4 Performance of existing duties

It has traditionally been the case that in most circumstances the performance of an existing duty cannot be consideration for a further promise. In terms of our definition of consideration the reason is relatively clear. Where I am already under a legal duty to perform an act or make a promise, I cannot be said to have been induced to do that thing by the further promise made by another, since the obligation to do it already existed.

It is traditional to subdivide the rule into three different types of case:

(a) performance of a duty imposed by law

(b) performance of an existing contractual duty owed to a third party

(c) performance of an existing contractual duty owed to the promisor (the context for which will necessarily be a promise to alter an existing contract between the parties).

Performance of a duty imposed by law (a) and performance of an existing contractual duty owed to the promisor (c) have traditionally been regarded as insufficient to act as consideration for a fresh promise. Performance of a contractual duty owed to a third party (b) has long been recognized as an exception, presumably because of the involvement of the third party although no single justification for this exception has been accepted.

The strictness of this refusal to accept performance of existing duties as consideration to support fresh promises has been mitigated in two ways:

1. **Going beyond the duty**—the courts have shown a great willingness to find additional benefit or detriment in actions which go beyond the legal duty (a) or existing contractual duty owed to the promisor (c).

2. **The *Roffey* principle**—as a result of ***Williams v Roffey Bros*** [1991] 1 QB 1, it may be possible to avoid the restrictive outcome in category (c) (performance of an existing contractual duty owed to the promisor) where there is a factual (or practical) benefit to the promisor arising from the making of a promise to pay more money to secure performance of an existing duty owed to that promisor. This is not, however, the same thing as saying that the performance itself generates the consideration, as is the case in category (b) cases. As will be seen, it is the *promisor's* promise to pay more which provides the consideration in the category (c) case.

4.4.1 **Performance of a duty imposed by law (category (a))**

The leading case in the area of public duties is ***Collins v Godefroy*** (1831) 1 B & Ad 950.

> The plaintiff was promised payment in return for his undertaking to give expert evidence at a trial at which he was in any case obliged to attend to give evidence because he had been summoned by subpoena. In those circumstances the promise of payment was unenforceable because the plaintiff had given no consideration for it. He was under an existing duty imposed by law to attend the trial, and accordingly had done no more than he was already legally obliged to do.

A more modern statement of the rule was given by the House of Lords in ***Glasbrook Brothers Ltd v Glamorgan CC*** [1925] AC 270, although on the facts their Lordships considered that there was consideration as the police had gone beyond the scope of the duty imposed by law.

> This case involved a claim by a local authority to recover payment for the provision of police to guard a mine during a strike. The defendants argued that the police were charged with a duty imposed by law to guard the mine as part of their general duty to keep the peace, prevent crime, and protect persons and property from criminal injury. However, at the time of the strike the colliery owners had insisted on a greater level of manning than the local police had deemed necessary. The House of Lords, by a bare majority, decided that the only duty on the local authority was to provide such policing as was considered necessary by the police authority.

The decision as to what was necessary was not open to review by the courts in a case of this kind. Provision of policing beyond what was deemed necessary was not therefore performance of an existing duty, and could amount to consideration for a promise to pay for the service provided. (See also s. 25(1) of the Police Act 1996 which now allows claims for 'special police services' made by 'request', applied in *Harris v Sheffield United Football Club Ltd* [1987] 2 All ER 838 and *West Yorkshire Police Authority v Reading Festival Ltd* [2006] EWCA Civ 524, [2006] 1 WLR 2005. These services would necessarily need to be beyond the scope of the public duty imposed on the police so that the case law continues to provide a useful illustration of the 'going beyond duty' principle.)

Similarly, in **Ward v Byham** [1956] 1 WLR 496 the majority of the Court of Appeal found consideration in actions which they considered to go beyond the scope of the duty owed by law.

> The father of an illegitimate child agreed to pay the mother £1 per week to maintain the child, provided the mother was able to show that the child was 'well looked after and happy' and that the child was allowed to choose for herself whether to go to live with her mother or to carry on being cared for by a neighbour of the father's, which had been the previous arrangement. The child went to live with the mother, but the father stopped the payments when the mother married.
>
> The Court of Appeal treated the case as one of performance of an existing duty because the mother was under a statutory duty to look after the child properly. The majority of the Court of Appeal, Morris and Parker LJJ, while acknowledging that the mother did owe an existing duty, found 'ample consideration' for the promise in the mother's undertakings to keep the child happy and to allow her to choose where to live. On the other hand, Denning LJ would have enforced the promise of maintenance on the basis that he considered that a promise to perform an existing duty could be a good consideration where, as here, there was a factual benefit to the father in securing that performance.

The approach of the majority did not attack traditional orthodoxy (i.e. that there is no legal benefit or detriment in performing an existing duty) since it involved identifying additional benefit or detriment in law through actions or promises outside the scope of the duty owed in law. Denning's approach was considerably more radical since it involved recognizing benefits in fact rather than in law. Nevertheless, in **Williams v Williams** [1957] 1 WLR 148, Denning LJ repeated his argument that:

> a promise to perform an existing duty is, I think, sufficient consideration to support a promise, so long as there is nothing in the transaction which is contrary to the public interest.

For example, to enforce a promise such as that in **Collins v Godefroy** would clearly be contrary to the public interest.

4.4.2 Performance of an existing contractual duty owed to a third party

The performance of an existing contractual duty owed to a third party may be consideration for a promise.

For example (see Figure 4.1), if A owes an existing contractual duty to B, A can use the performance of this duty to B (or his promise to perform it) as consideration to support a promise by

C to pay A a sum of money. (In relation to the contract A/C, B is clearly a third party.) A's performance of the contract A/B can provide the consideration for a promise made by C.

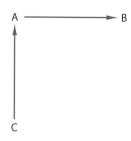

Figure 4.1

Early evidence of this exception may be found in **Scotson v Pegg** (1861) 6 Hurl & N 295.

> A entered into a contract with B to deliver coal to C. C then said to A that if A would deliver the coal to him, C would unload the coal at a fixed rate per day. C failed to keep his promise, and in response to legal action by A claimed that his promise was unsupported by consideration since A was already bound by his contract with B to deliver the coal to C. C was nevertheless found liable, and the court expressed the view that performance of an existing contractual duty owed to a third party (i.e., owed to B since the contract in question was the contract A/C) might be consideration for a separate promise (i.e., a promise by C).

It is not clear, however, whether this was the basis of the decision, or whether, on account of facts not disclosed in the report, A's promise to C carried an extra burden by comparison with his promise to B.

There may also be further support for the existence of this exception in **Shadwell v Shadwell** (1860) 9 CB NS 159, where a nephew had supplied consideration to support a promise to pay him £150 yearly by marrying his fiancée, whom he was under an existing contractual duty to marry because breach of promise to marry actions existed at this time. However, this decision is of doubtful authority on several grounds, including a possible absence of intention to create legal relations (see **5.2.1**) since it was a family agreement and the fact that the majority sought to find detriment to the nephew and a benefit to the uncle as a result of the nephew's marriage.

Whatever the authority of the earlier cases, the exception was subsequently confirmed by two Privy Council decisions, which are generally accepted as representing English law on this question. In **New Zealand Shipping Co. Ltd v A. M. Satterthwaite & Co. Ltd, The Eurymedon** [1975] AC 154, Lord Wilberforce, giving the majority opinion, said (at p. 168):

> An agreement to do an act which the promisor is under an existing obligation to a third party to do, may quite well amount to valid consideration and does so in the present case: the promisee obtains the benefit of a direct obligation which he can enforce. This proposition is illustrated and supported by *Scotson v Pegg*…which their Lordships consider to be good law.

In *The Eurymedon* the carrier of goods had by contract validly limited its liability to the shipper of the goods (contract 1). It was the carrier's responsibility to procure a stevedore to unload the goods (contract 2) but the court found that the stevedores enjoyed a quite independent contract with the shippers (contract 3) (on this aspect of the case, see **2.6.5** and **11.6.4**). (See Figure **4.2**.)

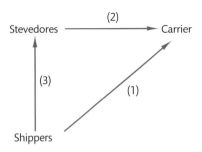

Figure 4.2

1. Contract 1 was the main contract between the shippers and the carriers whereby the carriers, their servants, agents, and independent contractors had the benefit of the exemption clause ('Himalaya clause').

2. Contract 2 was the contract whereby the carriers employed the stevedores to unload the goods at their destination.

3. Contract 3 needed to be 'created' by the court in order to make the exemption directly enforceable by the stevedores.

In order to establish that the promise of exemption was enforceable by the stevedores it had to be shown that they had provided consideration to support it. The only action of the stevedores which could constitute consideration was their act of unloading the goods, and this was a duty which they were already bound by their contract with the carrier (contract 2) to perform.

The Privy Council considered that the performance of this contractual duty owed to the carrier (contract 2) (a third party in relation to contract 3 between the shippers and stevedores) was a good consideration for the shippers' promise of exemption.

In *Pao On v Lau Yiu Long* [1980] AC 614, the Privy Council followed *The Eurymedon* on the question of consideration and performance of a duty owed to a third party. The Privy Council held that the plaintiffs had provided consideration for the promise of indemnity given by the defendants by promising to perform their existing contractual duty to the Fu Chip Company to retain 60 per cent of their shares. The case is therefore significant as an example of a situation where *promising* to perform an existing duty owed to a third party was held to be a valid consideration.

4.4.3 The basis of the 'pre-existing duty' rule and the justification for the exception

The main interest in the *Pao On* case may lie in the discussion by Lord Scarman of the purpose of the 'pre-existing duty' rule. Although the court was not prepared to commit itself to any particular view, it appeared sympathetic to the idea that the 'pre-existing duty' rule might be based in the prevention of duress by contracting parties against those to whom they owed contractual obligations (see [1980] AC 614 at p. 634; and see **4.4.4**).

Accordingly, it might be thought that in the case of promises by third parties the risk of such coercion would be considerably diminished so that no such public-policy need for the rule would exist in such a case. The Privy Council, however, went further, Lord Scarman stating:

> Where businessmen are negotiating at arm's length it is unnecessary for the achievement of justice, and unhelpful in the development of the law, to invoke such a rule of public policy…If a promise is induced by coercion of a man's will, the doctrine of duress suffices to do justice.

In fact, the **Pao On** case was an important stage in the development of a doctrine of economic duress (see **15.1.2**), which has made the possibility of success in a claim based on duress much greater. For this reason, Lord Scarman's argument above was broad enough in scope to apply not only to pre-existing duties as consideration for third-party promises, but also to the pre-existing duty cases in which traditionally there has been said to be no consideration.

This proposal had already been made by Denning LJ in **Williams v Williams** [1957] 1 WLR 148 (see **4.4.1**), when he stated that performance of existing duties should be a good consideration 'so long as there is nothing in the transaction which is contrary to the public interest'. The development of the modern doctrine of economic duress has since been accepted as justification for a more liberal interpretation of the consideration requirement but only in the context of category (c) cases (**Williams v Roffey Bros** [1991] 1 QB 1: see **4.4.4**), and even this has been limited further by denial of the application of this more generous interpretation in the context of alteration promises to accept less (**Roffey** involved an alteration promise to pay more).

4.4.4 Performance of a contractual duty owed to the promisor

The traditional principle is that performance of an existing contractual duty cannot be consideration for a further promise from the party to whom the existing duty is owed since there is no additional legal benefit or detriment.

The leading case was **Stilk v Myrick** (1809) 2 Camp 317, 170 ER 1168.

> A crewman had contracted to work a vessel on a voyage for a fixed sum, promising to do anything needed in all the emergencies of the voyage. During the voyage, two men deserted. The master offered extra payment to those remaining if they would work the ship home, and then on arrival refused to pay. The promise of extra payment was unenforceable, because desertion of crewmen was an emergency of the voyage so that there was already a duty to the employer to work the ship home in such a case. Therefore there was no consideration for the promise of further payment.

Most commentators accept that there is a considerable element of policy in the decision: to have enforced the promise was perceived to have been to risk exposing ships' masters to blackmail by the crew when far from England. Indeed, this was stated to be the *ratio* for the decision in Espinasse's report of **Stilk v Myrick** ((1809) 6 Esp 129, 170 ER 851), and although Espinasse was not regarded as the most reliable of reporters, the need to prevent extortion is a clear factor in both reports. Therefore, in **Stilk v Myrick**, the doctrine of consideration performed the function of a rule to prevent economic duress (see **15.1.2**).

In order to avoid this restrictive interpretation of the performance of an existing duty owed to the promisor as insufficient consideration, the courts sought to find additional contractual performance in order to be able to conclude that there was the necessary additional benefit or detriment to render the promise enforceable (***North Ocean Shipping Co. Ltd v Hyundai Construction Co. Ltd, The Atlantic Baron*** [1979] QB 705). It followed that the scope of the original contractual duty was also important in determining the existence of consideration, e.g. the more limited the scope of that duty, the easier it was to demonstrate that the promisee had gone beyond the scope of the duty and provided consideration.

Subsequently, however, in ***Williams v Roffey Bros*** [1991] 1 QB 1, whilst accepting the need to find consideration to support an alteration promise, the Court of Appeal considered that the consideration could be found in the form of a practical (or factual) benefit arising to the promisor from making the promise despite the fact that the promisee had done no more than he was already contractually bound to do under the terms of the existing contract. This decision does *not* provide that performance of an existing contractual duty is the consideration to support a fresh promise but it does mean that the fresh promise may well be enforceable where the promisee has done nothing more in exchange than perform his existing contractual duty. On this basis it is possible (in one sense, at least) to reconcile this decision with the principle in ***Stilk v Myrick***. Indeed, the Court of Appeal in ***Roffey*** denied that its decision had overruled ***Stilk v Myrick***. Glidewell LJ preferred to describe his approach as being to 'refine and limit the application of that principle'. That said, the net effect of ***Roffey*** must be to diminish the impact of the authority of ***Stilk v Myrick*** since it is clear that in that case there were factual benefits to the master and ship owner in ensuring that the ship was sailed home whilst short-handed. The only sensible distinction between the cases rests on the context for extortion in ***Stilk v Myrick*** and the finding in ***Williams v Roffey Bros*** that the promise was not extracted by duress (extortion or threats).

> The defendants in **Williams v Roffey Bros & Nicholls (Contractors) Ltd** were main contractors on a building contract, and they identified that the plaintiffs, who were subcontractor carpenters on the job, were in financial difficulty and at risk of not completing the work. Had the plaintiffs failed to complete the work, the defendants would have become liable to the building owner under an agreed damages clause (see **9.10**). The defendants therefore took the initiative to avoid the problem, by offering more money for the job to be completed on time. The plaintiffs accepted that offer, and then, when the additional payments were not made as promised, sought damages relying on the promise to pay more as being an enforceable promise.

The problem confronting the plaintiffs, arising out of ***Stilk v Myrick,*** was that they had given nothing in return for the promise of extra payment other than the performance they had undertaken to provide under the original contract. On the other hand, the commercial sense of the agreement was that the promise should be enforceable, (not having been extracted as a result of duress: see **15.1.2.3**), and this view prevailed with the Court of Appeal.

Thus, although no single majority emerges from the three judgments in the Court of Appeal, three strands of reasoning can be identified:

1. The policy element in ***Stilk v Myrick,*** which resulted in the consideration doctrine being applied in a very strict and formal way, is no longer present because of the emergence of the doctrine of economic duress, which allows for a more substantive appraisal of potentially unconscionable contracts (see **15.1.2**). Thus, the decision represents a relaxation of the strictness of the rules to identify consideration in the absence of evidence of duress (which would render the promise otherwise unenforceable).

2. The necessary consideration in a commercial case of this kind might be constituted by a factual (practical) benefit to the promisor, if the promisor was in fact induced to make the promise by the benefit *he perceived himself* to be receiving. There was a real (factual) benefit to the defendants in avoiding having to pay the sums due under the main contract in the event of late completion, and so the avoidance of the risk of breach by the subcontractors clearly induced the defendants to make their promise. In addition, the defendants achieved a further factual benefit by avoiding the difficulties of finding another subcontractor to complete the carpentry work.

3. By analogy with the second category of pre-existing duty cases (category (b), performance of a duty owed to a third party may be consideration for a contract with a separate promisor: see 4.4.2), no further consideration is required for the modification of an existing contract provided there is sufficient evidence of an intention that the alteration be legally binding.

Arguments 2 and 3 are conceptually very different, but it would be wrong to make much of this in the light of the ease with which a court may find a factual benefit if it so requires; consequently, the two arguments are functionally very closely related.

Although some doubts have been cast upon interpretations of **Williams v Roffey Bros**, which have proposed a very wide scope for the *ratio* of the case, it has not been suggested that the narrow *ratio* is in any sense unreliable. Indeed, in distinguishing **Williams v Roffey Bros** by restricting it to the context of extra payment for the originally agreed amount of work (so-called 'promises to pay more'), two differently constituted Courts of Appeal appear to have accepted the correctness of the decision in this respect (see **Re Selectmove Ltd** [1995] 1 WLR 474; **Re C (a debtor)**, *The Times*, 11 May 1994).

Nevertheless, the artificial nature of the doctrine was increasingly meant that the decision has been subjected to some criticism. In **South Caribbean Trading v Trafalgar Beheer BV** [2004] EWHC 2676 (Comm), [2005] 1 Lloyd's Rep 128, Colman J (*obiter*) considered that doing no more than the promisee was already contractually bound to do under the terms of its contract with the promisor should not constitute a sufficient consideration (**Stilk v Myrick**). He added:

> [108]   But for the fact that *Williams v Roffey Bros.* was a decision of the Court of Appeal, I would not have followed it. That decision is inconsistent with the long-standing rule that consideration, being the price of the promise sued upon, must move *from* the promisee...Lord Justice Glidewell substituted for the established rule as to consideration moving from the promise a completely different principle—that the promisor must by his promise have conferred a benefit on the other party. Lord Justice Purchas, at pp. 22–23 clearly saw the nonsequitur but was 'comforted' by observations from Lord Hailsham LC in *Woodhouse AC Israel Cocoa Ltd v Nigerian Product Marketing Co Ltd* [1972] AC 741 at pp. 757–758. Investigation of the correspondence referred to in those observations shows that the latter are not authority for the proposition advanced 'with some hesitation' by Lord Justice Purchas.

Nevertheless, the judge concluded that he would have been bound to follow **Williams v Roffey Bros** since it 'has not yet been held by the House of Lords to have been wrongly decided', although **Roffey** and a finding that factual benefit to the promisor enabled the promise to be enforceable could be avoided where there was evidence of duress.

It seems unlikely that at this stage the House of Lords would unravel the *Roffey* principle, although in terms of strict principle it must be considered as a 'creative' decision, since it is in line with the result sought to be achieved in respect of the enforceability of alteration promises. The only basis on which this unravelling is likely to happen would be following acceptance of a wider principle of estoppel to replace *Roffey* as the basis of enforcement of alteration promises—or, even more radical, enforceability based on reliance alone (see the discussion of these possibilities at 4.7.3).

The conclusion must therefore be that, at least in the context of alteration promises to pay more, consideration can be found in the factual benefit to the promisor arising from the alteration promise to pay more. In this situation, therefore, it should not be too difficult to establish the existence of a binding variation (or alteration promise), given that it appears that factual benefit is judged subjectively and it is unlikely that anyone would promise more to secure a result unless they subjectively considered this to be in their best interests.

Roffey consideration and the relationship with duress

 ## Key point

In *Roffey*, Glidewell LJ had sought to state the applicable legal principles in the following proposition:

1. if A has entered into a contract with B to do work for, or to supply goods or services to, B in return for payment by B and

2. at some stage before A has completely performed his obligations under the contract B has reason to doubt whether A will, or will be able to, complete his side of the bargain and

3. B thereupon promises A an additional payment in return for A's promise to perform his contractual obligations on time and

4. as a result of giving his A promise, B obtains in practice a benefit, or obviates a disbenefit and

5. **B's promise is not given as a result of economic duress or fraud on the part of A then**

6. the benefit to B is capable of being consideration for B's promise, so that the promise will be legally binding.

As discussed in Poole, 'Recession, changed circumstances and renegotiations: The inadequacy of principle in English law' (forthcoming), this can be interpreted as a single 'integrated principle' whereby the existence of duress in this alteration context will prevent a conclusion that there is consideration for the alteration promise despite the existence of factual benefits. In other words, absence of duress may be seen as a qualifying condition for such a conclusion. Of course, the result would be the same in that the alteration promise would be voidable for duress. However, it is not that simple to analyse since duress is a vitiating factor and it might be argued that unless there is a binding contract in principle (i.e., consideration exists) there is no contract to set aside for duress. It follows that logically the existence of consideration should be determined first and only then should the question of duress arise.

Nevertheless, this does not fit easily with any arguments suggesting that duress has replaced consideration as the key requirement to determine the enforceability of an alteration promise (or at least an alteration promise to pay more).

Adam Opel GmbH v Mitras Automotive Ltd [2007] EWHC 3205 (QB), [2008] Bus LR Digest D55 (economic duress paragraphs only), 18 December 2007, was a clear case of economic duress in the context of an alteration promise to pay more since, on learning that its contract to supply was to be terminated in six months' time, Mitras had sought an immediate increase in the price to be paid during the notice period and had threatened to suspend supplies if this was not agreed. The buyer had no realistic choice other to agree or its production would have come to a halt within days. When the notice period ended the buyer sought repayment arguing both that the promise to pay more was unenforceable as it was made under duress and that there was no consideration.

The judge, David Donaldson QC, sitting as a Deputy High Court Judge, focused on the duress argument and had no difficulty concluding that there was duress so that the agreement to pay more was voidable. He added (at [42]):

> The law of consideration is no longer to be used to protect a participant in such a variation. That role has passed to the law of economic duress, which provides a more refined control mechanism, and renders the contract voidable rather than void.

Quite apart from the terminology problems with the use of the word 'void' to explain absence of consideration when unenforceable is far preferable, the judge seemed to treat economic duress as a first hurdle. Having identified economic duress, he concluded without more, that it necessarily followed that 'GMR cannot rely on absence of consideration, whether as a supplement or an alternative to economic duress'. The judge did not, however, make clear whether (i) duress prevents *Roffey* consideration on the integrated analysis of Glidewell LJ, or (ii) whether there is in fact *Roffey* consideration for the alteration promise but that it does not matter given the finding of economic duress.

If duress is the central concept it is difficult to reconcile with Glidewell LJ's single test of consideration with its integrated requirement of **absence** of duress.

4.5 Alteration promises

4.5.1 The consideration requirement

As we can see from the discussion of contractual duties owed to the promisor (4.4.4), the role of consideration is not limited to the initial formation of contracts. Agreements between contracting parties not to continue with the contract, or to change (or alter) its terms, are normally unenforceable in the courts unless themselves contracts (see, e.g., *The Hannah Blumenthal* [1983] 1 AC 854). It follows that consideration is also required to support an alteration promise (*Stilk v Myrick* (1809) 2 Camp 317, 170 ER 1168; *Williams v Roffey Bros* [1991] 1 QB 1; and *Foakes v Beer* (1884) 9 App Cas 605).

In practice what happens may be very different. Parties on very good terms, and who regularly contract with each other, may be willing to uphold non-contractual variations and terminations of contracts. The problem with relying on the good relationship between the parties rather than on a legally enforceable agreement is that unforeseen circumstances may intervene to sour the good relationship, or to make its impact irrelevant. This is especially true where the original party is replaced by a trustee who is under a legal obligation to insist on strict legal rights, irrespective of any changes made by friendly arrangement. The classic situations of replacement by a trustee (or equivalent) are bankruptcy, receivership, or death of one of the parties.

4.5.2 Termination

As far as the termination of agreements is concerned, it is fairly easy to establish consideration in those cases where the contract is wholly or partially executory, i.e. where both parties still have some or all of their performance under the agreement left to execute. In this situation, if both parties give up their right to receive the remaining performance from the other party (so-called 'mutual release') then there is in that fact an exchange amounting to consideration. It does not matter that the performances outstanding are disproportionate, since the rule that consideration must be sufficient but need not be adequate (see 4.3.1) prevents examination of the equivalence of the exchange.

The Court of Appeal in *Compagnie Noga D'Importation et D'Exportation v Abacha (No. 4)* [2003] EWCA Civ 1100, [2003] 2 All ER (Comm) 915, was able to avoid the application of the principle in *Stilk v Myrick* (that performance of an existing contractual duty cannot be a good consideration for a fresh promise of payment) by concluding that there had been rescission (or termination) of an earlier agreement, followed by a new agreement ('replacement') rather than an unenforceable variation of the original agreement. It had been alleged that the new agreement of 16 August was unenforceable since it was not supported by any fresh consideration. However, the Court of Appeal held that an earlier agreement between the parties of 13 August, under which both had unperformed obligations, had been terminated by mutual release and the obligations under it had ended. This mutual release and the mutual promises in the new agreement were construed as the consideration for the new agreement of 16 August.

This construction, and the ability to identify mutual release and mutual promises, is illustrated further in the 'coffee substituted for tea' example, below 4.5.3.

Difficulties arise, however, where one party has performed fully. In this situation a release of the other party resembles a one-sided variation and requires further consideration if it is to be binding in contract.

4.5.3 Variation (or alteration)

Variation of the terms of a contract presents greater difficulty. A variation intended to be advantageous to both sides is automatically supported by consideration, since there is a mutual exchange of benefits (see 4.2.1). Sometimes what appears at first to be a one-sided variation can nevertheless, when properly analysed, be brought within the consideration doctrine. Consider the following example:

Example

A agrees to sell to B ten packets of biscuits, ten packets of tea, and ten loaves of bread for £40. Before either party has performed, B asks A to substitute five jars of coffee for five of the packets of tea. A agrees, saying that the price will remain the same. Is the variation enforceable? »

It might seem that the variation lacks consideration, since A is to perform something other than what was first agreed while B is only to pay what was originally asked. However, if the variation is seen as a two-stage (rather than single-stage) process, it is possible to discern consideration for the change being made:

(a) The first stage is where B agrees not to receive five packets of tea, in return for which A agrees not to receive whatever proportion of the total price is represented by the five packets. That stage represents one contract.

(b) Then A agrees to supply five jars of coffee, in return for which B agrees to pay whatever balance brings the total price back to £40. This is a second contract, and the variation is thereby enforceable.

The court may not consider whether a packet of tea is in fact worth the same as a jar of coffee as a result of the rule that consideration must be sufficient but need not be adequate.

Where, however, a variation benefits only one of the parties, some consideration additional to that of the original contract has traditionally been regarded as necessary for the variation to be binding. The Court of Appeal in *Williams v Roffey Bros* [1991] 1 QB 1 (see 4.4.4) confirmed the need for consideration to support an alteration (variation) promise, albeit making it easier to identify that consideration in some circumstances.

4.6 Alteration promises to pay more and alteration promises to accept less

Problems over consideration in contract variation cases are of two kinds:

1. One party wishes to obtain more money or greater reward than was originally agreed from the other party whilst providing the same performance (the enforceability of the other's promise to pay more).

2. One party wishes to obtain the agreed performance from the other party while giving something less than was agreed in return (the enforceability of the other's promise to accept less).

4.6.1 Promises to pay more

The decisions of *Stilk v Myrick* (1809) 2 Camp 317, 170 ER 1168 and *Williams v Roffey Bros* [1991] 1 QB 1 provide authority for the fact that such a promise must be supported by fresh consideration if it is to be enforceable by the promisee, and the fact that the promisee has rendered the performance originally required of him by the terms of the contract is insufficient to constitute that fresh consideration. However, as discussed above at 4.4, there appear to be two ways in which that fresh consideration can be provided:

1. it is possible to demonstrate that the promisee has gone beyond the scope of the original contractual duty and has thereby provided an additional benefit and/or incurred additional detriment (*North Ocean Shipping Co. Ltd v Hyundai Construction Co. Ltd, The Atlantic Baron* [1979] QB 705)

2. it is possible to find the necessary consideration in the fact that the promise gives rise to a factual benefit for the promisor (***Williams v Roffey Bros*** [1991] 1 QB 1). (This consideration is generated by the alteration promise itself and does not move from the promisee who has done no more than s/he was contractually bound to do under the contract. Thus, this consideration can involve practical benefit to the promisor without any corresponding additional *legal* detriment to the promisee—although there will be a factual detriment in performing the contractual duty already owed.)

The result is that consideration may be relatively easy to establish in the context of such an alteration promise, assuming that the promise was freely given and that practical (or factual) benefits are determined subjectively.

4.6.2 Promises to accept less

Promises to accept less than is owed under the existing contract have long troubled English courts. The problem is easily illustrated:

 Example

A sells his book to B for £10, payable next Tuesday; on Tuesday B has not got £10, but offers £8 which A accepts, promising (expressly or impliedly) that he will not seek to recover the remaining £2 from B. However, A later seeks to recover the balance of £2.

Is A's promise (to accept £8 in place of £10, and not to sue for the £2 balance) enforceable?

4.6.2.1 The need to supply fresh consideration

In ***Pinnel's Case*** (1602) 5 Co Rep 117a, it was held that a promise to accept less and not to sue for the balance (such as that made by A) was unenforceable unless B (as promisee) gave some new consideration for it. If B only part performed the existing obligation to repay the debt, that was insufficient to support the promise to accept less since B was doing no more than B was already bound to do.

The rule in ***Pinnel's Case*** was confirmed by the House of Lords in ***Foakes v Beer*** (1884) 9 App Cas 605.

In ***Foakes v Beer***, Dr Foakes was liable on a judgment debt to Julia Beer and it was agreed that if the judgment debt sum was repaid by agreed instalments then Julia Beer would not take any proceedings on the judgment. The judgment debt sum was repaid but Julia Beer claimed the interest on that judgment debt. The House of Lords considered that any promise by Julia Beer not to take any further proceedings on the judgment (e.g., by seeking interest) was not supported by consideration since Dr Foakes had done no more than he was already contractually bound to do. Accordingly, such a promise was unenforceable.

4.6.2.2 Finding the fresh consideration or other basis for enforceability of the alteration promise to accept less

On the other hand, provided something was given, the court is not entitled to enquire whether what was given was equal in value to the promise made (see 4.3.1). For example, the courts accepted that payment in kind ('a horse, a hawk or a robe'), if accepted by the creditor, could constitute the necessary consideration (***Pinnel's Case***). In addition, if additional benefit was conferred and/or detriment suffered, that would also constitute consideration for a promise to accept less, e.g. payment in advance at the creditor's request (***Pinnel's Case***) or at a different place at the creditor's request (although not if simply to suit the debtor, because there would be no additional benefit or detriment: *Vanbergen v St Edmund Properties* [1933] 2 KB 223).

Promises to accept less are also enforceable either if part of a composition agreement (e.g., agreement amongst all the creditors of a particular debtor to accept a certain percentage of their debts in full satisfaction: *Cook v Lister* (1863) 13 CB (NS) 543), or if the part payment is made by a third party as agent for the debtor and accepted in full settlement (***Hirachand Punamchand v Temple*** [1911] 2 KB 330; and see ***Bracken v Billinghurst*** [2003] EWHC 1333 (TCC), [2004] TCLR 4, for a modern example where the fact that the creditor had cashed a third-party cheque offered in full and final settlement of a debt provided the debtor with a complete defence to the creditor's claim for summary judgment on the debt, i.e. quick judgment on the basis that there is no real defence. Cashing the cheque amounted to acceptance of the third-party offer of part payment in full satisfaction). In ***Hirachand Punamchand v Temple*** Lieutenant Temple had borrowed money from the plaintiffs but the plaintiffs had cashed a draft for a smaller sum sent by the lieutenant's father (the third party to the debt contract) in full satisfaction of his son's debt. The Court of Appeal held that the plaintiffs could not then sue Lieutenant Temple for the balance. (This situation must be distinguished from part-payment by a debtor where the funds have been secured as a loan from a third party. This is a direct part payment by the debtor—see ***Treasure & Sons Ltd v Dawes*** [2008] EWHC 2182 (TCC), transcript available via Westlaw.)

The basis for these last two exceptions seems to be that it would be a fraud (on the other creditors, or on the third party) to go back on the promise. However, in both ***Hirachand Punamchand v Temple*** and ***Bracken v Billinghurst***, in the context of part payment by a third party, it was also considered that the debt was extinguished by the agreement with the third party to accept a smaller sum and so could not be revived for the purposes of suing the debtor for the balance on the debt.

4.6.2.3 Can practical benefit constitute the fresh consideration in the context of alteration promises to accept less?

In *Foakes v Beer* Lord Blackburn expressed some dissatisfaction with the conclusion that since payment of a smaller sum provided no additional benefit/detriment, it did not extinguish the debt so that the creditor could sue for the balance, arguing (at p. 622):

> All men of business…do every day recognise and act on the ground that prompt payment of a part of their demand may be more beneficial to them than it would be to insist on their rights and enforce payment of the whole. Even where the debtor is perfectly solvent, and sure to pay at the last, this is often so. Where the credit of the debtor is doubtful it must be more so.

Such reasoning recognizes that there may be a factual benefit in promising to accept less. Indeed, promises to accept less might seem to be no different in their nature to promises to pay more for the same performance, as in *Williams v Roffey Bros* (see Carter, Phang, and Poole, 'Reactions to *Williams v Roffey*' (1995) 8 JCL 248 and *Musumeci v Winadell Pty Ltd* (1994) 34 NSWLR 723; although compare O'Sullivan, 'In defence of *Foakes v Beer*' (1996) 55 CLJ 219).

If *Williams v Roffey Bros* had been held to be applicable to such promises, consideration might more easily have been found (arising from the practical benefit to the promisor) in a promise to accept less than the sum owed and promising not to claim for the balance. Nevertheless, in two cases heard by the Court of Appeal concerning promises to accept less, the Court of Appeal decision in *Williams v Roffey Bros* has been rejected in favour of adherence to the old-established authority of the House of Lords in *Foakes v Beer* (not cited to the Court of Appeal in *Williams v Roffey Bros*). In *Re C (a debtor)*, *The Times*, 11 May 1994, Bingham MR, speaking for the whole court, simply did not accept that, in the face of *Pinnel's Case* and *Foakes v Beer*, the *Williams v Roffey Bros* approach could be extended to promises to accept less than contractually owed. Whereas Peter Gibson LJ (*obiter*) in *Re Selectmove Ltd* [1995] 1 WLR 474, was clearly reluctant in conceding that he was bound by *Foakes v Beer*, and it seems he might otherwise have reached a different conclusion, his overall conclusion was that the Court of Appeal in *Selectmove* was bound by the decision of the House of Lords in *Foakes v Beer*.

These cases both involved debts to public bodies rather than variation of commercial contracts. Nevertheless, in the face of the doctrine of precedent, they clearly restrict further extension of *Williams v Roffey Bros* and have led to an unfortunate and arbitrary distinction, in terms of applicable principle and resultant enforceability, between contractual variations involving a promise to pay more and those contractual variations involving a promise to accept less. This result has also been implicitly accepted by the more recent decision of the Court of Appeal in *Collier v P. & M. J. Wright (Holdings) Ltd* [2007] EWCA Civ 1329, [2008] 1 WLR 643 (see **4.8.2.2**), per Arden LJ at [3], where *Roffey* was assumed to be inapplicable in the context of an alteration promise to accept less.

It is as well to note that *Foakes v Beer* was not applied in one first-instance decision where factual benefit was recognized.

> In *Anangel Atlas Compania Naviera SA v Ishikawajima-Harima Heavy Industries Co. Ltd (No. 2)* [1990] 2 Lloyd's Rep 526, the plaintiffs entered a contract to purchase a ship built by the defendants. The world shipping market fell into recession, and the plaintiffs discovered that the defendants were offering more advantageous terms to other clients. They sought and obtained the defendants' agreement that they should be accorded 'most favoured customer' status, so that in all respects, including price and terms of payment, they would be treated as favourably as any other customer. They subsequently sought to enforce this agreement, alleging that another customer had paid a lower price on more favourable payment terms. The defendants argued that the agreement was not supported by consideration. There was no suggestion that the plaintiffs' request for more favourable terms constituted economic duress. *Foakes v Beer* was not referred to in the judgment, but the practical effect of the agreement was to allow the plaintiffs to pay less than the sum originally agreed. By enforcing this agreement in express reliance on *Williams v Roffey Bros* and the notion of practical or subjective benefit, Hirst J seems to have avoided the problem posed by *Foakes v Beer*.

This apart, the reluctance of courts below the House of Lords to go against the clear authority of *Foakes v Beer* is understandable and proper. It has, nevertheless, had the effect of preserving the viability of the doctrine of promissory estoppel and has ensured that the law governing the enforceability of alteration promises is extremely complicated. It may be as well to summarize the current position:

Summary

1. *Williams v Roffey Bros* applies to alteration promises to pay more money so that (given the absence of economic duress) if there is a factual (or practical) benefit to the promisor arising from the promise, consideration to support that alteration promise can be found.

2. However, in stating that *Foakes v Beer* must apply to alteration promises to accept less, *Re Selectmove* and *Re C (a debtor)* have ruled out the possibility of finding consideration from a factual benefit to a creditor in agreeing to accept a smaller sum in full satisfaction.

3. It will therefore be necessary to look elsewhere for the consideration to support a promise to accept less (see discussion above), or, in the absence of consideration, the promise may have limited enforceability if the defence of promissory estoppel can be invoked.

4.7 Conclusions: The future of consideration

Although consideration appears to be firmly established in a central role in the English law of contract, and indeed appears to be the single element which distinguishes the common law contract from its continental civilian cousin, it would be wrong to conclude this section without acknowledging that for much of the past century consideration has been under attack from various quarters.

4.7.1 The reform agenda

In 1937, the Law Revision Committee (see its Sixth Interim Report, Cmd 5449) recommended a number of amendments to the detailed rules. Some of these proposals would have wrought a major change in our law, and could not be achieved without parliamentary intervention. For example, it was proposed that a promise in writing should be enforceable even if not supported by consideration. Other proposals have been at least partially achieved, e.g. the pre-existing duty rule (see 4.4); the rule that promisors in unilateral contracts should not be allowed to revoke once a promisee has started to perform (see 2.6.3); and the suggestion that where a promise is relied upon by the promisee it should be binding on the promisor (see generally 4.7.2 and 4.7.3 below). These changes have to some extent been brought about by judicial development, which is testimony to the continuing internal dynamism of the common law.

4.7.2 Professor Atiyah and the argument that enforceability should turn on reliance

Professor Atiyah has argued that there are historical grounds for saying that consideration is not the sole test used by the courts to determine whether a promise shall be enforceable, and that where justice required the courts have enforced promises on the basis of reliance by the promisee (see Atiyah, 'Consideration in contracts: A fundamental restatement' in Atiyah, *Essays in Contract Law* (Oxford University Press) 1986)). Such a notion, as we shall see (see 4.8.6.2), is consistent with developments in the United States.

More recently, the Court of Appeal of New Zealand in *Antons Trawling Co. Ltd v Smith* [2003] 2 NZLR 23 has accepted the existence of a binding variation to an employment contract based purely on the existence of reliance on the alteration promise without seeking to rely on the principle of factual benefit in *Williams v Roffey Bros.* It will be interesting to see how this reliance principle develops but it is important to appreciate that it is more limited than Professor Atiyah's argument for enforceability of *all* promises based on reliance. The *Antons Trawling* principle is limited to alteration promises (or modifications to existing contracts).

4.7.3 Other criticisms

These criticisms made by the Law Revision Committee and Professor Atiyah may be amongst the most eloquent, but they do not stand alone. The decision in *Williams v Roffey Bros* highlights the pragmatic approach to finding consideration which some courts are prepared to take in order to hold a particular promise to be binding in the light of the general context in which it was made. There was always likely to be a gradual progression away from the technical analysis of benefit and detriment towards the more impressionistic notion of inducement, thereby allowing the judges greater freedom to decide according to the flavour of the transaction whether agreements and promises should be treated as binding. Lord Wilberforce pointed the way forward in *The Eurymedon* [1975] AC 154 (see **4.4.2**), where he said of the transaction in dispute (at p. 167):

If the choice, and the antithesis, is between a gratuitous promise, and a promise for consideration…there can be little doubt which, in commercial reality, this is. The whole contract is of a commercial character, involving service on one side, rates of payment on the other, and qualifying stipulations as to both. The relations of all parties to each other are commercial relations entered into for business reasons of ultimate profit. To describe one set of promises, in this context, as gratuitous, or *nudum pactum*, seems paradoxical and is *prima facie* implausible. It is only the precise analysis of this complex of relations into the classical offer and acceptance, with identifiable consideration, which seems to present difficulty.

More particularly, it has long been considered that the need to establish consideration to support alteration promises may be too strict a requirement and fail to reflect the commercial realities of such alteration promises. This is evidenced in the development of the doctrine of promissory estoppel and in 1977 Professor Reiter in 'Courts, consideration and commonsense' ((1977) 27 Uni Toronto LJ 439 at p. 507) stated that insistence on the need to establish consideration in this context failed to recognize:

the illogicality of equating modifying with originating promises or to see that, insofar as consideration serves to exclude gratuitous promises, it is of little assistance in the context of on-going, arms-length, commercial transactions where it is utterly fictional to describe what is being conceded as a gift, and in which there ought to be a strong presumption that good commercial 'considerations' underlie any seemingly detrimental modification.

In the immediate aftermath of the decision in *Williams v Roffey Bros* [1991] 1 QB 1, there appeared to be clear evidence of such a practice, and the pragmatic nature of the decision, if not its technical basis, was warmly welcomed (see Adams and Brownsword (1990) 53 MLR 536 and Coote (1990) 3 JCL 23). The only issue at that time appeared to be to assess just how much the foundations of the doctrine of consideration had been shaken by this important decision.

The variety of reasons given for enforcing the promise of extra payment (see 4.4.4) makes it possible to identify both a narrow and a wide principle emanating from the decision. At the narrowest, it seems that the law relating to binding alterations of contracts has changed, so that a post-contractual promise relating to the main agreement (other than a promise to accept as full payment an amount less than the originally agreed price) will be enforced, subject to proof of the necessary intention and the absence of duress. It may also be argued that, on the basis of this decision, other areas of the law of contract, where the requirement of consideration may be said to be simply 'technical', might no longer prove troublesome, because the identification of a 'factual benefit' is always possible when the commercial context makes it implausible for the promise not to be regarded as binding (see, e.g. Coote (1990) 3 JCL 23, who argued that nobody would promise to pay more to achieve performance unless they regarded such a promise as beneficial to them; no one would 'throw good money after bad').

Of course, *Williams v Roffey Bros* is confined to the context of alteration promises. All three members of the Court of Appeal made it clear that they believed the particular context, which so influenced their reasoning, to be distinct from that of the formation of initial contracts. Accordingly, this principle will not be of any assistance in the context of the rule that a promise to keep an offer open is binding only if it is supported by consideration (see 2.5.3.1). Consequently, it would have been impossible to argue that the result of *Williams v Roffey Bros* would be that the doctrine of consideration would be abandoned altogether. Indeed, it would have been astonishing if such an interpretation were to have been suggested. There is no reason to think that English law should suddenly wish to make all gratuitous promises enforceable. The restrictive comments of the Court of Appeal in this important case were clearly designed to bring home the point that the doctrine of consideration remains central to mainstream contracts, and the decision reinforces the need to find consideration, albeit making it easier to establish in the context of promises to pay more. The Court of Appeal was at pains to stress this and would not otherwise have had to go to such lengths to identify the required consideration. Nevertheless, in *Anangel Atlas Compania Naviera v Ishikawajima-Harima Heavy Industries Co. Ltd (No. 2)* [1990] 2 Lloyd's Rep 526 at p. 545, Hirst J rejected the argument that *Williams v Roffey Bros* 'should be read as having only a very narrow ambit', although in the context the judge was not prepared to extend the *ratio* beyond the question of variation of an existing contract.

In subsequent cases (*Re Selectmove Ltd* [1995] 1 WLR 474; *Re C (a debtor)*, *The Times*, 11 May 1994), the Court of Appeal sought to place a limit on the scope of the *Roffey* ratio and these decisions appear to indicate that the courts are reluctant to abandon traditional rules of consideration, at least as far as release from debts is concerned.

More generally, it is as well to end this discussion of the impact of *Williams v Roffey Bros* with a note of caution about the developments arising out of it. Although the tone of the preceding analysis may have been to regard these developments as beneficial, any benefit is achieved at a price. The traditional consideration rules had the virtue of simplicity and the absence of difficult judgmental issues. The *Roffey* principle invests the judges with an enormous discretion over such cases, especially in ascertaining intention and in determining whether threats amount to economic duress (see 15.1.2). Before the old principles, and the occasional hard cases they engendered, are abandoned, we should be sure that the greater discretion of the new rule is in the best interests of the commercial community it must serve. In addition, it is important to consider whether there is, or should be, any *objective* evaluation of whether a benefit can be said to be a factual benefit where it is of *subjective* benefit to the party seeking to enforce an alteration promise to pay more.

It follows from the decision in *Re Selectmove* limiting the application of the *Roffey* principle to alteration promises to accept less means that the developments since the 1950s in the field of promissory estoppel seem likely to continue to be of relevance (see 4.8.2); and much of the academic argument (such as Chen-Wishart, 'Consideration: Practical benefit and the Emperor's new clothes' in Beatson and Friedmann (eds), *Good Faith and Fault in Contract Law* (Oxford University Press, 1995); and Hird and Blair, 'Minding your own business—*Williams v Roffey* revisited: Consideration reconsidered' [1996] JBL 254) has focused on arguments that, because of the technical difficulties in rationalizing the decision in *Williams v Roffey Bros*, the preferable approach to ensure the enforceability of alteration promises would be to adopt a flexible concept of estoppel as in the High Court of Australia (see *Waltons Stores (Interstate) Ltd v Maher* (1988) 164 CLR 387 and *Commonwealth of Australia v Verwayen* (1990) 170 CLR 394, discussed at 4.8.6.1). This approach involves a fundamental shift of emphasis away from the consideration doctrine and towards a more limited enforceability by means of the estoppel doctrine (discussed at 4.8.6). Alternatively, it may be preferable to follow the lead given by the Court of Appeal of New Zealand in *Antons Trawling Co. Ltd v Smith* [2003] 2 NZLR 23 (discussed at 4.7.2) and simply recognize that reliance alone is sufficient to justify enforcing an alteration promise.

> In *Antons Trawling Co Ltd v Smith*, the plaintiff, master of one of the defendants' fishing vessels, claimed that he had been promised a 10 per cent share of any additional fishing quota allocated to the defendants if he was able to demonstrate that there were sufficient fish to justify the government setting a larger quota. The government set a larger quota, and when the plaintiff sought to claim the promised 10 per cent of the fish caught under the additional quota the defendants claimed that he had not supplied any consideration to support their promise since it required him to do no more than was already required of him under the terms of his contract to explore for fish.
>
> The Court of Appeal of New Zealand held that where an alteration promise had been acted upon, in the absence of policy reasons to the contrary, the parties should be bound by the alteration since it was clear that the variation promise was intended to be acted upon and there was an intention to be legally bound by it.

Of course, the plaintiff still needed to show that he had acted on the promise and performed the task entitling him to the benefit of the alteration promise, i.e. to establish the existence of fish in sufficient commercial quantities ('the existence of a commercial fishery'). He had only achieved this in respect of one part of the larger quota.

Although this principle applies only to alteration promises, it has the potential to allow for the enforceability of *all* alterations promises (promises to pay more and promises to accept less) and so would eliminate the artificial and technical restrictions inherent in the current English law and the courts' refusal to extend the principle in *Williams v Roffey Bros* to alteration promises to accept less.

4.8 Absence of consideration and the defence of promissory estoppel

4.8.1 Development of the estoppel doctrine

Towards the end of the nineteenth century the courts developed a doctrine of equitable estoppel intended to prevent injustice arising out of the kind of situation where one party agrees to forgo his strict legal rights under the contract and this induces the other party to rely on this position but the first party then goes back on the arrangement and seeks to enforce his strict rights; for example, in the context of the part-payment example described above (**4.6.2**), where B has relied upon A's promise to accept £8 in full satisfaction of the £10 debt, and has, for example, spent the £2 balance but A is now seeking to enforce the original contract terms, claiming that any promise to forgo the balance is not supported by fresh consideration from B.

The application of the equitable estoppel doctrine meant that one-sided variations of contract might be *enforceable* in some circumstances despite the absence of consideration to support them. The best example of the operation of the doctrine is the leading case: ***Hughes v Metropolitan Railway Co.*** (1877) 2 App Cas 439.

> A lease contained a covenant requiring the lessee to repair upon notice from the lessor. Hughes, the lessor, gave notice requiring repair within six months. The railway company, the lessee, responded by offering to sell back to the lessor the company's remaining interest in the property under the lease. Negotiations continued for some two months before breaking down. Hughes subsequently claimed to be entitled to possession of the property on the basis that, since the company had failed to carry out the required repairs within six months of the original date of the notice requiring repair, the lease had been forfeited. The company claimed that there was a tacit understanding (or an implied promise) that the repairs need not be carried out if the negotiations came to a successful conclusion, and that in the meantime the period of notice would not start to run. In the House of Lords the existence of that implied promise was not really in doubt. Nevertheless, it was unsupported by consideration and therefore arguably unenforceable. However, the House of Lords refused to accept that argument.

The basis of their Lordships' decision is contained in the following, now famous, passage from the speech of Lord Cairns LC (at p. 448):

> It is the first principle upon which all Courts of Equity proceed, that if parties who have entered into definite and distinct terms involving certain legal results...afterwards by their own act or with their own consent enter upon a course of negotiations which has the effect of leading one of the parties to suppose that the strict rights arising under the contract will not be enforced or will be kept in suspense or held in abeyance, the person who might otherwise have enforced those rights will not be allowed to enforce them where it would be inequitable, having regard to the dealings which have thus taken place between the parties.

Thus, it is accepted that there is, in the name of equity, a doctrine which makes certain promises enforceable despite the absence of consideration. However, the nature and exact limits of this doctrine remain unclear. It should be noted that in many of the cases discussed in the following sections the expression 'promissory estoppel' is used, rather than 'equitable estoppel'. The change in terminology came about because of developments in the law starting in 1947. Those developments are discussed below.

4.8.2 The development of promissory estoppel

In the 1940s, the equitable doctrine established in ***Hughes v Metropolitan Railway Co.*** (1877) 2 App Cas 439 was taken into ground in which, some would argue, it had not been intended to operate.

4.8.2.1 The extension of the doctrine: Promissory estoppel and *Central London Property Trust Ltd v High Trees House Ltd*

Some years prior to the more direct attempt to enforce alteration promises in *Williams v Roffey Bros*, the courts had made a limited attack upon the rule (*Foakes v Beer*) that, in the absence of consideration, a part-payment promise was unenforceable. Rather than focusing on the identification of consideration, this attack focused on the question of enforceability based on reliance on the promise. The attack was led by Denning J in *Central London Property Trust Ltd v High Trees House Ltd* [1947] KB 130 ('*High Trees*'). In *High Trees*, Denning J suggested in an *obiter dictum* that where the conditions of promissory estoppel were satisfied, a creditor could not go back on a promise to accept less (and not to sue for the balance) where it would be inequitable to do so despite the absence of consideration to support the promise. In other words, the creditor could not go back on a promise not to enforce payment of the whole sum where the promise had been relied upon.

The case arose out of the classic situation (see 4.5.1) of a variation of strict contractual terms between parties enjoying a friendly relationship.

> In *High Trees* the tenant company was a subsidiary of the landlord company. The property in question was a block of flats over which the defendant tenant company had a 99-year lease, for which it paid a rent of £2,500 per year. At the outbreak of the Second World War many of the flats remained vacant, and the tenant company was unable to pay the full rent. The landlord company agreed to halve the rent (to £1,250 per year), and the tenant company paid that amount from 1940 onwards. By the beginning of 1945 the flats were fully let again. The landlord company was in receivership. The receiver believed that the company was entitled to arrears of rent for the whole period of the war, but brought a test case claiming full rent for the last two quarters of 1945.
>
> Denning J, relying on *Hughes v Metropolitan Railway Co.*, said that as a result of the equitable doctrine of estoppel, 'a promise to accept a smaller sum in discharge of larger sum, if acted upon, is binding notwithstanding the absence of consideration'. He noted with some satisfaction that his interpretation of the authorities achieved that which had been recommended by the Law Revision Committee in 1937, namely that a creditor's promise to accept part payment as full settlement should be binding.

Since the landlord company had sought only the rent for the last two quarters of 1945, this was held to be recoverable. Any estoppel had come to an end so that there was no difficulty in reverting to performance of the strict legal rights under the contract for the period covered by the claim. Denning J's comments concerning the rent for the period of the war when the flats could not be fully let, and the identification of an estoppel as operating in that period, are therefore *obiter* observations.

4.8.2.2 Assessment of the *High Trees* decision

There were two clear difficulties in the way of recognition of the operation of the doctrine of equitable estoppel in the context of part payment situations:

1. **The authority of *Foakes v Beer***

    It had previously been thought that there were clear authorities against the enforceability of alteration promises to accept less than the debt owed in the absence of fresh consideration to support that promise. In *Foakes v Beer* (1884) 9 App Cas 605, the House of Lords refused to enforce a promise not to seek interest on a debt when the promise was given without consideration (see 4.6.2.1) and *Foakes v Beer* was decided only seven years after

Hughes v Metropolitan Railway Co., without reference being made to that earlier decision. Although it can be argued that estoppel must be pleaded before the court may rely on it, it seems inconceivable that counsel in *Foakes v Beer* would have overlooked the decision in *Hughes* had counsel considered it relevant. In fact, *Hughes* deals with a different issue to that which arose in *Foakes v Beer* and in *High Trees.* In *Hughes* the principle was that, having implied that the tenant did not need to comply with the obligation to repair, the landlord could not treat the failure to comply as a breach of contract and forfeit the lease. In *Foakes v Beer* and *High Trees* the issue was whether the creditor (promisor) could change its mind and insist on performance of the contract in accordance with its terms, i.e. there was no question of the creditor alleging that the debtor was in breach of contract in complying with the amended terms.

Unsurprisingly, perhaps, it remains the case that courts demonstrate a reluctance to disregard the House of Lords' authority of *Foakes v Beer as the starting point* (see *Re Selectmove Ltd* [1995] 1 WLR 474 and *Ferguson v Davies* [1997] 1 All ER 315 at p. 323, per Henry LJ) where it is relevant on the facts. In *Collier v P. & M. J. Wright (Holdings) Ltd* [2007] EWCA Civ 1329, [2008] 1 WLR 643, the Court of Appeal applied *Foakes v Beer* in the context of an agreement by a creditor with a joint debtor whereby the creditor had agreed to accept only the proportionate share from that debtor and not to sue him for the remainder of the debt.

2. ***Jorden v Money* and the restriction of estoppel to representations of existing fact**

The other major obstacle to the decision in *High Trees* was *Jorden v Money* (1854) 5 HL Cas 185, in which the House of Lords ruled that the common law estoppel principle (which prevents a person from going back on a statement made once it has been relied upon) applied only to misrepresentations of *existing* fact, and did not apply to promises of *future* conduct such as a promise not to sue for the balance of a debt. On the other hand, this objection applies equally to *Hughes v Metropolitan Railway Co.* If that case is accepted as a valid exception to the rule in *Jorden v Money,* there would appear to be no reason why the *High Trees* case could not also be an exception.

It is possible to explain away these inconsistencies by ingenious arguments, as Denning J did in the *High Trees* case itself, resorting respectively to 'the fusion of law and equity' and an absence of intention to be legally bound. Nevertheless, the truth of the matter appears to be that, as originally conceived in *Hughes v Metropolitan Railway Co.,* equitable estoppel was not intended to apply to variations of price unsupported by consideration. Once, however, Bowen LJ had stated in *Birmingham and District Land Co. v LNW Railway Co.* (1888) 40 ChD 268 that the doctrine was not limited to forfeiture cases but applied to all variations of contractual rights; no meaningful distinction could be made between price terms and any others (although from the reasoning in *Re C (a debtor),* The Times, 11 May 1994, it appears that Sir Thomas Bingham MR would not agree). Denning J exploited this fact to the full by extending the equitable estoppel doctrine to its logical conclusion. Nevertheless, the subsequent cases are peppered with statements suggesting that the extension made by the *High Trees* decision is by no means firmly established in English law. Indeed, the House of Lords has not yet given its blessing to the doctrine of promissory estoppel. In both *Tool Metal Manufacturing Co. Ltd v Tungsten Electric Co. Ltd* [1955] 1 WLR 761 (per Lord Tucker at p. 784: see 4.8.5) and *Woodhouse A. C. Israel Cocoa Ltd v Nigerian Produce Marketing Co. Ltd* [1972] AC 741 (per Lord Hailsham at p. 758: see 4.8.3.1), the House of Lords expressly reserved the question of the existence, or at least the extent, of the doctrine.

4.8.3 **Requirements for promissory estoppel to operate**

4.8.3.1 A clear and unequivocal representation

The doctrine operates only where there is a clear and unequivocal representation that strict rights will not be enforced. In *Woodhouse A. C. Israel Cocoa SA v Nigerian Produce Marketing Co.* [1972] AC 741, Lord Hailsham said (at p. 756):

> The meaning is to exclude far-fetched or strained, but still possible, interpretations, while still insisting on a sufficient precision and freedom from ambiguity to ensure that the representation will…be reasonably understood in the particular sense required.

It seems that what is required is that only one reasonable meaning should be apparent from the representation made. In *Baird Textiles Holdings Ltd v Marks & Spencer plc* [2001] EWCA Civ 274, [2002] 1 All ER (Comm) 737, a claim based on estoppel failed because the alleged representation was considered to be no more than a bare assurance and insufficiently certain.

Nevertheless, it is apparent from *Hughes v Metropolitan Railway Co.* (1877) 2 App Cas 439 that if there is a sufficiently clear and unequivocal representation it need not be express, since in that case the representation was implied from the conduct of the lessor.

4.8.3.2 The doctrine operates as a defence and not as a cause of action

The major limitation on the promissory estoppel doctrine in English law is that it cannot be used to found a cause of action; that is, it may not be used in legal proceedings brought to force someone to uphold a promise. It can be used only to prevent someone going back on their promise and insisting on enforcement of their strict rights.

> In *Combe v Combe* [1951] 2 KB 215, during divorce proceedings the husband had promised to pay the wife a certain sum by way of maintenance. The wife gave no reciprocal promise to refrain from applying to the court for maintenance, so that (unusually) the husband's promise was not supported by consideration. The wife attempted to enforce the promise on the basis of 'promissory' estoppel, but her claim was refused by the Court of Appeal.

Denning LJ said (at pp. 219–20):

> Much as I am inclined to favour the principle…it is important that it should not be stretched too far, lest it should be endangered. That principle does not create new causes of action where none existed before…The doctrine of consideration is too firmly fixed to be overthrown by a side-wind. Its ill-effects have been largely mitigated of late, but it still remains a cardinal necessity of the formation of a contract, though not of its modification or discharge.

There are two separate points being made in this statement:

1. Promissory estoppel does not give rise to a cause of action

This limitation is sometimes expressed in the maxim that equitable or promissory estoppel is 'a shield not a sword' (per Birkett LJ in *Combe v Combe*). As an image the expression makes the point quite well, but it should not lead to the mistaken belief that the doctrine is available only to defendants and not to claimants. Promissory estoppel cannot found a cause of action where none would otherwise exist, but it may be used by a claimant in support of a cause of action which has an independent existence. Thus, if in *Hughes v Metropolitan Railway Co.* (1877) 2 App Cas 439 the lessor had actually retaken possession of the property, and upon breakdown of negotiations the lessee had sued to regain possession, the lessee would still have been able to rely on equitable estoppel to defeat the lessor's defence based on the lessee's failure to repair, since the cause of action would be based not on the implied promise to defer the time for repair, but on the right under the original lease to occupy the premises undisturbed for the agreed period.

The future of this limitation on promissory estoppel in English law is currently the subject of much debate in the light of comments made by Glidewell and Russell LJJ in *Williams v Roffey Bros* [1991] QB 1 suggesting that had promissory estoppel been pleaded they might have been prepared to reconsider the limitation. *Roffey* involved seeking to enforce a promise to pay more and this would have involved attempting to use promissory estoppel as a cause of action had it in fact been pleaded. In addition, no such limitation was imposed by the High Court of Australia in *Waltons Stores (Interstate) Ltd v Maher* (1988) 164 CLR 387, discussed at 4.8.6.1, in the context of a claim based on estoppel. In *Baird Textile Holdings Ltd v Marks & Spencer plc* [2001] EWCA Civ 274, [2002] 1 All ER (Comm) 737, there was an unsuccessful attempt to rely on the *Waltons Stores* general category of estoppel. However, the judgments disclose that this position might be reconsidered in the future if an appropriately argued case arises for determination by the House of Lords. This is discussed below at 4.8.6.3.

2. Promissory estoppel applies only in the context of alteration promises and does not do away with the need to establish consideration to support formation promises

In *SmithKline Beecham plc v Apotex Europe Ltd* [2006] EWCA Civ 658, [2007] Ch 71, Jacob LJ, with whose judgment Morritt C and Moore-Bick LJ agreed, stated that an estoppel could not be used to create a legal relationship in a third-party situation, and cited *Baird Textiles* as a recent example of an unsuccessful attempt to create a legal obligation where none existed before. In addition, Jacob LJ considered that 'an estoppel inherently must be raised by way of riposte' once the claimant has pleaded its case in order to argue that the claimant is prevented from pursuing that claim.

Thus, promissory estoppel in English law is not intended to replace the consideration requirement on the formation of a contract. In *Brikom Investments Ltd v Carr* [1979] QB 467, Roskill LJ stressed that 'it would be wrong to extend the doctrine of promissory estoppel, whatever its precise limits at the present day, to the extent of abolishing in this backhanded way the doctrine of consideration'.

4.8.3.3 Reliance and the fact that it must be inequitable to go back on the promise

The promissory estoppel doctrine depends upon some act of reliance by the promisee before it operates. There are those who believe that reliance demands that the promisee must have been induced by the promise to have acted to their detriment in some way (based arguably on the doctrine of strict estoppel, where such a requirement exists). Such a definition is suspiciously reminiscent of now outmoded definitions of consideration (see 4.2.1), and may arise out of a confusion with proprietary estoppel (see 4.9). In fact, it is not easy to see that the promisees in either *Hughes v Metropolitan Railway Co.* or *High Trees* acted to their detriment, other than that they acted in accordance with the subsequent promise rather than the original contract. The suspension of the strict rights under the contracts was, on the contrary, a benefit to the promisees in both cases. Equally in *Collier v P. & M. J. Wright (Holdings) Ltd* [2007] EWCA Civ 1329, [2008] 1 WLR 643 (see 4.8.2.2), the debtor had acted on the promise in an entirely beneficial way but Arden LJ concluded that a triable issue based on promissory estoppel had been established.

The reliance requirement for the operation of the doctrine of promissory estoppel was formulated so as to require the promisee to have 'altered his position' in reliance on the promise. In *E. A. Ajayi v R. T. Briscoe (Nigeria) Ltd* [1964] 1 WLR 1326 Lord Hodson interpreted this expression to mean that the promisee's position had to be altered in a detrimental way. However, in *W. J. Alan & Co. Ltd v El Nasr Export and Import Co.* [1972] 2QB 189, Lord Denning MR stated that he could find no support in the authorities for the view that there must be a detriment, and that all that was required was that the promisee must have 'conducted his affairs on the basis' of the promise so that 'it would not now be equitable to deprive him of its benefit'. Lord Denning therefore interpreted 'altered his position' to mean that the promisee 'must have been led to act differently from what he otherwise would have done'.

The one sense in which detriment is relevant to the doctrine is that there would be a detriment if the original contract were to be enforced unamended by the subsequent promise. Here, however, the sense of 'detriment' is nowhere near the same as that once used to define consideration. It does no more than contribute to the sense of justice inherent in the requirement that enforcement of the strict rights under the contract be 'inequitable' in the circumstances. Indeed, it may be that even the requirement of reliance is no more than the most likely way of demonstrating inequity, and is not in itself sufficient to trigger the doctrine.

In *Société Italo-Belge pour le Commerce et l'Industrie SA v Palm & Vegetable Oils (Malaysia) Sdn Bhd, The Post Chaser* [1982] 1 All ER 19, Robert Goff J insisted that the only requirement was that inequity be demonstrated. He said (at p. 27):

> But it does not follow that in every case in which the representee has acted or failed to act, in reliance on the representation, it will be inequitable for the representee to enforce his rights, for the nature of the action, or inaction, may be insufficient to give rise to the equity, in which event a necessary requirement stated by Lord Cairns LC for the application of the doctrine would not have been fulfilled.

In this case the promisees did rely on the representation made, but the promisors withdrew the suspension of strict rights very soon afterwards and before any real harm had been done, so that in the particular circumstances the judge found that it would not be inequitable to enforce the strict rights (and the promisors could therefore go back on their representation despite the fact that it had been acted upon).

These comments reflect what must be the functions of reliance as a requirement. One function must be evidential; the existence of reliance tends to confirm that the promise was made and was taken seriously. A second function reflects the statement by Lord Cairns LC in *Hughes v Metropolitan Railway Co.* (1877) 2 App Cas 439, that the doctrine applies to prevent the enforcement of strict rights where to enforce them 'would be inequitable having regard to the dealings which have thus taken place between the parties'. In other words, as indicated by the comments in *The Post Chaser*, the fact of reliance is at least one element to be taken into account in assessing whether enforcement would in all the circumstances be inequitable. Where the reliance is detrimental, it should be easier to establish that it would be inequitable to allow the promisor to go back on the promise.

4.8.4 Duress against creditors: Is it inequitable to go back on an alteration promise to accept less where that promise was extracted as a result of the exercise of duress?

It has already been suggested that a probable reason for the rule that consideration cannot be provided by the performance of an existing duty is the fear of duress by debtors against creditors (see 4.4.4). The decision in *Central London Property Trust Ltd v High Trees House Ltd* [1947] KB 130 results in the enforcement (albeit in a limited sense) of a promise to accept a smaller sum in full satisfaction for a larger sum owed. However, particularly in times of financial difficulty, it may be the case that the promise to accept less may have been obtained as a result of duress. This problem was confronted in *D. & C. Builders Ltd v Rees* [1966] 2 QB 617, where the debtor exploited the straitened circumstances of the creditor to extort a promise to accept immediate part payment of the debt in final settlement (the evidence was that the debtor's wife was aware of the creditor's circumstances). The plaintiff creditor then claimed the balance, and the question facing the Court of Appeal was whether there was a binding promise to accept less than the debt owed in full satisfaction of the debt. Lord Denning MR (who was in a minority on this reasoning, but not in the result of the case) found for the plaintiff creditor by relying on the statement of the doctrine by Lord Cairns LC in *Hughes v Metropolitan Railway Co.* Lord Denning MR said (at p. 625):

> The creditor is only barred from his legal rights when it would be *inequitable* for him to insist upon them…Where there has been a *true accord*…then it is inequitable for the creditor afterwards to insist on the balance…In the present case, on the facts as found by the judge, it seems to me that there was no true accord. The debtor's wife held the creditor to ransom.

In simple terms, there is nothing inequitable about not enforcing such a promise when the promise was obtained by duress. This approach matches that of Lord Scarman in *Pao On v Lau Yiu Long* [1980] AC 614, who said that there was no harm in allowing consideration to be constituted by performance of an existing duty provided that there was protection against duress (see 4.4.3). Similar reasoning was used to justify a more liberal approach to the doctrine of consideration in *Williams v Roffey Bros* [1991] 1 QB 1 (see 4.4.4). Of course, it follows that it is necessary to be able to make a clear distinction between pressure or threats which constitute duress and instances where there is no such pressure (see 15.1.2.3 for further discussion of the scope of economic duress).

4.8.5 The effect of promissory estoppel: Suspending or extinguishing the strict legal rights?

Where an alteration promise to accept less is supported by fresh consideration or is otherwise enforceable (4.6.2.2), the promise is binding for all time. This is a higher level of enforcement than is possible using the doctrine of promissory estoppel so that the fact that the courts have limited the application of the decision of the Court of Appeal in *Williams v Roffey Bros* [1991] 1 QB 1 to promises to pay more is extremely significant (*Re Selectmove Ltd* [1995] 1 WLR 474). The

Williams v Roffey Bros (factual benefit) approach to the identification of consideration would have rendered the equitable doctrine of promissory estoppel largely redundant in this context. Such a result might have been preferable since, if supported by consideration, a promise is legally enforceable for all time, whereas the effect of promissory estoppel appears to be more limited. In particular, it would seem that the doctrine operates only to suspend legal rights and not to extinguish them, so that it may be possible in the future to go back on a promise to accept less despite the operation of the doctrine of promissory estoppel. In *Hughes v Metropolitan Railway Co.* (1877) 2 App Cas 439, such a consequence was inevitable since it was impossible in the factual context to extinguish the property owner's right to have the property repaired. All that was in issue was the date by which the lessee needed to have complied with the duty to repair.

Subsequent cases suggest that a party making a promise not to enforce strict rights may withdraw that promise upon giving reasonable notice to the promisee.

> In *Tool Metal Manufacturing Co. Ltd v Tungsten Electric Co. Ltd* [1955] 1 WLR 761, the respondents were bound to pay royalties to the appellants under an agreement made in 1938 for the import, manufacture, use, and sale of hard metal alloys. They were also to pay compensation if the material manufactured exceeded a stated volume. At the outbreak of the Second World War, the appellants agreed to suspend the right to compensation. In 1945 the appellants claimed to have revoked that suspension, and to be entitled once more to receive it. That claim failed on the basis that reasonable notice needed to be given in order to resume the strict legal rights under the contract. In the later case this earlier action was held by the House of Lords to be sufficient notice to the respondents of termination of the suspension of the right to compensation.

In the *High Trees* case (see **4.8.2.1**), the promissory estoppel which Denning J found to exist on the facts, was stated to operate only for as long as the wartime conditions prevailed. It seems that the right to enforce the strict rights under the contract revived automatically once those conditions ceased to exist. It is not easy to see why that did not also happen in *Tool Metal*, although it might be argued that the giving of reasonable notice is a suitable mechanism to ensure that the other party is aware that the strict rights are to be revived and to ensure that it is therefore no longer inequitable to go back on the promise. It would also appear to generate more certainty (if only we knew what might constitute a period of 'reasonable' notice) and less injustice than a rule whereby estoppel might automatically come to an end, especially if there were to be disagreement about whether the estoppel conditions had ceased to exist. The safest way to resume strict legal rights must therefore be to give reasonable notice.

4.8.5.1 Single debts and periodic payments

The suspensory nature of the estoppel means that in cases involving single debt obligations, the operation of the estoppel merely gives the debtor more time to pay the balance. However, it may well be that where strict rights are suspended in a contract calling for repeated performances over a period of time (such as periodic payments, e.g. of rent), rights accruing during the period of suspension are not enforceable, and in that sense are extinguished. Thus, in the *Tool Metal Manufacturing* case, it seems to have been assumed that, after termination of the suspension, the appellants were not entitled to claim for compensation which would otherwise have been payable during the period of suspension of the right to compensation. Moreover, in the leading case of *Central London Property Trust Ltd v High Trees House Ltd* [1947] KB 130 (see **4.8.2.1**), there are *obiter dicta* of Denning J to the effect that periodic payments of rent which had fallen due during the period of suspension of rights could not be recovered once the suspension of rights had come to an end.

From statements made by Lord Denning in *Brikom Investments Ltd v Carr* [1979] QB 467 (at pp. 484–5), it seems that he believed that in some circumstances it might be impossible for the promisor to go back to the strict rights under the contract. He made a statement to similar effect in *D. & C. Builders Ltd v Rees* [1966] 2 QB 617 (at p. 624) suggesting that promissory estoppel might operate to extinguish legal rights. These comments can be explained if Lord Denning was referring to individual periodic payments, such as the rental payments during the bombing of London in the *High Trees* case and the royalty payments during the Second World War in the *Tool Metal* case.

4.8.5.2 The context may indicate that the strict contractual rights cannot be revived

Ogilvy v Hope Davies [1976] 1 All ER 683 provides an example of a situation where it was held to be inequitable to allow the vendors of property to insist on the strict date for completion and this operated as a permanent waiver. This was because they had led the purchaser to believe that they were not insisting on the strict legal position. The vendors of the property were selling it as trustees but failed to supply the purchaser with their own deed of appointment. This was required before the purchaser could make requisitions on title and on 15 August (fifteen days before the completion date) the vendors led the purchaser to believe that all the requisitions should be held up until they could be made comprehensively. Given that time was short when this statement was made and the deed was not in fact delivered until 20 August, the purchaser was entitled to assume that completion by 30 August would not be possible. It was inequitable, given the time period, to go back on that representation before 30 August. In this sense the completion date of 30 August was *permanently waived* and the vendors could not claim for any losses incurred as a result of the delayed completion.

Nevertheless, it seems unlikely that the courts will find that promissory estoppel extinguishes strict rights except where the context demands it. To this extent any suggestions that might be made that Arden LJ was suggesting otherwise in *Collier v P. & M. J. Wright (Holdings) Ltd* [2007] EWCA Civ 1329, [2008] 1 WLR 643 at [39], [42] must be greeted with caution. Arden LJ stated that any attempt to go back on the promise would be inequitable given reliance and a voluntary agreement to accept less. In addition, she continued: 'In addition, in these circumstances, the promissory estoppel has the effect of extinguishing the creditor's right to the balance of the debt.' With respect, this does not represent the traditional understanding of the law on the effect of promissory estoppel and would elevate the effect of promissory estoppel to the equivalent of consideration. It would then represent a direct and immediate challenge to *Foakes v Beer* since the two could not stand together. It may be possible to explain these comments in *Collier* as related only to cases where the part payment has been made, as opposed to promised, but that would not restrict the comment in any practical sense since this is invariably the case with part payment; it is still a *part* payment, albeit a full payment of that part and this is precisely the nature of the part payment in *Foakes v Beer*. Given that *Collier* is not an actual decision applying promissory estoppel, and only a finding that there was an arguable defence of promissory estoppel, the best advice may be to treat these comments as 'unfortunate' and wait for the position to be redressed, as inevitably it will be given the recent context for creditor/debtor relationships.

Of course, the enforceability of joined promises, both not to enforce strict rights and not to withdraw that first promise, has not been tested in the courts.

4.8.6 Conclusion: The future of promissory estoppel and the Australian use of estoppel to prevent unconscionable conduct

Despite doubts expressed about the doctrine in the House of Lords (see **4.8.2.2**), and fears that it might abolish in a backhanded way the doctrine of consideration (see **4.8.3.2**), promissory estoppel appears now to be well established as a doctrine of English law. Suggestions that it might become largely redundant by virtue of developments in relation to consideration (see **4.7.3**), which avoid the restriction afflicting promissory estoppel (i.e., that it cannot be used as a cause of action), have subsided as a result of the continuing significance of the decision of the House of Lords in *Foakes v Beer*. In fact, it appears that the emphasis has shifted *towards* promissory estoppel and the possibility that the Australian lead might be followed to develop a broader category of estoppel, or at least to relax the existing doctrine of promissory estoppel in English law.

4.8.6.1 *Waltons Stores v Maher*

In the Australian courts a general category of estoppel has been used to prevent unconscionable conduct. This estoppel has been utilized in circumstances where there was no pre-existing relationship between the parties and in order to enforce a promise directly.

In **Waltons Stores (Interstate) Ltd v Maher** (1988) 1 64 CLR 387, negotiations had taken place between the respondent and the appellant whereby the respondent was to demolish an existing building on land owned by the respondent and then build a new building, in accordance with the appellant's specifications, which would be leased to the appellant. The respondent thought that the agreement only needed to be executed and that this was to take place. The respondent therefore began the work of demolition. The appellant failed to execute the agreement, but did not inform the respondent until a considerable amount of the work had taken place.

The respondent argued that the appellant was estopped from going back on its implied promise to complete the contract. The appellant argued that estoppel could not operate because there was no pre-existing legal relationship and because estoppel could not be used as a cause of action.

The High Court of Australia held that the appellant knew that the respondent was exposed to a detriment in acting in reliance on the representation that the contract would be executed, and it was unconscionable to act in a way which encouraged that detriment. Accordingly, the appellant was estopped from denying that it was bound.

The decision (and hence this estoppel) is based on preventing 'detrimental reliance' and so would not be appropriate, in this form, in relation to cases where there was no detriment (e.g., **High Trees** itself).

In addition, the estoppel will not necessarily lead to full enforcement of the promise. The remedy available will be limited to the 'minimum equity needed to avoid the detrimental reliance' (see also the support for the 'minimum equity' principle in **Commonwealth of Australia v Verwayen** (1990) 170 CLR 395). Since the estoppel in **Waltons Stores** protects against detrimental reliance through the unconscionable conduct of a promisor, it might be thought that reliance damages would be the appropriate remedy rather than fulfilling the promisee's expectations, although there could be no universal rule (see Robertson, 'Reliance and expectation in estoppel remedies' (1998) 18 LS 360). However, in *Giumelli v Giumelli* (1999) 163 ALR 473 (see Edelman (1999) 15 JCL 179), the High Court of Australia took the view that this estoppel is not based solely on a requirement of detrimental reliance. The court therefore suggested that *prima facie* the expectation measure was appropriate in order to ensure that the promise is fulfilled (see also Cooke,

'Estoppel and the protection of expectations' (1997) 17 LS 258). Only in instances of detrimental reliance would a reliance-based remedy be appropriate.

There are signs, therefore, of an even greater relaxation of this 'estoppel' in the Australian courts, although further clarification is required on the details and the theoretical underpinning for this doctrine. In particular, if the basis for this equitable intervention is the existence of 'unconscionable conduct' it will be necessary to provide sufficient scope in this definition to justify intervention in scenarios typically covered by estoppel. In the context of proprietary estoppel the English House of Lords has recently expressly rejected unconscionability as the basis for raising the estoppel in the absence of a proprietary claim (***Cobbe v Yeoman's Row Management Ltd*** [2008] UKHL 55, [2008] 1 WLR 1752), which may present difficulties. There are other specific dangers associated with a general estoppel, since it will inevitably be uncertain and may cause problems in its application. However, even the Australian courts deny the existence of a single unified estoppel, while effectively merging the existing estoppels to such an extent that this is the inevitable conclusion.

4.8.6.2 Other examples of limited direct enforcement

§ 90(1) of the American Restatement (2d) Contracts (1979) also recognizes that promissory estoppel may give rise to a cause of action, and gives the courts a discretion to determine the appropriate remedy:

A promise which the promisor should reasonably expect to induce action or forbearance on the part of the promisee or a third person and which does induce such action or forbearance is binding if injustice can be avoided only by enforcement of the promise. ***The remedy granted for breach may be limited as justice requires***. [Emphasis added.]

4.8.6.3 The possibilities for relaxation of the strict requirements for promissory estoppel in English law

In ***Williams v Roffey Bros*** [1991] 1 QB 1, both Glidewell and Russell LJJ raised the possibility that estoppel might have been pursued as an argument on the facts. Counsel for the plaintiff clearly considered that, since the plaintiff was seeking to directly enforce a promise to pay more, an argument based on factual benefit was more likely to succeed than an argument based on estoppel as giving rise to a cause of action. However, Russell LJ commented that he would have 'welcomed' such an argument based on estoppel. It must be noted, however, that this was a very pragmatic Court of Appeal, and that another court might not be willing to entertain an argument which appears to conflict so directly with ***Combe v Combe***.

Indeed, ***Combe v Combe*** was relied upon by the Court of Appeal in ***Baird Textile Holdings Ltd v Marks & Spencer plc*** [2001] EWCA Civ 274, [2002] 1 All ER (Comm) 737, in reaching its conclusion that Baird could not successfully argue that there was an estoppel which gave it a right to require Marks & Spencer to continue to place orders for garments (the estoppel argument also failed because of the uncertainty of any representation: see 4.8.3.1). Counsel for Baird argued that ***Waltons Stores*** could be relied upon in order to create a cause of action. The argument was rejected on the basis that English law had not yet reached this position, although it was conceded that such an argument might succeed in a future case before the House of Lords. On the other hand, the actual decision in ***Waltons Stores*** might not provide strong authority for the use of a promissory estoppel as a cause of action. Mance LJ considered that *Waltons Stores* was a decision relating to formalities, i.e. there was agreement but it had not been executed. Given the existence of agreement, he considered that using estoppel in this situation might not constitute 'giving a cause of action in itself'; rather it operated to prevent Maher objecting to the binding nature of what was an agreed lease.

4.9 Proprietary estoppel

It has been suggested that the distinction between promissory and proprietary estoppel is not helpful (per Scarman LJ in *Crabb v Arun District Council* [1976] Ch 179), and that the proprietary estoppel doctrine is 'an amalgam of doubtful utility' (per Goff J in *Amalgamated Investment & Property Co. Ltd v Texas Commerce International Bank Ltd* [1982] QB 84 at p. 103). Nevertheless, the fact that under the doctrine of proprietary estoppel new rights giving rise to a cause of action may be created is sufficient to distinguish it from promissory estoppel, which is limited to a much criticized, purely defensive mode of operation.

Proprietary estoppel gives rise to an equitable right under which a non-owner may become entitled to land. This estoppel was originally regarded as being created by expenditure on, or use of, land with the acquiescence of the owner, in the mistaken belief, by the person making the expenditure or using the land, that they were the owner (*Dillwyn v Llewelyn* (1862) 4 De GF & J 517) (type 1 cases). However, the doctrine developed to such an extent that most of the recent cases have been (type 2 cases) whereby the doctrine has been extended to provide a remedy where the non-owner is encouraged by the true owner to believe that they either have an interest in the land, or that the true owner will grant them an interest in the land in due course and the non-owner acts to their detriment in reliance on this promise or encouragement (*Crabb v Arun District Council* [1976] Ch 179).

In this last form it is possible to see that proprietary estoppel may allow the achievement of a legal result which could in other circumstances be achieved by contract, although difficulties would exist in relation to fulfilling the formal requirements under s. 2 of the Law of Property (Miscellaneous Provisions) Act (LP(MP)A) 1989 if proprietary estoppel either is not regarded as sufficing since that would contradict the statutory requirements (see Lord Scott in *Cobbe v Yeoman's Row Management Ltd* [2008] UKHL 55, [2008] 1 WLR 1752) or the circumstances under which the estoppel arises are not considered to give rise to a constructive trust (s. 2(5) LP(MP)A 1989: see 5.4.4.1).

The doctrine affords the non-owner a cause of action to protect their interest, which might go as far as the court ordering the property to be conveyed to that party.

4.9.1 The requirements for proprietary estoppel

In *Re Basham* [1987] 1 All ER 405, the judge, Edward Nugee QC sitting as a High Court judge, set out the requirements for the doctrine in these general terms (at p. 410):

> Where one person (A) has acted to his detriment on the faith of a belief, which was known to and encouraged by another person (B), that he either has or is going to be given a right in or over B's property, B cannot insist on his strict legal rights if to do so would be inconsistent with A's belief.

These requirements have been refined and developed, particularly by the recent decisions of the House of Lords in *Cobbe v Yeoman's Row Management Ltd* [2008] UKHL 55, [2008] 1 WLR 1752 and *Thorner v Major* [2009] UKHL 18, [2009] 1 WLR 776.

4.9.1.1 Expectation and reliance

There must be knowledge or encouragement of A's belief, and in practice this must amount to a representation or assurance pertaining to an interest in identified property upon which it is reasonable for A to rely and which A can show that he believed to be binding and irrevocable.

Such a representation needs to be 'clear enough' for it to be reasonable to rely upon it in the belief that it is binding and irrevocable. What amounts to sufficient clarity will turn to a large extent on the context (*Macdonald v Frost (Executrix of the Estate of John Henry Frost, Deceased)* [2009] EWHC 2276 (Ch), 5 October 2009). This is necessarily difficult to establish in the context of future type 2 proprietary estoppel where the representation may relate to an assurance as to a future interest in identified property and there is necessarily a period of time between the representation and the point when that future interest should materialize (*Thorner v Major* [2009] UKHL 18, [2009] 1 WLR 776; see McFarlane and Robertson, 'Apocalypse averted: Proprietary estoppel in the House of Lords' (2009) 125 LQR 535). In *Thorner v Major* the House of Lords overturned the conclusion of the Court of Appeal applying the promissory estoppel test of whether there was sufficient evidence of a clear and unequivocal intention by a cousin that his younger cousin was to inherit a farm and concluding that the claim failed. The House of Lords considered that what was 'clear enough' depended on the context over a number of years and reinstated the trial judge's finding that the cousin had reasonably understood his older cousin's acts and conduct as an assurance that he would definitely inherit.

By comparison, in *Attorney-General of Hong Kong v Humphreys Estate (Queen's Gardens) Ltd* [1987] 1 AC 114 reliance was not reasonable because the party said to have made the representation had made clear at all times that its statements were 'subject to contract', so that when no contract could be agreed, no liability based upon proprietary estoppel could be imposed. Similarly, in the important and limiting decision of the House of Lords in *Cobbe v Yeoman's Row Management Ltd* [2008] UKHL 55, [2008] 1 WLR 1752, their Lordships held that proprietary estoppel could not operate because the basis for it was an incomplete agreement which depended on a contingency, i.e. that if C obtained planning permission for redevelopment of Y's land then Y would sell the land to C and they would split the profit. However, Y did not enter into the sale contract when C secured this permission. This is not a typical proprietary estoppel scenario since there is no proprietary interest being claimed; rather it is a claim to a contract which there was no legal duty to enter into and is similar to instances where a contract fails to materialize, which is the basis on which the House of Lords proceeded (i.e., *quantum meruit* for the value of the services provided and costs expended by C). This factual scenario does, however, have similarities to *Waltons Stores v Maher* (1988) 164 CLR 387 (see **4.8.6.1**), which may suggest problems for any future arguments based on applying this type of estoppel in England. It follows that any expectation arising in contractual negotiations for the sale of land is unlikely to be sufficient to found an estoppel.

4.9.1.2 There must be detrimental reliance as a result of this encouragement or assurance

Here the requirement appears to be strict, and not as fluid as it appears to be in the case of promissory estoppel (see **4.8.3.3**). For clear cases of detriment, see *Gillett v Holt*, where the plaintiff worked for a period exceeding thirty years, had been a surrogate family to the landowner and had taken no other action to benefit himself on the basis of the repeated assurances that the farm business would be his, and *Thorner v Major* [2009] UKHL 18, [2009] 1 WLR 776, where a cousin worked on another cousin's farm for no remuneration for over thirty years.

> In *Crabb v Arun District Council* [1976] Ch 179, the plaintiff sold part of his land, relying on a representation by the defendant that he had a right of access over the defendant's land to reach the land retained by him. No right of access was granted so that the land was landlocked. The Court of Appeal held that the plaintiff had clearly acted to his detriment in reliance on the representation, and the defendant was therefore estopped from denying the right of access.

4.9.1.3 Unconscionability

Recent case law has referred explicitly to the need for 'unconscionability' (*Gillett v Holt* [2001] Ch 210, *Jennings v Rice* [2002] EWCA Civ 159, [2003] 1 P & CR 8). In other words, it must be unconscionable to retract the assurances or to fail to give effect to them, e.g. by making a will which fails to reflect the prior assurances of the testator (*Murphy v Burrows* [2004] EWHC 1900 (Ch), [2005] 1 P & CR DG3: since there was another payment, 'viewed in the round', it was not unconscionable for the assurances to be retracted despite that fact that there had been detrimental reliance). However, this is merely one of the requirements and the decision of the House of Lords in *Cobbe v Yeoman's Row Management Ltd* [2008] UKHL 55, [2008] 1 WLR 1752 has made it clear that a claim for proprietary estoppel cannot be based solely on a claim of unconscionable conduct by the representor. A proprietary estoppel has to include a proprietary claim made by the claimant (to acquire property) and an answer to that claim that the person against whom the claim was made could be estopped from asserting (i.e. owner did not intend to transfer the land but cannot assert this given contrary assurances and the other's detrimental reliance). On the facts in *Cobbe*, this was entirely absent and there was nothing which the representor could be estopped from asserting. The Court of Appeal had been quite wrong, in the absence of such a proprietary claim based on expectation, to assert that an equity arose based only on the unconscionable conduct of the representor. This was described as 'a recipe for confusion'. The House of Lords was also keen to stress the confines of the doctrine of proprietary estoppel and that it should not be permitted to lead to undue uncertainty in commercial transactions.

4.9.2 The remedy

Where the conditions for the establishment of proprietary estoppel are fulfilled, the court has a wide discretion to satisfy the equity (i.e., to determine a remedy). It may order the full ownership (fee simple) to be transferred to the party encouraged to believe an interest was to be granted; but where appropriate, a more limited form of remedy may be granted (see *Inwards v Baker* [1965] 2 QB 507: right to occupy property for life). The crucial requirement is that there is proportionality between the award and the detriment suffered (see *Jennings v Rice* [2002] EWCA Civ 159, [2003] 1 P & CR 8 (CA). In *Gillett v Holt*, compensation in money (for being excluded from the farm business) formed part of the remedy. In *Murphy v Burrows*, had the estoppel been established, it was considered that financial compensation of just over one-sixth of the estate would have been an appropriate remedy in view of the need to ensure proportionality.

4.9.3 **Assessment**

The doctrine of proprietary estoppel is not without difficulty and has been on something of a rollercoaster ride in the House of Lords in recent years. The decision in ***Cobbe v Yeoman's Row*** may seriously restrict the practical scope of its application, although the fact that a cousin succeeded in ***Thorner v Major*** raises hopes that the doctrine has life left in it yet. It is still unclear why proprietary estoppel should create a cause of action when promissory estoppel does not, other than the differing contexts in which enforcement is liable to be sought. Neither is it clear whether it applies only to real property (land), or whether it extends to other property, although the decision in ***Cobbe v Yeoman's Row*** may suggest that it is limited to acquiring interests in real property.

Further reading

General and reform

Atiyah, 'Consideration: A restatement' in *Essays on Contract* (Oxford University Press, 1986).

Coote, 'Consideration and variations: A different solution' (2004) 120 LQR 19.

Treitel, 'Consideration: A critical analysis of Professor Atiyah's fundamental restatement' (1976) 50 Aust LJ 439.

Treitel, 'Agreements to vary contracts' in *Some Landmarks of Twentieth Century Contract Law* (Clarendon Press, 2002).

Roffey and existing duty

Adams and Brownsword, 'Contract, consideration and the critical path' (1990) 53 MLR 536.

Carter, Phang, and Poole, 'Reactions to *Williams v Roffey*' (1995) 8 JCL 248.

Chen-Wishart, 'Consideration: Practical benefit and the Emperor's new clothes' in Beatson and Friedmann (eds), *Good Faith and Fault in Contract Law* (Oxford University Press, 1995).

Coote, 'Consideration and benefit in fact and in law' (1990) 3 JCL 23.

Halson, 'Opportunism, economic duress and contractual modifications' (1991) 107 LQR 649.

Hird and Blair, 'Minding your own business—*Williams v Roffey* re-visited: Consideration reconsidered' [1996] JBL 254.

O'Sullivan, 'In defence of *Foakes v Beer*' (1996) 55 CLJ 219.

Promissory estoppel

Cooke, 'Estoppel and the protection of expectations' (1997) 17 LS 258.

Denning, 'Recent developments in the doctrine of consideration' (1952) 15 MLR 1.

Denning, *The Discipline of Law* (Butterworths, 1979).

Duthie, 'Equitable estoppel, unconscionability and the enforcement of promises' (1988) 104 LQR 362.

Edelman, 'Remedial certainty or remedial discretion in estoppel after *Giumelli*' (1999) 15 JCL 179.

Halson, 'The offensive limits of promissory estoppel' [1999] LMCLQ 256.

Robertson, 'Reliance and expectation in estoppel remedies' (1998) 18 LS 360.

Spence, *Protecting Reliance: The emergent doctrine of equitable estoppel* (Hart Publishing, 1999).

Thompson, 'Representation to expectation: Estoppel as a cause of action' [1983] CLJ 257.

Intention to be legally bound, formalities, and capacity to contract

5

Summary of the issues

To be enforceable as a contract the parties must have an intention to be legally bound (known as an intention to create legal relations). This is judged objectively through the use of two presumptions which are capable of being rebutted, although clear evidence is required to do so.

• In the context of social or domestic agreements, it is presumed that there was no intention to be legally bound. This position appears to be a matter of public policy but the presumption is not irrebuttable. However, it is unlikely to be rebutted in the absence of clear reliance, certainty of terms, and evidence of the seriousness of the promise.

• In the context of commercial agreements, it is presumed that the parties intended to be legally bound unless there are clear words indicating the absence of a promise or that the parties have agreed to be bound in honour only.

• In addition to the requirement to establish an intention to create legal relations, a promise will, in general terms, be unenforceable unless it is contained in a deed or is supported by consideration. (The requirements for a deed or consideration were discussed in **Chapter 4**.) Some contracts require particular formalities to be binding and **Chapter 5** examines these different requirements and the consequences of non-compliance with the formality requirements.

• The chapter concludes with a brief discussion of the capacity rules in contract (i.e. a party's ability in law to contract) and the effect of incapacity on a contract. The capacity rules, as a general rule, also have the effect of rendering the contract unenforceable, at least for the party affected by the lack of capacity. This part of the chapter focuses, in particular, on contracts made by minors (persons under 18 years of age).

• Minors have the capacity to make contracts for 'necessaries' and may be bound by certain contracts unless they are repudiated. Other contracts entered into by minors are invalid unless ratified on reaching 18. The Minors' Contracts Act 1987 contains additional interpretative provisions and provisions allowing for the court to order restitution of property to the other contracting party.

• The ability to contract of those lacking capacity due to 'an impairment of, or a disturbance in the functioning of, the mind or brain' is governed by the provisions of the Mental Capacity Act 2005. These provisions include the fact that a person so lacking capacity must pay a reasonable price for 'necessaries' and contain provisions for a Court of Protection and lasting powers of attorney.

- Companies and limited liability partnerships are separate legal persons. Whereas statute states that an LLP has unlimited capacity, the capacity of a company is dictated by its constitution, although statute protects innocent third parties where the company acts *ultra vires* (i.e., beyond its powers).

5.1 Intention to be legally bound: The context

It is generally accepted that legal systems must have some means of identifying those agreements which, although to all outward appearances qualify as contracts, are regarded as being beyond the reach of legal remedies. In essence, therefore, the concept of 'intention to create legal relations' is used by the courts as a device to enable them to deny enforceability to those agreements which they consider should not be legally binding and hence enforced. This, of course, is diametrically at odds with the concept of assessing the parties' intentions to see whether *they* intended to create legal relations.

 Example

Tom is a nineteen-year-old student, living at home with his parents during the vacation. He has no money, and approaches his father, Dick, for an allowance. Dick says that if Tom will clean the family car once a week, do the shopping, and keep the garden tidy, he will give him £30 per week. Tom agrees. Not many people would disagree with the conclusion that despite the outward appearance of agreement and *consideration* (a promise to do the various odd jobs about the house in exchange for a promise to pay an allowance), this arrangement should not be regarded as a contract, in the sense that the courts ought to be unwilling to enforce trivial family agreements.

For much of the nineteenth century, the period of development of modern contract law, the underlying theory was (as discussed at 1.4.2.2) that contracts were built upon the will of the parties. It is not surprising, therefore, that the test for identifying those contracts beyond the reach of the law was framed in terms of whether the parties intended legal relations (or intended to be bound in law). Nevertheless, today it is accepted that reference to the parties' intentions may be no more than a convenient short way of describing a test which is rather more complex than that. In fact, it is notoriously difficult to prove intention, since there is often no objective evidence which may be produced as conclusive proof. If every party seeking a legal remedy under a contract were put to the burden of establishing that both parties positively intended legal consequences to follow from their agreement, it would be a major stumbling block to the formation of valid contracts and commercially inefficient. For this reason the law has had to accept a much more restricted test of intention.

5.2 Presumed intention

The conventional view of intention to create legal relations is that agreements divide for these purposes into two general types: social/domestic agreements and commercial agreements. For each type there is a corresponding presumption (although for evidence of a recent broader contextual approach, see the decision of the Court of Appeal in *Edmonds v Lawson* [2000] QB 501, discussed at **5.3**). **For social/domestic agreements, the presumption is that there is no such intention to create legal relations, whereas for commercial agreements the presumption is that such an intention exists.** One difficulty with this otherwise straightforward scheme lies in the nature of presumptions, which are technical devices of the law of evidence. A presumption may be displaced by any actual evidence to the contrary. Such a precarious status is inconsistent with the role the particular presumptions are called upon to play in relation to intention to create legal relations, which is precisely to avoid instability of contracts caused by parties finding it too easy to avoid liability by denying the relevant intention.

From the cases which are discussed here, it should be apparent that in this particular context the presumptions are by no means easily displaced, and indeed it may seem that they are at times impossible to displace. The true situation seems to be that the term 'presumption' is not being used in its technical evidential sense here. Rather, when we say intention is presumed in relation to commercial agreements, we mean that a reasonable person in this situation would have expected legal consequences to flow from this agreement and, in the absence of some reason of policy against it, the court will enforce that reasonable expectation. Equally, when we say that there is a presumption of an absence of intention to create legal relations in social or domestic agreements (like Tom and Dick's, above), we mean that the reasonable expectation is that no legal consequences would flow from the agreement. Recognising reasonable expectations from the context also seems to be the basis for the decision in *Edmonds v Lawson* [2000] QB 501, discussed at **5.3**, where the presumptions were not applied.

It is true that some aspects of normal presumptions are present in those in use here, notably the fact that a presumption in favour of one conclusion places the burden of proof on the party seeking to establish the opposite. In other words, any party seeking to establish that a commercial agreement was not intended to be legally binding must persuade the court that that is the case, and failure to persuade will result in the opposite conclusion prevailing. Here the difference is that persuading the court may be very difficult; in legal terms, the burden of proof is very high.

The truth of the matter seems to be that the rule of presumed absence of intention is really based on a judicial policy of unwillingness to interfere in domestic disputes (sometimes referred to as 'freedom from contract'). In the words of Atkin LJ in the leading case of *Balfour v Balfour* [1919] 2 KB 571 at p. 579: 'In respect of these promises each house is a domain into which the King's writ does not seek to run.' By comparison, the inference is that, the effectiveness of contracting as a mechanism for planned exchanges in the commercial context would be seriously undermined if there was no assumption of an intention to be legally bound in the case of commercial contracts.

5.2.1 Social and domestic arrangements

The law relating to intention to create legal relations is most difficult in the case of non-commercial agreements. The difficulty stems partially from difficulties in identifying social and domestic arrangements, and partially from the desire to be able to enforce certain agreements even if they are social or domestic in character. It was in the case of *Balfour v Balfour* [1919] 2 KB 571, concerning an agreement between husband and wife, that Atkin LJ first clearly articulated the test based upon the intentions of the parties.

5.2.1.1 Husband and wife

The key authority is **Balfour v Balfour** [1919] 2 KB 571.

> The husband worked overseas, and it became clear that for reasons of health his wife could no longer live where he worked. On a return trip to England they agreed that he would return overseas while she stayed in England and that he would pay her £30 per month for her living expenses. Subsequently they became estranged, and the wife sued to enforce the promise of financial support. The Court of Appeal held that the promise was not legally enforceable because there had been no intention to create legal relations.

There is no doubt, as subsequent cases have shown (see **Merritt v Merritt** [1970] 1 WLR 1211), that if the maintenance agreement had been made upon breakdown of the marriage, rather than prior to breakdown when relations between the parties were entirely amicable, the agreement would have been enforceable even though entered into between husband and wife (see also **Soulsbury v Soulsbury** [2008] EWCA Civ 969, [2008] 2 WLR 834, per Ward LJ at [35]). It is not disputed that legal relations are intended in the latter situation on the basis that the fact of breakdown takes the agreement outside the sphere of domestic arrangements. In **Merritt v Merritt** [1970] 1 WLR 1211 (at p. 1213) Lord Denning MR stated:

> It is altogether different when the parties are not living in amity but are separated, or about to separate. They then bargain keenly. They do not rely on honourable understandings. They want everything cut and dried. It may safely be presumed that they intend to create legal relations.

Nevertheless, it will still be necessary for the language of a promise made on separation to be sufficiently certain if it is to be enforced. In **Gould v Gould** [1970] 1 QB 275, a separating husband's promise of payment 'so long as I can manage it' was not sufficiently certain to rebut the normal presumption of no intention to be legally bound.

These cases are further examples of the way in which many potential contractual rights crystallize at the time of formation of the agreement and cannot be affected by subsequent events. In **Balfour v Balfour**, the only relevant intention was that existing at the time of making the agreement, and the fact that subsequently the marriage had broken down and the wife intended to enforce the agreement could not change it from being beyond the scope of the law.

5.2.1.2 Rebutting the presumption

In the case of the presumption against intention to create legal relations, it is unlikely that courts would find any express statement of the parties to be conclusive, since it is here that the policy element of the doctrine is at its strongest. Thus, in the example of Tom and Dick (see **5.1**), it is unlikely that we would be any happier about the legal enforceability of their agreement had it contained a clause stating that it was intended to create legal relations. The policy against judicial intervention in such agreements would still prevail. Nevertheless, the courts have been willing to find social/domestic agreements enforceable in some cases, although it is not always easy to identify the evidence which caused the presumption to be rebutted. **Factors such as certainty of terms, seriousness, and reliance appear to be important.**

An instructive case involving the question of intention to create legal relations between *parent and child* is **Jones v Padavatton** [1969] 1 WLR 328.

The plaintiff sought to persuade her daughter to take up a new career by offering to pay her fees and provide her with a living allowance while she pursued studies to become a barrister. The plaintiff also bought a house, in which the daughter had rooms, the rest being let to tenants. Eventually, after more than one unsuccessful attempt at the examinations, mother and daughter fell out, and the mother sought to evict the daughter from the house. The majority of the Court of Appeal (Danckwerts and Fenton Atkinson LJJ) found that the daughter had no right to stay in the house because there was no enforceable contract between her and her mother. The majority relied on the speech of Atkin LJ in **Balfour v Balfour** [1919] 2 KB 571, in concluding that this was a domestic agreement and that the presumption of no intention to create legal relations had not been rebutted.

Although there was clear reliance by the daughter on the mother's promise, the terms of their arrangement were regarded as not being sufficiently certain. Salmon LJ agreed with the overall conclusion of the majority but for different reasons. In particular, Salmon LJ considered that when the agreement was entered into it was intended to have contractual force. He considered that it was impossible to think that the daughter had given up her secure and lucrative career without the protection of an enforceable promise of financial support. However, this agreement was only to last for a reasonable period of time, and he felt that this period had elapsed so that the mother was entitled to possession of the house.

There is much to commend the reasoning of Salmon LJ in this case. It suggests that while families' trivial agreements are beyond the scope of the law, when families come to agreements which will have a serious impact on the lives of their members, they are as entitled to the remedies of the courts as everybody else. Such a principle would seem to be inconsistent with the decision in **Balfour v Balfour**, however, in that it is difficult to deny that the agreement between the Balfours had a serious impact on their lives. Nevertheless, other cases do seem to support the idea that where the subject matter of the dispute is more than trivial, the courts will be more willing to find the requisite intention in order to ensure that a contractual remedy will be available.

Parker v Clark [1960] 1 WLR 286 concerned an agreement between family members.

The defendants, an elderly couple agreed with another couple (their niece and her husband, who were some years younger than them) that if the younger couple would sell their home and move in with them, sharing household expenses, the defendants would leave their house to the niece, her sister, and daughter. The younger couple, the plaintiffs, sold their own home and moved in with the older couple. However, the two couples later fell out, and the plaintiffs were told to find alternative accommodation. They sought damages for breach of contract. Devlin J held that the language of the correspondence, the surrounding circumstances, and the precise details governing the arrangement, indicated that the parties intended to create legal relations.

The presumption normally applicable in domestic arrangements had been rebutted. In particular, the judge could not believe that the plaintiffs would have taken the drastic step of selling their own house without the security of a legal right to live in the home of the other couple. On these facts there was seriousness, certainty of terms, and reliance.

By comparison, it is unlikely that an arrangement between family members, friends, or work colleagues, to share prizes or competition winnings, would be sufficient to rebut the presumption of no intention to be legally bound in the absence of a written document recording the terms of the arrangement and thereby indicating the seriousness of the parties' intent (*Wilson v Burnett* [2007] EWCA Civ 1170, (2007) 151 SJLB 1399 (official transcript available via Westlaw): no binding agreement to share bingo winnings; although compare *Simpkins v Pays* [1955] 1 WLR 975: coupon containing forecasts by each of the three parties who lived in the same house and evidence of agreement whereby they would share any winnings. In the latter case the plaintiff had established that the parties contemplated legal consequences).

5.2.1.3 Intention and reasonable expectation

The major difficulty with the view that social and domestic agreements will be held enforceable where they are more than trivial and have a serious impact on the parties, is that while it appears to coincide with what the courts often do, it is not entirely consistent with what the judges say they are doing. On the other hand, the orthodox language of intention appears to be based on a legal fiction, in that few (if any) parties turn their minds at the time of forming such agreements to the question of whether legal rights are being created. This is hardly surprising since such agreements are entered into in confident anticipation of continued good relations. It would be undesirable if the nobler feelings of parties to serious social or domestic agreements became an impediment to legal recourse in situations where their good relations have broken down. For this reason the courts must put themselves in the place of the parties at the time of the agreement, and ask whether it would have been reasonable to expect legal relations to result from the agreement in the undesirable event of amicable relations ending. In this way it is possible to avoid the 'rose-tinted' view of the parties at the time of making the agreement. It is not surprising, therefore, that the courts' willingness to find intention increases the more serious the promises made in the agreement, the more precisely they are expressed, and the greater the reliance on the agreement.

5.2.1.4 Policy considerations

Just as policy considerations weigh in the determination of intention to create legal relations in the commercial context (see **5.2.2**), they can also be important in the social or domestic context. In ***Balfour v Balfour*** [1919] 2 KB 571 there is clear recognition of a desire to prevent the courts becoming flooded with litigation concerning domestic agreements (see, for example, Atkin LJ's statement that 'the small Courts of this country would have to be multiplied one hundredfold if these arrangements were held to result in legal obligations').

In the context of agreements to provide lifts to work, the basic policy objective and the inevitable 'hazards of everyday life' ought to result in the conclusion that there is no intention to create legal relations (***Coward v Motor Insurers' Bureau*** [1963] 1 QB 259). However, the broader social need to ensure that such passengers are covered by insurance appears to have led the House of Lords in ***Albert v Motor Insurers' Bureau*** [1972] AC 301 to conclude that there was an intention to create legal relations (based on a determination that it was a business arrangement and therefore subject to the presumption applicable to commercial contracts).

The determination of contractual intention may even turn on the precise question before the court; see Hedley (1985) 5 OJLS 391 who claimed that the question in ***Coward v MIB*** was whether a driver could be compelled to carry others in future (executory arrangement), whereas in ***Albert v MIB*** the issue was whether there was an obligation to pay for services rendered (i.e., executed arrangement). Thus, the courts may be unwilling to declare that there is no contractual intention when faced with a question reflecting the existence of an executed social or domestic agreement.

5.2.2 **Commercial agreements**

It was suggested earlier (see 1.4.1) that one of the main economic purposes of contracts is to stimulate exchange. It would be undesirable, therefore, for the intention to create legal relations requirement to become a further hurdle in the way of a party seeking to enforce a commercial contract. For this reason, the presumption that intention exists in such contracts is extremely difficult to displace, so that only a party with solid evidence of a contrary intention would risk litigation.

5.2.2.1 Advertising: Advertising gimmick or promissory statement?

In relation to commercial agreements, advertisers may seek to rely on an absence of intention to create legal relations in order to avoid being held to the exact words of advertisements. If a beer producer chooses to promote its product by claiming that it enables those who drink it to achieve impossible feats beyond the reach of ordinary mortals, it is no doubt seen by reasonable people as a joke, and not as a serious claim to be elevated into a contractual promise or as having any contractual consequences. Such a statement is a mere advertising gimmick or 'puff'. Nevertheless, it may be possible to establish that an advertisement amounts to a promise because on the facts there is evidence of an intention to be legally bound. This is what happened in *Carlill v Carbolic Smoke Ball Co.* [1893] 1 QB 256.

> The company had claimed that their smoke ball, when used three times a week for two weeks, would provide infallible protection against influenza, and had promised to pay £100 to anyone able to show that they had contracted influenza after use of their smoke ball despite having used it in the prescribed manner. To demonstrate the good faith of this promise, the company stated that it had placed £1,000 in a specific bank account. Particularly in the light of this last fact, the Court of Appeal was unwilling to accept that the promise was no more than an advertising gimmick which was not intended to attract legal consequences. Accordingly, the plaintiff, who had contracted influenza despite using the smoke ball as instructed, was able to enforce the promise.

More recently, a similar argument of no intention to be bound in relation to an ABTA notice of protection was rejected by the majority of the Court of Appeal in *Bowerman v ABTA Ltd* [1996] CLC 451.

> The plaintiffs had booked a holiday through a tour operator, which was a member of ABTA. The tour operator had become insolvent and the question that arose for decision was whether the ABTA notice displayed on the premises of the tour operator amounted to a binding offer of protection so that customers were entitled to be reimbursed the full cost of the holiday.
>
> The majority of the Court of Appeal (Waite and Hobhouse LJJ) rejected an argument that this notice was non-promissory and therefore not binding. The majority considered that the notice was intended to be read, and would reasonably be read by customers, as constituting a binding offer which a customer could accept by booking a holiday with the tour operator.

Hobhouse LJ stated that the document 'is clearly intended to have an effect on the reader and to lead him to believe that he is getting something of value'. He added that, given this reasonable interpretation by the public, ABTA could not deny that it intended to accept any legal obligation to the customer, or say that it was not making any promise. If ABTA had wished to deny legal effect, it should have done so by the use of express words to this effect. However, as Hobhouse LJ recognized, from a commercial perspective ABTA would not have wished to do this, because 'to have included such words would have destroyed the value of the document in the eyes of the public and nullified the very effect which ABTA intended it to, and which it did, achieve—to induce the public to book with and entrust their money to ABTA members'.

This approach can be compared with the denial of legal effect contained in the dissenting judgment of Hirst LJ in *Bowerman v ABTA*, who considered that this was a non-promissory notice intended only to reassure the public. He placed emphasis on the language used as indicating a lack of contractual commitment, and considered that this position was supported by the decision of the Court of Appeal in *Kleinwort Benson v Malaysia Mining Corporation Bhd* [1989] 1 WLR 379 (see 5.2.2.2).

These cases indicate that whether a particular advertisement is regarded as promissory, and as intended to have legal effects, will depend upon the particular facts and it seems that the 'promissory hurdle' must be overcome before the presumption of an intention to be legally bound will apply in the commercial context.

As the difference of opinion in *Bowerman* indicates, judges may be in total agreement about the law applicable, but unable to agree upon its application to the facts. A similar difference of opinion occurred in the House of Lords in *Esso Petroleum Co. Ltd v Commissioners of Customs and Excise* [1976] 1 WLR 1.

> The company had organized a promotion in conjunction with the 1970 World Cup, whereby purchasers of four gallons of petrol received a free 'World Cup Coin'. The coins had no real value, but those collecting the coins would presumably buy Esso petrol in preference to other brands for the duration of the promotion. The Commissioners of Customs and Excise sought to recover purchase tax on the coins on the ground that they had been produced for general sale.
>
> In the House of Lords one argument was that the coins could only be 'for sale' if there was an intention to create legal relations in respect of the transfer of the coins between garage proprietors and customers purchasing petrol. Lords Simon and Wilberforce considered that there was such an intention, relying on the business context and the large commercial advantage Esso expected to derive from the scheme. On the other hand, Viscount Dilhorne and Lord Russell came to the opposite conclusion, relying on the language of the offer, the trivial value of the coins, and the fact that it was unlikely that any motorist denied a coin would bring an action in the belief that a legal remedy was available to him.

5.2.2.2 Comfort letter or guarantee?

The question of intention to create legal relations in commercial agreements was considered in *Kleinwort Benson Ltd v Malaysia Mining Corporation Bhd* [1989] 1 WLR 379 in the context of a 'letter of comfort'.

> The plaintiff bank agreed to make a loan facility available to M, a wholly owned subsidiary of the defendants. In the course of negotiations the parties had not been able to agree upon any security to be given for the loan, but the defendants had provided a 'letter of comfort', containing the key sentence: 'It is our policy to ensure that the business of M is at all times in the position to meet its liabilities to you under the above arrangements.' When the tin market collapsed, M ceased trading and went into liquidation without paying its very considerable debt to the plaintiffs. The plaintiffs then sued the defendants, claiming that this sentence in the 'letter of comfort' was a contractual promise, which had been breached.

At first instance the judge had approached the question of whether there was a contractual promise by considering whether there was an intention to create legal relations. He had applied the presumption applicable to commercial agreements in concluding that there was. **However, the Court of Appeal considered that the correct approach was first to consider whether, on the construction of the statement, it was promissory in its nature. On these facts the particular statement was no more than a statement of present intention and not a promise about the future conduct of the defendants. Therefore it had no contractual force.** In coming to this conclusion the court noted the fact that the parties had been unable to agree upon more formal security, and that the notion of a comfort letter was known by both sides to describe a document by which the defendants gave comfort to the plaintiffs, 'by assuming, not a legal liability to ensure repayment of the liabilities of the subsidiary, but a moral responsibility only'.

5.2.2.3 Rebutting the presumption in the context of commercial agreements: 'Honour clauses' and other express statements denying enforceability

As was indicated in the decision of the majority in *Bowerman v ABTA Ltd* (see 5.2.2.1), and assuming the necessary promissory statement, a presumption of intention to create legal relations will arise in the context of commercial agreements. However, this presumption may be rebutted by express words denying that the agreement is to have legal consequences and to be enforceable in the courts by stating that it is 'binding in honour only'. For example, football pools coupons contain such a statement (see *Jones v Vernon's Pools Ltd* [1938] 2 All ER 626). The leading case accepting the validity of such honour clauses is *Rose & Frank Co. v J. R. Crompton & Bros Ltd* [1925] AC 445.

> The plaintiffs were to be the defendants' agents to sell a certain kind of paper in the United States, and the document setting out the agency agreement contained a term usually referred to as the 'honourable pledge clause'. It purported to provide that the agreement was to be viewed as a definite expression of intention, but not as a formal or legal agreement subject to the jurisdiction of the courts. The parties continued their relationship for some time, and from time to time the plaintiffs would place a specific order which was met by the defendants. The defendants then suddenly announced that they would fulfil no more orders, and the plaintiffs sued to enforce the general agency agreement. The House of Lords upheld the 'honourable pledge clause', effectively saying that in the main agency agreement there was no intention to create legal relations and no legally binding contract.

On this basis, there could be no obligation on the plaintiffs to place orders and no obligation on the defendants to fulfil those orders. However, their Lordships treated actual transactions under this agency agreement as giving rise to 'ordinary legal rights', so that there was an obligation to deliver goods where orders had been accepted and an obligation to pay for those goods on delivery.

Case analysis

The presumption of intention can be seen as having been rebutted by the express clause in the agreement, but there is some logical difficulty about this view since ironically it would seem that the clause could have no legal force if the agreement in which it was contained was found not to be a contract. On its face the agreement, which had been signed by both parties, was perhaps good objective evidence of intention, but there must be some doubt about that, since the purpose of the clause appears to have been to avoid the impact of American laws on restrictive practices. As it seems clear that the main agency agreement would have been regarded as a contract but for this clause, it is also slightly surprising that the clause did not fall foul of the rule against ousting the jurisdiction of the courts (see 16.4.2).

The burden of proof

It might seem that there is little difference between the approach adopted in respect of intention to create legal relations in **Rose & Frank Co. v J. R. Crompton & Bros** and that adopted in **Kleinwort Benson**. However, although it was said to be of no practical significance in the outcome of the case, the Court of Appeal in **Kleinwort Benson** suggested that in its approach of relying simply on the construction of the words used, the onus of proof lay on the plaintiffs to show that the letter of comfort should be treated as a contractual promise. However, where the promise is clear, in the context of a commercial contract, the onus is on the party seeking to rebut the presumption that there is an intention to create legal relations to show that the contract is unenforceable. Thus, there is a difficult distinction between:

1. clauses which state that commercial agreements will not be legally enforceable (where the burden of proof is on the party denying legal enforceability to rebut the normal presumption of intention to create legal relations)

2. statements in commercial agreements which are non-promissory in nature and so without legal force (where the burden of proof is on the party asserting that the statement is promissory and therefore has legal force because of the operation of the presumption in the commercial context).

It is perhaps for this reason that the decision in **Kleinwort Benson** has been criticized in some quarters, because it makes it all too easy for firms to avoid legal responsibilities in the commercial context by establishing that statements are non-promissory (see *Banque Brussels Lambert SA v Australian National Industries Ltd* (1989) 21 NSWLR 502, noted Tyree (1989–1990) 2 JCL 279).

Implied agreements in the commercial context

Where it is alleged that an *implied* agreement has been reached, as was the case in **Baird Textile Holdings Ltd v Marks & Spencer plc** [2001] EWCA Civ 274, [2001] 1 All ER (Comm) 737, then despite the commercial context it is for the party alleging that there is a contract to establish the necessary intention to create legal relations. As Mance LJ stated (at [61]):

> An intention to create legal relations is normally presumed in the case of an express or apparent agreement…it is otherwise when the case is that an implied contract falls to be inferred from parties' conduct…It is then for the party asserting such a contract to show the necessity for implying it.

This was not established on the facts since the evidence pointed to the fact that it was a deliberate decision not to enter into any express contract in order to maintain flexibility in the commercial relationship. A similar conclusion was reached in *McPhail v Bourne* [2008] EWHC 1235 (Ch), transcript available via Westlaw, concerning an alleged agreement between the members of the band 'Busted' relating to song-writing credits, copyright, and income sharing. No intention to be legally bound had been established and it was unclear what the terms of this alleged agreement were.

Difficulties with evidence of contractual intent

In many cases direct evidence of intention will not be available, and the courts must draw such implications as they may from the surrounding circumstances.

The willingness to examine the wider background and circumstances in order to determine promissory statements and contractual intention is evident in the decision of the majority of the Court of Appeal in *Bowerman v ABTA Ltd* [1996] CLC 451. However, this is in marked contrast to the approach adopted by Hirst LJ (dissenting) who limited the evaluation to the wording of the document before him and concluded that the words used were non-promissory. The approach adopted can therefore be pivotal in the evaluation of intention.

In both *Rose & Frank Co. v J. R. Crompton & Bros* and *Kleinwort Benson Ltd v Malaysia Mining Corporation Bhd*, there existed a document which on its face indicated an apparent absence of legal intention, respectively in the 'honourable pledge clause' and the designation of the document containing the relevant assurances as a 'comfort letter'. This evidence is fairly conclusive. However, in *Orion Insurance Co. plc v Sphere Drake Insurance plc* [1990] 1 Lloyd's Rep 465 (first instance), [1992] 1 Lloyd's Rep 239 (Court of Appeal), Hirst J, at first instance, had concluded that in the light of the surrounding circumstances, a commercial agreement between two insurance companies lacked any intention to create legal relations despite the absence of an *express* statement to this effect The agreement in question was reached orally and subsequently recorded in writing. The plaintiffs, who sought to prove that the agreement was not legally enforceable, argued that the oral agreement had been agreed to be no more than a matter of goodwill, although no mention of this element was to be found in the written record. The Court of Appeal nevertheless upheld the judge's findings of fact, which led to the conclusion that there had been no intention to create legal relations. It was quite permissible to admit parol evidence (see 6.2.1) to show an absence of such intention. Moreover, although the presumption of legal intention is said not to be easily rebutted in commercial cases, it is clear that in the Court of Appeal's view the appropriate burden of proof remains the usual civil test of balance of probabilities.

Often it seems that a decision on the question of intention to create legal relations is a cloak for a more pressing question of policy. In *Ford Motor Co. Ltd v AUEFW* [1969] 2 QB 303, the court was faced with the question of whether a collective bargaining agreement between management and the trade union was legally binding. The matter was clearly commercial, and so the burden lay on the union, which sought to deny contractual intention. The court found in the union's favour. In so doing it relied on evidence from industrial relations experts, which was general rather than relevant to the particular agreement. Thus, the actual intentions of the parties seem to have been less relevant than the court's view that it was desirable as a matter of policy to keep such agreements out of the courts. The matter is now governed by s. 179 of the Trade Union and Labour Relations (Consolidation) Act 1992, which reverses the presumption otherwise prevailing in commercial cases.

5.3 **A contextual approach**

More recently, the Court of Appeal, in *Edmonds v Lawson* [2000] QB 501, considered the question of intention to create legal relations in the context of a claim by a pupil barrister that her pupillage constituted a contract of employment for the purposes of the National Minimum Wage Act 1998. The judge at first instance had found for the claimant, having concluded that there was an intention to create legal relations in relation to an offer of pupillage because it was a business (commercial) arrangement. This decision was potentially of great significance to the operation of the pupillage system. However, the Court of Appeal, while holding that there was an intention to create legal relations, and hence a binding contract, held that the pupillage was not a contract of apprenticeship (pupils are not 'workers'), so that pupil barristers were not covered by the legislation.

The approach adopted by the Court of Appeal is interesting in that it was far from clear which presumption should apply to the agreement. It could be argued that it was not commercial since pupils are not paid, but should an agreement for education be classified as social or domestic? Rather than being bound by such constraints, the Court of Appeal focused on the specific context to determine whether objectively there was the necessary contractual intention to be legally bound. In particular, it seems that the court was focusing on the seriousness of the arrangement for all the parties concerned as indicating the necessary intent. The Court of Appeal emphasized the process leading up to the making of an offer of pupillage and the benefit of recruiting the ablest pupils who might later go on to be considered for tenancy. Lord Bingham CJ (at p. 515) specifically stressed that whether either the pupil or chambers would sue in the event of default made no difference to the conclusion on the question of whether there was the necessary intention to be legally bound.

Conclusion

Difficulties can exist in identifying the type of contract for the purposes of the application of the presumptions. *Edmonds v Lawson* is a good illustration of the fact that, on occasions, it can be difficult to clearly identify a contract as either commercial or social/domestic and the very existence of the presumptions can force an artificial classification which fails to reflect the realities of the contractual context. This difficulty is further illustrated by the judge's conclusions on the facts of *Sadler v Reynolds* [2005] EWHC 309 (QB), 7 March 2005 (official transcript available via Westlaw):

> The claimant, a journalist and professional ghostwriter, sought damages for breach of an alleged oral contract to ghostwrite the autobiography of a well-known businessman claiming that the agreement had been made following a number of meetings (including one at which their wives had been present) and that the claimant had been charged with securing a reputable publisher, that the parties had agreed to share proceeds on a 50:50 basis and that he had come up with a number of ideas for the writing on the basis of this 'agreement'.
>
> The judge considered that, given the context and nature of the parties' dealings, this agreement fell somewhere between a transaction which was obviously commercial and a social agreement. On the facts she considered that the claimant had the onus of establishing an intention to create legal relations although this onus was not as heavy as in the case of a purely social relationship. The judge held that the claimant had discharged this burden of proof of legal intent since the defendant knew that the claimant was an experienced journalist and had previously been employed as a ghostwriter, they had a meeting to discuss the possibility of the claimant ghostwriting this 'auto' biography, and both planned to make money from the transaction.

The question was always seen in terms of the claimant having to establish the necessary intent rather then the intent being presumed (one way or the other). It might be thought that the judge was looking at the question of intent as supporting the claim that there was an agreement on these terms between the parties (see earlier the discussion of implied agreement and *Baird Textile Holdings Ltd v Marks & Spencer plc* [2001] EWCA Civ 274, [2001] 1 All ER (Comm) 737, at 5.2.2.3). However, it appears to have been easily accepted on the evidence that there was in fact an express agreement that the claimant would write the book. A claimant would normally need to establish an intention to be legally bound only where the agreement was social or domestic.

It seems difficult to justify the conclusion in *Sadler v Reynolds* that, irrespective of any social relationship between the parties, the agreement was anything other than a commercial agreement for profit to which the presumption should have applied. It is the nature of the agreement that should determine classification, rather than the identities of the parties (see, for example, *Snelling v John G. Snelling Ltd* [1973] 1 QB 87, discussed at **11.7.2**, concerning a business agreement between brothers). If the presumptions are abandoned in favour of a contextual approach then the claimant will have the burden of proof, which may be unfortunate in a commercial sense. The better approach is surely to apply the contextual approach only when it is not possible to classify the nature of the agreement as either commercial or social/domestic, as in *Edmonds v Lawson*, rather than in *Sadler v Reynolds* where there was no more than a social context for the making of a commercial agreement.

5.4 Formalities: Unenforceability by defect of 'form'

5.4.1 Introduction

Where the law states that a contract is enforceable only if recorded in a particular way, the rule is described as a requirement of form.

It is one of the commonest misconceptions of contract law among lay people that contracts are enforceable only if in writing. It is true that the job of the courts, and of lawyers advising clients, would be much easier if we were to insist that all contracts be put in writing. If we pause and consider the implications of this, it will soon be realized, however, that this would mean that each time anyone bought a loaf of bread or a drink in a pub, they would be obliged to countersign an invoice. There would be an intolerable burden on daily consumer intercourse. **For that reason, the general rule is that there is no requirement that contracts be made in writing, and the parties are left to their own good sense as to whether written evidence is necessary.**

In commercial dealings written evidence is almost inevitably available, but for the most part that is a matter of choice, not a matter of law. Where complex obligations of great value are undertaken on each side, so that any dispute may involve liability for very large sums of money, parties will inevitably choose to keep an accurate record of their agreement (and see **3.4.1** on rectification of written agreements).

In the seventeenth century, the law required a large number of contracts to be made in writing. Today, it may generally be said that the law insists on writing only where the subject matter or nature of the contract requires either absolutely certain evidence or some cautionary element to bring home to one of the parties the seriousness of the legal agreement being entered into. Thus, some consumer credit, hire purchase, and distance-selling agreements (defined in **5.4.4.3**) require a particular form of writing as a means of protecting consumers and in recent years there has been a growth in the formality requirements in the consumer context with a view to increasing the protection for consumers.

There are differing consequences for non-compliance with formalities, e.g. the contract may be void, ineffective, unenforceable, or the effect may be to deprive the transaction of the consequences which would normally follow.

The DCFR and formalities

The *Draft Common Frame of Reference* (DCFR) specifies no requirements as to form since the general approach is informality. Nevertheless the DCFR recognizes (Principle 55) that national laws may impose requirements of form. DCFR, II-1:106(2) does, however, state that where a contract is invalid only because it does not satisfy a requirement of form, and one party acts in the mistaken, but reasonable, belief that it is valid, then, if the other party knew it was invalid and knew or could reasonably be expected to know that the other party was acting to its potential prejudice in the mistaken belief that the contract was valid but allowed that other to continue to act (contrary to the principle of good faith and fair dealing), that other is liable for any loss suffered by the first (mistaken) party.

5.4.2 Instances where there are requirements of form

Requirements of form are of three types:

1. contracts required to be made by deed (see 5.4.3)
2. contracts required to be in writing (see 5.4.4)
3. contracts required to be evidenced in writing (see 5.4.5).

5.4.3 Contracts required to be made by deed

The common law made provision for a particularly formal kind of legal writing by means of the document made under seal (a deed). The more picturesque formalities associated with such documents have now disappeared, but these deeds must still be made in accordance with certain formal requirements, as set out in s. 1 of the Law of Property (Miscellaneous Provisions) Act 1989. These include the requirement of properly attested signature and delivery (s. 1(3)). Although the word 'deed' does not need to be used in the document, it must be clear on the face of the document that the parties intended the document to have this extra status of formality (s. 1(2) and see *HSBC Trust (Co.) UK Ltd v Quinn* [2007] EWHC 1543 (Ch), 9 July 2007).

The most common transaction which must be made in the form of a deed is the conveyance of a legal estate in land, e.g. a lease for more than three years (see ss. 52 and 54 of the Law of Property Act 1925). A deed is also the means by which to make enforceable a gratuitous promise which otherwise would have no legal effect (see 4.1), i.e. if there is a deed there is no requirement to plead and establish the existence of consideration. A further advantage is that a longer limitation period applies to a contract made in a deed (twelve years from the date of the breach of contract: Limitation Act 1980, s. 8(1)), whereas the period applicable to a simple contract (i.e., not contained in a deed) is six years (s. 5(1)). Although this form of enforceable promise is not often used for commercial transactions, there can be tax reasons which dictate its use, e.g. covenants to make gifts to charity.

Corporate deeds

Where a deed is required in the corporate context, s. 46 of the Companies Act (CA) 2006 provides for a document to be validly executed by a company if duly executed and delivered as a deed. Delivery is presumed to occur on execution unless it is clear that this was not the intention, e.g. if the intention was to sign and hold the deed until satisfaction of an outstanding condition.

To be validly executed as a deed (CA 2006, s. 44) the company document must be in writing and accord with the signature requirements set out in that section. The CA 2006 provides for signature by either two directors, by a director and a company secretary, or by one director in the presence of a witness who attests the signature. Alternatively the company's common seal may be affixed to the document if the company has elected to retain a seal (CA 2006, s. 45).

5.4.4 Contracts required to be made in writing

For some contracts it is an additional condition of enforceability, beyond the fact of consideration and intention to create legal relations, that the contract be in writing. In practical terms, among the most important of these are the following:

- contracts for the sale or disposition of an interest in land
- consumer credit agreements
- distance selling contracts
- marine insurance contracts
- bills of exchange and bills of sale.

5.4.4.1 Contracts for the sale or disposition of an interest in land

Such contracts must be made in writing, signed by both parties (as to signature, see the discussion of electronic signatures at 5.4.6). The Law of Property (Miscellaneous Provisions) Act 1989 repealed s. 40 of the Law of Property Act 1925, which required contracts for land to be **evidenced in writing**, and replaced it with a requirement that such contracts be **made in writing** incorporating all the terms.

Section 2 of the Law of Property (Miscellaneous Provisions) Act 1989

Section 2(1) of the 1989 Act provides:

> A contract for the sale or other disposition of an interest in land can only be made in writing and only by incorporating all the terms which the parties have expressly agreed in one document or, where contracts are exchanged, in each.

There is a growing body of case law determining:

- which transactions fall within s. 2
- how the requirements of s. 2 can be satisfied
- in particular, the position where the s. 2 formalities are not complied with.

Transactions falling within s. 2

The grant of an option to purchase land would fall within the scope of the section, but the exercise of such an option would not and so need not be signed by both parties (*Spiro v Glencrown Properties Ltd* [1991] Ch 537). Equally, an agreement, made in the course of negotiations for the sale of a house, not to enter into negotiations with any rival purchaser for a period of time (a 'lock-out' agreement) is not a disposition of an interest in land, and so does not fall within the scope of s. 2(1): ***Pitt v PHH Asset Management Ltd*** [1994] 1 WLR 327 and *Dandara Holdings Ltd v Co-operative Retail Services Ltd* [2004] EWHC 1476 (Ch), [2004] 2 EGLR 163.

Satisfying the requirements of s. 2

Incorporation of the terms in accordance with s. 2 of the 1989 Act can be achieved by setting them out in the contract document, or by reference to another document (s. 2(2)). In *Record v Bell* [1991] 1 WLR 853, it was held that where incorporation is alleged to have been achieved by reference to another document, in order to be effective for the purposes of s. 2 the contract of sale which both parties have signed must refer to and identify that other document.

Each party must sign a document incorporating the terms, although it need not be the same document which bears both signatures, especially where there is to be an exchange of contract documents (s. 2(3)). It is clear that where the terms of a secondary document are to be incorporated, it is the principal document that needs to be signed. In *Firstpost Homes Ltd v Johnson* [1995] 1 WLR 1567, the document, which it was claimed contained the contract between the parties, referred to an attached plan. The purchaser signed the plan but not the principal document, and the Court of Appeal found that the requirements of s. 2 were not satisfied.

Failure to comply with the s. 2 requirements

A purported contract made in contravention of these rules would be without effect. However, some protections exist:

1. Rectification

Rectification is provided for expressly by s. 2(4), is possible by order of the court where it results in the contract fulfilling the s. 2 requirements. This could not be achieved if there had to be a concluded contract *before* rectification since that would be impossible through failure to fulfil s. 2; however, as discussed in **3.4.1.1**, for rectification there need only be evidence that the written agreement does not reflect the terms actually agreed by the parties.

2. Collateral contract

This might be available to provide for aspects of the contract not covered by the written document. An example might be a house sale, in which it had been agreed that carpets would be included in the purchase price but where the sale of the carpets was not recorded in the contract document. That part of the sale might be regarded as a collateral contract, without doing violence to the principle established by s. 2. In *Tootal Clothing Ltd v Guinea Properties Management Ltd* (1992) 64 P & CR 452, the Court of Appeal found that an agreement by which a landlord undertook to contribute to the cost of shop fitting work to be carried out by the tenant was 'supplemental' to the main tenancy agreement, as designated by the parties, and was not, therefore, one of the terms which had to be recorded in writing.

3. Proprietary estoppel

The doctrine of proprietary estoppel has the potential to provide protection against unenforceability for failure to comply with s. 2 formalities. It applies, in particular, where one party has been encouraged by another to believe that they will be granted an interest in the property in question, and that party has acted to their detriment in reliance on that belief (discussed at **4.9** and see particularly ***Thorner v Major*** [2009] UKHL 18, [2009] 1 WLR 776). The doctrine affords such a party a new cause of action to protect their interest, which might go as far as the court ordering the property to be conveyed to that party. However, it is not expressly provided for in the statute, so that its application may risk being excluded as contrary to the Parliamentary intent (see, e.g. *McCausland v Duncan Lawrie Ltd* [1997] 1 WLR 38 and *United Bank of Kuwait plc v Sahib* [1997] Ch 107) and it is clear that the mere fact of an invalid agreement cannot found an estoppel as this would defeat the policy of the 1989 Act (*Attorney-General for Hong Kong v Humphreys Estate (Queen's Gardens) Ltd* [1987] AC 114 and *Cobbe v Yeoman's Row Management Ltd* [2008] UKHL 55, [2008] 1 WLR 1752).

Nevertheless, in *Kinane v Mackie-Conteh* [2005] EWCA Civ 45, [2005] WTLR 345, Arden LJ had said (at [29]) that it did not follow that the existence of a failed agreement prevented reliance on an estoppel since it was necessary to consider whether the claimant was relying on the invalid agreement or the unconscionable conduct of the defendant in encouraging the claimant to believe that the agreement was valid. Dixon ('Proprietary estoppel and formalities in land law and the Land Registration Act 2002' in Cooke (ed.), *Modern Studies in Property Law,* Vol. 2 (Hart Publishing, 2003)) referred to this as the 'double assurance theory' of estoppel in that the defendant represents (a) the right over his land and (b) that this right will exist despite a failure to comply with statutory formalities. Thus, the estoppel was considered as operating to remedy the unconscionability, i.e. to provide a remedy due to the failure of these assurances rather than on the basis of permitting an invalid agreement to be enforced. Such a conclusion must now be seriously in question following the interpretation and explanation of proprietary estoppel by the House of Lords in *Cobbe v Yeoman's Row Management Ltd* [2008] UKHL 55, [2008] 1 WLR 1752.

> In **Cobbe v Yeoman's Row Management Ltd** [2008] UKHL 55, [2008] 1 WLR 1752, C had reached an oral agreement in principle with Y that C would obtain planning permission for the redevelopment of land owned by Y and that, subject to it being obtained, Y would sell the land to C for redevelopment with the profit over a certain level being split equally between C and Y. The claimant (C) went to considerable expense and effort to obtain planning consent. Having done so, however, Y refused to enter into the contract of sale. Since the 'agreement' was unenforceable for lack of writing, C sought to rely on proprietary estoppel. The Court of Appeal had decided that proprietary estoppel operated because Y had acted unconscionably in leading C to believe that a contract would result. This estoppel did not undermine s. 2 because it was based on the unconscionable conduct of Y rather than the enforcement of an invalid contract. Since remedying unconscionability was the purpose of the estoppel, the Court of Appeal considered that the assurance given did not need to satisfy the test of contractual certainty. It merely needed to be sufficiently certain to give rise to an expectation.
>
> However, the House of Lords unanimously rejected the claim based on proprietary estoppel and held that the appropriate remedy was a *quantum meruit* (restitutionary) claim based on the value of the services provided and costs expended by C. There was no more than an incomplete agreement based on a contingency.

Significantly, for the purposes of a discussion of s. 2, Lord Scott addressed the question of whether an agreement to acquire an interest in land which does not comply with s. 2 can nevertheless be enforceable by means of proprietary estoppel. This was strictly *obiter* given the decision that there was no complete agreement to acquire an interest in land. Lord Scott (at [29]) stated:

> My present view…is that proprietary estoppel cannot be prayed in aid in order to render enforceable an agreement that statute has declared to be void. The proposition that an owner of land can be

estopped from asserting that an agreement is void for want of compliance with the requirements of s. 2 is, in my opinion, unacceptable. The assertion is no more than the statute provides. Equity can surely not contradict the statute.

Lord Walker stated (at [93]) that he did not think it necessary or appropriate 'to consider the issue on s. 2 of the 1989 Act'. Lord Brown stated that he agreed with both Lord Scott and Lord Walker. It is therefore unclear whether proprietary estoppel will have any future role to play in the s. 2 context.

Lord Scott's *obiter* proposition was followed and applied by Peter Smith J in *Hutchison v B. & D. F. Ltd* [2008] EWHC 2286 (Ch), [2009] L & TR 12, However, it is clear that **Cobbe** rests on a finding that where the agreement is incomplete (inchoate) and based only on the defendant's unconscionable behaviour, it cannot found a proprietary estoppel (*Kirker v Ridley*, unreported, 17 December 2008 (ChD) so that 'the House of Lords left unanswered the question whether a *complete* agreement for the acquisition of an interest in land that does not comply with the formalities prescribed by section 2 can become enforceable via the route of proprietary estoppel' (emphasis added) (Mark Herbert QC in *Herbert v Doyle* [2008] EWHC 1950 (Ch), [2009] WTLR 589). The judge in *Herbert v Doyle* therefore considered that despite Lord Scott's *obiter* statement 'it remains the case that, if all the requirements are otherwise satisfied for a claim based on proprietary estoppel to succeed, the claim will not fail solely because it also consists of an agreement which falls foul of section 2'.

Nevertheless, it must be recognized that there is a clear irony involved in pleading proprietary estoppel, which is based on an informal agreement as the basis for avoiding a formality requirement in statute. It could be that Lord Scott is correct in anticipating that this is not possible, particularly as statute reserves this role in express terms for the constructive trust (s. 2(5)).

4. Constructive trust

This is a device that has the advantage of being expressly included in the legislation. By s. 2(5), the constructive trust is specifically excluded from the s. 2 requirements and ought therefore to provide a way around a failure to comply with its formalities. It has become common practice, however, for both proprietary estoppel and the constructive trust to be pleaded in cases where s. 2 formalities are lacking and the agreement would otherwise be unenforceable. For example, in **Yaxley v Gotts** [2000] Ch 162, both proprietary estoppel and the constructive trust arose for consideration. The case concerned an oral agreement to transfer the ground floor of a house in exchange for renovation work and acting as managing agent. The judge at first instance had made an order for a lease on the basis of proprietary estoppel. The appeal was based on the argument that any oral contract was void as it did not comply with the s. 2 formalities, and proprietary estoppel was therefore inappropriate. The Court of Appeal, however, held that the agreement could be enforced using the constructive trust based on the common intentions of the parties and in order to avoid unconscionability. However, the Court of Appeal clearly considered that the constructive trust was a similar remedy to proprietary estoppel. Robert Walker LJ stated: '[a] constructive trust of that sort is closely akin to, if not indistinguishable from, proprietary estoppel. Equity enforces it because it would be unconscionable for the other party to disregard the claimant's rights.'

The suggestion therefore was that rights arising under proprietary estoppel arose from the context of unconscionability rather than from the agreement itself. This must now be seriously in doubt since in **Cobbe v Yeoman's Row Management Ltd** [2008] UKHL 55, [2008] 1 WLR 1752,

Lord Scott considered that proprietary estoppel does not provide an independent means by which a person can acquire a right, i.e. there must be a complete agreement and rights cannot be acquired simply because of the unconscionable conduct of a defendant. In addition, he did not consider that a constructive trust arose on the facts since the unconscionable behaviour alone would not justify such a finding given that Y owned the property and that it was apparent that an enforceable contract would not necessarily result from the obtaining of the planning permission given the speculative and contingent nature of the arrangement. Lord Scott referred specifically to rights acquired as part of a joint venture in order to establish the existence of a constructive trust. However, on the facts in *Cobbe* the argument was that a trust should be created in relation to a right which Y held *before* any negotiations with C. Lord Scott rejected this.

Post *Cobbe* the constructive trust will inevitably take on greater prominence as a means of avoiding the potentially unfair consequences that may follow from a failure to comply with s. 2 (e.g., *Re West Norwood Cemetery* [2005] 1 WLR 2176). However, the findings in *Cobbe* demonstrate all too clearly that a finding of constructive trust is not inevitable and will not arise in the event of any contingencies existing, e.g. in *James v Evans* [2001] CP Rep 36, [2000] 42 EG 173, the argument for a constructive trust failed because the negotiations had been conducted 'subject to contract'.

Despite the uncertainties presented by the decision in *Cobbe v Yeoman's Row*, it seems clear that where there is a *complete* agreement or a sufficiently clear and unequivocal assurance (*Thorner v Major* [2009] UKHL 18, [2009] 1 WLR 776) (as opposed to an incomplete agreement based on contingencies or a right alleged to be based only on the other's unconscionable conduct), proprietary estoppel can be shown to exist. The interesting questions are (i) whether proprietary estoppel so established can prevent s. 2 unenforceability (Lord Scott thinks not) and (ii) whether an established proprietary estoppel (based on a complete agreement) can be used as the basis for the constructive trust which can be relied upon to avoid s. 2 formalities problem. We know, however, from observations that he made in *Thorner v Major* [2009] UKHL 18, [2009] 1 WLR 776 at [20], that Lord Scott would prefer to see proprietary estoppel and the constructive trust kept separate.

5.4.4.2 Consumer credit agreements

Other important contracts required to be made in a particular form of writing are consumer hire purchase and credit sales agreements, which are regulated agreements under the Consumer Credit Act (CCA) 1974, s. 60. Such contracts must be in the form prescribed by regulation (Consumer Credit (Agreements) Regulations 1983, SI 1983/1553, as amended by SI 2004/1482). This means that the express terms must be set out in a prescribed order and various notices given, e.g. the notice of the right to cancel during the 'cooling-off' period. This document must be signed by both parties and a copy supplied to the debtor. Other formalities have been introduced through secondary legislation, e.g. the Consumer Credit (Disclosure of Information) Regulations 2004, SI 2004/1481, relating to information to be provided **before** the credit agreement is entered into.

Failure to comply with the formalities set out in the legislation may not be fatal to such an agreement but it will require a court order if the agreement is to be enforced (CCA 1974, s. 65(1)), and such an order will not be issued if the consumer did not sign the agreement, or did not receive a copy of the agreement or notice of his right to cancel. It was made clear in *McGuffick v Royal Bank of Scotland plc* [2009] EWHC 2386 (Comm), [2010] 1 All ER 634, [2010] 1 All ER (Comm) 48, that a creditor's rights and the debtor's liability to pay will continue to exist in the event of the unenforceability of a consumer credit agreement, at least where that unenforceability arises under s. 77(1) and (4). Section 77(1) requires a creditor to produce a copy of the executed agreement together with a statement of payments made and owing. If it fails to do so then the creditor is not entitled to enforce the agreement. This unenforceability was not the same as the total extinction of the rights under the consumer credit agreement so that, for example, a creditor can report the debtor to a credit reference agency in relation to the non-payment. The underlying purpose of these provisions is to provide protection for consumer debtors, in particular by providing them with information such as the details of the annual percentage rate charged for the credit, without permitting the formality requirement to become a technical defence operating to protect consumers against claims for non-payment. *McGuffick* may tip that balance slightly in favour of creditors since debtors in dispute as to formalities will need to continue to make payments or risk their credit status.

In *Wilson v First County Trust Ltd (No. 2)* [2003] UKHL 40, [2004] 1 AC 816, the question was whether a failure to comply with these legislative formalities in s. 60 of the CCA 1974, so that the court was barred from enforcing the agreement (s. 127(3)), amounted to an infringement under the Human Rights Act 1998 (see the discussion at 1.7). The Court of Appeal held that there was an infringement of the lender's rights under Art. 1 (protection of peaceful enjoyment of possessions), in this case the ability to enforce security for a debt, and under Art. 6 of the First Protocol of the Human Rights Convention (denial of a fair and public hearing to determine civil rights and obligations), which was scheduled to the 1998 Act. However, the House of Lords allowed the appeal by the Secretary of State for Trade and Industry on the basis, *inter alia,* that the agreement was made before the Act came into force and it could not have been Parliament's intention that the 1998 Act should have retrospective effect. In any event, s. 127(3) was not incompatible with Art. 6 since it did not prevent the court from determining whether or not the agreement was in fact enforceable. In addition, Art. 1 was not infringed since the underlying policy of the legislation was to protect consumers and Parliament was justified in these circumstances in depriving lenders of their usual rights of possession where those lenders failed to comply with the necessary formalities imposed to protect the consumer. (Subsequently s. 127(3) of the CCA 1974 was repealed by the CCA 2006, Sch. 4, para. 1 (in force since 6 April 2007).)

5.4.4.3 Distance-selling contracts

The Consumer Protection (Distance Selling) Regulations 2000, SI 2000/2334 (as amended by SI 2005/689), implemented the EC Distance Selling Directive 97/7/EC [1997] OJ L144/19. The regulations apply to any contract (except those excluded by reg. 5):

> concerning goods or services concluded between a supplier and a consumer under an organised distance sales or service provision scheme run by the supplier who, for the purposes of the contract, makes exclusive use of one or more means of distance communication up to and including the moment at which the contract is concluded. [Reg. 3(1).]

This includes contracts made by letter, press advertising with order forms, catalogues, telephone, fax, email, and Internet contracts.

Formalities are required for the conclusion of such contracts in that certain information must be given to the consumer prior to the conclusion of the contract (reg. 7(1)), such as the supplier's identity, price, delivery costs, and the existence of the right to cancel. This information can be given in a form 'appropriate to the means of distance communication used', e.g. telephone call or email. Regulation 8 requires much the same information to be given in writing or in another 'durable medium' (email should suffice, but a phone call would not) before or at the time of delivery of the goods or during the performance of the contract for services. The cancellation period is seven working days from the date of receipt of the goods or, in the case of services, from the date on which the contract was made (regs 11 and 12). In the case of services, the supplier must provide the consumer with information concerning how the right to cancel may be affected if the consumer agrees to performance commencing within the seven-day period following the conclusion of the contract. If that information is supplied before performance begins and the consumer agrees to performance commencing before the end of the cooling-off period then there is now no right to cancel. Certain contracts are excluded from the operation of the 2000 Regulations, namely contracts for the sale of an interest in land, including for construction of a building on land (although rental agreements are covered), financial services contracts, contracts concluded by means of automated machines, and contracts concluded at an auction.

The Proposal for a Directive on Consumer Rights, COM (2008) 614 final, 8 October 2008, which is part of the review of the consumer acquis, will strengthen consumer rights in relation to distance sales, e.g. the seven-day cooling-off period will be extended to fourteen days and there would be an extended definition of a distance sale thereby extending the scope of the consumer protection.

To some extent the 2000 Distance Selling Regulations overlap with the requirements imposed by regs 9 and 11 of the Electronic Commerce (EC Directive) Regulations 2002, SI 2002/2013 in the context of contracts concluded by electronic means (although the 2002 Regulations do not apply to contracts concluded by exchange of email). The service provider can be compelled to comply with the requirement in reg. 9(3) (terms and conditions to be provided in a way which allows the customer to store and reproduce them) and any other failure can result in an action for damages for breach of statutory duty. The customer has a right to rescind the contract if the service provider has not complied with reg. 11(1)(b) relating to information to allow the customer to identify and correct input errors.

More generally, enforcement of the consumer legislation is governed by Part 8 of the Enterprise Act 2002 and achieved via the securing of enforcement orders, normally by the Office of Fair Trading (OFT). In addition, it would appear that a failure to supply material information may constitute a misleading omission within reg. 6 of the Consumer Protection for Unfair Trading Regulations 2008, SI 2008/1277 and therefore constitute an offence under these regulations (reg. 10). There are specific rules contained in s. 218A of the Enterprise Act 2002 applicable to establishing evidence in relation to enforcement under that Act of infringements of the Unfair Trading Regulations.

5.4.4.4 Marine insurance contracts

By ss. 21 to 24 of the Marine Insurance Act 1906, a contract of marine insurance will not be admitted in evidence unless contained in a document ('policy') signed by the insurer. Thus, the whole contract must be in writing.

This is not strictly a condition of validity of such a contract, but only of its admissibility in evidence in trial proceedings. In fact, the contract itself is regarded as formed by assent given before the policy is drawn up. However, inadmissibility in evidence may be an insurmountable obstacle to enforcement.

5.4.4.5 Other instances

A bill of exchange must be in writing and signed (ss. 3(1) and 17(2) of the Bills of Exchange Act 1882). A typical example of a bill of exchange is a cheque (see **11.5.4**). If the instrument is not in writing, it will not be a bill of exchange and the usual characteristics of that instrument will be lost, e.g. negotiability.

A bill of sale is void unless made in a particular form (Bills of Sale Act (1878) Amendment Act 1882, s. 9). A bill of sale is a document recording a transaction transferring title to goods to someone else, but not possession (see s. 4 of the 1878 Act). The Acts of 1878 and 1882 were passed to prevent people obtaining credit on the security of goods which were in their possession but which they no longer owned.

5.4.5 Contracts required to be evidenced in writing

Contracts of guarantee are required to be evidenced in writing (Statute of Frauds 1677, s. 4). There must be 'some memorandum or note thereof' in writing, which is signed by the party to be charged. A guarantee is defined by s. 4 as a 'promise to answer for the debt, default or miscarriage of another person'. In other words, there is a promise by one person to meet the liabilities of another should that other become liable and fail to pay. It follows that it is considered appropriate to protect against alleged purely oral commitments to guarantee.

The definition of a guarantee is important because the formality rule is said not to apply to contracts of indemnity. Contracts of indemnity are defined as promises to pay for another whether or not there is liability on that other. Thus, in the case of indemnities the guarantor is taking on primary liability, whereas s. 4 applies only where the guarantor takes on secondary liability. However, this distinction has been subject to severe criticism (*Yeoman Credit Ltd v Latter* [1961] 1 WLR 828) and appears illogical in policy terms.

The s. 4 requirement continues to offer protection. In **Carlton Communications plc v The Football League** [2002] EWHC 1650 (Comm), 1 August 2002, it was claimed that Carlton and Granada, as shareholders of the parent company of ONdigital plc, were liable under an alleged guarantee for ONdigital's liabilities under a contract with the Football League. This argument failed because (1) there was no such guarantee, only a statement in a bid document that was 'subject to contract' and (2) there was no authority to give such a guarantee, and (3) even if there had been a guarantee, it would have been unenforceable under s. 4 of the Statute of Frauds 1677 because of the lack of a written document containing an unequivocal guarantee.

In **J. Pereira Fernandes SA v Mehta** [2006] EWHC 813 (Ch), [2006] 1 WLR 1543, the question was whether an email could satisfy the requirements of s. 4.

Mehta was a director of a company that had failed to pay for goods supplied by the Portuguese company. To settle the matter Mehta had sent an email offering a personal guarantee of £25,000 and repayment terms. The body of the email did not mention Mehta's name and there was no signature at the bottom. However, the service provider automatically indicated the email address of the sender in the email header of all messages sent and received. It was held that although (1) the email constituted a written memorandum of the guarantee for the purposes of s. 4 because it was in writing, the terms were clear and the evidence was that this offer had been accepted orally, (2) it could not satisfy the s. 4 requirements because the email contained no signature. The name of the sender inserted at the end of the body of the text would constitute a signature if it was clear that it had been inserted to give authenticity to the guarantee commitment; but the automatic insertion of the email address would not clearly be intended to operate as a signature, in the absence of evidence to the contrary, and could not suffice for these purposes because it was merely an 'incidental' inclusion. It followed that the guarantee was unenforceable.

The decision in **Mehta** seems correct on the facts and has contributed to some degree of clarity in relation to electronic contract formation since it is quite clearly the case that emails can satisfy any requirement for writing. It also provides guidance on satisfying any signature requirement.

The policy underlying s. 4 of the Statute of Frauds was confirmed by the House of Lords in **Actionstrength Ltd v International Glass Engineering SpA** [2003] UKHL 17, [2003] 2 AC 541 (discussed by Robertson (2003) 19 JCL 173) where a claim based on estoppel was made in an attempt to avoid the s. 4 formality requirement.

The alleged agreement was an oral agreement between the claimant (which was providing labour for International Glass) and Saint-Gobain Glass (for whom International Glass was building a factory) that in consideration of the claimant not withdrawing its labour from the site, Saint-Gobain would attempt to persuade International Glass to pay the claimant in full and on time, and failing this Saint-Gobain would withhold sums due to International Glass in order to pay the claimant directly. When the claimant sought to rely on this alleged oral agreement, Saint-Gobain claimed that the agreement amounted to a guarantee and was unenforceable since the s. 4 formalities had not been complied with. In response the claimant argued that Saint-Gobain was estopped from relying on s. 4 once the claimant had acted to its detriment on the faith of Saint-Gobain's oral promise.

The House of Lords could find no evidence for any estoppel in that there was no evidence that Saint-Gobain had represented either that there was no guarantee, or that the absence of writing would not be a problem. The only representation was the oral agreement, which was unenforceable in accordance with s. 4. In any event, their Lordships considered that to allow an argument based on estoppel would be inconsistent with the statute and would undermine its purpose. It would always be the case that the party seeking to enforce a guarantee would have performed first and would have acted to its detriment on the faith of the promise in the guarantee. Section 4 could not be defeated by an argument that the _unenforceable_ oral promise in the guarantee amounted to an _enforceable_ estoppel.

However, their Lordships considered that some estoppels might prevent reliance on the statutory formalities, e.g. if there was a representation that the statute would not be invoked or that the guarantee would be confirmed in writing.

5.4.6 Electronic signatures and the implications of e-commerce

5.4.6.1 Recognition of electronic signatures

Electronic signatures have been given legal recognition by the Electronic Communications Act 2000, s. 7 (implementing aspects of the Electronic Signatures Directive 1999/93/EC [2000] OJ L13/12). Section 7(1) refers to the admissibility of an electronic signature 'incorporated into or logically associated with a particular electronic communication or particular electronic data' and certification of that signature, as evidence in relation to the authenticity or integrity of the communication or data. In other words, an electronic signature may fulfil the same function as a hand-written signature in relation to electronic communications. This is vitally important for the effectiveness of Internet contracting. Authenticity is explained in s. 15(2) as relating to questions of whether the communication comes from that person, whether the communication is 'accurately timed and dated' and whether it is intended to have legal effect. The integrity issue relates to the question of whether the communication has been interfered with in any way. The Electronic Signatures Regulations 2002, SI 2002/318 provide for supervision and liability of 'certification-service-providers'.

The decision in *J. Pereira Fernandes SA v Mehta* [2006] EWHC 813 (Ch), [2006] 1 WR 1543 (see 5.4.5) has clarified the fact that signature can occur by including the sender's name in the email text provided it is clear that the name was intended to operate as a signature.

5.4.6.2 Facilitating the effectiveness of e-commerce

Section 8 of the Electronic Communications Act 2000 gives the Secretary of State the power by statutory instrument to remove restrictions in any other legislation which impede the effectiveness of electronic commerce (e.g., formalities, such as deeds or other writing, or a requirement that the post be used). In addition, Art. 9(1) of the E-Commerce Directive (2000/31/EC: see 2.4.2.3) provides that Member States must ensure that their legal system allows contracts to be concluded by electronic means, and that this means ensuring that any legal requirements which apply to the contractual process 'neither create obstacles for the use of electronic contracts nor result in such contracts being deprived of legal effectiveness and validity on account of their being made by electronic means'. Article 9(2) provides for various exceptions; in particular, Art. 9(2)(a) allows for exemptions in relation to 'contracts that create or transfer rights in real estate except for rental rights'. The problem with this is that it does not appear to exempt leases, so that, in future, leases may need to be capable of being created or transferred electronically. There is also an exemption in Art. 9(2)(c) for 'contracts of suretyship granted and on collateral securities furnished by persons acting for purposes outside their trade, business or profession', which would take some guarantees outside the electronic requirements. However, the provision specifies that the exemption will apply only if the guarantor was 'acting outside their trade, business or profession'. Therefore, business guarantees will also need to be capable of being effected electronically.

Although the E-Commerce Directive has been largely transposed by the Electronic Commerce (EC Directive) Regulations 2002, potential formalities conflicts were not addressed in time and the government instead gave a commitment to resolve any remaining legal obstacles to recognizing contracts concluded by electronic means. In December 2001 the Law Commission published its Advice on 'Electronic Commerce: Formal Requirements in Commercial Transactions' in which it concluded that it was only in 'very rare cases' that the statute formalities would conflict with the Art. 9 obligation but that where this was the case, for example the context of regulated agreements under the CCA 1974 where the copy of the executed agreement and notice of cancellation rights were required to be sent by post (CCA 1974, ss. 63 and 64), statutory revision could be effected to clarify the position. This apart, it was considered that requirements for 'writing' and 'signature' could generally be satisfied by emails and electronic signatures. Subsequently the Consumer Credit Act 1974 (Electronic Communications) Order 2004, SI 2004/3236, made the necessary changes to ss. 63(3) and 64(1) to allow for communication by an 'appropriate method', which includes the valid use of electronic communications if this has been agreed.

Changes to formalities in the context of registered land in order to set up an electronic system appear to go further than required by Art. 9. Section 91 of the Land Registration Act 2002 sets out the requirements for the framework to transfer and create interests in registered land by electronic means. The requirements specify that any relevant document in electronic form must contain the certified electronic signature of all persons authenticating the document. If the relevant conditions are met, this electronic document can be regarded as being in writing, as properly signed by all

194

persons whose electronic signature it contains, and by s. 91(5) it can take effect as a deed. This legislation is supplemented by the Land Registration (Electronic Conveyancing) Rules, SI 2008/1750.

5.5 Contractual capacity

The aim of the principles governing contractual capacity (ability to enter legally binding agreements) is to seek to balance the interests of those who are considered to need protection (in the form of a denial of capacity and hence the ability to contract) and the persons or firms who contract with them without knowledge of the relevant impediment.

5.5.1 Capacity of individuals

The paradigm of contractual capacity is embodied in the adult of sound mind, and any deviation from that state is cause to question a party's capacity to contract.

5.5.1.1 Mentally disordered and intoxicated persons

1. **Mental impairment**

The Mental Capacity Act 2005 governs the capacity of individuals. It provides that a person will lack capacity if he is 'unable to make a decision for himself in relation to the matter' at the time the contract is made (s. 2(1)). It does not matter whether the mental impairment is permanent or temporary (s. 2(2)). Section 3(1) describes the impairment in terms of the inability:

(a) to understand the information relevant to the decision,

(b) to retain that information,

(c) to use or weigh that information as part of the process of making the decision, or

(d) to communicate his decision (whether by talking, using sign language, or any other means).

The Act also provides for a Court of Protection applicable to those who lack capacity with the power to make declarations as to a person's capacity and ability to contract in specified situations (s. 15). There is also provision for lasting powers of attorney (s. 9 and the Lasting Powers of Attorney, Enduring Powers of Attorney and Public Guardian Regulations 2007, SI 2007/1253).

The mentally impaired person will remain liable to pay a reasonable price for 'necessaries' (s. 7(1)), which are defined as goods or services 'suitable to a person's condition of life and to his actual requirements at the time when the goods or services are supplied' (s. 7(2); see the Mental Capacity Act 2005 Code of Practice, para. 6.58 and the discussion of 'necessaries' in the context of minors' contracts, at **5.5.1.2**).

2. **Intoxicated persons and those whose understanding and awareness is otherwise impaired**

Where a person does not fall within the definition in this Act for mental impairment, but nevertheless it can be shown that at the time of contracting the person was incapable of understanding the nature of the actions in question or was intoxicated (*Matthews v Baxter* (1873) LR 8 Ex 132)

and the other contracting party knew or ought to have known of this at the relevant time (see *Imperial Loan Co. v Stone* [1892] 1 QB 599), the contract will be voidable (capable of being set aside by that party) subject to the usual rule concerning 'necessaries'. Where the other party does not know, or ought to have known of the mental impairment at the time of contracting, the contract will be binding and enforceable (**Hart v O'Connor** [1985] AC 1000: elderly man suffering from dementia).

5.5.1.2 Minors

A minor is a person under eighteen years of age. Contracts by minors are governed by a mix of common law and statutory rules, particularly the Minors' Contracts Act 1987.

A contract made by a minor is not void; and although the minor is not normally bound, the other party will be. There are, however, some exceptions to this principle, where the minor will be bound:

- contracts for necessaries
- those contracts which are binding on the minor *unless* repudiated by him before he reaches eighteen, or within a reasonable time of doing so (these might be referred to as 'voidable' contracts)
- if the minor to ratifies a non-binding contract on attaining his majority.

1. Contracts for necessaries

A minor must pay a reasonable sum for necessaries, defined by s. 3 of the Sale of Goods Act (SGA) 1979 as 'goods suitable to the condition in life of the minor…and to his actual requirements at the time of the sale'.

Necessaries are more than just what may be needed to keep body and soul together and reflect a minor's 'condition in life'. The classic case is *Nash v Inman* [1908] 2 KB 1.

In **Nash v Inman** the defendant, while still a minor, purchased clothing, including eleven fancy waist-coats, from the plaintiff. It was established that he already had a supply of clothing sufficient for his condition in life, and so the clothing purchased could not be regarded as necessaries.

The case illustrates the two difficulties inherent in the rule:

- The court has to make invidious judgments about what is appropriate to any particular 'condition of life'.
- More seriously, a salesperson may well be unable to judge, when confronted with a minor wishing to make a purchase, whether the good in question is a 'necessary' in the case of the particular minor.

The Law Commission once suggested that the concept of necessaries should be abandoned and replaced with a more narrowly defined concept of necessities (see Working Paper No. 81). This suggestion was not pursued by the final report (Law Com. No. 134).

Contracts of employment, of apprenticeship, or for instruction are also treated as contracts for necessaries. They are binding on minors unless more burdensome than beneficial (*Doyle v White City Stadium* [1935] 1 KB 110).

For example, in **De Francesco v Barnum** (1890) 45 ChD 430, the plaintiff brought an action for an injunction to prevent wrongful interference with his contract (under seal) with a minor who was apprenticed to him as a stage dancer. The contract provided that she was not to be paid unless actually employed by the apprentice master, and that she should not accept other employment without his consent. The girl took alternative employment with the defendant, and the plaintiff's action to restrain this interference in the contract of apprenticeship failed because the contract was invalid as unduly burdensome.

It is accepted that such contracts will contain onerous terms for minors. The rule is that such terms must not be out of proportion to the benefit accruing to the minor.

In the 'Wayne Rooney' case (***Proform Sports Management Ltd v Proactive Sports Management Ltd*** [2006] EWHC 2903 (Ch), [2007] Bus LR 93), the judge considered that the general rule applied rather than the exceptions so that the minor (Rooney) was not bound.

At the age of fifteen (i.e., when a minor) Wayne Rooney had entered into a player representation agreement with the claimant whereby the claimant company was to act as his executive agent and represent him. Rooney could not become a professional footballer until he reached seventeen (FA Rules) but was employed as a trainee. The claimant alleged that the defendant had also entered into a player representation agreement with Rooney whilst its contract was still operating. The claimant therefore brought an action against the defendant for unlawful interference with and/or procuring the breach of its contract with Rooney. The judge held:

(a) The agreement was not enforceable against Rooney as he was a minor and the general rule was that contracts were voidable at his option.

(b) The contract was not analogous to a contract for necessaries and could not be analogous to a contract of apprenticeship, education, or service (which would generally be enforceable against a minor) since Rooney was already with a football club and could not yet become a professional footballer. Therefore the contract with the agent did not enable him to earn a living or advance his skills.

It followed that the defendant could not be liable for the tort of inducing the breach of contract since this contract was voidable at the option of the person alleged to have been induced.

The liability of minors to pay for necessaries has generally been regarded as resting not on contract but on quasi-contract: it is payment for a benefit received. It follows that, an executory contract (i.e., unperformed) for necessaries would be unenforceable against a minor. The wording of s. 3 of the SGA 1979 is consistent with that conclusion. In the case of contracts of employment, however, the rule may be different.

In *Roberts v Gray* [1913] 1 KB 520, the defendant entered a contract to work for the plaintiff in what would today be called a billiards 'circus'. The defendant was still a minor. Shortly before the tour began the defendant withdrew, in breach of his contract. The plaintiff brought an action on the contract to recover expenses incurred in preparation for the tour. The contract was found to be enforceable against the minor although still executory.

2. Contracts valid unless repudiated at majority

Certain contracts made by minors are voidable but become valid when the minor attains majority unless repudiated at that time.

The rules governing these contracts are unaffected by the Minors' Contracts Act 1987, and such contracts continue to be governed by the common law rules. The most common types of contract within this category are contracts to acquire either shares in a company, or an interest in land. In each case, what is acquired is an enduring benefit to which certain obligations attach. To be effective, the repudiation must be accompanied by a surrender of the interest in question (see *North Western Railway v McMichael* (1850) 5 Ex 114). The contract must be repudiated either before attaining majority or within a reasonable time of attaining majority, although what is a reasonable time is a question of fact in each case (see *Edwards v Carter* [1893] AC 360). Money actually paid is not recoverable in such a case, except where there has been a total failure of consideration (see **Steinberg v Scala (Leeds) Ltd** [1923] 2 Ch 452).

3. Contracts ratified on reaching majority

Despite the general rule that other contracts are not binding on the minor, since the rule exists to protect minors and not to prevent contracts, following the repeal of s. 2 of the Infants Relief Act 1874, **the minor can choose to ratify the contract, expressly or impliedly, on reaching eighteen**.

Other contracts

Contracts which are not for 'necessaries' and which are not validated are unenforceable against the minor, although they are binding on the other party. Nevertheless, property may pass from the minor to the other party under them (*Chaplin v Leslie Frewin (Publishers) Ltd* [1965] 3 All ER 764). Moreover, the minor may not recover property or money which has passed under an unenforceable contract, except in circumstances where such recovery would be available to a person of full contractual capacity, such as total failure of consideration. Since property also passes to the minor under such contracts, in the case of contracts for goods such failure will not occur (*Rowland v Divall* [1923] 2 KB 500).

By contrast, there is the possibility of recovering property, which has passed under the unenforceable contract from the other party to the minor.

Restitutionary remedy against minors

Before the Minors' Contracts Act 1987, restitution was available against a minor in the case of fraud or in quasi-contract for so-called 'waiver of tort' (*Bristow v Eastman* (1794) 1 Esp 172). These rules are preserved by s. 3(2) of the 1987 Act, but are less favourable to a party seeking restitution against a minor than the discretionary rule introduced by s. 3(1). The provision will particularly benefit traders who supply goods to minors on credit, and who are then unable to obtain payment because the contract is unenforceable by virtue of the minor's age. (Of course, minors are not able to acquire a credit card so that the practical instances of acquiring goods on credit may be extremely limited.)

Under s. 3(1), the court may order the minor to return the property acquired if it is just and equitable to do so. 'Property' is not defined in this section, and so it is not clear whether it includes money obtained under such a contract. However, s. 3(1) applies to property acquired or any property representing it, and if property acquired has been converted into something else it is likely to have been converted into money. If that may be recovered under the Act, it would be strange if money acquired directly could not be. Another difficulty with the notion of property representing property acquired under the contract is where the proceeds are money, and it has been paid into a bank account from which withdrawals have been made, or where other goods have been purchased the value of which is greater than merely the proceeds of the property originally acquired. No doubt the resolution of these problems will be clouded by the exercise of the court's discretion over whether to order restitution at all.

Misrepresentation of age

A difficult problem arises where the minor represents that they are of full age. The law's policy of protecting minors still applies, so that the contract is unenforceable. It would be undesirable, however, for the minor to take advantage of their own wrongdoing. A rule of equity therefore requires the minor to restore goods acquired. The same rule cannot provide for the repayment of money loaned.

> In *R. Leslie Ltd v Sheill* [1914] 3 KB 607, when still a minor the defendant had borrowed £400 from the plaintiff moneylenders, but had misrepresented that he was of the age of contractual capacity. The plaintiffs brought an action to recover the principal sum and interest. The plaintiffs were unable to obtain restitution because that would have been equivalent to enforcing the contract which was not possible.

Where goods are acquired and sold, the proceeds of sale may be recovered by a tracing remedy (*Stocks v Wilson* [1913] 2 KB 235).

5.5.2 Companies incorporated under the Companies Act and limited liability partnerships

5.5.2.1 A company incorporated under the Companies Act

A company incorporated under the Companies Act 1985 has separate corporate personality, i.e. it is a legal entity independent of the identity of its respective members (see **Salomon v A. Salomon & Co. Ltd** [1897] AC 22). (This can be compared with general partnerships, which have no separate legal capacity and whose contracts are governed by general agency principles.) The capacity of the company to contract is therefore a separate question to the capacity of the individual owners or directors to bind the company when making contracts.

A company which acts outside the limitations of its constitution is said to be acting *ultra vires* (outside its capacity). Traditionally contracts which were *ultra vires* the company were held to be void (*Ashbury Railway Carriage and Iron Co. v Riche* (1875) LR 7 HL 653). The company's constitution is now contained in its articles of association (s. 17) and s. 31 provides that unless the articles specifically restrict the company's objects these objects will be unrestricted, thereby limiting the possibility of *ultra vires* action. In any event, s. 39 of the Companies Act 2006 removes the possibility for *ultra vires* in the external sense by stating that the validity of a company's acts is not to be questioned on the ground of lack of capacity because of anything in the company's constitution (i.e., the company's articles of association). Section 40 of the Companies Act 2006 protects persons 'dealing with a company in good faith' from being affected by the existence of any internal constitutional controls on the power of the directors to bind the company when making contracts. Persons dealing with the company in good faith need not be concerned about whether the directors are acting within the terms of the company's constitution. Such contracts will be valid and enforceable. *Ultra vires* is therefore only likely to have any relevance in terms of the internal relationship between the shareholders and the company (s. 40(4) and (5)).

5.5.2.2 Limited liability partnerships

Limited liability partnerships are bodies corporate (s. 1(2) of the Limited Liability Partnerships Act 2000), i.e. they have separate legal personality and they also have unlimited capacity (s. 1(3)). The power of members to bind the limited liability partnership is governed by agency principles (s. 6 of the Limited Liability Partnerships Act 2000).

5.5.3 DCFR and capacity

Issues of legal capacity are outside the scope of the DCFR, 1–1:101 and II-7:101.

Further reading

Intention to be legally bound

Brown, 'The letter of comfort: Placebo or promise?' [1990] JBL 281.

Hedley, 'Keeping contract in its place: *Balfour v Balfour* and the enforceability of informal agreements' (1985) 5 OJLS 391.

Hepple, 'Intention to create legal relations' [1970] CLJ 122.

Formalities

Robertson, 'The Statute of Frauds, equitable estoppel and the need for "something more"' (2003) 19 JCL 173.

Part 2

Content, interpretation, performance, and breach

The essence of a bilateral contract is the existence of obligations owed by each contracting party to the other. Most disputes about contracts, and in turn most litigation, are not concerned with whether a contract has come into existence, but involve questions relating to the performance and construction of the obligations created by the contract.

- Has a relevant pre-contractual statement become one of the 'promises' of the contract? (6.1)

- Are the parties subject to obligations other than those expressed in the terms of their agreement? (6.4)

- What standard of performance is demanded? (8.2.1.1)

- How is a particular obligation to be interpreted? (Chapter 6B)

- What are the consequences of breach of the terms of the contract? (8.4.2)

- Is it possible to avoid the consequences of breach? (Chapter 7)

All these questions are extremely important and are examined in Part 2 of this book (Chapters 6 to 8).

There is a further relevant consideration when examining whether it is possible to avoid the consequences of breach:

- What happens to the parties' obligations if, after the contract is made, some event occurs which is outside the control of the parties, but which makes further performance impossible? Does this provide an excuse for non-performance?

This question relates to the application of the doctrine of frustration (Chapter 12) and since this concerns the question of the contractual allocation of risk and how the law responds to impossibility, the discussion is deferred until examining impossibility in general (Chapters 12 and 13).

Content of the contract and principles of interpretation

Summary of the issues

This chapter examines how the terms of the parties' agreement are identified, i.e. how we identify the contractual promises to be performed, and assesses how the courts interpret the meaning of those terms.

- **The first issue relates to the status of statements made prior to the conclusion of the contract and why this matters.** Have those statements been incorporated as terms, are they misrepresentations (false statements of fact inducing the contract: see Chapter 14), or are they contractual terms? This depends on the intentions of the parties, as objectively ascertained, and whether they intended that any binding promise was being made as to the truth of the statement. The courts have developed a number of guidelines to assist in determining the parties' intentions.

- **If the alleged contact is in writing, the issues relate to whether that writing represents the parties' contract or whether there are other oral or written terms.** The parol evidence rule provides that where the contract is written, that writing represents the complete contract. However, this definition allows the rule to be sidestepped by defining the contract as partly written and partly oral. Alternatively, any oral terms can take effect as a collateral contract, which is separate to any written contract to which the parol evidence rule applies. However, entire agreement clauses are a common feature of contracts. Such clauses provide that the parties have not relied on any term (contractual promise) which is not contained in the written contract. Therefore entire agreement clauses prevent arguments that there are oral terms and/or that a collateral contract exists.

- **Terms must be incorporated into the contract** (and establishing incorporation is the first requirement to be able to rely on an exemption clause: see Chapter 7). Incorporation can be achieved by signature, although the consequences of such a principle can be harsh. Alternatively, incorporation can be achieved by notice. Reasonable steps must be taken to bring the existence of the term to the other party's attention before or at the time of contracting, and the term in question must be contained in a document which would be expected to contain contractual terms. If the term is onerous or unusual a higher standard of incorporation is required. Alternatively, if, for example, notice has been given too late on this occasion, it may still be possible for a term to be incorporated on the basis of a consistent course of dealing between the parties or on the basis of their common understanding.

- **Terms may be implied into contracts from custom, by statute (e.g., terms imposing obligations on sellers of goods contained in the Sale of Goods Act (SGA) 1979) or by the courts.** Courts imply terms in fact, i.e. to give effect to the intentions of the parties on the basis of necessity. On the other hand, some terms are implied in law into all contracts of a particular type as a 'necessary incident' of that category of contracts.

• The interpretation of contracts is of considerable practical importance and the applicable principles were set out in the speech of Lord Hoffmann in Investors *Compensation Scheme Ltd v West Bromwich Building Society*. In general terms, there has been a movement away from a literal interpretation of contracts. In the past it was generally only possible to go outside the document and examine the wider context in which the contract was made where there was some ambiguity in the words used. However, in *West Bromwich* Lord Hoffmann confirmed that it is appropriate to consider the wider 'matrix of fact' and to adopt a construction which makes 'business common sense', i.e. a more purposive approach. Although this may be the price to be paid for achieving an interpretation conforming to an objective view of the parties' actual intentions in the circumstances, there have been fears that this new approach is too uncertain and leaves too much discretion to the judges, e.g. how is the 'matrix of fact' to be defined? A particular concern in recent case law, however, has been whether the principle that pre-contractual negotiations are generally inadmissible for the purposes of contract interpretation can be sustained in the post *West Bromwich* context.

6A Content

6.1 Pre-contractual statements: Terms or mere representations?

6.1.1 Introduction

The important question here is whether pre-contractual statements (which are often oral) have become terms of the contract.

Pre-contractual statements are of three types:

- puffs
- representations
- terms.

The most common type of puff is the advertising gimmick. Puffs are statements which give rise to no legal consequences. They are statements which are not meant to be taken literally and there is no intention to be legally bound (see 5.2.2.1). *Carlill v Carbolic Smoke Ball Co.* [1893] 1 QB 256 is an example of an advertising gimmick where the statement was more than a puff, because there was evidence of an intention to be bound in the company's statement that £1,000 had been deposited with its bank.

6.1.2 Why distinguish representations and terms?

The basic distinction between a representation and a term is that a term involves a promise as to the truth of the statement, whereas a representation involves no such promise as to truth, although the statement in question does induce the making of the contract.

Both representations and terms give rise to legal consequences if the representation is false (misrepresentation, discussed in Chapter 14) or if the term is broken (breach of contract, discussed in Chapter 8). It is significant, however, that the legal consequences for misrepresentation and breach of contract are not the same.

Prior to the mid-1960s, the distinction between representations and terms was vitally important, because the remedy of damages for misrepresentation could be obtained only if it was established that the misrepresentation was fraudulent. Therefore, it was often vital to establish that a false pre-contractual statement was a term. However, since the House of Lords decision in *Hedley Byrne & Co. Ltd v Heller & Partners Ltd* [1964] AC 465 (see 14.4.3.1) and, in particular, the Misrepresentation Act 1967, damages have been available for non-fraudulent misrepresentations.

Nevertheless, there is still a distinction between a claim for misrepresentation and for breach of contract in relation to both the ability to claim damages and, more especially in a practical context, the measure of those damages.

6.1.2.1 The ability to claim damages

There is an automatic right to claim damages on proof of a breach of a term of the contract (see 8.4.1), whereas damages for misrepresentation may be *claimed* only on proof of fault (i.e., where the statement maker was fraudulent or negligent in making the statement). Damages cannot be **claimed** for innocent misrepresentation, although they may be awarded at the discretion of the court (Misrepresentation Act 1967, s. 2(2): see 14.6.5).

6.1.2.2 The different measure of damages

The most important distinction, however, remains the different measure of damages. In the event of a breach of contract, the normal measure of damages will be the expectation measure, i.e. the claimant is put into the position that the claimant would have been in had the contract been properly performed (and the breach not occurred) (see 9.2). On the other hand, the measure of damages for misrepresentation is tortious, i.e. it aims to put the claimant into the position that the claimant would have been in had the contract not been made (see 14.6).

This is not the only difference in terms of measure of damages, since the ability to recover for losses (the remoteness rule) is also very different, at least in terms of comparing typical claims. The applicable remoteness rule in the context of a claim for breach of contract (*Hadley v Baxendale* (1854) 9 Exch 341: see 9.9.2) is much stricter because it requires that the loss in question be within the reasonable contemplation of the parties when they made the contract as the probable result of its breach, and the interpretation of this principle by some members of the House of Lords (Lords Hoffmann and Hope) in *Transfield Shipping Inc. v Mercator Shipping Inc.* [2008] UKHL 48, [2009] 1 AC 61 (see 9.9.2.7), may mean it is stricter still in terms of the losses that a party in breach is likely to be responsible for. Lords Hoffmann and Hope considered that a party in breach should be responsible only for those losses in contract for which that party had assumed responsibility. By comparison, the remoteness rule for fraudulent misrepresentation (and under s. 2(1) of the Misrepresentation Act 1967 for negligent misrepresentation) is considerably more generous (although controversial in the context of negligent misrepresentation) from the perspective of the injured party, since all direct loss, regardless of foreseeability, is recoverable (14.6.2.1 and 14.6.4.1).

This difference between a contractual measure and the measure in either the tort of deceit or when seeking damages under s. 2(1) of the Misrepresentation Act 1967 may therefore be an important one where there are a number of consequential losses resulting from the making of a false pre-contractual statement. In such circumstances, and despite the need to plead fault in relation to a misrepresentation claim, recovery of damages for misrepresentation may be preferable to seeking to recover in a claim for breach of contract, where such losses may be too remote to be recovered.

6.1.3 Making the distinction between representations and terms

The test of whether a representation has become a term is very imprecise. It is essentially a question of the statement maker's intention, as objectively judged (see 2.1; and Lightman J in *Inntrepreneur Pub Co. v East Crown Ltd* [2000] 2 Lloyd's Rep 611 at p. 615).

 Question

> Was it the statement maker's intention to make a binding promise as to the truth of their statement so that if the statement were inaccurate it would result in automatic breach of the contract (see *Heilbut, Symons and Co. v Buckleton* [1913] AC 30)?

Another way of putting this question is simply to ask whether the intention of the statement maker was to guarantee the truth of their statement.

The problem is that there is often very little external evidence from which to identify this intention. In addition, there is an added complexity in the case law, because a statement can also amount to a contractual promise on the basis that it is a collateral warranty: a promise that reasonable care and skill has been exercised, as opposed to a guarantee of a particular result.

6.1.3.1 The guiding principles to assist in determining intention

Although the existence of the intention necessary for a statement to be incorporated into the contract as a term is regarded as a question of fact, some guiding principles emerge from examination of the cases.

As a starting point, where the agreement between the parties has been reduced into writing soon after the statement was made, and the statement is not part of the writing, there is a not unnatural presumption that the statement was not intended to be part of the contract (*Heilbut, Symons and Co. v Buckleton* [1913] AC 30). Lightman J in *Inntrepreneur v East Crown* went as far as referring to this as a '*prima facie* assumption…that the written contract includes all the terms the parties wanted to be binding between them'. Lightman J also stressed that 'the longer the interval' between the statement and the contract, 'the greater the presumption must be that the parties did not intend the statement to have contractual effect'.

However, this 'presumption' can be rebutted by reference to specific guidelines. The guidelines are a helpful starting point but, as Lord Moulton warned in *Heilbut Symons and Co. v Buckleton* [1913] AC 30, they cannot be decisive on the question of the parties' intentions:

> [T]hey cannot be said to furnish decisive tests, because it cannot be said as a matter of law that the presence or absence of those features is conclusive of the intention of the parties. The intention of the parties can only be deduced from the totality of the evidence and no secondary principles of such a kind can be universally true.

Unfortunately, the application of these guidelines does not always lead to the predicted result, and it is submitted that this is because the courts have generally tended to focus on only *one* of these guidelines instead of applying them all to a particular set of facts (although compare the decision in *Pritchard v Cook & Red Ltd*, unreported, 4 June 1998). Although the statement in *Dick Bentley Productions Ltd v Harold Smith (Motors) Ltd* [1965] 1 WLR 623 (see 6.1.3.4) was held to amount to a term because of the special knowledge of the statement maker, it was also the case that the buyer had made it clear that he wished to purchase a 'well vetted' car, so that the 'importance attached' test would also appear to have been satisfied.

6.1.3.2 Accepting responsibility or advising on verification

If the statement maker accepts responsibility for the truth of a statement, the statement is likely to be regarded as a term, because in accepting responsibility the statement maker is guaranteeing its truth (*Schawel v Reade* [1913] 2 IR 81: the plaintiff stopped examining a horse when told by the defendant that the horse was sound and that there was no need to continue the examination). On the other hand, if the statement maker asks or advises the other to check the reliability of the statement, e.g. by recommending that a survey be carried out or that the accounts be examined, that statement should be interpreted as a representation, because in such circumstances that person cannot be making a binding promise that the statement is true (*Ecay v Godfrey* (1947) 80 Lloyd's Rep 286: the defendant had asked the plaintiff if he would be having the motor cruiser surveyed so that the defendant could not be accepting responsibility for its condition).

6.1.3.3 Importance attached test

If it is made clear that the statement was so important to the recipient that the recipient would not have contracted had that statement not been made, that statement is likely to be interpreted as a term (or binding promise that the statement is true). It is important to appreciate that it is not merely a matter of the importance of the statement to the recipient; it must also be the case that this importance is clear to the statement maker before the statement is made, either because the recipient expressly makes the importance clear or because its significance is clear from the circumstances of contracting.

> In *Bannerman v White* (1861) 10 CB NS 844, the defendant asked whether sulphur had been used in the production of hops he was considering buying, stating that he was not interested in buying them if it had. He was assured that no sulphur had been used. However, the hops were found to contain sulphur, and the defendant claimed to be entitled to reject them, arguing that this amounted to a breach of term (i.e., breach of contract). His argument prevailed. Without the false statement there would have been no contract. This meant that the statement was not merely a pre-contractual inducement but amounted to a description of the subject matter of the sale, and was thus a term.

An appropriate general test would therefore be to ask whether the statement maker is taking personal responsibility for the statement. Where the term satisfies the importance attached test, it will be a factor indicating such personal responsibility. This can be seen in *Pritchard v Cook & Red Ltd*, unreported, 4 June 1998.

> The plaintiff had purchased a rally car from the defendant after having asked to see the specification for the car. The defendant had produced the specification, which had been supplied to him by the car's manufacturer, after copying the details onto his own headed notepaper. The written contract made no reference to this technical specification. Since the car did not accord with the specification, the plaintiff claimed damages, alleging breach of contract.

The Court of Appeal held that the technical specification was a term of the contract on the importance attached test, i.e. the plaintiff had specifically asked to see it and the evidence was that he would not have purchased the car without these details contained in the specification. By copying the specification onto his own headed notepaper, the defendant had taken personal responsibility for its accuracy.

6.1.3.4 Statement maker's special knowledge of the subject matter

Where the person making the statement has special knowledge of the subject matter of the contract, or holds himself out as having such knowledge, the courts may be more willing to treat the statement as a term of the contract. A party may hold himself out as having special knowledge by suggesting that there is no need to check the accuracy of the statement made (*Schawel v Reade* [1913] 2 IR 81). Thus, the guidelines can overlap in terms of pointing to the same outcome.

The relevance of special knowledge is well illustrated by contrasting two cases in which material facts about second-hand cars were falsely stated.

In *Oscar Chess Ltd v Williams* [1957] 1 WLR 370, a private seller represented his car to be a 1948 Morris. It was in fact a 1939 version of the same model, worth substantially less. The statement of the car's age was held not to be a term. The private seller had no special knowledge and had relied on the registration book for his belief. In addition, the buyers in this case were car dealers and were therefore in at least as good a position to discover the truth of the statement.

Therefore, the private seller did not assume any personal responsibility for the statement.

In *Dick Bentley Productions Ltd v Harold Smith (Motors) Ltd* [1965] 1 WLR 623, a car dealer stated that a car had an engine which had done only 20,000 miles. This was in fact untrue. The buyer sought damages alleging breach of contract. The statement as to mileage was treated as a term.

The apparent distinction between the cases is the status of the person making the representation. A private seller did not have the special knowledge which indicated an intention that the statement be treated as a contractually binding promise, but a car dealer did. In *Dick Bentley Productions Ltd v Harold Smith (Motors) Ltd* this distinction led Lord Denning MR to suggest that the presence of fault was the basis for the distinction. However, it seems wrong to suggest that fault is the only test, and arguably what Lord Denning was stating was simply that, on the facts, the obligation broken was an obligation to exercise reasonable care and skill. **The true test ought therefore to be that the dealer was in a better position to discover the truth and therefore impliedly took personal responsibility for the truth of statements made.**

It was argued in *Pritchard v Cook & Red Ltd* (see 6.1.3.3) that the defendant in that case was selling in a personal capacity and that *Oscar Chess v Williams* therefore applied to any statements made. However, the Court of Appeal distinguished *Oscar Chess* on the basis that in that case the seller had indicated that his statement was derived from the registration book so that he could not be taking personal responsibility for it. However, in *Pritchard v Cook & Red Ltd*, the defendant had clearly taken personal responsibility for the manufacturer's specification by copying it onto his own paper and not issuing a disclaimer.

6.1.4 Collateral warranties

In the past, before the time when damages were available in cases of non-fraudulent misrepresentation, it was frequently argued that a non-fraudulent pre-contractual statement was a term giving rise to liability in damages on the basis that it was a 'collateral warranty'. Whereas a statement is normally classified as a term on the basis that the intention is to guarantee the truth of the statement, the 'collateral warranty' is an implied promise that reasonable care and skill has been employed in making the statement. Such a promise will most frequently be implied where the statement in question is a forecast, made by an expert or other person with special knowledge of the subject matter. It follows that the courts have been able to treat such forecasts as contractual terms and impose liability in breach where the promise is broken (i.e., where there has been a failure to exercise reasonable care and skill).

In **Heilbut, Symons and Co. v Buckleton** [1913] AC 30, the House of Lords had stated that the courts should not be quick to find such collateral warranties, and that there must be clear evidence of an intention that the statements made should have contractual force. Despite these strictures, the courts have found the collateral warranty to be a useful device for achieving what they believed to be a just result, particularly in the period before damages for negligent mis-representation became available. In **Dick Bentley v Harold Motors** (above), the Court of Appeal held that the car dealer's statement amounted to a collateral warranty, giving rise to a remedy of damages as reasonable care and skill had not been taken in making the statement about the car's mileage.

In **Esso Petroleum Co. Ltd v Mardon** [1976] QB 801 the Court of Appeal held that a forecast by a person with forty years' experience of the potential throughput of a petrol station, which was intended to induce the defendant to take a tenancy of that petrol station, amounted to a collateral warranty that the forecast had been given using reasonable care and skill. The Court of Appeal also held that the forecast amounted to a negligent misstatement (see **14.4.3.1**).

Thus, when a person with special knowledge of the subject matter makes a statement, that statement is likely to be interpreted as a contractual promise on the basis that it constitutes a collateral warranty rather than because it can be said to be a guarantee of truth or result.

6.1.5 Conclusion

It is difficult to predict with absolute certainty which pre-contractual statements will be incorporated as terms and which will be regarded only as representations. It is hard to resist the conclusion that the courts enjoy the element of discretion which the current vague guidelines provide, and would not like to see them replaced by anything more certain. The basic test of contractual intention allows the court to pick and choose those representations which are to have contractual status without reference to tight identifiable criteria. Predictability suffers as a consequence of this rule, but it may be a price we are willing to pay for the element of fairness it may import.

6.2 Written contracts

6.2.1 The parol evidence rule

If a contract is wholly in writing, there is no difficulty in ascertaining its express terms—although there may be difficulties interpreting them (see discussion at **6B** below). However, a situation can arise where, although there is a written document, one party alleges that this is not the whole contract and that there is either some orally agreed term, or a term in some other written document. Thus, it is claimed that this first written document does not contain the entire contract.

Key point

The parol evidence rule states that *if the contract is written* then that writing is the whole contract and the parties cannot adduce extrinsic evidence, and especially oral evidence, to 'add to, vary or contradict that writing' (e.g., *Henderson v Arthur* [1907] 1 KB 10).

A related rule prevents, as a general principle, use of extrinsic evidence of negotiations and subsequent conduct to prove the meaning of words used in a written contract (see **6B**).

In disallowing any terms other than those recorded in writing, the parol evidence rule contributes greatly to contractual certainty, since others can rely on the written document as representing the entire agreement between the parties. Nevertheless, this can be achieved at the expense of apparent justice, since it may be clear that further terms have been agreed but have not been included in the writing. For this reason, the courts developed a series of exceptions to the rule, to the extent that it can no longer be said that the general rule is that extrinsic evidence is inadmissible to prove further terms (unless the contract contains an entire agreement clause: see **6.2.1.4**). It is clear that the parol evidence rule applies only to express terms, and does not operate to prevent the implication of terms into the contract (see **6.4**). Neither does it operate to prevent proof by extrinsic evidence of such defects in the contract as mistake (see **Chapter 3**) and misrepresentation (see Chapter 14).

Thus, in addition to parol evidence being admitted in order to imply terms, it can also be admitted in the following situations.

6.2.1.1 Rectification

Rectification is an equitable remedy which allows a document to be revised where there has been a transcription mistake in recording in writing a previous oral agreement (see **3.4.1**). Rectification could not apply without the existence of an exception to the parol evidence rule, since extrinsic evidence must be introduced to prove the content of the original oral agreement.

6.2.1.2 Contract partly written and partly oral

If it is held that the contract was intended to be partly written and partly oral, this necessarily means that it is not a wholly written contract, and therefore the parol evidence rule does not apply. It is perfectly permissible to introduce extrinsic evidence of oral terms in order to determine whether the contract is a contract wholly in writing to which the parol evidence rule applies. This means that the parol evidence rule has little substance, since it can always be avoided by introducing evidence of oral terms and concluding that the contract is not a written one. This led Professor Wedderburn ([1959] CLJ 58) to conclude that the rule was no more than a 'self evident tautology', i.e. it is always true.

In *J. Evans & Son (Portsmouth) Ltd v Andrea Merzario Ltd* [1976] 1 WLR 1078, the parties had been doing business together for some time. The plaintiffs shipped goods on trailers with the defendants, the trailers always being stored below deck on the ship. The defendants wanted to change to container transport, and the plaintiffs would agree to the change only if the containers were also shipped below deck. The defendants gave an oral assurance to that effect. However, the written contract purported to allow the defendants complete freedom in the handling and transportation of the goods. One container was stored on deck, and while in transit fell into the sea.

The Court of Appeal had no doubt that there had been a breach of contract. As Roskill LJ stated, where the contract is partly written and partly oral, 'The court is entitled to look at and should look at all the evidence from start to finish in order to see what the bargain was that was struck between the parties.'

Significantly, having accepted evidence that there was an oral term (or promise) that the goods would be shipped below deck, the Court of Appeal also held that the oral term overrode the inconsistent term of the written contract (allowing the defendants complete freedom in determining transportation of the goods). This was also the approach taken by the Court of Appeal in *Couchman v Hill* [1947] KB 554, where an oral assurance that a heifer was 'unserved' was held to override an exemption printed in the auctioneers' catalogue to the effect that there was to be no responsibility for the correct description, or any fault or defect in a lot.

6.2.1.3 Collateral contract

The courts have also been willing to allow the use of collateral contracts to sidestep the parol evidence rule. **The parol evidence rule will apply to the written contract but** where there is an oral promise which exists in parallel, the court may conclude that the oral promise is enforceable as a second (or collateral) oral contract. The promise can be enforceable as a contract since the consideration for the promise is the making of the main written contract. **Since this collateral contract is a separate *oral* contract, the parol evidence rule cannot apply to it.**

In theory, such a contract will be found to exist only if the promise it is alleged to contain is independent of the subject matter of the major contract (*Mann v Nunn* (1874) 30 LT 526). Equally, a collateral contract is supposed not to contradict the terms of the major contract (*Henderson v Arthur* [1907] 1 KB 10). Nevertheless, it seems clear that the courts have not allowed these limitations to restrict the operation of this device as a means of avoiding the parol evidence rule.

In ***City and Westminster Properties (1934) Ltd v Mudd*** [1959] Ch 129, a representation was made that a landlord would not enforce a covenant in a lease preventing the tenant from residing in the premises. The tenant would not have entered into the contract without that assurance. The oral assurance was held to be a contractual promise (on the basis of the importance attached test). The court found this promise to have been incorporated in a separate collateral contract, overriding the inconsistent covenant against residence contained in the main contract.

Lord Denning in the Court of Appeal in ***J. Evans & Son (Portsmouth) Ltd v Andrea Merzario Ltd*** [1976] 1 WLR 1078, concluded that the oral assurance (that goods would only be shipped below deck) constituted a separate collateral contract inducing the written contract and that the oral term of the collateral contract overrode the inconsistent term of the main written contract, which had allowed the defendants complete freedom in the handling and transportation of the goods.

6.2.1.4 The effect of an entire agreement clause

It should be possible to avoid the kind of argument which prevailed in ***City and Westminster Properties (1934) Ltd v Mudd*** and ***J. Evans & Son (Portsmouth) Ltd v Andrea Merzario Ltd*** by inserting what is known as an 'entire agreement clause' in the written agreement.

Key point

An entire agreement clause states that the document is intended and agreed to contain the entirety of the contract between the parties, and each party acknowledges that it has not relied upon any promise or undertaking in entering into the agreement which is not expressly contained in the written document.

The inclusion of such a clause ought to be sufficient to indicate the parties' intentions on the matter, namely that the contract is a purely written contract to which the parol evidence rule applies, so that it is not possible to adduce evidence of alleged oral terms in order to add to, vary, or contradict the written document. Certainly, the inclusion of such a clause should operate to prevent an allegation that the contract is partly written and partly oral. However, it had been suggested in *Chitty on Contracts,* 28th edn (Sweet and Maxwell, 1999), Vol. 1, at para. [12–102], that such a clause would not prevent extrinsic evidence of a collateral contract or warranty because 'the parol evidence rule does not extend to such cases'. Nevertheless, it is submitted that there can be only one purpose behind the inclusion of such a clause, and this was acknowledged by Lightman J in *Inntrepreneur Pub Co. v East Crown Ltd* [2000] 2 Lloyd's Rep 611.

In *Inntrepreneur v East Crown*, the claimant sought to enforce a covenant in a lease for a public house against the defendant. By the terms of this covenant the defendant had agreed to purchase its supply of beer from the claimant (a 'beer tie'). The defendant alleged that a collateral warranty had been given by the claimant whereby it had agreed to release the tie by 28 March 1998, and so the defendant counterclaimed that there was no such tie in existence after this date. One of the defences of the claimant to this allegation was that the contract contained an entire agreement clause, and the question was whether the clause prevented the defendant from relying on the alleged collateral warranty.

Lightman J held (following *Deepak Fertilisers and Petrochemical Corporation v Davy McKee (London) Ltd* [1999] 1 Lloyd's Rep 387) that even if a collateral warranty could be established, it was deprived of legal effect by the entire agreement clause. The clause made it clear that the terms which the parties had agreed to were only those contained in the written agreement.

Lightman J stated (at p. 614) that 'any promises or assurances made in the course of the negotiations (which, in the absence of such a clause, might have effect as a collateral warranty) shall have no contractual force save in so far as they are reflected and given effect in that document'. The clause precluded a party to a written agreement 'from threshing through the undergrowth and finding, in the course of negotiations, some (chance) remark or statement (often long forgotten or difficult to recall or explain) upon which to found a claim ... to the existence of a collateral warranty'. (An entire agreement clause is therefore more effective than labelling the pre-contract negotiations as 'subject to contract' since it has been held that the latter will not prevent a collateral contract being agreed: *Business Environment Bow Lane Ltd v Deanswater Estates Ltd* [2007] EWCA Civ 622, [2007] L & TR 26, [2007] NPC 79.)

A simple entire agreement clause as such does not extend to prevent a claim for misrepresentation, since it is merely a denial of contractual force. However, it is possible to draft a provision which also sets out to exclude liability for misrepresentation, although this would be subject to the reasonableness requirement in the Unfair Contract Terms Act (UCTA) 1977 (see 7.6.6) by virtue of s. 3 of the Misrepresentation Act 1967 (see 14.7). Section 3 of the 1967 Act relates only to misrepresentation, and therefore has no application to an entire agreement clause relating to contractual terms.

Written contracts now commonly contain a version of an entire agreement clause so that the practical significance of the decision in **Inntrepreneur v East Crown** cannot be overstated in terms its ability to confirm the primacy of the parties' written contract and to instil new life into the parol evidence rule, which had been considered to have little practical operation. The Law Commission in its 1986 report (Law Com. No. 154, Cmnd 9700) had concluded that there was little point in seeking reform of the rule since its effect was widely understood to be minimal.

The parol evidence rule was relied on by Lord Hobhouse in **Shogun Finance Ltd v Hudson** [2003] UKHL 62, [2004] 1 AC 919, discussed at **3.3.3.4**, as the basis for concluding that it was not possible to go outside the terms of the written offer of the hire purchase contract.

6.2.2 **The effect of signature**

6.2.2.1 Bound by signature in the absence of fraud or misrepresentation

In *L'Estrange v E. Graucob Ltd* [1934] 2 KB 394, Scrutton LJ stated (at p. 403):

> When a document containing contractual terms is signed, then, in the absence of fraud, or, I will add, misrepresentation, the party signing it is bound, and it is wholly immaterial whether he has read the document or not.

This rule is an important buttress of contractual certainty and is a reflection of the objective approach to contract formation, since if the parties sign a document they are objectively to be taken to be agreeing to its terms. However, its unbending application has sometimes appeared to cause hardship. In part that is because unscrupulous businessmen have exploited the rule seeking to take advantage of others, particularly consumers.

> In *L'Estrange v E. Graucob Ltd*, the plaintiff had bought a cigarette vending machine from the defendants. She had signed the defendants' order form, which contained a broad exemption from liability in very small print on poor quality paper. It was held that as the plaintiff had signed the written document she was bound by its terms, including the exemption, although she had not read it.

Although frequently criticized, the principle in *L'Estrange v Graucob* relating to the effect of signature, was affirmed in strong terms by the High Court of Australia in *Toll (FGCT) Pty Ltd v Alphapharm Pty Ltd* [2004] HCA 52 (noted Peden and Carter (2005) JCL 96). Amongst the reasons given for supporting the signature rule was the fact that signature is taken to indicate a willingness to be bound and is relied upon as having this effect (although this would seem to be self-fulfilling in that it is because it is recognized as having this effect that it does so). More significantly perhaps, the fact that there is now legislative protection against being bound by certain types of clauses provides a counterbalance (see **6.2.2.2**). As discussed above, the signature rule is also thought to promote contractual certainty. However, the High Court indicated that the rule might not apply where, in the light of the circumstances and nature of the document signed, the signature could not be taken as indicating an intention to be bound by its terms. This amounts to another piece of circular reasoning since this undermines the principle of contractual certainty.

Despite the acknowledged significance of signature, it is clear that signature will not bind where it was fraudulently obtained or obtained as a result of a misrepresentation as to the effect of what was being signed. For example, in *Curtis v Chemical Cleaning and Dyeing Co.* [1951] 1 KB 805, the receipt for a wedding dress excluded all liability for damage but the assistant had misrepresented its effect by asserting that liability was limited to damage to beads and sequins. The court took the view that its decision was consistent with *L'Estrange v Graucob Ltd*, in which it had been suggested that the strict approach to signed documents would not apply where the party claiming not to be bound was misled.

In *Peekay Intermark Ltd v Australia and New Zealand Banking Group Ltd* [2006] EWCA Civ 386, [2006] 2 Lloyd's Rep 511, [2006] 1 CLC 582, there was an unsuccessful argument based on misrepresentation seeking to avoid being bound by the signed writing (for discussion of the misrepresentation argument see 14.2.2.4).

An experienced customer had signed an investment contract without reading it on the basis that he claimed to have relied on an informal description of the product given over the telephone. The question for the court related to whether there had been a misrepresentation which had induced the contract and whether that misrepresentation operated despite the existence of the signature to the conflicting terms describing the product in the written document. The judge at first instance had considered that there was a misrepresentation and that it prevailed since the investor was entitled to assume that the terms in the writing made no material change to the product described orally. However, the Court of Appeal disagreed, stressing the fact that the true position appeared clearly on the face of the signed written document and that the investor had not been induced by any misrepresentation concerning the nature of the investment product. By signing whilst failing to read the final terms and conditions the claimant was taking the risk that the final contract terms would not be to his liking. (In any event there was an entire agreement clause (a risk disclosure statement) placing the burden on the investor to satisfy himself of the nature of the transaction and the risk exposure and this prevented him later seeking to deny this by raising allegations of misrepresentation: see 14.7.3.)

Moore-Bick LJ (at [43]) reinforced the significance of the principle in *L'Estrange v Graucob,* describing it as:

an important principle of English life which underpins the whole of commercial life; any erosion of it would have serious repercussions far beyond the business community. Nonetheless, it is a rule which is concerned with the content of the agreement rather than its validity. Accordingly…the contract may be rescinded if one party has been induced to enter into it by fraud or misrepresentation.

On these facts there was no such actionable misrepresentation.

6.2.2.2 Other limitations on the principle that signature binds

There are other limitations on this principle in *L'Estrange v Graucob Ltd*.

1. Statute now regulates exemption clauses and, more generally, unfair terms in consumer contracts (see UCTA 1977 (see 7.6), and the Unfair Terms in Consumer Contracts Regulations 1999, in particular Sch. 2, 1(b) and (i) may be relevant: see 7.7).

2. The document which is signed must be a document which would be expected to contain contractual conditions (e.g., *Grogan v Robin Meredith Plant Hire* [1996] CLC 1127: signing

a time sheet containing clauses could not amount to a binding variation of the contract terms because a time sheet was not a document which might be expected to contain such clauses).

6.2.2.3 Electronic signatures

In the context of electronic communications, signature includes an electronic signature (Electronic Communications Act 2000, s. 7, discussed at **5.4.6.1**).

6.3 Oral contracts: Incorporation of written terms

The law on the question of incorporation of terms has evolved almost entirely through litigation in respect of clauses excluding or limiting liability (see **Chapter 7**), especially those contained in standard-form contracts. Nevertheless, the principles are equally applicable to all express terms. In relation to exclusion and limitation clauses, the law on incorporation of terms is less crucial than it once was because other means of control of such devices now exist (i.e., statutory controls: see **7.5**) which make it less important for a claimant to establish that the clause in question was not part of the agreement. However, analysis of this kind was used in *Interfoto Picture Library Ltd v Stiletto Visual Programmes Ltd* [1989] 1 QB 433 to exclude a clause which purported to impose a severe penalty for late performance, on the basis that it had not been incorporated into the contract. Allegations that the clause in question has not been incorporated because it is onerous or unusual and has not been fairly and reasonably brought to the other party's attention, have been the focus of a number of contractual cases over recent years (see **6.3.1.5**).

In addition, any statements which it is claimed have been incorporated as terms must be made prior to the conclusion of the contract, and it is for this reason that the rules of offer and acceptance are important in this context (see **Chapter 2**).

There are various means of achieving incorporation:

- by signature (discussed at **6.2.2** in the context of signature to a written contract but a signature could equally appear on a written document alleged to be incorporated into an oral contract)
- by reasonable notice
- on the basis of a consistent course of dealing
- on the basis of the common understanding of the parties.

In addition, of course, as we have already seen at **6.1.3.3** and **6.2.1.3**, a pre-contractual statement can be incorporated as a term of the contract by means such as the importance attached test and the collateral contract device.

6.3.1 Incorporation of written terms into an oral contract: Reasonable notice

The practical difficulty is to establish precisely what terms have been agreed by the parties to an oral contract.

It may be alleged that terms on unsigned written documents (e.g., on a ticket or order form) have been incorporated as terms of an oral contract. In order for such terms to be effectively incorporated:

1. They must be set out in a document which would be expected to contain contractual terms.
2. Reasonable notice of the existence of the terms must have been given before or at the time of contracting.

6.3.1.1 Contractual document

In *Chapelton v Barry UDC* [1940] 1 KB 532, tickets for the hire of deckchairs were obtainable from the deck-chair attendant. The plaintiff obtained tickets from the attendant. He did not notice that the tickets contained a clause purporting to exempt the council from any liability for accidents or damage arising from the hire of the deckchairs. The Court of Appeal held that this term on the ticket could not be relied on by the council since the ticket was a mere voucher or receipt for money paid rather than a contractual document.

There are two important factors to bear in mind when seeking to assess whether a written document, such as a ticket, constitutes a contractual document:

1. The fact that a ticket or other document is called a receipt is not conclusive of the fact that it is non-contractual.
2. The time of the making of the contract appears to be important, since a document can constitute a contractual document only if it is delivered before the contract is formed.

On the facts in *Chapelton*, there was a binding contract when the deckchair was removed from the pile (the pile of deckchairs constituted a standing offer which was accepted when a customer removed a deckchair from the pile). Since the ticket was not part of this contractual process and might be obtained some time later, it could only be a receipt for money paid. Of course, if the ticket were always obtained from the attendant before selecting and removing the deckchair, it would seem to be a contractual document and its terms duly incorporated. (On the facts of *Chapelton* the attendant happened to be standing near the pile of deckchairs so that the ticket was obtained at that time but the Court of Appeal stressed that this might not have been the case and hirers of deckchairs might have sat on the chair for some time before the attendant came to issue the ticket and collect their money.) This sort of distinction is unhelpful in terms of determining the terms of a contract.

Thus, it is recognized that some documents record performance of an existing contractual obligation rather than forming part of the making of the contract and evidencing its terms. Such documents are therefore not regarded as contractual documents, essentially because the contract has already been made. In *Grogan v Robin Meredith Plant Hire* [1996] CLC 1127, it was stated that invoices, time sheets, or statements of account are not normally documents forming part of the making of a contract. However, it may well be the case that, rather than recording the existence of a contract, a particular invoice constitutes the offer to contract and clearly, in these circumstances, that invoice would be a contractual document, e.g. the delivery note in *Photolibrary Group Ltd (trading as Garden Picture Library) v Burda Senator Verlag GmbH* [2008] EWHC 1343 (QB), [2008] 2 All ER (Comm) 881, discussed below at 6.3.1.3 and 6.3.1.5, was held to constitute an offer.

6.3.1.2 Reasonable notice of the existence of the terms

1. What is meant by reasonable notice?

It is a question of whether reasonable notice (in an objective sense) of the *existence* of the terms was given to the offeree before the time of accepting the offer. However, it is important to appreciate that the offeree does not need actual subjective knowledge of the detail of the terms in question.

If the person receiving the ticket (or other written document) knows that it contains writing, that person will be bound by the terms contained in the document, provided that it is a contractual document and provided that it is common knowledge that such writing contains terms and conditions (per Mellish LJ in *Parker v South Eastern Railway* (1877) 2 CPD 416). Nowadays it is common knowledge that tickets and similar documents generally do contain such conditions, and the test will therefore be whether notice of the conditions has been provided to people in general (*Thompson v London, Midland and Scottish Railway* [1930] 1 KB 41). No account will therefore be taken of the fact that the individual claimant is illiterate or unable to understand the language in which the terms are drafted, at least where this factor is not known to the party supplying the ticket or other document (*Geier v Kujawa Weston and Warne Bros (Transport) Ltd* [1970] 1 Lloyd's Rep 364).

2. Can there be incorporation by reference? Is this reasonable notice?

It is clearly recognized that terms can be incorporated by reference to another document in which they can be found, e.g. in the *Thompson* case the face of the ticket said 'see back', and on the back it stated that the ticket was issued subject to conditions set out in the timetables, available for purchase at 6d. These conditions were held to be incorporated. Although this is an extreme case, because the timetables were extremely bulky and relatively expensive to purchase, the principle of incorporation by reference remains a valid one. This point is neatly illustrated by the facts and decision in *O'Brien v MGN Ltd* [2001] EWCA Civ 1279, [2002] CLC 33, discussed at 6.3.1.5, where the Court of Appeal held that the newspaper's rules governing scratch card games were incorporated into the contract although these rules had not been published in full in the newspaper on the day in question. It was sufficient that the scratch card made reference to the existence of the rules which had been published in back issues of the newspaper or could be obtained, on request, from the newspaper's offices. Indeed, it is common commercial practice to make reference to the existence of full terms and conditions contained in a separate document and obtainable on request.

However, in *Sterling Hydraulics Ltd v Dichtomatik Ltd* [2006] EWHC 2004 (QB), [2007] 1 Lloyd's Rep 8 (see also 2.4.2.3), the faxed acknowledgement of the purchase order stated only that delivery was 'based on our General Terms of Sale'. A blank page 2 should have contained the seller's terms and conditions. When the goods supplied proved defective, the seller claimed that the contract incorporated its standard terms and conditions containing exemption clauses. However, the judge held that these terms had not been incorporated. The difficulty was not with the words of reference to standard terms to be found elsewhere but with the failure to make a copy of these terms available at all, since this did not amount to 'adequate notice' (see also *J. Murphy & Sons Ltd v Johnston Precast Ltd* [2008] EWHC 3024 (TCC)).

6.3.1.3 Before or at the time of contracting

Reasonable notice must be given 'in time', i.e. before or at the time of contracting. It is for this reason that the principles of offer and acceptance are important in this context.

In *Olley v Marlborough Court Ltd* [1949] 1 KB 532, a hotel sought to exclude its liability for the loss of valuable personal possessions by a guest at the hotel by reference to an exclusion notice on the back of the hotel bedroom door. However, the contract had been made at the hotel reception desk before the offeree had any possible means of knowing about the purported exclusion of liability. The court therefore found the notice to be ineffective because it was too late to be incorporated as a term of the contract.

Similarly, in **Grogan v Robin Meredith Plant Hire** [1996] CLC 1127, the agreement for the hire of a driver and machine was made over the telephone, whereas the Contractors' Plant Association Conditions were not introduced until two weeks later when the driver presented his time sheet referring to the work as being undertaken on the basis of these conditions. The Court of Appeal held that this notice was too late.

In *Photolibrary Group Ltd (trading as Garden Picture Library) v Burda Senator Verlag GmbH* [2008] EWHC 1343 (QB), [2008] 2 All ER (Comm) 881 (also discussed at 6.3.1.5), terms on a delivery note supplied with various photographic transparencies were considered to be incorporated since this delivery, accompanied by the delivery note, was analysed as an offer which was accepted by the acceptance of the transparencies.

6.3.1.4 Tickets

It has been suggested that printed notices contained in tickets are an exception to the general principle, in that they may be effective to exclude liability although not actually delivered to the purchaser until after the moment of agreement between the parties.

In **Parker v South Eastern Railway** (1877) 2 CPD 416, the railway company operated a left-luggage office in which the plaintiff left a bag, paying the required fee and receiving a ticket in return. On the ticket were the words 'See Back', and on the back was a clause purporting to limit the company's liability in the case of lost luggage to £10. The plaintiff's bag was lost; its contents were worth more than £10. The court found the clause on the ticket sufficient to limit the company's liability as stated. Mellish LJ took the view that printing on a ticket would be incorporated into a contract provided that a reasonable person would appreciate that there was writing containing conditions on the ticket.

This view appears to neglect the issue of whether such notice as there was came too late, since it is common for the point of offer and acceptance to precede the issuing of the ticket. However, in *Thornton v Shoe Lane Parking Ltd* [1971] 2 QB 163, Lord Denning explained the process of offer and acceptance in ticket cases so that the result could coincide with the position in *Parker v South Eastern Railway* and other nineteenth-century ticket cases where incorporation was achieved. Lord Denning considered that the issue of the ticket is the offer, and acceptance occurs when the customer takes the ticket and retains it without objection. On this basis there is incorporation in time of any terms printed on the ticket. Lord Denning acknowledged that this interpretation was based on a 'fiction', because it assumes that the customer will examine the ticket and decide whether to accept the terms or return it without incurring any liability.

In **Thornton v Shoe Lane Parking Ltd**, there was a notice at the entrance to a barrier-operated car park which stated that parking was to be 'at owner's risk'. An automatic barrier controlled entry to the car park. When the motorist drove up to the barrier, a machine dispensed a ticket. This ticket stated that it was 'issued subject to conditions displayed on the premises'. Inside the car park there was a notice excluding liability for personal injury to customers.

The Court of Appeal held that the exemption on the ticket was too late, because the contract for the use of the car park was concluded when the motorist drove up to the barrier and activated the machine.

Lord Denning said he was not prepared to apply the nineteenth-century ticket cases in the context of a ticket issued by an automatic machine. Instead, he stated that the machine is making a standing offer which the customer accepts when he does whatever is required to activate the machine, e.g. by putting money into a slot. The net effect of this analysis was that anything on the ticket dispensed by the machine would not be incorporated because it would be too late.

6.3.1.5 The stricter approach for onerous or unusual terms

In *Thornton v Shoe Lane Parking* the notice at the entrance ('parking at owner's risk') was in time, but it was construed so as not to extend to exempt the car park from liability in respect of personal injury. This was because personal injury was said to be an unusual liability to exclude in these circumstances and therefore needed to be drawn to the customer's attention in explicit terms in order to be incorporated. Lord Denning considered that: 'In order to give sufficient notice, it would need to be printed in red ink with a red hand pointing to it, or something equally startling' (see also *J. Spurling Ltd v Bradshaw* [1956] 1 WLR 461).

This approach involves applying different standards of incorporation to different terms, and it was adopted by the Court of Appeal in *Interfoto Picture Library Ltd v Stiletto Visual Programmes Ltd* [1988] QB 433.

> The term in question involved a fee of £5 per day per transparency for their late return. The Court of Appeal regarded the clause as particularly onerous and unusual, and argued that such a clause would not be regarded as fairly and reasonably brought to the notice of the other party 'unless it was drawn to his attention in the most explicit way'. However, whereas Dillon LJ concluded that for this reason the clause was not incorporated, Bingham LJ considered that, although it was incorporated, it could not have any effect in the circumstances of the case.

Such unusual or onerous terms might need to be presented in a large size print or be placed in a box in a written document in order to satisfy this higher standard of incorporation.

? Question

What is the position if the argument relates to an alleged onerous or unusual term in a signed document which has not been sufficiently brought to the other's attention before signature?

In *Ocean Chemical Transport Inc. v Exnor Craggs Ltd* [2000] 1 All ER (Comm) 519, the Court of Appeal considered whether the *Interfoto* test had to be applied even where the other party had signed to acknowledge the terms. The Court of Appeal suggested that, in the light of the principle in *L'Estrange v Graucob Ltd*, that this would be the position only in an extreme case 'where a signature was obtained under pressure of time or other circumstances' **and** where the clause was particularly onerous or unusual in relation to the contract. However, it would seem that there are other more appropriate contractual doctrines to call in aid in such a situation, e.g. duress, undue influence, or the plea of *non est factum*.

The difficulties associated with this higher standard test for incorporation

1. Must the particular clause be onerous or unusual or must it be an onerous or unusual version of a clause of this type?

This question was answered differently by the members of the Court of Appeal in *AEG (UK) Ltd v Logic Resource Ltd* [1996] CLC 265.

(a) The majority: Hirst and Waite LJJ. The majority held that in a purchase contract to supply goods for export, a clause which stated that the purchaser was to return defective goods at his own expense was an onerous **and** unusual term, so that it would be incorporated only if 'fairly and reasonably brought to the attention' of the purchaser.

(b) *Hobhouse LJ (dissenting):* Hobhouse LJ gave a dissenting judgment on this issue on the basis that this type of clause was commonly found in printed conditions. Hobhouse LJ considered (at p. 277) that the correct approach would be to consider 'the kind of clause' in issue and to consider whether a particular clause was onerous or unusual only in the context of this kind of clause. He considered it wrong to apply the *Interfoto* test to the specific terms of the particular clause in question, on the basis that this amounted to 'completely distorting the contractual relationship between the parties and the ordinary mechanisms of making contracts'. He therefore distinguished both *Interfoto*, which was described as 'an extortionate clause', and *Thornton v Shoe Lane Parking*, where the clause related to personal injuries, regarded as something totally different to the subject matter of a car parking contract.

This significant difference between the approach of the majority in *AEG (UK) Ltd v Logic Resource Ltd* and Hobhouse LJ (dissenting) was resolved by the Court of Appeal in *Ocean Chemical Transport Inc. v Exnor Craggs Ltd* [2000] 1 All ER (Comm) 519. Evans LJ (with whose judgment the other members of the Court of Appeal agreed) stated (at p. 529):

> **It seems to me that the question of incorporation must always depend upon the meaning and effect of the clause in question.** It may be that the type of clause is relevant. It may be that the effect of the particular clause in the particular case is relevant. That, of course, was the division of opinion in the *AEG* case.

Thus, Evans LJ rejected the approach of Hobhouse LJ in *AEG v Logic Resource* and required the *particular* clause to be unusual or onerous rather than that it is a version of a type of clause that would satisfy this test.

2. Must the clause be onerous or unusual or both onerous and unusual?

The circumstances in which the higher standard of incorporation is called for require either that the clause in question should be onerous **or** unusual (albeit on the facts in *AEG v Logic Resource* the clause in question satisfied both elements of this test). This fact has not deterred statements such as that of Rix LJ (with whose judgment Mummery and Peter Gibson LJJ agreed) in *HIH Casualty & General Insurance Ltd v New Hampshire Insurance Co* [2001] EWCA Civ 735, [2001] 2 Lloyd's Rep 161 at [22], requiring that the clause in question be both unusual *and* onerous. If the application of the higher standard turns on the type of clause, then the type of clause should be both unusual and an onerous version of the type of term. However, on the basis of the decision in *Ocean Chemical Transport v Exnor Craggs Ltd*, where it is the particular clause which needs to be assessed, it would seem that either requirement ought to suffice, and an examination of the early authorities indicates that these requirements are viewed as alternatives.

3. Establishing that the clause is onerous or unusual

As the interpretation question in 1 above has now been resolved, the real difficulty with this difference in the standard to achieve incorporation will be to decide whether in fact a clause is onerous or unusual so that the higher standard of incorporation is required. This is a question of fact in each case and it is clear that there is often little agreement between individual judges as to whether the higher test needs to be satisfied.

In ***O'Brien v MGN Ltd*** [2001] EWCA Civ 1279, [2002] CLC 33, the majority (Hale and Potter LJJ) considered that there was nothing onerous or unusual in rule 5 of the newspaper's rules governing the operation of the scratch-card game, whereas Evans LJ clearly considered that this term needed to be given greater prominence (in part because he seems to have considered that it was a matter of chance whether a person had access to the rules). Rule 5 provided that where more prizes were claimed than were available, the prize would be awarded on the basis of a simple draw. The majority considered the rule to be sensible in the circumstances and was able to distinguish ***Interfoto*** (where the clause imposed an additional burden on the defendants) and ***Thornton v Shoe Lane Parking*** (where the clause sought to exclude liability for personal injuries). Hale LJ stated that this clause 'merely deprives the claimant of a windfall for which he has done very little in return'.

In any event, as Hale LJ stated in ***O'Brien v MGN***:

> the words 'onerous or unusual' are not terms of art. They are simply one way of putting the general proposition that reasonable steps must be taken to draw the particular term in question to the notice of those who are bound by it and that more is required in relation to certain terms than to others depending on their effect.

This is a common-sense statement of the principle but fails to assist with the problem of certainty and predictability on such an important question as the incorporation of contractual terms and is unlikely to resolve difficulties in drafting standard terms. On the other hand, there are signs of good sense, e.g. in ***Shepherd Homes Ltd v Enica Remediation Ltd*** [2007] EWHC 70 (TCC), [2007] BLR 135, it was held that a limitation of a construction contractor's liability to the contract price could not be said to be onerous or unusual. Generally speaking, the scope of terms that are regarded as 'usual terms in the trade' will tend to reduce the scope for argument that the term in question is onerous. The onerous or unusual argument was rejected in ***Photolibrary Group Ltd (trading as Garden Picture Library) v Burda Senator Verlag GmbH*** [2008] EWHC 1343 (QB), [2008] 2 All ER (Comm) 881, also discussed at 6.3.1.3, on the basis of facts that were similar to those in ***Interfoto*** (photographic transparencies), since there was a substantial course of dealing between the parties based on the terms in the delivery notes which set fees for loss of the transparencies and, since the fees set for loss were quite normal in the business, they could not be regarded as in any way unusual.

6.3.1.6 Internet contracts and reasonable notice

Before leaving this section, it is as well to consider the question of incorporation of terms and conditions into contracts concluded on the Internet. A supplier will need to ensure that the customer had reasonable notice of applicable terms and conditions **before contracting**. Normally this will be achieved by requiring the customer to click on an icon to signal agreement to the terms and conditions which are displayed (but seldom read) before the contract is concluded. The same need to ensure a higher degree of notice for onerous or unusual terms will also apply.

6.3.2 Consistent course of dealing

Even if notice of the terms was not given on the particular occasion, where the parties deal with each other on a regular basis on standard terms and conditions the terms may be incorporated into the particular contract on the basis of a previous course of dealing between the parties (*Hardwick Game Farm v Suffolk Agricultural Poultry Producers Association* [1969] 2 AC 31). Nevertheless, the party seeking to rely on a course of dealing for the incorporation of terms will have to sustain the burden of proving that the course of past conduct has been **sufficiently consistent** to give rise to the implication that in similar circumstances a similar contractual result will follow.

In *McCutcheon v David MacBrayne Ltd* [1964] 1 WLR 125, the plaintiff had used the defendants' ferry service for his car on several occasions in the past. Sometimes he had been asked to sign a note containing an exclusion clause, but sometimes he had not. On the occasion in question the ferry sank, and no note had been signed. The defendants were unable to rely on the course of dealing to incorporate an exclusion clause into the contract since it was inconsistent.

A more recent example of incorporation based on previous course of dealing is provided by the decision of the Court of Appeal in *Petrotrade Inc. v Texaco Ltd* [2000] CLC 1341.

The contract was entered into by telephone and the basic terms agreed. Subsequently, a telex was sent which contained Petrotrade's standard terms, including a clause providing for payment to be made without deduction or set-off. It was alleged that these terms were incorporated on the basis of the previous dealings between the parties. The Court of Appeal found that over the thirteen months prior to this contract there had been five other contracts between the parties for the sale of the same or similar products by Petrotrade, and where the transactions had been confirmed on the same terms including this anti set-off clause. Accordingly, given this previous course of dealing, both parties made the agreement on the basis that the contract would again be subject to these terms.

Similarly, in *Balmoral Group Ltd v Borealis (UK) Ltd* [2006] EWHC 1900 (Comm), [2006] 2 Lloyd's Rep 629, [2006] 2 CLC 220 (discussed further at 7.6.6.2), the course of dealing was established, although this was despite the fact that the number of prior orders had been small and for very different goods. The crucial factor (at [363]) was that Borealis had made it clear at the start of their trading relationship that it was only willing to supply on the basis of its own terms and prices as quoted. This position would have needed to be expressly reversed.

The decisions in course of dealing cases turn on their particular facts, but it should be easier to establish the necessary consistency in the course of dealing between commercial parties (as in *Petrotrade v Texaco* and *Balmoral v Borealis*) than as against a consumer. For example, in *Hollier v Rambler Motors (AMC) Ltd* [1972] 2 QB 71, the Court of Appeal held that a garage's standard terms were not incorporated into a repair contract with a customer because there was not a consistent course of dealing between the parties using these terms. The customer had used the garage for repairs on only three or four occasions in a five-year period.

6.3.3 Common knowledge

In very limited circumstances the courts may be willing to incorporate a term into a contract without actual notice and without any prior course of dealing. The courts will incorporate terms in these circumstances only where there is some common basis shared by the parties which justifies the presumption that the parties have a common understanding that the terms will apply. The common basis will usually be supplied by the fact that both parties belong to and are familiar with the terms of a particular trade, and indeed the terms in question may need to be standard conditions issued by a trade association.

An example of incorporation in this form can be found in *British Crane Hire Corporation Ltd v Ipswich Plant Hire Ltd* [1975] QB 303.

> This case involved a clause in a standard form hire contract between two businesses, which were both in the plant hire business. Although notice was given too late in relation to the particular contract, the terms were held to be incorporated because both parties knew of these printed conditions which were in common use in the plant hire business.

British Crane Hire can usefully be compared with *Grogan v Robin Meredith Plant Hire* [1996] CLC 1127, where the judge rejected an argument to the effect that, although notice of the terms had been given too late on this occasion (see 6.3.1.3), they could be incorporated based on the common understanding of the parties. The judge appeared to regard the terms in question as not being used so frequently and commonly as to be common knowledge within the industry. This seems doubtful in view of the decision in *British Crane Hire* (as the decision relates to the same set of standard terms), and the significant distinguishing factor may be the fact that the parties in *Grogan* were not operating in the same business; only one party was in the business of hiring plant, the other party laid pipes.

   British Crane Hire was also distinguished in *Ofir Scheps v Fine Art Logistic Ltd* [2007] EWHC 541 (QB), partly it seems on the basis that the parties were not in exactly the same business.

> The claimant had purchased a sculpture at auction which was being stored by the auction house. The claimant engaged the defendant to collect and store it. Although the defendant collected the sculpture, it then went missing and the defendant's view was that it must have been accidentally destroyed. The defendant alleged that the agreement with the claimant incorporated the defendant's standard terms and conditions, limiting its liability to a fixed figure. It alleged, relying on *British Crane Hire v Ipswich*, that this was common knowledge in the transport and storage business so that the claimant, which had considerable experience of arranging for transport of such works of art, must have been aware of it.
>
>   Teare J held that the terms were not incorporated since (1) the defendant had not provided the claimant with a copy of these terms or with a document referring to them and (2) there was no evidence that the claimant had any particular knowledge of them. *British Crane Hire v Ipswich* was distinguished, the judge noting (at [24]) that in that case '[b]oth parties to the hiring contract were in business of hiring out cranes'. Teare J also stressed the fact that the parties in *British Crane Hire* were of equal bargaining power, traded upon similar terms derived from the Contractors Plant Association form, and had in fact traded on two occasions in the immediate past on this basis. It was therefore possible to 'readily conclude that the defendants intended to trade on the plaintiffs' terms'.

6.4 Implied terms

6.4.1 Introduction

In many contracts, although the main primary obligations are contained in express terms, the parties do not express all the primary obligations or do not provide for every eventuality.

   The implication of terms might be considered controversial since it frequently amounts to filling the gaps in the contract so that the courts might be accused of making the contract for the parties (see 3.1.1) and/or interfering with contractual certainty, i.e. the ability to rely on the express terms of the contract as representing the parties' agreement without the risk of any 'extra' terms. However, the courts have traditionally justified the implication of terms to fill gaps on the basis of giving effect to the deemed intentions of the parties and/or on the basis of 'necessity'. Statute implies terms in some circumstances in order to give effect to policy objectives, e.g. the sale of goods legislation implies terms in favour of buyers as a protection device.

 ## Example

When a student goes into a shop to buy a new textbook, the bookseller and the student do not discuss or express any terms relating to the quality of the book to be sold. Nevertheless, if the book proved to have been bound with an important section missing, the student would be less than happy if he had no remedy against the bookseller. On the contrary, it is understood that what is being sold must be a book which is in the state a book of that description would normally be in. That understanding is incorporated into the contract by means of an implied term (in the particular case, a term derived from statute: s. 14(2) of the SGA 1979, imposing an obligation that the goods will be of satisfactory quality—see 6.4.2.4).

6.4.1.1 Implication of terms when construing a contract

Until **Attorney General of Belize v Belize Telecom Ltd** [2009] UKPC 10, [2009] 1 WLR 1988, it was generally thought that the courts implied terms in some cases in order to fill gaps in the express terms, i.e. as a process of addition. Lord Hoffmann's clarification of principle in **Attorney General of Belize v Belize Telecom Ltd** has now explained that the implication of terms was only ever an exercise of construction of the facts to seek the parties' intentions, i.e. identifying terms to give effect to intentions. Such terms are necessarily implied as 'one-off' terms, following a process of construction, in order to make sense of the contract in its context and ascribe to it a meaning which it would reasonably be understood to mean. These are so-called 'terms implied in fact': see 6.4.2.2.

6.4.1.2 Implication of terms irrespective of the parties' intentions in order to secure a policy objective/protection for a category of contracting parties

It is equally clear that some terms are implied irrespective of the intentions of the parties (so called 'terms implied in law': see 6.4.2.3).

In the example above of the sale of a book, the obligation to meet a certain quality standard is said to derive from an implied term, but it may not be certain that the bookseller intended such a term. Indeed, it may be more honest simply to say that in that situation a positive obligation of the law of contract is imposed on the seller, whatever his intentions (see Stephenson LJ in *Mears v Safecar Securities Ltd* [1983] QB 54). The notion of an **imposed** obligation is all the more persuasive because in our example it will be impossible for the seller to exclude liability for the obligation as against a consumer (UCTA 1977, s. 6(2): see 7.6.4.1).

This leaves open the question of the basis on which terms are imposed on the parties, i.e. the so-called policy question. Whatever the conceptual basis of implied terms of this type, in practice the courts have inevitably been drawn into a practice of seeking to ensure that contracts of a recognizable and frequently occurring type conform to general (reasonable) expectations of what obligations such contracts should contain.

6.4.1.3 Limitations on the ability to imply terms

It is important to realize, however, that while the courts today may be more willing to imply terms than once they were, there are important limits on the ability to make such an implication.

1. The courts should not make a contract for the parties when this would amount to amending the meaning that would reasonably be put on the contract terms in the contractual context. An omission of an express term may be deliberate (Lord Hoffmann in **Attorney General of Belize v Belize Telecom Ltd** [2009] UKPC 10, [2009] 1 WLR 1988 at [17]). The courts should not cross the line and 'write the parties' contract' for them (Lord Wright in **Hillas & Co. Ltd v Arcos Ltd** (1932) 147 LT 503: see 3.1.2).

2. It must be possible to formulate any term implied by the courts with sufficient precision for the court to be able to give effect to it (**Shell UK Ltd v Lostock Garage Ltd** [1976] 1 WLR 1187 and **Durham Tees Valley Airport Ltd v Bmibaby Ltd** [2009] EWHC 852 (Ch), [2009] 2 Lloyd's Rep 246).

3. In addition, an implied term cannot coexist with an express term which flatly contradicts it. However, where the exact scope of an express term leaves some latitude in its application (such as in the form of a discretion), it may be narrowed or widened by an implied term (per Browne-Wilkinson V-C in **Johnstone v Bloomsbury Health Authority** [1992] 1 QB 333 at pp. 350–1).

6.4.2 Methods by which terms are implied

Terms may be implied by:

- custom or as a result of trade usage or business practice
- the courts—either by implication into the particular contract to reflect the parties' objective intentions and to make the contract work (terms implied in fact) or by implication into all contracts of a particular type on the basis that the term is a necessary incident of that type of contract (terms implied in law)
- statute—implication into contracts of certain types, irrespective of the parties' wishes.

6.4.2.1 Terms implied by custom or trade usage

Terms may be implied on the basis of an established custom or usage of the relevant trade, unless such a term would be inconsistent with an express term of the contract. In order for a term to be implied by custom, the term must be clearly established and 'notorious', i.e. well known within the trade context. In **Hutton v Warren** (1836) 1 M & W 466, the court implied a term into an agricultural lease that upon quitting tenants were entitled to an allowance for seed and labour, on the basis of a custom which was said to be incorporated into all such contracts.

It was once thought that such terms were incorporated by virtue of what it might be assumed in all the circumstances must have been the intention of the parties, treating them as a species of term implied in fact. Today, the incorporation of customary terms, especially those in general use in a particular trade, may owe more to the courts' desire to regulate the content of contracts by encouraging the use of standardized terms. Such an approach would be more closely akin to that of terms implied in law.

For example, in **British Crane Hire Corporation Ltd v Ipswich Plant Hire Ltd** [1975] QB 303 (see also 6.3.3), the Court of Appeal held that the contract was subject to terms not seen by the offeree before the time of contracting These terms were a version of the 'Contractors' Plant Association' terms which were customarily used in the particular trade, and with which both parties would have been familiar since they were both in the plant hire business. The term in question related to liability for the cost of recovering a crane if it got bogged down in soft ground.

6.4.2.2 Terms implied in fact: Construing the contract and giving effect to the parties' intentions as objectively determined

Terms are implied in fact on the basis of an intention imputed to the parties from the actual circumstances as a process of construction of the contract in question. Thus, there is no question of imposing a legal obligation. The Privy Council made this clear in *Attorney General of Belize v Belize Telecom Ltd* [2009] UKPC 10, [2009] 1 WLR 1988. Lord Hoffmann explained that where there was no express term governing the event '[t]he most usual inference…is that nothing is to happen. If the parties had intended something to happen the instrument would have said so' (at [17]). This was considered to be the position on the facts in *Mediterranean Salvage and Towage Ltd v Seamar Trading and Commerce Inc., The Reborn* [2009] EWCA Civ 531, [2009] 1 CLC 909, since 'if the parties had intended the charterers to warrant the safety of a loading berth, they could and would have said so, as is very common in voyage charterparties', per Lord Clarke MR at [11].

The process of implication of a term in fact is one of construction of the content of the contract to identify the parties' intentions through the meaning 'which the instrument would convey to a reasonable person having all the background knowledge which could reasonably be available to the audience to whom the instrument is addressed' (detached objectivity: see 2.1.1). If the reasonable addressee would consider 'that the only meaning consistent with the other provisions of the instrument, read against the relevant background, is that something is to happen' if this event occurs, then the court will imply a term providing for what is to happen if that event occurs.

Significantly, Lord Hoffmann expressly stated that this implication 'only spells out what the instrument means', i.e. it is an application of the construction process, rather than a process by which the court adds something that was not already inevitably intended in this context. In particular, his Lordship stressed (at [16]) that a court 'has no power to improve upon the instrument which it is called upon to construe…It cannot introduce terms to make it fairer or more reasonable.'

Lord Cross in *Liverpool City Council v Irwin* [1977] AC 239 at p. 258 had also been clear on this latter point:

What the court is being in effect asked to do is to rectify a particular—often a very detailed—contract by inserting in it a term which the parties have not expressed. Here it is not enough for the court to say that the suggested term is a reasonable one the presence of which would make the contract a better or fairer one; it must be able to say that the insertion of the term is necessary.

This represented a firm rebuke of Lord Denning MR who, in the Court of Appeal in the *Liverpool City Council v Irwin* case, had suggested that such a term might be implied where it was just and reasonable in the circumstances. Such a test was firmly rejected by the House of Lords on appeal.

The word 'necessity' correctly reflects the approach since it indicates that the court 'must be satisfied that it is what the contract actually means'. The Court of Appeal in *Mediterranean Salvage and Towage Ltd v Seamar Trading and Commerce Inc., The Reborn* [2009] EWCA Civ 531, [2009] 1 CLC 909, was clear that necessity was still relevant to the process of construction. Lord Clarke MR commented (at [15]): 'Moreover, as I read Lord Hoffmann's analysis, although he is emphasizing that the process of implication is part of the process of construction of the contract, he is not in any way resiling from the often stated proposition that it must be necessary to imply the proposed term. It is never sufficient that it should be reasonable.' On these facts the implied term alleged was not necessary 'to make the contract work' (so presumably it could not have been understood as being part of the contract by the reasonable person).

In *Attorney General of Belize v Belize Telecom Ltd* the Privy Council was required to construe the articles of association of a company (i.e., the company's constitutional document). A provision of the articles provided for those holding a certain type of share and size of shareholding to be entitled to appoint and remove two specific directors relating to this shareholding. The appointments had been made by a qualifying shareholder. However, that shareholder later lost the type and size of shareholding required under this article and the question arose of whether the two directors appointed under it could be removed given that the only power to remove in the articles was entrusted by this article to a person holding the requisite shareholding and no one satisfied that criteria after the shareholder lost its entitlement. Could the articles be construed as providing for these directors to vacate their office if there was no longer any holder of the relevant type of shareholding? The Privy Council applied the construction test and concluded that such an implication should be made. There was no longer a shareholding of the type and size to authorize or justify such appointments so that these directors had to vacate their office.

The test for implication of terms in fact

The conditions thought necessary to imply a term in fact prior to *Attorney General of Belize v Belize Telecom Ltd* were summarized by Lord Simon in *BP Refinery (Westernport) Pty Ltd v Shire of Hastings* (1977) 180 CLR 266 at pp. 282–3: '(1) it must be reasonable and equitable; (2) it must be necessary to give business efficacy to the contract, so that no term will be implied if the contract is effective without it; (3) it must be so obvious that "it goes without saying" (4) it must be capable of clear expression; (5) it must not contradict any express term of the contract'. His Lordship conceded that these are conditions which may overlap. Lord Hoffmann in *Attorney General of Belize v Belize Telecom Ltd* concluded (at [27]), that they are:

best regarded, not as a series of independent tests which must each be surmounted, but rather as a collection of different ways in which judges have tried to express the central idea that the proposed implied term must spell out what the contract actually means, or in which they have explained why they did not think that it did so.

It therefore appears that the officious bystander test and the business efficacy test are no more than ways of justifying the conclusion on implication of terms in fact following the construction approach.

1. The 'officious bystander' test

The 'officious bystander' test derived from *Shirlaw v Southern Foundries (1926) Ltd* [1939] 2 KB 206, where MacKinnon LJ expressed it as follows:

> Prima facie that which in any contract is left to be implied and need not be expressed is something so obvious that it goes without saying; so that, if, while the parties were making their bargain, an officious bystander were to suggest some express provision for it in their agreement, they would testily suppress him with a common 'Oh, of course!'

This 'officious bystander' test imposed a very strict standard for the imposition of terms (Lord Wilberforce in **Liverpool City Council v Irwin**) and attempts to imply terms on this basis often failed because while one of the parties would clearly have assented to the term if it had been proposed, the same could not unquestionably be said of the other party.

> In **Shell UK Ltd v Lostock Garage Ltd** [1976] 1 WLR 1187, the petrol company had introduced a subsidised support scheme which was available to selected tied garages, including two of the defendant's competitors but not the defendant's garage. When the defendant broke the tie agreement by obtaining petrol from another petrol company, Shell sought an injunction and damages for breach of contract. In its defence, the defendant claimed that Shell was in breach of an implied obligation that it would not discriminate abnormally against the defendant in favour of competing and neighbouring garages.
>
> The majority of the Court of Appeal refused to imply such a term on the basis that it was not a necessary term. Although the defendant would clearly have considered such a term to be necessary, Shell might not have agreed to it if asked at the outset.

Another reason why the suggested term was not implied in the **Shell** case was that it could not 'be formulated with sufficient precision', and this would seem to be an inherent problem with terms implied in fact.

2. The 'business efficacy' test

This test provided for the law to imply a term with the object of giving the transaction such efficacy as both parties must have intended that it should have.

> In **The Moorcock** (1889) 14 PD 64 the plaintiffs had agreed with the defendants that the plaintiffs' ship should load and unload at the defendants' wharf on the Thames. Both parties knew that the ship would settle on the riverbed at low tide, but the defendants had not expressly guaranteed the good condition of the riverbed. The ship was damaged while at the wharf when it settled on hard ground rather than on mud. The question was whether there was an implied term in the contract to take reasonable care to see that the berth at the wharf was safe. The court found such a term to exist.

Bowen LJ said (at p. 68):

> An implied warranty, or as it is called a covenant in law, as distinguished from an express contract or express warranty, really is in all cases founded upon the presumed intention of the parties, and upon reason. The implication which the law draws from what must obviously have been the intention of the parties, the law draws with the object of giving efficacy to the transaction and preventing such a failure of consideration as cannot have been within the contemplation of either side.

In other words, the term is implied because without it the contract cannot be performed as the parties must have intended or in order to make the contract work.

> **Equitable Life Assurance Society v Hyman** [2002] 1 AC 408 is an example of a term implied in fact. The House of Lords implied a term, restricting the discretion of the Society's directors to award lower final bonuses, in order to ensure that there was no conflict with the reasonable expectations of the parties. When the 'with-profits' policies had been issued, both parties would have assumed that the purpose was to protect policyholders against a fall in market annuity rates and this was a positive selling point when the Society marketed these policies. The effect of the proposed action by the directors would have been to deprive the guarantee in such a policy of any substantial value. On this basis the implication of such a term was strictly necessary.

The applicable question post *Attorney General of Belize v Belize Telecom Ltd*

In *Attorney General of Belize v Belize Telecom Ltd* [2009] UKPC 10, [2009] 1 WLR 1988, Lord Hoffmann spelt out (at [21]) the single question determining implication of a term in fact:

> in every case in which it is said that some provision ought to be implied in an instrument, the question for the court is whether such a provision would spell out in express words what the instrument, read against the relevant background, would reasonably be understood to mean.

The test is therefore now one of construction only and the officious bystander and business efficacy tests are regarded merely as ways to explain what the contract means, and what it does not mean.

As if to reinforce the point that the application of other tests might not prove helpful, Lord Hoffmann added that '[t]here are dangers in treating these alternative formulations of the question as if they had a life of their own' since it might be forgotten that the central question is one of construction of the contract and whether it reflects what a reasonable person would understand it to mean.

The formulation of whether a term is 'necessary to give business efficacy to a contract' served only to underline points of construction, i.e. the need to examine what the instrument would be understood to mean by a reasonable person with knowledge of the relevant commercial background. If the instrument is a commercial contract that person would be expected to consider whether any other meaning would fail to give effect to the parties' business purposes (e.g., as in the *Equitable Life* case and the need to avoid frustration of the parties' reasonable expectations). The need to examine 'practical consequences' of adopting particular meanings in the commercial context was stressed by Teare J (at [44]–[45]) in *Inta Navigation Ltd v Ranch Investments Ltd* [2009] EWHC 1216 (Comm), [2009] 1 CLC 887, when he rejected a particular construction as producing 'a commercially unreasonable result'.

Equally, there was a very real danger, given the subjectivity of the officious bystander test or 'it goes without saying' test (i.e., if **the parties** had been asked, would **they** have said: 'of course; it goes without saying'), that attention would be diverted from the objectivity of construction in the central question of what the contract would reasonably be understood to mean. His Lordship also disliked the officious bystander test since it suggested that the need for such an implied term had to be 'immediately apparent', whereas a failure to make express provision for an event might be the result of a failure to think though all the eventualities in a complicated instrument. He added: 'In such circumstances, the fact that the actual parties might have said to the officious bystander "Could you please explain that again?" does not matter', if it is clear that only one answer would be consistent with the meaning of that instrument. In *In the matter of Lehman Brothers International (Europe) (in administration) v RAB Market Cycles (Master) Fund Ltd* [2009] EWHC 2545 (Ch), the judge accepted that the failure of Lehman Brothers was regarded as no more than a remote contingency and so did not feature as a major inclusion in express terms in agreements made by the firm. Nevertheless, it was clear how the agreements should be construed in order to give effect to the intention of the parties in the context of all the terms of the agreement and the new circumstances.

Finally, the fact that a proposed implied term is incapable of being expressed with any precision (see *Shell v Lostock Garages*) is merely another way of saying that 'a reasonable man would not have understood that to be what the instrument meant'.

Summary

Terms implied in fact must be:

1. implied on a 'one-off' basis into this particular contract
2. based on construing the contract so that it reflects what a reasonable person would understand it to mean
3. necessary to achieve that construction.

6.4.2.3 Terms implied in law

Terms implied in law do not depend upon any intention imputed to the parties. They consist of legal obligations generally imposed on one of the parties in a common contractual relationship, without reference to the particular circumstances. Some legal obligations are imposed by the courts and some, although originally imposed by the courts, have now been given statutory force.

Summary

Terms implied in law must be:

1. implied as a matter of policy into all contracts of a particular type
2. a 'necessary incident' of this type of contract, i.e. necessary because of the contract's subject matter
3. a reasonable term to imply.

The Court of Appeal in *Crossley v Faithful & Gould Holdings Ltd* went so far as to suggest that the decision to imply a term in law rested on questions of 'reasonableness, fairness and the balancing of competing policy considerations' rather than 'necessity'.

Lord Denning MR described the process of implication of terms in law in *Shell UK Ltd v Lostock Garages Ltd* [1976] 1 WLR 1187. He said that it occurs in all common contractual relationships, such as seller and buyer, master and servant, landlord and tenant, and so on. He continued at p. 1196:

In such relationships the problem is not solved by asking: what did the parties intend? Or, would they have unhesitatingly agreed to it, if asked? It is to be solved by asking: has the law already defined the obligation or the extent of it? If so, let it be followed. If not, look to see what would be reasonable in the general run of such cases…and then say what the obligation shall be.

The basis for the implication of terms in this way appears to be the desire to regulate certain common types of contract. It is done so that one party does not take unfair advantage of another, and so that adequate protection is given to both parties even when, as is often the case with such common contracts, little time is spent on detailed negotiation of the terms. Thus, the common contracts have taken on standard content by implication of terms in law. The finding of a term in one case may be binding in terms of precedent in subsequent cases. Such a position would be inconceivable in the case of terms implied in fact.

The leading case on terms implied in law (i.e., involving legal obligations imposed on a contracting party by the courts) is *Liverpool City Council v Irwin* [1977] AC 239.

The council let flats and maisonettes in a tower block to tenants. The lifts and rubbish chutes of the tower block constantly broke down. The tenancy agreement imposed certain obligations on tenants, but was silent about the obligations of the council to maintain the building. The tenants withheld their rent in protest at the council's failure to maintain the building properly. The council brought an action to obtain possession and the tenants counterclaimed for breach of an implied obligation to keep the block in proper repair.

The House of Lords was unwilling to imply a term in fact into the particular agreement. However, their Lordships were willing to imply, as a necessary incident of all tenancy agreements in which the tenants are granted the use in common of stairways, corridors, lifts, etc., an obligation on the landlord 'to take reasonable care to keep in reasonable repair and usability' the common parts (per Lord Wilberforce).

Lord Wilberforce suggested that the test was one of necessity and Lord Scarman in *Tai Hing Cotton Mill Ltd v Liu Chong Hing Bank Ltd* [1986] AC 80 at p. 107 and Lord Bridge in *Scally v Southern Health and Social Services Board* [1992] 1 AC 294 at p. 307, both refer to terms which are a 'necessary incident' of a ('definable category of', per Lord Bridge) contractual relationship. Lord Bridge's formulation was warmly approved by Lord Woolf in *Spring v Guardian Assurance plc* [1995] 2 AC 296.

Despite what may be seen as an unfortunate parallelism of language, it seems that 'necessary on the facts' (terms implied in fact) and 'necessary incident of a definable category of contractual relationship' (terms implied in law) must have different meanings. The notion of 'necessary incident' draws upon a much wider set of criteria to determine its meaning, and it must be supposed that ultimately terms implied in law on the basis of being a necessary incident of such contracts are founded upon reasonable expectation (see further, Phang, 'Implied terms in English law' [1993] JBL 242). Lord Woolf's short speech in *Spring v Guardian Assurance plc* provides an excellent demonstration of the implication of a term under this rule. He refers expressly to what is 'normal practice' in contracts of the particular kind, and to the fact that it would not be right to expect the party to enter into an engagement of that kind except on the basis of the proposed implied term. This is very much the language of reasonable expectation, which was also the terminology employed by the House of Lords in *Equitable Life Assurance Society v Hyman* [2002] 1 AC 408, although the reasonable expectation in the case of terms implied in law embraces much broader contextual considerations than might be applicable in the context of terms implied in fact on a on-off basis based on **the parties'** reasonable expectations. The implication of a term in law in *Scally v Southern Health and Social Services Board* [1992] 1 AC 294 was also based on 'wider considerations' outside the parties and their presumed intentions.

The difficulty in practice is to know what these broader 'expectations' and 'considerations' might include (see Peden, 'Policy concerns behind implication of terms in law' (2001) 117 LQR 459 and the suggestion that the courts take into account general issues of fairness and the impact on the parties of implication of the alleged term). Peden's comments were specifically relied upon by Dyson LJ in the Court of Appeal in *Crossley v Faithful & Gould Holdings Ltd* [2004] EWCA Civ 293, [2004] 4 All ER 447, in reaching the conclusion that it was better to focus on questions of 'reasonableness, fairness and the balancing of competing policy considerations' rather than the 'elusive concept of necessity'. On the facts the Court of Appeal rejected an argument for an implied term that an employer should take reasonable care of an employee's economic well-being (by advising the employee of the financial consequences of early retirement). Unsurprisingly, such a term was considered to involve too large an extension of the law in this area and to place an unfair and unreasonable burden upon employers. It is clearly much wider than the terms implied in *Mahmud v Bank of Credit and Commerce International SA (In Liquidation)* [1998] AC 20 (implied term that employer would not conduct a dishonest or corrupt business) and in *Scally* (all employees in a certain category had to be notified of their entitlement to certain benefits) and needed to be more closely confined by the factual scenario.

6.4.2.4 Terms imposed by statute

Certain obligations, which were at one time imposed by the courts, have now been given statutory force. Most important among these are terms relating to quality in sale or supply of goods contracts, and those relating to the standard of performance in contracts for services.

1. Quality obligation in sale of goods contracts

The **SGA 1979, s. 14** (as amended by the Sale and Supply of Goods Act 1994 and the Sale and Supply of Goods to Consumers Regulations 2002, SI 2002/3045) provides:

> (2) **Where the seller sells goods in the course of a business**, there is an implied term that the goods supplied under the contract are of satisfactory quality. [Emphasis added.]

For s. 14(2) and (3) to apply the seller must sell 'in the course of a business' (see discussion as to meaning, 7.6.1.1). The buyer could be an individual consumer or a business. The Act then defines satisfactory quality as meaning that the goods 'meet the standards that a reasonable person would regard as satisfactory, taking account of any description of the goods, the price (if relevant) and all the other relevant circumstances' (s. 14(2A)). Quality of goods includes 'their state and condition' as well as aspects (s. 14(2B)) such as: fitness for all the purposes for which goods of the kind in question are commonly supplied; appearance and finish; freedom from minor defects; safety; and durability.

However, by s. 14(2C):

> The term implied by subsection (2)…does not extend to any matter making the goods unsatisfactory—
>   (a) which is specifically drawn to the buyer's attention before the contract is made,
>   (b) where the buyer examines the goods before the contract is made, which that examination ought to reveal, or
>   (c) in the case of a contract for sale by sample, which would have been apparent on a reasonable examination of the sample.

2. Fitness for a particular purpose

Under s. 14(3), again where the seller sells good in the course of a business, where the buyer makes known to the seller a particular (as opposed to the common) purpose for buying the goods in question, there is a further implied term that the goods be fit for that particular purpose.

3. Other implied terms in sale of goods contracts

Section 13(1) of the SGA 1979 implies a term into **a contract for the sale of goods by description** that the goods will correspond with the description. This term is implied whether the seller is operating a business or is an individual consumer. **What is meant by 'a contract for the sale of goods by description' to which s. 13(1) applies?** In ***Harlingdon & Leinster Enterprises Ltd v Christopher Hull Fine Art Ltd*** [1992] 1 QB 564, the Court of Appeal held that the sale of a painting as a 'Gabriele Műnter' was not a sale by description. For a sale to be by description that description had to be influential in the sale so that it became a contractual term and it would be extremely difficult to establish a common intention that the description should be a term of the contract where the party had not shown that it had relied on that description. Since the buyer was the specialist dealer and had inspected the painting before buying, it could not be said to be within the parties' reasonable contemplations that the buyer was relying on that description. Thus the Court of Appeal preserved the distinction between terms and representations (see 6.1.2).

However, ***Beale v Taylor*** [1967] 1 WLR 1193 demonstrates that where a buyer has reasonably relied on a description, there will be a sale by description despite the fact that the buyer has inspected the goods. The defendant had offered his car for sale and described it as a 'Herald, convertible, white, 1961'. The plaintiff had examined the car and then purchased it. However, the car was in fact made up of two halves of different cars which had been welded together and although one half could be dated as 1961, the other half was older. The Court of Appeal considered that this was a sale by description of a '1961 Herald'. (This case should be compared with ***Oscar Chess Ltd v Williams*** [1957] 1 WLR 370, discussed at 6.1.3.4, where the statement as to a car's age was treated as a representation rather than a term as to description, possibly because the buyer was a garage rather than a private buyer.)

Section 15(2) of the SGA 1979 implies a term into a contract for sale by sample that 'the bulk will correspond with the sample in terms of its quality' and that 'the goods will be free from any defect, making their quality unsatisfactory, which would not be apparent on reasonable examination of the sample'.

There are also implied terms that the seller has title to the goods (s. 12(1)) and that the seller has disclosed all charges and encumbrances known to the seller but not known to the buyer (s. 12(4)).

There is a further implied term that the goods are free from any undisclosed encumbrances and that the buyer will otherwise enjoy quiet possession of the goods (s. 12(2)).

4. Contracts for work and materials

These are contracts where the provision of 'work' or a service is the central object of the contract but the contract also involves an incidental supply of materials (goods). Examples would be contracts to service or repair vehicles where new parts are used or a contract to instal central heating or a new bathroom where there is work but also a transfer of ownership of goods, e.g. the radiators, new bath or shower etc.

(a) *Goods or materials*

Similar implied terms to those relating to the goods in a sale of goods contract are implied into contracts for work and materials by the provisions of the Supply of Goods and Services Act 1982 (SGSA 1982) which deal with contracts for the transfer of property in goods. Thus, s. 3(2) implies a term relating to the transfer of goods by description, s. 4(2) satisfactory quality if supplied in the course of a business and s. 4(4) and (5) reasonably fit for a particular purpose made known prior to transfer.

(b) *The work (service) element*

The implied term applicable is that contained in SGSA 1982, s. 13 (contract for the supply of services), discussed below.

5. Contracts for the hire of goods

There are similar implied terms relating to the goods which are the subject of the hire (defined by SGSA 1982, s. 6) (see s. 8(2) (description), s. 9(2) (satisfactory quality), s. 9(4) and (5) (reasonably fit for the purpose), and s. 10(2) (sample)).

6. Contract for the supply of services: standard of performance

Under s. 13 of the SGSA 1982, there is an implied term that the supplier of services will carry out the service with reasonable care and skill. This standard is different from that applying to the sale or supply of goods. In the case of the latter the obligation to meet the required standard is absolute, and it will not be a defence to a claim of breach of the implied term of, for example, satisfactory quality, that the seller did his best to supply goods of that quality. In the case of the supply of services, however, the performance obligation will be met if the person performing the services uses reasonable care and skill. There is no guarantee that a particular result will be achieved (see 8.2.1).

6B Interpretation

6.5 Principles determining how to interpret contracts

6.5.1 Historical context : The four-corners rule

Just as statutes inevitably require interpretation by the courts to overcome the inherent inability of language to capture a single meaning representing the intention of Parliament, so for similar reasons the parties' contract may also require interpretation in order to ascertain its meaning before it is capable of being enforced. Since the modern rules of interpretation are based on the law of the nineteenth century, which in turn was based on a theory of contractual liability created by the will of the parties (see 1.4.2.2), the basic rule is that the court must find the intention of the parties. Construction has been confirmed as the determinative test for the implication of terms in fact (*Attorney General of Belize v Belize Telecom Ltd* [2009] UKPC 10, [2009] 1 WLR 1988: see 6.4.2.2). It is also the basis upon which decisions are made concerning the application of doctrines of mistake (3.2.1 and Chapter 13) and frustration (Chapter 12). Contracts also need to be construed to determine the nature and extent of their obligations, so that breach can be identified (Chapter 8) and exemption clauses need to be construed to determine whether they cover the loss, liability for which it is sought to exclude (see 7.4). It is difficult therefore to understate the importance of contractual construction to contemporary English contract law.

Traditionally, it was considered that, as a result of the parol evidence rule, the courts were, in general terms, limited in the search for intention to consideration of the contract document alone. In particular, as a general rule it has long been considered that it is not possible to have regard to the parties' negotiations or subsequent conduct. In *Lovell & Christmas Ltd v Wall* (1911) 104 LT 85 at p. 88, Cozens-Hardy MR said:

> It is irrelevant and improper to ask what the parties, prior to the execution of the instrument, intended or understood…[U]nless the case can be brought within some or one of [the] exceptions, it is the duty of the court, which is presumed to understand the English language, to construe the document according to the ordinary grammatical meaning of the words used therein, and without reference to anything which has previously passed between the parties to it.

However, there were **three recognized exceptions** where it was permissible to go outside the document and introduce extrinsic evidence to establish meaning.

1. The first exception is perhaps the most obvious, namely where the words in question have a technical (or other special) meaning. It is clear that this remains the position.

2. It was possible to examine the purpose and background to the document (the so-called 'matrix') in order to resolve a clear ambiguity.

3. It was possible to examine the purpose and background to the document (the matrix) where the literal meaning of the words used would lead to absurdity.

In *Prenn v Simmonds* [1971] 1 WLR 1381 at p. 1385, Lord Wilberforce stated that if the interpretation of the words used would destroy the very purpose of the contract and undermine it, 'that may be a strong argument for an alternative interpretation, if that can reasonably be found'. Although Lord Wilberforce appeared to make this comment in the context of the limitations of the so-called 'absurdity' exception, this comment was taken by the House of Lords in *Investors Compensation Scheme Ltd v West Bromwich Building Society* [1998] 1 WLR 898 as allowing a more liberal interpretation of contracts according with principles of commercial common sense (see Lord Steyn in *Mannai Investment Co. Ltd v Eagle Star Life Assurance Co. Ltd* [1997] 2 WLR 945).

6.5.2 *West Bromwich*: Contextual interpretation

Lord Hoffmann stated the current legal principles in the *Investors Compensation Scheme* case (at pp. 114–15) as follows:

(1) Interpretation is the ascertainment of the meaning which the document would convey to a reasonable person having all the background knowledge which would reasonably have been available to the parties in the situation in which they were at the time of the contract.

(2) The background was famously referred to by Lord Wilberforce as the 'matrix of fact'. Subject to the requirement that it should have been reasonably available to the parties and to the exception to be mentioned next, it includes *absolutely anything* which would have affected the way in which the language of the document would have been understood by a reasonable man.

(3) The law excludes from the admissible background the previous negotiations of the parties and their declarations of subjective intent. They are admissible only in an action for rectification. The law makes this distinction for reasons of practical policy and, in this respect only, legal interpretation differs from the way we would interpret utterances in ordinary life.

(4) The meaning which a document...would convey to a reasonable man is not the same thing as the meaning of its words. The meaning of words is a matter of dictionaries and grammars; the meaning of the document is what the parties using those words against the relevant background would reasonably have been understood to mean. The background may not merely enable the reasonable man to choose between the possible meanings of words which are ambiguous but even...to conclude that the parties must, for whatever reason, have used the wrong words or syntax...

(5) The 'rule' that words should be given their 'natural and ordinary meaning' reflects the common-sense proposition that we do not easily accept that people have made linguistic mistakes, particularly in formal documents. On the other hand, if one would nevertheless conclude from the background that something must have gone wrong with the language, the law does not require judges to attribute to the parties an intention which they plainly could not have had. [Emphasis added.]

Lord Hoffmann justified this approach by relying on what he described as 'the fundamental change which has overtaken this branch of the law, particularly as a result of the speeches of Lord Wilberforce'. However, the approach is far-reaching because it completely removes the traditional constraints of the parol evidence rule. In addition, the reference to the matrix of fact as including 'absolutely anything' which would have affected how the language was reasonably understood, was bound to prove controversial.

The approach now is that, unless the words have a technical meaning, they are to be construed in their natural and ordinary meaning set in the context of the contract as a whole. The contract must then be construed against the 'matrix of facts', i.e. all the information and background available to the parties at the time they made the contract, such as previous dealings and their contractual purpose, but excluding evidence of their negotiations (discussed below).

6.5.2.1 Meaning to reflect business common sense: Principles 4 and 5

The courts are required to construe contractual provisions to give such a meaning as reflects 'business common sense'. As Lord Diplock stated in *Antaios Cia Naviera SA v Salen Rederierna AB, The Antaios* [1985] AC 191 at p. 201:

> If detailed semantic and syntactical analysis of words in a commercial contract is going to lead to a conclusion that flouts business common sense, it must yield to business common sense.

In other words, if the contract as construed applying ordinary language and rules of syntax would lead to an unreasonable result, the assumption must be that the parties cannot have intended it. (This approach is similar to the much criticized approach of the House of Lords in *Schuler v Wickman Machine Tool Sales Ltd* [1974] AC 235, discussed at 8.5.3.2.)

In *Mannai Investments Co Ltd v Eagle Star Life Assurance* [1997] AC 749, Lord Steyn commented (at p. 771):

> In determining the meaning of the language of a commercial contract, and unilateral contractual notices, the law therefore generally favours a commercially sensible construction. The reason for this approach is that a commercial construction is more likely to give effect to the intention if the parties. Words are therefore interpreted in the way in which a reasonable commercial person would construe them. And the standard of the reasonable commercial person is hostile to technical interpretations and undue emphasis on niceties of language.

The *Investors Compensation Scheme* approach to contractual interpretation is open to criticism on a number of grounds; but in particular, because of its vagueness, it will inevitably lead to the much-dreaded uncertainty in the context of commercial contracts, especially for third parties. There is clearly no universal understanding, even among commercial judges, of what will constitute 'business common sense'. In addition, as Sir Christopher Staughton wrote ('How do the courts interpret commercial contracts?' [1999] CLJ 303 at p. 307), the need to examine the matrix of facts when determining contractual interpretation means that '[i]t is hard to imagine a ruling more calculated to perpetuate the vast cost of commercial litigation'.

The House of Lords took the opportunity to clarify matters in *Bank of Credit and Commerce International SA v Ali* [2001] UKHL 8, [2001] 2 WLR 735.

> This case concerned the terms of a release which the employee of BCCI was asked to agree to when being made redundant by the bank. The employee signed the release but subsequent case law permitted a particular form of claim that had not previously been thought to exist. This claim meant that former employees were able to bring claims for financial loss resulting from the stigma attached to having worked for the bank, which was found to have acted in breach of a duty of trust and confidence (*Mahmud v BCCI SA* [1998] AC 20, discussed at 9.9.4.6). The question was whether the former employee was barred from bringing such an action by the terms of the release. The majority of the House of Lords construed the terms of the release and concluded that, by examining all the surrounding circumstances, the parties could not have intended to provide for the release of rights and the surrender of claims which had never been within their contemplations.

237

Lord Clyde considered that the court had to determine:

> the meaning which the document would convey to a reasonable person having all the background knowledge which would reasonably have been available to the parties in the situation in which they were at the time of the contract

and that this would include matters of law as well as matters of fact. The release could not have been intended, on a reasonable construction, to cover future claims which might arise and which were not related to the termination of the employee's contract, such as future stigma losses.

Lord Hoffmann dissented on the application of the principles of interpretation (which he had set out in the *Investors Compensation* case) but reaffirmed them and took the opportunity to respond to the criticisms that had met his formulation of the matrix as including 'absolutely anything'. He stated (at [39]):

> I did not think it necessary to emphasise that I meant anything which a reasonable man would have regarded as relevant. I was merely saying that there is no conceptual limit to what can be regarded as background. It is not, for example, confined to the factual background but can include the state of the law…I was certainly not encouraging a trawl through 'background' which could not have made a reasonable person think that the parties must have departed from conventional usage.

Therefore, the crucial factor when identifying the matrix should be relevance. It is likely, as the case law serves to illustrate, that individual judges will disagree on this question of interpretation so that the uncertainties will remain. However, some commentators, such as McMeel [1998] LMCLQ 382, have argued that this is the necessary price to be paid for greater fairness in contractual construction and it is clear that the *West Bromwich* approach, particularly the ability to examine the commercial context and background, has had major implications for principle in other areas of contract law where a determination of intention as revealed by the context is required, e.g. the implication of terms in fact *Attorney General of Belize v Belize Telecom Ltd* [2009] UKPC 10, [2009] 1 WLR 1988: see 6.4.2.2.

6.5.2.2 Linguistic mistake where an interpretation based on ordinary language and syntax makes 'no commercial sense'

Chartbrook Ltd v Persimmon Homes Ltd [2009] UKHL 38, [2009] 3 WLR 267, concerned an agreement for the development of land. Persimmon was required to obtain planning permission and would then construct the scheme. On completion, Chartbrook would dispose of the units, Persimmon would receive the proceeds and use those proceeds to pay Chartbrook a price for the land based on the total land value and an ARP 'additional residential payment', which was defined in the contract. The parties' dispute arose because they gave different interpretations to the ARP and its calculation. Chartbrook claimed that it had been underpaid.

At first instance and in the Court of Appeal, the APR definition was interpreted on the basis of ordinary rules of syntax since 'the words made sense on their own'. However, the House of Lords allowed the appeal by Persimmon on the basis that the context and background indicated that 'something must have gone wrong with the language' (Lord Hoffmann), although accepting that a court did not easily accept that linguistic mistakes were made in formal documents. An interpretation based on the ordinary rules of syntax made no commercial sense and would not accord with what a reasonable person, having all the background knowledge that would have been available to the parties, would have understood the parties to have meant. Thus the House of Lords was able to correct an error through interpretation without having to resort to a claim for rectification.

Whilst the ordinary interpretation made no commercial sense in *Chartbrook*, in ***Bishops Wholesale Newsagency Ltd v Surridge Dawson Ltd*** [2009] EWHC 2578 (Ch), it was held that the natural meaning of the words prevailed. The judge, Judge Mackie QC, stated that when interpreting a contractual provision it was first necessary to decide that ordinary meaning of the language amounted to an error or absurdity before then deciding what reasonable people in the position of the parties at the time would reasonably have intended the words to mean. On these facts there was no doubt as to the ordinary meaning of the words chosen, no error or absurdity and the parties had been advised by solicitors when formulating and agreeing the contract terms. On these facts nothing had 'gone wrong with the language'. Whilst it was conceded that the particular term might appear generous on the natural meaning interpretation, that was not a basis for courts to adjudicate between parties about the commercial good sense of different meanings and interpretations of terms given that the intended meaning was clear.

6.5.3 Pre-contractual negotiations

6.5.3.1 The exclusionary rule

Prenn v Simmonds [1971] 1 WLR 1381 is authority of the House of Lords for 'the exclusionary rule', i.e. there is to be no recourse to pre-contractual negotiations to explain the meaning the parties must be taken to have intended for their contractual document.

- Lord Wilberforce said that 'such evidence is unhelpful' because only when the contract is finally made is there a consensus, and until that time the parties' respective intentions may change, or be refined. There can be no guarantee, therefore, that an intention appearing during negotiations has remained constant until the time of contracting.

- In such circumstances it is thought safer to rely on the words of the document alone since statements made in pre-contract negotiations will be necessarily more subjective.

- There is a further argument that admission of such evidence would led to uncertainty and unpredictability in terms of interpretation which would add to the costs involved in any dispute and litigation.

- It is also argued that if negotiations are not excluded there would be an adverse effect on third party rights, i.e. third parties taking an assignment of the contract or relying upon it as security could not be safe in making assumptions as to meaning without knowing what had taken place during these negotiations between the original parties.

6.5.3.2 Should 'the exclusionary rule' be reconsidered and pre-contractual negotiations become admissible as an aid to construction?

The UNIDROIT *Principles* (Art. 4(3)), *Principles of European Contract Law* (PECL) (Art. 5:102), and the *Draft Common Frame of Reference* (DCFR) II-8:102(1)(a), all permit reference to prior negotiations when determining the 'common intention of the parties' so it might be thought that a similar approach should be acceptable in English law. Lord Nicholls in his Chancery Bar Lecture 'My Kingdom for a horse: The meaning of words', published at (2005) 121 LQR 577, was critical of the non-admissibility of evidence of pre-contractual negotiations, considering this evidence to be inadmissible only if 'unhelpful', and that it would only be 'unhelpful' where the evidence merely illustrates separate positions and aspirations of the negotiating parties. However, if the evidence was that the parties had reached some agreement during the negotiations regarding the meaning of a word or phrase or of a particular clause then evidence of this would be helpful as, to use the words employed by Lord Nicholls (at p. 583), 'the best evidence of all'.

The more general question of whether 'the exclusionary principle' should be abandoned came before the House of Lords in **Chartbrook Ltd v Persimmon Homes Ltd** [2009] UKHL 38, [2009] 3 WLR 267 (6.5.2.2). The House of Lords, having found in favour of Persimmon on the construction issue, made *obiter* observations as a response to an argument that account should be taken of the pre-contractual negotiations, particularly two letters which Persimmon claimed supported its interpretation of the agreement. The main ground discussed for permitting such evidence to be admissible was that in some cases such evidence would clearly be 'helpful' and 'relevant'. Lord Hoffmann put it thus:

> Among the dirt of aspirations, proposals and counterproposals there may gleam the gold of a genuine consensus on some aspect of the transaction expressed in terms which would influence an objective observer in construing the language used by the parties in their final agreement. Why should the court deny itself the assistance of this material in deciding what the parties must be taken to have meant?

His Lordship expressly rejected an attempt to limit the exclusionary rule to instances where pre-contractual negotiations were irrelevant in determining intention but to admit it when the evidence is shown to be relevant (an argument not dissimilar to the parol evidence rule and its application as a self-evident tautology: see 6.2.1). The authorities did not support a qualification to the exclusionary rule based on relevance.

Lord Hoffmann concluded that since 'the rule of inadmissibility has been established for a very long time' and by a consistent line of authority, and (at [41]) 'there is no clearly established case for departing from the exclusionary rule', the fact that the rule might mean that 'parties are sometimes held bound by a contract in terms which, upon a full investigation of the course of negotiations, a reasonable observer would not have taken them to have intended' could be 'justified in the more general interest of economy and predictability in obtaining advice and adjudicating disputes', absent any empirical evidence pointing in the opposite direction. In any event, there were 'the safety nets' of rectification and estoppel by convention, i.e. the parties may claim that as a result of a mistake the final contract does not represent their common intention as to the meaning they intended their agreement to have (discussed at 3.4.1). Alternatively if the parties have negotiated an agreement upon a common assumption that particular words will bear a certain meaning then estoppel may operate to prevent a claim that the words should be given a different meaning.

However, Lord Hoffmann was clear that although the exclusionary rule excluded evidence of pre-contractual negotiations for the purpose of interpreting the parties intended meaning, such evidence was not thereby excluded if sought to be introduced for other purposes, e.g. to establish that a fact which might be relevant as background was known to the parties (see **Estor**

Ltd v Multifit (UK) Ltd [2009] EWHC 2565 (TCC) where the court used pre-contract information to identify the parties to the contract on this basis)—and clearly such evidence was admissible to support a claim for rectification or estoppel; indeed, this was frequently used by parties to bring the excluded pre-contractual evidence before the court. This evidence was not an exception to the rule but rather it operated outside the rule.

Baroness Hale, whilst purporting to agree with Lord Hoffmann and Lord Walker, conceded: 'But I have to confess that I would not have found it quite so easy to reach this conclusion [as to the meaning of ARP] had we not been made aware of the agreement which the parties had reached on this aspect of their bargain during the negotiations which led up to the formal contract.' These negotiations had been introduced quite legitimately in the context of the rectification claim but it is worrying that, whilst purporting to support the exclusionary rule, her Ladyship also conceded that she had taken account of this evidence in reaching her conclusion on the interpretation of the meaning of the disputed words. She concluded that '[i]n the end abolition may be the only workable legislative solution' but in the meantime the courts could determine in which cases such evidence is 'helpful', possibly by looking at whether in terms of the law of rectification a 'consensus' had been reached in the negotiations. If there was no consensus, then the evidence of the negotiations would necessarily be 'unhelpful'. There is something superficially attractive in this solution, assuming that it is intended to apply beyond rectification cases. However, it is less attractive when the position of third parties is considered since they are unlikely to have knowledge of prior negotiations, let alone whether those negotiations reached any consensus on the meaning of particular words or phrases.

6.5.4 Prior contracts

However, it is accepted that evidence of prior contracts, as opposed to prior contractual negotiations in this contract, is always admissible (*HIH Casualty & General Insurance Ltd v New Hampshire Co.* [2001] EWCA Civ 735, [2001] 2 Lloyd's Rep 161 at [83] and *KPMG LLP v Network Rail Infrastructure Ltd* [2007] EWCA Civ 363, [2007] Bus LR 1336).

6.5.5 Deleted words in contracts and documents

In *Mopani Copper Mines plc v Millenium Underwriting Ltd* [2008] EWHC 1331 (Comm), [2008] 2 All ER (Comm) 976, [2008] 1 CLC 992, Christopher Clarke J considered (at [120]), that where there was ambiguity in the words that remained in a document it was legitimate to look at deleted words in a document in order to determine what the parties had agreed that they had **not** agreed. Equally, deleted words in a printed document or form may resolve the ambiguity of a neighbouring paragraph that remains. This principle is said not to offend 'the exclusionary principle' relating to pre-contractual negotiations.

6.5.6 Subsequent conduct is generally inadmissible

Authority for this principle can be found in the decision in *James Miller & Partners Ltd v Whitworth Street Estates (Manchester) Ltd* [1970] AC 572. This is because conduct of a party after making the contract does not assist in objective identification of the meaning with which the parties used particular words at the time they made the contract.

Further reading

A Content

Bradgate, 'Unreasonable standard terms' (1997) 60 MLR 582.

Kramer, 'Implication in fact as an instance of contractual interpretation' [2004] CLJ 384.

Law Commission, Report No. 154, *Law of Contract: The parol evidence rule* (1986) Cmnd 9700.

Macdonald, 'Incorporation of contract terms by a "consistent course of dealing"' (1988) 8 LS 48.

Macdonald, 'The duty to give notice of unusual contract terms' [1988] JBL 375.

Macdonald, 'The Emperor's old clauses: Unincorporated clauses, misleading terms and the Unfair Terms in Consumer Contracts Regulations' (1999) 58 CLJ 413.

Peden, 'Policy concerns behind implication of terms in law' (2001) 117 LQR 459.

Peden and Carter, 'Incorporation of terms by signature: L'Estrange rules!' (2005) 21 JCL 96.

Phang, 'Implied terms revisited' [1990] JBL 394.

Phang, 'Implied terms, business efficacy and the officious bystander: A modern history' [1998] JBL 1.

Wedderburn, 'Collateral contracts' [1959] CLJ 58.

B Interpretation

Gee, 'The interpretation of commercial contracts' (2001) 117 LQR 358.

Kramer, 'Common sense principles of contract interpretation (and how we've been using them all along)' (2003) 23 OJLS 173.

McMeel, 'The rise of commercial construction in contract law' [1998] LMCLQ 382.

McMeel, 'Prior negotiations and subsequent conduct: The next step forward for contractual interpretation?' (2003) 119 LQR 272.

McMeel, *The Construction of Contracts: Interpretation, implication and rectification* (Oxford University Press, 2007).

Lord Nicholls, 'My kingdom for a horse: The meaning of words' (2005) 121 LQR 577.

Staughton, 'How do the courts interpret commercial contracts?' [1999] CLJ 303.

Exemption clauses and unfair contract terms

Summary of the issues

- An exemption clause is a clause which seeks either to exclude a party's liability for breach or to limit that liability to a specified amount. Exemption clauses may alternatively seek to exclude or limit the remedies that would otherwise be available for breach or seek to deny that any breach of contract or breach of a duty of care has arisen.

- Although such clauses have benefits, especially in commercial contracts, in allocating risks between the parties and avoiding duplicate insurance cover, both the courts and Parliament have sought to control their use.

- In order to be enforceable as an exemption clause, the clause in question must:

  1. be incorporated as a term

  2. cover the loss which has occurred in the circumstances in which it occurred

  3. not be rendered unenforceable under either the Unfair Contract Terms Act (UCTA) 1977 and/or (consumer contracts only) the Unfair Terms in Consumer Contracts Regulations (UTCCR) 1999. The UTCCR 1999 have a broader scope of application and strike at unfair terms generally (with the exception of so-called 'core terms') in consumer contracts.

- Incorporation of terms was considered in 6.3. The current chapter examines the question of construction of the clause and the legislative regulation of exemption clauses and unfair terms.

- Prior to UCTA 1977 the courts construed exemption clauses very strictly in order to protect consumers. Such a strict approach is no longer necessary as the legislation can fulfil this purpose and nowadays clauses are construed on their natural and ordinary meaning to see if they cover what has happened. Some of the restrictive construction devices may still be relied upon, e.g. negligence construction, but the courts are becoming increasingly willing to adopt a less technical and more liberal approach to such construction, reflecting the general approach to contractual interpretation (see Chapter 6B).

- Where UCTA 1977 applies, it will render the clause in question either totally unenforceable in the circumstances or enforceable only if shown to be reasonable. The applicable outcome is determined by the liability which it is sought to exclude or limit and, on occasion, by the type of loss that has occurred or whether it is sought to rely on the clause 'as against a person dealing as consumer'. In relation to the reasonableness requirement, there is a clear policy distinction in the decisions between the operation of clauses in the commercial and consumer contexts.

- The UTCCR 1999 implement a European Directive and provide regulation of unfair terms in consumer contracts (other than core terms such as the price, see *Office of Fair Trading v Abbey National plc* [2009]

UKSC 6 (bank charges case)). A term is unfair if 'contrary to the requirement of good faith it causes a significant imbalance in the parties' rights and obligations arising under the contract' to the detriment of the consumer. The regulations therefore introduced the notion of good faith into English law. Good faith, and its application in the context of the regulations, was examined by the House of Lords in *Director General of Fair Trading v First National Bank*.

• The regulations are interesting because they provide for pre-emptive challenges to unfair terms (i.e., without reference to an actual dispute) by bodies such as the Office of Fair Trading (OFT) and utility regulators. The aim is to prevent the continued use of terms regarded as unfair.

• The Law Commission examined the complex relationship between UCTA 1977 and the UTCCR 1999 and made recommendations in a report for reform, including a unified regime for consumer contracts with the aim of simplifying and clarifying the applicable principles and altering the burden of proof. In the context of business contracts, there is a recommendation for a special regime applicable to 'small businesses' whilst the approach to business-to-business (B2B) contracts is non-interventionist, reflecting the current approach to reasonableness in commercial contracts under UCTA 1977.

7.1 Introduction

7.1.1 Control of the substantive content of contracts

This chapter focuses on legal regulation of 'substantive unfairness' in contracts. In other words, the parties' ability to control the content of their contracts is not unrestricted, and both the courts and Parliament—most recently in order to implement European directives—have interfered to prevent the inclusion and use of terms that are regarded as 'unfair'.

Clauses which purport to exclude or to limit liability for breach of contract are the most common form of what are referred to in this chapter as 'exemption clauses'. It is important to note, however, that exemption clauses come in many different forms (see 7.1.4.1). The applicable rules remain generally the same.

Exemption clauses are an important feature of modern contracts, and in recent years have been the focus of much judicial, legislative, and academic attention. More recently, in the context of consumer contracts, there has been legislative regulation of both specific terms (e.g., the consumer credit legislation) and the broader category of terms on the basis of 'unfairness'. This broader regulation, contained in the Unfair Consumer Contracts Regulations 1999, SI 1999/2083, is particularly interesting because the intervention is expressly linked to the concept of 'good faith', which has long been recognized as an essential feature of contracting in many jurisdictions, although not in England and Wales. (There are specialist texts examining this area of law, most notably Macdonald, *Exemption Clauses and Unfair Terms*, 2nd edn (Tottel Publishing, 2006) and Lawson, *Exclusion Clauses and Unfair Contract Terms*, 9th edn (Sweet and Maxwell, 2008).) This chapter examines the reasons for, and the mechanisms of, control of exemption clauses and other mechanisms for the control of the fairness of contractual terms.

It is also important to appreciate that the restraint-of-trade doctrine and measures controlling anti-competitive agreements (discussed in Chapter 16) are further examples of the control of the content of contracts. This control is based both on reasonableness as between the parties and broader considerations of public policy, i.e. what is reasonable in the public interest. In addition, there may be a broader doctrine of unconscionability (based on the principle in *Fry v Lane* (1888) 40 ChD 312, discussed in 15.3.3) which will affect contractual content, and the 'penalty rule' and rules governing relief from forfeiture (discussed in 9.10) also represent an attempt to regulate contractual content.

7.1.2 Standard-form contracts and the purpose of exemption clauses

Since classical contract law saw contractual liability as something created by the operation of the will of the parties, rather than as liability imposed by law, it was inevitable that the classical law should accept the power of the parties to modify as they saw fit the nature of the liability created. Thus, while the usual result of the breach of a promise, which had been duly incorporated in a valid contract, was, at the very least, to create a secondary obligation to pay damages in compensation for any loss suffered, it was open to the parties to agree to contractual 'promises' that did not have this usual result. The more common means of modifying the usual liability were to exclude any obligation to pay compensation, or to limit the amount of compensation payable.

It should not be thought that such exemption clauses are necessarily bad, or that the classical law was excessively naive in allowing parties to abdicate all responsibility for their promises. The classical law *assumed* (in a way which today might be frequently challenged) that all parties to contractual negotiations would be bargaining freely, would be best placed to know their own interests, and would agree to such terms only if some, not necessarily immediately apparent, benefit would accrue from so doing.

These assumptions remain valid where the parties do in fact deal with each other on an equal footing. **In that situation, typified by the commercial contract, the exemption clause is an important device for allocating the risks of the contract between the parties.**

 Example

> Imagine a contract for the supply of machinery which depends upon the availability of raw materials from abroad. Both parties know that there is a slight risk that the usual, low-cost supplier will be slow to supply because of the unstable political conditions in its country. Alternative supplies are available at much higher cost. The seller of the machinery may quote two prices: let us say £2,500 for a guaranteed delivery date, by using the high-cost raw materials; and let us say £1,500 using the low-cost raw materials, but subject to an exclusion of liability for late delivery. The buyer may then choose which contract is preferable, knowing that the seller will not agree to bear the risk of late delivery if the cheaper contract is chosen.

There is no reason for the law to interfere with this kind of use of exemption clauses, and indeed to do so would be to undermine the economic basis of the parties' agreement.

Nevertheless, it is generally accepted today that there are situations in which exemption clauses are not freely negotiated, at which point the law may seek to interfere. These situations usually involve standard-form contracts. Such contracts are entered into on the basis of a standard set of contractual terms contained in a document drawn up by one of the parties. Standard-form contracts are not necessarily bad. They represent the reaction of lawyers to the increase in contractual activity engendered by the industrial revolution. As goods were mass produced, it became much more convenient to use 'mass produced' contracts, since the circumstances of one sale were normally very similar to another, meaning that the costs of individual drafting could be avoided. It became normal practice to include one or more exemption clauses in such standardized contracts. Sometimes the inclusion of these clauses reflected the practice of a particular trade in the allocation of risks between buyers and sellers, and so was entirely legitimate. The problem with standard-form contracts, however, is that they may present little choice to the party who has not drawn up the document. If that person wants the product, he may have to accept the terms drawn up by the other party; if the terms are unacceptable, that person will be resigned to not obtaining the product from this source. For this reason standard-form contracts are sometimes called 'contracts of adhesion'.

Thus, standard-form contracts may be used to **impose** an exclusion or limitation of liability which has not been negotiated, and for which the person whose normal contractual rights are diminished has received no alternative benefit. **The imposition of such exemption clauses may be particularly harmful in consumer contracts, where the disequilibrium between the bargaining positions of the parties may be substantial, and where the consumer may have no alternative but to accept the terms if such exemptions are commonplace throughout the particular industry, as is often the case.**

7.1.3 Judicial attitudes to exemption clauses

Judicial attitudes to exemption clauses have hardened over the last hundred years. It is still the case that individually negotiated contracts containing exemption clauses are generally assumed not to be harmful. The attitude to standard-form contracts may be summarized by reference to the speech of Lord Diplock in the House of Lords in *Schroeder Music Publishing Co. Ltd v Macaulay* [1974] 1 WLR 1308.

- Standard-form contracts which are used for convenience to express common commercial agreements, and which do so in terms normal to such contracts, are presumed to be fair and reasonable.

- Standard-form contracts in consumer transactions, and in other situations in which one party is said to have no alternative but to contract on the terms offered if that person is to contract at all, are not presumed to be fair and reasonable. Rather, they are viewed as the product of the superior bargaining position of one of the parties.

The courts often suspect that that superior bargaining position is being exploited at the cost of the other party, and for that reason will do everything in their power to avoid the consequences of such clauses. It is sometimes suggested that the judicial attitude to exemption clauses in cases of superior bargaining power is oversimplistic (Trebilcock in Reiter and Swan (eds), *Studies in Contract Law* (Butterworths, 1981), p. 481). The assertion that consumers have no alternative but to contract on such terms has been challenged, and it has been suggested that consumers do get (an admittedly non-negotiated) benefit from such contracts in the form of lower prices than would prevail if each contract had to be individually negotiated. Nevertheless, there is growing evidence that such clauses have been used in consumer contracts precisely in order to frighten off complainants, even when there is little or no prospect of the clause being upheld by the courts. In these circumstances it seems likely that, whatever the economists may say about the reasonableness and utility of exemption clauses in all types of contract, judicial attitudes will remain unsympathetic to their use in consumer contracts. That position has been reinforced by legislation (see 7.5).

7.1.4 Types and nature of exemption clauses

7.1.4.1 Types of exemptions

It would be impossible, and fruitless, to catalogue every known type of exemption clause. The wit and invention of contracts' draftsmen have been fuelled by the courts' attempts to control such clauses and have resulted in the regular discovery of new and ingenious forms of exemption clause, to which subsequently the courts have to react.

- Most common are the clauses purporting to exclude liability completely for part at least of what would otherwise be included in the contractual undertaking (e.g., excluding liability for consequential losses), and those clauses limiting liability to a particular sum (e.g., the price payable under the contract).

- Other common forms are those which limit the remedy available either by imposing a short time-limit during which claims for breach must be made, or by imposing onerous conditions on obtaining the remedy (such as payment of costs of transport of defective goods to and from the supplier's place of business).

- More difficult to control are clauses which, rather than exempting liability for breach, purport to modify the performance obligation, so that no breach occurs (see the discussion of terms which modify expected contractual obligations, at 7.6.4.2).

7.1.4.2 The nature of exemption clauses

Before examining the approach to legal regulation of such clauses, it is essential to first consider their nature. It is possible, and arguably more logical, to treat an exemption clause like any other term of the contract so that it operates to define the obligations of the parties. This was the approach adopted by Lord Diplock in *Photo Production Ltd v Securicor Transport Ltd* [1980] AC 827. However, the generally accepted view is that such clauses may operate as a defence to the liability which would otherwise exist. This is artificial in that it involves construing all of the other terms of the contract in order to identify the contractual obligations and duties owed, and then separately considering whether the exemption clause operates to exclude or limit that liability (see Yates, *Exclusion Clauses in Contracts,* 2nd edn (Sweet and Maxwell, 1992), pp. 123–33).

7.2 Exemption clauses as defences to liability

The common law provides no rule or doctrine whereby an exemption clause may simply be declared unenforceable on the ground that it is unfair or unreasonable (*Photo Production Ltd v Securicor Transport Ltd* [1980] AC 827: see 7.4.3). For many years, therefore, the courts' hostility to such clauses found expression in the application, often in strict or strained terms, of devices of the general law of contract to the particular problem of exemption clauses. The more common of such devices are discussed below. In theory, they are still applicable despite the enactment of statutory controls on certain exemption clauses; in practice, in many instances the courts have been able to adopt a more realistic and less artificial approach to the application of these devices because of the existence of the more direct means of control where these are available. However, in recent years there has been a tendency to rely upon the *Interfoto* principle (*Interfoto Picture Library Ltd v Stiletto Visual Programmes Ltd* [1989] QB 433), requiring a higher standard of incorporation for certain exemption clauses considered to be onerous or unusual, discussed at 6.3.1.5.

It is recognized that in order to be able to rely upon an exemption clause as a defence to liability, the party seeking to rely upon the clause has the burden of establishing that the exemption clause was incorporated and covers the liability which has occurred in the circumstances in which it occurred. The enforceability of the clause can then be defeated only if the clause is rendered unenforceable by statute.

7.3 Incorporation

The rules governing the incorporation of written terms into agreements have already been examined (see 6.2.2 and 6.3). As was noted there, the law on incorporation had developed almost exclusively through judicial attempts to avoid the impact of exemption clauses.

In the absence of signature, the general principle is that any clause which has not reasonably been brought to the notice of the offeree before the time of acceptance of the offer (and thus the making of the contract) will not be incorporated into the contract (see, e.g., *Thornton v Shoe Lane Parking Ltd* [1971] 2 QB 163: see 6.3.1.4). By means of this principle the courts have been able to prevent reliance upon contract terms which were printed in receipts or invoices and which had not come to the attention of the party in question when entering the agreement. The courts have also used the requirement that a higher degree of notice is required for unusual or onerous terms in order to prevent reliance on such terms which were not 'fairly and reasonably' brought to the attention of the other party (*Interfoto Picture Library Ltd v Stiletto Visual Programmes Ltd* [1989] QB 433: see 6.3.1.5; notably, Bingham LJ considered this to be an aspect of English law developing 'piecemeal solutions to demonstrated problem of unfairness' in a way which achieved the same result as the doctrine of good faith (or 'fair and open dealing') in other jurisdictions). In instances where a higher standard of incorporation is relevant, it is necessary to specifically draw the attention of the other party to the existence of the clause (e.g., by highlighting the exemption clause).

7.4 Construction

7.4.1 Devices of interpretation

At one time, this was the final mechanism open to a court which sought to protect the consumer from the consequences of an exemption clause in a contract. On occasions, therefore, there is clear evidence of rather strained and artificial constructions of such clauses; the classic example being the decision of the Court of Appeal in *Hollier v Rambler Motors (AMC) Ltd* [1972] 2 QB 71. Such artificial interpretations are no longer required because of the existence of statutory provisions to regulate the use of such clauses, and the basic construction test propounded by Lord Bridge in *George Mitchell (Chesterhall) Ltd v Finney Lock Seeds* [1983] 2 AC 803 at p. 811, namely:

whether the relevant condition, on its true construction in the context of the contract as a whole is effective to exclude or limit the liability in question. In other words, it is only necessary to construe the clause on its natural and ordinary meaning to see if it covers what has happened.

However, this said, there are a number of interpretation devices which indicate that the basic approach to construction can be a strict one. A party seeking to avoid liability must be able to prove the common intention of the parties by clear words, since the courts will otherwise assume that the normal incidents of contractual liability were intended. This strict interpretation takes several forms.

7.4.1.1 The courts will not imply any exemption greater than that contained in the words used

> In **Andrews Bros (Bournemouth) Ltd v Singer & Co. Ltd** [1934] 1 KB 17, the plaintiffs contracted to purchase 'new' cars from the defendant company. The contract contained a clause excluding 'all conditions, warranties and liabilities implied by common law statute or otherwise'. One of the cars was found to have done a substantial mileage on delivery to the plaintiffs and therefore clearly was not 'new'. The exclusion clause did not protect the defendants. It excluded implied terms, while the requirement that the cars be 'new' was an express term of the contract.

7.4.1.2 The courts operate what is known as the *contra proferentem* rule

Where the meaning of an exemption clause is ambiguous, that ambiguity will be resolved against the party seeking to rely on the clause (the *proferens*). In other words, the courts will adopt the meaning which is unfavourable to that party.

> In *Beck and Co. v Szymanowski and Co.* [1924] AC 43, the contract provided that delivered goods were deemed to be in satisfactory condition unless complaint was made within fourteen days of receiving them. The clause was ineffective to exclude liability for short delivery (i.e., for goods not delivered; a different breach) even though complaint was made more than fourteen days after receiving the goods.

Although this rule rests on the existence of ambiguity in the meaning of the exemption clause, the courts have been resourceful in finding such ambiguity when it has suited them to be able to cut down the impact of a clause.

> For example, in **Houghton v Trafalgar Insurance Co. Ltd** [1954] 1 QB 247, a car insurance policy did not give protection to cover damage occurring when the car was conveying 'any load in excess of that for which it was constructed'. An accident occurred when the car, designed to carry five people, was carrying six. The Court of Appeal considered that 'load' was ambiguous, and construed it against the insurers to limit it to excess weight rather than excess passengers.

The *contra proferentem* rule is expressly incorporated in the **Unfair Terms in Consumer Contracts Regulations 1999, SI 1999/2083, reg. 7(2)**:

> If there is doubt about the meaning of a written term, the interpretation which is most favourable to the consumer shall prevail.

However, this principle is excluded from operation in respect of pre-emptive challenges to clauses in standard forms (see discussion at 7.7.7).

7.4.1.3 Negligence construction: Exclusion clauses

In what is a particular and common example of the operation of the *contra proferentem* rule, the policy of the courts is to limit the scope of exclusion clauses (as opposed to limitation clauses) by restricting the scope of the exclusion. In particular, the courts have shown themselves unwilling to extend the scope of an exclusion clause to liabilities other than contractual (unless it is expressly stated to cover them), thereby ensuring that the claimant has an alternative remedy in tort to which the clause does not apply.

In the context of purported exemptions from liability for negligence this policy is given effect in the test proposed by Lord Morton in **Canada Steamship Lines v The King** [1952] AC 192 at p. 208:

(ii) If the clause contains language which expressly exempts the person in whose favour it is made (hereafter called 'the *proferens*') from the consequence of the negligence of his own servants, effect must be given to that provision…

(iii) If there is no express reference to negligence, the court must consider whether the words are wide enough, in their ordinary meaning, to cover negligence on the part of the servants of the *proferens*…

(iv) If the words used are wide enough for the above purpose, the court must then consider whether 'the head of damage may be based on some ground other than that of negligence'…The 'other ground' must not be so fanciful or remote that the *proferens* cannot be supposed to have desired protection against it; but subject to that qualification…the existence of a possible head of damage other than that of negligence is fatal to the *proferens* even if the words are *prima facie* wide enough to cover negligence on the part of his servants.

Before explaining this construction device there are two issues to consider:

- It is first necessary to add a note of caution on the application of these construction principles, especially in the light of the more liberal approach to contractual interpretation consequent on the principles developed in **Investors Compensation Scheme Ltd v West Bromwich Building Society** [1998] 1 WLR 898, discussed at Chapter 6B. In particular, this approach may mean that the courts will adopt a more relaxed approach to the application of Lord Morton's guidelines in the construction of exemption and indemnity clauses. This was confirmed in the speeches of the House of Lords in **HIH Casualty & General Insurance Ltd v Chase Manhattan Bank** [2003] UKHL 6, [2003] 1 All ER (Comm) 349. **The guidelines did not have the status of a set of rigid rules and were not to be applied in a way which would produce a result at odds with the commercial purpose of the contract. Nevertheless, it remains the case that clear words will be required to exclude a person's liability for the consequences of his own negligence.**

- Secondly, in order to understand Lord Morton's guidelines it is necessary to appreciate what is meant by liability in negligence in this context.

Contractual obligations require one of two standards of performance (discussed at 8.2.1), so that either:

- contractual liability may be strict (absolute obligations)

- contractual liability may be qualified (imposing a qualified contractual duty to exercise reasonable care and skill).

Negligence liability for the purposes of exemption clauses will include breach of a duty of care in tort but also includes breach of these qualified contractual obligations.

The *Canada Steamship* principle embodies the basic policy of the courts with regard to the construction of clauses excluding liability. This policy is to limit the scope of such clauses by restricting their operation so that, as a general rule, they exclude only strict contractual liability.

 Key point

In order to extend to exclude liability in negligence the clause in question would need to expressly extend to negligence liability, e.g. by using the word 'negligence' or a synonym of negligence. If this is the case, then effect will be given to this wording and the exclusion clause will exclude both strict contractual liability and negligence liability, as relevant.

However, if there is no express reference to negligence but the words used in the clause are wide enough to cover negligence liability, the exclusion will not cover negligence liability if there is some other liability to which the clause could extend on the facts, such as strict contractual liability.

The classic example of the application of this rule of construction is *White v John Warwick & Co. Ltd* [1953] 1 WLR 1285.

> The plaintiff was injured when the saddle on a bicycle hired from the defendants tipped and he fell on the road. The contract of hire exempted the defendants from liability for any personal injuries to the hirers of bicycles but made no express mention of negligence liability. Without the clause, the plaintiff might have succeeded against the defendants either for breach of contract, or for the defendants' negligence. (There was a breach of the strict contractual obligation to supply a bicycle fit for the purpose and also liability in negligence due to the failure to take care to ensure that the bicycle supplied was safe.) Since both types of liability had arisen on the facts, the Court of Appeal held that the exemption clause was effective to exclude liability in contract only, so that the plaintiff's action in negligence succeeded despite the clause.

Although the *Canada Steamship* test is a rule of construction, so that each case must be treated on its particular facts, some common threads emerge.

1. Negligence expressly mentioned

In accordance with Lord Morton's first test in the *Canada Steamship* case, to exclude liability for negligence as well as liability for breach of contract, express words ('negligence' or a synonym of negligence) must be used (see, e.g., *Monarch Airlines Ltd v London Luton Airport Ltd* [1997] CLC 698, where the words 'neglect or default' extended to exclude liability for negligence and breach of statutory duty). It might be considered sensible therefore to expressly extend the scope of the exclusion clause to cover liability in negligence. However, as Steyn LJ made clear in *E. E. Caledonia Ltd v Orbit Valve Co. plc* [1994] 1 WLR 1515 at p. 1523, it might not make commercial sense to insert such a reference as it would tend to frighten off the other party. Thus, '[o]missions of express reference to negligence tend to be deliberate'.

Since the policy of the courts is to require very clear words indeed before permitting a party to avoid liability for the consequences of their own negligence, a strict interpretation is evident both in relation to express references to negligence and whether the clause is capable, on the basis of the words used, of applying to negligence liability.

> For example, in *Stent Foundations Ltd v Gleeson plc* [2001] BLR 134, the clause stated: 'The Subcontractor shall be responsible for and indemnify the Contractor against any claims in respect of plant or tools of the Sub-Contractor or his workmen which may be lost or damaged by fire or any other cause…'. The judge dismissed an argument that the words used covered negligence liability. There was no express reference to negligence and, in addition, the words were not wide enough to cover such liability. The words 'any other cause' had to be interpreted restrictively in the light of the preceding words 'lost or damaged by fire', and fire was neutral on the question of fault. Accordingly, it was unnecessary to consider whether there was any other liability to which the clause could apply before concluding that negligence liability was not covered by this clause.

Another example of this strict interpretation of clauses as not excluding liability for negligence can be seen in the decision of the Court of Appeal in *E. E. Caledonia Ltd v Orbit Valve Co. plc* [1994] 1 WLR 1515.

> The plaintiffs made a payment to the estate of an engineer following his death in a fire on the plaintiffs' oil platform. The plaintiffs sought to recover this payment from the defendants (the engineer's employers) under the terms of an indemnity. The indemnity applied in respect of any claim, demand, cause of action, loss, expense, or liability arising from the death of such an employee in the performance of the contract. The death had been found to be the result of the plaintiffs' negligence and as a result of their breaches of health and safety regulations (i.e., breach of statutory duty so that liability is strict). The Court of Appeal held that the indemnity did not expressly cover negligence and that very clear words would be required in order for it to operate to protect a party from the consequences of that party's own negligence. In addition, as there was another liability (breach of statutory duty), the indemnity could not extend to cover the negligence. (On the facts, the Court of Appeal also held that the indemnity did not cover the breach of statutory duty because it amounted to a provision allocating full responsibility to each party for the consequences of its own actions.)

2. Negligence the only liability on the facts

Although not discussed by Lord Morton in *Canada Steamship*, it has been held that an exemption clause must be construed to cover negligence liability, despite the absence of any express reference to negligence, if the words of the clause are wide enough to cover negligence and negligence is the only liability which has arisen on the facts. (This would appear to follow from Lord Morton's point (iv) above.)

> For example, in *Alderslade v Hendon Laundry Ltd* [1945] 1 KB 189, the plaintiff sent items to the laundry which were not returned. The contract contained a clause restricting recovery for lost items to twenty times the laundering charge. Since the laundry's only liability for lost items lay in negligence (breach of a duty to take care), the limitation clause was redundant unless applicable to such liability. Therefore, the Court of Appeal held that the defendant was able to rely on the clause to limit its liability.

In *Macquarie Internationale Investments Ltd v Glencore (UK) Ltd* [2008] EWHC 1716 (Comm), [2008] 2 CLC 223, whilst Walker J accepted the *HIH* contextual approach, his finding that the clause was intended to cover negligence also matched the application of the *Canada Steamship* principles, since although negligence was not used explicitly, the words were wide enough to cover negligence and it was the only envisaged liability on the facts.

7.4.1.4 Construction of limitation clauses

Generally speaking, the approach of the courts to limitation clauses, as opposed to total exclusion clauses, has been more generous and such clauses tend to be construed more favourably. In particular, in order to limit liability for negligence the test is only that the clause should be 'most clearly and unambiguously expressed' (per Lord Wilberforce, *Ailsa Craig Fishing Co. Ltd v Malvern Fishing Co. Ltd* [1983] 1 WLR 964 at p. 966).

Lord Wilberforce set out the basis for this favourable treatment:

> Clauses of limitation are not regarded by the courts with the same hostility as clauses of exclusion: this is because they must be related to other contractual terms, in particular to the risks to which the defending party may be exposed, the remuneration which he receives, and possibly also the opportunity of the other party to insure.

This distinction in treatment has subsequently been endorsed at the highest level, e.g. by Lord Bridge in *George Mitchell v Finney Lock Seeds* [1983] 2 AC 803 at p. 814, by Steyn LJ in *E. E. Caledonia Ltd v Orbit Valve plc* [1994] 1 WLR 1515 at p. 1521, and by Evans LJ in *BHP Petroleum v British Steel* [2000] 2 All ER (Comm) 133 at p. 143. However, there are a large number of assumptions made about the circumstances in which limitation amounts are determined. It may be that it is at the stage of legislative regulation (and, in particular, the reasonableness and circumstances of drafting the clause) that the more favourable treatment should be given, rather than at the construction stage. In addition, it is possible to envisage a position where the limitation amount is drafted at such a low figure that it is not substantially different in effect to a total exclusion clause (see, e.g. comments by the High Court of Australia in *Darlington Futures Ltd v Delco Australia Pty Ltd* (1986) 161 CLR 500). It would be sensible, therefore, to avoid any blanket rule applicable to limitation clauses and leave examination of such clauses to the context of the legislation.

7.4.1.5 Inconsistent with an oral undertaking

A further device of interpretation relates to inconsistency. **If the exemption clause is inconsistent with an oral undertaking given before or at the time the contract was made, the exemption clause will be overridden and will not apply on the facts** (see *J. Evans & Son (Portsmouth) Ltd v Andrea Merzario Ltd* [1976] 1 WLR 1078, discussed at 6.2.1.2: oral undertaking that the goods would be stored below deck overrode the inconsistent printed conditions which would have rendered the oral promise illusory; and see also *Couchman v Hill* [1947] KB 554).

A further example is provided by *Mendelssohn v Normand Ltd* [1970] 1 QB 177.

> In this case a car park attendant had expressly promised to lock a car after parking it. This was considered to amount to an implied promise by the attendant to see that the contents of a car were safe and the Court of Appeal held that this implied promise took priority over a printed exemption which was inconsistent with it.

7.4.2 Fraud or misrepresentation

As discussed in Chapter 6, at 6.2.2, a party will be unable to rely on an exemption clause if that person has induced the other party to enter the contract by misrepresenting, fraudulently or otherwise, the meaning and effect of the clause.

> In *Curtis v Chemical Cleaning and Dyeing Co.* [1951] 1 KB 805, the defendants sought to rely on a clause exempting liability for 'any damage, however arising', which had been represented to the plaintiff as only excluding liability for particular risks, namely the beads and sequins on the wedding dress. The Court of Appeal held that the defendants could not rely on the clause to avoid liability when the dress was returned with a stain which appeared during cleaning, since that was a different type of damage to that covered in their representation to the plaintiff concerning the scope of the clause.

7.4.3 Fundamental breach

In the 1950s there developed out of the strict interpretation approach to exemption clauses, a doctrine suggesting that **as a matter of law** the courts would not allow an exemption clause to exclude or limit liability for a breach which deprived the non-breaching party of the main performance due to the party under the contract. Sometimes it was said that there were certain 'fundamental terms', liability for breach of which could never be exempted. Alternatively, it was said that certain types of breach were 'fundamental', in that they were so serious that liability for them could not be exempted. The authority for such a rule, or rules, was never very clearly explained, and such interference with the intentions of the parties as expressed in their contract was out of character for the common law.

In *Suisse Atlantique Société d'Armement Maritime SA v NV Rotterdamsche Kolen Centrale* [1967] 1 AC 361, the House of Lords attempted to put an end to this alleged rule of law.

> The case involved the charter of a ship for two years' consecutive voyages between the United States and Europe. The owners were to be paid according to the number of voyages made. Eight round trips were made in all, and the owners alleged that but for breach of the terms of the contract relating to loading and unloading a further six trips could have been made. The charterers said that the owners' damages were limited by a clause fixing compensation for delay to $1,000 per day. The owners claimed not to be bound by that clause because the charterers had committed a fundamental breach of the contract.

Viscount Dilhorne said (at p. 392):

> In my view, it is not right to say that the law prohibits and nullifies a clause exempting or limiting liability for a fundamental breach or breach of a fundamental term. Such a rule of law would involve a restriction on freedom of contract and in the older cases I can find no trace of it.

There can be little doubt that the other members of the House of Lords agreed with this statement, and intended their remarks to be consistent with it. Nevertheless, their attempt to bury the fundamental breach doctrine was not entirely successful.

- Their remarks were strictly *obiter*, since it was found that the clause in question was not an exemption clause at all but a liquidated damages clause (see **9.10.1**).
- Moreover, several passages in their Lordships' speeches suggested that there might be a residual rule of law applicable in the case of fundamental breach, especially where the non-breaching party elected to treat the contract as repudiated.
  - (a)   Lord Wilberforce said that it might be correct to say that there is a rule of law against the application of exemption clauses the effect of which is to deprive one party's

stipulations of all contractual force, reducing the contract to 'a mere declaration of intent'.

(b) And Lord Reid suggested that an election to treat a contract as repudiated caused the whole contract to cease to exist, including the exclusion clause, so that it would be ineffective to exclude loss.

Out of these fragments the Court of Appeal, led by Lord Denning MR, contrived to revive the doctrine of fundamental breach, at least in the case where the effect of breach was so serious that the non-breaching party had no real alternative but to elect to treat the contract as repudiated (see *Harbutts' 'Plasticine' Ltd v Wayne Tank and Pump Co. Ltd* [1970] 1 QB 447).

However, the House of Lords was given a further opportunity to clarify the law in ***Photo Production Ltd v Securicor Transport Ltd*** [1980] AC 827. This time there could be no doubt that the issue of the effect of fundamental breach on an exemption clause was squarely raised.

Under the contract in question, Securicor was to make patrol visits at night and at weekends to the premises of Photo Production. The contract contained a clause exempting Securicor from liability for the acts of its employees unless such acts could have been prevented by due diligence on the part of Securicor; and exempting Securicor from liability for loss caused by fire unless the loss was solely attributable to the negligence of a Securicor employee acting within the course of his employment. One night, the duty patrolman deliberately started a fire, and although it was not found that his intention was to destroy the factory, his action caused a loss of £615,000.

The House of Lords overruled *Harbutts' 'Plasticine' Ltd v Wayne Tank and Pump Co. Ltd* [1970] 1 QB 447 and said that the question of whether an exemption clause applied in the case of a very serious or 'fundamental' breach was no more than a question of the proper construction of the particular clause. It found that in this case the clause was drafted in such terms that liability was in fact excluded. The decision was justified on the basis that this was a commercial contract between parties in equal bargaining positions and the clause was therefore a risk allocation provision placing the burden of insurance on Photo Production.

The last vestiges of the fundamental breach rule of law were demolished by a careful analysis of the effect of a breach of condition or a serious breach of an innominate term (repudiatory breach), since the House of Lords (per Lord Diplock) took the view that repudiatory breach and fundamental breach were one and the same thing. The effect of such a breach is to give the non-breaching party the option of treating the contract as repudiated (discussed at **8.4.2**), so that there is no longer any need to perform the primary obligations. However, the contract itself does not come to an end. The secondary obligations (e.g., to pay damages for loss caused by breach) remain in existence, as would any exemption clause. The Court of Appeal in *Harbutts' 'Plasticine'* (and perhaps Lord Reid in *Suisse Atlantique*) had confused the ending of the primary obligations with the ending of all obligations.

The facts of ***Photo Production*** pre-dated the Unfair Contract Terms Act 1977, although the Act had been passed by the time the case reached the House of Lords. Lord Wilberforce indicated what he believed should be the policy of the common law towards exemption clauses after the passing of the Act, saying:

It is significant that Parliament refrained from legislating over the whole field of contract. After this Act, in commercial matters generally, when the parties are not of unequal bargaining power, and when risks are normally borne by insurance, not only is the case for judicial intervention undemonstrated, but there is everything to be said, and this seems to have been Parliament's intention, for leaving the parties free to apportion the risks as they think fit and for respecting their decisions.

255

Conclusion

The position at common law seems to be, therefore, that the only control over the use of exemption clauses duly incorporated into the contract is to determine whether as a matter of construction they apply to the breach in question. Thus, the only significance of a fundamental breach is that clear words will be required if the clause is to cover such a breach. Where the breach is deliberate and repudiatory in nature, express words seem to be required. In *Internet Broadcasting Corporation Ltd (t/a NETTV) v Mar LLC (t/a MARHedge)* [2009] EWHC 844 (Ch), [2009] 2 Lloyd's Rep 295 the judge stressed that it was not enough to point to the literal meaning of the words used; something more explicit was essential particularly where, as here, the losses would be uninsurable in the event of such a breach. In *Regus (UK) Ltd v Epcot Solutions Ltd* [2008] EWCA Civ 361, [2009] 1 All ER (Comm) 586, the Court of Appeal rejected an argument that the words 'in any circumstances' were wide enough to exclude recovery of losses for fraudulent or malicious damage, although concluding that there was no deliberate intention, through not repairing the office air-conditioning system, to cause loss to office customers.

There is little doubt that in the past the courts were willing to find ambiguity and difficulty simply in order to have a means of eliminating oppressive exemption clauses. It now seems that since oppressive clauses may be dealt with under the legislation (and/or by denying incorporation on the basis that the clause is onerous or unusual and has not been fairly and reasonably brought to the other's attention), there is no reason to adopt any artificial constructions or to stray beyond merely seeking the ordinary meaning of the words used. There are indications that the House of Lords has recognized that strict construction should not be 'strained construction' (per Lord Wilberforce in *Ailsa Craig Fishing Co. Ltd v Malvern Fishing Co. Ltd* [1983] 1 WLR 964; approved by Lord Bridge in *George Mitchell (Chesterhall) Ltd v Finney Lock Seeds Ltd* [1983] 2 AC 803).

7.5 Statutory control of exemption clauses

7.5.1 UCTA 1977

The enactment of the Unfair Contract Terms Act 1977 introduced a major addition to the mechanisms for controlling exemption clauses. The power to override exemption clauses found to be unreasonable had been introduced in the case of implied terms in the sale of goods by the Supply of Goods (Implied Terms) Act 1973 (see now s. 55 of the Sale of Goods Act (SGA) 1979). The 1977 Act, however, applies more extensive controls to a wide range of categories of contract, so that, for contracts within the scope of the Act, the courts for the first time had a general and direct means of control of the use of exemption clauses.

The application of UCTA 1977 may render an exemption clause either totally unenforceable, or unenforceable unless shown to be reasonable.

7.5.2 UTCCR 1999

Further changes to this statutory regime of control of exemption clauses were introduced by European Directive 93/13/EC on Unfair Terms in Consumer Contracts, now implemented in the **Unfair Terms in Consumer Contracts Regulations 1999, SI 1999/2083** (replacing the original implementing regulations of 1994, SI 1994/3159). In general terms, the regulations provide that 'unfair terms' in a contract concluded between a 'seller or supplier' and a 'consumer' will not be binding on the consumer. Thus, the regulations apply only in the context of 'consumer contracts' (defined at 7.7.1.1), but their application extends beyond exemption clauses to 'unfair terms' in general, whilst excluding certain 'core' terms from the scope of assessment for unfairness.

A detailed assessment of the differences between the scope of these two legislative measures can be found at 7.7.4. The next section will focus on an examination of UCTA 1977 before embarking upon a detailed examination of the UTCCR 1999 (at 7.7).

7.5.3 The Law Commission's recommendations for reform

However, before proceeding it is important to be aware that the **Law Commission,** in its report, *Unfair Terms in Contracts,* Law Com. No. 292, Cm. 6464 (February 2005), proposed a single unified regime to replace UCTA 1997 and UTCCR 1999 in the context of consumer contracts. In the context of business contracts, there is a recommendation for a special regime applicable to 'small businesses' while the approach to B2B contracts is non-interventionist, reflecting the current approach to reasonableness in commercial contracts under UCTA 1977. The report contains a draft bill. More specific consideration of issues of interest in the proposed recommendations are discussed at the applicable points of discussion of the existing law in order to highlight how the position will differ if the proposed legislation is enacted.

The report's recommendations and the draft bill provide a single regime for 'consumer contracts' covering unfair terms (and not just exemption clauses). This consumer regime will extend to negotiated terms as well as standard or non-negotiated terms and will alter the burden of proof that currently exists under the regulations so that the business will have the burden of showing that a term is fair and reasonable where the term is detrimental to the consumer (unless there is a pre-emptive challenge by the OFT or other body, when that body will have the burden of establishing that the term is unfair). This general provision (draft clause 4(1)) will not apply to a term which defines the main subject matter of a consumer contract as long as the term is transparent and substantially the same as the definition the consumer reasonably expected (an interesting legislative inclusion of reasonable expectations although one that will inevitably give rise to case law). Of particular significance is the clarity provided by express recognition that terms which currently are unenforceable under UCTA, s. 2(1) (death or personal injury resulting from negligence: see 7.6.2) and s. 6(2) (exclusion or limitation of liability for breaches of basic obligations in the sales legislation, e.g., satisfactory quality: see 7.6.4.1) will remain unenforceable. Although it should be possible to establish that such terms are unfair under the regulations, they are not automatically unfair.

In the business context, the report and draft legislation distinguishes between 'small businesses' and other businesses. 'Small businesses' are considered to warrant protection which should not be extended to other B2B contracts. Under the legislation small businesses will be able to challenge any standard term which has not been altered through negotiation, as long as it is not concerned with the main subject matter of the contract or the price. If the term is detrimental to the small business and the small business wishes to challenge it, it has the burden of establishing that the term is not 'fair and reasonable' (i.e., the reverse of the burden of proof for consumers). While it is commendable to wish to protect such businesses, there are difficulties in deciding where to draw the line and the draft bill contains complex definitions of small business in an attempt to avoid the difficulties encountered in other areas of law in ensuring that 'small businesses' are in fact 'small'. In any event, some important categories of contracts are excluded from this protection and, as small businesses are not covered by the pre-emptive challenges, they will need to possess sufficient resources to pursue court action challenging terms as unfair.

The approach to other B2B contracts is non-interventionist (see the discussion below 7.6.6.2 on the approach to the reasonableness requirement under UCTA 1977 in commercial contracts). This differs from the more radical suggestion on B2B contracts proposed in the consultation paper which had proposed to extend the UTCCR regulation into the area of B2B contracts. The s. 6(3) protection, against exemptions of the implied obligations under sales law if the term is not shown to be reasonable, is not contained in the draft bill in its current form. Instead, such a term in a B2B contract will only have to be shown to be fair and reasonable if one business deals on the other's written standard terms of business (draft clause 9). It is envisaged that the current case law on the meaning of 'written standard terms of business' will continue to 'assist' (*Unfair Terms in Contracts,* Law Com. No. 292, Cm. 6464, paras 4.45–4.57).

The test of 'fair and reasonable' is contained in clause 14 of the draft bill (now extended to apply to notices as well as contractual terms) and refers to the need to take into account 'the extent to which the term is transparent' (defined in clause 14(3) in presentational terms) and 'the substance and effect of the term, and all the circumstances existing at the time it was agreed' (substantive and procedural fairness and reasonableness). In examining this second aspect of the test the court is to have regard to the facts listed in clause 14(4). This list will replace the guidelines in Sch. 2 to UCTA and extends the relevant factors. Clause 14(6) refers to the Sch. 2 indicative list of consumer contract terms and small business contract terms which may be regarded as not being fair and reasonable. This list is based on Sch. 2 to UTCCR but is expressed in clearer terms and includes examples. The problem would seem to be the relationship between these, the Sch. 2 list and the various factors identified in clause 14(4).

Finally, there is an equivalent to s. 13 of UCTA 1977 to explain the extended meaning of terms which exclude or restrict liability. The provision covering negligence liability is in similar terms to s. 2 of UCTA (clause 1 of the draft Bill) although certain issues are clarified in the clause 2 exceptions.

This draft legislation will inevitably be a great improvement on the current law, although the difficulties of the exercise in relation to some issues which the Law Commission recognizes mean that it is unlikely to be a complete panacea. The 'good news' is that if the draft bill is enacted in its current form, much of the existing case law will remain relevant for purposes of interpretation, e.g. the case law discussing 'written standard terms of business' in s. 3 of UCTA 1977.

A history of legislative control over unfair terms can be found in the Law Commission Consultation Paper, *Unfair Terms in Contracts,* LCCP No. 166, 2002, at paras 2.10–2.16.

Whilst the government accepted the Law Commission's recommendations in principle, matters are now on hold since in October 2008, the European Commission published the EU Consumer Rights Directive, *Proposal for a Directive on Consumer Rights,* COM (2008) 614 final, 13 October 2008, as an outcome of the 'review of the consumer acquis'. This proposed directive will repeal four existing consumer directives, including unfair contract terms, and would set out more consistent rules for both business and consumers through use of a maximum harmonization clause, whereby Member States could not maintain or adopt provisions providing greater protection than those laid down in the directive. The Law Commissions' recommendations are therefore on hold at the moment.

7.6 The Unfair Contract Terms Act 1977

7.6.1 The scope of the Act

7.6.1.1 Business liability

UCTA 1977 applies (subject to certain exceptions) in the case of both contract and tort to 'business liability', which means liability for things done or to be done in the course of a business, and liability arising from the occupation of business premises (UCTA 1977, s. 1(3)). 'Business' is given a broad definition by the Act (UCTA 1977, s. 14), so that it embraces not only the normal meaning of commercial activity, but also the professions, government departments, and local or public authorities. The intention appears to have been to exclude from the general scope of the Act by this expression only private, occasional contracts. In the case of sale and hire purchase, the Act applies irrespective of whether the liability arises in the course of a business (UCTA 1977, s. 6(4)), although this exception is not as major as it may appear (see 7.6.4.1).

7.6.1.2 Clauses covered by the Act: s. 13

It must be stressed that UCTA 1977 does not provide a general power to strike out any term which the court considers to be unreasonable or unfair. Its main targets are exemption clauses; that is, clauses excluding or limiting liability. This definition is extended by s. 13(1) to include clauses making the enforcement of liability subject to compliance with a condition, clauses excluding or limiting any right or remedy that would otherwise be available, and clauses restricting or excluding rules of evidence or procedure.

Stewart Gill Ltd v Horatio Myer & Co. Ltd [1992] 1 QB 600, provides an example of a clause which purported to restrict a right or remedy otherwise available, and which therefore fell within the ambit of UCTA 1977.

> The clause in question purported to prevent the buyer from withholding payment by reason of a set-off or counterclaim in the event of a breach of contract by the supplier. It was claimed on behalf of the supplier that the reference in s. 13(1) to restrictions of rights or remedies and rules of procedure brought such clauses within the scope of the Act only where they achieved indirectly an exclusion or limitation of liability which, if expressly stipulated, would be subject to control under the Act; whereas in this case the restriction on the right of set-off did not exclude or limit the liability of the supplier, but only required the buyer to prosecute his claim in relation to defective goods in separate legal proceedings. This argument was unanimously rejected by the Court of Appeal, which held that the clause excluded the buyer's 'right' to set off its claims against the seller's claim for the price and also excluded the procedural rules applicable to a set-off.

The Act also applies to clauses which purport to modify the expected contractual obligation or duty, rather than to exempt liability for breach (UCTA 1977, s. 13(1)).

> For example, in **Smith v Eric S. Bush** [1990] 1 AC 831, the House of Lords held that a disclaimer clause in a mortgage valuation which stipulated that the valuation was provided without any acceptance of responsibility, fell within s. 13(1) of UCTA 1977 because it purported to prevent any duty of care from arising.

7.6.1.3 Clauses and contracts which are not covered by the Act

The 1977 Act does not, however, apply to arbitration clauses (UCTA 1977, s. 13(2)).

Certain other important categories of contracts are excluded from the scope of the major provisions of the Act.

- Schedule 1, para. 1 excludes from ss. 2–4 and s. 7, contracts of insurance, contracts relating to interests in land, contracts relating to intellectual property, contracts relating to companies (whether or not incorporated), and contracts relating to securities.
- Schedule 1, para. 2 excludes contracts of marine salvage, charterparties, and contracts of carriage of goods by sea from the same provisions other than s. 2(1), except where the provisions operate in favour of a person dealing as a consumer (see 7.6.4.1).
- Employment contracts are excluded by Sch. 1, para. 4, on similar terms.
- By s. 26, the Act does not apply to international supply contracts as defined in that section.

7.6.2 Liability for negligence: s. 2

'Negligence' is defined by the 1977 Act as breach of an obligation to take reasonable care or to exercise reasonable skill arising out of the express or implied terms of a contract (i.e., qualified contractual liability: 8.2.1), or existing as a common law duty (i.e., in tort) or arising out of the Occupiers' Liability Act 1957 (UCTA 1977, s. 1(1)).

As far as the law of contract is concerned, it should be remembered that many obligations arising out of contracts are strict. That is to say, the standard of performance demanded is not merely to take reasonable care or to exercise reasonable skill in attempting to achieve the purpose of the contract. Rather, the party performing can avoid breach only by actually achieving that purpose. Therefore, exemption clauses relating to such contractual terms are not subject to the controls applying to clauses which purport to exclude or limit liability for 'negligence' contained in s. 2 of the Act (although they may be subject to other controls relating to attempts to exclude or limit contractual liability, discussed at 7.6.4).

Nevertheless, some contractual obligations are not strict. Where the achievement of the result is dependent to some appreciable extent on factors beyond the control of the person providing the service, it would be nonsensical to **guarantee** that the result will be achieved (see 8.2.1.1). Thus, lawyers cannot guarantee that their clients will escape conviction when prosecuted; they can only undertake to use reasonable skill in seeking to prevent conviction. **Breach of such obligations is what is meant by 'negligence' liability in the context of contracts, and exemption clauses relating to such liability are governed by UCTA 1977, s. 2.**

Section 2(1) of the 1977 Act provides:

(1) A person cannot by reference to any contract term or to a notice given to persons generally or to particular persons exclude or restrict his liability for death or personal injury resulting from negligence.
(2) In the case of other loss or damage, a person cannot so exclude or restrict his liability for negligence except in so far as the term or notice satisfies the requirement of reasonableness.

The section is not limited in its application to exemption clauses contained in contracts. It would apply, for example, to a notice erected by the owner of land at an entrance to that land through which members of the public pass.

 ## Summary

Section 2(1) renders totally unenforceable any exclusions and limitations of liability for death or personal injury caused by negligence.   »

Section 2(2) UCTA 1977 provides that liability for other loss or damage (i.e., other than death or personal injury) resulting from negligence may be excluded, provided the contract term or notice satisfies the requirement of reasonableness (see 7.6.6). 'Other loss or damage' includes property damages and financial loss, e.g. as in *Smith v Eric S. Bush* [1990] 1 AC 831 where the loss was financial loss following a negligent survey.

7.6.3 Guarantees of consumer goods

Sometimes manufacturers (and possibly distributors) of consumer goods issue a 'guarantee' of goods sold by the retailer to the consumer. Often the guarantee purports to limit, or even exclude, the liability of the party issuing it for negligence which leads to the goods being defective. Such an exemption may take effect as a non-contractual notice, or may constitute a separate contract between manufacturer and consumer (although not a contract of sale). The danger of such guarantees is that, while they may offer an easier remedy for trivial defects than can be had by taking the goods back to the seller, such advantage is often gained by the sacrifice of more important rights in the case of serious loss such as might result from a defect causing personal injury. For this reason purported exemptions contained in consumer guarantees are of no effect (UCTA 1977, s. 5). Therefore, although s. 5 may overlap with s. 2 in some instances, the protection offered is such that the clause will always be totally unenforceable.

Section 5(3) provides that this section does not apply to exemptions contained in contracts of sale, hire purchase, work and materials, or hire, which are provided for elsewhere (see 7.6.4.1).

The Law Commission Consultation Paper of 2002 (*Unfair Terms in Contracts,* LCCP No. 166) provisionally recommended that the protection afforded by s. 5 was unduly complex, no longer required for the protection of consumers, and should be abolished. This recommendation is repeated in the Law Commission's report, *Unfair Terms in Contracts,* Law Com. No. 292, Cm. 6464 (2005), on the basis that s. 5 is superfluous, given the scope of s. 2 and the provisions of the Consumer Protection Act 1987, and therefore its retention would only add to the complexity of the legislation (see paras 3.12 and 3.48 of the report).

7.6.4 Contractual liability

In the case of attempted exemptions of strict contractual obligations (i.e., obligations which must be performed completely and precisely to an absolute standard), the 1977 Act contains two sets of provisions which may be applicable.

- There are specific provisions designed to deal with attempts to exclude or limit liability for breaches of the implied obligations relating to the goods in sale and supply contracts **(UCTA 1977, ss. 6 and 7).**

- There is also a general provision which may apply to attempts to exempt from liability for breaches of strict contractual obligations, but it will be applicable only if one of the qualifying conditions is met **(UCTA 1977, s. 3).**

7.6.4.1 The sale or supply of goods

As mentioned above, the Act contains special provisions, additional to those in s. 3, which apply to clauses purporting to exempt liability for breach of the terms relating to the goods which are implied by statute into contracts for the sale or supply of goods (see 6.4.2.4).

Section 6 applies to implied terms in the sale of goods. It should be noted that this section applies to all liability, and not merely to that incurred in the course of a business (UCTA 1977, s. 6 (4)). However, the important implied terms of quality in s. 14 of the SGA 1979 arise only in the case of sales made in the course of a business.

The Supply of Goods and Services Act 1982 implies terms similar to those of the 1979 Act into contracts for the supply of goods, that is, contracts under which title to goods passes but not by way of sale (e.g., work and materials contracts, such as a building contract under which goods are to be incorporated into the finished structure as part of the contract performance: see 6.4.2.4). Attempted exemptions of liability for breach of these implied terms are governed by UCTA 1977, s. 7.

Title

- In the context of a sale of goods contract, the implied condition that the seller has or will have the right to sell the goods (SGA 1979, s. 12) cannot in any circumstances be excluded by reference to a contract term (**UCTA 1977, s. 6(1)(a)**).

- Section 7(3A) of the 1977 Act provides that liability for breach of s. 2 of the Supply of Goods and Services Act 1982 (relating to the transfer of goods in a work and materials contract) cannot be exempted (Supply of Goods and Services Act 1982, s. 17(2)).

- However, liability for breach of s. 7 of the 1982 Act (implied obligation concerning the right to transfer possession of goods in a hire contract) can be exempted, but only if the clause satisfies the reasonableness requirement (UCTA 1977, s. 7(4)).

Description, satisfactory quality, and fitness for purpose

In the case of attempts to exempt liability for breaches of ss. 13–15 of the SGA 1979 (covering sale by description, satisfactory quality, fitness for purpose, and sale by sample), the position under UCTA 1977, s. 6 is different depending upon whether or not one of the parties **deals as consumer** (UCTA 1977, s. 12).

- Where one party deals as consumer, liability for breach of these implied terms cannot be exempted (**UCTA 1977, s. 6(2)(a)**).

- Where the party seeking to enforce liability is not a consumer, liability for breach of the implied terms may be exempted, but only in so far as the exemption clause satisfies the requirement of reasonableness (**UCTA 1977, s. 6(3)**).

The same distinction applies in the context of attempts to exclude the same obligations relating to description, satisfactory quality, fitness for purpose, and correspondence with sample in contracts for work and materials and hire contracts, i.e. these obligations cannot be excluded as against a consumer (**UCTA 1977, s. 7(2)**) but may be excluded as against a person dealing otherwise than as consumer where the clause in question is shown to be reasonable (**UCTA 1977, s. 7(3)**).

The Act therefore contains an important distinction between those dealing as consumers and others.

'Dealing as consumer'

A party **deals as consumer** if that party does not make (or hold themselves out as making) the contract in the course of a business while the other party does, and, in the case of a contract for goods where the consumer is not an individual, the goods are of a type ordinarily supplied for private use or consumption (**UCTA 1977, s. 12(1) and (1A)**, as amended by the Sale and Supply of Goods to Consumers Regulations 2002, SI 2002/3045).

Section 12(2) also provides that an individual buyer at an auction sale for second hand goods which is open to the public (s. 12(2)(a)) or a buyer who is not an individual where goods are sold by auction or by competitive tender (s. 12(2)(b)) will never be dealing as a consumer. By s. 12(3), if a person claims that the other is not dealing as consumer, that person has the burden of establishing this.

In the context of UCTA 1977 it has been established that the mere fact that a party is a business (e.g., a partnership or a registered company) will not necessarily mean that particular contracts which it enters into are made in the course of business. In *R. & B. Customs Brokers Co. Ltd v United Dominions Trust Ltd* [1988] 1 WLR 321, **the Court of Appeal held that a transaction would be made in the course of a business where it was integral to the nature of the business or, if only incidental to the carrying on of the relevant business, where there was a degree of regularity in entering into such transactions.**

> In *R. & B. Customs Brokers v UDT* the plaintiff company was a small company and operated as a freight forwarding agent. The company was owned and managed by a husband and wife. The company purchased a car under a conditional sale agreement from the defendant finance company. The car was to be used for both business and private use. However, the car proved to be defective and the plaintiff company brought an action against the defendant. The defendant sought to rely on an exemption clause in the contract excluding the implied conditions as to the quality of the car or its fitness for purpose unless the buyer was dealing as a consumer. Therefore the crucial question was whether the plaintiff company had purchased that car 'in the course of a business', which would exclude it from contracting as a consumer.
>
> The Court of Appeal relied on the meaning of these words as they had been interpreted in the context of the Trade Descriptions Act 1968, to the effect that a contract would be made 'in the course of a business' only if the contract in question was an integral part of the business, or such contracts were entered into with such regularity that it could be treated as integral. Applying this test, the court held that the plaintiff company was dealing as a consumer (and not in the course of a business) because purchasing cars was not integral to the company's business; and since they had bought only one or two cars in this way, there was also not the necessary regularity to render this a contract entered into in the course of a business.

Case analysis

This decision has rightly been criticized. It seems strange that much the same expression used in s. 1(3) of UCTA 1977 appears to have been interpreted on the basis of the identity of the party without embarking upon the sort of analysis of the transaction, which is called for under the *R. & B. Customs Brokers* test (see, e.g., *St Albans and District Council v International Computers Ltd* [1995] FSR 686: assumption that a local authority was contracting 'in the course of a business' because it fell within the s. 14 definition of a business). It may also be criticized as introducing potential uncertainty, and because it is far from clear that s. 12 was intended to give protection to companies in this way (see also comparison with UTCCR 1999, which are inapplicable to regulate terms used against a company and the adoption of the UTCCR 1999 definition of 'consumer' in the Sale and Supply of Goods to Consumers Regulations 2002: 7.7.1.1).

However, in terms of result, the *R. & B. Customs Brokers* decision may be no bad thing, in that it does allow for a measure of discretion to permit the protection of s. 6(2) (and also that of s. 3) to apply to small businesses that have not made the individual contract as an integral part of the business. Of course, some contracts will be integral, e.g. a garage business purchases cars for resale where the garage company would be a non-consumer when entering into such contracts. The effect of s. 12(1)(c), requiring that in the context of sale contracts the goods supplied must be of a type ordinarily supplied for private use and consumption, will also limit the scope of a finding that a company has purchased goods as a consumer. This subsection applies only where the buyer is not an individual.

The result in *R. & B. Customs Brokers* may be easier to justify on the basis that the car in question was purchased for both business and personal use. This means that it is possible to rationalize the decision as being in line with the position under UCTA 1977, s. 5 (exclusions in guarantees of consumer goods: see 7.6.3). Such exclusions are totally unenforceable if the goods prove defective 'while in consumer use' and by s. 5(2) goods are defined as being 'in consumer use' when they are being used 'otherwise than exclusively for the purposes of a business'. On the facts in *R. & B. Customs Brokers*, since the car was not exclusively for business use, it would have been 'in consumer use', and hence it is feasible to consider the purchasing company as a consumer for the purposes of s. 6(2) and s. 3 of the 1977 Act. On this basis, the position ought to be different if the car is purchased exclusively for the use of the husband and wife for business purposes. However, this is not the test in the *R. & B. Customs Brokers* case.

More recently, the Court of Appeal had to consider the meaning of the words 'in the course of a business' in the context of s. 14 of the SGA 1979 (see 6.4.2.4).

> In *Stevenson v Rogers* [1999] 2 WLR 1064, it was argued that the sale of a trawler by a fisherman was not 'in the course of a business' so that there was no implied term as to quality. The Court of Appeal held that, under the 1979 Act, a sale would be in the course of a business unless it was a purely private transaction outside the scope of any business carried on by the seller. Accordingly, there was such an implied term in this contract.

Significantly, the test applied by the Court of Appeal would bring the contract within the expression 'in the course of a business' where the sale is incidental to the seller's business. There was also no requirement to establish regularity.

There has been support for adopting the *Stevenson v Rogers* interpretation in the context of UCTA 1977 (see Macdonald (1999) 3 Web JCLI), especially because it is difficult to justify different results under the two statutes arising from analysis of the same transaction. There is a need for clear rationalization of the scope of 'consumer' in relation to the sales legislation and the *R. & B. Customs Brokers* approach associated with s. 12 of UCTA 1977. Nevertheless, in *Feldaroll Foundry plc v Hermes Leasing (London) Ltd* [2004] EWCA Civ 747, (2004) 101 (24) LSG 32, when the Court of Appeal was asked to prefer the definition in *Stevenson v Rogers* it applied the *R. & B. Customs Brokers* test. The question for consideration was whether a company could rely on the protection provided by UCTA 1977, s. 6(2) to those dealing as a consumer when it purchased a Lamborghini car for the use of the company's managing director. The Court of Appeal held that the *R. & B. Customs Brokers* test applied because the meaning of 'in the course of a business' arose in the context of the application of UCTA 1977. The court also stressed that the fact that Feldaroll was a public company did not prevent the application of *R. & B. Customs Brokers*. The result was that the claimant company was dealing as a consumer and could reject the defective car despite the existence of a term excluding implied conditions of satisfactory quality and fitness for purpose. Therefore, this decision has further entrenched the distinction between the test under UCTA 1977 and under the SGA 1979.

The Law Commission's recommendation on the meaning of a 'consumer contract'

The Law Commission's report, *Unfair Terms in Contracts,* Law Com. No. 292, Cm. 6464 (2005), which recommends a unified regime for consumer contracts, defines a 'consumer contract' as a contract between '(a) an individual ("the consumer") who enters into it wholly or mainly for purposes unrelated to a business of his, and (b) the person ("the business") who enters into it wholly or mainly for purposes related to his business' (clause 26 of the draft Bill). Thus, only natural persons will be consumers under the new scheme (as is currently the position under UTCCR 1999) and such a consumer must act for purposes outside the course of his business. The inclusion of the words 'wholly or mainly' address the classification problems where a contract is partly private and partly for business purposes. The Law Commission proposes that it should be for the courts to classify a contract as 'consumer' in accordance with what they regard as the **predominant purpose** of the contract.

The new scheme proposes special treatment for 'small businesses' (Part 5 of the report, clause 11 and clauses 27–9 of the draft Bill) enabling them to challenge standard terms that are not 'core' terms and which have not been individually negotiated. A term excluding liability for satisfactory quality as against a company where that term has not been negotiated would seem to be subject to the 'fair and reasonable' test if used against a small business (draft clause 11) or if the company is dealing on the other's written standard terms of business (draft clause 9), but not otherwise.

7.6.4.2 Section 3: General contractual liability

Section 3 of the 1977 Act applies to breaches of strict contractual obligations, other than the implied goods obligations covered by ss. 6 and 7, but only if one of the qualifying conditions is applicable.

The qualifying conditions in s. 3(1) are that either one party deals as consumer (see above discussion of the meaning of this expression in s. 12(1)), or one party deals on the other party's written standard terms of business.

Dealing on the other's written standard terms of business

The expression 'written standard terms of business' is not defined in the Act. Many contracts are in standard form, and s. 3 is clearly intended to apply to such contracts. It has not been clear, however, how much 'individualization' of such standard forms is permitted before the section ceases to apply. For example, many standard forms leave blanks in the clauses relating to quantity and to price which must be filled in for each particular contract. The policy behind the Act ought to mean that such forms are still within the meaning of the section. Traditionally, however, it has been less clear whether a standard form in which the original offeree had deleted certain terms and then sent it back (as a counter-offer), and which had then been accepted by the original offeror, would still be within the meaning of the section. In *Chester Grosvenor Hotel Co. Ltd v Alfred McAlpine Management Ltd* (1991) 56 BLR 115, Judge Stannard said:

What is required for terms to be standard is that they should be regarded by the party which advances them as its standard terms and that it should habitually contract in those terms. If it contracts also in other terms, it must be determined in any given case, and as a matter of fact, whether this has occurred so frequently that the terms in question cannot be regarded as standard, and if on any occasion a party has substantially modified its prepared terms, it is a question of fact whether those terms have been so altered that they must be regarded as not having been employed on that occasion.

The question of what constitutes written standard terms was considered at length by Judge Thayne Forbes, acting as an official referee in the High Court, in *Salvage Association v CAP Financial Services Ltd* [1995] FSR 654.

> There were two contracts. The first was contained in a document produced in advance by the defendants; the conditions of business stated were accepted without any attempt to renegotiate any of them. The defendants argued that they would have been willing to renegotiate, but the judge did not allow this to deflect him from finding that this contract was concluded on the defendants' written standard terms of business. The second contract took as its point of departure the first, but was further negotiated and, seemingly, amendments made.
>
> The mere fact that the parties started with a document prepared by one of them in advance did not make this a standard-form agreement. Whether this amounted to a standard-form agreement was a question of fact, taking into account the degree of negotiation and variation, and alternatively the degree of imposition of terms, in the light of the relative bargaining power of the parties. In this case, the second contract had moved sufficiently away from the original written standard terms of business for s. 3 not to apply.

In *St Albans City and District Council v International Computers Ltd* [1996] 4 All ER 481 (for full discussion see 7.6.6.2), the defendants had submitted their own standard form for negotiation. At first instance, Scott Baker J ([1995] FSR 686) considered that, if the terms are amended as a result of negotiations, assuming the amendments were not too substantial, the contract could remain as standard form as long as there was no negotiation over the 'relevant exempting terms'. Such negotiation would appear to be fatal. The Court of Appeal held, affirming the decision of Scott Baker J on this point, that the local authority had contracted on the defendants' written standard terms of business because the standard form 'remained effectively untouched'. In particular, Nourse LJ stressed the fact that s. 3 referred to 'dealing', which meant 'making a deal' and could thus be distinguished from any negotiations preceding it.

A very generous interpretation was adopted by Judge Bowsher QC in *Pegler v Wang (UK) Ltd* [2000] BLR 218. The problem on the facts was that it was not the contract itself, but the exclusion and limitation clauses inserted in it, which were standard-form clauses used by the defendant. The judge held that as the defendant considered these clauses to be non-negotiable, in relation to these material clauses the claimant had clearly contracted on the defendant's 'written standard terms of business'. On this interpretation, it was not necessary for the whole contract to be in standard form. What mattered was whether there had been negotiation of the relevant clauses. This decision suggests that it may be sufficient that the **only** standard clause is the exemption.

A less controversial example is provided by the first instance decision in *Watford Electronics Ltd v Sanderson CFL Ltd* [2000] 2 All ER (Comm) 984. Judge Thornton QC had to consider whether the addition of a clause committing the defendant to use its best endeavours to allocate appropriate resources to the project, precluded the application of s. 3 of UCTA 1977. The judge held that the test was whether the written standard form was relied upon 'without *material* variation' (emphasis added). He concluded that the standard term had not been varied because the amendment was no more than a vague and unenforceable obligation. However, even if the amendment had been enforceable, it would have to be considered against the totality of the standard conditions which otherwise remained unaltered. As such an amendment would have been narrow and insubstantial, the contract would still have been made on the basis of the defendant's written standard terms of business. (The decision on reasonableness was overturned on appeal to the Court of Appeal (see 7.6.6.2), but no appeal was heard on the general application of s. 3.)

The importance of establishing that the contract was made on 'the other's written standard terms of business' has become increasingly clear. Often the application of UCTA 1977 will turn on this finding.

Two conclusions emerge from the recent case law:

1. There must be no negotiation of the relevant exempting terms.

2. Any amendment of other terms will have to be considered against the totality of the standard conditions.

In its second report, preceding UCTA 1977, the Law Commission had made a deliberate decision not to recommend a definition of 'written standard terms of business' on the basis that any definition would provide businesses with the ability to draft to avoid it (Law Commission second report on *Exemption Clauses,* Law Com. No. 69 (1975), para. 157), but the current position is generating a good deal of judicial argument on the matter. There are also potential problems in the requirement that the standard terms be 'written' in terms of the nature of electronic contracting and the requirements of the Electronic Communications Act 2000 (see Macdonald and Poyton [2000] 3 Web JCLI).

The Law Commission's report of 2005, *Unfair Terms in Contracts,* Law Com. No. 292, Cm. 6464, has determined to preserve these definitional difficulties by retaining this as the qualifying condition for regulation of general contractual liability in the context of B2B contracts (see paras 4.45–4.57) on the basis that this test 'is as good as any that can be achieved'. This conclusion would seem to be correct but it will preserve the significance of the existing jurisprudence on the subject. In the context of the small business regime the qualifying test for the regime to apply is to be whether the term was put forward as one of the other party's standard terms of business and was not individually negotiated. This is an easier test to satisfy since it requires only a representation of standard form and judges the terms individually so that it should be relatively easy to establish whether the term in question has been individually negotiated (see para. 5.75).

The s. 3 test

Where a party deals as consumer, or on the other's standard terms, that other may not exclude or limit his liability for breach of contract by means of a term in the contract except in so far as the term satisfies the requirement of reasonableness (UCTA 1977, s. 3(2)(a)). (The 'reasonableness' test is considered below: see 7.6.6.)

The scope of s. 3

In general, exemption clauses operate to exclude or limit liability for breach. However, careful drafting of a contract may result in the performance obligation being such that a performance which might normally be regarded as defective does not amount to breach. In this case it is said that the term defines the performance obligation, rather than simply exempting liability for breach. Indeed, some commentators (notably Yates, *Exemption Clauses in Contracts,* 2nd edn (Sweet and Maxwell, 1992), pp. 123–33: see 7.1.4.2) **have argued** that in most circumstances exemption clauses should be read in the context of the whole agreement, rather than as separate from the rest of the agreement, so that most so-called exemption clauses are obligation-defining rather than liability-exempting. As discussed at 7.1.4.2, there is some support for this approach in the speech of Lord Diplock in *Photo Production Ltd v Securicor Transport Ltd* [1980] AC 827.

The approach assumes that where the parties have defined the obligations in a particular way, there is no reason to exert the kind of control thought to be desirable where one party seeks to exempt liability. The difficulty with this assumption is that it may fail to take account of the fact that many contracts are perceived as being standardized, so that there is a general expectation, independent of any particular contract, of the content of such contracts. To vary the terms from those generally expected may be just as undesirable as to exclude liability if the effect is to deprive one party of what was reasonably expected under the contract. It is only if contracts are exclusively the product of the will of the parties, rather than constructed from common intention and certain obligations imposed by law, that it would be reasonable to suggest that the proper expectation of the content of a contract can be determined by an examination of its particular terms and nothing else. Modern contract theory does not generally accept such a proposition. The orthodox approach, then, is to treat exemption clauses generally as separate from the rest of the contract, and therefore not as defining the obligations, and that approach is taken by UCTA 1977. The orthodox approach was also adopted by the Court of Appeal in *Phillips Products Ltd v Hyland* [1987] 1 WLR 659 (see also *Smith v Eric S. Bush* [1990] 1 AC 831). Slade LJ said (at p. 664):

> In our judgment, in considering whether there has been any breach of any obligation…the court has to leave out of account, at this stage, the contract term which is relied on by the defence as defeating the plaintiffs' claim for breach of such obligation or duty…

The 1977 Act attempts to restrict the use of unreasonable obligation-defining clauses.

By s. 3(2)(b) of the 1977 Act, a party may not claim to be entitled:

> (i)   to render a contractual performance substantially different from that reasonably expected of him; or
>
> (ii) …to render no performance at all,
>
> except in so far as the contract term satisfies the requirement of reasonableness.

Of course, these provisions apply only in the case of contracts where one party deals as consumer or on the other's written standard terms (UCTA 1977, s. 3(1); see above).

There is an important limitation on the scope for the application of s. 3(2)(b). In order for s. 3(2)(b) to apply it is the contractual performance of the party seeking to enforce the term which must have been substantially altered, e.g. to provide a different holiday itinerary.

> On the facts in *Paragon Finance plc v Nash* [2001] EWCA Civ 1466, [2002] 1 WLR 685, the argument was that the mortgagee's discretion to fix interest rates in relation to a loan agreement amounted to altering the 'contractual performance' within s. 3(2)(b) and was therefore subject to the reasonableness requirement in s. 3 of UCTA 1977. However, the Court of Appeal held that it was the performance of the mortgagors that was altered by the term permitting this discretion so that s. 3 did not apply.

Section 3(2)(b)(i) assumes that it is possible to identify a performance which is reasonably to be expected. This assumption might be realized in two ways.

- The contract might be of a recognized and standardized type.

 ## Example

A contract for the provision of domestic decorating services is rarely negotiated in detail. In particular, it is unlikely that the parties will discuss measures to be taken to protect existing decoration which is not to be replaced. Rather, the customer will assume that the decorator will take reasonable care to avoid damage to existing decorations, and such a term would normally be implied in law (Supply of Goods and Services Act 1982, s. 13). If the decorator's order form, which was signed by the customer, included a term making protection of existing decorations the responsibility of the customer, such a term would have defined the contractual obligations in a way other than would generally have been expected.

Section 3(2)(b)(i) does not say that it is not permitted to redefine the contractual obligations in such a way; it merely says that it is not permitted unless reasonable. This test might be satisfied relatively easily in such a case by showing that the customer was fully aware of the effect of the clause, and possibly by showing that the price charged was lower than would be charged where it was the decorator's contractual responsibility to take such precautions.

- Alternatively, there may be a conflict between the apparent main purpose of the contract and the performance one party is entitled to tender under the terms contained in the fine print of the agreement.

For example, in ***Anglo-Continental Holidays Ltd v Typaldos Lines (London) Ltd*** [1967] 2 Lloyd's Rep 61, the plaintiffs made particular holiday arrangements through a travel agent. The contract contained a clause stating that 'Steamers, sailing dates, rates and itineraries are subject to change without notice'. The Court of Appeal refused to allow the defendants to rely on the clause to escape liability for breach of contract when the original arrangements were changed unilaterally.

Russell LJ pointed out, however, that the clause was not an exemption clause but a clause defining the contractual liability. In his view, 'the propounder of that clause cannot be enabled thereby to alter the substance of the arrangement'. Under s. 3(2)(b)(i) of the 1977 Act, assuming the qualifying conditions of s. 3(1) were met, the issue would have been whether the clause was unreasonable in allowing changes to be made unilaterally from what had apparently been agreed under the main provisions of the contract.

Section 3(2)(b)(ii) is something of a red herring. If one party is defined by the contract as being under no obligations at all, the contract must surely fail for want of consideration (see 4.3). Where the absence of obligation affects only part of the contract, it can be dealt with under s. 3(2)(b)(i).

7.6.5 Special provisions

7.6.5.1 Indemnity clauses

An indemnity clause in a contract is a clause under which one party agrees to indemnify the other for any liability incurred. Such a clause may have the same effect as an exemption clause, and in any case often transfers liability away from the party who would normally be liable. Such a clause is effective against a person who deals as consumer only in so far as it satisfies the requirement of reasonableness (**UCTA 1977, s. 4**). On the other hand, a transfer of liability between potential defendants, neither of which deals as a consumer, is apparently a form of duty-defining clause which is not subject to control under the Act at all, on the basis that it leaves the claimant's right to a remedy untouched (***Thompson v T. Lohan (Plant Hire) Ltd*** [1987] 1 WLR 649).

7.6.5.2 Secondary contracts

Section 10 of UCTA 1977 is intended to prevent the evasion of the provisions of the Act by means of a secondary contract. Since the main provisions of the Act are concerned with terms in contracts which exclude or restrict liability arising under those contracts, it was feared that imposing such exclusions and restrictions by means of separate contracts might thwart the purpose of the Act. Section 10 attempts to close that loophole. A typical situation addressed by this provision would be where a maintenance contract, entered into in connection with the purchase of goods, purports to exclude or restrict rights arising under the purchase contract. In ***Tudor Grange Holdings Ltd v Citibank NA*** [1992] Ch 53, Browne-Wilkinson V-C held that s. 10 only applies to 'attempts to evade the Act's provisions by the introduction of such an exemption clause *into a contract with a third party*' (emphasis added). Consequently, in terms of the situation described above, s. 10 would apply where the maintenance service contract, which provides the vehicle for the exemption clause, is entered into with a party other than the supplier of the goods; it does not apply where the supplier is also the principal party to the maintenance agreement.

It must therefore be asked whether this interpretation of s. 10 leaves a loophole in cases where the secondary contract which exempts liability is entered into by both parties to the original contract. It is submitted that it does not, because the other provisions of the Act are drafted sufficiently widely to catch terms in secondary contracts between the original parties which purport to exempt liability under the original contract. That is, the Act does not presuppose or require that the foundation of liability and any purported exemption be contained in a single contract for its provisions to apply.

The careful construction of s. 10 of the 1977 Act by Browne-Wilkinson V-C in ***Tudor Grange Holdings Ltd v Citibank NA***, arose out of a challenge to a settlement of a claim.

> The plaintiffs claimed breach of contract by the bank, and argued that the bank's defence, based on a contractual settlement of the claim, was ineffective because the settlement was unenforceable under UCTA 1977, s. 10. However, as we have already seen, since the contract settling the claim was between the original parties to the banking contract, s. 10 did not apply.

Moreover, Browne-Wilkinson V-C saw the possibility of compromises or settlements being challenged under the Act as most undesirable as a matter of policy, and accordingly would interpret the Act as not extending to such transactions, relying upon what he took to be Parliament's intention and the mischief aimed at by the Act.

7.6.6 The 'reasonableness' requirement: s. 11

The requirement of reasonableness imposed by the 1977 Act is highly, and arguably unnecessarily, complex. In addition, although the policy objective appears to be fairly clear in the context of consumer contracts, it is far from straightforward in the context of commercial contracts, and discernible differences in policy can be identified in the case law (see Adams and Brownsword (1988) 104 LQR 94).

It is important to appreciate at the outset that the reasonableness requirement is not always the applicable test under the Act (see, e.g., UCTA 1977, s. 2(1)) and the temptation to apply it to all clauses must therefore be resisted.

Section 11(1) defines the test for determining reasonableness as whether the term is a fair and reasonable one to have been included in the light of circumstances known (or which ought to have been known) to the parties at the time of contracting. In other words, the court may not take into account subsequent events, and in particular the actual effect of breach, in determining whether the exemption clause was reasonable. Nevertheless, it seems that in practice the courts do have regard to the effect of the breach. Under UCTA 1977, s. 11(1), the courts may consider circumstances which should have been in the contemplation of the parties at the time of contracting. If a particularly serious breach has occurred, a court could hold that the parties should have realized the possibility of such a serious breach, and then find that it was unreasonable at the time of contracting to exclude liability for such consequences.

Section 11(5) provides that the burden of proving reasonableness lies on the party seeking to rely on the exemption clause.

7.6.6.1 The approach to assessing reasonableness

In *George Mitchell (Chesterhall) Ltd v Finney Lock Seeds Ltd* [1983] 2 AC 803, Lord Bridge set out the approach to be taken by the courts in assessing reasonableness. Although Lord Bridge rejected the notion that such a decision was 'an exercise of discretion', he accepted that the courts:

> must entertain a whole range of considerations, put them in the scales on one side or the other, and decide at the end of the day on which side the balance comes down.

It follows that each case must necessarily turn on its own particular facts, so that cases have limited significance in terms of their precedent value. In *Phillips Products Ltd v Hyland* [1987] 1 WLR 659, the Court of Appeal made this clear. Slade LJ, speaking for the whole court, said (at pp. 668–9):

> The question for the court is not a general question whether or not condition 8 is valid or invalid in the case of any and every contract of hire entered into between a hirer and a plant owner who uses the relevant CPA conditions. The question was and is whether the exclusion of Hamstead's liability for negligence satisfied the requirement of reasonableness imposed by the Act, in relation to *this particular contract*... It is important therefore that our conclusion on the particular facts of this case should not be treated as a binding precedent in other cases where similar clauses fall to be considered but the evidence of surrounding circumstances may be very different. [Emphasis in original.]

The significance of this denial of precedent value for judicial decisions on the reasonableness of exemption clauses soon became apparent when the same clause was treated quite differently (in a different fact situation by a differently constituted Court of Appeal) in *Thompson v T. Lohan (Plant Hire) Ltd* [1987] 1 WLR 649. (It is therefore preferable to speak of a clause being 'unenforceable' because of the application of the reasonableness test in UCTA 1977, rather than void.)

Nevertheless, in **Smith v Eric S. Bush** [1990] 1 AC 831, the House of Lords appears deliberately to have attempted to set down a general rule on the unacceptability of exclusions of liability by professional surveyors towards private house buyers. In confronting the question of reasonableness, Lord Templeman and Lord Griffiths both considered 'the general pattern of house purchases' and the impact of their finding on other transactions of the same type, while limiting their 'ruling' to domestic house purchases and reserving their position on exclusions of liability in respect of surveys of commercial property. The real significance of this decision appears to be that it represents a rare reported example of the application of the reasonableness requirement to a consumer contract and as a matter of policy the objectives of UCTA 1977 in this context are much clearer than is the case in the context of commercial contracts.

Until fairly recently, there were few reported decisions involving the reasonableness test. This was partly attributable to the fact that many of the consumer cases would be decided by the county courts, and also because editors of law reports presumably considered there to be little value in reporting case law which had no real value as a precedent. Although there are signs that this position may have changed because it is possible to identify trends and recurring factors in the case law, the decisions reported tend to have concerned commercial contracts. This is probably because of the size of the claims involved and the significance in financial terms of a finding that the exemption clause is reasonable or unreasonable. However, it may also be because the approach of the courts in the context of commercial contracts is more interesting since there is no clear-cut policy objective (as clearly exists in the consumer context).

The role of appellate courts

In *George Mitchell*, Lord Bridge also explained that in the light of the essentially fact-based exercise undertaken by the courts, and on the basis that the court at first instance will have heard all the evidence and witness statements relevant to the factors:

> the appellate court should treat the original decision with the utmost respect and refrain from interference with it unless satisfied that it proceeded upon some erroneous principle or was plainly and obviously wrong.

Watford Electronics Ltd v Sanderson CFL Ltd [2001] EWCA Civ 317, [2001] 1 All ER (Comm) 696 and *Regus (UK) Ltd v Epcot Solutions Ltd* [2008] EWCA Civ 361, [2009] 1 All ER (Comm) 586, are recent examples of cases where the Court of Appeal overturned a first instance finding on reasonableness.

7.6.6.2 Factors relevant in the assessment of reasonableness

1. Factors identified by the legislation

- Under **s. 11(4) of UCTA 1977**, there is a special test stated to be applicable to limitation clauses (i.e., clauses restricting liability to a specified sum of money). In such cases the court must have particular regard to whether the person seeking to limit their liability could expect to have resources available to meet such liability should it arise, and to the extent to which it was possible for that person to have obtained insurance cover for such liability. The cost and availability of insurance has been applied more generally as a factor (e.g., in *Photo Production Ltd v Securicor Transport Ltd* [1980] AC 827, the House of Lords stressed that the cost of the patrolling service was modest and that it was reasonable for the factory owners to cover this risk by taking out insurance cover).

- Under s. 11(2), in the case of exemptions of implied terms in the sale or supply of goods (UCTA 1977, ss. 6 and 7: see **7.6.4.1**), the court is referred to a set of guidelines on reasonableness, set out in **Sch. 2**. Among the factors to be taken into account are:
  - the relative strengths of the bargaining positions of the parties;
  - whether in agreeing to the exemption a party received an inducement (e.g., a lower price);
  - whether any condition for the enforcement of liability (e.g., claiming within seven days of performance) could practically be complied with; and
  - whether the goods were specially made at the request of the buyer.

In addition, Sch. 2(c) refers to the existence of knowledge of the existence and extent of the term. This refers to the reality of any consent to the term rather than the fact that the test of incorporation has been satisfied (*AEG (UK) Ltd v Logic Resource Ltd* [1996] CLC 265). The clearest evidence of consent to a term will be evidence that it is the result of negotiation (see *Britvic Soft Drinks v Messer UK Ltd* [2002] EWCA Civ 548, [2002] 2 Lloyd's Rep 368).

Although in theory this list of factors applies only in the context of exclusions of implied terms in sale and supply contracts, these factors have been applied more generally by the courts (as confirmed by Stuart Smith LJ in *Stewart Gill Ltd v Horatio Myer & Co. Ltd* [1992] 1 QB 600 at p. 608). Their application has now become a matter of course in case law involving an assessment of reasonableness; so much so, that judgments are frequently structured around an examination of the application of each in turn.

2. Factors identified by the courts

Bearing in mind the limitations of decided cases in this area as precedents, it is proposed to examine some of these cases in an attempt to identify recurring factors and themes which may be of assistance in terms of giving advice.

(a) Commercial contracts

In their article ((1988) 104 LQR 94), Adams and Brownsword identified two different approaches to reasonableness in the commercial context.

- The *Photo Production* approach of freedom of contract and the ability to allocate risks bearing in mind the availability of insurance cover—this approach has gained prominence in recent decisions: see, e.g., *Monarch Airlines Ltd v London Luton Airport Ltd* [1997] CLC 698 and *Watford Electronics Ltd v Sanderson CFL Ltd* [2001] EWCA Civ 317, [2001] 1 All ER (Comm) 696 (below).

- On the other hand, there is a more interventionist approach exemplified by the decision in *George Mitchell.*

In *George Mitchell (Chesterhall) Ltd v Finney Lock Seeds Ltd* [1983] 2 AC 803, the defendants had supplied cabbage seed at a contract price of approximately £200. The cabbages did not grow properly, causing lost production to the value of £61,000. The contract purported to limit liability for defective seeds to the amount of the contract price. (UCTA 1977 did not apply to this contract because it was entered into before 1 February 1978, but it was subject to the reasonableness test applicable under s. 55(3) of the

SGA 1979, which for these purposes was essentially similar to the UCTA 1977 test.) In the Court of Appeal ([1983] QB 284), in finding the clause to be unreasonable, Kerr LJ reasoned as follows (at pp. 313–14):

> The balance of fairness and reasonableness appears to me to be overwhelmingly on the side of the plaintiffs…Farmers do not, and cannot be expected to, insure against this kind of disaster; but suppliers of seeds can…I am not persuaded that liability for rare events of this kind cannot be adequately insured against. Nor am I persuaded that the cost of such cover would add significantly to the cost of seed. Further, although the present exemption clause has been in existence for many decades, the evidence shows that it was never negotiated. In effect, it was simply imposed by the suppliers, and no seed can in practice be bought otherwise than subject to its terms. To limit the supplier's liability to the price of the seed in all cases, as against the magnitude of the losses which farmers can incur in rare disasters of this kind, appears to me to be a grossly disproportionate and unreasonable allocation of the respective risks.

This decision can be compared with that in **R. W. Green Ltd v Cade Brothers Farms** [1978] 1 Lloyd's Rep 602.

> In **R. W. Green Ltd v Cade Brothers Farms**, a supply of potatoes had been infected with a virus but a limitation clause in the contract purported to limit liability to the price (£634), although the actual loss of profit on the crop was around £6,000. This limitation clause was held to be reasonable because the parties were of equal bargaining power, the clause had been negotiated between relevant trade bodies and had been in use for many years. In addition, the buyers could have paid more to obtain a guarantee against the virus.

In the commercial context the most important factors pointing to the reasonableness of a clause appear to be:

- equality of bargaining position
- whether the clause is a generally accepted clause in the industry in question and was negotiated by the trade bodies concerned
- whether, on this basis, it is essentially a clause allocating a particular risk between two commercial parties thereby avoiding the risk of duplicate insurance.

These factors were cited in **Monarch Airlines Ltd v London Luton Airport Ltd** [1997] CLC 698, in support of a finding that a clause, excluding the liability of the airport for unintentional damage to aircraft, was reasonable. They were also used in the context of a 'no set-off' clause in a commercial agreement in **Schenkers Ltd v Overland Shoes Ltd** [1998] 1 Lloyd's Rep 498. The clause in question was in common use (having been arrived at following negotiations between the relevant representative bodies). It was also well known in the trade and by these parties who were in roughly equal bargaining positions.

In **Watford Electronics Ltd v Sanderson CFL Ltd** [2001] EWCA Civ 317, [2001] 1 All ER (Comm) 696 (noted Peel (2001) 117 LQR 392), there was a claim for damages for breach of a contract to supply a bespoke integrated software system.

> The contract contained the defendant's standard terms, including a clause purporting to exclude any liability for indirect or consequential losses and a clause limiting liability in a general sense to the price paid under the contract (£104,600). The contract also contained entire agreement clauses (see **6.2.1.4**). The system proved to be faulty and the claimant sought damages amounting to £5.5m for breach of contract (namely loss of profits, the increased costs of working and reimbursement of the cost of replacement).

At first instance ([2000] 2 All ER (Comm) 984) the judge held the exemption clauses to be unreasonable in their entirety. However, the Court of Appeal considered that the judge had reached his conclusion on an incorrect basis as he had failed to consider the exemption clauses as separate clauses dealing with separate instances of liability (i.e., as a term excluding indirect losses and as a term limiting liability for direct loss). The judge had failed to consider reasonableness in relation to each clause. Accordingly, the Court of Appeal reversed the judge's decision so that the clauses were considered to be reasonable.

The Court of Appeal held that the **clauses were reasonable because the contract had been negotiated between experienced businessmen of equal bargaining power and skill. Both should have appreciated the party which was to bear the risk of loss and would anticipate that the price would reflect that risk.** Chadwick LJ stated (at [54]):

> In circumstances in which parties of equal bargaining power negotiate a price for the supply of product under an agreement which provides for the person on whom the risk of loss will fall, it seems to me that the court should be very cautious before reaching the conclusion that the agreement which they have reached is not a fair and reasonable one.

Chadwick LJ continued:

> experienced businessmen representing substantial companies of equal bargaining power…should…be taken to be the best judge of the commercial fairness of the agreement which they have made; including the fairness of each of the terms in that agreement…Unless satisfied that one party has, in effect, taken unfair advantage of the other—or that a term is so unreasonable that it cannot properly have been understood or considered—the court should not interfere.

This 'freedom of contract' or 'sanctity of contract' approach of the Court of Appeal is very much in line with that of the House of Lords in *Photo Production* and, as Peter Gibson LJ stated in his judgment (at [55]), in these circumstances there will be 'little scope for the court to unmake the bargain made by commercial men'. In *Granville Oil & Chemicals Ltd v Davies Turner & Co Ltd* [2003] EWCA Civ 570, [2003] 1 All ER (Comm) 819, Tucker LJ (with whose judgment Potter LJ and Hart J agreed) stated (at [31]):

> The 1977 Act obviously plays a very important role in protecting vulnerable consumers from the effects of draconian contract terms. But I am less enthusiastic about its intrusion into contracts between commercial parties of equal bargaining strength, who should generally be considered capable of being able to make contracts of their choosing and expect to be bound by their terms.

This non-interventionist approach to clauses in commercial contracts was also evident in *Frans Maas (UK) Ltd v Samsung Electronics (UK) Ltd* [2004] EWHC 1502 (Comm), [2005] 2 All ER (Comm) 783, where Gross J (at [158]–[159]) explicitly adopted Tucker LJ's comment in *Granville Oil*. In *Sterling Hydraulics Ltd v Dichtomatik Ltd* [2006] EWHC 2004 (QB), [2007] 1 Lloyd's Rep 8 (2.4.2.3 and 6.3.1.2) there were clauses which attempted to exclude all liability for defects in the seals, in particular for consequential loss, unless there was prompt reporting of defects when liability would be limited to price of the goods, or there was intentional or gross negligence by the supplier. However, apart from imposing a one-week limit for reporting claims based on hidden defects, the exclusion and limitation provisions were considered to be reasonable in view of the equal bargaining power. Limitation to the price was reasonable because it was a 'low value high volume contract' and, since the supplier was given no information as to the precise use for the seals, it could not have taken out insurance for the full risks.

In *Regus (UK) Ltd v Epcot Solutions Ltd* [2008] EWCA Civ 361, [2009] 1 All ER (Comm) 586, the Court of Appeal held that there was nothing unreasonable in a clause limiting liability for loss of profits and consequential losses in a commercial contract providing for serviced office accommodation since the parties were of equal bargaining power, had negotiated their contract and the evidence was that the customer used a similar clause in its own business. Customers were advised to take out insurance to cover their business losses and it was generally more appropriate for the customer to take out this insurance than the service supplier.

In recent years the courts have also considered the nature of the contract and the extent of the commercial risks involved when concluding that exemption clauses were reasonable. For example, the supply of computer software is a notoriously risky commercial operation and the potential scope of liability is extensive. It therefore appears that in the light of these facts the courts are prepared to permit exclusions of consequential (or indirect) losses as long as it is possible to recover for direct losses resulting from the breach. For example, in *SAM Business Systems Ltd v Hedley and Co* [2002] EWHC 2733 (QB), [2003] 1 All ER (Comm) 465, the judge held that as there was a money-back guarantee covering the price of the software (i.e., a limitation of liability in relation to direct loss), the exclusion of incidental or consequential losses was reasonable. The clause was also considered to be a common clause in relation to the supply of computer software.

By comparison, in the soft drinks cases (*Britvic Soft Drinks v Messer UK Ltd* [2002] EWCA Civ 548, [2002] 2 Lloyd's Rep 368 and *Bacardi-Martini Beverages Ltd v Thomas Hardy Packaging* [2002] EWCA Civ 549, [2002] 2 Lloyd's Rep 379) exclusion clauses in commercial contracts purporting to exempt from liability for the contamination of the supply of carbon dioxide to be used in the manufacture of soft drinks were considered to be unreasonable. This decision was based on the lack of negotiation of the clause, the fact that the contamination was due to the negligence of the supplier, and the fact that this particular event would not have been contemplated as a commercial risk. In *Balmoral Group Ltd v Borealis (UK) Ltd* [2006] EWHC 1900 (Comm) (discussed at 6.3.2) the judge held (at [418]–[426]) that since the clause required Balmoral to bear the entire risk of latent defects in Borealis's product, it was unreasonable and an inappropriate allocation of the risk. Balmoral had no choice other than to accept Borealis's terms and Borealis could have covered the risk in relation to its own products with insurance.

However, as the decision in *Overseas Medical Supplies Ltd v Orient Transport Services Ltd* [1999] CLC 1243 illustrates, it also remains possible for a clause to be unreasonable in a commercial contract where it undermines a contractual allocation of risk.

The plaintiff contracted with the defendant freight forwarders for the transportation to Iran and back of equipment for an exhibition. The contract provided that the defendant was to insure the equipment. However, the defendant failed to take out the insurance and, in response to a claim by the plaintiff when the equipment was lost, sought to rely on a limitation clause limiting recovery to an amount per kilo (approximately £600 when the actual loss was £8,590). The judge held that the limitation was reasonable in respect of liability for loss of the goods, but not in relation to liability for breach of the obligation to insure. The Court of Appeal agreed. The failure to insure, when taken with the limitation, would have meant that the customer lost both the goods and the insurance which would otherwise have compensated him. In addition, the plaintiff had no real choice other than to use the defendant, a specialist firm.

Equally, it may be possible to establish that although the contract is made in the commercial context, the positions of the parties are unequal so that the rationale underlying the non-interventionist approach in commercial contracts cannot apply. Thus, in ***Motours Ltd v Euroball (West Kent) Ltd*** [2003] EWHC 614 (QB), [2003] All ER (D) 165, the judge avoided the non-interventionist approach advocated for commercial contracts and concluded that a clause in standard conditions of a telephone service supplier excluding liability for consequential losses was unreasonable. He concluded that the parties were not of equal bargaining power and there had been no discussion or negotiations about the terms of the contract.

(b)   Consumer contracts

For the purposes of assessing the approach in the context of consumer contracts, it is necessary to consider the decision of the House of Lords in ***Smith v Eric S. Bush*** [1990] 1 AC 831.

> The House of Lords held that a disclaimer contained in a mortgage valuation given in respect of a domestic dwelling was unreasonable because of the lack of equal bargaining power (at least in the context of modest domestic purchases) and because the burden of insurance would be better placed on the valuers than on individual purchasers. It was no answer to argue that the purchasers could have paid more to obtain another, more detailed survey, since it was not a realistic option to pay twice for the same thing and purchasers of domestic dwellings could not afford this extra expense.

As might be expected, this is highly protectionist in its approach, although the House of Lords made clear that the position might well be different in the case of expensive dwellings or business premises.

Another interesting 'quasi-consumer' case example is the decision in ***St Albans City and District Council v International Computers Ltd*** [1995] FSR 686, noted Macdonald (1995) 58 MLR 585, [1996] 4 All ER 481 (CA), noted Hedley (1997) 56 CLJ 21. **Although the contract was made by a local authority and the clause in question was a limitation clause (as opposed to a total exclusion), there was a clear inequality of bargaining power and clear evidence of a protectionist approach being taken by the courts.**

> The contract concerned the supply of a computer database for the purposes of calculating local tax rates. A serious error caused the council a loss of more than £1m, while the contract purported to limit recovery to £100,000. The limitation clause was unreasonable, taking into account the unequal bargaining position of the parties, the extensive resources of the defendant and the small limitation figure relative to the potential actual loss. In addition, the defendant had adequate insurance, whereas reasonably priced insurance cover would probably not have been available to the plaintiff. In practice, the company's customers bore the cost of the insurance cover: on the other hand, if the clause had been effective, the loss would have been borne by the taxpayers.

7.6.6.3 The effect and scope of a finding of unreasonableness

Each substantive provision of the 1977 Act which subjects an exemption clause to the requirement of reasonableness is drafted in such a way as to make it clear that, if the requirement of reasonableness is not met, the clause may not be relied upon to exclude or restrict a liability which would otherwise arise under the contract. Thus, the simple effect of a finding of unreasonableness is to cause the contract to be applied and interpreted without reference to the offending element.

Difficulties may arise in respect of this 'simple' consequence where the exemption clause is in a composite form, relating to several different possible breaches of the contract in question, or purporting to exclude or restrict liability, remedies, or procedural rights in more than one way. In such a case the question arises whether a failure to satisfy the requirement of reasonableness in respect of one particular dimension of the clause will cause the whole clause to fail, or whether an offending element may be severed from the remainder of the clause, where that remainder does satisfy the requirement of reasonableness. The question was confronted directly in ***Stewart Gill Ltd v Horatio Myer & Co. Ltd*** [1992] 1 QB 600.

> The relevant clause purported to prevent the buyer withholding payment of any amount due to the supplier 'by reason of any payment credit set off counterclaim allegation of incorrect or defective Goods or for any other reason whatsoever which the customer may allege excuses him from performing his obligations'. The plaintiffs claimed the final instalment due under the contract, which the defendants had withheld because of a counterclaim in respect of an alleged breach. The plaintiffs therefore sought to rely upon the set-off and counterclaim element in the exemption clause to show that withholding the sum due was not allowed under the contract, even if the alleged breach by the plaintiffs could be established. The defendants argued that the element in the exemption clause relating to payments and credits was unreasonable, so that the whole clause failed.

Lord Donaldson MR (with whom Balcombe LJ agreed) appears to have been willing to believe that a clause preventing a right of set-off might be reasonable, but was unwilling to believe that it might be reasonable to prevent withholding payment where the plaintiffs owed the defendants money as a result of pre-existing payments or credits. The question therefore was whether the unreasonable part relating to payments and credits could be severed from the remainder of the clause. The court was unanimous that it could not:

- Lord Donaldson relied upon the wording of s. 11(1), which states that the requirement of reasonableness 'is that *the term* shall have been a fair and reasonable one' (emphasis added).

- Stuart-Smith LJ (with whom Balcombe LJ and Lord Donaldson agreed) relied upon the fact that the assessment of whether the clause is reasonable is to be made in the light of circumstances known to the parties at the time of contracting. He pointed out that it is impossible to know at the time of contracting which part of a composite and potentially severable exemption clause will be relied upon at some indeterminate time in the future, so that unless the entire clause is the subject of scrutiny and stands and falls as a whole, the reasonableness test cannot be applied as laid down by the Act.

Nevertheless, in ***J. Murphy & Sons Ltd v Johnston Precast Ltd*** [2008] EWHC 3024 (TCC), Coulson J commented (at [137]), that he did not think *Stewart Gill* was a case concerned with actual severance but 'whether the court should look only at part of the clause in question, rather than the entirety of the clause. Moreover, the dispute there came down to the consideration of a few words within a clause, which made severance, for all practical purposes, impossible'. Coulson J therefore concluded that it was perfectly consistent to break down a lengthy contractual term into parts and then assess whether 'those different parts are performing different functions'. Moreover, in ***Regus (UK) Ltd v Epcot Solutions Ltd*** [2008] EWCA Civ 361, [2009] 1 All ER (Comm) 586, the Court of Appeal commented (*obiter*) that if clauses are seen as independent, i.e. serving a different purpose (in this case a very specific limitation clause limited to recovery of 125 per cent of the fees or £50,000), they can be severed and enforced.

7.7 Unfair terms in consumer contracts

Directive 93/13 on Unfair Terms in Consumer Contracts [1993] OJ L95/29 was originally implemented in English law by the Unfair Terms in Consumer Contracts Regulations 1994, SI

1994/3159, which substantially reproduced the wording, if not the order of presentation, of the directive itself. However, no attempt was made to tackle any clear overlap or potential conflicts between the directive, the existing legislation (UCTA 1977), and common law rules. One of the frequent criticisms was that the implementation of the directive had been rushed (despite the fact that the deadline for its implementation was 31 December 1994 and the regulations did not take effect until 1 July 1995), and this may explain why there was no attempt to consolidate the directive and the existing law. Although the 1994 regulations have been repealed and replaced by the 1999 regulations, SI 1999/2083, the main difference of substance relates to so-called pre-emptive challenges to unfair terms by 'qualifying bodies' (see 7.7.7) and again there was no attempt to rationalize legislative regulation in this area. The potential therefore remains for the English courts to be presented with a series of complex questions about the interplay of the sometimes parallel, sometimes overlapping, and potentially conflicting rules.

In 2005 the Law Commission examined the complex relationship between UCTA 1977 and the UTCCR 1999 and made recommendations in a report, *Unfair Terms in Contracts*, Law Com. No. 292, Cm. 6464, for reform of the law in this area. The principal recommendation is for a unified regime for consumer contracts with the aim of simplifying and clarifying the applicable principles and altering the burden of proof. These recommendations are now on hold pending the possible implementation of *Proposal for a Directive on Consumer Rights*, COM (2008) 614 final, 13 October 2008, which would replace the Unfair Terms Directive (93/13/EEC).

7.7.1 Scope of the 1999 regulations

The purpose of the directive was said to be to harmonize the law relating to 'unfair terms in contracts concluded between a seller or supplier and a consumer'. **The Unfair Terms in Consumer Contracts Regulations 1999, SI 1999/2083** make this scope clear in reg. 4(1).

7.7.1.1 Consumer contracts

Regulation 3(1) defines a seller or supplier as 'any natural or legal person who…is acting for purposes relating to his trade, business or profession, whether publicly owned or privately owned', and 'consumer' is defined as 'any natural person who is acting for purposes which are outside his trade, business or profession'. Thus, the regulations are in this sense narrower than UCTA 1977 because they apply only to consumer contracts. The 1977 Act can apply to commercial contracts (e.g., s. 2, s. 3 (where one party contracts on the other's written standard terms of business), s. 6(3), and s. 7(3)).

The regulations will apply to guarantee contracts concluded by a consumer but only where the principal contract to which it relates, and was ancillary, had also been executed by a natural person who was not acting in the course of their trade or profession (***Barclays Bank plc v Kufner*** [2008] EWHC 2319, [2009] 1 All ER (Comm) 1: the defendant, guarantor, had given a guarantee as security for a loan made by the claimant bank to a company that was beneficially owned by the defendant. The loan agreement had been entered into by a company, which was not a consumer, and the guarantee had also not been executed by a consumer since the defendant had been acting for business purposes in seeking to establish a ship chartering business. It followed that the regulations did not apply on the facts.)

The regulations apply to contracts relating to land (***London Borough of Newham v Khatun*** [2004] EWCA Civ 55, [2004] 3 WLR 417: the UTCCR 1999 applied to local authorities carrying out their statutory duties to house homeless persons. The local authority was regarded as a seller or supplier within reg. 3 and the homeless persons were consumers). Similarly, in ***Freiburger Kommunalbauten GmbH Baugesellschaft & Co. KG v Hofstetter***, Case C-237/02 [2004] 2 CMLR 13, the European Court of Justice had considered that the directive applied to a contract for the purchase of a building under construction. The regulations also apply to arbitration agreements (ss. 89 and 90, Arbitration Act 1996).

The definition of 'consumer' in the regulations means that a company cannot qualify as a consumer since companies (and limited liability partnerships) are legal entities and not natural persons. However, in the context of arbitration agreements this position is expressly amended by s. 90 so that the UTCCR 1999 also apply to legal persons, or at least this is the case where the arbitration agreement is for a sum in excess of £5,000. Nevertheless, as a general rule, the regulations cannot apply to terms in contracts entered into between two companies. Technically, a sole trader and a general partnership would fall within the definition of 'natural persons', but in order to gain the protection of the regulations the individual or individuals in question would need to be acting for purposes which are outside their business purposes.

> This was the test applied in the context of a dispute as to whether an arbitration clause in a contract to refurbish a residential property fell within the regulations when made between a company and a business: *Heifer International Inc v Christiansen* [2007] EWHC 3015 (TCC), [2008] 2 All ER (Comm) 831. This contract related to a property purchased by the claimant company as a private residence for the company's Russian owner and his family and so was not made in the course of the company's business. Had the property been purchased by the company as an investment, the position would have been different.

The definition of 'in the course of a business' discussed earlier in the context of UCTA 1977 (see 7.6.4.1), may well be applicable here, so that if the contract in question is not an integral part of the business, or if only incidental to the carrying on of the business, the contract would need to be entered into with sufficient regularity to constitute a contract for business purposes (see ***R. & B. Customs Brokers & Co. Ltd v United Dominions Trust Ltd*** [1988] 1 WLR 321).

'Consumer' is therefore defined more generously under UCTA 1977, since in some circumstances a company may be 'dealing as a consumer' within s. 12(1) of that Act (see ***R. & B. Customs Brokers*** and discussion at 7.6.4.1).

Although where a consumer acts as agent for a non-consumer the contract will not generally be a 'consumer contract' within the regulations, it may nevertheless fall within the regulations where the 'agent' also undertakes personal liabilities in that contract made on behalf of another. ***Domsalla (T/A Domsalla Building Services) v Dyason*** [2007] EWHC 1174 (TCC), [2007] BLR 348, (also discussed at 7.7.3) concerned a dispute between a builder and a residential occupier under a contract to reinstate a house seriously damaged by fire. The occupier had entered into the contract with the builders as agent for the insurance company dealing with the claim. However, it was held that the regulations applied because the contract terms made the occupier liable to the builders both as principal and agent.

7.7.1.2 Not individually negotiated

In another sense, the 1999 regulations are narrower than UCTA 1977. UCTA may apply to negotiated terms, but the regulations will apply only where the term in question is 'not individually negotiated'.

7.7.1.3 Unfair terms

On the other hand, the regulations are also wider in one important respect, namely the fact that they apply to 'unfair terms' in general. For example, the regulations contain protection against unreasonable deposits and penalty clauses overlapping with existing common law control provided by 'the penalty rule' (see **9.10.2**), although the latter are not limited to consumer contracts or to contracts which are not individually negotiated. Although the regulations do apply to exemption clauses (see Sch. 2, para. 1(a) and (b) for examples), their coverage also extends beyond this to terms in general (although not those terms covered by reg. 4(2) and reg. 6(2), see below). UCTA 1977, on the other hand, applies only to exemption clauses (as defined by UCTA 1977, s. 13(1)).

7.7.1.4 Terms excluded from the scope of the regulations

1. Mandatory statutory or regulatory provisions

The regulations do not apply to contractual terms which 'reflect mandatory statutory or regulatory provisions' (reg. 4(2)(a)), the assumption being that if Member States have by legislative act given approval to particular contract terms, those terms cannot by definition be deemed to be unfair (see the preamble to the directive, recital 13). The preamble envisages that 'default' obligations such as s. 14(2) of the SGA 1979 (implied condition that goods sold be of satisfactory quality: **6.4.2.4**) would be excluded from the scope of the regulations. This would accord with the treatment of attempts to exclude or limit liability for breach of such terms as against a consumer under UCTA 1977, s. 6(2). Regulation 4(2)(b) also expressly excludes 'the provisions or principles of international conventions', such as the Warsaw Convention limitations on liability towards passengers in aircraft.

2. Core terms which define the main subject matter or relate to the adequacy of the contract price

The 1999 regulations expressly exclude from their scope those terms which define the main subject matter of the contract and questions relating to the adequacy of the contract price in relation to the performance to be provided by the other party, provided that such terms are in 'plain intelligible language' (reg. 6(2)).

In the first case on the regulations (albeit the 1994 version), *Director General of Fair Trading (DFGT) v First National Bank plc* [2001] UKHL 52, [2002] 1 AC 481, one of the arguments by the bank was that the regulations could not apply to the contested term since it was a 'core term' concerning the 'adequacy of the price or remuneration'.

> The term in question was a term in a consumer loan agreement which provided for interest to be paid after any judgment on the debt. Therefore, in the event of judgment on the debt, contractual interest remained payable despite the fact that the debtor paid the instalments due under the terms of the judgment. The House of Lords held (confirming the position adopted by the judge at first instance and the Court of Appeal) that the term was an incidental term dealing with the consequences of the borrower's default. It did not concern the adequacy of the interest earned by the bank as its remuneration for the loan. Accordingly, this was not a 'core term' and therefore the regulations applied.

Lord Bingham (with whose reasons the other members of the House agreed) stated (at [12]):

> The object of the Regulations and the Directive is to protect consumers against the inclusion of unfair and prejudicial terms in standard-form contracts into which they enter, and that object would plainly be frustrated if regulation 3(2)(b) [now reg. 6(2), UTCCR 1999] were so broadly interpreted as to cover any terms other than those falling squarely within it.

(The claim that the term was an unfair term under UTCCR 1999 is discussed below at 7.7.3.)

Subsequently, in ***Bairstow Eves London Central Ltd v Smith*** [2004] EWHC 263 (QB), [2004] 2 EGLR 25, it was held that reg. 6(2) ('core terms') is to be interpreted restrictively, thereby allowing more terms to be assessed for unfairness.

> The case concerned a term in an estate agency contract providing for commission at the rate of 1.5 per cent if paid in full within ten days of completion or agreed alternative payment date; otherwise commission was payable at 3 per cent on the sale price with interest at 3 per cent above base. The judge had concluded that this was not a 'core term' (i.e., did not concern the adequacy of the price or remuneration) and that the 3 per cent term was unfair and so not binding on the vendors. The estate agents appealed on the applicability of the regulations and on appeal it was held that the issue here was whether the core rate was 3 per cent with an option to pay 1.5 per cent (in which case reg. 6(2) was applicable) or whether the core rate was 1.5 per cent with a 'default' provision of 3 per cent. He concluded that the 1.5 per cent was contemplated as the price, with a default position of 3 per cent if the vendors failed to pay within ten days. Accordingly reg. 6(2) did not apply and the regulations as a whole were applicable. (The issue of unfairness was not appealed.)

Relying on the guidance in ***Director General of Fair Trading v First National Bank***, Gross J concluded:

> regulation 6(2) must be given a restrictive interpretation; otherwise a coach and horses could be driven through the Regulations. So, while it is not for the Court to re-write the parties' bargain as to the fairness or adequacy of the price itself, regulation 6(2) may be unlikely to shield terms as to price escalation or default provisions from scrutiny under the fairness requirement contained in regulation 5(1).

Nevertheless, the clause in question may be interpreted as a 'core term', e.g. because it relates to the subject matter of the contract, so that the regulations will not apply.

> For example, in ***Bankers Insurance Co Ltd v South*** [2003] EWHC 380 (QB), [2004] Lloyd's Rep IR 1, the defendant, South, had purchased holiday insurance for a trip to Cyprus. The policy contained an exclusion of liability for accidents 'involving your ownership or possession of any…motorised waterborne craft'. While South was driving a jet ski he was involved in a collision and the other person (the second defendant) was seriously injured. The second defendant commenced proceedings against South. The insurer sought a declaration that because of the exclusion it was not liable to indemnify South. It was held that the exclusion clause clearly covered the jet ski accident (its terms were in 'plain and intelligible' language) and since it related to the definition of the subject matter of the contract (within reg. 6(2) UTCCR 1999), the regulations did not apply and the term could not be assessed for fairness.
> In ***Baybut v Eccle Riggs Country Park Ltd***, *The Times*, 13 November 2006 (see 7.7.4.2), a term providing for a yearly licence to use a static caravan park was held to be 'a core term' within reg. 6(2) as defining the main subject matter of the contract.

The question of the application of reg. 6(2) to exclude the operation of the regulations was also considered in ***Office of Fair Trading v Foxtons Ltd*** [2009] EWHC 1681 (Ch), [2009] 29 EG 98 (CS). The case concerned a term in the standard terms of a letting agent which provided that commission was payable not only when a tenant was first introduced but also if the tenant renewed, extended, purchased the property or the landlord assigned its rights to a third party, even where none of these events was attributable to anything done by the letting agent. Was commission part of the contract price within reg. 6(2)? Mann J placed great reliance on the decision in *First National Bank* and also the decision of the Court of Appeal in *Office of Fair Trading v Abbey National plc* [2009] EWCA Civ 116, which has since been overturned on appeal by the Supreme Court. Mann J considered that it was a question of impression and how the term in question would be perceived by the typical consumer landlord as well as how it was perceived by Foxtons. Was the clause perceived to be a core provision, i.e. part of the core bargain, or was it perceived to be ancillary or incidental? The judge concluded that the term was not core, pointing to the fact that the term was hidden away in the document and that there would have needed to be clearer reference to the term from the outset and real negotiation between the parties. In any event, the judge paid particular attention to the fact that a core term would need to be expressed in plain and intelligible language, which this was not. This decision has all the hallmarks of a policy decision in order to be able to test the commission clauses for unfairness. Commission clearly relates to the key duties of the letting agent and would seem to be the price charged for that service. It follows that the decision on this point might be different in the light of the rather different approach subsequently adopted by the Supreme Court in the bank charges case.

The scope of reg. 6(2) had also been at issue in the 'bank charges' litigation since the banks had argued that the terms imposing such charges could not be considered as unfair terms since they fell within this exclusion. (Banking is generally free for those customers who stay in credit, but fixed fees and interest are payable by customers with overdrafts, particularly customers who have unauthorized overdrafts.) In *Office of Fair Trading v Abbey National plc* [2009] UKSC 6, [2009] 3 WLR 1215, the Supreme Court accepted this argument and therefore concluded that the regulations cannot apply to test the fairness, or otherwise, of bank charges levied on personal current account customers for unauthorised overdrafts.

At first instance and before the Court of Appeal ([2009] EWCA Civ 116, [2009] 2 WLR 1286) the banks had lost the argument and it was held that the regulations applied so that the OFT was entitled to assess the charges for fairness. This conclusion had been reached by interpreting reg. 6(2)(b) so as to give effect to directive 93/13 and the purpose of Art. 4(2) of that directive. This led the Court of Appeal to conclude that the bank charges were ancillary and not part of 'the core terms' of the contract to which reg. 6(2)(b) applied. On appeal the Supreme Court had only to determine whether these charges fell within the exclusion in reg. 6(2)(b) as being 'the price or remuneration, as against the service supplied in exchange'.

The Supreme Court rejected the distinction between sums that represented the core bargain and ancillary sums. There was no principled basis for treating some terms as more essential than others in this context (see Lord Walker at [41]). The question was only whether the charges represented the monetary price for the service provided in exchange under the contract. Not all terms would fall within this definition (*First National Bank, Bairstow Eves* were cited as examples) but these charges clearly did. They were part of the customer's package (per Lord Mance at [114]) and the price paid for banking services. Their Lordships were aware of the wider implications and Lord Walker noted that these charges amounted to 'over 30 per cent' of the revenue stream for banks from personal account customers, which suggested they must be part of 'the core or essential bargain'. It was also irrelevant that payment of these charges was contingent so that the majority of customers would not pay them (at [47]).

7.7.2 The term must not be individually negotiated

The control of unfair terms applies only to contractual terms which have not been individually negotiated. Of course, it is most often the case that consumer contracts are in such form. However, in any event the expression is given the very broadest definition in the 1999 regulations.

Regulation 5(2) provides a presumptive test of when a term is not individually negotiated, that is to say 'where it has been drafted in advance and the consumer has therefore not been able to influence the substance of the term'. It is also expressly provided (by reg. 5(3)) that a contract may as a whole be treated as a pre-formulated standard form despite the fact that certain aspects of a term or one specific term have been individually negotiated.

The intention is clear: the fact that the consumer has been able to influence the content of the contract in a minor way does not prevent the remainder of the contract not so influenced from being treated as not individually negotiated and so potentially containing unfair terms. (Compare with the approach to 'other's written standard terms of business' in UCTA 1977, s. 3(1)—see 7.6.4.2. Difficulties can arise under s. 3(1) of UCTA 1977 if a standard form is used as the basis for negotiation and there is some variation. No such difficulties can arise under the regulations.) **In addition, the burden of proving that a term was individually negotiated (and therefore outside the regulations) falls on the seller or supplier.**

Where the consumer has had an influence on the content of a term through individual negotiation, it is assumed that the term will not be unfair, so that the regulations apply only to the rest of the contract. Although the logic of this provision may be understood, it is possible to imagine individual negotiation itself being affected by the inequality of bargaining power between parties where one is a consumer, so that it may be a false assumption to believe that individual negotiation is a safeguard against unfairness.

The Law Commission's recommendation in its 2005 report, *Unfair Terms in Contracts,* Law Com. No. 292, Cm. 6464, accepts that since UCTA 1977 applies whether the clause is negotiated or not, e.g. UCTA 1977, s. 3, and the unified regime should not reduce the level of consumer protection, the consumer regime should apply to negotiated and non-negotiated terms (para. 3.55). This accords with the response of the UK government to the European Commission Review of the directive (UK Response to the European Commission, DTI, February 2001, responding to the *Commission Report on the Implementation of Council Directive 93/13/EEC on Unfair Terms in Consumer Contracts,* COM(2000) 248). By comparison, the small business regime will apply only to those terms put forward as standard terms and which have not been subsequently changed in favour of the small business as a result of negotiation (para. 5.75).

7.7.3 Determining unfairness and the meaning of good faith

Key point

The contractual term shall be regarded as unfair if 'contrary to the requirement of good faith, it causes a significant imbalance in the parties' rights and obligations arising under the contract, to the detriment of the consumer' (reg. 5(1)).

This provision is the key to the control mechanism adopted by the directive and introduces the concept of good faith into English law. **The most important factor to appreciate is that it is the consumer who will have the burden of proving unfairness under the regulations.**

To the detriment of the consumer

It appears that the notion of 'detriment to the consumer' is unlikely to cause great difficulty; it is subordinate to the notion of 'significant imbalance', and its only purpose is to indicate for whose benefit the control is to be exercised. In the unlikely event of an imbalance **in favour** of the consumer, the term would clearly not be 'unfair'.

Contrary to good faith, the clause or term causes a significant imbalance in the parties' rights and obligations

The key notion is a 'significant imbalance in the parties' rights and obligations arising under the contract' which is in some way contrary to the 'requirement of good faith'. These are vague and ill-defined criteria, and the regulations fail to make clear the relationship between them. In particular, the drafting of reg. 5(1) does not make clear whether the requirement of lack of good faith is additional to the condition of imbalance between the parties, or whether imbalance is to be regarded in itself as evidence of a lack of good faith. Neither the directive nor the regulations provide clear guidance on this matter, or on what constitutes a significant imbalance. Some assistance in relation to 'good faith' can be gained by referring to recital 16 of the preamble to the directive, which defines compliance with the requirement of good faith as being satisfied by dealing equitably and fairly with the consumer, whose legitimate interests must be taken into account. However, in its *Further Consultation Document,* September 1994, the then DTI stated: 'So far as the directive is concerned, good faith cannot be further elaborated on. It is more than a combination of the factors set out in Recital 16 to the Directive.'

In the 1994 regulations (now repealed and replaced by the 1999 regulations), the substance of recital 16 was repeated in the previous Sch. 2 to the regulations, but with the significant omission of any reference to the consumer's legitimate interests. In fact, the old Sch. 2 to the regulations was similar in content to Sch. 2 to UCTA 1977, with the exception of old Sch. 2(d), having regard to 'the extent to which the seller or supplier has dealt fairly and equitably with the consumer'. However, this assistance has been dropped altogether from the 1999 regulations (on the grounds that it was not included as a provision of the directive itself), and the only assistance provided is the general provision contained in reg. 6(1) (old reg. 4(2)) which refers to unfairness as being assessed 'taking into account the nature of the goods or services for which the contract was concluded and referring, at the time of the conclusion of the contract, to all circumstances attending the conclusion of the contract and to all the other terms of the contract or of another contract on which it is dependent'.

In summary, therefore, **unfairness is determined in the light of the subject matter, the circumstances surrounding formation and the other terms of the contract.** This guidance is very evidently rather general in its nature. Consequently, identification of the criteria for compliance with the terms of the regulations is a process of deduction from what is termed (in reg. 5(5)) an 'indicative and non-exhaustive list of the terms which may be regarded as unfair' and which is contained in Sch. 2 to the regulations.

The Schedule 2 list of indicative terms which may be unfair

The list is too long (seventeen items) to reproduce here, but it is possible to indicate its main themes. As might be expected, it includes terms which are plainly within the scope of UCTA 1977. Other items on the list appear well beyond the reach of the 1977 Act, such as terms 'enabling a seller or supplier to terminate a contract of indeterminate duration without reasonable notice except where there are serious grounds for so doing' (Sch. 2(1)(g)), and terms 'enabling the seller or supplier to alter the terms of the contract unilaterally without a valid reason which is specified in the contract' (Sch. 2(1)(j)). Such terms have not been subject to control under English law until now, although it might be argued that in some circumstances they might be classified as terms which modify expected contractual obligations and so are subject to the requirement of reasonableness under s. 3(2)(b)(i) of the 1977 Act (see 7.6.4.2) and some of them might fall within the application of the penalty rule (see 9.10.2).

From this list it appears possible to deduce that imbalance and lack of good faith are distinct elements in the test.

 Example

A power to alter terms unilaterally constitutes an imbalance in the rights and obligations of the parties: but that in itself is not deemed to be unfair. There must also be no valid reason specified in the contract for such unilateral alteration, and it appears to be the absence of valid reason which constitutes the lack of good faith.

Nevertheless, although the two-part mechanics of the test appear to be clearly established, the list also demonstrates the extent to which both imbalance and lack of good faith will always be questions of fact in each particular case, thereby leaving a very considerable element of discretion to the courts.

Interpretation by the courts

There has been considerable academic debate concerning the possible reaction of the English courts to the concept of good faith. Although English law did not formally recognize any concept of 'good faith' as such, the Chancery courts in the exercise of their 'equitable' jurisdiction, developed principles based on conscience and unconscionability which are closer to the notion of good faith in the civil law than any common law concepts. Equally, in the US, the Uniform Commercial Code has developed the idea of unconscionability into a significant regulatory device for contracts. In that context it is said that the purpose of the rule is to prevent oppression or unfair surprise. Since we are back to fairness, there is a danger of circularity and also a danger of confining unfairness to procedural matters. The reference to 'significant imbalance' would appear to be more closely concerned with substantive unfairness.

Professor Beale in 'Legislative control of fairness: The Directive on Unfair Terms in Consumer Contracts' in Beatson and Friedmann (eds), *Good Faith and Fault in Contract Law* (Oxford University Press, 1995), made the following comment concerning the meaning of 'good faith':

I suspect that good faith has a double operation. First, it has a procedural aspect. It will require the supplier to consider the consumer's interests. However, a clause which might be unfair if it came as a surprise may be upheld if the business took steps to bring it to the consumer's attention and to explain it. Secondly, it has a substantive content: some clauses may cause such imbalance that they should always be treated as unfair.

The first reported decision of the higher courts examining the regulations (1994 version) was the decision of the House of Lords in ***Director General of Fair Trading v First National***

Bank plc [2001] UKHL 52, [2002] 1 AC 481 (for facts see 7.7.1.4), noted Macdonald (2002) 65 MLR 763.

> The Director General of Fair Trading sought an injunction to prevent the continued use of this term, arguing that it was 'unfair' within the regulations. The judge at first instance had considered that the term was not 'unfair' whereas the Court of Appeal held that the term was unfair because of the imbalance of bargaining power and the fact that the term would create 'unfair surprise', i.e. following a judgment on the debt, the borrower would be required to pay the debt in instalments; but if he complied with that order, he would then find that he had to pay additional sums to cover the contractual interest when his attention had not been drawn to this fact.
>
> On appeal, the House of Lords held that the term was not unfair. Although it was accepted that a consumer who was subject to a judgment debt was affected to his detriment, this was not the result of the application of the challenged term, but the result of the applicable legislation and its failure to allow the contractual interest to be covered by the terms of the judgment on the debt. The term itself was a perfectly fair provision which enabled the lender to recover the principal and interest on the loan amount.

Lord Bingham noted that good faith is not 'a concept wholly unfamiliar to British lawyers. It looks to good standards of commercial morality and practice.' He equated good faith with 'fair and open dealing'. Lord Bingham stated (at [17]):

> The requirement of significant imbalance is met if a term is so weighted in favour of the supplier as to tilt the parties' right and obligations under the contract significantly in his favour. This may be by the granting to the supplier of a beneficial option or discretion or power; or by the imposing on the consumer of a disadvantageous burden or risk or duty...The requirement of good faith in this context is one of fair and open dealing. Openness requires that the terms should be expressed fully, clearly and legibly, containing no concealed pitfalls or traps. Appropriate prominence should be given to terms which might operate disadvantageously to the customer.

Lord Bingham appears to confine good faith to procedural aspects ('fair and open dealing') although he refers to the regulation as laying down a composite test, i.e. the 'significant imbalance' requirement imports considerations of the substantive fairness of the term judged in the context of the contract terms as a whole. However, whilst there was agreement that 'significant imbalance' relates to substantive considerations, it would also appear to be the case that good faith may entail both procedural and substantive issues and Lord Bingham appears to accept this since the examples he uses refer to issues of unconscionability and taking advantage of a position of vulnerability in bargaining.

Lord Steyn concluded that that '[a]ny purely procedural or even predominantly procedural interpretation of the requirement of good faith must be rejected' and considered that there was a large area of overlap between the requirements that the term cause a significant imbalance in the parties' rights and obligations, and the requirement that this should be contrary to the requirement of good faith. This amounts to acceptance that good faith can involve issues relating to substantive fairness.

Thus, it would seem to be the case that 'good faith' used in this context is an overarching concept which may be infringed in circumstances either of substantive or procedural unfairness where this results in significant imbalance in the parties' positions to the detriment of the consumer. References in reg. 6(1) to the position surrounding the making of the contract and its substantive fairness add support to such an interpretation.

In *Office of Fair Trading v Foxtons Ltd* [2009] EWHC 1681 (Ch), [2009] 29 EG 98 (CS), Mann J assessed whether the commission clauses were unfair and noted that there was a significant imbalance as a result of the term since the amounts of commission were significant and operated adversely over time, e.g. if commission was payable for a renewal the level of services given in exchange for the payment would be minimal. The judge then turned to procedural questions of 'openness and fairness' and concluded that unless the landlord knew the clause was there it would operate as an annual 'trap, or a time bomb' given that landlords are not focusing on renewal. It was doubtful that the typical consumer landlord would realize the clause was there and would not expect it so that the clause would have to be clearly presented and drawn to the attention of the consumer landlord.

In *Bryen & Langley Ltd v Boston* [2005] EWCA Civ 973, [2005] BLR 508, the Court of Appeal had to consider whether the adjudication provision in the Joint Standards Tribunal (JCT) standard form of contract was an unfair term within the UTCCR 1999. The Court of Appeal held that, although it was potentially unfair, for there to be a significant imbalance it was necessary to consider whether the term had been **imposed** on the consumer in circumstances which justified the conclusion that the supplier had failed to satisfy the requirements of fair dealing. The difficulty here was that the terms had not been imposed by the supplier but by the consumer's own agent (his quantity surveyor) who had imposed the JCT terms on the supplier in the invitation to tender. In other words, the consumer could not complain when the supplier had been asked to tender on the very terms which the consumer was now objecting to. In addition, as there was no procedural unfairness, i.e. lack of transparency, fair dealing, or good faith in the way in which the contract was made, the claim that the provisions were unfair terms within the UTCCR could not succeed. Much depends upon whether it is considered appropriate to look behind the standard form and to ask whether the consumer actually knew of, and read, the applicable provisions, before submitting them for adoption as the contract terms. This seems unrealistic, albeit that it may be in line with the European jurisprudence on the matter. The key question is whether the consumer **has been able** to influence the substance of the terms and, if the consumer has 'chosen' to adopt a standard form, it would seem that he will have had the opportunity to decide against adoption in all but the most exceptional circumstances. Other cases following this conclusion and reasoning are *Lovell Projects Ltd v Legg* [2003] 1 BLR 452 and *Westminster Building Co Ltd v Beckingham* [2004] EWHC 138 (TCC), 94 Con LR 107.

This case law can be compared with the factual scenario in *Picardi v Cuniberti* [2002] EWHC 2923 (Ch), [2003] BLR 487, where the adjudication provisions were held to be unfair terms having been imposed on the consumer by the supplier's architect. In *Mylcrist Builders Ltd v Buck* [2008] EWHC 2172 (TCC), [2009] 2 All ER (Comm) 259, [2008] BLR 611, Ramsey J held that an arbitration clause in a consumer contract was unfair (although compare the arbitration clause in *Heifer International Inc v Christiansen* [2007] EWHC 3015 (TCC), [2008] 2 All ER (Comm) 831, discussed at 7.7.1.1). In *Mylcrist* the problem was that the consumer was forced to submit to arbitration because any claim before the courts would have been stayed (s. 9 of the Arbitration Act 1996) and that this was expensive (£2,000) when compared with the size of the sum in dispute (£5,000). The judge concluded that a lay person would not necessarily appreciate the significance of an arbitration clause so that there had not been 'fair and open dealing' as required by the

UTCCR. Finally, this was not a case where the consumer was responsible for the instigating the standard form containing this clause.

In ***Domsalla (T/A Domsalla Building Services) v Dyason*** [2007] EWHC 1174 (TCC), [2007] BLR 348 (see 7.7.1.1), the occupier withheld payments and the builder therefore submitted the dispute to JCT adjudication.

- Although it was potentially unfair for the builders to rely on the adjudication provisions since the owner had no control over the contract and was required to enter into it on those terms by the insurers, the adjudication provisions did not substantially alter the balance of the parties' rights and obligations.

- However, since the occupier was not entitled, as would normally have been the case for an employer, to issue withholding notices (this was a matter for the insurers) and if the notices were not properly issued the owner would incur liability, the effect of the provisions on withholding notices could substantially affect the owner's rights so that these withholding provisions were unfair.

A further factor which influenced the first instance decision in ***Bryen & Langley Ltd v Boston*** [2004] EWHC 2450 (TCC), 98 Con LR 82, although not the decision of the Court of Appeal [2005] EWCA Civ 973, [2005] BLR 508 in rejecting the appeal, was the nature of the goods or services, i.e. a costly construction contract for which professionals had been employed, as compared with 'normal' consumer contracts such as minor household maintenance projects. It cannot be relevant to consider such questions when there is a statutory definition of consumer for these purposes, however strong the temptation to do so.

In the Law Commission's report, *Unfair Terms in Contracts* (2005), the proposed general test in the context of consumer contracts (applicable to those terms which are not automatically of no effect, such as excluding negligence liability for death or personal injury and excluding liability for breach of implied terms as to description, satisfactory quality, and fitness for purpose), is that terms are to be subject to a 'fair and reasonable' test (para. 3.90) which will not explicitly refer to 'good faith'. However, whether a term satisfies this test will depend upon the same considerations as were apparent in the deliberations of the House of Lords in ***Director General of Fair Trading v First National Bank plc***, namely '(a) whether it is transparent; (b) its substance and effect and (c) the circumstances in existence at the time the contract was made' (para. 3.101 and draft clause 14). A term may fail the test simply because it lacks transparency and it is significant that both procedural and substantive fairness are to be judged in the wider context, as in ***Director General of Fair Trading v First National Bank***.

The proposed legislation is to provide detailed guidance for the application of this test (see, e.g., the meaning of 'transparent' in draft clause 14(3) and the list of matters relating to substance and effect in draft clause 14(4)). This is also applicable in the context of B2B contracts, where the old UCTA provisions continue to apply, e.g. the s. 3 replacement, and in the context of the small business regime. The key distinction is that whereas in the consumer context it is the business that will bear the burden of showing that the term if fair and reasonable, that burden will fall on the business seeking to challenge a term in the context of the small business regime and the B2B contracts. Schedule 2 to the draft Bill contains a list of terms which may be regarded as not being fair and reasonable (Part 2). These are helpfully set out in plain English and the explanatory notes provide examples of the types of terms in question. Inevitably, this will greatly simplify and improve accessibility of the applicable law for consumers, but also for small businesses.

7.7.4 **Comparison of the regulation of exemption clauses under UCTA 1977 and the 1999 regulations**

This discussion relates only to regulation of exemption clauses in consumer contracts, where there may well be overlaps in the regulatory provisions available. The directive permits Member States to provide higher levels of consumer protection so that it is envisaged that there may be additional regulation. The consequence is that distinct bodies of rules, each with a different scope and a different test of what is acceptable in the consumer interest, currently apply to the same general issues of consumer protection. The result is that as things stand at present consumers are faced with two layers of complex regulation in a vital area of contracts.

7.7.4.1 Burden of proof

The significant difference between UCTA 1977 and the 1999 regulations is the burden of proof. Whereas under UCTA 1977 either the clause will be totally unenforceable or the burden of proving that the clause is reasonable will fall on the party seeking to rely on the clause, under the 1999 regulations the consumer (or 'qualifying body' in the case of claims under reg. 12) will have to prove that the term is 'unfair'.

7.7.4.2 Unenforceable clauses under UCTA 1977

If the clause in question purports to exempt liability in negligence for death or personal injury, it will be unenforceable under s. 2(1) of the 1977 Act. Under UTCCR 1999, this liability is specifically mentioned as an event which *may* be regarded as unfair under Sch. 2(1)(a), although the regulations would not apply if the term was individually negotiated. However, it would be most unlikely that this would be the case.

Therefore, the main difference under the Act is that the protection against the effect of such a clause is absolute, whereas under the regulations unfairness would have to be proved for the clause not to be binding on the consumer (reg. 8(1)); albeit that in practical terms the position under the Act and general policy considerations would make it fairly easy to discharge the burden of proof in relation to such a clause.

It would appear that the implied terms in sale and supply contracts relating to the goods cannot be 'unfair' under the regulations because they are mandatory provisions which are not capable of being excluded or limited (reg. 4(2) and ss. 6(2) and 7(2) of UCTA 1977). This was extended to all implied terms by Judge Pelling QC in ***Baybut v Eccle Riggs Country Park Ltd***, *The Times*, 13 November 2006 (transcript available via Westlaw). Although the UTCCR 1999 are not expressly limited to express terms, the judge considered it 'highly unlikely' (at [23]) that they were intended to have any application to implied terms. Implied terms under statute fall within s. 6(2) as 'mandatory statutory or regulatory provisions'. Terms implied by the courts at common law can be implied only if reasonable so that the judge considered they could not then be found to be 'unfair'. In addition, all the examples in Sch. 2 relate to express terms. However, terms implied by custom or on the basis of a course of dealing are not subject to the same test for initial reasonableness; it need only be established that they are clearly established and 'notorious' (see 6.4.2.1). It might therefore be argued that this category of implied terms might fall outside the scope of the ***Baybut*** prohibition. The yearly licence was fixed by express agreement and was 'a core term' within reg. 6(2) as relating to the definition of the main subject matter—so that the regulations did not apply in any event.

7.7.4.3 Other clauses

In relation to a clause exempting liability in negligence for loss or damage (to which UCTA 1977, s. 2(2) would apply), the consumer would need to establish that the clause was 'unfair' within reg. 5(1). Attempts to exclude contractual liability may be 'unfair', assuming that the term was not individually negotiated. This may involve reliance on the illustrative list of terms which may be regarded as unfair contained in Sch. 2. However, the consumer would still need to establish the unfairness (reg. 5(1)) on the particular facts.

In relation to clauses which modify or exclude the contractual obligation in a consumer contract and which would be subject to the reasonableness test under UCTA 1977, s. 3(2)(b), Sch. 2(1) to the 1999 regulations makes clear that, in respect of terms to which the regulations apply, certain terms which allow the non-consumer party to vary expected contractual obligations unilaterally (Sch. 2(1)(j) and (k)), or which result in an imbalance in the extent to which the parties are contractually bound (Sch. 2(1)(c) and (o)), may be regarded as unfair terms; although it would be for the consumer to prove that, contrary to the requirement of good faith, there was a significant imbalance in the parties' positions to the detriment of the consumer. In this respect protection for consumers under the regulations may prove less effective than under the Act.

Although the reasonableness test and the test for unfairness are not the same, they may well lead to the same result in practice. There is some established guidance on reasonableness under the 1977 Act (see 7.6.6.2). The OFT publishes guidance on unfair terms, which taken with the decision of the House of Lords in *Director General of Fair Trading v First National Bank plc* [2001] UKHL 52, [2002] 1 AC 481 (see 7.7.3) and subsequent case law, constitutes some guidance on the interpretation of unfairness under the regulations.

7.7.5 Plain, intelligible language

Under reg. 7(1), there is a duty placed on the seller or supplier to ensure that terms offered to the consumer in writing are 'expressed in plain, intelligible language'. This expression is not defined in the 1999 regulations, and its real value as a requirement may be doubted. The principal reason is that there is no real sanction for not using such language, except that where there is doubt 'the interpretation which is most favourable to the consumer shall prevail' (reg. 7(2), as applied in *Governors of the Peabody Trust v Reeve* [2008] EWHC 1432 (Ch), [2009] L & TR 6). This rule is similar to the existing rule in English law of *contra proferentem* interpretation of exemption clauses (see 7.4.1.2), although under the directive it applies to all terms. Since the only sanction is to be found in the construction of the language of the doubtful term, it is perhaps overstating the case to say that terms must be in plain language: the obligation cannot be effectively enforced. Regulation 7 therefore amounts to no more than a legislative exhortation to use plain language.

The Law Commission's report, *Unfair Terms in Contracts* (2005), includes a proposal for a rule of interpretation in favour of the consumer in cases of any doubt about the meaning of a term (para. 3.107; see clause 8 of the draft Bill), although not in relation to pre-emptive challenges. This replicates reg. 7(2) of the UTCCR 1999: see 7.4.1.2.

7.7.6 The consequences of a term being unfair

Where a term is unfair under the regulation it is unenforceable (or not binding) on the consumer (**reg. 8(1)**). As is noted at 7.7.5, this sanction does not apply to the obligation to use plain, intelligible language.

Where a term is unfair and so not binding on the consumer, the remainder of the contract 'shall continue to bind the parties if it is capable of continuing in existence without the unfair term' (**reg. 8(2)**). This appears to imply that where a term contains an unfair element the whole term is affected so that the contract must be read without the whole term. It will be seen later, in the context of illegality, that English law is willing to consider severing the offending parts from terms where that is grammatically possible and consistent with the public policy issues at stake (see 16.7.10). The severance rule might be thought to contribute to the preservation of contracts; the deletion of whole terms must increase the risk that the commercial balance of the contract will be upset, or that the contract will become too vague to be enforceable. This must be balanced against the overall purpose of consumer protection, which is perhaps more likely to be guaranteed if unfair terms are completely outlawed (see also 7.6.6.3 in the context of UCTA 1977).

The European Court of Justice considers that since the directive is a consumer protection measure, consumers do not need to plead unfairness under the regulations before the court will be prepared to make a finding of unfairness so that the term is not binding (*Océano Grupo Editorial SA v Murciano Quintero*, C-240/98–244/98, [2000] ECR I-494, [2002] CMLR 43 and *Mostaza Claro v Centro Móvil Milenium SL*, C-168/05 [2007] Bus LR 60, [2007] 1 CMLR 22). This position was said to be reinforced by the existence and terms of Art. 7 of the directive (pre-emptive challenges to unfair terms).

7.7.7 General challenges to unfair terms

Article 7 of the directive requires Member States to ensure that adequate and effective means exist to prevent the continued use of unfair terms, including powers under which persons or organizations having a legitimate interest under national law in protecting consumers shall be able to bring representative 'actions' to determine whether contractual terms drawn up for general use are unfair.

By **reg. 10(1)**, the Director General of the Office of Fair Trading (DGFT) has a duty to consider any complaint made to him alleging that a term is unfair, unless he considers the complaint to be 'frivolous or vexatious' or unless a 'qualifying body' has notified the DGFT that it agrees to consider the complaint. 'Qualifying bodies' are listed in Sch. 1 to the 1999 regulations and are divided into two types: Part 1 'qualifying bodies' include utility regulators, the Rail Regulator, and, as amended by the Unfair Terms in Consumer Contracts (Amendment) Regulations 2001, SI 2001/1186, the Financial Services Authority; the Part 2 qualifying body is the Consumers' Association. If a Part 1 qualifying body has notified the DGFT that it agrees to consider a complaint then that body will be under a duty to consider it (reg. 11(1)).

The DGFT (or any qualifying body if it has notified the DGFT) may apply for an injunction to prevent the use of unfair terms in consumer contracts. This covers both the existing contract and future contracts. (*Office of Fair Trading v Foxtons* [2009] EWCA Civ 288, [2010] 1 WLR 663: the majority (Moore-Bick LJ dissenting) interpreted Article 7 of the directive as permitting the court to grant an injunction to prevent the enforcement of a term that had been found to be unfair in relation to an existing contract, i.e. the power was not limited to the use of terms in future contracts.)

Regulation 10(3) recognizes that the seller or supplier in question may give an undertaking not to continue use of a term, and that such undertakings may be considered when making the decision whether or not to apply for an injunction. In practice, undertakings have staved off action in the majority of instances, although see, e.g., *Director General of Fair Trading v First National Bank plc* [2001] UKHL 52, [2002] 1 AC 481 and *Office of Fair Trading v Foxtons Ltd* [2009] EWHC 1681 (Ch), [2009] 29 EG 98 (CS).

In fulfillment of its duty of dissemination of information and advice (reg. 15), the OFT published regular bulletins and now publishes guidance, e.g. OFT 311 (revised version September

2008), which is structured in accordance with Sch. 2 to the regulations and gives information on complaints received as well as general policy. This guidance also contains examples of terms which the OFT considers to be unfair and in relation to which it has obtained undertakings to cease use and/or reformulate (for further information, refer to the OFT's website at <http://www.oft.gov.uk>). This guidance is likely to continue as the primary source of information on specific instances of 'unfairness'. It was explicitly referenced by the judge when reaching a conclusion on unfairness of a unilateral variation clause in a tenancy agreement in ***Governors of the Peabody Trust v Reeve*** [2008] EWHC 1432 (Ch), [2009] L & TR 6. However, it does not have the precedent value or standing of case law interpretation of the regulations and it will be interesting to see what happens as the body of case law on the regulations grows, and whether it is in conflict with the OFT's views on the same type of term (see, e.g., the question of the potential unfairness of entire agreements in consumer contracts, *OFT v MB Designs (Scotland)* 2005 SLT 691).

7.7.7.1 Enforcement

The enforcement procedures in the consumer context have been strengthened by Part 8 of the Enterprise Act 2002. Designated enforcers are given wide powers to apply to the courts for enforcement orders (which are similar to injunctions) against traders who do not comply with their legal obligations to consumers. These powers extend to domestic and community law which impacts on consumers, including UCTA 1977, the sale and supply legislation and the Misrepresentation Act 1967 (the Enterprise Act 2002 (Part 8 Domestic Infringements) Order 2003, SI 2003/1593) and the UTCCR 1999, the E-Commerce Directive, Distance Sales and Unfair Commercial Practices Directive (s. 212 of the Enterprise Act 2002, the Enterprise Act 2002 (Part 8 Community Infringements Specified UK Laws) Order 2003, SI 2003/1374 and 2006/3372).

It is possible that the Consumer Protection from Unfair Trading Regulations 2008, SI 2008/1277 (CPRs), implementing the EU Unfair Commercial Practices Directive (UCPD) 2005/29/EC, could apply to the use of unfair contract terms if there are terms which implement unfair commercial marketing and selling practices, e.g. misleading consumers about their rights such as cancellation rights. The CPRs create offences in respect of these unfair commercial practices. It is possible that the use of such terms could give rise to enforcement action under the CPRs in addition to, or in place of, the UTCCR 1999.

The Commission has also published a Green Paper suggesting the adoption of collective rights of consumer redress, 'Consumer Collective Redress', COM (2008) 794 final, with a view to permitting class actions by affected groups of consumers.

Finally, in two recent European decisions the European Court of Justice has held that in relation to a consumer contract a national court should, of its own motion, examine whether a contract term was potentially unfair even where the consumer had not sought to challenge the term as unfair (***Pannon GSM Zrt v Erzsébet Sustikné Győrfi***, C-243/08, [2010] 1 All ER (Comm) 640 and ***Asturcom Telecomunicaciones SL v Rodriguez Nogueira***, C-40/08, [2010] 1 CMLR 29: national court to assess of its own motion whether arbitration clause wasunfair).

7.7.7.2 The Law Commission

The Law Commission's draft Bill (clause 7) contains a similar pre-emptive scheme intended to prevent the use of unfair terms. However, the substantive details are set out in Sch. 1 to the draft Bill with the aim of avoiding clutter within the main body of the proposed legislation since these rules 'will seldom be required by individual consumers'.

Further reading

General

Lawson, *Exclusion Clauses and Unfair Contract Terms*, 9th edn (Sweet and Maxwell, 2008).

Macdonald, *Exemption Clauses and Unfair Terms*, 2nd edn (Tottel Publishing, 2006).

Trebilcock, 'An economic approach to the doctrine of unconscionability' in Reiter and Swan (eds), *Studies in Contract Law* (Butterworths, 1981).

Yates, *Exclusion Clauses in Contracts*, 2nd edn (Sweet and Maxwell, 1992).

Construction

Adams, 'Fundamental breach: Positively last appearance' (1983) 46 MLR 771.

Barendt, 'Exclusion clauses: Incorporation and interpretation' (1972) 35 MLR 644.

Gower, 'Exemption clauses: Contractual and tortious liability' (1954) 17 MLR 155.

Nicol and Rawlings, 'Substantive fundamental breach burnt out' (1980) 43 MLR 567.

Palmer, 'Limiting liability for negligence' (1982) 45 MLR 322.

Palmer, 'Negligence and exclusion clauses again' [1983] LMCLQ 557.

UCTA 1977

Adams and Brownsword, 'The Unfair Contract Terms Act: A decade of discretion' (1988) 104 LQR 94.

Hedley, 'Defective software in the Court of Appeal' (1997) 56 CLJ 21.

Macdonald, 'Exclusion clauses: The ambit of s. 13(1) of the Unfair Contract Terms Act 1977' (1992) 12 LS 277.

Macdonald, 'The Council, the computer and the Unfair Contract Terms Act 1977' (1995) 58 MLR 585.

Macdonald, 'In the course of a business': A fresh examination' (1999) 3 Web JCLI.

Macdonald and Poyton, 'A particular problem for e-commerce: Section 3 of the Unfair Contract Terms Act 1977' [2000] 3 Web JCLI.

Palmer and Yates, 'The future of the Unfair Contract Terms Act 1977' (1981) 40 CLJ 108.

Peel, 'Reasonable exemption clauses' (2001) 117 LQR 545.

UTCCR 1999

Beale, 'Unfair contracts in Britain and Europe' [1989] CLP 197.

Beale, 'Legislative control of fairness: The Directive on Unfair Terms in Consumer Contracts' in Beatson and Friedmann, *Good Faith and Fault in Contract Law* (Oxford University Press, 1995).

Bright, 'Winning the battle against unfair contract terms' (2000) 20 LS 331.

Collins, 'Good faith in European contract law' (1994) 14 OJLS 229.

Dean, 'Unfair contract terms: The European approach' (1993) 56 MLR 581.

DTI Consultation Paper, *European Commission Review of Directive 93/13/EEC on Unfair Terms in Consumer Contracts*, July 2000.

European Commission, *Report on Unfair Terms*, COM (2000) 248.

Macdonald, 'Mapping the Unfair Contract Terms Act 1977 and the Directive on Unfair Terms in Consumer Contracts' [1994] JBL 441.

Macdonald, 'Scope and fairness of the Unfair Terms in Consumer Contracts Regulations: *Director General of Fair Trading v First National Bank*' (2002) 65 MLR 763.

Macmillan, 'Evolution or revolution? Unfair terms in consumer contracts' [2002] CLJ 22.

Law Commission

Law Commission Consultation Paper, *Unfair Terms in Contracts*, LCCP No. 166 (2002).

Law Commission Report, *Unfair Terms in Contracts*, Law Com. No. 292, Cm. 6464 (February 2005).

Macdonald, 'Unifying unfair terms legislation' (2004) 67 MLR 69.

Breach of contract

Summary of the issues

A contract can be discharged by performance, agreement, frustration (see **Chapter 12**) or by breach. The primary focus of this chapter is breach, and particularly repudiatory breach, i.e. discharge (termination) of the contract for that breach. The chapter starts with some brief background relating the standard of performance required by contractual terms and therefore what is required to discharge the contract by performance. It also explains how parties can achieve discharge of the contract by agreement.

• In practice most contracts are discharged by performance. It is necessary to identify the standard of performance required in relation to each contractual obligation since a failure to perform to the required standard constitutes a breach. Contractual obligations are either strict or qualified.

• Contracts may be discharged by agreement but such an agreement to discharge must be legally enforceable and so must be supported by consideration, if not contained in a deed.

• A breach of contract will occur where, without lawful excuse, a party either fails or refuses to perform a contractual obligation imposed on that party by the terms of the contract or performs a contractual obligation in a defective manner.

• Every breach of contract will give rise to a right to claim damages. However, unless the breach constitutes a repudiatory breach, the contract will remain in force. If the breach is repudiatory the non-breaching party will have the option either to accept the breach as terminating the contract (in which case both parties' future obligations will be discharged) or to affirm the contract (in which event the contract remains in force for both parties).

• It is crucially important therefore to be able to identify repudiatory breaches and the classification of terms is important for this purpose. Breaches of certain types of terms (conditions) are, in the main, repudiatory breaches and breaches of innominate terms will be repudiatory breaches if the effects of the breach are serious. However, the process of identifying conditions and innominate terms is uncertain and there are risks for the non-breaching party in deciding to treat a breach as repudiatory as this may constitute wrongful repudiation.

• A breach of an entire obligation will also constitute a repudiatory breach but it is important to distinguish entire and severable obligations since breach of a severable obligation does not entitle the non-breaching party to elect to terminate the whole contract. There are recognized circumstances when it is possible to avoid the usual consequences of the entire obligation rule.

• Breach may be anticipatory, i.e. breach occurs before the time for performance because, for example, one party indicates that he will not be performing. The non-breaching party is entitled to take the other party at his word. He can elect to accept this breach by anticipatory repudiation as terminating the contract, in which event he need not wait until the date for performance before claiming damages. Alternatively, the non-breaching party can affirm and await the date for performance (give the breaching party a second chance). If the non-breaching party chooses to affirm he may, in certain circumstances, continue with his performance and claim the contract price although this is controversial since it is clear that the performance is not wanted by the guilty party. Affirmation also means that each party is expected to perform their obligations as they fall due so that there are some risks to the non-breaching party in selecting this route.

8.1 Background: What is the process of discharge?

1. The primary obligations of a contract are those which determine the performance obligations of the parties (see Lord Diplock in ***Photo Production Ltd v Securicor Transport Ltd*** [1980] AC 827).

2. Discharge of a contract is the process whereby the primary obligations (i.e., the obligations to perform: see 8.2.1) under a contract, which is validly formed, come to an end.

3. In many circumstances the secondary obligation to pay damages to compensate for losses also ends (e.g., discharge by frustration: see 12.8), but that is not always the consequence of discharge. In the case of discharge by breach, a secondary obligation to pay damages for loss caused (or a secondary obligation to pay the contract price) continues (see 8.4).

Most commonly, the discharge of a contract will occur on performance of both parties' primary obligations (see 8.2). However, as an alternative, a contract may be discharged by agreement of the parties. This chapter will briefly examine both discharge by performance and discharge by agreement before focusing on the central issue of the chapter, namely discharge for breach. It is important to bear in mind that there is another form of discharge of a contract, where the operation of the doctrine of frustration discharges both parties from performance of their future obligations. This doctrine is discussed in Chapter 12.

 Key point

Distinguishing the process of discharge of valid contracts from situations where a contract is void or is rescinded

It is vitally important to maintain a distinction between the discharge of **valid** contracts and the processes by which invalid contracts come to an end or are invalidated.

The situations where a contract is either void or voidable (so called vitiating factors) are largely discussed in Part 4.

A contract may be invalid (void or voidable) because it is affected by:

- mistake (see Chapters 3 and 13)
- misrepresentation (see Chapter 14)

- duress or by undue influence (see Chapter 15)
- illegality, including restraint of trade (see Chapter 16).

Void: Since a void contract is automatically of no effect from the very beginning, and hence gives rise to no obligation to perform, it is sufficient for the party asserting its invalidity to do nothing, and plead the invalidity as a defence to a claim for breach.

Voidable: Where a contract is voidable (e.g., for misrepresentation), the contract remains valid until set aside by the party who has the right to set it aside. This process is known as **rescission**.

The process of rescission is very different to the discharge of a contract, because if a voidable contract is rescinded, the contract is then treated as having no effect from the beginning, whereas discharge of the contract does not destroy the contract itself. It merely brings the primary obligations to an end (see above), i.e. future obligations are discharged.

8.2 Discharge by performance or agreement

8.2.1 Discharge by performance

A contract is discharged by the performance by both parties of all the primary obligations, express and implied, which they owed under the contract. An obligation will be performed only where the performance meets the standard of performance required. Consequently, a failure to reach the required standard will constitute breach.

8.2.1.1 The standard of performance

Contractual obligations require one of two standards of performance.

1. Strict contractual obligations

The general rule is that the performance obligation is strict, so that the contractual obligation must be completely and precisely performed. There is no defence for failure to meet this strict obligation. For example, if a seller fails to deliver the goods to the buyer on the contractual date set for delivery to occur, it will not help the seller to argue that it was let down by its supplier. There is a strict contractual breach by the seller in failing to deliver the goods on time, although the seller may have a remedy against its supplier under the terms of the separate contract with its supplier.

The only exception to this strict contractual liability is for what may be regarded as 'microscopic' deviations (the *de minimis* rule). However, if the failure to meet the strict performance standard falls outside *de minimis,* there will be a breach.

The obligations as to description, fitness for purpose, satisfactory quality, and correspondence with sample in a sale of goods contract (Sale of Goods Act (SGA) 1979, ss. 13–15: see 6.4.2.4) are strict contractual obligations. That is, any failure of performance to match the contractual undertaking, however slight, is still breach. For example, in *Arcos Ltd v Ronassen* [1933] AC 470, timber staves of half an inch in thickness were purchased to make into cement barrels. In fact most of the timber was one-sixteenth thicker than the contractual description, although it was still perfectly useable for the purpose of making cement barrels. Nevertheless, this amounted to a breach of contract. Since it amounted to a breach of condition (SGA 1979, s. 13: see 8.5.3.1 and 8.5.7), the buyer could reject the timber.

2. Qualified contractual obligations

In some circumstances the performance obligation is not strict but qualified. **If an obligation is qualified there is no requirement to achieve a guaranteed result; instead the obligation is only to exercise reasonable care and skill.**

An example of a qualified contractual obligation is s. 13 of the Supply of Goods and Services Act 1982 (see 6.4.2.4). At common law this standard of performance has long been regarded as the appropriate standard for professional people such as doctors and lawyers, whose work makes it impossible to guarantee a result. However, it is possible to undertake a strict standard of performance in relation to certain obligations, e.g. in *Platform Funding Ltd v Bank of Scotland plc* [2008] EWCA Civ 930, [2009] QB 426, the majority of the Court of Appeal (Sir Anthony Clarke MR dissenting) accepted that the normal duty owed by a surveyor was a duty of reasonable care and skill in carrying out the survey and checking for defects. It was, however, a strict undertaking that the surveyor would survey the correct property! Although the property to be surveyed will be named in the instructions, Sir Anthony Clarke MR emphasized the absence on these facts of any clear agreement that the surveyor was undertaking an absolute commitment that the correct property would be surveyed.

A further example of an implied qualified obligation is provided by the decision of the House of Lords in *Liverpool City Council v Irwin* [1977] AC 239 (obligation to take reasonable care to keep the common parts of a tower block in reasonable repair, and on the facts the local authority had met this standard of performance: see 6.4.2.3). Any failure to exercise reasonable care and skill (i.e., failing to meet the qualified standard) would amount to breach.

8.2.2 Discharge by agreement

8.2.2.1 General

A contract may be discharged by agreement between the parties. Where the discharge occurs with the free consent of both parties and without subsequent change of heart, there is no need for any particular form of agreement. The parties may simply abandon performance. In practice, however, in order to guard against a change of heart by the other party, it will be desirable to adopt some form of legally binding agreement to discharge all future performance obligations.

8.2.2.2 The requirement of consideration

In addition to demonstrating the existence of an agreement to discharge future obligations (*The Hannah Blumenthal* [1983] 1 AC 854), the parties must also demonstrate that this agreement to discharge is legally enforceable. The best way of so doing will be to establish the existence of a second contract to discharge the first, which will require the existence of consideration (see 4.5.2).

8.2.2.3 Mutual release

Where both parties have performance obligations remaining under the contract, mutual abandonment of those remaining obligations (mutual release) is enough to satisfy the requirement of consideration (i.e., each party agrees to give up their right to receive the other's performance), so that such discharge is legally enforceable (see 4.5.2).

The position is the same where **both** parties breach obligations under their contract and then agree to discharge it.

8.2.2.4 What is the position if one party's obligations have been performed but the other owes future performance?

Where one party's obligations have been performed so that only the other party needs to be discharged from further performance, the requirement of consideration may not be satisfied by mere abandonment of the contract. The parties may enter into a binding release in a deed, whereby the party whose obligations have been performed agrees to discharge the other from that other's performance obligations. No consideration is required because this agreement to discharge is contained in a deed (see 4.1).

Release and replacement

It is possible to have an agreement which amounts to **a release and replacement**. This involves the total discharge of the original contract followed by the substitution of a new contract between the parties, assuming that there is the necessary consideration present (*Morris v Baron and Co.* [1918] AC 1). The Court of Appeal in *Compagnie Noga D'Importation et D'Exportation v Abacha (No. 4)* [2003] EWCA Civ 1100, [2003] 2 All ER (Comm) 915 (discussed at 4.5.2), held that there was a mutual release from an earlier agreement followed by a replacement agreement. The mutual release and the mutual promises in the replacement agreement were construed as the consideration to support that new agreement.

Binding variation (accord and satisfaction)

Alternatively, there may be a separate agreement supported by new consideration (so-called **accord and satisfaction**) to discharge (or vary) a particular contractual term. For example, one party (A) may agree to release the other (B) from B's liability to pay damages for B's breach if B pays A pays £200 in compensation. However, it is clear that the 'satisfaction' (i.e., the consideration) cannot be a lesser form of what was due under the contract (*Pinnel's Case* (1602) 5 Co Rep 117a: see 4.6.2.1). In other words, payment of a smaller sum cannot discharge (or extinguish) the obligation to pay the full amount owed. This remains the position because the principle in *Williams v Roffey Bros & Nicholls (Contractors) Ltd* [1991] 1 QB 1 (which identifies consideration as constituted by a factual (or subjective) benefit to the promisor arising from an alteration promise) applies only to alteration promises to pay more and does not apply to alteration promises to accept less than the sum owed (*Re Selectmove Ltd* [1995] 1 WLR 474: see 4.6.2.3). Therefore, in order for there to be the necessary 'satisfaction' to support the variation in the contract terms, the promisee will need to supply something extra, such as agreeing to pay a smaller sum on an earlier date or at a different place at the creditor's request.

Estoppel or waiver

In the absence of the necessary consideration to support a release or variation of a contract term, a promise to discharge one or more obligations may have some limited effect because of the operation of the doctrine of promissory estoppel or as a 'waiver'. Since the development of the promissory estoppel doctrine (see 4.8.2), waiver has become indistinguishable (see 4.8). The courts have often used the two expressions interchangeably, since both are concerned with forbearance or giving up legal rights. As a result, it may be that it would be better if use of the term 'waiver' were dropped to avoid confusion. In any event, it will be recalled that the effect of promissory estoppel is said to be that it operates only to suspend contractual rights and not to extinguish or terminate them (see 4.8.5). Therefore, it might be considered that it has no relevance to the discharge of contracts. Nevertheless, since it may cause individual instalment obligations to be extinguished, e.g. as in *High Trees House* (see **4.8.2.1** and **4.8.5.1**), in this limited sense it can be said that a contract (or at least an obligation under that contract) may be discharged by estoppel.

8.3 Discharge (termination) by occurrence of a condition subsequent

A contract may also be discharged by the occurrence of a condition subsequent stipulated by the parties. A **condition subsequent** is a stipulation of a state of affairs which will cause existing contractual obligations to terminate (*Head v Tattersall* (1871) LR 7 Ex 7). A modern example of such a condition might be a provision in a long-term supply agreement that the contract should terminate when the price of the goods in question reaches a stated figure. Thus, the condition may be an event beyond the control of either of the parties (e.g., attainment of a certain point on a cost-of-living index), or may be entirely within the control of one of the parties (e.g., giving and serving a stipulated period of notice).

 Key point

A condition subsequent is a 'contingent' condition and such conditions impose no positive obligation to ensure absolutely that the condition does (or does not) materialize. It must, therefore, be distinguished from *promissory conditions*, under which one party undertakes that a certain result will be achieved, and guarantees that undertaking by its promise. In the case of a promissory condition (discussed at **8.5.2.1**), failure to achieve the promised result is a breach. Thus, a promissory condition is the type of condition which is used to express a primary obligation of the contract.

Where a contract on its face has no provision for termination then, in the absence of any indication of an intention that the contract be perpetual, the courts will imply a term that the contract is terminable upon reasonable notice (*Staffordshire Area Health Authority v South Staffordshire Waterworks Co.* [1978] 1 WLR 1387).

8.4 Breach and discharge by breach (repudiatory breach)

8.4.1 Identifying breach and remedies available for breach

A breach of contract will occur where, without lawful excuse (e.g., frustration: see **Chapter 12**), a party either fails or refuses to perform a performance obligation imposed upon it under the terms of the contract. Alternatively, a party may perform its contractual obligations but may do so defectively, in the sense of failing to meet the required standard of performance (see **8.2.1.1**).

In general terms, the non-breaching party is entitled to be compensated for the loss it suffers which was caused by this breach. This is because the failure to perform a primary obligation under the contract gives rise to a secondary obligation to pay damages or to pay the contract price (see

Lord Diplock in ***Photo Production Ltd v Securicor Transport Ltd*** [1980] AC 827). However, that right to damages may be effectively excluded or limited by an exemption clause in the contract (see Chapter 7), or the case may fall within the limited category of situations in which specific performance is available as a remedy (see generally, 10.2). This apart, the secondary obligation to pay damages or the contract price will arise on proof of breach.

The consequences of breach by one party for the other party's performance obligations depend largely upon the nature of the obligation breached (see 8.5.2.1) and upon whether the parties' performance obligations are 'concurrent conditions' (see 8.6.1).

8.4.2 Repudiatory breach and the election to terminate or affirm

Unless the breach of contract constitutes a repudiatory breach, the contract will remain in force and both parties must continue to perform their obligations under it. However, a repudiatory breach allows the non-breaching party to treat the contract as repudiated. This slightly cumbersome expression is the most accurate description of the effect of such breach. It is often said that such breach discharges or terminates the contract, but neither expression is technically accurate since the primary obligations do not automatically come to an end; and even if the primary obligations cease, secondary obligations under the contract exist after breach (***Photo Production Ltd v Securicor Transport Ltd***). It is sometimes said that such a breach entitles the non-breaching party to 'rescind' the contract and this choice of word appears to have been approved by some members of the House of Lords (e.g., Lord Roskill in the ***Photo Production*** case, and Lord Diplock in *Gill & Duffus SA v Berger & Co. Inc.* [1984] AC 382). Nevertheless, this meaning of 'rescind' is very different from the meaning of this expression which is applied in the context of misrepresentation (see 14.5.1), under which a contract is set aside and treated as if it had never existed from the very beginning. The use of 'rescission' in the context of breach has been attacked several times by Lord Wilberforce (in ***Johnson v Agnew*** [1980] AC 367, and in ***Photo Production***). To avoid confusion, it is better to restrict the notion of rescission to misrepresentation, and in the case of breach of contract to adopt the more cumbersome formulation used above.

The non-breaching party *may* treat the contract as repudiated but is not obliged to do so. Thus, in the event of a repudiatory breach of contract, the non-breaching party has the option (or 'election') to treat both parties' future obligations to perform as terminated or to affirm the contract (see ***Decro-Wall International SA v Practitioners in Marketing Ltd*** [1971] 1 WLR 361).

Summary

Termination: If the non-breaching party elects to accept the breach as terminating the contract, only the parties' future obligations are discharged. The contract itself survives and its terms may be relevant for the purposes of assessing remedies, e.g., any exemption clauses and/or agreed damages clause will remain and will be relevant to the assessment of damages.

Affirmation: The alternative option to termination is for the non-breaching party to affirm the contract. This obliges both parties to continue to perform all remaining obligations due under the contract.

Damages: In addition, irrespective of whether the non-breaching party decides to terminate or affirm, the breach will cause the secondary obligation to pay damages as compensation to arise.

It is crucially important to appreciate that if, after a repudiatory breach, the non-breaching party affirms the contract, effectively the 'slate is wiped clean' as far as future performance is concerned. Consequently, future defective or non-performance by the party electing to affirm the contract will in turn become a breach (e.g., **Motor Oil Hellas (Corinth) Refineries SA v Shipping Corporation of India, The Kanchenjunga** [1990] 1 Lloyd's Rep 391, HL, and see **Force India Formula One Team Ltd v Etihad Airways PJSC** [2009] EWHC 2768 (QB), [2010] ETMR 14). It may even be a repudiatory breach entitling the other party, who was originally at fault, to treat the contract as at an end.

8.4.2.1 Non-breaching party elects to treat the repudiatory breach as terminating the contract

Until such time as the non-breaching party elects to treat the contract as repudiated, it must be regarded as subsisting. **A difficult question of fact may be to ascertain whether the non-breaching party has elected to accept the repudiation and treat the contract as at an end.** A clear and unequivocal communication to that effect will resolve the matter. (Acceptances more general must be unequivocal and generally silence will not suffice: see 2.4.5.1.)

> **?** **Question**
>
> What if the non-breaching party simply does not perform its own contractual obligations? Is this sufficiently unequivocal to constitute acceptance of the repudiatory breach as terminating the contract, particularly bearing in mind that in general an 'acceptance' must be unequivocal and that silence will not suffice: 2.4.5.1)?

In **Vitol SA v Norelf Ltd, The Santa Clara** [1996] QB 108, the buyers had sent a telex which amounted to a repudiatory breach, and the question was whether that repudiation had been accepted by the sellers who had then not performed any of their own obligations, including tendering the bill of lading (which would be necessary to give rise to the obligation for the buyers to pay the price). The Court of Appeal had held that, as a matter of law, an election to accept the repudiation could not be inferred from the non-breaching party's inaction, with the result that the contract was found to be subsisting. However, this decision was reversed on appeal by the House of Lords ([1996] AC 800). In the opinion of Lord Steyn, whose speech was unanimously supported by the other members of the House of Lords, the question whether the election to treat the contract as repudiated had been communicated was a question of fact, depending on 'the particular contractual relationship and the particular circumstances of the case'. However, he was prepared to accept that 'a failure to perform may sometimes signify to a repudiating party an election by the aggrieved party to treat the contract as at an end'. Lord Steyn then gave two examples of situations where non-performance could be interpreted as an election to treat the contract as at an end.

1. In his first example, an employer informs a contractor that his services are no longer required and that the contractor need not return the next day. If the contractor never returns then, in the absence of any other explanation, this, in Lord Steyn's words, would 'convey a decision to treat the contract as at an end'.

2. The second example concerns an overseas sale with shipment of the goods on a specified vessel sailing on a specified date, where the seller is under a contractual duty to obtain the necessary export licence. If the buyer repudiates the contract before any loading starts and the buyer knows that the seller has not applied for the export licence, 'it may well be that an ordinary businessman…would conclude that the seller was treating the contract as at an end'.

In *Masri v Consolidated Contractors International UK Ltd* [2006] EWHC 1931 (Comm), the defendants sought to rely on *Vitol v Norelf* as founding their claim to have accepted the claimant's repudiatory breach as terminating the contract.

> The claimant sought to recover sums he claimed were owed to him in relation to the 1 per cent interest in an oil concession that he had been given under the terms of an agreement with the defendants. However, the claimant was in default under the terms of that agreement as he had failed to make the payments required from him. The defendants therefore alleged that the agreement had been terminated. Gloster J held that although the claimant had been in repudiatory breach of the agreement, there had been no acceptance of that repudiation. The evidence was that the repudiation had been waived but, even if that were wrong and there had been a decision to accept the breach as terminating the agreement, there had been no communication of this acceptance to the claimant.
>
> It had been argued that *Vitol v Norelf* could be relied upon to conclude that acceptance required no communication on the facts and could occur through conduct. However, the test is whether the conduct 'would have clearly and unequivocally conveyed to the reasonable person in the position of the repudiating party that the aggrieved party is treating the contract as at an end'. The evidence relied upon was (1) returning US$1.5 million at a time when the claimant knew that he had not provided the repeatedly requested guarantee and owed millions of dollars, and (2) the failure to make a call on the claimant in respect of his share of the development costs. However, the judge considered that a reasonable person in the position of the claimant would not have considered these actions as bringing the contract to an end and there was evidence that an exact record had been kept on the claimant's accumulated debts. This was inconsistent with a communicated acceptance of the repudiation.

(The Court of Appeal reversed the decision in this case on other grounds, namely the identification of the terms of the parties' agreement. Since there was no repudiatory breach, the question of termination of the contract for that breach did not arise for consideration before the appeal court: [2007] EWCA Civ 688, [2007] 2 CLC 49.)

8.4.2.2 Non-breaching party elects to affirm the contract

It is clear that in order for an affirmation to be valid, the non-breaching party must know of the facts giving rise to its right to accept the repudiatory breach as terminating the contract and of its right to choose between affirming the contract and treating the contract as discharged.

Must be unequivocal

The election to affirm must also be unequivocal and make it clear that the non-breaching party is committing to continuing with performance of the contract. In *Yukong Line Ltd of Korea v Rendsburg Investments Corporation of Liberia* [1996] 2 Lloyd's Rep 604, the response to a repudiatory breach indicated that it was 'totally unacceptable' and 'strongly requested' the party in breach 'to honour their contractual obligations' and confirm that this would occur. This response was held to be insufficient to convey an intention to continue with the contract. Moore-Bick J (at p. 608) stated:

> Considerations of this kind are perhaps most likely to arise when the injured party's initial response to the renunciation of the contract has been to call on the other to change his mind, accept his obligations and perform the contract. That is often the most natural response and one which, in my view, the court should do nothing to discourage. It would be highly unsatisfactory if, by responding in that way, the injured party was to put himself at risk of being held to have irrevocably affirmed the contract.

8.4.2.3 In what circumstances will the non-breaching party lose the right to accept the repudiatory breach as terminating the contract?

1. Estoppel

There is a danger that a party who has not yet affirmed but is still deliberating what to do, may lose the right to treat the contract as terminated because of the operation of estoppel (see *Clough v London and North Western Railway Co.* (1871) LR 7 Ex 26). In order for such an estoppel to operate, the position of the breaching party must have been prejudiced in the meantime. In **Peyman v Lanjani** [1985] Ch 457, May LJ (at pp. 495–6) adopted the following passage from the judgment of Sholl J in the Australian decision in *Coastal Estates Pty Ltd v Melevende* [1965] VR 433 at p. 443:

> If the defrauded party does not know that he has a legal right to rescind, he is not bound by acts which on the face of them are referable only to an intention to affirm the contract, unless those acts are 'adverse to' the opposite party, i.e., unless they involve something to the other party's prejudice or detriment…This is a form of estoppel, for the other party has in such a case acted upon a representation, made by the defrauded party's conduct, that the latter is going on with the contract.

The application of these principles is well illustrated by the facts of **Peyman v Lanjani**.

> The defendant entered into an agreement for the assignment to him of a lease, expressed to be non-assignable without the true consent of the landlord. The landlord's consent was obtained by deception. The plaintiff then agreed to purchase the lease from the defendant, and again an attempt was made to obtain the landlord's consent by deception, although the plaintiff was not a party to this. On discovering the deception, the plaintiff consulted the solicitor acting for both parties, who urged him to proceed with the purchase. The plaintiff therefore paid the first £10,000 of the purchase price. A month later the plaintiff consulted new solicitors, who advised him of his right to terminate the agreement on account of the defect in the defendant's title caused by the original deception.
>
> The Court of Appeal held that the plaintiff had not lost the right to treat the contract as repudiated. The payment of £10,000 was not an irrevocable election because it had been made before the plaintiff was aware of the full facts, including the fact that he had a right to treat the agreement as at an end. Neither did it give rise to an estoppel preventing the plaintiff from treating the contract as repudiated, most particularly because there was no detriment to the defendant.

If a party either delays or neglects to react to a repudiatory breach (in this case by over a year) it may be held to have affirmed the contract, and it seems that this may occur even if the contract contained a clause stating that delay, neglect, or forbearance in enforcing a provision will not constitute a waiver and will not prejudice a termination provision in the contract. The crucial question is whether the court considers that the party has, by conduct, elected to affirm the contract and to abandon the right to exercise the contractual termination provision (**Tele2 International Card Company SA v Post Office Ltd** [2009] EWCA Civ 9). If the party does exercise the termination provision when there is no right to terminate, its action will constitute an anticipatory repudiation and give rise to a claim for damages in favour of the party committing the original breach.

2. Acceptance of goods in a sale of goods contract

In the context of sale of goods, the option to terminate the contract for repudiatory breach will be lost once the buyer has accepted the goods (SGA 1979, s. 11(4)). Section 35(1) and (2) defines this acceptance to include express indication of acceptance or, once the goods have been delivered, any act by the buyer which is inconsistent with the seller's ownership after the buyer has had a reasonable opportunity to inspect the goods to determine their conformity with the contract, or to compare the bulk with the sample. A buyer is also deemed to have accepted the goods after the lapse of a reasonable time in which he has retained the goods without indicating an intention to reject them (s. 35(4)). The availability of a reasonable opportunity to inspect the goods is a material factor in determining whether the 'reasonable' time has passed so as to constitute a lapse of time. However, the buyer is not deemed to have accepted the goods by asking for or agreeing to repair (s. 35(6)(a)), or delivering the goods to a third party under a sub-sale (s. 35(6)(b)), or by accepting part of a delivery of goods (most probably a part unaffected by the breach) while claiming to be entitled to reject the rest (s. 35A(1)). In *J. H. Ritchie Ltd v Lloyd Ltd* [2007] UKHL 9, [2007] Bus LR 944, [2007] 1 WLR 630, the House of Lords considered that if the commercial buyer agrees to repair (so that under s. 35(6) there is no acceptance), there is a separate contract which suspends the right to reject. This contract places a duty on the repairer to disclose the nature of the defect so that the buyer can make an informed decision as to whether to reject later. (However, in relation to consumer buyers there is an initial choice to reject or affirm and a separate right to **require** the seller to repair or replace the non-conforming goods, unless repair or replacement is impossible or disproportionate in comparison to other remedies. The right to reject is then lost unless the repair or replacement cannot be achieved in a reasonable time or without significant inconvenience to the buyer: see ss. 48A–F, SGA 1979.)

Except as described above in the case of the sale of goods, the right to treat the contract as repudiated is not lost by mere lapse of time. Nevertheless, in a limited number of circumstances lapse of time might result in prejudice to the breaching party, or might be regarded as evidence of an intention to continue with the contract, in which case the right to treat the contract as repudiated would be lost (per Fenton Atkinson LJ in *Allen v Robles* [1969] 1 WLR 1193).

8.5 What constitutes a repudiatory breach of contract?

8.5.1 Renunciation and incapacitation

From the perspective of the non-breaching party, it is essential to be able to identify whether a repudiation has occurred. The repudiation must be—within evidential limits—unequivocal. Clearly, an express statement that no performance will be undertaken will suffice. Where the repudiation is deduced from conduct, it is not enough simply that performance is unlikely to match the contractual undertakings. It must be apparent that on the balance of probabilities the party in question either will not (renunciation) or cannot (incapacitation) perform its obligations (*Alfred Toepfer International GmbH v Itex Itagrani Export SA* [1993] 1 Lloyd's Rep 360). As Lord Wilberforce stated in *Woodar Investment Development Ltd v Wimpey Construction (UK) Ltd* [1980] 1 WLR 277 at p. 280:

in considering whether there has been a repudiation by one party, it is necessary to look at his conduct as a whole. Does this indicate an intention to abandon and to refuse performance of the contract?

The majority of the House of Lords in *Woodar v Wimpey* (for facts see **11.7.3.1**) held, on the facts, that there was no renunciation (i.e., repudiation) of the contract because, instead of the necessary communicated intention to abandon the contract, Wimpey was relying on a contractual term as justifying the right to terminate. This term gave a right to terminate where compulsory purchase had been commenced, and that was precisely what had occurred on the facts.

8.5.2 Type of term broken determines whether the breach is repudiatory

Outside instances of renunciation and incapacitation, breaches of certain types of terms constitute repudiatory breaches, giving rise to the option for the non-breaching party to accept the breach as terminating the contract, or to affirm. It is therefore necessary to determine the classification of terms for this purpose, to consider the type of term broken and whether this breach is repudiatory.

8.5.2.1 Classification of terms

For this purpose there are three basic types of terms:

- **conditions**
- **warranties**
- **innominate (or intermediate) terms.**

Different meanings for the term 'condition'

In ordinary language a 'condition' is a stipulation of something which must be fulfilled before further action will take place or results will be achieved. The law has attributed more specific meanings to the word, and it is important to distinguish between these meanings.

1. Contingent conditions

Conditions precedent and subsequent, which are sometimes collectively called 'contingent' conditions, impose no positive obligation to ensure absolutely that the condition does (or does not) materialize.

- A **condition precedent** is a stipulation of a state of affairs which must be achieved before any contractual liability, or possibly any further contractual liability, will be incurred. In some circumstances the parties agree that a contract shall come into existence between them upon the occurrence of some event which is uncertain, but remain free to withdraw from that agreement until the event occurs (*Pym v Campbell* (1856) 6 E & B 370). More usually, however, the main contractual obligations do not come into force until the condition is satisfied, but the parties are contractually bound not to withdraw from the conditional agreement (*Smith v Butler* [1900] 1 QB 694). In these circumstances the parties may be under an obligation not to impede the occurrence of the condition (*Mackay v Dick* (1881) 6 App Cas 251). Sometimes there may even be an obligation to use reasonable efforts to cause the event upon which the contract is conditioned to occur, and failure to use such efforts will constitute a breach (*Hargreaves Transport Ltd v Lynch* [1969] 1 WLR 215).

- A **condition subsequent** is a stipulation of a state of affairs which will cause existing contractual obligations to terminate (discussed at **8.3**), e.g. that the contract should terminate when the price of the goods in question reaches a stated amount.

These *contingent* conditions must, therefore, be distinguished from *promissory* conditions, under which one party undertakes that a certain result will be achieved, and guarantees that undertaking by its promise. Failure to achieve the promised result is a breach. Thus, a promissory condition is the type of condition which is used to express a primary obligation of the contract.

Where the word 'condition' is used without qualification, it is almost certainly being used in the sense of a promissory condition, and it is in that sense that it is being referred to here when breach of contract is discussed. The confusion of terminology can arise because these promissory obligations are themselves classified as **conditions**, warranties or innominate terms and the type of term broken determines the remedy available for breach.

2. Promissory conditions (terms): Distinguishing conditions, warranties, and innominate terms

- **Conditions** are important terms which are said 'to go to the root of the contract'; and if they are broken, the breach is generally regarded as repudiatory so that the non-breaching party will have the option of terminating the contract for the future or affirming it, in addition to the remedy of damages. Conditions can be directly contrasted with warranties.

- **Warranties** are less important terms which do not 'go to the root of the contract'; and the breach of such a term can be adequately compensated with a remedy of damages. Accordingly, breach of warranty is not a repudiatory breach and there can be no option for the non-breaching party to terminate or affirm. The only remedy for the non-breaching party will be damages.

- **Innominate (or intermediate) terms** defy rigid classification but appear to lie somewhere between a condition and warranty and might best be described as the type of term which may be broken in a number of different ways, not all of which would be serious. Therefore, whether a breach of an innominate term constitutes a repudiatory breach, giving rise to the option to terminate or affirm, will depend upon the effects of the breach and whether these effects are serious. If the effects are serious, the breach will be repudiatory and there is an option to terminate or affirm; whereas if the effects are not serious, the non-breaching party will be limited to a remedy of damages.

There is a further classification of obligations which can be made and which is relevant in determining if a repudiatory breach has occurred, namely the distinction between breach of an entire obligation and breach of a severable obligation. This distinction is discussed at 8.6 below.

8.5.3 **Is the term a condition?**

Breach of a condition (used in the specific sense) entitles the non-breaching party to treat both parties' future obligations under the contract as discharged, so that the contract is brought to an end for the future (see the discussion of discharge for breach at 8.4). For this reason, not all the terms of the contract are classed as conditions. The parties rarely intend that breach of relatively unimportant terms should cause the entire agreement to collapse. Equally, the courts will not lightly classify terms as conditions because of the fact that the consequence of breach of such terms is fixed and does not take account of the actual effects of the breach in question.

8.5.3.1 Statutory classification of conditions

The implied terms as to description, fitness for purpose, satisfactory quality, and correspondence with sample in the sales and supply legislation are classified as conditions (e.g., SGA 1979, ss. 13(1A), 14(6), and 15(3), as amended). It should follow that in the event of a breach the buyer should be entitled to reject the goods (terminate the contract for repudiatory breach) or affirm (as by acceptance of the goods, SGA 1979, s. 35). However, s. 15A(1) provides that where the buyer is a non-consumer and there is a breach of s. 13, 14, or 15, such a breach **may** instead be treated as a breach of warranty (so that the only remedy will be damages) if the breach is so slight that it would be unreasonable to reject the goods (i.e., unreasonable to exercise the normal remedy of terminating the contract). (For these purposes, 'consumer' has the same meaning as under the Unfair Contract Terms Act (UCTA) 1977: see the discussion of UCTA 1977, s. 12 at 7.6.4.1.) This legislative provision, which may be ousted by the terms of the contract (s. 15A(2)), introduces remedial flexibility in order to allow the courts to take account of the nature of the breach that occurs where the buyer is a non-consumer. It also follows that since this provision was introduced by the Sale and Supply of Goods Act 1994, there has been a distinction in terms of remedial treatment between consumer and non-consumer buyers. In *J. H. Ritchie Ltd v Lloyd Ltd* [2007] UKHL 9, [2007] Bus LR 944, [2007] 1 WLR 630, the House of Lords considered that if under the general provisions in the sales legislation (SGA 1979, s.35) the commercial buyer agrees to repair, there is a separate contract which suspends the right to reject (whereas in the consumer context repair will generally mean that rejection is lost). This contract places a duty on the repairer to disclose the nature of the defect so that the buyer can make an informed decision as to whether to reject. (See below for the position of the consumer buyer and the position on repair and rejection.)

This distinction has been accentuated by further legislative changes in the Sale and Supply of Goods to Consumers Regulations 2002, SI 2002/3045 (introduced to implement the Consumer Sales and Guarantees Directive, 1999/44/EC), which introduced new ss. 48A–F into the SGA 1979 and thereby extended the remedies available to consumer buyers in instances of breaches of these implied terms in sale contracts (description, satisfactory quality, fitness for purpose, and correspondence with sample). For these purposes 'consumer' is defined in the same way as in the Unfair Terms in Consumer Contracts Regulations 1999, as 'any natural person who…is acting for purposes which are outside his trade, business or profession' (reg. 2). Sections 48A–F of the SGA 1979 enable a consumer buyer to require the seller to repair or replace the non-conforming goods, unless repair or replacement is impossible or disproportionate in comparison to other remedies. Repair or replacement must be achieved within a reasonable time and without causing significant inconvenience to the buyer. If repair or replacement is impossible or disproportionate or the seller is in breach of either of the obligations to do so in a reasonable time or without significant inconvenience to the buyer, the buyer may instead rely on one of two additional remedies, i.e. require the seller to reduce the purchase price by an appropriate amount or 'rescind' (terminate) the contract.

The difficulty with this has been that since the directive envisaged repair or replacement as the first recourse for consumer remedies, there has been uncertainty in some quarters as to whether the right to reject was thereby lost. It is difficult to see this since the legislative amendments in ss. 48A–F of the SGA 1979 refer to 'additional remedies' and do not remove the general initial right of a consumer buyer to rescind (terminate) for the repudiatory breach (i.e., the breach of condition) and claim damages for any additional losses suffered as a result of the breach. The intention must be to provide for greater flexibility and relevance of remedy rather than to reduce existing consumer remedies. Nevertheless, if the buyer requests repair or replacement, the right to reject the goods will be lost unless, of course, the seller fails to comply within a reasonable time (compare with the position under SGA 1979, s. 35, *J. H. Ritchie Ltd v Lloyd Ltd* [2007] UKHL 9, [2007] Bus LR 944, [2007] 1 WLR 630, discussed at 8.4.2.3).

However, in October 2008 the European Commission published a *Proposal for a Directive on Consumer Rights*, COM (2008) 614 final, 13 October 2008, which includes a proposal to abolish any right to reject the goods. The Law Commission issued a Consultation Paper (*Consumer Remedies for Faulty Goods*, LCCP No. 188) in November 2008 and published its report, Law Com. No. 317, Cm. 7725, in November 2009. The Law Commission has recommended the retention of the right to reject as an initial remedy having, in most cases, a thirty-day duration. This is an extremely welcome recommendation and accords with consumer expectations, irrespective of the availability of rights to request repair and replacement. However, the problems will occur if the directive is implemented in its current form since it is a maximum-harmonization measure which would prevent a Member State from continuing or adopting laws giving greater consumer protection than that laid down in the directive.

8.5.3.2 Non-statutory classification as a condition

In the absence of a statutory classification of the term in question (see, e.g., SGA 1979, ss. 14(6) and 15(A), discussed at 6.4.2.4 and 8.5.3.1), the starting point for identifying conditions is the intention of the parties. Generally, description of a term as a condition, or as entitling a party to terminate the contract (or reject the goods) upon breach, will result in the court following the parties' own classification. In **Lombard North Central plc v Butterworth** [1987] 1 QB 527 the point was considered very carefully by Mustill LJ at pp. 535–7. He stated:

> A stipulation that time is of the essence, in relation to a particular contractual term, denotes that timely performance is a condition of the contract. The consequence is that delay in performance is treated as going to the root of the contract, without regard to the magnitude of the breach.

Nevertheless, the court may be unwilling to accept the parties' classification if the court considers that a breach of this term could not have been intended by the parties to give rise to the option to terminate the contract.

> In **L. Schuler A-G v Wickman Machine Tools Sales Ltd** [1974] AC 235, the House of Lords refused to treat as a condition a term which was expressly stated to be 'a condition of this agreement'. The clause went on to provide for weekly visits over a period of four and a half years to six named firms (some 1,400 visits in total). The House of Lords did not believe that the parties can have intended that a single failure to make one of the visits should entitle the other party to bring the contract to an end.

Lord Reid said (at p. 251):

> We must remember that we are seeking to discover intention as disclosed by the contract as a whole. Use of the word 'condition' is an indication—even a strong indication—of such an intention but it is by no means conclusive.
>
> The fact that a particular construction leads to a very unreasonable result must be a relevant consideration. The more unreasonable the result the more unlikely it is that the parties can have intended it…

309

Schuler v Wickman may therefore constitute an early example of contractual construction to give effect to the meaning which the parties must reasonably have intended on an objective assessment (***Investors Compensation Scheme Ltd v West Bromwich Building Society*** [1998] 1 WLR 898: see 6.5.2; and ***Attorney General of Belize v Belize Telecom Ltd*** [2009] UKPC 10, [2009] 1 WLR 1988: 6.4.2.2).

There is further evidence of this approach in the decision of the Court of Appeal in ***Rice (T/A The Garden Guardian) v Great Yarmouth Borough Council*** [2003] TCLR 1, (2001) 3 LGLR 4, *The Times*, 26 July 2000, although the problem in this case was that the term in question was not expressly stated to be a condition, rather the clause referred to a right to terminate.

> A clause of the four-year contract to provide leisure management and grounds maintenance services stated that 'if the contractor committed a breach of any of its obligations...the council may...terminate the contractor's employment...by notice in writing'. The Court of Appeal held that a literal interpretation of this would entitle the council to terminate 'for any breach of any term' and that this 'flies in the face of commercial common sense'. The breach in question would have to constitute a repudiatory breach in order to justify the ability to terminate.

In the light of this decision it would seem sensible to avoid such open termination provisions, and to spell out the status of individual potential breaches.

Termination provisions and the relationship with repudiatory breach

Express termination provisions are common in contracts and the Court of Appeal in ***Stocznia Gdynia SA v Gearbulk Holdings Ltd*** [2009] EWCA Civ 75, [2009] 3 WLR 677, has confirmed that the exercise of an express termination provision in a contract does not prevent the non-breaching party from treating the contract as repudiated at common law (and so recovering contractual damages based on lost expectation) rather than recovering on the basis provided for in the termination provision (in this case repayment of instalment sums received in anticipation of performance, together with interest). Equally, exercising that termination provision would not constitute affirmation of a repudiatory breach as there was no election involved. A termination provision might operate when there was no repudiatory breach but it would be envisaged that there would come a point at which a breach might be repudiatory, i.e. when the breach went to the root of the contract. It followed that since the delay in delivery on these facts was repudiatory (i.e. it went to the root of the contract), the purchaser could recover the instalment payments (restitution based on total failure of consideration: see 10.5.1) and damages for repudiation (lost bargain).

8.5.3.3 Assessment of the importance of the term to the contract as a whole

In ***Hong Kong Fir Shipping Co. Ltd v Kawasaki Kisen Kaisha Ltd*** [1962] 2 QB 26, Diplock LJ suggested that a condition exists only in the case of a term 'where every breach...must give rise to an event which will deprive the party not in default of substantially the whole of the benefit which it was intended that he should obtain from the contract'. That definition of a condition was rejected by Megaw LJ in the Court of Appeal in ***Bunge Corporation v Tradax Export SA*** [1980] 1 Lloyd's Rep 294, and his view was affirmed by the House of Lords ([1981] 1 WLR 711). It is too strict a test to say that every breach must deprive the other party of substantially the whole benefit for a term to qualify as a condition. Nevertheless, the formulation does give a good indication of the nature of terms which are conditions. They are those terms which contain the main obligations, and which are central to the existence of the contract. It follows that the determination of whether a clause is a condition may require the court to make a 'value judgment about the commercial significance of the term in question' (per Kerr LJ in *State Trading Corporation of India Ltd v Golodetz Ltd* [1989] 2 Lloyd's Rep 277 at p. 283, approved by Lord Ackner in *Compagnie Commerciale Sucres et Denrées v C. Czarnikow Ltd, The Naxos* [1990] 1 WLR 1337 at pp. 1347–8).

In *Bunge Corporation v Tradax Export SA* [1981] 1 WLR 711, Lord Wilberforce expressly approved the *dictum* of Roskill LJ in *The Hansa Nord* [1976] QB 44, to the effect that the courts should not be too ready to interpret contractual clauses as conditions. The usual alternative will be to classify the term as **innominate**, which may be more appropriate if the term is such that breach may involve either serious or trivial consequences; in such cases the courts are unwilling to allow the serious legal consequences of breach of condition (see 8.5.5) to operate in instances where the practical consequences of breach are trivial.

In *Barber v NWS Bank plc* [1996] 1 All ER 906, Sir Roger Parker in the Court of Appeal clearly had this distinction in mind when determining whether a term was a condition of the contract. The term in question related to an assertion by a finance company that it would be the owner of a particular car at the time of its eventual sale to a buyer. In concluding that it was a condition, two tests were used: first, the term was 'fundamental to the transaction' and secondly:

> This term is not one which admits of different breaches, some of which are trivial, for which damages are an adequate remedy, and others of which are sufficiently serious to warrant rescission. There is here one breach only. [Per Sir Roger Parker at p. 911.]

Expressions such as 'fundamental to the transaction' can be problematic because they mean different things to different judges. It is not difficult to see, however, how in this case the two tests led to the same conclusion.

8.5.3.4 Time stipulations in commercial contracts

Certain terms which are in common use in commercial contracts have acquired, by custom and the operation of the doctrine of precedent, definitive classification as conditions. The main explanation for this is the requirement of commercial certainty. Business people need to know the effect of a contractual term, and more particularly they need to know what the effect of breach will be. Therefore, when words have been interpreted in a certain way by the courts, it is generally desirable that that interpretation be consistently maintained. (This principle was reaffirmed by Lord Steyn in the decision of the House of Lords in *Jindal Iron & Steel Co. Ltd v Islamic Solidarity Shipping Co. Jordan Inc.* [2004] UKHL 49, [2005] 1 WLR 1363.) The certainty requirement is particularly true of time conditions (see *United Scientific Holdings Ltd v Burnley Borough Council* [1978] AC 904). A striking example of the strictness of the approach to time clauses is provided by the decision in *Union Eagle Ltd v Golden Achievement Ltd* [1997] AC 514. A delay of ten minutes caused the contract to be lost, and the only real issue before the Privy Council was whether relief could be granted (see further, 9.10.5.3).

Thus, in commercial, and particularly mercantile (or shipping), contracts the normal rule is that stipulations as to time of performance are crucial ('time is of the essence'), so that any breach entitles the other party to treat the contract as repudiated without assessing whether the term in question actually 'goes to the root of the contract'. As explained by Megaw LJ in the Court of Appeal in ***Bunge Corporation v Tradax Export SA*** [1980] 1 Lloyd's Rep 294 at p. 306:

> I think it can fairly be said that in mercantile contracts stipulations as to time not only may be, but usually are, to be treated as being 'of the essence of the contract', even though this is not expressly stated in the words of the contract. It would follow that in a mercantile contract it cannot be predicated that, for time to be of the essence, any and every breach of the term as to time must necessarily cause the innocent party to be deprived of substantially the whole benefit which it was intended that he should have.

This reasoning was applied by the courts in a series of cases.

> In ***The Mihalis Angelos*** [1971] 1 QB 164, a charterparty (contract to hire a ship) stated that the vessel was 'expected ready to load' on 1 July 1965 at Haiphong. The charterers purported to cancel the charter because their cargo was unavailable after the American bombing of the railway line to Haiphong. Such cancellation was not allowed under the terms of the contract. However, unknown to the charterers when they cancelled, at the time of entering the contract the owners had no reason to believe the ship would be ready to load on the date stated. The phrase 'expected ready to load' was held to be a condition, breach of which entitled the charterers to treat the contract as repudiated irrespective of the consequences of the breach.

This approach to time clauses was confirmed by the House of Lords in ***Compagnie Commerciale Sucres et Denrées v C. Czarnikow Ltd, The Naxos*** [1990] 1 WLR 1337, in which Lord Ackner cited with approval Lord Wilberforce's statement in ***Bunge Corporation v Tradax Export SA*** [1981] 1 WLR 711, that time clauses in mercantile contracts should 'usually' be treated as conditions.

Despite the strength of the authorities indicating that time stipulations in commercial or mercantile contracts will be treated as conditions, such a position cannot be regarded as conclusive in the light of the decision of the House of Lords in ***Torvald Klaveness A/S v Arni Maritime Corporation, The Gregos*** [1994] 1 WLR 1465, concerning the obligation to redeliver a vessel on time at the end of a time charterparty. The majority of the House of Lords considered this obligation to be an innominate term, and only Lord Templeman (dissenting) considered that as a time stipulation it amounted to a condition and was therefore of the essence of the contract. The majority was clearly concerned to achieve flexibility in terms of remedy in the event of a short delay, whereas Lord Templeman's speech emphasizes the commercial importance of this provision and the need for commercial certainty. This tension between flexibility and commercial certainty is evident throughout this area of law. The underlying basis for this decision appears to be the more general justification for innominate terms, namely the avoidance of a classification of a term as a condition in order to prevent a party using such a breach as justifying escape from the contract for other (normally economic) reasons (see, e.g., ***Reardon Smith Line Ltd v Hansen-Tangen*** [1976] 3 All ER 570). As Lord Mustill stated in ***Torvald Klaveness v Arni Maritime, The Gregos*** (at p. 1475):

> [A]lthough it is well established that certain obligations under charterparties do have the character of conditions I would not...wish to enlarge the category unduly, given the opportunity which this provides for a party to rely on an innocuous breach as a means of escaping from an unwelcome bargain.

In **Universal Bulk Carriers Pte Ltd v Andre et Cie SA** [2001] EWCA Civ 588, [2001] 2 Lloyd's Rep 65, the charterers were required to serve the relevant notice within a set period prior to the commencement of the laytime in order for laytime to commence. [Laytime is the period specified in the charterparty contract to enable the charterer to load or discharge the cargo and will be particularly important in a time charter]. The charterers failed to serve the notice in accordance with this time provision. The owners claimed that the term was a condition which had been accepted as terminating the contract so that they were no longer under any obligation to nominate a vessel to perform the charterparty. The charterers sought damages claiming that this failure on the part of the owners to nominate a vessel constituted a breach.

The Court of Appeal held that, having considered the appropriate test, namely whether the nature of the subject matter of the contract or the surrounding circumstances indicate that the clause was intended to be a condition, the clause relating to the laytime notice was not a condition. In the event that the charterers failed to serve the required notice, the contract could still be performed in accordance with its terms and therefore the serving of the notice could not have been intended as a pre-condition to performance of the owners' obligations.

In the light of these decisions it seems unlikely that the courts will automatically assume that a time stipulation in a mercantile contract is a condition, irrespective of the consequences of the breach, but will assess whether the clause fulfils the criteria to qualify as a condition on the facts.

Nevertheless, in instances where there are concurrent 'conditions' so that payment is a condition precedent to the delivery of a vessel in a mercantile contract, full compliance with that payment obligation is likely to be considered as a condition (*PT Berlian Laju Tanker TBK v Nuse Shipping Ltd* [2008] EWHC 1330 (Comm), [2008] 2 Lloyd's Rep 246, [2008] 2 All ER (Comm) 784), since the parties would not contemplate delivery without payment in full.

8.5.3.5 Time stipulations in non-commercial contracts

In non-commercial contracts, time is not generally regarded as being of the essence unless expressed to be so by the parties. In the absence of express agreement, failure to abide by a time clause does not entitle the other party to treat the contract as repudiated unless the delay goes to the root of the contract and deprives the non-breaching party of the whole benefit of the contract (*United Scientific Holdings Ltd v Burnley Borough Council* [1978] AC 904 and see *Hayes (t/a Orchard Construction) v Gallant* [2008] EWHC 2726 (TCC), [2008] All ER (D) 86 (Nov.)).

In some circumstances, however, even where the original contract makes no stipulation about the time for performance, time may be made of the essence by the service of a notice to complete (although the notice will not operate if it does not make this clear: *Shawton Engineering Ltd v DGP International Ltd* [2005] EWCA Civ 1359, [2006] 1 BLR 1).

In **British & Commonwealth Holdings plc v Quadrex Holdings Inc.** [1989] QB 842 at p. 857, Lord Browne-Wilkinson V-C stated that:

three requirements have to be satisfied if time for completion is to be made of the essence by the service of a notice, *viz.*: (1) the giver of the notice (the innocent party) has to be ready, willing and able to complete; (2) the other party (the guilty party) has to have been guilty of unreasonable delay before a notice to complete can be served; and (3) the notice when served must limit a reasonable period within which completion is to take place.

Lord Browne-Wilkinson's second requirement has provoked some comment. In the case in question, no time for performance was stipulated, and so unreasonable delay is very clearly a necessary condition for the legitimate service of notice. In cases where a time for performance is stipulated, without it being a condition, it used to be thought that unreasonable delay beyond the time stipulated was required before notice could be served. Lord Browne-Wilkinson clearly did not like the rule, but did not feel he could overturn it. In *Behzadi v Shaftesbury Hotels Ltd* [1992] Ch 1, the Court of Appeal held that notice could be served as soon as the date stipulated for performance had passed.

The assumption has been that service of such notice, followed by non-compliance, would allow the party serving the notice to treat the contract as repudiated. However, in **Re Olympia & York Canary Wharf Ltd (No. 2)** [1993] BCC 159, Morritt J said that the possibility of repudiation would arise only where the failure to comply with the time notice went to the root of the contract (see 8.5.3.3). This restrictive view reflected the judge's concern not to allow a unilateral variation of the contract, which in his view a time notice might otherwise amount to, since it would make time for performance a condition without that being the original agreement of the parties. This was accepted as being the governing principle in **Dalkia Utilities Services plc v Celtech International Ltd** [2006] EWHC 63 (Comm), [2006] 1 Lloyd's Rep 599 at [131]–[132]. On the facts the period of notice was considered unreasonable and, in any event, the breach on which the notice was based was not, even after expiry of the notice, of such a nature as to go to the root of the contract.

8.5.4 Is the term a warranty?

A warranty is a term of a contract containing a minor (or less important) primary obligation. Breach of such a term gives rise to a secondary obligation to pay damages, but does not constitute a repudiatory breach presenting the non-breaching party with the option of accepting the breach as terminating the contract or affirming.

The distinction between conditions and warranties is traditionally demonstrated by contrasting two cases with similar facts.

1. In **Poussard v Spiers** (1876) 1 QBD 410, a singer, hired to perform during the entire run of an operetta, did not arrive until after one week of the run, when a substitute had been taken on. It was held that the singer's obligation to appear as from the first night was a condition, the breach of which entitled the show's producer to dispense with her services.

2. However, in **Bettini v Gye** (1876) 1 QBD 183, a singer, hired to perform during an entire season, had agreed to arrive six days in advance for rehearsals, but was three days late. The court did not believe that the clause relating to rehearsals was so central to the main purpose of the contract as to constitute a condition. The singer's breach, therefore, did not allow the contract to be treated as repudiated, but only allowed recovery of damages for whatever loss had been suffered.

In the past the courts maintained that the distinction between conditions and warranties was to be made without considering the actual results of breach, and was to be determined on the basis of the relative importance of the term in the context of the contract as a whole at the date when it was drafted. Today, it is still the case that where the parties have expressly designated a term to be merely a warranty, or where the term is classed as a warranty by statute, the consequences of the actual breach ought not to be taken into account. But where there is no express classification of the term by either of these means, it seems unlikely that the court would classify a term as a warranty without first considering the result of the breach under the innominate term doctrine (see 8.5.5).

8.5.5 More flexibility at a price: Innominate or intermediate terms

8.5.5.1 Introduction of the innominate term

The innominate term was introduced in *Hong Kong Fir Shipping Co. Ltd v Kawasaki Kisen Kaisha Ltd* [1962] 2 QB 26, because although a classification of either condition or warranty had the advantage of certainty of remedy in the event of breach, once a term was classified as a condition it allowed the non-breaching party to rely on a trivial breach of that term in order to escape from the contract for other reasons, such as the fact that the contract had turned out to be a bad bargain. In other words, the certainty was inflexible.

> In *Hong Kong Fir Shipping*, clause 1 of a contract for the charter of a vessel for a period of two years (commencing in February 1957) described the vessel as 'being in every way fitted for ordinary cargo service'. When delivered to the charterers the vessel was unseaworthy, because her engines were old. On her first voyage under the charter she needed repairs, and the vessel was not properly seaworthy until mid-September 1957. However, in June the charterers had treated the breach as repudiatory and terminated the charter. The question for the Court of Appeal was whether the breach of clause 1 entitled the charterers to treat the contract as repudiated, or only entitled them to damages.

Diplock LJ said (at p. 70):

315

> There are, however, many contractual undertakings of a more complex character which cannot be categorised as being 'conditions' or 'warranties'. Of such undertakings all that can be predicated is that some breaches will, and others will not, give rise to an event which will deprive the party not in default of substantially the whole benefit which it was intended that he should obtain from the contract; and the legal consequences of the breach of such an undertaking, unless provided for expressly in the contract, depend on the nature of the event to which the breach gives rise and do not follow automatically from a prior classification of the undertaking as a 'condition' or a 'warranty'.

Such terms were christened 'innominate' (there being no technical name for them) or 'intermediate', since they lay somewhere between conditions and warranties in terms of relative importance. A finding that a term is innominate rather than a condition has been said to 'repress sharp practice' (Weir [1976] CLJ 33) since it will prevent a trivial breach of the term being used to justify termination and withdrawal from the contract for other reasons (e.g., *Reardon Smith Line Ltd v Hansen-Tangen* [1976] 1 WLR 989; and see also *The Gregos* [1994] 1 WLR 1465 (discussed above at 8.5.3.4).

8.5.5.2 Difficulties in identifying innominate terms

The analysis proposed by Diplock LJ in *Hong Kong Fir* was immediately welcomed by the courts (see, for example, Lord Wilberforce in *Reardon Smith Line v Hansen-Tangen* [1976] 1 WLR 989 at p. 998). Nevertheless, there has been some reaction against the uncertainty the doctrine can introduce into commercial contracts because of the need to wait and see whether the consequences of the breach are sufficiently serious to render it a repudiatory breach.

> In **Bunge Corporation v Tradax Export SA** [1981] 1 WLR 711, buyers agreed to purchase 15,000 tons of soyabean meal from the sellers. The contract provided for three shipments of 5,000 tons, one of which was to be made during June 1975. Under the contract the buyers were to provide a vessel at a nominated port, and were to give fifteen days' notice of expected readiness of the vessel. Therefore, for shipment in June notice had to be given by 13 June. Notice was in fact given on 17 June. The Court of Appeal and House of Lords both found the delay in giving notice to be a repudiatory breach of the contract. Lord Wilberforce said that certain contractual terms, especially those agreed by the parties to give rise upon any breach to a right to treat the contract as repudiated, were not amenable to being classified as innominate terms. He said that the contrary proposition would be 'commercially most undesirable...It would fatally remove from a vital provision in the contract that certainty which is the most indispensable quality of mercantile contracts.'

However, as noted at **8.5.3.4,** this did not prevent the majority of the House of Lords in *Torvald Klaveness A/S v Arni Maritime Corp, The Gregos* [1994] 1 WLR 1465, from determining that an obligation under a time charter to redeliver a vessel on time was only innominate.

The identification of innominate terms is therefore a process of elimination, in the sense that all terms which are not so important that breach will always entitle the non-breaching party to treat the contract as repudiated (conditions), and which equally are not so unimportant that their breach would never entitle the non-breaching party to treat the contract as repudiated (warranties), are innominate or intermediate terms. Hale LJ, in *Rice v Great Yarmouth Borough Council* [2003] TCLR 1, (2001) 3 LGLR 4, *The Times*, 26 July 2000 (for facts see **8.5.3.2**), defined an innominate term as 'one which can be broken in so many different ways and with such varying consequences that the parties cannot be taken to have intended that any breach should entitle the innocent party to terminate the whole contract'.

Upjohn LJ, in *Hong Kong Fir Shipping* [1962] 2 QB 26 at pp. 62–3, discussed the reasons why the seaworthiness clause in the charterparty in that case constituted an innominate term:

> Why is this basic and underlying condition of seaworthiness not, in fact, treated as a condition? It is for the simple reason that the seaworthiness clause is breached by the slightest failure to be fitted 'in every way' for service. Thus...if a nail is missing from one of the timbers of a wooden vessel, or if proper medical supplies or two anchors are not on board at the time of sailing, the owners are in breach of the seaworthiness stipulation. It is contrary to common sense to suppose that, in such circumstances, the parties contemplated that the charterer should at once be entitled to treat the contract as at an end for such trifling breaches.

The distinction between conditions and innominate terms is far from obvious on occasion. For example, in *BS & N Ltd (BVI) v Micado Shipping Ltd (Malta) No. 1, The Seaflower* [2001] 1 Lloyd's Rep 341, [2001] 1 All ER (Comm) 240, although the judge at first instance ([2000] CLC 795) held that a clause guaranteeing to obtain approval for a vessel was an innominate term, the Court of Appeal considered it to be a condition. This type of uncertainty does little to assist business people in determining their options, especially in view of the possible dangers of wrongful repudiation (see below).

8.5.5.3 The effect of breach of an innominate term

- Where the result of the breach is substantially to deprive the non-breaching party of the benefit they were intended to obtain under the contract, the breach of the innominate term will be treated as repudiatory (see, e.g., *Federal Commerce & Navigation Co Ltd v Molena Alpha Inc.* [1979] AC 757).

- Where, however, the effects of the breach caused loss to the non-breaching party but were not so serious as to deprive them of the benefit of the contract, the non-breaching party would be limited to the remedy of damages. For example, in *Hong Kong Fir Shipping*, after the repairs to the ship, seventeen months of the original charter of twenty-four months remained and therefore the effects of the breach were not considered to deprive the non-breaching party of substantially the whole benefit of the contract.

8.5.5.4 Flexibility but uncertainty: Dilemmas for the non-breaching party

The innominate term is a focal point of the tension that exists in the law of contract between the sometimes conflicting interests of certainty and fairness. The essential flexibility, or fatal uncertainty, of innominate terms stems from the fact that it is not possible to predict before the time of the breach what the effect of breach of such a term will be. It is therefore for the parties, if they value certainty so highly, to ensure by careful drafting of their contracts that the consequences of breach of every term are clearly stated, thereby seeking to avoid the possibility of the court treating a term as innominate. However, as noted above, it can be difficult to ensure effective classification of a term as a condition, e.g. *Schuler v Wickman Machine Tools* [1974] AC 235 (see 8.5.3.2) and the approach of the courts has, at times, been unpredictable, e.g. the approach to time stipulations in mercantile contracts (see *Torvald Klaveness v Arni Maritime, The Gregos* [1994] 1 WLR 1465: see 8.5.3.4).

Whilst there is much to be said in favour of removing the rigidity of the condition/warranty classification, the current uncertainty presents a difficulty for the non-breaching party who has to decide what action to take and whether to treat the breach as repudiatory.

Weir ([1976] CLJ 33) also criticized the innominate term, relying on the decision in *Cehave NV v Bremer Handelsgesellschaft mbh, The Hansa Nord* [1976] QB 44, on the basis that classification as an innominate term and the application of the effects of the breach test, can operate to 'reward incompetence', i.e. that the party who was originally in breach of contract may terminate in the belief that the term broken is a condition when in fact the term broken is only an innominate term and not repudiatory in the light of the seriousness of the breach. This action would constitute a wrongful repudiation, entitling the party who committed the original breach to the usual remedies.

The case concerned the sale of citrus pulp pellets to be used as animal feed at a price of £100,000. Shipment was to be made in good condition. On arrival it was discovered that some of the pellets were damaged and the buyers rejected the entire cargo on the basis that this amounted to a breach of condition; it was also the case that the market price for these pellets had fallen since the making of the contract. The sellers then resold the pellets to an importer and the importer resold them on the same day to the original buyers, who used the pellets for the original purpose as animal feed. The Court of Appeal held that the term 'shipment in good condition' was innominate and, since the cargo had been used for its intended purpose, the effects of the breach were not serious. Accordingly, the buyers had wrongfully repudiated because they had made the wrong decision on the applicable remedy (see 8.7.6, The risk of overreacting to a breach).

8.5.6 Conditions and non-conditions?

In practice, the essential distinction to be made is that between conditions and non-conditions, the effects of the breach test (**Hong Kong Fir**) being applied to all non-conditions. This appears to be because, except in the case of terms expressly designated as warranties, there is little point in distinguishing between innominate terms and warranties. The outcome in terms of remedy is the factor having practical importance and this can be determined by applying the effects of the breach test. This has led to the suggestion that there are two types of contractual terms: conditions (repudiatory) and non-conditions (which will be repudiatory only if the effects of breach are serious): see Reynolds (1981) 97 LQR 541. This also appears to be the approach adopted by Upjohn LJ in the **Hong Kong Fir** case. On the basis of this approach, the key determinant is whether a term is a condition. If it is not, it is a non-condition to which the **Hong Kong Fir** test applies.

Nevertheless Peel, *Treitel's Law of Contract*, maintains that it remains important to make the classification between conditions, warranties, and innominate terms because a breach of warranty can *never* be a repudiatory breach and so will never give rise to the option to terminate or affirm. However, it is extremely difficult to make classifications of terms and it can be argued that the classification can be achieved through the application of the effects of the breach test in **Hong Kong Fir**, i.e. if the effects of the breach are not serious then the remedy is limited to damages only—and, reasoning backwards, that would classify the term as a warranty.

8.5.7 Classification of implied terms as conditions, warranties, or innominate terms

Just as express terms may be classified according to their relative importance (see 8.5.2.1), so some **implied** terms are more important than others. The SGA 1979 employs the expression 'implied term', but it goes on to specify more precisely the type of obligation. So, the implied terms of satisfactory quality and fitness for purpose in s. 14 are said to be conditions (s. 14(6)). If s. 15A of the 1979 Act (inserted by the Sale and Supply of Goods Act 1994) applies to the sale, it may follow that the applicable remedy will be damages only rather than the usual option to terminate or affirm. Section 15A(1) provides that where the buyer is a non-consumer and there is a breach of s. 13, 14, or 15 (so-called breaches of condition), such a breach **may** instead be treated as a breach of warranty (so that the only remedy will be damages) if the breach is so slight that it would be unreasonable to reject the goods (i.e., unreasonable to exercise the normal remedy of terminating the contract). Section 15A can be expressly or impliedly ousted (s. 15A(2)).

Putting convoluted drafting into plain language: in consumer contracts these implied terms are conditions (although see the additional remedies available to consumer buyers as a result of ss. 48A–F, SGA 1979, inserted by the Sale and Supply of Goods to Consumers Regulations 2002, SI 2002/3045, discussed above at 8.5.3.1); in non-consumer contracts they may be treated as warranties if the breach is so slight that it would be unreasonable to reject the goods (for a discussion of the definition of 'consumer', see 7.6.4.1).

Not all implied obligations in the sales legislation are conditions; for example, the implied term that the goods in question are free of any charge or encumbrance and that the buyer has a right to quiet possession is expressed to be a 'warranty' (SGA 1979, s. 12(5A)). On the other hand, s. 13 of the Supply of Goods and Services Act 1982, which imposes an obligation of reasonable care and skill in the supply of services, refers only to an 'implied term'. It must be assumed that the statutory intention was for this term to be treated by the courts as innominate, on the basis that it is the type of term where breach may sometimes result in serious damage and sometimes trivial damage.

Except in the case of statutory implied terms, there is no reason for prior classification of implied terms, since the terms are not known to the parties until the time of litigation. There is, therefore, no requirement of certainty or predictability of the effect of breach of such terms since, being implied, they cannot be relied upon in the course of a party's planning. The court is free simply to indicate the type of term when specifying the term to be implied in any given case. It seems likely that in practice the courts will do so only after considering the consequences of the breach which has been found to have occurred (see, generally, 8.5.6).

8.6 Entire or severable obligations

8.6.1 Introduction: Explanation of concurrent obligations

Promissory conditions (obligations) are of three types (per Lord Mansfield in *Kingston v Preston* (1773) 2 Doug 689):

- independent obligations
- obligations which are a condition precedent
- concurrent obligations.

1. Independent obligations

Where an obligation is an independent obligation, its breach by party A will not entitle party B to cease performance of party B's obligations under the contract. Independent conditions are rare in modern contracts.

2. Conditions precedent

Alternatively, performance of one obligation may be a condition precedent of the other, so that party B is not obliged to perform until party A has performed its obligation under the contract.

3. Concurrent performance obligations

In this instance performance is more or less simultaneous, and it is not certain which party is obliged to act first. Accordingly, party B must be ready and willing to perform its obligations in order to be able to maintain a claim against party A for a breach by party A.

The latter two categories may both be described as dependent obligations. Of these, concurrent performance obligations are the more common.

Whether conditions are dependent or independent is to be determined by construction of the contract. The law is very unwilling to treat conditions as independent, since to do so removes an important security under the contract from the party to whom the obligation expressed in the condition is owed. That is, if the parties' obligations to perform are concurrent, each has an important lever they can use to ensure the other's performance, since each may withhold their own performance until the other party is ready and willing to perform. When it was stated that the effect of breach of condition was to entitle the non-breaching party to treat the contract as repudiated (see 8.5.2.1), it was assumed that the condition was a dependent condition.

An example of dependent concurrent conditions is afforded by the main primary obligations of the contract of sale, as expressed in s. 28 of the SGA 1979:

Unless otherwise agreed, delivery of the goods and payment of the price are concurrent conditions, that is to say, the seller must be ready and willing to give possession of the goods to the buyer in exchange for the price and the buyer must be ready and willing to pay the price in exchange for possession of the goods.

Where a condition is classed as independent it changes the effect of breach, so that the non-breaching party must continue to perform its obligations under the contract. Thus, to classify a condition as independent has much the same effect as classifying a term as a warranty (see 8.5.4). Possibly the only relevant modern example of an independent condition is the landlord's covenant to repair premises, which is said to be independent of the tenant's obligation to pay the rent (*Taylor v Webb* [1937] 2 KB 283; and see also **Liverpool City Council v Irwin** [1977] AC 239). As a result, the tenant may not withhold payment of rent in order to force the landlord to perform the landlord's obligation to repair.

8.6.2 Entire and severable obligations explained

Some contracts involve very simple exchanges. A consumer sale for cash in a shop, for example, involves the exchange of money for goods, with possibly no other terms than an implied condition of quality. In such a contract it is easy to see, assuming that the conditions are concurrent (see 8.6.1), that the whole of each party's side of the bargain is the necessary condition for the performance of the other side. Any breach would destroy the commercial point of the exchange, and so would entitle the non-breaching party to treat the contract as repudiated.

Many contracts, however, do not involve such simple exchanges. Sales on credit terms of industrial machines, long-term requirements contracts, construction contracts, among many others, all involve complex sets of obligations on both contracting parties. This complexity gave rise to the standard form, and the difficulties it creates in the formation of contracts (for example, see 2.4.2.3). In some such cases it is still true that **any breach would destroy the commercial point of the exchange, so that the whole of each party's side of the bargain is the necessary condition for the performance of the other. In such cases the obligations are described as 'entire' and breach of an entire obligation will constitute a repudiatory breach.**

However, in many complex commercial contracts it is possible to see that breach of an important term may not destroy the whole commercial point of the exchange. The obligations in such a contract are described as 'severable' (or 'divisible'), and the result is that breach of such an obligation does not entitle the non-breaching party to treat the whole contract as having been repudiated. It will entitle that party to damages, and may entitle the non-breaching party to avoid performance of an obligation which was dependent upon the obligation breached.

Nevertheless, it may be that a series of breaches of severable obligations could have a cumulative effect amounting eventually to a repudiation of the whole contract (e.g., *Alexander Corfield v David Grant* (1992) 59 BLR 102). In **Rice (T/A The Garden Guardian) v Great Yarmouth Borough Council** [2003] TCLR 1, (2001) 3 LGLR 4, *The Times*, 26 July 2000 (for facts, see 8.5.3.2), in the context of a long-term contract for leisure services where no single breach was repudiatory but there were a number of repeated breaches, the Court of Appeal held that the correct approach to determine whether there was a repudiatory breach would be to look at the contractor's performance over one year (of the four-year contract period) to determine whether the council was substantially deprived of the benefit that it had contracted for in that period. It was possible that there would be some aspects of the contract which were so important 'that the parties would be taken to have intended that any deprivation would be sufficient in itself' to justify termination. However, subject to this, the test required an examination of the cumulative past breaches to see whether they were such as to justify an inference that the contractor would continue to deliver a substandard performance in the future. On the facts the cumulative effect was considered to be insufficient.

8.6.2.1 Identifying severable obligations

A simple example of a contract consisting of severable obligations is a contract for sale and delivery of goods in instalments which are to be paid for separately. Section 31(2) of the SGA 1979 actually states that in the case of delivery by instalments which are to be paid for separately, 'it is a question in each case depending on the terms of the contract and the circumstances of the case whether the breach of contract is a repudiation of the whole contract or whether it is a severable breach giving rise to a claim for compensation'.

> In *Regent OHG Aisestadt v Francesco of Jermyn Street Ltd* [1981] 3 All ER 327, the contract called for the supply of sixty-two suits in a number of instalments. After delivery of several instalments which had been accepted, one instalment was defective, being one suit short. The buyers claimed to be entitled to treat the whole contract as repudiated on the basis of breach in respect of the single instalment (the shortfall of one suit being outside *de minimis*: see **8.2.1.1**).
>
> Mustill J rejected that argument. The obligation to supply was severable so that each instalment was a separate delivery. Therefore, a breach in respect of one instalment did not entitle the non-breaching party to treat the whole contract as repudiated.

The judge did not say, as seemingly he should have, that the breach did, however, entitle the buyers to reject the whole instalment affected by the short delivery (*Jackson v Rotax Motor and Cycle Co.* [1910] 2 KB 937).

8.6.2.2 Identifying entire obligations

The classic example of an entire obligation is *Cutter v Powell* (1795) 6 TR 320.

> A sailor was hired as mate for the voyage from Jamaica to England. He was to be paid a lump sum on completion of the voyage, and it appears that the payment was considerably in excess of the normal amount for such a voyage. He died before reaching England, and his widow sued to recover a reasonable sum as payment, relative to the period of the sailor's service before his death. The court refused her claim. Lord Kenyon CJ regarded the contract as 'a kind of insurance', with the result that the sailor's entitlement was 'all or nothing'. Moreover, the court was unwilling to allow the remedy of *quantum meruit* where there was an express contract governing relations between the parties.

Ashhurst J said (at p. 325):

This is a written contract, and it speaks for itself. And as it is entire, and as the defendant's promise depends upon a condition precedent to be performed by the other party, the condition must be performed before the other party is entitled to receive anything under it.

321

Thus, the result of failure to perform an entire obligation completely and precisely may be to deprive the party in breach of any payment for whatever performance there has been. It is for this reason that the courts are often unwilling to find that the obligations under a contract are entire. Nevertheless, certain types of contract are usually found to consist of entire obligations, especially lump-sum contracts for domestic building or other similar services (e.g., *Bolton v Mahadeva* [1972] 1 WLR 1009: lump-sum contract to install central heating in a private house). An advantage of the entire obligations rule in such cases is that it gives the consumer a useful means of ensuring that work is completed, since until it is completed no payment is due (see 8.6.4.1).

8.6.3 Entire and severable obligations in the same contract

Although the courts sometimes refer to entire or severable **contracts**, it is important to note that it is **obligations** which are either entire or severable, and not the contracts themselves. A contract may well consist of both entire and severable obligations. For example, although *Cutter v Powell* (1795) 6 TR 320 is the classic example of an entire 'contract', the court's reflections on the nature of entire obligations did not suggest that every minor breach of the deceased's duties as a mate during the voyage would have entitled the employer to deny him any payment for his services (per Somervell LJ in *Hoenig v Isaacs* [1952] 2 All ER 176).

A further example can be seen in the case of sale of goods contracts. The general rule is that the seller's obligation to deliver the correct quantity in a **consumer** sale of goods contract is entire so that an excess or shortfall will, subject to *de minimis*, entitle the buyer to refuse to accept the goods and pay for them. (As we saw at 8.6.2.1, this rule does not apply, however, to a contract for delivery in instalments. If one instalment is short, the buyer is not necessarily entitled to refuse to accept further deliveries.) However, obligations as to quality are not entire; although a breach of s. 14(2) or (3) of the SGA 1979 would be a repudiatory breach in a consumer sale of goods contract, that has nothing to do with the entire obligation rule.

8.6.4 Avoiding the entire obligation rule

Apart from the obvious means of avoiding the entire obligation rule, by classing the obligations in question as severable (see 8.6.2.1), two other means exist to prevent the party in breach being denied any payment where that party's performance, although not exactly matching their contractual undertaking, has nevertheless bestowed a substantial benefit on the non-breaching party.

8.6.4.1 Acceptance of the benefit by the non-breaching party

The party in breach of an entire obligation may be entitled to reasonable payment for the value of its actual performance if the non-breaching party accepts such performance as has been given and determines to keep whatever benefit may have been derived from it. 'Acceptance' in this sense does not mean an indication that the non-breaching party will not treat the contract as repudiated (which is the sense in which it is used in s. 11(4) of the SGA 1979: see 8.4.2.3); it means simply that the non-breaching party, while regarding the breach of the entire obligation as bringing the original contract to an end, wishes to keep a benefit conferred and is willing to pay the 'going rate' for it. In other words, although the contract may be discharged for the breach of the entire obligation, a new contract to pay a reasonable sum for the benefit which has been accepted will be implied.

> This principle is explained in **Sumpter v Hedges** [1898] 1 QB 673. The plaintiff builder had contracted to build two houses on the defendant's land for a lump sum of £565. After completion of just over half the work, the builder abandoned the project. He had in fact received some payment, but not the entire value of the work. The defendant completed the building work, using materials left on the site by the plaintiff. At first instance the plaintiff was awarded the value of the materials used by the defendant to complete the building, but was awarded nothing for the work done but not finished. The first-instance judgment was upheld on appeal.

In *Sumpter*, Collins LJ said (at p. 676):

> There are cases in which, though the plaintiff has abandoned the performance of a contract, it is possible for him to raise the inference of a new contract to pay for the work done on a *quantum meruit* from the defendant's having taken the benefit of that work, but, in order that that may be done the circumstances must be such as to give an option to the defendant to take or not to take the benefit of the work done.

Therefore, such payment depends upon finding a new, implied contract, and such a contract will not be found where the non-breaching party has no real choice as to whether to accept the benefit. In the case of a half-finished building erected on the non-breaching party's own land, there is no choice over whether to accept the benefit; the building cannot be knocked down and 'returned' to the builder in any meaningful way. The builder could not recover for his part-performance. On the other hand, building materials not incorporated into the unfinished building could have been returned, so that a positive choice had been made to keep them. On this basis the builder in *Sumpter v Hedges* was entitled to payment representing the reasonable value of these building materials.

It has been suggested that the fact that payment for an accepted benefit depends upon the availability to the beneficiary of a real choice of whether to accept it, has made this rule too strict and that there should be more general recovery in respect of benefits conferred (Law Commission Report No. 121, *Pecuniary Restitution on Breach of Contract* (1983)). A case such as **Bolton v Mahadeva** [1972] 1 WLR 1009 (see **8.6.2.2**) is a striking modern example.

> The plaintiff had agreed to install central heating for a lump sum of £560. It proved to be defective, but the plaintiff would not put it right, which would have cost a further £174. The plaintiff was not allowed any payment for the work done, although he had conferred a net benefit on the defendant of £386.

Nevertheless, as was pointed out in a note of dissent in the Law Commission's report, the main value of classifying an obligation as entire is that it places in the hands of the other party powerful means of ensuring proper performance of the obligation, namely, the refusal of payment. Were that possibility to be removed, it might do harm to the interests of a significant number of people who are probably among the least likely to be willing to resort to litigation; that is, since most complex construction contracts are now designed for performance in stages, with interim payments, and so are severable, most contracts involving entire obligations will be between small builders and domestic consumers. Therefore, entire obligations, which may once have been thought to have been oppressive to the less powerful in society (see **Cutter v Powell** (1795) 6

TR 320), may now serve a useful purpose in terms of consumer protection. The recommendation in the Law Commission's report, which would have reversed cases like *Bolton v Mahadeva*, has not been implemented (see Burrows (1984) 47 MLR 76 for discussion of these issues).

8.6.4.2 Substantial performance

The rigours of the 'entire obligation' rule may also be avoided by means of the doctrine of substantial performance. **Where performance is incomplete or defective (the breach), but the extent of the failure to match the contractual undertaking is trivial by comparison with the primary obligations which have been satisfactorily performed, the court may be prepared to find that there has been substantial performance.** The result is to prevent the non-breaching party from treating the contract as repudiated, although that party will still be entitled to damages, or to a set-off against the contract price, for any loss caused by the fact that there has been a breach of contract.

> In *Hoenig v Isaacs* [1952] 2 All ER 176, the plaintiff had agreed to decorate and furnish the defendant's flat for a lump sum of £750. Some progress payments were made, but upon completion of the work £350 was outstanding. The defendant claimed that the plaintiff could not recover this amount since this was an 'entire contract' (by which it was meant that the obligation was entire) and the plaintiff was in breach in that some of his workmanship was defective. It was found as a fact that some of the work was defective, but that it would cost in total no more than £55 to put it right. It is not surprising, in these circumstances, that the Court of Appeal was unwilling to find that the plaintiff was not entitled to further payment. This very minor breach would have resulted in a large windfall for the defendant as a result of not having to make full payment under the contract. Therefore, the Court of Appeal held that the plaintiff had substantially performed the contract and could recover, less a deduction to cover the cost of remedying the defects.

The result was not to overlook the plaintiff's breach, but to limit the consequences of that breach to the creation of a secondary obligation to pay damages rather than to allow it to operate to excuse the defendant from performing his obligations.

Although this doctrine plays a useful role in mitigating the effects of the entire obligation rule, it is limited to minor failures to match the contractual undertaking. In *Bolton v Mahadeva* [1972] 1 WLR 1009, for example, the breach was far too serious to fall within the substantial performance rule.

There are clear similarities between the doctrine of substantial performance and the category of innominate terms, the consequences of breach of which depend upon how serious the breach was (see 8.5.5). This similarity is by no means coincidental. In *Hoenig v Isaacs*, Somervell LJ traced the origin of the substantial performance doctrine to the judgment of Lord Mansfield in *Boone v Eyre* (1779) 1 H Bl 273, 126 ER 160 and in *The Hansa Nord* [1976] QB 44, Lord Denning MR traced the origin of the innominate term to the same source.

8.7 Anticipatory breach

8.7.1 Identifying a breach by anticipation and assessing its nature

It has been assumed in the discussion to date that breach is constituted either by non-performance, or by defective (including late) performance once the time for performance stipulated in the contract has arrived. However, where one party indicates in advance of the time for performance, either expressly or by conduct, an intention not to perform, or to perform in a manner inconsistent with the contractual undertaking, special rules apply; or, at least, the usual rules apply somewhat differently to this particular situation. Such an indication is sometimes called 'anticipatory breach', but should more properly be referred to as 'breach by anticipatory repudiation', since it is the announcement of intention rather than the non-performance which is in advance of the stipulated time.

In *Yukong Line of Korea v Rendsburg Investments Corporation of Liberia* [1996] 2 Lloyd's Rep 604, Moore-Bick J (at p. 607) accepted the following clear principle:

> A renunciation of the contract by one party, prior to the time for performance is not itself a breach but it gives the other party, the injured party, the right to treat it as a breach in anticipation and thus to treat the contract as discharged immediately. In other words, if a person says he will not perform, the law allows the other to take him at his word and act accordingly.

The application of this doctrine is well illustrated by the early leading case of *Hochster v De La Tour* (1853) 2 E & B 678, 118 ER 922.

> The defendants had contracted to employ the plaintiff as a courier as from 1 June 1852. However, on 11 May the defendants informed the plaintiff that his services would not be required. The plaintiff immediately commenced an action for breach of contract. The defendants argued that the plaintiff was not entitled to a remedy unless he could show that on the due date for commencement of performance of his services he was ready and willing to perform his side of the contract (i.e. concurrent obligations: see 8.6.1). The court rejected that argument, saying that the plaintiff was free to choose whether to await the time for performance, in which case he must then be ready and willing to perform, or to treat the contract as immediately repudiated, in which case the concurrent condition was discharged.

The main justification given for the rule was that it was better for both parties that the plaintiff should avoid the wasteful expenditure of preparing for a performance which he had already been told would not be accepted. It is clear that the court took the view that the right to an immediate remedy was based on the fact of repudiation, and not on any notional 'acceleration' of the contract date for performance. Lord Campbell CJ explained this finding on the basis of an implied term that between the time of contracting and the due date for performance neither party would 'do anything to the prejudice of the other inconsistent with' the contractual relationship which had been created. This rule is confirmed by subsequent cases. For example, even where performance is contingent upon a condition that may never materialize, anticipatory repudiation entitles the other party to an immediate remedy (*Frost v Knight* (1872) LR 7 Ex 111). Nevertheless, if it is clear beyond doubt that the contingency cannot materialize, so that the repudiation cannot be said to deprive the other party of any reasonably expected performance, no remedy will be available (*The Mihalis Angelos* [1971] 1 QB 164). In *The Mihalis Angelos* Megaw LJ stated:

> In my view, where there is an anticipatory breach of contract, the breach is the repudiation once it has been accepted, and the other party is entitled to recover by way of damages the true value of the contractual rights which he has thereby lost; subject to his duty to mitigate. If the contractual rights which

he has lost were capable by the terms of the contract of being rendered either less valuable or valueless in certain events, and if it can be shown that those events were, at the date of the acceptance of the repudiation, predestined to happen, then in my view the damages which he can recover are not more than the true value, if any, of the rights which he has lost, having regard to those predestined events.

8.7.2 Identifying anticipatory repudiatory breach

In the case of breaches by anticipation, it is necessary to decide whether the anticipatory breach is repudiatory in order to determine whether there is an option to terminate or affirm the contract. Communicating to the other party that the other's performance is not wanted evidences a clear intention to renounce the contract so that in many instances the anticipatory breach will be repudiatory on this basis. However, in other instances the classification of terms broken may be relevant. In ***Decro-Wall International SA v Practitioners in Marketing Ltd*** [1971] 1 WLR 361, the question arose whether late payment on a particular instalment, where such late payment was known to be likely to be repeated in the future, entitled the other party to treat the whole contract as repudiated. The plaintiff argued that a single late payment, which was likely to be repeated, amounted to an anticipatory repudiation of the whole agreement. The Court of Appeal accepted that the late payment was a breach, and that there was every likelihood of that breach being repeated in the future, but did not accept that the plaintiff was thereby discharged from further performance under the contract. The term in question was not sufficiently serious to amount to repudiation if broken, thereby justifying bringing the whole contract to an end.

8.7.3 The election to terminate or affirm for anticipatory repudiatory breach

On the basis that the breach is repudiatory, the usual election will apply so that the non-breaching party will have the option of accepting the breach as terminating the contract, or affirming and awaiting performance on the contractual date set for that performance to begin (***Fercometal SARL v Mediterranean Shipping Co. SA*** [1989] AC 788).

However, the non-breaching party's right of election upon receiving notice of the other's intention not to continue with the contract is not completely without limit. There is a limitation on the power of the non-repudiating party to elect to affirm the contract.

8.7.3.1 Limitation on the power of the non-repudiating party to elect to affirm the contract

In ***White & Carter (Councils) Ltd v McGregor*** [1962] AC 413, the appellants had agreed with the respondents to advertise the respondents' business on litter bins to be supplied to local authorities. On the same day, the respondents repudiated the agreement, but the appellants went ahead, performed their side of the contract for the full three years agreed and claimed the contract price. The House of Lords (by a majority of 3:2) held that they were entitled to recover the contract price. There was no requirement that they minimize (or mitigate) their loss by finding an alternative business or product to advertise on the litter bins.

This decision has proved controversial because of the wastage involved. Nevertheless, in ***Reichman v Beveridge*** [2006] EWCA Civ 1659, [2007] Bus LR 412, a landlord-and-tenant case, the tenant argued that having left the premises three years into a five-year lease, there was a duty placed on the landlord to mitigate in a claim for rent arrears following the abandonment, e.g. by finding a replacement tenant, marketing the premises and not rejecting offers from prospective tenants. However, the Court of Appeal accepted that there was no such duty to mitigate in an action in debt (i.e., the action for arrears of rent).

In view of the objections to wastage inherent in the *White & Carter* principle, subsequent courts have seized upon statements by Lord Reid in order to limit the potential scope of the principle (indeed, Megarry J in *Hounslow v Twickenham* [1971] Ch 233 considered them to be part of the *ratio* in *White & Carter*).

 Key point

Lord Reid said that the general power to affirm the contract could not be exercised by a person who had no 'legitimate interest, financial or otherwise, in performing the contract rather than claiming damages'. However, it would not be sufficient that it was merely 'unreasonable' to affirm; something more than this was required.

Thus, the guilty party can avoid the operation of the principle in *White & Carter* by establishing that the non-breaching party has no legitimate interest in continuing performance.

Lord Reid's statement was adopted and applied in *Clea Shipping Corp. v Bulk Oil International Ltd, The Alaskan Trader* [1984] 1 All ER 129. The principle is clearly aimed at preventing very obvious wastage when the other party does not require performance.

On the facts in *The Alaskan Trader*, it was held that the owners had acted 'wholly unreasonably' when, despite the charterers' rejection of a two-year charter after one year of the term when the vessel had to undergo extensive repairs, the owners had carried out repairs and kept the vessel and the crew ready to receive sailing instructions from the charterers.

In *Ocean Marine Navigation Ltd v Koch Carbon Inc., The Dynamic* [2003] EWHC 1936 (Comm), [2003] 2 Lloyd's Rep 693, when the charterers failed to redeliver the vessel on time, the owner claimed to be entitled to the hire under the terms of the contract, rather than being limited to damages for repudiatory breach, It was therefore necessary to consider Lord Reid's limitation of 'legitimate interest' and whether it was possible to affirm. The judge considered that the rationale for this limitation is to avoid saddling 'the other party with an additional burden with no benefit to himself'. However, it was accepted that it was serious to 'fetter' the non-breaching party's right of election (by restricting the election to terminating and claiming damages). Therefore, the limitation needed to be confined to 'extreme cases' where damages would be an adequate remedy and where an election to affirm and go on with the contract would be 'wholly unreasonable'; the word 'wholly' indicating that this exception applied only in extreme cases.

The judge considered the following to be the applicable principles governing the exceptional case where affirmation will be prevented:

[23]…(i) The burden is on the contract-breaker to show that the innocent party has no legitimate interest in performing the contract rather than claiming damages. (ii) This burden is not discharged merely by showing that the benefit to the other party is small in comparison to the loss to the contract-breaker.

Thus, the burden of preventing the usual election from operating will be on the contract-breaker and it requires more than simply evidence that the benefit to the non-breaching party is relatively small.

In **Reichman v Beveridge** [2006] EWCA Civ 1659, [2007] Bus LR 412 (discussed above), the specific argument was that the landlord could not choose to affirm and seek monies due under the contract following the anticipatory breach by the tenant because damages would be an adequate remedy and it was 'wholly unreasonable' (relying on Lord Reid's first limitation) to elect to affirm. However, the Court of Appeal held that (1) it was not wholly unreasonable for an innocent landlord to refuse to take steps to find a new, replacement tenant; and (2) damages might not be an adequate remedy because if the landlords did accept the action as forfeiting (terminating) the lease and re-let but at a lower market rent than available under the terms of the lease, damages could not be recovered for loss of that rent, there being no authority in English law allowing a landlord to recover loss of *future* rent (i.e., from forfeiture to expiry of lease) from a former tenant. The landlord would therefore not be acting unreasonably in concluding that he should not terminate the lease because, if the future rent was lower, he might not be able to recover the lost rent as damages. The tenant was the party in breach and should not be able to transfer the consequences to the landlord, i.e. a duty to forfeit and find new tenants. Thus, while the court stressed the limited nature of the principle in **White & Carter**—namely, affirmation and recovery in debt with no duty to mitigate—it found it to be applicable to this situation involving a relationship of landlord and tenant.

8.7.4 Affirmation following anticipatory repudiation

An election to affirm the contract means that all the obligations of both contracting parties remain alive. In order to constitute an affirmation of the renunciation there must be evidence of a clear and unequivocal intention to continue with the contract (see the earlier discussion of affirmation in *Yukong Line Ltd of Korea v Rendsburg Investments Corporation of Liberia* [1996] 2 Lloyd's Rep 604; 8.4.2.2, which is authority for the fact that a request to the renunciating party to change its mind and honour its obligations on the contractual date will not suffice for affirmation).

8.7.4.1 Is the election irrevocable or can the non-breaching party change its mind before the contractual date set for performance?

One of the reasons for the strict approach to identification of affirmation as requiring clear and unequivocal evidence of an intention to continue with the contract, is frequently stated to be that the election is irrevocable, i.e. having affirmed, the non-breaching party cannot change its mind in the period between affirmation and the contractual date for performance (although following non-performance on the contractual date there would be a new opportunity to elect to terminate or affirm for that actual repudiatory breach). As stated by Lord Ackner in *Fercometal v Mediterranean Shipping* [1989] AC 788:

there is no third choice…to affirm the contract and yet be absolved from tendering further performance unless and until [the breaching party] gives reasonable notice that he is once again able and willing to perform.

However, although this represents the general principle, it has long been recognized that where the breach is a continuing one (i.e., it continues after affirmation) and is repudiatory, the fact of the earlier affirmation will not prevent the non-breaching party from choosing to terminate in the period prior to that date set for contractual performance. This was recognized by Thomas J (*obiter*) in *Stocznia Gdanska SA v Latvian Shipping Co.* [2001] 1 Lloyd's Rep 537, when he stated (at p. 565; para. 172):

> To require an innocent party, who has by pressing for the contract affirmed it, to wait until there is an actual breach by the party in breach before he can bring the contract to an end might well...have required that innocent party to engage in performance that is entirely pointless and wasteful as the party in breach would, when he became under an obligation to accept performance, refuse to do so.

This approach is in line with the general approach of preventing wasteful performance which the other party does not want. It is a different emphasis (and different result), as Thomas J recognized, to the approach taken by Colman J in the *Stocznia* litigation ([1997] 2 Lloyd's Rep 228). Colman J considered it important that, following affirmation, the breaching party needs to be able to rely on the fact that it will have a further opportunity to perform, whereas Thomas J's approach focused on the position of the non-breaching party who would otherwise be bound to continue performance when it was clear that it continued to be unwanted. It was the existence of these two differing positions that made this such a difficult area of law. In terms of policy, it was necessary to determine whether the law favoured allowing unrestricted opportunity for the breaching party to rescue initial non-performance (i.e., the possibility of curing the 'breach') at, or before, the contractual date for performance, or favoured recognizing the realities of the parties' positions in the light of recurrent breach and therefore avoided the incurring of wasteful additional expenditure. In the latter scenario, in essence, there is no realistic possibility of cure. Although the award of damages would be aimed at compensating the non-breaching party for the loss suffered, such a party is under no duty to mitigate following the affirmation and this does seem extremely wasteful where the indications of non-payment are so clear (*White & Carter (Councils) Ltd v McGregor* [1962] AC 413).

In *Stocznia Gdanska SA v Latvian Shipping Co. (No. 3)* [also known as *Stocznia Gdanska SA v Latvian Shipping Co. (Repudiation)*] [2002] EWCA Civ 889, [2002] 2 All ER (Comm) 768, [2002] 2 Lloyd's Rep 436, on appeal from the decision of Thomas J, the Court of Appeal recognized (again *obiter*) that once affirmation had occurred, in the event of a continuing anticipatory repudiation in the period prior to the contractual date set for performance, the non-breaching party could terminate despite the earlier affirmation. The Court of Appeal therefore preferred the approach taken by Thomas J (*obiter*) on this issue and considered that affirmation of an anticipatory repudiation related only to past breaches 'leaving open the question of continuing or renewed anticipatory breach' (per Rix LJ). Of course, as the Court of Appeal recognized, this does leave open the question of defining a continuing breach, especially the status of silence. It was recognized that in the context of a continuing duty to perform following affirmation, such silence might be 'a speaking silence'.

The Court of Appeal also recognized that there was a period **prior** to the election when the non-breaching party was making up its mind whether to terminate or affirm. In this period the contract and the right to terminate were both kept alive. As Rix LJ noted, this period cannot extend indefinitely and inaction over a sufficiently lengthy period may be held to constitute affirmation. In addition, since the contract remains alive until the non-breaching party terminates, the non-breaching party will be subject to the same risks that affect the non-breaching party who formally affirms (see below).

8.7.4.2 Risks to the non-breaching party following the decision to affirm after the other party's anticipatory repudiation

Following affirmation, the non-breaching party is exposed to a number of risks in the period between affirmation and the contractual date for performance, which might seriously affect its position and remedies following the earlier renunciation. The existence of these risks lends support to the position adopted by the Court of Appeal in *Stocznia* since, if the non-breaching party does have to accept these risks, it is arguable that in this period the ability to terminate should continue to exist where the renunciation is continuing.

The risks placed on the affirming party in the period between affirmation and the date for performance are not insignificant. For example:

1. If the non-breaching party is itself in breach of contract, that party cannot argue, at least not unless estoppel operates, that the initial renunciation by the other party operates as an excuse for its own subsequent breach.

In *Fercometal SARL v Mediterranean Shipping Co. SA, The Simona* [1989] AC 788, charterers of a ship gave notice of cancellation of the contract which was not in accordance with the terms of the charterparty and amounted to repudiation. The shipowners did not accept the repudiation, but instead gave notice of readiness to load. This notice complied with the terms of the charterparty and constituted an affirmation, but was false, and so in turn constituted a breach. The charterers consequently rejected the notice and gave further notice of cancellation, which on this occasion complied with the terms of the charterparty. The shipowners sued the charterers. The House of Lords rejected this claim. Once the contract was treated as being still in force, it was 'kept alive for the benefit of both parties', and the party affirming could not both keep it alive and seek to justify his own non-performance by reference to the earlier repudiation.

2. Similarly, if the contract is frustrated (see **Chapter 12**) in the period between the affirmation and the due date for performance, the frustration will discharge the contract and the non-breaching party will lose the remedy of damages for the breach.

In *Avery v Bowden* (1855) E & B 714, the master of a ship had been told in advance of the last possible date for loading that there was no cargo available, which may have amounted to repudiation. He elected to affirm the contract, and remained in port hoping that a cargo would eventually be provided. Before the last possible date for performance of the contract, the contract was frustrated by the outbreak of the Crimean War, thus depriving the shipowners of a remedy they might have had for the failure to provide a cargo, had that repudiation been accepted as terminating the contract.

8.7.4.3 Limitation on the ability to claim the contract price having affirmed

In *White & Carter*, Lord Reid also discussed a further limitation (in addition to the legitimate interest requirement before being able to affirm) on the principle in that case. However, it is a limitation on the ability of the non-breaching party to claim the contract price, rather than a limitation on that party's ability to affirm following a breach by anticipatory repudiation. In this sense it is a different limitation to the need to have a 'legitimate interest' in continuing performance.

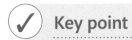

✓ Key point

This second limitation requires that the affirming party must be able to continue with their own performance of the contract without the cooperation of the breaching party in order to be able to claim the contract price (otherwise the affirming party will be limited to a remedy in damages).

Cooperation in this context includes both active and passive cooperation of the renouncing party (e.g., ***Hounslow London Borough Council v Twickenham Garden Developments Ltd*** [1971] Ch 233: following renunciation by the local authority employers, contractors had no right to insist on continuing to perform the contract because the work was being done on local authority property and they were unable to gain access to the site without the local authority's permission).

In the context of a sale of goods contract, the seller can bring a claim for the price only where property in the goods has passed from the seller to the buyer. This in turn is determined by the principles contained in ss. 17 and 18 of the SGA 1979. If the sale is for specific goods, property passes immediately to the buyer (s. 18, r. 1). Specific goods are 'identified and agreed upon at the time the contract is made' (SGA 1979, s. 61). On the other hand, if the sale is for 'unascertained or future goods by description', property cannot pass until the goods are 'unconditionally appropriated to the contract' with the buyer's consent (s. 18, r. 5). Unascertained goods include generic goods such as 1,000 gallons of diesel. Future goods are defined as 'goods to be manufactured or acquired by the seller after the making of the contract of sale', and so would include, for example, a yacht to be manufactured to the buyer's specification. Therefore, in the case of unascertained or future goods, the buyer who has indicated in advance that it does not want the goods, can prevent the seller who affirms from being entitled to claim the contract price because the buyer's assent is required for property in the goods to pass. In a practical sense, the buyer would refuse to accept delivery and therefore prevent property in the goods from passing (per Lloyd J in *The Alaskan Trader*).

However, the restriction in *White & Carter* that a claimant will be limited to a remedy in damages where he is unable to perform without the cooperation of the contract-breaker, applies only where the performance which has been prevented by the breach was a pre-condition to the payment obligation, i.e. the performance obligation was entire. In ***Ministry of Sound (Ireland) Ltd v World Online Ltd*** [2003] EWHC 2178 (Ch), [2003] 2 All ER (Comm) 823, the non-breaching party could perform only if CDs were supplied by the party in breach. However, since there was no link between the required performance and the right to receive the contractual payment, and since the contract had been affirmed and not terminated for repudiatory breach, in principle the contract term providing for payment could be enforced by a claim in debt. Thus, as there was no link between performance and payment it did not matter that performance was impossible without cooperation.

For further discussion of the *White & Carter* principle and its limitations, see Carter, Phang, and Phang, 'Performance following repudiation: Legal and economic interests' (1999) 15 JCL 97.

8.7.5 Accepting the anticipatory repudiatory breach as terminating the contract

As discussed at 8.4.2.1, it must be clear to the party in breach that the non-breaching party has accepted the conduct as terminating the contract; and although it is possible as a matter of law for this to occur simply by the non-breaching party failing to perform its own contractual obligations, whether it will do so is 'a question of fact depending on the particular contractual relationship and the particular circumstances of the case' (see generally *Vitol SA v Norelf Ltd, The Santa Clara* [1996] AC 800 at p. 811 per Lord Steyn: discussed at 8.4.2.1). In practice, however, it would seem to depend on whether the non-breaching party's failure to perform its own contractual obligations is explicable to a reasonable person only on the basis that the non-breaching party has accepted the repudiation as terminating the contract.

If the non-breaching party has terminated following the renunciation, it is clear that he can claim damages from that time and does not need to wait until the date fixed for performance under the contract (*Hochster v De La Tour* (1853) 2 E & B 678: for facts see 8.7.1). However, the non-breaching party would be under a duty to mitigate its loss as from the date of termination.

8.7.6 The risk of overreacting to a breach

A party faced with what it thinks is an actual or anticipatory repudiation must take careful stock before acting. If the non-breaching party is mistaken in thinking that the other party has repudiated the contract, its own purported election to accept this action as discharging future obligations may itself amount to a (anticipatory) repudiation (*Federal Commerce and Navigation Ltd v Molena Alpha Inc.* [1979] AC 757).

Some doubt was cast on this proposition by the House of Lords in *Woodar Investment Development Ltd v Wimpey Construction (UK) Ltd* [1980] 1 WLR 277. Lord Wilberforce said that a party's mistake as to their rights, in the absence of bad faith, would not lead the court to regard a purported termination of the contract as a repudiation. However, the other party may be unable to tell whether an apparent repudiation stems from a mistake as to rights, or from a simple decision not to proceed with the contract. *Woodar v Wimpey* is thus a source of considerable uncertainty in the law, and may best be regarded as limited to the situation in which the question is whether the conditions of an express termination clause have been met, when the other party would usually be able to determine the reason for the termination. Where the purported termination is for an alleged breach of condition (or its equivalent), the risk should remain with the party making the election.

Regrettably, this argument was not accepted by the Privy Council in *Vaswani v Italian Motors (Sales and Services) Ltd* [1996] 1 WLR 270. It was accepted that merely to assert a claim based on an erroneous but good faith interpretation of the contract would not amount to a repudiation. However, there would necessarily be a repudiation if the assertion went beyond any position consistent with being willing to continue with the contract. In many instances a party who, believing that a repudiatory breach has occurred, wishes to escape from the contract, will make it perfectly clear that they want no more to do with the contract (see *Hong Kong Fir Shipping Co. Ltd v Kawasaki Kisen Kaisha Ltd* [1962] 2 QB 26, and *Cehave NV v Bremer Handelsgesellschaft mbh, The Hansa Nord* [1976] QB 44, where the goods were wrongfully rejected). Lord Woolf in *Vaswani* expressly relied upon the statement of Lord Wilberforce in *Woodar v Wimpey* that 'repudiation is a drastic conclusion which should only be held to arise in clear cases of a refusal, in a matter going to the root of the contract, to perform contractual obligations'.

However, in *Vaswani*, the mistaken interpretation of the contract resulted in a demand for a purchase price significantly higher than that agreed originally or permissible under a price variation clause. It was not inconsistent with a willingness to continue the contract, apparently because the party making the excessive claim never indicated that it would be pointless to tender the correct sum (although they did say that failure to pay the amount claimed would result in loss of a deposit). Although the desire not to visit the drastic consequences of repudiation on a mistaken but good-faith party is understandable, it fails to take account of the altogether more difficult position of the other party, who may not be in a position to differentiate between mistaken good faith and repudiation.

To remove some of the uncertainty from that risk, English law would do well to imitate the provision of the American Uniform Commercial Code (UCC) which enables a party who has reasonable ground for insecurity with respect to the other's performance to demand an assurance of the performance due, and if it is not forthcoming within a reasonable time then to treat the contract as repudiated (UCC §2–609). There are similar provisions in the UNIDROIT *Principles of International Commercial Contracts* (Art. 7.3.4), the *Principles of European Contract Law* (PECL) (Art. 8:105), and the *Draft Common Frame of Reference* (DCFR) III-3:505. Such a procedure might have avoided some of the difficulty in ***Alfred Toepfer International GmbH v Itex Itagrani Export SA*** [1993] 1 Lloyd's Rep 360.

> The buyer agreed to buy one cargo of 22,000 tonnes of maize. However, the sub-buyers had nominated a ship that could carry only part of this as they had already ordered it to load some cargo beforehand at another port. The seller treated this as a repudiation by the buyer. However, the judge disagreed. The fact that the sub-buyers had nominated a ship that was unable to load the full cargo did not establish that the buyer had renunciated (or repudiated) the contract due to an inability to perform. It only established that the buyer **might** not be able to perform.

The seller's position, which was to say the least difficult, would have been improved had it been able to force the buyer to say what action it proposed to take.

The position of a party confronted by conduct which is ambiguous and may amount to a repudiation, is improved a little by the common-sense approach of Moore-Bick J in ***Yukong Line Ltd v Rendsburg Investments Corporation*** [1996] 2 Lloyd's Rep 604. On this approach, a party's legal position should not be adversely affected if the first steps taken are to verify the precise intentions of the other, since this will not necessarily amount to treating the breach as repudiatory and electing to affirm. In addition, the decision in ***Stocznia Gdanska SA v Latvian Shipping Co. (No. 3)*** [2002] EWCA Civ 889, [2002] 2 All ER (Comm) 768, also assists the position of the non-breaching party faced with the election to terminate or affirm since it recognizes the existence of a period in which the non-breaching party can make up its mind on the election. However, it will not be possible to delay unreasonably without risking a finding of affirmation.

Further reading

Classification of terms

Bojczuk, 'When is a condition not a condition?' [1987] JBL 353.

Girvin, 'Time charter overlap: Determining legitimacy and the operation of repudiatory breach of contract' [1995] JBL 200.

Treitel, 'Types of contractual terms' in *Some Landmarks of Twentieth Century Contract Law* (Clarendon Press, 2002).

Weir, 'The buyer's right to reject defective goods' [1976] CLJ 33.

Repudiatory breach and the election

Brownsword, 'Retrieving reasons, retrieving rationality? A new look at the right to withdraw for breach of contract' (1992) 5 JCL 83, **or** Adams and Brownsword, *Key Issues in Contract* (Butterworths, 1995), Ch. 6, 'Breach and withdrawal'.

Hedley, 'Eloquent silences and reasonable people' [1996] CLJ 430.

Law Commission, *Consumer Remedies for Faulty Goods*, Consultation Paper, LCCP No. 188 (2008) and Report, Law Com. No. 317, Cm. 7725 (2009), <http://www.lawcom.gov.uk/consumer_remedies.htm>.

Reynolds, 'Warranty, condition and fundamental term' (1963) 79 LQR 534.

Reynolds, 'Discharge of contract by breach' (1981) 97 LQR 541.

Shea, 'Discharge from performance of contracts by failure of condition' (1979) 42 MLR 623.

Treitel, 'Affirmation after repudiatory breach' (1998) 114 LQR 22.

Breach of entire obligation as repudiatory

Burrows, 'Law Commission Report on Pecuniary Restitution on Breach of Contract' (1984) 47 MLR 76.

Law Commission, Report No. 121, *Pecuniary Restitution on Breach of Contract* (1983).

Anticipatory breach

Carter, Phang, and Phang, 'Performance following repudiation: Legal and economic interests' (1999) 15 JCL 97.

Coote, 'Breach, anticipatory breach, or the breach anticipated?' (2007) 123 LQR 503.

Liu, 'Inferring future breach: Towards a unifying test of anticipatory breach of contract' [2007] CLJ 574.

Tabachnik, 'Anticipatory breach of contract' [1972] CLP 149.

Part 3

Enforcement of contractual obligations

Overview of the law on remedies for breach of contract

(a) The notion of enforcement: The compensation principle

The definition of contracts as 'legally enforceable agreements' (see **1.1**) assumes that mechanisms exist for the enforcement of those agreements which are identified by the law as creating legally enforceable performance obligations. The mechanisms of enforcement of contractual obligations are the subject of the next two chapters (**Chapters 9** and **10**). **Chapter 11** examines the question of enforcement by or on behalf of third parties and so is related to the general enforcement question.

In fact, very few contractual obligations are 'enforced' in the sense of compelling actual performance, or in the sense of deterring non-performance by the threat and imposition of penalties.

Although compulsion and penalty probably represent the popular notion of enforcement, the basic legal means of enforcement of contractual obligations is by compensation for loss caused; in other words, by the payment of damages for breach of contract (see **Chapter 9**). It is enforcement in the sense that the party who should have performed but did not, is compelled to pay the extra cost of obtaining substitute performance.

(b) No punishment for breach of contractual obligations

English law has traditionally denied any role for punishment in the enforcement of contracts. Although theorists have at times attributed the binding force of contractual undertakings to the moral obligation to keep one's promises, the law does not seek to punish promise-breakers, just as it is not directly concerned to enforce morality. Punishment is regarded as an instrument of social control, so that the law punishes criminals and may in limited circumstances award punitive (or 'exemplary') damages against those who are particularly callous or deliberate in the commission of torts (*Rookes v Barnard* [1964] AC 1129 and *Cassell & Co. Ltd v Broome* [1972] AC 1027), although even in tort the scope of recovery of exemplary damages is very limited (see *AB v South West Water Services Ltd* [1993] 1 All ER 609). It is unlikely that the decision in *Kuddus v Chief Constable of Leicestershire Constabulary* [2001] UKHL 29, [2002] 2 AC 122 will have extended the possibility of recovery of exemplary damages in a tort claim to any significant extent. There is little scope for such social control in English contract law, however; the focus is rather on enabling private transactions, and in the last resort on remedying grievances.

In addition, the award of exemplary damages in a contract claim would defeat the theory of efficient breach. For these reasons, among others, there is no penalty for breach of contract (*Perera v Vandiyar* [1953] 1 All ER 1109).

Where breach occurs but no loss is sustained, in most circumstances only nominal damages will be awarded (*Surrey County Council v Bredero Homes Ltd* [1993] 1 WLR 1361; although see **10.6.2** and **10.6.4**). The *Bredero Homes* case reveals essential truths about remedies for breach of contract. The breach was deliberate, and made with the intention of increasing the profitability of the transaction, which intention was duly realized. It might be thought that such conduct would invite censure from the courts, but, crucially, the non-breaching party could not be shown to have suffered a loss. The Court of Appeal was unanimous in refusing any award of damages, although the House of Lords in *Attorney-General v Blake* [2001] 1 AC 268, has since held that in very exceptional circumstances, it may be possible to obtain an order whereby the party in breach has to account for profits made as a result of the breach. The exact scope of this principle in *Attorney-General v Blake* is unclear but, because of the specific facts of the case, it would appear that it was not intended to have more general application and should be very tightly circumscribed. Nevertheless, there were signs in subsequent case law of attempts to test the limits of the discretion to award an account of profits in the commercial context (see *Esso Petroleum Co. Ltd v Niad Ltd*, unreported, 22 November 2001, *Experience Hendrix LLC v PPX Enterprises Inc.* [2003] EWCA Civ 323, [2003] 1 All ER (Comm) 830, [2003] EMLR 25, and *Lane v O'Brien Homes Ltd* [2004] EWHC 303 (QB), unreported, 5 February 2004). The relationship between the *Wrotham Park* principle and the account of profits in *Blake* has proved particularly controversial of late and, in particular, the suggestion that an account of profits is a compensatory remedy has meant some rethinking of the law in this area (*World Wide Fund for Nature v World Wrestling Federation Entertainment Inc.* [2007] EWCA Civ 286, [2007] Bus LR 1252, [2008] 1 WLR 445 (see **10.6.4.3**).

Another aspect of the non-punitive approach to contractual damages is the policy of the courts denying enforcement to contractual clauses purporting to impose penalties for non-performance (see **9.10.2**).

(c) Substitute performance rather than compelling actual performance

The political and economic liberalisms which were the foundations upon which nineteenth-century contract law was built (see **1.4.2.2**) were inconsistent with the idea of compelling a person to perform a contract against their will in circumstances in which suitable equivalent alternative performance was available. In the case of contracts for goods or services in which there is an available market, the non-breaching party can obtain substitute performance. The price the party in breach must pay for not being compelled to perform against their will is the extra cost of obtaining that substitute performance.

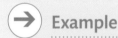 Example

. . . .

If A promises to cut B's hedge on Tuesday for £25, but then arranges to cut C's lawn on the same day for £30, making performance of the contract with B impossible, there is undoubtedly a breach of contract. A will not be punished, neither will A be forced to revoke the contract with C in order to perform the contract with B. B must find someone else to cut the hedge, and if the market price for the services of a hedge-cutter is higher than £25, A must pay the difference.

The contract has been enforced only in the sense that at the end of the day B will have received the promised contractual performance at the cost to him agreed in his contract with A.

This result can be justified in terms both of the relationship between the parties and of economic efficiency (or the so-called 'theory of efficient breach').

• No doubt B would not be happy to accept A's services, since B believes A to be unreliable; equally, it may be impossible to force A to perform at A's best if it would amount to performance given against A's will. In these circumstances substitute performance is probably more acceptable to both.

• Alternatively, if A is to pay B's extra costs, B will be no worse off by allowing A not to perform, while A may be better off if B's extra cost is less than the extra profit A will make on A's contract with C. That is, if B's substitute performance costs £28 then A must pay B £3 for B to be no worse off. A makes an extra profit, by contracting with C for £30, so that after paying B A will be £2 better off.

For one party to be better off while no party is worse off is, in economic terms, an efficient result. (This simple example assumes that B incurred no costs in finding substitute performance.)

It is therefore only where substitute performance is irrelevant or inadequate that the law will compel actual performance. Substitute performance is irrelevant where the contractual obligation that is unperformed is to pay the price (see 10.1), since compulsion of payment of the price is no different from compulsion to pay damages of the cost of substitute performance. However, substitute performance will be inadequate where the promised contractual performance is in some way unique, or at least exceedingly rare, so that substitution is impossible.

• For example, a contract to sell the 'Mona Lisa' is a contract for a unique item, and if breached the buyer could obtain no substitute. In such circumstances damages are inappropriate, and the court will compel actual performance (see 10.2).

• Substitute performance may also be inadequate where the contractual undertaking is in the form of a promise to refrain from some activity.

 Example

> If A pays £50 to B, A's neighbour, in return for B's promise to refrain from making loud noises during the period while A is revising for an examination, calculating A's loss should B disturb A's work may be impossible. A needs to be able actually to prevent the disturbance occurring.

Again, in such circumstances damages are inappropriate, and the court will compel actual performance (see 10.3).

(d) Compensation for losses: The interest to be compensated?

Except in those cases where substitute performance is irrelevant or inadequate, the method of enforcement of contractual obligations is by compensation for losses caused by their breach.

The claimant may have suffered loss in any of three broad areas of interest, and the interest to be compensated determines the measure of damages payable.

• The **expectation interest** refers to whatever is necessary to put the claimant into the position the claimant would have been in had the contract been performed. Compensation for lost profit is compensation of an expectation interest, as is payment of damages for the cost of substitute performance.

• The **reliance interest** refers to whatever is necessary to put the claimant into the position the claimant was in before the contract was made rather than seeking to compensate for loss of an anticipated gain.

Compensation for expenditure made towards performance of the contract is compensation of this reliance interest. This reliance interest is the same as the standard measure of damages for tort.

• The **restitutionary interest** refers to the restoration to the claimant of a benefit conferred on the defendant to which the defendant is not entitled. The basis for this recovery is that the defendant would otherwise be unjustly enriched at the claimant's expense. Compensation for work done in anticipation of entering a contract, which in fact never materializes, is compensation of a restitutionary interest, as is the return of an advance payment under a contract which is void for mistake, or discharged by frustration.

Damages for breach of contract

Summary of the issues

Damages are available as of right on proof of breach of contract. This chapter examines the aims of contractual damages and the factors influencing their quantification.

• **Contractual damages are compensatory and not punitive, i.e. they aim to compensate the claimant for losses suffered, as opposed to seeking to punish the defendant.**

• **The compensatory aim of contractual damages is to put the claimant in the position he would have been in had the contract been properly performed and had the breach not occurred.** This translates to an aim of seeking to protect the expectation of performance (known as the 'expectation interest' or the 'performance interest'), although in some circumstances the courts may award damages to compensate for reliance interest damages (expenditure wasted as a result of the breach).

• **It is important to correctly identify the expectation interest by reference to the loss suffered by the claimant on breach and to recognize that this loss may extend beyond the financial interest in performance to include purely subjective expectations in performance (the 'consumer surplus').** This lost expectation is normally measured in terms of difference in value between what was expected and what was received but if the claimant had a non-financial interest in performance such a measure may not properly compensate and so it is important to consider the circumstances in which the courts are prepared to award cost-of-cure damages. As there are dangers in the award of cost of cure (or replacement) damages, the courts have developed principles determining the availability of such an award in an attempt to balance the competing considerations.

• **Non-pecuniary losses are generally not recoverable in a claim for breach of contract. However, in some circumstances a modest sum may be awarded for the disappointment suffered through not receiving the promised performance.** These exceptional circumstances are assessed.

• There are other limitations on the claimant's ability to be fully compensated such as the 'duty' to take reasonable steps to minimize loss (**mitigation**), the fact that losses which are too remote a consequence of the breach cannot be recovered (**remoteness**), and the possibility that a damages award may be apportioned to take account of the claimant's own negligence (**contributory negligence**).

• **The parties may agree in advance on the damages to be payable in the event of breach (agreed damages clauses).** However, in certain circumstances the courts will strike down these clauses if they are penal. It is necessary to distinguish those clauses operating as penalties from those which constitute enforceable liquidated damages. In addition, there are a number of anomalies surrounding the operation of the penalty rule.

9.1 Basis of recovery of damages in a contract claim

In *Photo Production Ltd v Securicor Transport Ltd* [1980] AC 827 (see 7.4.3 and 8.4), Lord Diplock said at p. 849:

> Every failure to perform a primary obligation is a breach of contract. The secondary obligation on the part of the contract-breaker to which it gives rise by implication of the common law is to pay monetary compensation to the other party for the loss sustained by him in consequence of the breach...

Thus, damages for breach of contract are available as of right, on proof of breach. In some circumstances breach may also give the non-breaching party the option of bringing the outstanding primary obligations to a premature end (see 8.4.2). In this chapter, however, we shall consider the rules applicable to the secondary obligation to pay compensation (damages) for loss caused which arises whenever there is a breach of contract. Essentially we will be examining how these damages are quantified.

9.1.1 Compensation for loss suffered

The basic aim of contractual damages is to compensate the claimant for the loss the claimant has suffered as a result of the breach of contract. Therefore, in calculating these damages the traditional focus has been placed on the claimant's loss.

A claimant cannot recover more than his actual loss; and if the claimant suffers no loss, he will be constrained to recovering only nominal damages, although see the discussion in 11.7.3, concerning the ability to recover for substantial losses suffered by a third party.

9.1.2 Can the profit resulting from a deliberate breach of contract be recovered?

The compensatory principle also means that, since it is not part of the loss suffered by the claimant, the claimant cannot, as a general rule, recover any profit made by the defendant even if that profit resulted from a deliberate breach of contract by the defendant (*Surrey County Council v Bredero Homes Ltd* [1993] 1 WLR 961; although see the discussion at 10.6.4 relating to the possible recovery of profits and the decision in *Attorney-General v Blake* [2001] 1 AC 268). This has since been interpreted as a compensatory remedy rather than restitutionary (*WWF World Wide Fund for Nature v World Wrestling Federation Entertainment Inc.* [2007] EWCA Civ 286, [2008] 1 WLR 445, [2007] Bus LR 1252, [2008] 1 WLR 445.

9.1.3 **Are exemplary or punitive damages recoverable in a contract claim?**

Since contractual damages are compensatory rather than punitive, exemplary damages have not been available in a claim in contract (***Addis v Gramophone Co. Ltd*** [1909] AC 488). In *Rookes v Barnard* [1964] AC 1129, the House of Lords had limited the ability to recover exemplary damages in tort to three situations:

- oppressive conduct by government officials
- where the defendant's conduct is calculated to make a profit from his wrong
- where statute expressly so provides.

Until *Kuddus v Chief Constable of Leicestershire Constabulary* [2001] UKHL 29, [2002] 2 AC 122 it had also been the case that exemplary damages in a tort action were available only where the cause of action was one where exemplary damages had been permitted prior to the decision in *Rookes v Barnard*. In *Kuddus* this position was relaxed. However, any possible expansion of recovery of exemplary damages on this tortious basis should not extend to breach of contract claims. In ***Johnson v Unisys Ltd*** [2001] UKHL 13, [2003] 1 AC 518, it was stated quite clearly that such damages cannot be awarded in a claim for breach of contract and the Law Commission in its report, *Aggravated, Exemplary and Restitutionary Damages*, No. 247 (1997) did not suggest any reform of the law with respect to recovery in a claim based on breach of contract. In July 2009 the Ministry of Justice published a response to its consultation on this question ('The Law on Damages', CP 9/07) rejecting possible legislative intervention and confirming the government's wish to see no further encroachment on the distinction between punishment and compensation.

The decision in ***Attorney-General v Blake*** [2001] 1 AC 268, discussed at **10.6.4** (allowing an account of profits resulting from a breach of contract although limited to exceptional circumstances), cannot be taken as permitting general recovery of punitive damages in contract since the decision must be given a narrow interpretation (see discussion at **10.6.4.1**) and it is considered that in *Blake* Lord Nicholls was referring to the award as being compensatory (***WWF World Wide Fund for Nature v World Wrestling Federation Entertainment Inc.*** [2007] EWCA Civ 286, [2008] 1 WLR 445, [2007] Bus LR 1252, [2008] 1 WLR 445).

To award punitive damages in the context of a contractual claim would circumvent the 'theory of efficient breach', i.e. that, put simply, it makes commercial sense to allow a party to determine whether it is in its commercial interests to continue with performance or to breach the contract and pay compensatory damages. Therefore, to force performance under threat of the punishment of exemplary damages would detract from this theory of commercial efficiency. (This is discussed and explained in **Part 3(c)**, above.) In any event, it is possible in some circumstances to recover for non-pecuniary losses in a contractual claim so that compensation is recoverable for a wider category of loss than the purely economic.

9.2 **The aim of compensation**

The basic rule of recovery of compensation in the case of breach of contract is that the non-breaching party is to be put into the position it would have been in had the contract been performed as agreed (*Robinson v Harman* (1848) 1 Ex 850; and see ***Surrey County Council v Bredero Homes Ltd*** [1993] 1 WLR 961). This principle was also confirmed as fundamental in ***Golden Strait***

Corporation v Nippon Yusen Kubishika Kaisha, The Golden Victory [2007] UKHL 12, [2007] Bus LR 997, [2007] 2 WLR 691, per Lord Bingham (at [9]), Lord Scott (at [29]), and Lord Carswell (at [57]).

9.2.1 Compensation for what? Lost expectation

This general measure of loss was described above (**Part 3(d)**) as compensating the claimant's expectation interest, i.e. compensation for loss of the benefit of the promised performance (the expected gain under the contract).

Lost expectation may therefore comprise loss of a profit which would have been made but for the breach.

 Example

If A bought machinery from B with the intention of making goods and selling them at a profit to C, then B's failure to deliver the machines will result in A losing the profit to be made on the sale of the goods.

Subject to certain limitations (see **9.9**), quantification of such a loss should not present great difficulty.

However, lost expectation may also occur without any intention to profit from the contract, and in those circumstances quantification of the loss is more difficult. It may be measured either by reference to the diminished value to the claimant (see **9.3.2.1**), or by reference to the cost of achieving the agreed performance (see **9.3.3**).

9.2.2 Compensation for what? Wasted expenditure

In some cases the claimant may prefer, or may be obliged (see **9.3.4**), to recover compensation for his reliance interest (see **9.4**), such as out-of-pocket expenses arising from his performance of the contract, and other expenses which it was intended would be recovered if the contract had been performed.

There is no reason why both lost profit and out-of-pocket expenses should not both be recovered, provided there is no double compensation (see **9.5**).

9.2.3 Securing restitution of benefits conferred

Compensation of the claimant's restitutionary interest, i.e. restoration of a benefit conferred by the claimant on the defendant on the basis that otherwise the defendant would be unjustly enriched at the claimant's expense, is discussed at **10.4**.

9.3 Quantification of loss: Lost expectation

As discussed above, damages to compensate for expectation loss seek to protect the expectation of performance resulting from the promise by compensating for the loss of that expectation.

However, in order to achieve this compensation it is necessary to identify the expectation which has been lost and then to quantify it. Some of the problems in the case law can be attributed to attempts to achieve the quantification without first identifying the loss.

9.3.1 The scope of the performance interest

As will be discussed in more detail later, the 'performance interest' or contractual expectation is based on identifying and assessing the value of certain 'benefits' which the claimant expected to receive under the contract. These benefits may not be limited to an expectation of financial benefits but can include anticipated subjective benefits (known as 'the consumer surplus', see the discussion of *Ruxley Electronics v Forsyth* [1996] AC 344: see **9.3.3**; and *Farley v Skinner (No. 2)* [2001] UKHL 49, [2002] 2 AC 732: see **9.9.4.4**).

Damages for breach of contract should give effect to this 'performance interest' by awarding damages to compensate for:

- the loss of the expected financial benefit
- the loss of 'subjective benefits' or preferences which are considered to be part of the contractual expectation: see *Ruxley Electronics v Forsyth* and discussion in *Farley v Skinner (No. 2)*. (This is an aspect of the larger question of the circumstances in which it is possible to recover for non-pecuniary losses—see the discussion at **9.9.4**—e.g., as part of an expectation of contractual 'enjoyment' or peace of mind and recognition of loss of amenity.)

However, the performance interest may also include the interest in getting the performance itself, which should automatically result in a cost of cure measure (subject to reasonableness) to ensure that the performance is achieved. This can be distinguished from the interest in securing the benefits of the contract. See the discussion of Lord Griffiths's 'broad ground' in *Linden Gardens Trust Ltd v Lenesta Sludge Disposals Ltd* [1994] 1 AC 85 at p. 96 (see **11.7.3.2**). The 'broad ground' argument focuses only on the fact that the contracting party has not received 'the bargain for which he contracted'. For example, Lord Griffiths stated that a husband who contracts for repairs to his wife's house has suffered loss because he does not receive the bargain for which he contracted, although in terms of traditional losses, since the husband has no proprietary interest in the property, he suffers no tangible loss as a result of the breach.

Although the award in *Ruxley Electronics v Forsyth* was a loss-of-amenity award (loss of enjoyment), it seems clear that counsel for Mr Forsyth's primary argument was that Mr Forsyth did not get the performance he had contracted for, i.e. a pool of the required depth, so that cost-of-cure damages were required as the applicable remedy. This is supported by the evidence relating to the fact that Mr Forsyth did not dive and so his personal loss of enjoyment would have been minimal. Although rejecting the availability of this award on the facts, the House of Lords wanted to find some way to recognize the non-performance (failure to construct a pool of the depth set out in the contractual specification). This approach receives some support from the approach taken by Lord Scott in *Farley v Skinner (No. 2)* since Lord Scott distinguished *Ruxley* from the usual distress claims on the basis that the distress was not treated as a consequential loss following from the breach. In *Ruxley* the loss was treated as a loss of the entitlement to performance so that it involves a 'deprivation of contractual benefit' (although compare this with the decision of the High Court in *Birse Construction Ltd v Eastern Telegraph Co. Ltd* [2004] EWHC 2512 (TCC), [2004] 47 EG 164 (CS)).

Although there is additional support for this 'broad ground' in the speeches of Lords Goff and Millett in *Alfred McAlpine Construction Ltd v Panatown* [2001] 1 AC 518—and possibly in that of Lord Browne-Wilkinson (discussed at **11.7.3.2**)—the existence of such a performance interest entitling the contracting party to receive damages in the event of non-performance has yet to be fully accepted. Accordingly, the emphasis in this chapter is placed on loss caused to the claimant through the non-fulfilment of the promised expectation (benefits)—pecuniary and non-pecuniary losses, i.e. losses flowing from the breach rather than for the **fact** of the breach.

9.3.2 Calculation of expectation loss

- Expectation loss will normally be compensated on the basis of the difference in value measure, i.e. the difference in value between the promised performance and the actual performance. Difference in value damages are often calculated using the 'market price' rule. However, where there is no market, these damages will be calculated as the difference between the value of the performance as contracted for and the actual value of the performance received.

- Alternatively, in some circumstances, it may be possible to recover the cost of achieving the expected performance ('cost of cure').

9.3.2.1 Difference in value

1. The market-price rule

Identifying the market

Where the goods are freely available upon demand, there is no difficulty in identifying a 'market' and the price at which goods may be bought or sold. However, more limited circumstances may constitute a market. In **Shearson Lehman Hutton Inc. v Maclaine Watson & Co. Ltd (No. 2)** [1990] 3 All ER 723, Webster J said, in the context of a breach by the buyer (non-acceptance), that a market would exist in which to sell the goods where either: (i) the seller actually offers the goods for sale and there is one actual buyer on that day at a fair price or (ii) there is no actual offer for sale but there are sufficient traders potentially in touch with each other to evidence a market in which the actual or notional seller could, if they wished, sell the goods. The market price of the goods (which represents their real value) is then said to be either: (i) the 'fair price' obtained by the actual sale or (ii) in the absence of an actual sale, a fair price for the total quantity of goods sold on the market on the relevant date, or such price as might be negotiated 'within a few days with persons who were members of the market on that day and who could not be taken into account as potential buyers on the day in question only because of difficulties of communication'.

Assessment of damages for the seller's breach (non-delivery of goods) in a contract for the sale of goods: Sale of Goods Act (SGA) 1979, s. 51(3)

- The law assumes that the buyer will mitigate its loss (see **9.9.3**) by immediately going to the market and buying similar goods from another source.
- The buyer will then suffer a loss only if he has to pay more for the substitute goods on the open market than he had originally contracted to pay.
- The buyer's damages will, therefore, be assessed by subtracting the contract price from the market price at the time of breach (SGA 1979, s. 51(3)).
- Where the buyer had anticipated making a profit on the transaction by reselling the goods at a price higher than the market price, the buyer's damages are nevertheless restricted to the difference between market price and contract price since the buyer would have been able to make the resale, and thus the profit, by obtaining substitute goods on the market (*Williams v Reynolds* (1865) 6 B & S 495).

Assessment of damages for the buyer's breach (non-acceptance of goods) in a contract for the sale of goods: SGA 1979, s. 50(3)

- Where there is an available market, it is assumed that the seller will immediately be able to sell the goods to a substitute buyer, so that the seller will suffer a loss only if the market price is below the price the seller had originally contracted to receive.

- The seller's damages will, therefore, be assessed by subtracting the market price at the time of the breach from the contract price (SGA 1979, s. 50(3)).

Lost-volume sales

Where there is such a breach by the buyer, the market-price rule will often result in no loss to the seller being revealed; standard items are sold at standard prices, so that there will be no difference between market price and contract price.

Example

If A has three sacks of coal to sell, and contracts to sell them to B at the standard (market) price of £20 per sack, if B later wrongfully refuses to accept the coal, A will almost certainly be able to sell them to C at the same price. B will assert that it is entitled to benefit from A's mitigation of the loss (see 9.9.3) so that no damages are payable, while A will assert that it has lost the profit on the sale to B since it would have been able to sell another three bags of coal to C.

The expectation loss claimed by A is usually referred to as created by 'lost volume'.

(a) *Supply greater than demand*

The claim will succeed in cases where supply is greater than demand. That is, if A has unlimited access to supplies of coal then it is true that it could have made sales to both B and C, so that there is genuinely one lost sale, and A should recover the profit it would have made on that sale (*Thompson (W. L.) Ltd v Robinson (Gunmakers) Ltd* [1955] Ch 177: the case involved the sale of a new 'Vanguard' car. Such cars were readily available so that supply exceeded demand and the breach resulted in a lost sale).

(b) *Demand greater than supply*

However, where demand is greater than supply, the claim will not succeed. That is, if the three sacks of coal were A's last three available sacks, and no further supplies were obtainable, A could not have made sales to both B and C, and the sale to C was genuinely a substitute for the sale to B. In such a case there will be no lost profit (*Charter v Sullivan* [1957] 2 QB 117, also a new car sale).

These rules do not apply in the case of unique goods, since in that case there is no market for such goods and no scope for a substitute sale (*Lazenby Garages Ltd v Wright* [1976] 1 WLR 459: this case concerned the sale of a second-hand car, but there is scope for doubting whether every second-hand car is 'unique').

2. **Alternative measures of difference in value**

The market-price rule will not be used as the measure of loss either:

- where there is no available market
- where, in the circumstances, the non-breaching party is not expected to avail itself of the market to mitigate its loss.

(a) *No available market*

There may be no available market for a number of reasons, and it will be a question of fact in each case whether a market exists. A good example of absence of a market is where goods are specially manufactured to the order of the buyer, so that it is very unlikely that a different buyer would have ordered precisely the same goods. Another is where there is a serious disequilibrium between supply and demand. Thus, in ascertaining a seller's loss there may be no market price if supply so far outstrips demand that the seller cannot reasonably make an alternative sale. Equally, in ascertaining a buyer's loss, there may be no market price if demand so outstrips supply that the buyer cannot reasonably make an alternative purchase.

Where there is no market, the basic principle is that the market-price-rule formula (see above) should continue to be used, but the court must put its own estimation of the actual value of the goods in question into the formula in place of the market price. Such estimations will sometimes be highly speculative, although the court may have some evidence available from actual contracts of resale of the goods. In some circumstances measurement of the expectation loss is so uncertain that the claimant may prefer to claim reliance losses (see **9.4**).

(b) *Instances where the non-breaching party is not expected to go into the market*
(i) *Defective performance*

A claimant buyer will not be expected to avail itself of the market to mitigate a loss when it is obliged to keep the goods despite the breach, which will occur when the breach relates only to a warranty (see **8.5.4**), or is a non-serious breach of an innominate term (see **8.5.5**), or where the breach once entitled the buyer to reject the goods but that right has been lost (see **8.4.2.3**).

The buyer will still seek to be compensated for its lost expectation through the defective performance, which in this case will normally be represented by the difference in value of the goods as warranted (promised) in the contract and as actually delivered. Here again, the estimation of values may be somewhat speculative, although where there is a market, the warranted value will be taken to be the same as the market price.

An interesting question arises where the buyer's actual loss resulting from the supply of defective goods is less than the difference in value.

> In *Slater v Hoyle & Smith Ltd* [1920] 2 KB 11, the contract was for the sale of 3,000 pieces of cotton of a particular quality. The cotton delivered was not of this quality, but the buyers had already contracted to sell 2,000 of the pieces to a sub-buyer and the buyers managed to use some of the cotton supplied partially to perform this sub-sale. The price applicable to the sub-sale was higher than the market value of the cotton supplied. The Court of Appeal held that the buyers could obtain damages based on the difference between the value of the cotton as warranted and as supplied without taking account of the price received under the sub-sale.
>
> However, the majority of the Court of Appeal in *Bence Graphics International Ltd v Fasson (UK) Ltd* [1998] QB 87, distinguished *Slater* and said that damages should be the loss directly and naturally arising. Accordingly, the majority decided that where it is within the contemplation of the parties at the time of contracting that, after substantial processing, goods will be resold, the loss caused by the seller's breach of warranty will be measured by reference to the buyer's potential liability to sub-buyers.

Thus, the principle appears to be that recoverability turns on the scope of contemplations at the time of contracting. In other words, is the subsequent event within the contemplations of the parties and so part of the contemplated loss/gain? If it is not then it can be discounted as not being referable to the breach. The problem with this approach is that it uses remoteness to identify the loss when remoteness should determine only the ability to recover for an identified loss. On the other hand, it does reflect the actual position on loss suffered.

(ii) Late delivery

1. Where the delay in delivery constitutes a repudiatory breach and the buyer rejects the goods for this reason, damages are assessed as if the breach constituted non-delivery (SGA 1979, s. 51(3)).

2. However, where the delay in delivery is affirmed or does not constitute a repudiatory breach, the measure of damages will differ depending upon the intended purpose behind the purchase of goods. Damages will normally be assessed on the basis of the difference in market value where goods intended for income-generation (e.g., manufacturing machinery) are delivered late, and the lost expectation will be the profits lost during the period when the machinery should have been in operation (see ***Victoria Laundry (Windsor) Ltd v Newman Industries Ltd*** [1949] 2 KB 528; discussed at **9.9.2.2**). However, where the intention was to sell the goods in the market, the loss will be the difference between the market price on the date when the goods should have been delivered and the market price on the date when they were delivered.

(iii) Cancellation of a contract to supply

The normal measure of damages where a contract to supply is cancelled will be the lost net profit on the contract. (It may be possible, in addition, to recover for wasted expenditure incurred in seeking to perform prior to the date of cancellation: see **9.4**.) In exceptional circumstances, the supplier may, in addition to net profit, be able to recover an element of the gross profit to cover fixed overheads where it is not possible to defray these overheads by obtaining a substitute contract (***Western Webb Offset Printers Ltd v Independent Media Ltd*** [1996] CLC 77: in this case it was not possible to obtain a substitute contract due to a business recession).

9.3.3 Cost of cure

Cost of cure (or repair) is the other possible way of calculating expectation loss. In some circumstances, awarding cost of cure may be the only way of ensuring that the claimant's expectation under the contract is fulfilled.

9.3.3.1 Contractual purpose

In a contract for the sale of goods the buyer will probably want performance in order to put the goods into immediate use, or in order to resell them and make a profit on the sale. The seller's failure to deliver may be cured by the buyer obtaining substitute goods in the market. In such a case, difference in value, as measured by the market-price rule (see **9.3.2.1**), and cost of cure are one and the same thing. In other circumstances, the claimant may have wanted performance for other 'subjective' reasons, so that a damages award based on an objective difference in value will not compensate that claimant. Harris, Ogus, and Phillips ((1979) 95 LQR 581) refer to these 'subjective' reasons for wanting performance as 'the consumer surplus'.

 Key point

The 'consumer surplus' is defined as 'the excess utility or subjective value over and above the market value of the performance contracted for' and which would have been secured had the contract been properly performed. »

For example, if A contracts with B for B to build a wall on A's land in order to act as a boundary and reduce noise, but B fails to build the wall, it is arguable that the only way to compensate A (and achieve A's purpose under the contract) will be to award the cost of achieving that promised performance, i.e. building the wall.

The measure of cost of cure may be significantly greater than the measure of difference in value. The question, therefore, is whether the courts should give effect to the consumer surplus and award higher cost-of-cure damages.

In the famous American case *of Jacob and Youngs v Kent* 230 NY 239 (1921), the plaintiffs had inserted an express clause in the contract that a particular make of piping be used in the plumbing work during the construction of a house. A different make of piping of identical quality was in fact used. The court refused to allow damages on the basis of cost of cure, and allowed only the difference in value, which was purely nominal.

9.3.3.2 Balancing the competing issues

The courts have to balance two competing issues here:

- Awarding cost of cure may appear to be out of all proportion to the consequences of the breach, and there is a risk of unjust enrichment if the claimant is awarded cost-of-cure damages but then does not use this damages award to carry out the cure.

- On the other hand, if a building owner has specified a particular means of performance, the building contractor may save costs of performing by not complying with the specification but only have to pay a small difference in value measure of damages. This might send the wrong signals to the construction industry. In addition, if the cost of cure is not awarded, it can be argued that the building owner's performance interest has not been fulfilled.

In order to seek to achieve a balance between these two competing issues, the courts have imposed some limitations on the ability to recover cost-of-cure damages in such circumstances whilst showing a willingness to recognize 'the consumer surplus'.

9.3.3.3 Recognition of 'the consumer surplus'

There has been very clear recognition of this non-financial interest in performance, for example, in ***Radford v De Froberville*** [1977] 1 WLR 1262, ***Ruxley Electronics and Construction Ltd v Forsyth*** [1996] 1 AC 344, and ***Attorney-General v Blake*** [2001] 1 AC 268.

For example, in ***Attorney-General v Blake***, Lord Nicholls stated:

The law recognises that a party to a contract may have an interest in performance which is not readily measured in terms of money.

Thus, the mere fact that the claimant has stipulated for a particular kind of performance which others would regard as having no value, or as not enhancing the value of the property, will not of itself prevent the recovery of cost-of-cure damages. In ***Ruxley Electronics***, Lord Jauncey referred to the construction of a folly in a garden and stated that, if the folly collapsed, it would be irrelevant to the determination of the loss suffered to argue that the construction of the folly, which did not increase the value of the land, 'was a crazy thing to do'.

> In *Radford v De Froberville* [1977] 1 WLR 1262, the defendant had contracted to build a wall on her land to mark the boundary, but failed to perform. The plaintiff was entitled to the cost of building a wall on his own land to mark the same boundary, and it was irrelevant that a less costly structure such as a fence would have done the job equally well.

9.3.3.4 When will cost-of-cure damages be awarded?

Cost-of-cure damages will be recoverable only where both:

- **it is reasonable to award such damages in the sense that the cost of cure is not out of all proportion to the benefit to be obtained** (as in *Jacob and Youngs v Kent*, 230 NY 239 (1921))
- **the rebuilding has been completed or it is clear that there is an intention to use the damages award to carry out the rebuilding.** This is because, unless there is an intention to rebuild or cure, cost of cure will not be an actual loss needing to be compensated by a payment in damages.

These limitations were confirmed by the House of Lords in ***Ruxley Electronics***, although they can be traced back to ***Radford v De Froberville*** (reasonable on the facts to award cost of cure) and ***Tito v Waddell (No. 2)*** [1977] Ch 106 (the court was not convinced that the damages award would be used to cure the breach).

> In ***Ruxley Electronics and Construction Ltd v Forsyth*** [1996] 1 AC 344, the defendant employed the plaintiff to construct a swimming pool in his garden. It was to be of a maximum depth of seven feet, six inches. The finished pool was only six-feet deep at the point where people dive in. However, at first instance it was found that the pool, as constructed, was safe for diving. The failure to meet the contractual specification could be remedied only by demolishing the existing pool and starting again, at a cost of £21,560. At first instance the judge found that there was no difference in value between the pool as specified and that actually built. He awarded £2,500 for lost amenity. The Court of Appeal awarded the full cost of curing the defect.
>
> The House of Lords was unanimous in holding that, in the circumstances, the cost of cure was not recoverable, so that the Court of Appeal's decision was reversed and the original award for loss of amenity, which had not been challenged, was allowed to stand. Lord Lloyd referred to the judgment of Cardozo J in *Jacob and Youngs v Kent* in stating that as a general principle the cost of cure can be recovered only 'if it is reasonable for the plaintiff to insist on that course'. In assessing whether it was reasonable to allow the cost of cure it was appropriate to consider the personal preferences of the buyer in stipulating for a particular performance as this assisted in identifying the loss suffered. However, personal preferences 'cannot *per se* be determinative of what that loss is' (per Lord Jauncey).

The conclusion is that there is a line to be drawn between circumstances in which cure is reasonable and those in which it is not. In his speech in ***Ruxley Electronics*** Lord Bridge gave an example, which was also referred to by Lord Jauncey.

> A house is to be built and the owner specifies that one of the lower courses of brick should be blue. The house as built conforms to the specification except in relation to the colour of this course of bricks. Yellow bricks have been used instead of blue. To conform to the requirements of the owner would involve knocking down the house and rebuilding, at great cost.

This is an example where it would clearly be unreasonable to award cost of cure. Lord Jauncey contrasted this with the position where a building is constructed so defectively that it is of no use for its designed purpose; it would clearly be reasonable to award cost of cure in such a case. Of course, these examples are extremes and the majority of cases will fall somewhere in between.

This distinction is also well illustrated by **McGlinn v Waltham Contractors Ltd** [2007] EWHC 149 (TCC), [2008] Bus LR 233, the claimant had demolished and rebuilt a building where the building defect was aesthetic rather than structural and sought to recover the full cost. However, it was held that although the claimant was not limited to diminution in value and this was unquestionably a case where the correct measure of loss was reinstatement, he was entitled only to the repair cost as demolition and rebuilding were out of all proportion and he had not acted reasonably in demolishing. (Similarly, in *Tomlinson v Wilson* (QB) (TCC), 11 May 2007, a house extension was defective and the judge considered it unreasonable to award the cost of demolition and rebuilding since the building could have been repaired at a much lower cost. Damages for distress during the period of the repair would have been available as distress consequent on physical inconvenience. See 9.9.4.2.)

Ruxley Electronics was applied in **Birse Construction Ltd v Eastern Telegraph Co. Ltd** [2004] EWHC 2512 (TCC), [2004] 47 EG 164 (CS).

> The claimant built a residential college for the defendant. After completion the defendant complained that there were numerous defects. However, by this time the defendant had decided to sell the property and so took no steps to rectify these defects. The claimant brought an action to recover retention money which had been held back by the defendant and the defendant counterclaimed for damages. The issue for the court related to the measure and type of damages available. Since the proposed sale of the college had reached an advanced stage at the date of the hearing and it had been negotiated without any discount in the price to take account of the defects, the claimant argued that the defects had not caused the defendant any actual loss so that damages should be nominal. However, the defendant argued that it was entitled to substantial damages because (i) it had not received what it had contracted for and (ii) many of the defects had an adverse effect on the general appearance, comfort and amenity of the college so that loss of amenity damages should be awarded.

Judge Humphrey Lloyd QC applied *Ruxley* and awarded nominal damages of £2. He concluded:

(i) If the college were sold at an undiminished price, any financial loss to the defendant would have been avoided and in such circumstances it would be unreasonable to award damages based on the cost of repair, especially as there was no intention to repair the defects. The judge rejected the defendant's argument that it was irrelevant that there was no intention to carry out the remedial work.

(ii) The argument based on loss of amenity was 'hollow' considering that the defendant had taken no steps to rectify any of the defects in question and loss of amenity damages would therefore be refused. In other words, the judge considered that if the defects were that disturbing, a reasonable owner would have taken steps to rectify the position.

He stated:

> It is now clear from *Ruxley*… that the normal measure of damages for defective works is the cost of reinstatement (i.e., the cost of remedial works) but in every instance it has to be reasonable to apply it. Thus where that measure is out of proportion to the claimant's real loss then some other measure should be used. This is the case where there has been a modest effect on the utility of the works and where it would be reasonable to assess the loss on the basis of diminution in value. A pragmatic approach may have to be applied although the claimant is not to be too readily deprived of the ordinary measure of compensation.

The judge's approach is interesting because the result of this award was that the claimant did not need to pay for the consequences of its breach since there was no award of any kind, even for loss of amenity. It also suggests that Lord Griffiths's 'broad ground' (in *Linden Gardens Trust Ltd v Lenesta Sludge Disposals Ltd* [1994] 1 AC 85: see **11.7.3.2**) did not even come into the equation on these facts, i.e. damages for the fact of non-performance/defective performance. This appears to be because the judge took the opposite view, i.e. that the defendant had suffered no loss.

The House of Lords in *Ruxley* confirmed that it is important to take into account the intention to carry out the cure or repair since otherwise the cost of rebuilding is not a loss actually suffered—and it is this point which appears to have prevailed in **Birse Construction**. (Thus, intention is important for the purposes of identifying a loss; however, once a clear loss is identified, it is no concern of the courts to assess what the claimant will do with the damages award, per Lord Clyde in **Alfred McAlpine Construction Ltd v Panatown Ltd** [2001] 1 AC 518.)

The same principle of 'no loss' was applied in **Sunrock Aircraft Corporation Ltd v Scandinavian Airlines System Denmark-Norway-Sweden** [2007] EWCA Civ 882, [2007] 2 Lloyd's Rep 612: two leased aircraft had been returned unrepaired and the normal measure of damages would be the cost of repair. Instead of arranging for a repair the lessor had sold on the aircraft at a price which reflected the fact that there had been no diminution in the value of the aircraft. Nominal damages were therefore awarded.

The remedy of cost of cure must be appropriate to the defendant's liability

In addition to these general principles, we know that cost of cure will be awarded only where such a remedy is appropriate to the liability assumed by the defendant. For example, if the obligation undertaken is a qualified obligation (reasonable care and skill), awarding cost of cure would amount to treating it as if it were a strict contractual obligation. The House of Lords in **Farley v Skinner (No. 2)** [2001] UKHL 49, [2002] 2 AC 732, disapproved a distinction between strict and qualified obligations but only in the context of the availability of damages for distress and disappointment. Since the disapproval does not extend to recovery of the basic measure of damages, *Watts v Morrow* remains good law on this point.

In **Watts v Morrow** [1991] 1 WLR 1421, the purchasers of a house brought an action against a surveyor for breach of a contract to exercise care and skill in preparing a report on the house purchased. Defects were found which were not revealed by the defendant's report. The difference in value between what the plaintiffs paid and what the house would have been worth had the defects been known was put at £15,000. The plaintiff paid nearly £34,000 to remedy the defects and sought the larger sum in damages for breach of contract.

In the Court of Appeal, Ralph Gibson LJ (at p. 1436) said that to award damages for the cost of cure would amount to compensating the plaintiff for breach of a warranty by the defendant that the condition of the house was correctly described by the surveyor. No such warranty was given in a case such as this. Relying on the judgment of Denning LJ in *Philips v Ward* [1956] 1 WLR 471, Ralph Gibson LJ stated that compensation was limited to the amount which would 'put the plaintiff into as good a position as if the contract for the survey had been properly fulfilled'. Had the survey been properly carried out, either the plaintiff would not have bought at all (in which case there would have been no loss), or he would have bought at the lower value (so that the difference in value was the proper measure of the loss).

9.3.4 Expectation loss speculative and uncertain

There can be no doubt that the measurement of expectation loss may be a speculative and uncertain process, especially in cases where it must be assessed by reference to difference in value and where the assumed value of the market price is unavailable as a guide. Nevertheless, as a general principle, damages for lost expectation may always be recovered, subject to the various limitations considered below (see 9.9). The fact that measurement of the loss is difficult or speculative will not prevent the court attempting such measurement and awarding damages accordingly.

> In *Simpson v London and North Western Railway Co.* (1876) 1 QBD 274, the plaintiff sent specimens by rail for exhibition at a trade show, clearly indicating the date by which they had to arrive. They arrived after that date, and the plaintiff claimed damages for loss of the profits he would have made had he been able to exhibit his specimens. He was entitled to succeed, despite the speculative nature of his loss.

Thus, the court will attempt to put some value on an expectation even when what is lost is no more than an opportunity to take the risk of making a profit, rather than a certain loss of a speculative profit.

> For example, in *Chaplin v Hicks* [1911] 2 KB 786, there was an agreement between the defendant, a theatrical manager, and the plaintiff that, if the plaintiff would attend for an interview, he would select twelve out of fifty interviewees for employment. He then failed, in breach of contract, to give the plaintiff a reasonable opportunity to attend. She was able to recover damages for that lost opportunity, although there was no certainty that she would have been successful. In those circumstances the loss was said to depend upon the chances of her succeeding at interview, which were quantifiable. The court said, 'where by contract a man has a right to belong to a limited class of competitors, he is possessed of something of value, and it is the duty of the jury to estimate the pecuniary value of that advantage if it is taken from him'.

In some cases, however, the estimation of the lost expectation may be so speculative that the courts will refuse to award damages on the standard basis, and will instead only compensate the claimant's out-of-pocket expenses in attempting to perform the contract. The classic example of this principle is the Australian case of *McRae v Commonwealth Disposals Commission* (1951) 84 CLR 377 (see also 13.2.2).

> In *McRae v Commonwealth Disposals Commission*, the plaintiffs and defendants had contracted for the recovery of a shipwrecked oil tanker, said by the defendants to be lying at a specified place. The plaintiffs mounted an expedition to salvage the tanker, but no tanker could be found and it became apparent that none had ever existed. The plaintiffs claimed lost profit as the measure of their lost expectation resulting from the defendants' breach. The High Court of Australia considered that recovery of lost profit on the vessel would be too speculative since no details had been given at the time of contracting about the size of the tanker, or whether it still held its cargo of oil, and it could not be known whether the salvage operation would have been successful. Instead, the court awarded the plaintiffs' reliance loss, that is, the wasted cost of mounting the salvage expedition. They also recovered the price they had paid under the contract (the restitutionary interest: see discussion at 10.5.1).

The distinction between *McRae* and *Chaplin v Hicks* is that in *Chaplin v Hicks* there was a real or tangible loss of a chance of obtaining the prize, while in *McRae* the plaintiffs could not demonstrate that any profit would have been made so that the loss was purely speculative. This distinction was confirmed by the Court of Appeal in *Allied Maples Group Ltd v Simmons and Simmons (a firm)* [1995] 1 WLR 1602.

> The loss suffered by the plaintiff as a result of the defendant's breach depended on the hypothetical action of a third party, in that the plaintiff argued that if it had been properly advised by the defendant it would have had the opportunity of negotiating a better deal with target companies during an

acquisition. The Court of Appeal held that the plaintiff was entitled to succeed in its action since it had established on the balance of probabilities that there was a 'substantial chance' of negotiating a better deal and not merely a speculative chance. The plaintiff did not need to establish that the negotiations would definitely have succeeded.

9.4 Quantification of loss: Reliance loss

As discussed in **Part 3(d)**, reliance loss will arise where the claimant has expended money either in preparation for, or in partial performance of, the contract which is then wasted because of the breach. Damages which compensate for reliance loss are intended to compensate for this wasted expenditure.

9.4.1 When can (or must) reliance loss damages be claimed?

9.4.1.1 Reliance loss must be claimed where expectation loss it too speculative

Where expectation loss is too speculative to recover because it is impossible to say what the profit on the contract would have been, reliance loss will necessarily have to be claimed (see above at **9.3.4**, *McRae v Commonwealth Disposals Commission* (1951) 84 CLR 377: reliance loss measure imposed by the court). A further example is provided by the facts of *Anglia Television Ltd v Reed* [1972] 1 QB 60: reliance loss claimed because it was not possible to prove what the profits on the contract would have been.

In *Anglia Television Ltd v Reed*, the plaintiff television company had been forced to abandon its project to make a film when the lead actor withdrew from the project in breach of contract. The company was able to recover for wasted expenditure, including expenditure incurred before the contract with the actor had been made.

Thus, pre-contractual expenditure which has been lost as a result of the breach will also be recoverable as reliance loss provided that 'it was such as would reasonably be in the contemplation of the parties as likely to be wasted if the contract was broken' (see remoteness rule, at **9.9.2**).

9.4.1.2 Can a claimant choose whether to claim reliance loss rather than expectation loss?

In some circumstances the claimant may prefer to claim reliance loss rather than the expectation loss. In general, it appears that the claimant can choose to claim reliance loss subject to an important limitation.

The limitation

The essence of the limitation is that such a claim must not result in the compensation of a loss which is not the result of the defendant's breach.

✓ Key point

The claimant cannot claim damages for reliance loss if this would amount to compensating the claimant for having made a 'bad bargain'. To award reliance loss in these circumstances would amount to »

353

putting the claimant in a better position than the claimant would have been in had the contract been properly performed. In the case of bad bargains, the loss results from the claimant having made the contract rather than from its breach by the defendant.

Of course, this is just the situation where the claimant would want to recover for wasted expenditure, and the courts will therefore be extremely wary of such claims.

> In **C. and P. Haulage v Middleton** [1983] 1 WLR 1461, the plaintiff was entitled under a series of six-month contracts to the use of a garage for the purposes of his business. He had spent some money on equipping the garage for his needs, but under the contracts the equipment installed became the property of the garage owner once the plaintiff's use of the garage ceased. Ten weeks before the end of one of the six-month contracts, the garage owner ordered the plaintiff out of the garage in breach of contract. The local planning authority allowed the plaintiff to use his own garage for more than ten weeks, with the result that he saved the weekly rental on the garage. His profits were, therefore, greater than if the contract had not been breached. He brought an action to recover the costs of equipping the garage from which he had been ejected.
>
> The Court of Appeal rejected that claim on the ground that the cost of the equipment would have been lost had the contract been performed as agreed and lawfully terminated at the end of a six-month period. The loss did not, therefore, result from the breach but from the terms of the contract itself, and so was not to be compensated. The plaintiff could recover only nominal damages for the breach.

However, it is not the case that it needs to be shown that but for the breach this expenditure would have been recoverable out of the income produced by performance of the contract. Provided the contract would have resulted in the claimant breaking even on the venture, wasted expenditure is recoverable. It is irrelevant to such a claim that the claimant would not have made a net profit.

The burden of proof

The burden of proof on this issue is quite complex. In **Dataliner Ltd v Vehicle Builders and Repairers Association**, *The Independent*, 30 August 1995, the Court of Appeal held that the claimant had the burden of establishing on the balance of probabilities that, but for the defendant's breach, he would have recouped this expenditure (or broken even). On the facts in **Dataliner**, this meant establishing that but for the defendant's breach in failing to promote a trade show, the plaintiff would have recouped his expenses in attending by obtaining sales at the trade show. This is further illustrated by the decision in **Parker v S. J. Berwin and Co** [2008] EWHC 3017 (QB), [2009] PNLR 17; the court rejected the claimant's allegation that there was a 'legal presumption' that they would not have wasted their expenditure in relation to a proposed takeover of a football club had it not been for the defendant solicitors' inaction and lack of advice. The claimant alleged that it was for the defendant to prove otherwise. The judge rejected this. The burden was the claimant's. If the court had accepted that the defendant had this burden it would have involved the defendant seeking to prove that a successful bid for the club could not have been made, i.e. establishing a negative, namely that viable funding would not have been available to the claimant.

However, **where the nature of the breach makes it impossible for the claimant to establish that the expenditure would otherwise have been recouped, the burden shifts to the** defendant to establish that the claimant would not have recouped his expenditure irrespective of the breach.

> In *CCC Films (London) Ltd v Impact Quadrant Films Ltd* [1985] 1 QB 16, the contract was discharged by the defendant's breach, so that the plaintiff was deprived of the films which, it was anticipated, would have generated sufficient profits to cover the plaintiff's costs. Therefore, as a result of the defendant's breach, the plaintiff was unable to prove that he would otherwise have recovered his expenditure.

This burden of proof, although complex, is sensible because the claimant will normally be in the better position to discharge the burden of establishing that its costs would have been recouped. However, where the defendant's breach makes this impossible, the burden should shift to the defendant to prove that the claimant would not have recovered.

9.5 Quantification of loss: Avoiding double compensation

In *Anglia Television Ltd v Reed* [1972] 1 QB 60, Lord Denning MR said that a claimant may elect whether to claim for loss of profits or for wasted expenditure, but that the claimant cannot claim for both. That statement, taken out of context, may be misleading. Lord Denning MR did not indicate whether he was speaking of gross or net profits. It is true that a claimant may not claim both the reliance loss of wasted expenditure **and** the gross profit expected under the contract, since the claimant would expect to recover expenditure out of such gross profit, and to award both would be double compensation of the reliance loss (*Cullinane v British 'Rema' Manufacturing Co. Ltd* [1954] 1 QB 292). But if it is advantageous to the claimant to divide the claim between expenditure on performance and the lost net profit, there seems to be no good reason why the claimant should not do so, since the net profit is calculated by deducting expenditure from the gross profit (see *Hydraulic Engineering Co. Ltd v McHaffie, Goslett and Co.* (1878) 4 QBD 670, where such a claim was allowed). To award only net profit and the expenditure wasted would involve no double compensation.

 Example

> Contractor A submits a quotation to B to supply B with a bathroom. The quotation is based on the cost of the bath etc, the costs of installation and includes a profit figure. This would constitute the gross profit figure or price for the contract. Shortly after the work commences to remove the old bathroom suite, B cancels the contract.
>
> If the contract had been completed, A would have expected to incur the cost of the bathroom equipment and the labour cost and to have defrayed these costs out of the contract price, leaving the net profit on the contract. In the event of breach it is clear that A can claim the net profit as expectation loss.
>
> Can A also recover for other wasted expenditure? In a situation such as this where the breach occurs shortly after performance commences, A will be unable to claim the gross-profit figure since the full labour cost will not have been incurred and it should be possible to mitigate the loss attributable to the purchase of the bathroom suite, e.g. the builders merchant might accept return of the unused bathroom suite but would charge a re-stocking charge of between 10 and 25 per cent. Therefore »

A may wish to claim the actual labour cost, and any part of the cost of the bathroom suite which cannot be mitigated (e.g., the re-stocking charge), as reliance losses, i.e. losses incurred in performance of the contract which are now wasted as a result of the cancellation. This would not involve any double recovery in respect of the same loss.

9.6 Consequential loss

The courts sometimes speak of the award of damages for 'consequential loss' resulting from the breach of the contract. The phrase has no very precise meaning, but it usually indicates loss which does not result directly from the breach but which is still an inevitable consequence of the breach.

For example, in a contract for the sale of an animal feed hopper, if the ventilation of the hopper is defective there is a breach of the contract.

- The loss directly resulting is that the hopper is not worth as much as promised in the contract, and that loss may be compensated by an award of damages for the difference in value (assuming the hopper was not, or could not be, rejected: see 8.4.2) or for cost of cure (see 9.3.3).

- Where, in addition, the livestock became ill and the herd had to be destroyed through eating animal feed which had become mouldy due to the defective ventilation on the hopper, there is a *consequential* loss of the value of the herd resulting from the breach. In such a case the difference in value or cost of cure may be minimal, but the consequential loss is considerably greater (see *H. Parsons (Livestock) Ltd v Uttley Ingham & Co. Ltd* [1978] 1 QB 791, discussed at 9.9.2.5).

To describe the loss as consequential is, however, of little significance except to find a convenient label for a loss which purists do not regard as strictly **belonging to either the expectation or the reliance** categories. What must be remembered is that such loss raises particular questions of causation—namely, did the loss actually result from the breach which occurred (see 9.9.1.1)?—and, in particular, of remoteness of damage which relates to the ability to recover for that loss—namely, was this consequence of the breach within the contemplation of the parties at the time of contracting, so that the defendant in promising to perform can be taken to have promised not to cause such loss, or to have assumed responsibility for it (see 9.9.2)?.

9.7 Time for assessment of loss

The general principle is that damages are to be assessed at the time of breach (or when the loss is suffered), which usually occurs at the time when performance became due (*Miliangos v George Frank (Textiles) Ltd* [1976] AC 443 at 468 and *Johnson v Agnew* [1980] AC 367 at pp. 400–1). This is because it is the earliest date when the claimant could be expected to mitigate (i.e., to find the substitute performance) or take other appropriate remedial action.

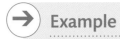

Example

The buyer's damages for the seller's non-delivery in a contract for the sale of goods are to be assessed according to the market price for the goods (see **9.3.2.1**) at the time when the goods ought to have been delivered (SGA 1979, s. 51(3)). This rule is based on the obligation placed on the claimant to mitigate its loss (see **9.9.3**), and assumes that the claimant will do so by taking immediate action.

However, it is accepted that the breach-date principle may not be appropriate in all cases, e.g. Lord Wilberforce in *Johnson v Agnew*, at p. 400 stated: 'But this is not an absolute rule: if to follow it would give rise to injustice, the court has power to fix such other date as may be appropriate in the circumstances.'

In *Golden Strait Corporation v Nippon Yusen Kubishika Kaisha, The Golden Victory* [2007] UKHL 12, [2007] 2 AC 353, the House of Lords by a majority of 3:2 held that damages may be reduced where subsequent events are known to the court at the date of the court hearing (and assessment of quantum) which have reduced the actual loss suffered.

The charterer had chartered the vessel from the shipowner under a time charterparty commencing in July 1998 and the earliest date for its termination was December 2005. The charter provided (clause 33) that if war broke out between named countries then both parties would be entitled to terminate. The charterer repudiated on 14 December 2001 by redelivering the ship and the shipowner accepted that repudiation on 17 December. The shipowner claimed to be entitled to damages measured by reference to the full term of the repudiated time charter (four years). However, in the meantime the Second Gulf War broke out in March 2003 and was an event that would have justified the charterer terminating the charter under clause 33. The charterer claimed that a party in breach could rely on subsequent events to reduce the damages so that no damages could be recovered after March 2003 (meaning that the damages would cover a period of fourteen months instead of four years), whereas the shipowner alleged that the loss should be measured at the date of acceptance of the repudiation in the interests of commercial certainty and finality, and that anything that happened afterwards was irrelevant.

The House of Lords held 3:2 (Lords Scott, Carswell, and Brown; Lords Bingham and Walker dissenting) that since contractual principles required the innocent party (shipowner) to be placed in the position that it would have been in if the contract had been properly performed, the most important principle was to compensate for actual loss suffered (not for more than was actually suffered) rather than commercial certainty and finality which is inherent in the breach-date rule. Although the assessment based on the breach-date rule would normally achieve that result, the courts should not apply it where it did not. It followed that the subsequent event, which occurred before the assessment of damages was made, could be taken into account.

This majority view of their Lordships followed the approach taken in the lower courts and is based on the principle that where there is knowledge, speculation is not required. There was indeed knowledge of the fact that the Gulf War had broken out in March 2003 but it had to be assumed that, had the charter continued, the war clause would have been exercised by the charterer in March 2003. It is also rather too convenient to rely on the principle of full compensation for actual loss where this operates to constrain additional recovery but to support principles that reduce damages and so constrain the ability of a claimant to be fully compensated for its actual loss (see **9.9**).

It is therefore a difficult decision for commercial lawyers whose primary focus is commercial certainty and who regard breach as crystallizing the loss at that date (see the important dissenting speeches of Lord Bingham and Lord Walker). The normal reaction, and expectation, in such instances would be for the owner to recharter the vessel in the market and to recover for any loss as the difference between this market rate and the rate under the charter for the remainder of the term.

The result of this decision is similar to treating termination for repudiatory breach as if the contract had been affirmed and the risk of subsequent events would then fall on the party who chose to affirm (*Fercometal Sarl v Mediterranean Shipping Co. SA* [1989] AC 788: see **8.7.4.2**—risk of subsequent frustration). It also has the unfortunate side-effect of implicitly encouraging the delay of the hearing for the assessment of quantum in such cases in the hope that a war clause or similar will be assumed to have been activated. On termination the loss should have become fixed, subject only to mitigation.

The *Golden Victory* was applied in the context of a major construction contract to give primacy to the compensation principle and limit recovery of damages by enabling the court to disregard certain obligations on the basis that the employer had already engaged another contractor to perform those obligation (*Multiplex Constructions (UK) Ltd v Cleveland Bridge UK Ltd* [2008] EWHC 2220 (TCC)). The judge treated this decision as permitting post-repudiation events to be taken into account when awarding damages recoverable for repudiation.

The principle in *The Golden Victory* now seems to have a life of its own. In *Force India Formula One Team Ltd v Etihad Airways PJSC* [2009] EWHC 2768 (QB), [2010] ETMR 14 the judge allowed Formula One to recover damages for wrongful termination which included points gained in the championship in subsequent seasons. There was no need to speculate about the contingency of the points arising in subsequent seasons, i.e. to make a claim based on loss of the chance of acquiring a bonus based on those points, since there was evidence that the points had in fact been gained. The judge could see no reason not to apply the principle in *The Golden Victory* in order to assess damages in the light of events subsequent to the breach. It is always possible to introduce evidence of loss but it is generally in relation to damages assessed at the date of the breach and not into the future.

- In any event, the general breach-date 'rule' is only presumptive so that, where it would be reasonable for the claimant to do something other than to take immediate steps to mitigate the loss, the court will postpone the time for assessment of damages until whatever date is more appropriate. For example, the non-breaching party may be allowed time to seek confirmation that no performance will be forthcoming, or that defective performance will be cured, before being expected to mitigate the loss.

In *Radford v De Froberville* [1977] 1 WLR 1262 (see **9.3.3.3**), it was suggested that when at first it seems probable that the defendant will make good his default, damages will be assessed at the time when that probability ceases to exist, since the duty to take steps of mitigation arises at that point.

Further, when damages are awarded in lieu of specific performance (see **10.2.4**), it is accepted that they are assessed at the time of the hearing.

In *Wroth v Tyler* [1974] Ch 30, the defendant had repudiated a contract for the sale of a house. The question was whether damages in lieu of specific performance should be assessed on the basis of the market price at the date if the breach (£7,500) or at the date of judgment (£11,500). In the particular circumstances the plaintiff, due to lack of funds, could not reasonably have done anything to mitigate the loss by purchasing a different house at the date of breach so that the date of judgment was chosen as the appropriate date for the assessment of damages.

In *Johnson v Agnew* [1980] AC 367, the vendors agreed to sell a house and land to the purchaser, but the purchaser failed to complete the transaction on the day appointed. The vendors then obtained an order for specific performance, but it was not drawn up for some five months, by which time specific performance had become impossible. The vendors sought discharge of the order for specific performance, and to recover damages in its place. The House of Lords found for the vendors, holding that damages were to be assessed at the date when specific performance became impossible.

In **Johnson v Agnew** Lord Wilberforce said (at p. 401):

> In cases where a breach of a contract for sale has occurred, and the innocent party reasonably continues to try to have the contract completed, it would to me appear more logical and just rather than tie him to the date of the original breach, to assess damages as at the date when (otherwise than by his default) the contract is lost.

Bear Stearns Bank plc v Forum Global Equity Ltd [2007] EWHC 1576 (Comm) is similar in terms of principle as the buyers had good reasons for not immediately going into the market to mitigate their loss since they had first sought specific performance of a sale of shares before abandoning it on discovering that the sellers had disposed of the shares to another. The judge therefore took the market price at a time later than the contractual date for performance.

- In some cases it may be impossible at the time of performance for the non-breaching party to discover that a breach has occurred.

 ## Example

It is breach of a contract of sale of goods to deliver goods which are defective, but the breach may remain undetected if the defect does not immediately manifest itself (e.g., a car with a latent fault which will inevitably cause it to break down after 1,500 miles of driving).

In such a case the damages will be assessed at the time when the breach could first reasonably have been discovered (*East Ham Corporation v Bernard Sunley & Sons Ltd* [1966] AC 406).

9.8 Effect of tax on quantification

Where the claim is for lost gross profit under a contract, the court must take into account the effect of tax liability before making its award. Where damages awarded in judicial proceedings for breach of contract are not subject to taxation but profits earned through the agreed performance of the contract would have been, the latter liability for tax must be accounted for. The court must not award more than the net amount which the claimant would have been able to keep as a result of performance of the contract, after tax had been deducted from the gross income.

This principle is best demonstrated by the decision of the House of Lords in **British Transport Commission v Gourley** [1956] AC 185. The case involved an action in tort for loss of earnings resulting from personal injury, but the reasoning applies equally to actions for breach of contract.

> The plaintiff suffered gross loss of earnings of nearly £38,000, which, had he received it as income, would have been reduced by liability for tax to under £7,000. The court awarded only the lower sum, since damages for loss of earnings are not taxable while income is.

This rule does not apply to loss of a capital asset, since there is no general liability for tax on the acquisition of capital assets. Neither does it apply to many claims for lost profit, since damages for lost commercial profits are themselves taxable as income.

9.9 Limitations on the ability to obtain compensation

9.9.1 Causation and contributory negligence

9.9.1.1 Causation

Damages will not be awarded to compensate loss which was not caused by the breach. We have already encountered an example of this principle in operation in the case of *C. and P. Haulage v Middleton* [1983] 1 WLR 1461 (see **9.4.1.2**).

> The user of a garage claimed his wasted expenditure in equipping the garage when the garage owner wrongfully terminated his contract to use the premises. The Court of Appeal rejected the claim, because ten weeks later the owner could have rightfully terminated the contract, whereupon the equipment would in any case have become the property of the garage owner. Therefore, the loss by wasted expenditure was not **caused** by the breach of contract, but by a term of the contract, which in this respect was inherently disadvantageous to the plaintiff.

In all cases the question whether the loss was caused by the breach will largely be a question of fact, on which it is difficult to give any guidance.

An effective cause of the claimant's loss

In contract claims the breach must be shown to be *an* effective cause of the claimant's loss, and it is not sufficient that the breach merely provided the claimant with an opportunity to sustain losses (*Galoo Ltd v Bright Grahame Murray* [1994] 1 WLR 1360).

In the majority of cases causation is not a difficult issue; greater difficulty arises from the question whether loss, which admittedly results from the breach, is too remote to be compensated (see **9.9.2**) and this would seem even more likely that there will be a change of emphasis from causation in favour of remoteness given the decision of the House of Lords in *Transfield Shipping Inc. v Mercator Shipping Inc., The Achilleas* [2008] UKHL 48, [2009] 1 AC 61, where the majority held that the test was whether there had been an 'assumption of responsibility' for the loss in question (see the discussion of *SAAMCO*, below). This would ignore the fact that causation is an ingredient in establishing liability whereas remoteness relates to whether the loss which has been caused by the breach can be recovered (i.e., a quantum question).

Other contributing causes

Causation may sometimes present difficulty when it appears that the loss was caused partly by the breach and partly by some other factor. The general rule is that where breach can be shown to be *an* actual cause of the loss, the fact that there is another contributing cause is irrelevant. The breach will entitle the non-breaching party to damages.

> For example, in *Wroth v Tyler* [1974] Ch 30 (see **9.7**), the plaintiff's loss was caused partially by the defendant's breach of contract and partially by the fact that the plaintiff lacked the financial resources to take active steps to mitigate the loss. The loss was nevertheless recoverable.
>
> Similarly, in *County Ltd v Girozentrale Securities* [1996] 3 All ER 834, the Court of Appeal said that the trial judge had been wrong, having identified two contributing causes to the loss sustained, to choose which of them was the effective cause by enquiring which had been of 'greater efficacy' in causing the loss. That the breach of contract might have had a lesser role in causing the loss did not mean that it was not a cause for the purposes of the recovery of damages. It was sufficient in a claim in contract that the cause in question was **an** effective cause of the loss.

However, where one of the contributing causes of the loss was an adverse movement in the market, the House of Lords decided that the full amount of the loss is not necessarily to be regarded as having been caused by the breach: see ***South Australia Asset Management Corporation (SAAMCO) v York Montague Ltd*** [1997] AC 191, reversing the decision of the Court of Appeal *sub nom Banque Bruxelles Lambert SA v Eagle Star Insurance Co. Ltd* [1995] QB 375.

> In **SAAMCO**, mortgage companies were induced to lend money by a negligent overvaluation of the property which was being purchased and which was the security for the loan. The borrower defaulted, and the lender's position was made even worse by a very sharp decline in property values. The essential question was whether the extra loss resulting from the fall in property values could be said to have been caused by the breach, and to be recoverable as damages. The additional amounts at stake were sometimes several million pounds. The Court of Appeal said they were recoverable: but for the negligent valuation, the lender would not have lent the money at all, and it was entitled to be compensated for all the loss suffered, including that resulting from the fall in the market.
>
> However, the House of Lords disagreed. The most significant element in the reasoning was that Lord Hoffmann did not regard the essential issue as one of causation at all. The issue was the extent of liability, which in turn depended upon just what the defendant had undertaken to do. In these cases, the defendants had only undertaken to provide information, not to provide advice about the transactions contemplated. Their liability was therefore limited to the direct consequence of the information being wrong, which was that the lenders had inadequate security, but did not include the disastrous consequences of the fall in the market. At best, that was an indirect consequence of the information being wrong, and the law does not impose liability for such loss unless there are grounds of policy to show strong disapproval, as in fraud (compare with **Smith New Court Securities Ltd v Scrimgeour Vickers (Asset Management) Ltd** [1997] AC 254: damages for fraudulent misrepresentation could include subsequent loss in value of shares due to other causes on the basis that locked into the transaction by the fraud, discussed at **14.6.2.2**).

Intervening acts of third parties

Where the act of a third party or parties is a factor contributing to the loss, in addition to the breach by the defendant, the question whether the act by the third party will excuse the breaching party from the obligation to pay damages is largely a question of whether the contract has been frustrated (see **Chapter 12**). The court is likely to be especially concerned to know whether the intervening act was so foreseeable that steps could have been taken to avoid it.

> For example, in ***The Eugenia*** [1964] 2 QB 226 (see **12.4.5** and **12.6.2**), the charterers of a vessel breached their contract by taking the vessel into the Suez Canal at a time when it was a 'dangerous' zone. The effect

of that breach was made many times worse by the act of a third party in closing the canal. Nevertheless, the charterers were not excused the obligation to pay compensation for their breach.

Intervening act of the claimant

Where the claimant is negligent and that negligence is a *novus actus interveniens*, this action provides a complete defence because it breaks the chain of causation.

> For example, in *Beoco Ltd v Alfa Laval Co. Ltd* [1995] QB 137, the defendants supplied a defective machine. It was inadequately repaired. The plaintiffs put the machine back into service without carrying out tests, and it exploded, causing much more serious damage and a loss of production. The Court of Appeal held that although at one time the plaintiffs had a right of recovery for breach of contract against the defendants because of the original defect, any loss resulting from that breach was extinguished by the explosion which destroyed the machine and was not therefore attributable to the defendants.

9.9.1.2 Contributory negligence

Where the claimant has been negligent but the claimant's negligence is not so great as to break the chain of causation, the position is quite complex. Contributory negligence by a claimant relates to issues of quantum and the possible apportionment of damages. At this stage liability is established and there are no issues of causation.

In the law of torts, where injury is caused by the negligence of the defendant and by the contributory negligence of the claimant, the damages payable by the defendant to compensate the claimant will be reduced proportionately to the amount by which the claimant's negligence contributed to the injury (Law Reform (Contributory Negligence) Act 1945). **The question is whether the provisions of that Act cover breach of contract.** The difficulty is the definition of 'fault' in s. 4 of that Act. 'Fault' is defined as meaning 'negligence, breach of statutory duty or other act or omission which gives rise to a liability in tort or would, apart from this Act, give rise to the defence of contributory negligence'.

The applicable principles in contractual claims were determined in ***Forsikringsaktieselskapet Vesta v Butcher*** [1986] 2 All ER 488 (decision of Hobhouse J) which was affirmed by the Court of Appeal ([1989] AC 852). **The availability of apportionment for the claimant's contributory negligence is dependent on the nature of the obligation broken by the defendant, i.e. whether the defendant's breach is strict or qualified.**

> In **Vesta v Butcher**, the plaintiffs were insurers of a fish farm. They had secured reinsurance of 90 per cent of the risk through the defendant brokers. It was a condition of the contract of reinsurance that the farm be subject to a 24-hour watch. The owners of the farm informed the plaintiffs that it was impossible to comply with the condition, and the plaintiffs in turn informed the defendants. The defendants took no action, and the plaintiffs failed to follow up their first telephone call. The farm lost 100,000 fish, and the reinsurers denied liability because of the absence of a 24-hour watch. The plaintiffs brought an action against the defendants for breach of contract, alleging negligence. The defendants pleaded the plaintiffs' contributory negligence in failing to follow up the first telephone call as a defence to this claim.

Hobhouse J divided contractual claim into three categories, and concluded that in at least one of these cases apportionment for contributory negligence was applicable.

Category 1: Where the contractual obligation is strict

Many claims for breach of contract depend upon contractual terms imposing a strict standard of performance on the defendant (see 8.2.1.1) so that performance is guaranteed. Hobhouse J stated that where the defendant has breached a term imposing a strict standard of performance (Category 1 case), there is no scope for the operation of the contributory negligence rule. This is because since the defendant's negligence, if any, is irrelevant to the defendant's liability for breach of such a term, any negligence by the claimant should also be irrelevant.

The Law Commission's working paper, *Contributory Negligence as a Defence in Contract* (No. 114, 1990), provisionally recommended that contributory negligence should apply to Category 1 cases (breach of strict obligation by the defendant), but this would undoubtedly have been an undesirable development in the law, since it would undermine the nature of strict liability. In its final report, *Contributory Negligence as a Defence in Contract* (No. 219, 1993), the Law Commission abandoned this proposal, and the ***Vesta v Butcher*** position that there is no apportionment in cases of breaches of strict contractual obligations, was reaffirmed by the Court of Appeal in ***Barclays Bank plc v Fairclough Building Ltd*** [1995] QB 214.

Category 2: Qualified contractual obligation to take care but no independent duty of care in tort

Where the contract term broken imposes only an obligation to exercise reasonable care and skill, a qualified contractual obligation (see discussion at 8.2.1.1), but there is no duty of care existing independently of the contract (Category 2 cases), it is a matter of debate whether the claimant's damages can be apportioned to take account of the claimant's contributory negligence. In *De Meza v Apple* [1974] 1 Lloyd's Rep 508, at first instance, it was stated that the 1945 Act did apply to such a case, but the matter was left open by the Court of Appeal.

Category 3: Qualified contractual obligation and duty of care owed in tort

Some contracts impose a duty to exercise reasonable care (qualified contractual obligation), the breach of which would in any case amount to an independent tort (Category 3 cases). ***Vesta v Butcher*** belonged to this category, and therefore Hobhouse J found no difficulty in holding that the 1945 Act did apply to such a claim (see also *Platform Home Loans Ltd v Oyston Shipways Ltd* [2000] 2 AC 190). As Neill LJ remarked in *AB Marintrans v Comet Shipping Co. Ltd, The Shinjitsu Maru No. 5* [1985] 1 WLR 1270, there is 'great force in the contention that the same rule should apply to claims whether they are based in contract or tort where the act complained of involves the breach of a duty of care'. In ***Forsikringsaktieselskapet Vesta v Butcher*** [1989] AC 852 in the Court of Appeal, Neill LJ accepted that this might be achieved under the analysis offered by Hobhouse J at first instance, although he expressed doubts about whether the wording of s. 4 of the 1945 Act was capable of such an interpretation. This objection might be met by a very minor amendment of the 1945 Act to include a definition of negligence as contained in s. 1(1) of the Unfair Contract Terms Act (UCTA) 1977, which covers 'any obligation, arising from the express or implied terms of a contract, to take reasonable care or exercise reasonable skill in the performance of the contract'.

In its 1993 report the Law Commission recommended that contributory negligence should apply in all cases of contractual negligence (i.e., where the defendant's breach of contract was a breach of a qualified contractual obligation: Categories 2 and 3). The Law Commission also recommended that the parties should be able to exclude apportionment for contributory negligence if they so wished. It was proposed that this could be achieved expressly or by implication, e.g. using an agreed damages clause would impliedly exclude apportionment for contributory negligence. However, it was proposed to implement these recommendations by means of a separate bill relating to contributory negligence in contract claims, rather than by amendment to the wording of the 1945 Act.

Summary of the current position

No progress has since been made with the Law Commission's proposals, although the decision of the Court of Appeal in *Barclays Bank plc v Fairclough Building Ltd* [1995] QB 214 is in line with the recommendations contained in the 1993 report in relation to breaches of strict contractual obligations (i.e., no contributory negligence). The position with regard to Category 3 cases seems reasonably settled. However, it will be interesting to see whether future courts will be prepared, pending legislation, to treat Category 2 and Category 3 cases in the same way and how they justify their actions under the 1945 Act.

Apportionment of damages for the claimant's contributory negligence

- Defendant's breach—Category 1: ✗.
- Defendant's breach—Category 2: ✓?
- Defendant's breach—Category 3: ✓.

9.9.2 Remoteness of damage

The defendant is not liable for all losses which result from the breach of contract. Some losses are too remote a consequence of the breach to be recoverable, in the sense that they are regarded as too improbable and therefore not within the scope of the contractual responsibility undertaken.

The remoteness rule in contract is therefore concerned with recoverability for identified loss and is designed to prevent the defendant having to compensate a loss attendant upon a risk which was not the defendant's to bear as he had not assumed responsibility for it. However, this is a statement of outcome, it does not tell us how we decide for which losses a defendant is to be responsible (or can be taken to have assumed responsibility to use the new form of wording adopted by some of their Lordships in *Transfield Shipping Inc. v Mercator Shipping Inc., The Achilleas* [2008] UKHL 48, [2009] 1 AC 61). The staring point for any discussion must be the test that determines this question, namely the statement of principle by Alderson B in *Hadley v Baxendale*.

The test

In *Hadley v Baxendale* (1854) 9 Ex 341 at p. 354, Alderson B said:

Where two parties have made a contract which one of them has broken, the damages which the other party ought to receive in respect of such breach of contract should be such as may fairly and reasonably be considered either arising naturally, i.e., according to the usual course of things, from such breach, of contract itself, or such as may reasonably be supposed to have been in the contemplation of both parties, at the time they made the contract, as the probable result of the breach of it.

This rule, which is the test of the remoteness of damage, is intended to ensure that the defendant was aware when making the contract that it had to avoid causing the kind of loss which occurred. The rule can be analysed in economic terms and is concerned with optimizing the allocation of risks between the parties to the contract.

- If a party knows that it must bear the risk of losses occurring naturally ('in the usual course of things'), that party can take preventative action with the aim of avoiding that loss.

- In addition, if a party knows that it must bear a particular risk then that party can take out appropriate insurance cover for that risk. Uncertainty over allocation of risk often leads to duplicate insurance which is economically inefficient.

- The fact that the breaching party will also be responsible for unusual losses where knowledge of the relevant facts has been disclosed, encourages the parties to address the risks and to give relevant information.

It is important to remember that remoteness is judged on the basis of contemplations (or knowledge) at the time of the contract, rather than at the time of the breach (*Jackson v Royal Bank of Scotland* [2005] UKHL 3, [2005] 1 WLR 377) and damages are therefore assessed on this basis.

9.9.2.1 Two limbs or a single remoteness rule?

Prior to the decision of the House of Lords in *Transfield Shipping Inc. v Mercator Shipping Inc., The Achilleas* [2008] UKHL 48, [2009] 1 AC 61, the test of remoteness of damage established in *Hadley v Baxendale* was frequently described as consisting of two rules, or a single rule with two limbs (*Victoria Laundry (Windsor) Ltd v Newman Industries Ltd* [1949] 2 KB 528). It was often applied on this basis in order to distinguish between the general damage in the first limb (not needing to be specifically pleaded in a breach of contract claim) and the special damage covered by the second limb (which did).

- **Under the first limb, damages may be recovered for loss arising 'according to the usual course of things' from the breach of contract (i.e., normal loss). The intention of this rule may be said to be the identification of those losses which *must inevitably* have been within the contemplation of the parties** as likely to result in the event of breach of contract. The likelihood of such losses is a reasonable deduction from the nature of the contract, and the defendant cannot simply assert that he did not know of that risk to avoid having to compensate such loss. Knowledge of such losses is therefore imputed, and consequently the loss must have been within the reasonable contemplations of both parties.

- **Under the second limb, damages may also be recovered which result from special circumstances, provided the defendant knows of those circumstances** (see, for example, *Seven Seas Properties Ltd v Al-Essa (No. 2)* [1993] 1 WLR 1083: no actual knowledge of the sub-sale and so could not recover lost profit on that sub-sale). **Only if there is knowledge of the relevant facts giving rise to the special damage can it be said that the loss was within the reasonable contemplations of *both* parties.**

In *Hadley v Baxendale*, Alderson B said (at pp. 354–5):

> Now, if the special circumstances under which the contract was actually made were communicated by the plaintiffs to the defendants, and thus known to both parties, the damages resulting from the breach of such a contract, which they would reasonably contemplate, would be the amount of injury which would ordinarily follow from a breach of contract under these special circumstances…

It is almost certain that Alderson B did not intend to establish two rules of remoteness of damage. Rather, there is a single test which requires greater knowledge on the part of the defendant as the degree of likelihood of the particular loss resulting from the breach diminishes.

- The single test is applied in *The Heron II* [1969] 1 AC 350 at p. 385.
- Evans LJ states in *Kpohraror v Woolwich Building Society* [1996] 4 All ER 119 at pp. 127–8:

> I would prefer to hold the starting point for any application of *Hadley v Baxendale* is the extent of shared knowledge of both parties when the contract was made…When that is established it may often be the case that the first and second parts of the rule overlap, or at least that it is unnecessary to draw a clear line of demarcation between them.

- Lord Hope in *Jackson v Royal Bank of Scotland* [2005] UKHL 3, [2005] 1 WLR 377 referred to the existence of a single principle of 'what was in the contemplation of the parties at the time they made the contract'. However, his Lordship then identified the loss as normal loss, arising naturally from the breach of confidence which was held to lead naturally onto the cancellation of the applicable supply contract.

Usual (or normal) loss and loss resulting from special circumstances (abnormal loss) are therefore no more than the polar positions of that single shared knowledge test. However, they assist greatly in coming to a determination under that single test of shared knowledge.

9.9.2.2 The operation of the limbs in practice

The operation of the two limbs to determine reasonable contemplations is well illustrated by the decision of the Court of Appeal in *Victoria Laundry (Windsor) Ltd v Newman Industries Ltd* [1949] 2 KB 528.

The defendant engineering company contracted to sell a boiler to the plaintiff laundry company. The boiler was to be delivered on 5 June. The defendants were aware of the nature of the plaintiffs' business and had been informed by letter that the plaintiffs intended to put the boiler to immediate use. The boiler was delivered late. The plaintiffs sought damages for the profit they would have earned through the use of the boiler in their business during the period of the delay and for the profit on a number of highly lucrative government contracts which they 'could and would have accepted'.

The Court of Appeal held:

(i) The plaintiffs were not entitled to recover for the loss of profit on the government contracts since the defendants had no knowledge of these contracts or of their terms.

(ii) However, that did not mean that the plaintiffs could not recover damages for general lost profit from the expansion of their business intended as a result of purchasing the boiler. Once the defendants knew that the boiler was intended for immediate use they should have been able to work out for themselves that late delivery was likely to lead to loss of business.

These general profits are usually treated as normal loss, and it is submitted here that this is the correct conclusion. Every loss depends on **some** fact, and the fact in question was not a special fact but very common (see, e.g., *The Heron II* [1969] 1 AC 350: fall in market price of sugar due to delay in shipment was normal loss but on the basis that the shippers **knew** they were shipping sugar for sugar merchants to a port where there was a sugar market). Arguably, therefore, if a business purchases machinery or equipment, the natural conclusion is that it is intended to be used immediately on receipt. Another view can be adopted, namely that the loss of profits in this case was dependent on knowledge of the special fact that the plaintiffs intended to put the boiler to immediate use in their business and so amounted to abnormal loss. If this is the case, had the defendants not known the boiler was intended for immediate use, the court might have found that even damages for loss of general profits were too remote. This type of distinction may be the approach that was adopted by Lord Rodger and Baroness Hale in *Transfield Shipping Inc. v Mercator Shipping Inc., The Achilleas* [2008] UKHL 48, [2009] 1 AC 61; see discussion at 9.9.2.7. It may be that a more contextual basis for determining whether a loss is normal loss should be adopted in future.

9.9.2.3 Loss depending on special facts

By comparison with the position in *The Heron II*, remoteness on the facts of *Hadley v Baxendale* was held to turn on a special fact and the lack of knowledge of that special fact.

> The plaintiffs, mill owners in Gloucester, engaged the defendant carriers to take a mill shaft to Greenwich as a pattern for a new shaft. In breach of contract, delivery was delayed so that the stoppage at the mill was extended. The plaintiffs claimed damages for their loss of profit caused by the delay. It was held that this loss of profit was not recoverable because it was too remote a loss. The loss did not arise naturally because the plaintiffs might have had a spare shaft.

The fact that the mill had a spare shaft would not be a natural inference from the circumstances, and on this basis this case can be distinguished from the *Victoria Laundry* loss of general profits. Thus, *Hadley v Baxendale* indicates the importance of informing the other party of circumstances which affect performance and the risk where full recovery is required. It also indicates the importance of identifying a loss as abnormal on the facts and in the context of the particular contract. This may be precisely what the House of Lords was seeking to do in *Transfield Shipping Inc. v Mercator Shipping Inc., The Achilleas* [2008] UKHL 48, [2009] 1 AC 61.

9.9.2.4 Identifying normal and abnormal losses

An examination of the case law reveals that it is often difficult to divide losses into two simple categories of:

- **normal losses** (those arising in the usual course of things)
- **abnormal losses** (those arising out of special circumstances).

It is significant that the approach evidenced in the case law is generally to restrict normal loss, thereby encouraging greater disclosure of the factual background (see, e.g., *Balfour Beatty Construction (Scotland) Ltd v Scottish Power plc* (1994) 71 BLR 20: actual knowledge of the construction process of continuous pour was required and could not be imputed).

However, the approach to 'normal loss' or 'direct loss' may depend on the context in which the question of construction arises. In the context of the remoteness rule there is a strong policy incentive to restrict the scope of normal loss in order to encourage disclosure of facts and risks. However, in the context of construction of exemption clauses which exclude liability for 'indirect or consequential loss', the policy considerations may suggest limiting the scope of 'indirect loss' in order to limit the scope of the exclusion so that a more generous interpretation of 'direct loss' is apparent. For example, in *Hotel Services Ltd v Hilton International Hotels (UK) Ltd* [2000] 1 All ER (Comm) 750, the question was whether such a clause exempted the supplier of defective electronic minibars from liability for the cost of their removal and the loss of profit on their use suffered by the hotel. The Court of Appeal held that neither of these losses depended on special facts. Both losses were **direct and natural consequences of the breach,** because it was obvious that if the minibars were dangerous they would have to be removed and it was clear that when in use such minibars would generate a profit.

9.9.2.5 Test for the likelihood of loss

It remains to determine what must be the likelihood of a loss resulting in order for it to be recoverable as being within the parties' reasonable contemplations at the time of contracting.

In *Victoria Laundry (Windsor) Ltd v Newman Industries Ltd,* Asquith LJ impliedly suggested that the test was the same as the test of foreseeability in the tort of negligence, since he said that the claimant may recover 'such part of the loss actually resulting as was at the time of the contract *reasonably foreseeable* as liable to result from the breach' (emphasis added). However, this formulation was called into question by the House of Lords in *The Heron II*. Lord Reid said that the claimant may only recover 'loss arising naturally' or 'in the usual course of things' (echoing Alderson B in *Hadley v Baxendale*); and the claimant may not recover loss which, although a real possibility, was likely to occur only 'in a small minority of cases'. Lord Reid went on to stress that the test of remoteness in contract is stricter than the test of remoteness in tort, for the reason that the communication of special circumstances is irrelevant to many torts but in contract allows the defendant to modify his contract or performance according to the known risks of the contract. The remoteness test must therefore encourage such communication.

In *H. Parsons (Livestock) Ltd v Uttley Ingham & Co. Ltd* [1978] 1 QB 791, the Court of Appeal was faced with the task of making sense of the very vague tests of remoteness then available.

> The contract was for the sale of an animal feed hopper. The ventilation of the hopper was defective, amounting to breach of the contract. The farmer's livestock became ill through eating animal feed which was mouldy because the ventilation was defective, so that the herd had to be destroyed. The particular illness and its consequence would have been considered an unlikely result of the breach in question at the time when the contract was made. The farmer claimed the loss of the value of the herd. The Court of Appeal concluded that the farmer could recover.

However, the approaches of the majority (Scarman and Orr LJJ) and Lord Denning MR differed.

1. Lord Denning

Lord Denning MR found the various formulations of the test of remoteness confusing and 'a sea of semantic exercises'. He accepted that sometimes the test is stricter than at others, but rather than distinguishing between contract and tort he distinguished between:

- claims for economic loss (such as lost profit)
- claims for physical loss (as in this case).

In the case of physical loss, he considered that the less strict test of remoteness applied. Provided some physical injury might be envisaged, its precise nature was irrelevant.

2. Scarman and Orr LJJ

Scarman LJ (with whom Orr LJ agreed) rejected Lord Denning's distinction between economic and physical loss, and ultimately decided that the remoteness tests in contract and tort were the same. This reasoning must be doubted, however, in view of Lord Reid's clear statement in *The Heron II* that the test in contract is stricter than the test in tort.

This issue has yet to be resolved although there must be a preservation of the distinction between remoteness in contract and tort.

- In favour of Lord Reid's approach in *The Heron II* is the argument that contracts enable the parties to allocate risks between themselves, and that such allocation will work only if the parties have proper information about the risks involved. The strict remoteness test in contract would encourage the provision of such information, since unless the information is provided, the loss will not be recoverable. Contract and tort remoteness tests should be different in degree to reflect the different contexts for the risk, and knowledge of that risk.

- The approach advocated by Lord Denning in *Parsons v Uttley Ingham* of distinguishing on the basis of loss has the advantage that it would prevent the result of the case depending upon the artificial classification of the claim as either contractual or tortious. It would also impose a stricter test on those claims which are inherently speculative (lost profits), while allowing a more lenient test for claims where the loss is more readily measured (physical loss). However, it begs another question, namely whether it is always possible to make such a clear distinction between financial and physical loss and whether it is necessarily the case that the remoteness tests for contract and tort should be assimilated.

9.9.2.6 Type/extent principle

Scarman and Orr LJJ decided *H. Parsons (Livestock) Ltd v Uttley Ingham & Co. Ltd* on the basis that since the type of loss was within the parties' contemplations, the extent of it need not be. This was also the basis for the decision in *Brown v KMR Services Ltd* [1995] 4 All ER 598.

> *Brown v KMR Services Ltd* arose out of the disastrous losses made by Lloyd's 'Names' and was one of several actions brought against those who had encouraged (or not discouraged) such 'Names' taking on excessive liabilities. The losses were, of course, financial, not physical; they were of a type which it could readily be 'foreseen' might be incurred as a result of the breach of contract, but their extent went well beyond that which might in any year arise 'in the usual course of things'. The losses were held to be recoverable because in this context the *type* of loss fell within the remoteness principle.

This reasoning highlighted some issues in terms aligning this principle with the outcome in decisions relating to financial loss where the courts have differentiated between kinds of financial loss or profit loss (e.g., in *Victoria Laundry v Newman Industries*: general loss of profits and profits on specific contracts were not treated as part of a generic class of loss of profits).

> For example, in *Kpohraror v Woolwich Building Society* [1996] 4 All ER 119, the question arose of the extent of liability for breach of a banking contract where the bank had wrongfully dishonoured the plaintiff's cheque. Counsel for the plaintiff sought to rely on *Brown v KMR Services Ltd* to establish that once the defendant knew that the account would be used in export-import transactions, the particular extent of financial loss in such transactions was of no concern and the full loss should be recoverable. The Court of Appeal baulked at such reasoning, perhaps not surprisingly since the cheque was for £4,550 while the total loss claimed was more than £57,000. In refusing to award such extensive compensation the court clearly proceeded on the basis that knowledge of the particular risk, or that generic risks of a similar extent might arise, was necessary for such loss to avoid being too remote.

9.9.2.7 The decision of the House of Lords in *Transfield Shipping*

This approach in **Kpohraror v Woolwich Building Society** has similarities with the preferred approach adopted by Lord Rodger and Baroness Hale in the recent decision of the House of Lords in **Transfield Shipping Inc. v Mercator Shipping Inc., The Achilleas** [2008] UKHL 48, [2009] 1 AC 61.

> Time charterers were nine days late in redelivery of the vessel. The owners had rechartered the vessel and when it was not redelivered on time the owners had agreed an extension of the cancelling date under the new (follow-on) charter but only on the basis that the new charterers received a reduction in the daily rate of the hire. The question was whether damages were limited by the remoteness principles to the difference between the charter rate and the market rate at the time of redelivery for the nine-day period of the overrun when the owners did not have the vessel because of the breach (as argued by the charterers) or whether the owners could claim damages based on the loss of hire on the next charter ($8,000 a day for 191 days of the follow-on charter). The owners alleged that the latter measure was the only way in which they could be compensated for their actual loss but the charterers argued that this was possible only where there was actual knowledge (second limb of **Hadley v Baxendale**).
>
> The arbitrator and judge had considered that this situation fell within the first limb (normal loss) so that the actual loss suffered was within reasonable contemplations. The Court of Appeal agreed on the basis that a time charterer would know that the owner was likely to have entered into a new charter to follow closely on from the redelivery of the vessel and impliedly took the risk of loss in relation to this if they were late in redelivering.
>
> However, the House of Lords disagreed and considered that damages were limited to the lower figure, namely the difference between the charter rate and the market rate at the time of redelivery for the nine-day period of the overrun. The charterers had assumed responsibility for the nine-day delay in returning the vessel but that they had not assumed responsibility for the entirety of the follow-on charter because they could neither control that loss nor quantify it.

Unfortunately in terms of clarity of the law, their Lordships did not adopt a single line of reasoning to justify this conclusion and unfortunately it is the first approach which may be adopted in future.

1. Lord Hoffmann and Lord Hope

The question to ask in terms of remoteness in contract was whether in objective terms the charterers had 'assumed responsibility' for the loss in question. Remoteness on this basis would turn not on questions of normal or abnormal loss but on whether the loss for which compensation is sought is of a 'kind' or a 'type' for which the contract-breaker ought fairly to be taken to have accepted responsibility. With respect, this is the law of tort and is mostly closely associated with Lord Hoffmann's speech in **SAAMCO (South Australia Asset Management Corp v York Montague Ltd)** [1997] AC 191. This may be envisaged as a way of recognizing what losses ought objectively to be treated as falling within the parties' contemplations and it is tempting to talk of this being constituted by those losses which the parties must have intended to assume responsibility for but it does not actually take us to that determination. It is similar to reasonable contemplations in that focus is on outcomes and not the process of getting there. It might just as effectively be argued that the parties assume responsibility for normal losses because these are expected, whereas abnormal losses would not assumed without a more express assumption of the risk involved. The question still needs to be addressed of for what losses does a party assume responsibility? The real issue in **Transfield** was the extent or type of the loss and whether the extent of a loss fell within the parties' reasonable contemplations but that principle could have been refined without taking a sledge hammer to existing principles of remoteness. The real problem appears to have been the finding, in general terms, by the courts below that this follow-on charter was normal loss and therefore the full extent of that normal loss ought to have been within remoteness. However, neither conclusion need follow. The motivation for this decision was accepted practice and understanding in the shipping industry that 'liability was restricted to the difference between the market rate and the charter rate for the overrun period'. Such an outcome could have been accommodated within the application of existing principles and approaches. How could the full extent of the loss be within the parties' reasonable contemplations when both would have been aware of this restriction and so could not be said to be contracting on a different basis unless there was express evidence of a contrary intention? The type/loss principle could have been abandoned as not reflecting the parties' objective intentions on losses for which there should be responsibility, or the House could have concluded that on the facts this was abnormal loss so that an express acceptance of the risk based on knowledge would be required. The only result of adopting the first approach is that there are likely to be arguments denying an assumption of responsibility for all and any losses as this has now become a question of fact in each instance. The clear market understanding in *Transfield* is likely to be a rarity. Defendants will need to establish all the background facts that they will rely upon as denying an assumption of responsibility. The result will be complex arguments on remoteness—both facts and law. There are also unhelpful references throughout to 'reasonable foreseeability' (tort) and duties of care, which have no place in the contractual context (*The Heron II*). The scope of recovery in contract must reflect the fact that the context and knowledge is necessarily tighter.

2. Lord Rodger and Baroness Hale

This approach has more to recommend it, with the exception of references to reasonable foreseeability. Lord Rodger concluded that neither party would reasonably have contemplated that an overrun of nine days would 'in the ordinary course of things' cause the owners the type of loss for which they claimed damages. It followed that this was not normal loss but the product of the 'extremely volatile market conditions' causing the owners' actions in relation to the discount. On this basis, the loss was too remote to be recoverable. There are similarities here with the approach adopted by the Court of Appeal in *Victoria Laundry* since the definition of loss is an extremely narrow one and it may be that this is the preferable method of analysing cases such as this one. Loss of profits on a follow-on charter ought generally to be normal loss. The extent of the loss, and even its precise origins, would not have been within the parties' imputed contemplations. That has generally led to recovery for the full extent of the loss (see *H. Parsons (Livestock) Ltd v Uttley Ingham & Co. Ltd* [1978] 1 QB 791 and *Brown v KMR Services Ltd* [1995] 4 All ER 598 and the type/extent principle). The type/extent principle was not regarded as being incorrect by either Lord Rodger or Baroness Hale.

3. Lord Walker

Whilst Lord Walker regarded the assumption of responsibility principle as 'helpful' in the tort context, he did not go as far as adopting it for contract. This must be correct since it does not assist in explaining how the assumption of responsibility is to be determined and it is clear that the test must remain different from the test in tort and be based on losses within reasonable contemplations. Lord Walker considered that the parties had simply not contracted on the basis that there should be unlimited recovery for losses associated with the follow-on charter, particularly as the charterers could have no control over the follow-on contract or the terms on which the owners had contracted. This is much closer to the approach adopted by Lord Rodger and Baroness Hale.

Conclusion

It is difficult to say where this leaves the remoteness test for recovery in contract. It may be that the type/extent principle ought to be reformulated in the context of reasonable contemplations so as to limit recovery. Alternatively, the same result can be achieved as was achieved by Lord Rodger and Baroness Hale by narrowly identifying the loss in the first instance. This is in line with *Victoria Laundry*, although difficult to assimilate with other decisions on the type/loss principle. What is, unfortunately, probably more likely to happen is that courts will seize on the assumption of responsibility principle and, by default, end up assimilating remoteness in contract and tort. This is to be regretted and it is to be hoped that the rationale for the contract test in *Hadley v Baxendale*, as explained and interpreted in the *Heron II*, will prevail. This decision may be no more than a desire to reflect the contracting context (evident elsewhere in recent decisions of their Lordships), but that can be accommodated without doing damage to the established basis of principle. One early sign is encouraging. In *ASM Shipping Ltd of India v TTMI Ltd of England, The Amer Energy* [2009] 1 Lloyd's Rep 293, in the context of an attempt to reopen the *Hadley v Baxendale* approach that had been taken to remoteness, Flaux J stated:

> To the extent that Lord Hoffmann was purporting to lay down some new test as to recoverability of damages in contract, he was in a minority. Although Lord Hope adopts a similar analysis at paras 30 and 36, he does so essentially by way of application of established principles. In any event it is important to note that even Lord Hoffmann acknowledges in paras 9 and 11 of his opinion that departure from the normal principles of foreseeability would be unusual. Although he refers to shipping as a market where limitations on the extent of liability arising out of general expectations in that market might be more common, I do not consider that he was intending to say that in all shipping cases (as opposed to the type of time charter case then under consideration) the rule in *Hadley v Baxendale* as subsequently refined, will no longer apply. If he was saying that, it was not a view shared by the majority and it would be heterodox to say the least.

This interpretation also received some support from Cooke J in *Classic Maritime Inc. v Lion Diversified Holdings Berhad* [2009] EWHC 1142 (Comm), [2010] 1 Lloyd's Rep 59, when he noted the disapproval of Flaux J and commented that it would be surprising if the House of Lords had altered the remoteness test for contract to 'assumption of responsibility'. Cooke J went on to apply the first limb in *Hadley v Baxendale* and approved references to 'reasonable contemplations'. On the basis that the loss in question was within the parties' contemplations, Cooke J considered that none of their Lordships in *Transfield* had said that the full extent of such a loss should not be recoverable.

Thus, the crucial factor is not that 'assumption of responsibility' and 'reasonable contemplations' are different tests, which Faux J denied in *The Amer Energy*, but whether it is possible post-*Transfield* to retain the limbs of normal loss and abnormal loss to assist in reaching a conclusion on this outcome. The comments in *Classic Maritime* and the application in *GB Gas Holdings Ltd v Accenture (UK) Ltd* [2009] EWHC 2734 (Comm), suggest that the limbs are not so easily overturned as they provide an established and helpful route to a conclusion. It is possible to analyse *Transfield* as a decision based on the loss falling outside the parties' reasonable contemplations because the contractual context required special knowledge of the facts pertaining to the follow-on contract.

9.9.3 Mitigation

A claimant is under a 'duty' to mitigate his loss in the sense that a claimant may not recover damages for losses which could have been avoided by taking reasonable steps.

In *British Westinghouse Electric and Manufacturing Co. Ltd v Underground Electric Railways Co. of London Ltd* [1912] AC 673, Viscount Haldane LC said (at p. 689):

> The fundamental basis is…compensation for pecuniary loss naturally flowing from the breach; but this first principle is qualified by a second, which imposes on a plaintiff the duty of taking all reasonable steps to mitigate the loss consequent upon the breach, and debars him from claiming in respect of any part of the damage which is due to his neglect to take such steps…[T]his second principle does not impose on the plaintiff an obligation to take any step which a reasonable and prudent man would not ordinarily take in the course of his business.

The mitigation principle is central to many other aspects of the law relating to damages. For example, we have already seen how the market-price rule for quantification of difference in value damages is based on an assumption of immediate mitigation of loss (see **9.3.2.1**).

9.9.3.1 Reasonable steps

The duty to mitigate is limited by the fact that a claimant is only required to take **reasonable steps** to minimize its loss. Thus, loss will not be recoverable if it could be avoided by taking reasonable steps. The market-price rule for quantifying difference in value damages embodies this limitation, in that where there is a market it is reasonable for the claimant to seek substitute performance via the market, and loss greater than that represented by the market price formula cannot be recovered.

What is reasonable will very largely depend upon the facts of individual cases. In *Pilkington v Wood* [1953] Ch 770, it was held that there was no duty to embark on 'a complicated and difficult piece of litigation' in order to attempt to remedy the consequences of the defendant's breach of contract. However, in some circumstances it may be reasonable to accept the performance offered by the defendant even when that performance amounts to breach of the original contract. If it remains the best substitute performance available then it will be unreasonable not to go to that source (*Payzu Ltd v Saunders* [1919] 2 KB 581). What is reasonable may also depend upon the circumstances of the claimant. In *Wroth v Tyler* [1974] Ch 30, the plaintiff was unable to mitigate because he lacked the financial resources to make a substitute purchase. His failure to mitigate was not unreasonable in the circumstances.

A claimant must not by unreasonable action on its part increase the loss resulting from the breach and reasonableness of the action is judged at the time when the need to take such action arises.

- If the claimant takes reasonable steps in an attempt to minimize the loss but these reasonable steps result in increased loss, the claimant can recover for that increased loss.

In *Banco de Portugal v Waterlow* [1932] AC 452, the defendant's breach resulted in large numbers of forged banknotes circulating in Portugal. The plaintiffs undertook to honour the face value of all such notes, although they were able to detect the forgeries. The plaintiffs' action increased the loss resulting from the breach, but was held to be reasonable because to have done otherwise would have caused a crisis of confidence in the paper currency. The assessment of reasonableness must be judged at the time and not with the benefit of hindsight. As Lord Macmillan stated, at p. 506: 'It is often easy after an emergency has passed to criticize the steps which have been taken to meet it, but such criticism does not come well from those who have themselves created the emergency. The law is satisfied if the party placed in a difficult situation by reason of the breach of a duty owed to him has acted reasonably in the adoption of remedial measures, and he will not be held disentitled to recover the cost of such measures merely because the party in breach can suggest that other measures less burdensome to him might have been taken.'

- **Conversely, if the mitigating act has the effect of wiping out the loss resulting from the breach, the claimant will be entitled to only nominal damages for that breach.**

In the *British Westinghouse* case, the appellants were to supply electricity turbines to the respondents' specification. The turbines never met that specification, and after a time were replaced by turbines of a different manufacture. These turbines were much more efficient to run, so that the savings over the original turbines were such that the replacement machines paid for themselves in a short time. The respondents claimed damages for the cost of replacing the original turbines, but the House of Lords refused that claim. The respondents had rightly mitigated their loss, and had been so successful that most of the losses had been eliminated. The respondents were not entitled to anything more than the compensation already received for the period of time when the original turbines were running inefficiently.

However, the rule that benefits from actions taken in mitigation of the loss must be set off against the loss, even to the point of eliminating it, applies only where there is a demonstrable link between the original breach, the mitigating steps, and the benefit accruing. A merely collateral benefit accruing as a result of a new contract entered into in an effort to mitigate would not be set off against loss claimed as a result of the breach (*Famosa Shipping Co. Ltd v Armada Bulk Carriers Ltd* [1994] 1 Lloyd's Rep 633).

9.9.3.2 Mitigation and anticipatory breach

The mitigation principle applies to breach by anticipatory repudiation (see 8.7) as it applies to ordinary breach, but in some instances the effect of its application is rather different.

- Where the non-breaching party accepts the repudiation as terminating the contract, loss sustained is subject to the mitigation principle from the moment of that acceptance and it is not possible to wait until the date for performance due under the contract.

- However, where the non-breaching party affirms the contract following an anticipatory breach, the rule that the loss must not be increased by taking unreasonable steps is reflected in the rule that a party may not affirm the contract and continue performance in the face of a repudiation unless that party has a legitimate interest in so doing (see 8.7.3.1). Where the contract is affirmed, the obligation to take steps to reduce the loss which will be sustained when the time for performance comes, arises only at the time for performance.

This rule is conceptually logical, in that the mitigation principle expects the claimant to take steps to reduce the loss resulting from breach. If the contract is affirmed there will be no breach until non-performance on the due date, and until then both breach and loss are only potential, so that there is no scope for the mitigation principle to apply. Nevertheless, this rule seems rather wasteful, since it allows the claimant to take no action even when it is clear that performance will not take place and it is also clear that some of the loss is avoidable. Avoiding such waste may be preferable to the conceptual purity of the existing rule (see also discussion at 8.7.3.1).

9.9.4 Non-pecuniary loss

9.9.4.1 General limitation

As a general rule, damages cannot be recovered in contract for losses which do not affect a pecuniary interest of the claimant, and to this extent contractual damages may under-compensate that claimant.

✓ Key point

In addition to financial loss a claimant might suffer disappointment, hurt feelings, or distress as a result of breach, but damages for such non-pecuniary losses are generally not recoverable in contract.

This general rule is said to stem from the House of Lords' authority of *Addis v Gramophone Co. Ltd* [1909] AC 488, where it was held that it was not possible to recover damages for the distress caused by the nature of a dismissal from employment (i.e., caused by the **manner of the breach**), as opposed to directly caused by the breach itself. This general principle was approved by the House of Lords in *Johnson v Gore Wood and Co. (a firm)* [2002] 2 AC 1.

In *Watts v Morrow* [1991] 1 WLR 1421, Bingham LJ explained that the general denial of liability for non-pecuniary loss was based 'on considerations of policy' rather than because such loss was not considered to be a foreseeable consequence of the breach.

9.9.4.2 Distress consequent on physical inconvenience

It follows from the statements above that damages for distress **are** recoverable where that distress is directly consequent on physical inconvenience caused by the breach. In *Perry v Sidney Phillips and Son* [1982] 1 WLR 1297, the Court of Appeal held that damages for distress caused by repairs necessitated following a negligent property survey were recoverable on the basis that this loss was foreseeable. This principle was also applied in *Watts v Morrow* [1991] 1 WLR 1421, to allow recovery for distress caused by the physical inconvenience of living in a property while repairs were carried out. A recent example is provided by the decision in *Haysman v Mrs Rogers Films Ltd* [2008] EWHC 2494 (QB). Damages for distress were payable when a film company that had contracted to use the claimant's home damaged the property, and particularly the driveway. These distress damages may be considered as damages for distress consequent on the physical inconvenience of the repair process but were also considered to fall within the 'peace of mind' exception.

This also appears to be the basis for recovery in *Hobbs v London and South Western Railway Co.* (1875) LR 10 QB 111.

The plaintiff and his family were taken to the wrong station by the railway company, necessitating a walk of several miles on a wet night. The plaintiff recovered damages for that inconvenience.

Had the plaintiff mitigated his loss by hiring a cab (which, assuming one could be found, would have been reasonable), his expenditure would clearly have been recoverable. Thus, although the loss was in fact non-pecuniary, it might just as well have been very specifically quantifiable in financial terms. It is where the loss bears no relation to a financial loss that the general principle is that courts will not award damages.

The House of Lords in *Farley v Skinner (No. 2)* [2001] UKHL 49, [2002] 2 AC 732, considered that, as an alternative basis for the award of damages on the facts, the claimant could have recovered damages for distress consequent on the physical inconvenience caused by the breach of contract.

Farley v Skinner (No. 2) involved a negligent survey report in relation to a house in the vicinity of Gatwick Airport. The plaintiff had specifically requested that the defendant investigate whether the house would be affected by aircraft noise and the surveyor had negligently reported that this noise would not be a problem. The plaintiff purchased the house and spent money on modernization but, on moving in, discovered that the house was close to a navigation beacon where aircraft were stacked prior to landing and as a result was badly affected by aircraft noise at such times. The plaintiff decided not to sell but sought damages for the breach of contract. It was found as a fact that there was no difference in value between the price paid for the house and its market value. However, the judge at first instance awarded £10,000 damages for distress consequent upon the plaintiff's physical discomfort caused by this noise. The majority of the Court of Appeal allowed the defendant's appeal on the basis that there was no physical inconvenience. (This would appear to miss the point since, in accordance with the terms of this exception, the distress must be **consequent on physical inconvenience caused by the breach**; it is not the case that the distress itself needs to be classified as physical.)

Although the House of Lords considered that the case fell within one of the exceptional situations where it was possible to recover damages for distress, their Lordships also considered (*obiter*) that the plaintiff might have recovered damages for distress consequent on physical inconvenience.

Lord Scott treated the **physical discomfort** suffered by the plaintiff as consequential loss so that the distress which followed was recoverable as being within the reasonable contemplations of the parties as liable to result from this breach. He stressed that it was the **cause** of the inconvenience or discomfort that was vital, rather than assessing whether the distress itself was physical or non-physical and this must be the correct approach. By comparison, distress or disappointment attributable only to the fact that the breach of contract has occurred is not recoverable, but if the breach leads to physical consequences and inconvenience, damages can be awarded to compensate for the distress which follows from those physical consequences.

9.9.4.3 Major or important object of the contract is to provide pleasure, relaxation, peace of mind, or freedom from molestation

In addition to distress consequent on physical inconvenience, there are other recognized instances where such damages may be recovered. These exceptions were recognized by the Court of Appeal in *Bliss v South East Thames Regional Health Authority* [1987] ICR 700, which also reinforced the authority of *Addis v Gramophone* as the central principle.

Dillon LJ stated that there were exceptions 'where the contract which has been broken was itself a contract to provide peace of mind or freedom from distress': see *Jarvis v Swans Tours Ltd* [1973] QB 233, *Hamilton-Jones v David and Snape (a firm)* [2003] EWHC 3147 (Ch), [2004] 1 WLR 924, and *Heywood v Wellers* [1976] QB 466.

In *Watts v Morrow* [1991] 1 WLR 1421, Bingham LJ (at p. 1445) explained the exceptional cases in the following statement, which has subsequently been accepted as the authoritative statement of the scope of these exceptions:

> But the rule is not absolute. Where the very object of a contract is to provide pleasure, relaxation, peace of mind or freedom from molestation, damages will be awarded if the fruit of the contract is not provided or if the contrary result is procured instead.

Loss of expectation of pleasure or of freedom from molestation

In these exceptional situations, where the contract is intended to confer a benefit other than a pecuniary gain, damages for disappointment can be justified on the basis of compensating for the loss of expectation of that benefit (or, to put it another way, protection of the 'performance interest'). Again, these exceptions can be seen as covering distress caused by the breach rather than the manner of the breach.

> For example, in *Jarvis v Swans Tours Ltd* [1973] QB 233, the plaintiff booked a winter holiday which the defendants promised in their brochure would be like a 'house-party', with special entertainment and proper facilities for skiing. The skiing facilities were in fact inadequate, the entertainment was far from special, and in the second week the 'house-party' consisted of the plaintiff alone. The Court of Appeal held that he was entitled to recover not merely the cost of the holiday, but a similar amount again as general damages for the disappointment suffered and the loss of the entertainment he had been promised in the brochure. Lord Denning MR pointed out that the plaintiff had entered the contract not merely to purchase the travel facilities and the board and lodging, but in order to enjoy himself, and he was entitled to compensation for the loss of that part of his expectation. However, in *Wiseman v Virgin Atlantic Airways Ltd* [2006] EWHC 1566 (QB), (2006) 103 (29) LSG 29, the court rejected a claim for damages for distress when the claimant was ridiculed, alleged to have a fake passport, and prevented by the airline from using his return ticket. (Other claims for the breakdown of a relationship and the expenses of others were too remote and a robbery that occurred before the claimant was able to fly home was not caused by the breach of contract. It merely provided the situation in which the robbery occurred.)
>
> *Heywood v Wellers* [1976] QB 446 concerned a contract employing a solicitor for the express purpose of obtaining a non-molestation injunction against a former male friend of the plaintiff. The solicitor was negligent so that no effective protection was achieved. The damages award included a sum to compensate the plaintiff for the distress consequent on this failure to ensure the peace of mind and freedom from molestation, which it was the purpose of the contractual duty to achieve. Similarly, in *Demarco v Perkins* [2006] EWCA Civ 188, [2006] PNLR 27, the claimant had lost a substantial chance of obtaining an annulment of his bankruptcy through the negligence of the defendant accountants and was able to recover for the distress suffered as 'a material element in a retainer was the provision of peace of mind and the avoidance of distress'. Distress damages of £6,000 were therefore awarded, discounted for the loss of chance to £5,100.

In *Yearworth v North Bristol NHS Trust* [2009] EWCA Civ 37, [2009] 3 WLR 118, the Court of Appeal held that contractual arrangements for the storage of sperm amounted to a contract for the provision of peace of mind in that the purpose of the contract was to preserve the ability for the men involved to become fathers when they were about to undergo cancer treatment that would impact their fertility. It followed that modest recovery of damages for distress was possible when the storage equipment failed.

Loss of amenity as a loss of expectation

A similar rationale appears to underlie those cases where the court awards damages on the basis of cost of cure, despite the fact that the difference in value is small relative to that cost, in order to meet the claimant's particular expectation or 'consumer surplus' (e.g., *Radford v De Froberville* [1977] 1 WLR 1262: see **9.3.3.4**).

In *Ruxley Electronics and Construction Ltd v Forsyth* [1996] 1 AC 344, Lord Mustill recognized the need to 'cater for those occasions where the value of the promise to the promisee exceeds the financial enhancement of his position which full performance will secure' (see **9.3.3.1** for the earlier discussion of 'the consumer surplus'). Lord Lloyd believed that in this case the owner's subjective appreciation of the benefit of the contract could be catered for by making a modest award (for loss of amenity) expressly in reliance on *Jarvis v Swans Tours Ltd* (and see *Jackson v Horizon Holidays Ltd* [1975] 1 WLR 1468). Lord Lloyd stated that he could live with this conclusion as 'a further inroad on the rule in *Addis*', although he preferred to regard it as 'a logical application or adaptation of the existing exception to a new situation'. The argument was that Mr Forsyth had contracted for a swimming pool for reasons of pleasure, and in this sense his expectation had not been fulfilled. However, the amount awarded as damages for loss of amenity was relatively small, and significantly less than the cost of cure.

The award of damages for loss of amenity was considered by Lord Steyn in *Farley v Skinner (No. 2)* [2001] UKHL 49, [2002] 2 AC 732 at [21], to 'have been authoritatively established' although in *Johnson v Gore Wood and Co. (a firm)* [2002] 2 AC 1, when the House of Lords commented on this aspect of the decision in *Ruxley Electronics v Forsyth*, Lord Bingham made it clear that he did not consider that it affected the general applicability of *Addis* on the facts before him (a claim for distress damages by a company shareholder in relation to the management of the company).

Despite having been 'authoritatively established', it is difficult to justify the conclusion that the award of loss of amenity is generally available outside the context of the 'pleasure' exception to *Addis* (see Poole (1996) 59 MLR 272) so that if the main purpose of the contract is not the provision of pleasure, e.g. commercial contracts, *Ruxley* cannot permit a loss of amenity award. This was confirmed explicitly in *Regus (UK) Ltd v Epcot Solutions Ltd* [2007] EWHC 938 (Comm), [2007] 2 All ER (Comm) 766. (The decision of the Court of Appeal [2008] EWCA Civ 361, related to reasonableness of the exemption clause under UCTA 1977.)

This case concerned a contract for serviced office accommodation. The air-conditioning system was defective and a third-party inspector had recommended urgent remedial work, costing £23,500, but this was not carried out. In its claim for damages for breach of contract, the accommodation user had sought, along with damages for loss of profits, damages for distress, inconvenience, and loss of amenity in connection with the defective air-conditioning system. However, the judge held that there was no authority permitting recovery for loss of amenity where the purpose of the contract was not to provide pleasure and that *Ruxley* could not apply here. In relation to *Ruxley* he stated (at [48]): 'As I read the decision…the House of Lords…upheld, for the most part in passing, an award of damages of £2,500 for loss of pleasurable amenity (i.e. fun) of a swimming pool. This was on the basis that the contract was one to provide pleasure and amenity analogous to *Jarvis* and the holiday cases, and thus very different from the business purpose of the contract in this case. Epcot does not however appear to claim damages for loss of any subjective or idiosyncratic pleasure or amenity and it would be unusual, if not impossible for a company to do so. For the most part a company's advances and setbacks are measured in financial terms. I emphasise that I was taken to no authority on this issue.'

9.9.4.4 The scope of the exceptions and cases falling outside

With the exception of these situations, the courts have refused to award damages for non-pecuniary loss and they have consistently refused to extend the recognized scope of these exceptions despite encouragement to do so from counsel in a number of cases.

The scope of the exceptions was believed to be limited by the need to show that the object of pleasure, peace of mind, or freedom from distress was **the very object** of the contract (i.e., the fundamental purpose of the contract) (see Macdonald (1994) 7 JCL 94 and Capper (2000) 116 LQR 553).

In *Watts v Morrow* [1991] 1 WLR 1421, the Court of Appeal, placing considerable reliance on the decision in *Hayes v James and Charles Dodd* [1990] 2 All ER 815, declined to give more than a very narrow scope to the category of contracts 'to provide peace of mind or freedom from distress', and refused to regard a surveyor as having any such contractual obligation towards the purchaser of a house for whom he had prepared a report on the basis that 'peace of mind' was not the subject matter of such a contract.

A further example is provided by *Alexander v Rolls Royce Motor Cars* [1996] RTR 95, where it was held that a contract for car repair was not a contract to provide freedom from worry and anxiety since this was not the subject matter of the contract.

This restrictive interpretation enabled the courts to discount the possibility of recovery of distress damages in the case of breaches of commercial contracts since the essential object of such contracts is not the provision of pleasure or peace of mind. Of course, as a matter of policy there is much to be said in favour of not permitting any extension of distress damages to commercial cases. In *Hayes v James and Charles Dodd* [1990] 2 All ER 815, Staughton LJ was very robust in dismissing such a claim for distress damages (in the context of a claim against solicitors dealing with a commercial conveyance where there had been a failure to advise that the business purchased would be landlocked). In his view the reason for disallowing the claim was not merely a question of remoteness of damage, but one of policy. The policy was to limit recovery for mental distress to 'certain classes of case' (see more recently *Johnson v Gore Wood and Co.* [2002] 2 AC 1, confirming this position and Lord Scott in *Farley v Skinner (No. 2)* [2001] UKHL 49, [2002] 2 AC 732 at [82]: if the only disappointment relates to a the failure to perform the contractual obligations and nothing more, then recovery is ruled out on policy grounds). Staughton LJ in *Hayes v James and Charles Dodd* referred to the dangers of allowing recovery of distress damages in commercial cases when he stated:

I would not view with enthusiasm the prospect that every shipowner in the Commercial Court, having successfully claimed for unpaid freight or demurrage, would be able to add a claim for mental distress suffered while he was waiting for his money.

However, this case law and comment also illustrated the reluctance to extend the scope of the exceptions. This may be explained in part by the difficulty of quantification of such losses, by the fear of unfounded claims (since such feelings are hard to prove or disprove), and by the fear of double compensation (in that disappointment, etc. may be adequately compensated by an award of damages for any pecuniary interest injured by the breach).

More liberal interpretation of 'the objects exception'

In the light of this general approach, the decision of the House of Lords in *Farley v Skinner (No. 2)* [2001] UKHL 49, [2002] 2 AC 732, represents a more liberal interpretation of the scope of the 'objects' exception since the House awarded distress damages on the basis that **the major or important object** of the contract was to provide pleasure, relaxation, or peace of mind. **This object no longer needs to the sole or 'very' object of the contract.**

> The crucial fact in *Farley v Skinner* (for full facts see **9.9.4.2**) was that the plaintiff had specifically requested the surveyor to report on the impact of aircraft noise so that the case could be distinguished from a general survey contract. As an alternative to the argument that damages were recoverable for distress consequent on physical inconvenience, the plaintiff argued that the 'objects' exception applied. However, the majority of the Court of Appeal had rejected this argument on the basis that 'the very object' of the contract was to undertake the survey with reasonable care and skill and not to provide peace of mind. The obligation to investigate the aircraft noise was not 'the very object' but a minor aspect of the overall contractual purpose.
>
> On appeal, the House of Lords held that because the plaintiff had specifically asked for confirmation on this matter, it was sufficient that the obligation to investigate the aircraft noise was a major or important part of this contract.

Evaluation of the scope of the exception in *Farley v Skinner (No. 2)*

In practical terms, this relaxation is unlikely to have much impact in the absence of some specific request to give an undertaking, such as occurred on the facts in *Farley v Skinner (No. 2)*.

In addition, Lord Scott considered that such an award of damages for distress would not arise at all if there was a difference in value as a result of the breach. Lord Scott justified this conclusion by stating that any other conclusion would involve double recovery. With respect, it is difficult to see that this necessarily follows since a claimant may suffer a reduction in the value of property **and** additional loss of satisfaction with the end product. In *Hamilton-Jones v David and Snape (a firm)* [2003] EWHC 3147 (Ch), [2004] 1 WLR 924 the court awarded damages for distress as an additional element of the damages award.

In *Farley v Skinner* it had also been argued that damages for distress could not be awarded in relation to a breach of a qualified contractual obligation, such as the duty to exercise reasonable care and skill in carrying out a survey (*Watts v Morrow* [1991] 1 WLR 1421). The House of Lords rejected such a restriction on the basis that it should not make any difference to the recovery of distress damages whether the claimant had negotiated for a guarantee or only a qualified contractual obligation.

Finally, their Lordships rejected the argument that the plaintiff had forfeited any right to claim non-pecuniary damages by failing to move out of the house; such action was reasonable in the circumstances so that the plaintiff had not failed in the duty to mitigate his loss.

Differences in approach in *Farley v Skinner*

There is a considerable divergence in approach, if not in outcome, between Lord Steyn (with whose reasons Lord Browne-Wilkinson agreed) and Lord Scott (who expressed the belief that he was agreeing with the reasoning of Lord Steyn).

Lord Scott appears to have been advocating a broader approach to the assessment of distress damages as part of the performance interest debate (see **9.3.1**). Indeed, his approach is not linked expressly to the objects exception. The loss of amenity award in *Ruxley* was treated as a direct consequence of the failure to fulfil the performance interest (referred to as 'deprivation of a contractual benefit') and compensatable on the normal basis. Lord Scott distinguished this case from a true distress damages case where distress is treated as a consequential loss. He then proceeded to analyse many of the damages for distress cases as being examples of 'deprivation of contractual benefit' to which normal principles for determining the measure of damages applied. This analysis also applied on the facts of *Farley v Skinner (No. 2)* because of the specific request and report on the aircraft noise.

This moves determination of recovery away from the 'object exception' and back to general principles of recovery. It ought to follow, therefore, that recovery for distress would be more generous on the 'deprivation of contractual benefit' analysis since the main limitation will be remoteness and not the scope of the contractual object.

Farley v Skinner applied

> In ***Hamilton-Jones v David and Snape (a firm)*** [2003] EWHC 3147 (Ch), [2004] 1 WLR 924, in addition to an award for her financial loss, the claimant was awarded £20,000 as damages for mental distress on the basis that 'a major or important object of the contract' was to ensure the claimant's peace of mind through the actions of the defendant solicitors with a view to preventing her estranged husband from removing the children from the country. The defendant failed in this duty and two of the children were removed from the jurisdiction. This could not be the sole purpose of the contract because under the applicable legislation that was the protection of the child. However, Neuberger J referred to this peace of mind purpose as 'a significant reason for the claimant instructing the defendants' and concluded therefore that it 'was at least "an important" object of the contract and part of the reason for contracting', which satisfied the test for recovery stipulated in ***Farley v Skinner***.

The judge made no attempt to apply Lord Scott's approach to the determination of recovery but relied on the traditional exceptions, as interpreted and extended in ***Farley v Skinner (No. 2)***. This case has therefore entrenched the approach in ***Farley*** but its real significance may lie in the size of the award of damages for distress since the usual figures awarded are on the low side, e.g. £2,500 in ***Ruxley Electronics v Forsyth*** (not challenged or debated as to figure on appeal) and £10,000 in *Farley v Skinner*. Lord Steyn noted that such awards 'should be restrained and modest' and Lord Scott considered £10,000 to be 'on the high side'. *Gemma Ltd v Gimson* [2004] EWHC 1982 (TCC), 97 Con LR 165, may represent the high point of likely recovery and is based on extreme inconvenience and distress over a ninety-week period. The couple (the building owners) were awarded £4,500 each with £250 to each of their four children), totalling £10,000.

A recent example demonstrating the liberality of the 'peace of mind' exception post ***Farley*** is provided by ***Haysman v Mrs Rogers Films Ltd*** [2008] EWHC 2494 (QB) (for facts see **9.9.4.2**). The judge considered that one of the important objects of the contract to use the claimant's house for filming was the peace of mind to the homeowner who was permitting this activity to take place. This would be stretching the scope of the exception in the absence of a similar provision to ***Farley*** involving an express undertaking to investigate, or in this case to protect. On the facts the film company had expressly promised to indemnify against damage to the property and to restore it to its original condition. This contract was distinguishable from an ordinary commercial contract and, although the contract itself may not have the purpose of pleasure or peace of mind, if pleasure or peace of mind can be shown to be a contract term or important part of the contract, the case may fall within the extended scope of the exception.

9.9.4.5 Challenging *Addis v Gramophone*

Although the decision in ***Addis v Gramophone*** was re-examined in ***Johnson v Unisys Ltd*** [2001] UKHL 9, [2003] 1 AC 518 (see **9.9.4.6**), the reconsideration was essentially focused on the question of whether, despite **Addis**, it is possible to claim damages for financial loss (i.e., loss of earnings/ loss of employment prospects) based on the manner of a wrongful dismissal.

- Lord Steyn expressly stated that the question before the House of Lords was no wider than this, i.e. it was not an authority on the question of damages for anxiety and mental stress resulting from the manner of the dismissal, and it would be 'wrong to express any view on it'.

- Lord Millett admitted that these facts did not represent 'an appropriate occasion on which to revisit' **Addis**, but explained that there could be no damages for injured feelings in the context of breaches of commercial contracts on the basis that such loss would be too remote. He also explained the 'exceptional' cases, such as **Jarvis v Swans Tours Ltd** [1973] QB 233, not as exceptions but as falling outside the principle in **Addis** altogether, because the loss (distress and disappointment) in such cases is the direct result of the breach itself, rather than the manner of the breach.

- Only Lord Hoffmann (with whose judgment Lord Bingham agreed) went as far as to suggest that if the question had been concerned with non-pecuniary loss (damages for distress, damage to reputation) resulting from the dismissal, he would have been prepared to 'circumvent or overcome the obstacle of *Addis*'.

Nevertheless, the fact that the **Addis** principle is no longer seen as permanently entrenched has been relied upon to justify the recent liberalization of the scope of the exceptions as part of a circular justification (see, for example, Neuberger J in **Hamilton-Jones v David and Snape (a firm)**, at [63], referring to the trend to extend the exceptions to **Addis** 'particularly…in claims by private consumers of goods and services'). This extension has, in turn, been considered to illustrate a more general unease with the scope of the principles in **Addis**.

9.9.4.6 Damages for loss of reputation

Traditionally it has not been possible, as a general rule, to recover contractual damages for loss of reputation. Quite apart from the inevitable difficulties of causation, the problem is that such a loss could not be formulated in terms of financial interests.

Addis v Gramophone Co. [1909] AC 488 has been interpreted as authority for the fact that a plaintiff wrongfully dismissed in a particularly abrupt way could not recover damages for injury to his reputation by the manner of his dismissal. Lord Loreburn went on to suggest that damages were not recoverable for the increased difficulty of obtaining alternative employment and this has also been interpreted as part of the *ratio* in the case, although in **Johnson v Unisys Ltd** [2001] UKHL 9, [2003] 1 AC 518, Lord Steyn regarded the headnote as 'arguably wrong' in so far as it states that it is never possible to sue for loss of employment prospects resulting from the manner of a dismissal. In a general sense, it is possible to distinguish this type of loss since it can be identified as financial loss and in general the law will allow damages for lost expectation (see **9.2.1**), and loss of this kind is sufficiently similar for it to be difficult to justify any distinction being made. It is on this question that there has been a radical re-evaluation.

Stigma compensation

Such damages for financial loss caused by difficulty in obtaining alternative employment (so-called 'stigma compensation') were awarded by the House of Lords in **Mahmud v Bank of Credit and Commerce International SA (in liquidation)** [1998] AC 20 (also known as *Malik v BCCI*) on the basis that the employer in the case was in breach of an implied term not to conduct the business in a dishonest and corrupt way. Exceptionally, on the facts of this case, it was reasonably foreseeable that such a breach would prejudice the future employment prospects of these employees. This was seen as an extremely limited decision because the claim in **Mahmud** was not a claim for true distress damages and it was not based on wrongful dismissal. It was limited to a claim for continuing financial loss ('special damage') due to an inability to obtain alternative employment resulting from breach of this particular implied term in the operation of the business.

In **Johnson v Unisys Ltd** [2001] UKHL 9, [2003] 1 AC 518, the claimant tried to use the principle in **Mahmud** but to extend it to such damages resulting from the manner of a wrongful dismissal. The Court of Appeal ([1999] 1 All ER 854) had considered that such a claim was precluded by **Addis** and that **Mahmud** could not apply to a claim based on **the manner of dismissal**. There is also a legislative regime for compensation for unfair dismissal under which compensation is capped at a maximum amount.

> In **Johnson v Unisys Ltd** the claimant had been summarily dismissed from his employment and had obtained the statutory maximum for unfair dismissal from an employment tribunal (at the time this was just under £11,700). He claimed that, as a result of the manner of the dismissal, he had suffered psychiatric illness and considerable distress and had been unable to obtain employment. Accordingly, he sought to recover £400,000 in lost earnings relying on the **Mahmud** argument, i.e. that by dismissing him in this way his employers had breached the implied term not to conduct themselves so as to damage the relationship of trust and confidence.

Basing the argument on breach of an implied term of trust and confidence does seem illogical, in that in the context of dismissal there will inevitably be this breakdown in the relationship, although it may be easier to argue if this obligation is limited to the manner of actually carrying out the dismissal.

> The majority of the House of Lords considered that the implied term of trust and confidence was an obligation in a continuing relationship rather than one relating to the termination of that relationship (although Lord Steyn would have extended the obligation to all aspects of the relationship and Lord Hoffmann would have considered a different implied term in relation to termination corresponding with a duty to act fairly). However, the principal difficulty for the majority in accepting any common law right to such damages lay in the fact that Parliament had already put in place a statutory regime governing this compensation. Only Lord Steyn did not consider this a difficulty, but agreed with the majority that the claimant could not recover at common law by citing the difficulties of establishing that the loss was not too remote and had actually been caused by the manner of the dismissal rather than the fact of dismissal.

It is unlikely, therefore, that an argument such as that in **Johnson v Unisys Ltd**, in relation to the dismissal process itself, will ever get very far because of these practical difficulties of proof (see *Bank of Credit and Commerce International SA (in liquidation) v Ali (No. 3)* [2002] EWCA Civ 82, [2002] 3 All ER 750, for evidence of the difficulties of causation even where the claim falls within **Mahmud**). The House of Lords has also made it clear that it is not possible to argue that the statutory unfair dismissal legislation permits any award for injured feelings: *Dunnachie v Kingston upon Hull City Council* [2004] UKHL 36, [2005] 1 AC 226.

The principle in **Mahmud** has therefore been confirmed as limited in its operation and it cannot currently apply to losses claimed to result from the manner of a wrongful dismissal. Nevertheless, in *Eastwood v Magnox Electric plc* [2004] UKHL 35, [2005] 1 AC 503, the House of Lords was able to distinguish **Johnson v Unisys Ltd**, since the breach causing loss (financial loss due to the psychiatric illness caused by the breach) had occurred prior to the dismissal process and so could be seen as independent of the subsequent unfair dismissal. This enabled a separate award of common law damages to be made in respect of this breach under the principle in **Mahmud** despite the existence of an award for the later unfair dismissal under the statutory scheme. Thus, the crucial question will be whether the breach in question was part of the dismissal procedure. If it is part of the dismissal procedure, it is covered by the unfair dismissal legislation which does not permit an award for injured feelings.

Although the actual decision in **Johnson v Unisys Ltd** is restrictive, it is clear that House of Lords wished to see further movement away from **Addis**, on the basis that the employer-employee relationship had moved on in the past ninety years (see Lord Steyn's speech), and Lord Hoffmann's suggestion of a willingness to get around **Addis** in the context of distress damages indicates that we may yet see further relaxation of the principle where the circumstances permit. Nevertheless, the House of Lords has also applied **Addis** in the context of a claim by company shareholders in *Johnson v Gore Wood and Co. (a firm)* [2002] 2 AC 1, although even in this decision Lord Cooke (at p. 109) suggested that **Addis** may not be a permanent feature of English law.

Instances where damages for loss of existing reputation are recoverable

There are a number of recognized instances of damage to an *existing* reputation.

- One such instance applies in the case of breach of a banking contract by the wrongful dishonouring of a cheque, which traditionally was limited to dishonouring the cheques of traders (*Wilson v United Counties Bank Ltd* [1920] AC 102).

In *Kpohraror v Woolwich Building Society* [1996] 4 All ER 119, the Court of Appeal extended this to non-trader clients of banks on the basis that the exception existed to protect the reputation for creditworthiness of the client. A reputation for creditworthiness is 'as important for their personal transactions' for individuals as it is for traders, given the existence of central registers of credit ratings. Individuals might also suffer loss if their reputations were damaged by the wrongful dishonouring of cheques. Accordingly, in today's society, there was no good reason for limiting this recovery to traders.

- Damages for loss of reputation may also be recoverable for breach of an advertising or publicity contract, where the main purpose of the contract is to promote and publicize. If the breach has the opposite effect, there is a failure of the main purpose of the contract. A good illustration of this is **Aerial Advertising Co. v Batchelors Peas Ltd (Manchester)** [1938] 2 All ER 788 (the 'one' contract law case that every law student seems to remember!).

The plaintiffs were to advertise the defendants' peas by flying over towns trailing a banner reading 'Eat Batchelors' peas'. In breach of contract, the pilot flew over the main square of Salford during the two minutes' silence on Armistice Day. This caused great upset and the defendants' products were boycotted, leading to a fall in sales.

9.10 Agreed damages provisions

As in many other areas of contract law, the nineteenth-century view that contractual obligations were founded in the will of the parties resulted in the rule that the common law provisions as to the award of damages might be displaced by express agreement. The *prima facie* rule is that if the parties provide in their contract for the amount of damages to be paid upon breach, that term of the contract will be enforced to the exclusion of whatever might be the common law measure of damages. Such clauses are common in commercial contracts, especially to deal with delay in performance.

There are advantages for both parties in the use of such clauses:

- The non-breaching party is spared the effort and possible expense of proving its loss, together with the added complexities of remoteness and mitigation, so that a claim for compensation will be relatively straightforward.

- In addition, the party who must perform has clear notice of the extent of the risk upon non-performance.

- The existence of such contractually agreed damages should avoid much of the disruption to the continuing relationship between the parties and the associated costs of a dispute on quantum, so that such clauses are generally regarded as efficient and desirable.

The courts have nevertheless been unwilling to allow their unfettered use on the basis that there is a danger that where the damages payable are set too high, the clause will have a punitive effect, which would be contrary to the essential purpose of enforcement of contractual obligations (see **Part 3(b)**). Further, there is a danger that disadvantageous terms as to damages might be forced by the stronger party on the other, rather than be freely negotiated.

Key point

The distinction between clauses which will be enforced and those which will not is expressed as a distinction between **liquidated damages clauses** (enforceable) and **penalty clauses** (unenforceable).

9.10.1 Liquidated damages clauses

The essence of a liquidated damages clause is that it should be a genuine attempt to pre-estimate the loss which will be suffered by breach (***Dunlop Pneumatic Tyre Co. Ltd v New Garage and Motor Co. Ltd*** [1915] AC 79). Once that definition is established, however, the identification of liquidated damages clauses is rather a process of elimination; that is, the clause will be enforced by the courts unless it falls foul of the rule against penalties (see **9.10.2**).

9.10.1.1 Effect of classification as a liquidated damages clause

Once a clause is classified as a liquidated damages clause, the liquidated sum will be payable whether the actual loss is greater or smaller than this stipulated sum.

In ***Cellulose Acetate Silk Co. Ltd v Widnes Foundry (1925) Ltd*** [1933] AC 20, the contract contained a term providing for damages for late performance to be paid 'by way of penalty' at a rate of £20 per week. The actual loss for a delay of thirty weeks was £5,850. The House of Lords held that despite the designation of this clause as a penalty, it was in fact a genuine pre-estimate of the likely loss resulting from delay and so was a liquidated damages clause. It therefore followed that the non-breaching party could recover only £600 (£20 × 30).

9.10.1.2 Distinguished from limitation clauses

One function of a liquidated damages clause may be to keep the compensation payable upon breach below the amount of the loss actually sustained. For the party who must perform, the advantage of knowing the precise extent of the risk of non-performance usually lies in knowing that the risk is limited. Thus, in *Cellulose Acetate Silk Co. Ltd v Widnes Foundry (1925) Ltd*, damages payable under the clause amounted to £600, while the actual loss was £5,850. Ironically, it was the non-breaching party who sought to avoid the clause on the ground that it was a 'penalty', a threat to compel him to perform, so that he could recover his actual loss.

Cases of this kind raise the question whether liquidated damages clauses are a class of exemption clause, subject to the panoply of controls now existing over such clauses (see generally 7.5). In *Suisse Atlantique Société d'Armement Maritime SA v NV Rotterdamsche Kolen Centrale* [1967] 1 AC 361 (see 7.4.3) it was suggested that such a clause was not a limitation clause, since it fixed the amount payable irrespective of loss, so that the sum would be payable even if the loss were less than the amount stipulated. A limitation clause simply puts a ceiling (or upper limit) on the loss recoverable, and if the loss is below that amount only the actual loss is recoverable. On the other hand, it would seem that a clause fixing damages at an amount below the lowest possible loss which can be envisaged at the time of contracting is a form of limitation clause. It may be that the area of overlap between limitation clauses and liquidated damages clauses requires further examination, and perhaps reform (see 9.10.4).

9.10.2 **Penalties**

A clause is a penalty if the sum fixed is not a genuine pre-estimate of the loss suffered in the event of breach but is designed as a threat to compel the other to perform by penalizing that other for non-performance.

An example of a penalty is the retransfer clause in *Jobson v Johnson* [1989] 1 WLR 1026.

> The defendant had contracted to purchase shares in a football club on terms whereby, if he defaulted on payment of any instalment of the purchase price, he was required to retransfer the shares for £40,000. The defendant defaulted when he had paid £140,000 of the purchase price. The Court of Appeal held that the retransfer clause was not a genuine pre-estimate of the loss on breach but a penalty payable on breach.

The classic statement of the approach to be adopted is the statement of Colman J in *Lordsvale Finance plc v Bank of Zambia* [1996] QB 752 at 762:

> Whether a provision is to be treated as a penalty is a matter of construction to be resolved by asking whether at the time the contract was entered into the predominant contractual function of the provision was to deter a party from breaking the contract or to compensate the innocent party for breach. That the contractual function is deterrent rather than compensatory can be deduced by comparing the amount that would be payable on breach with the loss that might be sustained if breach occurred.

9.10.2.1 Effect of classification as a penalty

Until this case it had largely been assumed that classification of a term as a penalty resulted in the clause being wholly unenforceable, and the non-breaching party being left to recover unliquidated damages at common law to compensate for their actual loss. However, in *Jobson v Johnson*, the Court of Appeal held that it was for the court, in the exercise of its equitable jurisdiction against penalties, to enforce the penal clause only to an extent commensurate with the actual loss sustained by the non-breaching party, i.e. the penalty is unenforceable beyond the actual loss suffered (per Nicholls LJ at p. 1040).

Of course, in many cases the distinction is of no relevance, for the quantification of damages payable would be the same in each case. But in *Jobson v Johnson* the Court of Appeal relied on the exact nature of this equitable jurisdiction to impose complex terms on the plaintiff's right to a remedy, involving an election between alternative modes of proceeding, which went way beyond the mere recovery of damages.

To summarize the position:

- If the actual loss is lower than the penalty amount, only the actual loss can be recovered because the penalty is invalid.
- It should follow that if the actual loss is greater than the penalty amount, the non-breaching party should be able to claim its higher actual loss.

This conclusion was given some support by the decision in *Wall v Rederiaktiebolaget Luggude* [1915] 3 KB 66 but provoked some considerable academic debate (see Hudson (1974) 90 LQR 31 and (1975) 91 LQR 25, Gordon (1974) 90 LQR 296, and Barton (1976) 92 LQR 20). Such a conclusion encourages the non-breaching party whose actual loss if higher than the penalty amount to argue that an agreed damages clause is an unenforceable penalty (see, e.g., the argument in *Cellulose Acetate Silk Co. Ltd v Widnes Foundry (1925) Ltd* [1933] AC 20).

In the context of consumer contracts (see 7.7), penalties may additionally be unenforceable as 'unfair' terms. Under the Unfair Terms in Consumer Contracts Regulations 1999, SI 1999/2083, Sch. 2(1)(e), a term may be unfair where it has not been individually negotiated if it requires 'any consumer who fails to fulfil his obligation to pay a disproportionately high sum in compensation'.

In *Munkenbeck and Marshall v Harold* [2005] EWHC 356 (TCC), unreported, 17 March 2005, a term providing for interest to be payable at 8 per cent over base in the event of late payment was held to be unfair within the regulations because it was considered to be onerous and unusual and caused an imbalance contrary to the good faith requirement since there was no similar term in respect of monies which might fall due to the consumer. However, the interest clause did not constitute a penalty as, in the light of the relevant rate of interest under the late-payment legislation, it could not be said that the figure in question did not represent a genuine pre-estimate of the damage likely to be suffered by the claimant architects in the event of non-payment by a client. Thus, on the facts, a liquidated damages clause was held to be an unfair term within the Unfair Terms in Consumer Contracts Regulations (UTCCR) 1999. (See further the discussion of the UTCCR 1999 at 7.7.)

9.10.3 Distinguishing liquidated damages and penalty clauses

The distinction between liquidated damages and penalty clauses is a vital one. It is essentially a question of construction depending upon the parties' intentions judged in the light of all the circumstances at the time of the contract. One of the main values of liquidated damages clauses is that they enable a precise figure to be put on the risk of breach, and therefore the court should intervene in such an agreement between the parties only where it appears that one is taking unfair advantage of the other.

Some guidelines to assist in determining this intention were laid down by Lord Dunedin in *Dunlop Pneumatic Tyre Co. Ltd v New Garage and Motor Co. Ltd* [1915] AC 79. The continuing authority of these guidelines was endorsed by the Privy Council in *Philips Hong Kong Ltd v Attorney-General of Hong Kong* (1993) 61 BLR 49.

- **The clause will be a penalty if the sum payable is 'extravagant and unconscionable' by comparison with the greatest loss which might be caused by the breach.**

In many cases this rule will be simple to apply. In *Philips Hong Kong Ltd v Attorney-General of Hong Kong*, it was held that comparisons must be made in respect of reasonably likely eventualities, and it would not be adequate proof that a clause amounts to a penalty to show a serious disparity between amounts recoverable and loss actually sustained in wholly unlikely, hypothetical situations. The Privy Council accepted that it would be very difficult to draft a clause which would never operate in a penal way. Lord Woolf also stressed that in a commercial contract, in the absence of blatant domination by one party over the other, the courts should not be as ready to conclude that a clause is penal because of the need for certainty in the commercial context.

This principle was confirmed in *McAlpine Capital Projects Ltd v Tilebox Ltd* [2005] EWHC 281 (TCC), [2005] BLR 271, where the judge noted the fact that since a penalty clause is an anomaly, the courts were predisposed to enforce agreed damages clauses as liquidated damages, particularly where the agreement was made in a commercial context between two parties of equal bargaining power.

In *Cenargo Ltd v Izar Construcciones Navales SA* [2002] EWCA Civ 524, [2002] CLC 1151, the Court of Appeal (*obiter*) adopted the approach in *Philips* and considered that in the commercial context, an agreed damages clause should not be tested against trifling breaches causing trifling loss. The clause in question should therefore be construed as applying only to major breaches, for which it would be a genuine pre-estimate of the loss. This decision further illustrates the policy objective in assessing agreed damages clauses in commercial contracts.

In *Murray v Leisureplay plc* [2005] EWCA Civ 963, [2005] IRLR 946, the Court of Appeal had to consider whether a clause in a service agreement providing for the payment of one year's gross salary in the event of termination of the employment without a year's notice constituted an unenforceable penalty clause. The conclusions of the Court of Appeal reinforce the position that in a commercial contract it will be difficult to argue that a clause is penal. The Court of Appeal held, relying on *Dunlop Pneumatic Tyre Co. Ltd v New Garage & Motor Co. Ltd* [1915] AC 79, that the correct approach to determining whether a clause was a liquidated damages amount or a penalty was to:

(1) identify the breach(es) of contract that the clause applied to, namely the failure to give a full one year's notice of termination
(2) identify the amount payable on breach (i.e., one year's gross salary)
(3) identify the amount that would be payable in unliquidated damages, taking account of the need to mitigate the loss suffered
(4) identify the parties' reasons for agreeing this clause and whether the amount payable was imposed as a deterrent to breach or constituted a genuine pre-estimate of the loss.

The employee would have to mitigate by giving credit for any salary he could reasonably have earned in the remainder of the one year period but the comparison between that figure and the one-year gross salary was not conclusive on the question of whether the clause was imposed as a deterrent. Instead, it was clear that the context for the agreement was commercial and the employee had been able to negotiate its terms. There were balancing advantages to the employer and balancing disadvantages to the employee and the employer had freely agreed to this figure as compensation without any discount for mitigation. Therefore the Court of Appeal concluded that, in all the circumstances, the employer had not discharged the burden of showing that the clause was not a genuine pre-estimate of the loss so that the clause was enforceable. This equal bargaining power (**Phillips Hong Kong**) approach can also be seen in **Tullett Prebon Group Ltd v El-Hajjali** [2008] EWHC 1924 (QB), [2008] IRLR 760, in the context of a clause in an employment contract providing for payment if a prospective employee failed to start work for the employer. There had been specific consideration of this term and the parties had been legally represented. There was no reason to interfere with the parties' agreement unless the stipulated sum was extravagant or unconscionable in amount compared with the greatest loss that could conceivably follow a breach.

In **M. & J. Polymers Ltd v Imerys Minerals Ltd** [2008] EWHC 344 (Comm), [2008] 1 Lloyd's Rep 541, [2008] 1 All ER (Comm) 893, on the evidence it was clear that the take or pay clause was commercially justifiable, did not amount to oppression, was negotiated and freely entered into between parties of comparable bargaining power, and did not have the predominant purpose of deterring a breach of contract or acting as a provision '*in terrorem*'. The parties' negotiations had taken place in a commercial context and it followed that the clause was not a penalty.

The same policy prevails in **Meretz Investments NV v ACP Ltd** [2006] EWHC 74 (Ch), [2007] Ch 197, where the question was whether a leaseback option clause (providing for the transfer of the property from one party to another in the event of breach through failure to develop in time) in an agreement for the sale of a development lease amounted to a penalty. It was capable in principle of being a penalty since it was not intended to compensate for loss and could be seen as an attempt to penalize the other for breach. However, Lewison J stated (at [349]): 'But that is only the starting point for the inquiry whether it is a penalty. To characterise a clause as a penalty, with the consequence that the court will refuse to enforce it, is a blatant interference with freedom of contract, and should normally be reserved for cases of oppression.' He continued, 'There is, in my judgement, nothing inherently oppressive in a contractual term which has the effect of precluding one party to the contract from continuing to enjoy benefits under the contract at a time when he is not adhering to his own obligations. That, as it seems to me, is the substance of the Lease-Back Option.' In addition, there were other factors which favoured the clause not being a penalty including the fact that it is common for a development lease to be capable of termination if the developer does not develop, the fact that only a small initial consideration had been given so that the best hope of a return was completion of the development, and the time limit on development was subject to various extension possibilities.

However, it is clear that there are limits and in **Jeancharm Ltd v Barnet Football Club** [2003] EWCA Civ 58, 92 Con LR 26, the Court of Appeal made it clear that where a clause in a commercial contract was very clearly not a genuine pre-estimate of the likely loss, the principle in *Philips* would not rescue it.

> The clause in question provided for interest at 260 per cent per annum for late payment to the supplier. The supplier sought to argue that it was necessary to assess this clause as one of several clauses allocating risks between the parties in a commercial contract and was balanced by the existence of a clause whereby it had to pay 20p per garment per day if the goods (football kits) were delivered late, i.e. this was not a situation of dominance by one commercial party over another. The Court of Appeal refused to accept that this approach in the commercial context made any difference to the fundamental principle that if a clause was very obviously not a genuine pre-estimate of loss then it was an invalid penalty.

Thus, the principle in **Philips** merely means that the courts will not tolerate attempts to avoid agreed damages clauses based on hypothetical possible breaches; by comparison, the offending clause in **Jeancharm** applied to a single type of actual and easily anticipated breach, namely late payment. Another example of a clause found to be a penalty in a commercial contract is provided by *Lansat Shipping Co Ltd v Glencore Grain BV, The Paragon* [2009] EWCA Civ 855, [2009] 2 Lyold's Rep 688, [2010] 1 All ER (Comm) 459: a provision for payment, as compensation for late redelivery, of a higher market rate for the period of overrun and also for the period of the last thirty days of the contracted period was penal. It was a threat to compel performance and not a genuine pre-estimate of the loss that would be caused by breach.

Current policy also clearly favours protection of consumers through a greater willingness to conclude that a clause amounts to an unenforceable penalty. A good example of this can be seen in the county court case of *Volkswagen Financial Services (UK) Ltd v Ramage*, 9 May 2007. There was an agreement to hire a new Audi coupé from VW for thirty-six months at £567.40 a month. The agreement was terminated for non-payment. Clause 8.2 provided for compensation or agreed damages of the total amount of rentals payable, less the amount paid or which had become due, less a rebate of rentals not yet due 'calculated at 4% per annum on rentals which have not become due'. VW claimed £13,365, which was made up of a claim for £10,428 as future rentals, arrears at the date of termination, and a recovery fee. The defendant claimed that clause 8.2 was a penalty and unenforceable. The judge at first instance had concluded that the clause was a genuine pre-estimate of loss and therefore a liquidated damages clause (on the basis that the calculation of the loss was not easy; see final bullet point on the *Dunlop* guidelines, below). In addition, it was considered that the courts should be slow to treat agreed damages as penalties, particularly since the defendant was an 'articulate and intelligent' consumer who had freely entered into the agreement.

On appeal it was held that since the clause allowed almost complete recovery of the hire despite the fact that the car was returned early and therefore had a much greater value than would have been the case if returned at the end of the term, it was a penalty and the characteristics of the defendant were irrelevant. It was important to consider any residual capital value of the asset hired when calculating the likely loss and the parties should ensure that this likely loss equated with the agreed damages sum. Since the value of the car on its return would vary depending on when in the hire term it was actually returned, a single simple formulation of genuine pre-estimate of loss was unworkable, i.e. a sliding scale would be required.

- **Where the breach consists of not paying a sum of money, and the amount payable under the clause upon breach is greater than the sum owed, the clause will be a penalty.**
- **Where the contract provides for the same amount to be payable as damages in the event of several different types of breach, some of which may result in serious and others only trifling damage, it is presumed that the clause is a penalty.**

The rationale of this presumption is simply that it is unlikely that each type of breach will result in exactly the same degree of loss, so that the clause does not represent a genuine attempt to pre-estimate the loss. On this basis, the presumption may be rebutted by showing that in all the circumstances the amount payable was a genuine pre-estimate of the loss resulting from each type of breach.

- Finally, Lord Dunedin pointed out that **the fact that the loss is difficult or impossible to pre-estimate does not of itself turn every liquidated damages clause into a penalty.**

In the *Dunlop* case itself, the contract contained a provision providing for a payment of £5 per tyre in 'liquidated damages' if any tyre was sold at below the list price. The House of Lords held that this was a liquidated damages clause despite the fact that precise quantification of Dunlop's loss in these circumstances would have been difficult and the £5 figure was only a rough and ready way of estimating it. The £5 figure was reasonable in the circumstances and represented 'the true bargain between the parties'.

The decision of Jackson J in ***McAlpine Capital Projects Ltd v Tilebox Ltd*** [2005] EWHC 281 (TCC), [2005] BLR 271, confirms that an objective test is applied when determining whether an agreed damages clause is penal. The test does not turn on the question of bona fides and the honesty of the party in question. In addition, it was important to stress that the genuine pre-estimate of loss did not have to coincide with the actual loss suffered in order to confirm the clause as liquidated damages, i.e. the estimate did not need to be correct. The clause will fail to be a genuine pre-estimate of the loss only if there is an unacceptable difference between the estimate and the likely damages. The judge's references to the 'reasonableness' of the pre-estimate rather then its genuineness would appear to be an unhelpful contribution. Jackson J appears to have used this expression to distinguish the issue of the bona fides of the party or parties who insert the figure but it appears to have the opposite effect of reintroducing it. The issue is merely whether any difference between the estimated figure included in the contract and the likely loss on breach is regarded as permissible, as opposed to a 'very wide gulf' which the judge considered had been the position in the cases where a clause had been held to be penal.

9.10.4 Critique of the scope of the penalty rule

9.10.4.1 Imbalance in the parties' positions or freely negotiated between commercial parties dealing at arm's length?

Sometimes it seems that the distinction between liquidated damages and penalty clauses is merely used to justify the court's decision about whether a particular clause should be enforced, and does not enable the parties to predict whether an agreed damages clause will be enforceable. Equally, the law may strike down a clause intended as an incentive to performance even when the clause has been freely negotiated between the parties.

A better approach might be to follow the example of UCTA 1977 (see generally 7.6), and to treat contracts differently according to whether they are freely negotiated or the clause has been imposed, by virtue of a standard form or the superior bargaining position of one of the parties. In the former case there seems no good reason to disallow a penalty clause, since it must be assumed that the party subject to its terms must have had good reason to agree to it. In the latter case, both penalty clauses and unreasonably low liquidated damages clauses might be disallowed.

As discussed above, there is some evidence of a willingness to adopt such an approach in the advice of the Privy Council in ***Philips Hong Kong Ltd v Attorney-General of Hong Kong*** (1993) 61 BLR 49, where Lord Woolf stressed the importance of not interfering with the freedom of parties to stipulate for themselves the damages recoverable upon breach, 'especially in commercial contracts'. On the other hand, he appeared to contemplate that courts should be more willing to interfere where the contract does not involve 'two parties who should be well capable of protecting their respective commercial interests'. Rather, where 'one of the parties ... is able to dominate the other as to the choice of the terms of the contract', the courts should be more vigilant in ensuring that damages recoverable under a contract clause are not extravagant (although see ***Jeancharm Ltd v Barnet Football Club*** [2003] EWCA Civ 58, 92 Con LR 26, where there was no evidence of 'domination' on the facts but the clause in question provided for an extravagant damages amount). Of course, in the context of consumer contracts, penalty clauses which have not been individually negotiated may be unenforceable as unfair terms essentially because of this imbalance in the parties' relationship (see 7.7 and **9.10.2.1**).

9.10.4.2 The penalty rule applies to sums payable on breach

It is also possible to criticize the fact that the penalty rule applies only where the sum specified as agreed damages is payable on breach. Therefore, if an agreed sum is penal in nature but payable on some event other than breach, it will remain payable (***Export Credit Guarantee Department v Universal Oil Products Co.*** [1983] 1 WLR 399). This is unsatisfactory and leads to all sorts of fine distinctions in practice, e.g. ***Alder v Moore*** [1961] 2 QB 57 where the promise was interpreted as a promise to repay £500 if the defendant played football again, rather than a promise not to play with a £500 penalty if the promise was breached. This is little more than an exercise in semantics, although the outcome was that the penalty rule did not apply and the £500 had to be repaid.

In ***Euro London Appointments Ltd v Claessens International Ltd*** [2006] EWCA Civ 385, [2006] 2 Lloyd's Rep 436, the key clauses in the standard terms of an employment agency relating to fees for introductions of applicants to the client provided that payment had to be made within seven days of the date of the invoice and that for a client to qualify for a refund of the fees in circumstances where the employment ended prematurely (within twelve weeks of being engaged) the client had to pay the agency's fees within seven days of the date of the invoice. There was a schedule of refunds applicable for this twelve-week period where the invoice had been paid within the seven-day period. The invoice was not paid and the two introductions had either left within the twelve-week period or been dismissed. The agency argued that in accordance with the refund clause the client was not entitled to the refunds and sought payment of the invoice sum. The district judge had held that the refund clause was a disguised penalty clause and could not be relied upon to claim a refund. However, the Court of Appeal disagreed and held that:

- The seven-day requirement was not an obligation (i.e., it required no payment of money in itself). It was merely a condition precedent to the ability to secure a refund. It followed that the refund clause could not be a penalty payable on breach.

- The two clauses were not interdependent. If the client failed to pay within the seven days there was no breach of any obligation in the refund clause. This could be seen by altering the time period in the invoice clause to say fourteen days and then examining the refund clause.

The Court of Appeal also considered, *obiter*, that the refund clause could not have been a penalty since its dominant purpose was not to deter a breach. It was compensatory, providing an allocation of the risk to the client over the twelve-week period.

Bank charges

In relation to the attempts to reclaim bank charges, one aspect of the argument put by the Office of Fair Trading (OFT) was that since the amount of the charge was not a genuine pre-estimate of the likely loss (i.e., administrative costs etc.) to the bank in the event that the customer is overdrawn, such charges amounted to an unenforceable penalty payable on breach. However, the argument put by the banks was that customers were not prohibited from becoming overdrawn so that payment of this charge did not arise through breach. In ***Office of Fair Trading v Abbey National plc*** [2008] EWHC 2325 (Comm), [2009] 1 All ER (Comm) 717, the OFT had argued that a term whereby the customer was prohibited from giving an instruction for payment when the customer did not have the funds and had no agreed overdraft, was penal in nature and imposed a charge upon breach. The banks argued that any charge would be payable when the overdraft was provided to cover this and not on the breach itself. Accordingly, they did not consider that it could be penal.

Andrew Smith J held that it did not follow that the penalty rule had no application to benefits received from wrongdoing short of a breach, e.g. obtaining an overdraft through the use of a cheque backed by a cheque guarantee card. The judge also considered that a sum could be penal if payable on an event that might not be a breach of contract, if the reality was that it became payable upon a breach. Nevertheless, he considered that the OFT arguments involved strained constructions of wording and held that the banks were entitled to declarations that the terms, and charges imposed under the terms, were not capable of amounting to penalties at common law. The judge had already rejected a claim in previous proceedings that the Unfair Terms in Consumer Contracts Regulations 1999 had removed the application of the common law penalty doctrine in the context of consumer contracts ([2008] EWHC 875 (Comm), [2008] 2 All ER (Comm) 625)). See also [2009] EWHC 36 (Comm) for declarations and, in some instances, refusal of declarations that conditions were not penal. (For arguments relating to unfair terms and the UTCCR 1999, see 7.7.1.4.)

Minimum payment clauses

This restriction is capable of causing particular difficulties in the context of minimum payment clauses in the event of termination of hire-purchase agreements.

- If the customer gives notice to terminate the agreement early, the contract may provide for the customer to make payment of a minimum sum as compensation for loss of the agreement. Since this is a non-breach event, the penalty rule will not apply to this payment.

- However, if the customer defaulted on his payments under the agreement, the penalty rule would apply to this breach and render the minimum payment clause unenforceable.

This was criticized in **Bridge v Campbell Discount Co. Ltd** [1962] AC 600 where it was referred to as 'a paradox' by Harman LJ.

In its Working Paper (*Penalty Clauses and Forfeiture of Monies Paid,* WP No. 61, 1975) the Law Commission recommended the abolition of this arbitrary distinction so that the penalty rule 'should be applied wherever the object of the disputed contractual obligation is to secure the act or result which is the true purpose of the contract'. However, no action was taken on this recommendation, and the House of Lords in **Export Credit Guarantee Department v Universal Oil Products Co.** [1983] 1 WLR 399 confirmed the restriction on the application of the penalty rule to breaches of contractual obligations.

Schedule 2(1)(e) to the Unfair Terms in Consumer Contracts Regulations 1999, SI 1999/2083, provides that in consumer contracts a term may be unfair if it requires any consumer 'who *fails to fulfil his obligation* to pay a disproportionately high sum in compensation' (emphasis added). It therefore appears that the same restriction applies in the consumer context.

9.10.5 Deposits, prepayments, and relief from forfeiture

Closely related to the rule against penalty clauses and the rules governing restitution of sums paid under contracts (see **10.5**) are those rules which govern claims to recover various forms of advance payment made in respect of a contract. The law in this area, like the law relating to penalty clauses, is not always logically defensible, and the different rules for different categories of payment set out below would benefit from a thorough revision, and from integration with a revised set of rules on penalty clauses.

9.10.5.1 Deposits

Money paid in advance which is expressly designated as a deposit is not normally recoverable in the event of breach of the contract by the paying party even if the payee has not suffered any loss as a result of the breach. Authority for this rule is well established; in **Howe v Smith** (1884) 27 ChD 89 the element of penalty embodied in the rule was invoked as a desirable incentive to performance, 'an earnest to bind the bargain'. In *Damon Compania Naviera SA v Hapag-Lloyd International SA* [1985] 1 All ER 475, the Court of Appeal, confirming the rule, also held that if the deposit remained unpaid at the time of the breach, the non-breaching party was entitled to bring an action to recover payment.

Although the rule against recovery of deposits may be equivalent to the enforcement of penalty clauses, in that the amount of the deposit may far exceed the actual loss to the party entitled to retain it, it had been thought (subject only to an *obiter* statement of Denning LJ in **Stockloser v Johnson** [1954] 1 QB 476 at p. 491) that the rule against penalties and the equitable jurisdiction to allow relief from forfeiture could not apply. The only exception appeared to be s. 49(2) of the Law of Property Act 1925, which provides that in contracts for the sale or exchange of interests in land the court may, if it thinks fit, order the repayment of any deposit.

However, in **Workers Trust and Merchant Bank Ltd v Dojap Investments Ltd** [1993] AC 573, the Privy Council imposed an important limitation on the general principle. Lord Browne-Wilkinson accepted that a deposit is not normally recoverable because it is given in earnest of performance. Nevertheless, he went on to say that 'it is not possible for the parties to attach the incidents of a deposit to the payment of a sum of money unless such sum is reasonable as earnest money'. In the particular case, a deposit of 25 per cent had been demanded when the prevailing local rate was 10 per cent. The Privy Council advised that the deposit was unreasonable, and that the deposit should be repaid subject to a set-off for any loss actually sustained.

Apart from this limited instance of unreasonable deposits, the penalty rule does not therefore apply to deposits. The Law Commission's Working Paper No. 61 (see 9.10.4) recommended that it should do so.

9.10.5.2 Prepayments not expressed to be deposits

Where part of the contract price has been paid in advance, **without that payment being expressed to be in the nature of a deposit or subject to express forfeiture**, the payment may be recovered upon termination of the contract, subject to any set-off there may be for performance rendered before the time of discharge (*Dies v British & International Mining & Finance Corporation Ltd* [1939] 1 KB 724 and *Rover International Ltd v Cannon Film Sales Ltd (No. 3)* [1989] 1 WLR 912). It is therefore vital to be able to distinguish between deposits (above) and mere prepayments, although *Dies v British & International Mining & Finance Corporation Ltd* is also authority for the proposition that in the event of doubt the payment will be treated as a prepayment rather than as a deposit to be forfeited on breach.

However, in some instances the prepayment may be completely consumed by performance, e.g. contracts for work and materials where the recipient of the advance payment is bound to incur costs in performing prior to completion. In both **Hyundai Heavy Industries Co. v Papadopolous** [1980] 1 WLR 1129 and **Stocznia Gdanska SA v Latvian Shipping** [1998] 1 WLR 574, concerning the construction of ships, the contractual obligations were held to include the design and construction of the ships as well as their delivery. Since much of the design and construction work had been completed, it was possible to bring an action to recover a prepayment which had become due (see the further discussion at **10.5.1.2**). Therefore, much may turn on the nature of the contract and the purpose behind the requirement for the making of prepayments.

9.10.5.3 Relief from forfeiture

Where breach results in the breaching party losing the benefit of all payments or rights under the contract in a manner which is disproportionate to the actual breach or the loss caused by it, the law may provide relief from that forfeiture, e.g. preventing payments made by a defaulting party from being lost. Such relief is closely related to the rule against penalties, although the technical requirements for its application are very different.

There is an equitable jurisdiction in the court to provide relief from forfeiture in some circumstances, but the courts take a very restrictive view of their powers in this area. Consequently, there are considerable advantages in being able to characterize a clause as amounting to a penalty, rather than merely leading to forfeiture, since relief of some kind is then immediately available (***Jobson v Johnson*** [1989] 1 WLR 1026: see **9.10.2**). There would seem to be no functional difference between a deposit (as described in **9.10.5.1**) and an express clause allowing forfeiture of prepayments. However, it appears that the jurisdiction to relieve against forfeiture does not extend to deposits as such (although Lord Browne-Wilkinson in ***Workers Trust*** clearly indicates that it does apply to forfeiture of 'unreasonable deposits').

The modern foundation for the equitable jurisdiction is ***Stockloser v Johnson*** [1954] 1 QB 476. The Court of Appeal held that a clause providing for forfeiture of prepayments would not be enforced if it was penal, and if to enforce it would be oppressive and unconscionable. The relief provided will usually be the allowance of more time in which to make an overdue payment, although sometimes the repayment of sums paid may be ordered. Relief will not be granted if the primary object of the transaction would thereby be defeated (*Shiloh Spinners Ltd v Harding* [1973] AC 691 at p. 723). However, more significantly, the House of Lords has ruled that the power to provide relief from forfeiture may be exercised only in relation to possessory or proprietary rights (*Scandinavian Trading Tanker Co. AB v Flota Petrolera Ecuatoriana* [1983] 2 All ER 763).

It seems that this restriction is part of a more general policy of limiting the scope of relief from forfeiture, largely for reasons of commercial certainty. The decision of the Privy Council in ***Union Eagle Ltd v Golden Achievement Ltd*** [1997] AC 514 provides a good illustration of this principle.

> Time was of the essence in relation to completion of the purchase of a flat, and there was a provision allowing for forfeiture of the deposit in the event of any failure to comply with the contract terms. The purchaser was ten minutes late in tendering the purchase price and sought relief against forfeiture in the form of an extension of the time for completion. The Privy Council refused this relief, citing the need for certainty.

In essence it was being asked to relieve against the immediate right to terminate the contract for failure to comply with the essential time condition when it was important, for reasons of certainty, for the vendor to know whether he could resell the flat. However, it would seem questionable whether that relief should also mean that the vendor can keep a reasonable deposit.

Further reading

General principles determining recovery of damages

Birks (ed.), *Wrongs and Remedies in the Twenty-first Century* (Oxford University Press, 1996).

Burrows, *Remedies for Torts and Breach of Contract*, 3rd edn (Oxford University Press, 2004).

Carter and Peden, 'Damages following termination for repudiation: Taking account of later events' (2008) 24 JCL 145.

Cartwright, 'Compensatory damages: Some central issues of assessment' in Burrows and Peel (eds), *Commercial Remedies: Current issues and problems* (Oxford University Press, 2003).

Coote, 'Breach, anticipatory breach, or the breach anticipated?' (2007) 123 LQR 503.

Friedmann, 'The performance interest in contract damages' (1995) 111 LQR 628.

Fuller and Perdue, 'The reliance interest in contract damages' (1936) 46 Yale LJ 52.

Harris, Ogus, and Phillips, 'Contract remedies and the consumer surplus' (1979) 95 LQR 581.

Law Commission Report No. 247, *Aggravated, Exemplary and Restitutionary Damages* (1997).

Liu, 'The date for assessing damages for loss of prospective performance under a contract' [2007] LMCLQ 273.

Loke, 'Cost of cure or difference in market value? Toward a sound choice in the basis for quantifying expectation damages' (1996) 10 JCL 189.

McKendrick, 'Breach of contract and the meaning of loss' [1999] CLP 37.

Mustill, '*The Golden Victory*: Some reflections' (2008) 124 LQR 569.

O'Sullivan, 'Loss and gain at greater depth: The implications of the *Ruxley* decision' in Rose (ed.), *Failure of Contracts: Contractual, restitutionary and proprietary consequences* (Hart Publishing, 1997).

Phang, 'Subjectivity, objectivity and policy: Contractual damages in the House of Lords' [1996] JBL 362.

Poole, 'Damages for breach of contract: Compensation and "personal preferences"' (1996) 59 MLR 272.

Webb, 'Performance and compensation: An analysis of contract damages and contractual obligation' (2006) 26 OJLS 41.

Limitations on the compensation principle

Bridge, 'Mitigation of damages in contract and the meaning of avoidable loss' (1989) 99 LQR 398.

Burrows, 'Contributory negligence in contract: Ammunition for the Law Commission' (1993) 109 LQR 175.

Capper, 'Damages for distress and disappointment: The limits of *Watts v Morrow*' (2000) 116 LQR 553.

Capper, 'Damages for distress and disappointment: Problem solved' (2002) 118 LQR 193.

Cartwright, 'Remoteness of damage in contract and tort: A reconsideration' (1996) 55 CLJ 488.

Enonchong, 'Breach of contract and damages for mental distress' (1996) 16 OJLS 617.

Kramer, 'The new test of remoteness in contract' (2009) 125 LQR 408.

Law Commission Working Paper No. 114, *Contributory Negligence as a Defence in Contract* (1990).

Law Commission Report No. 219, *Contributory Negligence as a Defence in Contract* (1993).

Macdonald, 'Contractual damages for mental distress' (1994) 7 JCL 94.

McKendrick and Graham, 'The sky's the limit: Contractual damages for non-pecuniary loss' [2002] LMCLQ 161.

Peel, 'Remoteness re-visited' (2009) 125 LQR 6.

Phang, 'The crumbling edifice? The award of contractual damages for mental distress' [2003] JBL 341.

Robertson, 'The basis of the remoteness rule in contract' (2008) 28 LS 172.

Agreed damages clauses

Barton, 'Penalties and damages' (1976) 92 LQR 20.

Beale, 'Unreasonable deposits' (1993) 109 LQR 524.

Gordon, 'Penalties limiting damages' (1974) 90 LQR 296.

Harpum, 'Equitable relief: Penalties and forfeitures' [1989] CLJ 370.

Hudson, 'Penalties limiting damages' (1974) 90 LQR 31 and (1975) 91 LQR 25.

Law Commission Working Paper No. 61, *Penalty Clauses and Forfeiture of Monies Paid* (1975).

Remedies providing for specific relief and restitutionary remedies

10

Summary of the issues

This chapter is divided into two parts.

The first part of the chapter considers those equitable remedies which provide for specific relief. **Specific relief is the general name for those remedies for breach of contract which compel actual performance rather than merely compensating for loss caused by breach.**

Compulsion of performance may take the form of claiming an agreed sum (see 10.1), or a claim seeking specific performance (see 10.2), or a claim seeking an injunction (see 10.3).

• **The claim or action for an agreed sum gives effect to the claimant's performance interest by ordering that the party in breach pay the liquidated sum (debt), which was his agreed performance under the contract. The claimant can seek this remedy only where it has performed the obligations which caused the debt obligation to arise.** This section also discusses the question of recovery of interest on the debt and the ability to recover for other losses resulting from the non-payment.

• **Specific performance is a court order compelling actual performance of agreed obligations (other than payment of the price).** As it is an equitable remedy it is available at the discretion of the court and, since English law regards damages as the primary remedy for breach, specific performance is available only when damages would be an inadequate remedy. There are a number of other restrictions on the court's ability to order specific performance.

• **An injunction is a court order restraining the defendant from a specified activity, e.g. breach of a negative stipulation in the contract such as a restraint of trade clause.**

The second part of the chapter contains a brief introduction to restitutionary remedies, namely recovery based on failure of consideration and *quantum meruit* (see 10.5). These are situations where one party has received a benefit at the expense of the other. **This is sometimes referred to as 'unjust enrichment by subtraction'.**

The controversial question of the availability of 'restitutionary damages for breach of contract', which focuses on whether the claimant can obtain restitution of a gain made by the defendant (in excess of any loss made by the claimant) as a result of a breach of contract, is discussed at **10.6.**

• **Restitutionary remedies seek to restore money paid or the value of a benefit conferred in circumstances where it would be unfair for the recipient to retain that benefit.** These remedies can apply in circumstances in which no contract exists and so are not limited to instances of breach of contract.

• **Money paid in advance may be recovered where there has been a total failure of consideration.** This may occur because an anticipated contract fails to materialize or because the contract has become frustrated or is affected by a fundamental initial mistake. Restitution may also be sought in cases of illegality. The exact meaning and scope of total failure of consideration is considered in this chapter.

• In certain circumstances it may be possible to recover the reasonable value of a performance as a *quantum meruit* claim on the basis that a benefit has been conferred on the other party for which no payment under a contract can be made.

• **In very exceptional circumstances the court may order a defendant to account for a gain resulting from a breach of contract in the form of an account of profits where the claimant has suffered no loss.** The scope of these exceptional circumstances and the nature of this remedy are discussed in this chapter. However, the recent trend has been to award so-called *Wrotham Park* damages based on the amount that would have been required to release the negative covenant that has been broken rather than an account of profits. The recent case law is examined, together with the relationship between these forms of recovery. Although recent case law appears to confirm that both are compensatory remedies rather than being based on restitution, for reasons of convenience they remain within this chapter).

10.1 Claiming an agreed sum

The most common form of claim for an agreed sum is a claim for the price. The purpose of the claim is to enforce the defendant's contractual obligation (the promise to pay). It rests on the fact that the claimant has performed its obligations which gave rise to that obligation to make payment, i.e. the money must be due to the claimant. It is therefore a claim in debt, rather than a claim for damages.

There are many advantages of such a claim, since the amount claimed is known from the beginning ('a liquidated sum'):

• Many of the difficulties relating to actions for damages—notably, remoteness of damage (see **9.9.2**) and mitigation (see **9.9.3**)—are avoided. In a debt claim, the amount of the debt is the amount recovered.

• In addition, because the issues at trial are frequently uncomplicated, there is a streamlined procedure for claims for unpaid debts (i.e., summary judgment: Civil Procedure Rules, r. 24).

In most cases the only difficulties, if there are any, are (1) questions of fact and (2) problems of enforcement. Questions of fact (1) arise where the defence offered is that the obligation to pay has been discharged by a defective performance by the claimant (see **8.4**). Enforcement problems (2) arise where the defendant has not paid because it lacks the means to pay.

Greater difficulties occur where the party in breach will not allow the other party to complete performance, which has the effect of preventing the latter bringing a claim for the price. The performing party will be confined to a claim for damages for its actual loss and will be subject to a duty to mitigate that loss.

10.1.1 Breach by anticipatory repudiation and claiming the agreed sum

In *White & Carter (Councils) Ltd v McGregor* [1962] AC 413, before the appellants had commenced performance of the contract, the respondents had announced that they no longer wished to go ahead with it. The appellants nevertheless elected to affirm the contract (which they were held to be entitled to do: see 8.7.3.1 where the facts are given) and continued their performance, claiming thereby to be entitled to the price. On the facts of this case, they were able to perform without the need for the other party's cooperation, so that there was nothing to prevent them performing despite the respondents' protestations that it was pointless. A majority of the House of Lords upheld the appellants' claim of the price, despite the absence of any attempt to minimize the loss (see **9.9.3**).

It therefore seems that, unlike the position in relation to a claim for unliquidated damages, there is no obligation to mitigate when claiming only for an agreed sum. This particular decision may have been justified on the ground either that in the particular circumstances mitigation was in any case impossible, or that the loss would have been very difficult to quantify as damages. Nevertheless, it raised the possibility that a party might be able to elect to continue performance without any substantive reason. If the performance remained unwanted by the other party then the cost of performance would be wasted. **For this reason, the right to elect to affirm the contract is limited to those cases where the party wishing to affirm has a legitimate interest in so doing (see 8.7.3.1) and the ability to perform without the cooperation of the party in breach.**

Where there is no legitimate interest in continuing to perform the contract rather than claiming damages (and assuming that the right to claim the price has not yet arisen because the necessary performance has not yet taken place), the non-breaching party will be forced to mitigate its loss and claim damages.

For example, in ***Clea Shipping Corp. v Bulk Oil International Ltd, The Alaskan Trader*** [1984] 1 All ER 129, the owners claimed that they could affirm and keep the vessel at the disposal of the charterers although the charterers had indicated that the vessel was not required. The judge held that this action was 'wholly unreasonable' so that the owners were not entitled to the payment of hire for the vessel during this period.

In essence, the owners had to mitigate their loss because they did not have the necessary interest in continuing with performance. Thus, mitigation may actually prevent a non-breaching party from performing and so having an entitlement to claim the agreed price. It seems, however, that mitigation could have no relevance where the claim for the price had already arisen.

10.1.2 Sale of goods

A particular problem may arise in the sale of goods when legal performance, which is constituted by the passing of property, is separated from the physical delivery of the goods, which may take place at a later date. This is because s. 49 of the Sale of Goods Act (SGA) 1979 provides that the seller can bring a claim for the price if the property in the goods has passed to the buyer.

Example

A sells his cow 'Rose' to B for £500, promising to deliver her to B's farm five days later. Since this is a contract for the sale of specific goods, property passes immediately to B (SGA 1979, s. 18, r. 1), with the result that A has performed everything necessary to bring a claim for the price (SGA 1979, s. 49(1)).

If B informs A before the time for delivery that he no longer wishes to buy 'Rose', it seems that A may still claim the price, obliging B to take on the responsibility of disposing of the cow. If B is a dealer then he may well be better able to dispose of the cow, in which case this rule is justified. However, in a similar case in which A is a dealer and B is only a consumer, it makes little sense to leave disposal of the unwanted goods to the party less likely to be able to sell them without difficulty.

Here again, the claim for the price appears to be inconsistent with the obligation on the claimant to mitigate the loss, which exists in the case of a claim for damages.

10.1.3 Non-payment: Recovery of additional loss and interest

10.1.3.1 At common law

At common law, in the absence of a contractual provision fixing interest on a debt, as a result of the decision in *London, Chatham and Dover Railway Co. v South Eastern Railway Co.* [1893] 1 AC 429, the general rule used to be that interest was not payable on late payment of debts. The result was that, at common law, a debtor discharged its obligation by paying the amount owed even if that payment was made late. The House of Lords in ***Sempra Metals (formerly Metallgesellschaft Ltd) Ltd v IRC*** [2007] UKHL 34, [2008] 1 AC 561, finally removed this common law immunity for debtors so that it is possible to recover interest losses on the usual basis for recovery, i.e. subject to the loss falling within the rules of remoteness. Lord Nicholls commented (at [94]): 'the House should now hold that, in principle, it is always open to a claimant to please and prove his actual interest losses caused by late payment of a debt, including whether this was simple or compound interest actual interest losses. These losses will be recoverable, subject to the principles governing all claims for damages for breach of contract, such as remoteness, failure to mitigate and so forth.' In *Sempra Metals* Lord Nicholls expressly recognized that the loss in question 'may be the cost of borrowing money' and that this cost 'may include an element of compound interest'. Alternatively, 'the loss may be loss of an opportunity to invest the promised money' which itself 'may need to include a compound element if it is to be a fair measure of what the plaintiff lost by the late payment'. Recognition of an ability to recover compound interest is important since previously recovery had been limited to simple interest only. The Law Commission had recommended that there should be a general power to award compound interest for debts or damages of £15,000 or more, and a presumption in favour of such an award unless the case involved less than a year's delay, when interest would be limited to simple interest (see Law Commission consultation paper, *Compound Interest*, LCCP No. 167 (2002) and Law Commission report, *Pre-Judgment Interest on Debts and Damages*, Law Com. No. 287 (2004). Although compound interest had been permitted in limited circumstances in the context of unjust enrichment by *Westdeutsche Landesbank Girozentrale v Islington LBC* [1996] 1 AC 669, in ***Sempra Metals (formerly Metallgesellschaft Ltd) Ltd v IRC*** [2007] UKHL 34, [2008] 1 AC 561, a majority of the House of Lords (3:2) held that a court had jurisdiction to award compound interest where the claimant sought a restitutionary remedy for the time value of money paid under a mistake; in this case premature payment of advance corporation tax on dividends in breach of European law.

However it is clear that all claims to interest as damages will need to be affirmatively pleaded and proved. Lord Nicholls stressed that '[g]eneral damages are not recoverable. The common law does not assume that delay in payment of debt will of itself cause damage. Loss must be proved'. Any claim to actual interest losses will need to be particularized, established, and shown to be within the parties' reasonable contemplations as liable to result from the breach (which may now mean that the debtor must be shown to have assumed responsibility for those losses, ***Transfield Shipping Inc. v Mercator Shipping Inc., The Achilleas*** [2008] UKHL 48, [2009] 1 AC 61).

In *Wadsworth v Lydall* [1981] 1 WLR 598, the plaintiff was the vendor of land who intended to use £10,000, to be paid by the purchaser before a stipulated date, as down-payment on the acquisition of other land. The defendant purchaser was aware of this intention, but paid only £7,200 by the stipulated date, so that the plaintiff had to borrow the balance for the down-payment. The plaintiff sought the interest payable on the sum borrowed to enable the down payment to be made as damages, and was held to be entitled to recover such damages.

Where it is not possible to prove the actual interest loss, the creditor will be required to resort to interest under statute.

10.1.3.2 Interest under statute

1. Interests on judgment debts

For some time now the courts have had a statutory discretion to award interest on judgments in claims for an agreed sum. This discretion covers both interest on debts for which judgment has been given, and interest on sums paid before judgment but after the proceedings have commenced (Supreme Court Act 1981, s. 35A or County Courts Act 1984, s. 69, as amended by the Administration of Justice Act 1982).

2. Payment of the debt is late but is made before proceedings are commenced

Until comparatively recently, there was no statutory provision dealing with the situation where the debtor paid late but before the commencement of proceedings, despite the fact that late payment of debts had become widespread and almost a matter of commercial practice.

The Late Payment of Commercial Debts (Interest) Act 1998 introduced a right to statutory interest. This Act made interest payable on late payment of debts arising from sale and supply contracts where both parties act 'in the course of a business'. (This phrase has caused difficulties in other contexts—see 7.6.4.1. The Act will have greater scope if the interpretation in *Stevenson v Rogers* [1999] 2 WLR 1064 is adopted.) The Act applies to all commercial contracts for the supply of goods or services made after 7 August 2002. Statutory interest runs from the contractual date for payment or, where there is no such date, thirty days after (whichever is the later of) either performance by the supplier or the giving of notice of the debt. Section 5 provides for the court to reduce the usual statutory right to interest (currently 8 per cent above Bank of England base rate) where the interest of justice so requires because of the conduct of the supplier. The policy of the Act is clear in the decision of the Court of Appeal in ***Ruttle Plant Hire Ltd v Secretary of State for Environment, Food and Rural Affairs*** [2009] EWCA Civ 97, [2009] BLR 301. The case concerned interpretation of the provisions of the Act in the context of the late payment of a debt owed by the government to a private contractor involved in foot and mouth disease decontamination. The Court of Appeal held that the Act did not require a perfect invoice giving notice of the debt in order for time to run. Money was owed when the job was done. An incorrect invoice would activate the protection of s. 5 in favour of the paying party on the basis that uncertainty had been caused by the supplier's invoice, but that did not justify the paying party withholding all monies due and expecting to avoid the high interest under the Act, only those sums pertaining to the uncertainty.

In order to implement EC Directive 2000/35/EC on combating late payment in commercial transactions, the Late Payment of Commercial Debts Regulations 2002, SI 2002/1674 inserted a new s. 5A into the 1998 Act. This applies to contracts made after 7 August 2003 and provides for a right to a fixed sum by way of compensation for the costs suffered by suppliers which arise from late payment. This amount depends on the size of the debt: if the debt is less than £1,000 the compensation is £40; if it is more than £1,000 but less than £10,000 the compensation sum is £70; and £100 is the compensation amount where the debt is more than £10,000.

Any contract term which purports to exclude or vary the statutory right to interest for late payment is unenforceable unless the contract provides a 'substantial remedy' for late payment.

A contractual remedy is regarded as 'substantial' unless it is insufficient either as a compensation for late payment, or as a deterrent to late payment, or if allowing the contractual remedy to operate in place of the statutory remedy would not be 'fair or reasonable'. This is judged by considering factors similar to those in Sch. 2 to the Unfair Contract Terms Act (UCTA) 1977, such as strength of bargaining positions, whether the term was imposed by one party to the detriment of the other and whether there was any inducement to agree to the term. In addition, in assessing the fairness and reasonableness of the alternative, the court is to consider 'the benefits of commercial certainty'. In order to prevent more complex attempts to avoid the 1998 Act, s. 10 also provides that any term purporting to postpone the date when the qualifying debt would be created (even if not contained in written terms of business) will be subject to UCTA 1977 test of reasonableness (see 7.6.6).

The 1998 Act is an important measure, but its effectiveness will need to be judged in the light of the evidence on whether businesses feel able to enforce their statutory right to interest against large public companies or public authorities with whom they have a long-term business relationship. The decision of the Court of Appeal in **Ruttle Plant Hire** is helpful in terms of explaining that over-reliance on technicalities and any attempts at unjustified evasion by the paying party are unlikely to be entertained as providing an excuse to avoid the rates and penalties provided by the Act.

10.2 Specific performance

An order of specific performance is a court order compelling actual performance of the substantive primary obligations under the contract (i.e., the obligations to perform rather than those merely to pay the price: see 10.1). The court ensures compliance with its order by deterring non-compliance with threats of punitive measures against the person to whom the order is addressed. These measures include committal to prison for contempt of court, sequestration of property, and fines.

At common law the only remedy for breach of contract was by way of damages to compensate for loss caused. The Chancery Court made specific performance available, by way of exception. It remains an exceptional remedy even after the amalgamation of law and equity, in that damages are available as of right upon breach if loss can be proved, while the availability of specific performance is subject to a number of restrictions, including that damages be an inadequate remedy. This position, in theory at least, can be compared to that in civil law systems where specific enforcement of the contract may be considered the primary remedy for breach of contract.

10.2.1 Inadequacy of damages

The principle whereby damages may compensate the non-breaching party's cost of obtaining substitute performance has already been explained (see **Part 3(c)**). In such circumstances damages may be said to be an adequate remedy, and it is for this reason that in the ordinary run of cases specific performance will not be awarded.

 Example

In many contracts for the sale of goods, it is possible to purchase substitute goods in the market, and therefore damages, to cover the cost of obtaining substitute performance, will be an adequate remedy (*Société des Industries Metallurgiques SA v The Bronx Engineering Co. Ltd* [1975] 1 Lloyd's Rep 465).

Nevertheless, it is open to a party to demonstrate that for some reason damages would be an inadequate remedy; the important point being that this burden is placed on the non-breaching party.

It is impossible to list every eventuality allowing specific performance, but the more common situations in which the remedy will be available can be identified:

- **The most obvious case is where substitute performance is unavailable.** Thus, where goods are in some way unique, no substitute for them will satisfy the buyer and in such circumstances specific performance is the better remedy (SGA 1979, s. 52). The example of a valuable painting has already been suggested (see **Part 3(c)**); another example of a unique good might be a family heirloom.

Perhaps more significantly, it appears that the courts may be willing to accept a commercial definition of the unavailability of substitute goods. In such circumstances rarity in absolute terms may not be necessary, if within the relevant time limits of the particular contract substitute performance cannot be obtained.

In **Sky Petroleum Ltd v VIP Petroleum Ltd** [1974] 1 All ER 954, the plaintiff company had contracted to purchase all its requirements of petrol and diesel fuel from the defendant at fixed prices for a ten-year period. During a time of worldwide shortages of petroleum products the defendant purported to terminate the contract, leaving the plaintiff with no realistic prospect of obtaining alternative supplies. The plaintiff sought an injunction to prevent termination of the contract. Goulding J accepted that by granting an injunction he would be specifically enforcing the contract, and that petrol and diesel fuel were not of themselves unique. Nevertheless, he granted the injunction because in the particular circumstances damages were an inadequate remedy, since 'for all practical purposes' substitute performance would not be available in time to prevent the plaintiff going out of business.

- **Contracts for the sale of land merit separate attention.** As a matter of law all land is unique, so that specific performance is available upon breach of a contract for the sale of land. This rule does not vary according to the facts of each case, so that even a contract to purchase a modest house, of a kind which may be duplicated several times in a single development, is regarded as subject to the remedy of specific performance. The rule extends not only to purchasers of land, but also to vendors. It is not clear that the purchaser's obligations to pay the purchase price and to take conveyance of the land are in every case unique, and it seems likely that the extension of specific performance to claims brought by the vendor is based in the principle of mutuality (see **10.2.3.2**).

- **Specific performance may also be granted when the quantification of damages is difficult for some reason** (for example, it was accepted in **Co-operative Insurance Society Ltd v Argyll Stores (Holdings) Ltd** [1998] AC 1 that damages would not be adequate because of difficulties in quantifying the plaintiff's loss over the full term of the lease, although the House of Lords refused specific performance for other reasons (see **10.2.2.1**)), and especially where there is a risk that the claimant will not be properly compensated if restricted to the remedy of damages.

- **For this reason, specific performance will also be available where for technical reasons damages would only be nominal, so that the sole means of protecting the claimant's expectation is by compelling performance.**

In **Beswick v Beswick** [1968] AC 58, a contract between uncle and nephew provided for the sale of the uncle's business to the nephew in return for payment of a pension to the uncle, which was to continue after the uncle's death as payment to his widow. After the uncle's death the nephew ceased making the payments. The widow was prevented from suing in her own right because of the application of the doctrine of privity (see **11.7.1**, although compare with the position now under the Contracts (Rights of Third Parties) Act 1999). However, she could succeed in an action as administratrix of her husband's estate. The difficulty was that the estate had suffered no loss as a result of the breach of contract, since Mr Beswick's interest, and so the estate's, ceased upon his death. The widow had suffered the loss in her personal capacity. However, her husband's estate could not recover damages on behalf of someone who was not a party to the contract (discussed at **11.7.3**). **Nevertheless, the House of Lords was able to avoid the obvious injustice of allowing the nephew to break his promise by awarding specific performance of the contract. On the facts, specific performance was the most appropriate remedy.**

- In some circumstances, specific performance may even be awarded simply because the defendant is unlikely to be able to come up with the money to pay damages (*Evans Marshall and Co. Ltd v Bertola SA* [1973] 1 All ER 992).

10.2.2 Contracts not specifically enforceable

Certain contracts, which might otherwise satisfy the tests for the availability of specific performance, cannot be enforced in this way because of the nature of the obligations undertaken.

10.2.2.1 Difficulties in supervision

It was once thought that contracts requiring considerable supervision of performance would never qualify for specific performance.

For example, in ***Ryan v Mutual Tontine Westminster Chambers Association*** [1893] 1 Ch 116, a lease contained a term by which the landlords undertook to provide a resident porter in constant attendance at a block of flats. The person appointed had other employment, and so was often absent from the flats. The court refused specific performance of this term of the lease because it would require a level of constant supervision beyond that which the court was able to provide.

This principle has been invoked in a number of different situations, including building contracts. Nevertheless, it may well be that the unavailability of specific performance on this ground can always be avoided by careful drafting. The decision in ***Ryan v Mutual Tontine Westminster Chambers Association*** was effectively distinguished in the similar case of *Posner v Scott-Lewis* [1986] 3 All ER 513, on the ground that, in the particular circumstances, what was necessary to comply with the contract could easily be defined and did not require excessive supervision. Thus, it is not that the court lacks the power to ensure that the terms of the contract are being carried into effect properly; rather, the difficulty usually stems from the fact that the contract does not state sufficiently precisely the performance intended by the parties.

Vagueness in an alleged contract does not necessarily make it unenforceable through the remedy of damages (although see **3.1.3**), but it may prevent the court supervising its performance. Thus, building contracts can be specifically enforced provided 'the particulars of the work are so far definitely ascertained that the court can sufficiently see what is the exact nature of the work' (per Romer LJ in *Wolverhampton Corporation v Emmons* [1901] 1 KB 515).

Megarry J in ***C. H. Giles & Co. Ltd v Morris*** [1972] 1 All ER 960, expressed dissatisfaction with any absolute restriction based on the difficulty of supervision, as much will clearly depend upon the drafting of the term in question and the background circumstances. These surrounding circumstances appear to have been crucial in the decision of the House of Lords in ***Co-operative Insurance Society***

Ltd v Argyll Stores (Holdings) Ltd [1998] AC 1 (discussed by Jones [1997] CLJ 488 and Phang (1998) 61 MLR 421), to refuse specific performance because of difficulties in supervising compliance.

> The defendant, a supermarket chain, had a lease of a unit in the plaintiff's shopping centre. It was a term of the lease that the defendant covenanted to keep the premises open for retail trade during the usual hours of business. Although the lease was for a 35-year term, after less than six years the defendant closed the supermarket and moved out of the centre. The plaintiff sought specific performance of the covenant to compel the defendant to continue to operate the supermarket. Despite that fact that damages would clearly have been an inadequate remedy on the facts (see **10.2.1**), the House of Lords refused to order specific performance on the basis that its effect would be to order the carrying on of an uneconomic business. Thus, the loss which might then be suffered by the plaintiff would be out of all proportion to the loss suffered due to the breach of the covenant. In addition, it would be difficult both to formulate a suitable order and to supervise it.

This decision may be compared with that in *Rainbow Estates Ltd v Tokenhold Ltd* [1998] 2 All ER 860, which concerned breach of a tenant's covenant to repair. This could be specifically enforceable because it would be an order to achieve a specified result (which was capable of supervision), rather than an order to carry on an activity (as in *Co-operative v Argyll*).

A further example is provided by *Vertex Data Science Ltd v Powergen Retail Ltd* [2006] EWHC 1340 (Comm), [2006] 2 Lloyd's Rep 591.

> V had agreed to supply P, the electricity supply company, with outsourcing services. The parties had not got on and P had issued a notice of termination alleging a number of persistent and material breaches. V sought an injunction to prevent P acting on its notice which would be equivalent to an order for specific performance. Tomlinson J held that it would not be appropriate to grant this relief since the agreement required extensive mutual cooperation and it would have the effect of compelling parties whose relationship had broken down to continue in a contractual relationship. In addition, the court would struggle to enforce such an order given that the contract did not indicate precisely the action required if P was to avoid preventing or hindering V from performing its contractual obligations (*Co-operative Insurance Society v Argyll*).

10.2.2.2 Contracts of personal service

More clearly excepted from the scope of the remedy of specific performance are contracts of personal service. The reason is usually said to be that it would be an infringement of liberty to oblige one party to work personally for the other (*De Francesco v Barnum* (1890) 45 ChD 430: facts given at **5.5.1.2**), or to have to employ a particular person.

> In *Page One Records Ltd v Britton* [1968] 1 WLR 157, 'The Troggs', a pop group, appointed the plaintiffs as their sole agent and manager for a period of five years. The contract contained an express negative covenant whereby the group agreed not to engage anyone else to act as their manager during that period. The judge refused to enforce this covenant by means of an injunction because such a group could not work at all without a manager. An injunction would therefore have had the same effect as an order of specific performance of the management contract. It would be wrong to force the group to continue to employ as their manager and agent any person in whom they had lost confidence.

See also *Warren v Mendy* [1989] 1 WLR 853: no injunction to compel a boxer to use the exclusive services of a particular manager. The position in question necessitated mutual trust and confidence, and it would therefore be wrong to force the boxer to employ as a manager a person in whom he had lost confidence.

There is now a statutory provision preventing specific performance (or a compelling injunction) against an employee in relation to the general obligation to work for an employer (Trade Union and Labour Relations (Consolidation) Act 1992, s. 236). **Thus, an injunction is extremely unlikely to be issued to force one person to employ another where the relationship is based on the maintenance of confidence.**

Although, in general, an injunction will not be issued to prevent a person working for any other person in breach of covenant, it may be granted where there is an express term of the contract preventing the party in question from taking up **specified** alternative employment.

> For example, in **Lumley v Wagner** (1852) 1 De GM & G 604, the plaintiff engaged the defendant to sing at his theatre, and the contract contained an express clause forbidding the defendant from singing anywhere else for the period of the contract. The defendant then entered another contract to sing elsewhere, and refused to perform under her contract with the plaintiff. Specific performance was not available to the plaintiff because the contract was for personal service, but the express negative covenant could be enforced by injunction thereby preventing the defendant from singing elsewhere.
>
> Similarly, in **Warner Brothers Pictures Inc. v Nelson** [1937] 1 KB 209, an injunction was granted to prevent the film actress, Bette Davis, appearing in any film or stage production for anyone other than Warner Brothers without their consent. The important point was that Warner Brothers did not seek enforcement of a positive performance obligation, which would have been refused. Counsel for Miss Davis had argued that if the injunction was granted she would effectively be placed in the position of having to work for Warner Brothers or starve. The judge rejected this argument on the basis that Miss Davis could earn money in other ways.

There is an evident tension here between avoiding forcing a person to work for a particular employer and yet giving effect to stipulations in his contract which were freely agreed to and which have significant financial implications for the employer. In practice, the courts are unlikely to apply the test in *Warner Bros* when considering whether to grant an injunction. It is far more likely that they will have regard to the circumstances in which the restraint is asked for, including matters such as the duration and likely effect on the reputation and general prospects of the person being restrained (see the discussion of restraint of trade clauses at **16.7**).

As **Vertex Data Science Ltd v Powergen Retail Ltd** [2006] EWHC 1340 (Comm), [2006] 2 Lloyd's Rep 591 (see **10.2.2.1**) illustrates, even where the parties are in a commercial and not a personal relationship, the courts are unlikely to order specific performance where the mutual confidence in the relationship has broken down.

10.2.3 Equitable limits: Discretion, mutuality, and volunteers

10.2.3.1 Discretion

Specific performance is an equitable remedy. This fact is significant in that equitable remedies are not available as of right, unlike the common law remedy of damages. Even where the claimant can demonstrate that his claim satisfies the conditions of availability of the remedy outlined above, the court has a discretion to refuse specific performance. Of course, the discretion is not entirely arbitrary. The extent of the discretion is that if the claim falls within certain loosely defined categories, the court may refuse to award specific performance if in the circumstances it believes that would be the right thing to do.

- **The court may consider the conduct of the claimant, and if the claimant has not behaved entirely properly it may refuse specific performance.** The claimant's conduct need not amount to a legal wrong; mere 'trickery' will suffice to allow the court to consider exercise of the discretion (*Quadrant Visual Communications Ltd v Hutchison Telephone (UK) Ltd* [1993] 1 BCLC 442) and specific performance will be refused where the claimant has been guilty of some unfairness or sharp practice (*Pateman v Pay* (1974) 232 EG 457). This principle is sometimes colourfully stated in the terms that 'he who comes to equity must come with clean hands'. Any provision of the contract which purports to prevent the application of the 'clean hands' rule will be ineffective: the parties cannot fetter the discretion of the court (*Quadrant Visual Communications Ltd v Hutchison Telephone (UK) Ltd*).

- **The remedy may also be refused where it would be unfair to the defendant or result in personal hardship** (e.g., *Patel v Ali* [1984] Ch 283). In ***Shell UK Ltd v Lostock Garage Ltd*** [1976] 1 WLR 1187, an injunction to prevent a tied garage from obtaining petrol from another supplier was refused on the ground that the plaintiff supplier had granted discounts to all garages in the area other than the defendant's, so that it had become impossible for the garage to compete. No injunction could therefore be granted while this discount scheme for other garages was in place.

10.2.3.2 Mutuality

Specific performance may also be refused where there is no mutuality of remedy between the parties. It was once thought that this requirement meant that specific performance would not be available if at the time of contracting it could not also have been available to the other party. There was little sense in such a strict rule, and there were a number of exceptions to it.

The rule was subsequently clarified by the Court of Appeal in ***Price v Strange*** [1978] Ch 337.

> The defendant promised to grant a lease to the plaintiff in return for the plaintiff's promise to do some internal and external repairs. The plaintiff's promise could not be specifically enforced. By the time of the trial the internal repairs had been completed, and the plaintiff had wrongfully been prevented from doing the external repairs by the defendant (who had carried them out herself). The court considered that the crucial time at which mutuality must be tested is the time of the trial. At that point the claimant must have performed all of its obligations, or these obligations must themselves be capable of specific performance, or non-performance of those obligations must be adequately compensatable by an award of damages (see **10.2.1**).

The purpose of the rule is to protect a defendant from the risk of being obliged to perform the actual contractual undertakings only to find that it will be inadequately compensated for the claimant's own non-performance. As such, it may be no more than a particular application of the undue hardship principle. In ***Price v Strange***, the plaintiff's contractual undertakings were not capable of specific performance, but by the time of the trial they had all been performed, so that there was no risk of hardship to the defendant in granting specific performance.

10.2.3.3 Volunteers

It is a general principle of equity that it will not 'assist a volunteer'. **That is, equitable rules and remedies will not be applied in the case of a person who has not given real consideration for a promise.** Thus, a promise which is binding under the common law because it was made under in a deed (see **4.1**), or which was given for a nominal and symbolic consideration such as a peppercorn (see **4.3.2**), cannot be specifically enforced (*Re Parkin* [1892] 3 Ch 510). However, there are signs that this principle may have been relaxed. Under the Contracts (Rights of Third Parties) Act 1999, a third party who satisfies the test of enforceability will be able to enforce a contractual term even where that third party has not provided any consideration to support it, assuming that the promise is supported by consideration provided by the promisee so that it is not a gratuitous promise. The third party will have any remedy that 'would have been available to him in an action for breach of the contract if he had been a party to the contract' (s. 1(5)). This would, in principle, include the remedy of specific performance, although the third party would technically be a volunteer in equity.

10.2.4 Damages in lieu of specific performance

By the Supreme Court Act 1981, s. 50, the High Court is empowered to award damages in lieu of specific performance. In the majority of cases the claimant will be unlikely to invite the court to exercise its power, since it is possible to claim damages and specific performance at the same time (Supreme Court Act 1981, s. 49). However, damages in lieu of specific performance may be awarded in circumstances in which common law damages would not be, although instances are likely to be rare. Where such damages are awarded they are to be assessed in the same way as common law damages for breach of contract (*Johnson v Agnew* [1980] AC 367), although see the discussion of time for assessment at **9.7**.

10.3 Injunction

An injunction is a court order restraining the defendant from a specified activity. Its use extends far beyond the law of contract, but in this context it may be used to prevent the breach of a negative stipulation in the contract. The example given earlier of such a stipulation was a promise in the form of a contract not to make loud noises during the period when the promisee was revising for an exam (see **Part 3(c)**) and see also restraint of trade provisions (see **16.7**). Such promises may be enforced by means of an injunction.

The requirement that damages be shown to be inadequate before specific relief will be granted does not apply strictly to ordinary injunctions. Nevertheless, the courts will not in most circumstances allow the claimant to exploit this difference to achieve by injunction what cannot be achieved by specific performance. We have already seen how this principle applies in the case of contracts of employment (see **10.2.2.2**). In other contracts the courts will be unwilling to enforce by injunction an express term which does no more than broadly prohibit breach of the positive stipulations in the contract, if the contract would not otherwise qualify for specific performance. Thus, injunctions are limited to specific restraints.

Normally, the activity to be restrained will be stipulated expressly in the contract, and the courts will be unwilling to imply a negative stipulation from the positive terms of the agreement. Such implication will occur, however, where the circumstances justify it. For example, where an exclusive dealing agreement is found not to be in restraint of trade (see **16.7.7**), the court may imply a negative term preventing conduct which is inconsistent with the purpose of such a contract (*Evans Marshall and Co. v Bertola SA* [1973] 1 All ER 992). Nevertheless, it is usual for such contracts to contain explicit negative stipulations.

10.3.1 Types of injunctions

- **Prohibitory injunctions** are granted to prevent future breach of contract.
- However, if the claimant wishes to compel the defendant to remedy an injury caused by a breach which has already occurred, that claimant must obtain a **mandatory injunction**.

The effect of such an injunction is to compel the defendant to undo work which has been done in breach of a negative stipulation in the contract.

 Example

A mandatory injunction might be granted to compel the defendant to cut down trees which had been planted in breach of a covenant not to restrict the claimant's view (*Wakeham v Wood* (1982) 43 P & CR 40).

Mandatory injunctions are subject to the same rules as specific performance. Damages must be an inadequate remedy, and grant of the injunction must not cause undue hardship to the defendant. This latter requirement may be waived where the breach was deliberately and knowingly committed (*Wakeham v Wood*).

10.4 Restitution

The modern law of restitution is firmly based in the notion of unjust enrichment (***Lipkin Gorman v Karpnale Ltd*** [1991] 2 AC 548).

Enrichment by subtraction

In the general field of contracts, unjust enrichment will usually take the form of a benefit accruing to one party which for some reason may be regarded as 'belonging' to another, and the purpose of a restitutionary remedy would be to restore the benefit to its 'rightful owner'—either on the basis that there has been a total failure of consideration or via a *quantum meruit* payment for the reasonable value of the performance. **Such cases are often referred to as instances of enrichment by subtraction from the claimant.**

 Example

A classic example would be the rendering of some performance, in anticipation of a contract being made, only to have that expectation come to nothing because of a failure to agree terms. The recipient of the performance has received a benefit which must have cost the other party something to provide, and it would be unjust to allow the benefit to be retained without payment of some kind.

In this context, restitutionary remedies do not provide a response to one party's failure to satisfy the other party's expectation under the contract. **Rather, they seek to restore money paid or the value of a benefit conferred in circumstances in which no contract exists, or in which there is no longer any obligation to perform under an admitted contract.** Thus, their availability is not solely dependent upon the existence of a breach of contract, although where there has been breach the non-breaching party may have to decide whether a claim for expectation loss or a restitutionary remedy would provide a better level of compensation.

Enrichment without subtraction

There may also be an enrichment, which in some circumstances might be considered unjust, where one party receives a benefit as a result of a wrong done to the other party, without there being any 'subtraction' from that party (or measurable loss suffered by the non-breaching party); and the question then posed is whether a remedy should be available in such a case (and the nature of such a remedy). This question is considered at **10.6**.

10.5 Enrichment by subtraction

10.5.1 Total failure of consideration

Even in the absence of breach, a party may recover money paid in anticipation of a contractual performance which the other party has failed to provide where there has been a total failure of consideration.

Performance may be impossible because the contract has been frustrated (**see Chapter 12**), or because unknown to the parties the subject matter of the contract had been destroyed before the time of contracting (see 13.3.1). In each case the promisee may recover money paid in advance despite the fact that the failure of performance does not amount to breach. Indeed, most claims for total failure of consideration do not arise out of breach by the other party. In the event of breach, the normal reaction will be to claim damages for lost expectation, but the restitutionary remedy is available as an alternative (see **10.5.3**).

10.5.1.1 Illegality

Special rules apply where there is no performance because the contract is illegal (see 16.6). However, these special rules apply only between the parties to the agreement which is tainted with illegality.

In **Lipkin Gorman v Karpnale Ltd** [1991] 2 AC 548, the House of Lords had to deal with a claim to recover money stolen from the plaintiffs and then paid to the defendants in good faith but under a contract which was void under s. 18 of the Gaming Act 1845 (see 16.3). In restating the modern law of restitution, Lords Goff and Templeman agreed that the essential question was whether the defendants had been unjustly enriched. That in turn depended upon whether, irrespective of their good faith in receiving the money, the defendants had given good consideration for it. It was held that they could not have given valuable consideration, because at that time the contract was void. The mere fact of honouring gaming debts did not amount to providing consideration; as a matter of law it was no more than a gift from the gambling club to the client. Consequently, the unjust enrichment was established, and the restitutionary claim succeeded, subject only to the defence of change of position, recognized as a general defence to restitutionary claims by the House of Lords in this case.

Similar reasoning has been applied to interest rate swap transactions which were void because they were *ultra vires* (beyond the power of) the local authorities involved (*South Tyneside Metropolitan Borough Council v Svenska International plc* [1995] 1 All ER 545). The courts have considered there to be no consideration in such cases (see *Westdeutsche Landesbank Girozentrale v Islington BC* [1994] 4 All ER 890 at p. 924, *Kleinwort Benson Ltd v Birmingham CC* [1997] QB 380 at pp. 386–7, *Guinness Mahon & Co. Ltd v Kensington and Chelsea RLBC* [1999] QB 215, and *Deutsche Morgan Grenfell Group plc v Inland Revenue Commissioners* [2006] UKHL 49, [2007] 1 AC 558).

However, in instances of payments made under a void contract as a result of a mistake of law (i.e., a mistaken belief that the contract is valid), the payments made can be recovered even where there is no total (or partial) failure of consideration (*Kleinwort Benson Ltd v Lincoln CC* [1999] 2 AC 349). A recent example of restitutionary recovery in an invalid swap transaction is provided by the decision in *Haugesund Kommune v DEPFA ACS Bank* [2009] EWHC 2227 (Comm).

10.5.1.2 Relationship to consideration as 'promise'

In relation to the formation of contracts 'consideration' was described as constituted not merely by an exchange of performances, but also by an exchange of promises. It might be thought, therefore, that where it is possible to show agreement there can never be a failure of consideration. However, where 'consideration' is used in the technical sense of giving rise to a restitutionary remedy upon total failure, it must be understood as referring to *performance* of whatever was promised in the agreement.

In *Fibrosa SA v Fairbairn Lawson Combe Barbour Ltd* [1943] AC 32 (see **12.8.1.1**), Viscount Simon LC explained (at p. 48):

> [I]n the law relating to the formation of contract, the promise to do a thing may often be the consideration; but, when one is considering the law of failure of consideration and of the quasi-contractual right to recover money on that ground, it is, generally speaking, not the promise which is referred to as the consideration, but the performance of the promise. The money was paid to secure performance and, if performance fails, the inducement which brought about the payment is not fulfilled. If this were not so, there could never be any recovery of money, for failure of consideration, by the payer of the money in return for a promise of future performance.

This standard explanation of the doctrine of total failure of consideration was affirmed by the Privy Council in *Goss v Chilcott* [1996] AC 788 at p. 797.

> In *Fibrosa SA v Fairbairn Lawson Combe Barbour Ltd* [1943] AC 32, the seller was prevented from completing performance of a contract by the outbreak of war, since the buyer was in enemy occupied territory. The buyer had paid part of the price in advance, and since it had received none of the promised performance, it was entitled to repayment of that money because there had been a total failure of consideration.
>
> In *Rover International Ltd v Cannon Film Sales Ltd (No. 3)* [1989] 1 WLR 912, the Court of Appeal held that there had been a total failure of consideration despite the fact that Rover had received the films in question. The total failure of consideration related to the fact that the promised performance for which they had contracted was the securing of a profit and this had been prevented.

It will therefore be a matter of determining what performance is owed under the terms of the contract. This was again confirmed by the House of Lords in *Stocznia Gdanska SA v Latvian Shipping Co.* [1998] 1 WLR 574. The House of Lords explained that for there to be a total failure of consideration, it did not need to be established that the promisee had received nothing under the contract; the issue was whether the other party had performed any part of its contractual duties in respect of which payment was due.

> The argument on the facts of this case was that because the defendants had not received the vessels being constructed under the contract, there was a total failure of consideration. The House of Lords

considered that the contractual obligations, for which payment was to be made, extended beyond delivery of the vessels and included design and construction. Accordingly, since some of this work had been completed, there was no total failure of consideration. This was reinforced by the fact that payment was to be made in instalments.

10.5.2 Partial failure of performance

The general rule is that where the promisee has received *some* of the performance to which the promisee is entitled under the contract, so that the failure is only partial, the promisee is not able to recover money paid in advance (*Whincup v Hughes* (1871) LR 6 CP 78).

The explanation for this rule is usually said to be that it is impossible to apportion the consideration between the performed and unperformed parts of the contract. For this reason, where performance is severable (see 8.6.2.1), so that the money paid can easily be split *pro rata* among the several parts, recovery of part of the money for partial failure of consideration will be allowed (*Ebrahim Dawood Ltd v Heath (Est. 1927) Ltd* [1961] Lloyd's Rep 512).

This rule was applied to slightly surprising effect in **Goss v Chilcott** [1996] AC 788 (discussed by Carter and Tolhurst (1997) 11 JCL 162).

In **Goss v Chilcott**, the appellants had borrowed a sum of money, but had been unable to repay any of the capital, and in fact paid only two instalments of interest. An action against them in contract was unavailable, for reasons which are not relevant here. The question was whether the capital was recoverable for total failure of consideration. The Privy Council rejected the argument that there was no failure of consideration because of the reciprocal exchange of promises at the time of making the contract. For these purposes, the existence of consideration required actual performance of some part of what had been promised (see **10.5.1**).

More difficulty was presented by the fact that two instalments of interest payments were made. In the light of these payments, it could be argued that there had been *some* performance, so that there had not been a *total* failure of consideration. However, the contract did not provide, as would usually be the case with a long-term loan, for the scheduled payments to combine both interest and some repayment of capital; they were only payments of interest due. As a result, Lord Goff said, it was possible to separate the elements of the contract; and, since there was no performance in respect of the capital, it could be recovered.

It may also be possible for a promisee to convert a partial failure of consideration into a total failure of consideration by returning any benefit received by such performance as has taken place. This may be a particularly desirable course of action if the promisee is of the opinion that a restitutionary remedy would be preferable to a claim for damages (see 10.5.3). In some circumstances, of course, restoration of the benefit will be impossible. Where building work has been done on the promisee's land, but not completed, the promisee cannot return the work done (*Sumpter v Hedges* [1898] 1 QB 673: see 8.6.4.1). If, however, it is impossible to return the performance received for some reason connected with the other party's breach, there will be no obstacle to recovery of payment on the basis of total failure of consideration.

In some circumstances restoration of any performance received will not convert partial into total failure of consideration because the promisee has had the benefit of use between the time of performance and the time of its return (*Hunt v Silk* (1804) 5 East 449). This rule may sometimes appear to conflict with cases in the sale of goods, where the courts will find total failure of consideration even when the goods in question have been in the possession of and used by the promisee over a substantial period of time. The reason is that in the sale of goods the essential performance is the provision of good title to the thing sold, and the courts take the view that use of the goods in question is irrelevant to the contract of sale (*Rowland v Divall* [1923] 2 KB 500). This rule makes good sense in the case of a dealer, who purchases to resell and who must therefore have title, but does not seem right in the case of a consumer, who purchases in order to use the goods in question.

The Law Commission in its Working Paper, *Pecuniary Restitution on Breach of Contract* (No. 65), had provisionally recommended that restitutionary recovery ought to be available in cases of partial failure of the consideration. However, the Law Commission changed its mind in its 1983 report (No. 121). This may be explicable in the light of the inventiveness of the courts in enabling recovery, despite what appears to be only a partial failure of consideration.

10.5.3 Restitution versus damages

Where the total failure of consideration is due to breach by the other party, the promisee will normally claim damages for loss of expectation, since the promisee will probably wish to recover the cost of mitigating its loss by resort to the market, and may wish to recover damages for lost profits. If the contract was an advantageous one then the expectation measure of damages will almost certainly be more attractive than recovering money paid. If, however, the claimant had made a bad bargain, so that a loss would have been made on the contract had it been performed, the claimant may be glad of the opportunity provided by the total failure of consideration to retrieve intact the investment made.

10.5.4 *Quantum meruit*

Quantum meruit **is a remedy under which a party who has provided a benefit, and who for some reason cannot obtain payment under a contract, may recover the reasonable value of the benefit provided.** It may apply where there is no contract, or where the contractual provisions as to remuneration are inapplicable.

10.5.4.1 *Quantum meruit* in the absence of contract

Where one party confers a benefit on another with the intention on both sides that that benefit will be paid for, then, in the absence of any contract between the parties, the party conferring the benefit will be able to recover reasonable remuneration from the recipient under the restitutionary remedy of *quantum meruit* (*Planche v Colburn* (1831) 8 Bing 10). This is a sum which is not based on any contract price because there is no agreed contract price. It will need to be calculated by reference to market rates. For an example of the operation of this principle, see ***British Steel Corporation v Cleveland Bridge & Engineering Co. Ltd*** [1984] 1 All ER 504 (see 3.1.4.1).

> The plaintiffs had begun work on the manufacture of steel nodes at the request of the defendants despite the facts that the parties had yet to reach agreement on all the elements of the contract. Both sides confidently expected to reach agreement without difficulty. Final agreement was never reached. The plaintiffs had delivered all but one of the nodes and claimed a *quantum meruit* for the work they had done. Their claim succeeded.

The ***Cleveland Bridge*** decision was rightly distinguished by Rattee J in ***Regalian Properties plc v London Dockland Development Corporation*** [1995] 1 WLR 212. In *Regalian* (unlike the *Cleveland Bridge* case) the plaintiffs had not carried out the work at the request of the defendants;

rather, they had done it in order to be able to win the contract from the defendants. The negotiations had been conducted on a 'subject to contract' basis so that such expenditure was at the plaintiffs' own risk, conferred no benefit on the defendants, and was not recoverable when they failed to obtain the anticipated contract.

Remuneration on the basis of *quantum meruit* may also be recoverable where performance is rendered under a contract which, unknown to both parties, is void.

> In **Craven-Ellis v Canons Ltd** [1936] 2 KB 403, the plaintiff had worked as managing director of a company without being appointed in the manner required by law. His contract was therefore void, but he was able to recover the reasonable value of his work.

Similar rules apply in the case of work done by companies under contracts which are void because at the time the contract was made the company had not been incorporated, and so had no legal existence (***Rover International Ltd v Cannon Film Sales Ltd (No. 3)*** [1989] 1 WLR 912).

10.5.4.2 *Quantum meruit* despite the contract

Where there is a contract between the parties, it is fundamental to the law of contract that payment is to be determined according to the terms of the contract. The courts must not interfere with the parties' agreement. However, in limited circumstances that general rule is displaced and the court will allow a *quantum meruit* remedy despite the existence of a contract.

- Where the contract fails to provide for the payment to be made, a reasonable price is payable. This rule has been embodied in statute (SGA 1979, s. 8; Supply of Goods and Services Act 1982, s. 15). The same rule may also apply where the contract provides a price-fixing mechanism which is regarded as a mechanism for fixing a fair price rather than an essential factor in its determination, and for some unforeseen reason this mechanism fails to work—***Sudbrook Trading Estate Ltd v Eggleton*** [1983] 1 AC 444 (see **3.1.4.4**).

- In the case of an entire obligation, partial performance does not entitle the party who breaches by abandoning performance before completion to any payment under the contract (see **8.6.2** and **8.6.2.2**). Where, however, the non-breaching party voluntarily accepts a benefit conferred by partial performance before the contract has been abandoned, the party who has breached may recover the reasonable value of the benefit conferred.

- Conversely, where the non-breaching party confers a benefit on the other party before the latter's breach, the non-breaching party may recover the value of that benefit under a *quantum meruit* rather than bringing a claim for damages (*Slowey v Lodder* (1901) 20 NZLR 321, affirmed by the Privy Council *sub nom Lodder v Slowey* [1904] AC 442). By so doing, the non-breaching party may be able to avoid the consequences of having made a bad bargain.

10.6 Enrichment without subtraction from the claimant: The remedy of the account of profits and its relationship with *Wrotham Park* damages

In this context the question is whether the claimant can recover where the defendant has been unjustly enriched as a result of a breach of contract but there is no measurable loss suffered by the claimant (i.e. no subtraction from the claimant). As explained at **9.1.2**, the difficulty is that a transfer (disgorgement) of the defendant's profit, where the claimant has suffered no loss, would appear to constitute punishment for a breach whereas the contractual remedy of damages is compensatory.

10.6.1 Rejection of such a general remedy

In **Surrey County Council v Bredero Homes Ltd** [1993] 1 WLR 1361 the council sold land to the defendant property developer, who covenanted not to build more than seventy-two houses on it. Without seeking a variation of the covenant (for which it would certainly have had to pay), the developer built an additional five houses. The council claimed damages based on its estimate of what the defendant would have had to pay as the 'price' for variation of the covenant. Inevitably, there was some sympathy for the council's case: the developer had deliberately breached the covenant in order to make a greater profit. On the other hand, the council could not be shown to have suffered a loss. Thus, there was an enrichment of the defendant without there being any subtraction from the plaintiff in this case. Normal contract damages were not recoverable, because the plaintiff was already in the position it would have been in had the contract not been breached. The question was simply whether the deliberate breach of the contract should in some way be sanctioned by making the defendant disgorge a part of its profit. The Court of Appeal did not think it should. Case law rejected this possibility. For example, in **Tito v Waddell (No. 2)** [1977] Ch 106, 332, Megarry V-C stated: 'The question is not one of making the defendant disgorge what he has saved by committing the wrong, but one of compensating the claimant.'

10.6.2 The *Wrotham Park* principle: Damages based on the price to release a negative stipulation or covenant

The only previous case in which recovery had been permitted in similar circumstances, *Wrotham Park Estate Co. Ltd v Parkside Homes Ltd* [1974] 1 WLR 798, was approved but distinguished by Steyn LJ (on the basis that it concerned an interference with property rights).

In **Wrotham Park Estate Co. Ltd v Parkside Homes Ltd,** the defendant had built houses on his land in breach of a restrictive covenant in favour of an adjoining estate. The estate owners sought an injunction but were unsuccessful. However, they were awarded damages based on the profit which the defendant made from the breach of covenant on the basis that this related to the sum the estate owners might reasonably have required to relax the covenant.

Wrotham Park was distinguished in **Surrey v Bredero** and the *Wrotham Park* principle was treated as being of limited application and relevance. It was interpreted by Dillon and Steyn LJJ as resting on wrongful interference with property rights (seemingly by analogy with tort cases of trespass, under which a person who uses land without permission must pay for that use, even if no harm has been done to the land: e.g., *Whitwham v Westminster Brymbo Coal and Coke Co.* [1896] 2 Ch 538). In addition, it was seen as a decision to award damages in lieu of an injunction, whereas in **Surrey v Bredero** the council had not sought specific enforcement. The Court of Appeal in **Surrey v Bredero** was also concerned in policy terms about the potential extension to permit a general right to damages based on disgorging the defendant's profit.

10.6.3 Arguments in favour of a more general ability to disgorge profits

It has been argued that a more general right to 'restitutionary damages' could solve many of the existing dilemmas in the application of principles governing breach of contract. For example, it has been suggested (see Poole (1996) 59 MLR 272, in the context of *Ruxley Electronics v Forsyth* [1996] 1 AC 344: see **9.3.3.4**) that in cases where there is no difference in value but cost of cure damages would be disproportionate (cases of 'skimped performance'), a suitable remedy would be to require the defendant contractor (say) to disgorge its savings in costs through constructing the swimming pool at less than the required depth. This would send a more appropriate signal to the construction industry and achieve a better balance of the respective interests.

In its 1997 report, *Aggravated, Exemplary and Restitutionary Damages,* No. 247, at paras 3.38–3.47, the Law Commission rejected suggestions advocating a legislative formulation for such 'restitutionary' damages on the basis that this would 'freeze' the position. Instead, the Law Commission recommended that the availability of such damages should be left to common law development. The conclusion that legislation is not considered necessary was reaffirmed when the Ministry of Justice published a response to its consultation on this question ('The Law on Damages', CP 9/07) in July 2009.

10.6.4 The decision in *Attorney-General v Blake*: Account of profits in very limited circumstances

The question was discussed again in *Attorney-General v Blake* [2001] 1 AC 268, and some common law development occurred, although the exact scope of this development is uncertain. At first sight this development appeared to be very limited (see Hedley (2000) 4 Web JCLI) but, almost inevitably, the decision was initially seized upon by counsel as supporting a broader principle. **The majority of the House of Lords considered that in 'exceptional circumstances', the non-breaching party could recover the profits made as a result of the other's breach of contract (by way of an account of profits) even where the breach of contract did not involve the use of, or interference with, a property interest of the claimant.**

Lord Nicholls (with whom Lords Goff, Browne-Wilkinson, and Steyn agreed) put the position as follows:

> When, exceptionally, a just response to a breach of contract so requires, the court should be able to grant the discretionary remedy of requiring the defendant to account to the plaintiff for the benefits he has received from his breach of contract. In the same way as a *plaintiff's interest in performance* may make it just and equitable for the court to make an order for specific performance or grant an injunction, so *the plaintiff's interest in performance* may make it just and equitable that the defendant should retain no benefit from his breach of contract. [Emphasis added.]

In other words, it was considered that such a remedy would give effect to the plaintiff's 'interest in performance', which subsequently has been interpreted to mean that such damages are compensatory in nature, see discussion below at **10.6.4.3**.

> Blake had worked for the intelligence services but had become an agent for the Soviet Union. He had been tried and imprisoned for treason, but had escaped from prison to Moscow, where he had written his autobiography. This book had been published in England and (although by this time none of the material it contained was confidential) publication was in breach of a term of Blake's former employment contract that he would not divulge official information. The Attorney-General wanted to prevent payment of the royalties to Blake.

The facts of **Blake** were exceptional because of the nature of the wrong involved (which may be analogous to breach of fiduciary duty), and the majority considered that it justified an order that the Attorney-General was entitled to an account of these profits.

Lord Nicholls expressly approved the reasoning in **Wrotham Park** and stated that 'in so far as the *Bredero* decision is inconsistent with the approach adopted in the *Wrotham Park* case, the latter approach is to be preferred'.

10.6.4.1 What will constitute 'an exceptional case'?

This still leaves open the question of precisely what will constitute an 'exceptional case'. The House of Lords laid down no detailed guidance and stated that 'no fixed rules can be prescribed' (per Lord Nicholls). The only real comments are the following statements by Lord Nicholls:

> The court will have regarded to all the circumstances, including the subject-matter of the contract, the purpose of the contractual provision which has been breached, the circumstances in which the breach occurred, the consequences of the breach and the circumstances in which relief is being sought.

This is not terribly helpful because it is far too general. Lord Nicholls added the following as a possible qualifying condition:

> A useful general guide, although not exhaustive, is whether the plaintiff has a legitimate interest in preventing the defendant's profit-making activity and, hence, in depriving him of his profit.

In his speech Lord Nicholls examined the two instances which had been suggested by the Court of Appeal as justifying restitutionary intervention: (i) 'skimped performance' (see above); and (ii) instances where the profit was made by the defendant doing the very thing he had contracted not to do. Lord Nicholls considered that neither instance could be covered by an account of profits; implying that instances of skimped performance might be addressed in other ways and that the second possibility was far too wide because it extended to all negative stipulations. It therefore seems that the possibility of recovering account of profit damages for skimped performance has been ruled out.

Lord Nicholls did, however, agree with Lord Woolf in the Court of Appeal that the following factors would **not** be a sufficient basis to justify the award of an account of profits:

- the existence of a cynical and deliberate breach
- the fact that the breach enabled the defendant to enter into a more profitable contract elsewhere
- that the defendant had put it out of his power to perform his contract with the claimant.

Thus, although **Blake** is an important decision in recognizing the possibility of disgorgement of a defendant's profit (in the limited sense of an account of profits), the circumstances in which this remedy might operate are uncertain. The majority clearly considered the practical scope of such a remedy to be extremely limited. Only Lord Hobhouse warned against the potential consequences of this apparent recognition of non-compensatory damages for breach of contract if applied to commercial contracts, arguing that such a step would require 'very careful consideration before it is acceded to'. In particular, Lord Hobhouse stressed the fact that such an award would by-pass the usual duty to mitigate in this context. However, this was always unlikely to deter the making of commercial claims including an account for profits, and this proved to be the case.

10.6.4.2 Claims for an account of profits in subsequent case law

1. *Esso Petroleum Co Ltd v Niad Ltd*

In ***Esso Petroleum Co Ltd v Niad Ltd***, unreported, 22 November 2001 (noted Beatson (2002) 118 LQR 377) Morritt V-C concluded that an account of profits was an available remedy on the facts, involving a breach of a commercial contract.

> The breach was a deliberate failure by the defendant, owner of a petrol service station, to implement a promotional scheme. In return for a discount on the price of petrol received from the claimant, the defendant agreed to report the petrol prices of local competitors and to charge the price recommended by the claimant oil company. However, the defendant kept the discount he received. The claimant wanted to know whether it was possible to secure an account of profits so that the defendant would be obliged to return the amount charged for petrol over and above the price recommended by the claimant. Morritt V-C discussed the decision in ***Blake*** and concluded that an account of profits would be an available remedy only in exceptional circumstances where:
>
> (i) **the usual remedies for breach of contract would be inadequate**
> (ii) **the claimant had a legitimate interest in preventing the defendant from profiting from the breach** (although these hardly seem appropriate criteria to limit recovery to exceptional cases and may well apply in many commercial cases).
>
> In particular, it is difficult to identify circumstances where a claimant who is owed a contractual performance would not have the necessary legitimate interest in securing that performance and preventing the defendant from profiting from the breach.
>
> On the facts, and applying these criteria, he concluded that this was such an exceptional case because (i) the claimant could not establish the lost sales which were attributable to the defendant's failure to implement the scheme and so damages for breach would have been limited to nominal damages only, and (ii) the claimant had the necessary legitimate interest because the defendant's breach of the terms of the scheme threatened to undermine it.

It can be argued that one of the difficulties with an account of profits, and a fact which should limit its application, is the need to establish a causal link between the breach and the profit/sales. However, in ***Esso v Niad*** the absence of this link is used as a ground justifying the availability of this remedy on the basis that damages were unavailable due to the very same causal difficulties. However, there was considered to be an alternative remedy on the facts, namely restitutionary recovery on the basis of unjust enrichment. This would allow recovery in full of the excess amount (the difference between the price charged and the recommended prices) and was clearly considered to be the more appropriate remedy by Morritt V-C.

The worrying aspect of the decision relates to the liberal interpretation of the ***Blake*** principles said to govern the circumstances in which the remedy of an account of profits was to be available.

2. *Experience Hendrix LLC v PPX Enterprises Inc.*

The Court of Appeal was then called upon to determine whether an account of profits could be ordered in a different commercial context.

> In **Experience Hendrix LLC v PPX Enterprises Inc.** [2003] EWCA Civ 323, [2003] 1 All ER (Comm) 830, [2003] EMLR 25, the claim for an account of profits related to a fairly typical commercial scenario where there have been breaches of an agreement containing a negative stipulation (in this case concerning licences of Jimi Hendrix music) and, although an injunction had been issued to prevent future losses, the claimant wanted to recover in respect of past breaches when there was no evidence of financial losses attributable to those past breaches. The claimant therefore sought to recover either (on the basis of **Blake**) for an account of the profit made through the exploitation of the Hendrix material in breach of the negative stipulation or, for a measure of damages which was more than nominal.

Mance LJ (with whose judgment the other members of the Court of Appeal agreed) explained the scope of the **Blake** decision using factors referred to by Lord Nicholls in the House of Lords in **Blake** which emphasized its exceptional (if not extreme) nature and therefore justified the account of profits:

> The exceptional nature of *Blake's* case lay first of all, in its context—employment in the security and intelligence service, of which secret information was the lifeblood, its disclosure being a criminal offence…Blake had furthermore committed deliberate and repeated breaches causing untold damage, from which breaches most of the profits indirectly derived in the sense that his notoriety as a spy explained his ability to command the sums for publication which he had done…Thirdly, although the argument that Blake was a fiduciary was not pursued beyond first instance, the contractual undertaking he had given was 'closely akin to a fiduciary obligation, where an account of profits is a standard remedy in the event of breach'.

Analysis of the case law

Experience Hendrix was not sufficiently 'exceptional' to justify an account of profits; features (i) (national security/secret information) and (iii) (fiduciary breaches) were clearly missing, although it was clear that the claimant had a legitimate interest in prevent the profit-making activity. (Given this approach, and conclusion, it is difficult to see what was so 'exceptional' about the facts of **Esso v Niad**.) The Court of Appeal in **Experience Hendrix** was clearly conscious of the implication of awarding an account of profits in a commercial context and purported to distinguish *Niad* on the basis that the defendant's breaches in that case had the effect of undermining the whole purpose of the agreed scheme. This might provide evidence to satisfy feature (ii) above ('deliberate and repeated breaches *causing untold damage*'), suggesting that the exceptional nature of the profits may be pivotal, but fails to explain why the absence of features (i) and (iii) was not considered fatal to the award of an account of profits in **Esso v Niad**.

The outcome in **Experience Hendrix** reflects the fact that the **Blake** account of profits is to be restricted to exceptional cases and the significance of the decision in **Experience Hendrix** appears to be that it has acted as a deterrent to future attempts to present a non-exceptional commercial case as 'exceptional' within the **Blake** principle. On the other hand, the availability of the **Wrotham Park** award enables courts to achieve an appropriate compromise between awarding nothing at all and awarding a full account of all the profits. In the case of breaches of negative stipulations in commercial cases, such as in **Experience Hendrix,** such an approach is helpful and preferable.

The price of release from the negative stipulation as a remedy of more general application

An important feature in **Experience Hendrix** would seem to have been the availability of another remedy (and this was also the position in **Esso v Niad**), since the Court of Appeal held that the defendant should pay the sum that might reasonably be demanded by the Hendrix estate to release the negative stipulation in the contract (on the basis of the **Wrotham Park** principle, see earlier discussion at **10.6.2**).

10.6.4.3 The debate about the nature of the remedies

1. Different forms of restitutionary remedy

Edelman suggested that the **Wrotham Park** principle and the principle in **Blake** should be distinguished on the basis that **Wrotham Park** was a case of 'restitutionary damages' (the amount required to relax the covenant which had been breached) and **Blake** was an account of the actual profits resulting from the breach, which is a 'disgorgement' remedy (Edelman, *Gain-Based Damages: Contract, tort, equity and intellectual property* (Hart Publishing, 2002)). Edelman argued that, where compensatory damages are not available, **Wrotham Park** restitutionary damages should be more generally available in breach of contract cases as a restitutionary remedy by subtraction. However, this view must now be considered as incorrect in the light of recent case law and more explicit explanation of the underlying basis for each remedy.

2. Different forms of compensatory remedy in cases of no identifiable financial loss

Brightman J in **Wrotham Park** had clearly considered that the price of the release as damages was essentially compensatory, i.e. compensation for lost expectation, since the position where there is a negative stipulation in a contract is to raise an expectation that the activity in question will not take place, e.g. building more houses than the planning permission permits, or publishing an autobiography which breaches a contractual undertaking not to divulge official secrets. However, there is also an expectation that it is possible to negotiate a release from the negative stipulation at a price. Therefore, assuming that the breach prevents the negotiation of a release, it defeats this expectation interest (i.e., the claimant's expectation that it will be possible to receive payment to agree to a release).

More conclusively, Chadwick LJ in the Court of Appeal in *WWF World Wide Fund for Nature v World Wrestling Federation Entertainment Inc.* [2007] EWCA Civ 286, [2008] 1 WLR 445, [2007] Bus LR 1252, [2008] 1 WLR 445, confirmed this position but also went much further and confirmed that both the **Wrotham Park** award and the account of profits in **Blake** were not 'gains-based' but compensatory in nature:

> When a court makes an award of damages on the *Wrotham Park* basis it does so because it is satisfied that it is a just response to circumstances in which the compensation which is the claimant's due cannot be measured (or cannot be measured solely) by reference to identifiable financial loss. Lord Nicholls' analysis in *Attorney-General v Blake* demonstrates that there are exceptional cases in which the just response to circumstances in which the compensation which is the claimant's due cannot be measured by reference to identifiable financial loss is an order which deprives the wrongdoer of all the fruits of his wrong. The circumstances in which an award of damages on the *Wrotham Park* basis may be an appropriate response, and those in which the appropriate response is an account of profits, may differ in degree. But the underlying feature, in both cases, is that the court recognises the need to compensate the claimant in circumstances »

where he cannot demonstrate identifiable financial loss. To label an award of damages on the *Wrotham Park* basis as a 'compensatory' remedy and an order for an account of profits as a 'gains-based' remedy does not assist an understanding of the principles on which the court acts. The two remedies should, I think, each be seen as a flexible response to the need to *compensate* the claimant for the wrong which has been done to him. [Per Chadwick LJ at [59]; emphasis added.]

In ***WWF World Wide Fund for Nature v World Wrestling Federation Entertainment Inc.*** [2007] EWCA Civ 286, [2008] 1 WLR 445, [2007] Bus LR 1252, [2008] 1 WLR 445, a dispute had arisen between the parties concerning the initials 'WWF' which were used by the Wrestling Federation but had long been associated with the Fund for Nature. The parties had entered into an agreement to compromise their litigation and regulate the future use of these initials which restricted the use that could be made of the initials by the Wrestling Federation. However, the Fund for Nature later alleged various breaches of this agreement and, although it had been refused an account of profits in earlier proceedings, the High Court had later concluded that in appropriate circumstances a claimant might be entitled to damages on the ***Wrotham Park*** basis (accepted to be compensatory) on the basis of the price to release the negative stipulation. The Wrestling Federation had appealed claiming that the ***Wrotham Park*** remedy was a juridically similar remedy to the account of profits which had been refused earlier in the proceedings. If this was the case it followed that the matter of the remedy had already been decided and was *res judicata*. The argument was that both were 'gains-based awards'.

The Court of Appeal held that since the account of profits had been refused it would be an abuse of process to give permission to seek damages on the ***Wrotham Park*** basis because these claims were juridically 'highly similar', although this was because they were both compensatory in nature (albeit compensation where there was no identifiable financial loss) and not because they were both restitutionary (or gains-based) remedies.

421

Thus, although the **Wrotham Park** award was unavailable in this case, the Court of Appeal made it clear that in a claim relating to a breach of restrictive covenant for an injunction and damages for past breaches, the court might award damages of the price for the release of the negative covenant (as the sum which the court considered would be reasonable for the covenantor to pay and the covenantee to accept for the hypothetical release of the covenant), in addition to an injunction, or **Wrotham Park** damages alone, despite the fact that the claimant (covenantee) was unable to establish any identifiable financial loss. This sum was to be assessed as at the date immediately before the breaches occurred and would cover the period until the injunction (covering future breaches) began to operate. The Court of Appeal was clear that this remedy was separate to the remedy of the injunction, and not dependent on it in any way. In other words, the decision in *Experience Hendrix* has been confirmed as providing the most appropriate remedy in these circumstances.

In **Devenish Nutrition Ltd v Sanofi-Aventis SA** [2007] EWHC 2394 (Ch), [2008] 2 WLR 637, [2008] Bus LR 600 (in the context of a rejected claim for an account of profits where there had been a breach of Art. 81 of the EC Treaty (unlawful cartels)), Lewison J considered it to be established that **Blake** was a case based on compensation rather than restitution and that Lord Nicholls had treated it as such, referring to the fact that 'the injured party's rights were invaded' and although he had suffered no loss, 'the common law has found a means to award him a sensibly calculated amount of money' as an exception to the usual basis for compensatory recovery. Thus the emphasis is on the claimant's position rather than the defendant's gain. Lewison J concluded: 'It is precisely because he [the claimant] has suffered no loss that the law's response is to seek a different way to compensate him for the invasion of his rights.' The judge therefore noted that '[i]f, on the other hand, the claimant can demonstrate identifiable financial loss then principle would suggest that the compensation he receives should be commensurate with the loss he demonstrates', whereas this cannot be the case in these situations of no identifiable loss which called for an original response from the courts. (The decision on the non-applicability of *Blake* in this context was endorsed by the Court of Appeal [2008] EWCA Civ 1086, [2009] 3 WLR 198, [2009] Bus LR 858. Interestingly, Arden LJ refers to *Blake* as a 'restitutionary award' (at [111]), despite *WWF* confirmation that it is compensatory, possibly because in *Devenish* ordinary compensatory damages were available and a preferable remedy.)

Thus, the common factor is the inability to identify a measurable financial loss caused by the breach. The law provides two solutions to address this which both aim to compensate the claimant for the loss of the contractual undertaking (i.e. the fact of breach). They differ in degree and availability. *Wrotham Park* damages are more generally available and can be applied to any breach which involves breaching a promise not to do something (negative stipulation). The *Blake* account of profits is an exceptional remedy. However, since the determination of the *Wrotham Park* measure seems to begin from a position of identifying profits saved, the two are clearly linked in heir focus and it is a matter of degree, i.e. in a *Blake* award the claimant should be able to recover all profits which it can be demonstrated resulted from the breach, in a *Wrotham Park* award the profits resulting from the breach are merely the starting point for a determination of the appropriate measure of recovery.

10.6.4.4 Measure

That both the account of profits and *Wrotham Park* damages are compensatory and therefore based on similar principles resolves a potential difficulty since the starting point for an assessment of the price to secure the release of a negative stipulation will tend to be the profit made or anticipated. This approach to the setting of the measure under *Wrotham Park* is well illustrated by the decision in *Lane v O'Brien Homes Ltd* [2004] EWHC 303 (QB), unreported, 5 February 2004 and it provides a useful indicator of how far the courts have come since *Surrey v Bredero*.

> *Lane v O'Brien Homes Ltd* involved a sale of land for residential development purposes. However, the sale was subject to an oral collateral contract setting a limit of three houses to be built. The defendant built four houses in breach of this collateral contract, and at first instance damages of £150,000 had been awarded on the basis of loss of the chance to negotiate a release from the restrictive term in the collateral contract. However, on appeal, Clarke J considered that the preferable basis for the award was the *Wrotham Park* principle, although this seems to amount to the same thing since there was no actual release and it was accepted that hypotheticals had to be employed to determine the likely price of the release.

The judge also made some interesting observations on the difficult question of measuring this price of the release allowing the extra house to be built. The starting point is to consider the potential profit to be made (in this case on the fourth house) and it was not the case that damages had to be limited to a small percentage of this profit, although this was the case in *Wrotham Park* itself. The profit on the actual sale of the fourth house was £280,000 so that damages of £150,000 can hardly be described as a small percentage of this figure.

It therefore appeared that *Wrotham Park* damages achieved much the same end as the *Blake* account of profits. Whereas that is controversial if the remedies are essentially very different, i.e. one compensatory and the other gain-based, it is surely to be expected that they will be similar if based on the same underlying premise of compensation in situations where there is 'no identifiable financial loss'.

Further reading

General

Burrows, *Remedies for Torts and Breach of Contract*, 3rd edn (Oxford University Press, 2004).

Law Commission Consultation Paper, LCCP No. 167, *Compound Interest* (2002).

Law Commission Report No. 287, *Pre-Judgment Interest on Debts and Damages* (2004).

Specific performance

Burrows, 'Specific performance at the crossroads' (1984) 4 LS 102.

Jones, 'Specific performance: A lessee's covenant to keep open a retail store' [1997] CLJ 488.

Kronman, 'Specific performance' (1978) 45 Uni of Chicago L Rev 351.

Phang, 'Specific performance: Exploring the roots of "settled practice"' (1998) 61 MLR 421.

Schwartz, 'The case for specific performance' (1979) 89 Yale LJ 271.

Enrichment by subtraction: Total failure of consideration and *quantum meruit*

Carter and Tolhurst, 'Restitution for failure of consideration' (1997) 11 JCL 162.

Law Commission Working Paper No. 65, *Pecuniary Restitution on Breach of Contract* (1975).

Law Commission Report No. 121, *Pecuniary Restitution on Breach of Contract* (1983).

Virgo, 'Recent developments in restitution of mistaken payments' [1999] CLJ 479.

Virgo, *The Principles of the Law of Restitution*, 2nd edn (Oxford University Press, 2006).

Blake and *Wrotham Park*

Beatson, 'Courts, arbitrators and restitutionary liability for breach of contract' (2002) 118 LQR 377.

Birks, 'Profits of breach of contract' (1993) 109 LQR 518.

Burrows, 'No restitutionary damages for breach of contract' [1993] LMCLQ 453.

Campbell, 'The treatment of *Teacher v Calder* in *A-G v Blake*' (2002) 65 MLR 256.

Campbell, 'The extinguishing of contract' (2004) 67 MLR 817.

Cunnington, 'Changing conceptions of compensation' (2007) 66 CLJ 507.

Cunnington, 'The assessment of gain-based damages for breach of contract' (2008) 71 MLR 559.

Edelman, *Gain-Based Damages: Contract, tort, equity and intellectual property* (Hart Publishing, 2002).

Goodhart, 'Restitutionary damages for breach of contract' [1995] RLR 3.

Hedley, 'Very much the wrong people: The House of Lords and publication of spy memoirs' (2000) 4 Web JCLI.

Law Commission Report No. 247, *Aggravated, Exemplary and Restitutionary Damages* (1997).

McKendrick, 'Breach of contract, restitution for wrongs and punishment' in Burrows and Peel (eds), *Commercial Remedies* (Oxford University Press, 2003).

11 Privity of contract and third party rights

Summary of the issues

• **The doctrine of privity of contract provides that a person who is not a party to a contract cannot acquire any rights under that contract or be subject to any of its burdens.** This doctrine remains the general rule in English law.

• The fact that a third-party beneficiary of a contract could not enforce the contractual benefits in its favour was generally regarded as unsatisfactory and a number of devices were developed in order to circumvent this aspect of the privity doctrine. In addition, a number of exceptions were developed where third-party rights were recognized. These devices and exceptions can be artificial and complex so that there were calls for reform of the third party beneficiary rule. However, these devices and exceptions remain, despite legislative reform.

• **The Contracts (Rights of Third Parties) Act 1999 allows the parties to a contract to grant enforceable rights (such as the ability to rely on an exemption or limitation) to third parties. It is not every third party who will be able to enforce a contractual provision in its favour, only those third parties who satisfy the test of enforceability in s. 1 of the Act.** Part of this test requires that the third party be expressly identified in the contract by name, description or as falling within a particular class, e.g. independent contractors.

• **Where the s. 1 test is satisfied, it will not matter that the third party may not have provided consideration for the promise it is seeking to enforce, as long as the promise is not gratuitous (i.e., as long as it is supported by consideration supplied by another).**

• The Act includes provisions dealing with the effect on third parties of variations and cancellations of the original contract terms and the question of enforcement by both the promisee and third party.

• **If the third party has not been given an enforceable right under the 1999 Act, it is still possible for the promisee to enforce the promise and seek to obtain a remedy on behalf of the third-party beneficiary, e.g. specific performance requiring that the promisor perform the promise for the benefit of the third party.** The difficulty in a promisee seeking to recover damages on behalf of a third party is that a party is generally restricted to recovering damages for his own loss. In some circumstances it seems that it is possible for a promisee to recover substantial damages to compensate for a loss suffered by a third party but these circumstances still appear to be evolving. One argument, giving a broad interpretation to the scope of the promisee's performance interest, has recently been the subject of much academic debate, and has wider potential implications for damages for breach of contract. However, the judges currently seem divided as to its merits.

- The 1999 Act does not affect the rule that a contract cannot impose an obligation (or burden) on a person who is not a party to the contract. Nevertheless, some specific exceptions exist at common law concerning restrictions on the use of property and burdens imposed on bailors by the terms of sub-bailments.

11.1 Background: Who can enforce the contract?

The examination of the law of contract in the preceding chapters of this book almost always assumed that the type of contract under consideration involved two parties who were each to perform a stipulated obligation towards the other. From that assumption it followed that the enforcement of the obligations promised in the contract was a principal concern of the contracting parties themselves, and the question whether any other person might be entitled to enforce performance of the contract did not occur. This concentration on the effect of bilateral contracts between the contracting parties is inevitable, since that is the area in which most contractual disputes occur. Nevertheless, it is easy to imagine situations in which one party has stipulated in the contract that performance be made towards some other person, and examples of this type of contract have been noted in passing (e.g. 4.4.2 and 10.2.1).

This chapter considers the rules of the law of contract, and related rules, applicable to contracts which stipulate a benefit for a third party. This type of contract may most easily be described in terms of a triangular relationship. (See Figure 11.1.)

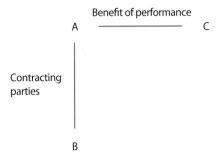

Figure 11.1

The contract is negotiated and made between A and B, but B stipulates that A's performance should be made to C (the third party). The questions which arise are:

- whether C may enforce A's promise to perform for C's benefit
- whether B may enforce A's promise for the benefit of C.

Related problems arise when B purports to stipulate not for a benefit to accrue to C from A's performance, but for C to perform B's obligations under the contract (so-called 'burdens' under the contract).

The general principle is that only the parties to the contract are bound by, or are entitled to a remedy for enforcement of the obligations under, the contract. This rule is known as the

doctrine of privity of contract. The effect of the doctrine may be demonstrated by reference to a classic case from the law of torts.

> In *Donoghue v Stevenson* [1932] AC 562, the appellant and a friend went into a café, where the friend ordered a bottle of ginger beer for the appellant. The drink came in an opaque bottle. Part of the contents was poured out and the appellant consumed it. When the rest was poured out, a partly decomposed snail was found. The appellant suffered nervous shock and illness, and wished to recover compensation. She was unable to proceed against the café owner in contract because the contract to purchase the ginger beer was made with her friend and the appellant was not a party to it. Accordingly, she chose to proceed against the manufacturer of the ginger beer and established a breach of a duty of care in tort.

The unavailability of an action in contract against either manufacturer or retailer led to the development, in *Donoghue v Stevenson*, of the modern tort of negligence, under which the claimant may recover compensation for loss suffered as a result of the defendant's breach of a duty of care.

11.2 The doctrine of privity of contract

The doctrine of privity of contract states that a person may not enforce a contractual promise and obtain remedies for its breach, even when the promise was expressly made for that person's benefit, if he is not a party to the contract. The corollary of this is that persons who are not a party to a contract may not have their rights diminished by that contract.

Both aspects of the doctrine have been subject to certain exceptions, although the exceptions to the latter rule (the 'burden' rule) are limited. Indeed, the rationale of the burden rule is easy to understand, since any other rule would be an infringement of individual liberty. However, the benefit rule is less readily explained (although see **11.3**). It was confirmed in English law in the early nineteenth century (*Price v Easton* (1833) 4 B & Ad 433). More modern authority for the rule is found in the decision of the House of Lords in ***Dunlop Pneumatic Tyre Co. Ltd v Selfridge & Co. Ltd*** [1915] AC 847.

> In ***Dunlop Pneumatic Tyre Co. Ltd v Selfridge & Co. Ltd***, the appellants had sold tyres to a distributor on terms that the distributor would not resell them at a price lower than the appellants' list price, and on terms that if sold to a trade buyer the distributor would obtain a similar undertaking from that buyer. The distributor resold some tyres to the respondents who gave the required undertaking, agreeing to pay £5 liquidated damages to the appellants for each tyre sold in breach of that undertaking. The respondents sold tyres below the list price, and the appellants sued to recover the agreed damages.

In a much-quoted passage, Viscount Haldane LC said (at p. 853):

> My Lords, in the Law of England certain principles are fundamental. One is that only a person who is a party to a contract can sue on it. Our law knows nothing of a *jus quaesitum tertio* arising by way of contract. Such a right may be conferred by way of property, as, for example, under a trust, but it cannot be conferred on a stranger to a contract as a right to enforce the contract *in personam*. A second principle is that if a person with whom a contract not under seal has been made is to be able to enforce it consideration must have been given by him to the promisor or to some other person at the promisor's request.

Viscount Haldane's statement of the privity doctrine has been taken as comprising two elements:

- one relating to the agreement component of a contract
- the other relating to the consideration component.

11.2.1 **The agreement component**

It will not normally be difficult to establish whether a person was a party to the agreement in question. It is a simple question of fact whether the person took part as a principal in the negotiations which resulted in agreement. Occasional difficulty may arise when a beneficiary under the contract has signed the contractual document, and it is disputed whether the beneficiary signed as a party to the agreement or merely as someone interested under the agreement (e.g., **Coulls v Bagot's Executor & Trustee Co. Ltd** (1967) 119 CLR 460: agreement containing a promise to pay a weekly royalty to Coulls and his wife had been signed by both but the majority of the High Court of Australia held that the wife was not a party to the contract).

11.2.2 **The consideration component**

The rule that consideration must move from the promisee appears to originate in the early privity case of *Tweddle v Atkinson* (1861) 1 B & S 393.

> After a marriage the partners' respective fathers entered into an agreement whereby each would pay a sum of money to the husband, and by that agreement the husband was to have the power to sue for the sums of money promised. After the death of his wife's father, the husband sued his father-in-law's estate to recover the sum promised. However, the action failed because the husband had given no consideration for the promise (although he was also not a party to the contract).

The rule that consideration must move from the promisee also appears to have been the *ratio* of the decision of the House of Lords in **Dunlop Pneumatic Tyre Co. Ltd v Selfridge & Co. Ltd** [1915] AC 847 (above). The need to establish consideration has resulted in all kinds of complexities in devices designed to avoid the application of the privity doctrine (e.g., agency; see, e.g., **11.5.2.2**).

11.2.2.1 Traditional explanation for this principle and the Law Commission's interpretation

The rule that consideration must move from the promisee was traditionally explained on the basis that a party not providing consideration is not part of the axis of inducement or mutual exchange, which is central to the enforceability of agreements. Nevertheless, it is not easy to discern any policy interest making such a rule necessary. As long as the promise in question is not gratuitous (i.e., the promisee has provided consideration for it), there is arguably no reason why the third party should have to provide consideration and this is the reasoning which appears to have been accepted by the Law Commission in its report, *Privity of Contracts: Contracts for the benefit of third parties,* Law Com. No. 242, Cm. 3329 (1996) (see Part VI, pp. 68–73), when concluding that the third-party beneficiary of a promise need not provide consideration.

In its consultation paper (LCCP No. 121, 1993), the Law Commission had considered that the consideration requirement did not pose a problem to its suggested reform of the third-party beneficiary rule because the rule only required that 'consideration must move from the *promisee*'.

However, the Law Commission later accepted that this had been interpreted as 'consideration must move from the *plaintiff* [*claimant*]' or person seeking to enforce the contract. Clearly the entire reform would be ineffectual if the third party could be prevented from enforcing the contract on the basis that it had not provided consideration. The Law Commission was satisfied that this problem was met by the central provision of the legislation giving a third party the right to enforce the contract and concluded that the clause 'can only be interpreted as also reforming the rule that consideration must move from the promisee'. There is no provision in the applicable legislation, the Contracts (Rights of Third Parties) Act 1999, spelling out the position on consideration but the case law indicates that the fact that consideration does not move from the third-party claimant will not defeat the legislative purpose.

11.2.2.2 Summary

Since the introduction of this legislation a third party seeking to enforce a contractual provision using the 1999 Act, cannot be defeated by a claim that the third party has not provided consideration to support the promise, as long as the promise is not gratuitous (i.e., as long as the promisee has supplied consideration).

It is unclear whether there has been any alteration in the need to provide consideration in situations falling outside the Act, e.g. joint promisees. In ***Coulls v Bagot's Executor and Trustee Co. Ltd*** (1967) 119 CLR 460 (see **11.2.1**), although the majority of the High Court of Australia considered that the widow was not a party to the contract, the minority (Barwick CJ and Windeyer J) considered that the fact that the widow had provided no consideration for the promise was not fatal to her ability to enforce the promise given that the husband had provided consideration to support it.

11.3 Criticisms and calls for reform

The reasons for the privity doctrine are unclear. In ***Trident General Insurance Co. Ltd v McNiece Brothers Proprietary Ltd*** (1988) 165 CLR 107, Toohey J (in the High Court of Australia) considered that the privity doctrine 'lacks a sound foundation in jurisprudence and logic'.

11.3.1 Justifications of the privity doctrine

1. It has sometimes been suggested that the doctrine rests on a principle of mutuality, to the effect that it would be unfair to allow a person to sue on a contract where that person cannot be sued by the other party (***Tweddle v Atkinson*** (1861) 1 B & S 393).

2. It has also sometimes been suggested that it would be undesirable to allow third-party rights to be created by contract, since that would restrict the freedom of the parties subsequently to amend or rescind their agreement (***Re Schebsman*** [1944] Ch 83).

3. Alternatively, it was suggested that third-party beneficiaries were frequently gratuitous recipients of the benefit in their favour, and so the rule was closely related to the doctrine of consideration.

Each of these explanations is open to objection, either on the ground that provided the contract is freely negotiated there is no particular reason why contracting parties should not undertake obligations which lack mutuality or which restrict their future freedom to act, or on the ground that the explanation does not account for the full extent of the rule.

11.3.2 **Criticism in the context of the intended third party beneficiary**

Whatever the explanation of the rule may be, it has been strongly and consistently criticized, at least in the context of contractual provisions in favour of third parties (e.g., Flannigan, 'Privity: The end of an era (error)' (1987) 103 LQR 564). Thus, whereas it has generally been accepted that there must be a privity doctrine to prevent total strangers from seeking to enforce a contract, it is more difficult to justify why, in situations where a contract is expressly made for the benefit of a third party (such as the husband in *Tweddle v Atkinson*), that third party should not be able to enforce that benefit. It is essentially in the context of enforcement by these third party intended beneficiaries that exceptions to privity have been recognized and various devices have been invented to avoid the operation of the doctrine.

In *Dunlop Pneumatic Tyre Co. Ltd v Selfridge & Co. Ltd* [1915] AC 847, Lord Dunedin, who felt compelled to agree with Viscount Haldane in finding against the appellants, said (at p. 855):

> I confess that this case is to my mind apt to nip any budding affection which one might have had for the doctrine of consideration. For the effect of that doctrine in the present case is to make it possible for a person to snap his fingers at a bargain deliberately made, a bargain not in itself unfair, and which the person seeking to enforce it has a legitimate interest to enforce.

As long ago as 1937 the Law Revision Committee (Sixth Interim Report, Cmnd 5449, p. 31), proposed that a third party should be able to enforce a contract where the contract expressly conferred a benefit on that third party. In *Beswick v Beswick* [1968] AC 58, Lord Reid referred to this proposal and said that that 'if one had to contemplate a further long period of Parliamentary procrastination, this House might find it necessary to deal with this matter'. In *Woodar Investment Development Ltd v Wimpey Construction (UK) Ltd* [1980] 1 WLR 277, Lord Scarman regretted that nothing had been done about this 'unjust rule', and he was not alone in his criticism. Lord Goff in *White v Jones* [1995] 2 AC 207 commented that 'our law of contract is widely seen as deficient in the sense that it is perceived to be hampered by the presence of an unnecessary doctrine of consideration and (through a strict doctrine of privity of contract) stunted through a failure to recognise a jus quaesitum tertio'.

The justifications for reform of the third-party beneficiary rule are well rehearsed and were set out and explained by the Law Commission in its report (pp. 39–50). The fundamental justifications for reform were also set out by Steyn LJ in *Darlington Borough Council v Wiltshier Northern Ltd* [1995] 1 WLR 68 at p. 76:

> The case for recognising a contract for the benefit of a third party is simple and straightforward. The autonomy of the will of the parties should be respected. The law of contract should give effect to the reasonable expectations of contracting parties…there is no doctrinal, logical, or policy reason why the law should deny effectiveness to a contract for the benefit of a third party where that is the expressed intention of the parties. Moreover, often the parties, and particularly third parties, organise their affairs on the faith of the contract. They rely on the contract. It is therefore unjust to deny effectiveness to such a contract. I will not struggle with the point further since nobody seriously asserts the contrary.

- **Intention**

  Whereas the intentions of the parties are usually given prominence in English contract law (see classical contract law, at 1.4.2.2), in respect of the operation of the privity doctrine those expressed intentions were ignored.

- **Reliance by third-party beneficiary**

  Not unreasonably, a third-party intended beneficiary may have relied upon the promise.

- **Attempts to avoid privity: complex, artificial, and uncertain**

  It is also the case that the various attempts to avoid the operation of privity in this context (see 11.6) have resulted in legal principles which are 'complex, artificial and uncertain'.

- **European position**

  Perhaps most significant is the fact that many of the jurisdictions in the European single market provide for the enforceability of stipulations for the benefit of third parties and the English position would cause harmonization difficulties for the European Union (see, e.g. Art. 6:110, *Principles of European Contract Law* (PECL): third party's right to enforce may be expressly or impliedly agreed by the parties; the *Draft Common Frame of Reference* (DCFR) II-9:301: the parties to a contract may, by the contract, confer a right or other benefit on a third party).

- **Commonwealth position**

  Significantly, the doctrine has also either been rejected or abrogated in many Commonwealth and common law jurisdictions (a good example is the New Zealand Contracts (Privity) Act 1982), so that the English position appeared to be out of line.

- **Commercial difficulties**

  However, perhaps the greatest impetus for reform stemmed from the fact that the third party rule led to difficulties in commercial life. The Law Commission specifically cited and explained the problems in relation to construction contracts and insurance contracts. (Unfortunately it appears that the legislative reform, with its associated uncertainties, has had the opposite effect to that intended—see also 11.4.2—as parties to such agreements are contracting out of the application of the legislation designed to enable third-party beneficiaries to rely on contractual provisions in their favour.)

However, for another view, see Smith, 'Contracts for the benefit of third parties: In defence of the third party rule' (1997) 17 OJLS 643, especially pp. 658–63.

11.3.3 The debate concerning the format for reform

The debate in the early to mid-1990s focused on the format for reform (see Tettenborn [1996] JBL 602: 'The interesting question is, in short, not whether we ought to reform privity, but how') and, in particular, whether reform should be achieved judicially on a case-by-case basis, or by means of legislation.

The Supreme Court of Canada in ***London Drugs Ltd v Kuehne & Nagel International Ltd*** (1993) 97 DLR (4th) 261, when faced with a situation which did not fall within the technical requirements of an existing exception (***New Zealand Shipping Co. Ltd v A. M. Satterthwaite & Co. Ltd, The Eurymedon*** [1975] AC 154: see 11.6.4), created a new exception in order to give effect to the 'true intentions of the contracting parties and commercial reality'. Iacobucci J advocated this 'incremental approach' to change in appropriate circumstances. (A further example of this approach can be seen in **Fraser River Pile & Dredge Ltd v Can-Dive Services Ltd** [2000] 1 Lloyd's Rep 199. The Supreme Court of Canada continued its 'incremental changes' and held that a third party who fell within the class of 'charterers' could rely on a 'waiver of subrogation clause' in an insurance policy notwithstanding the doctrine of privity of contract.)

However, as Iacobucci J made clear in his judgment in **London Drugs**, 'major reforms…must come from the legislature'; and in **Fraser River** he again stated (at p. 208, para. 43):

> Wholesale abolition of the doctrine would result in complex repercussions that exceed the ability of the Courts to anticipate and address. It is now a well-established principle that the Courts will not undertake judicial reform of this magnitude, recognizing instead that the legislature is better placed to appreciate and accommodate the economic and policy issues involved in introducing sweeping legal reforms.

There are distinct problems posed by judicial reform of the privity rule, as is evident from an examination of the decision of the High Court of Australia in **Trident General Insurance Co. Ltd v McNiece Brothers Proprietary Ltd** (1988) 165 CLR 107; judges may differ in their justifications for allowing third-party enforcement on the facts of the case. In **The Mahkutai** [1996] 3 All ER 502, Lord Goff identified some of the problems of judicial reform, namely, having to wait for an 'appropriate' case to arise and for the question of reform to be fully argued. However, the greatest danger of judicial reform is the uncertainty that it would generate (a particular problem in the commercial context), and the Law Commission cited this uncertainty as a reason in favour of its proposed legislative reform on the question of enforcement by third-party beneficiaries.

11.3.4 The scope of the legislative reform

 Key point

The Law Commission's proposed legislative reform was broadly adopted as the Contracts (Rights of Third Parties) Act 1999. However, it is important to appreciate that it does not abolish privity.

There are a number of reasons why its scope is limited:

1. Burdens were excluded from the scope of the Law Commission's reform and the Act does not therefore allow enforcement of burdens imposed on third parties. The exceptional situations when a 'burden' may be imposed on a third party are discussed at 11.8.

2. The 1999 Act deals only with enforcement of benefits by third parties and, although it came into force on 11 November 1999, it applies only to contracts entered into after 11 May 2000, unless the contract was made between 11 November 1999 and 10 May 2000 and expressly stated that the 1999 Act was applicable. Therefore the common law may remain applicable to some existing contracts.

3. Even where the Act does apply to the contract, it is not every third party who can enforce a contractual provision. The test of enforceability in s. 1 of the Act must be satisfied before a third party will have rights of enforcement. This test of enforceability is vital to the scope of the legislation and, as we will see, many of the existing decisions would be unaffected if the Act were to apply to the same set of facts. However, s. 7(1) of the Act makes it clear that existing exceptions to privity and devices to avoid privity will continue to operate in this situation.

It is therefore necessary to approach this topic by first examining the Act and its scope, and then examining what are now residual common law exceptions which may still be relevant in some situations falling outside the Act. It is to be hoped that the existence of the Act will not curtail judicial developments outside the scope of the Act, although it is extremely likely that the Act will have some effect on interpretation of common law devices falling outside its remit. It is also the case that the existing rights of promisees to secure remedies for the benefit of third parties are unaffected by the legislation. The Law Commission specifically left this question for judicial reform. The scope for the promisee to recover on behalf of the third party, and the limitations on this, are discussed at **11.7**.

11.4 The Contracts (Rights of Third Parties) Act 1999

11.4.1 Third party enforcement

In its report, the Law Commission had recommended that the privity doctrine be reformed by legislation in order to 'enable contracting parties to confer a right to enforce the contract on a third party', i.e. the right to enforce remedies for breach of contract that would have been available had the third party been a contracting party, and the right to enforce an exemption clause as if the third party was a party to the contract.

- This basic right is contained in s. 1(1) of the 1999 Act, which states that a person who is not a party to the contract may enforce a term of the contract in their own right if the test of enforceability in s. 1(1)–(3) is satisfied.

- Section 1(5) provides that for this purpose the third party will have 'any remedy that would have been available to him in an action for breach of contract if he had been a party to the contract (and the rules relating to damages, injunctions, specific performance and other relief shall apply accordingly)'.

- For the avoidance of doubt, s. 1(6) provides for a third party to be able to enforce an exemption or limitation clause in a contract (where the test of enforceability is satisfied). This is important to the reform as many of the difficult cases have concerned enforcement of these clauses by third parties and one of much criticized technical common law exceptions to privity was developed to deal with this situation (see **11.6.4**).

The fact that the third party has not provided consideration to support the promise will not prevent that third party enforcing the term (assuming that the promise is not gratuitous). This is not contained in the Act, but the entire reform would fail if the position was otherwise and the Law Commission made this clear in its report.

Interestingly, if a person is a party to the contract because they are a joint promisee but they have not provided consideration for the promise, the Act cannot apply because such a person is not a third party. Such a joint promisee might therefore be unable to enforce the contractual term in their favour on the basis that they have not provided consideration. It would be anomalous for a joint promisee to be in a worse position than a third party, and the Law Commission clearly envisaged that the courts would resolve this difficulty, presumably on the basis that the particular joint promisee does not need to provide consideration for the promise as long as it is supported by consideration provided by another joint promisee.

- By s. 3, the promisor will have the same defences and rights of set-off in a claim for enforcement brought by the third party as in a claim brought by the promisee. This is subject to any express clause in the contract giving additional or reduced defences in an enforcement claim by a third party. Section 3(6) specifically states that a third party seeking to enforce an exemption clause will be subject to the same controls on enforcement as would exist in the case of enforcement by a contracting party.

11.4.2 The test for third party enforceability

As discussed earlier, it was never intended that complete strangers should be able to enforce contractual provisions, only third parties who were intended to benefit under the relevant term of the contract. Accordingly, the test of enforceability must achieve this objective. Formulating such a test has proved to be difficult and the proposed test contained in the report was altered from that which had originally been proposed in the consultation paper on the basis that the original test was too restrictive, since it required not only that there be an intention that the terms should confer a benefit on the third party, but also that there was an intention that it should create a legal obligation enforceable by that third party (the so-called 'dual intention test'). This dual intention test was rejected and replaced with the test now contained in s. 1(1)–(3) of the 1999 Act.

There are two ways in which a third party may satisfy the test of enforceability and be able to enforce contractual terms under the Act:

1. **The contract may expressly state that the third party is to have a right to enforce the provision (s. 1(1)(a)).**

Under s. 1(3), the third party 'must be expressly identified in the contract by name, as a member of a class or as answering a particular description', although the third party need not be in existence at the time the contract is made. On the basis of current drafting practice, it will be rare that the s. 1(1)(a) test of enforceability will be satisfied. It requires a particular form of drafting which, if used in the past, did not achieve its objective. Ironically, there was such a provision on the facts in *Tweddle v Atkinson* (1861) 1 B & S 847, so that if this set of case facts were to arise again, the husband ought to be able to enforce the promise in his favour. Section 1(1)(a) does, however, indicate the most straightforward method for conferring a right of enforcement on third parties, where this is desired, and ought therefore to affect **future** drafting practice. Nevertheless, the evidence to date is that, rather than contracting to fall within the Act, many commercial parties are contracting to avoid its operation because of the uncertainties over some of its other provisions. Contracting so that the Act will not operate can be achieved by stating that the third party will not receive an enforceable right.

2. **As an alternative to the s. 1(1)(a) test, third parties will also fall within the Act and be able to enforce contractual provisions in their own right where they are expressly identified in the contract and 'the term purports to confer a benefit' on that third party (s. 1(1)(b)).**

For s. 1(1)(b) to apply it is vital to establish that the clause or agreement in question was 'intended to confer a benefit' on a 'third' party. Christopher Clarke J made this clear in his application in ***Dolphin & Maritime & Aviation Services Ltd v Sveriges Angfartygs Assurans Forening, The Swedish Club*** [2009] EWHC 716 (Comm), [2009] 1 CLC 460, [2009] 2 Lloyd's Rep 123. Dolphin, the claimant, was a recovery agent acting on behalf of underwriters and the cargo owners in relation to a vessel entered with the Swedish club which had been involved in a collision. Acting on behalf of the underwriters, Dolphin had entered into an agreement with the club whereby sums recoverable from the vessel's owner were to be paid to Dolphin. The underwriters had then settled directly with the club and the underwriters refused to pay Dolphin's commission. Dolphin had therefore sought to enforce the terms of its agreement with the club. However, it was held that the agreement with the club related only to the means by which the club's obligation to the underwriters was to be discharged, i.e. the means by which payment was to be made to the underwriters. The intended beneficiaries were the underwriters on whose behalf the payment was to be received and not Dolphin, albeit that Dolphin's position would be improved if the club had paid Dolphin (since the commission could have been deducted from this sum). This was merely a 'provision for payment of a sum to an agent on his principal's behalf' (not covered by s. 1(1)(b)) as opposed to 'an agreement by A and B that A will pay C (C not being A's agent or trustee)' (falling within s. 1(1)(b)).

The proviso to s. 1(1)(b): s. 1(2)

However, by s. 1(2): 'Subsection (1)(b) does not apply if on a proper construction of the contract it appears that the parties did not intend the term to be enforceable by the third party'.

This would appear to be the case in most construction contracts, so that it will not enable a building owner (third party to the contract between main contractor and subcontractor) to sue a subcontractor directly since the intention is that the owner should sue the main contractor. Inevitably this intention proviso will cause problems of certainty for commercial parties since this is not a simple test (although it is similar to the sole test used in the New Zealand Contracts (Privity) Act 1982, s. 4). (For further discussion, see Roe, 'Contractual intention under section 1(1)(b) and 1(2) of the Contracts (Rights of Third Parties) Act 1999' (2000) 63 MLR 887.)

The literal interpretation of the s. 1(2) proviso to s. 1(1)(b) indicates that it will defeat the test of enforceability in s. 1(1)(b) only where there is something in the contract which indicates that the parties had no intention to confer an enforceable benefit on the third party on whom the contract terms purport to confer a benefit. It follows logically that the third party does not need to prove a negative. If the contract is silent on the matter the s. 1(1)(b) test of enforceability will be satisfied.

The operation of the test of enforceability was considered in ***Nisshin Shipping Co. Ltd v Cleaves & Co. Ltd*** [2003] EWHC 2602 (Comm), [2004] 1 Lloyd's Rep 38.

Cleaves (C) had negotiated a number of time charters on behalf of the owners (N). Each charter contract provided for the payment of commission to C and contained an arbitration clause. N claimed that C was not entitled to the commission because it was in repudiatory breach of the agency agreement. C purported to refer the commission issue to arbitration and claimed to have the standing to be able to enforce the commission clause as a result of the application of s. 1(1)(b) of the 1999 Act, although it was not a party to the charter contracts. (It was accepted that the clauses did not expressly provide that Cleaves could enforce the commission clause directly against Nisshin.)

Colman J held:

1. The clause purported to confer a benefit on Cleaves.

2. Section 1(2) did not require that for s. 1(1)(b) to apply it had to be shown that the parties positively intended that the benefit should be enforceable by the third party; rather, it stated that s. 1(1)(b)

could not apply if it appeared that the parties did **not** intend the third party to have a right of enforcement. Thus, since the contract was silent on the matter, there was nothing to indicate that the parties did not intend C to have the right of enforcement and the s. 1(1)(b) test of enforceability was satisfied.

This decision therefore confirms the literal interpretation of the s. 1(2) proviso and has subsequently been confirmed by the Court of Appeal in *Laemthong International Lines Co. Ltd v Artis, The Laemthong Glory (No. 2)* [2005] EWCA Civ 519, [2005] 1 Lloyd's Rep 632.

A problem arose concerning the delivery of goods at the end of a voyage charter since delivery was to be on presentation of the bills of lading but these documents had not reached the receivers of the cargo prior to the arrival of the ship at the port of destination. Where the bills of lading were unavailable, the goods could be delivered to the receivers if a letter of indemnity (LOI) was provided by the receivers. The parties to the LOI were the charterers and receivers so that it amounted to a contract between the charters and the receivers. The LOI contained a promise by the receivers to indemnify the charterers, its servants or agents in respect of any liability resulting from the delivery of the goods at the receivers' request without production of the bill of lading. On the arrest of the vessel and production of the original bills of lading by the Yemen Bank and its claim to the value of the goods discharged, the question arose of whether the shipowners were covered by this LOI (charterers and receivers) as they were not parties to it but had delivered the cargo to the receivers. The shipowners sought to rely on s.1 of the 1999 Act.

The Court of Appeal held that the shipowners were to be regarded as 'agents' of the charterers for the purpose of delivery of the goods to the receivers. The terms of the LOI amounted to a promise to confer a benefit on the shipowner, acting as 'agent' and the receivers had failed to discharge the burden imposed by s. 1(2) of proving that this LOI was not intended by the parties (receivers and charterers) to be enforceable by the shipowner. As a result, the indemnity promise in the LOI was enforceable.

Clarke LJ, delivering the judgment of the court, stated:

The whole purpose of the receivers' LOI was on the one hand to ensure that the receivers received the cargo from the ship without production of the original bills of lading and on the other hand to ensure that the owners were fully protected from the consequences of arrest or other action which might be taken by the holders of the original bills of lading.

In *Prudential Assurance Co. Ltd v Ayres* [2007] EWHC 775 (Ch), the tenant had assigned the lease and provided a guarantee to the landlord for payment of the rent in the event that that the new tenant (the assignee), a partnership, failed to pay. However, the landlord and the new tenant (the assignee partnership) had then entered into a separate deed agreeing that the liability under the lease should be limited to the assets of the assignee partnership and not its individual partners and that the same limitation should apply in relation to 'any previous tenant' on a guarantee When the partnership became insolvent the landlord sought the unpaid rent from the original tenant in accordance with the guarantee. The original tenant sought to rely on the deed to which it was not a party. Lindsay J held that the tenant could enforce the deed through the application of s. 1(1)(b) of the 1999 Act. He considered that the tenant fell within the expression 'any previous tenant' used in that deed and that the deed purported to confer a benefit on that tenant. The judge noted that: 'There is within s. 1(1)(b) no requirement that the benefit on the third party shall be the predominant purpose or intent behind the term or that it denies the applicability of section 1(1)(b) if a benefit is conferred on someone other than the third party.' In addition, there was nothing to indicate that the tenant was not intended to be able to enforce this protection directly although he pointed out that: 'It would have been easy enough (but somewhat destructive of the overall purpose of [the deed]) so to provide had that been intended but nothing to that effect appears.' It followed that once the assets of the insolvent assignee partnership had been exhausted, nothing further could be recovered from the original tenant.

Although this decision was overturned by the Court of Appeal ([2008] EWCA Civ 52, [2008] 1 All ER 1266, this was on the construction of the deed, which it was held did not purport to convey any benefit on the original tenants in relation to the guarantee relationship between the landlord and the original tenant. Instead it purported to limit the rights of recovery of the landlord and the original tenant against the individual partners. Accordingly no application of the 1999 Act arose. Nevertheless, it is clear that the first instance comments of Lindsay J concerning the construction of s.1(1)(b) of the Act remain valid and were cited by Christopher Clarke J in the subsequent decision of *Dolphin & Maritime & Aviation Services Ltd v Sveriges Angfartygs Assurans Forening, The Swedish Club* [2009] EWHC 716 (Comm), [2009] 1 CLC 460, [2009] 2 Lloyd's Rep 123 (discussed above).

Section 1(3)

In a practical sense, this s. 1(1)(b) test will also be limiting because of the s. 1(3) requirement that applies to both limbs of s. 1(1) and requires that the third party be '*expressly* identified in the contract by name, as a member of a class or as answering a particular description' (emphasis added), although the third party need not be in existence at the time the contract is made. An analysis of existing case law will illustrate the limitations this imposes and the fact that it restricts the operation of the Act (see, e.g. **11.6.4.4**). This limitation operated to significant commercial effect in *Avraamides v Colwill* [2006] EWCA Civ 1533, [2007] BLR 76.

> A had employed C to refurbish A's bathroom. C's performance was defective and C was therefore liable to A. However, C then sold his business to B on terms whereby B assumed C's liabilities 'to pay in the normal course of time any liabilities properly incurred by C as at 31 March 2003'. Did this mean that A had the ability to enforce this agreement (between B and C) against B as a third-party beneficiary?
>
> The Court of Appeal held that since A as third party was not **expressly** identified in the contract B/C by name, it could not be said that the intention and effect of the agreement was that persons with rights against C could enforce those rights directly against B. In any event, as the judge recognized (at [20]), there was also a potential problem with the s. 1(2) proviso since the contract may well have been construed to mean that it was not the intention that any such 'liabilities' were to have direct rights of enforcement in relation to them.

This is a major limitation on the ability of the Act to give third parties enforceable rights. To enable A to recover the agreement would have needed to involve agreement to pay the current creditors of the company since A would then have fallen within that description (subject again to there being nothing in s. 1(2) to deny the intention to allow enforcement by those creditors).

In *Laemthong International Lines Co. Ltd v Artis, The Laemthong Glory (No. 2)* [2005] EWCA Civ 519, [2005] 1 Lloyd's Rep 632 (facts above), it was argued that the LOI did not expressly identify the owners by name but the Court of Appeal held that they must fall within the expression 'agents' of the charterer in the light of the rest of the wording of the LOI and the fact that they were instructed to deliver the cargo on behalf of the charterers.

The s. 1(3) requirement is therefore likely to lead to further argument and is the pivotal provision in relation to the scope of the legislation.

11.4.3 **Variation or cancellation**

One of the most controversial and difficult issues to be resolved when formulating such a legislative reform is the crucial question of whether the original parties should be able to vary or cancel the third party's benefit under the contract. This is a particular problem where the third party has relied on the rights in the contract.

- Section 2(1) provides that the contracting parties cannot vary or cancel the third party's rights without that third party's consent where the third party had communicated their assent to the term to the promisor (s. 2(2) explains this assent and ousts the postal rule in the case of assent by post), or the third party had relied on the term and the promisor knew this (or ought reasonably to have foreseen this).

It appears that any reliance will suffice for this purpose; this is extremely generous to the third party.

Thus, this section appears to offer generous and effective protection for third parties in this situation, or at least it would offer protection but for s. 2(3).

- Section 2(3) expressly allows contracting parties to opt out of this provision by stipulating for a different crystallization test (other than assent or reliance), or by reserving the right to vary or cancel the third party's right irrespective of reliance or acceptance by the third party.

- In accordance with the report recommendations, there is also a specific judicial discretion to vary or cancel irrespective of reliance or acceptance by the third party in certain circumstances (s. 2(4)–(7) of the Act).

These provisions shift control, and hence the balance, back in favour of the contracting parties.

11.4.4 **Overlapping claims**

Another potential difficulty posed by third-party reform concerns the question of overlap with remedies of the promisee against the promisor. **In other words, should the promisee lose the right of enforcement where the third party has such a right?** This would require an extremely complex piece of drafting and arguably would be undesirable and impossible to achieve. **On the other hand, if both retain a right of action, who would have priority?**

The Law Commission recommended that the promisor's duty to perform should be owed to both promisee and the third party, so that (unless otherwise agreed between the parties) the promisee should retain the right to enforce a contract even if it was also enforceable by the third party. Since each has a separate right of action, there should be no priority rule (although the appropriate course would be to join the third party if the promisee sues). In addition, although it did not require legislation to say so, if the promisor fulfilled its duty to the third party, the promisor was, to that extent, to be discharged from its duty to the promisee.

The legislation is minimalist and to the point:

- Section 4 preserves the promisee's right to enforce the promise.
- Section 5 expressly seeks to avoid double liability by explaining that where the promisee has recovered substantial damages (or agreed sum) for the third party's loss, the third party will not be entitled to a duplicate damages sum because 'the court…shall reduce

any award to the third party to such extent as it thinks appropriate to take account of the sum recovered by the promisee'.

This situation appears to be of great concern to students, who point out that if the promisee does recover damages for the third party, there is no provision of the Act requiring the promisee to pass those damages to the third party. The absence of a provision is explicable because this is a question of remedies of the promisee and therefore outside the scope of the legislation. The question of liability to account to the third party should therefore be dealt with at common law (see the discussion at **11.7.4**).

11.4.5 The application of the Unfair Contract Terms Act (UCTA) 1977

The drafters of this legislation appear to have been concerned to avoid making it complex or providing provisions on matters which might become too prescriptive. However, they did include one particularly controversial provision:

> **?** **Question**
>
> **To what extent does UCTA 1977 protect a third party who acquires rights under this Act?**
>
> By s. 7(2) of the 1999 Act, s. 2(2) of UCTA 1977 shall not apply to the breach of a qualified contractual obligation where the person seeking to challenge the contractual provision is a third party relying on s. 1 of the 1999 Act. However, s. 2(1) of UCTA 1977 will apply (as an existing right or remedy), so that any contractual provisions excluding liability for death or personal injury will remain ineffective when utilized by a third party. This was stated in the debate in the House of Lords to be 'consistent with the underlying policy of the Bill which is to enable contracting parties to confer rights on third parties but to allow them to retain control over the nature and extent of those newly conferred rights' (Lord Irvine, 11 January 1999). However, it is questionable whether UCTA should be restricted in this way so as to exclude its protection in the context of third parties (see Lord Borrie in debate in the House of Lords, 11 January 1999), although it is clear that the Unfair Terms in Consumer Contracts Regulations 1999 cannot apply to a third-party claim because the regulations apply only to contracts between a seller or supplier and a consumer.
>
> It is also made clear by s. 7(4) that s. 1 of the 1999 Act will not allow a third party to be treated as a contracting party for the purposes of any other enactment. Specifically, s. 3 of UCTA 1977 applies '*as between contracting parties* where one of them deals as a consumer or on the other's written standard terms of business' (emphasis added). Thus, if an exclusion clause operated to exclude or limit a third-party right, it would not be subject to regulation under s. 3 of UCTA 1977. In this sense, the third party is not treated in the same way as the promisee and it will be easier for contracting parties to exclude third parties' rights. This appears to be in conflict with the apparent purpose of the 1999 Act.

11.4.6 Miscellaneous matters

Section 6 contains an extensive list of exceptions where this Act will not apply, e.g. contracts of employment, negotiable instruments (see **11.5.4**), contracts for the carriage of goods by sea (other than in relation to the benefit of exemption clauses) (see **11.6.3**), and the s. 33 contract (Companies Act 2006).

Finally, it is important to remember that the existing exceptions to privity are expressly preserved by s. 7(1) of the Act. Thus, although the Law Commission's report envisaged that the reform would avoid the 'complexities of the devices presently used to circumvent the privity doctrine', these complexities will remain, at least where the device has not been overtaken by the availability of a direct right of enforcement in the legislation. In **Nisshin Shipping Co. Ltd v Cleaves & Co. Ltd** [2003] EWHC 2602 (Comm), [2004] 1 Lloyd's Rep 38 (for facts see **11.4.2**), the terms of the charter contracts had created an express trust of the promise to pay commission to C and this was enforceable by the charterers as trustees. However, the existence of this trust did not mean that C was therefore denied its direct right of enforcement under s. 1(1)(b) of the 1999 Act.

It is important, therefore, to consider these common law exceptions and their potential usefulness in the light of the new legislation. Some of these 'exceptions' are merely means of circumventing the application of the privity doctrine using other legal concepts (see **11.5**). Others are true exceptions to privity which exist within the law of contract. These are considered below (see **11.6**).

11.5 Means of circumventing the privity doctrine

This section examines those mechanisms which exist as independent legal concepts and enable a benefit to be conferred on a third party who was not apparently a party to the making of the contract. Tort claims are clearly outside the law of contract. The other mechanisms are related to contract but represent independent concepts.

11.5.1 Claim in tort

The appellant in **Donoghue v Stevenson** [1932] AC 562 (discussed at **11.1**), was able to avoid the effect of the privity doctrine by framing her action in tort. This may be possible as a means of avoiding the privity doctrine but only where the loss in question is personal injury or physical damage. However, a third party may be permitted to enforce the terms of a contract by bringing an action in tort only where it can be shown that the promisor owed a duty of care to the third-party claimant, e.g. in **White v Jones** [1995] 2 AC 207: claim based on negligence brought by intended beneficiaries of a will where the solicitor preparing the will had been negligent. The majority of the House of Lords considered that this conclusion that a duty of care was owed was necessary to ensure that the beneficiaries were not deprived of a claim, albeit that this amounted to circumventing privity by giving the intended beneficiaries the benefit of a contract to which they were not parties. On the facts it was not possible for the estate to bring a claim.

However, it is by no means always possible to avoid the doctrine in this way because the promisor may not owe the necessary duty of care to the third party and, in any event, a claim in tort will not normally result in the award of compensation for expectation loss (see **6.1.2.2**). The facts in *White v Jones* were unusual because the measure of damages, where there has been negligence in preparing a will, is the value of the benefit not received (expectation loss). Normally the tort measure will ensure recovery is limited to reliance losses.

In addition, the practical viability of a tort claim as a means of avoiding the privity doctrine is dependent upon it being possible to recover for economic loss in tort, e.g. the diminished value

439

of the work done. However, the law has placed some constraints on the recognition of a duty of care in such cases. In ***Junior Books Ltd v Veitchi Co. Ltd*** [1983] 1 AC 520, English law appeared to accept the idea of permitting third-party recovery for economic losses in a negligence claim although this availability would appear to turn on the specific facts.

> JB had engaged a main contractor to build a factory. The laying of the floor was subcontracted out to V Ltd on the instructions of JB's architect. The floor was laid defectively, began to crack up and had to be replaced. JB sued V Ltd in negligence to recover the cost of the new floor. This was dependent on JB establishing that V Ltd owed a duty to JB to lay the floor with reasonable care and skill. The House of Lords accepted the existence of such a duty and although this amounted to circumventing the contractual duty owed to the main contractor, it has been justified subsequently as turning on the fact that V Ltd had indicated to JB, via its architects, that it could be relied upon to lay the floor with reasonable care and skill and this had been relied upon by JB in nominating V Ltd as the subcontractor.

This position can be compared with the position in *Simaan v Pilkington Glass Ltd (No. 2)* [1988] QB 758, where there was no such indication that the contractor could be relied upon to meet this standard of performance and no such duty of care was recognized.

   This interpretation of the principle in *Junior Books Ltd v Veitchi Co. Ltd* was also applied in ***Henderson v Merrett Syndicates Ltd*** [1995] 2 AC 145 where the House of Lords accepted that the existence of a contractual relationship did not prevent the recognition of a duty of care in tort based on the fact that there had been a clear indication by the managing agent to the Lloyd's 'Name' through the underwriting agent, that the 'Name' could safely rely on the managing agent to manage the affairs of the Lloyd's syndicate with care and skill.

11.5.2 Assignment and agency

Both assignment and agency make important contributions to the commercial world. Although not strictly exceptions to the privity doctrine, they are contrary to the spirit of that rule, and were developed to meet the practical needs of those in business, for whom the privity doctrine proved unduly restrictive.

11.5.2.1 Assignment (or transfer) of contractual rights

Assignment is a legal device which enables one party (the assignor) to transfer the benefit of a performance, which that party has contracted to receive, to another person in such a way that the assignee (to whom the benefit is transferred) may enforce performance. (See Figure 11.2.)

   B (the assignor) transfers the benefit of the performance owed by A to B (e.g., payment of a debt of £50) onto C (the assignee). C can enforce the performance (debt) against A (the debtor). In this

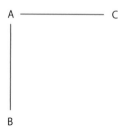

Figure 11.2

situation the original contract does not stipulate that the benefit of performance should go to a third party. Instead, after the contract A/B is made, B (the assignor/creditor) assigns the right to enforce the contract to C (as assignee). C then has a direct right of action against A (the debtor).

However, some rights cannot be assigned (e.g., if the contract which contains them is of personal nature or is a relationship of confidence) and some contracts contain prohibitions on assignment without consent. For example, in *Linden Gardens Trust Ltd v Lenesta Sludge Disposals Ltd* [1994] 1 AC 85 ('the St Martins Property' appeal) the ability to assign without consent was prohibited. See also *Barbados Trust Co. Ltd v Bank of Zambia* [2007] EWCA Civ 148, [2007] 1 Lloyd's Rep 495, [2007] 2 All ER (Comm) 445: assignment of debt needed prior written consent. However, a prohibition on assignment does not prevent a party declaring a trust over the benefit of the contract (i.e., the debt) (see 11.5.3). A trust is not akin to an equitable assignment since an assignment also requires an intention to transfer.

The drawback of assignment is that the assignee takes the benefit of performance 'subject to equities', i.e. the assignee cannot recover more from the debtor than the assignor might have recovered. Thus, defences available to the debtor against the assignor are equally valid against the assignee.

11.5.2.2 Agency

Agency is the legal device by which one person (the agent: A) may act on behalf of another (the principal: P) in the formation of a contract between that other and a third party. The agency doctrine in its standard form is not really an exception to the privity doctrine since there is no contractual relationship between the agent and the third party. Thus, the agent does not stipulate for a benefit to be conferred on the principal; rather, the principal is a party to the contract with the third party.

The agency argument was attempted—unsuccessfully—in *Dunlop Pneumatic Tyre Co. Ltd v Selfridge & Co. Ltd* [1915] AC 847 (for facts, see 11.2).

> The plaintiff, Dunlop, argued that Dew and Co had acted as their agents for the purposes of obtaining the undertaking from Selfridge that it would not sell tyres to trade buyers at less than the list price and it followed therefore that Dunlop could directly enforce this undertaking. However, Dunlop was unable to rely on the agency argument because it was unable to show that it had supplied any consideration to support such a promise.

Thus, in order to be able to enforce a third-party promise, the principal needs to show that it, rather than the agent, has supplied the consideration for that promise.

Nevertheless, agency has sometimes been used successfully as a means of avoiding the impact of the privity doctrine; see *The Eurymedon* device which was designed to enable a third party to rely on an exemption clause in a contract to which he was not a party (see 11.6.4) and where the necessary consideration for the promise was identified.

11.5.3 Trusts

The trust is a device developed by the Court of Chancery long before the Judicature Act 1875. It allows a party to pass property to a second party, while stipulating that the second party must hold the property for the benefit of a third. That stipulation is enforceable by the third party. In terms of the triangular relationship outlined in Figure 11.1, A (the trustee) receives property from B over which B has declared a trust in favour of C (the beneficiary or *cestui que trust*). C is then able to enforce the terms of the trust to prevent A dealing with the property other than in a manner which is to C's benefit. Although the relationship between the party declaring the trust (B) and the trustee (A) is not necessarily contractual, where it is, the device is inconsistent with the privity doctrine.

The Court of Chancery had developed the trust in response to issues of property and conscience arising out of such cases. Chancery took the view that a properly constituted trust had the effect of actually transferring and splitting the ownership of the property in question. The legal owner (i.e., under the common law rules) was the trustee; but the effect of the constitution of the trust was to make the third party the beneficial owner of the property. To allow the third party to enforce the trust was not, therefore, to allow the enforcement of a contractual right to acquire the property. The property belonged to the third party from the moment of constitution of the trust, and enforcement of the trust by the third party was necessary to prevent improper interference with that third party's right, which was similar in nature to a property right. In turn, the trustee could not as a matter of good conscience interfere with that right. The right of the beneficial owner could be lost only by virtue of the acquisition of the trust property by a bona fide purchaser for value who had no notice, actual or constructive, of the trust over the property (*Alcher v Rawlins* (1872) LR 7 Ch App 259).

In order for there to be a properly constituted trust, there must be property which is capable of being subjected to a trust. Property includes not only land and goods but also rights, such as a right under a contract, which are known as *choses in action*. There must be a declaration of, or disposition on, trust by a competent person which demonstrates a certain intention that a trust be created. There must also be certainty of property and of object, i.e. it must be possible to determine the property to which the trust attaches and the purposes for which the trust was created. Finally, the declaration or disposition must comply with any statutory requirements regarding evidence.

The most significant aspect of the trust as an exception to the privity doctrine arises where one party declares themselves to be a trustee on behalf of a third party of a right to performance owed to the third party by the other contracting party. That is, in terms of the triangular relationship outlined at Figure 11.1, where B declares **himself** *to* be trustee on behalf of C of the performance due to him under the contract from A. This situation is considered below (see **11.6.1**).

11.5.4 Negotiable instruments

The negotiable instrument is a device originally developed by the law merchant to overcome the privity doctrine and certain commercial disadvantages inherent in the device of assignment. Negotiable instruments are expressly excluded from the application of the 1999 Act by s. 6(1).

In the case of assignment (see 11.5.2.1), the assignee of a contractual right is at the very least inadequately protected unless notice of the assignment is given to the original debtor each time the right is assigned. Moreover, the assignee takes the right which has been assigned 'subject to equities', which means that any defences enjoyed by the original debtor against the assignor are equally valid against the assignee. Thus, an assigned right may not be worth its face value if the original debtor is entitled to a set-off against the assignor.

Example

Returning to the triangular relationship outlined in Figure 11.1, if B agrees to sell goods to A for £100, but the goods delivered are reduced in value to £80 by a breach of the quality term, the fact that B has assigned to C the right to recover payment from A will not entitle C to recover any more than the £80 which B could have recovered in his own right.

If, however, A's obligation to pay is recorded in a document ('instrument') which is recognized by the law as 'negotiable', B may transfer the right to recover the amount recorded in the instrument to C by simple delivery (i.e., by handing it over), or perhaps by indorsement and delivery (e.g., by signing it and then handing it over). There is no need to give notice of the transfer to the original debtor (A), and it may be transferred several times before the debt which it represents is collected from A. Moreover, the particular advantage of the negotiable instrument is that the transferee(s) do not take 'subject to equities', provided they receive the instrument for value and without notice of any defect in title which may have arisen before they became 'holder in due course' of the instrument.

Common forms of negotiable instrument are bills of exchange (of which the most familiar example is the cheque) and promissory notes (of which the most familiar example is the bank note). These are regulated by the Bills of Exchange Act 1882. It is beyond the scope of this book to list all other forms of negotiable instrument, but they include certain forms of bond and share certificates.

11.5.4.1 The requirements of negotiability

It is sometimes said that there are four requirements of negotiability:

1. that the right expressed in the instrument is to be transferable upon delivery (with indorsement where necessary)

2. that the holder of the instrument for the time being has the right to collect payment from the original debtor

3. that the holder for the time being, if taking for value and without notice, does not take subject to equities

4. that the instrument is of a type recognized by the law as negotiable.

However, the first three elements are not requirements but statements of the legal effect of the recognition that the instrument is negotiable. There is really only one requirement of negotiability, which is that the instrument is recognized as negotiable. But the mere fact that an instrument falls within a category of instruments generally regarded as negotiable does not prevent a particular instrument from being denied negotiability by express words (Bills of Exchange Act 1882, s. 8(1)). For example, cheques may be crossed 'not negotiable'. If they are crossed 'account payee' or 'account payee only', they are not negotiable, and are not even transferable.

11.5.4.2 The position of holder in due course

Negotiable instruments provide a means of circumventing the privity doctrine because the original contract debt is enforceable not only by the other contracting party, but also by any other person for the time being holding the instrument who has been constituted holder in due course. The position of the holder in due course is strengthened still further by the fact that if the party primarily liable on the instrument fails to pay, the holder in due course may if necessary bring a claim against all previous signatories of the instrument (Bills of Exchange Act 1882, s. 38(2)).

A party is holder in due course if that party receives the instrument for value and in good faith, provided it is complete and regular on its face (Bills of Exchange Act 1882, s. 29(1)), and is in a deliverable state (s. 31(3)–(4)). The requirement that the transfer be made for value is considerably more relaxed than the requirement of consideration in contracts generally.

- Provided value has been given at some time, the holder for the time being is deemed to have given value (s. 27(2) of the 1882 Act).

- Moreover, negotiable instruments are an exception to the general rule against past consideration (s. 27(1)(b): see **4.3.3.3**).

The requirement of good faith is the same as that in other parts of the law: the transferee must not have acquired the instrument by fraud, duress, undue influence, or other unacceptable behaviour, neither must the transferee have acquired it in the knowledge that it was already tainted with such defects before it came into the transferee's hands (s. 30(2) of the 1882 Act). The requirement that the instrument be complete and regular on its face poses little difficulty. It covers such defects as omission on the instrument of a payee or the amount payable. The requirement that the instrument be in a deliverable state is more complex. It relates to the need in certain circumstances for the instrument to be indorsed for the delivery to be effective. An instrument made payable to the bearer (a 'bearer bill') does not require indorsement in order to be negotiated, and so is always in a deliverable state. But an instrument made payable to a named person, or to a named person 'or order' (an 'order bill'), cannot be negotiated unless indorsed, and the fact of indorsement puts the bill in a deliverable state. Transfer of an order bill without indorsement would remove one of the essential characteristics of negotiability, i.e. that the holder acquires the instrument free from equities.

11.5.5 Collateral contract

The privity doctrine may be avoided by the collateral contract device, which gives a third party a right to enforce promises under a separate contract with the promisor.

> In ***Shanklin Pier Ltd v Detel Products Ltd*** [1951] 2 KB 854, the plaintiffs had hired a firm to paint their pier, and on the strength of a representation made by the defendants had instructed the firm to use the defendants' paint. The paint did not last anywhere near as long as the defendants had represented, but the contract for the purchase of the paint was between the firm of painters and the defendants, and so could not afford the plaintiffs a remedy. The court held that there was a collateral contract between the plaintiffs and the defendants to the effect that the paint would last for seven years. In this case the plaintiffs had furnished consideration for the defendants' undertaking by instructing the firm of painters to use the defendants' paint.

The collateral contract is of considerable practical significance in relation to commercial contracts as a means of avoiding the operation of the privity doctrine (see, e.g. *Andrews v Hopkinson* [1957] 1 QB 229: promise by car dealer enforced as a collateral contract with customer when the dealer's promise had induced the making of the separate contract of hire purchase between the customer and the finance company).

11.6 Exceptions to the privity doctrine

We have already considered devices, some of which may have had their origin in contract but all of which must now be regarded as conceptually independent, which may be used to circumvent the privity doctrine (see **11.5**). In this section we consider genuine exceptions to the privity doctrine.

11.6.1 Trust of rights created by contract

We saw above (see **11.5.3**) that the concept of privity is restricted to contracts and does not extend to trusts. A trust may attach to property of any kind, including a **chose in action**, which is a form of intangible property such as a right to enforce an obligation. It follows from that definition that a right under a contract is a chose in action, and thus may be subject to a trust.

The possibility is raised, therefore, that the promisee under a contract might declare themselves trustee of the benefit of the promise in question on behalf of a third party, and by that means avoid the privity doctrine.

This device was used successfully during the nineteenth century (*Lloyd's v Harper* (1880) 16 ChD 290), and its existence as a means of avoiding the privity doctrine was acknowledged by Viscount Haldane LC in **Dunlop Pneumatic Tyre Co. Ltd v Selfridge & Co. Ltd** [1915] AC 847, in the passage previously quoted (see 11.2).

11.6.1.1 Effect of a trust of a contractual right

Where a trust of a contractual right is found to have been created, the principal effect is to permit the third party to enforce the benefit.

> For example, in **Les Affréteurs Réunis SA v Leopold Walford (London) Ltd** [1919] AC 801, a charterparty between the shipowner and the charterer provided that the shipowner would pay a commission of 3 per cent to the broker who had negotiated the contract for the parties. When the shipowner failed to pay, the broker brought an action to recover the commission, although he was not a party to the contract.
>
> The House of Lords accepted that it was the practice of the shipping trade in such cases for the charterer to sue to enforce the promise of commission as trustee for the broker. Since the shipowner was willing to allow the case to be treated as having been brought upon such an action, the broker succeeded in recovering the commission.

The third party's claim to enforce the contract would normally need to be brought in the name of the trustee, but as **Les Affréteurs Réunis SA v Leopold Walford (London) Ltd** shows, the promisor may waive that requirement, in which case the third party may bring the claim in the third party's own name. If the trustee is unwilling to cooperate in bringing a claim to enforce the promise, the third party may start proceedings in their own name and join the trustee as co-defendant (**Vandepitte v Preferred Accident Insurance Corporation of New York** [1933] AC 70 at p. 79).

A further effect of the creation of a trust of a contractual right is to prevent the contracting parties from varying or rescinding the contract, since to do so would be an improper interference with the beneficiary's rights. An intention to reserve the right to vary in the future if so desired has been regarded as evidence contradicting the alleged intention to create a trust (**Re Schebsman** [1944] Ch 83).

11.6.1.2 Limits of the trust exception

Despite the apparent utility of the trust device as a means for avoiding the privity doctrine, it has fallen into disuse. **The reason is to be found in the requirements for the constitution of a trust (see 11.5.3), and especially in the requirement that there be a certain intention on the part of the person allegedly declaring the trust that a trust be created (*Vandepitte v Preferred Accident Insurance Corporation of New York* [1933] AC 70 and see *Nisshin Shipping Co. Ltd v Cleaves & Co. Ltd* [2003] EWHC 2602 (Comm), [2004] 1 Lloyd's Rep 38, discussed at 11.4.2 and 11.4.6, where the express trust did not displace a direct right of enforcement under the 1999 Act).**

The usual difficulty is that at the time of making the contract, and indeed at all times until the particular problem arises, the promisee has not thought at all about how the third party will enforce the benefit to be conferred.

In *Vandepitte v Preferred Accident Insurance Corporation of New York* [1933] AC 70, the plaintiff's action against an insurance company depended upon whether the insured held the promised cover under a policy of motor insurance on trust for his daughter who was a minor. Under the law of British Columbia the father was civilly liable for the torts of his minor children, so that it was almost inconceivable that he should feel it necessary to hold the benefit of insurance on his daughter's behalf since he was the person most likely to be sued, not his daughter. On that ground the Privy Council considered there to be no trust.

For some time the English courts have been unwilling to **imply** an intention to create a trust. In *Re Schebsman* [1944] Ch 83, Du Parcq LJ said:

[U]nless an intention to create a trust is clearly to be collected from the language used and the circumstances of the case, I think that the Court ought not to be astute to discover indications of such an intention.

In *Rolls-Royce Power Engineering plc v Ricardo Consulting Engineers Ltd* [2003] EWHC 2871 (TCC), [2004] 2 All ER (Comm) 129, it was held that a trust of a promise will be effective only if the party whose promise is held on trust either knew or had reason to know that the other contracting party was contracting as trustee. Therefore, the argument on these facts that the subsidiary had contracted as agent for the parent company could not succeed because there was no such knowledge of the parent company's interest in the contract and it was only subsequently that the subsidiary company's business was transferred to the parent.

In practice, therefore, unless there is an express declaration of the intention to create a trust it seems that the device of a trust of a contractual right will fail. It is likely that the 1999 Act would apply in circumstances where an express declaration of the trust of the benefit of a contractual promise arose (*Nisshin Shipping Co. Ltd v Cleaves & Co. Ltd*** [2003] EWHC 2602 (Comm), [2004] 1 Lloyd's Rep 38).** The potential benefit for the beneficiary of reliance on the express trust argument is that the beneficiary's rights are irrevocable, whereas a third party's rights are capable of being varied or rescinded by the contracting parties under the 1999 Act (s. 2).

11.6.2 Insurance

In principle the privity doctrine applies to contracts of insurance, but there are several statutory exceptions to the doctrine in the case of common contracts which provide for benefits to be payable to third parties.

- For example, under s. 148(7) of the Road Traffic Act 1988, an injured third party may recover compensation from the insurance company once the injured third party has obtained judgment against the insured.

- Under s. 11 of the Married Women's Property Act 1882, a spouse has an enforceable right to recover sums due on a policy of life insurance taken out by the other spouse on his or her own life.

11.6.3 **Carriage of goods by sea**

It is common in commercial transactions for one party (the shipper) to enter into a contract with another (the carrier) for goods to be taken and delivered to a third party (the consignee). The doctrine of privity of contract would prevent the consignee suing the carrier for damage caused to the goods in transit, since the consignee was not a party to the contract. In the nineteenth century, Parliament attempted to solve this problem by attaching the right to sue the carrier (originating in the shipper as a party to the contract of carriage) to the ownership in the goods, so that when the consignee became owner of the goods he acquired the right to sue the carrier for damage in transit (see the Bills of Lading Act 1855). More recently the complex nature of commercial transactions exposed weaknesses in this solution in the 1855 Act, especially where the consignee was for some reason regarded by law as exposed to the risk of loss in respect of the goods but had not acquired ownership (e.g., *Leigh and Sillavan Ltd v Aliakmon Shipping Co. Ltd* [1986] AC 785). By the Carriage of Goods by Sea Act 1992, Parliament attempted to remedy the situation. The 1855 Act was repealed, and under the 1992 Act the right to sue the carrier passed from shipper to consignee or lawful holder of a bill of lading (as defined by ss. 2 and 5) by operation of law, and independently of the passing of ownership. This statutory exception to the doctrine of privity of contract is said to be justified as a matter of commercial necessity.

The Contracts (Rights of Third Parties) Act 1999 does not apply to contracts for the carriage of goods by sea, which are expressly excluded from its application by s. 6(5)–(7).

11.6.4 *The Eurymedon* **device: Ability of third party to rely on an exemption clause**

11.6.4.1 Scope of the exception: Background

An exemption clause is a clause which purports to exclude or to limit liability for breach of contract. We have already examined the law relating to exemption clauses in two-party contract situations (see **Chapter 7**). However, some commercial transactions, especially those involving international trade and shipping, cannot easily be analysed in terms of the traditional bilateral contract. Since in the commercial field the attitude of the English courts has always been that contract law must be the servant, and not the master, of the needs and practices of those engaged in business (see **1.4**), the law must accommodate those needs and practices as best it can without over-insisting on the purity of the conceptual framework. It was precisely in the context of an attempt to protect a third party by means of an exemption clause that Lord Wilberforce made his now well-known statement about the occasional difficulty of 'forcing the facts to fit uneasily into the marked slots of offer, acceptance and consideration' (in ***New Zealand Shipping Co. Ltd v A. M. Satterthwaite & Co. Ltd, The Eurymedon*** [1975] AC 154: see **2.1.3**).

It was on the basis of the needs and practices of the business community that an exception to the privity doctrine, which allows the protection of third parties by means of an exemption clause, was allowed to develop. The ability to afford protection to third parties through exemption clauses was accepted as commercially efficient since in the commercial context such clauses operate as risk allocation devices. Given this commercial rationale based on the fact that such clauses are freely negotiated between commercial parties, the scope of the exception was unlikely to be extended to consumer contracts. It should be noted, however, that even where this exception applied and the exemption clause was found to be capable of protecting a third party, the clause remained subject to all the usual controls (see generally 7.5).

> In *Elder, Dempster and Co. v Paterson, Zochonis & Co. Ltd* [1924] AC 522, shipowners, who were not parties to a contract between the shippers of goods and the charterers of the vessel, which was evidenced by a bill of lading, claimed nevertheless to be protected by an exemption clause contained therein. The House of Lords upheld that claim. No reasons for the decision were given, other than that such a decision was consistent with the commercial realities of the situation, and that the alternative proposition—that the charterer was protected by the clause but the shipowners were not—was 'absurd'.

The difficulty of this decision was that it was clearly inconsistent with the privity doctrine, but did not explain how the doctrine had been avoided.

A very similar situation arose for consideration by the House of Lords in *Scruttons Ltd v Midland Silicones Ltd* [1962] AC 446. It was apparent that such purported extensions of exemption clauses to third parties, and especially to stevedores employed to load and unload cargoes, were commonplace in the commercial world, and that the particular action was regarded as a test case. The majority of the House of Lords confirmed that commercial contracts were not as a category exempt from the requirement in the general law of contract of privity between parties. **It was accepted that the privity doctrine might be avoided by means of a separate contract between the third party and the shipper of the goods, and that such a contract might arise by way of agency, but their Lordships would not find such a contract on this ground unless the requirements for a finding of agency were present, namely, there had to be authority to act as agent and consideration for the promise would need to be given by the third party (as principal in the agency relationship).**

Lord Reid (at p. 474) spelt out four conditions which would need to be satisfied before a third party could rely on an exemption clause in a contract to which that third party was not a party:

> I can see a possibility of success of the agency argument if (first) the bill of lading makes it clear that the stevedore is intended to be protected by the provisions in it which limit liability, (secondly) that the bill of lading makes it clear that the carrier, in addition to contracting for these provisions on his own behalf, is also contracting as agent for the stevedore that these provisions should apply to the stevedore, (thirdly) the carrier has authority from the stevedore to do that, or perhaps later ratification by the stevedore would suffice, and (fourthly) that any difficulties about consideration moving from the stevedore were overcome.

In this particular case there was nothing in the bill of lading to suggest that the exemption clause was intended to benefit the stevedores, and nothing to indicate that the carrier was contracting as agent for the stevedore to obtain the benefit of the clause. Nevertheless, the statement by Lord Reid provided a glimmer of hope to the business community who considered it commercially necessary to afford this protection to third parties involved in the performance of commercial contracts. As a result, attempts were made to draft contractual exemption clauses which would meet the requirements set out by Lord Reid.

One such clause (known as a 'Himalaya clause') fell to be considered by the Privy Council in *New Zealand Shipping Co. Ltd v A. M. Satterthwaite & Co. Ltd, The Eurymedon* [1975] AC 154.

As it was aimed at fulfilling Lord Reid's criteria, the clause is particularly long and complex, but its essential ingredients are that the clause expressly grants protection to a category of persons ('servants, agents and independent contractors') in a wide range of circumstances and expressly states that for the purposes of obtaining this protection the carrier is acting as agent or trustee on behalf of these persons who, to this extent, are to be regarded as parties to the contract.

It was established without difficulty that the clause satisfied the first three requirements of the agency argument put forward by Lord Reid.

11.6.4.2 Difficulties with Lord Reid's fourth criterion: Consideration to support the promise

The issue in *The Eurymedon* was whether there was any consideration for the contract between the stevedores and the shippers arranged through the agency of the carriers. The stevedores were already under a duty, by virtue of their contract with the carriers, to unload the cargo with due care, and the performance of that duty could also be consideration for the separate contract exempting the stevedores from liability to the shippers (see 4.4.2).

Although it was possible in *The Eurymedon* to find a contract between the shippers and the stevedores by virtue of the doctrine of agency, there was some difficulty about describing that contract as bilateral, since at the time when the carrier made the principal contract with the shipper the intended stevedore might be unaware of the actual contract envisaged (this would not affect the carrier's authority to act for the stevedore, which would have been given in general terms). The Privy Council overcame the difficulty by finding that the principal contract resulted in the shipper making an offer in the form of a unilateral contract whereby it would exempt from liability anybody undertaking to unload the cargo. This *Eurymedon* device was criticized because of its artificiality and complexity rather than because of its result.

11.6.4.3 Difficulties with Lord Reid's third criterion: Authority to act as agent

One reason why it was relatively easy in *The Eurymedon* to find that the carriers were acting as duly authorized agents for the stevedores was that the carriers and stevedores were part of the same group of companies. It was suggested (see *The Suleyman Stalskiy* [1976] 2 Lloyd's Rep 609) that where there was no previous relationship between the stevedore and the carrier the agency argument would not prevail over the privity doctrine. However, that suggestion was disapproved by Lord Wilberforce in a further Privy Council case on this point (**Port Jackson Stevedoring Pty Ltd v Salmond & Spraggon (Australia) Pty Ltd, The New York Star** [1981] 1 WLR 138). Lord Wilberforce thought that the *Eurymedon* principle should be regarded as being of general application, and should not depend upon fine distinctions based upon the nature of the relationship between carrier and stevedore. This reasoning appears to be correct. If it is the practice of the commercial world, when exemptions from liability are included in contracts, to seek to extend the benefit of such protection to third parties necessary to the performance of the contract, then there is no undue surprise to the other party if the first party claims also to contract as agent for such a third party, irrespective of whether there is any other relationship between them. In *Homburg Houtimport BV v Agrosin Private Ltd, The Starsin* [2003] UKHL 12, [2003] 2 WLR 711, Lord Bingham referred to the reasoning in *The Eurymedon* and *The New York Star* as 'a deft and commercially inspired response to technical English rules of contract, particularly those governing privity and consideration'.

Lord Wilberforce's plea in *The New York Star* to apply *The Eurymedon* generally, and not to seek to distinguish it based on fine distinctions of fact, was not followed by the English courts in the context of attempts by subcontractors to rely on clauses in the contract between the employer and main contractor. The English courts took the view that there could be no authority to act as agent for a person who had not been identified to that contract at the time it was entered into. Subcontractors would not generally be appointed until after the main contract was entered into and so could not have authorized the main contractor to contract on their behalf (*Southern Water Authority v Carey* [1985] 2 All ER 1077 and *Norwich City Council v Harvey* [1989] 1 All ER 1180; although in both cases the subcontractor was protected because the clause was interpreted as a risk allocation provision and as restricting the scope of the duty of care in tort).

This difficulty of non-existence in relation to the main contract was avoided by the High Court of Australia in *Trident General Insurance Co. Ltd v McNiece Brothers Proprietary Ltd* (1988) 165 CLR 107. The court allowed McNiece to obtain the protection of an insurance policy on the basis that it was a subcontractor of the insured and the policy purported to extend to cover subcontractors, even though McNiece was not a subcontractor at the time the policy contract was entered into. Commercial difficulties would arise if this broad interpretation was not adopted because third parties might well rely on the fact that they were covered by insurance and neglect to take out their own cover. Equally, if they did take out their own cover, it might result in double cover which would be inefficient.

More recently, presumably in the light of the position under the 1999 Act, the English courts have shown a greater willingness in the shipping context to interpret the *Eurymedon* principles in a manner which gives effect to the commercial expectations of the parties.

> For example, in *Owners of the Ship 'Borvigilant' v Owners of the 'Romina C'* [2003] EWCA Civ 935, [2003] 2 Lloyd's Rep 520, the Court of Appeal upheld the first instance decision of David Steel J ([2002] EWHC 1 759 (Admlty), [2002] 2 Lloyd's Rep 631) to the effect that NIOC had implied authority to contract with shipowners on behalf of other tug owners since the language of the tug requisition form referred to the fact that NIOC was contracting on behalf of such owners. It was not necessary for the form to expressly state that NIOC was contracting as agent and the language used indicated that NIOC must have had the authority of other tug owners to act in this way.

In the Court of Appeal Clarke LJ referred to Lord Reid's speech in *Scruttons v Midland Silicones* and added:

> Lord Reid did not say that the clause must expressly state that the carrier is contracting as agent for the stevedores. He simply said that the contract must make that clear…The question remains whether, construed as a whole, the contract provides that NIOC was entering into the contract, at least in part as the agent of the owner of any tug supplied by NIOC but not owned by NIOC. In my view, commercial good sense requires only one answer to that question, namely yes.

Clarke LJ (with whose judgment Dyson and Peter Gibson LJJ agreed) referred to the need (identified in *The New York Star*) to avoid 'a search for fine distinctions which would diminish the general applicability' of the *Eurymedon* principle.

The scope of the *Eurymedon* device was, and is, nevertheless quite limited. In *The Mahkutai* [1996] 3 All ER 502, the Privy Council refused to extend its scope to jurisdiction clauses, on the basis that, unlike exemption clauses which benefit one party only, jurisdiction clauses create mutual rights and obligations. A jurisdiction clause was a neutral clause, and not one included simply 'for the benefit' of one party.

11.6.4.4 The first requirement is key: It must be clear that the third party was intended to be protected by the clause

The most fundamental difficulty that could be faced in seeking to rely on *The Eurymedon* was experienced in *London Drugs Ltd v Kuehne & Nagel International Ltd* (1993) 97 DLR (4th) 261.

> There was a limitation clause in a storage contract which limited 'the warehouseman's liability'. However, the clause did not expressly cover the employees who in fact damaged the goods in storage. The Canadian Court of Appeal held that it covered the employees by impliedly extending the meaning of the clause although this amounted to extending Lord Reid's criteria in *Scruttons v Midland Silicones*. On appeal the Supreme Court of Canada considered that it was not possible to extend *The Eurymedon* in this way, and instead created a new exception to the privity doctrine in Canada. This exception was outside the scope of *The Eurymedon* and is limited to employees. It would apply where the clause expressly or impliedly extended the benefit of the clause to employees and the employees caused the loss in performing the very services provided for in the contract.

In *Fraser River Pile & Dredge Ltd v Can-Dive Services* [2000] 1 Lloyd's Rep 199, the *London Drugs* exception was put in broader terms, namely that the parties must have intended to extend the benefit to the third party and the activities performed by the third party must have been the very activities contemplated as coming within the scope of the contract or the contractual provision which was being relied upon. Thus, the only means of avoiding the limitation imposed by Lord Reid's first criteria was to create a specific exception.

The practical difficulties that may be experienced in attempting to establish the first of Lord Reid's criteria (that the clause makes it clear that the third party is intended to have the benefit of the protection of the clause) are also illustrated by the facts in *Homburg Houtimport BV v Agrosin Private Ltd, The Starsin* [2003] UKHL 12, [2003] 2 WLR 711. There was an extremely broad Himalaya clause in the bill of lading contract between the charterer and the shipper. Therefore, the shipowner was in principle within the scope of its protection as an independent contractor. However, the House of Lords held that the Hague Rules (an international convention) were incorporated into the bill of lading contract and these provisions invalidated the scope of the Himalaya clause (since they prescribed the exemptions and limitations available to the carrier of goods by sea). Accordingly, the shipowner could not rely on the protection afforded by the clause.

11.6.4.5 The effect of the 1999 Act on the ability of a third party to enforce an exemption clause

The ability of a third party to enforce a contract term (including an exemption clause: 1999 Act, s. 1(6)) is determined by the test of enforceability. Therefore, if the clause in question expressly provides that the third party, who is expressly identified in the contract by name or as a member of a class, is to have the right to enforce the exemption clause, the third party will clearly have that right (s. 1(1)(a)). However, the Himalaya clause in *The Eurymedon* (see **11.6.4.1**) does not expressly give this right. Instead, it states that the stevedore (as a member of the class of independent contractors) is to have the benefit of the clause and that the carrier is acting as his agent for this purpose. Section 1(1)(b) ought therefore to apply to this clause and factual context unless 'on a proper construction of the contract it appears that the parties did not intend the term to be enforceable by the third party'. This will depend on the wording of the contract as a whole. Accordingly, and on the basis that there is nothing to indicate that the parties did ***not*** intend the term to be enforceable by the third party (as to which see **11.4.2**), under the 1999 Act there should be a direct right of enforcement of the Himalaya clause in *The Eurymedon*. This should reduce much of the complexity of the law governing third-party enforcement of exemption clauses.

The 1999 Act may also provide a direct right of enforcement in situations such as those in *Southern Water Authority v Carey* and *Norwich City Council v Harvey* (see 11.6.4.3), because of the clarity of the risk-allocation clauses and because the Act specifically states that the third party (i.e., the subcontractor) 'need not be in existence when the contract is entered into' (**s. 1(3)**).

However, it would not be available in factual situations such as *Scruttons v Midland Silicones* because of the absence of an **express** identification of the third party as an intended beneficiary of the clause. The same problem would exist on the facts in *London Drugs v Kuehne and Nagel*, namely the fact that the clause does not **expressly** confer a benefit on the employees unless they can be said to be **expressly** identified as members of a class of 'warehouseman', when the reality is that this can be achieved only by fairly generous implication. *The Eurymedon* could not operate in either of these cases because the first criterion specified by Lord Reid is not satisfied. The 1999 Act effectively keeps this first requirement and dispenses with the remaining three, thereby eliminating the complexity. To illustrate this point, *London Drugs* can usefully be compared with *Fraser River Pile & Dredge Ltd v Can-Dive Ltd* [2000] 1 Lloyd's Rep 199, which **would** satisfy the s. 1(1)(b) test of enforceability in the 1999 Act. On the facts, the clause extended to third-party beneficiaries coming within the class of 'charterers', so that this constituted express identification in the waiver of subrogation clause.

11.7 Remedies available to the promisee

It would be possible to avoid the consequences of the privity doctrine if the promisee could bring a claim and recover remedies which enforced the third party's rights or compensated for the third party's loss.

The fundamental weakness in relying on this means of enforcement is that the third party will be dependent on the willingness of the promisee to bring a claim. In addition, this method of avoiding the consequences of privity will be less relevant as a result of the 1999 Act if the third party can achieve a remedy directly (although the promisee's right to enforce and recover on behalf of the third party is expressly retained: s. 5). Nevertheless, as we have seen, the 1999 Act does not provide third parties with rights of enforcement in all circumstances so that the remedies available to the promisee are still relevant to this discussion.

11.7.1 Specific performance

Specific performance is an order which would compel the promisor to carry out the promise so that the third party obtains the intended benefit under the contract. However, as discussed in 10.2.1, this remedy is discretionary and will not be granted where damages would be an adequate remedy. In *Beswick v Beswick* [1968] AC 58, the fact that the loss suffered by the promisee was negligible, so that damages would be purely nominal, was said to be good reason for awarding the discretionary remedy of specific performance (for the facts of this case, see 10.2.1). Mrs Beswick would now be able to enforce the nephew's promise directly under s. 1(1)(b) of the 1999 Act since the contract clearly purported to confer a benefit on her as a named individual (although it did not give her an express right to enforce the promise against the nephew). There also seems to be no evidence 'on the proper construction of the contract' that she was not intended to be able to enforce the term.

This remedy of specific performance is undoubtedly the best suited to achieving the promisee's original contractual intention of conferring a benefit on the third party, but it is not without limitations:

1. As a general remedy specific performance is subject to restrictions, such as the fact that damages must not be an adequate remedy (see also **10.2.1**).

2. Moreover, in *Beswick v Beswick* it was a happy coincidence that the widow had been appointed administratrix of the husband's estate, since she then had no problem in persuading the 'promisee' to bring the action for specific performance. Since it appears that the third party cannot compel the promisee to act (see **11.7.4**), the remedy of specific performance will be available only when it suits the promisee to enforce the contract.

3. In addition, it is suitable as a remedy only where the performance has yet to take place (or to take place fully). It will not be appropriate where the contract has been performed, albeit defectively, and the third party seeks a remedy.

11.7.2 Enforcement of negative undertakings

Where the contractual term breached is in the form of a negative undertaking (a promise to refrain from doing something), the obvious remedy is an injunction (see **10.3**), which is a form of specific relief similar to specific performance designed to prevent actions rather than to enforce performance. It would appear to be consistent with the reasoning in *Beswick v Beswick* [1968] AC 58 for an injunction to be available to a promisee in appropriate circumstances in the same way that specific performance was in that case.

Where the negative undertaking is a promise not to sue the third party, the correct procedure is not to seek an injunction but to ask the court to stay the proceedings which have been brought in contravention of the promise. In *Gore v Van der Lann* [1967] 2 QB 31, the Court of Appeal said that, even where there was a definite promise not to sue the third party, the promisee would be granted a stay of proceedings only if he had a sufficient interest in the enforcement of the promise. Such an interest would arise only if, for example, the promisee was under a legal obligation to reimburse the third party (the defendant to the action) in respect of any damages the third party had to pay to the claimant. However, in the subsequent case of *Snelling v John G. Snelling Ltd* [1973] 1 QB 87, the requirement of sufficient interest appears to have been ignored by the court.

> In *Snelling v John G. Snelling Ltd*, three brothers each loaned money to the family company, and subsequently agreed among themselves not to seek to recover such loans should any of them resign his directorship of the company. The plaintiff resigned and brought an action against the company to recover money loaned to it. The other brothers applied to be joined as defendants to the action, and then counterclaimed for a declaration that the plaintiff was not entitled to recover the sums in question. In theory, the plaintiff should have succeeded against the company, since the company could not enforce the stipulation made on its behalf. On the other hand, the brothers were entitled to succeed on their counterclaim. Ormrod J resolved this apparent impasse by staying the proceedings, since in reality the plaintiff had lost his action.

The two brothers were under no legal liability to the company should the third fail to keep his promise to refrain from recovering the money owing to him, so that it is not easy to see what was the sufficient interest which they had in seeking enforcement of the promise. The decision in *Snelling* would therefore appear to be more in line with the approach in *Beswick v Beswick*, i.e. that the nephew could not be allowed to ignore his express promise to pay Mrs Beswick on Mr Beswick's death. The brother in *Snelling* could not be permitted to do the very thing which he had contracted not to do.

453

It may be that the sufficient interest requirement is either an alternative (where there is no express promise not to sue), or of no effect at all (given that discussion of this issue in *Gore v Van der Lann* was strictly *obiter*).

11.7.3 Promisee's claim for damages

The difficulty with a claim for damages in relation to breach of a contract providing for a third-party benefit is that the promisee may usually recover damages only for the promisee's own loss. If the performance to be provided by the other party was intended entirely for the benefit of the third party, the law takes the view that there is no loss to the promisee resulting from the breach, so that damages will be purely nominal (*Beswick v Beswick* [1968] AC 58; although compare the opinion of Lord Pearce). Of course, if the promisee were to receive some benefit from the other party's performance in addition to the benefit intended for the third party, then that loss would be recoverable under the normal rules, but the promisee would still be unable to recover for the third party's loss. It seems, however, that if the promisee were to be under a legal obligation to compensate the third party in the event of non-performance by the other contracting party (e.g., as a result of a contract between promisee and third party), then that obligation would amount to a real loss to the promisee, and substantial damages would be recoverable on that account. It is open to question whether payment to the third party by the promisee on the strength of a perceived moral obligation to provide compensation would also be a recoverable loss.

11.7.3.1 Contracts made on behalf of a group for reasons of convenience

In recent years it has been suggested that the promisee should in any case be able to recover damages for the loss suffered by the third party. If the third party was then able to compel the promisee to hand over the damages recovered (see **11.7.4**), such a remedy would effectively side-step any privity problems (assuming that the promisee can be persuaded to bring the claim for damages in the first place). Such a claim by the promisee appears to have been allowed by the Court of Appeal in *Jackson v Horizon Holidays Ltd* [1975] 1 WLR 1468.

> In *Jackson v Horizon Holidays Ltd*, the plaintiff had booked a package holiday for himself and his family. The holiday fell well short of the standard promised. The plaintiff brought an action for breach of contract. The defendant holiday company challenged the trial judge's award of damages of £1,100, which was just less than the full cost of the holiday.
>
> In the Court of Appeal the award was upheld. Lord Denning MR said that the award was excessive as compensation for the plaintiff's loss alone, but was a correct assessment of the aggregate loss suffered by the whole family. The plaintiff was entitled to recover damages for loss suffered by the family members because he had contracted on their behalf. The other members of the Court of Appeal, although upholding the award, did not openly state that it represented compensation for loss suffered by the other members of the family as well as by the plaintiff.

Lord Denning MR regarded *Jackson v Horizon Holidays Ltd* as an example of a general principle allowing the promisee to recover damages on behalf of third-party beneficiaries. He claimed that it fell within the principle contained in an *obiter* statement by Lush LJ in *Lloyd's v Harper* (1880) 16 ChD 290 at p. 321: 'I consider it to be an established rule of law that where a contract is made with A for the benefit of B, A can sue on the contract for the benefit of B, and recover all that B could have recovered if the contract had been made with B himself.'

This reasoning and the width of this principle was disapproved (*obiter*) in ***Woodar Investment Development Ltd v Wimpey Construction (UK) Ltd*** [1980] 1 WLR 277.

> In ***Woodar Investments,*** the plaintiffs agreed to sell some land to the defendants for £850,000. It was a term of the contract that the defendants should pay £150,000 of the price to a third party. The defendants failed to go ahead with the purchase, and the plaintiffs claimed damages for what they said was a repudiatory breach.
>
> The House of Lords found that the defendants had not repudiated the contract, but went on to discuss the privity issue. While being far from satisfied with the privity doctrine (see **11.3.2**), their Lordships denied the existence of a general principle allowing the promisee to recover damages for loss suffered by the third-party beneficiary, and claimed that Lord Denning MR had taken the statement of Lush LJ out of its proper context limiting this principle to situations of agency or trust. They did not, however, overrule the actual decision in ***Jackson v Horizon Holidays Ltd.***

Lord Wilberforce thought that the decision probably belonged to a special category of cases 'calling for special treatment', where one party contracts for the benefit of a group for reasons of convenience. Transactions which may fall within this special category are 'contracting for family holidays, ordering meals in restaurants for a party, hiring a taxi for a group'.

It appears from this that the person contracting on behalf of the group would also need to suffer some loss in order to be able to recover for the members of the party. This would have been of no assistance on the facts in ***Woodar Investments***, because it was not a contract made on behalf of a group and there was no evidence that Woodar had suffered any loss as a result of the non-payment to the third party. In his speech Lord Scarman suggested that had Woodar been under an obligation to pay compensation to the third party following the non-payment, this might have been included within Woodar's loss (as promisee).

11.7.3.2 The *St Martin's Property* exception

Nevertheless, another exception to the general rule has been recognized in the commercial context, which allows the promisee to recover substantial damages on behalf of a third party although the promisee has not suffered any loss.

> In ***Linden Gardens Trust Ltd v Lenesta Sludge Disposals Ltd*** [1994] 1 AC 85 ('the *St Martin's Property*' appeal) the question arose of what compensation was recoverable where party A engaged party B to carry outwork on his property, in circumstances where both understood that A was very likely to transfer the property to party C. This transfer took place. B performed the work defectively and in breach of contract. In the absence of an assignment (which was contractually excluded) C could not sue, and it was argued that since A no longer had any interest in the property, its damages would be purely nominal. The House of Lords did not agree. Their Lordships' motivation appears to have been the desire to avoid the conclusion that the building contractor (B) would not have to pay substantial damages for the breach.

Relying on Lord Diplock's explanation (in ***The Albazero*** [1977] AC 774) of the decision in ***Dunlop v Lambert*** (1839) 6 Cl & F 600, Lord Browne-Wilkinson said (at pp. 114–15):

> The contract was for a large development of property which, to the knowledge of both [parties], was going to be occupied and possibly purchased by third parties...Therefore, it could be foreseen that damage caused by a breach would cause loss to a later owner and not merely to the original contracting party...In such a case, it seems to me proper, as in the case of the carriage of goods by land, to treat

> the parties as having entered into the contract on the footing that [the original owner] would be entitled to enforce the contractual rights for the benefit of those who suffered from defective performance …

The narrow ground

This reasoning is referred to as 'the narrow ground' for the decision in **Linden Gardens**. It is stated to be based on the principle explained by Lord Diplock in *The Albazero* [1977] AC 774 at 847:

> in a commercial contract concerning goods, where it is in the contemplation of the parties that the proprietary interests in the goods may be transferred from one owner to another after the contract has been entered into and before the breach which causes the loss or damage to the goods, an original party to the contract, if such be the intention of them both, is to be treated in law as having entered into the contract for the benefit of all persons who have or may acquire an interest in the goods before they are lost or damaged, and is entitled to recover by way of damages for breach of contract the actual loss sustained by those for whose benefit the contract is entered into.

This narrow-ground principle therefore allows A to retain the right to sue for substantial damages and recover for the loss suffered by C, on the basis that it was contemplated that someone other than A would suffer loss in the event of breach of the contract but be unable to sue.

The broad ground

Lord Griffiths advocated 'the broad ground' to support his conclusion that the building owner could recover substantial damages, and there was some sympathy with this approach from other members of the House of Lords (Lords Keith and Bridge, although Lord Browne-Wilkinson thought that further academic consideration of this ground was required). (For this academic discussion, see Palmer and Tolhurst (1997) 12 JCL 1, (1997) 12 JCL 97, and (1998) 13 JCL 143.) If the broad ground is accepted as a means of obtaining substantial damages on behalf of third parties, it has the potential drastically to alter the practical consequences of the application of the privity doctrine because the loss will be suffered by the promisee.

The broad-ground argument rests on the premise that in a contract for the supply of work and materials, it makes no difference whether the promisee has any proprietary interest in the subject matter of the contract; the crucial factor is whether there has been defective performance or non-performance, since the result of the breach is that the promisee does not receive 'the bargain for which he contracted'. That is the promisee's loss and the promisee can recover substantial damages on a cost of cure basis for that loss of expectation. (For further discussion of this broad-ground argument and recovery for loss of the 'performance interest', see McKendrick, 'Breach of contract and the meaning of loss' [1999] CLP 37, Coote, 'The performance interest, *Panatown*, and the problem of loss' (2001) 117 LQR 81; and the discussion at **9.3.1**.)

Subsequent case law

1. *Darlington Borough Council v Wiltshier Northern Ltd* [1995] 1 WLR 68

There was some support in the judgment of Steyn LJ in for the 'broad approach' advocated by Lord Griffiths. However, in that case it was the narrow ground in **Linden Gardens** which was applied by the Court of Appeal (in relation to a claim by the third party).

The contractor had contracted with Morgan Grenfell (which had become involved because of restrictions on local authority expenditure) to construct a recreation centre for the local authority on land owned by that local authority. Contractual rights had been assigned (transferred) to the council and the contractor was aware that that the centre was being built for the council. The local authority wanted to bring an action for defective performance of the construction contract, but could recover substantial damages only if Morgan Grenfell had assigned the right to substantial damages. Therefore, the question was the same as that in **Linden Gardens**, namely, could the contracting party recover substantial damages for breach of a contract when it had no property interest and had therefore suffered no loss?

The Court of Appeal applied the narrow-ground exception and held that there was a right to recover substantial damages, because it was clear to the contractor that the centre was being constructed for the local authority on local authority land and that the local authority would suffer loss in the event of breach.

This extends the application of the narrow ground to instances where the promisee has never had any ownership interest in the property affected by the breach. Steyn LJ pointed to the need, recognized previously by Lord Diplock and Lord Browne-Wilkinson in **Linden Gardens**, 'to provide a remedy where no other would be available to a person sustaining loss which under a rational legal system ought to be compensated by the person who has caused it'.

Although this is an interesting analysis to deal with the difficulty posed by subsequent assignment when the loss had already been incurred, the explanation of the principle that an assignee cannot recover more than the assignor, means that it may have been unnecessary for the Court of Appeal in **Darlington** to employ **The Albazero** in an effort to avoid it and enable the assignor to recover the third party's loss. It would have been easier to simply allow the assignor to recover substantial loss based on the position had there been no assignment and given that it retained ownership of the land and recreation centre.

2. *Offer-Hoar v Larkstore Ltd* [2006] EWCA Civ 1079, [2006] 1 WLR 2926, [2007] 1 All ER (Comm) 104

In this case the Court of Appeal had to consider whether a soil investigation consultant who had been employed by the original owner of the site was liable for a property developer's losses caused by a landslip in circumstances where the contractual rights had not been assigned until after the losses occurred. The argument was that since the original site owner did not own the property at the time of the landslip it had suffered no loss and could not assign more than it had, i.e. this was a 'black hole' problem. The Court of Appeal held that the property developer did have the right to sue the consultant for substantial damages for the loss suffered as a result of the landslip since the assignment was of a cause of action, including the remedy in damages, rather than an assignment of a loss, and that the remedy in damages was not to be limited to loss arising at the date of accrual of the cause of action. It followed that the principle, that an assignee cannot recover more than the assignor had the ability to assign/transfer, did not assist here since its purpose was to protect a contract breaker or debtor having to pay damages to the assignee that he would not have had to pay to the assignor had the assignment not taken place. It was not intended to enable the contract-breaker to escape all liability for its breach (black hole). The assignment on these facts did not expose the consultant to a claim for damages by the property developer that it would not have been exposed to by the original owner if no transfer had taken place.

3. *Catlin Estates Ltd v Carter Jonas* (a firm) [2005] EWHC 2315 (TCC), [2006] PNLR 15, [2006] 2 EGLR 139

Another example of a narrow-ground application is provided by the decision in **Catlin Estates Ltd v Carter Jonas (a firm).**

> The claimants sought damages against the defendant surveyors who were responsible for construction work under contracts between the claimant and the building contractor both in their own right and on behalf of the second claimant, the claimant company's sole shareholder and director. The claimant company had agreed to transfer the property to the shareholder but the transfer had not then been completed. The surveyors claimed that the claimant company had suffered no loss, as it had transferred the property, and could not recover substantial damages on behalf of the shareholder. It was held that since the legal title remained with the claimant company it had the right to bring proceedings for the breach of contract. In addition, since this was a private family company and the shareholder controlled it, the shareholder would have been the beneficiary of any damages award. It should not be possible for the surveyors to receive a 'get out of jail card free' because of the family arrangement to transfer the property, so that the company should be able to recover substantial damages for the sole shareholder. (As to the question of whether the shareholder had its own direct right of enforcement, see the discussion of this case below.)

4. *Alfred MacAlpine Construction Ltd v Panatown Ltd* [2001] 1 AC 518

By comparison, in **Panatown** the House of Lords refused to allow an employer to recover substantial damages for defective workmanship where the employer did not own the land in question and so had suffered no financial loss.

> Panatown had employed McAlpine to build an office block and a multi-storey car park. The construction site was owned throughout by an associate company of Panatown, UIPL. The distinguishing fact in this case was that the contractors (McAlpine) had also entered into a 'Duty of Care Deed' with UIPL (the site owner), which gave UIPL a direct remedy against the contractor for breaches of qualified contractual terms. Panatown claimed damages for defective performance of the construction contract. UIPL did not seek to bring an action under the Duty of Care Deed.
>
> The majority of the House of Lords held that, because of the existence of the Duty of Care Deed which gave the site owner a direct remedy, the narrow-ground exception in *Linden Gardens* could not apply; it was unnecessary because the third party had a direct right of action against the contractor. Accordingly, there was no need to depart from the general rule that substantial damages cannot be claimed by a promisee who has suffered no loss. (Compare with **Catlin Estates Ltd v Carter Jonas (a firm)** [2005] EWHC 2315 (TCC), [2006] PNLR 15, [2006] 2 EGLR 139, where it was held that even if the shareholder had a direct right of enforcement under the Defective Premises Act 1972, that would not have prevented the company recovering substantial damages under the *St Martin's Property* exception, since this restriction required the direct claim to be brought 'on the same conditions as the original claim' and the claim in contract was very different to the claim under the Defective Premises Act.)

The decision in **Panatown** therefore rests on its facts. However, it is a significant decision because the House of Lords modified the narrow ground in **Linden Gardens** and stated that it was not based on contractual intention and what the parties contemplated (as the Court of Appeal had considered [1998] CLC 636). Instead it was a solution imposed by law, although one which was excluded on the facts in **Panatown**. This approach avoided the difficult questions surrounding the determination of the intentions of the parties and, on this basis, it should follow that the narrow ground ought to apply whenever a third party suffers loss as a building owner and the employer's loss is purely nominal, either because he no longer owns the property in question or because he never owned it. It will only be in instances where there is direct redress (as in *Panatown* itself) that this operation of law will be necessarily excluded.

Consideration of the broad ground

1. *McAlpine v Panatown*

The House of Lords in *McAlpine v Panatown* also considered the broad ground which had been advocated by Lord Griffiths in *Linden Gardens.*

(a) The majority (who decided the case on the basis of the Duty of Care Deed) expressed grave doubts about the broad ground, although they accepted that the promisee would be able to recover in the event of defective performance if he spent money on repairing the defects, despite the fact that he was under no legal obligation to do so.

(b) On the other hand, there was support for the broad ground from the dissenting members of the House of Lords, Lords Goff and Millett. They dissented on the Duty of Care Deed because they considered it irrelevant. Their focus was on the loss suffered by the promisee (Panatown) as a result of the defective performance for which it had contracted, whereas the Duty of Care Deed dealt with the question of third-party enforceability.

(c) Lord Browne-Wilkinson (who was in the majority in that he considered that the Duty of Care Deed prevented the promisee's recovery) also appeared to accept the broad-ground argument because he attempted to link the two. He stated that because of the Duty of Care Deed, UIPL had a remedy against McAlpine so that Panatown had not suffered a loss of bargain (i.e., there was no damage to Panatown's performance interest).

(For further discussion of *McAlpine v Panatown*, see Coote, 'The performance interest, *Panatown*, and the problem of loss' (2001) 117 LQR 81.)

2. *Sabena Technics SA v Singapore Airlines Ltd* [2003] EWHC 1318 (Comm), unreported, 11 June 2003

On the other hand, in *Sabena Technics SA v Singapore Airlines Ltd*, there were signs of some reluctance to adopt the 'broad' ground. Colman J (at [140]) noted that 'the resolution of the differences of approach [i.e., the "narrow" ground and Lord Griffiths' "broad" ground] must be a matter for further consideration by the House of Lords' and he stressed the 'desirability of certainty in English commercial law'. The judge added that, in his opinion, this aim of commercial certainty would be best served by adopting the approach of the majority of their Lordships in *Panatown* (i.e., an ability to recover 'damages for the benefit of a third party for whom or on whose property the work was carried out and a parallel right of the third party to recover such damages from the contracting party').

3. *Rolls-Royce Power Engineering plc v Ricardo Consulting Engineers Ltd* [2003] EWHC 2871 (TCC), [2004] 2 All ER (Comm) 129

In *Rolls-Royce Power Engineering plc v Ricardo Consulting Engineers Ltd*, the judge did not follow the *McAlpine* interpretation of the narrow ground as being imposed by law rather then being based on contractual intention and contemplations. He insisted that any other interpretation would transform the exception into the general rule. Instead there needed to be 'special circumstances' to take the case outside the general rule (i.e., that a party may not recover substantial damages for breach of contract if he has suffered no loss). The judge stated that for the exception to operate it had to have been within the actual contemplation of the parties at the time the contract was made that an identified third party, or a third party who was a member of an identified class, would or might suffer damage in the event of a breach of that contract. He added that:

> if such knowledge at the date of the contract…were unnecessary, the result would be that a claim for substantial damages could be advanced on behalf of anyone whomsoever who contended that they had suffered loss as a result of a breach of contract, however remote their apparent connection to the performance of the contract. Such a possibility would destroy the general rule.

It is clear, therefore, that under the narrow ground, at the time of the contract, both parties must contemplate the transfer of the property and therefore that the other will suffer loss in the event of breach; see also Lindsay J in *Morgan Grenfell Development Capital Syndications Ltd v Arrows Autosports Ltd (No. 3)* [2004] EWHC 1015 (Ch), (2004) 148 SJLB 665 at [56]–[57].

The judge's reasoning in *Rolls-Royce* is convincing but does put clear ground between the 'narrow' ground and the 'broad' ground. If the narrow ground is imposed by law it becomes a default position and so is conceptually closer to the result which the 'broad' ground seeks to achieve.

Judge Seymour QC was reluctant to adopt Lord Griffiths's 'broad' ground which is hardly surprising given that *Rolls Royce* was heard in the High Court. In addition, he noted some practical difficulties with its application:

(a) The possible dangers of double liability for the same wrong, e.g. in tort to the person who has actually suffered loss and in contract as a notional loss to the actual claimant. However, the courts should be capable of dealing with such a possibility (see generally the discussion of overlapping claims at 11.4.4).

(b) The fact that although Lord Griffiths's approach might be applied where the damage is damage to, or failure to repair, property, it would be difficult to apply in the context of consequential losses since the nature and degree of consequential loss would tend to vary depending on the particular circumstances of the owner. Accordingly, it might be difficult to make an assessment of damages without reference to what actually happened to the other contracting party. (The question of recovery of consequential loss would, however, seem to be a separate question to the basic question of whether it is possible to recover substantial damages in principle. The consequential loss would need to be actual loss sustained by reference to an actual party and it might therefore be preferable to rely on the narrow ground for recovery if there are significant consequential losses suffered by a third party. The 'broad' ground would focus only on the 'performance loss' of the contracting party.)

(c) Given the lack of judicial unanimity with regard to the 'broad' ground and its potential scope of application, the judge concluded:

> In these treacherous waters I prefer to navigate by already published charts and to seek to apply the law as it has already clearly developed, rather than to speculate as to how it may develop in the future.

4. ***DRC Distribution Ltd v Ulva Ltd*** [2007] EWHC 1716 (QB)

In ***DRC Distribution Ltd v Ulva Ltd***, Flaux J discussed the broad-ground argument in the context of a sale of goods. First, he considered that it clearly did not represent the law and agreed with the comments of Lord Clyde in ***Panatown*** (at p. 534) that if the loss of expectation used in this sense amounted to a breach, it might cause a loss 'but it is not in itself a loss in any meaningful sense'. Second, however, the scope of the broad ground had been limited to contracts for the supply of services, such as building contracts, whereas sale of goods contracts did not fall into that category. Finally, he considered, relying heavily on the analysis in ***Panatown***, that the narrow ground was a rule of law which imputed to the parties the intention to enter into the contract for the benefit of the third party. However, that rule of law would be excluded where the contract terms and surrounding circumstances made it clear, as in ***Panatown*** through the terms of the Duty of Care Deed, that the parties cannot be treated as having contracted for the benefit of the third party.

There are therefore contradictory views on the nature of the narrow ground (and *The Albazero* exception) but Flaux J must be correct in following the analysis in ***Panatown***. The 'rule of law' analysis would apply the narrow ground as the default rule but it would be necessary to consider any evidence in favour of disapplying it on the facts.

11.7.4 Relations with the promisee

The third party's relations with the promisee are most likely to be an issue where after the time of contracting the promisee changes their mind about the intention to confer a benefit on the third party. The result of such a change of mind might be either a refusal to bring a claim against the promisor for specific performance, or, if damages were recoverable on behalf of the third party, a refusal to hand over the sum recovered. Lord Denning MR believed that the third party could prevent both such refusals. In the Court of Appeal in ***Beswick v Beswick*** [1966] Ch 538, he suggested that the third party could compel the promisee to bring the claim by starting proceedings and joining the promisee as co-defendant. However, the majority in the Court of Appeal rejected this procedure, and their view is the more orthodox.

In ***Jackson v Horizon Holidays Ltd*** [1975] 1 WLR 1468, Lord Denning suggested that when the plaintiff recovered damages on behalf of the third-party beneficiaries under the contract, he held these damages as money had and received for the use of the third parties, who in theory could therefore recover the money from him by legal action if he refused to hand it over. Subject to the proviso that such damages appear rarely to be recoverable (see 11.7.3), Lord Denning's suggestion would seem to be correct. In ***Darlington Borough Council v Wiltshier Northern Ltd*** [1995] 1 WLR 68, Dillon and Waite LJJ would have found, if necessary, that damages obtained by the original contracting party were held on a constructive trust for the true owner of the property, relying on an analogy with ***Lloyd's v Harper*** (1880) 16 ChD 290.

11.8 Privity and imposing obligations upon third parties

The privity doctrine provides that a third party cannot be made subject to a burden in a contract to which he is not a party. There are some recognized exceptions to this principle at common law, although, as noted at **11.3.4**, the Law Commission Report and the Contracts (Rights of Third Parties) Act 1999 do not extend to this aspect of the doctrine.

11.8.1 Bailment

Bailment involves the delivery of goods under a contract by a bailor to the bailee for some purpose, e.g., dry-cleaning, repairing, safekeeping, and their subsequent return to the bailor after that purpose has been fulfilled.

In some circumstances the bailor will be bound by the terms of a sub-bailment entered into by the bailee, including any exemption clauses in that sub-bailment.

> For example, in **Morris v C. W. Martin & Sons Ltd** [1966] 1 QB 716, the owner of a mink stole (the bailor) sent it to a furrier (the bailee) for cleaning. The bailee sent the stole to a sub-bailee for cleaning on terms whereby the goods were 'held at the customer's risk'. Could the sub-bailee rely on this exemption clause when sued by the bailor? Lord Denning (*obiter*) considered that as the bailor had agreed that the bailee should pass the stole to the sub-bailee for the cleaning, she had impliedly consented to the cleaning taking place on the terms of that sub-bailment.

This principle was accepted and applied by the Privy Council in **K. H. Enterprise v Pioneer Container, The Pioneer Container** [1994] 2 AC 324.

> The plaintiff cargo owners had contracted for the carriage of their goods. The contract terms entitled the carriers to subcontract the carriage on any terms and carriage had been subcontracted to the defendants. The question was whether the plaintiffs were bound by a clause in the contract between the carriers and the defendants which provided that any disputes were to be determined in Taiwan (an exclusive jurisdiction clause). The Privy Council held that the defendants were bound because they had consented to the cargo being sub-bailed on the defendant's terms.

The bailor will therefore be affected by terms in a contract to which the bailor is not a party where the bailor expressly or impliedly consented to those terms. It was also important to the recognition of bailment that the defendants in **The Pioneer Container** were aware that the cargo belonged to the plaintiffs and not to the carriers.

The Court of Appeal in **Sandeman Coprimar SA v Transitos Transportes Integrales SL** [2003] EWCA Civ 113, [2003] 2 WLR 1496, applied the same principle in an interesting factual context.

> The case concerned the transportation of seals which needed to be attached to Scotch whisky imports into Spain in order to indicate that excise duty had been paid. If the seals were not used the importer was liable as guarantor for the amount of the excise duty. The importer entered into a contract with TTI for the transportation of nine cartons of seals from Spain to Scotland. However, the carriage was subcontracted to Spain-TIR who subcontracted the final part of the carriage to BCT. The goods were delivered to BCT but then lost. As a result the importer became liable to the Spanish authorities under the terms of the guarantee. One of the issues before the Court of Appeal was whether Spain-TIR was liable as bailee and whether the Convention on the Contract for the International Carriage of Goods by Road (CMR) governed the relationship.
>
> The Court of Appeal held that since the importer (the bailor) had implicitly authorized the conclusion of a chain of contracts on CMR terms and had thereby consented to and authorized the sub-bailments on terms, all the terms agreed between TTI and Spain-TIR (bailee and sub-bailee) also applied between the bailor (the importer) and Spain-TIR. This was the position on the basis of bailment or under principles of contract since the terms were held to constitute a collateral contract between the importer and

sub-bailee. However, under the CMR terms the importer could not sue Spain-TIR (which was not the first or last carrier or responsible for the loss, having transferred the goods to BCT). The CMR terms also provided that the guarantee payment was not recoverable.

The case is significant as Lord Phillips MR stated that this conclusion could be achieved either on the basis of sub-bailment on terms or because there were collateral contracts in place.

11.8.2 Restrictions on the use of chattels

Under a doctrine peculiar to land law, founded in the old case of *Tulk v Moxhay* (1848) 2 Ph 774, third parties can be subject to burdens of restrictive covenants affecting land. The vendor of land can attach restrictive covenants to that land which 'run with the land' and regulate its future use. Such covenants are enforceable by adjacent landowners, and bind all subsequent purchasers.

It was suggested by the Privy Council in *Lord Strathcona Steamship Co. Ltd v Dominion Coal Co. Ltd* [1926] AC 108, that this principle also applied to restrictions affecting the use of chattels in contracts which did not concern land if the third party purchased the chattel in question with notice of the restriction. In *Lord Strathcona*, it was held that where purchasers of a vessel had purchased it with knowledge of the existence of a charter relating to its use, the charterers could obtain an injunction to prevent the new owners from ignoring that charter. However, in *Port Line Ltd v Ben Line Steamers Ltd* [1958] 2 QB 146, Diplock J refused to follow *Lord Strathcona* on the basis that it was wrongly decided due to an inappropriate analogy with the land law cases which required the party enforcing the restriction to have retained an independent proprietary interest which would benefit from the restriction. The charterers in *Lord Strathcona* had no such independent proprietary interest. Diplock J also stated that even if the principle did apply, it could do so only where the remedy sought was an injunction to restrain inconsistent use and where the purchaser took with **actual** notice of the restriction.

It may be the case that *Lord Strathcona* is actually an application of the tort of **knowing** interference with contractual rights. This appears to have been the view held by Browne-Wilkinson J when he followed *Lord Strathcona* in *Swiss Bank Corporation v Lloyds Bank Ltd* [1979] Ch 548. A third party commits a tort if that third party interferes in an intentional or reckless manner with a contract, e.g. intentionally procuring a contractual party to break their contract (*Lumley v Gye* (1853) 2 E & B 216). The issue of the injunction in *Lord Strathcona* would equate with this in preventing the new owner from acting inconsistently with an existing charter contract of which it was aware when it purchased the ship.

The point was reconsidered by Hoffmann J in *Law Debenture Trust Corporation plc v Ural Caspian Oil Corporation Ltd* [1993] 1 WLR 138.

The case concerned the claims for compensation of companies which had traded in Russia and whose assets had been confiscated as a consequence of the Russian revolution. The shares in these companies had been sold to L, subject to an undertaking by the purchaser that any compensation would be paid to the original shareholders and that a similar undertaking would be secured from future purchasers. The purchaser sold the shares on to H Ltd without obtaining the undertaking, and H Ltd later transferred the shares to C Ltd. The allegation was that both H and C had taken the shares with knowledge of the covenant. A significant sum in compensation was paid and the original shareholders sought to recover it.

Hoffmann J had to consider whether they had an arguable case to do so. He considered there to be an arguable case on the basis of interference with a remedy which would otherwise have been available, namely the fact that H knew of the breach of covenant and could therefore have been forced to transfer the shares back to L in order to prevent the obligation between the shareholders and L being defeated. The transfer by H to C had eliminated the possibility of this remedy and constituted a tort.

(The Court of Appeal ([1994] 3 WLR 1221) overturned the decision on this point on the basis that the tort could not exist unless the transfer between H and C constituted an actionable wrong, and none existed.)

Hoffmann J specifically rejected a claim based on the principle in *Lord Strathcona* on the ground that the shareholders were seeking to use the principle to obtain compliance with a positive covenant when the principle could only ever permit the issue of an injunction to ensure compliance with a negative covenant. Hoffmann J stated specifically (at p. 144):

> One thing is beyond doubt: [the principle] does not provide a panacea for outflanking the doctrine of privity of contract.

The result is that the decision has failed to resolve the uncertainties surrounding the relationship between the **Lord Strathcona** principle and the tort of knowing interference with contractual rights, although it appears that they can be claimed as alternatives and so may not be the same.

Further reading

Reform

Adams and Brownsword, 'Privity of contract: That pestilential nuisance' (1993) 56 MLR 722.

Adams, Beyleveld, and Brownsword, 'Privity of contract: The benefits and burdens of law reform' (1997) 60 MLR 238.

Burrows, 'Reforming privity of contract: Law Commission Report No. 242' [1996] LMCLQ 467.

Flannigan, 'Privity: The end of an era (error)' (1987) 103 LQR 564.

Kincaid, 'Privity reform in England' (2000) 116 LQR 43.

Law Commission Consultation Paper, LCCP No. 121, *Privity of Contracts: Contracts for the benefit of third parties* (1991).

Law Commission Report No. 242, *Privity of Contracts: Contracts for the benefit of third parties*, Cm. 3329 (1996).

Smith, 'Contracts for the benefit of third parties: In defence of the third party rule' (1997)17 OJLS 643.

The Contracts (Rights of Third Parties) Act 1999

Andrews, 'Strangers to justice no longer: The reversal of the privity rule under the Contracts (Rights of Third Parties) Act 1999' [2001] CLJ 353.

Burrows, 'The Contracts (Rights of Third Parties) Act and its implications for commercial contracts' [2000] LMCLQ 540.

Macmillan, 'A birthday present for Lord Denning: The Contracts (Rights of Third Parties) Act 1999' (2000) 63 MLR 721.

Phang, 'On justification and method in law reform: The Contracts (Rights of Third Parties) Act 1999' (2002) 18 JCL 32.

Roe, 'Contractual intention under section 1(1)(b) and 1(2) of the Contracts (Rights of Third Parties) Act 1999' (2000) 63 MLR 887.

Stevens, 'The Contracts (Rights of Third Parties) Act 1999' (2004) 120 LQR 292.

Treitel, 'The battle over privity' in *Some Landmarks of Twentieth Century Contract Law* (Clarendon Press, 2002).

St Martin's Property

Coote, 'The performance interest, *Panatown,* and the problem of loss' (2001) 117 LQR 81.

Duncan Wallace, 'Assignment of rights to sue: Half a loaf' (1994) 110 LQR 42.

McKendrick, 'Breach of contract and the meaning of loss' [1999] CLP 37.

Palmer and Tolhurst, 'Compensatory and extra-compensatory damages: The role of the "*Albazero*" in modern damages claims' (1997) 12 JCL 1 and 97.

Palmer and Tolhurst, 'Compensatory and extra-compensatory damages: *Linden Gardens* and the "Lord Griffiths" principle' (1998) 13 JCL 143.

Burden

Devonshire, 'Sub-bailment on terms and the efficacy of contractual defences against a non-contractual bailor' [1996] JBL 329.

Gardner, 'The proprietary effect of contractual obligations under *Tulk v Moxhay* and *De Mattos v Gibson*' (1982) 98 LQR 279.

Phang, 'Sub-bailments and consent: *The Pioneer Container*' (1995) 58 MLR 422.

Tettenborn, 'Covenants, privity of contract and the purchaser of personal property' (1982) 41 CLJ 58.

12 Discharge by frustration: Subsequent impossibility

Summary of the issues

• **A contract will be discharged by frustration where, after the formation of the contract, an event occurs which renders further performance of the contract impossible, illegal, or something radically different from what was contemplated by the parties when they made the contract.** Whether the event is frustratory will be determined by examining that event in the light of the terms and context of the contract in order to determine whether the performance has become impossible or fundamentally different from that anticipated by the contract terms.

• However, the frustration doctrine is a residual doctrine and will not apply where the parties have made express provision in the contract for the risk event which occurs (*force majeure* clauses). It also appears that the doctrine will not apply to events which were foreseeable but not provided for in the contract.

• The frustration doctrine cannot be relied upon by a party where the event in question is attributable to the fault of that party. Fault in this context includes breach of contract but also instances where the event in question results from the exercise of a choice by that party.

• **Where the frustration doctrine applies, a frustratory event will automatically discharge both parties from performance of their future obligations under the contract.** The legal position in relation to obligations which have already fallen due for performance, or been performed, will be determined in accordance with the provisions of the Law Reform (Frustrated Contracts) Act 1943.

• The 1943 Act provides for benefits to be dealt with on a restitutionary basis, i.e. advance payments are in general terms recoverable although the court may permit the recipient of the payment to retain some or all of that payment to cover its expenses, and where a valuable benefit has been conferred in performing the contract prior to the frustratory event, the court may award that party a just sum which cannot exceed the value of the benefit to the recipient. The Act's treatment of the pre-existing rights and obligations of the parties and the purpose underlying the 1943 Act is the subject of academic debate.

12.1 Introduction

As we saw in Chapter 8, in general, the performance obligation in contracts is strict (see 8.2.1.1): the promisor guarantees to achieve a stipulated result, and any failure to achieve that result constitutes a breach. Such a rule would cause injustice if, through no fault of either party, the promisor were prevented from performing and yet was held liable for the breach. Of course, where the performance obligation is to do no more than to exercise reasonable care and skill, the fact that the stipulated result is not achieved because of some extraneous factor will not matter, provided the promisor has exercised such care and skill. But where the performance obligation is strict, the promisor must overcome extraneous interference in his performance unless the law provides some doctrine of excuse.

In English law a doctrine of excuse is provided by the law relating to frustration (see generally, Treitel, *Frustration and Force Majeure,* 2nd edn (Sweet and Maxwell, 2004). The doctrine provides residual rules governing intervening events, the effect of which on further performance of the contract is so emphatic that the contract is automatically brought to an end. However, it is important to appreciate that the frustration doctrine is a residual doctrine and will therefore not apply if the parties have provided in their contract that the contract will terminate upon some contingency, or at least that the parties will not be liable for loss arising out of an incident which is beyond the control of the parties. Such clauses are usually referred to as *force majeure* clauses and are express risk allocation provisions. Where there is a *force majeure* clause in the contract, that clause will usually be enforced by the courts (e.g., *J. Lauritzen AS v Wijsmuller BV, The Super Servant Two* [1990] 1 Lloyd's Rep 1). It is possible that if such a clause were to allow a party to escape a liability which would otherwise usually be regarded as falling on that party under the contract, the clause might be subject to control under the Unfair Contract Terms Act (UCTA) 1977 (see 7.6).

12.2 History of the frustration doctrine

Until the middle of the nineteenth century English law had no general doctrine to excuse contractual performance. The leading case denying the existence of a doctrine of excuse for non-performance was **Paradine v Jane** (1647) Al 26, 82 ER 897.

> In an action in debt for rent due on certain land the defendant had argued by way of defence that he had been deprived of possession of the land by the action of an enemy army. The defence failed; the defendant had promised to pay rent, and if he sought to be excused in particular circumstances he should have made provision for the circumstances in his contract.

It need hardly be said that this reasoning was somewhat unrealistic, for if contracts were to contain express provision for every possible eventuality which might interfere in the contractual performance they would become very long documents indeed!

The important change in the law came in **Taylor v Caldwell** (1863) 3 B & S 826.

> In **Taylor v Caldwell,** the defendants had agreed to allow the plaintiffs to use their hall for four concerts for a fee of £100 for each day. After this contract was entered into but before the day of the first concert, the hall was destroyed by fire. The plaintiffs were without a venue for the concerts, for which preparations were well advanced. The plaintiffs sought to recover for their loss from the defendants, who pleaded the accidental destruction of the hall as an excuse for their non-performance. The contract contained no express provision for such an eventuality. The court found for the defendants.

The principle of cases like *Paradine v Jane* was said to be limited to 'positive and absolute' contracts, which were contracts in which one party had guaranteed their performance irrespective of all risks. Not all contracts were of that type. Blackburn J said (at pp. 833–4):

Where, from the nature of the contract, it appears that the parties must from the beginning have known that it could not be fulfilled unless when the time for fulfilment of the contract arrived some particular specified thing continued to exist, so that, when entering into the contract, they must have contemplated such existence as the foundation of what was to be done; there, in the absence of any express or implied warranty that the thing shall exist, the contract is not to be construed as a positive contract, but as subject to an implied condition that the parties shall be excused in case, before breach, performance becomes impossible from the perishing of the thing without default of the contractor.

From this carefully guarded statement of law has grown a general doctrine of excuse for non-performance. The 'absolute contracts principle' has become very much the exception, although it is possible for the parties to create an absolute contract by specifying that all the risks of performance are to fall on a named party (see **12.6**).

12.3 Legal nature of the frustration doctrine

12.3.1 Implied term theory

In *Taylor v Caldwell* (1863) 3 B & S 826, Blackburn J based his finding that performance had been excused upon an implied term of the contract between the parties that the concert hall should continue in existence until the time for performance. It is not particularly surprising that Blackburn J chose to base his reasoning on an implied term, since at that time the courts were adamant that it was not their role to interfere in the contracts of the parties (see **1.4.2.2**). Reasoning based on an implied term enabled the court to say that it was doing no more than enforcing what was the true agreement (or intentions) of the parties, including such terms as were so obvious that they had not been expressed (see **6.4.2.2**). The implied term basis for the frustration doctrine continued well into the twentieth century (e.g., *Krell v Henry* [1903] 2 KB 740 and *F. A. Tamplin Steamship Co. Ltd v Anglo-Mexican Petroleum Products Co. Ltd* [1916] 2 AC 397, per Lord Loreburn). There is no doubt that at that time what was intended was a term implied *in fact* between the parties (see **6.4.2.2**).

12.3.2 Moving away from the implied term reasoning

As the frustration doctrine developed and the courts were willing to apply the doctrine of excuse to an increasingly wide range of circumstances, the notion of the doctrine resting on a term implied in fact between the parties became something of a fiction. This was acknowledged by the House of Lords in *Davis Contractors Ltd v Fareham Urban District Council* [1956] AC 696. Both Lords Reid and Radcliffe pointed out that in many circumstances in which it was admitted that the frustration doctrine should apply, the test for the implication of a term in fact would not be satisfied. Thus, when asked whether in given circumstances the contract would be discharged the parties would not reply 'Oh, of course' (*Shirlaw v Southern Foundries (1926) Ltd* [1939] 2 KB 206: see **6.4.2.2**); rather, they would be likely to consider whether the risk was one which had been or ought to be allocated between them by their contract.

The modern view of the frustration doctrine is generally regarded as expressed in the speech of Lord Radcliffe, who said (at pp. 728–9):

> [P]erhaps it would be simpler to say at the outset that frustration occurs whenever the law recognises that, without default of either party, a contractual obligation has become incapable of being performed because the circumstances in which performance is called for would render it a thing radically different from that which was undertaken by the contract…But, even so, it is not hardship or inconvenience or material loss itself which calls the principle of frustration into play. There must be as well such a change in the significance of the obligation that the thing undertaken would, if performed, be a different thing from that contracted for.

Lord Radcliffe was anxious to make the point that, although in many cases it made no difference whether the legal basis was said to be an implied term or the application of an objective rule of contract law independent of the parties' intention, in some circumstances it might. If in implying a term the parties' intention was the guiding factor, in many circumstances the court would be unable to agree to the discharge of further performance since cases of this kind arise precisely when the parties have no intention because they have not addressed their minds to the issue. In Lord Radcliffe's view there was good authority that actual intention was not relevant (*Hirji Mulji v Cheong Yue Steamship Co. Ltd* [1926] AC 497). Today, Lord Radcliffe's concern is less important, because the law of implied terms has also been modernized, so that the courts now recognize a power to imply terms in law on the basis that such terms are considered a necessary incident of contracts of a particular type (see 6.4.2.3). Such terms are no more than obligations imposed on the parties independently of intention, and there may be little difference between Lord Radcliffe's basis for the frustration doctrine and a basis of a term implied *in law*. In either case, the difficulty of the absence of actual intention on the part of the parties is overcome.

12.3.3 The construction theory

In *Davis Contractors Ltd v Fareham Urban District Council*, Lord Reid concluded that:

> frustration depends, at least in most cases, not on adding any implied term, but on the true construction of the terms which are in the contract read in the light of the nature of the contract and of the relevant surrounding circumstances when the contract was made.

This construction approach rejects the artificiality of the implied term approach and requires an assessment of the events that have occurred in the light of the agreed terms of the contract (viewed in the context of the nature of the contract) in order to determine whether the agreed performance is now impossible or of a fundamentally different nature.

In *Great Peace Shipping Ltd v Tsavliris Salvage (International) Ltd* [2002] EWCA Civ 1407, [2003] QB 678 (a common mistake case discussed at 13.4.1.3), Lord Phillips MR traced the theoretical basis for the frustration doctrine and concluded (at [73]) that 'the theory of the implied term is as unrealistic when considering common mistake as when considering frustration'. Instead, both doctrines rested upon 'a rule of law under which, if it transpires that one or both of the parties have agreed to do something which it is impossible to perform, no obligation arises out of that agreement'. In **Gryf-Lowczowski v Hinchingbrooke Healthcare NHS Trust** [2005] EWHC 2407 (Admin), [2006] ICR 425 at [49], Gray J cited the following statement of Lord Simon in **National Carriers Ltd v Panalpina (Northern) Ltd** [1981] AC 675 at p. 700, as indicating the nature of frustration:

> Frustration of a contract takes place when there supervenes an event 'without default of either party and for which the contract makes no sufficient provision' which so significantly changes the nature (not merely the expense or onerousness) of the outstanding contractual rights and/or obligations from what the parties could reasonably have contemplated at the time of its execution that it would be unjust to hold them to the literal sense of its stipulations in the new circumstances; in such case the law declares both parties to be discharged from further performance.

More recently, Moore-Bick LJ in **CTI Group Inc. v Transclear** [2008] EWCA Civ 856, [2008] Bus LR 1729 (for facts see 12.6.1), explained the operation of the doctrine in the following words:

> it is essential to the doctrine of frustration that the performance of the contract in the new situation should be fundamentally different from that originally contemplated. In deciding whether that is the case it is necessary to have regard to the general nature of the contract as well as its specific terms, the context in which it was made and the contemplation of the parties as to the range of circumstances in which it might come to be performed.

12.4 Frustrating events

It is usually said that the question of whether an event frustrates the contract is a question of law. That may be a confusing statement. In the first place, it draws attention away from what is really inevitable, that in every case it is largely dependent upon the relevant facts whether or not a contract is frustrated. The question of law is whether the relevant facts render the performance demanded 'radically different' from the performance which was required by the contract terms (**Davis Contractors v Fareham Urban District Council** [1956] AC 696: see 12.3.3). It may also be confusing in that, since such cases are not heard by a jury but by a judge sitting alone, it might be thought that the distinction between law and fact is of little consequence. It is relevant, however, to the question of whether an appellate court will be willing to overturn the finding of a first-instance judge, or of an arbitrator. Nevertheless, it is crucial to realize that most frustration cases involve sometimes complex issues of fact which relate to the central question of whether the contractual performance required has been so changed by circumstances beyond the control of the parties that one party should be excused from that performance. It is, therefore, almost impossible to provide a comprehensive list of the circumstances in which a contract will be held to be frustrated. All that may be attempted is to outline some common categories of frustrating event.

12.4.1 Impossibility

Subject to any express allocation of the risk (see **12.6.1**), the most straightforward examples of frustrating events are those where performance in accordance with the express terms of the contract has become impossible.

12.4.1.1 Physical destruction of the subject matter

In some cases the impossibility is due to physical causes, as in the leading case of ***Taylor v Caldwell*** (1863) 3 B & S 826, where the destruction of the concert hall made performance impossible (see **12.2**).

12.4.1.2 Death of a party to a personal contract

Similar to the physical destruction of something which is essential to performance of the contract is the death of one of the parties in a personal contract. Many contracts, such as contracts for the sale of goods, do not require that the performance be made by any particular person, so that death does not prevent actual performance. But certain contracts, especially those for the performance of some skilled service, demand performance by a stipulated person, who is usually one of the parties to the contract. In such a case it is clear that death of that party makes performance of the contract impossible (*Stubbs v Holywell Railway Co.* (1867) LR 2 Ex 311).

12.4.1.3 Temporary impossibility

Temporary impossibility will frustrate the contract if the impossibility is of such a nature and likely duration that the resumed contractual performance would be radically different from that which was envisaged by the terms of the contract. A strike, whether by the other party or by a third party, may render performance impossible for part of the contract term and, if there is no express provision to provide for this eventuality (although unlikely in practice), it will be necessary to assess the impact of the strike on the performance contracted for.

> For example, in *Pioneer Shipping Ltd v BTP Tioxide Ltd* [1982] AC 724, a charterparty for six or seven voyages to be made during a nine-month period was reduced to half that number of voyages by a strike at the port where the ship was to be loaded. The contract was held to be frustrated because the performance actually possible bore no relation to the performance contracted for.

12.4.2 Unavailability of the subject matter

In some circumstances contractual performance is prevented because something essential to performance is unavailable. Performance is not strictly *impossible*, because the thing still exists, but for reasons beyond the control of the parties, it may not be put to the use which they had intended. For example, in ***Gamerco SA v ICM/Fair Warning (Agency) Ltd*** [1995] 1 WLR 1226 (for facts see **12.8.2.1**), the stadium at which the band 'Guns 'N' Roses' was to play was declared unsafe, and no other venue could be made available in time, so that the contract to promote the concert was frustrated.

Common examples of frustration of this kind arise in shipping contracts. Thus, where a ship has been requisitioned so that it will be unavailable to the charterer on the delivery date, the contract is frustrated (***Bank Line Ltd v Arthur Capel & Co.*** [1919] AC 435). It will also be the case that an illness will frustrate a personal employment contract where the contract calls for performance on a particular day and on that day the party in question is unable to perform.

> In *Robinson v Davison* (1871) LR 6 Ex 269, the defendant's wife had been engaged to play the piano at a concert but was unable to play on the particular day through illness. The defendant was able to plead his wife's illness as a defence to an action for breach of contract.

12.4.2.1 Temporary unavailability

Particular problems are caused when the unavailability of the subject matter of the contract is only temporary. For example, although it is clear that incapacitating illness on the single day for performance of the contract amounts to frustration (see *Robinson v Davison*, above), it is less easy to state with certainty the effect of prolonged illness on a contract of employment which may call for performance over a period of months or years. It is clear that such illness will excuse the employee's performance for the period of the illness, and it may give the employer the possibility of terminating the employment contract upon notice. However, whether it will immediately frustrate the contract, will depend upon the particular circumstances. In *Marshall v Harland & Wolff Ltd* [1972] IRLR 90, the relevant considerations were stated to include: the terms of the contract, the length of the contract, the nature of the employment (i.e., whether the employee was the only person employed in that capacity and the need of the employer to fill the post), the nature of the relevant incapacity, the period for which it had continued, the period of past employment, and the prospects of recovery.

An interesting set of facts arose in ***Gryf-Lowczowski v Hinchingbrooke Healthcare NHS Trust*** [2005] EWHC 2407 (Admin), [2006] ICR 425.

> The question in the case was whether a consultant surgeon's contract of employment had been discharged by frustration. Concerns had been raised about the claimant's performance and he had been on special leave for almost two years. It had been recommended that the surgeon should undergo 'reskilling' at another NHS trust before resuming his employment. He had managed to get an agreement 'in principle' with another trust for a suitable reskilling placement. However, the defendant trust then informed him that his contract of employment had been frustrated and subsequently sent a critical report to the other trust so that the offer of the placement there was withdrawn.
>
> Gray J held that given the specialist nature of the surgeon's work, the fact that termination of the employment would have had such a catastrophic effect on his employment prospects, and the fact that there remained a realistic possibility that a reskilling placement could be found, the surgeon's obligations under his contract were not incapable of being performed and the contract had not been frustrated. (In any event, the Trust could not rely on the doctrine of frustration as its own actions had led to the withdrawal of the reskilling placement with the other trust; see the discussion of fault at **12.7**.)

Similarly, if there is an agreed means to perform a charterparty using a particular ship and the ship in question is temporarily unavailable, the question will be whether the contractual performance when resumed will constitute performance of a fundamentally different contract.

> In ***Jackson v Union Marine Insurance Co. Ltd*** (1874) LR 10 CP 125, a ship was chartered to proceed with all possible dispatch from Liverpool to Newport, and there to load a cargo to be shipped to San Francisco. The ship ran aground one day out of Liverpool, and was not ready to load until eight months later. The contract had imposed no particular time limit for performance. The court held that there was an implied term that the ship should arrive in Newport in time for completion of the contract within a reasonable time, so that the contract was frustrated by such a long delay. It would have constituted 'a different voyage'.

Nevertheless, where the charter of the ship is expressed to run for a given length of time, temporary unavailability will frustrate the contract only if it takes up a disproportionate amount of the whole contract period. This may mean having to judge the period of a likely interruption, without knowing when it will end.

> For example, in *F. A. Tamplin Steamship Co. Ltd v Anglo-Mexican Petroleum Products Co. Ltd* [1916] 2 AC 397, the court had to determine whether the requisition of a ship in February 1915, which was under charter until December 1917, frustrated the contract. The court said that it did not, no doubt in the belief that the war which had occasioned the requisition would be over in time to allow a substantial period of the charter to be used as intended.

With hindsight it is easy to see that the court was unduly optimistic!

This approach of attempting to judge the period of interruption is similar to the approach adopted when assessing whether the nature of a breach of an innominate term is sufficiently serious to constitute a repudiatory breach of contract (***Hong Kong Shipping Co. Ltd v Kawasaki Kisen Kaisha Ltd*** [1962] 2 QB 26 per Diplock LJ at pp. 65–6: see 8.5.5). This may not prove to be entirely appropriate as a test for determining whether a common mistake is sufficiently fundamental (per Lord Phillips MR in ***Great Peace Shipping Ltd v Tsavliris Salvage (International) Ltd*** [2002] EWCA Civ 1407, [2003] QB 679 at [83]) but similar assessments in relation to interruptions, or potential interruptions, are often required in the context of temporary unavailability and the doctrine of frustration (e.g., ***Bank Line Ltd v Arthur Capel and Co.*** [1919] AC 435, *F. A. Tamplin Steamship Co. Ltd v Anglo-Mexican Petroleum Products Co. Ltd* [1916] 2 AC 397, and ***National Carriers Ltd v Panalpina (Northern) Ltd*** [1981] AC 675).

However, it is clear that the individual circumstances are vital to any decision and that the test of the likely length of any interruption may not be the sole determining factor and may, on the facts of a case, be outweighed by other features. ***Edwinton Commercial Corporation v Tsavliris Russ (Worldwide Salvage & Towage) Ltd, The Sea Angel*** [2007] EWCA Civ 547, [2007] 2 All ER (Comm) 634, concerned a charter for up to twenty days of a vessel to enable the salvage company to remove the oil from a stricken vessel. It was held that this was not frustrated by the unlawful detention (based on environmental grounds) of the chartered ship by the local port authorities for a three-month period towards the end of that twenty days when the salvage vessel had just unloaded its last shuttle cargo of retrieved oil. The Court of Appeal held that the test of comparing the probable length of the delay with the unexpired duration of the charter was not the decisive test on these facts since it was very different to cases of requisition, seizure, and entrapment due to war or major conflict where it was not possible to negotiate out of the situation. The timing issue was therefore only the starting point and one of many factors to consider. In particular, this was very different to a supervening event which postponed or interrupted the purpose of the contract since this purpose had been largely performed and the only consequences of the detention were financial, i.e. liability to pay hire continued for longer. It followed that this charter had not been frustrated.

Interestingly, the Court of Appeal also stressed that a relevant factor and underlying rationale for the frustration doctrine was the justice of the outcome and whether, on the facts, it would be just to relieve the salvage company of the consequences of their contract or unjust to maintain the contract. (This case is discussed further in relation to foreseeability at 12.6.3.)

12.4.2.2 Unavailability of the agreed means of performance

Where there is an agreed means of performance and this means is unavailable, the contract will be frustrated. For example, in ***Nickoll and Knight v Ashton, Edridge and Co.*** [1901] 2 KB 126, the unavailability of a particular ship which was specifically named in the contract, was held to frustrate the contract. The ship was also specified in *Jackson v Union Marine Insurance Co. Ltd* (1874) LR 10 CP 125 (see **12.4.2.1**) and the fact that the vessel (or choice of two vessels) was named in *J. Lauritzen AS v Wijsmuller BV, The Super Servant Two* [1990] 1 Lloyd's Rep 1 (see **12.7**) was at the root of the frustration question in that case.

However, what if, in a contract of sale, the seller's **anticipated** source of supply fails without the fault of the parties? Does this amount to a failure of the agreed means of performance so that the contract is frustrated? Where that source of supply is in no way a condition of the contract, but merely represents the seller's planned means of meeting its obligations, the contract will not be frustrated by failure of that source (*Blackburn Bobbin Co. Ltd v T. W. Allen & Sons Ltd* [1918] 2 KB 467). The reason is that, unless otherwise agreed, the risk of failure of a source of supply lies with the seller, which is expected to arrange alternative supplies if its planned supply is unavailable. There is no reason why the buyer should know of, or be affected by, the seller's planned mode of performance.

It is equally clear that even where **both** parties anticipate a particular performance unless this can be said to be an 'agreed' means of performance its unavailability will not render performance in accordance with the contract terms an impossibility.

> In *Tsakiroglou & Co. Ltd v Noblee Thorl GmbH* [1962] AC 93, although **both** parties envisaged that the shipment from Port Sudan to Hamburg would be made via the Suez Canal, there was no express stipulation naming this route as the agreed means of performance. Accordingly, it was not possible to excuse contractual performance simply because the Suez Canal had been closed.

Thus where the seller is concerned about sources of supply, and wishes to commit only in so far as the seller believes it has available sources, the seller may make the source of supply a condition of the contract.

> For example, in *Howell v Coupland* (1876) 1 QBD 258, the seller specified that the crop to be sold (200 tons of potatoes) was to be grown in a particular field. The crop in this field failed so that the seller was able to deliver only eighty tons. It was held that the seller was not liable for non-delivery of the remainder since it had become impossible to perform in accordance with the contract term.

Given this term of the contract, it would have been a breach of contract to supply from any other source, although the buyer might have agreed to a variation in the contract terms if the seller had proposed it.

The matter is, however, more complicated where the contract envisages *two* possible sources of supply, one of which is destroyed, but only after contract performance has been allocated to it, and where the other source will be exhausted by other contracts. In such circumstances, in the absence of a *force majeure* clause, it would appear that the party's choice of which contract to allocate to the source which was destroyed will operate to prevent the contract from being frustrated (*J. Lauritzen AS v Wijsmuller BV, The Super Servant Two* [1990] 1 Lloyd's Rep 1: see **12.7**).

12.4.3 Supervening illegality

In some cases although performance may remain physically possible, the contract is frustrated because since the time of contracting there has been a change in the law which makes further performance of the contract illegal. The most obvious instance of such illegality is where there has been subsequent legislation (*Denny, Mott and Dickson v James B. Fraser & Co. Ltd* [1944] AC 265).

Where the illegality exists before the time of contracting there is no scope for the operation of the doctrine of frustration, and the case falls to be determined according to the rules relating to illegal contracts (see **Chapter 16**). **However, it is possible for a contract to become illegal after it has been entered into, but before completely performed, and this may amount to frustration.** For example, it is against the law to trade with the enemy (Trading with the Enemy Act 1939). If at the time of contracting the other party is not 'the enemy' such a contract is not, of course, illegal; but it may become so by subsequent declaration of war. If war is declared before the time for performance, the contract will be frustrated (*Fibrosa SA v Fairbairn Lawson Combe Barbour Ltd* [1943] AC 32).

Similar considerations apply to temporary illegality as applied in the cases of temporary impossibility or unavailability. The period of the interruption, or likely interruption, must be assessed against the contract term and nature of the contracted performance.

> Thus, in **National Carriers Ltd v Panalpina (Northern) Ltd** [1981] AC 675, vehicular access to a warehouse, leased to the defendants from January 1974 for ten years, was blocked by order of the local authority in May 1979 and it was anticipated that access would be blocked for a further twenty months. The House of Lords held that in view of the length of the term and the period of the lease which would remain after this interruption, the defendants could not rely on frustration as a defence to an action for unpaid rent.

12.4.4 Frustration of the common purpose of both parties

In some circumstances, performance of the contract may still be possible but it would be a radically different performance from that originally envisaged by *both* parties. In other words, the event has destroyed the purpose of the contract for both parties, thereby frustrating the contract. The classic examples of this possible failure of the common purpose are the so-called 'coronation' cases, in which a series of contracts became devoid of purpose when the celebrations connected with the coronation of King Edward VII were cancelled because of the King's illness. However, this frustratory event is strictly interpreted since frustration of purpose might otherwise easily become a means to escape from a contract for economic reasons. **Therefore, the contract will not be frustrated unless the contract is wholly devoid of purpose for *both* of the parties.**

> In **Krell v Henry** [1903] 2 KB 740, the plaintiff sued the defendant for the balance due on a contract for the hire of rooms from which to view the coronation procession. The procession was cancelled after the hire contract was entered into. The Court of Appeal held that the contract was frustrated. Vaughan Williams LJ laid considerable emphasis upon the fact that it was known to both parties that the subject of the contract was not merely the hire of a room, but was the provision of a view of the coronation procession. On this basis, viewing the coronation procession was the 'foundation of the contract' for both parties so that its cancellation destroyed this common foundation. Vaughan Williams LJ distinguished this situation from a contract hiring a cab to go to Epsom on Derby Day. He stated 'I do not think that…the happening of the race would be the foundation of the contract' since, without additional qualification, it is simply a contract to drive to Epsom.

This case is usually compared with the decision in *Herne Bay Steam Boat Co. v Hutton* [1903] 2 KB 683.

> The contract in that case was for the hire of a boat to observe the King's review of the Navy and for a day's cruise round the fleet. The naval review was cancelled because of the King's illness but it was still possible to cruise round the fleet. The Court of Appeal held that the contract was not frustrated.

Analysis

Distinguishing these cases

The distinction between the cases appears to be that in *Herne Bay* the particular purpose was not the subject of the contract, i.e. the contract was not intended by the parties to stand or fall upon whether the naval review took place. The distinction is also sometimes explained in terms of the fact that part of the purpose in the latter case (the cruise round the fleet) was not frustrated (per Stirling LJ). The approach of the Court of Appeal in the *Herne Bay* case appears to be consistent with the approach of the courts to impracticability (see **12.4.5**), so that *Krell v Henry* may be something of an exceptional case.

12.4.5 Impracticability

Impracticability is the term used to describe circumstances in which, although contractual performance is technically still possible, it would impose a burden on one party quite different from that contemplated at the time of contracting. In the United States, the Uniform Commercial Code (UCC) has adopted a standard of impracticability rather than impossibility for all cases (UCC §2–615), with the express intention of replacing the absolute test of impossibility with a test of what is 'commercially impossible'. In other words, where performance under the contract is theoretically possible but commercially out of the question, the contract would be frustrated.

English law has largely been unwilling to accept that impracticability frustrates the contract, although there are indications that some extreme forms of impracticability might. The cases on unavailability are an example of this ambivalence. In *Jackson v Union Marine Insurance Co. Ltd* (1874) LR 10 CP 125 (see **12.4.2.1**), the contract could ultimately have been performed but was nevertheless held to be frustrated. In *Blackburn Bobbin Co. Ltd v T. W. Allen & Sons Ltd* [1918] 2 KB 467, however, the court was unwilling to find the contract frustrated despite the fact that not only had the seller's anticipated supply failed, but it was effectively impossible to get supplies of the kind of timber required.

The leading authority on impracticability in English law is *Davis Contractors Ltd v Fareham Urban District Council* [1956] AC 696.

The contractors agreed to build seventy-eight houses for the council over a period of eight months for a fixed price. A shortage of skilled labour caused the work to take a further fourteen months. The contractors argued that the contract had been frustrated by the delay, and that they were therefore entitled to payment on the basis of *quantum meruit* (see **10.5.4**), rather than the agreed price. The House of Lords held that the contract was not frustrated.

As has already been noted (see **12.3.2**), Lord Radcliffe said: 'it is not hardship or inconvenience or material loss itself which calls the principle of frustration into play'.

It is also accepted that the fact that performance of the contract will cost more than was originally anticipated is not, of itself, enough to frustrate the contract. This point is aptly illustrated by the facts and decision in *Amalgamated Investment & Property Co. Ltd v John Walker & Sons Ltd* [1977] 1 WLR 164.

The case concerned a contract for the purchase of property which had been advertised as suitable for redevelopment and which had been purchased for that purpose. It was held that the purchase contract had not been frustrated despite the fact that development was more or less impossible because the property had been listed as a building of special architectural or historic interest. Performance of the contract was not radically different from the performance contemplated by the parties since there was no contractual term that the property should continue to be available for development at the date of completion. It was simply a contract to purchase the specified property. The impact of the listing was economic, i.e. the property was worth £1.5m less than the purchase price because the listing affected the redevelopment value but it did not prevent the contract for purchase being carried out in accordance with its terms.

In *Thames Valley Power Ltd v Total Gas & Power Ltd* [2005] EWHC 2208 (Comm), [2006] 1 Lloyd's Rep 441, gas had been supplied under an agreement which contained a pricing mechanism and *a force majeure* clause and when the price of gas rose sharply so that supply under the terms of the pricing mechanism was uneconomic, the supplier issued a *force majeure* notice (i.e., stating that an event outside its control had occurred) with the result that it would cease supplies until the price fell. However, the rising cost of gas had made it less profitable to perform the supply contract obligations but had not made it impossible. The court therefore refused to relieve the supplier of its obligations.

This principle was also demonstrated by cases arising out of the closure of the Suez Canal, after the Anglo-French invasion in 1956.

In *The Eugenia, Ocean Tramp Tankers Corporation v V/O Sovfracht* [1964] 2 QB 226 (see also *Tsakiroglou & Co. Ltd v Noblee Thorl GmbH* [1962] AC 93), a charterparty provided for a voyage from Genoa via the Black Sea to India. The contract did not expressly provide, but both parties assumed, that the voyage would be made through the Suez Canal. The charterers claimed that the contract was frustrated by the closure of the canal. The Court of Appeal held that the contract was not frustrated.

However, the reasoning of the court suggests that some degrees of impracticability falling short of impossibility would frustrate the contract. Although the ship was actually trapped in the canal, the case was argued on the basis that it would have been possible not to enter the Canal and to complete the voyage by going the long way round via the Cape of Good Hope. The court might simply have said that since performance was not impossible the contract must stand. Instead, Lord Denning MR compared the total length in days of the voyage via Suez (108 days) with the length via the Cape (138 days), and found that the latter was not entirely disproportionate to the former. He said that the fact that performance was more onerous or more expensive was not enough to frustrate the contract, but that it would be frustrated where it would be 'positively unjust to hold the parties bound'. From this reasoning it may be implied that Lord Denning did not believe impossibility to be the only test of frustration.

As discussed above (see **12.4.2.2**), a party who is concerned that the cost of performance may in some circumstances prove greater than anticipated may protect himself by making express provision in the contract that performance in a particular way is a condition of the contract. Thus, in a case like *The Eugenia*, if the contract had stipulated that performance was to be via the Suez Canal, closure of the canal would have made performance impossible, rather than impracticable, and the contract would have been frustrated.

The issue of whether a contract is frustrated by impracticability is of particular importance during a period of severe inflation, such as that experienced by most western economies during the mid-1970s after the oil crisis. It is possible to view the increased cost of performance resulting from inflation as making the contractual performance something radically different from that which was originally undertaken. The law appears to exclude frustration in most cases (see *Thames Valley Power Ltd v Total Gas & Power Ltd* [2005] EWHC 2208 (Comm), [2006] 1 Lloyd's Rep 441 for an example) while admitting the possibility that a small number of cases might be so severely affected as to qualify. In ***British Movietonews Ltd v London & District Cinemas Ltd*** [1952] AC 166, Viscount Simon said (at p. 185):

> The parties to an executory contract are often faced, in the course of carrying it out, with a turn of events which they did not at all anticipate—a wholly abnormal rise or fall in prices, a sudden depreciation of currency, an unexpected obstacle to execution, or the like. Yet this does not in itself affect the bargain they have made. If, on the other hand, a consideration of the terms of the contract, in the light of the circumstances existing when the contract was made, shows that they never agreed to be bound in a fundamentally different situation which has now unexpectedly emerged, the contract ceases to bind at that point.

This statement is illustrative of the policy to use the frustration doctrine 'with great caution' and not allow it to 'become an escape route whenever there is an unexpected turn of events' (Adams and Brownsword, *Understanding Contract Law*, 5th edn (Sweet and Maxwell, 2007), p. 140).

12.5 **Contracts concerning land**

It has been a matter of doubt over many years whether the doctrine of frustration applies to contracts relating to interests in land. These doubts were expressed by the House of Lords in ***Cricklewood Property and Investment Trust Ltd v Leighton's Investment Trust Ltd*** [1945] AC 221 in the context of a lease. The purpose in taking the lease would clearly have been frustrated for a period, but in all probability not for very long by comparison with the full ninety-nine years of the lease. Therefore, the particular lease was held not to have been frustrated, but the House of Lords was divided in its reasoning. For two of their Lordships the frustration doctrine was potentially applicable but would rarely apply, since in most cases the frustration of purpose would be of short duration relative to the period of the lease. However, two members of the House of Lords considered that the frustration doctrine could never apply since a lease created a legal interest in land. It was this interest which constituted the subject matter of the lease contract, and the interest would survive even if it became impossible to use the leased premises.

The matter was reconsidered by the House of Lords in ***National Carriers Ltd v Panalpina (Northern) Ltd*** [1981] AC 675.

> A ten-year lease of a warehouse was deprived of its purpose for a period of twenty months by the closure of the only street allowing access by lorries. It was claimed that the lease had been frustrated. The House of Lords rejected that claim on the ground that after the disruption there would still be some three years of the lease to run.

A majority of their Lordships, however, accepted that in 'rare' circumstances a lease might be frustrated. Such occasions would be very infrequent for two reasons:

1. Since many leases run for terms of several years it is unlikely that a potentially frustrating event would take a sufficiently significant 'bite' out of the full term for actual frustration to occur.

2. The kind of major disaster which might frustrate even a long-term lease is usually provided for by an express term of the contract (see **12.6.1**).

It appears to be implicit in the reasoning in ***Amalgamated Investment & Property Co. Ltd v John Walker & Sons Ltd*** [1977] 1 WLR 164 (see **12.4.5**) that the doctrine of frustration may apply to contracts for the sale of land. Nevertheless, its operation in this context is subject to the fact that such contracts are affected by risk allocation rules (see **12.6**). Although the normal rule is that risk will pass on exchange of contracts, conveyancers may expressly delay the passing of risk until completion so that, for example, the risk of destruction of the property between contract and completion remains with the vendor and the vendor would need to ensure appropriate insurance cover. Even where there is no such express provision, this is still a matter of risk allocation, and the purchaser would cover the risk from exchange of contracts by taking out appropriate insurance.

12.6 Risk allocation and the foreseeability question

When circumstances intervene to frustrate a contract it may be said that a potential risk of the contract has materialized. Thus, if a party enters into a contract to hire a concert hall in several months' time, there is a risk that the concert hall will be destroyed in the meantime. The court must then decide whether that risk was to be borne by one or other of the parties (see also **12.7**). Thus, the mere fact that performance turns out to be impossible will not result in the contract being frustrated where one party took upon itself an obligation to perform in all the circumstances (see *Eurico SpA v Philipp Brothers* [1987] 2 Lloyd's Rep 215). In the absence of a very clear express provision, the courts may be faced with difficult questions of construction of the contract to determine what was undertaken.

12.6.1 Express risk allocation

Where one party is anxious not to have to bear a particular risk, that party may insert an express term in the contract, assuming that the other party agrees, allocating the risk to the other party. For example, where a manufacturer is anxious not to bear the risk of increased costs of performance in a long-term supply contract, the manufacturer may provide that the price to be paidw is to vary in proportion to some suitable index, such as an index of raw material costs. Equally, the contract may require one party to obtain an import or export licence. If the licence is refused by the authorities, it is then a question of construction whether the contract was frustrated or whether the party who failed to obtain it is liable for breach (see *Pagnan SpA v Tradax Ocean Transportation SA* [1987] 3 All ER 565).

In *Bangladesh Export Import Co. Ltd v Sucden Kerry SA* [1995] 2 Lloyd's Rep 1, BEI entered into contracts with SK for the import of sugar into Bangladesh. Import licences were required. The contract contained a term which said that licences were to be obtained by BEI, the buyer, and that 'the inability to obtain [an] import licence shall not be justification for declaration of ***force majeure***'. BEI took steps to obtain the necessary licences, but eventually licences were revoked and the imports prohibited. The Court of Appeal treated the express term as placing beyond doubt the possibility of frustration of the contract. The contract provided that the risk was to fall on BEI.

Thus, where the contract contains an express provision for the particular event which is alleged to have frustrated the contract, the courts will not intervene. The only limit on this rule is that as a matter of construction of the express terms of the contract a court may hold that the provision in question was not intended to apply to a supervening event of the gravity which actually occurred (**Metropolitan Water Board v Dick Kerr & Co. Ltd** [1918] AC 119) or in the circumstances that occurred (**Select Commodities Ltd v Valdo SA, The Florida** [2006] EWHC 1137 (Comm), [2007] 1 Lloyd's Rep 1). As Tomlinson J stated in *The Florida*, at [6]: 'a clause may give one or other party certain rights or protections in certain circumstances, but those circumstances can still result in frustration of the contract unless all of their effects on the rights and liabilities of both parties are dealt with comprehensively'. On the facts the clause (a liberty clause) did not comprehensively deal with the positions of the parties in the event of supervening illegality. The clause gave the charterers no right to insist on any alternative performance, it merely dealt with how the cargo should be dealt with if loaded before an event occurred. Where performance was rendered impossible before this, the clause could have no application and the frustration doctrine applied.

In the sale and supply context, the risk of inability to supply will normally rest with the seller of the goods so that it is clear that the seller's non-performance will be the seller's fault, and not frustration, despite the fact that the failure of the supply is not directly down to the seller. It is therefore for the seller to seek to transfer or off-set that risk by an express provision.

> In **CTI Group Inc. v Transclear SA** [2008] EWCA Civ 856, [2008] Bus LR 1729. C had wanted to break the cartel run by Cemex in the Mexican cement market and therefore sought to acquire a large quantity of cement to be stored in a vessel moored off the Mexican coast for shipment into the Mexican market. C entered into contracts with the seller (T), who had in turn intended to secure the supply from an Indonesian supplier and later from a supplier in Taiwan. However, each supplier in turn came under pressure from Cemex not to supply the cement so that the seller had no source of supply. The arbitrator considered that performance of the supply contracts had become commercially impossible so that this excused the seller from performance. However, C argued that this was at the seller's risk and so amounted to breach rather than frustration. At first instance it was held that although the contract between C and T had become impossible to perform, this was not a case of frustration since, as a matter of law, the risk of inability to supply was the seller's and it was for the seller to guard against that risk in dealings with the suppliers or by making delivery under the contract with the buyer conditional on the cement being available for delivery. The Court of Appeal agreed and dismissed the appeal. Delivery remained physically and legally possible, albeit that the seller's supplier had chosen not to make the goods available. That could not constitute frustration of the seller's contract.

12.6.2 Foreseeable risks but not provided for in the contract

It follows from the above that frustration applies only to contracts affected by events which have not been foreseen, in the sense that they have not been expressly provided for in the contract. In the law generally, however, the notion of foreseeability embraces not only things which have been provided for, but also those which a reasonable person would have foreseen even if the particular parties did not foresee them (e.g., the test for remoteness of damage: see **9.9.2**). This idea has been extended in some cases to the doctrine of frustration, so that it is said that not only does frustration not apply to contracts in which the parties have made express provision, but it also does not apply to contracts in which the parties *could have made* express provision, in the sense that the risk was foreseeable.

In **Davis Contractors Ltd v Fareham Urban District Council** [1956] AC 696, Lord Radcliffe treated the foreseeability of the risk as one of the main reasons for finding the contract not to have been frustrated. In such circumstances it is presumed that failure to allocate the foreseeable risk is evidence of an intention that the risk be allocated to lie where it falls 'naturally'. Thus, in the case of a manufacturer's long-term contract to supply goods, in the absence of indexation of the price, the risk of increased cost of performance falls naturally on the manufacturer since the contract is for a fixed price. The seller in a sale of goods contract will generally bear the risk of a failure in the source of supply (***CTI Group Inc v Transclear SA*** [2008] EWCA Civ 856, [2008] Bus LR 1729 (for facts see **12.6.1**).

Nevertheless, it may be doubted whether the fact that the risk is foreseeable will exclude the operation of the doctrine of frustration in every case.

1. Many risks are 'foreseeable' without the probability of their occurrence being so great that the parties ought to provide for them (see **12.6.3**). Contracts are not planned to provide for every extreme and remote eventuality. If this were the position, it would make contract drafting a very lengthy process and would be commercially very inefficient.

2. Moreover, in some cases it has been held that the fact that the parties actually foresaw a particular risk but made no express provision for it did not prevent the frustration doctrine intervening to stop the risk lying where it fell naturally.

In ***The Eugenia*** [1964] 2 QB 226 (the facts are given at **12.4.5**), Lord Denning MR said (at p. 239):

> It has frequently been said that the doctrine of frustration only applies when the new situation is 'unforeseen' or 'unexpected' or 'uncontemplated', as if that were an essential feature. But it is not so. It is not so much that it is 'unexpected', but rather that the parties have made no provision for it in their contract. The point about it, however, is this: If the parties did not foresee anything of the kind happening, you can readily infer that they have made no provision for it. Whereas, if they did foresee it, you would expect them to make provision for it. But cases have occurred where the parties have foreseen the danger ahead, and yet made no provision for it in the contract...see **W. J. Tatem Ltd v Gamboa** [1939] 1 KB 132.

In ***The Eugenia*** the parties knew of the danger that the Suez Canal might be closed but, unable to agree on what provision should be put in the contract, had agreed to 'leave the problem to the lawyers' should it materialize. If an actually foreseen but unprovided for risk may constitute a frustrating event, the same should be true of a risk which was foreseeable but not actually foreseen by these parties.

12.6.3 Foreseeability as an aid to construction

In the light of ***The Eugenia***, there cannot be a rule of law that frustration will not apply where the risk was foreseeable. The same would appear to be true even where the more qualified test of 'reasonably foreseeable' risk is used. In any case, that test is too vague to provide proper guidance.

Nevertheless, there is no denying the relevance of foreseeability to the question of allocation of risk. The courts are entitled to assess the degree of foreseeability of a risk in determining whether the parties intended the risk to lie where it falls naturally. The greater the probability of the risk materializing, the more likely it is that the parties did intend the inherent risk allocation of their contract. On the other hand, where the degree of probability is close to zero, the difficulty of determining the nature of the risk and of agreeing on its allocation may outweigh the likelihood of the risk maturing. As in ***The Eugenia***, the parties may prefer to leave the matter to be sorted out later. In those circumstances a presumption of allocation of the risk based on foreseeability would defeat the intentions of the parties, and it would be preferable to find the contract frustrated.

In ***Edwinton Commercial Corporation v Tsavliris Russ (Worldwide Salvage & Towage) Ltd, The Sea Angel*** [2007] EWCA Civ 547, [2007] 2 All ER (Comm) 634 (for facts see **12.4.2.1** above), it was clear that the risk of government detention of the salvage vessel was foreseeable given the environmental concerns about pollution from the stricken vessel. The Court of Appeal considered that it was essentially a question of using foreseeability as an aid to construction so that the less foreseeable an event the more likely it is that the end result will be frustration of the contract. On the facts in ***The Sea Angel*** the risk was foreseeable and the general risk had been covered by a special protection and indemnity clause in the charter. It followed that there could be no frustration.

Rix LJ summarized the position on foreseeable and foreseen events (at [127]) as follows:

> In a sense, most events are to a greater or lesser degree foreseeable. That does not mean that they cannot lead to frustration. Even events which are not merely foreseen but made the subject of express contractual provision may lead to frustration: as occurs when an event such as a strike, or a restraint of prices, lasts for so long as to go beyond the risk assumed under the contract and to render performance radically different from that contracted for. However...the less that an event, in its type and its impact, is foreseeable, the more likely it is to be a factor which, depending on other factors in the case, may lead on to frustration.

12.7 **Fault**

The doctrine of frustration applies only where the supervening event is beyond the control of the parties. It goes without saying that where performance has become impossible because of one party's breach, that party cannot claim that the contract is frustrated, and the other party may well be entitled to treat the contract as repudiated (in addition to recovering damages for any loss caused: see 8.4).

> In *The Eugenia* (discussed above at **12.4.5**), a clause in the contract provided that the chartered vessel was not to be taken into a war zone without the owner's consent. The vessel entered the Suez Canal in breach of this clause and became trapped when the canal was blocked. Therefore the charterers could not rely on the fact that they were trapped in the Suez Canal as frustrating the contract because this position was attributable to their own breach of contract.

The law goes further, however, and says that even in the absence of breach of contract, a party may not rely on the frustration doctrine when the supervening event results from some positive action of that party, i.e. is self-induced. The leading authority is ***Maritime National Fish Ltd v Ocean Trawlers Ltd*** [1935] AC 524, a decision of the Privy Council on appeal from Canada.

> Fishing boats using 'otter trawls' required a licence from the Minister of Fisheries. The defendants wished to operate five such boats, one of which was chartered from the plaintiffs. They duly applied for five licences, but were granted only three. They were invited by the minister to nominate the boats to which the licences would apply, and did not nominate the boat chartered from the plaintiffs. They then claimed that the charter of that boat was frustrated. Their claim was rejected. If they had wanted they could have

applied one of their three licences to the boat in question, so that it was their choice rather than the action of the minister which deprived the charter of the boat of its purpose. The supervening event was not beyond their control, and so did not frustrate the contract.

It might be assumed that if the defendants had chartered all their boats, so that two charters would have been without purpose whichever boats were nominated, the court might have been more willing to find that the two had been frustrated. However, *in J. Lauritzen AS v Wijsmuller BV, The Super Servant Two* [1990] 1 Lloyd's Rep 1 (discussed by McKendrick [1990] LMCLQ 153 and Hedley [1990] CLJ 209, and see the discussion in Peel, *Treitel's The Law of Contract,* 12th edn (Sweet and Maxwell, 2007), pp. 970–1), the Court of Appeal took a very strict line, and indicated that any act of choice by one of the parties would prevent the supervening event from being beyond that party's control, and so prevent the contract being frustrated. Once the impossibility of performance was attributable to the decision of one of the parties, whether or not amounting to breach of contract or negligence, it would be self-induced and so not frustration.

In **The Super Servant Two**, the defendants agreed to transport the plaintiffs' oil rig on one of two named barges. By an internal management decision, not communicated to the plaintiffs, the defendants allocated the task to the *Super Servant Two*, and allocated other tasks to the other named vessel. The *Super Servant Two* then sank, and the defendants claimed that the contract was frustrated, while the plaintiffs claimed that the contract was still physically capable of being performed but for the defendants' choice of vessel.

The Court of Appeal held that there was an alternative so that the sinking of *The Super Servant Two* did not automatically bring the contract to an end. It was the defendants' choice or election to allocate the other vessel to another contract. Accordingly, the defendants remained liable even though the loss was not due to any breach of contract or negligence.

The court does not appear to have considered whether that would be the case where the choice between the modes of performance lay entirely with the defendants, and the choice was made and communicated to the plaintiffs before the time of the allegedly frustrating event. The court also indicated that the defendants could have altered their risk by including a *force majeure* clause to provide for what was to happen in these circumstances, but had not done so. Therefore, the risk of being unable to perform and having no excuse rested on the defendants. This decision illustrates the courts' preference for the use of an express provision rather than reliance on the frustration doctrine and its associated consequences.

It follows from that analysis that a negligent act which results in impossibility of performance may not frustrate the contract. In **Taylor v Caldwell** (1863) 3 B & S 826, Blackburn J clearly believed that **if** the destruction of the concert hall had been caused by the negligence of the owners then they could not have been excused. In many cases, however, the issue may be decided simply on the basis of the burden of proof, since a party alleging that a contract is not frustrated because the impossibility is caused by the default of the other party must prove that default (**Joseph Constantine Steamship Line Ltd v Imperial Smelting Corporation Ltd** [1942] AC 154).

In *Joseph Constantine Steamship Line Ltd v Imperial Smelting Corporation Ltd*, the appellants chartered a ship to the respondents, with the intention that the ship should proceed to Australia to load. Before the ship could sail its boiler exploded, causing such a delay that there could be no doubt that the contract was discharged. The reason for the explosion was never discovered, although the respondents suspected that the appellants had been negligent and sought to argue that the frustration doctrine should not apply unless the appellants could prove that they had not been negligent.

The House of Lords rejected this argument. On the contrary, the burden of proving a negligent breach of the contract lay on the respondents, and in the absence of proof, the contract was discharged by frustration.

12.8 Legal effects of frustration

 Key point

The basic effect of frustration is automatically to bring the contract to an end for the future, irrespective of the wishes of the parties (***Hirji Mulji v Cheong Yue Steamship Co. Ltd*** [1926] AC 497). In this respect, discharge by frustration is significantly different from discharge by breach, where the party adversely affected may elect whether or not to treat the contract as repudiated (see **8.4.2**).

In the *Hirji Mulji* case a ship, the subject of a charterparty, was requisitioned, but the owners asked the charterers if they were willing to wait a little longer, because they believed the ship would soon be released. The charterers agreed, but when release eventually came, later than anticipated, they refused to take the vessel. The owners argued that the charterers had elected to affirm the contract, despite the potentially frustrating event. The House of Lords held that there was no scope for such an election. If the event were sufficiently serious to frustrate the contract, the effect was automatic discharge of all further obligations.

12.8.1 Financial implications of the common law rule

The original common law rule was that frustration caused all primary obligations (to perform) and secondary obligations (to pay damages) which had not accrued to terminate as from the time of the frustrating event, while obligations which had matured before the time of the frustrating event remained to be performed. Under this rule the distribution of loss resulting from frustration might appear quite arbitrary since the loss is said to 'lie where it falls'.

12.8.1.1 Money paid or payable in advance

Where the contract provided for a payment (not necessarily full payment) in advance of performance, the original common law rule was that money paid could not be recovered in the event of frustration, and if not actually paid would remain payable despite the frustration (***Chandler v Webster*** [1904] 1 KB 493).

However, the House of Lords in ***Fibrosa SA v Fairbairn Lawson Combe Barber Ltd*** [1943] AC 32, held that an advance payment could be recovered where there had been a total failure of consideration (see **10.5.1**).

The appellants ordered machinery from the respondents to be delivered to the appellants' factory in Poland. The appellants paid £1,000 in advance under the contract. The contract was frustrated by the German invasion of Poland, and the appellants sought the return of the £1,000. The respondents resisted their request because they had already expended large sums in partial performance of the contract. The appellants were successful in recovering their advance payment. There had been a total failure of consideration in the sense that the appellants had received none of the performance they had contracted for, and on that basis they were entitled to a restitutionary remedy to recover the money paid.

The problem with this analysis was that in remedying the hardship which would otherwise have fallen on the party making the advance payment, the House of Lords imposed as great a hardship on the recipient of the advance payment, who had incurred expenses in part performance. It was very likely that the contract had provided for advance payment as a form of insurance against precisely the kind of risk which materialized so that the court had interfered in the allocation of risk agreed between the parties, depriving the manufacturers of that insurance.

12.8.1.2 Payment on completion situations

Where the contract called for full performance on one side before payment by the other, the result of frustration was to leave the party who had partially performed before the time of the frustrating event without any payment for the work done.

> In **Appleby v Myers** (1867) LR 2 CP 651, the plaintiffs had contracted to install and maintain all machinery in the defendant's factory, payment to be made upon completion. Before the task of installation had been completed, the factory and machinery were destroyed by fire so that the contract was frustrated. Because the payment obligation was not due to be performed by the time of the frustrating event, the plaintiffs were not entitled to any payment for the work done.

In this case the defendants received no lasting benefit from the plaintiffs' performance, since the machinery was destroyed, but the same result would apply at common law where a lasting benefit was conferred. In *Cutter v Powell* (1795) 6 TR 320 (see **8.6.2.2**), the contract was frustrated by the seaman's death before completion of the voyage. His services before death were a benefit to his employer, but his estate was still unable to recover any payment since the contract provided for payment only on completion.

12.8.1.3 The need for reform

The common law rule on the effect of frustration was regarded as unsatisfactory for the above reasons, and so changes were made to the parties' pre-frustration obligations by the Law Reform (Frustrated Contracts) Act (LR(FC)A) 1943. Nevertheless, it is still important to understand the common law background, and to remember that the Act has no impact on the issue of whether a contract has been frustrated. It is also important to remember that **the automatic discharge of future obligations when frustration does occur is a common law principle.**

12.8.2 The Law Reform (Frustrated Contracts) Act (LR(FC)A) 1943

12.8.2.1 Money paid or payable in advance: s. 1(2)

Where the contract provides that all or part of the price shall be payable in advance then, by s. 1(2) of the LR(FC)A 1943, money actually paid is recoverable, and money payable but not yet paid at the time of the frustrating event need not be paid. It is not necessary to demonstrate a total failure of consideration for this rule to operate.

Section 1(2) is, however, subject to an important proviso intended to meet the objection to the *Fibrosa* case noted at **12.8.1.1** above.

 Key point

> Where the person entitled to the advance payment under the contract has incurred expenses directly related to the performance of the contract before the frustrating event occurs, the court has a discretion to allow the recipient of the advance payment to retain or recover such part of the advance payment as the court considers just having regard to all the circumstances.

The court's discretion is limited in two ways:

1. **The expenses which the court may determine that the recipient is entitled to retain from the advance payment cannot exceed the total amount payable in advance under the contract.** If the parties are to be assumed to have agreed to the advance payment as insurance for the party who has the substantial performance obligation, their estimate of the necessary insurance cover should be adhered to.

2. **In addition, the sum permitted by the court to cover these expenses may not exceed the value of the actual expenses incurred.**

The need for such provision is unclear, since it seems unlikely that a court should find it just to allow retention or recovery of a sum greater than the actual expenses incurred. The limitation appears to be intended to prevent the advance payment being regarded as automatically forfeit upon frustration, and may also be intended to prevent recovery of any allowance for profit as opposed to actual cost of performance, although in practice the distinction may be hard to draw (see LR(FC)A 1943, s. 1(4)). Thus s. 1(2) is not intended to allow the court a general discretion to permit recovery of expenses. In particular, it cannot be used at all, because it will not apply, to allow for the recovery of expenses where there is no advance payment.

One factor likely to affect the court's assessment of what is just in the circumstances is whether the expenses incurred may be recovered in some other way. For example, in the *Fibrosa* case, it may be that the machinery was not so peculiar to the appellants' needs that it could not be sold to an alternative buyer. Such a sale would 'mitigate' the loss caused by frustration (see **9.9.3**) so that the expenses should not be allowed to be retained or recovered out of the advance payment.

It has been suggested (see, e.g. Haycroft and Waksman [1984] JBL 207 and McKendrick, 'Frustration, restitution and loss apportionment' in Burrows (ed.), *Essays on the Law of Restitution* (Oxford University Press, 1991) that it might in many circumstances be 'just' to divide the loss between the parties, allowing retention or recovery of half of the expenses incurred. However, where the advance payment is a genuine form of insurance for one of the parties, freely negotiated between the parties, such an approach would seem to be undue interference in the parties' contract.

Until comparatively recently there was no reported decision on the operation of s. 1(2) and its proviso. However, the issue arose in *Gamerco SA v ICM/Fair Warning (Agency) Ltd* [1995] 1 WLR 1226.

A contract to promote a rock concert was frustrated by the closure of the stadium on safety grounds. Some US$412,000 had been paid in advance to the defendants, who were assumed, for want of concrete evidence, to have had preparatory expenses of US$50,000. The plaintiff promoters had themselves incurred expenses of around US$450,000. The only issue for Garland J was how to apply the proviso. He considered the suggestions which had been put forward concerning how this discretion should be exercised, namely 'total retention' and 'equal division', before coming to the conclusion that the invitation to do what he considered just left him 'a broad discretion…to do justice…and to mitigate the possible harshness of allowing all loss to lie where it has fallen'.

Putting this into practice, and mindful of the relatively low level of expenses incurred by the defendants by comparison with the losses faced by the promoters, the judge ordered repayment of the full amount paid in advance by the plaintiff promoters to the defendants, without deduction.

Garland J was reluctant to believe that the advance payment stipulated for was intended to be a form of insurance against loss under the contract. Consequently, the judge did not believe he was depriving the defendants of a bargained-for advantage under the contract. It is possible to imagine that the judge was influenced in part by the failure of the defendants to prove in detail the exact extent of their lost expenditure. (This result has, however, been criticized: see Carter and Tolhurst (1996) 10 JCL 264, who argue that there is no discretion to award a nil-expenses sum once expenses are proved.)

12.8.2.2 Performance conferring a valuable benefit and the award of a just sum: s. 1(3)

Where no advance payment is provided for under the contract, there is no entitlement to compensation for expenses incurred in performance of a contract which has been frustrated.

However, by s. 1(3) of the LR(FC)A 1943, if performance confers a valuable benefit on the other party before the frustrating event occurs, the court may award the performing party such sum as it considers just in the circumstances.

1. The sum may not exceed the value of the benefit to the party receiving it.

2. In assessing what would be just, the court must consider expenses incurred by the party receiving the benefit (including the question of whether an advance payment was made and whether the performing party was allowed to retain some or all of this to cover their expenses under the proviso to s. 1(2)).

3. The court must also consider the effect of the frustrating event on the benefit received.

The practical relevance of this provision is limited by the fact that the performance must have conferred a valuable benefit, in the sense of a tangible or long-term benefit. For example, there could be no s. 1(3) claim in *Gamerco v ICM* in respect of the plaintiffs' expenditure incurred in preparing the stadium for the concert because that expenditure had not resulted in any tangible benefit to the defendants at the time of discharge for frustration.

In addition, the drafting of s. 1(3) is complex, to say the least. Its operation was considered in *BP Exploration Co. (Libya) Ltd v Hunt (No. 2)* [1979] 1 WLR 783.

The important judgment is that of Robert Goff J at first instance, which was subsequently affirmed by the House of Lords ([1983] 2 AC 352).

The case arose out of a contract between the concessionaire of a potential oil field in Libya and the oil company who were to carry out the prospecting and development of the field. Four years after oil production began, the contract was frustrated by the Libyan government's nationalization of the plaintiff oil company's interest in the oil field. The oil company sought a just sum from the defendant concessionaire for benefits allegedly conferred by its performance under the contract before the time of nationalization.

Robert Goff J said (at p. 801):

> First, it has to be shown that the defendant has, by reason of something done by the plaintiff in, or for the purpose of, the performance of the contract, obtained a valuable benefit (other than a payment of money [to which s. 1(2) applies]) before the time of discharge. That benefit has to be identified, and valued, and such value forms the upper limit of the award. Secondly, the court may award to the plaintiff such sum, not greater than the value of such benefit, as it considers just having regard to all the circumstances of the case…

According to Robert Goff J, the correct approach is therefore for the court to:

1. identify and value the benefit to the party receiving it (this value forms the upper limit of any award under s. 1(3))

2. decide what just sum, up to that limit, to award to the party conferring that benefit.

What is the position if the frustration destroys the 'benefit'?

A key matter not entirely clear under s. 1(3) was whether the destruction of the benefit by the frustrating event, as in **Appleby v Myers** (1867) LR 2 CP 651 (see **12.8.1.2**), was relevant to the valuation of the benefit or to the assessment of the just sum. Robert Goff J said that the purpose underpinning the 1943 Act was the prevention of unjust enrichment, and he identified the benefit as being the end product of services rather than the services themselves. Therefore, if the end product was destroyed by the frustrating event, there would be no valuable benefit and there could be no award under s. 1(3) because there would be no unjust enrichment to remedy. Accordingly, in a case like **Appleby v Myers**, there would be no mechanism for recovery (in the absence of an advance payment under s. 1(2) and the exercise of the discretion under the proviso to allow retention of some or all of the advance payment to cover expenses). Thus, **Appleby v Myers** would be decided the same way under the 1943 Act.

It can be argued, however, that Robert Goff J's approach does not coincide with the true construction of the Act, since s. 1(3) speaks of a valuable benefit obtained **before the time of discharge**, which suggests that the valuation is to be made on the basis of circumstances existing immediately prior to the frustrating event. Moreover, s. 1(3)(b) provides that the effect of the frustrating event on the benefit is to be considered in assessing what 'the court considers just'. As Peel points out (*Treitel's Law of Contract,* 12th edn (Sweet and Maxwell, 2007), pp. 978–9), this alternative reading of the section leaves a wider discretion to the court without eliminating the possibility of following the narrower construction in appropriate circumstances. The court might award no sum at all if in its view that was what was just; but in other circumstances it would be able to award a just sum if justified. By linking destruction of the benefit to the setting of the upper limit to any award, rather than to the discretion to fix the sum payable, Robert Goff J perhaps unduly restricted that discretion.

12.8.2.3 Excepted contracts

The LR(FC)A 1943 does not apply to all contracts.

1. It does not apply where the parties have made express provision for the consequences of frustration (s. 2(3)).

2. Neither does it apply to wholly performed contractual obligations which may be severed from those which are affected by the frustrating event (s. 2(4)).

3. Certain types of contract for the carriage of goods by sea (s. 2(5)(a)), and contracts of insurance (s. 2(5)(b)), are excepted from the scope of the Act, since such contracts are themselves largely concerned with the allocation of risk, and it was not intended that the courts should interfere with such allocations.

4. Contracts for the sale of specific goods, which are frustrated by the goods perishing, are outside the terms of the Act (s. 2(5)(c)). The confusing wording of this final exception appears to reflect excessive caution on the part of the draftsman (see Atiyah, Adams, and MacQueen, *The Sale of Goods*, 12th edn (Pearson Longman, 2010), pp. 349–52).

Further reading

Treitel, *Frustration and Force Majeure*, 2nd edn (Sweet and Maxwell, 2004).

Coronation cases

Brownsword, 'Henry's lost spectacle and Hutton's lost speculation: A classic riddle solved?' (1985) 129 SJ 860.

McElroy and Williams, 'The Coronation cases' (1941) 4 MLR 241 and 5 MLR 1.

Self-induced frustration and the *Super Servant Two*

Hedley, 'Carriage by sea: Frustration and *force majeure*' [1990] CLJ 209.

McKendrick, 'The construction of *force majeure* clauses and self-induced frustration' [1990] LMCLQ 153.

Swanton, 'The concept of self-induced frustration' (1990) 2 JCL 206.

The Law Reform (Frustrated Contracts) Act 1943

Baker, 'Frustration and unjust enrichment' [1979] CLJ 266.

Carter and Tolhurst, 'Gigs n' restitution: Frustration and the statutory adjustment of payments and expenses' (1996) 10 JCL 264.

Clark, 'Frustration, restitution and the Law Reform (Frustrated Contracts) Act 1943' [1996] LMCLQ 170.

Haycroft and Waksman, 'Frustration and restitution' [1984] JBL 207.

McKendrick, 'Frustration, restitution and loss apportionment' in Burrows (ed.), *Essays on the Law of Restitution* (Oxford University Press, 1991).

McKendrick, 'The consequences of frustration: The Law Reform (Frustrated Contracts) Act 1943' in McKendrick (ed.), *Force Majeure and Frustration of Contract*, 2nd edn (Lloyd's of London, 1995).

Stewart and Carter, 'Frustrated contracts and statutory adjustment: The case for a reappraisal' [1992] CLJ 66.

Williams, *The Law Reform (Frustrated Contracts) Act 1943* (Stevens, 1944).

489

Part 4

Methods of policing the making of the contract

This Part considers those principles of the law of contract which prevent a contract apparently validly made from being enforced. Much of this policing has the effect of rendering the contract either void or voidable (see **3.2.2** and **8.1**) so that these doctrines are 'vitiating factors'. However, illegality (see **Chapter 16**) renders the contract unenforceable.

Chapter 13 examines non-agreement or 'common' mistake (initial impossibility) which, if the contract has made no provision for the risk in question, and if it is a fundamental common mistake, will render the contract void at common law. In the case of such mistakes, the parties are not denying that they reached agreement but allege that the contract was impossible from the outset so that the basis on which they entered into the agreement has been destroyed. This is linked to subsequent impossibility (frustration) discussed in **Chapter 12**. Both deal with impossibility and contractual risks, i.e. events outside the control of the parties. Frustration discharges the parties' future obligations under the contract, and is therefore similar in its effect to discharge for breach (see **Chapter 8**) but it is dealt with immediately prior to common mistake because both doctrines deal with the effect of impossibility in the absence of a contractual allocation of that risk. They need to be understood as dealing with the same type of problem, although the legal treatment of initial and subsequent impossibility is very different.

Until comparatively recently it was considered that a contract which was not void at common law for fundamental common mistake might nevertheless be voidable in equity. However, the Court of Appeal has decided that there is no such jurisdiction, thereby removing the previous remedial flexibility.

Chapter 14 examines the law of misrepresentation which renders contracts voidable if false statements (short of contractual promises) were made in order to induce the contract. **Chapter 15** examines the doctrines of duress and undue influence, which also regulate unfairness in the way in which the contract was made ('procedural unfairness'). These doctrines will also render the contract voidable if established. The related concept of whether there is a general doctrine of unfairness in bargaining or unconscionable bargaining is also discussed in this chapter. This chapter contains a new section examining the Consumer Protection from Unfair Terms Regulations 2008, SI 2008/1277, which prohibit unfair commercial practices which may be either misleading or aggressive in the B2C (business and consumer) relationship. Some provisions of these regulations will also overlap with instances of misrepresentations in the B2C context where a false statement induces the making of a contract, e.g. misleading information concerning after-sales service available or omitting or hiding material information.

Chapter 16 examines those instances where the law will regard the contract as tainted with illegality and therefore unenforceable. It also examines the effect of that illegality on the parties' positions, in particular the question of whether money or property passing under an illegal contract can be recovered and the consideration of the treatment of illegality by the Law Commission.

Non-agreement mistake

13

Summary of the issues

This chapter examines the legal treatment of those mistakes which are claimed to nullify consent on the basis that, although the parties have reached agreement, both parties entered into the contract under the same fundamental mistake.

• In order to protect the interests of third parties and to ensure certainty in transactions, the doctrine of common mistake in English law has traditionally been very narrowly defined. In any event, like the frustration doctrine, if the parties have allocated the risk of the event in the terms of their contract, that risk allocation clause will govern.

• There will be a fundamental common mistake in instances of true impossibility or failure of consideration, i.e. where both parties contract on the basis of a mistake as to the existence of the subject matter or as to ownership of the property which is the subject matter of the contract. However, a more restrictive approach has been taken to mistakes as to a quality of that subject matter since it is still technically possible to perform such a contract in accordance with its terms, despite the fact that the subject matter does not possess a quality which both parties believed it to have.

• There is authority of the House of Lords (*Bell v Lever Bros. Ltd*) confirming that such mistakes will only be treated as being fundamental (at common law) where the mistake is such as to render the subject matter 'essentially different' but this term is very narrowly defined and it is difficult to identify any instances where it would be satisfied.

• If a common mistake is sufficiently fundamental, it renders the contract automatically void so that any money or property transferred has to be returned. However, mistakes as to quality will generally not affect validity. This fact led Lord Denning to recognize an equitable jurisdiction to set aside a contract on terms on the basis of a common mistake which was recognized as being sufficiently 'fundamental' in equity, even if it was not sufficiently fundamental in law. Whilst this generated remedial flexibility in many cases of mistakes as to quality, it was difficult to reconcile with authority and to explain why a mistake could be fundamental in one sense (equity) but not in another (at common law). Fifty years later the equitable jurisdiction was denied by the Court of Appeal in *Great Peace Shipping*.

• The result is that the doctrine of common mistake in English law is even narrower than previously supposed and many instances where the parties consider the contract is affected by mistake are not recognized by law as being mistakes having legal consequences.

• Fine distinctions can arise in terms of the legal treatment of impossibility depending upon whether the impossibility is initial (common mistake) or subsequent (frustration doctrine). Common mistake renders the contract void, whereas frustration discharges future obligations and the Law Reform (Frustrated Contracts) Act 1943 provides for an adjustment of the parties' positions with regard to pre-existing obligations. However, in some instances it will be a matter of pure chance whether the impossibility is initial (already existing before the contract) or subsequent (occurring after it has been made).

13.1 Introduction

As discussed at **3.2.1**, there is no single coherent doctrine of mistake. This reflects the different contexts in which mistake may be said to exist. There are recognized categories of mistake:

1. **Mistakes which negative consent** (i.e., mistakes which prevent agreement):
   - cross-purposes (mutual) mistake (see **3.3.1**)
   - unilateral mistake as to term (see **3.3.1** and **3.3.2**).
2. **Mistakes which are said to nullify consent.**

(Terminology: These mistakes are most often referred to nowadays as 'common mistake', although in past decisions the courts sometimes referred to such mistakes as 'mutual mistakes'. This type of mistake should not, however, be confused with agreement cross-purposes mistakes, which were termed 'mutual mistake' in **Chapter 3** and the expression 'common mistake' will be used to refer to this type of mistake.)

The type of mistake discussed in this chapter is a non-agreement mistake (i.e., the parties are not denying that they reached agreement) but instead seek to 'nullify' that consent. It can be termed a 'common' mistake because it is claimed that in entering into the agreement the parties both made the **same mistake** and the true state of affairs was discovered only after objective agreement had apparently been reached.

(a) The common 'mistake' must have related to a matter which was 'fundamental' to their respective decisions to enter into the agreement.

(b) Any party who is seeking to rely on common mistake must have reasonable grounds for their belief (per Steyn J in *Associated Japanese Bank (International) Ltd v Credit du Nord* [1989] 1 WLR 255).

The existence and consequences of this type of mistake will arise for court decision where one of the parties (A) wishes to withdraw from the agreement (A/B) on this ground but the other (B) denies the existence of such a 'fundamental' common mistake, perhaps because the contract has proved advantageous to B.

Traditionally, the definition of 'fundamental mistake' for these purposes has been narrow so that the operation of the common mistake doctrine at common law has been very limited. This appears to be because such a mistake renders the contract void and therefore of no effect from the very beginning. Accordingly, as there is no contract, the parties are excused all performance. Not surprisingly, therefore, the courts have been anxious not to extend the operation of such a doctrine because of the effect of such a finding on both the positions of the parties and, in particular, on the position of innocent third parties (see the discussion at **3.2.2**).

Although some decisions of the Court of Appeal had determined that equity provided a more extended and flexible remedy in some circumstances (see **13.5**), this has now been denied by the

Court of Appeal in *Great Peace Shipping Ltd v Tsavliris (International) Ltd* [2002] EWCA Civ 1407, [2003] QB 679.

In addition, there is a further limitation on the operation of the doctrine of common mistake, since it cannot operate if one party has assumed the risk of the event in question (e.g., the non-existence of the subject matter) or if the contract was subject to a condition precedent, i.e. a contract shall not take effect unless the subject matter is in existence at the time of the agreement or a particular state of affairs exists (see 8.5.2.1).

13.2 Contractual allocation of risk

The risk that the assumed state of facts will not materialize may be allocated explicitly, or impliedly, to one or other party. Whether such an allocation of the risk of the relevant mistake to one or other of the parties has taken place must be determined **before** considering the possible operation of the doctrine of common mistake. As Steyn J stated in *Associated Japanese Bank (International) Ltd v Credit du Nord SA* [1989] 1 WLR 255 at p. 268:

> Logically, before one can turn to the rules as to mistake…one must first determine whether the contract itself, by express or implied condition precedent or otherwise, provides who bears the risk of the relevant mistake. It is at this hurdle that many pleas of mistake will either fail or prove to be unnecessary. Only if the contract is silent on the point is there scope for invoking mistake.

In *Kalsep Ltd v X-Flow BV, The Times*, 3 May 2001, the judge applied *Associated Japanese* and held that before concluding that an agreement was based on mistake, it was first necessary to determine whether the contract provided for either party to suffer the risk of the relevant mistake. On the facts, the risk was allocated by the contract so that the doctrine of mistake was excluded.

The fact that the doctrine cannot apply where the contract already allocates the risk of the event was also made clear in the judgment of Lord Phillips MR in *Great Peace Shipping Ltd v Tsavliris (International) Ltd* [2002] EWCA Civ 1407, [2003] QB 679. Lord Phillips stated (at [76]):

> the following elements must be present if common mistake is to avoid a contract: (i) there must be a common assumption as to the existence of a state of affairs; (ii) there must be no warranty by either party that that state of affairs exists; (iii) the non-existence of the state of affairs must not be attributable to the fault of either party; (iv) the non-existence of the state of affairs must render performance of the contract impossible; (v) the state of affairs may be the existence, or a vital attribute of the consideration to be provided or circumstances which must subsist if performance of the contractual adventure is to be possible.

Elements (ii) and (iii) identify instances of risk allocation, i.e. an assumption of responsibility by one of the parties.

13.2.1 **Express allocation of the risk**

The risk may be *expressly* undertaken by one party.

> In **William Sindall plc v Cambridgeshire CC** [1994] 1 WLR 1016 the contract to purchase land contained an express term stating that the land was sold 'subject to easements, liabilities and public rights affecting it'. The purchaser later discovered that, unknown to the parties, there was a foul sewer buried under the land. It sought to argue common mistake (for the argument relating to misrepresentation, see **14.6.5**).
>
> The Court of Appeal held that the contract term allocated the risk of such incumbrances to the purchaser so that the operation of the doctrine of mistake was excluded.

It follows that where an allocation of the risk has occurred, the fact that the contract as agreed cannot be performed may simply be something that the claimant purchaser has to accept as not being within the promise made by the other party (seller) so that no remedy is available (as in the *William Sindall* case). Alternatively, if the risk of non-performance has been allocated to the seller then the fact of non-performance will constitute a breach of the promise as to the existence of the subject matter and will amount to a breach of contract by that party (as in *McRae v Commonwealth Disposals Commission* (1951) 84 CLR 377, discussed below and at **13.3.1.2**, and, as to the measure of damages, at **9.3.4**).

13.2.2 **Implied allocation of the risk**

McRae v Commonwealth Disposals Commission (1951) 84 CLR 377 is a significant decision because the court implied a promise that the tanker was in the position specified and this implied promise was therefore the basis for the allocation of the risk of the tanker's non-existence.

> The Commission had invited tenders for a shipwrecked oil tanker, which was said by the Commission to contain oil and to be lying at a particular location. The plaintiffs' tender was accepted and they went to considerable expense in equipping a salvage expedition and sailing to the specified location. However, no tanker could be found, and it became apparent that none had ever existed. The Commission sought to resist the plaintiffs' claim for damages by arguing that, since the subject matter did not exist, the contract was void for mistake and they were not liable. The High Court of Australia held that there was a contract since the Commission had assumed contractual responsibility for the existence of the tanker. Since the tanker did not exist, the Commission was in breach of contract.

The existence of the tanker was not **expressly** promised by the Commission but the court was prepared to **imply** such a promise by attributing fault to the Commission in terms of the manner and context in which the assertion of the existence of the tanker had been made.

The judgment of the court reads:

[T]he Commission cannot in this case rely on any mistake as avoiding the contract, because any mistake was induced by the serious fault of their own servants, who asserted the existence of a tanker recklessly and without any reasonable ground. There was a contract, and the Commission contracted that a tanker existed in the position specified. Since there was no such tanker, there has been a breach of contract, and the plaintiffs are entitled to damages for that breach.

Having found there to be a contract, the court was able to award damages to the plaintiffs to compensate them for their expenses in conducting the salvage expedition. The plaintiffs were also able to recover the price paid (see 9.3.4).

The approach and decision in *Associated Japanese Bank (International) Ltd v Credit du Nord* [1989] 1 WLR 255 has taken on greater significance in recent cases since it has been accepted that in some contracts there may be an implied condition precedent that the goods exist at the time of the contract.

> Funds were raised against the security of certain non-existent machines on a 'sale and lease back', i.e. the non-existent machines were sold to the plaintiff bank for over £1m and then immediately leased back. The defendant bank had guaranteed the payments due under this lease. When the perpetrator of the fraud defaulted on the lease payments and disappeared with the £1m, the plaintiff bank sought to enforce the guarantee given by the defendant.
>
> However, it was held that the guarantee was subject to either an express or an implied condition precedent that the machines existed. Steyn J accepted that in order for the condition precedent to be implied the officious bystander test would need to be applied (see 6.4.2.2). Although this would be relevant only 'in comparatively rare cases' on these facts he considered that such an implied condition precedent existed. Since the machines did not exist the guarantee did not become effective and the defendant could not be liable under it.

More difficult is the effect that the non-existence has on the contract. If this is a true condition precedent then it should prevent the contract coming into existence, i.e. the contract is void. However, that may not seem suitable in terms of outcome and the parties' positions and the Court of Appeal in *Graves v Graves* [2007] EWCA Civ 660, [2007] 3 FCR 26, (2007) 151 SJLB 926, discussed further at 13.4.1.4, first implied a condition precedent into a tenancy agreement whereby the tenancy would end if housing benefit was not payable to the tenant (albeit by mistakenly employing a mistake-based test rather than the officious bystander test for the implication of a term), and then concluded that the tenancy was 'determined' for the future from the time when it became clear that no housing benefit was in fact payable. This enabled a flexible response in terms of the parties' positions which would not otherwise have been possible. However, this is problematic in terms of legal principle since the implication is that there **was** a valid contract which came to an end (i.e., a condition subsequent). This would be completely at odds with risk allocation for initial impossibility.

In *Butters v BBC Worldwide Ltd* [2009] EWHC1954 (Ch) Peter Smith J noted *Graves v Graves* had followed the approach to the implied condition precedent in the *Associated Japanese Bank* case. The parties had entered into a new licence agreement. However, it was alleged that this new licence had been entered into under a mistake concerning the validity of the termination clause in an earlier master licence and whether a proper termination of the master licence had occurred relying on that clause. On the facts the judge considered that, irrespective of the validity of the termination clause and its exercise, the master licence had been terminated when the new licence was entered into (mutual release and replacement: see 4.5.2). However, counsel alleged that it was a condition precedent to the new licence that this master licence was terminated and the judge accepted that the officious bystander test was appropriate to determine this question, although that was not the test applied in *Graves*. Nevertheless, the judge concluded that this was the wrong submission. The correct question to ask was whether there would be an implied condition precedent that if the master licence was not void that its validity would prevent that new licence from taking effect. On the facts there could be no implied condition precedent since the evidence was that the parties may have been aware of the issues relating to the validity but did not raise those issues when entering into the new licence and merely wanted to make a new start.

It is likely that we will see more of the implied condition precedent in future as a means of avoiding the strict consequences of mistake. Of course, the same conclusion (contract of no effect) should follow from a failure of an implied condition precedent but, as **Graves** demonstrates, it is possible to be flexible if the implied term is formulated appropriately, or (**Butters v BBC**) to avoid the implication of a condition precedent through an appropriate formulation of the required implied condition. Nevertheless, it is arguable that whereas **Associated Japanese** was explicitly claimed to be a mistake as to the existence of the 'subject matter', both **Graves** and **Butters** may in reality be mistakes about quality, i.e. whether the particular tenancy attracted housing benefit and whether a master licence was valid and subsisting or had been validly terminated.

13.3 Categories of common mistake at common law

The categories of common mistake at common law are based on a restrictive interpretation of mistakes which can be classified as 'fundamental' for this purpose.

These categories appear to equate with situations which are so acute that they constitute 'initial impossibility', i.e. unknown to the parties, the contract (as agreed) is impossible to perform. Usually this will be because the subject matter has ceased to exist *at* the time the contract was entered into (*res extincta*).

13.3.1 Mistake as to subject matter (*res extincta*)

In **Strickland v Turner** (1852) 7 Ex 208, a contract of annuity was void because, unknown to the parties, the annuity related to the life of a person who was already dead at the time the contract was entered into. A further example of this type of impossibility is provided by **Galloway v Galloway** (1914) 30 TLR 531. In this case a separation agreement was void because it was entered into in the mistaken belief that the parties were married to each other and therefore needed a formal separation. However, it transpired that the husband's previous spouse was still alive.

13.3.1.1 Perishing of specific goods

In the context of contracts for the sale of goods, the starting point for discussion is s. 6 of the Sale of Goods Act (SGA) 1979. Section 6 provides that 'where the contract is for the sale of specific goods' which have 'perished' by the time the contract is made, the contract is void. This section, as originally drafted in the SGA 1893, was said to be based on **Couturier v Hastie** (1856) 5 HL 673. However, it is doubtful that such a wide interpretation can be put on this decision.

> In **Couturier v Hastie,** a cargo of corn was shipped from a Mediterranean port to England. At a time when the cargo owner believed the corn to be in transit, the cargo was sold by him to the buyer. It later emerged that, because the cargo had begun to deteriorate, the master of the ship had sold it at a port en route **before** this contract of sale had been entered into. Neither party was aware of this position at the time of contracting. The seller argued that the buyer was liable to pay the price for the cargo on the basis that the buyer had purchased the cargo and all inherent risks.
>
> The House of Lords held that there was no such liability, because the contract was for the sale of existing goods but the seller no longer had the corn to sell at the time when the contract of sale was made.

It might be thought that this would mean that, if there was an implied term that the goods existed, the seller would be in breach. However, if the basis of the decision is that the contract was void for common mistake then there is no contract to breach. It has been assumed by subsequent commentators that the basis of the decision is common mistake, but the alternative interpretation (placing the risk of non-existence on the seller) is equally consistent with the decision in *Couturier v Hastie*.

The other problem with s. 6 is that it appears to require the goods to have existed at one time but to have subsequently 'perished' or ceased to exist. It is arguable, therefore, that s. 6 will not apply to situations where the goods **never** existed. (For further discussion, see Atiyah, '*Couturier v Hastie* and the sale of non-existent goods' (1957) 73 LQR 340.) At common law, it should equally be the case that a contract to purchase non-existent goods should be void for common mistake because there is no logical reason to distinguish it from goods which have perished. The shared misconception will be the same and it must surely be fundamental if the goods have **never** existed.

The case of *Associated Japanese Bank (International) Ltd v Credit du Nord* [1989] 1 WLR 255 (for facts see 13.2.2) might appear to be a further example of *res extincta*. In addition to the finding of an express or implied condition precedent (see 13.2.2), Steyn J considered that in any event the existence of the machines was of fundamental importance to the guarantee contract so that the guarantee contract was essentially different from what the parties believed it to be. The guarantee contract was therefore void for common mistake at common law. In fact, it can be argued, by analogy with *Bell v Lever Bros*, that the mistake was a mistake as to quality, i.e. that the lease related to machines which existed (see discussion of mistake as to quality, at 13.4). The difficulty with a *res extincta* conclusion is that it is the guarantee contract that was void but the subject matter of the guarantee was the lease and its obligations rather than the machines.

13.3.1.2 Assumption of contractual responsibility for the existence of the subject matter

The decision of the High Court of Australia in *McRae v Commonwealth Disposals Commission* (1951) 84 CLR 377 (for facts, see 13.2.2 above), concerned the sale of property which had never existed. However, the decision can be distinguished on the basis that the contractual risk of the non-existence was placed on the seller so that the non-existence constituted a breach of contract.

It is important, therefore, not to jump to the conclusion that, in a sale of goods contract, in the event of either non-existence or perishing of the subject matter the contract will always be void. It may be that the risk of existence has been placed on one of the parties so that there is a contract and the non-delivery of these goods will amount to a breach. A contractual assumption of risk excludes the operation of the doctrine of common mistake, in the same way that an applicable *force majeure* clause excludes the operation of the frustration doctrine. Equally, an argument that the existence of the subject matter is an implied condition precedent may mean that the contract never comes into existence (*Associated Japanese Bank*).

13.3.1.3 Impossibility: Common mistake and frustration

In a sense, therefore, this type of impossibility mistake has similarities with the factual context for frustration because both doctrines apply, in the absence of a contractual allocation of the risk in question, to instances of contractual impossibility (destruction of the subject matter: see 12.4.1). However, whereas the frustration doctrine applies where the impossibility occurs

499

after the contract was entered into, common mistake will apply where the impossibility is initial (i.e., unknown to the parties, the contract was impossible to perform at the time that it was entered into). This can lead to some fine distinctions of fact which result in significantly different consequences.

> In **Amalgamated Investment & Property Co. Ltd v John Walker & Sons Ltd** [1977] 1 WLR 164, the plaintiffs had agreed to purchase property from the defendants which had been advertised as suitable for redevelopment. Unknown to both parties, a decision had already been taken to list the property as a building of special architectural or historical interest, although the actual listing did not take place until after the purchase contract had been signed. The listing seriously affected the value of the property and the plaintiffs sought to have the contract set aside on the basis of mistake, or alternatively claimed that the contract had been frustrated. It was held that this was not a case involving a common mistake because the listing had not taken place until **after** the contract was made. In addition, the doctrine of frustration did not apply on the facts because this was a risk which was to be borne by the purchaser.

The fine distinction between circumstances requiring the operation of the doctrine of common mistake or the frustration doctrine can also be illustrated by comparing two cases involving very similar facts.

> In **Griffith v Brymer** (1903) 19 TLR 434, the contract was void for common mistake so that the advance payment had to be repaid. The contract in question was to hire a room to view the coronation procession of Edward VII. The contract was made at 11 a.m. on 24 June 1902 but, unknown to the parties, the decision to cancel the procession had been taken at 10 a.m. that morning.
>
> This can be compared with **Krell v Henry** [1903] 2 KB 740, involving a similar contract to hire a room to view the coronation procession, but this contract was entered into on 20 June so that the cancellation of the procession amounted to frustration. Since **Krell v Henry** was a case based on frustration, at common law the loss lay where it fell and the deposit could not be recovered. (For a discussion of how the position would differ under the Law Reform (Frustrated Contracts) Act 1943, see **12.8.2.1**.)

It is worth noting that **Griffith v Brymer** is not a case of impossibility due to the non-existence of the subject matter unless the contract purpose was specifically to hire rooms to view the procession. If it was merely to hire rooms, the contract would still be physically possible. However, the purpose of the parties had clearly become impossible in both cases given that the rooms were advertised for this purpose (see **12.4.4**).

13.3.1.4 Common theoretical basis: Common mistake and frustration

The basis for *res extincta* was also similar to the origins of the frustration doctrine which, as we saw in **Chapter 12**, was based on the implication of a term ('a condition') that the subject matter should continue to exist (e.g., *Taylor v Caldwell* (1863) 3 B & S 826: see 12.3.1). In other words, the existence of the subject matter at the time of the contract was interpreted as a condition precedent to the other party's obligation to perform (see *Associated Japanese Bank (International) Ltd v Credit du Nord* [1989] 1 WLR 255 and Smith (1994) 110 LQR 400). However, the theoretical basis for the frustration doctrine evolved in the twentieth century so that it is now based on a rule of law dependent upon the construction of the terms of the contract to determine whether the event which has occurred renders performance in accordance with those terms impossible (*Davis Contractors Ltd v Fareham Urban District Council* [1956] AC 696: see 12.3.2 and 12.3.3).

In *Great Peace Shipping Ltd v Tsavliris (International) Ltd* [2002] EWCA Civ 1407, [2003] QB 679, Lord Phillips MR (giving the judgment of the Court of Appeal) stated (at [61]) that the two doctrines had developed in parallel so that 'consideration of the development of the law of frustration assists with the analysis of the law of common mistake'. After reviewing the development of frustration, Lord Phillips concluded:

> the theory of the implied term is as unrealistic when considering common mistake as when considering frustration. Where a fundamental assumption upon which an agreement is founded proves to be mistaken, it is not realistic to ask whether the parties impliedly agreed that in those circumstances the contract would not be binding. The avoidance of a contract on the ground of common mistake results from a rule of law under which, if it transpires that one or both of the parties have agreed to do something which it is impossible to perform, no obligation arises out of that agreement.

In other words, if performance is impossible then as a matter of law the contract will be void for common mistake. However, in determining whether the contract is 'impossible' to perform it is necessary to construe the express contract terms and any implications arising from the surrounding circumstances, which Lord Phillips referred to as the 'contractual adventure'.

13.3.2 Mistake as to ownership (*res sua*)

In addition to *res extincta*, there is another category of fundamental common mistake at common law, namely mistakes concerning the ownership of property (*res sua*). Such a mistake occurs, for example, where a person contracts to purchase property which, unknown to both parties, the purchaser already owns.

501

> In *Cooper v Phibbs* (1867) LR 2 HL 149, Cooper agreed to lease a salmon fishery from Phibbs, both parties believing that the fishery belonged to Phibbs. In fact, Cooper was already entitled to enjoyment of the fishery as a life tenant. That is, although not absolute owner so that he could not dispose of the fishery, Cooper was effectively owner during his lifetime. He had no need to take the lease, and Phibbs had no power to grant it. It was held that the contract could be set aside (i.e., it was voidable), but the court allowed Phibbs compensation for money mistakenly spent on the fishery.

In *Bell v Lever Bros Ltd* [1932] AC 161, Lord Atkin relied on this decision of the House of Lords as an example of mistake operating to nullify a contract, and he expressly stated that the effect of such a mistake was to render the contract **void** and not merely voidable. The significance of this remark, which it is submitted is the correct position in law, will become clear below (see 13.5). Lord Atkin did not regard *Cooper v Phibbs* as depending on any special equitable doctrine. It may, however, provide some authority on which to base future arguments in favour of remedial flexibility to do justice on the facts.

13.4 Mistake as to quality at common law

13.4.1 Is it sufficiently fundamental?

A mistake as to quality made by both parties will not generally be sufficiently fundamental to render the contract void at common law since such a mistake does not render performance,

as originally agreed, impossible. The emphasis at common law appears to be placed on the sanctity of contract in the absence of clear impossibility.

13.4.1.1 Distinguishing mistakes as to quality and breaches of the satisfactory quality term: Identifying the context for a claim based on mistake

It is important at the outset to explain the distinction between mistakes as to quality and promises as to satisfactory quality which are implied in sales contracts where the seller sells in the course of a business (e.g., SGA 1979, s. 14(2)). 'Quality' in the context of mistake refers to some special quality as opposed to the basic overall minimum quality of the goods which is implied by s. 14(2) SGA. For example, mistakenly believing that the contract relates to a high grade of tea or to a particular manufacturer's pottery would not involve any breach of the satisfactory quality term.

13.4.1.2 *Bell v Lever Bros Ltd*

The leading case on mistake as to quality is ***Bell v Lever Bros Ltd*** [1932] AC 161.

> Bell and another were made executive officers of a subsidiary of Lever Bros. Subsequently, the subsidiary was closed down and a further contract made between Lever Bros and the executive officers, terminating their appointments in return for substantial compensation. It was then discovered that the officers had earlier engaged in private dealings in breach of their service contracts (which the officers themselves had forgotten about). Therefore, at the time of the contracts to terminate their appointments, Lever Bros. could have terminated the service contracts for these breaches, without having to pay any compensation. Accordingly, Lever Bros claimed that the termination contracts were void for mistake and the compensation repayable.
>
> The House of Lords (by a majority of 3:2) refused this claim. The mistake was merely as to a quality of the service contracts, namely whether they needed to be terminated by the payment of compensation, and did not render the contract void. (The consequence was that the compensation paid was not recoverable because the agreement under which the compensation was payable remained valid.)

Therefore, such mistakes will not generally be sufficiently fundamental in nature to render the contract void. Lord Atkin (giving what is generally acknowledged to be the leading speech for the majority) stated that **a mistake as to quality 'will not affect assent unless it is the mistake of both parties, and is as to the existence of some quality which makes the thing without the quality essentially different from the thing as it was believed to be'.**

In ***Associated Japanese Bank (International) Ltd v Credit du Nord SA*** [1989] 1 WLR 255, Steyn J regarded this statement by Lord Atkin as forming the *ratio* of the case and it was regarded as the determinative test by the Court of Appeal in ***Great Peace Shipping Ltd v Tsavliris (International) Ltd*** [2002] EWCA Civ 1407, [2003] QB 679 (for facts, see below). Lord Phillips MR, giving the judgment of the court, stated that the issue on the facts was whether the mistake as to the distance between the two vessels meant that the services to be provided would be 'something essentially different' to what the parties had agreed.

13.4.1.3 The test of 'essential difference'

As a broad test it might be considered that this test of essential difference would provide great scope for judicial discretion in evaluating the facts in mistake cases and that in many instances a mistake as to quality would render 'the thing without the quality essentially different from the thing as it was believed to be'. However, it would be wrong to jump to this conclusion and the case law does not support such an interpretation. In particular, this test would suggest a different result to that in *Kennedy v Panama, New Zealand and Australian Royal Mail Co.* (1867) LR 2 QB 580, although this case was one of the cases on which Lord Atkin relied in **Bell v Lever Bros**:

> The plaintiff had bought shares in a company in the belief, also held by the company, that the company had recently won a contract from the New Zealand government for the delivery of mail. However, the New Zealand government failed to ratify the agreement, and so the shares were worth much less. The court said that there was nevertheless a contract. Such a difference in quality, however severe, did not destroy the agreement. Nevertheless, it is difficult to accept that there was no essential difference in this case.

In addition, despite the existence of this broad principle of 'essential difference', Lord Atkin himself gave a number of examples (see [1932] AC 161 at p. 224) of mistakes which would not be sufficiently fundamental. These examples indicate that 'essential difference' will be very narrowly construed. Lord Atkin's examples included the following:

Example

A buys a picture from B; both A and B believe it to be the work of an old master, and a high price is paid. It turns out to be a modern copy. A has no remedy in the absence of representation or warranty.

In essence, Lord Atkin was saying that it will not suffice to state, 'If I had known the true facts I would not have entered into this contract.' If a quality is important to one of the parties, that party should ensure that its existence becomes a contractual promise or can form the basis for a claim in misrepresentation (a false statement of fact) (see 13.4.2). Lord Atkin justified this position (at p. 224) by stating that:

> it is of paramount importance that contracts should be observed, and that if parties honestly comply with the essentials of the formation of contracts—i.e., agree in the same terms on the same subject matter— they are bound, and must rely on the stipulations of the contract for protection from the effect of facts unknown to them.

Lord Atkin put forward another formulation for the test: 'Does the state of the new facts destroy the identity of the subject matter as it was in the original state of facts?' In Lord Atkin's example, the subject matter would still be identified as 'the old master'. It is interesting, however, to compare this with the suggested approach in Peel, *Treitel's The Law of Contract,* 12th edn (Sweet and Maxwell, 2007), pp. 322–3. Peel argues that the test should be whether the particular quality is so important to the parties that they actually use this quality in order to identify the subject matter, e.g. if in the example of the sale of 'the old master' the parties used the name of the artist to describe the subject matter itself. However, this argument was rejected by the Court of Appeal (*obiter*) in **Leaf v International Galleries** [1950] 2 KB 86, on the basis that there was no express term to this effect.

> In **Leaf v International Galleries**, the plaintiff had bought a painting believed to be by Constable, and it had also been represented as having been painted by Constable by the seller. Five years later, when the

plaintiff tried to sell the painting, it was discovered that the painting was not by Constable. The plaintiff therefore argued that the original contract of sale should be set aside. His action for misrepresentation failed because of the lapse of time (see 14.5.2.2), and in passing the Court of Appeal reiterated that no alternative remedy for mistake would be available as this was only a mistake as to quality. The fact that the mistake could be described as essential or fundamental did not change the fact that the contract as originally agreed continued to be capable of performance (and indeed had been performed).

Lord Evershed MR rejected the argument that the plaintiff had 'contracted to buy a Constable' by stating that '[w]hat he contracted to buy and what he bought was a specific chattel, namely, an oil painting of Salisbury Cathedral' and 'it remains true to say that the plaintiff still has the article which he contracted to buy'.

Similarly, in *Frederick E. Rose Ltd v William H. Pim Junior & Co. Ltd* [1953] 2 QB 450 (the full facts are given at **3.4.1.1**), the contract was for the sale and delivery of horsebeans, although both parties were under a mistake as to whether horsebeans were suitable for the plaintiffs' purposes in fulfilling a contract for the supply of 'feveroles'. It turned out that they were not, but the parties had agreed on the sale and purchase of horsebeans so that the contract as agreed was capable of performance and therefore was not void.

Lord Atkin's test in *Bell v Lever Bros* has generated a good deal of discussion concerning the meaning of 'essential difference'. There is one *obiter* statement in an English case which applies Lord Atkin's test more literally and suggests that the mistake as to a quality would have rendered the contract void. This is a statement by Hallett J in *Nicholson and Venn v Smith-Marriott* (1947) 177 LT 189, in the context of a sale of napkins and tablecloths described as the 'authentic property' of Charles I. In fact the linen was Georgian, and it was held that there was a breach of contract since this was a sale by description for Charles I linen. Hallett J stated that 'a Georgian relic…is an "essentially different" thing from a Carolean relic' so that the goods purchased were 'different things in substance from those which the plaintiffs sought to buy and believed they had bought'. This view was subsequently doubted by Denning LJ in *Solle v Butcher* [1950] 1 KB 671 and is generally regarded as weak support for arguing that a contract can be void for mistake as to quality in the light of the decision in the case that the description amounted to a contractual term, which would undoubtedly have influenced the finding of 'essential difference'.

The English approach can be compared with the approach exemplified by the decision of the Supreme Court of Michigan in *Sherwood v Walker* 33 NW 919 (1887), where the mistake, relating to whether the cow being sold was barren at the time of the sale, was held to relate to 'the very nature of the thing', i.e. it was held to relate to the subject matter being sold and not merely to a quality possessed by that subject matter. This case illustrates the difficulties of divorcing the question of value from the determination of 'essential difference'; e.g. one would undoubtedly pay a higher price for a painting by a famous artist. In *Sherwood v Walker*, the essential difference was that a cow in calf was worth considerably more than a barren cow, which would be sold for its meat. Therefore, a buyer would expect to pay a higher price for a cow in calf and, arguably, the only way to untangle the contract was to hold the contract to be void for common mistake. The English courts have not shown the same willingness to take account of price paid as indicating the existence of 'essential difference' in the subject matter (see, e.g., *Bell v Lever Bros Ltd*, where the compensation paid could not be recovered and more recently *Kyle Bay Ltd (T/A Astons Nightclub) v Underwriters Subscribing Under Policy Number 019057/08/01* [2007] EWCA Civ 57, [2007] 1 CLC 164: significant difference in amount could not be recovered because of the mistake).

It seems that it is this problem of 'result' which led Lord Denning in *Solle v Butcher* [1950] 1 KB 671 to find that a contract could be voidable in equity for mistake as to quality and be set aside on terms. However, the lack of any basis in precedent for such a jurisdiction in equity has since been confirmed by the Court of Appeal in **Great Peace Shipping Ltd v Tsavliris (International) Ltd** [2002] EWCA Civ 1407, [2003] QB 679 (see discussion below at 13.5).

The decision in **Great Peace Shipping Ltd v Tsavliris (International) Ltd** also confirmed the restrictive interpretation of Lord Atkin's statement of principle in **Bell v Lever Bros** and therefore the limited category of mistakes which will be sufficiently fundamental mistakes to render the contract void.

> The contract alleged to be affected by a common mistake was a contract whereby the vessel, *Great Peace*, was engaged for a minimum hire period of five days to sail towards the *Cape Providence* (another vessel), which had suffered structural damage, and to stand-by in case it was required for the purpose of saving life. At the time of entering into the contract, both parties were mistaken about the distance between these vessels (and therefore how long it would take for the *Great Peace* to rendezvous with the damaged vessel). Both parties thought that the vessels were only about thirty-five miles apart when the true distance was nearer 410 miles. On discovering the true position, the salvage company which had engaged the *Great Peace* secured the services of an alternate vessel and cancelled the contract hiring the *Great Peace*. The owners of the *Great Peace* sought the minimum five-day hire payable under the terms of the contract but the salvage company alleged that the contract was either void for common mistake or voidable in equity.
>
> The Court of Appeal held that the crucial test to determine if the contract was void was whether the common mistaken assumption of fact, relating to the proximity of the two vessels, meant that performance of the contract in accordance with its terms would be essentially different from the performance contemplated by the parties, i.e. were the services which the vessel could provide essentially different from those agreed upon? Since the *Great Peace* would have arrived in time to provide the intended service for a number of days, and given that the salvage company had not immediately cancelled the contract on discovering the true position, **performance of the contractual adventure was not impossible.** Accordingly, the contract was not void for common mistake and the salvage company was liable to pay the five-day hire charge.

Thus, 'essential difference' in **Great Peace** was equated with impossibility and it must follow that it will therefore be extremely difficult to identify a common mistake as to quality which will be sufficiently fundamental to render the contract void, albeit that the impossibility is not limited to strict compliance with the contractual terms but extends to whether the contractual adventure is impossible. Some of these difficulties are apparent in the post-**Great Peace** case law.

In **Brennan v Bolt Burdon** [2004] EWCA Civ 1017, [2005] QB 303 the key question was the effect of mistakes as to law since it was argued that a compromise agreement had been made under such a common mistake of law. The Court of Appeal accepted that in principle a mistake as to law could render a contract void for common mistake but there was no true mistake of law on these facts since at the time of the compromise the law was merely **in doubt**, rather then clearly wrong. When entering into compromise agreements each party accepted the risk that their view of the law might turn out to be mistaken and Sedley LJ stressed the need for certainty of compromise agreements and the ability to rely on their terms. He said:

> A shift in the law cannot be allowed to undo a compromise of litigation entered into in the knowledge of both of how the law now stood and of the fact—for it is always a fact—that it might not remain so.

Although the Court of Appeal did not completely rule out the possibility that compromise agreements could be void for mistake as to law, it was difficult to envisage how a mistake of law would ever render performance impossible (as required by the test in **Great Peace**). On the facts, this compromise was at all times capable of being performed. Sedley LJ expressed some difficulty with the **Great Peace** test in the context of mistakes of law and concluded that 'a different test may be necessary'. He considered that a more appropriate test might be whether 'had the parties appreciated that the law was what it is now known to be, there would still have been an intelligible basis for their agreement'.

In *Kyle Bay Ltd (T/A Astons Nightclub) v Underwriters Subscribing Under Policy Number 019057/08/01* [2007] EWCA Civ 57, [2007] 1 CLC 164, the issue again concerned the validity of a compromise agreement which had been entered into with the respondent insurance underwriters.

> The mistake related to the type of insurance cover believed to be in place for a nightclub. When the nightclub was destroyed by fire it became clear to the appellants that a different type of cover was in place to that requested by them and they were advised to agree to compromise the claim for £205,000, about a third less than they would have been entitled to had the cover they had in fact applied for been in place. However, it later transpired that the policy had been of the type they had requested so that a larger sum should have been payable under the claim and the settlement had been entered into on the basis of a mistake. However, the judge had held that the mistake was not sufficient to render the compromise agreement void and the Court of Appeal agreed on the basis that the subject matter was not rendered 'essentially and radically different' since the settlement compromise remained capable of performance at all times.
>
> The only mistake related to the fact that the nature of the cover was assumed to be on one basis rather than another. However, this was a detail of the basis on which the policy was written and 'did not go to the validity of the policy, the parties, the property, the nature of the business or the risks covered'. Neuberger LJ stated (at [26]): 'The difference between the actual and assumed subject matter of the settlement can in my view certainly be characterised as significant, but it is not an "essential...and radical..." difference.'
>
> In particular, the fact that the appellants received about a third less than they should have done although 'a significant, even a substantial, reduction' was not an 'essentially or radically different sum from its entitlement'.

13.4.1.4 Are the 'essential difference' and impossibility tests to be equated?

In *Champion Investments Ltd v Ahmed* [2004] EWHC 1956 (QB), the judge concluded that a mistake concerning the applicable rate of interest (1) was not essentially different to what the parties believed **and** (2) did not render performance of the contract impossible. The implication, therefore, is that there may be two hurdles in the path of a claimant alleging common mistake as to quality. Alternatively, this may be equating essential difference and impossibility and so applying one test.

In *Kyle Bay Ltd (T/A Astons Nightclub) v Underwriters Subscribing Under Policy Number 019057/08/01* [2007] EWCA Civ 57, [2007] 1 CLC 164, the Court of Appeal had first raised the question of whether the mistake concerning the insurance settlement agreement would satisfy the *Great Peace* test of rendering performance of the settlement impossible, and of course concluded that it would not. (It is difficult to envisage a situation when a compromise or settlement agreement would be impossible to perform but it could have been entered into on a very different basis to the actual position between the parties.) Neuberger LJ referred to the fact that Sedley LJ, in

Brennan v Bolt Burdon, had considered that the impossibility test might therefore be inappropriate in this context, although recognizing that it was essentially down to how the mistake was defined. Neuberger LJ went on to add that, if these doubts were justified, the right test was that in **Bell v Lever Bros** and **Associated Japanese**, i.e. the test of 'essentially and radically different'. Although this may suggest that the tests may have different spheres of application, Neuberger LJ helpfully pointed to the fact that the **Great Peace** had appeared to equate the tests. It may be that the most appropriate test will be applied in the particular context, assuming that the tests will not produce different results. It should not be necessary, however, to have to establish both tests as separate and independent requirements, as the judge at first instance had assumed was necessary in **Kyle Bay** [2006] EWHC 607 (Comm) at [43].

Unfortunately, different results would have followed from the application of the tests in **Graves v Graves** [2007] EWCA Civ 660, [2007] 3 FCR 26, (2007) 151 SJLB 926.

> An ex-husband had agreed to let his ex-wife live as a tenant in a property he owned. Both parties mistakenly, but justifiably, thought that 90 per cent of the rent would be paid through housing benefit. However, this was not the case since the couple's child also lived with the ex-wife. The ex-wife was unable to pay the rent and the ex-husband brought proceedings for possession. The Court of Appeal relied on the statement of Steyn J in the **Associated Japanese Bank** case and stated that the preliminary hurdle was to determine 'whether the contract itself, by express or implied condition precedent…provides who bears the risk of the relevant mistake'. However, Thomas LJ (giving a judgment agreed by Hughes and Coleridge LJJ) concluded that in order to establish an implied condition precedent that the tenancy contract would end if housing benefit was not payable, it needed to be shown that the tenancy was impossible to perform (obviously not the case) **or** 'essentially and radically different' in kind as a result of the non-availability of the housing benefit. The Court of Appeal concluded that the agreement was different in kind to that originally contemplated so that the condition could be implied. Therefore the agreement came to an end. The court then went on to adjust the parties' positions in relation to the deposit and the rent paid for occupation in the interim.

507

The Court of Appeal therefore applied a test applicable to a determination of whether a contract was void for common mistake in order to decide whether there was an implied condition precedent. The applicable test for the implication of such a term ought to have been the officious bystander test (see 6.4.2.2), a point made clear in **Butters v BBC Worldwide Ltd** [2009] EWHC 1954 (Ch) (and see also Capper [2008] LMCLQ 264). As a result of the implication of a condition precedent which had failed, rather than an argument based on mistake as to quality that would have been doomed to failure, the outcome was that the tenancy came to an end from the moment the position on housing benefit came to light. The wife could not therefore recover all of her deposit and rent paid (which would have followed if the contract had been void for mistake). Nevertheless, if the emphasis shifts to arguments based on the implication of an implied condition precedent as an alternative to an argument of mistake, it may not provide an easy solution since the officious bystander test is not easy to satisfy. Much will depend on how the term to be implied is constructed as to whether it is possible to say that both parties would have said, without hesitation, that the term is 'so obvious that we did not bother to write it down', e.g. could it be said that a landlord would always assume that the existence of housing benefit was a necessary term of the tenancy agre ment so that the tenancy should come to an end if this was not the case?

There is much scope for arguments of overlap between the factual context in **Bell v Lever Bros** and **Graves v Graves**, i.e. although both parties mistakenly thought housing benefit was available in relation to the tenancy, its non-availability did not make performance of the contract (or the adventure) impossible unless a very generous interpretation is taken of the context for the agreement. The reliance on the implied condition precedent could well be the result of a need to do justice on the facts which is not possible in cases of mistakes as to quality but was possible using the Court of Appeal's analysis.

13.4.1.5 Overall conclusion

In practical terms it is likely that cases of common mistake will be limited to instances involving a total failure of consideration (where one party is unable to deliver what the other party has contracted to receive), such as *res extincta* or *res sua*. This seems clear from the decision in ***EIC Services Ltd v Phipps*** [2004] EWCA Civ 1069, [2005] 1 WLR 1377 in which the Court of Appeal held that a bonus issue of shares was void because the absence of the applicable shareholder approval meant that any bonus shares would have to be nil paid. However, the fundamental premise on which bonus shares were issued was that the company had profits available for distribution which would extend in amount to pay up the bonus shares. Thus, because of the effects of the defects, the end result of nil-paid bonus shares was fundamentally different in nature to what had been contemplated.

The fact that Lord Phillips chose to extend impossibility to 'the contractual adventure' allows for some possibility of leeway in interpretation. In ***Apvodedo NV v Collins*** [2008] EWHC 775 (Ch), transcript available via Westlaw, Henderson J (at [43]) considered that if literally interpreted impossibility may be too strict a test and added: 'the true test may rather be whether the non-existence of the state of affairs renders performance of the contract *in accordance with the common assumption* impossible', and added 'much would depend on precisely how the "contractual adventure" was identified…'. The judge relied heavily on the decision in ***Associated Japanese Bank***, which turned on the conclusion that the existence of the machines was an express or implied condition precedent to the guarantee contract. Steyn J had also considered that the existence of the machines was of fundamental importance to the guarantee contract so that the guarantee contract was essentially different from what the parties believed it to be. The guarantee contract could therefore be void for common mistake at common law.

Future claims may show a greater willingness to rely on the decision in ***Associated Japanese Bank*** as justifying alternative claims based on an implied condition precedent and an allegation that the contract is void for common mistake alleging an interpretation of 'contractual adventure' as including an assumption about the existence of a state of affairs.

13.4.2 Relationship with other possible claims

It is important to make clear the relationship between mistake and the express undertakings or statements of the parties. The fact that a mistake as to quality does not result in the contract being a nullity means, as Lord Atkin made clear in ***Bell v Lever Bros Ltd***, that the claimant's only remedies lie in establishing either an express term of the contract by which the promisor undertakes to guarantee that the quality in question is present, or a pre-contractual representation that the desired quality is present. In these cases, absence of the desired quality will provide a remedy respectively for breach of contract or for misrepresentation. In other words, in these situations either by their contract, or as a result of the pre-contractual negotiations, the parties have allocated the risk that the quality will not be present to one or to the other (see, e.g., ***Nicholson and Venn v Smith-Marriott*** (1947) 177 LT 189 (sale by description within s. 13, SGA 1979) and ***Leaf v International Galleries*** [1950] 2 KB 86).

In these instances it would be inappropriate for the courts to intervene by means of the doctrine of common mistake, and it must be remembered that common mistake may be very much a last-ditch argument (especially as the equitable jurisdiction to set aside on terms has now been denied by the Court of Appeal in *Great Peace Shipping Ltd v Tsavliris (International) Ltd* [2002] EWCA Civ 1407, [2003] QB 679) since more effective remedies may be obtainable for breach of contract or for the misrepresentation. This principle is sometimes expressed in terms of the rule that mistake must not be the 'fault' of either party.

Common mistake as a last-ditch argument may need to be attempted, however, where there is no contractual promise or pre-contractual statement relating to the quality, or there is no possibility of an implied condition precedent.

13.5 Is there an equitable jurisdiction to set aside a contract for a common mistake as to quality although the mistake does not render the contract void at common law?

As discussed above, there has been some dissatisfaction with the rule that common mistakes, falling short of those which make performance of the contract as agreed impossible, do not render the contract void. Common mistakes as to quality might be considered to be fundamental in the sense that, in the absence of the mistake, the parties would not have entered into the contract. Thus, a mistake over the authenticity of a painting is no doubt one which is central to the contract. It can be argued that it involves a very narrow interpretation to say that the contract (for the sale of a specific painting) can still be performed and is therefore not void.

As suggested at 3.2.2, the explanation for the narrow interpretation is that any other rule would leave third-party interests unduly exposed to disputes between parties to transactions over which the third party has no control. Nevertheless, this explanation raised the possibility that a remedy for common mistake as to quality might be acceptable if it operated between the original parties to a transaction but did not operate to defeat third-party interests. This effect would be achieved if the impact of mistake on the contract were to make it merely voidable rather than void (see 3.2.2). Lord Denning had sought to achieve just such a rule and it is necessary to trace that development before assessing the decision of the Court of Appeal in *Great Peace Shipping Ltd v Tsavliris (International) Ltd* [2002] EWCA Civ 1407, [2003] QB 679 which, on the basis of *Bell v Lever Bros*, has since denied the existence of such a jurisdiction in equity.

13.5.1 Lord Denning's attempts to introduce the equitable jurisdiction

Denning LJ (as he then was) first reformulated the law relating to common mistake in *Solle v Butcher* [1950] 1 KB 671.

> The defendant agreed to lease a flat to the plaintiff for seven years at £250 per annum. The parties only arrived at this figure for the rent because both believed that the property was not subject to rent control under the Rent Acts. The plaintiff subsequently discovered that the property was subject to rent control, and the rent payable would have been only £140 per annum. Nevertheless, had the defendant served

509

the necessary statutory notices, the basic rent could have been increased to approximately £250 to take account of repairs and improvements to the property. The plaintiff sought to recover the overpaid rent over a two-year period, and sought a declaration that he was entitled to continue in occupation for the rest of the lease at an annual rent of £140. The defendant counterclaimed for the lease to be set aside for mistake.

The Court of Appeal gave the plaintiff the choice between surrendering the lease, or continuing in possession but paying the full amount of rent allowable (i.e., about £250) once the necessary statutory notices had been served.

In effect, these terms amounted to enforcement of the original contract term, and arguably this may have been because it was the plaintiff (surveyor) who had supplied the defendant with the information on the rent he could charge.

In **Solle v Butcher**, Denning LJ began his analysis of the law of mistake by referring to the statement of the law by Lord Atkin in **Bell v Lever Bros Ltd** [1932] AC 161, and by accepting the orthodox interpretation of what Lord Atkin said (see 13.4.1.2). He went on to suggest, however, that **Bell v Lever Bros Ltd** is not the whole law on common mistake and said that there was a doctrine of equity, not referred to in the House of Lords in **Bell v Lever Bros Ltd**, by which a contract may be set aside on terms on the basis of common mistake, including in circumstances where the mistake is only one of quality. (Subsequent commentators have expressed surprise that such a talented House of Lords, addressed by such eminent counsel, should have failed to take account of this equitable doctrine if such existed. The most likely explanation is that the doctrine was Denning LJ's own creation and the evidence suggests that this was the case.)

13.5.2 Assessing the evidence to support such an equitable jurisdiction

The argument in favour of a doctrine allowing for a mistake as to quality to be voidable in equity rests on a series of cases, of which a representative sample of two will illustrate that there is little foundation in precedent for it, however desirable the doctrine may have appeared. Perhaps the most important case is **Cooper v Phibbs** (1867) LR 2 HL 149. It was suggested above (see 13.3.2, where the facts are stated) that this was an example of the *res sua* principle of common mistake, which Lord Atkin in **Bell v Lever Bros Ltd** [1932] AC 161 treated as making the contract void. Denning LJ pointed out that, despite this comment, in **Cooper v Phibbs** Lord Westbury had stated that the contract was **voidable**; that the action was brought in the Chancery Court, where, had the contract been void at common law, that would have been the end of the matter; and that the court set the contract aside only after imposing terms on the parties. He therefore concluded that **Cooper v Phibbs** provided evidence to support the existence of an equitable jurisdiction to set aside the contract for mistake.

The circumstantial evidence is impressive, but can be explained as being consistent with Lord Atkin's interpretation of the case on the following grounds:

1. The essential fact is that the plaintiff had to show that he was really the owner of the fishery in question. As life tenant he was not full legal owner but had only an equitable interest. Before the Judicature Act 1873, such an interest would be recognized only in the Chancery Court.

2. Nevertheless, the rule of mistake applied by the Chancery Court was the common law rule that a contract to acquire an interest in one's own property is void as being impossible of performance.

3. The court imposed terms because the would-be lessor had spent money on the land, and was entitled to be compensated for the improvements made, probably on the basis of some form of proprietary estoppel (see **4.9**).

The second case relied on by Denning LJ was *Huddersfield Banking Co. Ltd v Henry Lister & Son Ltd* [1895] 2 Ch 273.

> The bank was a secured creditor of the defendant company, its security being the business property and all fixed assets. The defendant company was in liquidation, so that a receiver held all the company's assets on trust for the creditors. The plaintiff bank agreed to the sale of certain machinery, having determined that it was not fixed. It turned out that it had been improperly loosened, and so should have been treated as a fixed asset and thus part of the plaintiff bank's security. The plaintiff applied to have the agreement set aside.

The reason the bank had to apply to the Chancery Court was that the agreement was made under its auspices as supervisor of the liquidation. However, the court treated the agreement not as voidable but as void. The court relied on two cases (*Cooper v Phibbs* and *Strickland v Turner* (1852) 7 Ex 208: see **13.3.1**), which have both been analysed as examples of the application of the common law common mistake rule. The reason why the contract was void in this case was that at the time when the agreement for the sale of the unfixed machinery was made, there was no unfixed machinery to sell. There is no suggestion that an equitable doctrine of mistake was operating.

It appeared reasonably clear, therefore, that the legal foundation for the proposed equitable doctrine of common mistake was largely insubstantial. Nevertheless, there was significant Court of Appeal authority to support the existence of the equitable jurisdiction, as well as statements indicating that the doctrine was recognized by eminent members of the judiciary, including Steyn J (in *Associated Japanese Bank (International) Ltd v Credit du Nord SA* [1989] 1 WLR 255), who subsequently became a member of the House of Lords. In addition, the doctrine was not without merit. It was certainly much closer to the continental conception of mistake found in the writings of Pothier (see **3.2.1**) than the other elements of the narrow English doctrine.

13.5.2.1 Post-*Solle v Butcher*: Support from the Court of Appeal and High Court

The supposed equitable doctrine was applied or accepted in a number of judicial decisions after *Solle v Butcher*.

> For example, in *Grist v Bailey* [1967] Ch 532, Goff J set aside a contract for the purchase of a house believed to be subject to a protected tenancy whereas in fact it was available with vacant possession, making a difference of some £1,400 to the value of the property. The contract was set aside because the mistake was regarded as being sufficiently fundamental in equity and it was set aside on terms whereby the vendor undertook to give the purchaser the chance to buy the property at the true value.
>
> Similarly, in *Magee v Pennine Insurance Co. Ltd* [1969] 2 QB 507, the majority of the Court of Appeal set aside a contract of settlement of an insurance claim on the ground that the parties had been mistaken about the insured's entitlement to claim as a result of material misstatements in the original insurance proposal. (It is interesting that the terms in this case did not require the insurance company to return the insurance premium.) In this case there was a spirited dissenting judgment from Winn LJ, who considered the case indistinguishable on its facts from *Bell v Lever Bros Ltd*.

13.5.2.2 Steyn J in *Associated Japanese Bank (International) Ltd v Credit du Nord*

Perhaps most significantly, there was clear recognition of the equitable jurisdiction in the judgment of Steyn J (as he then was) in *Associated Japanese Bank (International) Ltd v Credit du Nord*

[1989] 1 WLR 255, although Steyn J clearly recognized that Lord Denning's interpretation of the majority judgments in *Bell v Lever Bros Ltd* was rather selective. Steyn J stated (at pp. 267–8):

> No one could fairly suggest that in this difficult area of the law there is only one correct approach or solution. But a narrow doctrine of common law mistake (as enunciated in *Bell v Lever Bros. Ltd*), supplemented by the more flexible doctrine of mistake in equity (as developed in *Solle v Butcher* and later cases), seems to me to be an entirely sensible and satisfactory state of the law.

Recognizing the tension that had appeared between the common law and equitable approaches to common mistake, Steyn J had sought to clarify the relationship and had concluded that the equitable jurisdiction was intended to mitigate the harshness of the strict approach at common law and would be relevant only where the mistake was not sufficiently fundamental to set aside the contract at common law. Although he did not need to clarify the circumstances in which the equitable jurisdiction would apply (the contract on these facts being void for mistake at common law), Steyn J appears to have regarded the doctrine in a positive light, e.g. in terms of flexibility and achieving a balance between fairness between the parties and protection of subsequently created third party rights.

However, a number of obvious discrepancies remained:

1. It was difficult to see why, if there was an equitable jurisdiction to set aside on terms, that jurisdiction had not been exercised (or even mentioned) in *Bell v Lever Bros*, where fairness between the parties might have suggested the return of all or part of the compensation payment.

2. How could a mistake be **insufficiently fundamental** at common law to render the contract void but **sufficiently fundamental** in equity for it to be set aside on terms?

The only possible conclusion was that 'fundamental' was being used in different senses.

In *William Sindall v Cambridgeshire County Council* [1994] 1 WLR 1016 at p. 1042, Evans LJ (*obiter*) attempted to explain this distinction:

> It must be assumed, I think, that there is a category of mistake which is 'fundamental' so as to permit the equitable remedy of rescission, which is wider than the kind of 'serious and radical' mistake which means that the agreement is void and of no effect in law…The difference may be that the common law rule is limited to mistakes with regard to the subject matter of the contract, whilst equity can have regard to a wider and perhaps unlimited category of 'fundamental' mistake.

The suggestion therefore was that a 'fundamental' common mistake in equity required only that the mistake be material to the parties' positions. In any event, this explanation was hardly convincing although a reasonable attempt at justifying a position already arrived at.

13.5.3 The denial of the equitable jurisdiction to set aside on terms: *Great Peace Shipping Ltd v Tsavliris Salvage (International) Ltd*

In *Great Peace Shipping Ltd v Tsavliris (International) Ltd* [2002] EWCA Civ 1407, [2003] QB 679 (for facts see 13.4.1.3), the alternative argument for the salvage company was that even if the mistake was not such as to render the contract void at common law, it was voidable in equity. However, both the judge at first instance, Toulson J, and the Court of Appeal denied the existence of any such equitable jurisdiction. Lord Phillips concluded:

> [118]   [T]he House of Lords in *Bell v Lever Bros. Ltd*…considered that the intervention of equity, as demonstrated in *Cooper v Phibbs*…, took place in circumstances where the common law would have ruled the contract void for mistake. We do not find it conceivable that the House of Lords overlooked an equitable right in *Lever Bros*. to rescind the agreement, notwithstanding that the agreement was not void for mistake at common law. The jurisprudence established no such right. Lord Atkin's test for common mistake that avoided a contract, while narrow, broadly reflected the circumstances where equity had intervened to excuse performance of a contract assumed to be binding in law.

The Court of Appeal also agreed with Toulson J that Lord Denning's approach in **Solle v Butcher** 'is not to supplement or mitigate the common law: it is to say that *Bell v Lever Bros. Ltd* was wrongly decided'. Lord Denning had been wrong to rely on **Cooper v Phibbs** as supporting his position since the nature of the mistake in that case was to render the contract void at law. In addition, there could be no solid jurisprudential basis for recognition of a category of equitable mistake of the kind alleged since it had not proved possible in the subsequent case law to identify a test for distinguishing mistakes at law and in equity (per Lord Phillips at [153]; for evidence for an attempt to make this distinction see Evans LJ in **William Sindall v Cambridgeshire County Council** [1994] 1 WLR 1016 at p. 1042: see 13.5.2.2). Lord Phillips therefore concluded that there was only one category of 'fundamental' mistake:

> We do not find it possible to distinguish, by a process of definition, a mistake which is 'fundamental' from Lord Atkin's mistake as to quality which 'makes the thing [contracted for] essentially different from the thing [that] it was believed to be'.

On this basis it was impossible to reconcile **Bell v Lever Bros Ltd** and *Solle v Butcher*.

The result was that there was nothing to mitigate the 'all or nothing' conclusion at common law that the contract was valid.

In **Statoil ASA v Louis Dreyfus Energy Service LP, The Harriette N** [2008] EWHC 2257, [2008] 2 Lloyd's Rep 685, [2009] 1 All ER (Comm) 1035 (see also 2.1.2 and 3.3.2.1) Aikens J reviewed the authorities before denying the existence of any equitable jurisdiction to rescind in the context of a claim to set aside a contract in the context of an alleged unilateral mistake as to an assumption made about a settlement contract. He stated (at [105]): 'If there is no such jurisdiction in the case of a common mistake, I fear I am unable to see how, in logic, one can devise a rationale for an equitable jurisdiction in the case of a unilateral mistake, at least where there has been no misrepresentation by the other party.'

13.5.4 Consequences of the denial of the equitable jurisdiction

While this conclusion may have the advantage of producing a neat and conceptually sound result and is one which in terms of legal analysis must be correct, it does mean that the common mistake doctrine is extremely limited. In addition, the outcome would appear to be based on 'all or nothing', i.e. either the contract is void and of no effect at all, or it remains valid.

Lord Phillips recognized this position when he stated:

[161]   We can understand why the decision in *Bell v Lever Bros. Ltd* did not find favour with Lord Denning MR. An equitable jurisdiction to grant rescission on terms where a common fundamental mistake has induced a contract gives greater flexibility than a doctrine of common law which holds the contract void in such circumstances.

In fact, it is not strictly true to state that equity has no possible jurisdiction where the contract is void at common law since **Cooper v Phibbs** provides evidence of equity's ability to intervene in such circumstances. The difficulties relate to situations, such as that in **Great Peace Shipping**, where the mistake is not sufficiently fundamental to render the contract void. There is no remedial flexibility because this is the point at which the line has been drawn. Lord Phillips did suggest that legislative intervention might be called for 'to give greater flexibility to our law of mistake than the common law allows' but he seems to be confining this comment to instances where the contract is void at common law. The New Zealand legislation provides a possible model for legislation which provides for a more flexible doctrine of mistake with flexibility of remedy (see Chandler, Devenney, and Poole [2004] JBL 34). In addition, the Singapore Court of Appeal in **Chwee Kin Keong v Digilandmall.com Pte Ltd** [2005] 1 SLR 502, albeit in the context of a unilateral mistake, criticized the decision in **Great Peace Shipping** denying the existence of the equitable jurisdiction. The court considered that the reason for this denial was 'the absence of any test to determine how the equitable jurisdiction should be applied to rescind a contract which was distinct from that which rendered a contract void in law' (at [68]) but concluded that '[b]y its very nature, the manner in which equity should be applied must depend on the facts of each case and the dictates of justice' (at [74]).

It will be interesting to see how the courts react to the denial in **Great Peace Shipping** of the equitable jurisdiction as it will undoubtedly leave less room for manoeuvre. It is likely that other legal principles will be increasingly relied upon to introduce the necessary degree of flexibility, e.g. implied condition precedent (see **Graves v Graves** and **Butters v BBC Worldwide Ltd**), or misrepresentation. The difficulties that might arise are well illustrated by the factual scenario in **Nutt v Read** (2000) 32 HLR 761, *The Times*, 3 December 1999 (see also (1999) 96 (42) LSG 44).

The claimants had agreed to sell a chalet on a caravan park to the defendants. It was also agreed that the defendants were to pay a monthly rent to occupy the pitch (the tenancy agreement). The defendants failed to pay this rent and the claimants sought to eject them from the site. The defendants' defence was that the agreement had been entered into under a common mistake, namely that both parties mistakenly believed that the chalet could be sold separately from the site pitch on which it stood. The position was complicated by the fact that the defendants had made some improvements to the chalet increasing its value from £12,500 to £28,750.

The two agreements were treated as separate, so that the judge at first instance held the agreement for the sale of the chalet to be void for fundamental mistake, i.e. the common fundamental mistaken assumption that the chalet could be sold separately from the pitch it occupied. Accordingly, the purchase price had to be returned to the defendant because the agreement was impossible in law.

However, as the Court of Appeal made clear, since the contract was void for mistake, there was no entitlement to compensation for the money spent on improvements.

At the time of this decision the courts recognized the existence of an equitable jurisdiction to set aside a contract on terms and the judge at first instance had rescinded the separate tenancy agreement. On appeal, the Court of Appeal confirmed that the tenancy agreement could be rescinded since the parties were under the common misapprehension that the pitch could be used independently of the chalet upon it. However, the issue of rescission on terms had not been appealed so that, although the Court of Appeal accepted that the claimants might have been ordered to pay compensation to the defendants for the improvements, it did not make such an order.

If similar facts were to arise post-***Great Peace Shipping Ltd v Tsavliris (International) Ltd*** [2002] EWCA Civ 1407, [2003] QB 679, the possibility of rescinding in equity would not exist so that it is likely that the court would treat this arrangement as a single agreement which was void at common law. This would allow the return of the purchase price but would not allow for any flexibility in terms of compensation for the improvements to the property returned. It might therefore be necessary to search for evidence of misrepresentation in order to achieve what the court might consider to be an acceptable result on the facts or, to use the common belief that the chalet could be sold separately to the pitch so that the separate tenancy of the pitch was required, in order to justify an argument that the continuation of this state of affairs was an implied condition precedent of the sale contract

The DCFR and initial mistake

Fundamental common mistake will render the contract voidable, rather than void, under the *Draft Common Frame of Reference* (DCFR) provisions and, more generally, the DCFR provides for greater flexibility in terms of the treatment of such mistakes. DCFR II-7:201 provides for either party to a common mistake to avoid the contract where the mistake is 'fundamental'; this is regarded as established where the party seeking avoidance alleges either that but for the mistake it would not have made the contract or that it would have done so only on fundamentally different terms. Avoidance is not possible, however, if there is fault, i.e. if the mistake was inexcusable in the circumstances or the risk of the mistake was assumed, or should have been assumed, by the party seeking avoidance. In cases of common mistake, DCFR II-7:203(3) provides for a discretion in the court to seek to rescue the contract in some form through an ability to respond to a request by either party to adapt the contract in order 'to bring the contract into accordance with what might reasonably have been agreed had the mistake not occurred'.

Further reading

Atiyah, '*Couturier v Hastie* and the sale of non-existent goods' (1957) 73 LQR 340.

Capper, 'More muddle on mistake: *Graves v Graves*' [2008] LMCLQ 264.

Cartwright, '*Associated Japanese Bank v Credit du Nord*' [1988] LMCLQ 300.

Cartwright, *Misrepresentation, Mistake and Non-Disclosure*, 2nd edn (Sweet and Maxwell, 2006).

Chandler, Devenney, and Poole, 'Common mistake: Theoretical justification and remedial inflexibility' [2004] JBL 34.

Macmillan, 'How temptation led to mistake: An explanation of *Bell v Lever Bros. Ltd*' (2003) 119 LQR 625.

Smith, 'Contracts: Mistake, frustration and implied terms' (1994) 110 LQR 400.

Treitel, 'Mistake in contract' (1988) 104 LQR 501.

14 Misrepresentation

Summary of the issues

This chapter examines the legal remedies for actionable misrepresentations, i.e. false statements of fact which induce the contract. A misrepresentation gives rise to different remedies to breaches of contract (i.e., breaches of contractual terms). In particular, the measure of damages is determined using different principles and, whereas a misrepresentation renders the contract voidable so that the contract will be treated as if it had never been made, a breach of contract will not affect the existence of the contract (in the absence of a repudiatory breach which has been accepted as terminating the contract, when future contractual obligations will be discharged: see 8.4.2.1).

• An actionable misrepresentation is an unambiguous false statement of fact made to the claimant and which induces the claimant to enter into the contract with the statement maker. In certain situations conduct can amount to a misrepresentation.

• There is generally no duty of disclosure in English law so that silence will not generally give rise to a claim in misrepresentation, in the absence of deliberate concealment. However, there are some recognized exceptions to this position when a duty of disclosure will arise and the failure to disclose will constitute a misrepresentation.

• The false statement must be a false statement of fact as opposed to a statement of opinion or future intention but in some circumstances what appear to be opinions or statements of intention are in fact statements of fact.

• The false statement of fact must have induced the contract in the sense that it must be material to the decision to contract, be known to the representee, be intended to be acted upon, and have been acted upon.

• If such an actionable misrepresentation has been established, the contract is voidable so that, in principle, the remedy of rescission is available to the claimant, i.e. if rescinded the contract is treated as if it had never been made. However, there are a number of bars to rescission.

• Damages may be available for misrepresentation in order to put the claimant into the position that it would have been in if the misrepresentation had not been made. There are three types of misrepresentations (dependent upon the state of mind of the statement maker): fraudulent, negligent, and innocent. If the misrepresentation is fraudulent, damages are in the tort of deceit, whereas the possibility of recovering damages for negligent misrepresentation was not recognized until the mid-1960s. However, it is now possible to recover damages for negligent misstatement at common law (i.e., in tort), or under s. 2(1) of the Misrepresentation Act 1967, which provides a statutory claim to damages where the burden of proving negligence is reversed. It is not possible to *claim* damages for innocent misrepresentation but damages may be awarded by the court instead of the remedy of rescission under s. 2(2) of the Misrepresentation Act 1967.

- By s. 3 of the Misrepresentation Act 1967, clauses attempting to exclude or limit liability for misrepresentation are subject to the reasonableness requirement. There is some debate, however, about which types of clauses fall within the scope of s. 3.

14.1 Introduction

14.1.1 Misrepresentation and its effect on the parties' positions

Misrepresentation comprises the law relating to the effect on a contract (and hence the parties' positions) where that contract was entered into on the basis of a false statement made during the course of contractual negotiations. A contract made as the result of a misleading representation is, subject to the limitations described in this chapter, voidable at the instance of the person to whom the misrepresentation was made (the misrepresentee). In other words, the primary remedy for misrepresentation will be for the misrepresentee to rescind the contract (set it aside). That person may also (or in the alternative) be able to recover damages as compensation for loss sustained.

Once the essential conditions for recovery for misrepresentation have been established (see 14.2), the combination of remedies available (see 14.5 and 14.6) depends upon the type of misrepresentation in question, whether fraudulent, negligent, or innocent (see 14.4). The law applicable is a complex blend of common law, equity, and statute.

14.1.2 Relationship of misrepresentation and other areas of law

Although misrepresentation is a separate body of law, requiring individual treatment, it enjoys close relations with, and indeed sometimes overlaps with, several other important areas of contract law. When confronted with a factual scenario, which at first sight appears to raise issues of misrepresentation, it is important to consider whether any other principles of law are also relevant, and especially to consider whether the application of those other principles of law might provide a better remedy for the party affected.

1. Misrepresentations which are also terms

Since misrepresentation relates to misleading statements made in the course of contractual negotiations, it is possible for such a statement to take on even greater significance and, by operation of the rules of offer and acceptance and incorporation of terms (see generally Chapter 6), to become an express term of the contract (see 6.1.4 and 6.3). The consequences of a statement being classified as a term are explained below (see 14.3), but the most obvious is that the falsity of the statement will result in a breach of the contract, giving rise to remedies quite different from those available for misrepresentation (see generally Chapter 6, at 6.1.2).

2. Claim based on mistake

The circumstances giving rise to a claim of misrepresentation may also substantiate a claim of mistake (Chapter 13). For example, to enter a contract masquerading as some other person is a fraudulent misrepresentation, while it may also give rise to relief on grounds of a (unilateral) mistake of identity (see 3.3.3). The advantage of mistake over misrepresentation in the majority of situations is that, if established, mistake renders the contract void and not merely voidable (see 3.2.2), so that the party seeking relief may be able to recover property even after it has passed into the hands of a third party.

3. Negligent misstatement in the law of tort

Contractual misrepresentation is very closely linked to negligent misstatements in the law of tort, and a set of facts may raise the possibility of claims for both negligent misstatement in tort and negligent misrepresentation in contract (see, e.g., *Esso Petroleum Co. Ltd v Mardon* [1976] QB 801: 14.4.3.1). It is important, therefore, in order to give the most appropriate advice, to be fully aware of the differences between these claims and the remedies available in each case.

4. Statute

When considering action to be taken in the event of discovering a misleading pre-contractual statement, it is important to remember regulatory legislation, which is also intended to police such behaviour. In the case of the Trade Descriptions Act 1968 and the Property Misdescriptions Act 1991, the making of false statements is an offence, but there is no complementary civil liability incurred (although the law of misrepresentation as described in this chapter may well apply). In the case of the Package Travel, Package Holidays and Package Tours Regulations 1992, SI 1992/3288, there is no civil liability arising out of the main regulations relating to false and misleading statements, but reg. 4 provides that organizers or retailers must compensate consumers for loss resulting from the supply of misleading information. In addition, the Fraud Act 2006 contains a new general criminal offence of fraud that can be committed in three ways: fraud by false representation (s. 2), fraud by failing to disclose information in circumstances where there is a duty of disclosure (s. 3; for these circumstances see the discussion in relation to contract at 14.2.1.2), and fraud by abuse of position (s. 4).

Finally, the Consumer Protection from Unfair Trading Regulations 2008, SI 2008/1277 (CPRs), which came into force on 26 May 2008, implement the EU Unfair Commercial Practices Directive (UCPD), 2005/29/EC (see also discussion at 1.6.2.1 and 15.3.1). The CPRs might be considered to cover similar ground to the law of misrepresentation and disclosure since they prohibit unfair commercial practices (marketing and selling practices) and specifically misleading actions (including false or deceptive information) (reg. 5) and misleading material omissions (reg. 6) in a business-to-consumer (B2C) contract. However the CPRs create offences (enforceable via the Enterprise Act 2002, Enterprise Act 2002 (Part 8 Community Infringements Specified UK Laws) Order 2003, SI 2003/1374, as amended) but do not provide any form of civil remedy for consumers.

There are also measures that apply outside the consumer context in B2B contracts, e.g. the Business Protection from Misleading Marketing Regulations 2008, SI 2008/1276, implementing directive 2006/114/EC concerning misleading and comparative advertising. These regulations are also relevant in this context as they prohibit advertising which misleads traders or is likely to injure a competitor. Again, they create criminal offences and do not impose any civil obligations or remedies.

More generally, it is important to be able to place misrepresentation in the wider context of regulation of contracts. Misrepresentation is an example of a doctrine designed to police the formation process (i.e., the circumstances surrounding the making of the contract) and achieve 'procedural fairness' by providing remedies for fraudulent and negligent misrepresentation, as opposed to fairness in terms of the content of the contract ('substantive fairness'—see, e.g., regulation of unfair terms (Chapter 7) and the penalty rule (9.10.2)). Other examples of doctrines aimed at achieving procedural fairness are the doctrines of duress and undue influence (discussed in Chapter 15).

14.2 Actionable misrepresentations

For a claim based on misrepresentation to succeed, there must have been an unambiguous, false statement of existing fact, which induced the claimant to enter into the contract.

14.2.1 False statement of fact

14.2.1.1 False and unambiguous

It might be assumed that identifying the fact that the statement is false would be an easy matter. However, falsity is sometimes a matter of degree. In *Avon Insurance plc v Swire Fraser Ltd* [2000] 1 All ER (Comm) 573, [2000] CLC 665, Rix J adopted the test applicable under s. 20(4) of the Marine Insurance Act 1906, namely whether the statement is 'substantially correct' so that any difference between what was represented and the correct position would not have been likely to induce a reasonable person to make the contract.

This is linked to the requirement that the misrepresentation be unambiguous. A party making a representation, which on a reasonable construction is true, will not be liable for misrepresentation simply because the representee has put some other construction on it which is not true.

In *McInerny v Lloyds Bank Ltd* [1974] 1 Lloyd's Rep 246, the purchaser of a business defaulted on the contract, causing loss to the plaintiff seller. The seller claimed to have been induced to enter the contract by a statement in a telex sent at the purchaser's request to the seller by the defendant bank. The statement in question was an opinion expressed to the purchaser about whether the seller would be likely to find the financing arrangements acceptable, and could not reasonably be construed as advising the seller to agree to the deal proposed. The Court of Appeal held that the bank was not liable for an unreasonable interpretation put on its statement by the plaintiff seller.

Thus, conduct will give rise to a claim for misrepresentation only if the meaning attached to the conduct by the claimant is a reasonable conclusion to be drawn from the defendant's actions.

14.2.1.2 Statement

Conduct

The requirement for a 'statement' has in one sense been interpreted fairly broadly, because the courts have shown a willingness to find the existence of a misrepresentation based on conduct, without the need for words. For example in *Curtis v Chemical Cleaning & Dyeing Co. Ltd* [1951] 1 KB 805 (see 7.4.2), Denning LJ stated:

any behaviour, by words or conduct, is sufficient to be a misrepresentation if it is such as to mislead the other…If it conveys a false impression, that is enough.

In *Gordon v Sellico* (1986) 278 EG 53, the plaintiff purchased the property in question following an inspection. However, the vendor was held to have fraudulently concealed dry rot and this was held to constitute a representation that the property did not suffer from dry rot.

Gordon v Sellico was relied upon in *Taylor v Hamer* [2002] EWCA Civ 1130, [2003] 1 EGLR 103. *Taylor v Hamer* concerned the removal of flagstones following the purchaser's inspection of the property, and the concealment of this fact by the making of an untruthful response to a pre-contract enquiry so that the purchaser was misled. (On the facts the existence of the flagstones was a term of the contract so their absence amounted to a breach for which damages for breach of contract were available.) In both cases the principle of *caveat emptor* (let the buyer beware) did not apply because of the actions and statements of the vendor which were intended to, and did, mislead the purchasers.

    Gordon v Sellico can usefully be compared with *Horsfall v Thomas* (1862) 1 H & C 90 (see also 14.2.2.2) where although there was a representation by conduct, the necessary inducement to contract was missing.

In *Horsfall v Thomas* concealing a serious defect in a gun by inserting a metal 'plug' amounted to representation by conduct. However, since the purchaser did not inspect the gun before purchase, he could not have been induced by the representation, and therefore there was no actionable misrepresentation.

A more recent example of a misrepresentation by conduct is provided by the facts in *Spice Girls Ltd v Aprilia World Service BV* [2000] EMLR 478.

The defendant, a motor scooter manufacturer, had agreed to sponsor the tour of the pop group, the Spice Girls. The group had participated in a photo shoot and other promotional material before the agreement was signed at a time when it was found that they knew that one member of the band had declared an intention to leave the group before the expiry of the term of the sponsorship agreement. The defendant sought damages for misrepresentation.

    Arden J held that taking part in the promotions amounted to a misrepresentation by conduct, namely a misrepresentation that the group did not know and had no reasonable grounds to believe that any member of the group had the intention to leave before the end of the agreement. (See also exception to duty of disclosure, below.)

This authority was relied upon in *Crystal Palace Football Club (2000) Ltd v Dowie* [2007] EWHC 1392 (QB), [2007] IRLR 682.

The defendant football manager's contract contained a provision requiring compensation of £1m to be paid if he left before the end of the contract term in order to take up employment at a premiership club. The claimant football club had entered into a compromise agreement with the defendant whereby the club agreed to release him without compensation. Crystal Palace was playing in the championship at the time and had failed to gain promotion. Eight days later the defendant was appointed as the manager of a premiership club, Charlton Athletic. The claimant therefore alleged that the defendant had deceived it into releasing him without compensation by falsely representing that he wanted to leave to move north for family reasons and had had no contact with Charlton.

It was held that the defendant had represented that he had no contact from Charlton at the relevant time and so was impliedly representing that he had no present intention to join Charlton, whereas he did have such an intention. He therefore knew the representations to be false and these misrepresentations had induced the making of the compromise agreement to forego the compensation payment.

Silence or non-disclosure

In another sense the requirement that there be a false 'statement' has been strictly interpreted. In most situations because of the principle of *caveat emptor* ('let the buyer beware'), mere silence or non-disclosure does not amount to an unambiguous, false representation, and therefore will not give rise to a claim for misrepresentation. Of course, as can be seen from the discussion at 14.2.2.2, where the non-disclosure goes beyond merely remaining silent and involves taking active steps to conceal a defect, it may amount to misrepresentation (see *Horsfall v Thomas* (1862) 1 H & C 90).

The general rule is usually said to be that there is no duty to disclose facts which if known might affect the other party's decision to enter the contract (*Keates v The Earl of Cadogan* (1851) 10 CB 591). The rule reflects the attitude of classical contract law that the parties must look after their own interests in making contracts. It may also be justified by saying that a general duty of disclosure would be too vague, since it would be impossible to specify precisely what should be disclosed. For example, in *Sykes v Taylor-Rose* [2004] EWCA Civ 299, [2004] 2 P & CR 30, in pre-liminary enquiries the vendor of a house was required to disclose 'any other information that you think the buyer might have a right to know'. This was held not to extend to include the fact that a child murder had been committed in the house some years earlier. The question of what should be disclosed was to be judged subjectively and the vendor honestly believed the purchaser had no right to be told.

Nevertheless, the general rule is subject to certain exceptions.

1. Half-truths

It is a misrepresentation to make statements which are true but which are misleading because they do not reveal all the relevant facts. Thus, to describe property which is the subject of negotiations for sale as fully let, without disclosing that the tenants have given notice to quit, is a misrepresentation (*Dimmock v Hallett* (1866) LR 2 Ch App 21).

2. Change of circumstances

Where a truthful statement of fact is made but is subsequently rendered misleading by a change of circumstances, there is a duty to correct what has become a false impression.

In *With v O'Flanagan* [1936] Ch 575, the defendant wished to sell his medical practice, and gave infor-mation to the plaintiff about the income to be derived from the practice. This information was true at the time it was given. The defendant then fell ill and the income from the practice fell away to almost nothing. The sale took place five months after the original information had been given, and without the defendant disclosing that the income had fallen dramatically. On discovering the state of the practice, the plaintiff successfully sought rescission of the contract of sale. He was entitled to continue to believe the truth of the statement made until the time of the sale or until it was corrected, so that failure to cor-rect it amounted to a misrepresentation.

In *Spice Girls Ltd v Aprilia World Service BV* [2000] EMLR 478, it was held that there was a duty to cor-rect the representation by conduct, namely, that the group did not know of the intention of one member to leave before the period of the sponsorship agreement ended. Nothing had been done to correct this continuing representation.

It is less clear whether a change of circumstances causing a person to amend an opinion voiced in the course of negotiations imposes a duty to disclose the change of opinion. It might be thought that since in some circumstances an opinion is treated as a statement of fact (see 14.2.1.3), in those same circumstances at least there would be a duty of disclosure where the opinion changed. Indeed, an argument could be made for extending the duty further, since an opinion will be treated as a statement of fact where there are no reasonable grounds for the opinion held. A change of circumstances would bring a once honestly held opinion into that category, and would appear to justify a duty of disclosure.

The same argument appears to apply to statements of future intention when the intention changes but is not disclosed before the time of contracting. However, despite some authority to the contrary (*Traill v Baring* (1864) 4 DJ & S 318, 46 ER 941), it has traditionally been considered that there is no duty to disclose a change of intention.

In *Wales v Wadham* [1977] 1 WLR 199, the plaintiff and the defendant, formerly husband and wife, agreed in the course of divorce proceedings that the plaintiff would pay the defendant £13,000 from his share of the sale of their house in return for her promise not to seek a maintenance award. The defendant had stated several times that she would not remarry. By the time of this agreement she had changed that intention, but did not reveal the fact to the plaintiff, who subsequently claimed that he would not have entered into the agreement had he known she was to remarry.

His action for rescission failed. The defendant was under no obligation to communicate her subsequent change of intention since her original statement of intention was honestly held at that time and did not amount to a representation of fact (see 14.2.1.3 for a discussion of the effect of statements of intention).

However, a recent case suggests that this traditional interpretation needs some refining. There may be liability if a representor who is taken to be making a continuing representation changes his mind but then fails to disclose that change of intention to the representee. In *Inclusive Technology v Williamson* [2009] EWCA Civ 718, [2009] EG 110, in the context of a statutory termination notice of a tenancy which indicated an intention to refurbish where the landlord later changed his mind but did not inform the tenant, the Court of Appeal held that compensation was payable on the basis that this representation only had meaning if it was a continuing representation into the future. As such it carried with it a duty to speak. By comparison, the statement in *Wales v Wadham* could never be taken as a 'statement that she would never change her mind'. In *Wales v Wadham* the statement was no more than an opinion and not a continuing representation into the future.

3. Fiduciary or confidential relationship

A fiduciary relationship is a relationship of special confidence between certain classes of people, imposing particular duties of care on those to whom confidence is entrusted. Typical examples of such relationships are solicitor and client, agent and principal, and between partners in a partnership. In such a relationship there is a duty of disclosure of all material facts. There is a close relationship between this duty of disclosure and the doctrine of undue influence, as can be seen from the case of *Tate v Williamson* (1866) LR 2 Ch App 55 (see 15.2).

4. Contracts *uberrimae fidei*

Certain types of contract impose a duty of disclosure irrespective of the nature of the relationship between the parties. They are called contracts *uberrimae fidei* (of utmost good faith), and the most common example is the contract of insurance. The insured is under a duty to disclose all material facts at the time of making the contract of insurance, and failure to disclose such facts entitles the insurer to refuse to pay when a claim is made (i.e., the insurance contract is voidable at the option of the insurers). The rule may be explained as necessary to enable the insurer to make a proper assessment of the risk it is to underwrite, and the duty is placed on the insured because it is claimed that the insured is the person in possession of the relevant information. However, it does mean that a person seeking insurance is placed in a difficult position because of the need correctly to identify those facts which are material and therefore to be disclosed.

In *Pan Atlantic Insurance Co. Ltd v Pine Top Insurance Co. Ltd* [1995] 1 AC 501, the House of Lords considered the circumstances in which an insurer could avoid liability on grounds of non-disclosure. The majority (in agreement with the principal speech of Lord Mustill) found that a non-disclosure would be material if it would have some (not necessarily decisive) effect on the mind of a prudent underwriter. Their Lordships were unanimous in deciding that materiality was only half the test since it also had to be shown that the non-disclosure induced the making of the contract (see 14.2.2.1).

Where there is a duty of disclosure and a fraudulent failure to disclose the information, a criminal offence may be committed (Fraud Act 2006, s. 3) if there was an intention to make a gain or cause a loss to another.

14.2.1.3 Statement of fact

If there is a false statement, it must also be a statement of fact as opposed to a statement of belief or opinion or a statement of future conduct or intention. This is because a fact can be true or false and because a representee is only justified in relying on facts. However, it is worth noting at the outset of this discussion that if a statement is made fraudulently (see 14.4.1.1), it is likely to be treated as a statement of fact.

Statements of law will usually constitute statements of fact because they are rarely abstract statements and are usually statements concerning the application of the law to certain facts (see the discussion at point 3 below).

1. Statements of opinion or belief

As a general rule, a statement of opinion is not a statement of fact.

> For example, in *Bisset v Wilkinson* [1927] AC 177, the owner of land told a prospective purchaser that, in his opinion, if properly worked, the land would support 2,000 sheep. However, to the knowledge of the purchaser, the owner had not worked the land himself as a sheep farmer, and the statement was no more than an honest estimate, made without particular expertise, as to the capacity of the land. The fact that the land did not have such a capacity did not therefore result in the owner's statement constituting a misrepresentation.

The significant factor was that the statement maker was in no better position to know the facts than the purchaser—and the purchaser knew this.

> In *Economides v Commercial Union Assurance Co. plc* [1997] 3 WLR 1066, it was held that there was no misrepresentation when a son incorrectly stated the value of his parents' belongings for the purposes of a contents insurance policy. They were not his belongings so that he was not in any better position than the insurers to know their true value.

Significantly, it was also held that there is no duty imposed upon such a person to carry out inquiries to establish an objectively reasonable basis for that statement of belief, i.e. to obtain independent valuations. To hold otherwise would clearly have been inconsistent with *Bisset v Wilkinson* and with the decision in *Hummingbird Motors Ltd v Hobbs* [1986] RTR 276, to the effect that statements of opinion by a person with no special knowledge of the subject matter will not constitute misrepresentations even if the belief is unreasonable.

However, what of the situation where the statement maker is in a better position to know the truth? Where the statement maker is in a better position to know the true position, that statement maker is representing that his statement is based on a reasonable belief and that he has reasonable grounds for making it. It follows that if the statement maker had no such reasonable belief or reasonable grounds, the false statement will constitute a misrepresentation.

In *Smith v Land & House Property Corporation* (1884) 28 ChD 7, the vendor described the tenant of property sold as 'a most desirable tenant', which was far from being the case. It was argued on the vendor's behalf that his statement had been no more than an expression of opinion but this argument was rejected by Bowen LJ, who said that *a statement of opinion by a person who is in the best position to know the true position would often be a statement of fact because there is an implicit assertion that the statement maker knows of facts that justify that opinion.*

What about *forecasts by experts*? It may be that the rule that statements of opinion are not generally representations of fact is no more than a particular application of the rule that a representation is not actionable unless made with the intention that it be relied upon by the representee (see 14.2.2.3). Thus, it is common practice to preface a remark by saying, 'It is only my opinion', when it is intended that no reliance should be placed upon it. In some circumstances a statement will be made which can only be an opinion, in that conclusive proof of its truth is unavailable at the time when the statement is made. **Nevertheless, the courts are prepared to impose liability for misrepresentation if the statement was made negligently, by an apparent 'expert', and with the intention that it be relied upon.**

In *Esso Petroleum Co. Ltd v Mardon* [1976] QB 801 a forecast was made by an Esso representative who possessed many years experience and therefore was considered to possess special skill and knowledge in relation to the subject matter of his forecast. This forecast of the potential throughput of a petrol station was intended to be relied upon by the prospective tenant and therefore amounted to a statement of fact that reasonable care and skill had been used in its preparation.

Although this statement was considered to be a statement of fact, the actual decision in the case is that the forecast amounted to a breach of contract (collateral warranty) or that there had been a breach of the duty of care in tort (negligent misstatement).

2. Statements of future conduct or intention

A misrepresentation as to the future is not, in general, a representation of existing fact, and is therefore not actionable. Thus, a person may state an intention at a point in time to follow a certain course of conduct in the future. It is not misrepresentation if that person is prevented from following that course of conduct or later changes his mind.

In *Inntrepreneur Pub Co. v Sweeney* [2002] EWHC 1060 (Ch), [2002] 2 EGLR 132, the defendant, landlord of a public house, had made a statement predicting that the tenant would be released from a beer tie by the end of March 1998. This statement of intention was honestly made and based on good grounds since the defendants' policy at that time was to release pubs from the ties in accordance with an undertaking to this effect which had been given to the Secretary of State for Trade and Industry.

Nevertheless, if the representation is a continuing one, the decision in *Inclusive Technology v Williamson* [2009] EWCA Civ 718, [2009] EG 110, suggests there is a duty to correct a change in intention and that a failure to do so may give rise to liability in some circumstances.

In addition, **if at the time of stating the intention the person did not in fact have any such intention, then that would be treated as misrepresentation, since a present intention is a fact which can be falsely described.**

In *Edgington v Fitzmaurice* (1885) 24 ChD 459, the directors of a company offered debentures for sale, saying that the purpose of the issue of debentures was to raise money for alterations and additions to premises, and for other purposes implying an expansion of the company's business. In fact, the money was needed to meet the company's liabilities. Bowen LJ noted that a representation as to the future would not normally form the basis of an action for misrepresentation, but had no hesitation in finding that where the state of a man's mind can be ascertained (although it may well not be easy to prove), it is 'as much a fact as the state of his digestion'. As a result, a misstatement as to the state of a man's mind is an actionable misrepresentation, and the directors in *Edgington v Fitzmaurice* were held liable.

3. Statements of law as applied to particular facts can be a statement of fact

Until recently it had traditionally been considered that a misstatement of law would not found a claim for misrepresentation. However, the correct position was that an abstract misstatement of law (made without reference to particular facts) could not found an actionable misrepresentation (e.g., 'rent control does not apply to premises which have been substantially altered so that they are in effect new premises'). It is more common for the representation to combine law and facts, e.g. *Solle v Butcher* [1950] 1 KB 671, so that it is a statement of the **effect** of the law in a given situation (e.g., 'the alterations done to these premises have made them new premises in the eyes of the law, so that rent control will not apply'). Such a statement, if false, is often described as a misrepresentation of private rights, and has traditionally been actionable.

In *Pankhania v Hackney London Borough Council* [2002] NPC 123, it was held that, since the decision of the House of Lords in *Kleinwort Benson Ltd v Lincoln City Council* [1999] 2 AC 349 (when the House overturned the principle that mistakes of law could not form the basis for a restitutionary claim for money paid), it was no longer the case that a misstatement of law could not be actionable.

The alleged representation preceding the purchase of a property used as a car park concerned a statement that the occupier of the car park was a contractual licensee whose occupation could be terminated on three month's notice. This was in fact incorrect and the car park user was protected as a business tenant under the Landlord and Tenant Act 1954. The judge, Rex Tedd QC, held that this was an actionable misrepresentation of law and awarded damages for misrepresentation under s. 2(1) of the Misrepresentation Act 1967.

However, in this case the statement of law relates to the application of the law to certain facts and therefore has traditionally been actionable on that basis.

14.2.2 Induces the other party to contract

For the representation to be said to have induced the contract, four conditions must be satisfied:

1. The representation must be material.
2. It must be known to the representee.
3. It must be intended to be acted upon.
4. It must be acted upon.

14.2.2.1 Material representation

A representation will induce a contract only if it is material. It must represent a fact which would positively influence a reasonable person, considering entering the contract, to decide positively in favour of so doing.

In many circumstances the requirement of materiality may be something of a formality, serving only to exclude trivial misstatements from actionability, or to enable the court to infer actual inducement (see 14.2.2.4). Thus, where a statement is made with the intention of inducing a contract (see 14.2.2.3), and is such as would influence a reasonable person to agree (that is, is **material**), it is not difficult to infer actual inducement (*Smith v Chadwick* (1884) 9 App Cas 187 at p. 196, and *Avon Insurance plc v Swire Fraser Ltd* [2000] 1 All ER (Comm) 573 at p. 633). Alternatively, if a representee does not act unreasonably in actually being induced to contract, it may be assumed that the representation was material.

14.2.2.2 Known to the representee

A representation cannot be said to have induced a contract unless it was known to the representee.

> Thus, in **Horsfall v Thomas** (1862) 1 H & C 90, active concealment was held to be a misrepresentation, but the plaintiff's failure to inspect the subject matter (a gun) meant that the misrepresentation never came to his attention, and so did not induce the contract.

Consistent with the general law of agency, a representation made to an agent is 'known' to the principal, whether actual knowledge exists or not (e.g., *Strover v Harrington* [1988] 1 All ER 769).

In addition, a representation made by one party to another, which induces a third party to enter a contract, is actionable by the third party provided the first party knew or ought to have been aware that the representation would be likely to be communicated to the third party (***Pilmore v Hood*** (1838) 5 Bing NC 97 and *Yianni v Edwin Evans and Sons* [1981] 3 All ER 593). This principle was applied in ***Clef Aquitaine Sarl v Laporte Materials (Barrow) Ltd*** [2000] 3 WLR 1760.

> In **Clef Aquitaine Sarl v Laporte Materials (Barrow) Ltd**, the first plaintiff company had been induced to enter into distribution agreements by a fraudulent misrepresentation based on the price list. However, the second plaintiff company had subsequently taken over the agreements (by novation). It was held that the second plaintiffs could rely on the misrepresentation because the defendants knew that the first plaintiffs were '[notionally] repeating to the [second plaintiffs] the misrepresentations which [the defendants] had made' but had 'stood by and allowed them to complete the novations without disillusioning them'.

14.2.2.3 Intended to be acted upon

To be actionable, a misrepresentation must be intended to be acted upon.

> In *Peek v Gurney* (1873) LR 6 HL 377, the promoters of a company issued a prospectus containing material misstatements. The intention had been to induce people to apply for the allotment of shares on formation of the company. The plaintiffs claimed to have been induced by the statements in the prospectus to purchase shares in the market. They were unable to recover their losses since there had been no intention on the part of those issuing the prospectus that it should be relied upon by those dealing in the shares subsequent to the original allotment.

As noted above (see 14.2.1.3), the qualification of a statement as merely an opinion is often taken to indicate that it is not intended that the statement be relied upon.

14.2.2.4 Actually acted upon

To establish that the representation induced the contract, it may not be enough merely to show that it was made and known about, that it was material, and that the representee entered into the contract. It is open to the representor to attempt to prove that the representee did not actually rely on the misrepresentation in deciding to enter the contract, but was persuaded by some other factor.

In *Peekay Intermark Ltd v Australia and New Zealand Banking Group Ltd* [2006] EWCA Civ 386, [2006] 2 Lloyd's Rep 511, [2006] 1 CLC 582 (for facts see **6.2.2.1**), the question was whether the claimant had been induced to sign an investment contract by relying on the informal (and incorrect) description of the product given over the telephone. The Court of Appeal held that it had been established that there was no inducement, stressing the fact that the claimant was 'an experienced investor' and the loose terms in which the product was described orally (so that it was not possible to obtain any clear understanding of the precise nature of the product without reference to the written terms and conditions in the signed writing, which the claimant had signed without reading). The claimant had therefore been induced to sign the written contract not as a result of anything the defendant bank had stated orally but as a result of his own assumption that the investment product in the written contract corresponded with the oral description. (See also the discussion at **14.7.3** in relation to the risk disclosure statement which the claimant had also signed.)

It seems, however, that in practical terms this will be possible only where the alleged misrepresentation is not fraudulent (***Barton v County NatWest Ltd*** [1999] Lloyd's Rep Bank 408). If the misrepresentation is fraudulent and material, it will give rise to a presumption of intention that the statement be acted upon and inducement (***Dadourian Group International Inc. v Simms (Damages)*** [2009] EWCA Civ 169, [2009] 1 Lloyd's Rep 601). Arden LJ summarized the position (at [99]) as follows:

(1) it is a question of fact whether a representee has been induced to enter into a transaction by a material misrepresentation intended by the representor to be relied upon by the representee; (2) if the misrepresentation is of such a nature that it would be likely to play a part in the decision of a reasonable person to enter into a transaction it will be presumed that it did so unless the representor satisfies the court to the contrary (see Morritt LJ in *Barton v County NatWest Ltd* [1999] Lloyd's Rep Bank 408 at page 421, para 58); (3) the misrepresentation does not have to be the sole inducement for the representee to be able to rely on it: it is enough if the misrepresentation plays a real and substantial part, albeit not a decisive part, in inducing the representee to act; (4) the presumption of inducement is rebutted by the representor showing that the misrepresentation did not play a real and substantial part in the representee's decision to enter into the transaction; the representor does not have to go so far as to show that the misrepresentation played no part at all; and (5) the issue is to be decided by the court on a balance of probabilities on the whole of the evidence before it.

Point (3) makes it clear that fraudulent misrepresentation will be considered to have induced the contract even if it is not the only factor to have contributed to the decision to enter the contract. It must merely be 'actively in the mind' of the misrepresentee when the contract is made as one of the reasons inducing the contract (***Ross River Ltd v Cambridge City Football Club Ltd*** [2007] EWHC 2115 (Ch), [2008] 1 All ER 1004, [2008] 1 All ER (Comm) 1028), although it need not be decisive.

In *Edgington v Fitzmaurice* (1885) 24 ChD 459 (see 14.2.1.3), the representee entered the contract partly as a result of fraudulent misrepresentations made, and partly as a result of his own mistake in thinking that the benefits of the contract were greater than was really the case. Nevertheless, the remedy of rescission was available to the representee.

Similarly, in *Morris v Jones* [2002] EWCA Civ 1790, unreported, 6 December 2002, a fraudulent misrepresentation that a basement flat had been 'tanked' could still be relied upon by the claimant, the prospective purchaser of the leasehold, as a factor inducing the contract despite the fact that the claimant had received three reports identifying problems of dampness in the property.

In cases of fraud, once it is concluded that the misrepresentation was intended to be acted upon and was relied upon by the misrepresentee in deciding to enter into the transaction in question, speculation as to how the representee would have acted if s/he had been told the truth is strictly irrelevant (*Downs v Chappell* [1997] 1 WLR 426 and *Dadourian Group International Inc v Simms (Damages)* [2009] EWCA Civ 169, [2009] 1 Lloyd's Rep 601), as is an argument that the representee would have made the contract even if the representation had not been made.

Is there still inducement where the representee chooses to test the truth of the statement and conducts their own investigations? With the exception of instances of fraudulent statements (*S. Pearson & Son Ltd v Dublin Corporation* [1907] AC 351), if the representee chooses to test the truth of the statement made by making their own investigations then the representee may be held to have relied upon their own judgement and not upon the misrepresentation.

In *Attwood v Small* (1838) 6 Cl & F 232, the plaintiffs sought to rescind a contract for the purchase of a mine, citing in evidence false statements made by the defendant seller about the mine's potential. However, the plaintiffs had sought to verify the seller's claims by appointing their own agent to examine the mine, and the agent had reported in similar terms. The House of Lords held that the contract could not be rescinded since the plaintiffs had relied on their own expert and not on the word of the seller. The fact that the expert had failed to discover the truth did not make the seller liable.

It is important not to overstate the scope of this principle since, as noted above, it will not operate if the misrepresentation is fraudulent. (See, e.g., *Clinicare Ltd v Orchard Homes & Developments Ltd* [2004] EWHC 1694 (QB), unreported, 14 July 2004: fraudulent statement that lessor was not aware of the property having been affected by dry rot at any time. Later the lessor's construction director had stated that there had been dry rot in the staircase but this had been replaced. The claimant's own surveyor reported that there was evidence of dry rot and further investigation was required, but the claimant subsequently entered into the lease which had imposed a full repairing obligation. Held: the decision to ignore the surveyor's advice was in part induced by the misrepresentation.)

In addition, as this decision illustrates, in order for *Attwood v Small* to operate it would appear that the misrepresentee must have relied entirely on the results of their own investigations and not at all on the misrepresentor's statement. This is unlikely to be the case, and ironically this will be particularly applicable where the investigations reveal a discrepancy between the misrepresentation and the independent report.

Is there still inducement if the representee fails to take advantage of an opportunity to discover the truth? The mere fact that the representee fails to take advantage of an opportunity to discover the truth, for example by inspection of goods or property, does not prevent reliance on the misrepresentation. Such a person will still be induced by the misrepresentation.

> In *Redgrave v Hurd* (1881) 20 ChD 1, an elderly solicitor wished to sell his house and a share in his practice. He told a prospective younger partner that the income of the practice was about £300 a year, showing him ledgers covering some £200 a year and stating that the balance was made up by income not shown in the ledgers but derived from other work represented by a bundle of papers which were available. The prospective partner did not examine the bundle of papers; had he done so, he would have discovered that the income they represented was minimal. At first instance, it was held that failure to take the opportunity of inspecting the papers indicated that there had been no reliance on the misstatement. However, on appeal that finding was unanimously overturned and it was held that the contract could be rescinded for the misrepresentation.

The decision in *Redgrave v Hurd* must now be read in the light of the developing law governing negligent misrepresentation and the application thereto of the doctrine of contributory negligence (see 14.6.7). However, that cannot disturb the fact of inducement by the misrepresentation and the availability of rescission. Any contributory negligence will affect only the measure of the damages award.

The *Redgrave v Hurd* principle was applied in the analysis of the Court of Appeal in *Peekay Intermark Ltd v Australia and New Zealand Banking Group Ltd* [2006] EWCA Civ 386, [2006] 2 Lloyd's Rep 511, [2006] 1 CLC 582 (see 6.2.2.1 and above) since it was noted that the defendant bank could not argue that the claimant was bound because he *should have* read the final terms and conditions before signing. Constructive notice will not suffice to prevent inducement; the knowledge of the true position must be actual.

14.3 Representations which become terms

As noted above (see 14.1.2), a misrepresentation may in some circumstances become a term of the contract. In other words, the representation can be incorporated as a term. For detailed consideration of the circumstances in which representations become terms, see 6.1.

At one time it was particularly important to attempt to establish that a representation had become a term of the contract because, unless fraud could be established (see 14.4.1.1), the remedies for misrepresentation compared very unfavourably with the remedies for breach (see 6.1.2). However, since it has been recognized that damages for negligent misrepresentation are available (see 14.4.3), identifying the fact that a representation has become a term is not as essential in terms of remedy. Moreover, it is no longer the case that the fact that a representation has become a term extinguishes the right to rescission for misrepresentation (Misrepresentation Act 1967, s. 1). Nevertheless, it will still be important to be able to determine whether a representation has become a term of the contract (see the discussion at 6.1.2):

- Damages are available for misrepresentation only on proof of fault, whereas damages are available as of right for breach of a term.
- A different measure of loss applies to misrepresentation from that applying to breach and the remoteness rules are different in breach of contract and misrepresentation claim.

Where a representation becomes a term, the injured party will have two possible claims: in breach of contract, and in misrepresentation. A skilful lawyer may be able to manipulate the distinctions between remedies for breach of contract and remedies for misrepresentation to his client's advantage (e.g., by formulating a claim for damages under s. 2(1) of the Misrepresentation Act 1967 where there are significant consequential losses or claiming expectation damages for breach of contract where the contract would have been a 'good bargain'). However, it is not possible both to rescind for misrepresentation and to claim damages in contract (expectation measure: see 9.2.1) since the effect of rescission is to treat the contract as if it had never been made and it is therefore not possible to obtain damages for its breach.

14.4 Types of misrepresentation

The remedies available for misrepresentation depend upon the type of misrepresentation, i.e. upon the state of mind of the statement maker in making the statement which induced the contract. There are three types of misrepresentation: fraudulent, negligent, and innocent. (This should not be confused with the fact that there are four possible **damages awards** for misrepresentation: tort of deceit, tort of negligent misstatement, s. 2(1), and s. 2(2) of the Misrepresentation Act 1967.)

The distinction between the three types of misrepresentation is particularly important in determining the damages for misrepresentation but also has some relevance in the context of the remedy of rescission.

In this section the elements of each type of misrepresentation are considered, while the remedies of rescission and damages are considered in 14.5 and 14.6.

14.4.1 Making the basic distinction

14.4.1.1 Fraud

Fraud was defined by the House of Lords in **Derry v Peek** (1889) 14 App Cas 337 as a false statement, 'made knowingly, or without belief in its truth, or recklessly, careless whether it be true or false'.

The essential ingredient for fraud is the absence of an honest belief that the statement is true. It is on this basis that it is possible to distinguish recklessness (fraud) and mere lack of care (negligence). Lord Herschell, who provided the above definition, went on to say that, in order to constitute fraud, recklessness must amount to an absence of belief in the truth of the statement made. In **Thomas Witter Ltd v TBP Industries Ltd** [1996] 2 All ER 573 at p. 587, Jacob J construed Lord Herschell's remarks as requiring a disregard for the truth' amounting to 'dishonesty'. In other words, a statement maker would be reckless if they had no knowledge whether the statement was true or false but asserted that it was true and thereby took a risk.

Change of circumstances misrepresentation: Fraudulent or negligent?

In **Thomas Witter Ltd v TBP Industries Ltd** [1996] 2 All ER 573, it was alleged that a failure to disclose a change in accounting method (see **With v O'Flanagan** [1936] Ch 575) amounted to a change of circumstances misrepresentation. It is certainly easy to jump to the conclusion that such a failure to disclose a change of circumstances will be deceitful. However, Jacob J explained that the failure to disclose might be attributable to a failure to realize that there is a duty to disclose. It is important, therefore, to consider whether the failure was in fact deliberate or dishonest (in which case it will amount to a fraudulent misrepresentation, as in **Banks v Cox** [2002] EWHC

2166 (Ch), unreported, 25 October 2002: deliberate failure to inform prospective purchasers of change in the social services budget which would impact on the nursing home business and other factors which had affected the business since the last set of accounts had been prepared), or whether there is no dishonesty and the failure to disclose the change in circumstances is merely negligent. The failure of a firm of architects to inform the client that the project leader for the contract had resigned and yet letting them sign the contract was established as a fraudulent misrepresentation in ***Fitzroy Robinson Ltd v Mentmore Towers Ltd*** [2009] EWHC 1552 (TCC), 125 Con LR 171, [2009] NPC 90, on the basis that the architects knew the importance that the clients attached to the project leader's continuing involvement and that disclosure might lead the client to go elsewhere.

Such a misrepresentation (involving a failure to disclose change of circumstances) would, it seems, have to be at least negligent, because under s. 2(1) of the Misrepresentation Act 1967 the burden of disproving negligence requires the misrepresentor to prove that the facts represented were true 'up to the time the contract was made'. In instances involving a failure to disclose a change of circumstances, the misrepresentor will be unable to discharge this burden.

14.4.1.2 Negligent misrepresentation

Fraud can be distinguished from a negligent statement where the statement maker believes the statement to be true (i.e., the statement maker is honest) but has been careless in reaching that conclusion. In other words, the statement maker is in breach of a duty of reasonable care and skill in making the statement.

14.4.1.3 Innocent misrepresentation

If the statement maker honestly believes that their statement is true and has reasonable grounds for that belief, the statement will be classified as an innocent misrepresentation.

14.4.2 Fraudulent misrepresentation and remedies available

At one time being able to establish fraud was crucial, since damages could not otherwise be claimed for misrepresentation. Today, a right to damages also exists in the case of negligent misrepresentation (see 14.4.3), but the distinction is still important in some cases, since proof of fraud **may** permit a greater measure of recovery (see 14.6.2) and takes the situation outside the scope of the court's discretion to award damages instead of rescission under s. 2(2) of the Misrepresentation Act 1967 (see 14.4.4).

Fraud provides the strongest combination of remedies for misrepresentation. Rescission and damages are available, and it is generally accepted that in the case of fraud the courts will compensate all loss which is a direct result of the transaction (***Doyle v Olby (Ironmongers) Ltd*** [1969] 2 QB 158). Damages for fraudulent misrepresentation are discussed in detail at 14.6.2.

A note of caution

Although it was suggested above that there are still advantages, in terms of the remedies available, to a representee who can establish the existence of fraud rather than mere negligence, against those advantages must be weighed the fact that the courts regard fraud as a very serious allegation, may demand more than the usual civil burden of proof from the party seeking to demonstrate its existence and may penalize in costs a party failing to make out such a claim. On the other hand, the remedies for negligent misrepresentation are often as good as those for fraud, and under s. 2(1) of the Misrepresentation Act 1967 (damages claim), the burden of proof is reversed so that it is the representor who has to establish that he was **not** negligent (see 14.4.3.2). In these circumstances, bringing a claim alleging fraud is not something which should be undertaken lightly.

14.4.3 Negligent misrepresentation: The available remedies

Misrepresentations which were made without due care, but were not reckless in the sense of being fraudulent, were once treated as 'innocent' misrepresentations. As a result, although rescission was available, no damages could be recovered. It was a rule which was regarded by many lawyers and commentators as unsatisfactory, and led to sometimes artificial interpretations to the effect that a representation had been incorporated in a contract, in order to allow the recovery of damages for what would then be breach (see 6.1.4). Eventually the position changed, but as a result of almost simultaneous, parallel common law and statutory developments, the law relating to negligent misrepresentation has become unnecessarily complicated. **In addition to the availability of the remedy of rescission (assuming none of the bars to rescission apply), these developments have resulted in *two possible claims for damages* being available in many instances to a party to whom a negligent misstatement has been made:**

- a claim in tort for negligent misstatement
- a claim for damages under s. 2(1) of the Misrepresentation Act 1967.

14.4.3.1 Negligent misstatement at common law

In *Hedley Byrne & Co. Ltd v Heller & Partners Ltd* [1964] AC 465, the House of Lords extended the common law tort of negligence to the field of negligent statements which cause loss.

> The plaintiffs had been asked for credit by a company, and had sought advice on the financial standing of the company from its bankers, the defendants. The defendants, who had known the purpose of the plaintiffs' request, had carelessly said that the company was financially sound. The House of Lords stated that the defendants owed a duty of care to the plaintiffs, but that since in the particular case the advice had been given expressly 'without responsibility', there was no liability.

In *McCullagh v Lane Fox and Partners Ltd* [1996] 1 EGLR 35, Hobhouse LJ considered that the question was whether any duty of care arose and that turned on whether the defendant had 'assumed responsibility' for the statement made (thereby following Lord Goff in *Henderson v Merrett Syndicates Ltd* [1995] 2 AC 145 at p. 181). The impact of the disclaimer, according to Hobhouse LJ, is to negative the assumption of responsibility for the statement: 'It … tells the recipient of the representation … that the maker is not accepting responsibility for the accuracy of the representation.' To be effective any disclaimer must satisfy ss. 2 and 11 of the Unfair Contract Terms Act (UCTA) 1977 (see further 7.6.2).

Therefore, at common law, the essential question is whether a duty of care (to do all that is reasonable to ensure that the statement made is correct) arises on the facts. The House of Lords said that the duty exists where there is a 'special relationship' between the parties, although their Lordships were not clear as to what constituted a special relationship. It seems certain at least that particular types of adviser, commonly regarded as professional (such as solicitors, barristers, accountants, surveyors, etc.), have a special relationship with their clients and so owe the duty of care to those to whom they give advice.

In *Caparo Industries plc v Dickman* [1990] 2 AC 605, the House of Lords reaffirmed that liability for negligent misstatement may be imposed, but was anxious to make clear that it would be imposed only where a close degree of interrelationship between the party making the statement and the party subsequently complaining could be found to exist. In particular, those making statements do not owe a duty of accuracy to the whole world, or to anyone who may happen to have the statement communicated to them. Lord Oliver stated:

> The necessary relationship between the maker of a statement or giver of advice (the adviser) and the recipient who acts in reliance on it (the advisee) may typically be held to exist where (1) the advice is required for a purpose, whether particularly specified or generally described, which is made known, either actually or inferentially, to the adviser when the advice is given, (2) the adviser knows, either actually or inferentially, that his advice will be communicated to the advisee either specifically or as a member of an ascertainable class, in order that it should be used by the advisee for that purpose, (3) it is known, either actually or inferentially, that the advice so communicated is likely to be acted on by the advisee for that purpose without independent inquiry and (4) it is so acted on by the advisee to his detriment.

The House of Lords clearly intended to place a restrictive interpretation on the doctrine, and that lead was followed in subsequent cases (e.g., *James McNaughton Papers Group Ltd v Hicks Anderson and Co.* [1991] 2 QB 113 and *Morgan Crucible Co. plc v Hill Samuel Bank Ltd* [1991] 1 Ch 259). More recently the courts have placed this analysis within the broader test of 'assumption of responsibility' for a statement (e.g., *Henderson v Merrett Syndicates Ltd* [1995] 2 AC 145, *White v Jones* [1995] 2 AC 207, *Spring v Guardian Assurance* [1995] 2 AC 296, *Williams v Natural Life Health Foods Ltd* [1998] 1 WLR 830, and *Merrett v Babb* [2001] EWCA Civ 214, [2001] QB 1174).

It appears that the English courts may be willing to find a special relationship wherever the person giving advice holds themselves out as possessing some expertise or special skill, and knows that the other party will rely on the advice given, irrespective of whether the person giving the advice is in fact a 'professional' adviser. Liability will then apply if it was reasonable for the other party to rely on the statement of the person giving the advice. This depends on the context so that statements made in the commercial context are more likely to give rise to a duty of care than those made in an informal social setting.

> In **Esso Petroleum Co. Ltd v Mardon** [1976] QB 801 (see **6.1.4**) the Court of Appeal found the duty of care to exist where an expert valuer for the oil company made a representation about the petrol sales potential of a garage to a prospective tenant. The statement maker clearly possessed special skill and knowledge concerning the subject matter of the contract. In addition, since the valuer was experienced and knew much more about the business than did the tenant, he could reasonably foresee that the tenant would rely on his judgement and it was reasonable for the prospective tenant to rely on his statements.

As **Esso v Mardon** illustrates, the common law negligent misstatement doctrine is *not limited to* representations which result in a contract between representor and representee (**Hedley Byrne & Co. Ltd v Heller & Partners Ltd:** *representation resulted in a contract with a third party) but can apply to representations which induce a contract between representor and representee.* Since the doctrine can apply to representations which induce a contract between representor and representee, in these factual situations there may be two, overlapping, possible damages claims: negligent misstatement in tort and under s. 2(1) of the Misrepresentation Act 1967.

However, the real difficulty with the claim for damages for negligent misstatement at common law is that the misrepresentee has the burden of proving both the existence of the duty of care (special relationship) and that the duty of care has been broken. This is very different if the claim is framed under s. 2(1) of the Misrepresentation Act 1967.

14.4.3.2 Section 2(1) of the Misrepresentation Act 1967: Damages claim

 Key point

Section 2(1) of the 1967 Act provides:

Where a person has entered into a contract after a misrepresentation has been made to him by another party thereto and as a result thereof he has suffered loss, then, if the person making the misrepresentation would be liable to damages in respect thereof had the misrepresentation been made fraudulently, that person shall be so liable notwithstanding that the misrepresentation was not made fraudulently, unless he proves that he had reasonable ground to believe and did believe up to the time the contract was made that the facts represented were true.

Scope of s. 2(1) claims

This statutory claim of damages for negligent misrepresentation is in one sense wider than that existing at common law, since it does not depend upon the existence of any kind of special relationship. In another sense, however, it is narrower, since it applies only where the representee has been induced to enter a contract with the representor by the misrepresentation (although it is clear that the courts will not permit an overly restrictive identification of the party to whom the representation needs to be addressed and with whom the contract needs to be made: *Cheltenham Borough Council v Laird* [2009] EWHC 1253 (QB), [2009] IRLR 621). Thus, a case like *Hedley Byrne & Co. Ltd v Heller & Partners Ltd* [1964] AC 465 (see 14.4.3.1) does not fall within the ambit of the section because the negligent misstatement did not result in a contract between the party giving the advice and the party seeking it.

It is potentially narrower in another sense, in that it may not apply to the exceptional cases of representation by silence (see 14.2.1.2), on the ground that such a misrepresentation is not 'made' within the terms of s. 2(1). There is an *obiter* statement to that effect in *Banque Financière de la Cité SA v Westgate Insurance Co. Ltd* [1989] 2 All ER 952 at p. 1004, although such an approach appears unduly literal and may be inconsistent with the general purpose of s. 2(1).

The burden of proof

Where the representation does fall within the ambit of the section, it is likely that the representee will choose to base the claim on s. 2(1) of the 1967 Act rather than the common law since the burden of proof is reversed as regards negligence. Once the claimant has established the existence of a false statement which induced the claimant to enter the contract, it is for the defendant to show that in making the representation 'he had reasonable ground to believe and did believe up to the time the contract was made that the facts represented were true'. This reversal of the burden of proof is a considerable advantage to the claimant.

It is also not merely a matter of disproving negligence. As a result of the decision of the Court of Appeal in *Howard Marine & Dredging Co. Ltd v A. Ogden & Sons (Excavations) Ltd*

[1978] QB 574, the defendant has to prove positively that he or she had reasonable grounds for their belief.

> In *Howard Marine & Dredging Co. Ltd v Ogden & Sons (Excavations) Ltd*, the defendants wished to hire barges and had been given details of capacity of the barges by the plaintiffs' marine manager. His statement had been based on figures in the Lloyd's Register but the Register was incorrect and the correct figures were available from documents in the plaintiffs' possession. When the defendants discovered the true capacity they refused to pay the full hire. The plaintiffs sought the outstanding hire and the defendants claimed damages under s. 2(1) of the Misrepresentation Act 1967. The majority of the Court of Appeal held that the plaintiffs had failed to prove that their marine manager had reasonable grounds to believe that the statement was true since there was no objectively reasonable ground for relying on the Register rather than the ships' documents. However, Lord Denning MR (dissenting) thought that the burden had been discharged and that negligence had been disproved since it was reasonable to rely on the Register.
>
> In *Spice Girls Ltd v Aprilia World Service BV* [2000] EMLR 478, Aprilia was held to be entitled to receive damages because under s. 2(1) the onus was on the Spice Girls to show that they had reasonable grounds to believe and did believe at the date of the agreement that the representation was true. Since it was found that they knew that one member intended to leave, they were not able to discharge that burden.

Thus, in cases in which it is not clear whether the defendant representor acted reasonably, at common law the claim for damages will fail; but in the same circumstances under s. 2(1) of the 1967 Act the claimant will succeed (*Howard Marine & Dredging Co. Ltd v A. Ogden & Sons (Excavations) Ltd* [1978] QB 574).

The fiction of fraud in s. 2(1)

Section 2(1) of the Misrepresentation Act 1967 is rather clumsily drafted, being based on what has been described as the 'fiction of fraud' (Atiyah and Treitel (1967) 30 MLR 369). Liability is said to exist where it would exist had the misrepresentation been made fraudulently, even though in the particular case it was not made fraudulently.

It is far from clear why this formulation was used. It may be that it was intended to indicate that the same measure of damages as for fraud should apply (see 14.6.4), although this appears unlikely. It is not thought that it is intended to import any of the other special rules applying to fraud, e.g. loss of profits recovery in *East v Maurer* (see 14.6.2.3; although see *Pankhania v Hackney LBC (Damages)* [2004] EWHC 323 (Ch), [2004] 1 EGLR 135 where Geoffrey Vos QC appeared to accept that in principle the *Smith New Court* principle could be applied to a s. 2(1) claim for damages because of the fiction of fraud, although it was inapplicable on the facts since there was no continuing misrepresentation or lock-in). This question of the scope of the fiction of fraud is discussed further in Poole and Devenney, 'Reforming damages for misrepresentation: The case for coherent aims and principles' [2007] JBL 269.

It seems more likely that the intention was to indicate the basic circumstances for liability in damages by no more than an analogy with the established circumstances for the availability of damages for the tort of deceit.

There also seems to be some confusion concerning what needs to be pleaded to claim damages under s. 2(1). Fraud should not be pleaded (unless there is a separate and alternative claim for damages in the tort of deceit). Under s. 2(1) the claimant need only establish the actionable misrepresentation for damages to be recoverable unless the defendant can establish that she had reasonable grounds for her belief that her statement was true. An inability to establish this does not mean that the misrepresentation is fraudulent, rather the misrepresentation would then be negligent.

535

The fiction of fraud merely means that alleging and proving fraud is not required to recover the **measure of damages** applicable for fraudulent misrepresentation. One reason for seeking recovery in the tort of deceit rather than s. 2(1) is the ability to recover for **all losses resulting from having made that contract**, rather than being limited to **all losses resulting from the fact that the individual representation is false** (Lord Steyn in *Smith New Court*: see 14.6.2.2). They are not necessarily the same thing so that the potential scope of recovery in fraud is wider.

14.4.4 Innocent misrepresentation: The available remedies

An innocent misrepresentation must today be regarded as a false statement which was made neither fraudulently nor negligently. In fact, as a result of the wording of s. 2(1) of the Misrepresentation Act 1967, it would appear that for the purposes of a claim for damages, an innocent misrepresentation is restricted to those circumstances where the representee not only believed the statement to be true, but is also able to prove that he or she was not negligent, i.e. that he or she had reasonable grounds for the stated belief (see 14.4.3.2).

The victim of an innocent misrepresentation is entitled to rescission of the contract, assuming none of the bars to rescission apply (see 14.5.2), and to an indemnity intended to help restore the parties to the position before the contract was made (see 14.6.6).

There is *no right* to damages for innocent misrepresentation. However, the court has a discretion under s. 2(2) of the Misrepresentation Act 1967 to award damages in lieu of (instead of) rescission. The weight of authority supports the view that this discretion is available only where the right to rescission has not been lost (*Floods of Queensferry Ltd v Shand Construction Ltd (No. 3)* [2000] BLR 81, *Government of Zanzibar v British Aerospace (Lancaster House) Ltd* [2000] 1 WLR 2333, [2000] CLC 735, and (*obiter*) in *Pankhania v Hackney London Borough Council* [2002] EWHC 2441 (Ch), [2002] NPC 123 at [74]: see 14.6.5.1), although this might result in there being no available remedy in a case of innocent misrepresentation.

14.5 Remedies for misrepresentation: Rescission

In addition to the positive remedies of rescission (see 14.5.1), damages (see 14.6), and indemnity (see 14.6.6), it is important to remember that misrepresentation affords a defence to a claim for breach of contract brought by the representor. This defence may be subject to the same limitations as the right to rescind (see 14.5.2). The possibility of a remedy of account of profits in cases of fraudulent misrepresentation short of a breach of fiduciary duty was left open in *Renault UK Ltd v Fleetpro Technical Services Ltd* [2007] EWHC 2541 (QB), [2008] Bus LR D17 (seeking to interpret *Murad v Al-Saraj* [2005] EWCA Civ 959, [2005] WTLR 1573) although the indications are that such a remedy is considered to be exceptional (see 10.6.4).

14.5.1 Availability of rescission

In principle rescission is available for all types of misrepresentation. **The effect of misrepresentation is to make a contract voidable, not void (see 1.5.3), and a claim for rescission is a claim to have the contract set aside, restoring the parties to the position they were in before the contract was made.**

In theory, rescission may be achieved without recourse to legal action, but in practice a party is likely to prefer to have the backing of a court order, especially where it is intended to recover property. The essential requirement of rescission, apart from satisfying the conditions of liability, i.e. establishing the actionable misrepresentation (see 14.2), is that notice be given to the other party. Where it is impossible to trace the other party the requirement of giving notice may be waived, provided all necessary steps have been taken to recover the goods.

> For example, in *Car and Universal Finance Co. Ltd v Caldwell* [1961] 1 QB 525, the owner of a car had been fraudulently persuaded to sell it to a rogue, who resold it to the finance company and then disappeared with the proceeds. Once aware of the true facts, the owner notified the police and the Automobile Association and asked for their help in recovering the car. These actions were found to have been enough to rescind the contract, and since they preceded the sale to the finance company, the finance company had not acquired good title to the car.

This principle and result may be explained in terms of the injustice of denying rescission simply because a rogue perpetrated a deliberate fraud and then absconded, so that notice could not be given. On the other hand, allowing rescission in those circumstances may cause hardship to a third party who has innocently acquired goods, if, as here, it is found that the rescission occurred before the third party acquired them.

14.5.2 Loss of the right to rescind

The remedy of rescission may be lost (or barred) if any of the following apply. These bars to rescission (with the exception of s. 2(2) of the Misrepresentation Act 1967) apply to all instances where the remedy of rescission is available, e.g. for duress or undue influence (see *Halpern v Halpern* [2007] EWCA Civ 291, [2007] 2 Lloyd's Rep 56, [2007] 1 CLC 527 for application of *restitutio in integrum* to duress).

14.5.2.1 Affirmation

The right to rescind is lost if the contract is affirmed by the representee after discovering the true state of affairs (*Long v Lloyd* [1958] 1 WLR 753). Affirmation is an indication to the representor that the intention is to continue with the contract, despite the misrepresentation and knowledge of the right to rescind (*Habib Bank v Tufail* [2006] EWCA Civ 374, [2006] 2 P & CR DG14, per Lloyd LJ at [20]). Affirmation may be indicated by express words, or by conduct.

> In *Long v Lloyd*, the plaintiff purchased a lorry which had falsely been represented to be in good condition. On its first journey several serious faults were discovered; they were drawn to the attention of the seller who offered to pay half the cost of repairs. On a second journey the lorry broke down again, revealing more serious faults. The plaintiff was held to have lost the right to rescind the contract. The first journey did not constitute affirmation, since the buyer was entitled to a 'test drive' to check the accuracy of the representation. The second journey, however, was made in the knowledge that the vehicle when sold was not in good condition, and therefore amounted to affirmation of the contract.

The result on the facts was that the plaintiff had no remedy at all for misrepresentation, since damages were unavailable at this time for such non-fraudulent misrepresentations.

14.5.2.2 Lapse of time

In some cases the right to rescind is lost through lapse of time. The bar to rescission through lapse of time represents one instance where it is relevant to consider the type of misrepresentation when determining the ability to rescind.

- In the case of fraudulent misrepresentations, time will run from the time when the fraud either was, or could with reasonable diligence have been, discovered.

- However, if the misrepresentation is non-fraudulent (i.e., negligent or innocent), time will run from the date of the contract. A good illustration of the operation of this principle is provided by the facts and decision in ***Leaf v International Galleries*** [1950] 2 KB 86 (see 13.4.1.3).

> In ***Leaf v International Galleries*** a painting, which had been misrepresented as having been painted by Constable, was sold to the plaintiff. Five years later the misrepresentation was discovered, and the plaintiff purchaser sought to rescind the contract of sale. His action failed because of the lapse of time since the sale. The misrepresentation in this case was innocent (which at the time embraced both negligent and wholly innocent misrepresentation) so that time ran from the date of the contract.

For a recent example of the remedy of rescission being lost due to lapse of time (delay), see ***Government of Zanzibar v British Aerospace (Lancaster House) Ltd*** [2000] 1 WLR 2333, [2000] CLC 735 (see 14.6.5.1).

14.5.2.3 *Restitutio in integrum*

The right to rescind is lost if *restitutio in integrum* is no longer possible; that is, if it is no longer possible to restore the parties to their positions before the contract was made.

Such will be the case where the nature of the subject matter has been changed (***Clarke v Dickson*** (1858) EB & E 148: misrepresentation induced the purchase of shares in a company which was subsequently wound up), or it has declined in value. For example, a contract for the purchase of a bottle of wine, induced by a misrepresentation about its quality, cannot be rescinded once the wine has been opened and drunk. It has been confirmed that this principle applies to rescission for duress (***Halpern v Halpern*** [2007] EWCA Civ 291, [2007] 2 Lloyd's Rep 56, [2007] 1 CLC 527).

> ***Halpern v Halpern*** concerned a compromise agreement alleged to have been reached between a number of the deceased's sons and daughter (the appellants) and another son and grandson (the respondents) relating to inheritance issues and an arbitration before a Beth Din. One term of the compromise was that all documents produced during the arbitration had to be destroyed or handed over to the appellants. The appellants raised the issue of duress in relation to this compromise agreement when sued for damages for its breach and the respondents claimed that since the relevant documents had been destroyed the compromise could not be rescinded because it would not be possible to make restitution and thereby put the parties back into the position they were in before the compromise. The appellants contended that an inability to give counter-restitution should not be a bar to a claim based on rescission for duress.
>
> The Court of Appeal held that rescission for duress was no different in principle to rescission for other vitiating factors, such as misrepresentation.

The problem with this decision is that the inability to make counter-restitution was directly attributable to a condition of the agreement said to be affected by the duress, which surely calls for some different outcome on the facts, if not in terms of legal principle. The Court of Appeal noted that given this situation 'it would be surprising if the law could not provide a suitable remedy', although did not specify at this stage (before the full facts were known) what this remedy would be or its basis in law other than securing 'practical justice'. However, it is conceded by the Court of Appeal that 'the primary objective may not always need to be to restore *both* parties to their previous positions' and the envisaged means is the principle in ***Erlanger v New Sombrero Phosphate Co.*** (For an example of the imposition of terms to achieve what was 'practically just' see *Redstone Mortgages plc v Welch and Jackson* [2009] 36 EG 98, 22 June 2009, Birmingham County Court.)

This equitable principle applies to mitigate the strictness of the position on the ability to make counter-restitution. The Chancery Court did not allow minor imperfections in the restoration of the original position to stand in the way of the remedy. For example, in ***Armstrong v Jackson*** [1917] 2 KB 822, a major depreciation in value of shares sold under a misrepresentation did not bar rescission, since it was possible to return the shares. In ordering rescission, the court may impose terms, for example to account for profits and to allow for deterioration, in order to do what has been described as 'what is practically just' (per Lord Blackburn in ***Erlanger v New Sombrero Phosphate Co.*** (1878) 3 App Cas 1218 at p. 1278). The court is much more likely to be willing to overlook imperfections in the process of restoring the original positions in the case of fraudulent than in the case of negligent or innocent misrepresentations (per Lord Wright in ***Spence v Crawford*** [1939] 3 All ER 271 at p. 288).

Rescission as 'an all or nothing' process

Although in ***TSB Bank plc v Camfield*** [1995] 1 WLR 430, the Court of Appeal held (in the context of a guarantee) that rescission was total and partial rescission on terms was not possible, the High Court of Australia in *Vadasz v Pioneer Concrete (SA) Pty Ltd* (1995) 130 ALR 570, preferred a more flexible approach. The guarantee in *Vadasz v Pioneer Concrete (SA) Pty Ltd* covered all monies owing in respect of both existing and future debts, when it had been represented that it would cover only future debts. The High Court of Australia was prepared to rescind the guarantee as regards the existing debt but to enforce it in relation to future indebtedness. The Privy Council in *Far Eastern Shipping Co. Ltd v Scales Trading Ltd* [2001] 1 All ER (Comm) 319 discussed these cases but found that, on the facts, it was unnecessary to decide between the competing authorities.

However, in the most recent English authority, ***De Molestina v Ponton*** [2002] 1 All ER (Comm) 587, Colman J emphatically rejected the concept of partial rescission as being contrary to the very nature of rescission. It might reasonably be argued, as counsel attempted to do in ***De Molestina v Ponton***, that partial rescission is not too far removed from the instances of equitable intervention to permit rescission on terms (e.g., payment to account for minor deterioration) in cases where substantial restitution is possible (per Lord Blackburn in ***Erlanger v New Sombrero Phosphate Co.*** (1878) 3 App Cas 1218 at p. 1278: see above). However, Colman J considered (at [6.3]) this to be entirely different to partial rescission since it was concerned with adjustments 'to take account of changes to property or benefits derived from the contract by one side or another during the period between the making of the contract and the proceedings for rescission'. He added:

> The scope of the equitable discretion in a rescission claim is confined to adjustments to achieve substantial restitution to accommodate events that have occurred after the contract has come into force and does not extend to the general reconstruction of the bargain to achieve an objectively overall fair result.

For argument to the contrary focusing on the existence of a different equitable jurisdiction, see Poole and Keyser, 'Justifying partial rescission in English law' (2005) 121 LQR 273.

On the facts in **De Molestina v Ponton** the problems of partial rescission were avoided because the judge provisionally considered that the three share distribution agreements were distinguishable from various other agreements and therefore could be rescinded without interfering with those other agreements. It has long been accepted that, although it is not possible in English law to rescind part of a contract and affirm the other part, if the parts can be severed so that they form separate and independent contracts, each contract can be separately rescinded. This is essentially what happened in **Barclays Bank v Caplan** [1998] FLR 532 in relation to guarantees which could be cleanly separated from one another (see 15.2.8.1).

Rescission of contracts to purchase a business

It appears from the decision in **Thomas Witter v TBP Industries Ltd** [1996] 2 All ER 573, that rescission of a contract to purchase a business may be particularly difficult to achieve because, in the opinion of Jacob J, it may well not be the same business by the time the question of the availability of rescission comes before the courts. The judge stressed that it was almost inevitable that there would have been changes in personnel and third-party mortgages would be affected. It might reasonably be considered that this approach would prove an encouragement to resist rescission of the sale of a business. In the case of fraudulent misrepresentations where the misrepresentee is locked in and cannot easily sell the business, the damages award will, subject to mitigation, take account of any fall in the value of the business down to the date of judgment (**Smith New Court Securities Ltd v Scrimgeour Vickers (Asset Management) Ltd** [1997] AC 254) and so be the more popular remedy. Jacob J also rejected the argument that it was for the misrepresentor to avoid rescission by demonstrating that third parties would be actually affected on the facts. Thus, this case also illustrates another bar to rescission, namely third-party interests.

The effective date of rescission

Whether these factors should impact in this way depends upon whether rescission is regarded as a self-help remedy so that it takes effect from the date of the misrepresentee's election to rescind or whether, as Jacob J in **Thomas Witter** assumed, at the date of the hearing. This difference in approach has significant implications since if the operative date is the date of the misrepresentee's election, any transactions between the operative date and the judicial 'declaration' of its validity are in danger of being unravelled. However, if the operative date is the date of the court order, then it is possible to take account of factors occurring in the period between the act of rescission and the trial date. The question of the nature of rescission as a remedy (i.e., as dependent on party action or order of the court) was taken by counsel for the defendants (appellants) at first instance in **Halpern v Halpern** [2006] EWHC 1728 (Comm), [2007] QB 88. However, the judge, Nigel Teare QC, stated (at [26]–[27]) that he would not resolve this debate because it was not necessary to do so on the preliminary issue, which was concerned with the need to give counter-restitution.

14.5.2.4 Third-party interests

Rescission is a personal remedy so that the right to rescind will be lost if third-party rights intervene (see 1.5.3). Since a contract affected by misrepresentation is only voidable, not void, a person acquiring goods under such a contract may pass good title at any time before rescission to an innocent third-party purchaser who has no notice of the misrepresentation (Sale of Goods Act (SGA) 1979, s. 23, and see 3.2.2.2).

In *Crystal Palace Football Club (2000) Ltd v Dowie* [2007] EWHC 1392 (QB), [2007] IRLR 682, for facts see 14.2.1.2, rescission was unavailable because of third-party interests since it would have the effect of retrospectively reviving the defendant's employment with the club when both had moved on (i.e., the defendant had since been employed elsewhere (Coventry), and Crystal Palace had a new manager). The defendant could not work for two clubs at the same time and the rights of his new club needed to be taken into account. Instead, it was appropriate to order damages or other financial relief as compensation.

Many of the recent cases in which wives have sought to avoid contracts in which they have agreed to provide security in the form of the matrimonial home in order to cover their husband's business debts, rest as much on misrepresentation as they do on undue influence. Consequently, the discussion at 15.2.8.2 relating to undue influence by a third party and the question of notice may be relevant in this context (*Royal Bank of Scotland v Etridge (No. 2)* [2001] UKHL 44, [2002] 2 AC 773).

14.5.2.5 Misrepresentation Act 1967, s. 2(2)

In the case of negligent and innocent misrepresentation, the right to rescind will be lost if the court exercises its discretion to award damages in lieu of (instead of) rescission under s. 2(2) of the Misrepresentation Act 1967 (see 14.6.5).

14.6 Damages for misrepresentation

14.6.1 Background

The original common law position was that damages were available only for fraudulent misrepresentation, by way of a tortious action for deceit (see 14.6.2). A non-fraudulent misrepresentation might be rescinded in equity, but gave rise to no common law right to damages. Instead, as part of the process of rescission, an indemnity might be awarded (see 14.6.6).

It is still the case that a wholly innocent misrepresentation gives no general *right* to damages (but see the discretion to award damages in lieu of rescission under s. 2(2) of the Misrepresentation Act 1967, at 14.4.4). However, as discussed above (see 14.4.3), the development of the tort of negligence (see 1.2) eventually gave rise to an action for damages for negligent misstatement which exists in tandem with the statutory right to damages for negligent misrepresentation (see 14.4.3).

Rescission and damages

With the exception of s. 2(2) of the Misrepresentation Act 1967 (see 14.4.4), the right to damages is additional to the right to rescission. Provided there is no double recovery, a representee is entitled to rescission **and** damages. This would be appropriate where, e.g., despite rescission the misrepresentee was not restored to his original position because of expenditure incurred as a consequence of entering into the voidable contract. In such a situation the claimant would **also** need to claim damages for misrepresentation (and the courts would have to consider the application of the relevant remoteness rule to the loss in question).

Damages where rescission has been lost

If the remedy of rescission has been lost, it follows that (apart from misrepresentations to which s. 2(2) of the Misrepresentation Act 1967 applies) the remedy of damages will remain and will represent the only mechanism for restoring the misrepresentee to their original position. It is clear that the right to damages will remain where a party goes ahead (affirms) the contract with knowledge of the misrepresentation and so loses the right to rescind (e.g. *Production Technology Consultants Ltd v Bartlett* [1988] 1 EGLR 182).

14.6.2 Measure of damages in the tort of deceit

Since the claim for damages in respect of fraudulent misrepresentation (see 14.4.1.1) is the tortious claim for deceit, the measure of damages is the usual tortious measure of out-of-pocket loss, rather than the contractual measure of expectation loss (explained 9.2.1). Thus, the representee is to be put into the position they would have been in had the representation not been made (***Derry v Peek*** (1889) 14 App Cas 337).

14.6.2.1 Remoteness and recovery

The remoteness rule in claims in the tort of deceit allows the misrepresentee to recover for all direct loss incurred as a result of the transaction which was induced by the fraudulent misrepresentation, regardless of foreseeability (***Doyle v Olby Ironmongers Ltd*** [1969] 2 QB 158). In ***Doyle v Olby*** the plaintiff had been fraudulently induced to buy a business and was entitled to recover as damages not only the price paid for the business but also subsequent investments (as consequential losses), subject only to giving credit for the benefits he received from the business.

The sum payable as damages is usually calculated by reference to the difference between the amount paid and the actual value of the subject matter of the contract judged at the date of the contract (***Smith New Court Securities Ltd v Scrimgeour Vickers (Asset Management) Ltd*** [1997] AC 254 at pp. 265 and 267, per Lord Browne-Wilkinson). So, if as a result of a misrepresentation, £2,500 was paid for a car that was actually worth only £1,500 at the date of the contract, damages would be assessed at £1,000.

In addition, as noted above, in the case of fraud the courts award damages for all loss, including consequential loss such as expenses incurred as a result of entering the contract (***Doyle v Olby (Ironmongers) Ltd*** [1969] 2 QB 158).

14.6.2.2 All losses flowing from the 'transaction'

In ***Smith New Court Securities Ltd v Scrimgeour Vickers (Asset Management) Ltd*** [1997] AC 254, the difference in value rule and the ***Doyle v Olby*** 'all loss directly flowing' rule came into potential conflict because of the particular facts.

> The defendant induced the plaintiff to purchase shares in a company by a misrepresentation found to have been fraudulent. Thereafter, a further massive fraud by a third party against the company in question was discovered, causing the value of the shares to plummet. Since the plaintiff had purchased the shares as a long-term 'market making' investment, and had paid more than their market value even at the date of the contract, there was no possibility of immediately reselling the shares.
>
> The question for the House of Lords was whether the plaintiff could recover the difference between the price paid for the shares and their eventual sale price which reflected the massive third-party fraud (around £11m), or whether the plaintiff was limited to recovering the difference between the price paid and the actual value of the shares at the date of the contract (just over £1m). Put another way, the issue was which of the parties should have to bear the effects of the third party's fraud. If difference in value at the date of the contract was the correct measure, the actual value of the shares at **the date of the transaction** between plaintiff and defendant would be assessed without taking account of the third-party fraud, which had not then been discovered. However, it was equally persuasively arguable that the

catastrophic loss was a direct consequence flowing from the defendant's fraud, since the plaintiff would not have been exposed to the risk at all but for the inducement that fraud provided.

The House of Lords decided that the risk was the defendant's, and allowed the plaintiff full recovery of its claim. According to Lord Browne-Wilkinson, the general rule is that loss is to be assessed at the date of the transaction. However, that rule was 'not to be inflexibly applied where to do so would prevent [the misrepresentee] obtaining full compensation for the wrong suffered'.

Accordingly, the general rule had to give way if 'the plaintiff is, by reason of the fraud, locked into the property' ([1997] AC 254 at p. 267). The same would also be true if the fraudulent misrepresentation continued to operate after the date of the contract so that the misrepresentee was 'induced to retain the asset'. Therefore, since the fraud induced the plaintiff to make a long-term investment, without the immediate prospect of reselling the shares, the loss was to be assessed as the actual loss suffered (i.e., the difference between price paid and the price at which the shares were eventually sold).

Lord Steyn adopted a less technical analysis: the only question was what loss did the plaintiff truly suffer? The transaction date valuation rule generally reveals this, but where on the facts it does not, it need not be used.

Thus, the policy is that where the statement maker has been fraudulent, the statement maker should be responsible for all the losses resulting from the other party having made the contract (i.e., losses from the 'transaction'). This greater potential liability might be seen as a deterrent to fraudulent inducements and this was the interpretation placed on the decision in *Doyle v Olby* by Lord Browne-Wilkinson.

The decision in *East v Maurer* [1991] 1 WLR 461 (for facts see below) represents a further application of recovery of the difference between the price paid and the price at which the property was eventually sold, plus consequential sale expenses. However, it is also the case that losses other than capital losses can be recovered on the *Smith New Court* basis if there is a lock-in or continuing misrepresentation after the date of the contract, e.g. the consequential losses arising from running a business purchased as a result of a continuing fraudulent misrepresentation (*Man Nutfahrzeuge AG v Freightliner* [2005] EWHC 2347 (Comm)) or applying a different date for the assessment of the capital loss when purchasing a business based on a 'lock-in' (*4 Eng Ltd v Harper* [2008] EWHC 915 (Ch), [2009] Ch 91).

In *Dadourian Group International Inc v Simms (Damages)* [2009] EWCA Civ 169, [2009] 1 Lloyd's Rep 601, the Court of Appeal held that the costs of pursuing proceedings in the New York courts and arbitration proceedings would not have been incurred if the respondent had not found itself in a dispute having acted in reliance on the misrepresentation and therefore were recoverable as losses flowing directly from the misrepresentation under the *Smith New Court* principle.

In *Invertec Ltd v De Mol Holding BV* [2009] EWHC 2471 (Ch), the claimant company had purchased the entire issue share capital of a company following fraudulent misrepresentations that the company was solvent, able to pay its debts as they fell due and up to date with its corporation tax liability. Damages were payable to put the claimant into the position that it would have been in, including full recovery for the price paid for the shares and sums paid under a consequential management services agreement that was tied to the purchase of the shares. However, the judge rejected the claim that the purchasers were 'locked into' the transaction, believing that rescission was possible on the facts or that the company could have been put into administration or liquidation. The decision to keep trading by lending further sums to the company was 'a commercial decision' and based on the mistaken belief that the company could trade its way out of the insolvency. This was, at [284], 'over-optimistic' but 'the over-optimism was not caused by the fraudulent misrepresentations'. (Compare with *Smith New Court* where there was value left in the company and where the House of Lords was prepared to conclude that there was a 'lock in'.) (See **14.6.2.5** for the discussion of the mitigation argument.)

The scope of consequential loss recoverable in a claim in deceit can be considerable—e.g. ***Kinch v Rosling*** [2009] EWHC 286 (QB) where a businessman was deceived by a solicitor over the funding for a takeover of a football club. The consequential losses suffered by the businessman caused him to be declared bankrupt and he was able to recover damages in respect of these losses and £10,000 damages for the humiliation and distress associated with the bankruptcy (compare distress claims in the contractual context: see **9.9.4**).

14.6.2.3 Loss of profits

The Court of Appeal in ***East v Maurer*** [1991] 1 WLR 461 (noted Marks (1992) 108 LQR 386), held that it was possible in principle to recover for loss of profits following a fraudulent misrepresentation on the basis of the ***Doyle v Olby (Ironmongers) Ltd*** formula allowing for recovery of 'all the actual damage directly flowing from the fraudulent inducement', even though loss of profits is normally associated with a claim in contract for expectation loss.

However, the Court of Appeal also held that loss of profits in the context of fraudulent misrepresentation could not be calculated on an expectation basis (i.e., as if the representation was true) because that would amount to converting the representation into a contractual promise (i.e., a term) that the statement was true. Instead, the loss of profits was to be calculated on a tortious basis, namely the profit which might have been made had the representation not been made at all.

Of course, this raises all sorts of questions relating to calculation of this loss of profits, and it is far too uncertain and speculative without further refinement. The Court of Appeal in ***East v Maurer*** therefore calculated the loss of profit as the profit the plaintiffs would probably have made if they had purchased another **hypothetical** hair salon at that price (and the Court of Appeal calculated this figure as £10,000).

East v Maurer was approved, in respect of fraud cases, by Lord Steyn in ***Smith New Court Securities Ltd v Scrimgeour Vickers (Asset Management) Ltd*** [1997] AC 254 at p. 282. On Lord Steyn's analysis, the recovery of **hypothetical lost profit** is 'classic consequential loss', and is to be distinguished from the contractual measure of damage, which would allow recovery of the profit as represented in fact. (For a further example of a judgment awarding loss of profits see ***Banks v Cox*** [2002] EWHC 2166 (Ch), unreported, 25 October 2002.)

Claims based on what the misrepresentee would otherwise have done ought to be based on evidence of the hypotheticals and there ought to be an actual alternative in order to establish the loss. The Court of Appeal in ***Davis v Churchward***, unreported, 6 May 1993 (noted Chandler (1994) 110 LQR 35) considered the question of recovery of loss of profits for fraudulent misrepresentation relating to the purchase of a public house. In this case, however, the court compared the public house purchased with an **actual** public house and came to the conclusion that, as there was no difference between the actual turnover in both, there could be no recovery for lost profits. The same approach can be seen in ***Dadourian Group International Inc. v Simms (Damages)*** [2006] EWHC 2973 (Ch). In a claim based on fraudulent misrepresentation, the claimant sought to recover loss of the profits resulting from being deprived from entering into a sale agreement with 'some other purchaser'. The judge rejected this claim on the facts, although not in general terms of the availability of loss of profit damages. He stressed that there would need to be evidence of another purchaser in the market and the claim would need to take account of the duty to mitigate. On the facts the claimant had failed to mitigate by simply scrapping the manufacturing equipment rather than attempting to market and sell it elsewhere. (The decision was affirmed by the Court of Appeal, [2009] EWCA Civ 169, [2009] 1 Lloyd's Rep 601, discussed at 14.2.2.4, but the arguments on appeal related to other findings, e.g. whether the costs of legal proceedings were recoverable.)

However, this contrasts with the acceptance in *4 Eng Ltd v Harper* [2008] EWHC 915 (Ch), [2009] Ch 91 and *Parabola Investments Ltd v Browallia Cal Ltd* [2009] EWHC 901 (Comm) that lost profits can be recovered in a deceit claim despite an inability to identify a specific alternative (and profitable) contract that would have been entered into had it not been for the fraudulent misrepresentation. This suggests that the principle in *Davis v Churchward* is incorrect and it seems that the usual rules of establishing loss may have no application in the context of fraud.

On the basis of *East v Maurer*, as applied in *Downs v Chappell* [1997] 1 WLR 426, because recovery for loss of profits for fraudulent misrepresentation is not based on the representation being true, in order to be entitled to claim loss of profits the misrepresentee must, it would seem, have been making a loss in practice (as opposed to less than the profit figure represented). In both *East v Maurer* and *Davis v Churchward* the purchasers suffered a net loss and so the question of loss of profits was considered. By comparison, in *Downs v Chappell* the purchaser was making a profit, albeit that the profit was not as high as represented, so that no loss of profits claim could be entertained. In practical terms this would limit the availability of this head of damages for fraudulent misrepresentation. However, in *Clef Aquitaine Sarl v Laporte Materials (Barrow) Ltd* [2000] 3 WLR 1760 (discussed below), a claim to recover a difference in profit level was permitted and the Court of Appeal stated that there was no general rule that profits could not be recovered in a 'no loss' situation.

14.6.2.4 Causation in terms of liability and distinguishing the identification of loss for purposes of determining quantum

In *Downs v Chappell* [1997] 1 WLR 461 the Court of Appeal held that, in the context of a fraudulent misrepresentation claim, once the facts of inducement by a material misrepresentation causing detriment had been established, it was irrelevant and unnecessary to consider what the misrepresentee would have done but for the representation (or had he been told the truth), i.e. the general causation question (see also discussion at 14.2.2.4).

This would not be the usual approach to questions of causation in tort but is justified in the context of fraud on the basis that a fraudulent misrepresentor should not be permitted to argue that the misrepresentee would have acted in the same way in any event. The difficulty with this argument is that the same test was also applied in relation to the second defendants, the first defendant's accountants, who were held liable in negligence.

This position on causation is somewhat different where the court is seeking to determine if the alleged loss was caused by the fraudulent misrepresentation when such hypotheticals (what the claimant would otherwise have done) are relevant (see, e.g., *East v Maurer* [1991] 1 WLR 461). In this context an interesting question arose in *Clef Aquitaine Sarl v Laporte Materials (Barrow) Ltd* [2000] 3 WLR 1760. **If the contract entered into as a result of a fraudulent misrepresentation is profitable for the misrepresentee, can that misrepresentee nevertheless claim damages in deceit on the basis that they would otherwise have entered into a more profitable contract on better terms?**

On the facts in *Clef Aquitaine Sarl v Laporte Materials (Barrow) Ltd*, the plaintiff company had agreed to purchase goods from the defendant. The defendant had fraudulently stated that the price list applicable represented the lowest prices at which the defendant's salesmen could sell the goods. The plaintiff managed to resell the goods at a profit, but wanted damages representing the difference between the price paid and the price that probably could have been negotiated but for the misrepresentation. In essence, the issue was whether 'all the damage (actual loss) directly flowing from the transaction' encompassed this situation. The argument against this was that it represented an attempt to create a contractual (loss of bargain) claim.

The Court of Appeal held that there was no absolute rule to the effect that damages in deceit could be recovered only if the transaction was loss making. If the plaintiff could prove that he would have entered into a different and more favourable transaction with the misrepresentor or a third party but for the deceit, he could recover for his loss on that basis.

Simon Brown LJ considered that allowing recovery on these facts gave effect to 'the overriding compensatory rule', i.e. that it represented damages for loss of an opportunity which the plaintiff would otherwise have had to agree better terms. Thus, it appears that, in the case of fraudulent misrepresentation, the misrepresentee can recover for lost opportunities as a result of entering the contract. This would include the profits that might have been made by purchasing another similar business at the same price.

Ward LJ noted the difficulties of distinguishing between a tortious approach (putting the misrepresentee in the position he would have been in had the misrepresentation not been made) and the contractual approach (putting him into the position he would have been in had a true statement been made). In particular, he noted the difficulties of drawing a line between recovery for loss of bargain (which was contractual and ruled out in this context) and recovery for the loss of a bargain which might have been made if the truth had been known. (See criticisms of this decision in Poole and Devenney [2007] JBL 269.) The nature of the potential for confusion is evident if the focus is placed on what would have happened if the fraudulent misrepresentation had not been made, e.g. how speculative is it possible to be in assessing loss, as opposed to causation?

By comparison, *Parabola Investments Ltd v Browallia Cal Ltd* [2009] EWHC 901 (Comm), Flaux J was prepared to accept that a claim can be made for an expectation loss of profit in a deceit claim, i.e. the extra profit that would have been made if the fraud had not occurred on the basis that it fell within the general principle in **Smith New Court** (loss flowing from the transaction and overriding compensatory principle). However, it must be asked whether the loss is in fact that 'direct' a consequence. Flaux J also considered that the **Smith New Court** principle applied to a loss of profits claim in deceit so that the loss of the extra profits that might have been made could be recovered right down to the date of judgment. If this is applied by analogy in the context of damages under s. 2(1) of the Misrepresentation Act 1967 (fiction of fraud: see 14.6.4), it would be a startling conclusion. The total amount of damages in this case were assessed ([2009] EWHC 1492 (Comm)) at nearly £19.3m.

In *4 Eng Ltd v Harper* [2008] EWHC 915 (Ch), [2009] Ch 91, the judge accepted that damages for loss of the chance to purchase an alternative company also fell within the general principle in **Smith New Court** and therefore could be recovered. David Richards J stated:

If the loss of the chance is damage directly caused by the defendants' deceit, it is as much within the scope of damages for deceit as payments or liabilities in fact made or incurred by the claimant or as damages for the loss of profits in a hypothetical alternative business established on the balance of probabilities as in *East v Maurer* [1991] 1 WLR 461 … It does not seem to me to be an objection that the loss is assessed as a loss of chance, not as a loss established on the balance of probabilities. It is true that it does not previously appear to have been decided that damages for loss of a chance are recoverable for deceit, but there is in my judgment no objection in principle. If damages for loss of a chance are recoverable in negligence, why should they not also be recoverable in deceit?

If loss of chance damages exists in this context there should be a discount applied for the chance that no suitable alternative hypothetical purchase can be found, but none was applied in either **East v Maurer** or **Clef Acquitaine** (possibly because such hypothetical examples are unnecessary). On the other hand, if we accept that loss of profits on an expectation basis can be recovered, loss of the chance of better profits is a logical next step.

14.6.2.5 Duty to mitigate

In **Smith New Court Securities Ltd v Scrimgeour Vickers (Asset Management) Ltd** [1997] AC 254 Lord Browne-Wilkinson also stated that the misrepresentee had a duty to mitigate its loss once it discovered the fraud.

> In **Downs v Chappell** [1997] 1 WLR 461, there was a fraudulent misrepresentation relating to the value of a bookshop business. The business was purchased for £120,000, and eventually sold for less than £60,000. However, the misrepresentee had earlier refused two offers of £76,000. The Court of Appeal held that damages were limited to £44,000, namely, the difference between £120,000 and £76,000. The plaintiff was entitled to damages for his loss to the date when he could have avoided further losses. The offer of £76,000 had been unreasonably refused and broke the chain of causation. As a result, the further loss (an extra £16,000) was not direct loss flowing from the misrepresentation.

The test for mitigation is the same as that applicable for breach of contract claims (i.e., a duty to take reasonable steps to minimize the loss: see **9.9.3**) (**Standard Chartered Bank v Pakistan National Shipping Corp**. [1999] 1 Lloyd's Rep 747: if the loss could reasonably have been avoided, it would not be regarded as having been caused by the misrepresentation). In affirming this first instance decision, the Court of Appeal in **Standard Chartered Bank v Pakistan National Shipping (Assessment of Damages)** [2001] EWCA Civ 55, [2001] 1 All ER (Comm) 822, confirmed that in the tort of deceit the concepts of mitigation and causation could not be separated and were 'two sides of the same coin' (per Potter LJ at [41]). Since mitigation requires only that reasonable steps are taken to minimize the loss, in **Banks v Cox (Costs)** [2002] EWHC 2166 (Ch), unreported, 25 October 2002, the claimants were not required to put the nursing home, for which they had paid £250,000, on the market at the suggested price of £120,000, since even if they sold the property at the lower figure that amount would not have covered their indebtedness to their bank. However, in **Invertec Ltd v De Mol Holding BV** [2009] EWHC 2471 (Ch) (for facts see **14.6.2.2**) the judge considered that as the true position on the insolvency of the company purchased was soon revealed, the decision to keep trading 'was not a reasonable attempt at mitigation, but a commercial gamble' and the defendants could not be the insurers of that gamble if it went wrong.

14.6.2.6 Exemplary damages and fraudulent misrepresentation

As discussed at **9.1.3**, the decision in **Kuddus v Chief Constable of Leicestershire Constabulary** [2001] UKHL 29, [2002] 2 AC 122, has opened the possibility for the expansion of instances where exemplary or punitive damages may be recoverable in a tort claim. It might be thought possible that this might in future extend to certain claims in the tort of deceit where the facts call out for a punitive response—and, presumably, where there is no separate criminal liability. However, in **Doe v Skegg** [2006] EWHC 3746 (Ch) the judge's comments may suggest that this is unlikely. He noted (at [33]) that one reason why a claim in fraud might be pursued despite the measure of damages available in a claim for damages under the Misrepresentation Act 1967 s. 2(1), is that 'it is thought more likely that a claim to exemplary damages will succeed where there has been a finding of fraud, although…the test for whether or not exemplary damages is to be awarded is wholly different to the test for fraud'.

14.6.3 Damages for negligent misrepresentations: Damages in tort for negligent misstatement

Clearly, damages for negligent misstatement (tort) at common law under the principle in **Hedley Byrne v Heller** [1964] AC 465 are tortious, and the remoteness test is whether the loss is a reasonable foreseeable consequence (albeit foreseeable only as a remote consequence) of the tort (**The Wagon Mound (No. 1)** [1961] AC 388).

Unlike the position with regard to fraudulent misrepresentation, it is clear that liability is limited to the position assessed at the date of the wrong. In **South Australia Asset Management Corporation v York Montague Ltd** [1997] AC 191, in the context of a negligent survey, the House of Lords held that damages had to be assessed as the difference between the price paid and the actual value of the property at the date of the purchase contract. The surveyor was responsible only for the consequences of the information in his survey being inaccurate and could not be made responsible for subsequent falls in property values. (The same principle will apply as a general rule to a claim for breach of contract. Comparison with the position for fraudulent misrepresentation (**Smith New Court Securities v Scrimgeour Vickers** [1997] AC 254) might therefore encourage a claim to be made in misrepresentation rather than contract in order to allow recovery of damages for losses subsequently incurred as a result of entering into the transaction.)

14.6.4 Damages for negligent misrepresentation under the Misrepresentation Act 1967, s. 2(1)

Section 2(1) of the Misrepresentation Act 1967 does not expressly state the applicable measure of damages. However, since the section is based on what is known as 'the fiction of fraud' (see 14.4.3.2), it seems the statutory right to damages, as the common law right (see 14.4.3.1), is based in tort and so the tortious (out-of-pocket) measure applies. In the past, the case law had not been entirely consistent on this question and occasionally the courts did allow recovery of expectation loss. However, the point now appears to have been finally settled by the Court of Appeal decision in **Royscot Trust Ltd v Rogerson** [1991] 2 QB 297 (noted Hooley (1991) 107 LQR 547 and Wadsley (1992) 55 MLR 698). **Royscot Trust** has proved to be a very controversial case, but not in respect of the basic measure of damages being tortious (i.e., out-of-pocket loss) since if the common law and statutory claims for negligent misstatement are truly alternatives, the basic measure of damages should be the same.

14.6.4.1 Fiction of fraud and the remoteness test under s. 2(1): *Royscot Trust Ltd v Rogerson*

Instead, the decision has proved controversial because of the literal interpretation of s. 2(1) of the Misrepresentation Act 1967 (the 'fiction of fraud') adopted by the Court of Appeal. In other words, the Court of Appeal stated that damages under s. 2(1) of the 1967 Act are to be assessed in the same way as damages for fraudulent misrepresentation, even though the misrepresentation is not fraudulent. In particular, the court refused to go against the express literal words of the statute (this 'fiction of fraud') in the context of the applicable remoteness test in order to apply the general test of foreseeability for negligence, but allowed the more generous test in fraud (*Doyle v Olby*: all direct loss regardless of foreseeability) to govern.

This aspect of the decision in *Royscot Trust* is easy to criticize because it treats negligent misrepresentations (honest statements) in the same way as fraudulent ones (dishonest statements). It also means that the remoteness tests applicable under the common law claim (*Hedley Byrne v Heller*) for negligent misstatement and under s. 2(1) of the 1967 Act for negligent misrepresentation are very different. Taken to its logical conclusion, the 'fiction of fraud' ought also to mean that the principle in *Smith New Court v Scrimgeour Vickers* [1997] AC 254 (see 14.6.2.2) on the measure of damages, and *East v Maurer* [1991] 1 WLR 461 on loss of profit damages for fraudulent misrepresentation, ought to apply with equal force to the assessment of damages under s. 2(1). This would seem a staggering conclusion, especially when the significance of the fraud in *Smith New Court* is considered.

It must be doubtful whether the same policy considerations should apply to negligent misrepresentations (see Hooley, 'Damages and the Misrepresentation Act 1967' (1991) 107 LQR 547). Nevertheless, in *Spice Girls Ltd v Aprilia World Service BV (Damages)* [2001] EMLR 8, Arden J had to assess damages under s. 2(1) of the Misrepresentation Act 1967 and held that she was bound to follow *Royscot Trust*. It was accepted that the damages had to be calculated as if the misrepresentation was fraudulent and on the basis of compensating Aprilia for losses flowing from the contract (i.e., the *Smith New Court* approach). Thus all direct loss and consequential loss was recoverable, but not payment of sponsorship fees made to the Spice Girls before the contract was concluded, since this payment had not been induced by the misrepresentation.

The position has become so acute that in *Avon Insurance plc v Swire Fraser Ltd* [2000] 1 All ER (Comm) 573, Rix J considered that because of application of the fraud rules to negligent misrepresentations under s. 2(1), a court should not be too willing to find there to be an actionable misrepresentation where the court had some room for the exercise of judgment. The judge continued (at p. 633, para. 201):

> If, on the other hand, the rule in *Royscot Trust Ltd* case were one day to be found to be a misunderstanding of the 1967 Act, and the way were to become open to treat an innocent misrepresentation under section 2(1) as though it was a case of negligence in *Hedley Byrne*, so that in the typical case of the provision of negligent information it would be possible to tailor the damages to the risk undertaken by the negligent representor…then there would be nothing to be said against adopting a more closely focused approach to the proof of misrepresentation.

In *Cheltenham Borough Council v Laird* [2009] EWHC 1253 (QB), [2009] IRLR 621, Hamblen J (at [524]) considered there was 'a real possibility of it being reversed' if *Royscot Trust* were to come before a higher court, citing the reasons discussed above. There are also clear signs of judicial discontent in those higher courts, although as yet no action.

In **Smith New Court Securities Ltd v Scrimgeour Vickers (Asset Management) Ltd** [1997] AC 254 at pp. 267 and 283, both Lords Browne-Wilkinson and Steyn noted the serious doubts about the correctness of the decision in **Royscot Trust Ltd v Rogerson**, but did not expressly overrule it since it was not necessary to the decision in the case. Lord Steyn did, however, make clear that in his view fraud and negligence should be treated differently, in that whereas remoteness for fraudulent misrepresentation allows for the recovery of all losses resulting from having entered into the contract, its application in the context of negligent misrepresentation would be limited to allowing for recovery of losses resulting from that negligent statement (which may be significantly narrower). (See the discussion of this distinction in *Man Nutfahrzeuge AG v Freightliner* [2005] EWHC 2347 (Comm), [193]–[197] concluding that the intention was to impose liability for losses 'arising out of the inaccuracy of any of the representations' 'but not against the entire consequences of entering into the agreement insofar as they could not be said to flow from the inaccuracy of the particular representation'.) This may be highly significant where there is more than one misrepresentation.

This area clearly cries out for reform (see Poole and Devenney, 'Reforming damages for misrepresentation: The case for coherent aims and principles' [2007] JBL 269). It may be that the courts are waiting for the Law Commission to investigate the Misrepresentation Act 1967 prior to legislative reform (see comments advocating this course of action by Jacob J in **Thomas Witter v TBP Industries Ltd** [1996] 2 All ER 573). However, until such time as the position is altered and *Royscot* is overruled, the remoteness test under s. 2(1) will be the test of all direct loss resulting from the misrepresentation, so that essentially the test will be to establish that the loss was **caused by the misrepresentation.** Where there is a causal link between the misrepresentation and the loss, the loss will therefore be recovered. The applicable test for this causal link will involve determining whether any subsequent action was reasonable and to be expected in the circumstances.

> In **Naughton v O'Callaghan** [1990] 3 All ER 191, the judge allowed recovery of the difference between the price paid for a thoroughbred colt, intended to be run as a race horse, and its actual value after the horse's value had fallen dramatically due to poor racing performances. The plaintiff's actions in training and racing the horse were exactly the conduct that would have been expected, and were reasonable in the circumstances given that the colt had been purchased as a racehorse.

Similarly, if the negligent misrepresentation induces the purchase of a business, it will have to be considered whether any consequential expenditure amounts to a reasonable and expected expense, taking into account the circumstances and, in particular, the nature of the business, or whether it is attributable to the independent whim of the purchaser. Thus, if the loss is caused not by the misrepresentation but by the misrepresentee's independent intervening action, it will not be recoverable (**Hussey v Eels** [1990] 2 QB 227).

14.6.4.2 Mitigation and s. 2(1)

The duty to mitigate loss (discussed above in the context of the fiction of fraud) also applies to claims for damages under s. 2(1) of the Misrepresentation Act 1967 (see **Pankhania v Hackney LBC (Damages)** [2004] EWHC 323 (Ch), [2004] 1 EGLR 135: it is a question of whether the claimant acted reasonably in terms of the steps taken subsequent to discovery of the misrepresentation).

14.6.5 Damages in lieu of rescission

Key point

Section 2(2) of the Misrepresentation Act 1967 provides:

Where a person has entered into a contract after a misrepresentation has been made to him otherwise than fraudulently, and he would be entitled, by reason of the misrepresentation, to rescind the contract, then, if it is claimed, in any proceedings arising out of the contract, that the contract ought to be or has been rescinded, the court or arbitrator may declare the contract subsisting and award damages in lieu of rescission, if of the opinion that it would be equitable to do so, having regard to the nature of the misrepresentation and the loss that would be caused by it if the contract were upheld, as well as to the loss that rescission would cause to the other party.

The aim of this provision is to prevent the use of the remedy of rescission in the case of trivial misrepresentations for which compensation would be an adequate remedy. This is because rescinding a contract has serious consequences, i.e. meaning the contract has no effect and any money or property which has changed hands will need to be returned (*William Sindall plc v Cambridgeshire CC* [1994] 1 WLR 1016 at p. 1045, per Evans LJ; see Beale (1995) 111 LQR 60).

It should be noted that s. 2(2) does not apply to fraudulent misrepresentation, since the law never treats fraud as trivial, and in practice it is most likely to be relevant where the misrepresentation is wholly innocent. The remedy is entirely within the discretion of the court, neither party having the right to insist upon its application. In exercising that discretion the court must weigh:

- the seriousness of the misrepresentation
- whether the representee will suffer greatly if not allowed to rescind
- whether the representor would suffer unduly if rescission were allowed (*William Sindall plc v Cambridgeshire CC* [1994] 1 WLR 1016 at pp. 1036–7, per Hoffmann LJ).

This exercise was carried out by the trial judge and then affirmed by the Court of Appeal in *UCB Corporate Services Ltd v Thomason* [2005] EWCA Civ 225, [2005] 1 All ER (Comm) 601.

In *UCB Corporate Services Ltd v Thomason*, a husband and wife were liable to the bank under two guarantees. As a result of misrepresentation (failure to disclose the full extent of the couple's assets) the bank entered into a waiver agreement releasing the liability under the guarantee. On discovering the misrepresentation, the bank sought to rescind the waiver agreement.

The Court of Appeal considered that the trial judge had been correct to conclude that the loss caused by the misrepresentation was the lost chance of recovering more money had it known the truth and therefore not agreed to the waiver, and not the amount of the guaranteed debt. This might result in little additional loss to the bank (the misrepresentee). On the other hand, if rescission was permitted it would have exposed the misrepresentors to a large liability, albeit that in practice that might not have been enforceable given the financial resources of this couple. The Court of Appeal therefore affirmed the decision of the trial judge to refuse to permit rescission.

This decision seems questionable since the likely actual loss is considered in relation to the assessment of the loss caused by the misrepresentation if the contract is upheld, whereas this is disregarded for the purposes of assessing the impact of allowing rescission.

An example of the kind of situation covered by the section might be an innocent misrepresentation, inaccurate by only one year, concerning the age of a secondhand cooker. Assuming the misrepresentation was sufficiently material to have induced the sale, it might be thought that the remedy of rescission would be unduly harsh in these circumstances; but for s. 2(2), it would be the only remedy available.

14.6.5.1 Must the remedy of rescission still be available if the s. 2(2) discretion is to be exercised?

It has traditionally been considered that the discretion to award damages instead of rescission could be exercised only if the right to rescind had not been lost (or barred), because the section as drafted appears to require that rescission be possible. Section 2(2) clearly refers to the discretion as existing where the injured party would otherwise be entitled to rescind. However, the consequence of the application of such a principle is that no useful remedy will exist, rescission having been lost and there being no discretion to award damages in its place. This interpretation was therefore criticized, but not really doubted, by Atiyah and Treitel ((1967) 30 MLR 369) at the time the Act was passed.

The conventional interpretation was challenged by Jacob J in *Thomas Witter Ltd v TBP Industries Ltd* [1996] 2 All ER 573 at p. 590 (see Beale (1995) 111 LQR 385). The judge clearly found such a limit on the discretion to award damages in lieu of rescission to be unattractive. He suggested that it might have been drafted in this way simply to require that the contract should have been open to rescission **at some point**, without requiring rescission to be a continuing possibility. He was offered support by counsel who had carried out a search of *Hansard* to discover what Parliament's intention had been. In the House of Commons, the Solicitor General had clearly indicated that the intention was to provide a remedy of damages where the right to rescission had been lost (Hansard HC, 20 February 1967, cols 1388–9). Jacob J needed no further encouragement and he duly found that 'the power to award damages under section 2(2) does not depend upon an extant right to rescission—it only depends upon a right having existed in the past'.

However, this approach has not been followed in a number of recent cases.

1. Judge Humphrey Lloyd QC in *Floods of Queensferry Ltd v Shand Construction Ltd* [2000] BLR 81 at p. 93, considered that for the discretion to be exercisable, the remedy of rescission had to exist at the date of the hearing.

2. In *Government of Zanzibar v British Aerospace (Lancaster House) Ltd* [2000] 1 WLR 2333, [2000] CLC 735, Judge Raymond Jack QC, sitting as a High Court judge, adopted the same approach (at pp. 2341–4) relying on the express words of the subsection, and refusing to follow *Thomas Witter v TBP Industries Ltd* on this point.

3. In *Pankhania v Hackney London Borough Council* [2002] EWHC 2441 (Ch), [2002] NPC 123, Rex Tedd QC (*obiter*) also considered that the s. 2(2) discretion could not apply unless the right to rescind was available at the date of the exercise of the discretion. The judge explained this in the light of the overall purpose of s. 2(2), which was to mitigate the harsh effects of rescission where this remedy was out of proportion to the misrepresentation and its effects. It was not intended 'to provide a remedy where there was none' prior to the Misrepresentation Act 1967.

Although this may be correct, it does have the unfortunate consequence that in some circumstances (admittedly limited) a misrepresentee may be left with no effective remedy (i.e., if the remedy of rescission has been lost and damages are not available because the misrepresentor had reasonable grounds to justify the statement made so that s. 2(1) damages cannot be claimed).

The significant differences of interpretation (and hence of result) in relation to this question of the availability of rescission and the s. 2(2) discretion again highlight the need for some reconsideration of the Misrepresentation Act 1967 (see 14.6.4.1).

14.6.5.2 The measure of damages under s. 2(2)

It may be that the measure of damages awarded in lieu of rescission is more restricted than either the out-of-pocket or lost expectation measures. The inference from s. 2(3) of the 1967 Act is that it is anticipated that damages under s. 2(2) will be lower than damages under s. 2(1), since the former are to be taken into account in assessing the latter, and this much is accepted by Hoffmann LJ (*obiter*) in *William Sindall plc v Cambridgeshire CC* [1994] 1 WLR 1016 at p. 1037.

However, if the purpose of the damages is to compensate for the loss of the right to rescind, it would seem that that loss is best measured as the difference between the contract price paid (which cannot now be recovered) and the actual value of the thing, which is the tortious measure of damages. This was the approach suggested *obiter* by the Court of Appeal in *William Sindall plc v Cambridgeshire CC*. Hoffmann LJ said that s. 2(2) allowed the court to uphold the contract and compensate the claimant for the loss suffered on account of the property not having been what it was represented to be. Section 2(2) damages could not be the difference between the price paid and the market value of the property on the basis that this was a loss flowing from having entered the contract. **That would be the appropriate measure for fraud, but s. 2(2) damages are different and represent the loss caused by the misrepresentation if the contract is upheld.** Evans LJ said (at p. 1044) that under s. 2(2), the loss caused by upholding the contract would be compensated by the award of 'the cost of remedying the defect, or alternatively…the reduced market value attributable to the defect'. It will not therefore extend to the loss caused due to entering into the contract, only the loss caused by upholding the contract.

On the facts in *Sindall* (see 13.2.1), the Court of Appeal considered (*obiter*) that the loss that would be caused to the misrepresentee if rescission were refused (and the contract was upheld) was not the full extent of the loss due to entering into the contract, i.e. taking account of the dramatic fall in the price of land, since that was not a loss caused by the misrepresentation if the contract was upheld. Instead, the misrepresentee's loss on this basis would be the cost of diverting the sewer which had been discovered, the loss of one plot and interest charges for any consequent delay.

For Hoffmann LJ in *Sindall*, the difference between s. 2(1) and s. 2(2) lay in the availability of damages for consequential loss, which would not be awarded under s. 2(2). This view was also supported by Jacob J in *Thomas Witter v TBP Industries Ltd* [1996] 2 All ER 573. It is submitted that this is the correct view of the section in view of the purpose of s. 2(2) damages, although Evans LJ in the *Sindall* case seems to contemplate the award of damages to compensate for consequential losses 'if appropriate'.

14.6.6 Indemnity

As was noted earlier (see 14.4.4), there is no general right to damages for a wholly innocent misrepresentation. Instead, where rescission is available it may be possible to recover an indemnity, which falls short of any measure of damages. **An indemnity provides compensation for** expenditure occurring as a result of 'obligations which have been created by the contract' into which the representee has been induced to enter (Bowen LJ in *Newbigging v Adam* (1886) 34 ChD 582 at p. 593).

The difference between an indemnity and damages may be demonstrated by reference to the facts of **Whittington v Seale-Hayne** (1900) 82 LT 49.

> The plaintiffs were induced to take a lease of a farm, intending to use it for poultry, by an innocent misrepresentation that the water supply was healthy. This proved not to be the case; a farm manager became ill and the poultry died. The plaintiffs were ordered by the local council to renew the drains, and they lost profits and spent money on medical care, rent, rates, outbuildings, and other business expenses. They sought to recover an 'indemnity' for all these costs. They were able to recover compensation for rent, rates, and renewing the drains, since these were obligations created by the fact of taking the lease. However, they could not recover the other expenses; these were items of damages, but did not qualify for an indemnity. They were expenses resulting from operating a poultry farm, and there was no **obligation** to run a poultry farm **created by** the contract.

14.6.7 Contributory negligence

Now that damages for negligent misrepresentation may be awarded, the question arises whether the misrepresentee's own negligence, which has contributed to his decision to enter the contract, operates to reduce the misrepresentee's damages award.

There is no scope for the application of contributory negligence where the misrepresentations were fraudulently made (**Alliance and Leicester Building Society v Edgestop Ltd** [1994] 2 All ER 38, *Corporation National del Cobre de Chile v Sogemin Metals Ltd* [1997] 1 WLR 1396). If the statement maker has been fraudulent, they should not be protected against the consequences of their statements by claiming that the misrepresentee was negligent. This point was confirmed by the House of Lords in **Standard Chartered Bank v Pakistan National Shipping Corporation (No. 2)** [2002] UKHL 43, [2003] 1 AC 959.

> On the facts of this case it was alleged that it was the claimant's own deceit which had partly caused the loss suffered. Payment for goods for export was to be made by means of a letter of credit. However, although the cargo was not shipped on time, the sellers had falsely stated the shipment date in the documents and payment had been authorized against these documents by SCB (the confirming bank) although it knew that the documents were presented after the expiry of the credit. SCB then sought reimbursement from the issuing bank by falsely stating that the documents had been presented in time. The issuing bank refused payment because of unrelated discrepancies in the documents. SCB then sought damages for deceit from the sellers who claimed that SCB's loss was partly attributable to their own deceit on the issuing bank.
>
> The House of Lords rejected this argument on the basis that the Law Reform (Contributory Negligence) Act 1945 did not apply to fraudulent misrepresentations since the Act was not intended to alter the previous position at common law.

Older authorities suggest that contributory negligence has no effect in the case of non-fraudulent misrepresentation (**Redgrave v Hurd** (1881) 20 ChD 1: see 14.2.2.4). These cases, however, predate the establishment of a separate category of negligent misrepresentation and the Law Reform (Contributory Negligence) Act 1945. In the general tort of negligence, s. 1(1) of the 1945 Act provides for apportionment of damages to take account of the claimant's contributory negligence.

Common law liability for negligent misstatement is clearly tortious (see 14.6.3), so that the 1945 Act will apply to claims based on *Hedley Byrne v Heller*.

Since negligent misstatement at common law and the statutory claim for damages under s. 2(1) of the Misrepresentation Act 1967 are alternatives, and the basic aim of damages in both cases is tortious, it might be thought that in the case of a claim for damages under s. 2(1), the misrepresentee's damages ought also to be reduced to take account of his contributory negligence. However, the *Royscot Trust* 'fiction of fraud' would suggest that damages under s. 2(1) should be assessed as if the misrepresentation were fraudulent. On this basis, there should be no apportionment for contributory negligence if the claim is brought solely under s. 2(1) since there is no apportionment for the misrepresentee's contributory negligence where the misrepresentor is fraudulent.

However, this latter interpretation would lead to all sorts of fine distinctions, especially since in *Gran Gelato Ltd v Richcliff (Group) Ltd* [1992] Ch 560 Nicholls V-C stated that where there are concurrent claims under *Hedley Byrne* and s. 2(1), the claimant's damages could be reduced in respect of both claims where there was contributory negligence by the claimant. He stated (at p. 573):

> It would be very odd if contributory negligence were available as a defence to a claim for damages based on a breach of a duty to take care in and about the making of a particular representation, but not available to a claim for damages under the 1967 Act in respect of the same representation.

It should therefore make no difference to the position if the claim is framed only under s. 2(1). A different interpretation would allow the 1945 Act to be avoided by claiming damages under s. 2(1) only, despite it being the case that the facts might also justify a claim based on *Hedley Byrne*.

Interestingly, in *Gran Gelato*, Nicholls V-C decided not to make any reduction in the damages awarded, on the ground that the defendants intended that the plaintiffs should act in reliance on the misrepresentation, so that they could not complain when liability was imposed precisely because the plaintiffs did act in the way the defendants intended. The judge suggests that his approach is supported by the decision in *Redgrave v Hurd*, but we have already seen that the relevance of that decision to the issue of damages for negligent misrepresentation is questionable. In fact, it has already been suggested (see 14.2.2.3) that a misrepresentation will not be taken to have induced the contract unless it was intended to be acted upon. Accordingly, this limitation on the application of contributory negligence inevitably appears to apply whenever liability can be established!

14.7 Excluding or limiting liability for misrepresentation

It is possible, in some circumstances, to exclude liability for pre-contractual misrepresentations, by means of an express term in the contract which was allegedly induced by the misrepresentation. In many respects such exclusions are subject to the same constraints as exclusions of contractual liability (see Chapter 7). For example, the clause will be interpreted restrictively, and will apply only if it covers the representation in question. So, in *Toomey v Eagle Star Insurance Co. Ltd (No. 2)* [1995] 2 Lloyd's Rep 88, Colman J found that a clause which purported to exclude the remedy of rescission, but which did not expressly refer to rescission on the basis of negligent misrepresentation, applied only to wholly innocent misrepresentation, and did not apply to negligent misrepresentation in the sense of the 1967 Act. Similarly, a clause which excludes or limits liability for misrepresentation will have no operation to a misrepresentation which has become a term (Jacob J in *Thomas Witter v TBP Industries Ltd* [1996] 2 All ER 573). In addition, there are also statutory controls on the use of such clauses, namely the Unfair Contract Terms Act (UCTA) 1977 and the Unfair Terms in Consumer Contracts Regulations 1999 (see 7.5).

In the context of misrepresentation, a clause which excludes or limits liability for misrepresentation in a consumer contract (see 7.7.1.1) may be voidable as an unfair term under the Unfair Terms in Consumer Contracts Regulations 1999 (see 7.7.6) and, more generally, **s. 3 of the Misrepresentation Act 1967** (as amended by UCTA 1977, s. 8) provides as follows:

If a contract contains a term which would exclude or restrict—

(a) any liability to which a party to a contract may be subject by reason of any misrepresentation made by him before the contract was made; or

(b) any remedy available to another party to the contract by reason of such a misrepresentation,

that term shall be of no effect except in so far as it satisfies the requirement of reasonableness as stated in section 11(1) of the Unfair Contract Terms Act 1977; and it is for those claiming that the term satisfies that requirement to show that it does.

In *Trident Turboprop (Dublin) Ltd v First Flight Couriers Ltd* [2009] EWCA Civ 290, [2009] 3 WLR 861, the Court of Appeal held that since s. 3 of the 1967 Act was worded in terms which rendered an exclusion clause ineffective unless it complied with the controls set out in the UCTA 1977, it made the latter the controlling instrument. Therefore it would not be right to treat the Misrepresentation Act as imposing restrictions in a case in which UCTA provided none, i.e. international supply contracts which are excluded from the application of UCTA 1977, s. 26.

14.7.1 The scope of s. 3

1. This section applies to both negligent and innocent misrepresentations (as a matter of policy, exclusions of liability for a person's own fraud are not permitted, see *S. Pearson & Son Ltd v Dublin Corporation* [1907] AC 351, below).

2. Section 3 will apply to clauses which purport to deny that any actionable misrepresentation has been made at all (*Cremdean Properties Ltd v Nash* (1977) 244 EG 547: no statement of truth being made). It is difficult to distinguish these clauses from those clauses which state that the supplier of information does not verify its accuracy or completeness and does not accept responsibility for the information supplied. Toulson J in *IFE Fund SA v Goldman Sachs International* [2006] EWHC 2887 (Comm), [2006] CLC 1043, [2007] 1 Lloyd's Rep 264 at [68]–[69] stated that 'the question is one of substance and not form'. He gave some examples of statements made by the seller of a car: (a) 'I have serviced the car since it was new, it has had only one owner and the clock reading

is accurate but those statements are not representations on which you can rely' and (b) 'The clock reading is 20,000 miles, but I have no knowledge whether the reading is true or false'. The statements in (a) would be representations and would fall within the statutory control in s. 3, despite the statement that they are not representations (*Cremdean Properties v Nash*). However, the qualifying words in (b) do not amount to an attempt to exclude liability for a false representation as to mileage but relate to the scope of the statement made. On the facts in this case the statements relating to non-verification and non-acceptance of responsibility for reviewing the information supplied related to the scope of the representations so that the statutory control did not apply. (This point was not the subject of appeal to the Court of Appeal [2007] EWCA Civ 811, [2007] 2 Lloyd's Rep 449, [2007] 2 CLC 134.)

3. Thus, it may be possible to avoid the impact of UCTA 1977 on clauses excluding liability for misrepresentation by careful drafting. For example, if the term in question limits or excludes the authority of an agent to make representations which will bind the principal, that amounts to a clause restricting the authority of agents and does not therefore come within the definition of an exclusion or limitation clause under UCTA 1977 (*Overbrook Estates Ltd v Glencombe Properties Ltd* [1974] 1 WLR 1353). Such clauses are, for example, fairly common in contracts for the sale of new homes, in an effort to exclude liability for any statements made by site agents.

Nevertheless, in the context of consumer contracts to which the Unfair Terms in Consumer Contracts Regulations 1999 apply, it may be that a clause 'limiting the seller's or supplier's obligation to respect commitments undertaken by his agents or making his commitments subject to compliance with a particular formality', such as approval of the principal, may be an unfair term and voidable under the regulations (Sch. 2(1)(n)). Whether this is in fact considered to be the case may depend on whether the word 'commitment' is interpreted narrowly, so as to be limited to a contractual undertaking, or whether it covers a representation by such an agent which induces the making of the contract but which does not become incorporated as a term.

14.7.2 The reasonableness requirement and s. 3

If s. 3 applies, the exclusion clause will be effective only if the party seeking to rely on it to avoid liability can satisfy the burden of proving that, at the time of contracting, it was reasonable, having regard to the circumstances within the contemplation of the parties (UCTA 1977, s. 11(1)). The operation of the reasonableness test is considered in more detail in relation to clauses excluding contractual liability (see 7.6.6).

However, it is possible to make two general points concerning attempts to exclude liability for misrepresentation:

1. A clause is more likely to be unreasonable where the statement maker is seeking to exclude liability for representations based on facts which are only within the knowledge of the statement maker and not that of the other party, e.g., *Howard Marine & Dredging Co. Ltd v A. Ogden & Sons (Excavations) Ltd* [1978] QB 574.

2. As a more general point, the law will not accept the exclusion of liability for a person's own fraud (*S. Pearson & Son Ltd v Dublin Corporation* [1907] AC 351), although it is possible to exclude liability for the fraud of employees and others, assuming clear words are used

to do so (***HIH Casualty and General Insurance Co. Ltd v Chase Manhattan Bank*** [2003] UKHL 6, [2003] 1 All ER (Comm) 349).

This raises a general point of construction since it **may** follow, therefore, that where the clause purports to exclude liability in respect of **all** types of misrepresentations (fraudulent, negligent, and innocent), it may be considered to be unreasonable because it **could** apply to exclude liability for fraud (***Thomas Witter v TBP Industries Ltd*** [1996] 2 All ER 573; although a different conclusion was reached on this point by Judge Raymond Jack QC in ***Government of Zanzibar v British Aerospace Ltd*** [2000] 1 WLR 2333 at pp. 2346–7). (This is yet a further point which would benefit from consideration by a higher court.)

Although not a higher court, this matter was considered by the High Court in **Six Continent Hotels Inc. v Event Hotels GmbH** [2006] EWHC 2317 (QB), (2006) 150 SJLB 1251.

> The claimant hotel company sued the defendant hotel company for unpaid fees for use of the Holiday Inn trademark. The defendant counterclaimed alleging misrepresentations to the effect that other German franchisees did not pay lower fees and that any new franchisees would pay higher fees. There was a term which stated: 'Each of the parties agree that it shall not commence any lawsuit or assert any claim…against the other party…based on actions, discussions or agreements…which occurred prior to the signing of this Agreement.' Counsel for the defendant argued, relying on **Thomas Witter**, that this clause could not be relied upon to cover any type of misrepresentation because it was drafted so widely as to be capable of covering fraudulent misrepresentations—and the coverage of fraud could not be severed. However, Gloster J, although holding that there were no misrepresentations, preferred the approach in **Government of Zanzibar v British Aerospace Ltd** [2000] 1 WLR 2333 to the effect that since any clauses excluding liability could not as a matter of construction cover fraud (**S. Pearson & Son Ltd v Dublin Corporation** [1907] AC 351), the clause in question could not have that intent. It followed that since any misrepresentations would not have been fraudulent (which would have precluded reliance on the clause), the clause could apply to non-fraudulent misrepresentations and was not therefore automatically unreasonable under s. 3.
>
> If s. 3 did apply, the court considered that the clause would satisfy the reasonableness requirement because the agreements were sophisticated agreements between commercial parties and there was no inequality of bargaining power. The parties desired commercial certainty and the price being paid reflected the agreed risks (*Grimstead & Son (E. A.) Ltd v McGarrigan*, unreported, 27 October 1999, per Chadwick LJ).

14.7.3 **Entire agreement clauses covering representations**

Contracts frequently contain a statement that the written document comprises all the terms of the contract between the parties and often add a statement that no representations have been made which are not contained in the written terms. These clauses are often referred to as 'entire agreement' clauses. The effect of such clauses has been the subject of judicial explanation by Lightman J in ***Inntrepreneur Pub Co. v East Crown Ltd*** [2000] 2 Lloyd's Rep 611, discussed at 6.2.1.4.

Lightman J distinguished between the first part of the clause, which stated that the agreement represented the 'entire agreement between the parties', and the second part of the clause providing that the party had 'not relied upon any advice or statement of the Company or its solicitors' before executing the agreement (so called 'non-reliance' clauses). He considered that whereas the first part (or 'entire agreement') clause defined where the terms of the contract could be found (i.e., in the written document only), the second part of the clause purported to exclude the existence of any liability for actionable misrepresentation and was therefore subject to s. 3 of the Misrepresentation Act 1967.

Lightman J said (at p. 614):

> an entire agreement provision does not preclude a claim in misrepresentation, for the denial of contractual force cannot affect the status of a statement as a misrepresentation.

The same approach was also adopted by Judge Raymond Jack QC in *Government of Zanzibar v British Aerospace (Lancaster House) Ltd* [2000] 1 WLR 2333. The judge distinguished the entire agreement clause [A] from clause [B], which excluded liability for misrepresentation.

On the facts in *Inntrepreneur Pub Co. v East Crown Ltd* (see 6.2.1.4), s. 3 of the Misrepresentation Act 1967 applied to the part of the clause seeking to exclude liability for misrepresentation and therefore had to be shown to be reasonable in order to be relied upon. Ironically, there may therefore be some point in 'threshing through the undergrowth' (at p. 614) in search of a misrepresentation in preference to a pre-contractual promise.

Important obiter comments of the Court of Appeal in *Watford Electronics Ltd v Sanderson CFL Ltd* [2001] EWCA Civ 317, [2001] 1 All ER (Comm) 696, appear to have complicated matters further in the context of 'non-reliance' clauses (providing that 'no statement or representations by either party have been relied upon') by treating such clauses, at least in the context of commercial contracts where commercial certainty is important, as operating as an estoppel against later allegations of misrepresentation based on reliance. Such an approach is justified as reflecting the nature of the commercial risks being assumed by the terms of the contract and these terms reflect the parties' intentions. However, in effect, this approach would provide protection for non-fraudulent misrepresentations in the commercial context and it might also be argued that the very purpose of the legislation in this area is to regulate the use of agreed exemption clauses which appear in clear terms to be attempting to exclude or limit the liability of one of the parties. It is difficult to see why non-reliance clauses should be treated differently. Nevertheless, Chadwick LJ considered that it 'would be bizarre' to attribute to the parties 'an intention to exclude a liability which they must have thought could never arise'. He explained the position on the evidential estoppel (at [40]) as follows:

> It is true that an acknowledgement of non-reliance does not purport to prevent a party from proving that a representation was made, nor that it was false. What the acknowledgement seeks to do is to prevent the person to whom the representation was made from asserting that he relied upon it. If it is to have that effect, it will be necessary…for the party who seeks to set up the acknowledgement as an evidential estoppel to plead and prove that the three requirements identified by this Court in *Lowe v Lombank Ltd* [1960] 1 WLR 196 are satisfied. That may present insuperable difficulties; not least because it may be impossible for a party who has made representations which he intended should be relied upon to satisfy the court that he entered into the contract in the belief that a statement by the other party that he had not relied upon those representations was true. But the fact that, on particular facts, the acknowledgement of non-reliance may not achieve its purpose does not lead to the conclusion that the acknowledgement is 'in substance an exclusion clause to which section 3 of the Misrepresentation Act is applicable'.

Thus, in the event that the misrepresentee alleges misrepresentation it is for the alleged misrep-resentor to seek to establish the estoppel based on the non-reliance clause. The balancing factor is that it is not easy to establish the estoppel on the facts, e.g. *Quest 4 Finance Ltd v Maxfield* [2007] EWHC 2313 (QB), [2007] 2 CLC 706, where the defendants argued that a warranty for a loan to the company should be set aside because they were induced by a misrepresentation that personal guarantees were not required and that the warranty would apply only in cases of fraud. The claimant argued the defendants were estopped from relying on statements in the claimant's brochure because of a declaration of non-reliance. However, on the facts the claimant could not rely on the 'non-reliance' declaration since it could not show that it had believed this declaration to be true and that there had been no reliance by the defendants. Therefore no estoppel operated.

The Court of Appeal's decision in *Watford Electronics Ltd v Sanderson CFL Ltd* means that a non-reliance clause (1) gives rise in appropriate cases to a contractual estoppel preventing the denial of the earlier acknowledgement of non-reliance as the basis for a claim in misrepresenta-tion, and (2) will not be subject to s. 3 because the non-reliance prevents an actionable misrepre-sentation from arising. These consequences are, of course, interrelated.

This aspect of the decision in *Watford Electronics* was applied and explained in *Peekay Intermark Ltd v Australia and New Zealand Banking Group Ltd* [2006] EWCA Civ 386, [2006] 2 Lloyd's Rep 511, [2006] 1 CLC 582 (for facts see 6.2.2.1 and 14.2.2.4). When signing the written contract the claimant had also signed a Risk Disclosure Statement stating that he understood the transaction and its terms and conditions and had 'independently satisfied' himself. It fol-lowed that the effect of such a clause 'in principle' was to give up any right to assert that the claimant had been induced to contract by misrepresentation and the clause therefore operated as a contractual estoppel (*Watford Electronics*) (per Moore-Bick LJ at [57]), although as the defendant had succeeded separately on the 'no inducement' argument these comments were necessarily *obiter*.

Thus s. 3 is applicable only if there has been an actionable misrepresentation and attempt to exclude or limit liability for it (*Cremdean Properties v Nash*). Where there is no actionable misrepresentation because the parties have agreed there is no reliance, and are estopped from denying that position, the statutory control is irrelevant and conflicts with party agreement. Why this distinction should be made is far from clear. The judge in *Peart Stevenson Associates Ltd v Holland* [2008] EWHC 1868 (QB) appeared to treat the approaches as being in conflict but did not think it necessary to 'decide between the two approaches in the circumstances of the present case'. The special factor in this case was that the misrepresentation was fraudulent so that the non-reliance clause was considered unreasonable. In any event the second and third requirements in *Lowe v Lombank Ltd* required to found the estoppel (see Chadwick LJ in *Watford Electronics* extracted above), were not satisfied.

Further reading

General

Cartwright, *Misrepresentation, Mistake and Non-Disclosure*, 2nd edn *(Sweet and Maxwell, 2006)*.

Rescission

Poole and Keyser, 'Justifying partial rescission in English law' (2005) 121 LQR 273.

Misrepresentation Act 1967

Atiyah and Treitel, 'Misrepresentation Act 1967' (1967) 30 MLR 369.

Beale, 'Damages in lieu of rescission for misrepresentation' (1995) 111 LQR 60.

Beale, 'Points on misrepresentation' (1995) 111 LQR 385.

Brown and Chandler, 'Deceit, damages and the Misrepresentation Act 1967, s. 2(1)' [1992] LMCLQ 40.

Cartwright, 'Damages for misrepresentation' [1987] Conv 423.

Chandler, 'Fraud: Damages and opportunity costs' (1994) 110 LQR 35.

Chandler and Higgins, 'Contributory negligence and the Misrepresentation Act 1967, s. 2(1)' [1994] LMCLQ 326.

Halson, 'Damages for the tort of deceit' [1997] LMCLQ 423.

Handley, 'Exclusion clauses for fraud' (2003) 119 LQR 537.

Hooley, 'Damages and the Misrepresentation Act 1967' (1991) 107 LQR 547.

Marks, 'Loss of profits in damages for deceit' (1992) 108 LQR 386.

Oakley, 'Measure of damages for misrepresentation' [1992] CLJ 9.

Oakley, 'Contributory negligence of a fraudulent representee' [1994] CLJ 218.

Parker, 'Fraudulent bills of lading and bankers' commercial credits: Deceit, contributory negligence and directors' personal liability' [2003] LMCLQ 1.

Poole and Devenney, 'Reforming damages for misrepresentation: The case for coherent aims and principles' [2007] JBL 269.

Wadsley, 'Measures in misrepresentation: Recent steps in awarding damages' (1992) 55 MLR 698.

15 Duress, undue influence, and unconscionable bargains

Summary of the issues

This chapter will examine two recognized doctrines of English law which provide a means for a claimant to avoid a concluded contract on the basis that threats or unfair pressures or influence were exerted to persuade the claimant to contract. In addition, it questions whether it is possible to recognize any general doctrine of fairness in English contract law and assesses the circumstances in which the courts have intervened to prevent one party taking advantage of another.

• The first of the recognized doctrines is the doctrine of duress which takes the form of some form of coercion or threat to the person, property, or to a person's financial interests (economic duress). The doctrine of economic duress is now seen as the primary mechanism to prevent promises obtained by extortion from being enforceable but it is a comparatively new doctrine and is still being developed.

• To succeed in a claim (or defence) based on economic duress it must be established that there is some illegitimate pressure or threat, which amounts to a significant cause inducing the claimant to contract because the claimant has no real practical choice other than to agree. In addition, the victim of duress will need to protest at the time or shortly thereafter. However, the exact meaning of these ingredients is unclear, particularly the meaning of illegitimate pressure and the effect of so-called lawful act duress.

• Undue influence is an equitable doctrine which can arise in two ways—actual undue influence (which is similar to duress because it arises from illegitimate pressure and abuse exerted by one party over the other) and circumstances where there is an evidential presumption that influence has been exercised which may become an evidential presumption of *undue* influence where there is something in the transaction 'which is suspicious or calls for an explanation' (i.e., of such a size or nature as to raise suspicions). In the case of presumptive undue influence, the conclusion of influence may arise automatically in the case of certain types of protected relationships but needs to be established on the facts in other cases on the basis that there is a relationship of trust and confidence between the particular parties. Where undue influence is established as between the contracting parties, the victim can have the transaction set aside.

• Where a wife gives security in order to support the debts of her husband (i.e., her contract is with the lender—someone other than the person exercising the influence), the lender will be affected by the actions of the person exercising the undue influence (e.g., her husband) where that lender is fixed with constructive notice of that other's undue influence. This will occur where the lender is 'put on inquiry' (and may occur in all cases where a wife stands surety for her husband's debts and not for any joint purpose). Lenders are required to take precise steps (involving ensuring that the practical implications of the proposed transaction have been explained to the wife) or the lenders risk losing their security.

- The final issue in this chapter concerns whether there is a general doctrine in English law which justifies interference on the basis of fairness in relation to the parties' bargaining positions. It appears that inequality of bargaining power per se will not be sufficient but that principles do exist to prevent an abuse of position of strength and to protect those in weaker positions, such as consumers. Parliament has had a role to play in terms of regulating substantive unfairness, including a new provision in the Consumer Credit Act (CCA) 1974 (introduced by the CCA 2006) enabling the courts to interfere in 'unfair credit agreements' (ss. 140A–D CCA 1974). There is also considerable existing European-led legislation to protect consumers. The Consumer Protection from Unfair Trading Regulations 2008, SI 2008/1277, implementing the Unfair Commercial Practices Directive, (2005/29/EC, OJ L149/22) prohibit certain forms of behaviour that fall within the remit of this chapter.

General background

This chapter examines doctrines relating to circumstances surrounding the making of the contract. In the context of consumer contracts, Parliament has stepped in to protect consumers against various high-pressure sales techniques, in particular, by allowing consumers a 'cooling off' period during which time the agreement can be cancelled (see, e.g., CCA 1974, the Cancellation of Contracts Made in a Consumer's Home or Place of Work etc. Regulations 2008, SI 2008/1816, and other cancellation rights (e.g., Consumer Protection (Distance Selling) Regulations 2000, SI 2000/2334, as amended by SI 2005/689)).

There are also recognized general doctrines applying to instances where unfair and illegitimate pressure or threats have been applied, or unfair advantage has been taken by one party over the other in order to persuade a party to contract or to agree a variation of the contract on disadvantageous terms. Where this is the case and either the doctrine of duress or undue influence applies, the contract is voidable (i.e., it can be set aside by the victim or complainant). The doctrine of duress, in particular, is likely to be highly relevant in the context of commercial contracts. However, there is a fine line to be drawn here, because some commercial pressure in negotiating is both normal and acceptable.

15.1 Duress

15.1.1 The limited early doctrine

The common law always accepted that some forms of coercion in the making of contracts resulted in the victim of the coercion being afforded a remedy, in that the contract would be set aside and any money paid could be recovered. However, the forms of coercion recognized as having such an effect were very limited. There was no doubt that duress to the person had such an effect, whether it took the form of threatened or actual violence (*Barton v Armstrong* [1976] 1 AC 104), or a threat of imprisonment (*Williams v Bayley* (1886) LR 1 HL 200), although the latter rule arose only after the intervention of equity. As such, the doctrine was of little significance, since the number of cases of duress to the person has always been small.

It has also been settled that a threat to seize another's property or to damage it (duress to property), will justify a claim of duress and result in the ensuing contract being set aside (see Lord Goff in *Dimskal Shipping Co. SA v International Transport Workers' Federation, The Evia Luck* [1991] 4 All ER 871 at p. 878).

In addition, in the mid-1960s the courts, led by Lord Denning MR, started to pay far greater attention to the requirement of fairness in bargaining. Thus, in ***D. and C. Builders v Rees*** [1966] 2 QB 617 (see 4.8.4), Lord Denning refused to apply the promissory estoppel doctrine to enforce a promise to accept a payment in final settlement of a debt, on the express ground that the promise had been extracted by unfair pressure and the creditor had been 'held to ransom' since the debtor knew of the creditor's financial difficulties and had sought to take advantage. The result of these developments has been the emergence of a new and far more significant doctrine of economic duress.

15.1.2 Economic duress

The idea that mere economic duress (threats to a person's financial or business interests) might be a ground upon which a contract could be set aside was first canvassed by Kerr J in ***Occidental Worldwide Investment Corporation v Skibs A/S Avanti, The Siboen and The Sibotre*** [1976] 1 Lloyd's Rep 293. The typical situation raising the possibility of a claim of economic duress is where one party threatens breach of contract unless the contract is renegotiated, and the other agrees rather than face disastrous consequences as a result of breach. The area is fraught with difficulty, however, since companies who deal with each other on a regular basis will often agree quite voluntarily to renegotiate a contract, and such agreements are the essence of the level of cooperation necessary in the business world. It would be unfortunate if they were threatened by the economic duress doctrine. On the other hand, changes to the law relating to consideration, particularly in the area of variation of commercial contracts (see ***Williams v Roffey Bros & Nicholls (Contractors) Ltd*** [1991] 1 QB 1: see 4.4.4), have increased the need for such a clear and recognized doctrine in English law.

In the past, contract changes achieved by means of unfair pressure or extortion could be resisted on the formal ground of absence of consideration. (See ***Stilk v Myrick*** (1809) 2 Camp 317, 6 Esp 129 (see 4.4.4), and ***Atlas Express Ltd v Kafco (Importers & Distributors) Ltd*** [1989] 1 All ER 641, where absence of consideration was the alternative ground for the decision.) A restrictive approach to the definition of consideration was required to achieve this (i.e., the performance of an existing duty could not be a good consideration because there was no additional legal benefit or detriment). However, in ***Williams v Roffey Bros*** (see 4.4.4) the Court of Appeal cited the availability of the doctrine of economic duress as the mechanism for preventing the enforceability of promises obtained as a result of extortion in order to justify its more relaxed approach to finding consideration. The result of this development is that the emphasis appears to have shifted from the doctrine of consideration to the doctrine of economic duress in order to prevent promises obtained by extortion, or improper threats, from being enforceable. It is vital, therefore, that the doctrine be clearly defined. However, as we shall see, the doctrine is a comparatively recent development in English law and, as such, is still developing.

15.1.2.1 Establishing economic duress

In ***Pao On v Lau Yiu Long*** [1980] AC 614 (see also 4.3.3), the Privy Council approved the doctrine of economic duress and attempted to identify its essential ingredients.

Lord Scarman identified two essential conditions for the operation of the doctrine:

1. 'coercion of the will that vitiates consent'

2. the pressure or threat must be illegitimate.

In ***DSND Subsea Ltd v Petroleum Geo Services ASA*** [2000] BLR 530, Dyson J identified the ingredients of actionable duress, as they have subsequently developed:

> [T]here must be pressure, (a) whose practical effect is that there is compulsion on, or lack of practical choice for, the victim, (b) which is illegitimate, and (c) which is a significant cause inducing the claimant to enter into the contract.

15.1.2.2 Coercion of the will that vitiates consent

The question in ***Pao On v Lau Yiu Long*** was whether there had been the necessary coercion of the will vitiating consent.

> Under the terms of a contract, the plaintiffs were to sell their shares in a company which owned a building under construction to the Fu Chip Company and were to receive shares in the Fu Chip Company in return. The defendants, the majority shareholders in the Fu Chip Company, had been concerned that if the plaintiffs chose to sell all these shares at one time, there would be a fall in the value of their shareholdings. The plaintiffs therefore agreed with the company that they would not sell 60 per cent of their shares for one year. The plaintiffs then threatened not to perform this promise unless the defendants agreed to indemnify them against any loss in the value of their shares in this one-year period. Fearing delays, and a loss of confidence in their company if the deal were not completed, the defendants signed an indemnity agreeing to compensate the plaintiffs if the value of these shares fell below $2.50 a share. The share price fell and the plaintiffs sought to rely on the indemnity. However, the defendants claimed that the indemnity had been obtained as a result of duress.
>
> Lord Scarman, giving the advice of the Privy Council, said that there was nothing wrong in principle in recognizing economic duress as a factor making contracts voidable. The essence of the rule, he said, was that 'there must be a coercion of will such that there was no true consent…it must be shown that the contract entered into was not a voluntary act'.
>
> It was essential to distinguish between mere commercial pressure, which is an everyday incident of the hard-nosed bargaining which goes on in the business world, and duress. On the facts in ***Pao On***, Lord Scarman emphasized the question of whether there was a realistic alternative open to the defendants. It was held that the defendants had coolly analysed the options and had taken a commercial decision that the risk to the company of non-performance was greater than the risk of the need to pay under the indemnity. Accordingly, there was no coercion of the will and no duress.

No realistic choice other than to agree

However, it would seem incorrect to argue that duress is based upon consent being vitiated so that the agreement is not voluntary. Atiyah ((1982) 98 LQR 197) strongly criticized this requirement. More recently, Lord Goff in ***Dimskal Shipping Co. SA v International Transport Workers' Federation, The Evia Luck*** [1991] 4 All ER 871 at p. 878, stated that he doubted whether it was helpful to speak of a person's will being coerced. The victim of duress knows exactly what they are doing and submits intentionally. In the criminal law, the House of Lords has been clear in saying that the defence of duress does not depend upon the absence of a voluntary act, but rather depends upon intentional submission in the face of no other practical alternative (*Lynch v DPP for Northern Ireland* [1975] AC 653). **The same must be true of contract, so that duress does not negate the existence of consent but is based upon a finding that the victim had no**

other realistic option available other than to agree. This reasoning is borne out by the fact that duress renders a contract voidable, and not void. In ***Universe Tankships Inc. of Monrovia v International Transport Workers' Federation, The Universe Sentinel*** [1983] 1 AC 366, Lords Diplock and Scarman admitted that duress in contract law does not involve the destruction of will but intentional submission to the inevitable.

In the light of this debate, the first ingredient for duress in ***Pao On*** has been reformulated as 'no realistic choice', rather than in terms of 'coercion of the will vitiating consent' (see, e.g., the statement of Dyson J in ***DSND Subsea Ltd v Petroleum Geo Services ASA*** [2000] BLR 530, which refers to compulsion and lack of practical choice).

B. & S. Contracts & Design Ltd v Victor Green Publications Ltd [1984] ICR 419, provides a useful example of a situation where there was no practical choice other than to agree.

> The plaintiffs were to erect exhibition stands for the defendants who had let these stands to various exhibitors. However, a week before the date of the exhibition, the plaintiffs' workers refused to work unless a pay demand was met. The defendants therefore paid £4,500 in order to avoid serious losses, which would have resulted from the claims against them by disappointed exhibitors. However, the defendants then deducted this figure from the contract price paid to the plaintiffs. The plaintiffs claimed the balance. The Court of Appeal held that the defendants had been affected by duress because they had no realistic choice other than to pay. An action for breach of contract against the plaintiffs, although technically possible, was unrealistic because it would have been too damaging.

In ***Carillion Construction Ltd v Felix (UK) Ltd*** [2001] BLR 1 it was held that threats to withhold deliveries when under a contractual obligation to use best endeavours to prevent delay, amounted to illegitimate threats and it was held to be unrealistic to expect the other party to seek a mandatory injunction. Similarly, in ***Atlas Express Ltd v Kafco (Importers & Distributors) Ltd*** [1989] 1 All ER 641, the defendant had no realistic choice other than to sign a revised contract for carriage of its goods because it could not, at such short notice, have obtained alternative carriage for the goods; and without the ability to deliver, it would have lost the contract to supply its major customer (Woolworth). In ***Adam Opel GmbH v Mitras Automotive Ltd*** [2007] EWHC 3205 (QB), [2008] Bus LR Digest D55, there was a threat to stop supplies of a component needed in the manufacture of vans unless the increased price and compensation were paid. There were no alternatives, production would have halted within twenty-four hours and there would have been significant consequences for other suppliers of parts for these vans. Accordingly there was no realistic choice other than to pay.

15.1.2.3 Illegitimate pressure or threat

1. Pressure or threat

In a claim for economic duress there must be pressure or a threat. This can lead to fine distinctions of fact. For example, in ***Williams v Roffey Bros*** [1991] 1 QB 1, it was vitally important that the impetus for the promise to pay more money came from the main contractor and so had not been obtained as a result of threats of non-performance from the subcontractor. It is less clear, however, what the position would be where one contracting party simply advises the other of difficulties or the possibility of non-performance. It would seem to be a question of fact as to whether this amounts to 'pressure' in all the circumstances.

2. The pressure or threat must be illegitimate

The pressure or threat must also be illegitimate. It is unclear where the line between legitimate and illegitimate pressures or threats is to be drawn. In ***DSND Subsea Ltd v Petroleum Geo***

Services ASA [2000] BLR 530, Dyson J stated that 'illegitimate pressure must be distinguished from the rough and tumble of the pressures of normal commercial bargaining'.

Some pressure is clearly legitimate and it is vitally important to the scope of the doctrine of economic duress that the line between legitimate and illegitimate pressure should be drawn with some certainty.

An example of clear illegitimate pressure is provided by the facts of ***Vantage Navigation Corporation v Suhail and Saud Bahwan Building Materials LLC, The Alev*** [1989] 1 Lloyd's Rep 138.

> The charterers had defaulted on the payment of hire for the vessel but the plaintiffs, the shipowners, were obliged by the contract to carry the cargo on board the vessel to its destination. Nevertheless, they threatened not to ship the cargo unless the defendants, the cargo owners, paid the plaintiffs the sum demanded. The defendants agreed but subsequently succeeded in a plea of duress. The pressure exerted by the plaintiffs was illegitimate since the plaintiffs had no rights over the goods and could not refuse to deliver the cargo.

In ***Universe Tankships Inc. of Monrovia v International Transport Workers' Federation, The Universe Sentinel*** [1983] 1 AC 366, the issue of the legitimacy of the pressure exerted hinged upon the interpretation of the Trade Union and Labour Relations Act 1974.

> The case concerned threats by a trade union to 'black' vessels, in the sense that no tugs would be provided to assist the vessels to leave harbour unless the ship owner made a payment to the trade union. If the vessels were unable to leave the harbour, the losses would have been considerable, so the shipowner paid and then claimed the return of this money. The trade union argued that their actions were protected as actions 'in contemplation of a trade dispute' under the 1974 Act.
>
> The majority of the House of Lords considered that the threats were illegitimate because the trade union was not protected by this legislation.
>
> The minority (Lords Scarman and Brandon) thought that the trade union was protected by the legislation, so that the threat was *prima facie* lawful. However, a lawful threat would constitute duress if used, as here, to further an illegitimate purpose such as blackmail.

In ***R v HM Attorney-General for England and Wales*** [2003] UKPC 22, [2003] EMLR 24, the Privy Council cited, with approval, the comments of Lord Scarman in ***The Universe Sentinel*** on the question of identification of illegitimate pressure. Lord Scarman had stated that it was necessary to examine both the nature of the pressure and the nature of the demand which the pressure is applied to support, so that a threat of unlawful action would generally be regarded as illegitimate pressure, whereas a threat of lawful action would not necessarily mean that the pressure was legitimate, e.g. blackmail using a lawful threat.

> In ***R v HM Attorney-General for England and Wales***, an SAS member alleged that he had been subjected to duress when he signed a confidentiality agreement to cover the period after he left the SAS. It was alleged that he had been threatened with return to his ordinary unit if he did not sign the agreement. However, *this threat was considered to be a lawful threat* since the MOD had the ability to make such a transfer and the SAS was reasonably entitled to regard anyone unwilling to accept the confidentiality agreement as unsuitable to be a member of the SAS. Therefore there was no duress and the decision to sign was no more than a matter of choice for the individual soldier, albeit one where there was 'overwhelming pressure' to sign.

Is there a category of lawful act duress?

In the 1990s the Court of Appeal had to address the question of whether there is a more general category of **lawful act duress, i.e. whether lawful (if ultimately unreasonable) demands can amount to illegitimate pressure.**

In **CTN Cash and Carry Ltd v Gallagher Ltd** [1994] 4 All ER 714, the defendants had mistakenly sent a shipment of cigarettes to the wrong place of business for the plaintiffs. The plaintiffs undertook to remedy the situation, but before the cigarettes could be moved there was a burglary and they were stolen. The defendants genuinely but mistakenly believed that the cigarettes were at the plaintiffs' risk, and so invoiced them for the price, threatening to withdraw credit facilities if the price was not paid. Under the terms of their arrangement the credit facilities could lawfully be withdrawn at any time. Faced with a choice between two evils, the plaintiffs opted to pay the price, and subsequently reclaimed the money paid on the basis that the payment had been made under duress. In finding for the defendants, Steyn LJ pointed to three key elements:

- the arm's length commercial dealings between two trading companies
- the lawful nature of the threat
- the *bona fide* belief in their entitlement on the part of the defendants.

To allow a claim based on lawful act duress in such circumstances would inevitably cause uncertainty in commercial dealings.

Steyn LJ was reluctant to say that 'lawful act duress' could never be established, but it seems that a commercial concern engaged in apparently arm's length bargaining will find it very difficult to base a claim on lawful act duress. It is arguable that the same might not be true in the context of a consumer contract.

In **GMAC Commercial Credit Ltd v Dearden**, unreported, 28 May 2002, a claim based on lawful act duress was firmly rejected on the basis that the pressure applied was normal commercial pressure.

The defendants were directors of a company to which the claimant had provided finance facilities. The defendants had been required to give personal guarantees in exchange for modifications to this finance agreement. Further funds were released on the basis that the guarantees would be entered into, and when an overpayment was made the claimant agreed to delay repayment if the guarantees were signed that day. The defendants later alleged that the guarantees had been obtained as a result of economic duress since they had signed the guarantees due to concern about the company's financial reputation with its customers and suppliers. The judge held that the pressure was normal and legitimate in such commercial arrangements. The claimant had exerted normal commercial pressure in order to enforce its contractual rights and had done so in good faith. Accordingly, the defence of economic duress failed.

Is the existence of good or bad faith a factor?

The suggestion is that good or bad faith of the person making the threat is a relevant factor.

- This would certainly appear to be an ingredient in the conclusion that there is no duress where the threat is legitimate.

- However, the bona fides would seem to be less relevant where the threat is illegitimate. The state of mind of a party breaching a contract (or threatening to breach a contract) is not otherwise treated as a relevant factor in English law. Mance J in **Huyton SA v Peter Cremer GmbH and Co.** [1999] 1 Lloyd's Rep 620, accepted that although the courts would be reluctant to reopen compromises reached in good faith, good faith on the part of a party making an illegitimate threat would not always give protection against a claim based on duress.

3. Causation: The illegitimate pressure must constitute a significant cause inducing the other party to contract

Any improper pressure must be 'decisive or clinching' (per Mance J (*obiter*) in **Huyton SA v Peter Cremer GmbH & Co.** [1999] 1 Lloyd's Rep 620). Thus, it must be established that the victim would not otherwise have made such a contract, or would not otherwise have contracted on those terms. (Compare with the position on causation for fraudulent misrepresentation: see 14.2.2.4.)

15.1.2.4 The need to protest at the time or shortly thereafter

The remedy for duress will be lost unless the victim of duress ensures that it takes action to 'protest at the time, or shortly thereafter' and seeks to reopen the issue (Kerr J in **Occidental Worldwide Investment Corporation v Skibs A/S Avanti, The Siboen and the Sibotre** [1976] 1 Lloyd's Rep 293).

The application of this requirement is well demonstrated by the decision in **North Ocean Shipping Co. Ltd v Hyundai Construction Co. Ltd, The Atlantic Baron** [1979] QB 705.

> In **The Atlantic Baron,** the defendants threatened to breach a contract for the construction of a tanker unless the plaintiffs agreed to pay 10 per cent on top of the contract price. Consideration for this agreement was furnished by the defendants agreeing to provide a corresponding increase in their letter of credit as security of performance. The plaintiffs agreed to make the extra payment because if the tanker had not been available they would have lost a very valuable charter. Eight months after delivery of the tanker the plaintiffs attempted to recover the extra payment. Mocatta J held that the defendants' demand would have amounted to economic duress making the contract voidable. However, the failure to protest or reopen the issue for such a long time amounted to constructive affirmation of the contract. Therefore, the plaintiffs were no longer entitled to a remedy based on duress.

However, the difficulty with this requirement is that it leaves the victim of alleged duress with a difficult choice when deciding what course of action to take. To sit back and fail to perform, relying on the duress as a defence to any claim by the other party, runs the risk of being interpreted as affirmation of the contract. On the other hand, if the danger perceived by the victim is sufficient to persuade that person to enter the contract despite its disadvantageous terms, it will also very likely be the case that the victim will not want to risk causing the other party to abandon performance by making an ill-timed protest. It seems that the courts will have to accept that the economic duress itself will prevent anything but mild protest until performance is complete. At that time the victim will have to take almost immediate action to avoid constructive affirmation of the contract. (In **The Atlantic Baron**, of course, it was considered that once the plaintiffs had taken possession of the tanker there was no further danger in registering a protest, and therefore waiting for eight months before doing so amounted to the affirmation.)

15.1.2.5 Application of other bars to rescission in duress claim

It appears that a claimant who can succeed in establishing duress may be at risk of losing the ability to rescind on other grounds (see bars to rescission, 14.5.2). For example, the Court of Appeal in **Halpern v Halpern** [2007] EWCA Civ 291, [2007] 2 Lloyd's Rep 56, [2007] 1 CLC 527 (for facts and discussion, see 14.5.2.3) held that rescission would be lost if the claimant could not make restitution. A compromise could not be rescinded because documents had been destroyed, although this action had taken place as a direct result of the terms of the agreement proved to be voidable for duress. The court accepted the fact that no real distinction should lie between duress (common law remedy) and undue influence (equity) as they both deal with instances of improper threats or pressures, e.g. the overlap of duress and undue influence in a claim based on actual undue influence. Whilst confirming the basic principle, the Court of Appeal seemed troubled by the facts and noted that 'it would be surprising if the law could not provide a suitable remedy'.

15.1.2.6 Conclusion

Although the number of judicial decisions examining economic duress has grown over recent years, key elements of the doctrine clearly require further elaboration. In *Huyton SA v Peter Cremer GmbH & Co.* [1999] 1 Lloyd's Rep 620 at p. 637, Mance J noted that the ingredients for establishing a claim in economic duress were 'minimum ingredients, not ingredients which, if present, would inevitably lead to liability'. He continued by stating that:

> The recognition of some degree of flexibility is not...fairly open to the reproach that it introduces a judicial 'discretion'. The law frequently has to form judgments regarding inequitability or unconscionability, giving effect in doing so to the reasonable expectations of honest persons.

It is nevertheless helpful to have some recognized and clearly defined ingredients for the operation of the doctrine of duress, especially as since *Williams v Roffey Bros* it now appears to be seen as the primary mechanism in English law preventing the enforceability of alteration promises obtained by extortion (see, e.g., *Adam Opel GmbH v Mitras Automotive Ltd* [2007] EWHC 3205 (QB), [2008] Bus LR Digest D55 (economic duress paragraphs only), 18 December 2007, discussed at **4.4.4**).

15.2 Undue influence

15.2.1 Nature of the undue influence doctrine

Undue influence is an equitable doctrine which provides relief from contracts entered into under improper pressure not amounting to duress. The courts will intervene where there is some relationship between the parties which has been exploited and abused to gain an unfair advantage. The precise basis of the court's intervention is a matter of debate (see in particular, Birks and Chin, 'On the nature of undue influence' in Beatson and Friedmann (eds), *Good Faith and Fault in Contract Law* (Oxford University Press, 1995)).

Undue influence might be thought to be clearly within the scope of the public policy concern for fairness in contract bargaining, and that rationale was put forward by Nourse LJ in *Goldsworthy v Brickell* [1987] 1 All ER 853 at p. 856. Lord Browne-Wilkinson appeared to have some sympathy for this view in *CIBC Mortgages plc v Pitt* [1994] 1 AC 200 at p. 209. His Lordship saw an obvious parallel between the undue influence cases and cases on abuse of confidence. The latter are based on public policy, and his Lordship expressed some doubt whether the two lines of cases were founded on distinct principles. However, as his Lordship recognized, in *National Westminster Bank Ltd v Morgan* [1985] AC 686, the House of Lords had expressed the view that undue influence was not based on considerations of public policy.

Undue influence appears to be based on a taking advantage of a relationship and the focus therefore rests on seeking to explain 'why' the complainant acted in the way they did, e.g. in transferring their property to the other. The focus should be on the complainant rather than focusing on the motives of the alleged influencer or even whether they were conscious of any wrongdoing (***Hammond v Osborn*** [2002] EWCA Civ 885, [2002] WTLR 1125: see 15.2.4.2). What matters is whether the end result involves a taking advantage of the relationship.

Whether a transaction has been brought about by undue influence is a question of fact so that case law has limited value in terms of precedent. The law governing undue influence is concerned with evidence and burdens of proof.

15.2.2 **Classification of undue influence**

Subsequently the courts clarified the nature of the requisite exploitation of a relationship required to establish that the contract could be set aside for undue influence. Lord Browne-Wilkinson in ***Barclays Bank plc v O'Brien*** [1994] 1 AC 180 approved a classification of types of undue influence put forward by the Court of Appeal in ***Bank of Credit and Commerce International SA v Aboody*** [1990] 1 QB 923 in terms of a distinction between actual undue influence (so-called 'Class 1') and presumed undue influence (where undue influence was presumed to have been exerted because of a relationship of trust and confidence between the parties). Presumed undue influence was subdivided into Class 2A cases (certain relationships where this presumption arose automatically) and Class 2B cases (where on the facts the relationship was such that the presumption of undue influence applied).

This classification has undergone some revision as a result of the decision of the House of Lords in ***Royal Bank of Scotland plc v Etridge (No. 2)*** [2002] UKHL 44, [2002] 2 AC 773 and, in particular, the nature of presumed undue influence has been re-evaluated and the manifest disadvantage requirement has been reviewed. The House of Lords considered that the law on 'presumed undue influence' had not been stated accurately in that the 'presumption' is no more than an evidential presumption that *influence* has been exercised. The evidential presumption did not extend to concluding that the influence was also 'undue'; that was a separate matter and required that there be something suspicious in the transaction or something which called for an explanation on the facts, e.g. the size or nature of the transaction. If this was the case then presumed undue influence would be established.

In the light of the decision in ***Royal Bank of Scotland plc v Etridge (No. 2)***, the basic categories of undue influence remain, i.e. there are three distinguishable categories:

- **actual undue influence**
- **two classes of evidential undue influence (protected relationships and other cases established on the facts)**:
  (a) Where the relationship falls within the recognized category of protected relationships, there is an automatic evidential presumption of **influence**. It is then only necessary to establish that the influence is 'undue', i.e. the existence of a wrong (abuse of trust or unfair advantage was taken, as demonstrated by the fact that the transaction is suspicious or calls for an explanation), before concluding that **undue influence** was exercised. Lord Nicholls in ***Royal Bank of Scotland plc v Etridge (No. 2)*** indicated that this evidence of the 'wrong' was linked to the 'manifest disadvantage' requirement in that if the transaction was shown to be manifestly disadvantageous to the claimant that was evidence suggesting that advantage had been taken of the position of influence.

  (b) Outside the class of protected relationships, the evidential presumption of influence may arise on the facts where one of the parties can be shown to have placed trust and confidence in the other. However, the difference in this instance is that this presumption of influence can be rebutted by the other party establishing that no such influence was in fact exercised. Again, it would be necessary to establish that the transaction was suspicious or called for an explanation in order to raise the presumption of undue influence (i.e., advantage taken of the position).

This is different to the pre-**Etridge** position but only in the sense that (1) the presumption arising from the relationship between the parties will establish influence (and not that the influence was undue); and (2) the presumption of influence is rebuttable if the relationship falls outside the protected class of relationships, but irrebuttable where the relationship is protected; and (3) the 'manifest disadvantage' requirement has been clarified and distinguished from the requirement for a third-party surety to be put on inquiry (i.e., that the transaction is not on its face to the financial advantage of the party alleging undue influence).

15.2.3 Actual undue influence

Cases of actual undue influence can be equated with the type of pressure required to establish duress (e.g., **Gill v RSPCA**, 19 October 2009: in order to establish that a will had been procured by undue influence it was necessary to establish coercion). In **Etridge** Lord Nicholls described this unacceptable conduct as 'overt acts of improper pressure or coercion such as unlawful threats' and added that 'today there is much overlap with the principle of duress as this principle has subsequently developed'.

In cases within this category the allegation is that actual influence was in fact exercised to take advantage of the claimant and it induced the complainant to enter into the transaction. In the past, cases of this type of domination frequently involved dubious spiritual advisers.

> In *Morley v Loughnan* [1893] 1 Ch 736, action was brought by executors to recover £140,000 paid by the deceased to a member of a religious sect. Wright J, in finding for the plaintiffs, said that there was no need to show a special relationship between deceased and defendant, because 'the defendant took possession, so to speak, of the whole life of the deceased, and the gifts were…the effect of that influence and domination'.

Another example is **Williams v Bayley** (1866) LR 1 HL 200 (which nowadays would probably be decided on the basis of duress: see 15.1.1).

> *Williams v Bayley* concerned a mortgage over a colliery which had been executed by the plaintiff following threats to prosecute the plaintiff's son for forgery. It was held that the plaintiff could avoid the mortgage on the basis of undue influence.

CIBC Mortgages plc v Pitt [1994] 1 AC 200 was treated by the House of Lords as a case involving actual undue influence.

> The defendant had been induced to agree to a second mortgage on the family home as security for a loan to finance share purchases. She had not wanted to go ahead with the scheme, but had given in to a campaign of sustained pressure. The principal issue for decision in that case was whether her claim of undue influence could succeed without her being able to prove that the transaction was to her manifest disadvantage. The House of Lords held that in a (Class 1) case of actual undue influence, the transaction need not be one that is disadvantageous to the party affected (overruling *Bank of Credit and Commerce International SA v Aboody* [1990] 1 QB 923 on this point).

Manifest disadvantage had been held to be a necessary ingredient of **presumed** undue influence (Class 2) by the House of Lords in **National Westminster Bank Ltd v Morgan** [1985] AC 686. But it had no relevance in the case of actual undue influence. According to Lord Browne-Wilkinson, this is because actual undue influence is a 'species of fraud', and 'like any other victim of fraud, a person who has been induced by undue influence to carry out a transaction which he did not freely and knowingly enter into is entitled to have that transaction set aside as of right'.

Since actual undue influence is akin to fraud, it follows that it is not a defence, where actual undue influence has been proved, to claim that the person influenced would have entered into the transaction anyway. Thus, the causation test is the same as that applicable in cases of duress to the person (*Barton v Armstrong* [1976] AC 104: see 15.1.1) rather than that applicable to economic duress (*Huyton SA v Peter Cremer GmbH & Co* [1999] 1 Lloyd's Rep 620: see 15.1.2.3).

This position was made clear by the Court of Appeal in *UCB Corporate Services Ltd v Williams* [2002] EWCA Civ 555, [2003] 1 P & CR 12.

> In *UCB Corporate Services Ltd v Williams* the wife was found to have been the victim of fraudulent misrepresentation and actual undue influence by her husband. The judge at first instance had rejected her claim to set aside the charge in favour of the claimant lender on the basis that she would have signed the charge even if she had known the full facts and the risks involved. The Court of Appeal allowed the wife's appeal since it was not relevant to ask whether the wife would have entered into the transaction in any event. It was sufficient that the actual undue influence was *a* factor inducing her to execute the charge.

Conclusion

Thus, these cases of actual undue influence, which are sometimes referred to as the 'domination' cases, do not require the complainant to show that there was any kind of special relationship or that there was a manifest disadvantage resulting from the transaction. On the other hand, complainants have the difficult task of proving that their free will to enter or to decline a particular contract was in some way overcome by the influence of another. It is clear from the speech of Lord Nicholls in *Royal Bank of Scotland plc v Etridge (No. 2)* [2002] UKHL 44, [2002] 2 AC 773 (see [32]–[33]) that it will not be easy to establish actual undue influence in the context of husband and wife relationships but that misrepresentations of fact will suffice as the basis for a claim. Lord Nicholls stated:

> Undue influence has a connotation of impropriety. In the eye of the law, undue influence means that influence has been misused. Statements or conduct by a husband, which do not pass beyond the bounds of what may be expected of a reasonable husband in the circumstances, should not, without more, be castigated as undue influence. Similarly, when a husband is forecasting the future of his business, and expressing his hopes or fears, a degree of hyperbole may be only natural. Courts should not too readily treat such exaggerations as misstatements. Inaccurate explanations of a proposed transaction are a different matter.

15.2.4 Evidential presumption of influence

In *Daniel v Drew* [2005] EWCA Civ 507, [2005] 2 FCR 365, the Court of Appeal held that whereas actual undue influence was something that had to be done to twist the mind of the donor, in cases of presumed undue influence it was more a case of what had not been done, namely ensuring that the transaction was the exercise of the free and independent will of the donor. However, as stated in *Turkey v Awadh* (below), the presumption of undue influence must arise before considering the question of whether it can be rebutted on the facts through demonstrating that the transaction was the result of the exercise of free and independent will.

The decision in ***Royal Bank of Scotland plc v Etridge (No. 2)*** has clarified the nature of the presumption of undue influence. It used to be considered that undue influence would be presumed where the relationship between the parties fell within certain recognized relationships or on the facts was shown to be a relationship where one party placed trust and confidence in the other. However, the House of Lords has now made it clear that it is only the existence of influence which may be presumed in such instances (although irrebuttably in the case of the recognized protected relationships). It is still necessary to establish the existence of the wrong, i.e. abuse or taking advantage of that relationship, albeit that the fact that the transaction is manifestly disadvantageous will raise suspicions of the wrong or 'undue' influence.

These requirements were clearly stated by the Court of Appeal in *Turkey v Awadh* [2005] EWCA Civ 382, [2005] 2 P & CR 29, [2005] 2 FCR 7:

(1) It was first necessary to determine whether the facts raised the presumption of undue influence. This involved two stages or two presumptions:

    (a) It required either the existence of a protected relationship or required facts that would persuade the court that the party in question was in a position to influence the will of the other in relation to the transaction, i.e. establishing a relationship of trust and confidence on the facts.

    (b) The transaction must then be shown to be one which cannot be explained by reference to the ordinary motives by which people are accustomed to act, i.e. suggesting that it is unlikely that the other would have entered into it unless 'his will was overborne'.

(2) It was finally necessary to consider whether the defendant could rebut the presumption by establishing that there was no abuse of trust.

Turkey v Awadh concerned an agreement whereby the claimant's daughter and her husband agreed to transfer a long leasehold interest in their house to the defendant in exchange for him agreeing to clear the mortgage on the property and various other debts. The Court of Appeal held that the presumption of undue influence did not arise because the transaction could be readily explained by the nature of the parties' relationship. Similarly, the transaction (father's removal of son as trustee in family company) in *Hogg v Hogg* [2007] EWHC 2240 (Ch), [2008] 1 P & CR DG7, [2008] WTLR 35, was held to be explicable in accordance with ordinary motives so that no presumption of undue influence arose.

15.2.4.1 What has happened to the manifest disadvantageous requirement?

In ***National Westminster Bank Ltd v Morgan*** [1985] AC 686, it was suggested that it is necessary to show that there was a manifest disadvantage to the complainant on the basis that the presumption of undue influence is derived from the reasoning that a party making an unfettered decision would not freely choose to enter into a manifestly disadvantageous contract. In *CIBC Mortgages plc v Pitt* [1994] 1 AC 200, Lord Browne-Wilkinson appeared to be less than certain that even in cases resting upon presumed undue influence that there was an absolute requirement to establish manifest disadvantage, but he was not required to rule upon the matter in that case. The requirement of 'manifest disadvantage' in cases of presumed undue influence was reconsidered by the Court of Appeal in **Barclays Bank plc v Coleman** [2000] 3 WLR 405 but it was bound to apply it. Nourse LJ (delivering the leading judgment) commented that 'a serious question mark' has been put 'over the future of the requirement of manifest disadvantage in cases of presumed undue influence' and the matter needed reconsideration by the House of Lords.

In the Court of Appeal in **Royal Bank of Scotland v Etridge (No. 2)** [1998] 4 All ER 705, Stuart-Smith LJ had made the point that evidence of manifest disadvantage is 'a powerful evidential factor' and in the House of Lords Lord Nicholls confirmed that **manifest disadvantage to the claimant would be *evidence* that the influence exercised was 'undue' or at least raised suspicions.** However, a broader assessment was called for, based on the statement of Lindley LJ in *Allcard v Skinner* (1887) LR 36 ChD 145 at p. 185:

> Where a gift is made to a person standing in a confidential relation to the donor, the Court will not set aside the gift if of a small amount simply on the ground that the donor had no independent advice. In such a case, some proof of the exercise of the influence of the donee must be given. The mere existence of such influence is not enough in such a case... But if the gift is so large as not to be reasonably accounted for on the ground of friendship, relationship, charity, or other ordinary motives on which ordinary men act, the burden is upon the donee to support the gift.

Each case will turn on its own facts but certain gifts may represent evidence which can be used to support an inference that the influence was undue, i.e. if a transaction is suspicious in the light of the nature of the relationship, it will tend towards establishing a presumption of **undue influence**.

It follows from this interpretation that manifest disadvantage is not a 'requirement' and that the courts will need to move away from the previous discussion in the case law which had centered on identification of advantage and disadvantage. Indeed, the Court of Appeal in **Macklin v Dowsett** [2004] EWCA Civ 904, [2004] 2 EGLR 75, has subsequently confirmed that there is no longer a manifest disadvantage **requirement**. The Court of Appeal focused instead on whether the transaction was readily explicable by the relationship of the parties or whether it was suspicious and called for an explanation. The court concluded that it did call for an explanation since it gave Macklin the option to require Dowsett to surrender a life tenancy in property in return for a payment of only £5,000.

This is good news since the previous case law revealed much confusion between this requirement and the requirements for a lender to be put on inquiry in a situation where the undue influence had been exercised by a third party (see the discussion at 15.2.8.2). Lord Nicholls considered that the expression 'manifest disadvantage' had given rise to misunderstanding because it had been used in a sense outside that intended by Lord Scarman in *National Westminster Bank Ltd v Morgan* and outside the principle in *Allcard v Skinner.* The problem had arisen in third-party surety cases involving wives who had given security over the matrimonial home to guarantee their husband's overdraft with his bank. Such cases had frequently involved arguments focusing only on the claimant wife's position concerning whether such a transaction was manifestly disadvantageous and, given that this was viewed as an absolute requirement, the courts took the view that the fact that a wife might benefit indirectly, in the sense that the household finances would be stronger if further funds were released to the husband's business, could not be considered as a sufficient 'advantage' in itself. In other words, the issue had focused on whether **any** advantage would prevent a conclusion of disadvantage. In addition, this issue had been caught up in the entirely separate consideration of whether a lender was affected by constructive notice of the husband's undue influence because the transaction on its face was 'not to the financial advantage of the wife'.

The broader approach in *Allcard v Skinner* focuses on the transaction and the nature of the relationship to determine whether it is suspicious so that an explanation is called for. Whereas evidence that the transaction is clearly not to the claimant's advantage will assist in establishing evidence of that suspicion, it will not be conclusive in itself.

Some confusion appears to remain in terms of explicit reference to 'the manifest disadvantage requirement' in establishing the presumption of undue influence in some of the case law since *Etridge*.

For example in *Leeder (aka Newey) v Stevens* [2005] EWCA Civ 50, (2005) 149 SJLB 112, *The Times*, 14 January 2005, the claimant had transferred a property into joint names in exchange for her long-term partner paying the remaining £5,000 on the mortgage. The deed of transfer enabled the defendant partner to force a sale. The Court of Appeal considered that the relationship of trust and confidence had been established on the facts and that this transaction called for an explanation based on the fact that it was 'manifestly disadvantageous'. Therefore the presumption of undue influence had arisen. It had not been rebutted since no independent legal advice had been received.

This may be no more than the reference to manifest disadvantage as **evidence** that the transaction is suspicious but the courts will need to be very careful not to reintroduce manifest disadvantage as a requirement. A correct statement of the principle was made by Lewison J in *Thompson v Foy* [2009] EWHC 1076 (Ch) at [99]: 'Disadvantage to the donor is not a necessary ingredient of undue influence…However, it may have an evidential value, because it is relevant to the questions whether any allegation of abuse of confidence can properly be made, and whether any abuse actually occurred.'

 ## Summary

Thus, in *Etridge* Lord Nicholls was stating that there is no longer a requirement to establish manifest disadvantage. Instead, the emphasis is on whether the nature and size of the transaction can be readily explained by the parties' relationship or calls for some explanation because it raises suspicions. Lord Nicholls suggested that the fact that the transaction was manifestly disadvantageous to the claimant may be evidence to support a conclusion that the transaction is suspicious so that the influence was *undue* and the transaction needs to be explained.

Equally, and more likely in practice, the fact that a transaction is not disadvantageous but perfectly rational in the circumstances, may support a conclusion that no 'undue' influence has been exercised and there is nothing in the transaction which is not readily explicable in terms of the parties' relationship and the context for the agreement. For example, in *Dailey v Dailey* [2003] UKPC 65, [2003] 3 FCR 369, a wife was unable to demonstrate that the presumption of influence arose on the facts or that there was anything in the transaction that was not readily explicable in terms of the parties' relationship, since the transaction involved a transfer to the husband for full value as part of proceedings for ancillary relief.

Lord Hope (at [24]) explained:

> Care needs to be taken to distinguish between cases where the wife has entered into a transaction with her husband which is gratuitous and those where the agreement is for her to receive full value for the property or interest which she is to transfer to him. In the former case, as Lindley LJ explained in *Allcard v Skinner* (1887) 36 ChD 145, 185, the burden is on the donee to support the gift if it is so large as not to be reasonably accounted for on the ground of the relationship. A transaction which is entered into for full value needs no such explanation. There is no presumption to rebut. That is not to say that a transaction of this type is immune from the exercise of undue influence. But if it is to be set aside on this ground it is for the party who makes the allegation to prove that undue influence was in fact exercised.

In other words, in such circumstances the donor would need to establish actual undue influence in order to succeed.

15.2.4.2 The influence must be 'undue'

The influence must be 'undue'. The fact that there must be some 'wrong' committed by the defendant was stressed by Lord Hoffmann in *R v HM Attorney-General for England and Wales* [2003] UKPC 22, [2003] EMLR 24. However, a 'wrong' means misconduct in the form of taking advantage of the relationship to advance one's own position while not ensuring that the claimant was exercising a free and informed choice in agreeing to the transaction. There has been some confusion on this point in recent case law, e.g. in *Macklin v Dowsett* [2004] EWCA Civ 904, [2004] 2 EGLR 75, the Court of Appeal rejected the notion that it was necessary to establish any wrong or misconduct. The correct position is that in cases of presumed undue influence this 'wrong' will be presumed from evidence of a transaction not easily explicable by the terms of the parties' relationship, e.g. suspicious in type or amount. In *Goodchild v Bradbury* [2006] EWCA Civ 1868, [2007] WTLR 463, Chadwick LJ explained the position as follows:

> A gift which is made without informed consideration by a person vulnerable to influence, and which he could not have been expected to make if he had been acting in accordance with the ordinary motives which lead men's actions, needs to be justified on the basis that the donor knew and understood what he was doing.

In *Hammond v Osborn* [2002] EWCA Civ 885, [2002] WTLR 1125, the Court of Appeal held that a defendant could not avoid such a finding by establishing the absence of an intention to commit a wrong, i.e. an absence of bad faith.

> In *Hammond v Osborn* an elderly donor had made a number of sizeable gifts (totalling £300,000) to the defendant, his neighbour who had been taking care of him. The gifts represented over 90 per cent of his liquid assets and exposed him to a considerable tax liability. The necessary relationship of trust and confidence was shown to exist on the facts and the presumption of undue influence was established because there was clearly something suspicious about gifts of this size in the circumstances. The presumption was not rebutted because no advice on the wisdom and implications of these actions had

been received. It was not sufficient to avoid this presumption by establishing the absence of bad faith on the part of the defendant.

It may be relatively easy to establish that the transaction raises suspicions, e.g. *Goodchild v Bradbury* [2006] EWCA Civ 1868, [2007] WTLR 463, concerned the gift of land by a frail and elderly gentleman (while in hospital suffering from a stroke) to his great-nephew and the subsequent sale of that land by the great-nephew to a property developer (for only £1,800). The evidence was that the property developer had arranged the solicitor who acted for the great-nephew in the transfer of the land from the great-uncle. The Court of Appeal held that a presumption of influence had arisen because of the circumstances of the transfer, although superficially a wedding gift.

The key question was whether the great-uncle was vulnerable because the relationship had the potential for abuse and the gift was not one that could be explained by reference to the ordinary motives by which people are accustomed to act. The uncle placed trust and confidence in the nephew and the evidence was that the sale of adjacent land for development would devalue the value of the great-uncle's remaining property. It was therefore for the nephew to show that the uncle was fully aware of what he was doing and that he had intended to make this gift. However, the uncle had not received any advice on this gift from his solicitor. Both transfers were therefore set aside for undue influence.

It seems clear that the size of the transactions is important in providing evidence of suspicion that advantage has been taken.

In *Watson v Huber* [2005] All ER (D) 156 (Mar.), 9 March 2005, the claimant had transferred a total of £900,000 to her half-sister with whom she had been living since the death of the claimant's husband. The necessary trust and confidence was established on the facts because the defendant looked after the claimant's financial affairs and operated an account in joint names. In addition, the number and size of the 'gifts' called for an explanation. The presumption was not rebutted. The judge stated that it would be 'unconscionable' to withhold the relief sought given the circumstances of this case, i.e. complete trust and confidence and the sheer size of the amount transferred.

In *Hodson v Hodson* [2006] EWHC 2878, the transferor, the frail mother of two adopted sons, had executed an enduring power of attorney in favour of these sons, jointly and severally (i.e., they could act independently in her affairs). She lived with one of the sons and his wife and was wholly dependent on them. Her property was transferred into the name of the daughter-in-law and shares were also transferred our of the mother's name. The judge stressed the scale of these transfers and the fact that they left the mother with no assets. In these circumstances, and given the fact that the money was spent on expensive cars and boats and in supporting the son's ailing business, a proper explanation was required. In particular, the scale of the transfers could not be explained by the nature of the relationship. There was no evidence to rebut the presumption so raised and the judge made a finding of undue influence.

15.2.5 Evidential undue influence: Protected relationships

There are certain relationships which the law regards as special, and as always incorporating elements of trust and confidence, so that **influence** can be automatically assumed. Typical of such relationships are solicitor and client (*Markham v Karsten* [2007] EWHC 1509 (Ch), [2007] BPIR 1109), doctor and patient, and parent and child (although not between adult child and elderly parents where a relationship of trust and confidence must be established on the facts: *Avon*

Finance Co Ltd v Bridger [1985] 2 All ER 281). Relations between husband and wife are said not to give rise to a special relationship, and so do not automatically raise any presumption of influence (*Midland Bank plc v Shephard* [1988] 3 All ER 17). The relationship of banker and customer is also outside this class of protected relationships (previously known as Class 2A) (*National Westminster Bank Ltd v Morgan* [1985] AC 686).

The result of the decision of the House of Lords in *Royal Bank of Scotland plc v Etridge (No. 2)* is that if the relationship in question falls within this category of protected relationships, the presumption of influence is automatic and irrebuttable. However, it will still be necessary to establish that the influence was undue and evidence of this may include the nature of the transaction in the context of the relationship in question (i.e., the *Allcard v Skinner* principle). If evidence suggests that the transaction is suspicious and the influence is **undue**, the presumption of undue influence will arise and it will then be open to the party alleged to have exercised the undue influence to establish that no undue influence was in fact exercised, e.g. by demonstrating that independent advice was received.

15.2.6 Evidential undue influence: Other cases established on the facts

Where the relationship does not fall into any of the recognized special categories automatically giving rise to the presumption of **influence**, it is still possible for a complainant to show that the particular relationship was in fact one based on trust and confidence so that the evidential presumption of influence will arise on the particular facts. However, the other party can seek to rebut the presumption of influence by evidence that no such trust and confidence existed.

In any event, there will be no presumption of undue influence unless the transaction is suspicious and calls for an explanation in the light of this relationship of trust and confidence.

15.2.6.1 Bank and customer

This method of establishing undue influence has been applied to the relationship between bank and customer. In *National Westminster Bank Ltd v Morgan* [1985] AC 686, Lord Scarman accepted that the relationship between bank and customer may be one of confidence, but that in the particular situation the bank 'had not crossed the line' into the realm of confidence.

However, in *Lloyds Bank Ltd v Bundy* [1975] QB 326, the Court of Appeal held that the facts did justify a presumption of (undue) influence between banker and customer.

- There was a special relationship of confidence because of the fact that old Mr Bundy had banked at this branch for many years and relied on the bank manager for all his financial advice.

- The manager was aware of this confidence placed in him.

- In addition, whereas the transaction in *Lloyds Bank Ltd v Bundy* was very evidently not in the interests of old Mr Bundy, the transaction in *National Westminster Bank Ltd v Morgan* was beneficial to Mrs Morgan because it allowed her to stay in her home, which would otherwise have been repossessed by the then mortgagee.

In the light of the different approach adopted in *Royal Bank of Scotland plc v Etridge (No. 2)*, the relationship in *Lloyds Bank v Bundy* would give rise to a presumption of influence and the general nature and size of the transaction, assessed in the context of Mr Bundy's position, would be evidence suggesting that 'undue' influence had been exercised and therefore requiring an explanation from the bank. It would then be for the bank to seek to rebut the presumption of undue influence.

Of course, where the relationship between bank and customer is the ordinary commercial one, and not a special relationship of confidence, it must be remembered that the bank may still owe an ordinary duty of care to give accurate advice which may be the basis of liability towards a customer (see *Cornish v Midland Bank Ltd* [1985] 3 All ER 513, and also 14.4.3.1).

15.2.6.2 Husband and wife

It has also been accepted that such relationships of trust and confidence based on the facts (previously Class 2B) may exist between husbands and wives, and indeed between other cohabitees or persons between whom there is an emotional involvement. In particular it was recognized by Lord Browne-Wilkinson in **Barclays Bank plc v O'Brien** [1994] 1 AC 180 at pp. 190–1 that:

> In those cases which still occur where the wife relies in all financial matters on her husband and simply does what he suggests, a presumption of undue influence within class 2B can be established solely from proof of such trust and confidence without proof of actual undue influence…[T]he sexual and emotional ties between the parties provide a ready weapon for undue influence: a wife's true wishes can easily be overborne because of her fear of destroying or damaging the wider relationship between her and her husband if she opposes his wishes.

Whilst it remains the position that there is no automatic presumption of undue influence in cases of husband and wife, the tone of speech of Lord Nicholls in **Royal Bank of Scotland plc v Etridge (No. 2)** [2002] UKHL 44, [2002] 2 AC 773, may suggest a more restrictive approach to concluding that a presumption of undue influence has arisen in the context of husband and wife. Although the presumption of influence may be shown to arise on the facts, for example, because the wife (or person in a similar cohabiting relationship) places total trust and confidence in the husband and does as she is told, the transaction must also be shown to raise suspicions that this influence is 'undue'. Therefore, there will also need to be some feature of the transaction which calls for explanation so as to provide evidence that the husband has abused the trust. Only in such cases will the presumption of undue influence apply.

Lord Nicholls stated that not all cases where a wife guarantees her husband's debts on the security of the matrimonial home will give rise to a presumption of undue influence by her husband. He added:

> Wives frequently enter into such transactions. There are good and sufficient reasons why they are willing to do so, despite the risks involved for them and their families. They may be enthusiastic. They may not. They may be less optimistic than their husbands about the prospects of the husband's business. They may be anxious, perhaps exceedingly so. But this is a far cry from saying that such transactions as a class are to be regarded as *prima facie* evidence of the exercise of undue influence by husbands.

The real change would appear to be in relation to the move away from a requirement of 'manifest disadvantage' to the broader test in **Allcard v Skinner** (1887) LR 36 ChD 145 at p. 185: see 15.2.4.1. Whereas the manifest disadvantage requirement focuses solely on the claimant's position and led to unfortunate discussions of whether to distinguish direct and indirect advantages to the claimant wife (see the discussion at 15.2.4.1), the broader approach in *Allcard v Skinner* focuses on the transaction and the nature of the relationship to determine whether it is suspicious so that an explanation is called for. Whereas evidence that the transaction is clearly not to the claimant's advantage will assist in establishing evidence of that suspicion, it will not be conclusive in itself. The result is that this evidence of undue influence is likely to focus more on the extremes and is therefore likely to reduce the discussions concerning indirect advantages to the claimant. However, without evidence of clear disadvantage, in the light of Lord Nicholls's comments, it is likely that in future a much broader view will be taken of the wife's position and greater allowance will be made for her emotional motivation so that a transaction may not be considered as unusual or as raising any suspicions.

15.2.6.3 Other cohabitees

As Lord Browne-Wilkinson recognized in *Barclays Bank plc v O'Brien* [1994] 1 AC 180 at p. 198, this discussion relating to husband and wives is also applicable whenever there is an emotional relationship between cohabitees, whether married or unmarried, heterosexual or homosexual. In *Massey v Midland Bank plc* [1995] 1 All ER 929, Steyn LJ extended the category further by including a couple enjoying a long-term emotional and sexual relationship, who had children but who did not in fact cohabit. The presumption of influence has also been held to apply between a son and his elderly parents (*Avon Finance Co. Ltd v Bridger* [1985] 2 All ER 281). No such presumption was established between a daughter and her mother in *Thompson v Foy* [2009] EWHC 1076 (Ch) since the judge considered there was no evidence of a complete relationship of trust and confidence, only the trust that a mother places in her daughter that she would repay money borrowed for a deposit. (The mother had also failed to establish actual undue influence by the daughter.)

15.2.6.4 Army (via commanding officer) and soldier

In *R v HM Attorney-General for England and Wales* [2003] UKPC 22, [2003] EMLR 24 (for facts see 15.1.2.3), the alternative argument to the claim based on duress was that undue influence had been exercised in obtaining the signature to the confidentiality agreement.

> It was alleged that the soldier placed trust and confidence in his commanding officer so that the presumption of influence arose on the facts. However, the Privy Council (Lord Scott dissenting) rejected this argument and stressed the contradiction between on the one hand relying on a relationship of trust and confidence and yet pleading duress in securing the signature. ('People do not usually trust those who coerce them', per Lewison J in *Thompson v Foy* [2009] EWHC 1076 (Ch).) In any event, the Privy Council concluded that any influence would not be undue since, as there was no illegitimate pressure sufficient to constitute duress (discussed at 15.1.2.3), the transaction could not amount to unfair exploitation of the parties' relationship.

15.2.7 Rebutting the presumption

In order for the presumption to arise in the first place there must be both a presumption of influence (automatic or established to have arisen on the facts) and evidence relating to the transaction which suggests that **undue** influence may have been exercised or at least raises such a suspicion (**Royal Bank of Scotland plc v Etridge (No. 2)**). The result is that the presumption of undue influence will not be assumed simply on the basis of an evidential presumption of influence.

The presumption of undue influence may in principle be rebutted, although in the case of the protected relationships (previously Class 2A) it is not possible to rebut the presumption of influence, only the fact that **undue** advantage has been taken of that position to influence (i.e., that the influence was improper or undue).

Rebuttal will require the defendant to show that the complainant was not in fact induced to enter the contract through the defendant's improper influence, but rather entered into it quite freely and fully aware of the situation. In many cases this may be achieved by showing that the complainant chose to go ahead even after receiving independent advice about the true nature of the transaction.

> In *Wadlow v Samuel (PKA Seal)* [2007] EWCA Civ 155, (2007) 151 SJLB 331, the issue was whether a management agreement entitled Seal's former manager to commission covering two albums recorded during the period of this agreement. After the release of the albums the management agreement had been terminated by a settlement agreement which had provided that the manager was entitled to the management agreement commission despite the fact that the agreement in question had been terminated. It was alleged that the management agreement was affected by undue influence on the part of the manager and that this meant that the settlement agreement was also voidable. However, the Court of Appeal held that the settlement agreement had been freely entered into by Seal since he had received independent legal advice and the context for the agreement was fundamentally different from the factual context for the making of the management agreement, e.g. breakdown of trust and confidence, and more balanced contract terms including a number of concessions by the manager.

However, in **Royal Bank of Scotland plc v Etridge (No. 2)** (at [20]) Lord Nicholls suggested that independent advice would not be conclusive:

> But a person may understand fully the implications of a proposed transaction, for instance, a substantial gift, and yet still be acting under the undue influence of another. Proof of outside advice does not, of itself, necessarily show that the subsequent completion of the transaction was free from the exercise of undue influence. Whether it will be proper to infer that outside advice had an emancipating effect, so that the transaction was not brought about by the exercise of undue influence, is a question of fact to be decided having regard to all the evidence in the case.

15.2.8 Effect of undue influence

Contracts affected by undue influence are voidable, not void. As with duress, this consequence seems to support the view that the doctrine is not concerned with the reality of consent, but with the protection of victims of improper behaviour. Since a tainted contract is only voidable, the victim must bring a claim for rescission to avoid it, and property passes under it. The effect of undue influence must be considered in more detail according to whether the undue influence is alleged between the contracting parties or whether third-party undue influence is involved.

15.2.8.1 Effect of undue influence between the contracting parties

1. Affirmation and acquiescence

The right to rescission may be lost if the complainant has affirmed the contract in some way after the undue influence has ceased. In particular, failure to act within a fairly short time of the undue influence ceasing may be interpreted as constructive affirmation.

In **Allcard v Skinner** (1887) LR 36 ChD 145, the plaintiff, under the influence of her spiritual adviser, joined an order called the 'Sisters of the Poor', to which her spiritual adviser was confessor. During the eight years she was a member the plaintiff gave some £7,000 to the defendant, who was head of the order. Six years after leaving the order she sought to recover the balance of that sum remaining unspent (about £1,700). The gift to the defendant was held to have been made under undue influence, because the plaintiff had not been independently advised. The plaintiff was, nevertheless, unable to recover the balance of her money because she had allowed such a long time to elapse before claiming, during which time she had been unaffected by the undue influence and when independent advice was presumably available to her.

In *Habib Bank Ltd v Tufail* [2006] EWCA Civ 374, [2006] 2 P & CR DG14, Lloyd LJ distinguished affirmation and acquiescence, since affirmation requires knowledge of the right to rescind. An example of acquiescence is provided by the decision in *Wadlow v Samuel (PKA Seal)* [2007] EWCA Civ 155, (2007) 151 SJLB 331 (for facts see **15.2.7**), the claim to rescind for undue influence in relation to the management agreement was made more than fifteen years after that contract had been made. Accordingly it was affected by *laches* (delay) and acquiescence and it would be inequitable to set it aside.

2. Partial rescission

An interesting question is whether partial rescission is possible, i.e. is it possible to separate parts of the contract affected by either misrepresentation or undue influence and enforce the remainder, or will the entire contract have to be rescinded?

In *TSB Bank plc v Camfield* [1995] 1 WLR 430, it had been argued that the charge in question should be set aside only to the extent that it provided security for a debt in excess of £15,000, the amount that the wife considered was her maximum liability. However, the Court of Appeal held that it had no power to impose terms and, insisting that rescission had to be total, set aside the charge in its entirety.

In *Vadasz v Pioneer Concrete (SA) Pty Ltd* (1995) 130 ALR 570, the High Court of Australia was prepared to enforce the part of a guarantee covering future debt, but not that part covering the existing debt, on the basis that it had been represented that the guarantee would cover only future debt. The High Court regarded this as no more than holding the party in question to what he was prepared to agree to independently of any misrepresentation.

Although this authority may be limited to rescission of guarantees, it is submitted that this approach would be generally preferable since it allows the court to do justice and recognize the realities of the parties' positions.

The question of which authority was to be preferred was discussed by the Privy Council in *Far Eastern Shipping Co. Public Ltd v Scales Trading Ltd* [2001] 1 All ER (Comm) 319, but determination of this question was not necessary for the Privy Council's decision on the facts before it and recent English authority, **De Molestina v Ponton** [2002] 1 All ER (Comm) 587, supports the view that partial rescission is contrary to the very nature of rescission; see further the discussion of this case law at **14.5.2.3**. Nevertheless, on the facts in **De Molestina v Ponton** the judge had provisionally considered that it was possible to distinguish the various agreements and so rescind some of them. It is also possible, although regarded as exceptional, to sever objectionable parts of an instrument and enforce the remainder. However, it is clear from *Barclays Bank plc v Caplan* [1998] FLR 532, that this will be possible only where the parts can be separated cleanly without affecting the substance of the part enforced, i.e. first guarantee separated from later guarantees.

3. Restitutionary relief

It is very likely that some form of restitutionary relief will be required in association with rescission of the contract (***Dunbar Bank plc v Nadeem*** [1998] 3 All ER 876). Where complete restitution is not possible because, for example, property values have gone down, the net balance is to be divided *pro rata* between the parties according to their original contributions to the transaction (***Cheese v Thomas*** [1994] 1 WLR 129). Where the normal remedy of restoring the parties to their original positions, with an account of profits, is impossible—for example because property has passed into the hands of a third party—the court has jurisdiction to impose a 'common-sense and…fair remedy' in order 'to achieve practical justice between the parties', at least where the undue influence involves a breach of fiduciary duty (per May J in ***Mahoney v Purnell*** [1996] 3 All ER 61 at p. 88, relying on *O'Sullivan v Management Agency and Music Ltd* [1985] QB 428). In the particular case, practical justice was achieved by 'an award…akin to damages' giving to the plaintiff as compensation a sum equal in value to what had been given up under the tainted transaction, but making an allowance for sums received thereunder.

15.2.8.2 Effect of third-party undue influence

It may be alleged that a contract is affected by the undue influence of a third party and that on that basis the contract is voidable. If the contracting party has knowledge of the undue influence practised by a third party in order to persuade the victim to contract, that contracting party will be affected by the undue influence. This is highly topical since the doctrine of undue influence has been invoked on many occasions over the last twenty years in an attempt to avoid an interest acquired by a bank as an indirect result of undue influence (either actual influence or, more usually, old Class 2B presumed undue influence on the facts) between husband and wife (or other cohabitees).

Where one cohabiting partner has misled or influenced the other into granting rights over the 'matrimonial' home to a bank by way of surety in respect of the first party's business liabilities, the victim will understandably be reluctant to give up the home if the business fails. The courts have had to try to find a balance between the rights of parties who risk being dispossessed and the rights of banks who have legitimately sought to protect their investments in business ventures and who might be forced to rethink their lending policies in relation to couples if they were always liable to lose their security at a later date.

Barclays Bank v O'Brien

After a number of false starts, in ***Barclays Bank plc v O'Brien*** [1994] 1 AC 180, Lord Browne-Wilkinson held that the key to determining the position of the bank lay in the doctrine of notice, and the significance of the decision of the House of Lords was that it provided the first attempt at guidance for lenders concerning how they might avoid being fixed with notice of a contracting party's undue influence. **Of course, it would be surprising to find that a bank had actual notice of undue influence; the critical issue therefore is whether the bank has constructive notice (i.e., in the circumstances the bank ought to have known of the undue influence and so is fixed with notice).** It is important to appreciate that whatever the position of the bank, if such a claim is to succeed the husband's undue influence must be established (actual or using the evidential presumption) before any question of the lender being affected can arise. This is separate to the question of whether the bank is fixed with constructive notice of that undue influence.

The House of Lords in **Barclays Bank plc v O'Brien** held the notice question involved two steps:

- A bank would be put on inquiry if it knew of the relationship and the transaction was not obviously of any financial advantage or benefit to the wife (or other cohabitee) so that there was a 'substantial risk' that a wrong had been committed.

- Once put on inquiry, the bank was fixed with constructive notice of the undue influence exercised by the contracting party, unless the bank had taken reasonable steps to satisfy itself that the wife had entered into the transaction freely and with knowledge of the true facts.

O'Brien provided that the bank could satisfy this requirement by warning the wife (at a meeting not attended by the husband) of the amount of her potential liability and the risks involved and by advising the wife to obtain independent legal advice.

Royal Bank of Scotland plc v Etridge (No. 2)

In **Royal Bank of Scotland plc v Etridge (No. 2)** [2002] UKHL 44, [2002] 2 AC 773, these principles were reformulated and the House of Lords stressed the need to balance the interests of protecting those giving the security, while ensuring that lenders could rely on that security if they had followed the appropriate procedures. Lord Nicholls stated:

> The law must afford both parties a measure of protection. It cannot prescribe a code which will be proof against error, misunderstanding or mishap. But it can indicate minimum requirements which, if met, will reduce the risk of error, misunderstanding or mishap to an acceptable level. The paramount need in this important field is that these minimum requirements should be clear, simple and practically operable.

He also recognized that the requirements did not provide a guarantee that wives would not be subjected to undue influence. The requirements were merely 'concerned to minimize the risk' that a wife had entered into the transaction as a result of her husband's undue influence.

It is important to note that the wife (or other surety) has the burden of proving that the bank or lender had the necessary constructive notice, and the formulation of any claim will need to make clear the facts upon which the notice argument is based (*Barclays Bank plc v Boulter* [1999] 4 All ER 513).

1. Putting the lender on inquiry

Although the decision in **O'Brien** was clearly intended to clarify the law, it resulted in a lengthy catalogue of decisions interpreting its declared principle.

For example, in **CIBC Mortgages plc v Pitt** [1994] 1 AC 200, the question was whether the circumstances of the particular case were such as to put the bank on inquiry so that the necessary steps needed to be taken in order for the bank to avoid being fixed with constructive notice of the husband's undue influence. **The House of Lords decided that the bank was not put on inquiry because the form applying for the loan indicated that it was a joint loan for the purpose of paying off the outstanding joint mortgage and to purchase a holiday home.** In fact, the loan was to enable the husband to speculate on the stock market and he had pressurized his wife into declaring that it was for these other purposes. However, on the face of the application form there was some apparent financial benefit to the wife. Accordingly, the bank could not be fixed with constructive notice of the husband's actual undue influence.

There was nothing particularly suspicious about the transaction in this case; indeed, if the bank had been on notice in this case then arguably banks would be on notice in every case involving husband and wife clients. However, this decision did make it clear that it was the form of the transaction which governed, and the court would not look behind the form at the substance of the transaction.

What was the position if the loan was used partly for joint purposes and partly to guarantee the husband's business debts? *Dunbar Bank plc v Nadeem* [1998] 3 All ER 876 differed from *CIBC v Pitt* because the allegation of actual undue influence failed. It was therefore necessary to rely on presumed undue influence by the husband, which required that the transaction be shown to be manifestly disadvantageous to the wife. On the facts this was held not to be the case because the wife obtained a beneficial interest in the matrimonial home as a result of the transaction. This requirement of 'manifest disadvantage', which was required to establish the existence of presumed undue influence had to be distinguished from the requirement, in the context of third-party undue influence and notice, that the transaction on its face was not to the advantage of the complainant (thereby putting the bank on inquiry and in danger of losing its security (*Bank of Cyprus (London) Ltd v Markou* [1999] 2 All ER 707 at p. 717)).

The latter question is entirely dependent on how the facts are presented to the bank (e.g., *CIBC v Pitt*) although on the facts in *Bank of Cyprus (London) Ltd v Markou* the court looked beyond the facts on paper, i.e. that the wife was a shareholder in the husband's company, and considered the bank's knowledge of the realities of the situation, namely that the company was wholly controlled by the husband and the wife had no active role.

One of the complexities may now have been eliminated following the decision of the House of Lords in *Royal Bank of Scotland plc v Etridge (No. 2)* [2002] UKHL 44, [2002] 2 AC 773, which has greatly simplified the so-called 'threshold' when the bank is put on inquiry. Lord Nicholls considered that *O'Brien* should be interpreted as providing that 'a bank is put on inquiry whenever a wife offers to stand surety *for her husband's debts*' (emphasis added). He went on to extend this to instances where husbands stand surety for the debts of their wives and to all unmarried couples whether or not they were cohabiting.

Such a position would eliminate the need to assess the precise nature of the relationship between the parties, as the only issue would be knowledge of the relationship. Since it refers to standing surety 'for her husband's debts', it is unlikely to eliminate some of the difficulties associated with joint purposes so that it will still be necessary in some instances to assess the declared purpose for the requested loan. However, in a simple case where the wife stands surety for the husband's debts, the bank will be automatically put on inquiry and questions concerning indirect benefits to the wife do not arise. Where funds are advanced jointly, the position will continue to be governed by the decision in *CIBC v Pitt*, i.e. the bank will not be put on inquiry. The only situation where the bank would be put on inquiry would be where the bank had knowledge that, despite the declared joint purposes, the loan is solely for the husband's purposes. Lord Nicholls described instances of loans to the husband's company where the wife had a shareholding in that company (e.g., as in *Bank of Cyprus (London) Ltd v Markou*) as being 'less clear cut'. However, he considered that the bank would be put on inquiry in all such cases, even where the wife was an officer of the company since there were obvious dangers in such a situation and 'the shareholding interests, and the identity of the directors, are not a reliable guide to the identity of the persons who actually have the conduct of the company's business'.

Despite these comments, it is far from clear that Lord Nicholls regarded such considerations as being vital in a practical sense because, in the context of 'non-sexual relationships', he considered that banks should not be required to evaluate the extent of influence of one party over the other, and added that 'the only practical way forward is to regard banks as put on inquiry in every case where the relationship between the surety and the debtor is non-commercial' (known as 'the wider principle'). (For an example of such a relationship see *Wright v Cherrytree Finance Ltd* [2001] EWCA Civ 449, [2001] 2 All ER (Comm) 877: pre-***Etridge*** case concerning widow and son-in-law in debtor/surety relationship.) **This suggests that whenever security is given in a non-commercial setting, a lender would be well advised to assume that it is put on inquiry and to take the appropriate steps to avoid being fixed with constructive notice.** Lord Nicholls added that he regarded this as 'a modest burden' and, given the need for certainty, this would appear to be entirely sensible as a course of action and should not prove too expensive a price to pay. To this extent, ***Etridge*** both simplifies the law and extends the protection available to such sureties. The decision also goes further in clarifying the steps that a bank needs to take to ensure it is protected.

2.   Steps to avoid being fixed with constructive notice of third-party undue influence

The ***O'Brien*** requirement that the bank should first advise the wife in a private interview proved troublesome because banks were, not surprisingly, reluctant to give direct advice for fear that this would form the basis for a later claim based, for example, on misrepresentation. In practice, therefore, and despite ***O'Brien***, the banks omitted this step and simply required the wife to seek legal advice. A body of case law developed which had the effect of shifting the responsibility for the giving of advice to solicitors and enabling the banks to be protected by the issue of a solicitor's certificate stating that the nature and effect of the documents had been explained to the wife (e.g., *Bank of Baroda v Rayarel* [1995] 2 FCR 631). It was also held that the bank was not concerned with matters concerning the solicitor's independence (*Massey v Midland Bank plc* [1995] 1 All ER 929, *Banco Exterior Internacional v Mann* [1995] 1 All ER 936, *Barclays Bank plc v Thomson* [1997] 4 All ER 816).

The House of Lords in **Royal Bank of Scotland plc v Etridge (No. 2)** [2002] UKHL 44, [2002] 2 AC 773, has now explained, in precise terms, the steps that the bank needs to take. The House of Lords considered that it was neither desirable nor practical to expect banks or solicitors to be satisfied that no undue influence has been exercised; that would involve questioning which was far too intrusive and would prove expensive.

Lord Nicholls said that:

> the furthest a bank can be expected to go is to take reasonable steps to satisfy itself that the wife had had brought home to her, in a meaningful way, the practical implications of the proposed transaction.

He concluded that the wife would then enter the transaction 'with her eyes open so far as the basic elements of the transaction are concerned'. It was not necessary that the bank itself fulfills this task and if the bank preferred, it could be undertaken by a solicitor. The expectation, based on existing practice, is that this will be the course of action selected by the banks.

The speech of Lord Nicholls is also significant in emphasizing that in the general sense it is not for the solicitor to veto the transaction; the decision on whether to proceed must lie with the wife (once the practical implications have been explained to her). However, Lord Hobhouse warned against confusing comprehension of a document (which is all that is required on the approach of Lord Nicholls) with agreement given freely in the knowledge of the true facts (which

Lord Hobhouse considered was necessary to negative undue influence). Lord Hobhouse was particularly concerned about situations where the husband's influence extended to the process where the wife received the explanation of the transaction and its implications. In such instances the wife might well comprehend (and so be informed) but would still not be able to give a 'free consent'.

Summary

As a result of the decision of the House of Lords in *Etridge*, in general terms, the bank need only take reasonable steps to satisfy itself that the practical implications of the proposed transaction have been explained to the wife and can rely on confirmation from the solicitor that this has been done, unless the bank knows or ought to realize that appropriate advice was not received. The bank is not expected to have any knowledge of the advice given by the solicitor and the solicitor is not accountable to the bank for the advice given to the wife. If the advice given were deficient in any respect, then the wife would need to seek redress from the solicitor, by means of an action based on negligent advice.

Their Lordships also considered that there should be no requirement that the solicitor should be wholly independent, i.e. a different solicitor to that engaged by the husband, on the basis that a requirement for a separate and independent solicitor might prove prohibitively expensive. The solicitor would owe duties directly to the client and if the solicitor was concerned that there was a real risk of conflict of interest which might inhibit the advice given, the solicitor would need to stop acting for the wife.

15.2.9 Post-*Etridge* case law: Acceptance of the 'wider principle'

The actual application of the principles emerging from the decision of the House of Lords decision in *Royal Bank of Scotland plc v Etridge (No. 2)* [2002] UKHL 44, [2002] 2 AC 773, appears to indicate that a bank will be put on inquiry in all cases involving a non-commercial relationship between surety and debtor (the 'wider principle' referred to by Lord Nicholls).

> In *First National Bank plc v Achampong* [2003] EWCA Civ 487, [2004] 1 FCR 18, [2003] NPC 46, at first instance the wife had succeeded in establishing that the bank was put on inquiry because of the nature of the relationship, the fact that the loan was for the purposes of the husband's business, and that she derived no benefit from it. However, on appeal, the Court of Appeal indicated that this type of investigation was unnecessary in order to conclude that the bank was put on inquiry. In other words, the Court of Appeal considered (*obiter*) that the 'wider principle' would be applicable. In addition, the Court of Appeal held that the bank had not avoided being fixed with constructive notice of the husband's undue influence simply because it knew that the wife had a solicitor. The problem was that the solicitor had not confirmed that he had informed the wife of the risk associated with standing surety (see also *Lloyds TSB Bank plc v Holdgate* [2002] EWCA Civ 1543, [2003] HLR 25, (2002) 146 SJLB 232).

In general terms, in order to be protected the bank would need to know that the wife's solicitor had been instructed to provide the necessary independent advice and the bank must have received the solicitor's confirmation that the advice had been given.

Perhaps a more interesting case, because it concerned alleged undue influence in a mother/son relationship, is ***Chater v Mortgage Agency Services Number Two Ltd*** [2003] EWCA Civ 490, [2004] 1 P & CR 4. The issues in the case concerned whether the son had subjected the mother to undue influence and whether the lender was put on inquiry.

> A mother and son had jointly borrowed money via a mortgage using the security of the mother's house, which was also transferred into their joint names. The purpose was to support the son's business. She later alleged undue influence in that she had placed trust and confidence in her son and had relied upon his assurances. In addition, she alleged that the lender was fixed with notice of this undue influence because it had failed to require her to take independent advice from a solicitor. The Court of Appeal applied the approach advocated by the House of Lords in **Etridge**. This required that undue influence be established on the facts. The court accepted that the mother had placed trust and confidence in her son in relation to the management of her financial affairs. The second factor was whether there had been a transaction calling for an explanation (applying the broader **Allcard v Skinner** approach rather than looking at disadvantage and any possible advantage in the transaction). There were a number of features of the transaction which the Court of Appeal viewed as calling for an explanation: the purpose of the loan had not been accurately described on the application form (i.e., it had been described as for home improvements), the mortgage was for a twenty-five-year term although the mother was sixty-one years old, and there was also a daughter and the mother had expressed an intention to treat both children equally. This provided *prima facie* evidence that the son had abused the influence he had in the relationship and the burden then shifted to the son to seek to counter the inference of undue influence. There being no satisfactory explanation from the son, the undue influence was established.
>
> However, the Court of Appeal concluded that the lender was not put on inquiry. This question turned solely on the information available to the lender, i.e. what it knew or ought to have known. This was not a debtor/surety or a husband/wife case (so that the 'wider principle' applied in **Achampong** (above) could not be utilized) and as far as the lender was concerned it was a joint application for a joint loan and the lender had no way of knowing that this was not true (and so similar to **CIBC v Pitt** [1994] 1 AC 200). It was also the case that the proceeds had been issued in the form of a joint cheque. The lender would only have been put on inquiry if aware that the loan had been made for the purposes of the son's business.

It follows from the application of this 'wider principle' that a bank is unlikely to be put on inquiry where the relationship between the surety and the debtor is commercial (e.g. *Bank of Scotland plc v Makris*, 15 May 2009, transcript available via Westlaw). In the commercial context the need for the protection does not exist, since as Lord Nicholls stated in **Etridge**: 'Those engaged in business can be regarded as capable of looking after themselves and understanding the risks involved in the giving of guarantees.'

15.2.10 Exceptional cases where the wrong is glaringly obvious

In ***Royal Bank of Scotland plc v Etridge (No. 2)*** [2002] UKHL 44, [2002] 2 AC 773, Lord Nicholls referred to 'exceptional circumstances where it is glaringly obvious that the wife is being grievously wronged' and that in such cases 'the solicitor should decline to act further'; the implication being that if the bank failed to investigate further it would be fixed with constructive notice. Although these 'exceptional circumstances' are not explained, the example given is so extreme (poor man transferring all his property to his solicitor) as to suggest that it is unlikely to apply in many instances. Nevertheless, this principle might apply in less obvious circumstances as long as there is clear evidence that undue influence is more than likely as opposed to circumstances which merely raise a suspicion.

However, Lord Nicholls specifically stated that he could not agree with the statement made by the Court of Appeal in **Etridge** ([1998] 4 All ER 705), which came to be known as the '*Etridge* exception' and which provided that where the transaction was 'one into which no competent solicitor could properly advise the wife to enter' the bank would be fixed with constructive notice even in instances where legal advice had been given. This would clearly go against the policy of achieving certainty so that, where banks had complied with the required steps, they could rely on the sanctity of their security.

Unsurprisingly, this principle (the '*Etridge* exception' in the Court of Appeal) was seized upon in subsequent cases to support an argument that the security was unenforceable because the lender had failed to take all the steps required in these circumstances. The Court of Appeal in *Barclays Bank plc v Goff* [2001] EWCA Civ 635, [2001] 2 All ER (Comm) 847, expressed some unease with the potential scope of the exception formulated by the Court of Appeal in **Etridge**.

Pill LJ stated (at para. 66) that:

> family members do sometimes enter into unwise arrangements to assist their nearest and dearest. I do not consider that the exception was intended to cover all cases in which a solicitor would be expected to decline to give positive advice to enter into the transaction or to all cases in which the solicitor would be expected to advise that the transaction was unwise.

He went on to stress the extreme nature of the facts of **Credit Lyonnais Bank** (see below), which was referred to as involving a transaction which 'shocks the conscience of the court' (per Millett LJ). The decision in **Portman Building Society v Dusangh** [2000] 2 All ER (Comm) 221 (see 15.3.4) also applied a test involving whether the conscience of the court is shocked by the transaction. In other words, the transaction must give rise to 'moral outrage' (per Ward LJ).

Although the principle of the Court of Appeal in **Etridge** was discredited by the House of Lords, as Lord Nicholls recognized, there will be some extreme cases where intervention by the courts is called for because the wrong is so obvious and the surety so obviously in need of protection.

It would seem that **Credit Lyonnais Bank Nederland NV v Burch** [1997] 1 All ER 144 provides an example of such a transaction where the court clearly considered that it needed to intervene to protect the defendant surety (i.e., the 'moral outrage' ground).

In **Credit Lyonnais Bank**, the defendant was a junior employee of a company and was a family friend of the plaintiff, the company's main shareholder. The plaintiff asked her to provide security to cover the company's overdraft, which involved charging her flat and giving an unlimited guarantee to the bank. Although the bank had advised her to obtain independent legal advice, she had not done so. When the company went into liquidation, the bank sought possession of the defendant's flat. The bank argued that it had discharged its responsibility by advising the defendant to take legal advice and could not be responsible for her failure to do so. The Court of Appeal held that, as the bank knew the nature of the employment relationship, it should have realized that undue influence was **probable**. Therefore, it should have ensured that the defendant obtained the independent legal advice and explained the potential extent of her liability. Accordingly, the bank was fixed with notice of the undue influence and the transaction was set aside.

In ***O'Brien***, Lord Browne-Wilkinson had stated that where undue influence was **probable** in the circumstances, the bank would need to ensure that independent advice was obtained so that ***Credit Lyonnais Bank*** and 'the glaringly obvious exception' may be no more than applications of this principle. The suggested link between cases of undue influence and unconscionability is discussed in 15.3.2 below.

15.3 A doctrine of unconscionable bargaining?

15.3.1 Inequality of bargaining power

At the root of both the doctrines of duress and undue influence lie considerations of fairness between the parties and a desire to prevent one party taking unfair advantage of the other. In ***Lloyds Bank Ltd v Bundy*** [1975] QB 326, Lord Denning MR argued that these doctrines were not really independent doctrines but rested on 'a single thread' of 'inequality of bargaining power'. Lord Denning MR stated (at p. 339):

> English law gives relief to one who, without independent advice, enters into a contract upon terms which are very unfair or transfers property for a consideration which is grossly inadequate, when his bargaining power is grievously impaired by reason of his own needs or desires, or by his own ignorance or infirmity, coupled with undue influences or pressures brought to bear on him for or for the benefit of the other.

Thus, the doctrines of duress and undue influence were seen as part of a general power of equity to intervene where there has been an abuse of unequal bargaining power between the parties. (As noted above at 15.2.6.1, the majority of the Court of Appeal in this case based their decision on a finding of undue influence by the bank because of the special relationship of confidence between bank and customer which had arisen on the facts.)

In ***National Westminster Bank Ltd v Morgan*** [1985] AC 686, Lord Scarman referred with approval to the conventional analysis provided by Sir Eric Sachs in ***Lloyd's Bank v Bundy***. Lord Denning's broader principle was firmly rejected. Lord Scarman has also expressly disapproval of such a doctrine in ***Pao On v Lau Yiu Long*** [1980] AC 614 (see 15.1.2.2) on the basis that it 'would render the law uncertain' because it would have to be determined on the facts of each case whether the use of the bargaining position was unfair.

Nevertheless, it may be that there is scope for a single principle as the basis for policing the fairness of bargains in the light of their content. In ***Schroeder Music Publishing Co. Ltd v Macaulay*** [1974] 1 WLR 1308 (see 16.7.8) Lord Diplock used the idea of inequality of bargaining power to assess what he considered to be fair between the parties. The same principle may be found in the test of reasonableness of an exclusion clause set out in Sch. 2 to the Unfair Contract Terms Act (UCTA) 1977 (see 7.6.6.2), which includes a reference to 'the strength of the bargaining positions of the parties relative to each other'. Clearly, there is also more direct consumer protection legislation, such as the Consumer Credit Act 1974, and the Unfair Terms in Consumer Contracts Regulations 1999 which regulate unfair terms (see 7.7) but take account of all the circumstances surrounding the making of the contract.

Outside the scope of legislation, there are limited signs that English law might be prepared to recognize a general right of intervention to prevent a weaker party (see, e.g., ***Alec Lobb (Garages)***

Ltd v Total Oil GB Ltd [1985] 1 WLR 173). In *Lloyd's Bank Ltd v Bundy*, Lord Denning MR was careful to avoid defining inequality of bargaining power only in terms of the obvious disparity between commercial enterprises and individual consumers. He defined it as existing whenever a party's bargaining power is 'grievously impaired by reason of his own needs or desires, or by his own ignorance or infirmity'. In this sense even economic duress against a large corporation would fall under the inequality of bargaining power principle. A weak bargaining position might be caused by other commercial commitments. In order to succeed, however, the corporation would also have to show abuse of that position by exertion of undue pressure on the part of the other contracting party. One of the criticisms made of Lord Denning's doctrine by Lord Scarman in subsequent cases (*Pao On v Lau Yiu Long* [1980] AC 614 and *National Westminster Bank Ltd v Morgan* [1985] AC 686) is that it exposes a risk that any contract, resulting from bargaining in which one party had the upper hand, might be overturned by the courts, thereby causing great uncertainty. However, it seems that any such doctrine would have to be based on the concept of 'abuse' of the unequal bargaining power and not merely its existence.

Something very like a doctrine of abuse of unequal bargaining power already exists in §2–302 of the American Uniform Commercial Code, which reads:

> (1) If the court as a matter of law finds the contract or any clause of the contract to have been unconscionable at the time it was made the court may refuse to enforce the contract, or it may enforce the remainder of the contract without the unconscionable clause, or it may so limit the application of any unconscionable clause as to avoid any unconscionable result.

The Code itself does not define 'unconscionable', but the commentary published with it says that the section is aimed at preventing 'oppression and unfair surprise' and is not intended to disturb normal allocations of risk resulting from disparities in bargaining power. It is a question to be determined by the court in each case whether the behaviour of one party has crossed the line between the free play of market forces and oppression. The relevance of bargaining power in the doctrine is that what may in some circumstances amount to oppression, will be regarded between parties of more equal bargaining power as legitimate negotiating tactics. Australia also has a recognized doctrine of unconscionability as a ground for intervention (*Commercial Bank of Australia Ltd v Amadio* (1983) 151 CLR 447).

The closest that English law comes to such intervention is:

1. The Unfair Terms in Consumer Contracts Regulations 1999, SI 1999/2083, where a term will be unfair if 'contrary to the requirement of good faith' it 'causes a significant imbalance in the parties' rights and obligations under the contract to the detriment of the consumer'. Many of the terms which are listed as indicative of unfairness in Sch. 2 are based on this imbalance; and in *Director General of Fair Trading v First National Bank plc* [2001] UKHL 52, [2002] 1 AC 481, the House of Lords assessed the unfairness of terms by reference to both procedural and substantive unfairness resulting in the contractual rights being tilted significantly in the supplier's favour or imposing a disadvantageous burden, risk, or duty on the consumer. This unfairness is therefore linked with the concept of inequality of bargaining power and a taking advantage of that position, which represent key ingredients in a wider doctrine of unconscionability. Unfairness on its own (or inequality of bargaining power) is not sufficient; there must also be this element of abuse.

2. The 'unfair relationship' provision in ss. 140A–D of the Consumer Credit Act 1974, as amended (the replacement for the largely ineffectual 'grossly' extortionate bargaining provision) is also potentially very significant indeed. The new provision is much wider than its predecessor and enables the court to make an order if it finds that the relationship between creditor and debtor arising out of a credit agreement, or that agreement taken with any related agreement, is unfair to the debtor. This unfairness can result from one or more of the following:

(a) any of the terms of the agreement, e.g. restrictions on termination rights or onerous charges

(b) the way in which the creditor has exercised or enforced any of its rights

(c) any other thing done by the creditor, whether occurring before or after the making of the agreement.

The court is also permitted to take into account all sorts of issues such as the debtor's age and financial circumstances, and any high-pressure selling techniques by the creditor. When an unfair relationship is established, the creditor may be ordered to repay sums paid, or the debt may be written off or the terms of the agreement may be varied.

3. The European directive concerning unfair business-to-consumer commercial practices (the Unfair Commercial Practices Directive or UCP; 2005/29/EC, OJ L149/22) (see also 1.6.2 and 14.1.2) was implemented by the Consumer Protection from Unfair Trading Regulations 2008, SI 2008/1277. These regulations prohibit unfair commercial practices (reg. 3) and this includes aggressive commercial practices (reg. 7) which cause or is likely to cause the making of a contract because it significantly impairs or is likely to impair consumer freedom of choice as a result of 'harassment, coercion or undue influence'. 'Undue influence' in this context is defined as 'exploiting a position of power in relation to the consumer so as to apply pressure, even without using or threatening to use physical force, in a way which significantly limits the consumer's ability to make an informed choice'. Interestingly, coercion is defined as threats to the person so this definition of undue influence includes economic duress. Contravention constitutes a criminal offence (reg. 11). The directive was stated to be 'without prejudice to contract law' (Art. 3(1)) and in particular to 'the rules on the validity, formation or effect of a contract', so that neither the directive nor the Unfair Trading Regulations provide any civil remedies for individual consumers in such circumstances. This is, however, a measure which is subject to the provisions contained in the Enterprise Act 2002 (see discussion at 7.7.7.1). It follows that the criminal prohibitions can be the subject of enforcement action.

15.3.2 The link between unconscionability and undue influence

There have also been increasing references in recent cases involving allegations of undue influence to a link between unconscionability and undue influence (*Credit Lyonnais Bank v Burch* [1997] 1 All ER 144 and *Dunbar Bank plc v Nadeem* [1998] 3 All ER 876). However, other cases have refuted such a link on the basis that undue influence is 'concerned with the prior relationship between the contracting parties and whether that was the motivation or reason for which the bargain was entered into' (per Buxton LJ in *Irvani v Irvani* [2000] 1 Lloyd's Rep 412). In other words, undue influence might be regarded as 'plaintiff-sided' (or 'claimant-sided'), whereas unconscionability might be regarded as 'defendant-sided' because it is concerned with abuse of position by the defendant.

Ward LJ in **Portman Building Society v Dusangh** [2000] 2 All ER (Comm) 221 considered the sides to the debate (Capper (1998) 114 LQR 479, and Birks and Chin, 'On the nature of undue influence' in Beatson and Friedmann (eds), *Good Faith and Fault in Contract Law* (Oxford University Press, 1995)), but did not consider it necessary to determine which position was correct. Instead, he regarded unconscionability as a legal wrong for the purposes of the application of **O'Brien**, i.e. in the same way as undue influence and misrepresentations were legal wrongs. Ward LJ also cited Mason J in the High Court of Australia in **Commercial Bank of Australia v Amadio** (1983) 151 CLR 447 at p. 461 to the effect that all of the reasons for setting aside contracts on equitable grounds 'constitute species of unconscionable conduct'. Mason J had also stated that:

Relief on the ground of 'unconscionable conduct' is usually taken to refer to the class of case in which a party makes an unconscientious use of his superior position or bargaining power to the detriment of a party who suffers from some special disability or is placed in some special situation of disadvantage…Although unconscionable conduct in this narrow sense bears some resemblance to the doctrine of undue influence, there is a difference between the two. In the latter the will of the innocent party is not independent and voluntary because it is overborne. In the former, the will of the innocent party, even if independent and voluntary, is the result of the disadvantageous position in which he is placed and of the other party unconscientiously taking advantage of that position.

This passage was also cited with approval by Mantell LJ (at [33]) in *Barclays Bank plc v Goff* [2001] EWCA Civ 635, unreported, 3 May 2001, although Mantell LJ recognized that the two remedies might both arise on the facts of a particular case (such as **Credit Lyonnais Bank**).

15.3.3 The principle in *Fry v Lane*

In English law the recognition of a principle of unconscionability has its origins in **Fry v Lane** (1888) 40 ChD 312. **This doctrine derives from a right of equity to set aside transactions at a considerable undervalue and without independent advice against the 'poor and ignorant'.** The presumption of fraud, which arises in these circumstances, may be rebutted by evidence that the bargain was 'fair, just and reasonable'. This principle has gradually been extended in its scope (e.g., **Cresswell v Potter** [1978] 1 WLR 255), so that 'poor and ignorant' is a matter of relative perspective and old age appears to come within its ambit (**Boustany v Pigot** (1993) 69 P & CR 298). In **Credit Lyonnais Bank v Burch** [1997] 1 All ER 144, Nourse LJ would, it seems, have been prepared to extend the doctrine still further, i.e. to a junior employee influenced by employer and family friend. However, the key ingredient of any doctrine of unconscionability, as explained in **Boustany v Pigot**, is not that the transaction is unreasonable or unfair, but there has been an 'abuse' of the position. Millett LJ in **Credit Lyonnais Bank** referred to the need for 'some impropriety, both in the conduct of the stronger party and in the terms of the transaction itself'. In **Kalsep Ltd v X-Flow**, *The Times*, 3 May 2001, it was stressed that a party seeking to set aside an agreement as an unconscionable bargain had to show more than just improvidence. Pumfrey J stated that although it would be difficult:

[I]t is necessary to prove impropriety, and that is to say not merely harshness but impropriety, both in the terms of the agreement and in the manner in which the agreement was arrived at.

On the facts there was no evidence of any coercion or other improper pressure, although the judge accepted that it was an 'exceptionally improvident agreement, ignorantly and foolishly entered into'. **It seems, therefore, that to succeed in a claim based on unconscionability, there must be procedural *and* substantive 'impropriety' which extends beyond mere unfairness.**

15.3.4 Unconscionability arguments in the case law

In ***Portman Building Society v Dusangh*** [2000] 2 All ER 221, the Court of Appeal refused to grant relief based on an argument of unconscionability of the bargain.

> The defendant was aged seventy-two. He was illiterate in English and spoke the language poorly. The claimant building society granted him a mortgage, guaranteed by his son, covering 75 per cent of the value of his property over twenty-five years in order to release the equity in the property. The money was given to the defendant's son to enable him to purchase a supermarket. The son was later declared bankrupt so that the guarantee was worthless. The building society sought to enforce their security, but the defendant claimed that because of the nature of the agreement it could be set aside as an unconscionable bargain, both in respect of unconscionable conduct by the son exploiting his father's weakness which affected the building society, and in respect of unconscionable conduct by the building society itself based on the principle in ***Fry v Lane***.
>
> The Court of Appeal rejected the argument based on the son's unconscionable conduct, distinguishing ***Credit Lyonnais Bank***, because the building society had not exploited the situation and had not acted in a 'morally reprehensible manner' (per Simon Brown LJ). The father had merely sought to assist his son in what he hoped would be a profitable venture. Ward LJ stated that 'it may be that the son gained all the advantage and the father took all the risk, but this cannot be stigmatized as impropriety. There was no exploitation of father by son such as would prick the conscience and tell the son that in all honour it was morally wrong and reprehensible.'

Undue influence was potentially relevant because of the finding that unconscionability was 'a legal wrong' within ***O'Brien***. However, there was no undue influence on the facts, the transaction was not manifestly disadvantageous and legal advice had been received.

In addition, the case would not have fallen within the ***Etridge*** exception identified by the Court of Appeal in that case (see **15.2.10**) where the lender would have been placed under a higher duty of inquiry and the solicitor ought to have refused to act. The transaction was not one which no competent solicitor could have advised the defendant to enter. If the same facts were to arise today, it would equally not be 'glaringly obvious' that the surety was being 'grievously wronged' (per Lord Nicholls in the House of Lords in ***Royal Bank of Scotland plc v Etridge (No. 2)*** [2002] UKHL 44, [2002] 2 AC 773 at [62]) so that the lender would be protected by taking the reasonable steps prescribed by the House of Lords in that case (see the discussion at **15.2.8.2**).

In addition, although the defendant fell within the 'poor and ignorant' requirement for the operation of the principle in ***Fry v Lane*** and the transaction was an improvident one, Simon Brown LJ stated that building societies were not required to police transactions to ensure the wisdom of parents' actions in seeking to assist their children.

15.3.5 Conclusion

The development of a doctrine of unconscionability is therefore likely to be hampered by the practical reality that few cases will justify intervention by the courts; and where they do so, they are also likely to give rise to a claim based on undue influence which may be conceptually more certain and therefore easier to satisfy. For example, in **Credit Lyonnais Bank v Burch**, there was no plea of unconscionable bargain, although the Court of Appeal considered there to be a sufficient basis for intervention on this ground. On the facts in **Portman v Dusangh**, there was no evidence of undue influence and the required unconscionable conduct was also missing.

15.3.6 **DCFR and UNIDROIT**

The *Draft Common Frame of Reference* (DCFR) has provisions covering duress and abuse of trust/ unfair exploitation. DCFR II-7:206 provides for avoidance of a contract induced by 'coercion or by the threat of an imminent and serious harm which it is wrongful to inflict, or wrongful to use as a means to obtain the conclusion of the contract'. However, in order to act as the inducement the threatened party must have had no reasonable alternative in the circumstances. DCFR II-7:207 provides for avoidance where that party was either dependent on the other or had a relationship of trust with the other, 'was in economic distress or had urgent needs, was improvident, ignorant, inexperienced or lacking in bargaining skill'. The other party must have had actual or constructive knowledge of these circumstances and exploited or taken advantage of the position 'by taking an excessive benefit or grossly unfair advantage'. The DCFR does allow for flexibility in terms of remedy by giving the court power to adapt the contract and also (II-7:13) allowing for recognition of partial avoidance (see discussion of partial rescission in English law: 14.5.2.3). There is also provision for damages for loss in instances where the contract can be avoided (II: 7214).

These DCFR provisions are based on the virtually identical provisions in the *Principles of European Contract Law* (PECL), Arts. 4:108, 4:109, 4:116, and 4:117. There are also provisions with different wording but similar effect in the UNIDROIT *Principles of International Commercial Contracts*, Arts 3.9 (Threat), 3.10 (Gross disparity/taking excessive or unjustifiable advantage), 3.16 (partial avoidance), and 3.18 (damages in instances where there is the right of avoidance).

Further reading

General and unconscionability

Atiyah, 'Contract and fair exchange' in *Essays on Contract* (Oxford University Press, 1986).

Brownsword, *Contract Law: Themes for the twenty-first century*, 2nd edn (Oxford University Press, 2006), Ch. 4.

Enonchong, *Duress, Undue Influence and Unconscionable Dealing* (Sweet and Maxwell, 2005).

Thal, 'The inequality of bargaining power doctrine: The problem of defining contractual unfairness' (1988) 8 OJLS 17.

Tijo, 'O'Brien and unconscionability' (1997) 113 LQR 10.

Tiplady, 'The judicial control of contractual unfairness' (1983) 46 MLR 601.

Waddams, 'Unconscionability in contracts' (1976) 39 MLR 369.

Duress

Atiyah, 'Economic duress and the overborne will' (1982) 98 LQR 197.

Beatson, 'Duress as a vitiating factor in contract' (1974) 33 CLJ 97.

Macdonald, 'Duress by threatened breach of contract' [1989] JBL 460.

Phang, 'Whither economic duress? Reflections on two recent cases' (1990) 53 MLR 107.

Phang, 'Economic duress: Recent difficulties and possible alternatives' [1997] RLR 53.

Smith, 'Contracting under pressure: A theory of duress' (1997) 56 CLJ 343.

Undue Influence (including relationship with unconscionability)

Bamforth, 'Unconscionability as a vitiating factor' [1995] LMCLQ 538.

Bigwood, 'Undue influence in the House of Lords: Principles and proof' (2002) 65 MLR 435.

Birks and Chin, 'On the nature of undue influence' in Beatson and Friedmann (eds), *Good Faith and Fault in Contract Law* (Oxford University Press, 1995).

Capper, 'Undue influence and unconscionability: A rationalisation' (1998) 114 LQR 479.

Capper, 'Banks, borrowers, sureties and undue influence: A half baked solution to a thoroughly cooked problem' [2002] RLR 100.

Chen-Wishart, 'The *O'Brien* principle and substantive unfairness' [1997] CLJ 60.

Hooley and O'Sullivan, 'Undue influence and unconscionable bargains' [1997] LMCLQ 17.

McMurty, 'Unconscionability and undue influence: An interaction?' [2000] Conv 573.

Phang and Tijo, 'The uncertain boundaries of undue influence' [2002] LMCLQ 231.

16 Illegality

Summary of the issues

This chapter is concerned with a brief introduction to two issues: (1) identifying contracts which are tainted by illegality or otherwise contrary to public policy, and (2) examining the effect on the parties' positions of this illegality.

• A contract may be illegal from the outset or the illegality may arise in the course of performance of what would otherwise be a valid contract. Where the contract is illegal in its performance, the courts may allow the party who was not party to that illegal performance to enforce it, e.g. by obtaining damages.

• Contracts may be illegal as a result of statute, e.g. express statutory prohibitions. At common law the courts have declared a wide range of contracts to be illegal or contrary to public policy, such as contracts to commit crimes or contracts prejudicial to sexual morality. In addition, the courts have struck down restraints of trade where they infringe the public interest in promoting free competition and where they are unreasonable as between the parties.

• As a general rule the courts do not enforce illegal contracts and will not permit recovery of benefits conferred in the performance of an illegal contract. However these principles are subject to some exceptions and this area of the law was much criticized so that in 1999 the Law Commission made a series of provisional recommendations for reform. Nevertheless when the Law Commission published its consultative report on the illegality defence in January 2009, whilst reaffirming its criticisms of the law, it recommended that any improvement to the law 'can best be left to development through the case law' based on the application of the policy factors which underpin the illegality defence. The Law Commission has, however, provisionally recommended legislation to deprive a *Tinsley v Milligan* party of a beneficial interest in some circumstances.

• In the context of the ability to enforce an illegal contract, there are a number of exceptions. For example (and as noted above) where a contract is illegal in its performance, the innocent party who was unaware of the illegality may enforce the contract. Alternatively, the court may consider that the punishment imposed for breach of a statutory provision is sufficient in its own right and does not render unenforceable the performance of a contract in breach of that provision. A defendant may have warranted that he will perform lawfully, so that when he fails to do so the claimant can seek damages for breach of that collateral warranty. It may also be possible to sever the illegal part of an agreement and enforce the remainder.

- There are also some exceptions to the non-recovery of benefits rule.

  (a) The courts will allow recovery where the parties are not *in pari delicto* (not equally guilty), e.g. one of the parties was unaware of the illegality.

  (b) The claimant may be able to recover money or property transferred if he repents within the *'locus poenitentiae'*. There is uncertainty concerning whether the claimant must 'genuinely' repent and whether it is possible to repent after performance has started.

  (c) Finally, recovery may be possible if the claimant can establish his right to the money or property transferred without having to rely upon the illegal contract (see, e.g., **Tinsley v Milligan**), although the Law Commission considers reform appropriate in this area.

16.1 Introduction

As a general principle it can be said that the courts will not enforce contracts which are tainted with illegality (*ex turpi causa non oritur* action: no action can arise from an illegal or immoral act).

There are two basic questions to consider:

1. What will constitute an illegal contract?

2. What will be the effect of that illegality?

In respect of this second question there are a number of more specific questions:

- Will the illegality operate as a defence to a contractual claim or a claim in restitution to recover money paid or other benefit conferred under the contract?

- Will it act as a defence to a claim to enforce a proprietary right created or transferred by such a contract?

- Alternatively, will there be any relief available to a party to an illegal contract?

The type of illegality will inevitably influence the attitude of the courts to the question of whether relief is possible.

16.1.1 Public policy

The notion of illegality covers a wide spectrum of factors which deprive contracts of legal force. These factors fall within the compass of the category of public policy where the public interest prevails over whatever may be the intentions of the parties.

In its Consultation Paper, *Illegal Transactions: The effect of illegality on contracts and trusts* (LCCP No. 154, 1999), the Law Commission used a wide definition of illegal contracts as including:

any contract which involves (in its formation, purpose or performance) a legal wrong (other than the mere breach of the contract in question) or conduct otherwise contrary to public policy. [Para. 7.70.]

16.1.2 **Illegality and the judicial response**

The factual situations giving rise to judicial intervention on the ground of illegality are so varied that they defy conceptual classification. Some traditional categories may be used for ease of exposition, but these categories are only descriptive, and few if any legal consequences derive from them. Contracts in restraint of trade are usually treated as a type of illegal contract. They are treated under a separate heading in this chapter partly to ease the organization of material, but also because the associated public policy issues extend beyond the general need to protect the public interest.

The attitude of the courts to claims of illegality is well summarized by the following passage from the judgment of Bingham LJ in ***Saunders v Edwards*** [1987] 2 All ER 651 at pp. 665–6:

> Where issues of illegality are raised, the courts have (as it seems to me) to steer a middle course between two unacceptable positions. On the one hand it is unacceptable that any court of law should aid or lend its authority to a party seeking to pursue or enforce an object or agreement which the law prohibits. On the other hand, it is unacceptable that the court should, on the first indication of unlawfulness affecting any aspect of a transaction, draw up its skirts and refuse all assistance to the plaintiff, no matter how serious his loss or how disproportionate his loss to the unlawfulness of his conduct.
>
> …[O]n the whole the courts have tended to adopt a pragmatic approach to these problems, seeking where possible to see that genuine wrongs are righted so long as the court does not thereby promote or countenance a nefarious object or bargain which it is bound to condemn.

In its 2009 consultative report, ***The Illegality Defence*** (LCCP No. 189), the Law Commission stated:

> The illegality defence should be allowed where its application can be firmly justified by the policies that underlie its existence. These include: (a) furthering the purpose of the rule which the illegal conduct has infringed; (b) consistency; (c) that the claimant should not profit from his or her own wrong; (d) deterrence; and (e) maintaining the integrity of the legal system. [Part 2: para. 2.35.]

The House of Lords in ***Tinsley v Milligan*** [1994] 1 AC 340 at p. 358, condemned any approach to illegality of contracts which suggests that the courts simply have a discretion as to whether to grant or refuse relief. However, in its 1999 consultation the Law Commission had recommended that the courts should have such a discretion (albeit within stated guidelines) to decide whether illegality should act as a defence to a claim in contract, in restitution or in respect of property rights (Law Commission, *Illegal Transactions: the effect of illegality on contracts and trusts,* LCCP No. 154 (1999), discussed in more detail at **16.6.3**). In the 2009 consultative report, *The Illegality Defence* (LCCP No. 189), the Law Commission had retreated from this recommendation (para. 3.122) with the exception of recommending legislation to implement a 'structured discretion to deprive a beneficial owner of his or her interest in the trust in limited circumstances' (i.e., ***Tinsley v Milligan*** resulting trust (para. 6.100), discussed at **16.6.2.3**). The proposed legislation is to be contained in the Law Commission's final report which is due in spring 2010. The reason justifying intervention in this area is that ***Tinsley*** is a decision of the House of Lords which lower courts are bound to follow and has been the subject of considerable academic and judicial criticism.

16.2 Statutory illegality

16.2.1 Express prohibition

Sometimes statute expressly prohibits the type of contract in question, in which case it is clear that neither party can enforce the contract, even if one of them is innocent.

> In *Re Mahmoud and Ispahani* [1921] 2 KB 716, the statute prohibited unlicensed dealing in linseed oil. The defendant misrepresented to the plaintiff that he had a licence, but subsequently refused to accept delivery arguing that the contract was illegal because he did not possess the required licence. Despite the plaintiff's innocence, the contract could not be enforced.

This principle was applied by the Court of Appeal in *Mohamed v Alaga and Co. (a firm)* [2000] 1 WLR 1815.

> The agreement (whereby a firm of solicitors would pay an introduction fee from its legal aid fees to a person introducing refugees requiring legal services) was expressly prohibited by subordinate legislation. Public policy precluded relief under the contract or by means of a claim in restitution for the services of introduction. However, the Court of Appeal did grant leave for the claim to be amended to a claim for a *quantum meruit* for services rendered (interpreting) as the plaintiff was blameless (in the sense that he was not aware of the breach of rules) and no public policy was infringed by allowing him to recover for these services.

This case was distinguished in *Awwad v Geraghty and Co. (a firm)* [2000] 3 WLR 1041, where the firm of solicitors was trying to recover a fee chargeable under the terms of a contract prohibited by subordinate legislation. On these facts, the Court of Appeal held that any claim for a *quantum meruit* also failed because such a claim was trying to achieve the same purpose, i.e. recovery of a fee which was contrary to public policy.

Some statutes are interpreted by the courts as being intended to regulate the activities of a particular class of persons, in which case only the party belonging to that class is disbarred from enforcing the contract, e.g. in *Bloxsome v Williams* (1824) 3 B & C 232, it was held that the Sunday trading laws were not aimed at all persons making contracts but only at **traders**.

16.2.2 Contracts not expressly or impliedly prohibited but performed by one party in illegal manner

> In *Archbolds (Freightage) Ltd v Spanglett Ltd* [1961] 1 QB 374, the defendants agreed to carry a cargo of whisky to London for the plaintiffs, who were unaware that the defendants did not have the required licence. The whisky was stolen, and when the plaintiffs claimed damages for the loss the defendants pleaded illegality. The plaintiffs were allowed to sue on the contract for the defendants' loss of the goods en route. The contract was not expressly or impliedly prohibited by statute (i.e., not illegal on its formation) and so was not illegal. It was performed by the defendants in an illegal manner, but the plaintiffs were not party to that illegal performance and so could enforce it.

However, it is clear from *Anderson Ltd v Daniel* [1924] 1 KB 138 that the illegal performer cannot enforce the contract. Equally, if the other party either knows of the illegal performance, or participates in it, that party will not be able to enforce the contract (*Ashmore, Benson, Pease & Co. Ltd v A. V. Dawson Ltd* [1973] 1 WLR 828: defendants carried tube banks in contravention of legislation specifying the maximum weight of lorries but since the plaintiff's representative had been present at loading and had raised no objection, the plaintiff was unable to recover damages when the tube bank was damaged during the journey).

16.2.3 Penalty provided by the statute is considered sufficient sanction

In some cases the penalty provided for by the statute is thought to be sufficient sanction for the infringement in question, so that the contract may be enforced by both innocent and guilty parties.

> In **St John Shipping Corporation v Joseph Rank Ltd** [1957] 1 QB 267, statute made it an offence to load a ship to such an extent that the load line was below the water. The offence was punishable by payment of a fine. When the plaintiff charterers committed this offence the defendants sought to withhold freight on the basis that it was an illegal contract. However, Devlin J held that the statute did not actually prohibit contracts of carriage performed in breach of the load line rule.

A similar conclusion was reached in *Hughes v Asset Managers plc* [1995] 3 All ER 669, where penalties were imposed on those dealing with share purchases without the necessary licence but the purchase contracts made by such persons were not void as illegal contracts.

16.3 Gambling contracts: Legally enforceable

'Gambling' means gaming, betting, and participating in a lottery (Gambling Act 2005, s. 3) and 'gaming' means participating in a game of chance for a prize (s. 6). The 2005 Act reversed s. 18 of the Gaming Act 1845 which had provided that gambling contracts were null and void so that there could be no action in the courts relating to recovery of any such bet or winnings. Section 335(1) of the 2005 Act instead provides that 'the fact that a contract relates to gambling shall not prevent its enforcement'. It follows that any money paid or property deposited under a gambling contract is no longer irrecoverable merely on the basis that it is a gambling contract (and so null and void). The only exceptions will be in relation to 'unlawfulness' (s. 335(2)), i.e. any other rule of law preventing the gambling contract from being lawful, e.g. if contrary to public policy, and if the Gambling Commission exercises its power to 'void' particular bets (s. 336).

16.4 Public policy under the common law

It is traditional for judges to deprecate resort to public policy (Burrough J in *Richardson v Mellish* (1824) 2 Bing 229 at p. 252) and to point to the adverse effect on freedom of contract of allowing public policy arguments to prevail (Jessel MR in *Printing and Numerical Registering Co. v Sampson* (1875) LR 19 Eq 462 at p. 465). Nevertheless, the different heads of public policy under which courts have declared contracts to be unenforceable are numerous, and despite judicial statements there is no reason to think that they may not increase still further and change over time. Listed below are the more common heads of public policy so far identified.

16.4.1 Contracts to commit crimes or civil wrongs

A contract to commit a crime is self-evidently illegal (see *Bigos v Boustead* [1951] 1 All ER 92: contract contrary to exchange control regulations). Equally, it is contrary to public policy for a criminal or the criminal's estate to benefit from the crime (*Beresford v Royal Insurance Co. Ltd* [1938] AC 586; the Proceeds of Crime Act 2002, as just one example, provides for confiscation orders in relation to the proceeds of crime). In **Gray v Thames Trains Ltd** [2009] UKHL 33, [2009] 3 WLR 167, the House of Lords applied a rule of law that was based on public policy and which was an aspect of the principle of *ex turpi causa* to preclude a person from recovering compensation for losses suffered in consequence of his own criminal act or for damage that was the consequence of a sentence imposed on him for a criminal act. It followed that the claimant, who had committed manslaughter as a result of psychological problems (post-traumatic stress disorder) caused by the negligence of the defendant train operator (namely the Ladbroke Grove train crash), was therefore precluded from recovering general damages and loss of earnings flowing from his crime.

Contracts to defraud the revenue are also illegal (**Alexander v Rayson** [1936] 1 KB 169: contract designed to make the value of property seem less to the rating authority; and *Q v Q* [2008] EWHC 1874 (Fam), [2009] 1 FLR 935, [2009] WTLR 1591: agreement with illegal purpose of cheating the Revenue of inheritance tax). However, a company incorporated to evade the payment of VAT was nevertheless able to enforce a sale of goods contract which was lawful in itself. The fraud in relation to the VAT would be committed only when there was a failure to account for it at the end of the accounting period (**21st Century Logistic Solutions Ltd (in Liquidation) v Madysen Ltd** [2004] EWHC 231 (QB), [2004] 2 Lloyd's Rep 92). It followed that the fraudulent intent was too remote from the lawful contract which merely provided the opportunity to commit the fraud. In *Q v Q* the judge distinguished *21st Century Logistic* on the basis that the illegality in *Q v Q* was the purpose of the transaction, just as the intention to defraud the trustee in bankruptcy was the central purpose in **Barrett v Barrett** [2008] EWHC 1061 (Ch), [2008] 2 P & CR 17 (discussed at **16.6.2.3**).

16.4.2 Contracts prejudicial to the administration of justice

Contracts which oust the jurisdiction of the courts are illegal provided no attempt is made to oust the supervisory role of the courts. (A provision in an agreement between parties to the sale of land to exclude s. 49(2) of the Law of Property Act 1925 (providing a discretion to order repayment of a deposit) was illegal and void as it purported to oust the jurisdiction of the court: *Aribisala v St James (Grosvenor Dock) Ltd* [2007] EWHC 1694 (Ch), [2007] 3 EGLR 39. However, arbitration clauses in contracts are enforceable (*Scott v Avery* (1855) 5 HL Cas 811.)

Maintenance agreements between husband and wife in which one party agrees not to apply to the court for maintenance have been held to be contrary to public policy (*Hyman v Hyman* [1929] AC 601), but the impact of that decision is considerably reduced by legislation (Matrimonial Causes Act 1973, s. 34) since the agreement is void in the sense that the wife is not bound by a promise not to apply to the court. However, the promise to pay may be treated as enforceable (see **4.8.3.2**). In **Soulsbury v Soulsbury** [2007] EWCA Civ 969, [2008] 2 WLR 834, the particular agreement was distinguishable and did not oust the jurisdiction of the court since it amounted to an agreement to pay £100,000 on the death of the ex-husband where the first wife had not enforced any arrears or applied for further matrimonial relief. There was nothing in the agreement which prevented the wife going back to the court, but if she did so it would render the fulfillment of the condition subsequent impossible.

It had been considered that any agreement which made financial arrangements for a separation which had not yet occurred would be contrary to public policy and void. However, in **MacLeod v MacLeod** [2008] UKPC 64, [2009] 3 WLR 437, the Privy Council considered that agreements made after marriage which provide for future separation (so-called 'post nups') could be given effect to by the courts under s. 34 of the Matrimonial Causes Act 1973. Baroness Hale (giving the judgment of the Board) considered that it was not for the Privy Council to reverse the long-standing rule that pre-nuptial agreements were contrary to public policy and thus not valid or binding in a contractual sense. Pre-nuptial agreements are currently the subject of an examination by the Law Commission. In **Radmacher v Granatino** [2009] EWCA Civ 649, [2009] 2 FLR 1181, [2009] 2 FCR 645, whilst the fact that such agreements remained void was regarded as 'increasingly unrealistic', it was for the Law Commission to report and Parliament to introduce legislation if this was considered necessary to redress this status. Nevertheless, on the facts, the Court of Appeal was prepared to give such an agreement such weight in ancillary relief proceedings as was necessary to achieve fairness between the parties. In addition, the Court of Appeal expressed some doubts about whether it could really be said that such agreements were contrary to public policy. If there was any provision which ousted the jurisdiction of the courts it would be void, if severable.

16.4.3 Contracts prejudicial to the family

There are statutory prohibitions on relinquishing the obligations of a parent (e.g., Children Act 1989, s. 2). A surrogacy agreement (whereby it is agreed that the surrogate mother will relinquish parental responsibility in favour of another) is unenforceable under s. 1A of the Surrogacy Arrangements Act 1985, as amended by s. 36 of the Human Fertilisation and Embryology Act 1990.

16.4.4 Contracts prejudicial to (sexual) morality

It is sometimes said that contracts contrary to public morals are unenforceable. The rule is probably limited to sexual morality and attitudes to this question have been transformed in recent years. In the nineteenth century, a strict approach was taken to sexual morality so that a promise of payment in order to induce a woman to become a man's mistress was unenforceable (*Benyon v Nettlefold* (1850) 3 Mac & G 94) and contracts ancillary to immoral purposes were also regarded as being contrary to public policy (*Pearce v Brooks* (1866) LR 1 Ex 213: contract of hire of a carriage for the known purpose of prostitution).

The change in attitudes to sexual morality over recent years is evidenced in a number of cases where the courts have rejected the public-policy argument and held the contracts to be valid, e.g. *Armhouse Lee Ltd v Chappell, The Times,* 7 August 1996 (contract for advertising of telephone 'sex lines' was not contrary to public policy so that the operator of the lines had to pay for the advertising) and *Sutton v Mischon de Reya* [2003] EWHC 3166 (Ch), [2004] 1 FLR 837 (deed of cohabitation between two people in a master/slave sexual relationship was not contrary to public policy). The fact that the attitude to unmarried cohabitees has been relaxed is further illustrated by the approach of the House of Lords in **Tinsley v Milligan** [1994] 1 AC 340 (the agreement between the couple was not challenged as being contrary to public policy on the basis that they were unmarried cohabitees).

16.4.5 Public corruption

Contracts which further corruption in public life are illegal. The rule is most commonly applied in the case of sales of public offices or honours.

> In *Parkinson v College of Ambulance Ltd* [1925] 2 KB 1, the plaintiff was encouraged to believe that if he were to make a substantial donation to a certain charity, the officers of the charity would be able to obtain a knighthood for him. The sum of £3,000 was agreed and paid, but no knighthood was forthcoming. The plaintiff sued to recover the amount paid, but was unable to succeed because the contract was found to be illegal (see also the Honours (Prevention of Abuses) Act 1925).

16.5 General effect of illegality

The effect of illegality varies according to the gravity with which the illegality is viewed by the court. The general principle is that illegal contracts are unenforceable (*Holman v Johnson* (1775) 1 Cowp 34), reaffirmed by Lord Goff and Lord Browne-Wilkinson in **Tinsley v Milligan** [1994] 1 AC 340 at pp. 355 and 363. Therefore:

1. **A claimant will not succeed if the claim is based on an illegal contract, or if the illegality of the contract must be pleaded to support the claim (*Barrett v Barrett* [2008] EWHC 1061 (Ch), [2008] 2 P & CR 17).**

2. **A claimant will not succeed if to do so would result in him benefiting from his own illegal contract.**

3. **However, a claimant may clearly succeed if the claim does not require any reliance on the illegal contract.** This would be the case where:

    (a) the claim made is not contractual at all (e.g., *Saunders v Edwards* [1987] 2 All ER 651: claim in tort for fraud giving rise to a contract which was tainted with illegality)

    (b) the illegality does not affect the contract upon which the claim was based but some related transaction (e.g., *Euro-Diam Ltd v Bathurst* [1988] 2 All ER 23: claim on a contract of insurance in respect of goods stolen in the course of a transaction tainted with illegality)

    (c) it is not necessary to plead the illegality because the party is merely asserting a property right (per Lord Browne-Wilkinson in **Tinsley v Milligan**: claim to have an equal share in property, despite the house having been put in only one name as a device to contribute to a fraud on the Department of Social Security; see further 16.6.2.3).

4. **Nevertheless, recovery on a collateral contract may be possible.** Sometimes, although it seems only exceptionally, in order to ensure that 'genuine wrongs are righted' the courts will go so far as to allow recovery on a collateral contract, thereby avoiding, by use of a fiction, the problem of allowing a claim founded upon an illegal contract. **However, this is of limited utility since a remedy under a collateral contract must not be the equivalent of enforcing the illegal contract.**

> In **Strongman (1945) Ltd v Sincock** [1955] 2 QB 525, a builder was informed by his client that the client would obtain the necessary licences, which the client then failed to do. A contract to build without a

licence was absolutely prohibited by statute. Although the builders could not recover the contract price because the contract was prohibited, the assurance that the client would obtain the necessary licences was considered to constitute an enforceable collateral contract to obtain them. The Court of Appeal held the client liable for breach of this collateral contract.

> This (fictitious) kind of enforceable collateral contract must be kept separate from other transactions collateral to illegal contracts. For example, security given in respect of payment for, or performance of, an illegal contract is tainted by the illegality of the main transaction (*Fisher v Bridges* (1854) 3 El & Bl 642).

5. Where one party is not involved in the illegal intention, as for example in the case of a class-protecting statute (*Bloxsome v Williams* (1824) 3 B & C 232: see 16.2.1), that party may enforce the contract or recover under a restitutionary remedy.

6. Finally, where one party adopts an illegal mode of performance without there ever having been any illegal intention at the time of contracting, that party may still enforce the contract, provided it does not have to rely on the illegal element.

In *Skilton v Sullivan, The Times*, 25 March 1994, the Court of Appeal allowed recovery of the price under a contract of sale (despite the fact that the seller had presented an invoice which falsely described the goods in order to delay payment of VAT), on the basis that the seller could establish liability to pay by relying only on the contract itself.

16.6 Recovery of money or property

16.6.1 No recovery where the parties are equally guilty

The general rule stated in *Holman v Johnson* (1775) 1 Cowp 341 (see 16.5) applies equally to claims brought to recover money or property passing as a result of an illegal contract as it does to enforcement of the contract itself. Thus, where the parties are equally guilty even a restitutionary remedy is barred.

This principle denying recovery was challenged in **Shanshal v Al-Kishtaini** [2001] EWCA Civ 264, [2001] 2 All ER (Comm) 601, as being contrary to the Human Rights Act 1998, and specifically Art. 1 of the First Protocol to the European Convention on Human Rights. Courts are 'public authorities' for the purposes of this legislation and therefore must ensure that the laws applied are compatible with Art. 1. Article 1 provides, *inter alia*, that 'no one shall be deprived of his possessions except in the public interest'.

The illegal contracts in this case were contracts entered into in breach of UN sanctions on trade with Iraqi citizens. The claimant sought repayment of money lent in breach of this law but the Court of Appeal rejected the claim. The Court of Appeal held that it was arguable whether the Human Rights Act applied at all since the unenforceability of a claim on the basis of illegality was not a deprivation of possessions within Art. 1. However, in any event, the case clearly fell within the public-interest exception so that the illegality defence did not infringe Art. 1.

In the light of this decision, it is likely that the principle prohibiting recovery of money or property transferred under an illegal contract will be considered as in the public interest and therefore as not involving any breach of the Human Rights Act 1998.

16.6.2 **Exceptions**

The principle prohibiting recovery is not absolute and may be avoided in a number of situations where either the parties are not regarded as being equally guilty, or the illegality need not be pleaded in order to obtain the remedy.

16.6.2.1 Where one party withdraws from the illegal transaction

Restitution may be available where one party withdraws before the illegal purpose is carried into effect (the so-called doctrine of *locus poenitentiae*). It appears that repentance is not necessary (*Tribe v Tribe* [1996] Ch 106).

In *Taylor v Bowers* (1876) 1 QBD 291, Mellish LJ suggested that withdrawal is allowed at any time before completion. However, in **Kearley v Thomson** (1890) 24 QBD 742, it was suggested that restitution would be denied once performance of the illegal purpose had started, irrespective of whether it was ever completed. The same reasoning was applied by the Court of Appeal (*obiter*) in **Collier v Collier** [2002] EWCA Civ 1095, [2003] 1 P & CR D3, where the illegal purpose, the transfer of leases from father to daughter in order to defeat the claims of the father's creditors, had already taken place. The **Kearley v Thomson** principle appears to be more consistent with the public policy requirements inherent in the control of illegal contracts.

For similar reasons, the withdrawal from the transaction must be voluntary. In *Bigos v Boustead* [1951] 1 All ER 92, restitution was refused because the plaintiff had 'withdrawn' from the transaction only after the illegal purpose had been frustrated by the duplicity of the other party. A slightly different version of this rule emerged in *Tribe v Tribe* [1996] Ch 107.

> In **Tribe v Tribe** the illegal purpose was never carried into effect because the 'need' for the illegal scheme (which was designed to defraud creditors by transferring property to another) was avoided. When it became clear that the illegal scheme was not required, the transferor claimed the property back. To the defence that the transaction was illegal so that restitution was not allowed, the transferor replied that he had withdrawn before it was carried into effect and the Court of Appeal accepted this argument.

This appears to be a surprising conclusion since the first element of the illegal transaction had been performed, i.e. the transfer of the property. The best explanation is probably that the transfer was not **necessarily** referable to an illegal purpose, and so should not be regarded as commencing the illegal performance. Such reasoning is technical and artificial; there is little doubt that the court was also influenced by the view it took of the conduct of the party (the son of the transferor) who sought to retain the property, contrary to what had been their original plan.

16.6.2.2 Fraud, duress, or undue influence

Where one party is induced to enter into an illegal contract by fraud, duress, or undue influence, that party is clearly not as guilty as the other. While it would be undesirable in such circumstances to enforce the contract, some remedy may be provided by permitting the victim to recover money or property passed as a result of the contract.

> In *Hughes v Liverpool Victoria Legal Friendly Society* [1916] 2 KB 482, the plaintiff was fraudulently induced to take out a policy of insurance on the life of someone in which she had no insurable interest. She was able to recover the premiums paid.

16.6.2.3 Proprietary remedy which does not rely on the illegal contract

Restitution will be allowed where the defendant is merely asserting a property right and need not rely on the fact that the contract is illegal.

In the case of the sale of goods, it is established that property passes despite the illegality (*Singh v Ali* [1960] AC 167). Therefore, a proprietary remedy would not be available in a sales case since there would be no property right to assert (see 1.5). However, where something less than full title is passed, as in the case of a lease, bailment, or pledge, there may be scope for restitution. Nevertheless, if, in order to assert that property has not passed to the other party, it is necessary to plead the illegality of the transaction under which physical possession was transferred, then no remedy is available (*Taylor v Chester* (1869) LR 4 QB 309). A common form of bailment is the hire-purchase agreement.

In ***Bowmakers Ltd v Barnet Instruments Ltd*** [1945] KB 65, goods were delivered to the defendants under an illegal hire-purchase agreement. The defendants had failed to make payments and had sold some of the goods. The plaintiffs claimed damages for conversion; that is, they brought an action to recover the value of the goods, asserting their property right. The Court of Appeal allowed this claim. The right to the goods which had been sold could be asserted by virtue of the law of bailment without reference to the terms of the contract.

However, the decision has been criticized for also allowing recovery for the goods retained by the defendants, since any right to their value, resulting from the failure to make the payments, must have depended on the terms of the contract, on which the court was not entitled to rely.

Tinsley v Milligan and the resulting trust (the 'reliance principle')

In ***Tinsley v Milligan*** [1994] 1 AC 340 (noted Berg [1993] JBL 513 and Enonchong (1995) 111 LQR 135), Lord Browne-Wilkinson, speaking for the majority in the House of Lords, took the view that an action brought to assert a joint interest in a house, which had been put into the name of only one of the parties in order to assist in a fraud against the Department of Social Security, did not involve any reliance on an illegal contract but was simply an action to enforce a property right in the form of a trust. He did not believe that the fact that the property right asserted was in the form of an equitable rather than a legal interest had any impact on the case. Lord Browne-Wilkinson accepted that at some time in the past an equitable property right might have required different treatment, but was persuaded that the fusion of law and equity allowed the plaintiff to avoid the consequences of the illegal contracts rule by relying on a property right whether legal **or** equitable. By comparison, Lord Goff, in the minority, took the view that an equitable property right could not be used in this way to avoid the consequences of the illegal contracts rule, because of the distinct maxim of equity that 'he who comes to equity must come with clean hands'.

Tinsley v Milligan was applied by the Court of Appeal in ***Mortgage Express v Robson*** [2001] EWCA Civ 887, [2001] 2 All ER (Comm) 886, to recognize an equitable interest in a property which had been jointly purchased with monies which represented the equity in previous properties purchased with mortgages which had been fraudulently obtained by the claimant's husband. The equitable interest was based on the contribution to the purchase price by the claimant and her husband, together with the claimant's contributions to improvements to the property. Although this case was factually different to ***Tinsley v Milligan*** (property acquired for unlawful purpose, whereas this case concerned a contribution from an unlawful source), the Court of Appeal did not consider this to be important. Instead, the important factor was that the claim was founded on the property right rather than the earlier illegal transactions. There was a similar outcome of a resulting trust in relation to a transfer into accounts of grandchildren in *Silverwood v Silverwood* (1997) 74 P & CR 453.

The decision in **Tribe v Tribe** [1996] Ch 107 (for facts, see 16.6.2.1, and noted Creighton (1997) 60 MLR 102 and Virgo [1996] CLJ 23) suggested that the **Tinsley v Milligan** or resulting trust analysis was ineffective between close family members (parent and child or husband and wife), since the transfer of property would not give rise to a resulting trust as it did in **Tinsley v Milligan** but rather would be subject to **the presumption of advancement**, i.e. it would be presumed that the intention was to make a gift to the transferee. That presumption could be rebutted only by disclosing the illegal purpose, so that any claim would be denied (see, e.g., **Q v Q** [2008] EWHC 1874 (Fam), [2009] 1 FLR 935, [2009] WTLR 1591: agreement to transfer title in property to sons to be held on trust but with the illegal purpose of cheating the Revenue of inheritance tax). Ironically, of course, if the parties are in any other relationship they can rely on the **Tinsley** resulting trust and need not lead any evidence of the illegality.

In **Tribe v Tribe**, that consequence was avoided by the plaintiff showing to the satisfaction of the Court of Appeal that he had withdrawn from the illegal purpose before it was carried into effect. By comparison, in **Collier v Collier** [2002] EWCA Civ 1095, [2003] 1 P & CR D3, the Court of Appeal (*obiter*) rejected the argument based on the doctrine of *locus poenitentiae* on the facts (see 16.6.2.1) and considered that if the facts had been as alleged (and the transfer of leases by the father to the daughter had been a gift) the presumption of advancement would have applied. The father would therefore have been unable to establish his equitable interest without relying on the illegal agreement.

The decision of the High Court of Australia in **Nelson v Nelson** (1995) 132 ALR 133 (discussed by Phang (1996) 11 JCL 53 and Creighton (1997) 60 MLR 102), appeared to represent a more flexible view of the presumption of advancement.

> The illegal purpose involved the purchase and transfer of a house by the mother to the son and daughter in order to enable a statutory subsidy to be obtained with which to purchase a second house. The son and daughter then sold the house in their names and it was claimed that the proceeds were held on trust for the mother. Although the court recognized that there was no resulting trust and the presumption of advancement applied, that presumption was rebutted. The result was that the mother could recover the proceeds of that house if she repaid the subsidy since the policy of the statute infringed did not require that such recovery should be denied.

This would suggest that the motivation may have been to avoid the outcome in terms of the parties' positions of the application of principle. (In this respect **Nelson v Nelson** can usefully be compared with the decision of the Court of Appeal in **Collier v Collier** when Mance LJ expressed 'no great liking for the result' whereby the father was unable to recover the property transferred to the daughter although the daughter had been involved in the illegal purpose.)

Confusion has been added by the decision of the House of Lords in *Stack v Dowden* [2007] UKHL 17, [2007] 2 AC 432, which may suggest that in some cases where there is joint legal ownership, joint equitable ownership should be assumed (a common-intention constructive trust), so that the resulting trust and presumption of advancement may no longer have any relevance in such a context. It is unclear, however, whether this decision will replace the resulting trust and presumption of advancement where legal title is held by one person only, as is likely to be the case where allegations of illegality are in issue. It follows, however, that to rebut the conclusion of a common-intention constructive trust in relation to the beneficial interest, it would be necessary to do so without relying on any illegality.

A trust argument failed in **Barrett v Barrett** [2008] EWHC 1061 (Ch), [2008] 2 P & CR 17 for this reason.

In *Barrett v Barrett*, Thomas Barrett had purchased a property as legal owner. When in June 1993 he became bankrupt the property vested in his trustee in bankruptcy. His brother, John, negotiated with the trustee to purchase the house. Thomas later claimed that John held the proceeds of sale of this house on trust for him because they had agreed at the time of the purchase from the trustee that the house would effectively remain as Thomas's house and that he would pay all the bills and contribute to the mortgage payments on it.

There could be no argument that the agreement was other than an agreement for an illegal purpose, i.e. its purpose was to defeat the interest of he trustee. However, Thomas argued that, relying on *Tinsley v Milligan* and a resulting trust, he could establish his beneficial interest in the property by bringing evidence of his contributions to the mortgage payments and that he therefore did not need to rely upon the illegal purpose in the agreement.

This argument was firmly rejected by David Richards LJ and *Tinsley* was distinguished on the basis that Thomas could not establish evidence of direct payments towards the purchase of the property, so that no resulting trust could arise. Payments towards the mortgage would not suffice as they might have been no more than payments in lieu of rent. To establish the beneficial interest as a constructive trust it would have to be shown that the contributions to the mortgage payments constituted part of an agreement to give a beneficial interest and Thomas could not establish this without relying on the illegal purpose, which was the essence of the agreement with John.

16.6.3 Reform

In *Tinsley v Milligan* [1994] 1 AC 340 at pp. 363–4, Lord Goff advocated reform of this area of the law on the basis that the present rules are 'indiscriminate in their effect, and are capable therefore of producing injustice'. The Law Commission examined this issue in its 1999 Consultation Paper, *Illegal Transactions: The effect of illegality on contracts and trusts* (LCCP No. 154), and also concluded that the law was 'unnecessarily complex', 'uncertain', and 'may give rise to unjust decisions'. It therefore recommended that the present rules (reliance principle, presumption of advancement, and the withdrawal exception) be replaced by giving the courts a discretion to decide whether to enforce the illegal contract or permit a claim in restitution, or to recognize property rights either created or transferred under an illegal contract. The discretion was to be circumscribed, in the broadest sense, by requiring the courts to consider a number of factors: the seriousness of the illegality involved; the knowledge and intention of the party claiming relief; whether denying the claim would deter the illegality; whether denying the claim would further the purpose of the rule which rendered the transaction illegal; and whether denying the claim would be proportionate to the illegality involved (para. 7.43).

It was also proposed that this discretion should not exist for contracts which do not involve any legal wrong but are illegal because they are otherwise contrary to public policy.

These factors are important because they emphasize the policy objectives underlying illegality. However, almost inevitably, they would still have allowed a good deal of discretion to the courts in individual cases and hence promote uncertainty in this area of the law. See Buckley, '"Illegal transaction": Chaos or discretion?' (2000) 20 LS 155 and Enonchong, 'Illegal transactions: The future? (LCCP No. 154)' [2000] RLR 82.

In its 2009 consultative report, *The Illegality Defence* (LCCP No. 189), the Law Commission abandoned any thoughts of a general discretion and re-emphasized the importance of meeting policy objectives when responding to illegality, considering that it was not possible to devise a workable system of rules to determine when the illegality defence should operate in this context. The preferred approach was to assess each case to see whether 'the application of the illegality defence can be justified on the basis of the policies that underlie that defence'. It followed that a balancing exercise was called for which weighed up the policies and assessed whether depriving a claimant of its rights was a proportionate response to meet those policy objectives.

The Law Commission did, however, make a specific recommendation for a statutory discretion to determine the effect of illegality on some trusts (Part 6) accepting that '[t]he division of the legal and equitable interests offers a unique opportunity to conceal the true beneficial ownership for illegitimate purposes' and the law in this area was arbitrary, potentially unfair, and uncertain in terms of its operation. The details of this discretion are due to be published with the final report and draft Bill (see Davies, 'The illegality defence: Two steps forward, one step back?' [2009] Conv 182).

16.7 Contracts in restraint of trade

Unlike the elements of the illegality doctrine previously dealt with, contracts in restraint of trade require reference both to:

- the public policy which seeks to protect the public interest over the parties' individual interests
- the public policy which deems it unfair to enforce the agreement between the parties.

Thus, such contracts may be subject to the intervention of the court on the ground either of protecting the general public interest, or of maintaining fairness between the parties. Moreover, whereas the illegality doctrine causes the public interest to be brought into conflict with the countervailing interest in freedom of contract, in the case of restraint of trade, the intervention takes place precisely to protect the public interest in freedom of contract.

Contracts in restraint of trade are contracts whereby one or both parties agree to limit their individual freedom to contract. The common law will not tolerate such limitations if the public interest in free competition is adversely affected, or if the limitation is unfair between the parties.

16.7.1 General principles

During the nineteenth century the restraint-of-trade doctrine barely existed since freedom of contract was considered the more important policy to pursue (*Printing and Numerical Registering Co. v Sampson* (1875) LR 19 Eq 462). This attitude neglected, or at least lagged behind, the progress of industrialization and commercial agglomeration which had taken place. However, in *Nordenfelt v Maxim Nordenfelt Guns and Ammunition Co. Ltd* [1894] AC 535, the House of Lords restated the restraint-of-trade rule, and its decision in that case is the foundation of the modern law.

Nordenfelt v Maxim Nordenfelt Guns and Ammunition Co. Ltd concerned a restraint upon the seller of an ammunition-and-arms-manufacturing company, which prevented him engaging in such business anywhere in the world for twenty-five years.

The leading speech is that of Lord Macnaghten. His statement of the law may be summarized as follows:

There is an initial presumption that contracts in restraint of trade are void. The courts may of their own motion refuse to enforce such a contract. The presumption may be rebutted only by showing special justifying circumstances. Whether the circumstances alleged to justify the restraint do so, is a question of law for the court. For a restraint to be justified it must be reasonable both in the interests of the parties and in the public interest. Generally, the burden of proof in relation to what is reasonable between the parties rests on the party seeking to enforce the contract. If that burden is sustained, the party resisting enforcement has the burden of showing that the restraint is contrary to the public interest.

Thus, of the two streams of public policy in relation to contracts in restraint of trade, fairness between the parties is predominant, since once that has been established the presumption switches to one of validity.

16.7.2 Reasonable between the parties

What is reasonable between the parties must be determined in each individual case. However, the decision of the House of Lords in *Herbert Morris Ltd v Saxelby* [1916] AC 688 provides guidance on how the issue is determined.

In *Herbert Morris Ltd v Saxelby* the defendant was employed as engineer by the plaintiffs, a leading manufacturer of hoisting machinery. His contract of employment contained a seven-year restraint on carrying on a wide range of related trades anywhere in the United Kingdom should he leave the plaintiffs' employment. The plaintiffs sought to enforce the clause. They failed.

The House of Lords identified two different types of contract in restraint of trade in which different policy considerations apply.

- In the sale of a business, restraints are permitted which seek to preserve the value of the 'goodwill' of the business by preventing the vendor setting up in competition with the purchaser.

- In contracts of employment it would not normally be reasonable to prevent a former employee from working in any capacity for a competitor, but restraints to prevent the loss of trade secrets or the poaching of customers to whom the employee had access are permitted.

In each case, the identification of a legitimate interest to be protected is only the first stage in the process of justification. It must also be shown that the duration and geographical extent of the restraint are not out of proportion to the interest identified.

While at first sight it may seem difficult to imagine how any restraint can be reasonable to the party upon whom it is imposed, it is essential to consider the whole contract in its economic context. In many cases, but for the restrictive terms, the contract as a whole might never have been made, or at least the person accepting the restraints might not have succeeded in obtaining such favourable terms. It was acknowledged, therefore, in *Esso Petroleum Co. Ltd v Harper's Garage (Stourport) Ltd* [1968] AC 269, that what is fair between the parties can be assessed only in the light of the consideration paid.

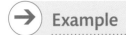

Example

> If in the sale of a business the vendor seeks to place a high value on the goodwill of the business, the purchaser will be entitled to restraints to ensure that the vendor cannot subsequently undermine that value by competing for former customers. Such restraints might not be permitted at all if no value was allocated to the goodwill.

16.7.3 Reasonable in the public interest

Although it would be rare for any restraint to have any perceptible effect on the competitive structure of the market as a whole, the public interest is an important consideration, especially in those cases falling outside the employment contract and the sale of the business type of restraint identified in *Herbert Morris Ltd v Saxelby* [1916] AC 688. When two companies, as a result of arm's length bargaining, agree not to compete with each other, it may be assumed that both think that the contract is reasonable. In such a case it is the public which is likely to suffer, and control by the courts in the public interest is essential.

16.7.4 Employment contracts

Restraints in employment contracts are usually subject to attack only in so far as they purport to operate after the period of employment has terminated.

Moreover, if the contract is terminated by a repudiatory breach by the employer, and the employee accepts the repudiation and treats the contract as at an end, restrictive covenants cease to bind the employee (per Simon Brown and Morritt LJJ in *Rock Refrigeration Ltd v Jones* [1997] 1 All ER 1, relying upon *General Bill Posting Co. Ltd v Atkinson* [1909] AC 118, HL). Thus, in the terminology devised by Lord Diplock in *Photo Production Ltd v Securicor Transport Ltd* [1980] AC 827, restrictive covenants are primary conditions and so terminate once the repudiation is accepted. As discussed at 8.4.1, secondary obligations which govern what happens after termination survive repudiatory breach. Since restrictive covenants in employment contracts are designed to govern post-termination conduct, there is obviously an argument for them to be classified as secondary obligations. The refusal to do so appears to reflect the general policy against such clauses.

The common legitimate interests which may be protected are trade secrets and clients or customers to whom the employee may have had access during the course of the employment. However, the restraint must not go beyond the scope of the type of activity carried on by the particular employee.

> In *Home Counties Dairies Ltd v Skilton* [1970] 1 WLR 526, a milk roundsman agreed not to sell milk or dairy produce to his former employer's customers. The restraint was found reasonable only upon an interpretation of 'dairy produce' limiting it to the kind of products with which he had dealt during the course of his employment.
>
> In *Mason v Provident Clothing & Supply Co. Ltd* [1913] AC 724, the restraint purported to prevent the employee entering into a similar business within twenty-five miles of London. His employment had been in a small shop in Islington, and for that reason the restraint was too wide to be reasonable.

16.7.5 **Sale of a business**

In the case of sale of a business, equality of bargaining power is more likely to exist between the parties, and so fairness between the parties might be thought to be a less crucial, and the public interest a more prominent, concern.

The classic case is *Nordenfelt v Maxim Nordenfelt Guns and Ammunition Co. Ltd* [1894] AC 535. The House of Lords identified the goodwill of the business as the interest entitled to protection. Lord Macnaghten stressed that the public have 'an interest in every person's carrying on his trade freely', and that restraints which are fair between the parties must not be 'injurious to the public'.

It is slightly surprising that there appear to be no cases of this kind where the public interest has been found to be the reason for the contract being void. Courts have usually referred to the public interest as an important factor to be considered, but have not matched their words with action. It may be that courts have not been sufficiently vigilant in this area since the changes supposedly wrought by the decision in *Nordenfelt*'s case.

16.7.6 **Cartels**

Cartels are agreements between supposedly competing undertakings at the same level in the commercial chain. They are sometimes known as horizontal agreements. At least at the time of contracting it must be assumed that the parties believe they are beneficial to them both, and there is little chance of an inequality of bargaining power being exploited. **On the other hand, where cartels consist of agreements not to compete, the conventional economic wisdom (and political judgement) is that the public may well be harmed if competition is unnaturally impaired.**

Cartels are now largely controlled by statutory regulation; the relevant rules are now contained in the Competition Act 1998, in particular the Chapter 1 prohibition which is to be interpreted in line with case law under Art. 81 of the Treaty of Rome. For example, s. 2(2)(a) of the Act prohibits agreement which 'directly or indirectly fix purchase or selling prices or any other trading conditions'. However, such an agreement will be prohibited only if it has an 'appreciable' effect on competition.

The fact that cartels meeting particular criteria are considered as contrary to the public interest can be seen in the fact that dishonestly engaging in a cartel with a competitor company can be a criminal offence (ss. 188 and 189 of the Enterprise Act 2002).

16.7.7 **Exclusive dealing agreements**

Exclusive dealing agreements are agreements between undertakings at different stages in the commercial chain which provide for a closer tie between the undertakings than a mere contract of supply. They are sometimes known as vertical agreements. They may well have advantages for both parties in terms of forward planning, but where one party is a retailer and the other a manufacturer, the security of supply for the retailer may be provided at too high price. The leading case is *Esso Petroleum Co. Ltd v Harper's Garage (Stourport) Ltd* [1968] AC 269.

In *Esso Petroleum Co. Ltd v Harper's Garage (Stourport) Ltd* the parties made a contract, known as a solus agreement, under which the garage owners agreed to purchase petrol only from the company. In the case of one garage the tie was to last for four years and five months, and in return the garage owners received a discount on the price of petrol supplied to them. In the case of a second garage the tie was to last for twenty-one years, and in return the garage owners received a mortgage loan of £7,000.

The House of Lords made it clear that there is no overall ban on such contracts. An investigation must be made in every case into whether there is a legitimate interest to be protected, and if so whether the restraints imposed are reasonable to protect the interests in question. On the particular facts, their Lordships found the shorter restraint to be reasonable, but the twenty-one-year restraint was unreasonable and unenforceable.

There are *obiter* statements in the **Esso** case suggesting that an agreement for these kinds of restraints, if contained in a lease, would always be considered valid. It was apparently feared that to say otherwise might cause unnecessary interference in the law of real property relating to restrictive covenants. That opinion has been questioned by subsequent commentators, and it was made clear in *Alec Lobb (Garages) Ltd v Total Oil (GB) Ltd* [1985] 1 WLR 173 that the restraint-of-trade doctrine did apply, in principle, to leases. However, on the facts the particular exclusive dealing agreement linked to the lease was reasonable.

16.7.8 Restraints on professional sportspeople and entertainers: exclusive service agreements

In some circumstances restraints are imposed to ensure that a person provides services for only one recipient. Such contracts are common in the world of professional sport and entertainment. The individual who is restricted may not have a contract of employment with the beneficiary of the restriction, but the individual is nevertheless unable to supply their services to anybody else. They are often referred to as 'exclusive service agreements'. This category includes those agreements where employers agree to regulate employment in a particular sector, and especially agree not to employ those who have previously worked for other parties to the agreement. Such agreements may be equivalent in effect to the restraints contained in contracts of employment (see 16.7.4), and for that reason they are within the restraint-of-trade doctrine.

In *Greig v Insole* [1978] 1 WLR 302, the organizers of international and English county cricket sought to exclude from their matches those players who participated in games promoted by a private cricketing 'circus' established in a battle over television rights. The plaintiff, who until this time had been captain of the England team, successfully challenged the ban imposed on the ground that it interfered with freedom of employment.

The most striking cases are those where the bodies responsible for the organization of professional sport impose a rule upon their members intended to prevent large clubs poaching the best players from small clubs. Often such rules are alleged to be justified in the interests of the sport-watching public. The employees of the clubs can find that they are unable to make the best commercial exploitation of their skills. The cases make it clear that such rules are in restraint of trade and thus invalid (*Eastham v Newcastle United Football Club Ltd* [1964] Ch 413).

There have also been a number of cases concerning exclusive service agreements between musicians/pop groups and their management.

In *Schroeder Music Publishing Co. Ltd v Macaulay* [1974] 1 WLR 1308, an unknown songwriter entered into a contract with a music publisher whereby they engaged his exclusive services for five years; and if royalties exceeded £5,000 the contract was to be automatically extended for a further five years. The contract was terminable at the option of the music publisher (who had copyright in all compositions),

615

but not at the option of the songwriter. The publisher was not obliged to publish any songs. The song-writer sought to escape the confines of the contract after achieving considerable popular success, alleging that the agreement was contrary to public policy. The House of Lords held that such agreements fell within the restraint-of-trade doctrine. The restrictions in this agreement were one-sided and removed all incentive to creativity. Accordingly, the agreement was an unreasonable restraint of trade.

16.7.9 Statutory control of anti-competitive agreements

In the domestic context restrictive agreements are subject to statutory control in accordance with the Competition Act 1998. However, the United Kingdom is also subject to the competition law of the EC, namely Arts 81 and 82 of the Treaty of Rome. (That treaty, and all law made under it, is part of English law by virtue of the European Communities Act 1972.) Competition law is the subject of specialist texts, such as Furse, *Competition Law of the EC and UK,* 6th edn (Oxford University Press, 2008) and Whish, *Competition Law,* 6th edn (Oxford University Press, 2008).

16.7.10 Severance of the offending parts

In some circumstances illegal contracts remain enforceable by both parties provided changes are made by removing the offending parts. The rule is especially relevant in the case of contracts in restraint of trade, which is why it is dealt with at this point.

Severance is allowed only if it is consistent with the public policy which made the contract containing the offending part illegal. If the whole contract is tainted by the illegality, severance cannot save it.

The illegal portion of the contract must be capable of being verbally and grammatically separated from the rest. **This principle is usually called the 'blue pencil' test.**

In *Goldsoll v Goldman* [1915] 1 Ch 292, the plaintiffs were dealers in imitation jewellery, and entered into an agreement with the defendant, a competitor, to the effect that the defendant would no longer compete with them in any capacity, either in his own right, or as an agent or employee of others, for a period of two years. The clause purported to cover 'the county of London, England, Scotland, Ireland, Wales, or any part of the United Kingdom of Great Britain and Ireland and the Isle of Man or France, the United States of America, Russia or Spain, or within twenty-five miles of Potsdamerstrasse, Berlin, or St Stefans Kirche, Vienna'. The Court of Appeal was willing to enforce the contract but for the unreasonable geographical extent of the restraint, and did so after severing the words from 'or France' to the end of the clause.

The illegal part of the contract must not be the main subject matter, since its severance would totally unbalance the agreement, making it essentially different from the original bargain.

In *Bennett v Bennett* [1952] 1 KB 249, a husband and wife separated, and the wife commenced divorce proceedings in which she applied for a maintenance order against her husband. Before the trial she entered into an agreement with the husband by which he undertook to pay her an annuity and to convey property to her, in return for which she promised not to pursue any claim for maintenance in the courts. The husband did not keep his side of the bargain. The promise not to seek maintenance was illegal (see 16.4.2), so that the whole of the consideration to be furnished by the wife failed, i.e. the various covenants.

Even where the illegal part is not the main subject matter of the contract, the courts will not sever it and enforce the rest if to do so would alter entirely the scope and intention of the agreement. This rule appears to be the most satisfactory explanation of *Attwood v Lamont* [1920] 3 KB 571, which is otherwise not easily distinguished from *Goldsoll v Goldman*.

> In *Attwood v Lamont*, the respondent was the owner of a department store which carried out tailoring and general outfitting. The appellant was employed as a cutter in the tailoring department, and his contract of employment contained a clause restraining him from working at any time in the future within ten miles of the store in the 'business of a tailor, dressmaker, general draper, milliner, hatter, haberdasher, gentlemen's, ladies' or children's outfitter'. The restraint was found to be too wide, since the appellant's only significant skill was as a tailor, and the question arose whether the other functions on the list might be severed. The Court of Appeal held that the rest of the clause could not be severed, and that this was a covenant 'which must stand or fall in its unaltered form'.
>
> Whether in any particular case the scope and intention of an agreement will be so altered by severance is a question of fact.

In *Carney v Herbert* [1985] 1 All ER 438, the Privy Council identified two limits on severance:

1. The significance of the illegal term or terms in relation to the whole of the transaction is to be judged not at the time of contracting, but at the time of trial. Consequently, the fact that a party would not have been willing to enter the contract but for the illegal term may be irrelevant.

2. Where the parties enter into a lawful contract, and there is an illegal ancillary provision with exists solely for the benefit of the claimant, which the claimant may waive without prejudicing the substance of the claim, the court will normally permit the provision to be severed, provided there will be no overriding affront to the public conscience.

On the other hand, the courts have expressed considerable reluctance to go out of their way to rescue employers from the consequences of having drafted restrictive covenants in terms that were excessively broad (*Living Design (Home Improvements) Ltd v Davidson* [1994] IRLR 69; *J. A. Mont (UK) Ltd v Mills* [1993] IRLR 172). Quite properly, the effect of these decisions ought to be to force employers to draft clauses properly and reasonably in the first place.

16.7.11 Remedies where a restraint is valid

Where it is sought to enforce a valid restraint-of-trade clause, the party for whose benefit the clause was included will usually be more concerned to prevent breach of the clause than to recover damages. Indeed, since restraints which are reasonable are often quite short in duration, the party benefited by the clause will require immediate protection (by the time the matter comes to a full trial the period of restraint may be close to expiry). Such immediate protection may be provided by the grant of an interim injunction (for jurisdiction of courts to grant interim injunctions, see Senior Courts Act 1981, s. 37(1) and County Courts Act 1984, s. 38; see also Civil Procedure Rules, r. 25 and Practice Direction 25).

Where the covenant is *prima facie* valid—i.e. reasonable in geographical area, scope, and duration—as in *Office Overload Ltd v Gunn* [1977] FSR 39, the court will grant the injunction. However, there will frequently be some dispute or doubt about the claimant's case. In *Lawrence David Ltd v Ashton* [1991] 1 All ER 385, the Court of Appeal held that, in such circumstances, the test to be applied in respect of an application for an interim injunction would be the usual test set out in *American Cyanamid Co. v Ethicon Ltd* [1975] AC 396. According to that test, such an injunction would be granted only where:

- there was a serious issue to be tried

- damages at the time of full trial would not be an adequate remedy

- the balance of convenience was in favour of granting it.

In *Lansing Linde Ltd v Kerr* [1991] 1 All ER 418, the Court of Appeal held that in respect of the first part of the test, where the full hearing would be held only at or about the time of the expiry of the period of restraint, an interim injunction would be granted only where there was not only a serious issue to be tried but the claimant was more likely than not to succeed at the full trial. Once the case for an injunction is made out, the claimant will normally be granted an injunction covering the whole scope of the restraint clause.

Injunctions to restrain breaches of restrictive covenants in employment contracts may be combined with an injunction restraining the misuse of confidential information obtained as a result of the employment. In the case of the latter type of injunction, the *American Cyanamid* principles will also apply (*Lock International v Beswick* [1989] 1 WLR 1668).

Further reading

General

Buckley, *Illegality and Public Policy,* 2nd edn (Sweet and Maxwell, 2009).

Categories of illegality

Buckley, 'Implied statutory prohibition of contracts' (1975) 38 MLR 535.

The illegality defence and reform

Beatson, 'Repudiation of illegal purpose as a ground for restitution' (1975) 91 LQR 313.

Berg, 'Illegality and equitable interests' [1993] JBL 513.

Buckley, 'Illegal transaction: Chaos or discretion?' (2000) 20 LS 155.

Coote, 'Another look at *Bowmakers v Barnet Instruments*' (1972) 34 MLR 38.

Creighton, 'The recovery of property transferred for illegal purposes' (1997) 60 MLR 102.

Davies, 'The illegality defence: Two steps forward, one step back?' [2009] Conv 182.

Dickson, 'Restitution and illegal transactions' in Burrows (ed.), *Essays on the Law of Restitution* (Clarendon Press, 1991).

Enonchong, 'Title claims and illegal transactions' (1995) 111 LQR 135.

Enonchong, 'Illegal transactions: The future? (LCCP No. 154)' [2000] RLR 82.

Furmston, 'The Illegal Contracts Act 1970: An English view' (1972) 5 NZULR 151.

Law Commission Consultation Paper No. 154, *Illegal Transactions: The effect of illegality on contracts and trusts* (1999).

Law Commission Consultative Report, No. 189, *The Illegality Defence* (2009).

New Zealand Illegal Contracts Act 1970.

Phang, 'Of illegality and presumptions: Australian departures and possible approaches' (1996) 11 JCL 53.

Rose, 'Reconsidering illegality' (1996) 10 JCL 271.

Virgo, 'Withdrawal from illegal transactions: A matter for consideration' [1996] CLJ 23.

Restraint of trade

Smith, 'Reconstructing restraint of trade' (1995) 15 OJLS 565.

Woodley and Wilson, 'Restraint, drafting and the rule in *General Billposting*' [1998] JBL 272.

Index

631